T0180237

Lecture Notes in Computer Science 12622

More information about this subseries at http://www.springer.com/series/7412

Hiroshi Ishikawa · Cheng-Lin Liu ·
Tomas Pajdla · Jianbo Shi (Eds.)

Computer Vision – ACCV 2020

15th Asian Conference on Computer Vision
Kyoto, Japan, November 30 – December 4, 2020
Revised Selected Papers, Part I

 Springer

Editors
Hiroshi Ishikawa
Waseda University
Tokyo, Japan

Tomas Pajdla
Czech Technical University in Prague
Prague, Czech Republic

Cheng-Lin Liu
Institute of Automation of Chinese Academy
of Sciences
Beijing, China

Jianbo Shi
University of Pennsylvania
Philadelphia, PA, USA

ISSN 0302-9743   ISSN 1611-3349   (electronic)
Lecture Notes in Computer Science
ISBN 978-3-030-69524-8   ISBN 978-3-030-69525-5   (eBook)
https://doi.org/10.1007/978-3-030-69525-5

LNCS Sublibrary: SL6 – Image Processing, Computer Vision, Pattern Recognition, and Graphics

This Springer imprint is published by the registered company Springer Nature Switzerland AG
The registered company address is: Gewerbestrasse 11, 6330 Cham, Switzerland

Preface

The Asian Conference on Computer Vision (ACCV) 2020, originally planned to take place in Kyoto, Japan, was held online during November 30 – December 4, 2020. The conference featured novel research contributions from almost all sub-areas of computer vision.

We received 836 main-conference submissions. After removing the desk rejects, 768 valid, complete manuscripts were submitted for review. A pool of 48 area chairs and 738 reviewers was recruited to conduct paper reviews. As in previous editions of ACCV, we adopted a double-blind review process to determine which of these papers to accept. Identities of authors were not visible to reviewers and area chairs; nor were the identities of the assigned reviewers and area chairs known to authors. The program chairs did not submit papers to the conference.

Each paper was reviewed by at least three reviewers. Authors were permitted to respond to the initial reviews during a rebuttal period. After this, the area chairs led discussions among reviewers. Finally, an interactive area chair meeting was held, during which panels of three area chairs deliberated to decide on acceptance decisions for each paper, and then four larger panels were convened to make final decisions. At the end of this process, 254 papers were accepted for publication in the ACCV 2020 conference proceedings.

In addition to the main conference, ACCV 2020 featured four workshops and two tutorials. This is also the first ACCV for which the proceedings are open access at the Computer Vision Foundation website, by courtesy of Springer.

We would like to thank all the organizers, sponsors, area chairs, reviewers, and authors. We acknowledge the support of Microsoft's Conference Management Toolkit (CMT) team for providing the software used to manage the review process.

We greatly appreciate the efforts of all those who contributed to making the conference a success, despite the difficult and fluid situation.

December 2020

Hiroshi Ishikawa
Cheng-Lin Liu
Tomas Pajdla
Jianbo Shi

Organization

General Chairs

Ko Nishino	Kyoto University, Japan
Akihiro Sugimoto	National Institute of Informatics, Japan
Hiromi Tanaka	Ritsumeikan University, Japan

Program Chairs

Hiroshi Ishikawa	Waseda University, Japan
Cheng-Lin Liu	Institute of Automation of Chinese Academy of Sciences, China
Tomas Pajdla	Czech Technical University, Czech Republic
Jianbo Shi	University of Pennsylvania, USA

Publication Chairs

Ichiro Ide	Nagoya University, Japan
Wei-Ta Chu	National Chung Cheng University, Taiwan
Marc A. Kastner	National Institute of Informatics, Japan

Local Arrangements Chairs

Shohei Nobuhara	Kyoto University, Japan
Yasushi Makihara	Osaka University, Japan

Web Chairs

Ikuhisa Mitsugami	Hiroshima City University, Japan
Chika Inoshita	Canon Inc., Japan

AC Meeting Chair

Yusuke Sugano	University of Tokyo, Japan

Area Chairs

Mathieu Aubry	École des Ponts ParisTech, France
Xiang Bai	Huazhong University of Science and Technology, China
Alex Berg	Facebook, USA
Michael S. Brown	York University, Canada

Additional Reviewers

Sathyanarayanan
   N. Aakur
Mahmoud Afifi
Amit Aides
Noam Aigerman
Kenan Emir Ak
Mohammad
   Sadegh Aliakbarian
Keivan Alizadeh-Vahid
Dario Allegra
Alexander Andreopoulos
Nikita Araslanov
Anil Armagan
Alexey Artemov
Aditya Arun
Yuki M. Asano
Hossein Azizpour
Seung-Hwan Baek
Seungryul Baek
Max Bain
Abhishek Bajpayee
Sandipan Banerjee
Wenbo Bao
Daniel Barath
Chaim Baskin
Anil S. Baslamisli
Ardhendu Behera
Jens Behley
Florian Bernard
Bharat Lal Bhatnagar
Uttaran Bhattacharya
Binod Bhattarai
Ayan Kumar Bhunia
Jia-Wang Bian
Simion-Vlad Bogolin
Amine Bourki
Biagio Brattoli
Anders G. Buch
Evgeny Burnaev
Benjamin Busam
Holger Caesar
Jianrui Cai
Jinzheng Cai

Fanta Camara
Necati Cihan Camgöz
Shaun Canavan
Jiajiong Cao
Jiale Cao
Hakan Çevikalp
Ayan Chakrabarti
Tat-Jen Cham
Lyndon Chan
Hyung Jin Chang
Xiaobin Chang
Rama Chellappa
Chang Chen
Chen Chen
Ding-Jie Chen
Jianhui Chen
Jun-Cheng Chen
Long Chen
Songcan Chen
Tianshui Chen
Weifeng Chen
Weikai Chen
Xiaohan Chen
Xinlei Chen
Yanbei Chen
Yingcong Chen
Yiran Chen
Yi-Ting Chen
Yun Chen
Yun-Chun Chen
Yunlu Chen
Zhixiang Chen
Ziliang Chen
Guangliang Cheng
Li Cheng
Qiang Cheng
Zhongwei Cheng
Anoop Cherian
Ngai-Man Cheung
Wei-Chen Chiu
Shin-Fang Ch'ng
Nam Ik Cho
Junsuk Choe

Chiho Choi
Jaehoon Choi
Jinsoo Choi
Yukyung Choi
Anustup Choudhury
Hang Chu
Peng Chu
Wei-Ta Chu
Sanghyuk Chun
Ronald Clark
Maxwell D. Collins
Ciprian Corneanu
Luca Cosmo
Ioana Croitoru
Steve Cruz
Naresh Cuntoor
Zachary A. Daniels
Mohamed Daoudi
François Darmon
Adrian K. Davison
Rodrigo de Bem
Shalini De Mello
Lucas Deecke
Bailin Deng
Jiankang Deng
Zhongying Deng
Somdip Dey
Ferran Diego
Mingyu Ding
Dzung Anh Doan
Xingping Dong
Xuanyi Dong
Hazel Doughty
Dawei Du
Chi Nhan Duong
Aritra Dutta
Marc C. Eder
Ismail Elezi
Mohamed Elgharib
Sergio Escalera
Deng-Ping Fan
Shaojing Fan
Sean Fanello

Moshiur R. Farazi
Azade Farshad
István Fehérvári
Junyi Feng
Wei Feng
Yang Feng
Zeyu Feng
Robert B. Fisher
Alexander Fix
Corneliu O. Florea
Wolfgang Förstner
Jun Fu
Xueyang Fu
Yanwei Fu
Hiroshi Fukui
Antonino Furnari
Ryo Furukawa
Raghudeep Gadde
Vandit J. Gajjar
Chuang Gan
Bin-Bin Gao
Boyan Gao
Chen Gao
Junbin Gao
Junyu Gao
Lin Gao
Mingfei Gao
Peng Gao
Ruohan Gao
Nuno C. Garcia
Georgios Georgakis
Ke Gong
Jiayuan Gu
Jie Gui
Manuel Günther
Kaiwen Guo
Minghao Guo
Ping Guo
Sheng Guo
Yulan Guo
Saurabh Gupta
Jung-Woo Ha
Emanuela Haller
Cusuh Ham
Kai Han
Liang Han

Tengda Han
Ronny Hänsch
Josh Harguess
Atsushi Hashimoto
Monica Haurilet
Jamie Hayes
Fengxiang He
Pan He
Xiangyu He
Xinwei He
Yang He
Paul Henderson
Chih-Hui Ho
Tuan N.A. Hoang
Sascha A. Hornauer
Yedid Hoshen
Kuang-Jui Hsu
Di Hu
Ping Hu
Ronghang Hu
Tao Hu
Yang Hua
Bingyao Huang
Haibin Huang
Huaibo Huang
Rui Huang
Sheng Huang
Xiaohua Huang
Yifei Huang
Zeng Huang
Zilong Huang
Jing Huo
Junhwa Hur
Wonjun Hwang
José Pedro Iglesias
Atul N. Ingle
Yani A. Ioannou
Go Irie
Daisuke Iwai
Krishna Murthy
   Jatavallabhula
Seong-Gyun Jeong
Koteswar Rao Jerripothula
Jingwei Ji
Haiyang Jiang
Huajie Jiang

Wei Jiang
Xiaoyi Jiang
Jianbo Jiao
Licheng Jiao
Kyong Hwan Jin
Xin Jin
Shantanu Joshi
Frédéric Jurie
Abhishek Kadian
Olaf Kaehler
Meina Kan
Dimosthenis Karatzas
Isay Katsman
Muhammad Haris Khan
Vijeta Khare
Rawal Khirodkar
Hadi Kiapour
Changick Kim
Dong-Jin Kim
Gunhee Kim
Heewon Kim
Hyunwoo J. Kim
Junsik Kim
Junyeong Kim
Yonghyun Kim
Akisato Kimura
A. Sophia Koepke
Dimitrios Kollias
Nikos Kolotouros
Yoshinori Konishi
Adam Kortylewski
Dmitry Kravchenko
Sven Kreiss
Gurunandan Krishnan
Andrey Kuehlkamp
Jason Kuen
Arjan Kuijper
Shiro Kumano
Avinash Kumar
B. V. K. Vijaya Kumar
Ratnesh Kumar
Vijay Kumar
Yusuke Kurose
Alina Kuznetsova
Junseok Kwon
Loic Landrieu

Dong Lao	Feng Liu	Niki Martinel
Viktor Larsson	Hao Liu	Jonathan Masci
Yasir Latif	Hong Liu	Tetsu Matsukawa
Hei Law	Jing Liu	Bruce A. Maxwell
Hieu Le	Jingtuo Liu	Amir Mazaheri
Hoang-An Le	Jun Liu	Prakhar Mehrotra
Huu Minh Le	Miaomiao Liu	Heydi Méndez-Vázquez
Gim Hee Lee	Ming Liu	Zibo Meng
Hyungtae Lee	Ping Liu	Kourosh Meshgi
Jae-Han Lee	Siqi Liu	Shun Miao
Jangho Lee	Wentao Liu	Zhongqi Miao
Jungbeom Lee	Wu Liu	Micael Carvalho
Kibok Lee	Xing Liu	Pedro Miraldo
Kuan-Hui Lee	Xingyu Liu	Ashish Mishra
Seokju Lee	Yongcheng Liu	Ikuhisa Mitsugami
Sungho Lee	Yu Liu	Daisuke Miyazaki
Sungmin Lee	Yu-Lun Liu	Kaichun Mo
Bin Li	Yun Liu	Liliane Momeni
Jie Li	Zhihua Liu	Gyeongsik Moon
Ruilong Li	Zichuan Liu	Alexandre Morgand
Ruoteng Li	Chengjiang Long	Yasuhiro Mukaigawa
Site Li	Manuel López Antequera	Anirban Mukhopadhyay
Xianzhi Li	Hao Lu	Erickson R. Nascimento
Xiaomeng Li	Hongtao Lu	Lakshmanan Nataraj
Xiaoming Li	Le Lu	K. L. Navaneet
Xin Li	Shijian Lu	Lukáš Neumann
Xiu Li	Weixin Lu	Shohei Nobuhara
Xueting Li	Yao Lu	Nicoletta Noceti
Yawei Li	Yongxi Lu	Mehdi Noroozi
Yijun Li	Chenxu Luo	Michael Oechsle
Yimeng Li	Weixin Luo	Ferda Ofli
Yin Li	Wenhan Luo	Seoung Wug Oh
Yong Li	Diogo C. Luvizon	Takeshi Oishi
Yu-Jhe Li	Jiancheng Lyu	Takahiro Okabe
Zekun Li	Chao Ma	Fumio Okura
Dongze Lian	Long Ma	Kyle B. Olszewski
Zhouhui Lian	Shugao Ma	José Oramas
Haoyi Liang	Xiaojian Ma	Tribhuvanesh Orekondy
Yue Liao	Yongrui Ma	Martin R. Oswald
Jun Hao Liew	Ludovic Magerand	Mayu Otani
Chia-Wen Lin	Behrooz Mahasseni	Umapada Pal
Guangfeng Lin	Mohammed Mahmoud	Yingwei Pan
Kevin Lin	Utkarsh Mall	Rameswar Panda
Xudong Lin	Massimiliano Mancini	Rohit Pandey
Xue Lin	Xudong Mao	Jiangmiao Pang
Chang Liu	Alina E. Marcu	João P. Papa

Toufiq Parag
Jinsun Park
Min-Gyu Park
Despoina Paschalidou
Nikolaos Passalis
Yash Patel
Georgios Pavlakos
Baoyun Peng
Houwen Peng
Wen-Hsiao Peng
Roland Perko
Vitali Petsiuk
Quang-Hieu Pham
Yongri Piao
Marco Piccirilli
Matteo Poggi
Mantini Pranav
Dilip K. Prasad
Véronique Prinet
Victor Adrian Prisacariu
Thomas Probst
Jan Prokaj
Qi Qian
Xuelin Qian
Xiaotian Qiao
Yvain Queau
Mohammad Saeed Rad
Filip Radenovic
Petia Radeva
Bogdan Raducanu
François Rameau
Aakanksha Rana
Yongming Rao
Sathya Ravi
Edoardo Remelli
Dongwei Ren
Wenqi Ren
Md Alimoor Reza
Farzaneh Rezaianaran
Andrés Romero
Kaushik Roy
Soumava Kumar Roy
Nataniel Ruiz
Javier Ruiz-del-Solar
Jongbin Ryu
Mohammad Sabokrou

Ryusuke Sagawa
Pritish Sahu
Hideo Saito
Kuniaki Saito
Shunsuke Saito
Ken Sakurada
Joaquin Salas
Enrique Sánchez-Lozano
Aswin Sankaranarayanan
Hiroaki Santo
Soubhik Sanyal
Vishwanath Saragadam1
Yoichi Sato
William R. Schwartz
Jesse Scott
Siniša Šegvić
Lorenzo Seidenari
Keshav T. Seshadri
Francesco Setti
Meet Shah
Shital Shah
Ming Shao
Yash Sharma
Dongyu She
Falong Shen
Jie Shen
Xi Shen
Yuming Shen
Hailin Shi
Yichun Shi
Yifei Shi
Yujiao Shi
Zenglin Shi
Atsushi Shimada
Daeyun Shin
Young Min Shin
Kirill Sidorov
Krishna Kumar Singh
Maneesh K. Singh
Gregory Slabaugh
Chunfeng Song
Dongjin Song
Ran Song
Xibin Song
Ramprakash Srinivasan
Erik Stenborg

Stefan Stojanov
Yu-Chuan Su
Zhuo Su
Yusuke Sugano
Masanori Suganuma
Yumin Suh
Yao Sui
Jiaming Sun
Jin Sun
Xingyuan Sun
Zhun Sun
Minhyuk Sung
Keita Takahashi
Kosuke Takahashi
Jun Takamatsu
Robby T. Tan
Kenichiro Tanaka
Masayuki Tanaka
Chang Tang
Peng Tang
Wei Tang
Xu Tang
Makarand Tapaswi
Amara Tariq
Mohammad Tavakolian
Antonio Tejero-de-Pablos
Ilias Theodorakopoulos
Thomas E. Bishop
Diego Thomas
Kai Tian
Xinmei Tian
Yapeng Tian
Chetan J. Tonde
Lei Tong
Alessio Tonioni
Carlos Torres
Anh T. Tran
Subarna Tripathi
Emanuele Trucco
Hung-Yu Tseng
Tony Tung
Radim Tylecek
Seiichi Uchida
Md. Zasim Uddin
Norimichi Ukita
Ernest Valveny

Nanne van Noord
Subeesh Vasu
Javier Vazquez-Corral
Andreas Velten
Constantin Vertan
Rosaura G. VidalMata
Valentin Vielzeuf
Sirion Vittayakorn
Konstantinos Vougioukas
Fang Wan
Guowei Wan
Renjie Wan
Bo Wang
Chien-Yi Wang
Di Wang
Dong Wang
Guangrun Wang
Hao Wang
Hongxing Wang
Hua Wang
Jialiang Wang
Jiayun Wang
Jingbo Wang
Jinjun Wang
Lizhi Wang
Pichao Wang
Qian Wang
Qiaosong Wang
Qilong Wang
Qingzhong Wang
Shangfei Wang
Shengjin Wang
Tiancai Wang
Wenguan Wang
Wenhai Wang
Xiang Wang
Xiao Wang
Xiaoyang Wang
Xinchao Wang
Xinggang Wang
Yang Wang
Yaxing Wang
Yisen Wang
Yu-Chiang Frank Wang
Zheng Wang
Scott Wehrwein

Wei Wei
Xing Wei
Xiu-Shen Wei
Yi Wei
Martin Weinmann
Michael Weinmann
Jun Wen
Xinshuo Weng
Thomas Whelan
Kimberly Wilber
Williem Williem
Kwan-Yee K. Wong
Yongkang Wong
Sanghyun Woo
Michael Wray
Chenyun Wu
Chongruo Wu
Jialian Wu
Xiaohe Wu
Xiaoping Wu
Yihong Wu
Zhenyao Wu
Changqun Xia
Xide Xia
Yin Xia
Lei Xiang
Di Xie
Guo-Sen Xie
Jin Xie
Yifan Xing
Yuwen Xiong
Jingwei Xu
Jun Xu
Ke Xu
Mingze Xu
Yanyu Xu
Yi Xu
Yichao Xu
Yongchao Xu
Yuanlu Xu
Jia Xue
Nan Xue
Yasushi Yagi
Toshihiko Yamasaki
Zhaoyi Yan
Zike Yan

Keiji Yanai
Dong Yang
Fan Yang
Hao Yang
Jiancheng Yang
Linlin Yang
Mingkun Yang
Ren Yang
Sibei Yang
Wenhan Yang
Ze Yang
Zhaohui Yang
Zhengyuan Yang
Anbang Yao
Angela Yao
Rajeev Yasarla
Jinwei Ye
Qi Ye
Xinchen Ye
Zili Yi
Ming Yin
Zhichao Yin
Ryo Yonetani
Ju Hong Yoon
Haichao Yu
Jiahui Yu
Lequan Yu
Lu Yu
Qian Yu
Ruichi Yu
Li Yuan
Sangdoo Yun
Sergey Zakharov
Huayi Zeng
Jiabei Zeng
Yu Zeng
Fangneng Zhan
Kun Zhan
Bowen Zhang
Hongguang Zhang
Jason Y. Zhang
Jiawei Zhang
Jie Zhang
Jing Zhang
Kaihao Zhang
Kaipeng Zhang

Lei Zhang
Mingda Zhang
Pingping Zhang
Qian Zhang
Qilin Zhang
Qing Zhang
Runze Zhang
Shanshan Zhang
Shu Zhang
Wayne Zhang
Xiaolin Zhang
Xiaoyun Zhang
Xucong Zhang
Yan Zhang
Zhao Zhang
Zhishuai Zhang
Feng Zhao
Jian Zhao
Liang Zhao
Qian Zhao
Qibin Zhao

Ruiqi Zhao
Sicheng Zhao
Tianyi Zhao
Xiangyun Zhao
Xin Zhao
Yifan Zhao
Yinan Zhao
Shuai Zheng
Yalin Zheng
Bineng Zhong
Fangwei Zhong
Guangyu Zhong
Yaoyao Zhong
Yiran Zhong
Jun Zhou
Mo Zhou
Pan Zhou
Ruofan Zhou
S. Kevin Zhou
Yao Zhou
Yipin Zhou

Yu Zhou
Yuqian Zhou
Yuyin Zhou
Guangming Zhu
Ligeng Zhu
Linchao Zhu
Rui Zhu
Xinge Zhu
Yizhe Zhu
Zhe Zhu
Zhen Zhu
Zheng Zhu
Bingbing Zhuang
Jiacheng Zhuo
Mohammadreza
    Zolfaghari
Chuhang Zou
Yuliang Zou
Zhengxia Zou

Contents – Part I

3D Computer Vision

3D Computer Vision

Weakly-Supervised Reconstruction of 3D Objects with Large Shape Variation from Single In-the-Wild Images

Shichen Sun[1], Zhengbang Zhu[1], Xiaowei Dai[1], Qijun Zhao[1,2(✉)], and Jing Li[1]

[1] College of Computer Science, Sichuan University, Chengdu, China
qjzhao@scu.edu.cn
[2] School of Information Science and Technology, Tibet University, Lhasa, China

Abstract. Existing unsupervised 3D object reconstruction methods can not work well if the shape of objects varies substantially across images or if the images have distracting background. This paper proposes a novel learning framework for reconstructing 3D objects with large shape variation from single in-the-wild images. Considering that shape variation leads to appearance change of objects at various scales, we propose a fusion module to form combined multi-scale image features for 3D reconstruction. To deal with the ambiguity caused by shape variation, we propose side-output mask constraint to supervise the feature extraction, and adaptive edge constraint and initial shape constraint to supervise the shape reconstruction. Moreover, we propose background manipulation to augment the training images such that the obtained model is robust to background distraction. Extensive experiments have been done for both non-rigid objects (birds) and rigid objects (planes and vehicles), and the results prove the superiority of the proposed method.

1 Introduction

Knowing 3D shapes of objects is of significant importance in many tasks, e.g., scene understanding [1] and surgical navigation. While inferring the 3D shape of an object from a single view of the object seems effortless for the human vision system, it is still quite difficult for computer vision systems. Some researchers implement 3D object reconstruction by using multi-view geometry based approaches [2–4], which estimate 3D object shapes by exploring the motion or appearance clues among the multiple views of objects. These methods are limited by the availability of multi-view images of objects, and are consequently not always applicable in different scenarios. In this paper, we focus on 3D object reconstruction from single images.

Learning-based approaches are nowadays dominant in 3D object reconstruction. These methods use 3D volumes [5], point clouds [6], or meshes [7] to represent 3D objects, among which meshes can provide finer shape details and

Electronic supplementary material The online version of this chapter (https://doi.org/10.1007/978-3-030-69525-5_1) contains supplementary material, which is available to authorized users.

H. Ishikawa et al. (Eds.): ACCV 2020, LNCS 12622, pp. 3–19, 2021.
https://doi.org/10.1007/978-3-030-69525-5_1

Input   Our Results   CMR [13] Results

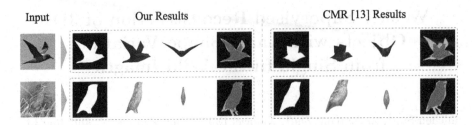

Fig. 1. Our proposed 3D object reconstruction method can infer more accurate 3D shapes especially for objects with large shape variation and images with cluttered background. For easy comparison, we overlay ground truth masks (in grey color) with the reconstructed ones (in cyan color), and highlight their common regions in red color. (Color figure online)

effectively support various shape editing and are thus preferred in many applications. Most of these methods [8–10] require ground truth 3D shapes as supervision during learning. Some of them [11] first learn morphable models based on the ground truth 3D shapes and then estimate 3D shapes for input images by fitting the morphable models. Others [12] learn mappings from 2D images to 3D shape deformations that are needed to transform the initial shape estimate towards its true value. Despite the impressive results obtained by these methods, collecting ground truth 3D shapes of objects is not always affordable or feasible. As a result, learning for 3D object reconstruction without supervision of ground truth 3D shapes is attracting increasing attention.

When ground truth 3D shapes are not available for the training 2D images, 3D object reconstruction learning can be supervised by various prior-based constraints or by features on 2D images. While priors such as smoothness [13] and low-rank [14] have been proven effective for unsupervised 3D object reconstruction, features like keypoints, silhouettes, foreground masks, texture values, and perceptual features [15] are widely used to enforce the coincidence between the input image and the image rendered from the estimated 3D object. To apply such supervision, existing methods [16] simply extract from the input image a latent feature representation, which is assumed to encode the shape, texture and camera parameters associated with the input image, and based on which the 3D object in the image is regressed. Despite the impressive results obtained by them, they work poorly when the objects have large shape variation or when the images have distracting background, as shown in Fig. 1. We believe that this is due to their inefficient utilization of data (or features) and constraints. For instance, when enforcing the coincidence, existing methods consider only locations of keypoints and apply geometric constraints like foreground mask constraint at the output layers only. As a consequence, they are poor both at dealing with invisible keypoints that are caused either by occlusion or by large pose variations of objects and at capturing rich shape deformations of objects.

This paper aims to boost the 3D reconstruction performance for objects with large shape variation and for images with cluttered background. To this end, we propose a novel learning framework by exploiting the training data and the geometric constraints in more efficient manners. Specifically, considering that shape variation leads to appearance change of objects at various scales, we propose a fusion module to combine multi-scale features extracted from the input image, based on which the 3D object is estimated. Considering the ill-posed nature of reconstructing 3D objects from single 2D images and the ambiguity caused by shape variation, we propose side-output mask constraint to supervise the feature extraction, and adaptive edge constraint and initial shape constraint to supervise the shape reconstruction. Moreover, we augment the training images via manipulating their background to improve the robustness of the obtained model to background distraction. We validate the superiority of our proposed method by extensive experiments for reconstructing both non-rigid objects, i.e., birds, and rigid objects, i.e., vehicles and planes.

2   Related Work

In this section, we first discuss the shape representations used in 3D object reconstruction, and then review the 3D reconstruction methods for animals, typical categories of objects with large shape variation.

Shape Representations: Early deep-learning-based methods [17,18] directly predict the final output shapes using voxel in low-resolution due to the high computation cost of 3D convolution operators. Based on the fact that the core difference between high-resolution and low-resolution shapes lies in the boundary surface details and detailed shape information, methods in [10,19] take octree, a sub-category of volume, as representation to implement high-resolution reconstruction in a computationally-efficient manner. Compared to volume, point cloud represents 3D shapes in a more flexible and expressive way. Fan *et al.* [20] firstly propose a framework to generate 3D shapes based on point cloud. Many other methods [21–24] then choose point cloud as representation and focus on how to alleviate the shape ambiguity and improve accuracy. Nevertheless, the predicted point clouds are still of low accuracy. Consequently, more and more methods [3,7,9,12,16,25–27] have replaced point cloud with mesh as the representation of 3D shapes. Mesh, particularly triangular mesh composed of node and triangular face, describes shapes in a more comprehensive way, enabling not only topology constraints but also alignment between shapes. Therefore, we will use mesh to represent 3D objects in this paper.

3D Animal Reconstruction: Little work has been done on 3D animal reconstruction. The seminal work in [28] learns a deformable model of animals from several images. The method is however restricted by precise manual annotations and not ready for strongly articulated objects. Method in [29] takes a set of segmented images as input, and adopts a patch-based approach to implement reconstruction. This way, articulated and relatively accurate 3D animal shapes can be reconstructed. In order to model 3D animal shape as a whole, method in [30] captures shape deformation by defining the stiffness value of local regions. To ease the lack of 3D scans, method in [31] instead uses 3D scans of toy animals to learn a parametric model called SMAL. Later, method in [32] makes the initial parametric model fit the characteristic of the individual shape of the given animal before optimization such that some species unseen in training set could have a better reconstruction. Most recently, a learning-based approach called SMALST [33] integrates SMAL model into a regression network. The method uses the existing SMAL model to spawn training data in various poses, shapes, camera parameters and backgrounds, which are naturally equipped with ground truth 2D annotations. Without relying on parametric model, Kanazawa *et al.* [13] learn from a collection of images of a specific category of objects (e.g., birds) a regression network that can deform an initial shape toward the true shape of the object instance in the input image. Common drawbacks of these methods include (i) exploiting features in a coarse manner without considering the impact of shape variation on object appearance, (ii) inefficient utilization of geometric constraints resulting in ambiguity in the reconstructed shape and low coincidence between the obtained 3D object and the input image, and (iii) poor generalization to in-the-wild images with messy background. As we will show in this paper, our proposed method can effectively get rid of these drawbacks and substantially improve the 3D object reconstruction accuracy.

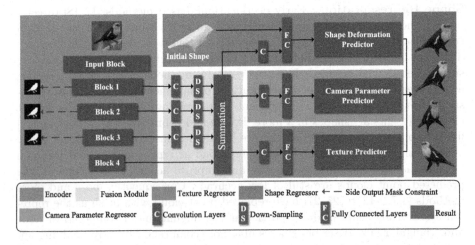

Fig. 2. Schematic diagram of the proposed method of unsupervised 3D object reconstruction from single images.

3   Method

3.1   Overview

Figure 2 shows the overall framework of our proposed single-image-based unsupervised 3D object reconstruction method. The input is a single RGB image of an instance of the target object category (e.g., birds). Note that during test the method does not require any annotation. To reconstruct the 3D model of the object instance, shape deformation, in addition to the UV-flow (i.e., texture feature; see ref. [13] for detail) and camera parameters, is estimated with respect to an initial shape. First, latent representations at multiple scales are extracted by using a backbone deep encoder network, and combined by using a fusion module. Shape deformation, UV-flow and camera parameters are then predicted all by inference from the fused features but with respective regressors. Multi-scale features are used such that richer appearance change induced by shape variation can be captured in 3D reconstruction. It is worth highlighting that the initial shape is also taken as input by the shape deformation regressor, which serves as additional constraint on the search of correct shape deformation. The 3D shape of the object in the input image can be finally obtained by applying the estimated shape deformation to the initial shape, while the texture value of each vertex in the 3D object shape can be obtained according to the estimated UV-flow and the input RGB image.

To determine the parameters involved in the encoder and regressor networks, a set of images of the target category of objects is required as training data. These training images are annotated with keypoints and foreground masks, but do not have ground truth 3D shapes. The training is supervised based on the re-projection of the reconstructed 3D object onto 2D image plane and by coincidence constraints and various prior constraints. In the rest of this section, we introduce in detail the key components of our proposed method for coping with shape variation and cluttered image background, including inference with multi-scale features, shape-sensitive geometric constraints, and training data augmentation via background manipulation.

3.2   Inference with Multi-scale Features

Existing 3D object reconstruction methods mostly extract latent representation at a single scale, i.e., the feature of the deepest layer of the encoder, based on which shape deformation, texture, and camera parameters all are predicted. In contrast, many other tasks have proven the necessity of using features at multiple scales. Specific to 3D object reconstruction, especially for objects with large shape variation, we argue that it is important to fuse multi-scale features for 3D object inference because shape variation could lead to object appearance change at a variety of scales. We thus propose to fuse the multi-scale features extracted from different layers of the encoder network for predicting 3D objects.

Unlike the method in [34] that concatenates multiple features to estimate 3D objects, we propose a convolution-based fusion module to combine multi-scale features. This is because the concatenation method dramatically increases the number of parameters which makes the network difficult to converge, especially without 3D supervision in our case. To solve this problem, in our proposed fusion module, the feature maps of lower layers are first convoluted and down-sampled to the same size as the feature map of higher layer, and afterwards the feature maps of different layers are added up via element-wise summation to produce the fused feature. Obviously, our proposed fusion module, while itself has very few parameters, does not affect the complexity of the regression network.

3.3   Shape-Sensitive Geometric Constraints

Keypoints, silhouette, and foreground mask are routinely used by existing unsupervised 3D object reconstruction methods as geometric constraints by enforcing the coincidence of these geometric features between the input image and the image generated from the reconstructed 3D object. Yet, as we will show below, the way of existing methods to apply geometric constraints can not effectively supervise the extraction of shape-sensitive features or avoid shape ambiguity. Therefore, we propose the following three shape-sensitive geometric constraints to enhance the ability of learned 3D object reconstruction model to handle objects with large shape variation.

Side Output Mask Constraint. While existing methods train the 3D object reconstruction network in an end-to-end manner, the geometric constraints applied on the final output might be of low efficiency in supervising the training of the encoder that is located at the frontal end of the entire network. Moreover, as being discussed above, multi-scale features extracted by different layers of the encoder are employed to regress the 3D object. Therefore, it is demanded to make the features capture as much shape information as possible. To this end, we propose to directly predict foreground mask from the feature extracted by the intermediate layer of the encoder. We use these side output foreground masks to evaluate the mask coincidence as additional supervision for training the encoder, which is defined as follows.

$$
L_{sidemask} = \sum_{i=1}^{N} \sum_{k=1}^{N_b} \sum_{(x,y)} [-M_{gt,i}(x,y) \log(M_{pred,i}^{k}(x,y)) \\
- (1 - M_{gt,i}(x,y)) \log(1 - M_{pred,i}^{k}(x,y))],
\tag{1}
$$

where $M_{gt,i}$ and $M_{pred,i}$ denote the ground truth mask and predicted mask, respectively, N is the total number of training images, N_b is the number of intermediate blocks that are considered in side output mask constraint, and (x,y) denotes the pixel on the mask.

Edge Constraint. Using mean squared error (MSE) to measure the coincidence of keypoints, existing methods face the difficulty in coping with ambiguous shapes. As shown in Fig. 3, two predictions of the four keypoints share the same MSE, but they are obviously not of the same optimality with respect to the ground

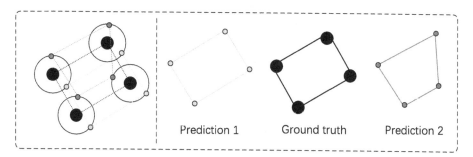

Fig. 3. Existing unsupervised 3D object reconstruction methods use mean squared error (MSE) to measure the coincidence of keypoints. MSE can not deal with ambiguous shapes: the two predictions share the same MSE; however, Prediction 1 is obviously better than Prediction 2. Introducing edge constraint can alleviate this problem.

truth. This is partially due to the missing edge or inter-keypoint constraint that can capture the shape topology. Motivated by the recent progress in human body pose estimation [35], we define the following edge loss to enforce the topology coincidence of the keypoints.

$$L_{edge} = \sum_{i=1}^{N} \sum_{j=1}^{N_E^i} \|E_{i,j} - \hat{E}_{i,j}\|_2^2, \quad E_{i,j} \in \mathcal{DT}(X_i), \qquad (2)$$

where E and $\hat{E}$ are, respectively, the ground truth and estimated edges connecting two keypoints, $\mathcal{DT}(*)$ denotes the operation creating the edge set for a set of visible keypoints via Delaunay Triangulation, i refers to the ith of the N training images, j refers to the jth of the N_E^i edges on the ith image, and X_i is the set of visible 2D keypoints on the ith image. Different from the edge loss defined in human body pose estimation which uses pre-specified keypoint connectivity, we adaptively generate edges for each image based on the visible keypoints on it. This way, our method can effectively deal with objects with large pose variation.

Initial Shape Constraint. Although existing unsupervised 3D object reconstruction methods mostly infer shape deformation (with respect to an initial shape estimate) rather than the shape itself, they calculate the shape deformation based purely on the extracted feature of the input image without considering the initial shape at all. We believe that explicitly utilizing the initial shape when predicting the shape deformation can serve as another constraint and thus help to improve the prediction accuracy. For this sake, we propose to concatenate the vertex coordinates of the initial shape with the extracted feature and feed the expanded feature vector into the shape deformation regressor. This is effective especially for largely deformed objects, e.g., birds with open wings.

3.4   Training Data Augmentation via Background Manipulation

In this paper, we employ a pre-trained ResNet-18 [36] as the backbone encoder network, and train the entire 3D object reconstruction network in an end-to-end manner with the following overall loss function,

$$
\begin{aligned}
Loss = &\lambda_1 L_{edge} + \lambda_2 L_{sidemask} + \lambda_3 L_{kp} + \lambda_4 L_{sil} \\
&+ \lambda_5 L_{cam} + \lambda_6 L_{smooth} + \lambda_7 L_{def} + \lambda_8 L_{texture}.
\end{aligned}
\tag{3}
$$

Here, L_{kp}, L_{sil}, and L_{cam} are defined as the MSE loss between ground truth and predicted values of keypoints, silhouettes, and camera parameters, respectively. The predicted 2D key-points are computed by reprojecting 3D key-points back to the image plane. We use NMR [37] to get the predicted silhouettes and texture under the observed view. L_{smooth} and L_{def} as defined in [13] are used to constrain the inferred shape to be natural; specifically, L_{smooth} is the discrete Laplace-Beltrami operator and L_{def} is to penalize large deformation. $L_{texture}$, a perceptual loss [38], is used to constrain the prediction of texture.

As we attempt to apply our proposed method to reconstructing 3D objects from in-the-wild images, we have to consider the impact of clutter background. Taking bird images as example, we observe that foreground birds could appear quite similar to the background in real-world images because of the natural camouflage of birds. Such camouflage would distract the trained reconstructor during testing as the foreground is not annotated on the test image. To solve this problem, we propose to augment the training data with images that are generated from the original training images by erasing or substituting the background (note that foreground has been annotated on the training images). We will experimentally show the effectiveness of such augmentation though it is very simple to apply.

4   Experiments

4.1   Implementation Details

The network is implemented in Pytorch and optimized using Adam with batch size as 16 and learning rate as 1e−5. The values of hyperparameters in Eq. (3) are set as $\lambda_1 = 5.0, \lambda_2 = 5.0, \lambda_3 = 60.0, \lambda_4 = 5.0, \lambda_5 = 5.0, \lambda_6 = 50.0, \lambda_7 = 10.0, \lambda_8 = 0.5$. We assume that objects are at the center of images. In our experiments, we crop the images according to the bounding boxes of objects such that the objects locate at image center.

4.2   Datasets and Protocols

We evaluate our proposed method with comparison to state-of-the-art (SOTA) methods for reconstructing both non-rigid objects and rigid objects. For non-rigid objects, we take birds as the target 3D objects, and use the CUB-200-2011 dataset. For the sake of fair comparison with the SOTA bird reconstruction method, namely CMR, in [13], we follow the same setup of data division into training, validation, and test sets. Each bird image is annotated with 9–15 keypoints, foreground mask as well as camera parameters. As for rigid objects, we consider vehicles and planes, and use the PASCAL 3D+ dataset [39] with the same data division as for the counterpart methods.

Due to the lack of ground truth 3D shapes, as being normally done in the literature [13,15], we also use the two metrics of Intersection over Union (IoU) and Percentage of Correct Keypoints (PCK) to assess the reconstruction accuracy. However, IoU puts more weight on the interior of reconstructed objects, while neglecting to some extent the discrepancy of boundary. For a more comprehensive evaluation of the reconstruction performance, therefore, we propose to use the structural similarity (SSIM) as another metric to measure the similarity between the input image and the rendered image. SSIM as a perceptual metric can effectively measure the structural difference, which is essential in evaluating the reconstructed 3D objects.

In the following experiments, we conduct model analysis and ablation study on the CUB-200-2011 dataset, and compare the proposed method with state-of-the-art methods on both CUB-200-2011 dataset and PASCAL 3D+ dataset.

4.3   Model Analysis

We compare different implementations of the proposed method to evaluate the impact of (i) number of side output mask constraints, (ii) definition of edges in edge constraint, (iii) background manipulation methods in data augmentation, and (iv) down-sampling methods in feature fusion.

Number of Side Output Mask Constraints. We consider four cases $\{S_i|i = 1, 2, 3, 4\}$ where S_i denotes applying side output mask constraint for the first i blocks following the input block (ordered from shallow to deep) in the encoder network. Figure 4 presents the mean IoU with regard to the number of side output mask constraints. The results demonstrate that more side output mask constraints can generally improve the reconstruction accuracy, but the performance gain becomes saturated as more deep blocks are included.

Definition of Edges. In this experiment, besides our proposed edge definition (DT), we consider three other definitions of edges, i.e., two prior-knowledge-based manual definitions (M1 and M2) and the full set of edges between visible keypoints (FC). The results are shown in Table 1. As can be seen, edge loss can effectively improve the reconstruction accuracy, and defining edges adaptively according to visible keypoints is better than using fixed edge definitions. Moreover, considering the computational cost, the proposed edge definition is more preferred than using the full set of edges.

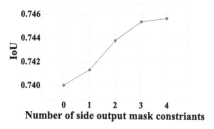

Fig. 4. Impact of number of side output mask constraints.

Background Manipulation Methods. Table 2 shows the results when different background manipulation methods are applied for data augmentation. We can see that while manipulating background of training images is effective in improving the reconstruction accuracy, the best way is to substituting the background pixel values with the average values of the background pixels across all the training images.

Down-Sampling Methods. In this experiment, we implement and compare three down-sampling methods for feature fusion: sampling (choose the value of center pixel in the sampling grid), average pooling, and max pooling. Table 3 gives the results. Note that according to the above evaluation results, we apply the edge constraint ('edge'), side output mask constraint ('so') as well as initial shape constraint ('isc') to the baseline in this experiment. As can be seen, the reconstruction accuracy is further improved after feature fusion. Moreover, among the three down-sampling methods, max pooling achieves the best results. We argue that max pooling has the ability to preserve the prominent feature benefiting the reconstruction, whereas average pooling would distract the regressor from the prominent feature, leading to poor results.

Table 1. Impact of edge definitions. DT is the proposed one. M1 and M2 are two manual definitions (see supplementary material for detail) that are fixed for all images no matter which keypoints are visible. FC denotes the full set of edges between visible keypoints. Time shows the additional time required for evaluating the edge loss.

Method	Time	IoU	PCK.1	PCK.15	SSIM
Baseline	–	0.740	0.783	0.916	0.8568
Baseline + edge (DT)	**0.01062**	0.747	0.848	0.943	**0.8587**
Baseline + edge (M1)	0.02320	0.742	0.813	0.922	0.8574
Baseline + edge (M2)	0.05936	0.745	0.828	0.938	0.8580
Baseline + edge (FC)	0.12469	**0.748**	**0.855**	**0.952**	0.8581

Table 2. Impact of background manipulation methods in data augmentation. Black, White, and Mean denote replacing the background pixel values with black $(0, 0, 0)$, white $(255, 255, 255)$, and the average values of the background pixels across all the training images, respectively.

Method	IoU	PCK.1	PCK.15	SSIM
Baseline	0.740	0.783	0.916	0.8568
Baseline + Black	0.743	0.854	0.951	0.8573
Baseline + White	0.750	0.852	0.949	0.8601
Baseline + Mean	**0.753**	**0.855**	**0.952**	**0.8605**

4.4   Ablation Study

In this experiment, we evaluate the contribution of different components to the performance gain of the proposed method. For this purpose, we gradually integrate the following components: initial shape constraint ('isc'), edge constraint ('edge'), side output mask constraint ('so') and multi-scale feature fusion ('msf'). Note that in this experiment the best implementation for 'edge', 'so' and 'msf' is employed according to the model analysis results. Table 4 summarizes the ablation study results, which clearly demonstrate that all the proposed components effectively improve the reconstruction accuracy.

Table 3. Impact of down-sampling methods in feature fusion. Three down-sampling strategies, Sampling at center pixels (Sampling), Average pooling (AvgPool) and Max pooling (MaxPool), are implemented.

Method	IoU	PCK.1	PCK.15	SSIM
Baseline	0.740	0.783	0.916	0.8568
Baseline + isc	0.742	0.798	0.933	0.8572
Baseline + isc + edge + so	0.749	0.851	0.953	0.8597
Baseline + isc + edge + so + Sampling	0.756	0.862	0.954	0.8620
Baseline + isc + edge + so + Avgpool	0.754	0.858	0.952	0.8607
Baseline + isc + edge + so + Maxpool	**0.757**	**0.866**	**0.957**	**0.8631**

Table 4. Ablation study results. 'isc', 'edge', 'so' and 'msf' denote, respectively, initial shape constraint, edge constraint, side output mask constraint and multi-scale feature fusion.

Model	IoU	PCK.1	PCK.15	SSIM
Baseline	0.740	0.783	0.916	0.8568
Baseline + isc	0.742	0.798	0.933	0.8572
Baseline + isc + edge + so	0.749	0.851	0.953	0.8597
Baseline + isc + edge + so + msf	**0.757**	**0.866**	**0.957**	**0.8631**

4.5   Comparison to State-of-the-Arts

We lastly compare our method with the state-of-the-art (SOTA) method CMR [13] on CUB-200-2011 dataset. The overall results in terms of PCK and IoU are presented in Fig. 5. It can be observed that the proposed method consistently outperforms CMR. The average results in terms of different metrics are shown in Table 5. Some examples of reconstructed 3D birds are shown in Fig. 6. As can be seen, our proposed method can generate visually more pleasant shapes, particularly for the torso and wings of birds.

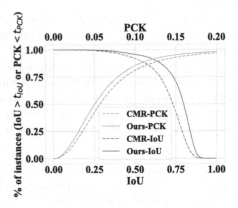

Fig. 5. Comparison with the SOTA method CMR [13] on CUB-200-2011. X-axis represents threshold (t_{PCK} or t_{IoU}) and Y-axis is the proportion of test instances whose PCK/IoU is lower/higher than the threshold.

We also evaluate our method for the reconstruction of vehicles and planes. We use the images in PASCAL VOC [39] and ImageNet [13] for training. An off-the-shelf segmentation framework [40] is used to obtain the silhouettes (and thus foreground masks) for the images. We report the IoU results of our method and the counterpart methods on the test PASCAL 3D+ dataset in Table 6. Our method improves the reconstruction accuracy for both categories of objects with a large margin. Some reconstructed planes and vehicles are visualized in Fig. 7.

Table 5. Comparison with the state-of-the-art method CMR [13] for 3D bird reconstruction on CUB-200-2011.

Method	IoU	PCK.1	PCK.15	SSIM
CMR	0.703	0.812	0.93	0.8439
Ours	**0.766**	**0.854**	**0.953**	**0.8657**

Table 6. Comparison of our method with state-of-the-art methods on the PASCAL 3D+ dataset [39] in terms of IoU. '+pose' indicates that the method requires ground truth camera parameters as input during test.

Method	Planes	Vehicles
CSDM [41]	0.398	0.600
DRC + pose [42]	0.415	0.666
CMR [13]	0.460	0.640
VPL + pose [15]	0.475	0.679
Ours	**0.584**	**0.853**

Fig. 6. Reconstruction results of our method and the CMR method [13] on CUB-200-2011. For easy comparison, we overlay ground truth masks (in grey color) with the reconstructed ones (in cyan color), and highlight their common regions in red color. (Color figure online)

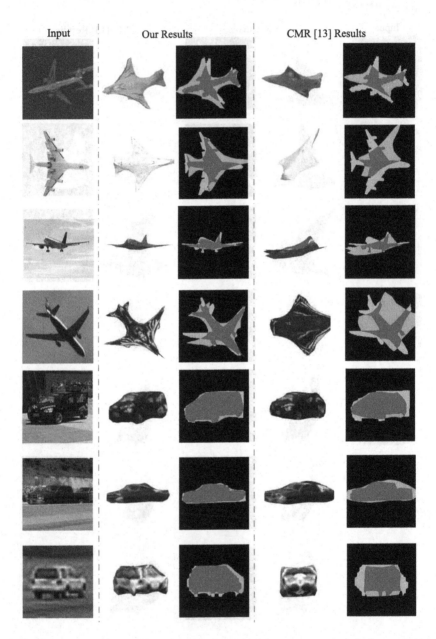

Fig. 7. Reconstruction results of our method and the CMR method [13] on PASCAL 3D+. For easy comparison, we overlay ground truth masks (in grey color) with the reconstructed ones (in cyan color), and highlight their common regions in red color. (Color figure online)

5   Conclusion

In this paper, we have made an attempt to boost the accuracy of reconstructing 3D objects with large shape variation from single in-the-wild images when 3D supervision is not available during training. Specifically, it provides an efficient and effective fusion module for aggregating multi-scale features for 3D reconstruction, and trains the entire reconstruction network with shape-sensitive geometric constraints including edge constraint, side output mask constraint, and initial shape constraint. Moreover, by augmenting the training data via manipulating the background in training images, our method can better deal with real-world images with distracting background.

Acknowledgments. This work is supported by the National Natural Science Foundation of China (61773270, 61971005).

References

1. Zhang, P., Liu, W., Lei, Y., Lu, H., Yang, X.: Cascaded context pyramid for full-resolution 3D semantic scene completion. In: IEEE International Conference on Computer Vision (ICCV), pp. 7801–7810 (2019)
2. Kar, A., Häne, C., Malik, J.: Learning a multi-view stereo machine. In: Guyon, I., et al. (eds.) Advances in Neural Information Processing Systems (NeurIPS), pp. 365–376 (2017)
3. Lin, C.H., et al.: Photometric mesh optimization for video-aligned 3D object reconstruction. In: IEEE Conference on Computer Vision and Pattern Recognition (CVPR), pp. 969–978 (2019)
4. Sridhar, S., Rempe, D., Valentin, J., Bouaziz, S., Guibas, L.J.: Multiview aggregation for learning category-specific shape reconstruction. In: Advances in Neural Information Processing Systems (NeurIPS), pp. 2348–2359 (2019)
5. Shen, W., Jia, Y., Wu, Y.: 3D shape reconstruction from images in the frequency domain. In: IEEE Conference on Computer Vision and Pattern Recognition (CVPR), pp. 4471–4479 (2019)
6. Yang, G., Huang, X., Hao, Z., Liu, M.Y., Belongie, S., Hariharan, B.: PointFlow: 3D point cloud generation with continuous normalizing flows. In: IEEE International Conference on Computer Vision (ICCV), pp. 4541–4550 (2019)
7. Pan, J., Han, X., Chen, W., Tang, J., Jia, K.: Deep mesh reconstruction from single RGB images via topology modification networks. In: IEEE International Conference on Computer Vision (ICCV), pp. 9964–9973 (2019)
8. Richter, S.R., Roth, S.: Matryoshka networks: predicting 3D geometry via nested shape layers. In: IEEE Conference on Computer Vision and Pattern Recognition (CVPR), pp. 1936–1944 (2018)
9. Smith, E., Fujimoto, S., Romero, A., Meger, D.: Geometrics: exploiting geometric structure for graph-encoded objects. In: Chaudhuri, K., Salakhutdinov, R. (eds.) International Conference on Machine Learning (ICML), pp. 5866–5876 (2019)
10. Tatarchenko, M., Dosovitskiy, A., Brox, T.: Octree generating networks: efficient convolutional architectures for high-resolution 3D outputs. In: IEEE International Conference on Computer Vision (ICCV), pp. 2088–2096 (2017)

11. Blanz, V., Vetter, T.: A morphable model for the synthesis of 3D faces. In: International Conference on Computer Graphics and Interactive Techniques (SIGGRAPH), pp. 187–194 (1999)
12. Wang, N., Zhang, Y., Li, Z., Fu, Y., Liu, W., Jiang, Y.G.: Pixel2Mesh: generating 3D mesh models from single RGB images. In: European Conference on Computer Vision (ECCV), pp. 52–67 (2018)
13. Kanazawa, A., Tulsiani, S., Efros, A.A., Malik, J.: Learning category-specific mesh reconstruction from image collections. In: European Conference on Computer Vision (ECCV), pp. 371–386 (2018)
14. Cha, G., Lee, M., Oh, S.: Unsupervised 3D reconstruction networks. In: The IEEE International Conference on Computer Vision (ICCV), pp. 3849–3858 (2019)
15. Kato, H., Harada, T.: Learning view priors for single-view 3D reconstruction. In: IEEE Conference on Computer Vision and Pattern Recognition (CVPR), pp. 9778–9787 (2019)
16. Liu, S., Saito, S., Chen, W., Li, H.: Learning to infer implicit surfaces without 3D supervision. In: Advances in Neural Information Processing Systems (NeurIPS), pp. 8293–8304 (2019)
17. Choy, C.B., Xu, D., Gwak, J.Y., Chen, K., Savarese, S.: 3D-R2N2: a unified approach for single and multi-view 3D object reconstruction. In: Leibe, B., Matas, J., Sebe, N., Welling, M. (eds.) ECCV 2016. LNCS, vol. 9912, pp. 628–644. Springer, Cham (2016). https://doi.org/10.1007/978-3-319-46484-8_38
18. Girdhar, R., Fouhey, D.F., Rodriguez, M., Gupta, A.: Learning a predictable and generative vector representation for objects. In: Leibe, B., Matas, J., Sebe, N., Welling, M. (eds.) ECCV 2016. LNCS, vol. 9910, pp. 484–499. Springer, Cham (2016). https://doi.org/10.1007/978-3-319-46466-4_29
19. Wang, P.S., Liu, Y., Guo, Y.X., Sun, C.Y., Tong, X.: Adaptive O-CNN: a patch-based deep representation of 3D shapes. ACM Trans. Graph. (TOG) **37**, 1–11 (2018)
20. Fan, H., Su, H., Guibas, L.J.: A point set generation network for 3D object reconstruction from a single image. In: IEEE Conference on Computer Vision and Pattern Recognition (CVPR), pp. 605–613 (2017)
21. Insafutdinov, E., Dosovitskiy, A.: Unsupervised learning of shape and pose with differentiable point clouds. In: Advances in Neural Information Processing Systems (NeurIPS), pp. 2802–2812 (2018)
22. Kurenkov, A., et al.: DeformNet: free-form deformation network for 3D shape reconstruction. In: Advances in Neural Information Processing Systems (NeurIPS), pp. 858–866 (2017)
23. Lin, C.H., Kong, C., Lucey, S.: Learning efficient point cloud generation for dense 3D object reconstruction. In: AAAI Conference on Artificial Intelligence (AAAI) (2018)
24. Wei, Y., Liu, S., Zhao, W., Lu, J., Zhou, J.: Conditional single-view shape generation for multi-view stereo reconstruction. In: IEEE Conference on Computer Vision and Pattern Recognition (CVPR), pp. 9651–9660 (2019)
25. Groueix, T., Fisher, M., Kim, V.G., Russell, B., Aubry, M.: AtlasNet: a papier-mâché approach to learning 3D surface generation. In: IEEE Conference on Computer Vision and Pattern Recognition (CVPR), pp. 216–224 (2018)
26. Mescheder, L., Oechsle, M., Niemeyer, M., Nowozin, S., Geiger, A.: Occupancy networks: learning 3D reconstruction in function space. In: IEEE Conference on Computer Vision and Pattern Recognition (CVPR), pp. 4460–4470 (2019)

27. Xu, Q., Wang, W., Ceylan, D., Mech, R., Neumann, U.: DISN: deep implicit surface network for high-quality single-view 3D reconstruction. In: Advances in Neural Information Processing Systems (NeurIPS), pp. 490–500 (2019)
28. Cashman, T.J., Fitzgibbon, A.W.: What shape are dolphins? Building 3D morphable models from 2D images. IEEE Trans. Pattern Anal. Mach. Intell. (PAMI) **35**(1), 232–244 (2013)
29. Ntouskos, V., et al.: Component-wise modeling of articulated objects. In: IEEE International Conference on Computer Vision (ICCV), pp. 2327–2335 (2015)
30. Kanazawa, A., Kovalsky, S., Basri, R., Jacobs, D.W.: Learning 3D deformation of animals from 2D images. In: Computer Graphics Forum, pp. 365–374 (2016)
31. Zuffi, S., Kanazawa, A., Jacobs, D., Black, M.: 3D menagerie: modeling the 3D shape and pose of animals. In: IEEE Conference on Computer Vision and Pattern Recognition (CVPR), pp. 6365–6373 (2017)
32. Zuffi, S., Kanazawa, A., Black, M.J.: Lions and tigers and bears: capturing non-rigid, 3D, articulated shape from images. In: IEEE Conference on Computer Vision and Pattern Recognition (CVPR), pp. 3955–3963 (2018)
33. Zuffi, S., Kanazawa, A., Berger-Wolf, T., Black, M.J.: Three-D Safari: learning to estimate zebra pose, shape, and texture from images "in the wild". In: IEEE International Conference on Computer Vision (ICCV), pp. 5359–5368 (2019)
34. Wen, C., Zhang, Y., Li, Z., Fu, Y.: Pixel2Mesh++: multi-view 3D mesh generation via deformation. In: IEEE International Conference on Computer Vision (ICCV), pp. 1042–1051 (2019)
35. Zhao, L., Peng, X., Tian, Y., Kapadia, M., Metaxas, D.N.: Semantic graph convolutional networks for 3D human pose regression. In: IEEE Conference on Computer Vision and Pattern Recognition (CVPR), pp. 3425–3435 (2019)
36. He, K., Zhang, X., Ren, S., Sun, J.: Deep residual learning for image recognition. In: IEEE Conference on Computer Vision and Pattern Recognition (CVPR), pp. 770–778 (2016)
37. Kato, H., Ushiku, Y., Harada, T.: Neural 3D mesh renderer. In: IEEE Conference on Computer Vision and Pattern Recognition (CVPR), pp. 3907–3916 (2018)
38. Zhang, R., Isola, P., Efros, A.A., Shechtman, E., Wang, O.: The unreasonable effectiveness of deep features as a perceptual metric. In: IEEE Conference on Computer Vision and Pattern Recognition (CVPR), pp. 586–595 (2018)
39. Xiang, Y., Mottaghi, R., Savarese, S.: Beyond PASCAL: a benchmark for 3D object detection in the wild. In: IEEE Winter Conference on Applications of Computer Vision (WACV), pp. 75–82 (2014)
40. Wu, Y., Kirillov, A., Massa, F., Lo, W.Y., Girshick, R.: Detectron2 (2019). https://github.com/facebookresearch/detectron2
41. Kar, A., Tulsiani, S., Carreira, J., Malik, J.: Category-specific object reconstruction from a single image. In: IEEE Conference on Computer Vision and Pattern Recognition (CVPR), pp. 1966–1974 (2015)
42. Tulsiani, S., Zhou, T., Efros, A.A., Malik, J.: Multi-view supervision for single-view reconstruction via differentiable ray consistency. In: IEEE Conference on Computer Vision and Pattern Recognition (CVPR), pp. 2626–2634 (2017)

HPGCNN: Hierarchical Parallel Group Convolutional Neural Networks for Point Clouds Processing

Jisheng Dang and Jun Yang[✉]

Lanzhou Jiaotong University, Lanzhou 730070, China
yangj@mail.lzjtu.cn

Abstract. To achieve high performance but less complexity for point clouds processing, we introduce HPGCNN, an efficient and lightweight neural architecture. The key component in our approach is the Hierarchical Parallel Group Convolution (HPGConv) operation. It can capture both the discriminative independent single-point features and local geometric features of point clouds at the same time to enhance the richness of the features with less redundant information by designing two hierarchical parallel group convolutions, which is helpful to recognize elusive shapes. To significantly further reduce complexity and natively prevent overfitting, we use global average pooling and a full connected layer instead of the traditional three full connected layers for classification. Moreover, to further capture the contextual fine-grained features with higher-level semantics, we introduce a novel multi-semantic scale strategy to progressively increase the receptive field of each local area through the information communication of local areas of different scales. Extensive experiments show that our HPGCNN clearly surpasses state-of-the-art approaches for point clouds classification dataset ModelNet40 and large scale semantic segmentation datasets ShapeNet Parts, S3DIS, vKITTI and SemanticKITTI in terms of accuracy and complexity.

1 Introduction

3D point clouds recognition and segmentation is the key technology of 3D point clouds processing and analysis, which is widely used in the fields of autonomous driving [1,2], intelligent robotics [3,4], environment perception [5,6], shape synthesis and modeling [7], etc. However, the irregularity and disorder of 3D point clouds have hindered the development of 3D point clouds recognition and segmentation technology. 3D point clouds recognition and segmentation have become a hot and difficult research topic in the field of computer vision and computer graphics. In order to improve the accuracy of 3D point clouds recognition and segmentation, a large number of methods, mostly composed of traditional methods and deep learning methods, have been proposed. Traditional methods [8,9] are used to design the feature descriptors of 3D point clouds manually, researchers rely on their existing domain knowledge to extract the features of

© Springer Nature Switzerland AG 2021
H. Ishikawa et al. (Eds.): ACCV 2020, LNCS 12622, pp. 20–37, 2021.
https://doi.org/10.1007/978-3-030-69525-5_2

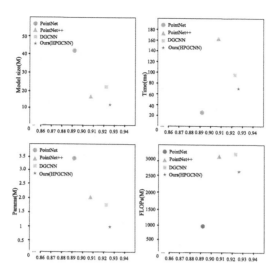

Fig. 1. Comparison with the state-of-the-art approaches in terms of accuracy, parameters, forward time and model size.

the 3D point clouds which are used further for the task of point clouds recognition and segmentation. Although these methods are effective when used on small datasets, their generalization ability is too poor to be suitable for other large scale datasets. Over the past few years, Convolutional Neural Network(CNN) has demonstrated its powerful abstraction ability of semantic information in computer vision field. Due to the complexity of the internal structure of 3D point clouds, deep learning methods used for 3D models recognition and segmentation still face with great challenges, there have been many achievements in this research area though.

However, currently most deep learning methods focus mainly on how to improve the recognition accuracy with little attention being paid to and few people considering such important issues as the model complexity, the computational complexity and eliminating redundancy of convolution operation is rarely mentioned for point clouds processing and analysis. In the point clouds processing domain and especially for some resource-constrained applications, such as autonomous driving which needs to process large scale point clouds with limited resources, the less redundancy information there is the better. Besides, as mentioned earlier, existing convolution kernels lack the ability to capture both the discriminative local geometric features and the independent single-point features of the point clouds at the same time, resulting in the features extracted that are inadequate. In fact, the local geometric features fully mine the fine-grained details of the local area, but it only focuses on the relative relationship between the point pairs, ignoring the absolute position relationship of each point in the 3D space, which destroys the independent single-point structure features of each point extracted from the most original three-dimensional coordinates information of the independent points without considering the neighborhood points. Therefore, a powerful convolution kernel should simultaneously take into account both discriminative local geometric features and independent single-point features to significantly improve the integrity of the features. We are most interested in improving the ability of the convolution kernel to extract more complete features while reducing the redundancy of the convolution kernel, which is beneficial to achieve a better balance among three aspects: model complexity, computation complexity and recognition accuracy. The redundancy comes from two extents: the local geometric features of local point clouds and the independent single-point features of each independent point. Therefore, we present a novel module built of a stack of blocks called Hierarchical Parallel Group Convolution (HPGConv). Our main contributions are summarized as follows:

- We propose an effective convolution operation, the hierarchical parallel group convolution, which can reduce the redundancy of the convolution kernel, and has the ability to encode both the discriminative local geometric features and the independent single-point features of the point clouds at the same time to enhance the completeness of features.
- Instead of adopting the traditional three fully connected layers used for classification in CNN, we adopt the global average pooling with a fully connected layer strategy to reduce the complexity and natively prevent overfitting in the overall structure.
- We introduce a novel multi-semantic scale strategy to progressively increase the receptive field of local areas of different scales, thereby effectively capturing contextual fine-grained features with higher level semantics.
- We propose a hierarchical parallel group convolutional neural network aimed at both in depth redundancy reduction and in width exploitation of the more discriminative independent single-point features and local geometric features for point clouds analysis. Extensive experiments on classification and segmentation tasks verify the effectiveness of our approach.

2   Related Work

(1) **Volumetric-based Methods.** In literatures [10–13], the irregular point clouds is transformed into regular 3D volumetric grids, and then 3DCNN is used to extract feature descriptor directly from the 3D volumetric grids to complete the point clouds classification and segmentation tasks. However, the sparsity of the 3D volumetric grids results in a large amount of memory consumption. To solve the problem of data sparsity, [14–16] adopt sparse structures like octrees or hash-maps that allow larger grids to enhance performance. Although they achieve leading results on point clouds classification and segmentation, their primary limitation is the heavy computation cost, especially when processing large-scale point clouds.

(2) **Projection-based Methods.** Projection-based methods [17–20] first project/flatten the 3D point clouds onto 2D views, and then the 2D views are input to classic 2D deep learning networks to extract their features to

leverage the success of 2D CNNs. For large-scale scene point clouds segmentation, these methods have some problems such as surface occlusion and density variation. Tatarchenko et al. [21] projects the local neighborhood onto the local tangent plane, and then processes them with two-dimensional convolution. However, projection-based methods have the problems of data redundancy and geometric structure information loss.

(3) **Methods based on geometric deep learning.** Geometric deep learning [22–24] is the approach for processing non-Euclidean structural point clouds using deep neural networks. Qi et al. [25] proposes the PointNet which uses Multi-Layer Perceptron (MLP) to extract the features of each point in the point clouds and then, in preparation for achieving the goal of 3D point clouds recognition, obtains the global feature descriptor by aggregating the features of all the points through a max pooling layer. In literature [26], PointNet++ hierarchically extracts features by arranging local point clouds. In literature [27], the local geometric features can be captured while the permutation invariance is guaranteed by establishing the dynamic graph CNN. The PointCNN network proposed in literature [28] learns an X-transformation from the input point clouds which is a generalization of the CNN leveraging of the spatial-local correlation from the data representing in the point clouds. A novel convolutional network structure called SpiderCNN [29] extracts deep semantic features by extending convolutional operations from regular grids to irregular point sets. PCNN [30] provides a flexible framework for adapting standard image-based CNNs to the point clouds setting using extension and restriction operations. Liu et al. [31] proposes the relation-shape convolution operation to encode the geometric relations of the points explicitly, thus resulting in good shape awareness. The graph convolutional neural network proves the advantage of graph representation method in non-Euclidean data processing tasks, it mainly contains of spectral representation [32–34] and surface representation [23, 26, 35–37]. These methods combine the features of local surface patches and are not affected by patch deformation in Euclidean space, so local geometric features can be fully explored. For large scale scene point clouds processing, Hu et al. [38] adopts random sampling and local features aggregation module which significantly speed up the processing of large scale point clouds. SPG [39] preprocesses the large scale point clouds as super graphs to learn per superpoint semantics.

3   Hierarchical Parallel Group Convolutional Neural Network

In this section, we explain the architecture of our Hierarchical Parallel Group Convolution (HPGConv for short) which is shown in Fig. 2 and Hierarchical Parallel Group Convolutional Neural Network (HPGCNN for short) which is shown in Fig. 3.

3.1 Hierarchical Parallel Group Convolution

Our HPGconv consists of two group convolutions: the Hierarchical MLP Group Convolution (HMGConv for short) and the Hierarchical Graph Group Convolution (HGGConv for short).

Hierarchical MLP Group Convolution. In the HMGConv, the parameters of MLP are divided into respective M groups, and it can be denoted as $\mathbf{W}^k = \left\{ \mathbf{W}_{11}^k, \mathbf{W}_{22}^k, ..., \mathbf{W}_{MM}^k \right\}$. In order to overcome the problem that information cannot communicate between the different-level feature maps of different groups of the standard group convolution and leverage the inter-group information more effectively, we hierarchically fuse feature maps of different groups. Specifically, we fuse the feature map $\mathbf{x}^k$ of $(m+1)^{th}$ group with the output $\mathbf{W}_{mm}^k \mathbf{x}^k$ of mth group on the channel dimension after the feature map of the mth group directly go through the $\mathbf{W}_{mm}^k$, and then feed the feature map into $\mathbf{W}_{(m+1)(m+1)}^k$. The output $\mathbf{x}^{k+1}$ of kth layer HMGConv to capture independent single-point features is given as follows,

$$
\mathbf{x}_M^{k+1} = diag(\mathbf{W}_{mm}^k {}_{m=1}^{M}) \times \mathbf{x}^k =
\begin{bmatrix}
\mathbf{W}_{11}^k & 0 & 0 & 0 \\
0 & \mathbf{W}_{22}^k & 0 & 0 \\
\vdots & \vdots & \vdots & \vdots \\
0 & 0 & 0 & \mathbf{W}_{MM}^k
\end{bmatrix}
$$

$$
\times
\begin{bmatrix}
\mathbf{x}^k & 0 & 0 & 0 \\
0 & \mathbf{x}^k = \mathbf{x}^k + \mathbf{W}_{11}^k \mathbf{x}^k & 0 & 0 \\
\vdots & \vdots & \vdots & \vdots \\
0 & 0 & 0 & \mathbf{x}^k = \mathbf{x}^k + \mathbf{W}_{(M-1)(M-1)}^k \mathbf{x}^k
\end{bmatrix}
\tag{1}
$$

where k denotes the kth convolution layer. We fuse the features of all the groups sufficiently to facilitate information communication by stacking group convolutions together and then through shuffling the feature channels. As a result of information communication, each group of the updated groups contains information from the other groups. We carry out the channel shuffle $\mathbf{P}^T$ by performing matrix reconstruction and matrix transpose operations in turns.

$$
\mathbf{y}_M = \mathbf{P}^T \mathbf{x}_M^{k+1} = R_P * T_P * R_P * \mathbf{x}_M^{k+1}
\tag{2}
$$

where R_P and T_P indicate the matrix reconstruction and the matrix transpose operations respectively.

Hierarchical Graph Group Convolution. Although our HMGConv fully explores the discriminative independent single-point features, it lacks the ability to capture the local geometric features, so we propose the HGGConv. A local area is constructed by searching the k nearest points, neighboring the sampling point, to calculate edge features $\mathbf{y}_j$ and fusion features $\mathbf{y}_{ij}$:

$$
\mathbf{y}_j = (\mathbf{x}_{ij} - \mathbf{x}_i), \mathbf{x}_i \in \mathbb{R}^F; \forall \mathbf{x}_{ij} \in Neighbors(\mathbf{x}_i)
\tag{3}
$$

$$
\mathbf{y}_{ij} = (\mathbf{x}_i, \mathbf{x}_{ij} - \mathbf{x}_i), \mathbf{x}_i \in \mathbb{R}^F; \forall \mathbf{x}_{ij} \in Neighbors(\mathbf{x}_i)
\tag{4}
$$

Similarly, the parameters of the graph convolution are divided into G groups to extract the discriminative local geometric features in each group. We also hierarchically fuse the extracted high-level features of the previous group with the input features of the next group to enhance the interaction of feature maps between different groups,

$$
\mathbf{x}_G^{k+1} = diag(\mathbf{W}_{gg}^k{}_{g=1}^G) \times \mathbf{x}^k = \begin{bmatrix} \mathbf{W}_{11}^k & 0 & 0 & 0 \\ 0 & \mathbf{W}_{22}^k & 0 & 0 \\ \vdots & \vdots & \vdots & \vdots \\ 0 & 0 & 0 & \mathbf{W}_{GG}^k \end{bmatrix}
$$

$$
\times \begin{bmatrix} \mathbf{x}_i^k & 0 & 0 & 0 \\ 0 & \mathbf{y}_j^k = \mathbf{y}_j^k + \mathbf{W}_{11}^k \mathbf{x}_i^k & 0 & 0 \\ \vdots & \vdots & \vdots & \vdots \\ 0 & 0 & 0\ \mathbf{y}_{ij}^k = \mathbf{y}_{ij}^k + \mathbf{W}_{(G-1)(G-1)}^k \mathbf{y}_j^k \end{bmatrix}
\tag{5}
$$

Mentioned earlier, the channel shuffling facilitates information communication between different groups.

$$
\mathbf{y}_G = \mathbf{P}^T \mathbf{x}_G^{k+1} = R_P * T_P * R_P * \mathbf{x}_G^{k+1}
\tag{6}
$$

Finally, we fuse the discriminative independent single-point features with the local geometric features to enhance the feature richness.

$$
\mathbf{x}^{k+1} = \mathbf{y} = Concat(\mathbf{y}_M, \mathbf{y}_G) = Concat(\mathbf{P}^T(\mathbf{x}_M^{k+1} + \mathbf{x}_G^{k+1}))
$$
$$
= Concat(\mathbf{P}^T(diag(\mathbf{W}_{mm}^k{}_{m=1}^M) + diag(\mathbf{W}_{gg}^k{}_{g=1}^G) \times \mathbf{x}^k
\tag{7}
$$

In summary, our HPGConv block can be formulated as

$$
\mathbf{x}^{k+1} = \mathbf{x}^k(\mathbf{W}_M + \mathbf{W}_G),
\tag{8}
$$

where $\mathbf{W}_M$ and $\mathbf{W}_G$ denote the parameters of the HMGConv and the HGGConv. We let $\mathbf{W} = (\mathbf{W}_G + \mathbf{W}_M)$ be the composite convolution kernel, then we get the following formula,

$$
\mathbf{x}^{k+1} = \mathbf{W}\mathbf{x}^k
\tag{9}
$$

which implies that an HPGConv block is equivalent to a regular convolution with the convolution kernel being the product of two sparse kernels. The computational complexity (FLOPs) and model complexity (parameters) of the HPGConv can be calculated by Eqs. 10 and 11 respectively,

$$
params = \frac{F_{input} \times W}{g} \times \frac{F_{output}}{g} \times g
$$
$$
= \frac{F_{input} \times F_{ouput} \times W}{g}
\tag{10}
$$

$$
FLOPs = \frac{N \times (1+k) \times F_{input} \times F_{output} \times W}{g}
\tag{11}
$$

Since we group the input channel and output channel separately, both of the input channel and the output channel are reduced to 1/g. Then, the increase of results will be limited by the fusion operation to only g times. Therefore, the final output of the parameters and FLOPs will be reduced to 1/g. Our HPG-Conv is an efficient and universal convolution operation with fewer redundant parameters that can enhance the encoding of more discriminative information to capture both the local geometric features and the independent single-point structural features at the same time for accomplishing accurate elusive shape. Our HPGConv can be integrated into multiple existing pipelines for point clouds processing easily.

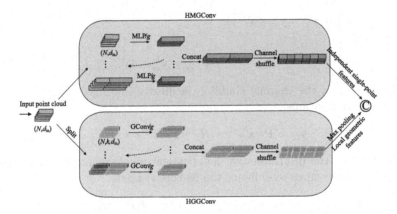

Fig. 2. HPGConv operation.

3.2 Hierarchical Parallel Group Convolutional Neural Network

Our Hierarchical Parallel Group Convolutional Neural Network (HPGCNN) architecture for point clouds classification and segmentation is shown in Fig. 3. In addition to HPGConv, it also contains two components: (1) multi-semantic scale, (2) global average pooling with a fully connected layer.

Multi-semantic Scale. Similar to PointNet++ [27], we adopt the Farthest Point Sampling (FPS) to iteratively select M, $(M < N)$, points from the point clouds. Then, we use the KNN algorithm to build local areas by searching a fixed number of nearest neighboring point for each sampling point according to the sorted Euclidean distance in 3D space. In order to capture the multi-scale local geometric features, for each sample point in the point clouds, we construct multi-scale local area structure by finding the top $[K_1, ..., K_t, ..., K_T]$ nearest neighbors. Taking into account the fact that there is no information interaction between local areas of different scales, we introduce multi-semantic scale strategy to input the high-level features extracted from the previous scale local area into the next scale local area to extend its receptive field. This allows the local areas of different scales to have larger receptive field which in turn leads to obtaining the higher semantic-level features that are beneficial to the acquirement of the multi-level contextual semantic information.

Global Average Pooling with a Fully Connected Layer. To achieve classification more efficiently, we first introduce the strategy of global average pooling with a fully connected layer instead of traditional three fully connected layer. Specifically, the average value of feature maps is invariant to the order of input points and we use global average pooling as the symmetric function. One advantage of the global average pooling is that it combines the global information of the feature maps by calculating the average value which strengthens the correspondence between the feature maps and the category, and is closer to the semantic category information. Another advantage is that the removal of the two fully connected layers results in a significant reduction in the model complexity and the computational complexity, thus overfitting the overall structure is natively avoided at this layer, and the cumbersome dropout layer [40] is no longer needed. As a final tribute to the global average pooling, we can say that by summing out the spatial information, it is more robust to the spatial translations of the point clouds.

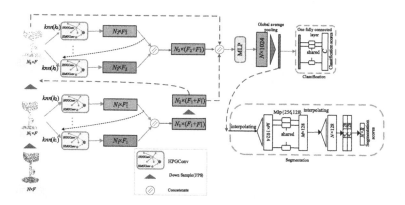

Fig. 3. Overview of HPGCNN.

4   Experiments

4.1   Shape Recognition

For the 3D point clouds recognition task, we carry out our experiments on standard public dataset ModelNet40 [10]. Table 1 shows the comparison results, obtained out of the ModelNet40 dataset, between our model and the recent state-of-the-art methods in terms of both accuracy and complexity, HGGC represents hierarchical graph group convolution. Figure 1 shows the efficiency of our model compared to other state-of-the-art methods. As can be seen from Table 1, our model outperforms the advanced DGCNN approach by 0.4% in terms of accuracy and reduces the amount of parameters, FLOPs, forward time and model size by 44.4%, 18.8%, 24.9% and 45.2% respectively. The effectiveness of our HPGCNN is evident from the results. We can also observe that our strategy of replacing the traditional three fully connected layers with the global average pooling and one fully connected layer is effective because the strategy successfully reduces the model and the computation complexity while maintaining a considerable recognition accuracy. Although our HGGC achieves the best performance in model complexity and computational complexity, it only focuses on local geometric features, drowning independent single point features, and weakens feature richness, leading to a decline in recognition ability. It is also worth mentioning that combining the HPGConv with the Deep Convolution (DConv) produces better results. In Fig. 4, we adopt T-distributed Stochastic Neighbor Embedding (T-SNE) to show that our HPGConv has the ability to extract more discriminative features, points with the same color belong to the same category. It can be seen that the extracted features by our HPGConv are much more discriminative than original point clouds and features extracted by DGCNN after training 250 epochs.

Table 1. Recognition results on the ModelNet40 dataset

Methods	mA (%)	OA (%)	Params (million)	size (MB)	FLOPs (million)	Time (ms)
VoxNet [11]	83.0	85.9	–	–	–	–
PointNet [25]	86.0	89.2	3.4	41.8	918.6	**24**
PN++ [26]	–	90.7	2.0	17.7	3136.0	163.2
KC-Net [41]	–	91.0	–	–	–	–
SpecGCN [42]	–	91.5	2.1	–	1112.0	11254.0
Kd-Net [43]	–	91.8	–	–	–	–
DGCNN [27]	90.2	92.2	1.8	22.1	3212.0	94.6
PCNN [30]	–	92.3	8.2	93.8	–	–
SpiderCNN [29]	90.7	92.4	–	36.9	–	–
PointCNN [28]	88.1	92.2	0.7	43.6	1682.0	–
Ours (HPGC-3FC)	90.1	92.4	1.6	22.9	2621	72.7
Ours (HGGC)	88.6	91.9	**0.5**	**6.5**	**771**	43.8
Ours (HPGC)	90.3	92.5	0.6	7.3	1079	59.6
Ours (HPGC+DC)	**90.4**	**92.6**	1.0	12.1	2609	71.0

Ablation Study. We have also carried out experiments on the ModelNet40 dataset with various settings of our model taken into consideration. Table 2 shows the performance of our model with different numbers of group of HMGConv and HGGConv. It can be observed that, when the numbers of group of HMGConv or the numbers of group of HGGConv increases till it reaches specified number and then decreases, our model has higher recognition accuracy OA and lower model complexity and computation complexity, this is because of the

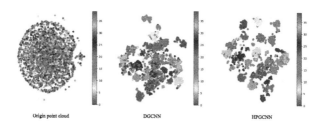

Fig. 4. Visualization of original point clouds and extracted discriminative 1024-dimensional features by HPGConv.

Table 2. Comparison of accuracy and complexity of different numbers of the groups

		OA	FLOPs	Time	Size	Params
$G = 1$	$M = 1$	92.3	4039	92.2	24.0	1.8
$G = 2$	$M = 2$	92.6	2609	71.0	12.1	1.0
$G = 3$	$M = 3$	92.4	500	50.0	7.2	0.35

fact that the presence of multiple groups helps capture more useful discriminative information with fewer parameters. In the case of our model ($G = 2$, $M = 2$), the FLOPs, the parameters, the model size and forward time are reduced by 35.4%, 55.6%, 49.6% and 23.0% respectively and the OA increases by 0.3% when compared to no grouping operation ($G = 1$, $M = 1$), which verifies the effectiveness of our HPGConv. However, we notice that the presence of the groups in a much larger number ($G = 3$, $M = 3$) degenerates the performance of our model. The reason is probably that only limited useful feature information is encoded by each individual group when we split the feature channels to too many groups. Beside the aforementioned settings, we try out our model with other different settings and the experimental results are shown in Table 3. It can be seen that the performance of HPGCNN is better when we adopt hierarchical strategy. Because it can increase the information interaction between groups to take advantage of the inter-group information. Multi-semantic scale strategy is better than traditional multi-scale strategy, which can increase the receptive field of local point clouds of different scales to capture contextual features with higher level semantic information, help to recognize fine-grained details.

Table 3. Ablation study of our model

Hierarchical	Multi-scale	Multi-semantic scale	OA (%)
			92.3
	√		92.4
		√	92.5
√	√	√	92.6

4.2 Semantic Segmentation

In order to test the effectiveness of our HPGCNN further for the fine-grained shape analysis of point clouds, we evaluate the performance of our model on the four public large scale semantic segmentation datasets ShapeNet Parts [44], S3DIS [45], vKITTI [46] and SemanticKITTI [47]. In all experiments, we implement the models with Tensorflow on one RTX 2080 GPU.

(1) **Evaluation on ShapeNet Parts.** Table 4 presents the quantitative results of different approaches on ShapeNet Parts. It can be seen that our HPGCNN has certain advantages in terms of the mIoU and FLOPs, specially the FLOPs is significantly lower than all other mainstream approaches. This because our HPGConv can significantly reduce the redundancy of the convolution kernel to encode more discriminative information.

Table 4. Comparison of segmentation accuracy of different approaches on the ShapeNet Parts dataset

Methods	mIoU (%)	FLOPs (million)
PointNet [25]	83.7	17841
PointNet++ [26]	85.1	–
DGCNN [27]	85.1	9110
LDGCNN [48]	85.1	28656
HPGCNN (ours)	**85.4**	**4527**

(2) **Evaluation on S3DIS.** Table 5, 6 and 7 show quantitative comparison of our HPGCNN with other state-of-the-art methods on large scale point clouds dataset, we can also see that our HPGCNN performs better when the tasks involved are large-scale point clouds processing. The OA of our HPGCNN when invoked on the S3DIS dataset reaches 90.0%, surpassing all the existing advanced approaches by a large margin and the mIoU is second only to KPconv. Notably, HPGCNN also achieves superior performance on six out of the twelve classes. The qualitative results are visualized in Fig. 5, it is easy to observe that prediction results of our HPGCNN is closer to Ground Truth. Compared to the most advanced approach SSP+SPG, our HPGCNN effectively improves the ability to recognize fine-grained details of elusive small object categories, such as the edges of the boards and the beams. Although global overall structural information and local geometric details of these elusive classes are very similar, to correctly recognize them requires a combination of global single point features and local geometric features.

(3) **Evaluation on vKITTI.** As shown in Table 6, our HPGCNN outperforms all existing advanced methods in terms of both mIoU and OA by a large margin on vKITTI dataset. Compared with the most advanced approach

Table 5. Comparison of segmentation accuracy of different approaches on the S3DIS dataset (6-fold cross validation)

Methods	OA (%)	mIoU (%)	Ceil	Floor	Wall	Beam	Col	Wind	Door	Chair	Table	Book	Sofa	Boad	Clut.
PointNet [25]	78.5	47.6	88.0	88.7	69.3	42.4	23.1	47.5	51.6	42	54.1	38.2	9.6	29.4	35.2
MS+CU [49]	79.2	47.8	-	-	-	-	-	-	-	-	-	-	-	-	-
G+RCU [49]	81.1	49.7	90.3	92.1	67.9	44.7	24.2	52.3	51.2	47.4	58.1	39	6.9	30	41.9
PointNet++ [26]	-	-	-	-	-	-	-	-	-	-	-	-	-	-	-
DGCNN [27]	84.4	56.1	-	-	-	-	-	-	-	-	-	-	-	-	-
3P-RNN [50]	86.9	56.3	-	-	-	-	-	-	-	-	-	-	-	-	-
RSNet [51]	-	56.5	92.5	92.8	78.6	32.8	34.4	51.6	68.1	60.1	59.7	50.2	16.4	44.9	52.0
SPG [39]	85.5	62.1	89.9	95.1	76.4	62.8	47.1	55.3	68.4	73.5	69.2	63.2	45.9	8.7	52.9
LSANet [52]	86.8	62.2													-
PointCNN [28]	88.1	65.4	94.8	97.3	75.8	63.3	51.7	58.4	57.2	71.6	69.1	39.1	61.2	52.2	58.6
PointWeb [53]	87.3	66.7	-	-	-	-	-	-	-	-	-	-	-	-	-
ShellNet [54]	87.1	66.8	-	-	-	-	-	-	-	-	-	-	-	-	-
HEPIN [55]	88.2	67.8	-	-	-	-	-	-	-	-	-	-	-	-	-
KPConv [56]	-	**70.6**	93.6	92.4	**83.1**	63.9	54.3	**66.1**	**76.6**	57.8	64	**69.3**	**74.9**	**61.3**	60.3
SSP+SPG [57]	87.9	68.4	91.7	95.5	80.8	62.2	**54.9**	58.8	68.4	78.4	69.2	64.3	52.0	54.2	59.2
RandLA-Net [38]	87.2	68.5	-	-	-	-	-	-	-	-	-	-	-	-	-
Ours	**90.3**	69.2	**95.4**	**97.5**	81.2	**73.7**	44.8	55.6	71.3	**86.5**	**76.3**	68.9	30.0	52.3	**66.0**

SSP+SPG, the OA and mIoU of HPGCNN improves by 7.4% and 9.1% respectively. Figure 6 illustrates our qualitative visualization of six samples by randomly selecting one scene from each of the six city scene sequences. It can be seen that our HPGCNN has achieved surprising segmentation results out of all the six scene sequences. In particular, our approach can correctly recognize the boundary between the two elusive categories terrain and road, although the overall shape of these items is greatly similar and they differ in terms of their local details. The reason is that our HPGConv can capture both global single-point structural features and fine-grained local geometric features to complement each other, making the extracted features more sufficient.

(4) **Evaluation on SemanticKITTI.** In Table 7, we compare HPGCNN with other state-of-the-art methods on SemanticKITTI dataset. Our approach takes fewer points as input, outperforms others by a large margin with fewer parameters, and obtains the best results in 6 of 19 categories. Note the high quality results on our method in relevant elusive classes such as fence, as well as in challenging classes such as motorcyclist. Furthermore, Fig. 7 illustrates our qualitative visualization of four samples on the validation split. It can be seen that our HPGCNN predict perfectly. The reason is that our HPGConv is designed to encode more of the discriminative fine-grained independent single-point features and the local geometric features simultaneously, which can enhance feature richness, and that the multi-semantic scale strategy can exploit the contextual fine-grained information along with the rich semantics.

Table 6. Comparison of segmentation accuracy of different approaches on the vKITTI dataset with 6-fold cross validation

Methods	OA (%)	mIoU (%)
PointNet [25]	79.7	34.4
Engelmann et al. in [58]	79.7	35.6
G+RCU [49]	80.6	36.2
3P-RNN [50]	87.8	41.6
SSP+SPG [57]	84.3	52.0
Ours	**91.7**	**61.1**

Table 7. Comparison of segmentation accuracy of different approaches on the SemanticKITTI dataset [47]. Only the recent published methods are compared and all scores are obtained from the online single scan evaluation track. Accessed on 23 June 2020

Methods	input	mIoU(%)	Params	road	sidewalk	parking	other-ground	building	car	truck	bicycle	motorcycle	other-vehicle	vegetation	trunk	terrain	person	bicyclist	motorcyclist	fence	pole	traffic-sign
PointNet [25]		14.6	3.00	61.6	35.7	15.8	1.4	41.4	46.3	0.1	1.3	0.3	0.8	31.0	4.6	17.6	0.2	0.2	0.0	12.9	2.4	3.7
SPG [39]		17.4	**0.25**	45.0	28.5	1.6	0.6	64.3	49.3	0.1	0.2	0.2	0.8	48.9	27.2	24.6	0.3	2.7	0.1	20.8	15.9	0.8
SPLATNet [16]		18.4	0.8	64.6	39.1	0.4	0.0	58.3	58.2	0.0	0.0	0.0	0.0	71.1	9.9	19.3	0.0	0.0	0.0	23.1	5.6	0.0
PointNet++ [26]	50k pnt	20.1	6	72.0	41.8	18.7	5.6	62.3	53.7	0.9	1.9	0.2	0.2	46.5	13.8	30.0	0.9	1.0	0.0	16.9	6.0	8.9
TangentConv [21]		40.9	0.4	83.9	63.9	33.4	15.4	83.4	90.8	15.2	2.7	16.5	12.1	79.5	49.3	58.1	23.0	28.4	8.1	49.0	35.8	28.5
RandLA-Net [38]		50.3	0.95	90.4	67.9	56.9	15.5	81.1	**94.0**	**42.7**	19.8	21.4	**38.7**	78.3	60.3	59.0	**47.5**	48.8	4.6	49.7	44.2	38.1
SqueezeSeg [59]		29.5	1	85.4	54.3	26.9	4.5	57.4	68.8	3.3	16.0	4.1	3.6	60.0	24.3	53.7	12.9	13.1	0.9	29.0	17.5	24.5
SqueezeSegV2 [60]		39.7	1	88.6	67.6	45.8	17.7	73.3	81.8	13.4	18.5	17.9	14.0	71.8	35.8	60.2	20.1	25.1	3.9	41.1	20.2	36.3
DarkNet21Seg [47]	64*2048 P	47.4	25	91.4	74.0	57.0	26.4	81.9	85.4	16.6	**26.2**	26.5	15.6	77.6	48.4	63.7	31.8	33.6	4.0	52.3	36.0	50.0
DarkNet53Seg [47]		49.9	50	**91.8**	**74.6**	**64.8**	27.9	84.1	86.4	25.5	24.5	**32.7**	22.6	78.3	50.1	64.0	36.2	33.6	4.7	55.0	38.9	**52.2**
PointASNL [61]	8k pnt	46.8	-	87.4	74.3	24.3	1.8	83.1	87.9	39.0	0.0	25.1	29.2	84.1	52.2	**70.6**	34.2	**57.6**	0.0	43.9	**57.8**	36.9
HPGCNN(Ours)	10k pnt	**50.5**	0.8	89.5	73.6	58.8	**34.6**	**91.2**	93.1	21.0	6.5	17.6	23.3	**84.4**	**65.9**	70.0	32.1	30.0	**14.7**	**65.5**	45.5	41.5

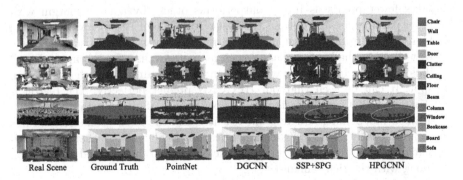

Real Scene   Ground Truth   PointNet   DGCNN   SSP+SPG   HPGCNN

Chair, Wall, Table, Door, Clutter, Ceiling, Floor, Beam, Column, Window, Bookcase, Board, Sofa

Fig. 5. Visualization of semantic segmentation results on the S3DIS dataset.

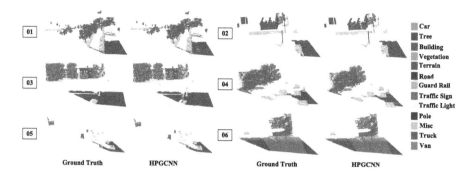

Fig. 6. Visualization of semantic segmentation results on the vKITTI dataset.

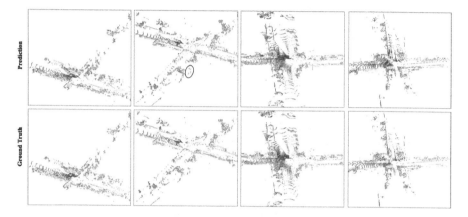

Fig. 7. Visualization of semantic segmentation results on the SemanticKITTI [47]. Red boxes show the failure cases.

5   Conclusion

In this paper, we present hierarchical parallel group convolutional neural network that, in addition to reducing the redundancy problem of the standard convolution operation, exploits the local and global representations in the depth and width of the network so that they can be complementary to each other and enhance the ability to recognize elusive classes. Furthermore, the strategy, we put forward, of combining the global average pooling with a fully connected layer to complete the classification task also proved effective and successful in further reducing the complexity as well as in avoiding overfitting. A multi-semantic scale strategy is also introduced to effectively capture context fine-grained information with higher level semantics. Extensive experiments on multiple benchmarks demonstrate the high efficiency and the state-of-the-art performance of our approach.

References

1. Qi, C.R., Liu, W., Wu, C., Su, H., Guibas, L.J.: Frustum PointNets for 3D object detection from RGB-D data. arXiv preprint arXiv:1901.09346 (2017)
2. Liu, Z., et al.: Real-time 6D lidar slam in large scale natural terrains for UGV. In: IEEE Intelligent Vehicles Symposium (IV), pp. 662–667 (2018)
3. Rusu, R.B., Marton, Z., Blodow, N., Dolha, M.E., Beetz, M.: Towards 3D point cloud based object maps for household environments. Robot. Auton. Syst. **56**, 927–941 (2008)
4. Biswas, J., Veloso, M.: Depth camera based indoor mobile robot localization and navigation. In: Robotics and Automation (ICRA), pp. 1697–1702 (2012)
5. Zhou, Y., Tuzel, O.: VoxelNet: end-to-end learning for point cloud based 3D object detection. In: Proceedings of the IEEE Conference on Computer Vision and Pattern Recognition, pp. 4490–4499 (2018)
6. Golovinskiy, A., Kim, V.G., Funkhouser, T.: Shape-based recognition of 3D point clouds in urban environments. In: Computer Vision, pp. 2154–2161 (2009)
7. Golovinskiy, A., Kim, V.G., Funkhouser, T.: Shape-based recognition of 3D point clouds in urban environments (2009)
8. Chua, C.S., Jarvis, R.: Point signatures: a new representation for 3D object recognition. Int. J. Comput. Vision **25**, 63–85 (1997)
9. Rusu, R.B., Blodow, N., Beetz, M.: Fast point feature histograms for 3D registration. In: ICRA, pp. 1848–1853 (2009)
10. Zhirong Wu, Shuran Song, A.K.: 3D ShapeNets: a deep representation for volumetric shape modeling. In: IEEE Conference on Computer Vision and Pattern Recognition (CVPR), pp. 1912–1920 (2015)
11. Maturana, D., Scherer, S.: VoxNet: a 3D convolutional neural network for real-time object recognition. In: 2015 IEEE/RSJ International Conference on Intelligent Robots and Systems (IROS), pp. 922–928 (2015)
12. Yizhak, B.S., Michael, L., Anath, F.: 3DmFV: 3D point cloud classification in real-time using convolutional neural network. IEEE Robot. Autom. Lett. **3**, 3145–3152 (2018)
13. Xavier Roynard, J.E.D.: Classification of point cloud scenes with multi scale voxel deep network. arXiv preprint arXiv:1804.03583 (2018)
14. Riegler, G., Ulusoy, A.O., Geiger, A.: OctNet: learning deep 3D representations at high resolutions. In: Proceedings of the IEEE Conference on Computer Vision and Pattern Recognition, pp. 6620–6629 (2017)
15. Graham, B., Engelcke, M., Der Maaten, L.V.: 3D semantic segmentation with submanifold sparse convolutional networks. In: Proceedings of the IEEE Conference on Computer Vision and Pattern Recognition, pp. 9224–9232 (2018)
16. Su, H., et al.: SPLATNet: sparse lattice networks for point cloud processing. In: Proceedings of the IEEE Conference on Computer Vision and Pattern Recognition, pp. 2530–2539 (2018)
17. Su, H., Maji, S., Kalogerakis, E., Learnedmiller, E.: Multi-view convolutional neural networks for 3D shape recognition. In: Proceedings of the IEEE International Conference on Computer Vision, pp. 945–953 (2015)
18. Alexandre Boulch, B.L.S.: Unstructured point cloud semantic labeling using deep segmentation networks. In: Proceedings of the Workshop on 3D Object Retrieval (2017)
19. Lawin, F.J., Danelljan, M., Tosteberg, P., Bhat, G., Khan, F.S., Felsberg, M.: Deep projective 3D semantic segmentation. In: International Conference on Computer Analysis of Images and Patterns, pp. 95–107 (2017)

20. Feng, Y., Zhang, Z., Zhao, X., Ji, R., Gao, Y.: GVCNN: group-view convolutional neural networks for 3D shape recognition. In: Proceedings of the IEEE Conference on Computer Vision and Pattern Recognition, pp. 264–272 (2018)

21. Tatarchenko, M., Park, J., Koltun, V., Zhou, Q.: Tangent convolutions for dense prediction in 3D. In: Proceedings of the IEEE Conference on Computer Vision and Pattern Recognition, pp. 3887–3896 (2018)

22. Bronstein, M.M., Bruna, J., Lecun, Y., Szlam, A., Vandergheynst, P.: Geometric deep learning: going beyond Euclidean data. IEEE Signal Process. Mag. **34**, 18–42 (2017)

23. Guo, Y., Bennamoun, M., Sohel, F., Lu, M., Wan, J.: 3D object recognition in cluttered scenes with local surface features: a survey. IEEE Trans. Pattern Anal. Mach. Intell. **36**, 2270–2287 (2014)

24. Guo, Y., Bennamoun, M., Sohel, F., Lu, M., Wan, J.: An integrated framework for 3D modeling, object detection, and pose estimation from point clouds. IEEE Trans. Instrum. Meas. **64**, 683–693 (2015)

25. Charles, R.Q., Su, H., Kaichun, M., Guibas, L.J.: PointNet: deep learning on point sets for 3D classification and segmentation. In: Proceedings of the IEEE Conference on Computer Vision and Pattern Recognition, pp. 77–85 (2017)

26. Qi, C.R., Yi, L., Su, H., Guibas, L.J.: PointNet++: deep hierarchical feature learning on point sets in a metric space. In: Advances in Neural Information Processing Systems (2017)

27. Wang, Y., Sun, Y., Liu, Z., Sarma, S.E., Bronstein, M.M., Solomon, J.: Dynamic graph CNN for learning on point clouds. ACM Trans. Graph. **38**, 146 (2019)

28. Li Y, Bu R, S.M.: PointCNN: convolution on x-transformed points. In: Advances in Neural Information Processing Systems, pp. 820–830 (2018)

29. Xu Yifan, Fan Tianqi, X.M.: SpiderCNN: deep learning on point sets with parameterized convolutional filters. In: Proceedings of the European Conference on Computer Vision, pp. 87–102 (2018)

30. Atzmon, M., Maron, H., Lipman, Y.: Point convolutional neural networks by extension operators, vol. 37, p. 71. arXiv preprint arXiv:1803.10091 (2018)

31. Liu, Y., Fan, B., Xiang, S., Pan, C.: Relation shape convolutional neural network for point cloud analysis. In: Proceedings of the IEEE Conference on Computer Vision and Pattern Recognition, pp. 8895–8904 (2019)

32. Zhang, Y., Rabbat, M.: A graph CNN for 3D point cloud classification. In: IEEE International Conference on Acoustics, pp. 6279–6283 (2018)

33. Defferrard, M., Bresson, X., Vandergheynst, P.: Convolutional neural networks on graphs with fast localized spectral filtering. In: Advances in Neural Information Processing Systems, pp. 3844–3852 (2016)

34. Yi, L., Su, H., Guo, X., Guibas, L.J.: SyncSpecCNN: synchronized spectral CNN for 3D shape segmentation. In: Conference on Computer Vision and Pattern Recognition, pp. 6584–6592 (2017)

35. Masci, J., Boscaini, D., Bronstein, M.M., Vandergheynst, P.: Geodesic convolutional neural networks on Riemannian manifolds. In: Proceedings of the IEEE International Conference on Computer Vision Workshops, pp. 832–840 (2015)

36. Simonovsky, M., Komodakis, N.: Dynamic edge-conditioned filters in convolutional neural networks on graphs. In: IEEE Conference on Computer Vision and Pattern Recognition (CVPR) (2017)

37. Monti, F., Boscaini, D., Masci, J., Rodola, E., Svoboda, J., Bronstein, M.M.: Geometric deep learning on graphs and manifolds using mixture model CNN. In: Proceedings of the IEEE Conference on Computer Vision and Pattern Recognition, pp. 5425–5434 (2017)

38. Hu, Q., et al.: RandLA-Net: efficient semantic segmentation of large-scale point clouds. arXiv preprint arXiv (2019)
39. Landrieu, L., Simonovsky, M.: Large-scale point cloud semantic segmentation with superpoint graphs. In: Proceedings of the IEEE Conference on Computer Vision and Pattern Recognition, pp. 4558–4567 (2018)
40. Wang, C., Samari, B., Siddiqi, K.: Local spectral graph convolution for point set feature learning. In: Proceedings of the European Conference on Computer Vision (ECCV), pp. 56–66 (2018)
41. Shen, Y., Feng, C., Yang, Y., Tian, D.: Mining point cloud local structures by kernel correlation and graph pooling. In: Proceedings of the IEEE Conference on Computer Vision and Pattern Recognition, pp. 4548–4557 (2018)
42. Wang, C., Samari, B., Siddiqi, K.: Local spectral graph convolution for point set feature learning. In: Proceedings of the European Conference on Computer Vision (ECCV), pp. 52–66 (2018)
43. Klokov R, L.V.: Escape from cells: deep Kd-networks for the recognition of 3D point cloud models. In: Proceedings of the IEEE International Conference on Computer Vision, pp. 863–872 (2017)
44. Yi, L., et al.: A scalable active framework for region annotation in 3D shape collections. ACM Trans. Graph. (TOG) **35**, 210 (2016)
45. Armeni, I., et al.: 3D semantic parsing of large-scale indoor spaces. In: Proceedings of the IEEE Conference on Computer Vision and Pattern Recognition, pp. 1534–1543 (2016)
46. Gaidon, A., Wang, Q., Cabon, Y., Vig, E.: Virtual worlds as proxy for multi-object tracking analysis. In: Proceedings of the IEEE Conference on Computer Vision and Pattern Recognition (2016)
47. Behley, J., et al.: SemanticKITTI: a dataset for semantic scene understanding of lidar sequences. In: IEEE International Conference on Computer Vision, pp. 9297–9307 (2019)
48. Zhang, K., Hao, M., Wang, J., De Silva, C.W., Fu, C.: Linked dynamic graph CNN: learning on point cloud via linking hierarchical features. arXiv Computer Vision and Pattern Recognition (2019)
49. Engelmann, F., Kontogianni, T., Hermans, A., Leibe, B.: Exploring spatial context for 3D semantic segmentation of point clouds. In: IEEE International Conference on Computer Vision Workshop, pp. 716–724 (2017)
50. Ye, X., Li, J., Huang, H., Du, L., Zhang, X.: 3D recurrent neural networks with context fusion for point cloud semantic segmentation. In: Proceedings of the European Conference on Computer Vision (ECCV), pp. 415–430 (2018)
51. Huang, Q., Wang, W., Neumann, U.: Recurrent slice networks for 3D segmentation of point clouds. In: Proceedings of the IEEE International Conference on Computer Vision, pp. 2626–2635 (2018)
52. Chen, L., Li, X., Fan, D., Cheng, M., Wang, K., Lu, S.: LSANet: feature learning on point sets by local spatial attention. arXiv Computer Vision and Pattern Recognition (2019)
53. Zhao, H., Jiang, L., Fu, C., Jia, J.: PointWeb: enhancing local neighborhood features for point cloud processing. In: Proceedings of the IEEE International Conference on Computer Vision, pp. 5565–5573 (2019)
54. Zhang, Z., Hua, B., Yeung, S.: ShellNet: efficient point cloud convolutional neural networks using concentric shells statistics. In: Proceedings of the IEEE International Conference on Computer Vision, pp. 1607–1616 (2019)

55. Jiang, L., Zhao, H., Liu, S., Shen, X., Fu, C.W., Jia, J.: Hierarchical pointedge interaction network for point cloud semantic segmentation. In: ICCV, pp. 1607–1616 (2019)
56. Thomas, H., Qi, C.R., Deschaud, J., Marcotegui, B., Goulette, F., Guibas, L.J.: KPConv: flexible and deformable convolution for point clouds. arXiv Computer Vision and Pattern Recognition (2019)
57. Landrieu, L., Boussaha, M.: Point cloud oversegmentation with graph-structured deep metric learning. arXiv Computer Vision and Pattern Recognition (2019)
58. Engelmann, F., Kontogianni, T., Schult, J., Leibe, B.: Know what your neighbors do: 3D semantic segmentation of point clouds. In: Leal-Taixé, L., Roth, S. (eds.) ECCV 2018. LNCS, vol. 11131, pp. 395–409. Springer, Cham (2019). https://doi.org/10.1007/978-3-030-11015-4_29
59. Wu, B., Wan, A., Yue, X., Keutzer, K.: SqueezeSeg: convolutional neural nets with recurrent CRF for real-time road-object segmentation from 3D lidar point cloud. In: ICRA, pp. 1887–1893 (2018)
60. Wu, B., Zhou, X., Zhao, S., Yue, X., Keutzer, K.: SqueezeSegV2: improved model structure and unsupervised domain adaptation for road-object segmentation from a lidar point cloud. arXiv Computer Vision and Pattern Recognition (2018)
61. Yan, X., Zheng, C., Li, Z., Wang, S., Cui, S.: PointASNL: robust point clouds processing using nonlocal neural networks with adaptive sampling. In: Proceedings of the IEEE Conference on Computer Vision and Pattern Recognition (2020)

3D Object Detection and Pose Estimation of Unseen Objects in Color Images with Local Surface Embeddings

Giorgia Pitteri[1]([✉]), Aurélie Bugeau[1], Slobodan Ilic[3], and Vincent Lepetit[2]

[1] Univ. Bordeaux, Bordeaux INP, CNRS, LaBRI, UMR5800, 33400 Talence, France
{giorgia.pitteri,aurelie.bugeau}@u-bordeaux.fr
[2] LIGM, IMAGINE, Ecole des Ponts, Univ Gustave Eiffel, CNRS,
Marne-la-Vallee, France
vincent.lepetit@enpc.fr
[3] Siemens Corporate Technology, Munich, Germany
sobodan.ilic@siemens.com

Abstract. We present an approach for detecting and estimating the 3D poses of objects in images that requires only an untextured CAD model and no training phase for new objects. Our approach combines Deep Learning and 3D geometry: It relies on an embedding of local 3D geometry to match the CAD models to the input images. For points at the surface of objects, this embedding can be computed directly from the CAD model; for image locations, we learn to predict it from the image itself. This establishes correspondences between 3D points on the CAD model and 2D locations of the input images. However, many of these correspondences are ambiguous as many points may have similar local geometries. We show that we can use Mask-RCNN in a class-agnostic way to detect the new objects without retraining and thus drastically limit the number of possible correspondences. We can then robustly estimate a 3D pose from these discriminative correspondences using a RANSAC-like algorithm. We demonstrate the performance of this approach on the T-LESS dataset, by using a small number of objects to learn the embedding and testing it on the other objects. Our experiments show that our method is on par or better than previous methods.

1 Introduction

Deep Learning (DL) provides powerful techniques to estimate the 6D pose of an object from color images, and impressive results have been achieved over the last years [1–6], including in the presence of occlusions [7–9], in the absence of texture, and for objects with symmetries (which create pose ambiguities) [10,11]. However, most of recent works focus on supervised approaches, which require that for each new object, these methods have to be retrained on many different registered images of this object. Even if domain transfer methods allow for training such methods on synthetic images instead of real ones at least to some extent, such training sessions take time, and avoiding them is highly appealing.

© Springer Nature Switzerland AG 2021
H. Ishikawa et al. (Eds.): ACCV 2020, LNCS 12622, pp. 38–54, 2021.
https://doi.org/10.1007/978-3-030-69525-5_3

Fig. 1. Overview of our method. We detect and estimate the 3D poses of objects, given only an untextured CAD model, without having to retrain a deep model for these objects. Given an input RGB image, we predict local surface embeddings (LSEs) for each pixel that we match with the LSEs of 3D points on the CAD models. We then use a PnP algorithm and RANSAC to estimate the 3D poses from these correspondences. We use the predicted masks to constrain the correspondences in a RANSAC sample to lie on the same object, in order to control the complexity. The LSE prediction network is trained on known objects but generalizes well to new objects. Similarly, we train Mask-RCNN on known objects, and use mask R-CNN to segment the objects in the image. Because we train Mask-RCNN in a *class-agnostic* way, it also generalizes to new objects without retraining. Note that we use masks of different colors for visualization only.

Recently, a few methods were proposed for 3D pose estimation for objects that were not seen during training, only exploiting an untextured CAD model provided for the new objects. This is an important problem in industrial contexts, but also very challenging as aligning an untextured CAD model to a color image remains very difficult, especially without pose prior. In DeepIM [12], the authors propose a pose refiner able to perform such alignment given some initial pose, however it has been demonstrated on very simple synthetic images with constant lighting. [13] proposes to learn to detect corners by using training images of a small set of objects, and estimates the object pose by robustly matching the corners of the CAD model with the corners detected in the input image. However, this requires the object to have specific corners and a skilled user to select the corners on the CAD model. Very recently, [14] proposes a single-encoder-multi-decoder network to predict the 6D pose of even unseen objects. Their encoder can learn an interleaved encoding where general features can be shared across multiple instances. This leads to encodings that can represent object orientations from novel, untrained instances, even when they belong to untrained categories. Even if the idea is promising, to achieve competitive results, they need to use depth information and refine the pose with an ICP algorithm.

In this paper, we investigate 6D object pose estimation in an industrial scenario with the challenges this implies: We want to handle symmetrical, textureless, ambiguous, and unseen objects, given only their CAD models. By contrast with some previous works, we also do not assume that the ground truth 2D bounding boxes for the objects are available. As shown in Fig. 1, our approach combines machine learning and 3D geometry: Like previous works [6,11,15,16], we establish dense correspondences between the image locations and 3D points on the CAD model, as they showed that this yields to accurate poses. However, there is a fundamental difference between these works and ours: They can train a machine learning model in advance to predict the 3D coordinates of the pixels in a given image. In our case, we want to avoid any training phase for new objects. We therefore rely on a different strategy: We introduce an embedding capturing the local geometry of the 3D points lying on the object surface. Given a training set for a small number of objects, we learn to predict these embeddings per pixel for images of new objects. By matching these embeddings with the embeddings computed for 3D points on the object surface, we get 2D-3D correspondences from which we estimate the object's 6D pose using RANSAC and a PnP solver.

This approach is conceptually simple, robust to occlusions, and provides an accurate 6D pose. However, to be successful, some special care is needed. First, the embeddings need to be rotation invariant. Second, because of the symmetries and this rotation invariance, many correspondences between pixels and 3D points are possible *a priori* and the complexity of finding a set of correct correspondences can become exponential. We control this complexity in two ways. We focus on image locations with the most discriminative embeddings as they have less potential correspondences. We also observe that Mask R-CNN [17] is able to predict the masks of new objects when trained without any class information, and thus can segment new objects without re-training. We use this to constrain the sets of correspondences in RANSAC to lie on the same mask, and thus drastically decrease the number of samples to consider in RANSAC.

In the remainder of the paper, we review the state-of-the-art on 3D object pose estimation from images, describe our method, and evaluate it on the T-LESS dataset [18], which is made of very challenging objects and sequences.

2   Related Work

In this section, we first review recent works on 3D object detection and pose estimation from color images. We also review methods for using synthetic images for training as it is a popular solution for 3D pose estimation. Finally, we review the few works that consider the same problem as us.

2.1   3D Object Detection and Pose Estimation from Color Images

The use of Deep Learning has recently significantly improved the performance of 6D pose estimation algorithms. Different general approaches have been proposed. One approach is to first estimate 2D bounding boxes for the visible objects, and predict the 6D pose of each object directly from the image region in the bounding box [1–3,5,10]. The pose can be predicted directly using quaternions for the rotation example, or via 3D points or the reprojections of 3D points related to the object, or by learning a code book using AutoEncoders. This last method has the advantage to work well with symmetrical objects, which are common in industrial contexts. Another approach, aiming to be more robust to occlusions, is to predict for each pixel offsets to the reprojections of 3D points related to the object [7, 19, 20].

Closer to our own approach, several works first predict for each pixel its 3D coordinates in the object's coordinate frame [4, 6, 11, 15, 16, 21–24]. This yields 2D-3D correspondences from which the object's 3D pose can be estimated using a PnP algorithm, possibly together with RANSAC for more robustness. In our case, we cannot directly predict the 3D coordinates of pixels as it can be done only for the objects or categories used for training. Instead, we learn to predict an embedding for the 3D local geometry corresponding to each pixel, and we rely on this embedding to match the pixel to its corresponding 3D point on the CAD models of new objects.

2.2 Training on Synthetic Images for 6D Pose Estimation

One popular approach to 6D pose estimation given only a CAD model and no, or few, real training images is to exploit synthetic images. There is however a domain gap between real and synthetic images, which has to be considered to make sure the method generalizes well to real images.

A very simple approach is to train a convolutional network for some problem such as 2D detection on real images and use the first part of the network for extracting image features [1, 25]. Then, a network taking these features as input can be trained on synthetic images. This is easy to do, but it is not clear how many layers should be used exactly. Generative Adversarial Networks (GANs) [26] and Domain Transfer have been used to make synthetic images more realistic [27–35]. Another interesting approach is domain randomization [36], which generates synthetic training images with random appearance by applying drastic variations to the object textures and the rendering parameters to improve generalization.

These works can exploit CAD models for learning to detect new objects, however they also require a training phase for new objects. In this work, we do not need such phase.

2.3 6D Pose Estimation Without Retraining

Very few recent works already tackled 6D pose estimation without retraining for new objects. One early approach targeting texture-less objects is to rely on templates [37]. Deep Learning has also been applied to such problem, by learning to compute a descriptor from pairs or triplets of object images [38–41]. Like ours, these approaches do not require re-training, as it only requires to compute the descriptors for images of the new objects. However, it requires many images from points of view sampled around the object. It may be possible to use synthetic images, but then, some domain transfer has to be performed. But the main drawback of this approach is the lack of robustness to partial occlusions, as the descriptor is computed for whole images of objects. It is also not clear how it would handle ambiguities, as it is based on metric learning on images. In fact, such approach has been demonstrated on the LineMod, which is made of relatively simple objects, and never on the T-LESS dataset, which is much more challenging.

More recently, DeepIM proposed a pose refiner able to refine a given initial pose. In [12], this refiner was applied to new objects, but only on very simple synthetic images with constant lighting. [13] proposes to learn to detect corners by using training images of a small set of objects and estimates the object pose by robustly matching the corners of the CAD model with the corners detected in the input image. This method requires objects to have specific corners and to offline select corners on the CAD model. Even more recently, [14] proposes an extension of [10] able to generalize to new objects. Thanks to the single-encoder-multi-decoder architecture, they are able to learn an interleaved encoding where general features can be shared across multiple instances of novel categories. To achieve competitive results, they need to use depth information and refine the pose with an ICP algorithm.

Our approach is related to [13], but considers any 3D location on the objects to get matches, not only corners. We compare against [13] and [14] in the experimental section.

3   Method

We describe our approach in this section. We first explain how we compute the local surface embeddings and how we obtain correspondences between the CAD models and the images. We then describe our pose estimation algorithm.

3.1   Local Surface Embeddings

To match new images with CAD models, we rely on embeddings of the local surfaces of the objects. To be able to match these embeddings under unknown poses, they need to be translation invariant and rotation invariant. Achieving translation invariance is straightforward, since we consider the local geometry centered on 3D points. Achieving rotation invariance is more subtle, especially because of ambiguities arising in practice with symmetrical objects. This is illustrated in Fig. 2(b): We need to compute the same embeddings for local geometries that are similar up to a 3D rotation.

More exactly, given a 3D point $\mathbf{P}$ on the surface of an object, we define the local geometry as the set of 3D points $\mathbf{M}_n$ in a spherical neighborhood centered on $\mathbf{P}$ and of radius r. In practice, on T-LESS, we use $r = 3\,\mathrm{cm}$. To compute a rotation-invariant embedding, we transform these points from the object coordinate system to a local patch coordinate system using a rotation matrix computed from the decomposition of the covariance matrix of the 3D points $\mathbf{M}_n$ after centering on $\mathbf{P}$ [42]:

$$C = \sum_n \mathbf{v}_n \cdot \mathbf{v}_n^\top , \tag{1}$$

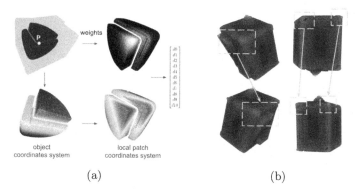

(a)   (b)

Fig. 2. (a): Computation of the LSEs for a given point **P** on a CAD model. We transform the 3D points in the neighborhood of **P** into a rotation-invariant local system and weight them before computing their moments. (b): Visualization of the rotation-invariance property on different parts of the same object. Similar local geometries yield similar LSEs. Through this paper, we represent the LSEs using only their 3 first values mapped to the red, green, blue channels except for Fig. 3 that shows all the values. (Color figure online)

where $\mathbf{v}_n = (\mathbf{M}_n - \mathbf{P})$ using a Singular Value Decomposition (SVD):

$$C = L^\top \Sigma R . \tag{2}$$

R is an orthogonal matrix, but not necessarily a rotation matrix, and small differences in the local geometry can result in very different values for R. We therefore apply a transformation to R to obtain a new matrix $\bar{R}$ so that $\bar{R}$ is a suitable rotation matrix. It can be checked that applying $\bar{R}$ to the $\mathbf{v}_i$ vectors will achieve rotation invariance for the local surface embeddings.

Let's denote by r_1, r_2, and r_3 the rows of R, and by $\bar{r}_1$, $\bar{r}_2$, and $\bar{r}_3$ the rows of $\bar{R}$. Applying R to the normal n of the object's surface at **P** yields a 3-vector $R \cdot n$ close to either $[0,0,1]^\top$ or $[0,0,-1]^\top$, depending on the orientation of R selected for the SVD. For normalisation, we choose that $\bar{R} \cdot n$ should always be closer to $[0,0,1]^\top$. We therefore compute $o = r_3^\top \cdot n$. If o is positive, we take $\bar{r}_3 = r_3$, otherwise we take $\bar{r}_3 = -r_3$. As a result, $\bar{R} \cdot n$ is always closer to $[0,0,1]^\top$ that to $[0,0,-1]^\top$. Finally, we take $\bar{r}_1 = r_1$ and $\bar{r}_2 = -\bar{r}_1 \wedge \bar{r}_3$, where $\wedge$ denotes the cross-product, which ensures that $\bar{R}$ is a rotation matrix.

We explain now how we define the local surface embeddings. For our experiments, we use the local moments of the local 3D points for simplicity but any other embeddings such as [43] could also work. Let us denote by $[x_n, y_n, z_n]$ the vectors $\bar{R}\mathbf{v}_n$, then local surface embeddings can be computed as:

$$\text{LSE}_{i,j,k}(\mathbf{P}) = \sum_n w_n x_n^i y_n^j z_n^k , \tag{3}$$

where $w_n = \exp(-\|\mathbf{v}_n\|^2/\sigma^2)$ is a weight associated to each point based on its distance from **P** (we use $\sigma = 5$ in practice) and i, j, k are exponents in the range

| Input image | $i=0, j=2, k=1$ | $i=0, j=2, k=0$ | $i=0, j=2, k=2$ |

| $i=2, j=0, k=1$ | $i=2, j=0, k=0$ | $i=0, j=0, k=2$ | $i=2, j=0, k=2$ |

Fig. 3. Visualization of some LSEs coordinates for an example image.

$[0, 1, 2]$. Theoretically it is possible to take all the combinations of exponents but we empirically found that the most discriminative values are computed using: $i \in \{0, 2\}$, $j \in \{0, 2\}$, $k \in \{0, 1, 2\}$, which gives 11 values for the full vector $\text{LSE}(\mathbf{P})$ as taking $i = j = k = 0$ gives a constant value and is not useful. Finally, we normalize the values of $\text{LSE}(\mathbf{P})$ to zero mean and unit variance so they have similar ranges. Figure 3 displays the embeddings for an example image.

3.2 Predicting the Local Surface Embeddings for New Images

Given a new CAD model, it is trivial to compute the local surface embeddings on points on its surface. Given a new input image, we would like to also compute the embeddings for the object points visible in this image. We use a deep network to perform this task. To do so, we create a training set by generating many synthetic images of known objects under various poses. We also compute the LSEs for all the pixels corresponding to a 3D point of one of the objects. We then train a U-Net-like architecture [44] to predict the LSEs given a color image. More details on the architecture and its training are provided in the experimental section.

This training is done once, on known objects, but because the embeddings depend only on the local geometry, the network generalizes well to new objects, as shown in Fig. 4.

3.3 Pose Estimation Algorithm

The pseudocode for our detection and pose estimation algorithm is given as Algorithm 1. Given a new image, we compute the LSEs for each of its pixels using the network described in Sect. 3.2 and establish correspondences between image pixels and object 3D points. However, the number of possible correspondences can quickly become very large, which would yield a combinatorial explosion

(a)   (b)   (c)

Fig. 4. Generalization of the LSE prediction network to new objects. (a) Input RGB image with objects seen during the training of the network (blue boundaries) and new objects (red boundaries). The LSE predictions (c) are close to the LSE Ground truth (b) for both the known and new objects. (Color figure online)

in the number of set of correspondences needed in RANSAC. We control the complexity in two different ways.

First, we focus on the most discriminative embeddings. Points on planar regions are very common and would generate many correspondences. We discard them by thresholding the embedding values: Points with very low absolute embedding values for the LSEs are removed. Figure 5(a) shows how pixels are selected.

Second, we force the correspondences in each sample considered by RANSAC to belong to the same object. Even when objects are not known in advance, it is possible to segment them: To do so, we use Mask-RCNN [17] to predict the masks of the objects. We fine-tuned it on our synthetic images already used for training the LSE predictor, as described in Sect. 3.2 in a class-agnostic way since we want to generalize to new objects. We found out that it works very well with new objects even for cluttered backgrounds, as shown in Fig. 6. This also allows us to easily discard pixels on the background from the possible correspondences.

We match the embeddings predicted for the pixels of the input image against the embeddings computed for the 3D points on the CAD model based on their Euclidean distances. In our implementation, we use the FLANN library [45] to efficiently get the k nearest neighbors of a query embedding. In practice, we use $k = 100$. This usually returns points in several clusters, as close points tend to have similar embeddings. We therefore go through the list of nearest neighbors sorted by increasing distances. We keep the first 3D point and remove from the

---

Algorithm 1. Pose estimation algorithm.

1: $\mathcal{C} \leftarrow$ CAD models for the new objects
2: $\mathcal{E}(C) \leftarrow \text{LSE}_{\text{CAD}}(C)$, the LSEs of 3D points for each CAD model C
3: $I \leftarrow$ input image
4: $\mathcal{F} \leftarrow \text{LSE}_{\text{pred}}(I)$, the predicted LSEs for the input image
5: $\mathcal{O} \leftarrow \text{Mask-RCNN}(I)$, the masks predicted by Mask-RCNN
6: $\mathcal{M} \leftarrow \{m_i\}_i$, the set of 2D-3D matches based on $\mathcal{E}(C)$ and $\mathcal{F}$. Each match m_i is made of an image location $\mathbf{p}$ and 3D points on the CAD models: $(\mathbf{p}, [\mathbf{P}_1, \mathbf{P}_2, ..., \mathbf{P}_{m_i}])$
7:
8: **procedure** POSE_ESTIMATION_O_C(O, C)
9:     $s_{\text{best}} \leftarrow 0$
10:    **for** iter $\in [0; N_{\text{iter}}]$ **do**
11:       $n \leftarrow$ random integer in $[6; 10]$
12:       $M \leftarrow n$ random correspondences $(\mathbf{p}, \mathbf{P})$,
13:          where $\mathbf{p} \in O$ and $\mathbf{P}$ is matched to $\mathbf{p}$ in $\mathcal{M}$
14:       **pose** $\leftarrow$ PnP(M)
15:       $s \leftarrow$ SCORE(**pose**, $C, \mathcal{E}(C), \mathcal{F}, O$)
16:       **if** $s > s_{\text{best}}$ **then**
17:          $\mathbf{pose}_{\text{best}} \leftarrow$ **pose**
18:          $s_{\text{best}} \leftarrow s$
19:    Refine $\mathbf{pose}_{\text{best}}$
20:    **return** $\mathbf{pose}_{\text{best}}$, SCORE($\mathbf{pose}_{\text{best}}, \mathcal{E}(C), \mathcal{F}, O, C$)
21:
22: **procedure** POSE_ESTIMATION
23:    **for** each mask $O \in \mathcal{O}$ **do**
24:       ▷ $s_{\min}$ is the minimum score for a match with a CAD model:
25:       $s_{\text{best}}(O) \leftarrow s_{\min}$
26:       **for** each CAD model C **do**
27:          **pose**, $s \leftarrow$ POSE_ESTIMATION_O_C(O, C)
28:          **if** $s > s_{\text{best}}$ **then**
29:             $s_{\text{best}} \leftarrow s$
30:             $\mathbf{pose}_{\text{best}}(O) \leftarrow$ **pose**
31:             $C_{\text{best}}(O) \leftarrow C$

---

list the other points that are also close to this point, and we iterate. This provides for each pixel a list of potential corresponding 3D points separated from each other.

When working on industrial objects like the ones in T-LESS, some pixels can be matched with several 3D points, as shown in Fig. 5(b), because of the rotation invariance property of the local LSEs and the similarities between local parts of different objects.

We finally use LO-RANSAC (Locally Optimized RANSAC) [46] with a PnP algorithm (we use [47] followed by a Levenberg-Marquardt optimization) to compute the poses of the visible objects. We take random $n \in [6; 10]$ for each RANSAC sample. At each iteration, we compute a score for the predicted pose as a weighted sum of the Intersection-over-Union between the mask from

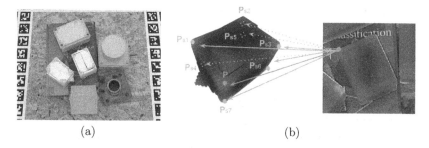

(a)   (b)

Fig. 5. Focusing on the most discriminative pixels. (a): In green, pixels with discriminative LSEs. We only consider them for correspondences with the CAD models. (b): A pixel can be matched with multiple 3D points on symmetrical objects because of the rotation invariance property of the LSEs. (Color figure online)

Fig. 6. Generalization of Mask-RCNN to unknown objects. We train Mask-RCNN in a class-agnostic way on a set of known objects. It generalizes well to new objects, and we use these masks to constrain the pose estimation. Note that we use masks of different colors for visualization only. Mask-RCNN cannot identify the new objects individually as it was not trained on them, it can only detect objects in a class-agnostic way. (Color figure online)

Mask-RCNN and the mask obtained by rendering the model under the estimated pose, and the Euclidean distances between the predicted LSEs and the LSEs for the CAD model after reprojection. We keep the pose with the largest score and refine it using all the inlier correspondences to obtain the final 6D pose.

4 Evaluation

In this section, we present and discuss the results of our pose estimation algorithm on the challenging T-LESS dataset [18], made of texture-less, ambiguous and symmetrical objects with no disciminative parts. It is well representative of the problems encountered in industrial context.

4.1 Dataset

To train our LSE prediction network, we generate synthetic images using the CAD models provided with T-LESS for a subset of objects in this dataset. The exact subset depends on the experiment, and we will detail them below. Similar to the *BlenderProc4BOP* [48] introduced in the BOP challenge [49], these images are created with Cycles, a photorealistic rendering engine of the open source software Blender by randomly placing the training objects in a simple scene made of a plane randomly textured and randomly lighted. We used both these synthetics and real images for training the network combined with data augmentation to take care of the domain gap between our synthetic images and the real test images. More specifically, we use $15K$ synthetic images and $\sim 7K$ real images—all the training images provided by T-LESS for the objects that are used for training the LSE prediction and Mask-RCNN. To create the ground truth embeddings, for each training image, we backproject the pixels lying on the objects to obtain their corresponding 3D points and their LSEs. Neither the embedding prediction network nor Mask-RCNN see the test objects during training.

4.2 LSE Prediction Network Architecture and Training

The architecture of the network predicting the LSEs for a given input image is a standard U-Net-like [44] encoder-decoder convolutional neural network taking a 720×540 RGB image as input. The encoder part is a 12-layer ResNet-like [50] architecture; the decoder upsample the feature maps up to the original size using bilinear interpolations followed by convolutional layers. We train the network with the Adam optimizer and a learning rate set to 10^{-4}. We also use batch normalization to ensure good convergence of the model. Finally, the batch size is set to 8 and we train the network for 150 epochs.

4.3 Metrics

We evaluate our method using several metrics from the literature. Analogously to other related papers [2,3,6,13], we consider the percentage of correctly predicted poses for each sequence and each object of interest, where a pose is considered correct based on the ADD metric (or the ADI metric for symmetrical objects) [37]. This metric is based on the average distance in 3D between the model points after applying the ground truth pose and the estimated one. A pose is considered correct if the distance is less than 10% of the object's diameter.

Following the BOP benchmark [49], we also report the *Visible Surface Discrepancy* (VSD) metric. The VSD metric evaluates the pose error in a way that is invariant to the pose ambiguities due to object symmetries. It is computed from the distance between the estimated and ground truth visible object surfaces in the following way:

$$err_{\text{VSD}}(\hat{S}, \bar{S}, S_I, \hat{V}, \bar{V}, \tau) = \underset{p \in \hat{V} \cup \bar{V}}{\text{Mean}} \begin{cases} 0, & \text{if } p \in \hat{V} \cap \bar{V} \wedge |\hat{S}(p) - \bar{S}(p)| < \tau \\ 1, & \text{otherwise} \end{cases} \quad (4)$$

where $\hat{S}$ and $\bar{S}$ are distance maps obtained by rendering the object model in the estimated and ground-truth poses respectively. The distance maps are compared

Table 1. Our quantitative results on T-LESS test Scenes #02, #03, #04, #06, #08, #10, #11, #12, #13, #14, #15 as used in [13]. We report results also for Objects #9 in Scenes #11 and #12 and for Object #26 in Scene #15 even though [13] does not. See text for details.

Scene	02	03	04	04	06	08	10	11	11	12	12	13	15	15	14	
Obj	7	8	26	8	7	20	20	8	9	7	9	20	29	26	20	Avg
[13]	**68.3**	**57.9**	28.1	21.2	36.8	10.0	27.8	**58.8**	–	23.1	–	26.6	48.0	–	10.0	34.7 (±18.5)
Ours	61.0	44.1	**55.6**	**39.1**	**44.8**	**38.2**	**38.3**	40.8	**46.1**	**41.2**	**45.8**	**39.5**	**77.0**	**63.6**	**24.9**	**46.7** (±12.0)

with the distance map S_I of the test image I to obtain the visibility masks $\hat{V}$ and $\bar{V}$, *i.e.* the sets of pixels where the object model is visible in image I. We report the mean VSD recall of 6D object poses at $err_{VSD} < 0.3$ with tolerance $\tau = 20$ mm and $>10\%$ object visibility.

4.4   Results

The complexity of the test scenes in T-LESS varies from several isolated objects on a clean background to very challenging ones with multiple instances of several objects with a high amount of occlusions and clutters. We compare our method against the two works that already consider 6D object detection and pose estimation for unknown objects on T-LESS, CorNet [13] and the MP-Encoder method of [14]. As the codes for these two methods are not available at the time of writing, we use the same protocols as in these works and report the results from the papers.

Comparison with CorNet [13]. We use here the same protocol as in [13]: We split the objects from T-LESS into two sets: One set of known objects (#6, #19, #25, #27, and #28) and one set of unknown objects (#7, #8, #20, #26, and #29), and we compare the 3D detection and pose estimation performance of our method and CorNet for the unknown objects in T-LESS test scenes #02, #03, #04, #06, #08, #10, #11, #12, #13, #14, and #15. We use synthetic images of the known objects for training the LSE prediction network. Results are reported in Table 1. We outperform CorNet on most of the objects, except on objects #7 and #8. This is because these objects have some 3D points with local geometry very different from the training objects (at the connections of the different parts). As a result, the predicted LSEs for these parts are not very accurate, generating wrong matches. Figure 8 shows some qualitative results for the unknown objects in the test images.

Comparison with MP-Encoder [14]. We use here the same protocol as in [14]: The objects from T-LESS are split into a set of known objects (#1–#18) and one set of unknown objects (#19–#30), and we compare the 3D detection and pose estimation performance of our method and MP-Encoder for the unknown objects in T-LESS test scenes following the BOP benchmark [49]. We use synthetic images of the known objects for training the LSE prediction network. Note that we report here the number of Table 3 from the [14] paper as the other reported

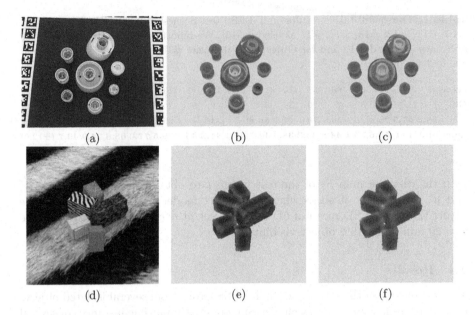

Fig. 7. Top row: Image with objects with rounded shapes (a). Ground truth and predicted LSEs (b) and (c). Bottom row: Image with random textures applied to some T-LESS objects (d). Ground truth and predicted LSEs (e) and (f).

Table 2. Mean *Visible Surface Discrepancy* (VSD) recall using the protocol of [14]. This metric evaluates the pose error in a way that is invariant to the pose ambiguities due to object symmetries. It is computed from the distance between the estimated and ground truth visible object surfaces.

	VSD recall
MP-Encoder [14]	20.53
Ours	**23.27**

results assume that the ground truth bounding boxes, the ground truth masks, or depth information are provided. Results are reported in Table 2. While our method performs slightly better, the performances are close and tells us that both methods are promising. The main difference is that the MP-Encoder relies on an embedding completely learnt by a network while our method incorporates some geometrical meaning that makes our approach more appealing for industrial purposes. Note that, as shown in Fig. 7, our LSE network can handle objects with rounded shape without being limited to objects with prominent corners as [13].

Fig. 8. Qualitative results on the unknown objects of the test scenes from T-LESS. Green bounding boxes denote ground truth poses, blue bounding boxes correspond to our predicted poses. (Color figure online)

4.5 Robustness to Texture

Our focus is on untextured objects, as industrial objects typically do not exhibit textures like the T-LESS objects. However, our LSEs can be predicted for textured objects as well. To show this, we retrained our LSE prediction network on synthetic images of the T-LESS objects rendered with random textures. The LSEs prediction for some test images are shown in the bottom row of Fig. 7.

5 Conclusion

We introduced a novel approach for the detection and the 3D pose estimation of industrial objects in color images. It only requires the CAD models of the objects and no retraining is needed for new objects. We introduce a new type of embedding capturing the local geometry of the 3D points lying on the object surface and we train a network to predict these embeddings per pixel for images of new objects. From these local surface embeddings, we establish correspondences and obtain the pose with a PnP+RANSAC algorithm. Describing the local geometries of the objects allows to generalize to new categories and the rotation invariance of our embeddings makes the method able to solve typical ambiguities that raise with industrial and symmetrical objects. We believe that using local and rotation invariance descriptors is the key to solve the 6D pose of new textureless objects from color images.

References

1. Kehl, W., Manhardt, F., Tombari, F., Ilic, S., Navab, N.: SSD-6D: making RGB-based 3D detection and 6D pose estimation great again. In: International Conference on Computer Vision (2017)
2. Rad, M., Lepetit, V.: BB8: a scalable, accurate, robust to partial occlusion method for predicting the 3D poses of challenging objects without using depth. In: International Conference on Computer Vision (2017)
3. Tekin, B., Sinha, S.N., Fua, P.: Real-time seamless single shot 6D object pose prediction. In: Conference on Computer Vision and Pattern Recognition (2018)
4. Jafari, O.H., Mustikovela, S.K., Pertsch, K., Brachmann, E., Rother, C.: IPose: Instance-Aware 6D Pose Estimation of Partly Occluded Objects. CoRR abs/1712.01924 (2017)
5. Xiang, Y., Schmidt, T., Narayanan, V., Fox, D.: PoseCNN: a convolutional neural network for 6D object pose estimation in cluttered scenes. In: Robotics: Science and Systems Conference (2018)
6. Zakharov, S., Shugurov, I., Ilic, S.: DPOD: dense 6D pose object detector and refiner. In: International Conference on Computer Vision (2019)
7. Oberweger, M., Rad, M., Lepetit, V.: Making deep heatmaps robust to partial occlusions for 3D object pose estimation. In: European Conference on Computer Vision (2018)
8. Peng, S., Liu, Y., Huang, Q., Bao, H., Zhou, X.: PVNet: Pixel-Wise Voting Network for 6DoF Pose Estimation. CoRR abs/1812.11788 (2018)
9. Hu, Y., Fua, P., Wang, W., Salzmann, M.: Single-stage 6D object pose estimation. In: The IEEE/CVF Conference on Computer Vision and Pattern Recognition (2020)
10. Sundermeyer, M., Marton, Z.-C., Durner, M., Triebel, R.: Augmented autoencoders: implicit 3D orientation learning for 6D object detection. Int. J. Comput. Vis. **128**(3), 714–729 (2019). https://doi.org/10.1007/s11263-019-01243-8
11. Park, K., Patten, T., Vincze, M.: Pix2pose: pixel-wise coordinate regression of objects for 6D pose estimation. In: Proceedings of the IEEE International Conference on Computer Vision, pp. 7668–7677 (2019)
12. Li, Y., Wang, G., Ji, X., Xiang, Yu., Fox, D.: DeepIM: deep iterative matching for 6D pose estimation. Int. J. Comput. Vis. **128**(3), 657–678 (2019). https://doi.org/10.1007/s11263-019-01250-9
13. Pitteri, G., Lepetit, V., Ilic, S.: CorNet: generic 3D corners for 6D pose estimation of new objects without retraining. In: International Conference on Computer Vision Workshops (2019)
14. Sundermeyer, M., et al.: Multi-path learning for object pose estimation across domains. In: Conference on Computer Vision and Pattern Recognition (2020)
15. Brachmann, E., Michel, F., Krull, A., Yang, M.M., Gumhold, S., Rother, C.: Uncertainty-driven 6D pose estimation of objects and scenes from a single RGB image. In: Conference on Computer Vision and Pattern Recognition (2016)
16. Wang, H., Sridhar, S., Valentin, J.H.J., Song, S., Guibas, L.J.: Normalized object coordinate space for category-level 6D object pose and size estimation. In: Conference on Computer Vision and Pattern Recognition (2019)
17. He, K., Gkioxari, G., Dollar, P., Girshick, R.: Mask R-CNN. In: International Conference on Computer Vision (2017)
18. Hodan, T., Haluza, P., Obdrzalek, S., Matas, J., Lourakis, M., Zabulis, X.: T-LESS: an RGB-D dataset for 6D pose estimation of texture-less objects. In: IEEE Winter Conference on Applications of Computer Vision (2017)

19. Hu, Y., Hugonot, J., Fua, P., Salzmann, M.: Segmentation-driven 6D object pose estimation. In: Conference on Computer Vision and Pattern Recognition, pp. 3385–3394 (2019)
20. Peng, S., Liu, Y., Huang, Q., Zhou, X., Bao, H.: PVNet: pixel-wise voting network for 6DoF pose estimation. In: Conference on Computer Vision and Pattern Recognition, pp. 4561–4570 (2019)
21. Taylor, J., Shotton, J., Sharp, T., Fitzgibbon, A.: The vitruvian manifold: inferring dense correspondences for one-shot human pose estimation. In: Conference on Computer Vision and Pattern Recognition, pp. 103–110 (2012)
22. Wang, Y., Tan, X., Yang, Y., Liu, X., Ding, E., Zhou, F., Davis, L.S.: 3D pose estimation for fine-grained object categories. In: European Conference on Computer Vision Workshops (2018)
23. Li, Z., Wang, G., Ji, X.: CDPN: coordinates-based disentangled pose network for real-time RGB-based 6-Dof object pose estimation. In: Proceedings of the IEEE/CVF International Conference on Computer Vision (2019)
24. Hodan, T., Barath, D., Matas, J.: EPOS: Estimating 6D Pose of Objects with Symmetries. arXiv preprint arXiv:2004.00605 (2020)
25. Hinterstoisser, S., Lepetit, V., Wohlhart, P., Konolige, K.: On Pre-Trained Image Features and Synthetic Images for Deep Learning. arXiv (2017)
26. Goodfellow, I.J., et al.: Generative adversarial nets. In: Advances in Neural Information Processing Systems (2014)
27. Bousmalis, K., Trigeorgis, G., Silberman, N., Krishnan, D., Erhan, D.: Domain separation networks. In: Advances in Neural Information Processing Systems, pp. 343–351 (2016)
28. Müller, F., et al.: GANerated hands for real-time 3D hand tracking from monocular RGB. In: Conference on Computer Vision and Pattern Recognition (2018)
29. Bousmalis, K., Silberman, N., Dohan, D., Erhan, D., Krishnan, D.: Unsupervised pixel-level domain adaptation with generative adversarial networks. In: Conference on Computer Vision and Pattern Recognition (2017)
30. Zhu, J.Y., Park, T., Isola, P., Efros, A.A.: Unpaired image-to-image translation using cycle-consistent adversarial networks. In: International Conference on Computer Vision (2017)
31. Ganin, Y., et al.: Domain-adversarial training of neural networks. J. Mach. Learn. Res. (2016)
32. Long, M., Cao, Y., Wang, J., Jordan, M.I.: Learning transferable features with deep adaptation networks. In: International Conference on Machine Learning (2015)
33. Hoffman, J., Tzeng, E., Darrell, T., Saenko, K.: Simultaneous deep transfer across domains and tasks. In: Csurka, G. (ed.) Domain Adaptation in Computer Vision Applications. ACVPR, pp. 173–187. Springer, Cham (2017). https://doi.org/10.1007/978-3-319-58347-1_9
34. Lee, H.Y., Tseng, H.Y., Huang, J.B., Singh, M., Yang, M.H.: Diverse image-to-image translation via disentangled representations. In: European Conference on Computer Vision (2018)
35. Zakharov, S., Planche, B., Wu, Z., Hutter, A., Kosch, H., Ilic, S.: Keep it unreal: bridging the realism gap for 2.5D recognition with geometry priors only. In: International Conference on 3D Vision (2018)
36. Tobin, J., Fong, R., Ray, A., Schneider, J., Zaremba, W., Abbeel, P.: Domain randomization for transferring deep neural networks from simulation to the real world. In: International Conference on Intelligent Robots and Systems (2017)
37. Hinterstoisser, S., et al.: Gradient response maps for real-time detection of textureless objects. IEEE Trans. Pattern Anal. Mach. Intell. (2012)

38. Wohlhart, P., Lepetit, V.: Learning descriptors for object recognition and 3D pose estimation. In: Conference on Computer Vision and Pattern Recognition (2015)
39. Balntas, V., Doumanoglou, A., Sahin, C., Sock, J., Kouskouridas, R., Kim, T.K.: Pose guided RGBD feature learning for 3D object pose estimation. In: International Conference on Computer Vision (2017)
40. Zakharov, S., Kehl, W., Planche, B., Hutter, A., Ilic, S.: 3D object instance recognition and pose estimation using triplet loss with dynamic margin. In: International Conference on Intelligent Robots and Systems (2017)
41. Bui, M., Zakharov, S., Albarqouni, S., Ilic, S., Navab, N.: When regression meets manifold learning for object recognition and pose estimation. In: International Conference on Robotics and Automation (2018)
42. Eggert, D., Lorusso, A., Fisher, R.: Estimating 3D rigid body transformations: a comparison of four major algorithms. Mach. Vis. Appl. **9**, 272–290 (1997)
43. Deng, H., Birdal, T., Slobodan, I.: PPF-FoldNet: unsupervised learning of rotation invariant 3D local descriptors. In: European Conference on Computer Vision (2018)
44. Ronneberger, O., Fischer, P., Brox, T.: U-Net: convolutional networks for biomedical image segmentation. In: Navab, N., Hornegger, J., Wells, W.M., Frangi, A.F. (eds.) MICCAI 2015. LNCS, vol. 9351, pp. 234–241. Springer, Cham (2015). https://doi.org/10.1007/978-3-319-24574-4_28
45. Muja, M., Lowe, D.: Fast approximate nearest neighbors with automatic algorithm configuration. In: International Conference on Computer Vision (2009)
46. Chum, O., Matas, J., Kittler, J.: Locally optimized RANSAC. In: German Conference on Pattern Recognition (2003)
47. Lepetit, V., Moreno-noguer, F., Fua, P.: EPnP: an accurate $o(n)$ solution to the PnP problem. Int. J. Comput. Vis. (2009)
48. Denninger, M., et al.: Blenderproc. arXiv preprint arXiv:1911.01911 (2019)
49. Hodan, T., et al.: BOP: benchmark for 6D object pose estimation. In: European Conference on Computer Vision, pp. 19–34 (2018)
50. He, K., Zhang, X., Ren, S., Sun, J.: Deep residual learning for image recognition. In: Conference on Computer Vision and Pattern Recognition (2016)

Reconstructing Creative Lego Models

George Tattersall$^{(\boxtimes)}$ ⓘ, Dizhong Zhu ⓘ, William A. P. Smith ⓘ,
Sebastian Deterding ⓘ, and Patrik Huber ⓘ

University of York, York, UK
gedtattersall@gmail.com,
{dizhong.zhu,william.smith,sebastian.deterding,patrik.huber}@york.ac.uk

Abstract. Lego is one of the most successful toys in the world. Being
able to scan, analyse and reconstruct Lego models has many applications,
for example studying creativity. In this paper, from a set of 2D input
images, we create a monolithic mesh, representing a physical 3D Lego
model as input, and split it in to its known components such that the
output of the program can be used to completely reconstruct the input
model, brick for brick. We present a novel, fully automatic pipeline to
reconstruct Lego models in 3D from 2D images; A-DBSCAN, an angular
variant of DBSCAN, useful for grouping both parallel and anti-parallel
vectors; and a method for reducing the problem of non-Manhattan reconstruction to that of Manhattan reconstruction. We evaluate the presented
approach both qualitatively and quantitatively on a set of Lego duck
models from a public data set, and show that the algorithm is able to
identify and reconstruct the Lego models successfully.

1 Introduction

Lego is one of the most successful toys in the world today. Its affordances have
made it widely recognised as a means of expressing, fostering, and studying creativity [1,2]. Using Lego models to study human creativity often requires scanning the physical models in some form in order to be able to formally reconstruct
and analyse them. One recent example is Ferguson et al. [3,4]. To explore novel
methods for computationally assessing human creativity, they created a "Lego
duck task" which involves constructing diverse ducks from the same set of six
Lego bricks. Their aim was to use computational formalisations of dissimilarity
to assess which ducks were more divergent, novel, and thus, creative. Such computational analysis logically requires a computational representation of the Lego
models. To this end, Ferguson et al. created a corpus of duck models, archived as
multiview images of the creations [4]. They used a variational auto-encoder on
the images to generate neural representations of the ducks. While their results

Electronic supplementary material The online version of this chapter (https://
doi.org/10.1007/978-3-030-69525-5_4) contains supplementary material, which is available to authorized users.

H. Ishikawa et al. (Eds.): ACCV 2020, LNCS 12622, pp. 55–70, 2021.
https://doi.org/10.1007/978-3-030-69525-5_4

Fig. 1. From left to right: real world Lego duck model, monolithic visual hull of duck from 2D image data, resulting reconstruction of the proposed approach.

were promising, such a machine learning approach limits possible formal analyses, as the computational representation remains 'opaque' to human inspection, which is why they recommended future work to explore the generation of more transparent, human-readable computational representations of models.

In this paper, we aim to go further than current 3D scanning methods by identifying the arrangement of a set of known Lego components to obtain a complete, brick by brick, 3D reconstruction of the original scanned Lego model. We propose a fully automatic pipeline to reconstruct semantic 3D Lego models from 2D images, comprising the following novel ingredients: angular DBSCAN, a novel variant of the clustering algorithm DBSCAN [5] using angular displacements that is suitable for grouping both parallel and anti-parallel vectors and a method for reducing the problem of non-Manhattan reconstruction to that of Manhattan reconstruction. Figure 1 shows an example model, the reconstructed visual hull, and the output of our proposed method, consisting of a 3D arrangement of the individual blocks that make up the original model.

2   Related Work

Although little research has been undertaken on the programmatic reconstruction of Lego models, there is a large area of research on identifying and reconstructing cuboids and buildings from point clouds. There exists also a small body of work on various mathematics of Lego permutations, Lego construction and Lego detection. No attempts have been made to reconstruct Lego *models* in 3D.

Manhattan-World Reconstruction: Kim and Hilton [6] showed in 2015 a pipeline that detects and reconstructs cuboids from multiple stereo pairs of spherical images, under the assumption of a Manhattan-world. They describe dealing with planes that are too similar to each other, eliminating unreliable planes and plane intersection refinement. They calculate the similarity between sets of parallel planes by: first calculating overlap and difference in position; merging similar planes by taking a parallel bounding box; and finally replacing the original planes with the newly created one. Their plane intersection refinement aims to create perfect cuboids from sets of noisy, Manhattan compliant planes by using intelligently picked tolerances to edit the plane parameters so that they exactly meet at corners to form cuboids.

Li et al. [7] deal with noisy input data in the form of 3D point clouds extracted from aerial photography. They present a *generate and select strategy*, formulated as a labelling problem, and solve it using a Markov Random Field. Their solution appears to work well for representing inputs as a densely packed set of blocks. In their setup, there is also the problem of missing walls, which is the identification of internal walls missing from the input data, but possibly recoverable from auxiliary data - such as 2D images. They also provide some insight into a solution to the problem of missing walls. They use Hough transforms to identify cuboid faces from their initial input images, which would be impossible to extract via analysis of 3D surfaces alone.

Non-Manhattan-World Reconstruction: With a point cloud as input, Cao and Wang [8] have developed a robust way to find cuboids of any rotation with impressive accuracy. They first seed cubes randomly in the point cloud and then use a Levenberg–Marquardt algorithm [9], paired with their method for calculating distance between each cube and the point cloud to optimise their output. They expand each cube to fit the ground truth as best as it can, paired with a smoothing variable that combines cuboids which it feels should not be disjoint. It seems to work best on inputs which extend out in *all* dimensions, but can still perform well with some changes to their smoothing variable if this condition is not met. Schnabel et al. [10] produced breakthrough research in the area of 3D reconstruction of arbitrary models using their RANSAC [11] approach. Their algorithm runs a single subroutine with 5 different types of shapes, attempting to find areas of the input point cloud where they each fit best. The research stresses that although their approach is fast and robust it does not find these shape proxies for every part of the input surface, leaving holes and overlaps between the disjoint shapes which have been found.

Lego Theory: There is a body of research (Durhuus and Eilers [12], Nilsson [13], Abrahamsen and Eilers [14]) that is focused on investigating Lego under certain heavy constraints such as Manhattan world assumption or known heights and widths of input models, with the aims of investigating the permutations, complexity, entropy and other properties of Lego models. There seems to be no exact formula to follow for computing the number of Lego permutations, especially with non-Mahattan models. The research does, however, show an exponential growth when computing the number of models which can be made using n Lego. Because of this, it is unlikely that any kind of brute force method would be feasible for Lego detection, construction or reconstruction without introducing some constraints on the search space.

Lego Detection: There have been many attempts to recognise and categorise individual Lego and Duplo bricks from 2D images using computer vision, deep learning and machine learning methods, including the work of Mattheij [15], the software of Nguyen [16] and West [17], and in material from Lego Education[1]. These are all able to do well at identifying individual bricks in images with only the target brick and a solid background. However, none of them leverage any advantage that a 3D input can provide, or attempt to process models with multiple connected bricks. Chou and Su [18] attempt to identify entire models as opposed to single bricks. There is no reconstruction involved in their research, however they develop a pipeline using a Microsoft Kinect and RANSAC to extract their target and then use a convolution neural network to identify whether the model is equivalent to another.

Lego Construction: The *Lego Construction Problem* was set by Lego to answer the question: "Given any 3D body, how can it be built from LEGO bricks?" [19]. The Lego Construction Problem looks for ways to construct any 3D input using Lego, so that the surface is similar enough to the original. While the Lego Construction Problem is not entirely applicable to the problem at hand, Kim et al. [19] has some discussion on the difficulties of dealing with the problem's large search space and they evaluate various methods for tackling this, such as using brick colour to aid in detection and ways of reducing the possible number of Lego that can be detected. Peysakhov and Regli [20] feature in the previous paper showing a method of unambiguously representing and abstracting a Lego model as a graph. Their graph representation is a directed graph where each node is a unique Lego, and each edge describes which studs connect Lego.

3   Method

In this section, we present our novel pipeline to reconstruct Lego models in 3D. 3D simplifies representation and provides invariance, modelling the intrinsic structure of our models. The low dimensionality is also crucial for measuring creativity, since we can only hope to capture a few hundred models from a few hundred people, so learning models from this data needs to be highly sample efficient to prevent overfitting.

The underlying idea of our pipeline is to reduce all of the Lego identification requirements to that of the simpler identification of Manhattan compliant meshes. Manhattan compliant Lego models have strict rules on how they can be constructed, leading to a finite number of possible models. By reducing the problem to a Manhattan world we aim to take advantage of this inherent structure to deduce the full reconstruction in an efficient manner. Together with the lack of available training data, this makes the problem an ideal fit for a more classical computer vision approach, rather than learning based methods. Furthermore, our approach allows full control of the types and number of Lego bricks used.

In the first step, we generate the visual hull of a model from the 2D input images. Next, we use any prior knowledge about the colours or patterns on the Lego to extract any information we can about their locations. The next three steps extract face information from the monolithic mesh, use the information to

---

[1] https://education.lego.com/en-us/lessons/ev3-cim/make-a-sorting-machine.

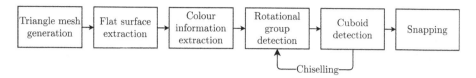

Fig. 2. Flowchart of the proposed pipeline.

reduce non-Manhattan compliant areas of the mesh to Manhattan ones, and then perform an adaptation of the *Block World Reconstruction* of Kim and Hilton [6] to identify remaining Lego. The final stage fixes any inaccuracies by snapping Lego together as they would be in the real world. An overview of the pipeline is shown in Fig. 2. The following sections will describe the steps in detail.

3.1   Triangle Mesh Generation

The input to our algorithm consists of a set of 2D RGB images of a physical Lego model, captured from viewpoints that uniformly sample a circle around the vertical Y-axis. Shape-from-X methods based on feature matching, such as structure-from-motion e.g. COLMAP [21,22], fail on such images due to the lack of texture on the lego bricks. Instead, we assume calibrated cameras and apply a standard space carving method [23,24] to these images to extract a volumetric visual hull. We convert the volumetric representation to a triangle mesh by applying the marching cubes algorithm (Fig. 3(a)). Finally, on the triangle mesh we apply Laplacian smoothing to reduce the roughness of the surface created by the voxel discretisation (Fig. 3(b)).

3.2   Flat Surface Extraction

To get any kind of meaning from the monolithic mesh, we must extract face information. To do this we perform a discrete differentiation on the monolithic mesh, labelling each triangle of the mesh with the dihedral angles between itself and each of its connecting triangles. From this we find which groups of triangles form flat surfaces by removing any triangles which have one or more dihedral angles over a certain threshold (Fig. 3(c) and (d)). We name the set of all flat surfaces F where each element is a set of triangles which make up a flat surface.

This method holds up very well for bricks due to the input meshes only containing right angles or flat surfaces. The Laplacian smooth used in the pre-processing also assists in ensuring robust identification of flat surfaces.

3.3   Colour Information Extraction

Lego plates are short in height relative to a standard brick. This means that the planar faces of the brick sides may be below the resolution of the generated mesh. If that is the case, we handle plates explicitly using a separate process.

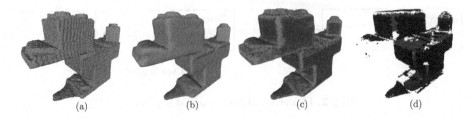

Fig. 3. Left to right: (a) input without any smoothing; (b) input after a Laplacian smooth; (c) mesh differentiation with yellow indicating areas of high curvature, and red indicating areas of low curvature; (d) groups of flat surfaces. (Color figure online)

To simplify this task, we assume that plates share the same colour and that this is different from the colour of the other bricks.

We extract all triangles from the mesh with the chosen colour, indicating a plate, and compute the bounding box of each cluster of triangles. We can then remove the associated triangles from the mesh and use the found cuboid faces in the *Cuboid Detection* of Sect. 3.5.

We can also use a similar filter to identify patterned bricks, and to extract the pattern information. This information can later be used to apply textures to appropriate bricks once found.

3.4 Rotational Group Detection

To identify the areas of the monolithic mesh which break the Manhattan assumption we first need to identify a set, P_F, of subsets of F such that each subset, p, contains only flat surfaces which are parallel to each other. We then need to find our set of rotational groups, $\Pi_F = \{(p_0, p_1) | p_0, p_1 \in P_F, p_0 \perp p_1)\}$.

By definition all elements of P_F should be disjoint with all other elements in P_F as well as $\bigcup_{p \in P_F} p$ being equal to F. We can formulate this as a clustering problem on the average normal of elements in F. By doing this we can leverage existing clustering algorithms [25].

Density-based spatial clustering of applications with noise [5] (DBSCAN) is a popular clustering algorithm in cases where the number of clusters to be found is unknown, unlike approaches such as k-means [26]. The fact that cuboids are made up of parallel and perpendicular sides means that DBSCAN clusters should all have a high density where we need them to, e.g. at least two flat surfaces being anti-parallel. This, in addition to its natural noise removal property, makes it a good choice for this application. DBSCAN is often used for clustering points in 3D euclidean space, for which the metric is almost always euclidean distance. While this would cluster together parallel vectors effectively, it would always fail to cluster anti-parallel vectors.

Angular DBSCAN: We subsequently develop *Angular DBSCAN* (A-DBSCAN), using $\left|cos(2\theta + \frac{\pi}{2})\right|$ as the density metric, as opposed to the usual

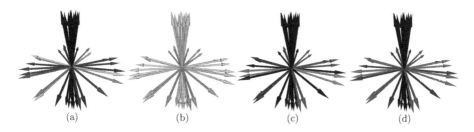

Fig. 4. From left to right: (a) vectors from six Lego with ground truth groupings; (b) vectors with no groupings (input to DBSCAN); (c) vector groupings after euclidean displacement or cosine distance DBSCAN; (d) vector groupings after Angular DBSCAN. $\epsilon = \frac{\pi}{20}$. Each colour represents a cluster.

euclidean distance or cosine distance, with the aim of removing the erroneous results produced by vector magnitude and anti-parallelism (Fig. 4). We modify the prerequisite definitions of DBSCAN from Schubert et al. [27] as follows:

- A vector V is a 'core vector' if at least $minVecs$ vectors have an angle less than ϵ between them and V, including V.
- A vector W is a 'direct neighbour' of a core vector, V, if vector W has an angle less than ϵ between V and itself.
- A vector W is a 'neighbour' of V if there is a path from V to W, where each vector in the path is a 'direct neighbour' of the previous vector.
- All other vectors are noise.

Here, with *angle between two vectors*, we mean the absolute acute angle, $|\cos(2\theta + \frac{\pi}{2})|$. The modified algorithm then becomes:

1. Identify the neighbouring vectors of every vector, and identify the core vectors.
2. Identify the connected components of core vectors on the neighbours graph, ignoring all non-core vectors.
3. Assign each non-core vector to a cluster within ϵ range, otherwise assign it to noise.

The output contains clusters of vectors identified using A-DBSCAN which, when mapped back to their original flat surfaces, split F into the elements of P_F. All other vectors will be returned as noise, and their original flat surfaces can be assigned as such.

Angular Pairing: At this point, given our input bricks each have 2 sets of parallel faces which are perpendicular to the Y-axis, $\#P_F \leq 12$. This makes it viable to run a brute force search on P_F, identifying perpendicular pairs, removing them from the search as we progress. The identified pairs make up our rotational groups Π. See Fig. 5 for an example.

Fig. 5. From left to right: (a) input mesh with red removed; (b) A-DBSCAN clusters by colour; (c) rotation groups Π, by colour. (Color figure online)

3.5 Cuboid Detection

Manhattan World Reduction: The first stage of detecting cuboids is to use the previously identified rotational groups to duplicate the monolithic mesh into $\#\Pi$ copies, followed by rotating each copy such that all flat surfaces in any given rotational group are Manhattan compliant within one of the copies. Splitting the meshes also allows the rest of the algorithm to run in parallel.

Brick Face Extraction: To extract the planar faces of our input, we take inspiration from part of Kim and Hilton's *Block world reconstruction* [6] as we act on the now Manhattan aligned mesh sections. In contrast to Kim and Hilton, we can disregard the scene scale parameter used in their approach as we know exactly the sizes we need from the sizes of Lego. In place of their 2D to 3D plane reconstruction methods, the prior steps in this section have already generated Manhattan compliant flat surfaces. If we name the set of flat surfaces in the current rotational group Ω, then for each item, Ω_i, we can look at its normal vector and calculate which global axis it aligns closest to, one of X, Y or Z. We call the identified axis A_i.

To extract plane segments, if we were to simply take a bounding box of each Ω_i, we would be affected by the absence of triangles which were on the connection between faces during the previous mesh differentiation, resulting in a plane segment which would be smaller than the face it is meant to represent. Instead we can compare Ω_i to the original input mesh and dilate Ω_i to rectify the previous erosion caused by removing areas of high curvature. Projecting the dilated Ω_i onto A_i results in a good silhouette of the model's face, from which we can then take a fuller bounding box (see Fig. 6). Doing this for all Ω_i gives us a set of axis-aligned plane segments, S_p. Subsequently, we merge similar planes as in Kim and Hilton, reducing the noise caused by rough scans.

Hidden Face Extraction: We define *hidden* faces to be faces of Lego bricks which are hidden in the internal space of the input visual hull, and so cannot be explicitly seen in images or extracted from the input mesh. We can however see faint lines defining these planes from the outside. This occurs when two bricks of the same colour are placed next to each other. In this part, we aim to

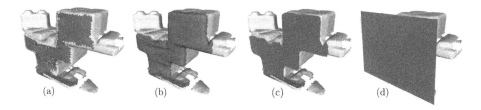

Fig. 6. From left to right: (a) input mesh with flat surface; (b) dilated flat surface against mesh; (c) flat surface projected to the identified axis A_i; (d) flat surface bounding box projected to A_i.

reconstruct the faces which correspond to these faint lines, to remove ambiguity in our reconstructions.

In Li et al. [7], Hough transforms are used to identify lines on the surface of their images, and to then extrapolate a face, perpendicular to the surface on which the line was identified. Instead of using Hough transforms we use Line Segment Detector (LSD) from Grompone von Gioi et al. [28], a more modern approach of line detection, which performs well on low contrast surfaces, has a linear time performance, and requires no parameter tuning.

To find connecting lines between two bricks at the same elevation, we apply LSD to each of the n input images of the model, and filter out any non-vertical lines. Next, we check that the pixels either side of the lines, within a tolerance, have a predominantly similar hue. Finally, to remove detection of corners, we can check that there is a low standard deviation in the hue of the pixels on either side of the line. Once we have our lines in 2D space, we tag them with a colour in the images in which they were found, and then retrieve the 3D information once the images have undergone the visual hull process (see Fig. 7(a)). Because we know that the tagged triangles all represent vertical lines, a 3D line can be created from the minimum and maximum of the y coordinates of the tagged triangles and the average of the x and z coordinates.

Using our identified set of 3D lines, we can find the extracted face which is most consistently closest to the line. Taking the identified face's normal vector, we can extrude a new plane segment from the 3D line in the direction of the normal by 16 units. Finally we perform a merging of new quads which are close to each other or overlapping, replacing two close quads with their bounding box. We chose to extrude by 16 units, as that will be adequate for sides of length 16 and 8, and will allow for 32 unit faces as long as there is a visible line on the other side of the brick which can be merged. Figure 7 depicts the process.

Column Identification and Cuboid Detection: To complete the individual identification of a Lego, $\mathbb{L}$, we first identify pairs of parallel planes from the set of axis-aligned plane segments S_p which have a significant overlap as well as a distance between them equal to either the length or width of $\mathbb{L}$. We next build columns with width and length equal to that of $\mathbb{L}$. Columns are identified by comparing each previously identified X-aligned pairing with each identified

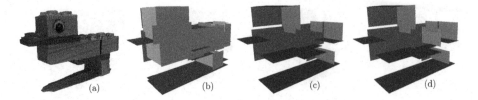

Fig. 7. From left to right: (a) input mesh with detected seam superimposed in blue; (b) extracted faces from input mesh; (c) inside of extracted faces, showing no internal face; (d) extracted hidden face highlighted yellow. (Color figure online)

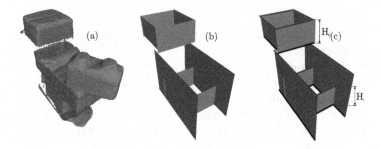

Fig. 8. From left to right: (a) input mesh; (b) identified 2×2 brick columns composed of two green and two purple planes each; (c) red and black edges indicate the maximum and minimum y coordinates of each plane, H_0 and H_1 are the distances between the minimum of the maxima y coordinates and the maximum of minima y coordinate of each column. (Color figure online)

Z-aligned pairing. We have a column when: we find two pairings where each plane segment intersects both plane segments of the other pairing, within a tolerance; the width and length of the column equal that of $\mathbb{L}$; $H \geq height(\mathbb{L})$ where H is the distance between the minimum of the maxima y coordinates of each plane and the maximum of the minima y coordinates of all planes in the column Fig. 8 depicts this process.

The final step of identifying cuboids is to take each identified column and find where the cuboid (or cuboids) are positioned within the column. Because of the lack of plane information between vertically connected bricks we can only identify top level or bottom level cuboids. We choose to find the top-most cuboid in a column, and to do so we search through all planes which have an identified axis A_i of Y, taking note of all which have a substantial overlap with the cross-section of the column. We then select the top most Y-plane.

At this stage we have five of the six faces of a Lego $\mathbb{L}$ identified, and therefore can extrapolate the final face by copying the top Y plane and subtracting the height of the Lego. Together with the rotation from the A-DBSCAN, $\mathbb{L}$ has now been fully identified, and we can continue with the next Lego.

3.6   Chiselling

To continue identifying the remaining bricks we can *chisel* through the model by removing input mesh information close to identified bricks, and injecting extrapolated bottom planes into the model where the identified top level Lego were found. This can be done recursively until we identify all bricks, or it does not find any new brick on a pass. At the end of the process we can report the exact number of Lego found.

3.7   Snapping

Various inaccuracies occur during the reconstruction, mostly due to inaccuracies in the input mesh. In an effort to improve upon this, we implement a snapping algorithm that loops over each Lego stud, searching for connections of the opposite type, and matching the closest stud as long as it is within $minDist$, where $minDist$ is set to the height of the thinnest Lego.

Doing this produces a graph similar to Peysakhov and Regli [20], connecting Lego by their studs. We can then use this graph to offset the position of each Lego to better snap to each other, while maintaining relative rotations.

4   Evaluation and Results

4.1   Angular DBSCAN

Choosing the correct value for the threshold ϵ is very important. If ϵ is too large, all vectors will be assigned to a single group. While, if ϵ is too small, each vector will be assigned to either its own group or noise, depending on the value of $minVecs$. Since most Lego are cuboid, each group of vectors should be composed of only orthogonal vectors. This sets a maximum ϵ of $\frac{\pi}{4}$ before ϵ covers all possible vectors at least once. To identify the optimal ϵ for the proposed A-DBSCAN on Lego we generated 6 groups of 6 orthogonal vectors to simulate the vectors produced by 6 Lego. We then apply a random rotation around the y-axis to each group to simulated rotations of Lego, and finally we add slight random noise to each vector. We then performed 1000 runs of the A-DBSCAN on these vectors for each value of epsilon between $\frac{\pi}{40}$ and $\frac{\pi}{4}$ in steps of $\frac{\pi}{20}$. We also simulate chiselling by removing vector groups which have been correctly identified, and performing a recursive step on the remaining vectors.

From Fig. 9, we can see that any $\epsilon \leq \frac{\pi}{20}$ does not identify nearly enough vectors correctly, while any $\epsilon \geq \frac{\pi}{20}$ shows a recursion depth which we wouldn't expect for groups of vectors this dense. To ensure we have not only grouped vectors together which were grouped together in the input, but also make sure we don't have too few groups, we need to find the ϵ which maximises both the mean percentage of vectors grouped together correctly, as well as the mean recursion depth. We highlight $\epsilon = \frac{\pi}{20}$ as the optimal result, with a mean percentage of vectors group together correctly of 98.37% and mean recursion depth of 1.856 (which implies there will usually be at least 2 groupings). These results are what we expect from this many vectors.

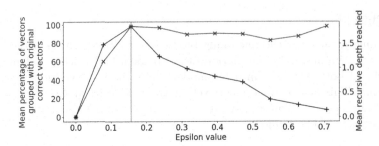

Fig. 9. DBSCAN epsilon tested for percentage of 'successful' groupings and the mean recursive depth reached.

4.2   Lego Reconstruction

Dataset: We evaluate our proposed approach on the data of Deterding et al. [3, 4], which has been collected with the goal of evaluating human creativity using Lego. It consists of a set of 162 Lego ducks, composed of the same 6 Lego. Each model is photographed on a turntable, resulting in 24 images.

Identified Bricks: First, we evaluate the percentage of inputs successfully converted into six unique Lego. Overall, roughly 44.3% of the models were completely reported as being identified correctly. 75% of 2×1 bricks were identified, 73.6% of 2×2 bricks, 84.6% of 2×3 slates, and 55% of 2×4 bricks. 140 out of the 162 ducks were used for the evaluation.

From the above results, we see that the identification of 2×4 bricks is considerably lower than any other Lego. This may be due to the large volume of the brick providing much more space to be affected by various forms of noise in the system. The larger faces of the 2×4 brick, paired with it often being used as a central Lego to a duck (as oppose to a top, bottom or side Lego) mean that it normally has more of its face area obscured by other bricks. If the attached bricks are not correctly identified then it may cause the central 2×4 brick to remain unidentified.

The overall relatively large number of non-perfectly reconstructed models is caused mainly by considerable artifacts of the reconstructed volumetric visual hull, which is an issue on nearly half of the reconstructed meshes. This is due to the test data's scan resolution, as well as the visual hull algorithm's resolution. Improving that would benefit all subsequent steps, and potentially removing the need of using colour information to identify plates (Sect. 3.3).

Mesh Similarity: Second, we compare the final reconstructed Lego models with the reconstructed visual hull from the 2D input images. We first apply rigid iterative closest point [29] to align the two meshes. Then, for every vertex, v, in our input mesh, of which there are hundreds of thousands, we find the smallest distance between v and the output mesh (a mesh with only hundreds

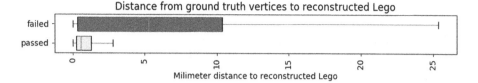

Fig. 10. Summary of vertex-wise distance to ground truth analysis.

of vertices). We then plot the range, interquartile range and mean of the set of ducks where we found six bricks, and the set where we found any less. This is shown in Fig. 10. We can see that there is a correlation between the algorithm reporting a pass or fail, as described in the previous subsection, and the distances between input and output meshes being small and large respectively.

For more context, a 1×1 Lego (smaller than any of our Lego) would be 8 mm on both of its sides, so when the algorithm reports a pass the output mesh will rarely be more than a 1×1 Lego away from the input, while it can leave gaps of over 5 times as far when it has reported a fail. An advantage of our algorithm being conservative in its searching, only identifying Lego if there is concrete reasoning to do so, as well as the bricks used to build the model being known beforehand, is that it allows us to know when we have passed fairly consistently. These results show that the system should rarely produce a false positive.

Visual Analysis: Finally, we qualitatively analyse the proposed method. Figure 11 shows example outputs from each stage of the algorithm, with the final result. In row (A), we show an example duck with hidden faces between vertically connected bricks. The chiselling was able to successfully identify all blocks, and it works well on most ducks. Row (B) shows a duck with multiple rotational groups, which were successfully detected, and subsequently the *Cuboid detection* is performed on both groups separately. Row (C) shows an example of a 2×2 and a 2×4 brick next to each other, and the proposed method successfully being able to identify and separate both bricks.

While our method performed very well on approximately half of the models in the dataset, there are two main reasons why it did not work well on the others. First, the initial mesh generation does not produce a high enough resolution mesh to capture the sides of plates or small holes in models, or left out large chunks of the model caused by a too large baseline between the 2D input images. Second, some ducks use an unorthodox construction method where the *sides* of plates would be rotated and snapped *between* studs (sometimes called 'pony-ear' or 'pony-leg' connections), which our method is not able to process. An example of such a model is shown in row (D).

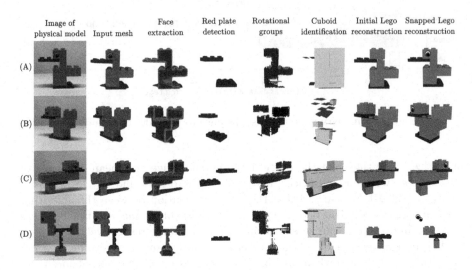

Fig. 11. Example reconstructions. Rows (A)–(C): successful reconstructions, row (D): failed reconstruction with pony-ear connections that our method is not able to process.

5   Conclusion

In this paper, we have demonstrated our novel pipeline that takes in a tightly coupled, non-Manhattan compliant Lego mesh and identifies the exact positions of each Lego used to construct it. We introduced Angular DBSCAN, A-DBSCAN, to reduce the non-Manhattan reconstruction to that of a Manhattan one, as well as a method combining image and mesh data to calculate hidden plane information. To the best of our knowledge, ours is the first piece of work in literature that reconstructs Lego models in 3D, and decomposes them into their exact bricks. The results show large potential for use in practise, for example for studying human creativity, but also in the broader study of 3D shape recognition.

The proposed system is conservative in its approach, only identifying Lego if there is concrete reasoning to do so. This, paired with the fact it takes the bricks used in the models construction, allow it to identify successfully whether or not it has passed in its identification of a model's construction with very high accuracy. The main limitation on what models can be used as input is that the current system cannot deal with models which contain 'pony ears' or 'pony leg' connections. This challenge will be tackled in future work. Finally, future work could be to explore the use of deep learning for parts of our pipeline.

Acknowledgements. This work was supported by the Digital Creativity Labs funded by EPSRC/AHRC/Innovate UK (EP/M023265/1), and the PLAYTrack project, supported by a research grant from the LEGO Foundation.

References

1. Gauntlett, D.: The LEGO system as a tool for thinking, creativity, and changing the world. In: Lego Studies: Examining the Building Blocks of a Transmedial Phenomenon, pp. 1–16 (2014)
2. Pike, C.: Exploring the conceptual space of LEGO: teaching and learning the psychology of creativity. Psychol. Learn. Teach. **2**, 87–94 (2002)
3. Deterding, S.: Brains, bricks, ducks, AI: New ways of assessing human and computational creativity. osf.io (2020). https://doi.org/10.17605/OSF.IO/2SGM9
4. Ferguson, M., et al.: Automatic similarity detection in LEGO ducks. In: Eleventh International Conference on Computational Creativity, ICCC 2020. Association for Computational Creativity (ACC) (2020)
5. Ester, M., Kriegel, H., Sander, J., Xu, X.: A density-based algorithm for discovering clusters in large spatial databases with noise. In: Simoudis, E., Han, J., Fayyad, U.M. (eds.) Proceedings of the Second International Conference on Knowledge Discovery and Data Mining, KDD 1996, Portland, Oregon, USA, pp. 226–231. AAAI Press (1996)
6. Kim, H., Hilton, A.: Block world reconstruction from spherical stereo image pairs. Comput. Vis. Image Underst. **139**, 104–121 (2015)
7. Li, M., Wonka, P., Nan, L.: Manhattan-world urban reconstruction from point clouds. In: Leibe, B., Matas, J., Sebe, N., Welling, M. (eds.) ECCV 2016. LNCS, vol. 9908, pp. 54–69. Springer, Cham (2016). https://doi.org/10.1007/978-3-319-46493-0_4
8. Cao, C., Wang, G.: Fitting cuboids from the unstructured 3D point cloud. In: Zhao, Y., Barnes, N., Chen, B., Westermann, R., Kong, X., Lin, C. (eds.) ICIG 2019. LNCS, vol. 11902, pp. 179–190. Springer, Cham (2019). https://doi.org/10.1007/978-3-030-34110-7_16
9. Levenberg, K.: A method for the solution of certain non-linear problems in least squares. Q. Appl. Math. **2**, 164–168 (1944)
10. Schnabel, R., Wahl, R., Klein, R.: Efficient RANSAC for point-cloud shape detection. Comput. Graph. Forum **26**, 214–226 (2007)
11. Fischler, M.A., Bolles, R.C.: Random sample consensus: a paradigm for model fitting with applications to image analysis and automated cartography. Commun. ACM **24**, 381–395 (1981)
12. Durhuus, B., Eilers, S.: On the entropy of LEGO. J. Appl. Math. Comput. **45**, 433–448 (2014)
13. Nilsson, R.M.: On the number of flat LEGO structures. Master's thesis, University of Copenhagen (2016)
14. Abrahamsen, M., Eilers, S.: On the asymptotic enumeration of LEGO structures. Exp. Math. **20**, 145–152 (2011)
15. Mattheij, J.: Neural nets vs. lego bricks [resources]. IEEE Spectr. **54**, 17–18 (2017)
16. Nguyen, H.M.: kinect-duplo-sensing: a ROS package for identifying Duplo blocks with the Microsoft Kinect sensor (2014). https://github.com/cheehieu/kinect-duplo-sensing
17. West, D.: A high-speed computer vision pipeline for the universal LEGO sorting machine (2019). https://towardsdatascience.com/a-high-speed-computer-vision-pipeline-for-the-universal-lego-sorting-machine-253f5a690ef4
18. Chou, C., Su, Y.: A block recognition system constructed by using a novel projection algorithm and convolution neural networks. IEEE Access **5**, 23891–23900 (2017)

19. Kim, J.W.: Survey on automated LEGO assembly construction. In: WSCG 2014: Poster Papers Proceedings: 22nd International Conference in Central Europen Computer Graphics, Visualization and Computer Vision in Co-operation with EUROGRAPHICS Association (2014)
20. Peysakhov, M., Regli, W.C.: Using assembly representations to enable evolutionary design of LEGO structures. AI EDAM **17**, 155–168 (2003)
21. Schönberger, J.L., Frahm, J.M.: Structure-from-motion revisited. In: Conference on Computer Vision and Pattern Recognition (CVPR) (2016)
22. Schönberger, J.L., Zheng, E., Frahm, J.-M., Pollefeys, M.: Pixelwise view selection for unstructured multi-view stereo. In: Leibe, B., Matas, J., Sebe, N., Welling, M. (eds.) ECCV 2016. LNCS, vol. 9907, pp. 501–518. Springer, Cham (2016). https://doi.org/10.1007/978-3-319-46487-9_31
23. Lorensen, W.E., Cline, H.E.: Marching cubes: a high resolution 3D surface construction algorithm. In: Stone, M.C. (ed.) Proceedings of the 14th Annual Conference on Computer Graphics and Interactive Techniques, SIGGRAPH 1987, Anaheim, California, USA, 27–31 July 1987, 163–169. ACM (1987)
24. Kutulakos, K.N., Seitz, S.M.: A theory of shape by space carving. Int. J. Comput. Vis. **38**, 199–218 (2000)
25. Xu, D., Tian, Y.: A comprehensive survey of clustering algorithms. Ann. Data Sci. **2**(2), 165–193 (2015). https://doi.org/10.1007/s40745-015-0040-1
26. Lloyd, S.P.: Least squares quantization in PCM. IEEE Trans. Inf. Theory **28**, 129–136 (1982)
27. Schubert, E., Sander, J., Ester, M., Kriegel, H., Xu, X.: DBSCAN revisited, revisited: why and how you should (still) use DBSCAN. ACM Trans. Database Syst. **42**, 19:1–19:21 (2017)
28. von Gioi, R.G., Jakubowicz, J., Morel, J., Randall, G.: LSD: a line segment detector. IPOL J. **2**, 35–55 (2012)
29. Besl, P.J., McKay, N.D.: A method for registration of 3-D shapes. IEEE Trans. Pattern Anal. Mach. Intell. **14**, 239–256 (1992)

Multi-view Consistency Loss
for Improved Single-Image 3D
Reconstruction of Clothed People

Akin Caliskan[1]($\boxtimes$)(iD), Armin Mustafa[1]($\boxtimes$)(iD), Evren Imre[2]($\boxtimes$)(iD),
and Adrian Hilton[1]($\boxtimes$)(iD)

[1] Center for Vision, Speech and Signal Processing University of Surrey,
Guildford, UK
{a.caliskan,a.mustafa,a.hilton}@surrey.ac.uk
[2] Vicon Motion Systems Ltd., Oxford, UK
evren.imre@vicon.com

Abstract. We present a novel method to improve the accuracy of the
3D reconstruction of clothed human shape from a single image. Recent
work has introduced volumetric, implicit and model-based shape learning frameworks for reconstruction of objects and people from one or more
images. However, the accuracy and completeness for reconstruction of
clothed people is limited due to the large variation in shape resulting from
clothing, hair, body size, pose and camera viewpoint. This paper introduces two advances to overcome this limitation: firstly a new synthetic
dataset of realistic clothed people, *3DVH*; and secondly, a novel multiple-
view loss function for training of monocular volumetric shape estimation,
which is demonstrated to significantly improve generalisation and reconstruction accuracy. The 3DVH dataset of realistic clothed 3D human models rendered with diverse natural backgrounds is demonstrated to allows
transfer to reconstruction from real images of people. Comprehensive comparative performance evaluation on both synthetic and real images of people demonstrates that the proposed method significantly outperforms the
previous state-of-the-art learning-based single image 3D human shape estimation approaches achieving significant improvement of reconstruction
accuracy, completeness, and quality. An ablation study shows that this
is due to both the proposed multiple-view training and the new *3DVH*
dataset. The code and the dataset can be found at the project website:
https://akincaliskan3d.github.io/MV3DH/.

1 Introduction

Parsing humans from images is a fundamental task in many applications including AR/VR interfaces [1], character animation [2], autonomous driving, virtual try-on [3] and re-enactment [4]. There has been significant progress on 2D

Electronic supplementary material The online version of this chapter (https://
doi.org/10.1007/978-3-030-69525-5_5) contains supplementary material, which is available to authorized users.

© Springer Nature Switzerland AG 2021
H. Ishikawa et al. (Eds.): ACCV 2020, LNCS 12622, pp. 71–88, 2021.
https://doi.org/10.1007/978-3-030-69525-5_5

human pose estimation [5,6] and 2D human segmentation [7,8] to understand the coarse geometry of the human body. Following this, another line of research has advanced 3D human pose estimation from monocular video [9–11]. Recent research has investigated the even more challenging problem of learning to estimate full 3D human shape from a single image with impressive results [12–15]. For clothed people in general scenes accurate and complete 3D reconstruction remains a challenging problem due to the large variation in clothing, hair, camera viewpoint, body shape and pose. Figure 1 illustrates common failures of existing single-view reconstruction approaches [12–14] where the reconstructed model does not accurately reconstruct the pose or shape from a different view. The proposed multiple view training loss successfully addresses this problem.

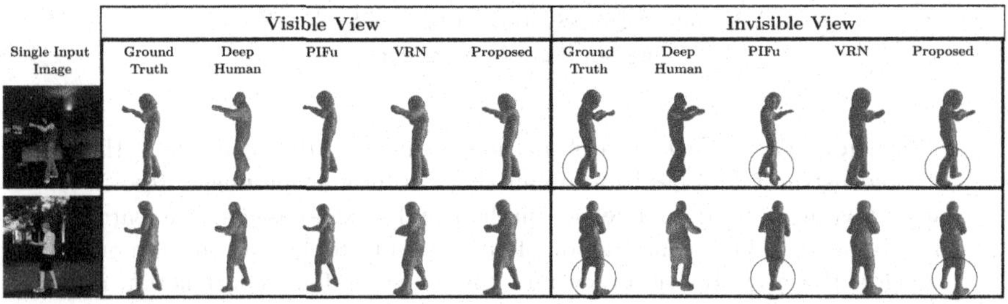

Fig. 1. Single view 3D reconstruction of clothed people from Deephuman [14], PIFu [13], VRN [15] and the proposed method.

In previous studies [16–21], learning-based human reconstruction from multi-view or depth camera systems in controlled environments has achieved a high level of shape detail. However, the ultimate challenge is monocular 3D human reconstruction from a single image. To address this problem, parametric model-based 3D human shape estimation methods have been proposed [22–24]. However, existing parametric models only represent the underlying naked body shape and lack important geometric variation of clothing and hair. Augmented parametric model representations proposed to represent clothing [25] are limited to tight clothing which maps bijectively to body shape and does not accurately represent general apparel such as dresses and jackets.

Recent model-free approaches have achieved impressive results in 3D shape reconstruction of clothed people from a single image using learnt volumetric [14,15,26], point cloud [27], geometry image [28] and implicit [13] surface representations. Learnt volumetric [15,18,26] and implicit [13] surface representations have achieved human reconstruction with clothing detail. Comparative evaluation of existing approaches (Sect. 4.2), shows that using a 3D voxel occupancy grid shows better accuracy than implicit functions because of encoding the complete topology of the human body. For example in PIFu [13], lack of global coherence is due to the sampling schema during training. Learning detailed shape representations of clothed humans requires a training dataset that represents the wide variety of clothing and hairstyles together with body shape, pose, viewpoint and scene variation for people observed in natural images. Previous studies presented various datasets to learn 3D human reconstruction from a single image. However, they have limited variation in human pose [13,15] or details in surface geometry [14,19], which limits learning accurate 3D human reconstruction. To address this problem [28] proposed a large synthetic training data of clothed people. However, despite the number of training samples, the rendered images have an unrealistic appearance for skin, hair and clothing texture.

In this paper, we improve the accuracy of clothed 3D human shape reconstruction from a single image, as shown in Fig. 1. To overcome the limitations of previous training data, we introduce the *3DVH* dataset, which provides 4 million realistic image-3D model pairs of people with a wide variety of clothing, hairstyles and poses giving detailed surface geometry and appearance rendered in both indoor and outdoor environment with realistic scene illumination. To improve the reconstruction accuracy we propose learning a volumetric shape representation using a novel multi-view loss function which ensures accurate single-view reconstruction of both visible and occluded surface regions. The novel loss function learns to incorporate surface photo-consistency cues in the single-view reconstruction which are not present in the observed image or 3D ground-truth shape reconstruction. The contributions of this work are:

– A novel learning based framework for 3D reconstruction of clothed people from a single image, trained on multi-view 3D shape consistency.
– A dataset of realistic clothed 3D human models with a wide variety of clothing, hair, body shape, pose, viewpoint, scenes and illumination.

The proposed approach gives a significant improvement in the accuracy and completeness of reconstruction compared to the state-of-the-art methods for single image human reconstruction [13–15] evaluated on real and synthetic images of people. The 3DVH dataset will be released to support future research.

2 Related Work

2.1 Single View 3D Human Reconstruction

Estimation of 3D human reconstruction from a single image requires a large amount of prior data to learn accurate predictions due to the large variation in clothing, pose, shape, and hair for people. Initial monocular human reconstruction methods use parametric human model such as SMPL [29,30] to estimate the body and shape parameters in an iterative manner using either 2D joint locations and silhouettes [22] or 3D joints and mesh coordinates [12]. To address the requirement of accurate 2D/3D joint labelled data, Kanazawa et al. [23] directly regress the shape parameters using weakly labelled 2D human body joints. To improve the accuracy of the models, an iterative optimization stage was added to the regression network [24]. Even though parametric model-based methods are able to reliably estimate the human body from a single image in the wild, estimated shapes are a naked human body without hair, clothing and other surface details. Recent approaches have extended this to tight-fitting clothing [31].

Table 1. Comparison of single view 3D reconstruction methods.

	3D representation	Training data	Clothed 3D reconstruction	Single(S)/ Multiple(M) supervision
Bodynet [19]	Explicit-Voxel	Surreal [19]	No	M
VRN [15]	Explicit-Voxel	–	No	S
SiCloPe [26]	Implicit	RenderPeople	Yes	S
DeepHuman [14]	Explicit-Voxel	THUman [14]	No	S
3DPeople [28]	Explicit-Geo. Img	3DPeople [28]	Yes	S
Mould.Hum. [27]	Explicit-Point Clo.	3D-Humans [27]	Yes	S
PIFu [13]	Implicit	RenderPeople	Yes	S
Ours	**Explicit-Voxel**	**3DVH**	**Yes**	**M**

Two categories of methods have been proposed to address this issue and perform model-free non-parametric reconstruction of clothed people: the first category of methods estimate the parametric human model with clothing on top [25,32] and the second category of methods directly estimates the shape from clothed human. This section focuses on the second category of model-free methods, Table 1. Model-free methods such as Bodynet [19] and Voxel Regression Network (VRN) [15] draw a direct inference of volumetric 3D human shape from a single image. However, the training dataset in Bodynet lacks geometric details of human body shape like hair and clothing, resulting in the reconstruction preserving the parametric body model shape. As shown in Table 1, Bodynet is supervised from multi-view images. However, different from our method, Bodynet uses multi-view silhouettes to learn 3D reconstruction. In VRN the training dataset lacks variation in shape, texture and pose limiting the generalisation capability. SiCloPe [26] introduces a method to predict multi-view silhouettes from a frontal image and 3D pose of a subject, the 3D visual hull is inferred from these silhouettes. However, this method achieves accurate reconstructions only for a limited number of human poses. Another recent line of research [28] obtained geometric image inference from a single image using a generative adversarial network. A concurrent work [14] predicts voxel occupancy from a single image using the initial SMPL model. This is followed by coarse-to-fine refinement to improve the level of detail in the frontal volumetric surface. However, both of these methods achieve limited accuracy in the reconstruction of clothing and hair detail. Other recent approaches to single image human reconstruction fit the parametric SMPL model to the input image and predict the surface displacements to reconstruct clothed human shape [33]. Front and back view depth maps are merged to obtain a full shape reconstruction [27].

PIFu [13] recently introduced pixel-wise implicit functions for shape estimation followed by mesh reconstruction, achieving impressive results with a high level of details on the surface. However, the method cannot handle wide variations in human pose, clothing, and hair. In summary, existing methods either obtain reconstruction for limited human poses or are unable to reconstruct clothing and hair details. The proposed method gives 3D reconstruction of human shape with a wide variety of clothing, body shape, pose, and viewpoint. Comparative evaluation with previous approaches on synthetic and real images demonstrate significant improvement in reconstruction accuracy and completeness.

2.2 Datasets for 3D Human Reconstruction

Datasets are fundamental to learn robust and generalized representation in deep learning. For 2D tasks such as 2D human pose estimation [5,6] or segmentation [7,8], it is relatively straight forward to annotate ground-truth landmarks. However, this becomes more challenging for 3D tasks such as annotating 3D joint locations which requires advanced motion capture systems [9–11] or obtaining ground-truth human body surface shape which requires sophisticated multi-camera capture system [34,35]. Additionally, these datasets require constrained indoor environments to obtain high quality results, which limits the amount of available data for training. Synthetic datasets have been introduced in the literature to address these issues [36].

Table 2. Existing dynamic 3D human datasets and *3DVH* are listed here. **3D-** Number of 3D models, **Img-** 2D images, **Cam** - Number of views, **BG** - Number of different backgrounds in the dataset, and **Act** - Human Actions. - represents missing details in the related publication. K and M stands for thousand and million respectively.

	#of data				#of act	GT data			3D human	
	3D	Img	Cam	BG		3D	Depth	Normal	Cloth	Hair
Odzemok [34]	250	2K	8	1	1	✓	✗	✗	✓	✓
Vlasic [35]	2K	16K	8	1	10	✓	✗	✗	✓	✓
Dressed Hu. [37]	54	120K	68	1	3	✓	✗	✗	✓	✓
MonoPerfCap [38]	2K	2K	1	8	53	✓	✗	✗	✓	✓
Surreal [19]	–	6.5M	1	–	–	✓	✓	✓	✗	✗
THUman [14]	7K	7K	1	–	30	✓	✓	✗	✗	✗
3DPeople [28]	–	2M	4	–	70	✗	✓	✓	✓	✓
3DVH	33K	4M	120	100	200	✓	✓	✓	✓	✓

Table 2 lists the properties and details of existing datasets. Varol et al. [36] proposed the *Surreal* synthetic human dataset with 3D annotated ground-truth and rendered images. 3D human meshes are generated by overlapping tight skin clothing texture on the SMPL [29] model. This leads to a lack of details in hair and clothing. Similar to this, [14] propose the *THUman* dataset, with 3D human models created using DoubleFusion [20] from a single depth camera and fitted with a parametric SMPL model. [39] provides natural images and SMPL

[29] models fitted to the associated images. However, these datasets give limited quality of reconstruction due to the lack of detail in the parametric model. 3D human model datasets were also introduced in [13,26], with a limited range of pose and geometric details for clothing and hair. Recently, [28] proposed synthetic *3DPeople* dataset with renderings of 3D human models with clothing and hair. However this dataset does not provide realistically rendered images and ground-truth (GT) 3D models (Table 2). The proposed dataset, *3DVH*, renders 3D models onto image planes using High Dynamic Range (HDR) illumination from real environments with ray casting rendering, leading to realistic camera images with GT 3D human models. The details of our rendering and the difference from the *3DPeople* dataset is explained in Sect. 3.4. *3DVH* is the largest dataset of high-quality 3D Human models and photo-realistic renderings on multiple camera views >$4m$ image-model pairs.

3 Single-View Human Shape with Multi-view Training

This section explains the novel method proposed for single-view 3D human reconstruction and training dataset generation. A single image of a person with arbitrary pose, clothing, and viewpoint is given as input to the pipeline, and the network predicts the 3D voxelized output of clothed human shape including both visible and occluded parts of the person.

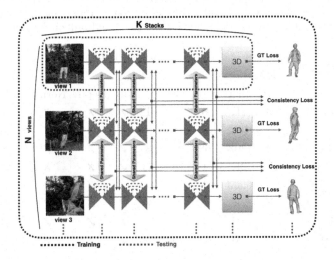

Fig. 2. The learning architecture of the proposed method. Stacked hourglass networks are trained with shared parameters (blue dashed lines), and two loss functions are computed (Sect. 3.3). However, one view is given as input to one stacked hourglass network for testing (red dashed lines) to predict voxel occupancy grid. (Color figure online)

In contrast to previous single-view 3D reconstruction approaches [19,40], the proposed approach is trained using a novel loss function on multiple view images of a person, as shown in Fig. 2. Each viewpoint image is passed through its own convolutional network and the parameters are shared between the networks. The proposed single view reconstruction network learns to reconstruct human shape observed from multiple views, giving a more complete reconstruction from both visible and invisible human body parts in the image. The network for single image 3D volumetric reconstruction consists of K stacked hourglass networks. For training with an $N-$view loss function, we train N single image networks in parallel with shared parameters. The error between the estimated 3D voxel occupancy and ground-truth 3D model is computed for each viewpoint, and view-dependent 3D occupancy grids are transformed from one camera to all other camera coordinate systems to evaluate the multi-view loss in 3D domain. This loss term enables the network to learn feature extraction robust to camera view changes and to predict multi-view consistent 3D human reconstruction from a single image. The proposed network is scalable to N views, and a detailed ablation study on the performance of the network with number of views is provided (Sect. 4.4).

3.1   Learning Architecture

The proposed learning architecture is illustrated in Fig. 2. Inspired by previous work [41], we use a stacked hourglass network architecture with skip connections to propagate information at every scale. Each hourglass network estimates the voxel occupancy as slices. The learning architecture consists of multiple parallel stacked hourglass networks with shared parameters. This allows the introduction of a multi-view loss function. In each hourglass module, there is a 2-dimensional convolution layer followed by a ReLU as an activation function, group normalization and res-net module (full details in the supplementary material). Due to the small memory requirements, we use a small batch size with group normalization [42] instead of batch normalization for efficient convergence. This network architecture is different from previous use of hourglass networks [15], as follows: the proposed hourglass module uses a single scale res-net [41] together with group normalization [42] instead of a multi-scale res-net and batch normalization respectively. In addition, we propose a novel multi-view learning framework with a $N-$view consistency loss combined with 3D losses. The *3DVH* dataset and the code will be made available for research and evaluation.

3.2   3D Human Representation

Representation of 3D content is crucial in single view reconstruction methods, as the design of the learning architecture is based on the representation. Previous studies investigate two groups of model-free 3D representations: implicit and explicit. As shown in Table 2, voxel [14,15], depth maps [27], and implicit surface representations [13] are used to represent 3D human shape. In implicit representation [13], pixel-aligned local feature extraction and the occupancy grid prediction for individual 3D point results in losing global topology of the 3D human body during inference due to the sampling-based training scheme.

This makes it challenging to resolve ambiguities in occluded human body parts, causing inaccurate 3D reconstruction (Fig. 1). Similarly, in [27], back and front depth map representation of the 3D human body disconnects the human body parts during inference, leading to incomplete 3D prediction. Hence we use a complete volumetric voxel occupancy based representation in the network. The network infers voxel occupancy for both visible and occluded body parts allowing shape reconstruction with self-occlusions. To obtain a smooth surface human reconstruction, iso-surface of the voxel occupancy grid are extracted using marching cubes.

3.3   The Proposed Loss Functions

The proposed learning architecture is supervised from the ground truth 3D human models rendered from multiple views and self-supervised with $N - 1$ other views. The 3D loss function $\mathcal{L}_{3D}$ computes the error between the estimated 3D voxel occupancy grid $(\hat{\mathcal{V}}_{ij})$ and 3D ground-truth $(\mathcal{V}_{ij})$ for the ith stack and for the jth camera view of the same subject. As stated in Eq. 1, the binary cross entropy [43] is computed after applying a sigmoid function on the network output. In particular, we used weighted binary cross entropy loss and γ is a weight to balance occupied and unoccupied points in the voxel volume:

$$\mathcal{L}_{3D} = \sum_{j=1}^{K} \sum_{i=1}^{N} \mathcal{L}(\mathcal{V}_{ij}, \hat{\mathcal{V}}_{ij}) \tag{1}$$

$$\mathcal{L}(\mathcal{V}_{ij}, \hat{\mathcal{V}}_{ij}) = \sum_{x} \sum_{y} \sum_{z} \gamma \mathcal{V}_{ij}^{xyz} \log \hat{\mathcal{V}}_{ij}^{xyz} + (1 - \gamma)(1 - \mathcal{V}_{ij}^{xyz})(1 - \log \hat{\mathcal{V}}_{ij}^{xyz})$$

where $\mathcal{V}^{xyz}$ stands for occupancy value of a voxel grid, $\mathcal{V}$, at position (x, y, z). Training a network with only binary cross entropy loss gives limited reconstruction quality for the occluded parts of the 3D human body, as shown in Fig. 8. In order to improve 3D model accuracy, we propose a second loss function, *multi-view consistency loss* $(\mathcal{L}_{MVC})$ between multiple camera views of the same scene. With a multi-view training loss, the proposed representation can learn features robust to camera view changes and self-occlusion. 3D voxel occupancy grids estimated per-camera view are transformed to $N - 1$ other camera coordinate system and the error is computed between the overlapped 3D voxel grids. The multi-view loss function is defined in Eq. 2, the $L2$ loss is computed between voxel occupancy estimates, $\hat{\mathcal{V}}$, from one camera and $N - 1$ other camera views for K stacks.

$$\mathcal{L}_{MVC} = \sum_{j=1}^{K} \sum_{i=1}^{N} \sum_{\substack{l=1 \\ l \neq i}}^{N} \hat{\mathcal{L}}(\hat{\mathcal{V}}_{ij}, \hat{\mathcal{V}}_{lj}) \tag{2}$$

$$\hat{\mathcal{L}}(\hat{\mathcal{V}}_{ij}, \hat{\mathcal{V}}_{lj}) = \sum_{x} \sum_{y} \sum_{z} \| \hat{\mathcal{V}}_{ij}^{xyz} - \hat{\mathcal{V}}_{lj}^{\mathcal{P}(xyz)} \|_2$$

where $\mathcal{P}(\mathcal{X}) = \mathcal{R}\mathcal{X} + \mathcal{T}$ is the transformation operator defined with *rotation matrix*, $\mathcal{R}$, and *translation vector*, $\mathcal{T}$ for *a 3D point*, $\mathcal{X}$. The combined loss function is the weighted sum of the 3D loss and multi-view consistency loss:

$$L = L_{3D} + \lambda L_{MVC} \tag{3}$$

The value of λ is chosen experimentally and remains constant for all tests as explained in Sect. 4.

3.4 3DVH Dataset

To improve the generalisation of human reconstruction with respect to clothing, hair and pose, we introduced a new dataset, *3DVirtualHuman (3DVH)* which is the first multi-view and multiple people 3D dataset to train monocular 3D human reconstruction framework. A comparison of the number of data samples, variation in human actions, ground-truth data, and details of 3D human models between the existing datasets and *3DVH* is shown in Table 2. *3DVH* is the largest synthetic dataset of clothed 3D human models with high level of details and realistic rendered images from multiple views.

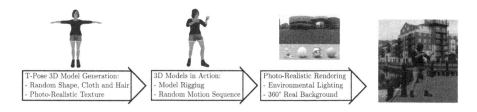

Fig. 3. Proposed *3DVH* dataset generation framework.

As illustrated in Fig. 3, the *3DVH* dataset is generated in three main steps: textures and clothed 3D human model generation; motion sequence application on these models; and multiple-view realistic rendering of the models. In the dataset, 3D human models with a wide variation in hair, clothing and pose are generated [44] for random motion sequences [45] to enable more complete and accurate 3D shape estimation.

Fig. 4. Example images and associated 3D ground-truth models from the proposed *3DVH* dataset.

In order to estimate high-fidelity and accurate 3D models on real images, the synthetic rendering should be as realistic as possible [13]. However existing synthetic datasets give unrealistic renderings with 3D human models with limited surface characteristics, such as surface normal maps [36]. To address this issue, we generate gloss, normal, diffuse and specular maps along with the 3D models to overcome the limitations of previous datasets [28] which use a point based light source, we use these appearance maps with spherical harmonics from 100 indoor/outdoor scenes from High Dynamic Range Image (HDRI) database [46] to apply realistic environmental illumination/lightning on the 3D models and render them into 120 cameras uniformly placed along a circular rig around the subjects. In *3DVH*, images are rendered using ray-tracing with environmental lighting, specular and normal maps to achieve realistic results. Previous synthetic datasets [28] use rasterization technique with single point light sources resulting in a lower non-realistic visual quality. Further detail on the facial appearance and hair could be included to achieve full photo-realism. In the supplementary document, various synthetic renderings are provided to show that the proposed dataset improves the realism. For every time frame, we randomly change the background HDR image to increase the data variety. The proposed dataset contains $4M$ image - 3D model pairs which are used for single-image 3D human reconstruction with 512×512 image resolution. Samples from the *3DVH* dataset are shown in Fig. 4. Multiple views are generated for each time instant to enable multi-view supervision in training the proposed network. 120 views for a single person at a time instant with the same background are generated. For comparison and evaluation in the paper we have trained the proposed network on 6 views. An ablation study is provided in Sect. 4.4 to evaluate the accuracy and completeness of the reconstruction with change in the number of views ($N \leq 6$) during training.

The *3DVH* dataset will be made available to support research and benchmarking, which complies with the Adobe FUSE licensing terms for release of generated 3D models. We will release a framework with **3DVH** Dataset for users to reproduce all source 3D models. The generated RGB images, depth, segmentation and normal maps will be made available to download.

4   Experimental Evaluation

This section presents the implementation details together with qualitative and quantitative results on the test set of the *3DVH* dataset and real images of people with varying poses and clothing. We evaluate the proposed method on 30,000 test images randomly chosen from the test split of the *3DVH* dataset. For each test image, we give the network a single RGB image and associated foreground segmentation mask. For a given test sample, the proposed method estimates the voxel occupancy grid from a single image. This is followed by surface mesh generation from the voxel grid by applying marching cubes.

4.1 Implementation Details

The proposed network is trained on the *3DVH* dataset, which is split into training, validation and test sets. The size of the input image is $512 \times 512 \times 3$ (as required by the network filters) and output voxel grid resolution is $128 \times 128 \times 128$. In ground-truth data, the points inside and outside the occupied volume are assigned to 1 and 0 values, respectively. During training, batch size and epochs are set to 4 and 40 respectively. The value of λ in Eq. 3 is experimentally set to $2e - 1$. With these settings the network is trained for 3 days using an NVIDIA Titan X with 12 GB memory. Our method is trained on low memory GPUs restricting the resolution to 128^3, however we can run our method with the resolution of 256^3 with the same memory and reduced batch size, or, high memory GPU devices could be used. Also, reducing the model complexity by decreasing the number of stacks in the hourglass network will reduce memory requirements with a slight decrease in accuracy. The Adam optimizer is used with a learning rate $lr = 2.5e - 4$ with the decimation of step-size in every 20 epoch. Refer to supplementary material for full implementation details.

4.2 Comparison

The proposed network is compared qualitatively and quantitatively with three recent state-of-the-art deep learning-based methods for single image 3D human reconstruction: DeepHuman [14], PIFu [13] and VRN [15]. To allow fair comparison, we retrain VRN and PIFu with the *3DVH* dataset using the code provided by the authors and use the pre-trained network of Deephuman (training code unavailable). The 3D reconstruction results of these methods are illustrated as they are produced by the papers' codes. The results are illustrated in mesh data format. Qualitative and quantitative comparison of the proposed approah against state-of-the-art methods are shown in Fig. 5 and 6, along with the ground-truth. We compute two error metrics using the ground-truth 3D models to measure the global quality of shape reconstruction: Chamfer Distance (CD) and 3D Intersection of Union (3D IoU) [47]. Figure 6 shows the comparison of results with ground-truth through the error comparison models with the Chamfer distance error coloured from blue to red as error increases. Colorbar shows the error in centimeter scale.

Qualitatively the proposed approach achieves significantly more complete and accurate reconstruction than previous approaches DeepHuman, PIFu, and VRN. VRN [15] produces over-complete 3D models with lack of reconstruction details and DeepHuman [14] fails on reconstruction of surface details with inaccurate reconstruction on clothing and erroneous estimation of limb positions resulting in shape distortion. Comparison of the proposed method and DeepHuman [14] is not a fair comparison, because DeepHuman requires additional a registered SMPL mesh to reconstruct 3D human. However, the proposed method does not requires prior registered SMPL model to predict 3D reconstruction. PIFu [13] gives limited accuracy for occluded (or invisible) body parts, as illustrated in rendered 3D reconstructions for both visible and invisible views in Fig. 5 and 6 and the Chamfer error metric illustration in Fig. 6. PIFu method is overfitted to its training dataset which is consisting of the people with mostly standing up pose. So, PIFu gives incomplete and inaccurate 3D reconstruction results for arbitrary human pose cases (Fig. 5) resulting in shape distortion. This is also shown in another study [48] that proposed method in PIFu [13] focuses on more cloth details and is less robust against pose variations. Note that PIFu's results can be superior in terms of high frequency details on the 3D surface because of the implicit 3D representation used in the method. The goal of single image 3D human shape estimation is to reconstruct the complete surface not just the visible part of the surface. As illustrated in Fig. 1, previous methods fail to accurately reconstruct occluded body parts or body poses when observed from different views. The proposed method solves the complete 3D reconstruction for both surface accuracy and completeness in arbitrary human pose as illustrated in Figs. 1, 5 and 6. Overall, our method using a multiview training loss demonstrates better completeness and accuracy in both visible and occluded parts for arbitrary human poses and clothing. These results indicate that human meshes recovered by the proposed method have better global robustness and alignment with the ground truth mesh. Note limbs are correctly reconstructed even when not visible in the single input image. This is due to the novel network architecture with multi-view supervision combined with training on the *3DVH* dataset of high-variety of human poses, clothing and hair styles. The proposed method correctly estimates reconstruction of clothing, shape and pose even when limbs are occluded.

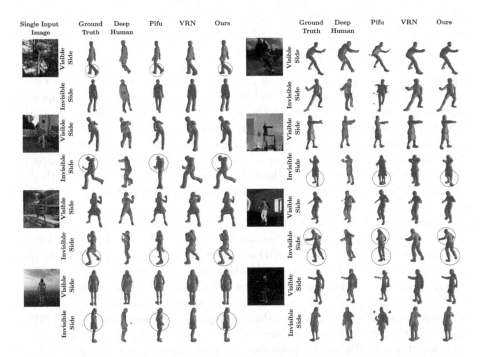

Fig. 5. Reconstruction results of Deephuman [14], PIFu [13], VRN [15] and the proposed method with 6-view training and ground-truth 3D human model. Reconstruction results are illustrated for both visible and invisible sides.

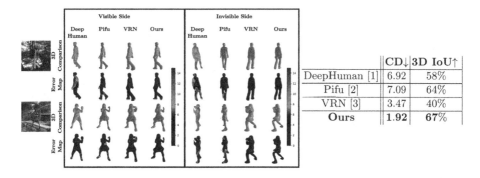

	CD↓	3D IoU↑
DeepHuman [1]	6.92	58%
Pifu [2]	7.09	64%
VRN [3]	3.47	40%
Ours	**1.92**	**67%**

Fig. 6. [Left]Reconstruction results of Deephuman [14], PIFu [13], VRN [15] and the proposed method with 6-view training and ground-truth 3D human model. Also, this figure shows associated per vertex chamfer distance from reconstruction to ground-truth model. Both 3D reconstruction results and error maps are illustrated for visible and invisible sides. **[Right]**Comparison of the proposed method with the state-of-the-art methods for different error metrics. **CD:** Chamfer Distance, **3D IoU**: 3D Intersection of Union For more details, please refer to the text.

4.3   Generalization to Real Images of People

In order to see the generalization of the proposed method, we design an experiment on real images. For this purpose, we used the THUman Dataset [14] which is a collection of real images of dynamic humans for a wide range of subjects and human poses for which ground-truth 3D reconstructon is available. This dataset provides 7000 data items in high variety of pose and clothing for more than 200 different human subjects. As with all previous methods [13–15], the proposed method uses the person pre-segmented from the background. Given this segmentation, the proposed method can reconstruct people in arbitrary indoor or outdoor scenes. In the experiments, the network weights are trained on *3DVH*, followed by fine tuning on the training split of the THUman dataset. The proposed single image reconstruction presented in Fig. 7 compares the reconstruction results of the proposed method with DeepHuman [14] and PIFu [13] on the test split of the THUman dataset. The DeepHuman network is trained only on the train split of *THUman* dataset. As shown in Fig. 7, the proposed

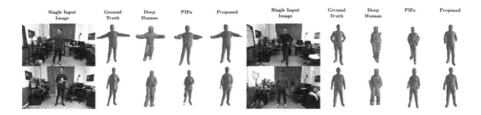

Fig. 7. The results of the proposed single image reconstruction method, PIFu [13] and DeepHuman [14] on real images.

method gives significantly more accurate 3D reconstructions from a single image compared to DeepHuman for a wide range of human poses, clothing and shape. The proposed method is able to estimate shape reliably even in the case of self-occlusions, where DeepHuman fails. The proposed method also shows more complete 3D reconstruction than PIFu with accurate 3D reconstruction of limbs. This is due to the multi-view supervision in the proposed method and the robust features learned from the *3DVH* dataset.

4.4   Ablation Study

The proposed single image human reconstruction exploits multiple views (N) to learn and predict a more complete reconstruction (Sect. 3). This section presents an ablation study with respect to the number of views and novel loss function, to evaluate how this affects the quality of the 3D human shape reconstruction. The proposed method is trained on the train split of the *3DVH* dataset with variable number of views $N = \{2, 4, 6\}$. The views are selected such that the cameras are equidistant along a circular camera rig in order to capture full human body shape. Each trained model is then tested on the test examples of the *3DVH* dataset and Chamfer distance (CD) and 3D intersection-over-union (3D IoU) errors are estimated, Fig. 8. The single image 3D reconstruction accuracy increases with the increase in the number of views used for training (Fig. 8). This demonstrates that the network gives better reconstruction with more supervision. We further trained and tested the proposed network with $N > 6$. However, marginal improvements were noticed because of the redundancy in the information across views.

# of Views	CD ↓	3D IoU ↑
2	4.64	32%
4	3.17	48%
6	1.92	67%

Fig. 8. Results of the proposed method with different loss functions (Sect. 3.3) and different number of view used in training. This figure shows the 3D reconstruction results of the network trained with both 3D ground-truth loss ($\mathcal{L}_{3D}$) and multi-view consistency loss ($\mathcal{L}_{MVC}$) and the results with only 3D ground-truth loss ($\mathcal{L}_{3D}$) for $N = \{2, 4, 6\}$ number of views. The table (right) also demonstrates the comparison of performance of the proposed method for different number of views.

We also investigated the effect of the proposed multi-view loss function on the accuracy of the reconstruction results in Fig. 8. The proposed network is trained with the train split of the *3DVH* dataset using 3D loss $\mathcal{L}_{3D}$ (Sect. 3.3) with 2-view supervision and complete loss $\mathcal{L} = \mathcal{L}_{3D} + \mathcal{L}_{VC}$ with $N = \{2, 4, 6\}$. Figure 8 demonstrates that the 3D reconstructions from the network trained with complete loss, $\mathcal{L}$, achieves more accurate and complete 3D human shape. This demonstrates that the proposed multi-view consistency loss makes a significant contribution to the results. More results are in the supplementary document.

Limitations: Although the proposed single image human reconstruction demonstrates significant improvement in the reconstruction quality over state-of-the-art methods, it suffers from the same limitations as previous methods. The approach assumes complete visibility of the person in the scene and can not handle partial occlusions with objects, as with previous approaches the method also requires a silhouette of the person along with the single image for 3D reconstruction.

Conclusion and Future Work: This paper introduces a novel method for single image human reconstruction, trained with multi-view 3D consistency on a new synthetic *3DVH* dataset of realistic clothed people with a wide range of variation in clothing, hair, body shape, pose and viewpoint. The proposed method demonstrates significant improvement in the reconstruction accuracy, completeness, and quality over state-of-the-art methods (PIFu, DeepHuman, VRN) from synthetic and real images of people. The multi-view consistency loss used in network training together with the novel *3DVH* dataset of realistic humans are both demonstrated to significantly improve the reconstruction performance achieving reliable reconstruction of human shape from a single image with a wide variation in pose, clothing, hair, and body size. Multi-view consistency loss enables reliable reconstruction of occluded body parts from a single image. For future work, we will exploit using multi-view loss for implicit 3D representations together with temporal information from a single-view video exploiting temporal coherence in the reconstruction to further improve the accuracy and details in the reconstruction.

References

1. Guo, K., et al.: The relightables: volumetric performance capture of humans with realistic relighting. ACM Trans. Graph. (TOG) **38**, 1–19 (2019)
2. Mustafa, A., Russell, C., Hilton, A.: U4D: unsupervised 4D dynamic scene understanding. In: ICCV (2019)
3. Dong, H., et al.: Towards multi-pose guided virtual try-on network. In: Proceedings of the IEEE International Conference on Computer Vision, pp. 9026–9035 (2019)
4. Liu, L., et al.: Neural rendering and reenactment of human actor videos (2018)
5. Cao, Z., Simon, T., Wei, S.E., Sheikh, Y.: Realtime multi-person 2D pose estimation using part affinity fields. In: CVPR (2017)
6. Alp Güler, R., Neverova, N., Kokkinos, I.: DensePose: dense human pose estimation in the wild. In: Proceedings of the IEEE Conference on Computer Vision and Pattern Recognition, pp. 7297–7306 (2018)
7. He, K., Gkioxari, G., Dollár, P., Girshick, R.: Mask R-CNN. In: Proceedings of the IEEE International Conference on Computer Vision, pp. 2961–2969 (2017)

8. Yang, L., Song, Q., Wang, Z., Jiang, M.: Parsing R-CNN for instance-level human analysis. In: Proceedings of the IEEE Conference on Computer Vision and Pattern Recognition, pp. 364–373 (2019)
9. Kocabas, M., Karagoz, S., Akbas, E.: Self-supervised learning of 3D human pose using multi-view geometry. In: Proceedings of the IEEE Conference on Computer Vision and Pattern Recognition, pp. 1077–1086 (2019)
10. Xiang, D., Joo, H., Sheikh, Y.: Monocular total capture: posing face, body, and hands in the wild. In: Proceedings of the IEEE Conference on Computer Vision and Pattern Recognition, pp. 10965–10974 (2019)
11. Tome, D., Russell, C., Agapito, L.: Lifting from the deep: convolutional 3D pose estimation from a single image. In: Proceedings of the IEEE Conference on Computer Vision and Pattern Recognition, pp. 2500–2509 (2017)
12. Pavlakos, G., Zhu, L., Zhou, X., Daniilidis, K.: Learning to estimate 3D human pose and shape from a single color image. In: Proceedings of the IEEE Conference on Computer Vision and Pattern Recognition, pp. 459–468 (2018)
13. Saito, S., Huang, Z., Natsume, R., Morishima, S., Kanazawa, A., Li, H.: PIFu: pixel-aligned implicit function for high-resolution clothed human digitization. In: Proceedings of the IEEE International Conference on Computer Vision, pp. 2304–2314 (2019)
14. Zheng, Z., Yu, T., Wei, Y., Dai, Q., Liu, Y.: DeepHuman: 3D human reconstruction from a single image. In: Proceedings of the IEEE International Conference on Computer Vision, pp. 7739–7749 (2019)
15. Jackson, A.S., Manafas, C., Tzimiropoulos, G.: 3D human body reconstruction from a single image via volumetric regression. In: Proceedings of the European Conference on Computer Vision (ECCV) (2018)
16. Mustafa, A., Kim, H., Guillemaut, J.Y., Hilton, A.: General dynamic scene reconstruction from multiple view video. In: The IEEE International Conference on Computer Vision (ICCV) (2015)
17. Leroy, V., Franco, J.S., Boyer, E.: Shape reconstruction using volume sweeping and learned photoconsistency. In: The European Conference on Computer Vision (ECCV) (2018)
18. Gilbert, A., Volino, M., Collomosse, J., Hilton, A.: Volumetric performance capture from minimal camera viewpoints. In: Proceedings of the European Conference on Computer Vision (ECCV), pp. 566–581 (2018)
19. Varol, G., et al.: BodyNet: volumetric inference of 3D human body shapes. In: Proceedings of the European Conference on Computer Vision (ECCV), pp. 20–36 (2018)
20. Yu, T., et al.: DoubleFusion: real-time capture of human performances with inner body shapes from a single depth sensor. In: Proceedings of the IEEE Conference on Computer Vision and Pattern Recognition, pp. 7287–7296 (2018)
21. Caliskan, A., Mustafa, A., Imre, E., Hilton, A.: Learning dense wide baseline stereo matching for people. In: Proceedings of the IEEE International Conference on Computer Vision Workshops (2019)
22. Bogo, F., Kanazawa, A., Lassner, C., Gehler, P., Romero, J., Black, M.J.: Keep It SMPL: automatic estimation of 3D human pose and shape from a single image. In: Leibe, B., Matas, J., Sebe, N., Welling, M. (eds.) ECCV 2016. LNCS, vol. 9909, pp. 561–578. Springer, Cham (2016). https://doi.org/10.1007/978-3-319-46454-1_34
23. Kanazawa, A., Black, M.J., Jacobs, D.W., Malik, J.: End-to-end recovery of human shape and pose. In: Proceedings of the IEEE Conference on Computer Vision and Pattern Recognition, pp. 7122–7131 (2018)

24. Kolotouros, N., Pavlakos, G., Black, M.J., Daniilidis, K.: Learning to reconstruct 3D human pose and shape via model-fitting in the loop. In: Proceedings of the IEEE International Conference on Computer Vision, pp. 2252–2261 (2019)
25. Bhatnagar, B.L., Tiwari, G., Theobalt, C., Pons-Moll, G.: Multi-Garment Net: learning to dress 3D people from images. In: 2019 IEEE/CVF International Conference on Computer Vision (ICCV), pp. 5419–5429 (2019)
26. Natsume, R., et al.: SiCloPe: silhouette-based clothed people. In: Proceedings of the IEEE Conference on Computer Vision and Pattern Recognition, pp. 4480–4490 (2019)
27. Gabeur, V., Franco, J.S., Martin, X., Schmid, C., Rogez, G.: Moulding humans: non-parametric 3D human shape estimation from single images. In: Proceedings of the IEEE International Conference on Computer Vision, pp. 2232–2241 (2019)
28. Pumarola, A., Sanchez, J., Choi, G., Sanfeliu, A., Moreno-Noguer, F.: 3DPeople: modeling the geometry of dressed humans. In: International Conference on Computer Vision (ICCV) (2019)
29. Loper, M., Mahmood, N., Romero, J., Pons-Moll, G., Black, M.J.: SMPL: a skinned multi-person linear model. ACM Trans. Graph. (Proc. SIGGRAPH Asia) **34**, 248:1–248:16 (2015)
30. Anguelov, D., Srinivasan, P., Koller, D., Thrun, S., Rodgers, J., Davis, J.: SCAPE: shape completion and animation of people. In: ACM SIGGRAPH 2005 Papers, pp. 408–416 (2005)
31. Ma, Q., et al.: Learning to dress 3D people in generative clothing. In: IEEE/CVF Conference on Computer Vision and Pattern Recognition (CVPR) (2020)
32. Yu, T., et al.: SimulCap: single-view human performance capture with cloth simulation. In: 32nd IEEE Conference on Computer Vision and Pattern Recognition (CVPR 2019), Long Beach, CA, USA. IEEE (2019)
33. Alldieck, T., Pons-Moll, G., Theobalt, C., Magnor, M.: Tex2Shape: detailed full human body geometry from a single image. In: Proceedings of the IEEE International Conference on Computer Vision, pp. 2293–2303 (2019)
34. Multiview video repository: Center for Vision Speech and Signal Processing (CVSSP). University of Surrey, UK (2020). https://cvssp.org/data/cvssp3d/
35. Vlasic, D., Baran, I., Matusik, W., Popović, J.: Articulated mesh animation from multi-view silhouettes. In: ACM SIGGRAPH 2008 Papers, pp. 1–9 (2008)
36. Varol, G., et al.: Learning from synthetic humans. In: Proceedings of the IEEE Conference on Computer Vision and Pattern Recognition, pp. 109–117 (2017)
37. Yang, J., Franco, J.-S., Hétroy-Wheeler, F., Wuhrer, S.: Estimation of human body shape in motion with wide clothing. In: Leibe, B., Matas, J., Sebe, N., Welling, M. (eds.) ECCV 2016. LNCS, vol. 9908, pp. 439–454. Springer, Cham (2016). https://doi.org/10.1007/978-3-319-46493-0_27
38. Xu, W., et al.: MonoPerfCap: human performance capture from monocular video. ACM Trans. Graph. **37**, 27:1–27:15 (2018)
39. Lassner, C., Romero, J., Kiefel, M., Bogo, F., Black, M.J., Gehler, P.V.: Unite the people: closing the loop between 3D and 2D human representations. In: Proceedings of the IEEE Conference on Computer Vision and Pattern Recognition, pp. 6050–6059 (2017)
40. Tulsiani, S., Efros, A.A., Malik, J.: Multi-view consistency as supervisory signal for learning shape and pose prediction. In: Proceedings of the IEEE Conference on Computer Vision and Pattern Recognition, pp. 2897–2905 (2018)

41. Newell, A., Yang, K., Deng, J.: Stacked hourglass networks for human pose estimation. In: Leibe, B., Matas, J., Sebe, N., Welling, M. (eds.) ECCV 2016. LNCS, vol. 9912, pp. 483–499. Springer, Cham (2016). https://doi.org/10.1007/978-3-319-46484-8_29
42. Wu, Y., He, K.: Group normalization. In: Proceedings of the European Conference on Computer Vision (ECCV), pp. 3–19 (2018)
43. Jackson, A.S., Bulat, A., Argyriou, V., Tzimiropoulos, G.: Large pose 3D face reconstruction from a single image via direct volumetric CNN regression. In: Proceedings of the IEEE International Conference on Computer Vision, pp. 1031–1039 (2017)
44. Adobe: Fuse (2020). https://www.adobe.com/products/fuse.html
45. Adobe: Mixamo (2020). https://www.mixamo.com/
46. HDRI: Heaven (2020). https://hdrihaven.com/
47. Jatavallabhula, K.M., et al.: Kaolin: a PyTorch library for accelerating 3D deep learning research. arXiv:1911.05063 (2019)
48. Huang, Z., Xu, Y., Lassner, C., Li, H., Tung, T.: ARCH: animatable reconstruction of clothed humans. In: IEEE/CVF Conference on Computer Vision and Pattern Recognition (CVPR) (2020)

Learning Global Pose Features in Graph Convolutional Networks for 3D Human Pose Estimation

Kenkun Liu, Zhiming Zou, and Wei Tang$^{(\boxtimes)}$

University of Illinois at Chicago, Chicago, IL, USA
{kliu44,zzou6,tangw}@uic.edu

Abstract. As the human body skeleton can be represented as a sparse graph, it is natural to exploit graph convolutional networks (GCNs) to model the articulated body structure for 3D human pose estimation (HPE). However, a vanilla graph convolutional layer, the building block of a GCN, only models the local relationships between each body joint and their neighbors on the skeleton graph. Some global attributes, e.g., the action of the person, can be critical to 3D HPE, especially in the case of occlusion or depth ambiguity. To address this issue, this paper introduces a new 3D HPE framework by learning global pose features in GCNs. Specifically, we add a global node to the graph and connect it to all the body joint nodes. On one hand, global features are updated by aggregating all body joint features to model the global attributes. On the other hand, the feature update of each body joint depends on not only their neighbors but also the global node. Furthermore, we propose a heterogeneous multi-task learning framework to learn the local and global features. While each local node regresses the 3D coordinate of the corresponding body joint, we force the global node to classify an action category or learn a low-dimensional pose embedding. Experimental results demonstrate the effectiveness of the proposed approach.

1 Introduction

The objective of 3D human pose estimation (HPE) is to predict the positions of human body joints in the camera coordinate system from a single RGB image. This task gains a lot of attention in the last few years [1–10] since it has various applications in human-computer interaction, action recognition and motion capture. 3D HPE is essentially an ill-posed problem because one pose in the 2D image coordinate system may correspond to multiple poses in the 3D camera coordinate system. But this ambiguity can be alleviated to a large extent by exploiting the structure information of the human body [11,12].

Two streams of approaches for 3D HPE have been investigated. The first stream of methods aim to build an end-to-end system that predicts the 3D coordinates of body joints directly from the input image [3,13]. Early approaches [14,15] are based on hand-designed features but they are likely to

© Springer Nature Switzerland AG 2021
H. Ishikawa et al. (Eds.): ACCV 2020, LNCS 12622, pp. 89–105, 2021.
https://doi.org/10.1007/978-3-030-69525-5_6

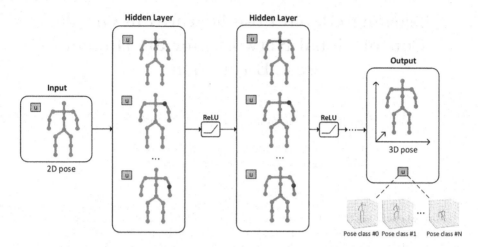

Fig. 1. Illustration of a graph convolutional network (GCN) with a global node u for 3D human pose estimation. The input is the 2D body joint locations predicted by an off-the-shelf 2D pose detector with a zero-initialized global feature vector. The GCN repeatedly transforms and aggregates features of local and global nodes to learn increasingly powerful representations. Finally, it predicts the 3D pose as well as the output of an auxiliary task, e.g., an action label of the pose.

fail in some challenging scenarios, e.g., depth ambiguity, viewpoint variation and occlusion. In recent years, the development of convolutional neural networks pushes the edge of this problem and significantly improves the estimation accuracy with the help of large-scale image data [16–20]. The second stream of approaches divide the 3D HPE into two subtasks, i.e., the prediction of 2D joints locations and 2D-to-3D pose regression [1,11,12]. Martinez et al. [1] prove that 3D coordinates of human body joints could be accurately estimated merely from the output of a 2D pose detector.

To model the articulated body structure, graph convolutional networks (GCNs) [21,22] have been introduced to solve the 2D-to-3D pose lifting problem [5,11,23]. GCNs are generalized from CNNs to construct a non-linear mapping in a graph domain. Different from CNNs, which act on image patches, GCNs update the features of each node from its neighbouring nodes in a graph. In this way, the prior of the graph structure is fed into the GCN model.

Though GCNs have shown decent results in 2D-to-3D pose lifting [5,11, 23], they have one potential limitation. A vanilla graph convolutional layer, the building block of a GCN, only models the local relationships between each body joint and their neighbors. Some global attributes, e.g., the action or viewpoint of the person, can be critical to 3D HPE, especially in the case of occlusion or depth ambiguity. Unfortunately, the importance of global features to 3D HPE is largely ignored by prior work.

This paper introduces a new 3D HPE framework by learning global pose features in GCNs, as illustrated in Fig. 1. Specifically, we first add a global node to the graph and connect it to all the body joint nodes. On one hand, the global node aggregates features from all body joints to model the global attributes. On the other hand, the feature update of each body joint depends on not only their neighbors but also the global node. To facilitate the learning of meaningful global attributes, we propose a heterogeneous multi-task learning framework. Specifically, we introduce auxiliary learning tasks for the global node. While each local node regresses the 3D coordinates of the corresponding body joint, we force the global node to classify an action category or learn a low-dimensional pose embedding.

Extensive ablation study indicates that (1) learning global features in a GCN can improve its performance and (2) solving the auxiliary learning tasks together with 3D HPE is beneficial.

In sum, the contribution of this paper is threefold.

- To our knowledge, this is the first work to learn global pose features in a GCN for 3D HPE. We add a global node to the skeleton graph and connect it to every body joint node so that each local node has access to global information during feature update.
- We propose a heterogeneous multi-task learning framework to facilitate the learning of effective global representations in a GCN. We introduce two auxiliary learning tasks, i.e., action classification and pose embedding, to achieve this goal.
- We perform extensive ablation study to investigate whether the extra global node and the auxiliary tasks help 3D HPE. Experimental results indicate that the proposed approach can outperform some state-of-the-art methods.

2   Related Work

3D Human Pose Estimation. The last two decades have seen the rapid development of 3D HPE. Early work builds 3D HPE systems on handcrafted features and geometric constraints [24–26]. Recently, state-of-the-art methods are based on deep neural networks. Chen et al. [27] propose a weekly-supervised encoder-decoder framework that can learn geometry-aware representations using only 2D annotations. Wang et al. [12] design a new network architecture to learn the bi-directional dependencies of body parts. 3D HPE can also be divided into two subtasks, i.e., 2D HPE and 2D-to-3D lifting. For example, Martinez et al. [1] use a fully connected network to regress the 3D body joint locations from the output of an off-the-shelf 2D pose detector. This simple baseline is very effective and outperforms the state-of-the-art one-stage approaches.

The works most related to ours are [5,11,23,28,29], which also apply GCNs for 3D pose regression. Zhao et al. [11] propose a semantic GCN to learn semantic information not explicitly represented in the graph. Ci et al. [23] extend the GCN to a locally connected network to improve its representation capability. Cai et al. [5] introduce a local-to-global network to learn multi-scale features for the graph-based representations. Liu et al. [28] study different weight sharing methods in the graph convolution. Zou et al. [29] introduce a high-order GCN for 3D HPE. However, the main contribution of this paper is to learn global pose features in a GCN, which these prior approaches ignore. Furthermore, while they only focus on the task of 3D HPE, we introduce a heterogeneous multi-task learning framework with auxiliary tasks to facilitate the learning of global features. And we generate labels for global node supervision by ourselves. The global features in our setting can be directly used for other follow-on tasks.

Graph Convolutional Networks. GCNs generalize CNNs by performing convolutions on graph data. They have been widely used to solve problems like the citation network [21] and molecular property prediction [30]. There are two categories of GCNs: spectral approaches and non-spectral (spatial) approaches [22]. The former are defined in the Fourier domain by calculating the eigen-decomposition of graph Laplacian [31], while the latter apply neural message passing to features defined on a graph [30]. Our approach falls into the second category. Battaglia et al. [32] generalize previous work into a unified graph network and also discuss the use of global node. While they focus on graph or node classification, our model is specially designed for 3D HPE. More importantly, we introduce a heterogeneous multi-task learning framework to learn global pose features via auxiliary tasks.

3   Approach

In this section, we first revisit the vanilla GCN, which models the local relationship between each node and their neighbors. Then, we propose to learn global pose features in a GCN and introduce a heterogeneous multi-task learning framework. Finally, we discuss the network architecture for 3D HPE.

3.1   Revisit GCN

Let $\mathcal{G} = (\mathcal{V}, \mathcal{E})$ denote a graph where $\mathcal{V}$ is a set of N nodes and $\mathcal{E}$ is the collection of all edges. We can represent the collection of all edges via an adjacency matrix $\mathbf{A} \in \{0,1\}^{N \times N}$. Let $\mathbf{x}_i \in \mathcal{R}^D$ denote a D-dimensional feature vector corresponding to each node i. $\mathbf{X} \in \mathcal{R}^{D \times N}$ collects all feature vectors, whose i-th column is $\mathbf{x}_i$. Then a graph convolutional layer [21], the building block of a GCN, updates features defined on the nodes through the following operation:

$$\mathbf{X}' = \sigma(\mathbf{W} \mathbf{X} \hat{\mathbf{A}}) \tag{1}$$

where $\mathbf{X}' \in \mathbb{R}^{D' \times N}$ is the updated feature matrix, D' is the dimension of the updated feature vector of each node, $\sigma(\cdot)$ is an activation function, e.g., ReLU, $\mathbf{W} \in \mathbb{R}^{D' \times D}$ is a learnable weight matrix. $\hat{\mathbf{A}} = \tilde{\mathbf{D}}^{-\frac{1}{2}}(\mathbf{A} + \mathbf{I})\tilde{\mathbf{D}}^{-\frac{1}{2}}$ is a normalized version of $\mathbf{A}$. Adding an identity matrix $\mathbf{I}$ to $\mathbf{A}$ means to include self-connections in the graph so that the update of a node feature vector also depends on itself. $\tilde{\mathbf{D}}$ is the diagonal node degree matrix of $\mathbf{A} + \mathbf{I}$ and helps the graph convolution to retain the scale of features.

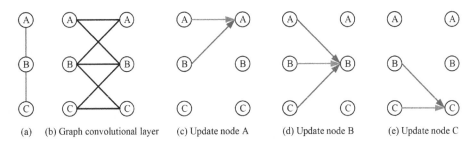

| (a) | (b) Graph convolutional layer | (c) Update node A | (d) Update node B | (e) Update node C |

Fig. 2. Illustration of the feature update in a graph convolutional layer. Blue arrows and red arrows respectively correspond to self-connections and other-connections. (a) A simple graph consisting of three nodes. (b) The updated features of each node (the right side) depend on the input features of itself and its neighboring nodes (the left side). (c) (d) (e) respectively show the feature update of nodes A, B and C. (Color figure online)

A GCN takes as input a feature vector associated with each node and repeatedly transforms them via a composition of multiple graph convolutions to get increasingly more powerful representations, which are used by the last layer to predict the output.

Let $\hat{a}_{ij}$ be the entry of $\hat{\mathbf{A}}$ at (i, j). $\mathcal{N}_i$ and $\hat{\mathcal{N}}_i \equiv \mathcal{N}_i \cup \{i\}$ denote the neighbors of node i excluding and including the node itself respectively. This means $j \in \hat{\mathcal{N}}_i$ if and only if $\hat{a}_{ij} \neq 0$. Then Eq. (1) can be written equivalently as below.

$$\mathbf{x}'_i = \sigma\left(\sum_{j \in \hat{\mathcal{N}}_i} \mathbf{W}\mathbf{x}_j \hat{a}_{ij} \right) \tag{2}$$

where $i \in \{1, ..., N\}$, $\mathbf{x}'_i$ is the i-th column of $\mathbf{X}'$ and also the updated feature vector of node i.

We empirically find using different weight matrices for the self-node and neighbors can significantly improve the performance:

$$\mathbf{x}'_i = \sigma\left(\mathbf{Q}\mathbf{x}_i \hat{a}_{ii} + \sum_{j \in \mathcal{N}_i} \mathbf{W}\mathbf{x}_j \hat{a}_{ij} \right) \tag{3}$$

where $\mathbf{Q}$ is the weight matrix corresponding to the self-transformation. We will use this formulation as our baseline GCN in the experiments.

Figure 2 demonstrates a graph convolutional layer for a simple 3-node graph and presents how each node is updated according to its neighbouring nodes. Within a single graph convolutional layer, only those nodes which are directly connected with a node could transmit information to it. There is no explicit mechanism for the GCN to learn global features that could be critical to 3D HPE. We will introduce our solution to this problem in the next section.

3.2 Learning Global Pose Features

Some global pose features, e.g., the action, viewpoint or scale of a person, can help reduce uncertainty in 3D HPE. For example, the action of a person, e.g.,

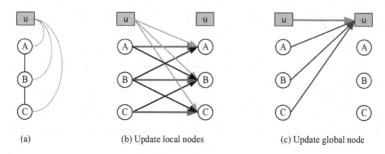

| (a) | (b) Update local nodes | (c) Update global node |

Fig. 3. Illustration of the feature update for local nodes and the global node. Arrays of the same color means applying the same weight matrix. (a) A simple graph composed of three nodes: A, B and C. **u** is the added global node, which is connected to all local nodes. (b) The feature update of local nodes. (c) The feature update of the global node.

walking or sitting, provides strong constraints on the relative locations of body joints, which eases pose estimation. This motivates us to learn global pose features in a GCN for 3D HPE.

Graph Convolution with a Global Node. To achieve this goal, we add a global node to the graph and connect it to all local nodes, e.g., the body joint nodes. The global features are obtained by aggregating all body joint features to model the global pose attributes. The feature update of each body joint depends on not only their neighbors but also the global node. Specifically, a graph convolutional layer with a global node is defined as:

$$\mathbf{x}_i' = \sigma(\mathbf{Q}\mathbf{x}_i \hat{a}_{ii} + \sum_{j \in \mathcal{N}_i} \mathbf{W}\mathbf{x}_j \hat{a}_{ij} + \mathbf{T}\mathbf{x}_u) \tag{4}$$

$$\mathbf{x}_u' = \sigma(\frac{1}{N} \sum_{j=1}^{N} \mathbf{R}\mathbf{x}_j + \mathbf{S}\mathbf{x}_u) \tag{5}$$

where $i \in \{1, \cdots, N\}$ indexes a local node and u represents the global node, $\mathbf{Q}, \mathbf{W}, \mathbf{T}, \mathbf{R}, \mathbf{S}$ are different weight matrices. Since the global node and local nodes carry different types of features, we assign different transformation matrices to them.

Equation (4) is the feature update rule for local nodes, which is the summation of three terms. The first term is the feature transformation of the i-th node itself, corresponding to the self-connection. The second term aggregates the transformed features of the neighboring nodes. The last term transforms the global features. Equation (5) is the update function for global features, which sums up two terms. The first term aggregates features from all local nodes. The second term is the feature transformation of the global node itself, corresponding to the self-connection of the global node.

Figure 3 demonstrates the feature updates of local nodes and the global node. The global node takes information from all local nodes and also contributes to the

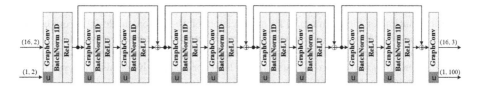

Fig. 4. This figure shows the GCN architecture we apply in our experiments. The building block is a residual block composed of two graph convolutional layers with 128 channels. This block is repeated four times. Each graph convolutional layer (except for the last one) is followed by a batch normalization layer and a ReLU activation layer.

feature update of local nodes. This gives local nodes access to global information during inference.

Heterogeneous Multi-task Learning. While the output of each local node is supervised by the 3D coordinate of the corresponding body joint, it remains unclear how to deal with the output of the global node during training. One solution is to simply ignore the update of global features in the last layer. In this case, gradients could still propagate from the loss of local nodes to the global features in previous layers to update the weights during training. This is because the update of local features at the current layer relies on the global features at the previous layer. During inference, we only need to check the output of the local nodes to get the 3D human pose prediction. But one potential limitation of this solution is that the lack of supervision for the global node may lead to inferior learning of global pose features.

To address this problem, we propose a heterogeneous multi-task learning framework. While local nodes still output 3D locations of body joints, the global node is responsible for an auxiliary task. Note the auxiliary task should be related to the main task, i.e., 3D HPE, and facilitate the learning of global pose features. In this paper, we consider two different kinds of auxiliary tasks: action classification and pose embedding.

Action classification means to classify the 3D pose to be predicted into an action label, e.g., running or jumping. The output of the global node is the probability distribution over action classes. Due to the lack of action annotations in the dataset, we need to generate some pseudo labels. Specifically, we use K-means to cluster the ground truth 3D poses in the training data to obtain their class labels and each cluster corresponds to an action class. Then, these action labels can be used to supervise the output of the global node during training, e.g., via a cross-entropy loss.

Pose embedding means to learn a low-dimensional representation of the pose. The output of the global node is a real-value embedding vector. We use a 2-layer decoder to reconstruct the 3D human pose from the embedding. The reconstruction error serves as the loss function of the global node. The decoder network is learned end-to-end with the embedding.

Table 1. Ablation study on the effectiveness of learning global pose features. **GN** is the abbreviation of global node. The supervision of the global node is through the **action classification** task (100 action classes). **Unsupervised GN** means the global node output is directly discarded in the training phase while **supervised GN** means the global node is supervised by action labels generated by K-means. All errors are measured in millimeters (mm).

Method	Channels	Params	MPJPE	P-MPJPE	Loss
Baseline GCN	205	0.69 M	41.87	33.53	**0.000079**
GCN (w/**unsupervised GN**)	128	0.69 M	41.44	31.83	0.000124
GCN (w/**supervised GN**)	128	0.69 M	**40.44**	**31.38**	0.000165
Baseline GCN	410	2.71 M	41.73	32.56	**0.000036**
GCN (w/**unsupervised GN**)	256	2.69 M	41.27	31.16	0.000058
GCN (w/**supervised GN**)	256	2.69 M	**38.72**	**30.75**	0.00009

3.3   Network Architecture

We adopt the network architecture shown in Fig. 4 for 3D HPE. The action classification is taken as the auxiliary task here. Following Martinez et al. [1] and Defferrard et al. [33], we stack multiple cascaded blocks, each of which is made up of two graph convolutional layers interleaved with batch normalization and ReLU. After that, we wrap every block as a residual block. Both the input and the output of the GCN are composed of two parts corresponding to local nodes and the global node, respectively. Specifically, the input is the 2D coordinates of the body joints and a zero-initialized vector. The output is the 3D body locations and the pose classification result. The overall loss is a summation of an $L2$-norm loss for 3D HPE and another loss for the auxiliary task, i.e., a cross-entropy loss for action classification and an $L2$-norm loss for pose embedding.

4   Experiments

4.1   Datasets and Evaluation Protocols

We conduct our experiments on the widely used dataset Human3.6M [34] and dataset MPI-INF-3DHP [35], and follow the previously used evaluation methods.

Human3.6M. This is the most popular indoor dataset for 3D HPE. It contains 3.6 million images filmed by 4 synchronized high-resolution progressive scan cameras at 50 Hz [34]. There are 11 subjects in total performing 15 daily activities such as walking, sitting, greeting and waiting. However, only 7 subjects are annotated with 3D poses. For fair comparison, we follow previous work [11,23, 36], i.e. 5 subjects (S1, S5, S6, S7, S8) of the 7 annotated subjects are used for training while the rest 2 subjects (S9 and S11) are used for testing. We train and test our GCN models on all 15 actions.

Two protocols are widely used for evaluation. **Protocol-1** is the mean per-joint position error (MPJPE), which computes the averaged Euclidean distance

Table 2. Ablation study on the number of action classes. **GN** is the abbreviation of global node. The supervision of the global node is through the **action classification** task. The column of **Classes** indicates different numbers of action classes. **Supervised GN** means the global node is supervised by action labels generated by K-means. All errors are measured in millimeters (mm).

Method	Classes	Channels	Params	MPJPE	P-MPJPE
GCN (w/**supervised GN**)	50	128	0.69 M	40.95	31.67
GCN (w/**supervised GN**)	100	128	0.69 M	40.44	**31.38**
GCN (w/**supervised GN**)	200	128	0.71 M	**40.25**	31.60
GCN (w/**supervised GN**)	50	256	2.66 M	40.03	30.98
GCN (w/**supervised GN**)	100	256	2.69 M	**38.72**	**30.75**
GCN (w/**supervised GN**)	200	256	2.74 M	39.82	30.91

error per joint between the prediction and the corresponding ground truth in millimeters. **Protocol-2** computes the same error after the alignment of the root joint of the prediction in accordance with the ground truth using a rigid transformation. The abbreviation of Protocol-2 is P-MPJPE.

MPI-INF-3DHP. This dataset is constructed by the Mocap system, containing both indoor and outdoor scenes with 3D pose annotations. We dismiss its training set, and only use the test set consisting of 2929 frames from six subjects conducting seven actions to evaluate the generalization capacity of our model. The results from this dataset are reported using the metrics 3D PCK and AUC [35].

4.2   Ablation Study

To avoid the influence of 2D human pose detector, we use 2D ground truth as the input for local nodes and initialize the global node with a zero vector. We adopt Adam [37] as the optimization method with an initial learning rate 0.001 and a decay rate 0.96 100K iterations. We initialize weights of GCNs using the method introduced in [38]. Following Zhao et al. [11], we set 128 as the default number of channels of each graph convolutional layer. We choose the optimal weight of the auxiliary loss via cross-validation: 0.001 for the cross-entropy loss used in action classification and 0.0001 for the $L2$-norm loss used in pose embedding. Equation (3) is taken as our baseline GCN.

Learning Global Pose Features. We first merely add a global node (**GN**) to our baseline GCN. When training and testing the GCN, there is no supervision for the global node. Then, we add the auxiliary task of action classification to supervise the learning of global features. Table 1 shows the results. To make sure that all models have the same number of parameters, we increase the number of channels for the baseline GCN. We can see that the baseline GCN has the lowest regression loss, but its error is higher than other two models. We infer this is mainly caused by overfitting. In this table, the GCN with a supervised global

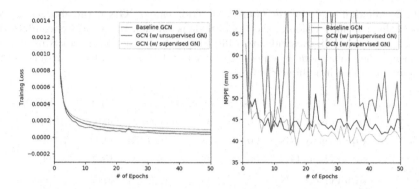

Fig. 5. The trend of the 3D HPE loss and the validation MPJPE during training. The number of parameters of each model is approximately 2.69M. **Unsupervised GN** means the global node output is directly discarded in the training phase while **supervised GN** means the global node is supervised by action labels generated by K-means.

Table 3. Ablation study on the embedding dimension. **GN** is the abbreviation of global node. The supervision of the global node is through the **pose embedding** task. The column of **Embedding** indicates different embedding feature dimensions. **Supervised GN** means the global node is supervised by the reconstruction loss of the embedding. All errors are measured in millimeters (mm).

Method	Embedding	Channels	Params	MPJPE	P-MPJPE
GCN (w/**supervised GN**)	10	128	0.67 M	**40.52**	**31.42**
GCN (w/**supervised GN**)	20	128	0.67 M	40.73	31.62

node performs the best given the same number of parameters. As we double the feature channels of hidden layers, the trend is more obvious. Thus, merely adding a global node could improve the performance of the baseline GCN, especially in P-MPJPE. With supervision, the GCN with a global node could perform better both in Protocol-1 and Protocol-2. The results shown in this table verify the effectiveness of both the global node and its supervision.

Furthermore, we plot the training loss and 3D HPE error descending curves, as shown in Fig. 5. Here, the training loss corresponds to the 3D HPE part of total training loss, excluding the loss from the global node. We can see from the figure that the training loss is becoming higher as we add a global node and then its supervision. The reason behind this is that adding a global node and its supervision would increase the importance of the global node, forcing the model to optimize global features. And we can see from the right-sided figure that the 3D HPE error is smaller and more stable when we add a global node and then the global node supervision. These results indicate that learning the global features and the auxiliary task improves the generalization ability of the GCN on 3D HPE.

Table 4. Quantitative comparisons on the Human 3.6M dataset under **Protocol-1**. The MPJPEs are reported in millimeters. The best results are highlighted in bold. **Legend:** (+) uses extra data from MPII dataset. (†) uses temporal information. (*) uses pose scales in both training and testing.

Protocol # 1	Dire.	Disc.	Eat	Greet	Phone	Photo	Pose	Purch.	Sit	SitD.	Smoke	Wait	WalkD.	Walk	WalkT.	Avg.
Hossain et al. [7] ECCV'18 (†)	44.2	46.7	52.3	49.3	59.9	59.4	47.5	46.2	59.9	65.6	55.8	50.4	52.3	43.5	45.1	51.9
Pavllo et al. [36] CVPR'19 (†)	45.2	46.7	43.3	45.6	48.1	55.1	44.6	44.3	57.3	65.8	47.1	44.0	49.0	32.8	33.9	46.8
Cai et al. [5] ICCV'19 (†)	44.6	47.4	45.6	48.8	50.8	59.0	47.2	43.9	57.9	61.9	49.7	46.6	51.3	37.1	39.4	48.8
Pavlakos et al. [3] CVPR'17 (*)	67.4	71.9	66.7	69.1	72.0	77.0	65.0	68.3	83.7	96.5	71.7	65.8	74.9	59.1	63.2	71.9
Martinez et al. [1] ICCV'17	51.8	56.2	58.1	59.0	69.5	78.4	55.2	58.1	74.0	94.6	62.3	59.1	65.1	49.5	52.4	62.9
Tekin et al. [39] ICCV'17	54.2	61.4	60.2	61.2	79.4	78.3	63.1	81.6	70.1	107.3	69.3	70.3	74.3	51.8	63.2	69.7
Yang et al. [20] CVPR'18 (+)	51.5	58.9	50.4	57.0	62.1	65.4	49.8	52.7	69.2	85.2	57.4	58.4	43.6	60.1	47.7	58.6
Pavlakos et al. [16] CVPR'18 (+)	48.5	54.4	54.4	52.0	59.4	65.3	49.9	52.9	65.8	71.1	56.6	52.9	60.9	44.7	47.8	56.2
Fang et al. [40] AAAI'18	50.1	54.3	57.0	57.1	66.6	73.3	53.4	55.7	72.8	88.6	60.3	57.7	62.7	47.5	50.6	60.4
Zhao et al. [11] CVPR'19	48.2	60.8	51.8	64.0	64.6	53.6	51.1	67.4	88.7	57.7	73.2	65.6	48.9	64.8	51.9	60.8
Sharma et al. [41] ICCV'19	48.6	54.5	54.2	55.7	62.2	72.0	50.5	54.3	70.0	78.3	58.1	55.4	61.4	45.2	49.7	58.0
Ci et al. [23] ICCV'19 (+)(*)	46.8	52.3	44.7	50.4	52.9	68.9	49.6	46.4	60.2	78.9	51.2	50.0	54.8	40.4	43.3	**52.7**
Ours	48.4	53.6	49.6	53.6	57.3	70.6	51.8	50.7	62.8	74.1	54.1	52.6	58.2	41.5	45.0	54.9

The Auxiliary Task of Action Classification. We use action classification as the auxiliary task to supervise the global node. The output of the global node is a probability distribution on the action classes. We cluster all 3D poses in the training set into 50, 100 and 200 action classes, respectively. A larger number of action classes generally leads to a more difficult classification task. We visualize some clustering centers in Fig. 6. Obviously, these actions are very different from each other: some of them are sitting while some of them are standing. We compare the performance of GCNs whose auxiliary task is to classify different numbers of action categories. The results are shown in Table 2. We find that when the number of feature channels is relatively small, the performance of these GCNs is robust to the number of action classes. But when the number of feature channels is doubled, categorizing poses into 100 classes helps the 3D HPE the most.

The Auxiliary Task of Pose Embedding. We also consider pose embedding as an auxiliary task. The output of the global node is an embedding vector whose dimension is smaller than that of a 3D pose vector (48 for 16 body joints). In our experiments, we compare the results obtained by setting the embedding dimension to 10 and 20, respectively. Table 3 shows that the dimension of the embedding only affects the performance slightly.

Table 5. Quantitative comparisons on the Human 3.6M dataset under **Protocol-2**. The P-MPJPEs are reported in millimeters. The best results are highlighted in bold. **Legend:** (+) uses extra data from MPII dataset. (†) uses temporal information. (*) uses pose scales in both training and testing.

Protocol # 2	Dire.	Disc.	Eat	Greet	Phone	Photo	Pose	Purch.	Sit	SitD.	Smoke	Wait	WalkD.	Walk	WalkT.	Avg.
Hossain et al. [7] ECCV'18 (†)	36.9	37.9	42.8	40.3	46.8	46.7	37.7	36.5	48.9	52.6	45.6	39.6	43.5	35.2	38.5	42.0
Pavllo et al. [36] CVPR'19 (†)	34.2	36.8	33.9	37.5	37.1	43.2	34.4	33.5	45.3	52.7	37.7	34.1	38.0	25.8	27.7	36.8
Cai et al. [5] ICCV'19 (†)	35.7	37.8	36.9	40.7	39.6	45.2	37.4	34.5	46.9	50.1	40.5	36.1	41.0	29.6	33.2	39.0
Sun et al. [18] ICCV'17	42.1	44.3	45.0	45.4	51.5	53.0	43.2	41.3	59.3	73.3	51.0	44.0	48.0	38.3	44.8	48.3
Martinez et al. [1] ICCV'17	39.5	43.2	46.4	47.0	51.0	56.0	41.4	40.6	56.5	69.4	49.2	45.0	49.5	38.0	43.1	47.7
Fang et al. [40] AAAI'18	38.2	41.7	43.7	44.9	48.5	55.3	40.2	38.2	54.5	64.4	47.2	44.3	47.3	36.7	41.7	45.7
Li et al. [9] CVPR'19	35.5	39.8	41.3	42.3	46.0	48.9	36.9	37.3	51.0	60.6	44.9	40.2	44.1	33.1	36.9	42.6
Ci et al. [23] ICCV'19 (+)(*)	36.9	41.6	38.0	41.0	41.9	51.1	38.2	37.6	49.1	62.1	43.1	39.9	43.5	32.2	37.0	**42.2**
Ours	38.4	41.1	40.6	42.8	43.5	51.6	39.5	37.6	49.7	58.1	43.2	39.2	45.2	32.8	38.1	42.8

Table 6. Quantitative comparisons on the Human 3.6M dataset under **Protocol-1**. All approaches take 2D ground truth as input. The MPJPEs are reported in millimeters. **Legend:** (+) uses extra data from MPII dataset. (*) uses pose scales in both training and testing.

Protocol # 1	Dire.	Disc.	Eat	Greet	Phone	Photo	Pose	Purch.	Sit	SitD.	Smoke	Wait	WalkD.	Walk	WalkT.	Avg.
Zhou et al. [10] ICCV'19 (+)	34.4	42.4	36.6	42.1	38.2	39.8	34.7	40.2	45.6	60.8	39.0	42.6	42.0	29.8	31.7	39.9
Ci et al. [23] ICCV'19 (+)(*)	36.3	38.8	29.7	37.8	34.6	42.5	39.8	32.5	36.2	39.5	34.4	38.4	38.2	31.3	34.2	36.3
Martinez et al. [1] ICCV'2017	37.7	44.4	40.3	42.1	48.2	54.9	44.4	42.1	54.6	58.0	45.1	46.4	47.6	36.4	40.4	45.5
Zhao et al. [11] CVPR'19	37.8	49.4	37.6	40.9	45.1	**41.4**	40.1	48.3	50.1	**42.2**	53.5	44.3	40.5	47.3	39.0	43.8
Ours	**36.2**	**40.8**	**33.9**	**36.4**	**38.3**	47.3	**39.9**	**34.5**	**41.3**	50.8	**38.1**	**40.1**	**40.0**	**30.3**	**33.0**	**38.7**

Comparing Table 2 and Table 3, using different auxiliary tasks affects the performance differently. Generally, the auxiliary task of action classification is more beneficial to the task of 3D HPE and the semantic meaning of the global node output is clear, but we need to generate pseudo action class labels by ourselves. As for the auxiliary task of pose embedding, it does not require extra generated labels. However, the output of the global node does not have explicit meanings and an extra decoder network which is composed of simple fully connected layers is needed. In addition, the global node output can also be used for other purposes. For example, it can be pose features for the task of human shape restoration or action recognition, for which pose information is significant.

Table 7. Quantitative comparisons on the MPI-INF-3DHP dataset. The auxiliary task for the global node in our method is 100-class pose classification.

	Training data	GS (PCK)	noGS (PCK)	Outdoor (PCK)	ALL (PCK)	ALL (AUC)
Martinez et al. [1]	H36m	49.8	42.5	31.2	42.5	17.0
Yang et al. [20]	H36m+MPII	–	–	–	69.0	32.0
Zhou et al. [17]	H36m+MPII	71.1	64.7	72.7	69.2	32.5
Pavlakos et al. [16]	H36m+MPII+LSP	76.5	63.1	77.5	71.9	35.3
Ci et al. [23]	H36m	74.8	70.8	77.3	74.0	36.7
Wang et al. [12]	H36m	–	–	–	71.9	35.8
Li et al. [9]	H36m+MPII	70.1	68.2	66.6	67.9	–
Zhou et al. [10]	H36m+MPII	75.6	71.3	**80.3**	75.3	38.0
Ours	H36m	**79.0**	**79.3**	79.8	**79.3**	**45.9**

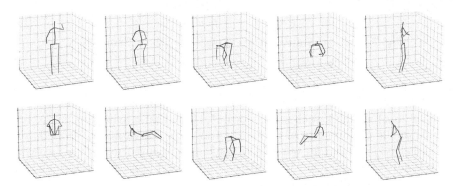

Fig. 6. These 3D poses are visualized K-means clustering centers when we categorize poses in the training set of Human3.6M into 50 action classes. Each pose category roughly represents a typical action, like waving, bending, lying and so on.

4.3   Comparison with the State of the Art

Results on Human3.6M. Following Pavllo et al. [36], we use 2D poses provided by a pre-trained 2D pose detector composed of cascaded pyramid network (CPN) [42] for benchmark evaluation. We use the GCN with a global node and an auxiliary task of 100-category action classification due to its overall best performance. We set the initial learning rate as 0.001, the decay factor 0.95 per 4 epochs and the batch size 256. We also apply dropout with a factor of 0.2 for each graph convolutional layer. It takes about 4 h to train our model for 50 epochs on a single GPU of Nvidia RTX 2080Ti. Table 4 and Table 5 compare our results and other state-of-the-art results under two protocols, respectively. In Protocol-1, the 3D pose error of our method is 54.9 mm, which is lower than many recent state of the arts [11,40,41]. When trained on ground-truth 2D poses, our model outperforms other methods [1,11] by a notable margin, as shown in Table 6. In Protocol-2, our method is comparable with previous state of the art [23] despite

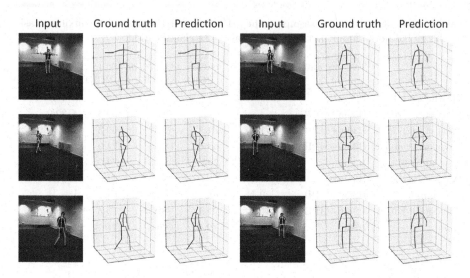

Fig. 7. Some qualitative results of our approach on Human3.6M.

they use extra data from MPII dataset for training and exploit the information of pose scale in both training and testing. Note that we do not incorporate any additional modules, such as non-local [5,11] and pose refinement [5], to further boost the performance of our method in these two protocols. In addition, the global node output in our model could be employed for follow-on tasks, like action recognition. Some qualitative results of our approach on Human3.6M dataset are presented in Fig. 7.

Results on MPI-INF-3DHP. Following [9], we apply our model trained on the training set of Human3.6M to the test set of MPI-INF-3DHP. The 2D joints provided by the dataset are taken as input. Table 7 shows the results. As we can see from the table, our method outperforms other recent methods in "**GS**" and "**noGS**". Though [10] has slightly higher PCK in "**Outdoor**", overall our method achieves the best performance in contrast with previous state of the arts [9,10,16,23] which attempt to address the generalization issue across different datasets. Notably, some of them even use more than one dataset to train their models. Since our model has not seen any pose contained in MPI-INF-3DHP, the results validate the generalization capacity of our model to new datasets.

5   Conclusion

In this paper, we introduce a novel 3D HPE approach by learning global pose features for 3D HPE. We also propose a heterogeneous multi-task learning framework to facilitate the learning of global features. With extensive ablation study and benchmark comparison, we make the following conclusions. (1) A global node is beneficial to GCNs for 3D HPE. (2) With supervision, a global node could learn global features better. (3) Both auxiliary pose classification and pose embedding are helpful to the supervision of a global node.

Acknowledgments. This work was supported in part by Wei Tang's startup funds from the University of Illinois at Chicago and the National Science Foundation (NSF) award CNS-1828265.

References

1. Martinez, J., Hossain, R., Romero, J., Little, J.J.: A simple yet effective baseline for 3D human pose estimation. In: Proceedings of the IEEE International Conference on Computer Vision, pp. 2640–2649 (2017)
2. Moon, G., Chang, J.Y., Lee, K.M.: Camera distance-aware top-down approach for 3D multi-person pose estimation from a single RGB image. In: Proceedings of the IEEE International Conference on Computer Vision, pp. 10133–10142 (2019)
3. Pavlakos, G., Zhou, X., Derpanis, K.G., Daniilidis, K.: Coarse-to-fine volumetric prediction for single-image 3D human pose. In: Proceedings of the IEEE Conference on Computer Vision and Pattern Recognition, pp. 7025–7034 (2017)
4. Qiu, H., Wang, C., Wang, J., Wang, N., Zeng, W.: Cross view fusion for 3D human pose estimation. In: Proceedings of the IEEE International Conference on Computer Vision, pp. 4342–4351 (2019)
5. Cai, Y., et al.: Exploiting spatial-temporal relationships for 3D pose estimation via graph convolutional networks. In: Proceedings of the IEEE International Conference on Computer Vision, pp. 2272–2281 (2019)
6. Arnab, A., Doersch, C., Zisserman, A.: Exploiting temporal context for 3D human pose estimation in the wild. In: Proceedings of the IEEE Conference on Computer Vision and Pattern Recognition, pp. 3395–3404 (2019)
7. Rayat Imtiaz Hossain, M., Little, J.J.: Exploiting temporal information for 3D human pose estimation. In: Proceedings of the European Conference on Computer Vision (ECCV), pp. 68–84 (2018)
8. Dong, J., Jiang, W., Huang, Q., Bao, H., Zhou, X.: Fast and robust multi-person 3D pose estimation from multiple views. In: Proceedings of the IEEE Conference on Computer Vision and Pattern Recognition, pp. 7792–7801 (2019)
9. Li, C., Lee, G.H.: Generating multiple hypotheses for 3D human pose estimation with mixture density network. In: Proceedings of the IEEE Conference on Computer Vision and Pattern Recognition, pp. 9887–9895 (2019)
10. Zhou, K., Han, X., Jiang, N., Jia, K., Lu, J.: HEMlets Pose: learning part-centric heatmap triplets for accurate 3D human pose estimation. In: Proceedings of the IEEE International Conference on Computer Vision, pp. 2344–2353 (2019)
11. Zhao, L., Peng, X., Tian, Y., Kapadia, M., Metaxas, D.N.: Semantic graph convolutional networks for 3D human pose regression. In: Proceedings of the IEEE Conference on Computer Vision and Pattern Recognition, pp. 3425–3435 (2019)
12. Wang, J., Huang, S., Wang, X., Tao, D.: Not all parts are created equal: 3D pose estimation by modeling bi-directional dependencies of body parts. In: Proceedings of the IEEE International Conference on Computer Vision, pp. 7771–7780 (2019)
13. Tekin, B., Katircioglu, I., Salzmann, M., Lepetit, V., Fua, P.: Structured prediction of 3D human pose with deep neural networks. arXiv preprint arXiv:1605.05180 (2016)

14. Agarwal, A., Triggs, B.: 3D human pose from silhouettes by relevance vector regression. In: Proceedings of the 2004 IEEE Computer Society Conference on Computer Vision and Pattern Recognition, CVPR 2004, vol. 2, p. II. IEEE (2004)
15. Zhao, X., Ning, H., Liu, Y., Huang, T.: Discriminative estimation of 3D human pose using gaussian processes. In: 2008 19th International Conference on Pattern Recognition, pp. 1–4. IEEE (2008)
16. Pavlakos, G., Zhou, X., Daniilidis, K.: Ordinal depth supervision for 3D human pose estimation. In: Proceedings of the IEEE Conference on Computer Vision and Pattern Recognition, pp. 7307–7316 (2018)
17. Zhou, X., Huang, Q., Sun, X., Xue, X., Wei, Y.: Towards 3D human pose estimation in the wild: a weakly-supervised approach. In: Proceedings of the IEEE International Conference on Computer Vision, pp. 398–407 (2017)
18. Sun, X., Shang, J., Liang, S., Wei, Y.: Compositional human pose regression. In: Proceedings of the IEEE International Conference on Computer Vision, pp. 2602–2611 (2017)
19. Sun, X., Xiao, B., Wei, F., Liang, S., Wei, Y.: Integral human pose regression. In: Proceedings of the European Conference on Computer Vision (ECCV), pp. 529–545 (2018)
20. Yang, W., Ouyang, W., Wang, X., Ren, J., Li, H., Wang, X.: 3D human pose estimation in the wild by adversarial learning. In: Proceedings of the IEEE Conference on Computer Vision and Pattern Recognition, pp. 5255–5264 (2018)
21. Kipf, T.N., Welling, M.: Semi-supervised classification with graph convolutional networks. arXiv preprint arXiv:1609.02907 (2016)
22. Zhou, J., et al.: Graph neural networks: a review of methods and applications. arXiv preprint arXiv:1812.08434 (2018)
23. Ci, H., Wang, C., Ma, X., Wang, Y.: Optimizing network structure for 3D human pose estimation. In: Proceedings of the IEEE International Conference on Computer Vision, pp. 2262–2271 (2019)
24. Agarwal, A., Triggs, B.: Recovering 3D human pose from monocular images. IEEE Trans. Pattern Anal. Mach. Intell. **28**, 44–58 (2005)
25. Rogez, G., Rihan, J., Ramalingam, S., Orrite, C., Torr, P.H.: Randomized trees for human pose detection. In: 2008 IEEE Conference on Computer Vision and Pattern Recognition, pp. 1–8. IEEE (2008)
26. Ionescu, C., Li, F., Sminchisescu, C.: Latent structured models for human pose estimation. In: 2011 International Conference on Computer Vision, pp. 2220–2227. IEEE (2011)
27. Chen, X., Lin, K.Y., Liu, W., Qian, C., Lin, L.: Weakly-supervised discovery of geometry-aware representation for 3D human pose estimation. In: Proceedings of the IEEE Conference on Computer Vision and Pattern Recognition, pp. 10895–10904 (2019)
28. Liu, K., Ding, R., Zou, Z., Wang, L., Tang, W.: A comprehensive study of weight sharing in graph networks for 3D human pose estimation. In: Vedaldi, A., Bischof, H., Brox, T., Frahm, J.-M. (eds.) ECCV 2020. LNCS, vol. 12355, pp. 318–334. Springer, Cham (2020). https://doi.org/10.1007/978-3-030-58607-2_19
29. Zou, Z., Liu, K., Wang, L., Tang, W.: High-order graph convolutional networks for 3D human pose estimation. In: BMVC (2020)
30. Gilmer, J., Schoenholz, S.S., Riley, P.F., Vinyals, O., Dahl, G.E.: Neural message passing for quantum chemistry. In: Proceedings of the 34th International Conference on Machine Learning, vol. 70, pp. 1263–1272. JMLR.org (2017)
31. Bruna, J., Zaremba, W., Szlam, A., LeCun, Y.: Spectral networks and locally connected networks on graphs. arXiv preprint arXiv:1312.6203 (2013)

32. Battaglia, P.W., et al.: Relational inductive biases, deep learning, and graph networks. arXiv preprint arXiv:1806.01261 (2018)
33. Defferrard, M., Bresson, X., Vandergheynst, P.: Convolutional neural networks on graphs with fast localized spectral filtering. In: Advances in Neural Information Processing Systems, pp. 3844–3852 (2016)
34. Ionescu, C., Papava, D., Olaru, V., Sminchisescu, C.: Human3.6M: large scale datasets and predictive methods for 3D human sensing in natural environments. IEEE Trans. Pattern Anal. Mach. Intell. **36**, 1325–1339 (2013)
35. Mehta, D., et al.: Monocular 3D human pose estimation in the wild using improved CNN supervision. In: 2017 Fifth International Conference on 3D Vision (3DV). IEEE (2017)
36. Pavllo, D., Feichtenhofer, C., Grangier, D., Auli, M.: 3D human pose estimation in video with temporal convolutions and semi-supervised training. In: Proceedings of the IEEE Conference on Computer Vision and Pattern Recognition, pp. 7753–7762 (2019)
37. Kingma, D.P., Ba, J.: Adam: a method for stochastic optimization. arXiv preprint arXiv:1412.6980 (2014)
38. Glorot, X., Bengio, Y.: Understanding the difficulty of training deep feedforward neural networks. In: Proceedings of the Thirteenth International Conference on Artificial Intelligence and Statistics, pp. 249–256 (2010)
39. Tekin, B., Márquez-Neila, P., Salzmann, M., Fua, P.: Learning to fuse 2D and 3D image cues for monocular body pose estimation. In: Proceedings of the IEEE International Conference on Computer Vision, pp. 3941–3950 (2017)
40. Fang, H.S., Xu, Y., Wang, W., Liu, X., Zhu, S.C.: Learning pose grammar to encode human body configuration for 3D pose estimation. In: Thirty-Second AAAI Conference on Artificial Intelligence (2018)
41. Sharma, S., Varigonda, P.T., Bindal, P., Sharma, A., Jain, A.: Monocular 3D human pose estimation by generation and ordinal ranking. In: Proceedings of the IEEE International Conference on Computer Vision, pp. 2325–2334 (2019)
42. Chen, Y., Wang, Z., Peng, Y., Zhang, Z., Yu, G., Sun, J.: Cascaded pyramid network for multi-person pose estimation. In: Proceedings of the IEEE Conference on Computer Vision and Pattern Recognition, pp. 7103–7112 (2018)

SGNet: Semantics Guided Deep Stereo Matching

Shuya Chen[1], Zhiyu Xiang[2]($\boxtimes$), Chengyu Qiao[1], Yiman Chen[1], and Tingming Bai[1]

[1] College of Information and Electronic Engineering, Zhejiang University, Hangzhou, China
[2] Zhejiang Provincial Key Laboratory of Information Processing, Communication and Networking, Zhejiang University, Hangzhou, China
xiangzy@zju.edu.cn

Abstract. Stereovision has been an intensive research area of computer vision. Based on deep learning, stereo matching networks are becoming popular in recent years. Despite of great progress, it's still challenging to achieve high accurate disparity map due to low texture and illumination changes in the scene. High-level semantic information can be helpful to handle these problems. In this paper a deep semantics guided stereo matching network (SGNet) is proposed. Apart from necessary semantic branch, three semantic guided modules are proposed to embed semantic constraints on matching. The joint confidence module produces confidence of cost volume based on the consistency of disparity and semantic features between left and right images. The residual module is responsible for optimizing the initial disparity results according to its semantic categories. Finally, in the loss module, the smooth of disparity is well supervised based on semantic boundary and region. The proposed network has been evaluated on various public datasets like KITTI 2015, KITTI 2012 and Virtual KITTI, and achieves the state-of-the-art performance.

1 Introduction

As a low cost 3D sensing module, stereo vision is widely used in lots of applications like robot navigation [1] or unmanned vehicles [2]. The main challenge of stereo vision lies in stereo matching, i.e., obtaining an accurate disparity map for the scene given a pair of stereo images.

Although the stereo matching performance has been greatly improved in recent years due to the development of deep learning [3,4], there still exists problems caused by the lack of reliable scene clues, large changes in illumination, object occlusion or low texture. As a bio-prototype of stereo vision, our eyes can judge the distance of objects by combining multiple clues, such as object categories, the integrity of objects, the judgment of foreground/background and so on. To some extent, it is capable of fusing more global semantic information to help the distance determination.

© Springer Nature Switzerland AG 2021
H. Ishikawa et al. (Eds.): ACCV 2020, LNCS 12622, pp. 106–122, 2021.
https://doi.org/10.1007/978-3-030-69525-5_7

In computer vision, semantic segmentation is an important high-level task in scene understanding [5,6]. The goal is to assign a correct category label to each pixel in the image and provide a high level understanding of the scene. These years have seen some successful fusion of semantics into different low level tasks such as optical flow [7], monocular depth estimation [8–10], depth completion [11] and stereo matching [12–14], etc. Generally, there are two ways to incorporate semantics. Fusion of convolutional semantic features is the most popular way [7–9,12–14], since semantic features are heterogeneous high level ones different from low level features, it can be complementary for stereo matching. The second way uses the geometric layout of semantic results [9,10,14], since both of semantic and disparity maps can display the general layout and object boundaries.

In this paper, we present a novel semantics guided deep stereo matching network (SGNet) with new semantic constraints embedded. As shown in Fig. 1, the entire model is built upon PSMNet [15], a mature 3D cost volume based deep stereo matching network. We design three novel modules which embed semantic feature consistency, semantic label based optimization and semantic smooth priori into disparity computation, respectively. Based on the observation that if two pixels in the stereo pair don't have the same semantic labels, they are unlikely to be the correct matching, a confidence module is designed. This module computes the consistency between the correlation obtained from the semantic and disparity features upon input images and takes it as the confidence level of the disparity cost volume. Then a residual module is proposed to further optimize the initial disparity results from the regression step. In this module, the initial disparity map is divided into multiple channels according to their semantic categories where depthwise convolution is adopted to obtain a semantic-dependent disparity residual. Finally, with a priori similarity between the semantics and disparity layout, two loss functions are proposed in the loss module to guide the smooth of disparity under the semantic supervision.

In summary, our contributions are:

(1) A novel semantic guided deep stereo matching network with residual based disparity optimization structure is proposed. Within the residual module, semantics based depthwise convolution operation is presented to obtain category-dependent disparity residual in order to refine the initial disparity;
(2) A confidence module based on semantic-disparity consistency is proposed to help the initial disparity regression. Two improved loss functions based on the similarity between semantic and disparity map are also presented to guide the smooth of disparity prediction;
(3) The entire module is implemented end-to-end and comprehensively evaluated in various public datasets. The experimental results achieve state-of-the-art performance, demonstrating the success of our semantic guidance policy.

2   Related Work

Traditional stereo matching algorithms usually consist of four steps [16]: matching cost computation, cost aggregation, disparity computation and refinement. Local algorithms like SSD [16] and SAD [17] aggregate the cost within windows and select the disparities with minimal cost. Global algorithms construct a global cost function to seek final disparities instead of using the aggregated cost, some examples are graph cuts [18] and belief propagation [19]. However, these methods need hand-crafted features and are still limited in ill-posed regions.

In contrast, learning based methods have a strong feature representation capability to deal with the problems in stereo matching. Early deep learning algorithms [3,4] only replace parts of steps in traditional pipelines. Different from these approaches which still require human involvement, end-to-end algorithms are becoming more popular in recent years. The structure of end-to-end networks can be roughly divided into two categories according to the different forms of computing matching cost, i.e., correlation based and 3D cost volume based methods. The former requires less memory and can directly obtain the similarity between extracted feature maps. The latter preserves more complete features and can usually achieve better performance.

Correlation Based Methods. FlowNet [20] first introduces the correlation layer which directly calculates the correlation between two images by inner product and demonstrates its success in optical flow computation. Upon FlowNet [20], DispNet [21] is proposed for the task of stereo matching. Based on DispNet [21], CRL [22] constructs a two-stage model, the initial disparity is corrected by using the residual multiscale signal in the second stage. AANet [23] adopts multiscale correlation layers and proposes intra-scale and cross-scale modules to further refine the disparity.

3D Cost Volume Based Methods. GC-Net [24] manages to employ contextual information with 3D cost volume and adopts 3D convolution to regress disparity directly. Yu et al. [25] propose a learnable matching cost volume. PSM-Net [15] introduces a pyramid pooling module to incorporate global and local features, and adopts stacked hourglass structures to regularize cost volume. To further fuse the constraints of image edges, EdgeStereo [26,27] trains an edge detection sub-network to refine the disparity by concatenating the edge features and the edge-aware loss. GA-Net [28] designs a semi-global aggregation layer and a local guided aggregation layer inspired by SGM [29]. HSM [30] proposes a network for high-res images by a coarse-to-fine hierarchy and adopts three asymmetric augmentation about imaging condition, calibration and occlusion.

Our method also takes advantages of both correlation and 3D cost volume presentation. We construct 3D cost volume to regress the initial disparity and adopt the correlation layer to embed the constraints from semantics.

Methods Combined with Semantics. Semantic segmentation is a high-level pixel-wise classification task, which can provide valuable semantic information to many low level tasks. It has been successfully incorporated into many tasks, e.g., optical flow [7], depth estimation [8–10] and depth completion [11].

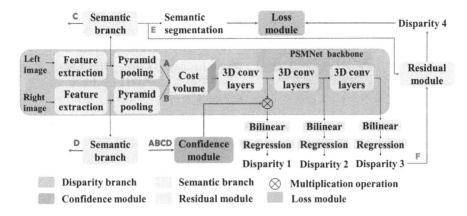

Fig. 1. Architecture of the proposed SGNet.

However, few semantics-combined stereo matching networks are published until recently. SegStereo [12] concatenates semantics with correlation features. DispSegNet [13] proposes an unsupervised algorithm which concatenates semantics with initial disparity to refine the prediction. SSPCV-Net [14] constructs heterogeneous and multiscale cost volumes combined with semantic features and proposes a 3D multicost aggregation module. It also uses gradient-related loss to constrain the smooth of disparity. These methods mainly embed semantics from the aspects of semantic features and geometric layouts.

Our solution utilizes the consistency between the semantic and disparity correlation as the cost confidence instead of directly adopting the concatenation operation to fuse the semantic features, as in [12] and [13]. In addition, we explicitly use the semantic category in our residual module by dividing the disparity map into multiple category channels and compute the category-dependent disparity residual. In spired by EdgeStereo [27] and SSPCV-Net [14] which adopt gradient-related loss to guide disparity prediction, we further supervise the smooth of disparity by boundary and inner region of semantic maps under the specialized category-dependent constraints.

3   Approach

3.1   Architecture Overview

The architecture of the proposed SGNet for stereo matching is illustrated in Fig. 1. It's built upon PSMNet [15], which uses 3D cost volume to compute stereo matching and possesses competitive performance. Given the left and right images, this baseline first gets high-dimensional features by the weight-sharing encoder layers. Then a pyramid pooling layer is followed to obtain the multiscale features and fuse them. The features are then translated in horizontal (x-disparity) direction and concatenated to construct 3D cost volume with different disparities. Disparity output is obtained by regression with stacked hourglass

Residual module:

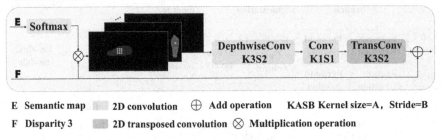

E Semantic map   2D convolution   ⊕ Add operation   KASB Kernel size=A , Stride=B

F Disparity 3   2D transposed convolution ⊗ Multiplication operation

Fig. 2. Structure of the residual module.

structures. Three outputs with gradually supervised refinement are used, each of which is the sum of the disparity value weighted by predicted probabilities. In [15], the last output, i.e., $disp3$ in Fig. 1, is regarded as the final output.

The baseline PSMNet [15] is taken as the disparity branch in our SGNet. Apart from it, a semantic branch is added after the feature extraction layer. It shares some shallow layers with the disparity branch and has independent high-level layers so that the unique characteristics of semantics can be extracted.

To embed semantic guidance into disparity computing process, three novel modules are added to the baseline network, i.e., residual module, confidence module, and loss module. The residual module takes $disp3$ as initial input, which is divided into multiple channels according to the semantic categories and further optimized by category-dependent convolution. The confidence module is combined with the $disp1$'s cost volume. It takes the semantic and disparity features from left and right images and produces the consistency confidence between the semantic and disparity correlation. This confidence will help better regress initial disparities. The loss module takes the final prediction $disp4$ and semantics as input and is responsible for embedding the semantics boundary and inner smooth constraints on supervisory loss.

3.2 Semantic Branch

Semantic segmentation and disparity networks share the shallow layers. The independent semantic branch employs two more residual blocks with 256 channels for deeper feature extraction. Similar to disparity branch, pyramid pooling module is also used for acquisition of local and global semantic features. Finally, the semantic results are obtained through a classification layer. Such structure has two advantages: (1) the disparity and semantics share the shallow layers making the network more efficient on learning the common features of two tasks. (2) The structure of semantic branch is similar to the disparity branch, so the whole network structure is more unified.

Confidence module:

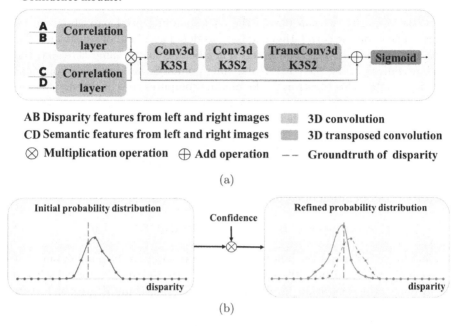

(a)

(b)

Fig. 3. Illustration of (a) network structure and (b) effects of the confidence module.

3.3   Residual Module

The motivation of this module is from the observation that the disparities within an object or category are mostly smooth. However, for different categories the degree of smooth may not be the same. For example, the surface of the road is generally flat with smooth, while the surface of other categories like trees may be much more uneven. Therefore, carrying out different convolution operations according to their semantic categories may help better learn the continuity of disparity for each category.

The residual module takes the semantic probability map and $disp3$ as input. $disp3$ with size $H \times W$ is multiplied with the semantic probability map with size $H \times W \times C$, where C is the number of classes. Since the semantic probabilities are between 0 and 1 representing the possibilities of each category, the operation results in category-wise raw disparity map with size $H \times W \times C$ for optimization. In other words, each channel of the map is the raw disparity under a certain category, as illustrated in Fig. 2.

Depthwise convolution is then performed for each channel. A pointwise convolution is followed to integrate all category channels. Finally a transposed convolution is used to compute the disparity residual.

3.4   Confidence Module

Given the disparity, we can obtain the corresponding pixel pairs between two images. The semantic correlation can be considered as a kind of constraint. That is, as for one pair, if these two pixels don't belong to the same category, then they are unlikely to be the correct matching points. So we propose a confidence module to embed this constraint. The module computes the consistency between the correlation on disparity and semantics and takes it as the confidence of $disp1$'s cost volume. Only when both of disparity and semantic correlations are high, the confidence value of the corresponding disparity candidate is high.

The network structure of confidence module is shown in Fig. 3(a). The semantic features as well as the disparity features with size of $H/4 \times W/4$ are fed into the correlation layer respectively to compute the correlation for each candidate disparity. The operation of correlation [20] is shown in Eq. 1.

$$Correlation(x, y, d) = \frac{1}{N_c} inner <f_1(x,y), f_2(x-d,y)>. \tag{1}$$

where $inner <>$ denotes the inner product operation, N_c is the number of feature channels, f_1 and f_2 denote the left and right feature maps. Compared with 3D cost volume, this operation intuitively shows the matching degree of features under different disparities. We apply this operation on disparity or semantic features respectively.

The output of the correlation layers in Fig. 3(a) represent semantic and disparity correlations respectively. They are then multiplied and fed into three consecutive 3D convolution layers with a residual structure to compute the consistency between these two different correlations. Finally a sigmoid function is employed to constrain the range of the output confidence.

As shown in Fig. 1, there are three levels of regression output in PSMNet [15]. Multiplying the obtained confidence values to $disp1$'s cost volume is a good choice because it's better to improve the disparity in the early stage. The effect of the confidence module on the disparity regression is illustrated in Fig. 3(b). The initial cost volume or the probability distribution along disparity dimension of a pixel may be inaccurate, with the probability peak drifted from the ground truth. After the correction from the confidence, the distribution can be adjusted and closer to the ground truth.

3.5   Loss Module

Loss for Single Tasks. For disparity estimation, we mainly use $smooth \ L_1$ loss since it is insensitive to outliers and the gradient change is relatively small.

$$L_{disp} = \frac{1}{N} \sum_{i=1}^{N} smooth(d_i, d_i^*). \tag{2}$$

In Eq. 2, d_i and d_i^* are the predicted disparity and corresponding groundtruth respectively, N is the number of valid pixels. During training, we supervise $disp1$, $disp2$, $disp4$, and output $disp4$ during testing, as shown in Fig. 1.

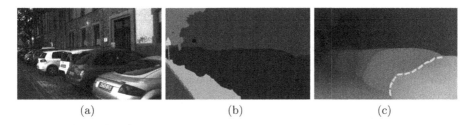

(a)   (b)   (c)

Fig. 4. Illustration of layout similarity of semantics (b) and disparity image (c) given an example scene from KITTI [31] (a). Although they have similar smooth layout, there are some inconsistent areas between the two images. For example, the red boundary in (b) and yellow boundary in (c) do not appear in the counterpart image. (Color figure online)

As for semantic loss L_{sem}, we adopt the cross-entropy loss to train the semantic branch as shown in following:

$$L_{sem} = -\frac{1}{N}\sum_{i=1}^{N}\sum_{c=1}^{C}y(i,c)log(p(i,c)). \tag{3}$$

where p is the predicted semantic probability, y is the corresponding groundtruth, C is the number of classes and N is the number of valid pixels.

Semantic Guided Disparity Loss. Semantic and disparity map are to some extent similar in geometric layouts. Therefore, the semantic ground truth can be utilized to guide the disparity map with a reasonable smooth constraint.

(1) Guided by Semantic Boundary

For most of the semantic foreground, such as vehicles, pedestrians or other objects, if semantic boundaries exist, so does disparity map. But it doesn't hold everywhere. For example, for parts of the background areas, such as "road", "sidewalk" or "parking", there are no obvious boundaries between two adjacent categories in disparity map, as shown in Fig. 4. The semantic boundary between the road and parking marked by red dashed lines doesn't appear in the disparity map. Therefore, we only supervise the disparity boundaries which has strong co-appearing relationships with semantics according to their categories.

We tend to punish on the pixels whose positions in ground truth semantics are boundary areas while in the predicted disparity map are not. The loss function motivated by [14] is constructed in Eq. 4, where a mask m_b is used to handle the valid area.

$$L_{bdry} = \frac{1}{N}\left(\sum_{i,j}|\varphi_x^2\left(sem_{i,j,m_b}\right)|e^{-|\varphi_x^2\left(d_{i,j,m_b}\right)|} + \sum_{i,j}|\varphi_y^2\left(sem_{i,j,m_b}\right)|e^{-|\varphi_y^2\left(d_{i,j,m_b}\right)|}\right). \tag{4}$$

In Eq. 4, sem_{i,j,m_b} and d_{i,j,m_b} are the semantic groundtruth and predicted disparity at $p(i,j)$ with $m_b(i,j) = 1$ respectively, φ_x^2 and φ_y^2 are the second-order gradient along the horizontal and vertical direction respectively, N is the number of valid pixels whose $m_b(i,j) = 1$.

Taking images in KITTI 2015 dataset as examples, the mask can be defined as:

$$m_b(i,j) = \begin{cases} 1, & p(i,j) \notin \text{"road", "sidewalk", "vegetation", "terrain",} \\ 0, & otherwise. \end{cases} \quad (5)$$

(2) Guided by Semantic Smooth

Smooth constraint in ground truth semantics can be another powerful supervision for disparity prediction. However there are also inconsistent areas where the semantics are smooth while the disparity are not. As shown in Fig. 4(c), the object boundary represented by yellow dashed line doesn't exist in the semantic map.

Our solution is a threshold based method. When the gradient of disparity is greater than a threshold λ, it indicates that there exist true boundaries so we don't enforce the semantic smooth constraint on it. In Eq. 6, we mostly punish on the pixels which are smooth in the semantic map while unsmooth in the disparity map, with the mask m_s to define the valid area.

$$L_{sm} = \frac{1}{N} \left(\sum_{i,j} |\varphi_x^2 (d_{i,j,m_s})| e^{-|\varphi_x^2 (sem_{i,j,m_s})|} + \sum_{i,j} |\varphi_y^2 (d_{i,j,m_s})| e^{-|\varphi_y^2 (sem_{i,j,m_s})|} \right). \quad (6)$$

$$m_s(i,j) = \begin{cases} 1, & \text{gradient of disparity map at } p(i,j) \text{ less than } \lambda, \\ 0, & otherwise. \end{cases} \quad (7)$$

Finally, integrating all of the above loss together, the total loss in our model is:

$$L = L_{disp} + w_{sem} * L_{sem} + w_{bdry} * L_{bdry} + w_{sm} * L_{sm}. \quad (8)$$

with

$$L_{disp} = w_{disp1} * L_{disp1} + w_{disp2} * L_{disp2} + w_{disp4} * L_{disp4}. \quad (9)$$

4   Experiments and Analysis

Our SGNet model is implemented by Pytorch [32] and we adopt Adam ($\beta_1 = 0.9$, $\beta_2 = 0.999$) to optimize the model. The learning rate is first set to 0.001 then set to 0.0001 in the later stage. The batch size is 2 in training and validation process due to the limited GPU resources. Input images are randomly cropped to size 160×320 for Virtual KITTI and 256 × 512 for the other datasets, and

Table 1. Results of different combining operations in confidence module. "Disp-cor" and "Sem-cor" denotes the correlation of disparity features and semantic features respectively.

Combination mode	$3px$ (%)	EPE (pixel)
Disp-cor + Seg-cor	1.362	0.6269
Disp-cor × Seg-cor	**1.299**	**0.6198**
Disp-cor × Disp-cor × Seg-cor	1.319	0.6212
Disp-cor × Seg-cor × Seg-cor	1.309	0.6238

Table 2. Results of different setting in loss module on KITTI 2015 validation set.

w_{bdry}	w_{sm}	λ	$3px$ (%)	EPE (pixel)
0.5	0.5	2	1.330	0.6274
0.5	0.5	3	**1.299**	**0.6198**
0.5	0.5	4	1.326	0.6226
0.7	0.5	3	1.336	0.6252
0.5	0.7	3	1.336	0.6235

the maximum disparity is set to 192. Some parameters in loss function are set according to [15] as $w_{disp1} = 0.5$, $w_{disp2} = 0.7$, $w_{disp4} = 1$, $w_{sem} = 1$, and w_{bdry}, w_{sm}, λ are determined experimentally.

During training or testing, following datasets are used:

(1) Scene Flow [21]

Scene Flow [21] is a synthetic dataset consisting of 35454 training images and 4370 testing images with dense ground truth disparity maps. In our experiments, this dataset is only used for pre-training. Since it doesn't contain semantic labels, only the stereo matching branch is pre-trained.

(2) KITTI stereo 2015 & 2012 [31,33]

KITTI [31,33] are the datasets with real-world street views which use lidar to obtain sparse groundtruth disparity. KITTI 2015 [31] includes 200 training images with semantic labels and 200 testing images. In the ablation experiments, 160 images are taken as the training set, and the remaining 40 images are taken as the validation set. KITTI 2012 [33] includes 194 training images without semantic labels and 195 testing images.

(3) Virtual KITTI [34]

Virtual KITTI 2 [34] is a dataset of virtual urban scenes that contains dense depth maps and semantic labels. The "15-deg-left" subsequence in sequence 2 is sampled as the validation set with 233 images, and the same subsequences in the remaining sequences are used as the training set which includes 1893 images.

Table 3. Ablation experiments of different modules on KITTI 2015 and Virtual KITTI dataset. "Baseline" refers to the disparity branch PSMNet [15], "C", "R" and "L" denote the confidence module, the residual module and the semantic guided loss module.

Model	Confidence module	Residual module	Loss module	3px (%)	EPE (pixel)	Run time (s)
SceneFlow + KITTI2015						
Baseline				1.415	0.6341	0.671
Baseline-C	✓			1.371	0.6275	–
Baseline-R		✓		1.368	0.6253	–
Baseline-CR	✓	✓		1.328	0.6203	–
Baseline-CRL	✓	✓	✓	**1.299**	**0.6198**	0.674
VirtualKITTI						
Baseline				4.108	0.6237	–
Baseline-CRL	✓	✓	✓	**3.874**	**0.5892**	–

In the main ablation experiments, our model is pretrained on the Scene Flow dataset then finetuned on KITTI 2015. Since both of KITTI 2015 and 2012 are the real-world datasets with urban scenes, when submitting to the benchmark, we train the pretrained model on mixed KITTI 2015 and KITTI 2012 datasets for 500 epochs to learn the generalization of features, and finally finetune it only on KITTI 2015 or KITTI 2012 dataset for another 200 epochs. During the training, only KITTI 2015 dataset provides the semantic labels.

Averaged end-point-error (EPE) and percentage of outliers with error more than k-pixel or 5% disparity (kpx) are used as performance metrics for all of the following experiments.

4.1   Ablation Studies

In this ablation studies, our model is first pre-trained on the Scene Flow dataset for 15 epochs with learning rate of 0.001, then fine-tuned on KITTI 2015 training set with learning rate of 0.001 in the first 600 epochs and 0.0001 in the next 100 epochs. As for Virtual KITTI, our model is trained from scratch with learning rate of 0.001 in the first 200 epochs and 0.0001 in the next 100 epochs.

Parameter Selection. We conduct experiments on different settings or hyper parameters for the modules to determine the best configuration.

As for the confidence module, we test the way of combination between disparity and semantic correlation, as shown in Table 1. Compared with addition operation, the model with multiplication reduces the $3px$ metric from 1.362% to 1.299%. Considering the possible different weights ratio of disparity and semantics, we also test the operation of multiplying disparity or semantic correlation one more time, which only results in worse performance. So we just select a single multiplication as the correlation combination.

As for the loss, some varying choices of the weight w_{bdry}, w_{sm} and the threshold λ are shown in Table 2. When setting $w_{bdry} = w_{sm} = 0.5$ and varying the

Table 4. Comparison on KITTI 2015 benchmark.

Model	All pixels			Non-occluded pixels		
	D1-bg	D1-fg	D1-all	D1-bg	D1-fg	D1-all
Models without semantics						
DispNetC [21]	4.32	4.41	4.34	4.11	3.72	4.05
MC-CNN-acrt [3]	2.89	8.88	3.89	2.48	7.64	3.33
GC-Net [24]	2.21	6.16	2.87	2.02	5.58	2.61
CRL [22]	2.48	3.59	2.67	2.32	3.12	2.45
PSMNet [15]	1.86	4.62	2.32	1.71	4.31	2.14
GwcNet-g [35]	1.74	3.93	2.11	1.61	3.49	1.92
EdgeStereo-V2 [27]	1.84	**3.30**	2.08	1.69	**2.94**	1.89
AANet+ [23]	1.65	3.96	2.03	1.49	3.66	1.85
Models with semantics						
SegStereo [12]	1.88	4.07	2.25	1.76	3.70	2.08
SSPCVNet [14]	1.75	3.89	2.11	1.61	3.40	1.91
SGNet (ours)	**1.63**	3.76	**1.99**	**1.46**	3.40	**1.78**

value of λ, the results show $\lambda = 3$ is a good choice to identify the real boundaries. Given $\lambda = 3$, change w_{bdry} and w_{sm}, the best performance is obtained when $w_{bdry} = w_{sm} = 0.5$. Therefore we set $w_{bdry} = w_{sm} = 0.5$ and $\lambda = 3$ for all of the following experiments.

Ablation of Modules. On the baseline disparity branch, we further evaluate the effectiveness of different modules by adding them separately as shown in Table 3. When only confidence or residual module is added, $3px$ error and EPE are reduced about 0.045% and 0.007 pixels respectively. Adding both modules can further decrease the error. On both KITTI 2015 and Virtual KITTI dataset, the best performance is achieved when all of the three modules are added. We also test the inference time of "Baseline" and "Baseline-CRL" on one Nvidia TITAN 1080TI. Although more modules together with a semantic branch are added, the inference time of our SGNet is still very close to the baseline.

In addition, the semantic performance of "Baseline-CRL" is evaluated with $mIoU = 48.12\%$ and $mAcc = 55.25\%$ in validation set.

4.2   Comparing with Other Methods

Results on KITTI 2015 Benchmark. We submit the best model trained on all KITTI 2015 training set to the online benchmark. The results are shown in Table 4, where "All pixels" and "Non-occluded pixels" separately represent the different range of pixels for evaluation, "D1" is the percentage of outliers with error more than 3-pixel or 5% disparity ($3px$), "bg", "fg" and "all" denote the

Fig. 5. Qualitative error maps on KITTI 2015 test set. The deeper blue color means the lower error, while the deeper red means the higher error. More noticeable differences can be observed in the area inside red box. (Color figure online)

Table 5. Comparison on KITTI 2012 benchmark.

Model	2px		3px		4px		5px	
	Noc	All	Noc	All	Noc	All	Noc	All
Models without semantics								
DispNetC [21]	7.38	8.11	4.11	4.65	2.77	3.20	2.05	2.39
MC-CNN-acrt [3]	3.90	5.45	2.43	3.63	1.90	2.85	1.64	2.39
GC-Net [24]	2.71	3.46	1.77	2.30	1.36	1.77	1.12	1.46
PSMNet [15]	2.44	3.01	1.49	1.89	1.12	1.42	0.90	1.15
AANet+ [23]	2.30	2.96	1.55	2.04	1.20	1.58	0.98	1.30
EdgeStereo-V2 [27]	2.32	**2.88**	1.46	**1.83**	1.07	**1.34**	**0.83**	**1.04**
Models with semantics								
SegStereo [12]	2.66	3.19	1.68	2.03	1.25	1.52	1.00	1.21
SSPCVNet [14]	2.47	3.09	1.47	1.90	1.08	1.41	0.87	1.14
SGNet (ours)	**2.22**	2.89	**1.38**	1.85	**1.05**	1.40	0.86	1.15

estimated area over background, foreground and all area, respectively. State-of-the-art models with or without considering semantics are listed for comparison.

As shown in Table 4, our model achieves the lowest error in most important "D1-all" metrics on both "All pixels" and "Non-occluded pixels", surpassing the other non-semantic or semantic guided methods in the list by a notable margin.

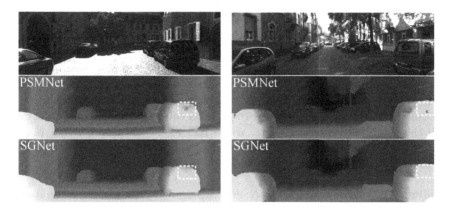

Fig. 6. The qualitative results on KITTI 2012 test set.

In particular, it improved about 0.3% on "D1-all" comparing with its baseline PSMNet [15], which demonstrates the effectiveness of our semantic guided policy.

Some qualitative comparisons on error map with PSMNet [15] and Seg-Stereo [12] are shown in Fig. 5. Generally, our model produces smoother predictions with lower error across the entire image. Some noticeable improvements can be found in the area bounded by the red boxes.

Results on KITTI 2012 Benchmark. We also fine-tune the model on KITTI 2012 dataset. Since no semantic labels are provided in KITTI 2012, the semantic branch is only trained by images on KITTI 2015. We then submit the prediction results to KITTI 2012 benchmark for evaluation. The results are shown in Table 5, where "Noc" and "All" represent the percentage of erroneous pixels only in non-occluded areas or in total, respectively.

Again, our model outperforms the baseline PSMNet [15] almost in all metrics except for $5px$ error on "All" pixels, where equal values are obtained. As expected, our model also performs better than most of the other non-semantics or semantics based method. Comparing with EdgeStereo-V2 [27], which embeds edge features and corresponding loss into the model, our method obtains better value on most non-occluded areas. We believe the performance of our model can be further improved if semantics ground truth are available in the training data.

Some qualitative comparisons with PSMNet [15] are shown in Fig. 6. Thanks to the effective guidance of semantics, our model can eliminate some holes inside objects and make the region more smoothing, as shown in the area inside the white boxes in Fig. 6.

5   Conclusion

Semantics as additional scene clues can provide valuable information for better stereo matching. In this paper we propose a semantic guided stereo matching network which optimizes the disparity computation from three semantics-related perspectives. In the confidence module, we employ the consistency between correlations on disparity and semantic features to adjust the cost volume. Within the residual module, semantics based depthwise convolution operation is presented to obtain category-dependent disparity residual in order to refine the initial disparity. An improved loss function module based on the similarity between semantic and disparity map is also presented to guide the smooth of disparity outputs. The entire model can be trained end-to-end and run with similar computing time with the baseline. Experiments on various KITTI dataset and benchmarks are carried out and state-of-the-art performances are achieved, which demonstrate the success of our semantic guide policy.

Funding. The work is supported by NSFC-Zhejiang Joint Fund for the Integration of Industrialization and Informatization under grant No. U1709214.

References

1. Schmid, K., Tomic, T., Ruess, F., Hirschmüller, H., Suppa, M.: Stereo vision based indoor/outdoor navigation for flying robots. In: Proceedings of the IEEE/RSJ International Conference on Intelligent Robots and Systems, pp. 3955–3962. IEEE (2013)
2. Chen, C., Seff, A., Kornhauser, A., Xiao, J.: DeepDriving: learning affordance for direct perception in autonomous driving. In: Proceedings of the IEEE International Conference on Computer Vision, pp. 2722–2730. IEEE (2015)
3. Žbontar, J., LeCun, Y.: Stereo matching by training a convolutional neural network to compare image patches. J. Mach. Learn. Res. **17**, 2287–2318 (2016)
4. Shaked, A., Wolf, L.: Improved stereo matching with constant highway networks and reflective confidence learning. In: Proceedings of the IEEE Conference on Computer Vision and Pattern Recognition, pp. 4641–4650. IEEE (2017)
5. Long, J., Shelhamer, E., Darrell, T.: Fully convolutional networks for semantic segmentation. In: Proceedings of the IEEE Conference on Computer Vision and Pattern Recognition, pp. 3431–3440. IEEE (2015)
6. Zhao, H., Shi, J., Qi, X., Wang, X., Jia, J.: Pyramid scene parsing network. In: Proceedings of the IEEE Conference on Computer Vision and Pattern Recognition, pp. 2881–2890. IEEE (2017)
7. Cheng, J., Tsai, Y.H., Wang, S., Yang, M.H.: SegFlow: joint learning for video object segmentation and optical flow. In: Proceedings of the IEEE International Conference on Computer Vision, pp. 686–695. IEEE (2017)
8. Zhang, Z., Cui, Z., Xu, C., Jie, Z., Li, X., Yang, J.: Joint task-recursive learning for semantic segmentation and depth estimation. In: Proceedings of the European Conference on Computer Vision, pp. 235–251 (2018)
9. Jiao, J., Cao, Y., Song, Y., Lau, R.: Look deeper into depth: monocular depth estimation with semantic booster and attention-driven loss. In: Proceedings of the European Conference on Computer Vision, pp. 53–69 (2018)
10. Chen, P.Y., Liu, A.H., Liu, Y.C., Wang, Y.C.F.: Towards scene understanding: unsupervised monocular depth estimation with semantic-aware representation. In: Proceedings of the IEEE Conference on Computer Vision and Pattern Recognition, pp. 2624–2632. IEEE (2019)

11. Zou, N., Xiang, Z., Chen, Y., Chen, S., Qiao, C.: Simultaneous semantic segmentation and depth completion with constraint of boundary. Sensors **20**, 635 (2020)
12. Yang, G., Zhao, H., Shi, J., Deng, Z., Jia, J.: SegStereo: exploiting semantic information for disparity estimation. In: Proceedings of the European Conference on Computer Vision, pp. 636–651 (2018)
13. Zhang, J., Skinner, K.A., Vasudevan, R., Johnson-Roberson, M.: DispSegNet: leveraging semantics for end-to-end learning of disparity estimation from stereo imagery. IEEE Robot. Autom. Lett. **4**, 1162–1169 (2019)
14. Wu, Z., Wu, X., Zhang, X., Wang, S., Ju, L.: Semantic stereo matching with pyramid cost volumes. In: Proceedings of the IEEE International Conference on Computer Vision, pp. 7484–7493. IEEE (2019)
15. Chang, J.R., Chen, Y.S.: Pyramid stereo matching network. In: Proceedings of the IEEE Conference on Computer Vision and Pattern Recognition, pp. 5410–5418. IEEE (2018)
16. Scharstein, D., Szeliski, R., Zabih, R.: A taxonomy and evaluation of dense two-frame stereo correspondence algorithms. Int. J. Comput. Vis. **47**, 7–42 (2001). https://doi.org/10.1023/A:1014573219977
17. Kanade, T., Kano, H., Kimura, S., Yoshida, A., Oda, K.: Development of a video-rate stereo machine. In: Proceedings of the 1995 IEEE/RSJ International Conference on Intelligent Robots and Systems. Human Robot Interaction and Cooperative Robots, vol. 3, pp. 95–100. IEEE (1995)
18. Boykov, Y., Veksler, O., Zabih, R.: Fast approximate energy minimization via graph cuts. IEEE Trans. Pattern Anal. Mach. Intell. **23**, 1222–1239 (2001)
19. Klaus, A., Sormann, M., Karner, K.: Segment-based stereo matching using belief propagation and a self-adapting dissimilarity measure. In: 18th International Conference on Pattern Recognition (ICPR 2006), vol. 3, pp. 15–18. IEEE (2006)
20. Dosovitskiy, A., et al.: FlowNet: learning optical flow with convolutional networks. In: Proceedings of the IEEE International Conference on Computer Vision, pp. 2758–2766. IEEE (2015)
21. Mayer, N., et al.: A large dataset to train convolutional networks for disparity, optical flow, and scene flow estimation. In: Proceedings of the IEEE Conference on Computer Vision and Pattern Recognition, pp. 4040–4048. IEEE (2016)
22. Pang, J., Sun, W., Ren, J.S., Yang, C., Yan, Q.: Cascade residual learning: a two-stage convolutional neural network for stereo matching. In: Proceedings of the IEEE International Conference on Computer Vision Workshops, pp. 887–895. IEEE (2017)
23. Xu, H., Zhang, J.: AANet: adaptive aggregation network for efficient stereo matching. In: Proceedings of the IEEE/CVF Conference on Computer Vision and Pattern Recognition, pp. 1959–1968. IEEE (2020)
24. Kendall, A., et al.: End-to-end learning of geometry and context for deep stereo regression. In: Proceedings of the IEEE International Conference on Computer Vision, pp. 66–75. IEEE (2017)
25. Yu, L., Wang, Y., Wu, Y., Jia, Y.: Deep stereo matching with explicit cost aggregation sub-architecture. In: Thirty-Second AAAI Conference on Artificial Intelligence (2018)
26. Song, X., Zhao, X., Hu, H., Fang, L.: EdgeStereo: a context integrated residual pyramid network for stereo matching. In: Jawahar, C.V., Li, H., Mori, G., Schindler, K. (eds.) ACCV 2018. LNCS, vol. 11365, pp. 20–35. Springer, Cham (2019). https://doi.org/10.1007/978-3-030-20873-8_2

27. Song, X., Zhao, X., Fang, L., Hu, H., Yu, Y.: EdgeStereo: an effective multi-task learning network for stereo matching and edge detection. Int. J. Comput. Vis. **128**, 910–930 (2020). https://doi.org/10.1007/s11263-019-01287-w

28. Zhang, F., Prisacariu, V., Yang, R., Torr, P.H.: GA-Net: guided aggregation net for end-to-end stereo matching. In: Proceedings of the IEEE Conference on Computer Vision and Pattern Recognition, pp. 185–194. IEEE (2019)

29. Hirschmuller, H.: Stereo processing by semiglobal matching and mutual information. IEEE Trans. Pattern Anal. Mach. Intell. **30**, 328–341 (2008)

30. Yang, G., Manela, J., Happold, M., Ramanan, D.: Hierarchical deep stereo matching on high-resolution images. In: Proceedings of the IEEE Conference on Computer Vision and Pattern Recognition, pp. 5515–5524. IEEE (2019)

31. Menze, M., Geiger, A.: Object scene flow for autonomous vehicles. In: Conference on Computer Vision and Pattern Recognition (2015)

32. Paszke, A., et al.: PyTorch: an imperative style, high-performance deep learning library. In: Advances in Neural Information Processing Systems, pp. 8024–8035 (2019)

33. Geiger, A., Lenz, P., Urtasun, R.: Are we ready for autonomous driving? The KITTI vision benchmark suite. In: Conference on Computer Vision and Pattern Recognition (2012)

34. Gaidon, A., Wang, Q., Cabon, Y., Vig, E.: Virtual worlds as proxy for multi-object tracking analysis. In: Proceedings of the IEEE Conference on Computer Vision and Pattern Recognition. IEEE (2016)

35. Guo, X., Yang, K., Yang, W., Wang, X., Li, H.: Group-wise correlation stereo network. In: Proceedings of the IEEE Conference on Computer Vision and Pattern Recognition, pp. 3273–3282. IEEE (2019)

Reconstructing Human Body Mesh from Point Clouds by Adversarial GP Network

Boyao Zhou[1]([✉]), Jean-Sébastien Franco[1], Federica Bogo[2], Bugra Tekin[2], and Edmond Boyer[1]

[1] Inria-Univ. Grenoble Alpes-CNRS-Grenoble INP-LJK,
Montbonnot-Saint-Martin, France
{boyao.zhou,jean-sebastien.franco,edmond.boyer}@inria.fr
[2] Microsoft, Zürich, Switzerland
{febogo,bugra.Tekin}@microsoft.com

Abstract. We study the problem of reconstructing the template-aligned mesh for human body estimation from unstructured point cloud data. Recently proposed approaches for shape matching that rely on Deep Neural Networks (DNNs) achieve state-of-the-art results with generic point-wise architectures; but in doing so, they exploit much weaker human body shape and surface priors with respect to methods that explicitly model the body surface with 3D templates. We investigate the impact of adding back such stronger shape priors by proposing a novel dedicated human template matching process, which relies on a point-based, deep autoencoder architecture. We encode surface smoothness and shape coherence with a specialized Gaussian Process layer. Furthermore, we enforce global consistency and improve the generalization capabilities of the model by introducing an adversarial training phase. The choice of these elements is grounded on an extensive analysis of DNNs failure modes in widely used datasets like SURREAL and FAUST. We validate and evaluate the impact of our novel components on these datasets, showing a quantitative improvement over state-of-the-art DNN-based methods, and qualitatively better results.

1 Introduction

Template-based human shape matching is a problem of broad interest in computer vision, for a variety of applications relevant to Augmented and Virtual Reality, surveillance and 3D media content production. It is relevant to various tasks such as dense shape alignment or tracking, shape estimation and completion from sparse or corrupt shape data.

B. Zhou–MSR-INRIA Joint Center.

Electronic supplementary material The online version of this chapter (https://doi.org/10.1007/978-3-030-69525-5_8) contains supplementary material, which is available to authorized users.

© Springer Nature Switzerland AG 2021
H. Ishikawa et al. (Eds.): ACCV 2020, LNCS 12622, pp. 123–139, 2021.
https://doi.org/10.1007/978-3-030-69525-5_8

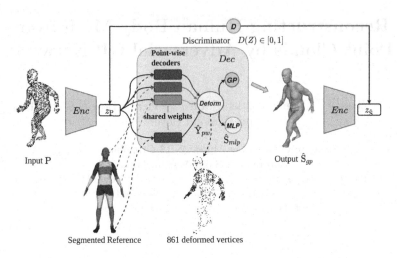

Fig. 1. Overview of our adversarial GP network.

This problem has been addressed with several classic approaches that either directly find dense correspondence using intrinsic surface embeddings [1–3] or use human body templates as geometric proxy to guide the matching [4–8]. Both approaches usually involve some form of non-convex optimization that is susceptible to ambiguities and local minima, and hand-crafted features to estimate the correspondence.

Aiming for noise and initialization resilience and improvement in feature description has motivated an avenue of research in learning-based correspondence approaches to the human shape matching problem. These methods have the property to automate feature extraction and matching by mining large datasets, and can estimate correspondences by building automatic feature classifiers with e.g. random forests [9], or simultaneously learn feature extraction and correspondence using DNNs [10–14].

Many of these learning approaches rely on some form of human a priori knowledge. Most methods propose matching to an explicit shape deformation model, for which a reduced parameterization is predicted [15–17] or whose mapping to the data is learned [18,19] from observations.

Among the most successful approaches of inspiration to this work are those matching human shapes using an implicit deformation model which is entirely learned with no manually set components, as applied to humans [20] or generic objects [21]. By encoding matching to an underlying template as the expression of a learned global feature in a latent space automatically discovered by an auto-encoder, the model can be entirely automated and trained end-to-end for generic matching of two shapes, as opposed to the previously described methods. As they use point-based DNN architectures [22], these approaches can be applied to point cloud inputs without any surface consistency. All these properties afford greater robustness and generalization abilities, and allow this family of methods to outperform the latter on standard benchmarks. However in this process a weaker human shape and consistent surface prior is encoded than previous approaches, which leads to noisy, and sometimes non-realistic predicted human shapes, as confirmed by an analysis of the failure cases of these approaches. Some of the failures are mitigated using a post-processing step which consists in optimizing the shape matching features inferred by the DNN in the latent space, which improves the final result.

In this work, we explore within this family of approaches how local and global shape priors, commonly not encoded with point-wise architecture, can be reintroduced while maintaining the benefits of such an architecture (e.g. PointNet [22]). We base our approach on a point-based auto-encoder similar to [20], but with several key differences. To alleviate inference noise, we introduce a Gaussian Process decoder layer which inherently encodes surface smoothness and surface point coherence on the shape with lower point dimensionality on the surface, only to the price of a small pretraining phase. Second, more global consistency is built in the model by adding fully connected layers at the end of the decoder, which is made possible by the surface dimensionality reduction previously discussed. Third, to avoid inferring drastically non human shapes, we introduce an adversarial training phase inspired by [23] which enforces consistency of human shape encodings in our latent space and helps to avoid overfitting. With these improved network characteristics and training procedures, we show that our approach provides results that are on par or better than state-of-the-art on the FAUST intra and inter challenges and illustrate the quality gain of our approach through an exhaustive ablation study illustrating the benefits of these three contributions.

2   Related Work

There exists a rich literature on registration and reconstruction of 3D data (see [24, 25] for a survey). Here, we focus our analysis on methods for registering human body shapes, following the classic distinction between template-free and template-based methods. We then briefly discuss how Gaussian Processes have been combined with DNNs in previous work, and the use of adversarial training in the context of 3D vision.

Template-Free Methods. Correspondences between non-rigid objects can be established by defining an intrinsic surface representation, which is invariant to bending. In the embedding space defined by this representation, the registration problem boils down to a non-convex optimization one. Examples of intrinsic representations are Generalized Multi-Dimensional Scaling (GMDS) [1], heat kernel maps [2], Möbius transformations [3]. Recent work tries to learn such representations, and therefore object-to-object correspondences, from data. While early approaches rely on random forests [9], subsequent ones employ DNNs [10,11]. For example, Deep Functional Maps [12,13] combine a deep architecture with point-wise descriptors [14] to obtain dense correspondences between pairs of shapes. These methods aim at matching arbitrary shapes. However, when focusing on particular instances like the human body, one can introduce more powerful class-specific shape priors.

Template-Based Methods. When registering noisy and incomplete 3D human body data, one commonly relies on a predefined 3D body template acting as a strong shape prior. At registration time, the template surface is deformed in order to match the data. Many approaches rely on a statistical body model [4,5] and define an objective function which is minimized via non-linear least squares [6–8]. However, these objective functions use hand-crafted error terms and are not as powerful as data-driven approaches. Recently, the wider availability of huge datasets of 3D body shapes [7,26] fostered the development of DNN-based methods. Mesh Variational Autoencoders [15] learn a latent space for 3D human body representation, but their input is limited to fixed-topology shapes. LBS-AE [16] proposes a self-supervised approach for fitting 3D models to point cloud. The method relies on DNNs to learn a set of Linear Blending Skinning [27] parameters. FARM [18] establishes correspondences between shapes by automatically extracting a set of landmarks and then using functional maps. Deep Hierarchical Networks [17] learn a 3D human body embedding which can then be fitted to data, leveraging a set of manually selected landmarks. Basis Point Sets [19] propose an efficient point cloud encoding, which can then be combined with DNNs [28] for shape registration and completion tasks.

GP and DNNs. Gaussian Processes (GP) are popular in statistical learning for their generalization capabilities. In 3D vision, Lüthi *et al.* [29] propose GPMMs, a morphable model based on GP, with applications to face modeling and medical image analysis. Recently, some studies [30,31] try to interpret how DNNs can simulate the learning process of GP. For example, Deep GP [32] focuses on probabilistic modeling of GP with DNNs, training the network via marginal likelihood. In this work, we leverage the interpolation and smoothness capabilities of GP in the context of 3D surface reconstruction.

Adversarial Training. After the introduction of Generative Adversarial Networks (GANs) [33], adversarial training has been widely used in computer vision. In 3D vision, HMR [34] applies adversarial learning to estimate 3D human body shape and pose from 2D images. CAPE [35] uses it to learn a model of people in clothing. Fernández Abrevaya *et al.* [36] and Shamai *et al.* [37] use adversarial training to model faces in 3D. Hu *et al.* [23] compare adversarial and L2-norm regularization for the task of image registration. To the best of our knowledge, our work is the first to propose adversarial training as a regularization term in the context of 3D registration.

In general, our work builds on 3D-CODED [20], which uses a PointNet-like [22] architecture to extract permutation-invariant point features. However it applies the point-wise decoders which are independent of each other. Thus we propose to strengthen the relationship of nearby points by using our GP layer and MLP layers. AtlasNet2 [38] aims at improving upon 3D-CODED reconstructions by using a learnable template. However AtlasNet2 results exhibit artifacts similar to the ones of 3D-CODED in some challenging cases. In order to make the network predictions more robust, we propose to use adversarial training.

3   Method

Our approach takes as input an unordered set of n 3D points $P \in \mathbb{R}^{n \times 3}$ and maps this set into a deformed instance $S \in \mathbb{R}^{res \times 3}$ of a reference mesh with a fixed resolution res. The number n of input points can vary. This to allow for partial or incomplete shape description as typical with laser scan or depth data. In order to learn such a mapping we use a point-wise encoder-decoder architecture trained on standard human body datasets. This architecture presents two innovations to better enforce shape consistency: first a regularization layer that builds on Gaussian Process (GP) and second a global adversarial loss. The sections below detail the different components of our framework.

3.1   Network Architecture

As shown in Fig. 1, our architecture encodes points P into a latent shape representation $\mathcal{Z}_p \in \mathbb{R}^{1024}$ which is then decoded into a deformation vector field Y defined over a mesh template to produce the shape S. Our objective is to balance global and local information with shape-wise and point-wise considerations. To this end, a PointNet [22] like encoder is used as a backbone to extract the 1024-dimension latent shape feature $\mathcal{Z}_p$. On the decoder side, we first expect this global shape feature $\mathcal{Z}_p$ to predict the deformation of a subset of representative points on the reference mesh in a point-wise manner. More global considerations are then applied on this subset of points with both Gaussian Process interpolation and fully connected layers. Furthermore, to better constrain the latent representation during training, the output vertices of the predicted deformed reference mesh S are fed into the encoder to verify whether they yield a latent feature $\mathcal{Z}_s$ close to the latent feature $\mathcal{Z}_p$ of the ground truth shape vertices.

Encoder. We extract the global feature $\mathcal{Z}_p$ with a simplified version of Point-Net [22]. The input points P are first processed by 3 hidden layers of size 64, 128 and 1024, respectively, followed by a max-pooling operator applied to the resulting point-wise features. Then, two linear layers of size 1024 lead to the latent space $\mathcal{Z}_{\mathcal{P}}$. All layers use batch normalization and $ReLU$ (rectified linear unit) activation.

Decoder. The decoder takes as input the shape feature $\mathcal{Z}_p$ extracted by the encoder together with l 3D locations x_i of vertices distributed on the reference mesh. Point-wise decoders with shared weights are first used on the combinations $(x_i, \mathcal{Z}_p)$. These decoders are composed of 3 hidden layers going from size 1027 to 513 and 256. The resulting features are projected into l individual vertex deformations y_i using 2 times hyperbolic tangent activation functions. Following point-wise decoders, two computation flows are applied in parallel on the resulting predicted vertex deformations y_i. One goes to GP layers that enforce local spatial consistency between vertices and the other goes to a fully-connected MLP layer that enforces a global constraint over vertices. We take the output of the GP flow as the final deformed instance.

3.2   Local and Global Spatial Consistency

Gaussian Process Interpolation. As mentioned before the decoder part includes a vertex interpolation technique based on Gaussian Process [39]. To this aim, we assume here that deformations y_i of the reference mesh at vertex locations x_i are, up to a bias $\varepsilon \sim \mathcal{N}(0, \sigma)$, non linear functions $y_i = f(x_i) + \varepsilon$, which distributions are jointly Gaussian, with mean and covariance defined by the kernel k:

$$k(x_i, x_j) = \gamma \exp(-\frac{\|x_i - x_j\|^2}{r}). \tag{1}$$

Under these assumptions, the joint distribution of l partial vertex observations Y and an unobserved vertex y_* over the deformed reference mesh can be expressed as:

$$\begin{bmatrix} Y \\ y_* \end{bmatrix} \sim \mathcal{N} \left(0, \begin{bmatrix} K(X,X) + \sigma^2 I, & K_*^T(x_*, X) \\ K_*(x_*, X), & k(x_*, x_*), \end{bmatrix} \right) \tag{2}$$

where $K(,)$ denotes the covariances over the associated vertices x_i on the reference mesh:

$$K(X,X) = \begin{bmatrix} k(x_1, x_1) & \dots & k(x_1, x_l) \\ \vdots & \ddots & \vdots \\ k(x_l, x_1) & \dots & k(x_l, x_l) \end{bmatrix}, \quad K_*(x_*, X) = \begin{bmatrix} k(x_*, x_1) & \dots & k(x_*, x_l) \end{bmatrix}. \tag{3}$$

The posterior probability $P(y_*|Y)$ can be inferred as a Gaussian distribution $\mathcal{N}(m(y_*), var(y_*))$ with:

$$m(y_*) = K_*(K + \sigma^2 I)^{-1} Y \tag{4}$$

$$var(y_*) = k_* - K_*(K + \sigma^2 I)^{-1} K_*^T \tag{5}$$

where, to simplify our notation, $K_* = K(x_*, X)$, $K = K(X, X)$ and $k_* = k(x_*, x_*)$. Taking the mean of this distribution as the predicted value we finally get:

$$y_* = K_*(K + \sigma^2 I)^{-1} Y. \tag{6}$$

In practice, to accelerate the GP computation and improve the reconstruction precision, we apply the above statistical reasoning individually over body parts instead of the full body. We follow for that purpose [40] and segment the body topology into 19 small patches, including two patches on the elbow (see Fig. 1). In addition, we do not consider absolute vertex locations as y_i but relative displacements with respect to the reference mesh instead. Note that we have finally 3 parameters: γ, r and σ for each body part. Thus we can use cross validation, more particularly in our case, *kernel selection*, to tune the GP parameters before the time-consuming gradient descent optimization during the neural network training.

In addition, the selected subset of l observation vertices impacts the final reconstruction of the full mesh. In order to select the most informative vertices for that purpose, we pre-tune 19 kernels and select the observation vertices using 10 random meshes from the FAUST training dataset. We start at 10% resolution of the template, i.e. 689 vertices, and progressively add vertices to minimize the reconstruction error, finding an optimal value of 861 vertices.

Our network predicts therefore the deformations of this subset of $l = 861$ vertices, which are then completed by our GP layer. The GP layer consists of 19 body part components that exploit Eq. (6) with pre-computed kernel matrices. As explained before, the vertex of template is deformed by a point-wise decoder. While this is similar in spirit to [20] and [38], our approach differs in 2 aspects: (i) Instead of considering random points over the mesh surface during training, our approach focuses on a fixed subset of points – this allows us to better exploit the local spatial consistency of the reference mesh deformations; (ii) Instead of directly predicting the deformed template vertices, our point-wise decoder predicts the deformations (residuals) with respect to the template. The rationale here is that the residual space is generally easier to learn than the original coordinate space. In Fig. 1, we show the segmented reference mesh and the 861 selected vertices deformed by the prediction of the point-wise decoder. Since the prediction is in the same order as the reference mesh, we can directly map the body part segmentation on the prediction of point-wise decoder.

Fully Connected Layer. The previous GP layer enforces local spatial constraints between mesh vertices by assuming joint Gaussian distributions that can be pre-learned from a few meshes. In order to complete this with more global considerations over the vertices of a shape, we also employ a fully-connected multi-layer perceptron as another interpolation flow. This MLP takes as input the $l = 861$ deformed vertices as predicted by the point-wise decoder. It is composed of a hidden layer of dimension 2048, followed by 2 times hyperbolic tangent activation functions, and one linear layer to interpolate to the resolution of the reference mesh, in practice 6890 vertices with the SURREAL synthetic data.

3.3   Training Loss

In order to train our network we define a loss function $\mathcal{L}_r$ that accounts for the 3 outputs yielded by the decoder. The point-wise decoder computes the deformation field y_i over the subset of l mesh vertices on the reference mesh, while the GP and MLP layers output the deformed instances in the same resolution as the reference mesh. Hence:

$$\mathcal{L}_r(\hat{Y}_{pw}, Y_l, \hat{S}_{gp}, \hat{S}_{mlp}, S) = L(\hat{Y}_{pw}, Y_l) + L(\hat{S}_{gp}, S) + L(\hat{S}_{mlp}, S) \qquad (7)$$

where $L(\cdot, \cdot)$ denotes the standard mean-square error, $\hat{Y}_{pw}$, $\hat{S}_{gp}$, $\hat{S}_{mlp}$ are the point-wise decoder, GP and MLP layer predictions respectively, Y_l is the ground truth deformation field over the reference mesh reduced to the l vertices predicted by the point-wise decoder and S is the ground truth deformed instance. In practice, we remark that the mesh obtained with the MLP layer is often blurry. However, the associated global constraint in the reconstruction loss appears to be beneficial in our experiments.

Adversarial Loss. In addition to the loss presented in the previous section, we investigate in this work the contribution of introducing an adversarial strategy [33] in the proposed framework. While the previous loss function enforces local and more global spatial consistency, it does not encode knowledge on what a regular shape should be. Hence artifacts can occur when considering data outside the training set, as in Fig. 4 with test data. In order to better detect abnormal outputs, we therefore propose an additional adversarial loss.

Recall that, given an arbitrary input point cloud P, the encoder generates a latent feature $\mathcal{Z}_p$. From this latent feature, the decoder generates a deformed version, $\hat{S}$, of the reference mesh. In principle, feeding the encoder with this set $\hat{S}$ should yield a latent feature $\mathcal{Z}_{\hat{s}(p)}$ statistically similar to $\mathcal{Z}_p$. We therefore express the adversarial loss as:

$$\mathcal{L}_a(P, \hat{S}) = \mathbb{E}_p[log(D(\mathcal{Z}_p)] + \mathbb{E}_{\hat{s}(p)}[log(1 - D(\mathcal{Z}_{\hat{s}})] \tag{8}$$

where $D(\cdot)$ is the discriminator trained to detect abnormal latent features. It projects the 1024-dimension point feature into 512 and then 256 dimensions with two hidden layers, and outputs a probability. The two hidden layers are activated by an *ELU* (Exponential Linear Unit) function followed by batch normalization; the output is activated by a *sigmoid* non linearity. The final loss for our network training is a combination of $\mathcal{L}_r$ and $\mathcal{L}_a$:

$$\mathcal{L}_t = \lambda_1 \mathcal{L}_r + \lambda_2 \mathcal{L}_a. \tag{9}$$

The training algorithm proceeds by iteratively updating the encoder-decoder and the discriminator as depicted below. The protocol followed in practice is detailed in Sect. 4.

Algorithm 1: Training Algorithm

Input: Ground truth deformed instances S of the reference mesh
Initialization;
for *Training iterations* **do**

> 1. Sample a mini-batch of point cloud $P \in S$;
> 2. Compute the reconstruction $\hat{S}(P)$;
> 3. Update $D(\cdot)$ by taking a learning step on loss $\mathcal{L}_a(P \sim real, \hat{S} \sim fake)$ (8);
> 4. Update then encoder and decoder by taking a learning step on loss $\mathcal{L}_t(\hat{S} \sim real)$ (9);

end

---

4   Experimental Results

In this section, we first describe the datasets and the corresponding evaluation protocols. We then compare our approach against the state-of-the-art methods and provide a detailed analysis of our framework.

4.1   Datasets

We evaluate our framework for reconstructing human body meshes from point cloud data on the standard SURREAL [26] and FAUST [6] datasets.

The SURREAL dataset is a large-scale synthetic dataset that consists of textured human body shapes in different 3D poses. We follow the protocol introduced in [20] to generate our training data that consists of 230,000 meshes.

The FAUST dataset provides 100 training and 200 testing human body scans of approximately 170000 vertices. They may include noise and holes, typically missing parts on the feet. The FAUST benchmark defines two challenges: the one on intra-, the other on inter-subject correspondences. We use the FAUST dataset only for testing purposes and do not use the provided scans for training.

4.2   Evaluation Protocol

We use the symmetric Chamfer distance between the predicted and ground-truth human shape to evaluate our framework on the SURREAL validation dataset. For our experiments on the FAUST dataset, we use the official test server to measure our accuracy. Throughout our experiments, we use the same training/test splits as 3D-CODED [20]. We perform a line-search to find the initial orientation and the initial translation that gives the smallest Chamfer distance during testing FAUST.

4.3   Implementation Details

We implement our Adversarial GP network in PyTorch and train for 25 epochs from scratch. In practice, we set $\lambda_1 = 10$ and $\lambda_2 = 0.05$. We use the Adam optimizer with a learning rate of 0.001 for the Discriminator and 0.0005 for Encoder and Decoder. We set the batch size to 32. We follow 3D-CODED [20] to add random translation between -3 cm and 3 cm to increase the robustness during training.

4.4   Comparison with Baselines

We report reconstruction and registration accuracy on the SURREAL [26] and FAUST [6] datasets and compare our results to the state-of-the-art results of [20] and [38] in Table 1.

We further use the following baselines and versions of our approach in the evaluation:

- *MLP*: A multi-layer perceptron with 2 layers as described in Section 3.2 operating on the output deformations of the point-wise decoder.
- *GP*: Gaussian Process layer as described in Sect. 3.2 operating on the output deformations of the point-wise decoder.
- *Adversarial GP*: Adversarial network coupled with the Gaussian process and MLP layers that operates on the output deformations of the point-wise decoder (see Sect. 3.3).

Table 1. Results on the SURREAL validation set for human body reconstruction and on the FAUST-inter correspondence challenge. As in [20,38], we report the symmetric Chamfer distance ($\times 10^{-3}$) for SURREAL validation. For FAUST, we report the Euclidean correspondence error in (cm). In FAUST, we apply the same refinement technique as in 3D-CODED to our MLP, GP and Adversarial GP.

Method	SURREAL-chamfer	FAUST-inter
3D-CODED [20]	1.33	2.88
AtlasNet2-Deformation [38] 3D	1.17	2.76
AtlasNet2-Points 3D	1.11	3.05
AtlasNet2-Deformation 10D	1.01	2.77
AtlasNet2-Points 10D	1.01	2.85
Ours (MLP)	0.54	2.94
Ours (GP)	**0.35**	**2.73**
Ours (Adversarial GP)	0.50	2.76

We further compare our results to [20,38] qualitatively to demonstrate the effectiveness of our method in Fig. 3 and Fig. 4.

Reconstruction. We report our surface reconstruction results in comparison to [20,38] on the SURREAL and FAUST datasets in Table 1. While providing accurate reconstructions, [20] relies on point-to-point distance minimization, therefore lacking global context. To remedy this and encode global context, we apply an MLP on point-wise predictions. This would help encode global context, but in return, would ignore local dependencies. Our GP layer, on the other hand, aims at finding a local context on each body part. As can be seen in Table 1, the GP layer yields the most accurate reconstruction results on the SURREAL validation set and in the FAUST Inter-Subject challenge. In Fig. 3, we also show qualitative results on SURREAL validation of the variants of our approach (MLP, GP, Adversarial GP) in comparison to 3D-CODED [20] and AtlasNet2 [38]. Our method yields better reconstruction accuracy than [20] and [38] and provides realistic surface reconstructions.

Table 2. Results for the FAUST intra- and inter-subject challenges for human body registration.

Method	Intra (cm)	Inter (cm)
3D-CODED [20]	1.985	2.878
Stitched puppets [8]	1.568	3.126
LBS-AE [16]	2.161	4.08
FARM [18]	2.810	4.123
BPS [19]	2.327	4.529
FMNet [13]	2.436	4.826
Convex-Opt [41]	4.860	8.304
Our GP	2.349	2.734
Our Adversarial GP	1.904	2.759

Registration. Our output mesh is reconstructed from an input point cloud and is aligned with a template shape. Therefore, our method could further compute registration to the human body by finding the closest point on the reconstruction. We evaluate our method on the FAUST [6] challenge, that includes 100-pairs of shapes to be matched. In FAUST, the input is real scan data in different orientations and translations and scans typically include noise and holes. In Table 2, we report the results of all published studies to date on the FAUST challenge. We do not include the results of DHNN as it requires manual selection of additional landmark points which is used to guide the optimization.

Importance of Adversarial Training. Although our GP network provides accurate reconstruction and registration results, we have observed in practice that it sometimes results in artifacts, as can be seen in a few cases in Fig. 4. Our adversarial GP, on the other hand, is able to correct these artifacts and results in physically plausible human shape reconstructions, as demonstrated in Fig. 4. This is in part due to the fact that adversarial training prevents overfitting to the SURREAL training data and achieves good generalization across datasets.

Table 3. Numeric comparisons. We report the symmetric Chamfer distance ($\times 10^{-3}$) on the SURREAL validation dataset and Euclidean correspondence error (cm) in FAUST -intra/-inter challenges for the variants of our model. We further compare adversarial training to L2 weight decay (regularization term $\lambda = 5 \times 10^{-4}$) and dropout. See more qualitative results in the supplementary material.

Method	SURREAL-chamfer	FAUST-intra	FAUST-inter
Adv+GP (w.o. MLP)	0.52	2.585	2.913
MLP+GP (w.o. Adv)	**0.37**	2.042	2.858
MLP+GP+L2 weight decay	5.40	6.068	7.58
MLP+GP+Dropout	0.38	2.236	2.984
Adv+MLP+GP (Adv GP)	0.50	**1.904**	**2.759**

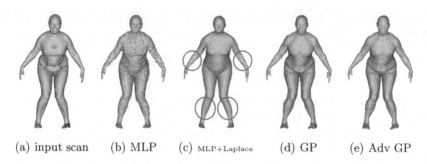

(a) input scan   (b) MLP   (c) MLP+Laplace   (d) GP   (e) Adv GP

Fig. 2. Smoothness of GP. From left to right, (a) input scan, reconstruction in standard resolution of (b) MLP, (c) MLP smoothened by the Laplacian operator, (d) GP, and (e) Adversarial GP.

We have observed that using the MLP network along with the GP layer further regularizes the training of our Adversarial GP framework. Therefore, in practice, we also employ an MLP during training of our Adversarial GP.

In Table 3, we further analyze the influence of adversarial loss on the reconstruction and registration. Using an adversarial loss yields more accurate results on the FAUST dataset. While resulting in lower accuracy on the SURREAL dataset, adversarial training helps to prevent overfitting by ensuring that the distributions of the input data and reconstruction are similar. In Fig. 4, we demonstrate that adversarial training in practice results in physically more plausible and realistic shapes. To demonstrate the effectiveness of adversarial training as a regularization mechanism, we further compare it to standard regularization techniques of L2-weight decay and dropout in Table 3.

Influence of Gaussian Kernel Regularization. In Fig. 2, we present qualitative reconstruction results obtained with different decoders to further support our quantitative analysis in Table 1. While the MLP decoder results in a blurry shape, Laplacian denoising results in a shrinkage in the volume, especially in the limbs. GP and Adversarial GP, on the other hand, provide high-fidelity reconstructions.

Table 4. Comparison to 3D-CODED [20] and AtlasNet2 [38] with and without refinement. We report Euclidean correspondence errors on the FAUST-inter challenge in (cm). The refinement is based on optimizing the global feature to minimize the symmetric Chamfer distance. We follow [20] to register the scan to a high-resolution template.

Method	3D-CODED	AtlasNet2	GP	Adversarial GP
Without refinement	6.29	4.72	**4.71**	4.964
With refinement	3.048	–	**2.734**	2.873
With refinement+ high-res template	2.878	2.76	2.815	**2.759**

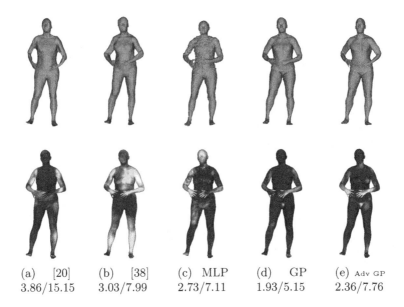

(a) [20]   (b) [38]   (c) MLP   (d) GP   (e) Adv GP
3.86/15.15   3.03/7.99   2.73/7.11   1.93/5.15   2.36/7.76

Fig. 3. Qualitative evaluation for human shape reconstruction. From left to right, reconstruction in standard resolution of (a) 3D-CODED [20], (b) AtlasNet2 [38], (c) Our MLP, (d) our GP and (e) our Adversarial GP. And we report the heatmaps and mean/max Euclidean reconstruction error in (cm) for this instance.

Refinement. During evaluation, we follow the same refinement strategy of 3D-CODED [20], that minimizes the Chamfer distance between reconstructions and inputs. Consequently, a nearest neighbor search is performed to find correspondences and match shapes. To highlight the benefit of refinement, we show in Table 4 our results in comparison to [20] and [38] with and without refinement. Refinement results in better accuracy for our method, as expected, and our approach provides better results in comparison to [20] and [38] in all cases. When we use a high resolution template for the nearest neighbor step, we gain an additional accuracy improvement for Adversarial GP, but not for GP. The result could not be always improved by using a high resolution template due to the fact that the FAUST-inter challenge computes the Euclidean distance between the prediction and sparse landmarks. Since the Euclidean distance is more tolerant of the artifacts in Fig. 4 than geodesic distance, Adversarial GP can not make great improvement in FAUST challenge.

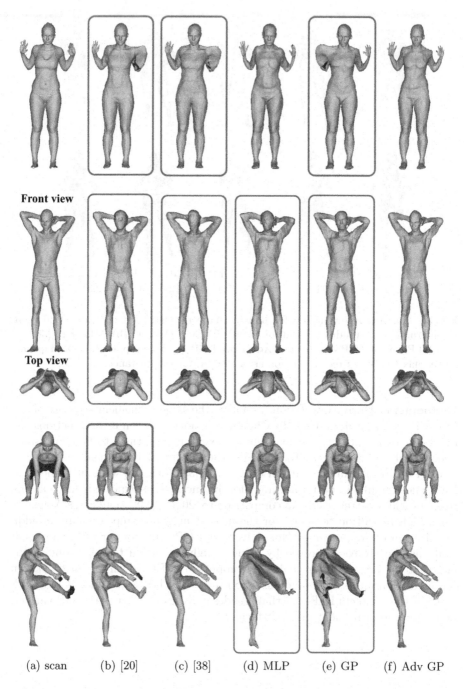

Fig. 4. Challenging cases in FAUST. From left to right, (a) input scan, reconstruction in high resolution of (b) 3D-CODED [20], (c) AtlasNet2 [38], (d) Our MLP, (e) our GP and (f) our Adversarial GP. We highlight the failure cases with red box. (Color figure online)

5   Conclusion

We have presented an encoder-decoder neural network architecture to reconstruct human body meshes from point cloud data, by learning dense human body
correspondences. Our architecture enforces surface consistency with a specialized
Gaussian process layer. Our adversarial training framework allows for generalization across datasets and reconstructs high-fidelity human meshes. Future work
will apply the proposed framework to problems like motion sequence alignment
and tracking.

References

1. Bronstein, A.M., Bronstein, M.M., Kimmel, R.: Generalized multidimensional scaling: a framework for isometry-invariant partial surface matching. Proc. Nat. Acad.
   Sci. **103**, 1168–1172 (2006)
2. Ovsjanikov, M., Mérigot, Q., Mémoli, F., Guibas, L.: One point isometric matching
   with the heat kernel. Comput. Graph. Forum **29**, 1555–1564 (2010)
3. Kim, V., Lipman, Y., Funkhouser, T.: Blended intrinsic maps. ACM Trans. Graph.
   (TOG) **30**, 1–12 (2011)
4. Anguelov, D., Srinivasan, P., Koller, D., Thrun, S., Rodgers, J., Davis, J.: SCAPE:
   shape completion and animation of people. ACM Trans. Graph. (TOG) **24**, 408–
   416 (2005)
5. Loper, M., Mahmood, N., Romero, J., Pons-Moll, G., Black, M.J.: SMPL: a skinned
   multi-person linear model. ACM Trans. Graph. (TOG) **34**, 248:1–248:16 (2015)
6. Bogo, F., Romero, J., Loper, M., Black, M.J.: FAUST: dataset and evaluation for
   3D mesh registration. In: Proceedings of the IEEE Conference on Computer Vision
   and Pattern Recognition, pp. 3794–3801 (2014)
7. Bogo, F., Romero, J., Pons-Moll, G., Black, M.J.: Dynamic FAUST: registering
   human bodies in motion. In: Proceedings of the IEEE Conference on Computer
   Vision and Pattern Recognition, pp. 6233–6242 (2017)
8. Zuffi, S., Black, M.J.: The stitched puppet: a graphical model of 3D human shape
   and pose. In: Proceedings of the IEEE Conference on Computer Vision and Pattern
   Recognition, pp. 3537–3546 (2015)
9. Rodolà, E., Bulò, S., Windheuser, T., Vestner, M., Cremers, D.: Dense non-rigid
   shape correspondence using random forests. In: Proceedings of the IEEE Conference on Computer Vision and Pattern Recognition, pp. 4177–4184 (2014)
10. Monti, F., Boscaini, D., Masci, J., Rodola, E., Svoboda, J., Bronstein, M.M.: Geo-
    metric deep learning on graphs and manifolds using mixture model CNNs. In:
    Proceedings of the IEEE Conference on Computer Vision and Pattern Recogni-
    tion, pp. 5115–5124 (2017)
11. Wei, L., Huang, Q., Ceylan, D., Vouga, E., Li, H.: Dense human body correspon-
    dences using convolutional networks. In: Proceedings of the IEEE Conference on
    Computer Vision and Pattern Recognition, pp. 1544–1553 (2016)
12. Halimi, O., Litany, O., Rodola, E., Bronstein, A.M., Kimmel, R.: Unsupervised
    learning of dense shape correspondence. In: Proceedings of the IEEE Conference
    on Computer Vision and Pattern Recognition, pp. 4370–4379 (2019)
13. Litany, O., Remez, T., Rodola, E., Bronstein, A., Bronstein, M.: Deep functional
    maps: structured prediction for dense shape correspondence. In: Proceedings of the
    IEEE International Conference on Computer Vision, pp. 5659–5667 (2017)

14. Tombari, Federico., Salti, Samuele, Di Stefano, Luigi: Unique signatures of histograms for local surface description. In: Daniilidis, Kostas, Maragos, Petros, Paragios, Nikos (eds.) ECCV 2010. LNCS, vol. 6313, pp. 356–369. Springer, Heidelberg (2010). https://doi.org/10.1007/978-3-642-15558-1_26

15. Tan, Q., Gao, L., Lai, Y.K., Xia, S.: Variational autoencoders for deforming 3D mesh models. In: Proceedings of the IEEE Conference on Computer Vision and Pattern Recognition, pp. 5841–5850 (2018)

16. Li, C.L., Simon, T., Saragih, J., Póczos, B., Sheikh, Y.: LBS autoencoder: self-supervised fitting of articulated meshes to point clouds. In: Proceedings of the IEEE Conference on Computer Vision and Pattern Recognition, pp. 11967–11976 (2019)

17. Jiang, B., Zhang, J., Cai, J., Zheng, J.: Disentangled human body embedding based on deep hierarchical neural network. IEEE Trans. Vis. Comput. Graph. **26**, 2560–2575 (2020)

18. Marin, R., Melzi, S., Rodolà, E., Castellani, U.: FARM: functional automatic registration method for 3D human bodies. In: Computer Graphics Forum, vol. 39, pp. 160–173. Wiley Online Library (2020)

19. Prokudin, S., Lassner, C., Romero, J.: Efficient learning on point clouds with basis point sets. In: Proceedings of the IEEE International Conference on Computer Vision, pp. 4332–4341 (2019)

20. Groueix, T., Fisher, M., Kim, V.G., Russell, B., Aubry, M.: 3D-coded : 3D correspondences by deep deformation. In: Proceedings of the European Conference on Computer Vision, pp. 235–251 (2018)

21. Groueix, T., Fisher, M., Kim, V.G., Russell, B., Aubry, M.: AtlasNet: a Papier-Mâché approach to learning 3D surface generation. In: Proceedings of the IEEE Conference on Computer Vision and Pattern Recognition, pp. 216–224 (2018)

22. Qi, C.R., Su, H., Mo, K., Guibas, L.J.: PointNet: deep learning on point sets for 3D classification and segmentation. In: Proceedings of the IEEE Conference on Computer Vision and Pattern Recognition, pp. 652–660 (2017)

23. Hu, Y., et al.: Adversarial deformation regularization for training image registration neural networks. In: Frangi, Alejandro F., Schnabel, Julia A., Davatzikos, Christos, Alberola-López, Carlos, Fichtinger, Gabor (eds.) MICCAI 2018. LNCS, vol. 11070, pp. 774–782. Springer, Cham (2018). https://doi.org/10.1007/978-3-030-00928-1_87

24. Biasotti, S., Cerri, A., Bronstein, A., Bronstein, M.: Recent trends, applications, and perspectives in 3D shape similarity assessment. Comput. Graph. Forum **36**, 87–119 (2016)

25. van Kaick, O., Hamarneh, G., Cohen-Or, D.: A survey on shape correspondence. Comput. Graph. Forum **30**, 1681–1707 (2011)

26. Varol, G., et al.: Learning from synthetic humans. In: Proceedings of the IEEE Conference on Computer Vision and Pattern Recognition, pp. 4627–4635 (2017)

27. Magnenat-Thalmann, N., Laperrire, R., Thalmann, D.: Joint-dependent local deformations for hand animation and object grasping. In: Proceedings of Graphics Interface, vol. 88.,Citeseer (1988)

28. Huang, G., Liu, Z., Van Der Maaten, L., Weinberger, K.Q.: Densely connected convolutional networks. In: Proceedings of the IEEE Conference on Computer Vision and Pattern Recognition, pp. 4700–4708 (2017)

29. Lüthi, M., Gerig, T., Jud, C., Vetter, T.: Gaussian process morphable models. IEEE Trans. Pattern Anal. Mach. Intell. **40**, 1860–1873 (2017)

30. Wilson, A.G., Knowles, D.A., Ghahramani, Z.: Gaussian process regression networks. In: Proceedings of the International Conference on Machine Learning. (2011)
31. Wilson, A.G., Hu, Z., Salakhutdinov, R., Xing, E.P.: Deep kernel learning. In: Artificial Intelligence and Statistics, pp. 370–378 (2016)
32. Damianou, A., Lawrence, N.: Deep gaussian processes. In: Artificial Intelligence and Statistics, pp. 207–215 (2013)
33. Goodfellow, I., et al.: Generative adversarial nets. In: Advances in Neural Information Processing Systems, pp. 2672–2680 (2014)
34. Kanazawa, A., Black, M.J., Jacobs, D.W., Malik, J.: End-to-end recovery of human shape and pose. In: Proceedings of the IEEE Conference on Computer Vision and Pattern Recognition, pp. 7122–7131 (2018)
35. Ma, Q., et al.: Learning to dress 3D people in generative clothing. In: Proceedings of the IEEE Conference on Computer Vision and Pattern Recognition, pp. 7122–7131 (2020)
36. Fernández Abrevaya, V., Boukhayma, A., Wuhrer, S., Boyer, E.: A decoupled 3D facial shape model by adversarial training. In: Proceedings of the IEEE International Conference on Computer Vision, pp. 1–10 (2019)
37. Shamai, G., Slossberg, R., Kimmel, R.: Synthesizing facial photometries and corresponding geometries using generative adversarial networks. ACM Trans. Multimed. Comput. Commun. Appl. **15**, 1–24 (2019)
38. Deprelle, T., Groueix, T., Fisher, M., Kim, V., Russell, B., Aubry, M.: Learning elementary structures for 3D shape generation and matching. In: Advances in Neural Information Processing Systems, pp. 7435–7445 (2019)
39. Williams, C.K., Rasmussen, C.E.: Gaussian Processes for Machine Learning. MIT Press, Cambridge (2006)
40. Basset, J., Wuhrer, S., Boyer, E., Multon, F.: Contact preserving shape transfer for rigging-free motion retargeting. In: MIG 2019 - ACM SIGGRAPH Conference Motion Interaction and Games, pp. 1–10 (2019)
41. Chen, Q., Koltun, V.: Robust nonrigid registration by convex optimization. In: Proceedings of the IEEE International Conference on Computer Vision, pp. 2039–2047 (2015)

SDP-Net: Scene Flow Based Real-Time Object Detection and Prediction from Sequential 3D Point Clouds

Yi Zhang[1], Yuwen Ye[1], Zhiyu Xiang[2]([⊠]), and Jiaqi Gu[1]

[1] College of Information and Electronic Engineering, Zhejiang University,
Hangzhou, China
[2] Zhejiang Provincial Key Laboratory of Information Processing, Communication
and Networking, Zhejiang University, Hangzhou, China
xiangzy@zju.edu.cn

Abstract. Robust object detection in 3D point clouds faces the challenges caused by sparse range data. Accumulating multi-frame data could densify the 3D point clouds and greatly benefit detection task. However, accurately aligning the point clouds before the detecting process is a difficult task since there may exist moving objects in the scene. In this paper a novel scene flow based multi-frame network named SDP-Net is proposed. It is able to perform multiple tasks such as self-alignment, 3D object detection, prediction and tracking simultaneously. Thanks to the design of scene flow and the scheme of multi-task, our network is capable of working effectively with a simple network backbone. We further improve the annotations on KITTI RAW dataset by supplementing the ground truth. Experimental results show that our approach greatly outperforms the state-of-the-art and can perform multiple tasks in real-time.

1 Introduction

Object detection is a fundamental task for the safety of autonomous driving [1]. Robust object detection in 3D point clouds faces the challenges caused by sparse range points. Accumulating multiple frame data could densify the point clouds and greatly benefit the detection task. YOLO4D [2] shows that temporal information can improve the accuracy of 3D object detection by applying LSTMs [3]. FAF [4] pre-registers the multi-frame point clouds, uses 3D convolution for multi-frame feature extraction, and implements a multi-task network based on 3D object detection. However, pre-registration of point clouds requires location information or special algorithms like ICP [5] which introduce extra sensor requirement or pre-computation. In fact, accurately aligning is a difficult task since there may exist moving objects in the scene. Traditional point registration methods like ICP assume the static scene and cannot tackle this problem.

Y. Zhang and Y. Ye—Equal contribution.

© Springer Nature Switzerland AG 2021
H. Ishikawa et al. (Eds.): ACCV 2020, LNCS 12622, pp. 140–157, 2021.
https://doi.org/10.1007/978-3-030-69525-5_9

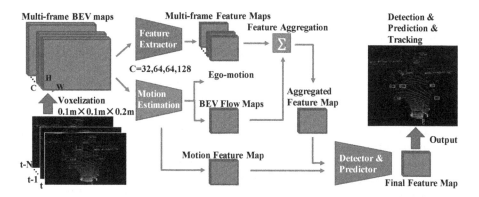

Fig. 1. Architecture of proposed network. We take multi-frame point clouds as input and perform multiple tasks jointly.

Besides detection, deeply understanding the scene's dynamics requires further prediction and tracking of the objects. When the observing platform itself is also moving, self-localization is also required to describe all of the motion dynamics in a unified world frame. These tasks are usually implemented separately. We believe it would be beneficial to fulfill them within a multi-task network. However, some challenges exist in realizing this idea. On the one hand, tracking by network requires multi-frame input, which means larger computation burden and difficulty of real-time implementation. If we still want the network to perform in real-time, only those with simple backbones can be considered. On the other hand, dealing with this complex multi-frame situation requires the network be sufficiently strong, so that all of the tasks can be correctly carried out. The dilemma reveals the real challenge when developing a real-time multi-frame multi-task network for perceiving the dynamic environment.

In this paper we propose SDP-Net, a novel fast and high-precision multi-frame multi-task network based on the bird's eye view (BEV) scene flow. It is able to complete the tasks of self-alignment, 3D object detection, prediction and tracking jointly from BEV. As shown in Fig. 1, we directly construct BEV maps from the multi-frame point clouds, and estimate the flow map and the ego-motion from them. After feature aggregation guided by BEV flow map, we detect objects, predict their motion and perform object tracking. The entire network uses 2D convolutions and shares features across multiple tasks to get real-time performance. We conduct the experiments on KITTI [6,7] RAW dataset and apply automatic method and manual fine-tuning to complete the annotations of unlabeled objects. Experimental results show that we can extract the motion information of objects effectively, and perform these tasks accurately. Importantly, we can perform accurate object detection even based on a simple backbone, achieving the state-of-the-art performance and outperforms the similar networks by a large margin. The entire approach can run at 12 FPS, meeting the real-time requirement. In summary, the key contributions of this paper are:

- We propose a BEV scene flow based multi-frame alignment method, which could estimate the correspondences of 3D features between consecutive frames and adaptively aggregate multiple frame information to benefit the 3D object detection task;
- We propose a multi-frame multi-task network based on the proposed BEV scene flow. Multiple related tasks like self-alignment, ego-motion estimation, object detection, object prediction and tracking are integrated in a unifying framework. These tasks complement each other and contribute achieving better performance than a single task;
- We improve the KITTI [6,7] RAW dataset by supplementing the ground truth, increasing the number of annotations by 10.58% for more accurate and reliable evaluation. We only use the provided ground truth in KITTI RAW dataset to guarantee the quality of the supplemented annotations;
- Our method is implemented end-to-end and verified on KITTI RAW dataset. The experimental results demonstrated that our network can run in real-time and achieve the superior performance on the tasks as detection and tracking.

2   Related Work

2.1   Single-Frame 3D Object Detection

In recent years, 3D object detection in a single frame has made great progress. MV3D [8] and AVOD [9] merge the information of RGB image and LIDAR point clouds to detect 3D objects. VoxelNet [10] and SECOND [11] detect objects by extracting voxel features in point clouds. F-PointNet [12] generates 2D object region proposals in RGB images to get the frustum point clouds, then applies PointNet [13] for 3D object detection. PointRCNN [14] uses PointNet++ [15] to extract features and optimizes the detection by box refinement. To improve the real-time performance, Complex-YOLO [16] build BEV map from 3D point clouds and apply YOLOv2 [17] to build a fast single-stage 3D object detector. PIXOR [18] and PIXOR++ [19] use occupancy maps of the point clouds as input, and perform 3D object detection with higher precision. PointPillars [20] applies PointNet to encode point clouds, and uses SSD [21] for object detection. MODet [22] extracts features in BEV and adopts prediction errors regression to improve accuracy. STD [23] uses spherical anchor and predict IoU branch to get great performance localization and classification. Fast Point R-CNN [24] combines RefinerNet to do a further fusion. PV-RCNN [25] and SA-SSD [26] combine voxel and points features to further improve the detection accuracy.

2.2   Multi-frame 3D Object Detection

The performance of object detection can be improved by utilizing temporal information. In the field of 2D video object detection, T-CNN [27] and MCMOT [28] use post-processing techniques to improve the detection results. Associated LSTM [29] and Bottleneck-LSTM [30] extract the multi-frame features with

LSTMs. FGFA [31] shows that the features of multiple frames can be fused through the guidance of optical flow to improve the detection performance. 3D object detection can benefit from similar ideas. Complexer-YOLO [32] applies multi-object tracking based on 3D object detection to increase accuracy and robustness. YOLO4D aggregates the 3D LIDAR point clouds over time as a 4D tensor, then applies LSTMs on YOLO3D [33] to extract temporal features and shows the advantages of incorporating the temporal dimension. FAF [4] pre-registers the multi-frame point clouds before input, then extracts multi-frame feature through 3D convolutions, and outputs the results of 3D object detection, prediction and tracking simultaneously. However, according to the same authors' work [19], FAF [4] still has lower object detection accuracy when compared with a faster 3D single-frame detector such as PIXOR. The reason partly lies in the misalignment error of moving objects in the scene, which is difficult to be removed by rigid body registration methods like ICP.

2.3   Object Prediction and Tracking

For moving objects, prediction and tracking can be further applied to describe the objects' behaviour in near future. When the observing platform itself is also moving, self-localization is also required to describe all of the motion dynamics in a unified world frame. Usually, these tasks are fulfilled separately.

Self-localization with 3D Point Clouds. Most of localization methods are presented in the field of SLAM. Given point clouds of different frames, DeepMapping [34] estimates poses and converts the registration problem to the unsupervised binary occupancy classification. L3-Net [35] uses PointNet to extract features, and applies 3D convolution and RNNs to output poses. [36] uses LIDAR Intensity Map to build embeddings, and estimates the localization by convolutional matching between the embeddings. PointFlowNet [37] estimates the 3D scene flow to endow the detected object with spatial velocity.

Prediction and Tracking. In order to predict the future location of objects, [38] proposes a system based on acceleration motion model and maneuver recognition respectively. [39] classifies vehicle motion with a Bayesian network for trajectories prediction. Given the detection results of the current and the past frames, the motion model or the appearance features is widely applied in data association [40,41]. Besides Hungarian algorithm [42], deep association networks [43,44] can also be employed. In order to track objects in 3D space, [45] proposes a 2D-3D Kalman filter to use the information of the image and 3D points jointly. AB3DMOT [46] extends the state space of Kalman filter with 3D object parameters, and performs fast and accurate object tracking without CNNs.

3D object detection, prediction and tracking are highly relevant tasks. Instead of completing these tasks separately, it would be a better way to fulfill them within a multi-task network. Inspired by [4], we take advantages of temporal information within multiple frames and perform object detection, prediction and tracking simultaneously. Different from [4], we estimate the BEV scene flow from multiple frames directly and do not require the frames to be pre-aligned. We can also perform an extra task of self-localization for the ego-vehicle.

3   SDP-Net

3.1   Network Structure

As shown in Fig. 1, the entire network is mainly composed of four modules, i.e., feature extraction, motion estimation, feature aggregation, and object detection and prediction. We build binary occupancy BEV map from point clouds of each frame, then perform feature extraction and motion estimation. During motion estimation, we estimate the BEV flow maps of multiple frames and output the 2D ego-motion relative to the previous frame. In feature aggregation module, we warp the feature maps of the past frames according to the corresponding BEV flow maps, and get the aggregated feature map with adaptive weights. In the module of object detection and prediction, we fuse the aggregated feature map and the object motion information, detect objects in the current frame and predict their motion offset in the future frames. Finally, the tracking can be carried out by association with simple overlap area of the current detection and the past predictions. In the following we describe our input representation first, and then introduce each module of the network in detail.

Point Cloud Processing. By constructing a BEV map, we can represent 3D space effectively and use 2D convolution for fast feature extraction. We take the point clouds from the current and the past N frames as input, and construct BEV maps separately. Following [22], we make a rough ground plane estimation to correct the height of point clouds. Then, we perform voxelization on point clouds, and build binary representation of each voxel. For each frame, we construct a binary occupancy tensor with a voxel size of $0.1 \text{ m} \times 0.1 \text{ m} \times 0.2 \text{ m}$ to speed up the following computation. When there is a point in the corresponding voxel, the value of the voxel is 1, otherwise the value is 0.

Feature Extractor. In the feature extraction stage, we apply a fairly simple network for real-time purpose. As shown in Fig. 1, for each BEV map, we perform only 4 convolutional layers and 3 max-pooling layers with 32, 64, 64 and 128 channels respectively, which result in an 8× downsampled feature map.

BEV Flow Based Motion Estimation. Point clouds are sparse and unevenly distributed in 3D space, it is difficult to make fast and accurate scene flow estimation for each 3D point. Considering that most of the objects in the scene stay in the ground, we focus on estimating the horizontal motions only. Given all of the binary voxel pillars in the scene, we focus on obtaining accurate motion flow for voxels on objects.

As shown in Fig. 2, the BEV flow map describes the relative motion of the pixels on each object in X and Y directions. For each pixel in the BEV flow map, if it belongs to an object, the value is the corresponding motion offset; otherwise it belongs to the background and the value is required to be zero. For computing efficiency, an 8× downsampled flow map is used.

The resulting BEV flow maps represent the motion of objects between the current and the past N frames. Based on them, the features of objects in the past frames can be warped into the current frame by:

$$F^{(t-n)\rightarrow t}(p) = F^{t-n}(p + flow^{t-n}(p)). \tag{1}$$

where $1 \leq n \leq N$, $F^{(t-n)\rightarrow t}$ is the resulting feature map warped from frame $t - n$ to t, and $flow^{t-n}(p)$ is the computed flow offset of the pixel p between frame t and $t - n$. For possible non-integer coordinates, bilinear interpolation is used for warping.

The detailed network structure of motion estimation module is illustrated in Fig. 3. Instead of performing estimation for every two frames, we concatenate the BEV maps of the current and the past N frames and extract features directly. Then, we estimate the BEV flow maps relative to the past N frames and the ego-motion on two branches simultaneously. On the BEV flow map estimation branch, we use pyramid structure to fuse features at different scales with up to 32× down-sampling. Then, after 3 layers of further convolution with 64, 32 and $N \times 2$ channels, a tensor of $H/8 \times W/8 \times (N \times 2)$ corresponding to the BEV flow maps of the past N frames is obtained. The BEV flow map of each frame has 2 channels, which represent the motion offset relative to current frame in X and Y directions respectively. Another branch of this module is to estimate the ego-motion. On this branch, we perform convolution and fully-connected operations based on the 64× downsampled feature map, and estimate the motion offset $(dx, dy, d\theta)$, which represents the translation and rotation of ego-vehicle.

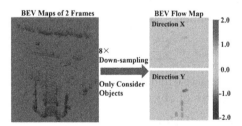

Fig. 2. BEV map (left) and the corresponding flow map (right). Voxel pillars of two neighboring frames are marked in blue and red respectively in BEV map. The BEV flow map contains the motion of the pixels on each object in direction X and Y. (Color figure online)

BEV flow branch and self-localization branch are essentially extracting the motion information of the foreground and background respectively. They share most of the layers in the sub network, which can speed up their convergence. We can have the ground truth for these two tasks from the labeled objects and GPS respectively for supervised training.

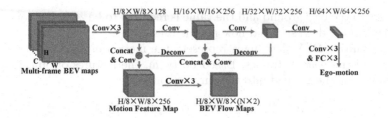

Fig. 3. Detailed structure of motion estimation module.

Feature Aggregation. Because the same object have different coordinates on the successive feature maps, direct aggregation will cause severe misalignment. We use BEV flow maps to guide the warping of multi-frame features in BEV and align the features of the same object as shown in Eq. (1).

In order to further suppress the impact of residential alignment error, we apply adaptive weights to the warped feature maps before aggregation. We use a 3-layer convolution operation with shared parameters on the warped feature maps, extract 1024-dimensional feature vectors at each pixel, and calculate the cosine similarity [31] with the feature vectors of current frame. Then, the normalized weights are computed as:

$$w^{t-n}(p) = \frac{exp(s^{t-n}(p))}{\sum_j exp(s^{t-j}(p))}. \tag{2}$$

where $0 \leq n \leq N$, $0 \leq j \leq N$, $s^{t-n}(p)$ is the cosine similarity between the 1024-dimensional feature vectors of current frame t and past frame $t-n$ at coordinate p, w^{t-n} is the normalized weight map of frame $t-n$. Finally, the aggregated feature map $\bar{F}$ can be computed as:

$$\bar{F} = \sum_n w^{t-n} * F^{(t-n) \to t}. \tag{3}$$

where $*$ represents elementwise multiplication. By accumulating multi-frame features together, the features of objects are strengthened.

Object Detection, Prediction and Tracking. We simultaneously detect objects and predict their motion offset in the next M frames in the object detection and prediction stage. As shown in Fig. 4, we apply pyramid structure and dense-block [47] on the aggregated feature map for further feature extraction. The output of the detection branch is the object classification confidence c_{obj}, location offset (t_x, t_y), object size (l, w) and object orientation $(sin\theta, cos\theta)$, which are further defined as [22]:

$$t_x = \frac{x_{gt} - x_{grid}}{grid}, t_y = \frac{y_{gt} - y_{grid}}{grid},$$
$$l = log(l_{gt}), w = log(w_{gt}), \theta_{gt} = atan2(\frac{sin\theta}{cos\theta}). \tag{4}$$

where $(x_{gt}, y_{gt}, l_{gt}, w_{gt}, \theta_{gt})$ is the ground truth, (x_{grid}, y_{grid}) is the grid location of each pixel in feature map, and *grid* is the size of each pixel in feature map. In practice, *grid* is set to 0.8 m.

We further introduce the *Motion Feature Map*, i.e., the feature block before the final *BEV Flow Map* in Fig. 3, to produce the prediction of the objects' location in the upcoming frames. FAF [4] uses several predefined anchors and describes the prediction with location offset, size and heading on future frame. In contrast, we don't use any anchors and only predict the relative motion of objects for the sake of efficiency. The motion offset is described as:

$$d_{tx}^{t+m} = t_x^{t+m} - t_x, d_{ty}^{t+m} = t_y^{t+m} - t_y, d_\theta^{t+m} = \theta^{t+m} - \theta. \tag{5}$$

where $1 \leq m \leq M$, (t_x, t_y, θ) and $(t_x^{t+m}, t_y^{t+m}, \theta^{t+m})$ represent the corresponding positions of the same object in the current frame t and the future frame $t + m$.

With the current detection and the past predictions at hand, it is straight forward to carry out the object tracking by simply checking the Intersection-Over-Union (IoU) on them. We first track the current objects based on the prediction of frame $t - 1$ with a certain IoU threshold. If no association could be set up, we further check the corresponding predictions from frame $t - 2$ to $t - M$ in order to set up the association.

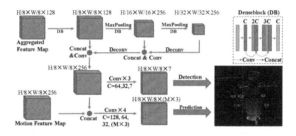

Fig. 4. Detailed structure of object detection and prediction module.

3.2 Loss Function

SDP-Net implements motion estimation, object detection, prediction and tracking jointly in BEV. Therefore, as shown in Eq. (6), the loss function L is mainly composed of motion estimation loss L_{motion}, object detection loss L_{det}, and object prediction loss L_{pred}. The weights among them are determined experimentally with $\lambda_1 = 0.125$, $\lambda_2 = 0.1$, $\lambda_3 = 1.25$.

$$L = \lambda_1 L_{motion} + \lambda_2 L_{det} + \lambda_3 L_{pred}. \tag{6}$$

Motion Estimation Loss. The motion estimation loss L_{motion} consists of BEV flow estimation loss L_{flow} and ego-motion loss L_{pose}:

$$L_{motion} = L_{flow} + L_{pose}. \tag{7}$$

We apply L2 loss and increase the weights of pixels with objects for L_{flow}:

$$L_{flow} = \frac{1}{N_t} \sum_p \lambda_4 |\widehat{flow}(p) - flow(p)|^2. \tag{8}$$

where N_t is the total number of pixels in the BEV flow map, $\widehat{flow}(p)$ and $flow(p)$ separately represent the estimation and ground truth on the coordinate p. In practice, if coordinate p belongs to an object, $\lambda_4 = 3$, if not, $\lambda_4 = 0.01$. Note that we get the ground truth of flow from supplemented annotations of KITTI RAW dataset instead of GPS, which will be described in Sect. 4.1.

We use smooth L1 loss for L_{pose} as:

$$L1(x) = \begin{cases} 0.5x^2, & if |x| \leq 1, \\ |x| - 0.5, & otherwise. \end{cases} \tag{9}$$

$$L_{pose} = L1(|\widehat{dx} - dx|) + L1(|\widehat{dy} - dy|) + \lambda_5 L1(|\widehat{d\theta} - d\theta|). \tag{10}$$

where $(\widehat{dx}, \widehat{dy}, \widehat{d\theta})$ and $(dx, dy, d\theta)$ represent the estimation and ground truth respectively, and we set $\lambda_5 = 100$ in practice.

Object Detection Loss. Object detection loss consists of classification loss L_{cls} and regression loss L_{reg}. We use focal loss as [48] for classification to alleviate the impact from sample imbalance, and consider all of the pixels in feature map to get L_{cls}. We use smooth L1 loss for regression. Total object detection loss:

$$L_{det} = L_{cls} + \frac{1}{N_p} \sum L_{reg}. \tag{11}$$

where N_p is the number of pixels corresponding to the positive samples and L_{reg} is the smooth L1 loss of $(t_x, t_y, l, w, sin\theta, cos\theta)$ for object regression.

Object Prediction Loss. We estimate object motion offset $(d_{tx}, d_{ty}, d_\theta)$ on the same pixels as object detection in feature map. We apply smooth L1 loss and consider all the positive samples in the future M frames:

$$L_{pred} = \frac{1}{N_p} \sum \sum_m [L1(|\widehat{d_{tx}^{t+m}} - d_{tx}^{t+m}|) + L1(|\widehat{d_{ty}^{t+m}} - d_{ty}^{t+m}|) + \lambda_6 L1(|\widehat{d_\theta^{t+m}} - d_\theta^{t+m}|)]. \tag{12}$$

where N_p is the number of pixels corresponding to the positive samples, $1 \leq m \leq M$, and we set $\lambda_6 = 100$ in practice.

4   Experiments

4.1   Dataset and Implementation Details

KITTI RAW Dataset. We use KITTI RAW dataset for network training and evaluation. The KITTI RAW dataset contains 37 labeled sequences collected in different scenes with a total of 12,486 frames. The annotations of each frame include RTK-GPS data, RGB images, 64-line LIDAR point clouds and object labels with tracking information. The KITTI RAW dataset contains

34278 labeled vehicles, which makes up the vast majority of labeled object type. The other objects like bicycles and pedestrians are unevenly distributed in the sequence and have only 1550 and 2574 labels respectively, which are not enough for network training and objective evaluation. Therefore, like FAF and PIXOR, we only consider vehicles in the experiments.

Ground Truth Supplementing. The KITTI RAW dataset does not annotate objects that look highly occluded in the RGB images, although many of them can still be observed in BEV space. Since one motivation of our network is to improve the detection of those hard objects by multi-frame fusion, failing to label these occluded objects will confuse the network and degrade the credibility of evaluation. Therefore, we develop a method to complete these missed ground truth. We use GPS of ego-vehicle to project the ground truth bounding boxes from the next frame back to the current frame. If the projected bounding box contains more than 3 points in the current frame while has less than 0.1 of IoU with any of the bounding boxes in the current frame, it means the same object in the current frame are missed due to the partial occlusion and can be supplemented. Then, we manually check the increased annotations and adjust the incorrect bounding boxes to eliminate the annotation error. Finally, we successfully expand the total number of vehicles from 34278 to 37906, with an increase of 10.58%. As shown in Fig. 5, for the original KITTI annotations, a certain number of objects that can be clearly observed in BEV space are missed. After ground truth supplementing, most of these highly occluded objects are found back and added. It makes our supplemented raw dataset a more difficult benchmark than the original KITTI.

Fig. 5. Two examples of ground truth supplementing. The original annotations are marked with yellow, while the supplemented are marked with red in BEV. The RGB images below show the corresponding scenarios, respectively.

Training Setup. Besides current frame, we consider the 4 recent frames of point clouds within the range of forward length $Y \in [0, 51.2\,\mathrm{m}]$, width $X \in [-28.8\,\mathrm{m}, 28.8\,\mathrm{m}]$ and height $Z \in [-2\,\mathrm{m}, 1\,\mathrm{m}]$. Thus our input is a $512 \times 576 \times 15 \times 5$ binary tensor which consists of X, Y, Z and time. And we predict objects' motion in 5 future frames. Then, we randomly split the KITTI RAW dataset for training and evaluation. The training set contains 24 sequences with a total of 7410 frames and the test set contains 13 sequences with a total of 5076 frames. We use NVIDIA GTX1080Ti GPU and Intel i7 CPU for both network training and evaluation. We set the initial learning rate to 0.001, the batch size to 4, the decay step to 150k, and the decay rate to 0.5. We follow [22] to apply data augmentation in training. We train the motion estimation module for 30 epochs first, then fix the module parameters, and train other modules for 60 epochs.

4.2 Evaluation Results

In the following, we evaluate the task performance of BEV flow estimation, ego-motion estimation, object detection and object tracking, respectively.

BEV Scene Flow Estimation. Some qualitative results of the estimated BEV flow maps as well as the corresponding detected objects are shown in Fig. 6, where we can see that the BEV flow of each object is well learned. The accuracy of the scene flow will dertermine the alignment of the multi-frame feature, which will further affect the performance of object detection. We compare our BEV flow estimation with the ICP or GPS based point clouds registration, as well as direct aggregation without any registration (Dir-Agg). The metric of mean alignment error of objects on the feature map is used, and the results are shown in Table 1. As expected, direct feature aggregation on original multi-frame point clouds produces large alignment error. Methods based on point clouds registration (ICP) can reduce the error by aligning the static foregrounds. Our method performs the best thanks to its capability of aligning the features in both static and moving objects at the same time. It even results in smaller error than the method based on GPS which shows poor performance in aligning moving objects.

Table 1. The mean alignment error of voxels in object.

Method	Dir-Agg	ICP	GPS	Ours
Mean alignment error (pixels)	2.04	0.84	0.76	0.67

Ego-Motion Estimation. We further output the self-motion offset results from the motion estimation branch. We calculate the mean error of all 13 sequences on KITTI RAW test set. The resulting translational and rotational errors of ICP are 0.26 m and 0.003 rad., comparing with ours 0.13 m and 0.003 rad., respectively. It indicates that our module can effectively estimate ego-motion from multiple frames.

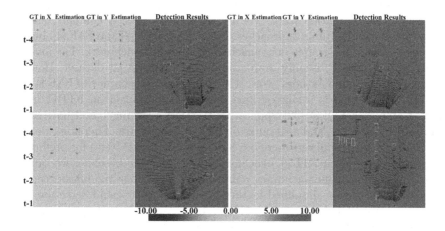

Fig. 6. Illustration of four groups of results each of which consists of a composite BEV flow image (left) and the object detection results for the current frame (right). In the BEV flow image the ground truth and the estimated flow map in X and Y direction relative to the time from $t-1$ to $t-4$ are further illustrated separately side by side. The object detection results are shown here just for reference, where the ground truth is labeled in red and the output of our network are marked with green. (Color figure online)

Table 2. Performance comparison of different methods on KITTI BEV benchmark.

Method	Times (ms)	mAP(%)		
		Easy	Moderate	Hard
PIXOR [18]	35	83.97	80.01	74.31
C-YOLO [32]	60	77.24	68.96	64.95
SDP-Net-s	**12**	**86.57**	**81.93**	**75.83**

Table 3. Performance comparison of different methods on KITTI RAW test set.

Method	Input	Modality	Times (ms)	mAP(%)		
				Easy	Moderate	Hard
F-Net [12]	Single-frame	Lidar&Img	170	89.60	82.49	70.90
MODet [22]	Single-frame	Lidar	50	90.20	87.49	84.27
SDP-Net-s	Single-frame	Lidar	**12**	86.05	81.91	79.00
ICP-based	Multi-frame	Lidar	ICP+59	90.01	84.73	82.60
SDP-Net	Multi-frame	Lidar	82	**91.51**	**88.29**	**84.74**

Object Detection. We first compare our approach with other methods and then conduct the ablation study. We are not able to directly compare our approach with the multi-frame approaches such as YOLO4D [2] and FAF [4], because they are neither open-source nor ranked on the public benchmark. The most relevant approach, FAF, is only evaluated on the TOR4D [4] dataset. However, according to the same authors' work [19], the detection accuracy of FAF is lower than PIXOR, which is a single-frame detector and ranked on KITTI benchmark. Complexer-YOLO [32] applies multi-object tracking based on a single-frame object detector, and also ranks on KITTI benchmark. Therefore, we build and train a single frame version of our model, termed SDP-Net-s for preliminary comparing purpose on KITTI benchmark. To build this baseline, we take the single-frame point clouds as input, removing all of the rest modules except the main backbone with a simplified feature pyramid structure and detection head. Then, we train SDP-Net-s on the KITTI benchmark dataset and compare it with these methods. As shown in Table 2, it can be found that our single-frame baseline has competitive performance compared with these two methods.

With this idea in mind, we further compare our approach with other multi-frame and single-frame approaches on our supplemented KITTI RAW test set. We follow the evaluation criteria of KITTI benckmark to set the IoU threshold to 0.7 and obtain the mean average precision (mAP) on three difficulty levels (easy, moderate and hard). In the hard level, all of the labeled objects are considered.

For the multi-frame approach, we build an ICP-based network for comparison. We remove the flow estimation module in our network and pre-register different frames of point clouds with ICP before input. Then, we apply the same feature extractor and adaptive weights to perform object detection. For the single-frame approaches, we train and evaluate F-PointNet [12] and MODet [22] which have more complex backbones than our approach. Considering that F-PointNet does not have an open-source 2D object detector, we use ground truth of 2D bounding boxes to get the frustum point clouds during training and evaluation. MODet is a single-stage high-precision object detector which has the state-of-the-art performance with higher detection accuracy compared to Point-RCNN [14] and PointPillars [20] on KITTI BEV benckmark.

As shown in Table 3, comparing with our single-frame baseline SDP-Net-s, F-PointNet performs worse in hard level, where lots of occluded or distant objects exist. The ICP-based network pre-registers the point clouds and has a certain improvement over our single-frame baseline. Our full approach SDP-Net outperforms the ICP-based approach by a large margin. It can adaptively aggregate the multi-frame features with unregistered point clouds input. Although residual networks with deeper network backbone are used in MODet [22], our approach still get better performance than it with a simpler backbone.

We further list mAPs of these methods according to the state and distance of objects, as shown in Table 4. For static objects, ICP-based method can perform accurate feature alignment, which is better than the single-frame method. But for moving objects, it has poor performance because of feature misalignment.

Our approach uses BEV flow map to guide feature aggregation and achieves the best detection performance for most of the moving and static objects.

Table 4. Performance comparison on different objects on KITTI RAW test set.

Method	Input	mAP(%)			
		Static& < 30 m	Static& > 30 m	Moving& < 30 m	Moving& > 30 m
F-Net [12]	Single-frame	83.93	48.94	70.67	45.17
MODet [22]	Single-frame	90.67	**66.57**	88.23	57.79
SDP-Net-s	Single-frame	87.34	56.60	84.20	53.58
ICP-based	Multi-frame	90.71	62.71	82.04	52.76
SDP-Net	Multi-frame	**91.54**	66.38	**89.28**	**60.75**

Table 5. Ablation study of SDP-Net on KITTI RAW test set.

Input	BEV flow map	Adaptive weights	mAP(%)		
			Easy	Moderate	Hard
Single-frame	\	\	86.05	81.91	79.00
Multi-frame	\	Applied	83.00	81.19	79.23
Multi-frame	Applied	\	88.36	84.53	82.79
Multi-frame	Applied	Applied	**91.51**	**88.29**	**84.74**

Ablation Study. We conduct the ablation study for SDP-Net by with or without BEV scene flow estimation or adaptive weights aggregation module. As shown in Table 5, without the guidance of BEV flow maps, the multi-frame performance is even lower than the single frame due to the feature misalignment. The adaptive weights can also help with the detection task by further reducing the residual misalignment error.

Prediction and Tracking. While detecting objects of the current frame, we also predict their motion in the next 5 frames. We compute the average distance error between the center of the predicted objects and the ground truth. The resulting mean errors in the next 5 frames are 0.18 m, 0.22 m, 0.27 m, 0.34 m and 0.39 m, respectively, which validate the accuracy of object prediction task.

We further track the objects based on the detection and prediction results, as described in Sect. 3.1. Some qualitative results are illustrated in Fig. 7, where we can see the tracking task is fulfilled robustly. We further quantitatively evaluate the tracking performance with the metric of Multiple Object Tracking Accuracy (MOTA), Multiple Object Tracking Precision (MOTP), Mostly-Tracked (MT) and Mostly-Lost (ML) following KITTI protocol, and set IoU to 0.5 for association and 0.8 score for thresholding. As shown in Table 6, our approach can perform object tracking with better performance than AB3DMOT [46].

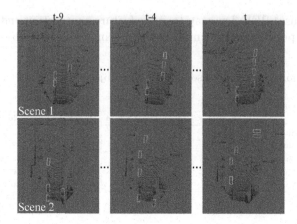

Fig. 7. Two scenes of object tracking, where the successive tracking results are listed in a row with time $t-9$, $t-4$ and t, respectively. The same object in each scene is marked with the same color.

Table 6. Results of object tracking on KITTI RAW test set.

Method	MOTA	MOTP	MT	ML
AB3DMOT [46]	78.89	84.69	74.22	6.52
SDP-Net	**82.29**	**84.96**	**81.05**	**4.66**

5 Conclusions

In this paper, we propose a novel scene flow based multi-frame multi-task network for 3D object detection and tracking. To the best our knowledge, ours is the first work which can adaptively integrating the multi-frame temporal laser data to enhance the object detection and prediction in real-time. We estimate the scene dynamics through BEV flow and then adaptively aggregate the features from multiple frames. Multiple related tasks such as ego-motion estimation, object detection, prediction and tracking are jointly performed in real time within our network. We achieve the superior performance than the state-of-the-art on the improved and more difficult KITTI RAW test set. In the future, we plan to test our approach on more datasets with more object categories, and incorporate more complex networks like PointNet for better feature extraction.

Funding: The work is supported by NSFC-Zhejiang Joint Fund for the Integration of Industrialization and Informatization under grant No. U1709214.

References

1. Levinson, J., et al.: Towards fully autonomous driving: systems and algorithms. In: IV (2011)

2. El Sallab, A., Sobh, I., Zidan, M., Zahran, M., Abdelkarim, S.: YOLO4D: a spatio-temporal approach for real-time multi-object detection and classification from lidar point clouds. In: NIPS Workshops (2018)
3. Hochreiter, S., Schmidhuber, J.: Long short-term memory. Neural Comput. **9**, 1735–1780 (1997)
4. Luo, W., Yang, B., Urtasun, R.: Fast and furious: real time end-to-end 3d detection, tracking and motion forecasting with a single convolutional net. In: 2018 IEEE/CVF Conference on Computer Vision and Pattern Recognition, pp. 3569–3577. IEEE (2018)
5. Besl, P.J., McKay, N.D.: Method for registration of 3-D shapes. In: Sensor Fusion IV: Control Paradigms and Data Structures, vol. 1611, pp. 586–606. International Society for Optics and Photonics (1992)
6. Geiger, A., Lenz, P., Urtasun, R.: Are we ready for autonomous driving? the KITTI vision benchmark suite. In: 2012 IEEE Conference on Computer Vision and Pattern Recognition. IEEE (2012)
7. Geiger, A., Lenz, P., Stiller, C., Urtasun, R.: Vision meets robotics: the KITTI dataset. Int. J. Robot. Res. **32**, 1231–1237 (2013)
8. Chen, X., Ma, H., Wan, J., Li, B., Xia, T.: Multi-view 3D object detection network for autonomous driving. In: CVPR. IEEE (2017)
9. Ku, J., Mozifian, M., Lee, J., Harakeh, A., Waslander, S.L.: Joint 3D proposal generation and object detection from view aggregation. In: IROS. IEEE (2018)
10. Zhou, Y., Tuzel, O.: VoxelNet: end-to-end learning for point cloud based 3D object detection. In: CVPR. IEEE (2018)
11. Yan, Y., Mao, Y., Li, B.: SECOND: sparsely embedded convolutional detection. Sensors **18**, 3337 (2018)
12. Qi, C.R., Liu, W., Wu, C., Su, H., Guibas, L.J.: Frustum PointNets for 3D object detection from RGB-D data. In: CVPR. IEEE (2018)
13. Qi, C.R., Su, H., Mo, K., Guibas, L.J.: PointNet: deep learning on point sets for 3D classification and segmentation. In: 2017 IEEE Conference on Computer Vision and Pattern Recognition (CVPR). IEEE (2017)
14. Shi, S., Wang, X., Li, H.: PointRCNN: 3D object proposal generation and detection from point cloud. In: 2019 IEEE/CVF Conference on Computer Vision and Pattern Recognition (CVPR). IEEE (2020)
15. Qi, C.R., Yi, L., Su, H., Guibas, L.J.: PointNet++: deep hierarchical feature learning on point sets in a metric space. In: NIPS (2017)
16. Simony, M., Milzy, S., Amendey, K., Gross, H.M.: Complex-YOLO: an euler-region-proposal for real-time 3D object detection on point clouds. In: ECCV (2018)
17. Redmon, J., Farhadi, A.: YOLO9000: better, faster, stronger. In: IEEE Conference on Computer Vision and Pattern Recognition, pp. 6517–6525. IEEE (2017)
18. Yang, B., Luo, W., Urtasun, R.: PIXOR: real-time 3D object detection from point clouds. In: CVPR. IEEE (2018)
19. Yang, B., Liang, M., Urtasun, R.: HDNET: exploiting HD maps for 3D object detection. In: CoRL (2018)
20. Lang, A.H., Vora, S., Caesar, H., Zhou, L., Yang, J., Beijbom, O.: PointPillars: fast encoders for object detection from point clouds. In: 2019 IEEE/CVF Conference on Computer Vision and Pattern Recognition (CVPR). IEEE (2019)
21. Liu, W., et al.: SSD: single shot multibox detector. In: Leibe, B., Matas, J., Sebe, N., Welling, M. (eds.) ECCV 2016. LNCS, vol. 9905, pp. 21–37. Springer, Cham (2016). https://doi.org/10.1007/978-3-319-46448-0_2
22. Zhang, Y., Xiang, Z., Qiao, C., Chen, S.: Accurate and real-time object detection based on bird's eye view on 3D point clouds. In: 3DV (2019)

23. Yang, Z., Sun, Y., Liu, S., Shen, X., Jia, J.: STD: sparse-to-dense 3D object detector for point cloud. In: ICCV. IEEE (2019)
24. Chen, Y., Liu, S., Shen, X., Jia, J.: Fast point R-CNN. In: 2019 IEEE/CVF International Conference on Computer Vision (ICCV), pp. 9774–9783 (2019)
25. Shi, S., et al.: PV-RCNN: point-voxel feature set abstraction for 3D object detection. In: Proceedings of the IEEE Conference on Computer Vision and Pattern Recognition. IEEE (2020)
26. He, C., Zeng, H., Huang, J., Hua, X.S., Zhang, L.: Structure aware single-stage 3d object detection from point cloud. In: Proceedings of the IEEE Conference on Computer Vision and Pattern Recognition. IEEE (2020)
27. Kang, K., et al.: T-CNN: tubelets with convolutional neural networks for object detection from videos. IEEE Trans. Circ. Syst. Video Technol. **28**, 2896–2907 (2017)
28. Lee, B., Erdenee, E., Jin, S., Nam, M.Y., Jung, Y.G., Rhee, P.K.: Multi-class multi-object tracking using changing point detection. In: Hua, G., Jégou, H. (eds.) ECCV 2016. LNCS, vol. 9914, pp. 68–83. Springer, Cham (2016). https://doi.org/10.1007/978-3-319-48881-3_6
29. Nam, H., Han, B.: Learning multi-domain convolutional neural networks for visual tracking. In: CVPR. IEEE (2016)
30. Liu, M., Zhu, M.: Mobile video object detection with temporally-aware feature maps. In: 2018 IEEE/CVF Conference on Computer Vision and Pattern Recognition (CVPR). IEEE (2018)
31. Zhu, X., Wang, Y., Dai, J., Yuan, L., Wei, Y.: Flow-guided feature aggregation for video object detection. In: 2017 IEEE International Conference on Computer Vision (ICCV). IEEE (2017)
32. Simon, M., et al.: Complex-YOLO: real-time 3D object detection on point clouds. In: CVPR Workshops (2019)
33. Ali, W., Abdelkarim, S., Zidan, M., Zahran, M., El Sallab, A.: YOLO3D: end-to-end real-time 3D oriented object bounding box detection from LiDAR point cloud. In: ECCV (2018)
34. Li, D., Chen, F.: DeepMapping: unsupervised map estimation from multiple point clouds. In: 2019 IEEE/CVF Conference on Computer Vision and Pattern Recognition (CVPR). IEEE (2020)
35. Lu, W., Zhou, Y., Wan, G., Hou, S., Song, S.: L3-Net: towards learning based LiDAR localization for autonomous driving. In: 2019 IEEE/CVF Conference on Computer Vision and Pattern Recognition (CVPR). IEEE (2020)
36. Barsan, I.A., Wang, S., Pokrovsky, A., Urtasun, R.: Learning to localize using a LiDAR intensity map. In: CoRL (2018)
37. Behl, A., Paschalidou, D., Donne, S., Geiger, A.: PointFlowNet: learning representations for rigid motion estimation from point clouds. In: 2019 IEEE/CVF Conference on Computer Vision and Pattern Recognition (CVPR). IEEE (2019)
38. Houenou, A., Bonnifait, P., Cherfaoui, V., Yao, W.: Vehicle trajectory prediction based on motion model and maneuver recognition. In: IEEE/RSJ International Conference on Intelligent Robots and Systems. IEEE (2013)
39. Schreier, M., Willert, V., Adamy, J.: Bayesian, maneuver-based, long-term trajectory prediction and criticality assessment for driver assistance systems. In: IEEE International Conference on Intelligent Transportation Systems. IEEE (2014)
40. Wojke, N., Bewley, A., Paulus, D.: Simple online and realtime tracking with a deep association metric. In: ICIP (2017)
41. Choi, W.: Near-online multi-target tracking with aggregated local flow descriptor. In: ICCV. IEEE (2015)

42. Kuhn, H.W.: The Hungarian method for the assignment problem. Naval Res. Logistics Q. **2**, 83–97 (1955)
43. Xu, Y., Ban, Y., Alameda-Pineda, X., Horaud, R.: DeepMOT: a differentiable framework for training multiple object trackers. arXiv preprint arXiv:1906.06618 (2019)
44. Voigtlaender, P., et al.: MOTS: multi-object tracking and segmentation. In: CVPR. IEEE (2019)
45. Osep, A., Mehner, W., Mathias, M., Leibe, B.: Combined Image- and world-space tracking in traffic scenes. In: 2017 IEEE International Conference on Robotics and Automation (ICRA). IEEE (2017)
46. Weng, X., Kitani, K.: A baseline for 3D multi-object tracking. arXiv preprint arXiv:1907.03961 (2019)
47. Huang, G., Liu, Z., Van Der Maaten, L., Weinberger, K.Q.: Densely connected convolutional networks. In: CVPR. IEEE (2017)
48. Ma, C., Huang, J.B., Yang, X., Yang, M.H.: Hierarchical convolutional features for visual tracking. In: ICCV. IEEE (2015)
49. Ross, T.Y.L.P.G., Dollár, G.K.H.P.: Focal loss for dense object detection. In: IEEE Transactions on Pattern Analysis and Machine Intelligence. IEEE (2017)
50. Ren, S., He, K., Girshick, R., Sun, J.: Faster R-CNN: towards real-time object detection with region proposal networks. In: NIPS (2015)
51. Lee, N., Choi, W., Vernaza, P., Choy, C.B., Torr, P.H., Chandraker, M.: DESIRE: distant future prediction in dynamic scenes with interacting agents. In: 2017 IEEE Conference on Computer Vision and Pattern Recognition (CVPR). IEEE (2017)
52. Alahi, A., Goel, K., Ramanathan, V., Robicquet, A., Fei-Fei, L., Savarese, S.: Social LSTM: human trajectory prediction in crowded spaces. In: 2016 IEEE Conference on Computer Vision and Pattern Recognition (CVPR). IEEE (2016)
53. Deo, N., Rangesh, A., Trivedi, M.M.: How would surround vehicles move? A unified framework for maneuver classification and motion prediction. IEEE Trans. Intell. Veh. **3**, 129–140 (2018)
54. Kim, B., Kang, C.M., Kim, J., Lee, S.H., Chung, C.C., Choi, J.W.: Probabilistic vehicle trajectory prediction over occupancy grid map via recurrent neural network. In: ITSC (2017)
55. Baser, E., Balasubramanian, V., Bhattacharyya, P., Czarnecki, K.: FANTrack: 3D multi-object tracking with feature association network. In: IV (2019)
56. Frossard, D., Urtasun, R.: End-to-end learning of multi-sensor 3D tracking by detection. In: ICRA. IEEE (2018)

SAUM: Symmetry-Aware Upsampling Module for Consistent Point Cloud Completion

Hyeontae Son and Young Min Kim[✉]

Department of ECE, Seoul National University, Seoul, South Korea
{sonhyuntae,youngmin.kim}@snu.ac.kr

Abstract. Point cloud completion estimates the complete shape given incomplete point cloud, which is a crucial task as the raw point cloud measurements suffer from missing data. Most of previous methods for point cloud completion share the encoder-decoder structure, where the encoder projects the raw point cloud into low-dimensional latent space and the decoder decodes the condensed latent information back into the list of points. While the low-dimensional projection extracts semantic features to guide the global completion of the missing data, the unique local geometric details observed from partial data are often lost. In this paper, we propose a shape completion framework that maintains both of the global context and the local characteristics. Our network is composed of two complementary prediction branches. One of the branches fills the unseen parts with the global context learned from the database model, which can be replaced by any of the conventional shape completion network. The other branch, which we refer as a Symmetry-Aware Upsampling Module (SAUM), conservatively maintains the geometric details given the observed partial data, clearly utilizing the symmetry for the shape completion. Experimental results show that the combination of the two prediction branches enables more plausible shape completion for point clouds than the state-of-the-art approaches (Code available on https://github.com/countywest/SAUM).

Keywords: Point cloud completion · Point upsampling · Symmetry · Two-branch network

1 Introduction

The real-world 3D measurements enable direct interaction with the physical environment and various applications, such as robotic grasping [1] and SLAM [2]. However, they rely on accurate 3D shapes, which require inferring the unknown geometry given partial measurements. Recent approaches learn a shape prior

Electronic supplementary material The online version of this chapter (https://doi.org/10.1007/978-3-030-69525-5_10) contains supplementary material, which is available to authorized users.

© Springer Nature Switzerland AG 2021
H. Ishikawa et al. (Eds.): ACCV 2020, LNCS 12622, pp. 158–174, 2021.
https://doi.org/10.1007/978-3-030-69525-5_10

knowledge from the database of 3D shapes to complete the 3D shape. They train a neural network that generates the complete shape given a partial shape motivated by the success of CNN-based computer vision technology. A straight-forward method is to represent the 3D shape with a dense 3D grid of voxels [3–5] and use 3D CNNs which are robust to the irregularity of inputs [6]. However, the 3D grid representation requires memory cubic to the resolution, whereas the 3D shape actually occupies only a sparse set of the dense grid. The memory inefficiency results in a coarse grid resolution, and the completed shape suffers from the quantization effects that loses the fine-grained geometric features [7].

Point-based approaches, on the other hand, represent the 3D shape in terms of points sampled on the surface of the geometry. It is not only memory efficient but also can be directly applied to the real-world 3D measurements to compensate for the prevalent scarcity of the raw point cloud data. Generating point clouds has been suggested for various tasks such as 3D reconstruction from a single image [8,9], super-resolution of point clouds [10–13], representation learning [14–17], and shape completion [18–26]. Most of them follow the conventional encoder-decoder structure. Given a list of 3D point coordinates, the encoder compresses the high-dimensional data into a low-dimensional global feature vector, whereas the decoder converts the compressed feature vector back into the 3D point cloud representing the shape. Despite the wide range of possible architecture choices, the decoder is designed to regress the 3D point clouds solely from the encoded global feature vector, which inherently focuses on regenerating the global semantics of the input data. While the generated geometry is approximately similar to the inputs, often the fine details are lost or hallucinated.

Our initiative is to create a point cloud shape completion pipeline that preserves the local details which can be observed from the partial measurements. In the case of images, the low-level features are successfully preserved using the U-Net architecture [27] for tasks such as semantic segmentation. The encoder-decoder structure for images are given as symmetric layers; the layers of the encoder network progressively reduce the spatial resolution of the given image to create more abstract representation and the decoder layers gradually increase the resolution back to the original image size. The U-Net model uses so-called "skip connections" between the symmetric layers existing in the encoder and the decoder. As a result, the original feature maps in the early layers of encoders are directly connected to the late-stage decoder layers, which can help the high-frequency details pass to the output directly. However, the skip connections cannot be applied to the networks for point cloud completion; a point cloud is not a regular grid and the numbers of points in input and output are usually not the same.

Instead, we create two complementary branches where one creates the global semantics and the other compensates for existing local details. We refer to the second branch as a **Symmetry-Aware Upsampling Module (SAUM)**, applicable to all of the existing encoder-decoder structured shape completion methods. SAUM is designed to generate locally consistent point clouds by fully utilizing the high-frequency features, and is also able to find the symmetric points of the input point clouds without enforcing symmetry explicitly. The SAUM can be easily combined as a parallel branch to the existing encoder-decoder architecture and overcome the fundamental limitation. Our experiments show that SAUM qualitatively increases the shape fidelity especially on the narrow structures with fine details, and quantitatively boosts the performance of various existing methods.

2   Related Works

Our framework uses the existing point cloud completion network as a backbone and attaches an additional branch to guide the locally consistent shape completion. We first review the existing point cloud completion, followed by point upsampling, which is the task that preserves the structure but enhance the quality by upsampling. We also compare our network with previous two-branch architecture dealing with 3D reconstruction.

Point Cloud Completion. Point cloud completion has gained recent attention as 3D acquisition becomes readily available with commodity depth sensors. There are two mainstreams for point cloud completion: supervised point completion [18,19,22,24–26,28] where the incomplete-complete pairs of point cloud data are given, and unsupervised point completion [20,21,23] without the explicit pairing of data.

The supervised network is trained to minimize the distance between the generated shape and the ground truth complete shape where Chamfer distance or Earth Mover's distance is generally chosen as the metric to compare two point clouds. The basic framework is encoder-decoder structure motivated from autoencoder, where the initial list of 3D points are encoded to make a global feature vector (GFV) from which the decoder generates point cloud.

Unsupervised shape completion uses a generative network motivated by the l-GAN framework [14] for utilizing the learned prior knowledge of the complete shapes. In addition to the distance between the input and output shapes, the unsupervised shape completion is trained with additional losses such as discriminator loss for generating plausible shape and latent space loss for the semantic similarity [20,21,23]. Even with the assistance of a generative network, the basic framework is encoder-decoder structure as the supervised case.

While the previous works share the encoder structure originated from Point-Net [29], different choices for decoder architecture have been introduced for shape completion; namely fully connected layers [14], tree-based [17,19], or 2D manifold-based [9,15] networks. Despite the progress in the decoder architecture, the encoder-decoder framework is fundamentally limited as the shape is generated from condensed global information without local guidance. As a result, the outputs are often blurry and inconsistent with the input shapes, instead of fully utilizing the clear geometric features given from the input. Our work attaches an additional network to the existing decoder architecture to complement the performance of existing shape completion and achieve the local consistency.

Point Upsampling. Point cloud upsampling increases the number of samples given the sparse set of points. While the task is not a shape completion, it creates high-resolution data capturing the local details, which resembles our complementary goal. PU-Net [10] pioneered the deep-learning-based point cloud upsampling. They proposed the "feature expansion" method implemented by separated convolutions. Another key contribution in the paper is proposing the repulsion loss to distribute the points more uniformly to alleviate the tendency for the generated points to stick to each other. Wang et al. [12] and Li et al. [13] used feature expansion but with different methods, namely code assignment inspired by the 2D manifold-based decoders [9,15]. Wang et al. [24] proposed the cascaded networks using the point upsampling networks for the point completion task. One of the strong cues they introduced is the mirror operation assuming the reflection symmetry, successfully generating recurring local structures. Their network requires additional pre-trained auto-encoder to capture the shape prior. On the other hand, our shape completion implicitly learns intrinsic symmetry without any assumptions or additional networks. We adopted the feature expansion used in the PU-Net [10] to shape completion task, and the results show that it could find the local structure of the shapes without additional loss term.

Two-Branch Network. Several works attempted to create complementary networks to deal with both local and global contexts of the point cloud shape. PSGN [8] first suggested the two-branch network generating point clouds, and suggested the different nature of the fully-connected networks and convolutional neural networks. Ours adopted the two-branch network for utilizing the local features by SAUM and the global semantic information by the existing decoders. Conceptually, our two-branch network emulates the skip-connection that observes details of original data [27] and global guidance [4]. Authors of [4] implemented global guidance by using the channel-wise concatenation of the global and local features and insisted it plays a key role in the consistent shape completion. The key difference between ours and their methods is the axis of the feature maps when concatenating them. Unlike the channel-wise feature concatenation in the skip-connection and the global guidance, ours uses point-wise concatenation of the generated outputs, which can be interpreted as the union of the point sets. The reason for the difference is the irregular nature of the point cloud representation which cannot be handled as a grid-like structure directly, whereas Han et al. [4] handle shapes in voxel grids and projected images.

3   Two-Branch Network

Given a set of incomplete point cloud P_{in}, our shape completion network creates a set of points P_{out} that is uniformly sampled on the overall shape surface. We present a two-branch network that is composed of the conventional encoder-decoder framework and the symmetry-aware upsampling module (SAUM), as shown in Fig. 1.

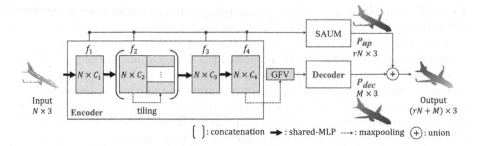

Fig. 1. The overall architecture of the two-branch network using SAUM. SAUM outputs rN points utilizing the multi-level local information. This module can be easily attached to the existing encoder-decoder architecture and the final output is a simple combination of outputs from two branches.

One of the challenges with neural network architecture using point cloud is that the structure is irregular with a varying number of inputs, N. The encoder aggregates the information from the varying number of points with maxpooling operation and find a global feature vector (GFV) with a fixed dimension. Then the decoder can use a fixed structure to regress to M points, P_{dec}. The additional SAUM branch upsamples the input P_{in} by the factor of r using multi-level features of the individual points resulting in P_{up} with rN points.

The final completed output is a set union of the two branches

$$P_{out} = P_{up} \cup P_{dec}, \qquad (1)$$

where the P_{dec} is the output of the decoder comprised of M points and the P_{out} is the combination of our two prediction branches. As a result, the two-branch network will create $rN + M$ points.

The two-branch network is jointly trained in a supervised setting, minimizing the reconstruction loss for the completed shape compared to the ground truth. The two most popular choices to evaluate the distance between two point sets are the Chamfer distance (CD) and the Earth Mover's distance. We adopted the Chamfer Distance as the reconstruction loss because it can be calculated even if the sizes of two point sets are different. Given two sets of 3D point cloud P_1 and P_2, the Chamfer Distance is defined as

$$CD(P_1, P_2) = \frac{1}{2}\Big(\frac{1}{|P_1|}\sum_{x \in P_1}\min_{y \in P_2}\|x - y\| + \frac{1}{|P_2|}\sum_{y \in P_2}\min_{x \in P_1}\|x - y\|\Big). \qquad (2)$$

We compare the raw output points P_{out} against the ground truth without further sampling, and train the entire network to minimize the reconstruction loss.

In the following, the network structures for the two branches are further explained.

3.1   Encoder-Decoder Network

Most of the previous approaches dealing with shape completion use the encoder-decoder framework, which we also utilize as one of the two branches to capture the global context from the partial data. The encoder follows the conventional structure motivated by the PointNet architecture. Specifically, features are extracted from individual points with d consecutive shared MLP layers, and we used four shared MLPs as shown in Fig. 1. Starting from the N points with three coordinates each, each MLP transforms them into $C_1, \cdots, C_d$ dimensional features, respectively. We denote the extracted $N \times C_i$ feature from the i-th layer of the encoder as f_i. Then the information from N points at the final depth d layer is combined into a single C_d dimensional vector with max-pooling operation, to which we refer as GFV.

The encoder used in our experiments is the same as Yuan *et al.* [18], which uses tiling the intermediate global feature (Fig. 1). The encoder structure is shared across different choices of decoders, and from the GFV, the decoder then regresses a list of M three dimensional points. The fine details are diluted as the global information is compressed into a single GFV.

3.2   Symmetry-Aware Upsampling Module (SAUM)

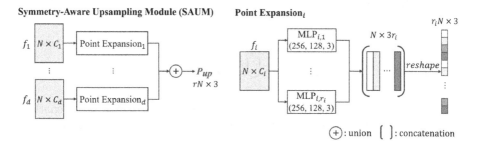

Fig. 2. SAUM architecture. The input is a list of encoder feature map $N \times C_1, \cdots, N \times C_d$, and the output is a set of rN points where $r = \sum_{i=1}^{d} r_i$ (left). SAUM is comprised of the d Point Expansion modules each of which maps the per-point features to upsampled points (right).

To complement the global context captured by the encoder-decoder network, we design a network that contains the multi-layer information of local context captured from intermediate layers of the encoder. SAUM is inspired by the U-Net architecture, which is widely used to transfer low-level features from the encoder to the decoder. The point cloud is not a regular grid structure and the direct connection between the encoder and decoder is not possible. Instead, we use the intermediate features from the encoder and create upsampling networks to find the underlying structure from various levels of abstraction.

Specifically, given the intermediate feature f_i from i-th layer, the $N \times C_i$ dimensional feature is mapped to $r_i N$ points by our *point expansion* module (Fig. 2, left). Inspired by the feature expansion operator [10], the point expansion (written as PE) module for f_i is composed of r_i units of the sequential shared MLP (Fig. 2, right):

$$PE_i(f_i) = RS([MLP_{i,1}(f_i), \cdots, MLP_{i,r_i}(f_i)]), \tag{3}$$

where

$$MLP_{i,j} = C_{i,j}^3(C_{i,j}^2(C_{i,j}^1)). \tag{4}$$

$C_{i,j}^k(\cdot)$ is a single shared MLP block, which is implemented as a 1×1 convolution, meaning that k-th block for the j-th upsampling branch of the i-th feature maps. We designed the last convolution $C_{i,j}^3(\cdot)$ for the output to have 3-dimensional channels so that it can generate a point cloud with size $N \times 3$. Thus, point expansion consists of independent upsampling branches as a special case of the feature expansion [10]. In short, we effectively use three consecutive 1×1 convolution to convert the f_i into three dimensional points for r_i units. $[\cdot]$ operator means the channel-wise feature concatenation, so the output for f_i is a tensor of size $N \times 3r_i$. $RS(\cdot)$ is a reshape operation to convert a $N \times 3r_i$ tensor to a $r_i N \times 3$ point cloud. In the end, the $PE_i(f_i)$ consists of r_i point sets which are the expanded from the i-th layer.

The final output of SAUM is P_{up} which is an union of the each expanded point set $PE_i(f_i)$

$$P_{up} = \bigcup_{i=1}^{d} \{PE_i(f_i)\}. \tag{5}$$

where the union operator $\bigcup$ can be implemented as a point-wise concatenation. Thus, P_{up} is comprised of the upsampled points of each layer, whose size is $rN \times 3$ where $r = \sum_{i=1}^{d} r_i$.

4 Experimental Setting

In this section, we discuss the datasets and the implementation details to test the performance of our suggested shape completion network.

4.1 Datasets

PCN Dataset. The PCN dataset [18] is composed of pairs of partial point cloud and corresponding complete point cloud derived from the eight categories of ShapeNet dataset [30]. Specifically, the eight categories are: airplane, cabinet, car, chair, lamp, sofa, table, and vessel and the number of the training models is 30974. The complete point clouds are created by uniformly sampling from the complete mesh, and the partial point clouds are generated by back-projecting 2.5D depth images into 3D to simulate the real-world sensor data. We used the same train/valid/test split provided by the original PCN dataset.

TopNet Dataset. The TopNet dataset [19] is composed of 28974 training models and 800 validation samples. The key difference to the PCN dataset is the number of points of ground truth: PCN dataset contains 16384 points whereas TopNet is comprised of 2048 points. Since TopNet dataset does not provide the ground truth for test data, we used the provided validation set for testing and picked 600 samples from the training data to use it as a validation set.

KITTI Dataset. The KITTI dataset, provided by [18], consists of the real-world LIDAR scans of 2401 cars. Unlike the previous two datasets, the partial point clouds in KITTI have no ground truth. Therefore we trained the networks with the car category in the ShapeNet and tested the performance in KITTI.

4.2   Implementation Details

We tested the performance of shape completion with and without the additional SAUM branch given the conventional encoder-decoder network. In all experiments we used the PointNet-based encoder that makes the best performances in [18] and [19]. We experimented on the four decoders to represent existing shape completion methods as baseline models: **FCAE** [14], **AtlasNet** [9], **PCN** [18], and **TopNet** [19]. We used $N = 2048$ for input point cloud by random sub-sampling/oversampling the points and designed all of the decoders to generate $M = 16384$ points for PCN dataset and $M = 2048$ points for TopNet dataset.

Our two-branch network is implemented by attaching our module to the baseline architectures mentioned above and jointly trained in an end-to-end manner. We chose the upsampling ratio r to be eight and two for the PCN dataset and the TopNet dataset respectively. Specifically, we set the $r_i = 2$ for $i = 1, \cdots, 4$ for PCN dataset and the $r_1 = r_2 = 1$ for TopNet dataset. The convolutional layers of the feature expansion ($C_{i,j}^1, C_{i,j}^2, C_{i,j}^3$ in Eq.(4)) are (256, 128, 3) for all experiments. For training the PCN [18], we followed the existing two-staged generation but attached SAUM only to the final output.

We implement the networks using TensorFlow and trained them on Nvidia RTX 2080 Ti and Titan RTX. All of the models are trained using Adam optimizer [31] with $\beta_1 = 0.9$ and $\beta_2 = 0.999$ for up to 300K steps with a batch size 32. The learning rate was initially chosen to be 10^{-4} and decayed by 0.7 every 50K steps. The best model was chosen based on the reconstruction loss calculated in the validation set.

4.3   Evaluation Metrics

For the evaluation of the consistent completion, we used three metrics: Chamfer Distance (CD), Earth Mover's Distance (EMD), and F-Score. We used the Eq. (2) for calculating the CD. While CD is a widely used metric to compare a pair of point sets, it is limited to represent the shape fidelity as points scattered without the correct geometric details can achieve a lower value in sum. The EMD is more sensitive metric to capture the detailed shape similarity, and is defined as:

$$EMD(P_1, P_2) = \min_{\phi: P_1 \to P_2} \frac{1}{|P_1|} \sum_{x \in P_1} \|x - \phi(x)\|_2, \tag{6}$$

where $\phi(x)$ represents the bijection from P_1 to P_2.

To demonstrate that our suggested network indeed better captures the fine structure, we adopt the F-Score suggested by recent works [28, 32] as a supplementary metric. F-Score is motivated by the IoU metric in object detection and is defined as

$$\text{F-Score(d)} = \frac{2 \cdot \text{precision}(d) \cdot \text{recall}(d)}{\text{precision}(d) + \text{recall}(d)}, \tag{7}$$

with

$$\text{precision}(d) = \frac{1}{N_{P_{out}}} \sum_{p \in P_{out}} \mathcal{I}[\min_{p' \in P_{gt}} \|p - p'\| < d] \tag{8}$$

and

$$\text{recall}(d) = \frac{1}{N_{P_{gt}}} \sum_{p' \in P_{gt}} \mathcal{I}[\min_{p \in P_{out}} \|p - p'\| < d] \tag{9}$$

where $\mathcal{I}[\cdot]$ represents an indicator function. Conceptually, precision represents the portion of the correct prediction of the reconstructed point cloud, and recall represents the reconstructed portion from the ground truth shape. The F-Score is high when both precision and recall are high.

For the KITTI dataset, which has no ground truth shape, we cannot apply the previous metrics. Instead, we adopt the Fidelity [18], which is the average distance from each point in the input to its nearest neighbor in the output for the validation of the local consistency.

5   Results

The quantitative results of SAUM-attached point cloud completion are shown in the Table 1 for PCN, TopNet, and KITTI datasets. Note that, for the fair comparison, we used farthest point sampling to sample the equal number of points for the reconstruction and the provided ground truth (16384 for PCN and 2048 for TopNet) in all of the following quantitative evaluations (Table 1, 2, 3) and visualizations (Fig. 3, 4, 6) because our network doesn't generate same number of points with the ground truth. For the distance threshold d defined in the F-Score, we chose the value roughly around the mean Chamfer Distance, $d = 10 \times 10^{-3}$ for the PCN dataset and $d = 20 \times 10^{-3}$ for the TopNet dataset respectively. The ground truth shape does not exist for the KITTI dataset, and we evaluated the Fidelity which measures how well the input is preserved [18].

Table 1. Quantitative results on the three datasets. The average CD multiplied by 10^3, EMD multiplied by 10^2, F-Score and, Fidelity are reported. The lower the CD, EMD, and Fidelity, the better. The higher the F-Score, the better. Better results are in bold.

Dataset	PCN			TopNet			KITTI
Metric	CD	EMD	F-Score	CD	EMD	F-Score	Fidelity
FCAE	9.799	17.128	0.651	22.036	14.731	0.597	0.03305
FCAE+SAUM	**8.668**	**9.015**	**0.745**	**20.295**	**8.573**	**0.654**	**0.01931**
AtlasNet	9.739	18.295	0.669	21.903	10.751	0.612	0.03505
AtlasNet+SAUM	**8.725**	**8.436**	**0.747**	**20.649**	**8.004**	**0.654**	**0.01820**
PCN	9.636	8.714	0.695	21.600	10.319	0.620	0.03382
PCN+SAUM	**8.900**	**6.631**	**0.741**	**20.400**	**7.847**	**0.665**	**0.01822**
TopNet	9.637	12.206	0.668	21.700	10.813	0.612	0.03595
TopNet+SAUM	**8.316**	**10.471**	**0.756**	**20.305**	**7.827**	**0.666**	**0.01684**

The results indicate that the attachment of SAUM boosts the performance of all existing decoders for all metrics and datasets. The improvement of EMD and F-Score, which are known to be more informative evaluation measure [14, 32], is significant with our module.

Figure 3 visualizes shape completion results of various input categories. We can observe that the existing shape completion methods (shown in red) generate approximately similar shape, but fail to preserve fine details for all of the four implementations tested. For example, the airplane tails or decorative curves at the lamp are diluted, and the points are scattered around the empty space between armrests, table legs, and mast of the ship. When there exist narrow structures or holes, points are scattered around the region, filling the space which should have been empty or deleting fine details. This phenomenon is called as the blindness of CD metric, discussed in [14]. In contrast, the SAUM-attached models (shown in green) better catch detailed local information and suffer less from the problem of the blindness of CD metric, because SAUM increases the number of points capturing the local structure. Figure 4 compares the reconstruction results against the ground truth, and indicates that the SAUM-attached networks have greater shape fidelity (lower distance to the nearest neighbor (NN)) compared to the decoder-only networks. This suggests SAUM increases the precision and the recall, and in the end increases the F-Score.

Figure 5 depicts the complementary nature of the two branches. We show the shape completion of the individual branches before the set union in addition to the final output compared against the ground truth. The upsampling of SAUM (blue) complements the global shape acquired from the decoder (red) and mainly preserves the observed details. It is interesting that our network is only trained with the reconstruction loss defined by CD, and we did not explicitly enforce the structural prior, but SAUM clearly utilizes the geometric structure of the input shape, such as reflective and rotational symmetry as shown in airplane wings or

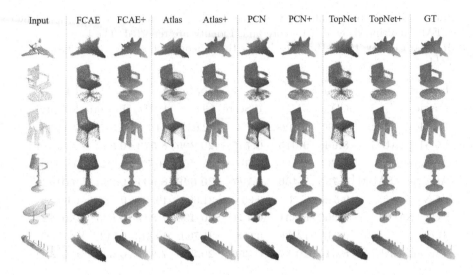

Fig. 3. Point cloud completion results of the various baselines and SAUM-attached models (post-fixed by +) on the PCN dataset. (Color figure online)

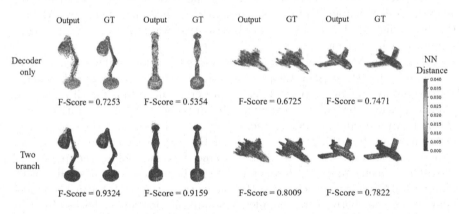

Fig. 4. Visualization of the output of neural networks and the ground truth. Each point is colored by the distance to the closest point in the other point cloud (nearest neighbor distance). The F-Score is high when both precision and recall are high, namely the ratio of blue points are high in the visualization for both of the output and the ground truth. TopNet was used for the decoder model for the lamps (left two columns) and PCN for the airplanes (right two columns).

chair legs. Note that feature expansion tends to generate points located near the original points in the upsampling task, but when applied to the completion task, it can also generate symmetric points without additional loss term. However, SAUM is not sufficient to generate global semantics of the underlying shape from partial data. Conventional decoders are trained to regress to complete shapes based on the semantic prior which compensate for the shortcomings of SAUM.

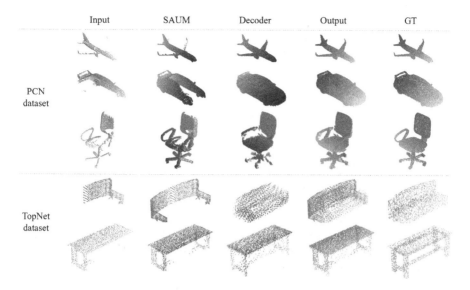

Fig. 5. Visualization of generated points from different branches, namely SAUM (blue) and decoder (red), and the union of them (green). PCN was used for the decoder. (Color figure online)

In our implementation, the joint training of SAUM and a decoder specifically utilizes the output of the decoder to predict the residual of SAUM. As a result, the two branches benefit from the complementary nature and the decoder relieves the burden of predicting complete shapes from SAUM.

Self-consistency Test. Loss of detailed geometry with existing decoders is a prevalent phenomenon regardless of the amount of incompleteness. It is due to the last maxpooling layer[24] in the encoder limiting only a fixed number of critical points and therefore the expressive power of the GFV. Even with an input that has no missing region, existing methods suffer from the bottleneck phenomenon of the performance, namely output blurry shape as ever. On the other hand, SAUM whose architecture focuses the local features can preserve the input geometry.

Motivated by the observation, we propose a self-consistency test to evaluate the consistency of the networks by using the ground truth shape as the input and comparing it with the output. We experimented with the pre-trained networks of the existing methods and SAUM-attached models on the PCN dataset. Figure 6 shows that the existing decoders cannot preserve the input geometry especially for the thin parts [18] while our SAUM not only keeps the fine details but also mitigates the decoder's hedging. Quantitative results on self-consistency test are reported in Table 2 with the same metric as shape completion: CD, EMD and F-Score. For each metric, we also reported the improvement ratio compared to the results of the original shape completion task (Table 1). The results show that the improvement ratios of SAUM-attached models are much greater than those of

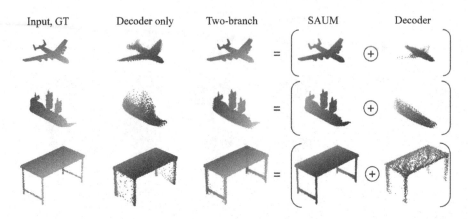

Fig. 6. Results of the self-consistency test on the PCN dataset. Note that the input is not partial shape but complete shape. TopNet was used for the decoder model for these visualizations.

Table 2. Self-consistency test on the PCN dataset. The average CD multiplied by 10^3, EMD multiplied by 10^2, F-Score for $d = 10 \times 10^{-3}$, and their improvement ratio compared to the cases of the partial input (Table 1) are reported. The lower the CD and EMD, the better and the higher the F-Score, the better. Better results are in bold.

Methods	CD	EMD	F-Score
FCAE	8.936 (8.81% ↓)	16.851 (1.62% ↓)	0.692 (6.30% ↑)
FCAE + SAUM	**6.610 (23.74% ↓)**	**3.523 (60.92% ↓)**	**0.869 (16.64% ↑)**
AtlasNet	8.801 (9.63% ↓)	17.457 (4.58% ↓)	0.718 (7.32% ↑)
AtlasNet + SAUM	**6.469 (25.86% ↓)**	**3.543 (58.00% ↓)**	**0.877 (17.40% ↑)**
PCN	8.743 (9.27% ↓)	8.231 (5.54% ↓)	0.730 (5.04% ↑)
PCN + SAUM	**6.483 (27.16% ↓)**	**3.717 (43.95% ↓)**	**0.868 (17.14% ↑)**
TopNet	8.754 (9.16% ↓)	11.653 (4.53% ↓)	0.709 (6.14% ↑)
TopNet + SAUM	**6.131 (26.27% ↓)**	**3.420 (67.34% ↓)**	**0.892 (17.99% ↑)**

the decoder-only models. The augmentation of SAUM can go beyond the inherent limitation of the representation power for the conventional encoder-decoder architecture, help to resolve the bottleneck problem, and lead to consistent shape completion.

Ablation Study. In our implementation, the base-line encoder uses encoder having four layers ($d = 4$) as suggested by previous works, and it is augmented with SAUM that is composed of the point expansion modules upsampling the points by the integer multiples of N given the intermediate features f_i ($i = 1, \cdots, d$). We change the attachment of the two-branch network and test with different upsampling ratio r and examine the quality of completed shape as an ablation study. The results using the PCN dataset are shown in Table 3. We

Table 3. Ablation study on the PCN dataset. The average CD multiplied by 10^3, EMD multiplied by 10^2 and F-Score for $d = 10 \times 10^{-3}$ are reported. The lower the CD and EMD, the better and the higher the F-Score, the better. The best performance results are in bold.

Methods	CD	EMD	F-Score
SAUM (×4) only	10.928	33.164	0.589
SAUM (×8) only	**9.832**	**23.081**	**0.658**
FCAE	9.799	17.128	0.651
FCAE+SAUM (×4)	8.816	14.383	0.721
FCAE+SAUM (×8)	**8.668**	**9.015**	**0.745**
AtlasNet	9.739	18.295	0.669
AtlasNet+SAUM (×4)	8.756	13.477	0.732
AtlasNet+SAUM (×8)	**8.725**	**8.436**	**0.747**
PCN	9.636	8.714	0.695
PCN+SAUM (×4)	**8.898**	7.366	0.737
PCN+SAUM (×8)	8.900	**6.631**	**0.741**
TopNet	9.637	12.206	0.668
TopNet+SAUM (×4)	8.785	11.376	0.731
TopNet+SAUM (×8)	**8.316**	**10.471**	**0.756**

first tested the performance of SAUM only without the encoder-decoder, and the performance is worse than most of the encoder-decoder baseline. Therefore, SAUM cannot generate plausible shape by itself, suggesting that the balance of SAUM and the existing decoders is important for consistent point cloud completion. As before, the attachment of SAUM enhances the quality of shape completion when applied jointly for all of the baseline networks. We also compare the effect of different upsampling ratio with $r = 4$ and $r = 8$. SAUM can complement the local consistency of the existing methods, improving the consistency with increasing r. The performance gain is more significant for EMD than CD, and we argue the EMD better captures the shape fidelity.

6   Conclusion

We propose SAUM, the symmetry-aware upsampling module that can be augmented to existing shape completion methods. Conventional shape completion methods are comprised of a decoder structure that generates unseen points based on semantic information condensed within a global feature vector and often fails to preserve local information. SAUM, on the other hand, utilizes the fine structure from the partial observation in addition to the latent symmetric structure. We suggest a two-branch architecture where the baseline decoder is attached with SAUM, which greatly improves the performance of the baseline. The two branches are complementary and in union generate globally consistent and completed shape, while maintaining the observed local structures.

Acknowledgements. This work was supported by the New Faculty Startup Fund from Seoul National University, KIST institutional program [Project No. 2E29450] and the National Research Foundation of Korea (NRF) grant funded by the Korea government (MSIT) (No. 2020R1C1C1008195).

References

1. Varley, J., DeChant, C., Richardson, A., Ruales, J., Allen, P.K.: Shape completion enabled robotic grasping. In: 2017 IEEE/RSJ International Conference on Intelligent Robots and Systems, IROS 2017, Vancouver, BC, Canada, 24–28 September 2017, pp. 2442–2447 (2017)
2. Cadena, C., et al.: Past, Present, and future of simultaneous localization and mapping: toward the robust-perception age. IEEE Trans. Robotics **32**, 1309–1332 (2016)
3. Dai, A., Qi, C.R., Nießner, M.: Shape completion using 3D-encoder-predictor CNNs and shape synthesis. In: 2017 IEEE Conference on Computer Vision and Pattern Recognition, CVPR 2017, Honolulu, HI, USA, 21–26 July 2017, pp. 6545–6554 (2017)
4. Han, X., Li, Z., Huang, H., Kalogerakis, E., Yu, Y.: High-resolution shape completion using deep neural networks for global structure and local geometry inference. In: IEEE International Conference on Computer Vision, ICCV, pp. 85–93 (2017)
5. Stutz, D., Geiger, A.: Learning 3D shape completion from laser scan data with weak supervision. In: 2018 IEEE Conference on Computer Vision and Pattern Recognition, CVPR 2018, Salt Lake City, UT, USA, 18–22 June 2018, pp. 1955–1964 (2018)
6. Mao, J., Wang, X., Li, H.: Interpolated convolutional networks for 3D point cloud understanding. In: The IEEE International Conference on Computer Vision (ICCV) (2019)
7. Wang, Z., Lu, F.: VoxSegNet: volumetric CNNs for semantic part segmentation of 3D shapes. IEEE Trans. Vis. Comput. Graph. **26**, 2919–2930 (2019)
8. Fan, H., Su, H., Guibas, L.J.: A point set generation network for 3D object reconstruction from a single image. In: 2017 IEEE Conference on Computer Vision and Pattern Recognition, CVPR, pp. 2463–2471 (2017)
9. Groueix, T., Fisher, M., Kim, V.G., Russell, B.C., Aubry, M.: A Papier-Mâché approach to learning 3D surface generation. In: The IEEE Conference on Computer Vision and Pattern Recognition (CVPR) (2018)
10. Yu, L., Li, X., Fu, C., Cohen-Or, D., Heng, P.: PU-Net: point cloud upsampling network. In: 2018 IEEE Conference on Computer Vision and Pattern Recognition, CVPR, pp. 2790–2799 (2018)
11. Yu, L., Li, X., Fu, C.-W., Cohen-Or, D., Heng, P.-A.: EC-Net: an edge-aware point set consolidation network. In: Ferrari, V., Hebert, M., Sminchisescu, C., Weiss, Y. (eds.) ECCV 2018. LNCS, vol. 11211, pp. 398–414. Springer, Cham (2018). https://doi.org/10.1007/978-3-030-01234-2_24
12. Wang, Y., Wu, S., Huang, H., Cohen-Or, D., Sorkine-Hornung, O.: Patch-based progressive 3D point set upsampling. In: IEEE Conference on Computer Vision and Pattern Recognition, CVPR, pp. 5958–5967 (2019)

13. Li, R., Li, X., Fu, C.W., Cohen-Or, D., Heng, P.A.: PU-GAN: a point cloud upsampling adversarial network. In: The IEEE International Conference on Computer Vision (ICCV) (2019)
14. Achlioptas, P., Diamanti, O., Mitliagkas, I., Guibas, L.J.: Learning representations and generative models for 3D point clouds. In: Proceedings of the 35th International Conference on Machine Learning, ICML, pp. 40–49 (2018)
15. Yang, Y., Feng, C., Shen, Y., Tian, D.: FoldingNet: point cloud auto-encoder via deep grid deformation. In: 2018 IEEE Conference on Computer Vision and Pattern Recognition, CVPR, pp. 206–215 (2018)
16. Yang, G., Huang, X., Hao, Z., Liu, M.Y., Belongie, S., Hariharan, B.: PointFlow: 3D point cloud generation with continuous normalizing flows. In: The IEEE International Conference on Computer Vision (ICCV) (2019)
17. Shu, D.W., Park, S.W., Kwon, J.: 3D point cloud generative adversarial network based on tree structured graph convolutions. In: The IEEE International Conference on Computer Vision (ICCV) (2019)
18. Yuan, W., Khot, T., Held, D., Mertz, C., Hebert, M.: PCN: point completion network. In: Proceedings of 2018 International Conference on 3D Vision (3DV) (2018)
19. Tchapmi, L.P., Kosaraju, V., Rezatofighi, H., Reid, I., Savarese, S.: TopNet: structural point cloud decoder. In: The IEEE Conference on Computer Vision and Pattern Recognition (CVPR) (2019)
20. Gurumurthy, S., Agrawal, S.: High fidelity semantic shape completion for point clouds using latent optimization. In: IEEE Winter Conference on Applications of Computer Vision, WACV, pp. 1099–1108 (2019)
21. Sarmad, M., Lee, H.J., Kim, Y.M.: RL-GAN-Net: a reinforcement learning agent controlled GAN network for real-time point cloud shape completion. In: The IEEE Conference on Computer Vision and Pattern Recognition (CVPR) (2019)
22. Liu, M., Sheng, L., Yang, S., Shao, J., Hu, S.: Morphing and sampling network for dense point cloud completion. In: The Thirty-Fourth AAAI Conference on Artificial Intelligence, AAAI 2020, The Thirty-Second Innovative Applications of Artificial Intelligence Conference, IAAI 2020, The Tenth AAAI Symposium on Educational Advances in Artificial Intelligence, EAAI 2020, New York, NY, USA, 7–12 February 2020, pp. 11596–11603. AAAI Press (2020)
23. Chen, X., Chen, B., Mitra, N.J.: Unpaired point cloud completion on real scans using adversarial training. In: 8th International Conference on Learning Representations, ICLR 2020, Addis Ababa, Ethiopia, 26–30 April 2020. OpenReview.net (2020)
24. Wang, X., M.H.A.J., Lee, G.H.: Cascaded refinement network for point cloud completion. In: IEEE/CVF Conference on Computer Vision and Pattern Recognition (CVPR) (2020)
25. Huang, Z., Yu, Y., Xu, J., Ni, F., Le, X.: PF-Net: point fractal network for 3D point cloud completion. In: IEEE/CVF Conference on Computer Vision and Pattern Recognition (CVPR) (2020)
26. Wen, X., Li, T., Han, Z., Liu, Y.S.: Point cloud completion by skip-attention network with hierarchical folding. In: IEEE/CVF Conference on Computer Vision and Pattern Recognition (CVPR) (2020)
27. Ronneberger, O., Fischer, P., Brox, T.: U-Net: convolutional networks for biomedical image segmentation. In: Navab, N., Hornegger, J., Wells, W.M., Frangi, A.F. (eds.) MICCAI 2015. LNCS, vol. 9351, pp. 234–241. Springer, Cham (2015). https://doi.org/10.1007/978-3-319-24574-4_28

28. Xie, H., Yao, H., Zhou, S., Mao, J., Zhang, S., Sun, W.: GRNet: gridding residual network for dense point cloud completion. CoRR abs/2006.03761 (2020)
29. Qi, C.R., Su, H., Mo, K., Guibas, L.J.: PointNet: deep learning on point sets for 3D classification and segmentation. In: 2017 IEEE Conference on Computer Vision and Pattern Recognition, CVPR, pp. 77–85 (2017)
30. Chang, A.X., et al.: Shapenet: an information-rich 3D model repository. CoRR abs/1512.03012 (2015)
31. Kingma, D.P., Ba, J.: Adam: A Method for Stochastic Optimization. In: 3rd International Conference on Learning Representations, ICLR (2015)
32. Tatarchenko, M., Richter, S.R., Ranftl, R., Li, Z., Koltun, V., Brox, T.: What do single-view 3D reconstruction networks learn? (2019)

Faster Self-adaptive Deep Stereo

Haiyang Wang[1], Xinchao Wang[2], Jie Song[1], Jie Lei[1], and Mingli Song[1(✉)]

[1] Zhejiang University, Hangzhou, China
{haiyang.wang,sjie,ljaylei,brooksong}@zju.edu.cn
[2] Stevens Institute of Technology, Hoboken, NJ, USA
xinchao.wang@stevens.edu

Abstract. Fueled by the power of deep learning, stereo vision has made unprecedented advances in recent years. Existing deep stereo models, however, can be hardly deployed to real-world scenarios where the data comes on-the-fly without any ground-truth information, and the data distribution continuously changes over time. Recently, Tonioni et al. proposed the first real-time self-adaptive deep stereo system (MADNet) to address this problem, which, however, still runs at a relatively low speed with not so satisfactory performance. In this paper, we significantly upgrade their work in both speed and accuracy by incorporating two key components. First, instead of adopting only the image reconstruction loss as the proxy supervision, a second more powerful supervision is proposed, termed Knowledge Reverse Distillation (KRD), to guide the learning of deep stereo models. Second, we introduce a straightforward yet surprisingly effective Adapt-or-Hold (AoH) mechanism to automatically determine whether or not to fine-tune the stereo model in the online environment. Both components are lightweight and can be integrated into MADNet with only a few lines of code. Experiments demonstrate that the two proposed components improve the system by a large margin in both speed and accuracy. Our final system is twice as fast as MADNet, meanwhile attains considerable superior performance on the popular benchmark datasets KITTI.

Keywords: Stereo matching · Self-supervised · Real-time

1 Introduction

Environment depth information is key to many applications such as autonomous driving and mobile robotics. Compared with technologies such as LIDAR, Structured Light and Time-of-Flight, stereo is competitive in practical application scenarios due to its lower cost, higher resolution and better universality for almost

This work is supported by National Natural Science Foundation of China (61976186), the Major Scientfic Research Project of Zhejiang Lab (No. 2019KD0AC01) and Alibaba-Zhejiang University Joint Research Institute of Frontier Technologies.

Electronic supplementary material The online version of this chapter (https://doi.org/10.1007/978-3-030-69525-5_11) contains supplementary material, which is available to authorized users.

© Springer Nature Switzerland AG 2021
H. Ishikawa et al. (Eds.): ACCV 2020, LNCS 12622, pp. 175–191, 2021.
https://doi.org/10.1007/978-3-030-69525-5_11

Fig. 1. Disparity maps predicted by AoHNet on KITTI sequence [9]. Given the source images (a), AoHNet exploits the traditional stereo method [10] as a second supervision (b) to quickly adapt to the new real scenario (c).

any environment. Many traditional stereo algorithms have been proposed in recent decades. However, most of these algorithms are limited to specific conditions (e.g., occlusions, texture-less areas, photometric distortions). Since Mayer et al. [1] proposed the first end-to-end stereo network DispNet, using convolutional neural networks (CNNs) to regress depth maps from images directly has become a dominant paradigm for stereo matching and is followed by many state-of-the-art stereo methods [2–5].

However, existing deep learning-based stereo methods always suffer from the domain shift problem where accuracy drops dramatically when the domain of testing data is different from that of training data [6]. Fine-tuning on the target domain can solve the above problem, but obtaining aligned label data often requires a large cost. [6,7] propose to generalize deep stereo to novel domains without the need of labels. However, they assume that the data of the target domain is available in advance while in the real world the data domain usually changes over time. Recently, Tonioni et al. [8] proposed the first real-time self-adaptive deep stereo system (MADNet) towards addressing the above problem. They cast the adaption as a continuous learning process and proposed a lightweight, fast and modular architecture (MADNet) together with a tailored training algorithm, termed Modular ADaptation (MAD) to improve the running speed. To bypass the unsupervised problem, they adopt image reconstruction loss as the proxy objective to train the model.

In this work, we significantly upgrade their method in both accuracy and speed based on two key insights. Firstly, MADNet only adopts image reconstruction loss as the proxy supervision. Albeit effective to some degree, this proxy objective requires a relatively long time (about 900 frames) to adapt the deep stereo model to a new scenario. To address this problem, a second supervision objective is proposed, termed Knowledge Reverse Distillation (KRD), to enhance the adaption process of the deep stereo model. In KRD, our goal is somewhat opposite to traditional KD: we leverage the noisy predictions from lightweight traditional models (teachers) as supervision to guide the learning of the deep stereo model (student), and make the student surpass the teacher. As the KRD loss is more calibrated to the goal than image reconstruction loss, the adaption process with the KRD loss takes less time (about 400 frames in our experiments) than with solely the image reconstruction loss. Figure 1 shows that with the supervision of KRD, AoHNet can quickly adapt to the new real scenario from a synthetic scenario and solve most of the mistakes within 50 frames.

Secondly, it can be found that the ceaseless fine-tuning of the deep stereo model in the online environment has two huge weaknesses. One is dropping the network running speed to a third, which is unbearable for real-world applications. The other is hurt the accuracy of the system, as the model will become over-fitted if it continues to train in the adapted environment. Thus we devise an extremely lightweight yet surprisingly effective Adapt-or-Hold (AoH) mechanism. The AoH mechanism is implemented by a Deep Q-Network (DQN) based on reinforcement learning. In every frame, the DQN directly decide whether to adapt or hold according to the input state. As it is really micro so incurs nearly no additional overhead into the system. Experiments conducted on KITTI [9] demonstrate that with AoH mechanism, our method achieves superior accuracy than MADNet. Even the deep stereo model adapts itself on only 10% of the frames, which meanwhile speeds up our system to about 29 FPS, one time faster than MADNet.

In summary, we make the following contributions:

- We introduce the Knowledge Reverse Distillation, a more powerful supervision than image reconstruction loss, to transfer deep stereo models to new scenarios without any ground-truth information.
- We propose an Adapt-or-Hold mechanism that allows the deep stereo model to hold or adapt itself automatically in the online environment. This mechanism improves not only the speed but also the accuracy of the system.
- Experimental results demonstrate that the proposed online system works about one time faster than its predecessor MADNet, meanwhile attains significantly superior accuracy on the popular benchmark KITTI.

2   Related Work

Here we briefly review some of the most related topics, including traditional stereo algorithms, supervised stereo algorithms, self-supervised depth estimation and deep reinforcement learning.

Traditional Stereo Algorithms. Researches have recently proposed many methods for the stereo matching, which finds its application in a wide domain of computer vision tasks [11–14]. Such algorithms usually involve four steps: i) matching cost computation, ii) cost aggregation, iii) disparity optimization/computation, and iv) disparity refinement. Scharstein et al. [15] divided these algorithms into two parts: local algorithms and global algorithms. Local algorithms firstly define a support window and an evaluation function, and then aggregate matching costs over the window. Global algorithms usually establish a loss function that combines matching cost terms and smoothness terms on the whole image, and then solves it using graph-based methods [16–18]. Thus, they often perform better than the local algorithm in quality and stability. However, global algorithms often rely on multiple iterations, which are challenging to be done in real-time. An excellent trade-off between accuracy and execution time is represented by ELAS [10] which is a Bayesian approach proposing a generative probabilistic model for stereo matching. It can compute accurate disparity of images at frame rates close to real-time.

Supervised Stereo Methods. Zbontar and LeCun [19] firstly applied deep learning in stereo vision by replacing the matching cost computation with a Siamese CNN learning similarity on small image patches. However, it still needs a series of post-processes. DispNet [1] was the first end-to-end stereo network that broke the pipeline in [15] by regressing the depth map from two images directly. GCNet [20] leverages the knowledge of the problem's geometry to form a cost volume and learns to incorporate contextual information using 3-D convolutions over this volume. Other works [2–5] following end-to-end stereo architectures outperform previous methods by building more complex architectures. However, the methods above all focus on accuracy with little consideration of speed and require a lot of training data with ground truth, which is not suitable in practical application scenarios [21–26].

Self-supervised Depth Estimation. Depth estimation in a self-supervised way is popular recently as it overcomes the shortcoming of requiring a large number of annotations. Some methods [27–29] make use of image reconstruction loss to drive the network in an unsupervised way. This loss is calculated from warping different views, coming from stereo pairs or image sequences. [6] proposed to adopt the off-the-shelf stereo algorithms together with a confidence estimator network CCNN [30] to fine-tune the network offline. A Deep Recurrent Neural Network with LSTM blocks [31] was proposed, which was able to adapt between different scenarios seamlessly, but it doesn't take speed into account for requiring 0.8–1.6 s for inference. Tonioni et al. [8] proposed the first real-time self-adaptive deep stereo system which only used image reconstruction loss. However, as shown in [32], the photometric loss is not a good choice for stereo problems. Different from [8], we propose an additional supervision obtained by the traditional algorithm to enhance the adaption process. What's more, a straightforward and efficient way is proposed to extract the high confidence pixels of the traditional algorithm without the need for additional networks.

Deep Reinforcement Learning. Since the first deep reinforcement learning model [33], termed Deep Q-Network (DQN), successfully learn control policies in Atari game, deep reinforcement learning has attracted the attention of many researchers. [34] adds a Target Q network to compute the target values, which reduces the correlations between the action-values and the target values. Other methods such as prioritized experience replay [35], double DQN [36], dueling DQN [37] are proposed to improve the performance of deep reinforcement learning. Because of the excellent performance of deep reinforcement learning in control policy problems, we make use of it to decide whether the stereo model needs to be fine-tuned or not in the online environment.

3   Methodology

Starting with a pre-trained deep stereo model (e.g., pre-trained on the synthetic data [1]), our goal is to deploy this stereo model to real-world applications where 1) no ground-truth information is available along with the raw data; 2) the

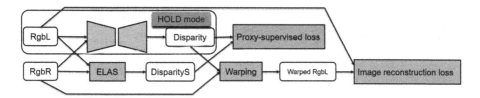

Fig. 2. An illustration of the self-supervised adaption framework. The white rectangles represent image data, the orange rectangle represents the network to be trained, the blue rectangles represent the traditional algorithm and the green rectangles represent the loss functions. (Color figure online)

data distribution in the current scenario is different from that of the training data used for pre-training the deep stereo model; 3) the scenarios may change continuously over the time. Thus, a *real-time, self-supervised* and *self-adaptive* system is needed to tackle all the aforementioned problems.

3.1   The Overall Framework

The overall framework of the proposed system is illustrated in Fig. 2. In order to avoid the loss of speed and accuracy caused by adapting the network all the time, we devised the AoH mechanism to enable the system to work in two modes: the ADAPT mode and the HOLD mode.

When the deep stereo model has been fully adapted to the current scenario, our system works in the HOLD mode. In this mode, the deep stereo model conducts only the inference process: fed with paired frames, outputting the stereo predictions. As no back-propagation is involved, the system works especially fast in this mode. If the scenario changes, the system will switch to the ADAPT mode. In this mode, the system will not only infer the stereo information of the current frames but also adapt itself to the new scenario by computing the loss and perform back-propagation. To speed up the adaption process of the deep stereo model for being rapidly switched to the more efficient HOLD mode, we propose the KRD objective to facilitate the adaption of the deep stereo model.

Now, the detailed description of the proposed KRD objective and the AoH mechanism is provided.

3.2   Knowledge Reverse Distillation

KRD is devised to remedy the incapability of the image reconstruction loss for adapting the deep stereo model to new scenarios. The goal of KRD is that by learning from the noisy predictions of the lightweight teacher, the student can overcome the shortcomings of the teacher so thus surpass the teacher after learning. We adopt the ELAS algorithm [10] as the teacher. ELAS is a lightweight, fast and general-purpose stereo algorithm that does not require any adaptation to be deployed in different scenarios. Though ELAS generates accurate disparity

Fig. 3. Examples of proxy labels computed by ELAS, left image (a), disparity map processed only by left-right consistency detection (b), and the sparse disparity map after low-texture areas removal (c).

at most pixels, there are still many unreliable predictions. A network trained on the raw output of the traditional algorithm would learn the inherent short-comings of it. Therefore, two remedies are proposed to help the student stereo model overcome the weakness of ELAS and finally surpass it in performance. Firstly, a lightweight confidence measure is proposed to quantify the reliability of predictions of every pixel efficiently. With this confidence measure, predictions with low confidence will be masked so that they will not contribute to the total loss. Secondly, we don't abandon the image reconstruction loss as well. The deep stereo model is supervised by both the KRD loss and image reconstruction loss. The synergy between these two losses pulls the model out of their weaknesses. Now, a more detailed description of these two remedies will be given.

Confidence Measure. Specifically, we mask two types of predictions (shown in Fig. 3): 1) those do not pass the left-right consistency detection, like the pixels removed in (b); and 2) those of pixels which lie in low-texture regions, e.g.., the sky in (c). The texture is calculated as the sum of the Sobel filter values of the pixels within the defined window, which is defined in [10]. The predictions of low-texture regions are masked for two considerations. On the one hand, Elas has the same disadvantages as traditional algorithms, that is, poor performance in the low-texture areas. For example, the area near the street lamp on the left and the sky area connected to the tree on the right in Fig. 3, which can not be detected in left-right consistency detection. On the other hand, from the perspective of model learning, pixels in low-texture regions are usually large in amount and their stereo predictions provide redundant supervision. A large amount of redundant supervision will overwhelm the objective, making the student learning bias to low-texture regions.

Given an input stereo pair I_l and I_r, we obtain the left and right disparity maps D_l and D_r. For all pixels p in the original disparity map D_l, if the texture of the pixel $texture(p)$ is lower than the threshold β or the left-right consistency detection $|D_l(p) - D_r(p - D_l(p))|$ is larger than the threshold δ, the disparity values are masked:

$$M(p) = \begin{cases} 0, & texture(p) \leq \beta \\ 0, & |D_l(p) - D_r(p - D_l(p))| \geq \delta. \\ 1, & otherwise \end{cases} \tag{1}$$

Synergy Between KRD and Image Reconstruction Loss. We adopt both the KRD loss and the image reconstruction loss to adapt our stereo model to new scenarios. The overall objective is:

$$L = L_R + \lambda L_{KRD}, \tag{2}$$

where L_{KRD} represents the KRD loss and L_R represents the image reconstruction loss. λ is the hyper-parameter trading off these two loss. The KRD loss is defined to be the average ℓ_1 distance between disparity maps from our model D and ELAS algorithm D_{ELAS}:

$$L_{KRD} = \frac{1}{|M|} |M \odot (D - D_{ELAS})|. \tag{3}$$

M is the binary matrix introduced in Eq. 1, and $|M|$ denotes the number of all valid pixels in D_{ELAS}. Image reconstruction loss is obtained by computing the discrepancy between the left image I_l and the reconstructed left image I_l' from the right image and the left disparity map. Following [28], we use a combination of ℓ_1 and single scale SSIM [38] as our image reconstruction loss L_R.

$$L_R = \frac{1}{N} \sum_p \alpha \frac{1 - SSIM(I_l(p), I_l'(p))}{2} + (1 - \alpha) \cdot |I_l(p) - I_l'(p)|. \tag{4}$$

N denotes the number of all pixels in the image and p represents each pixel.

3.3   The Adapt-or-Hold Mechanism

Keeping the model always adapting in the online environment heavily reduces the real-time responsiveness of our system. Worse, it also decreases the accuracy of the system. Here we introduce the proposed AoH mechanism which enables our system to automatically switch between the ADAPT mode and the HOLD model, which significantly improves the system in both speed and accuracy.

Markov Decision Process. We define AoH mechanism as a Markov Decision Process that contains state, action, and reward. According to the input state, the agent chooses one action from action space and gets the corresponding reward. Here are the definitions. The state should contain enough information to enable the agent to select a good action. Image reconstruction loss can reflect whether the model parameters are suitable in the online environment, and the computation is small compared with KRD. Therefore, we define the state as the image reconstruction loss of the last ten frames. The action space is clearly defined as two discrete options, ADAPT or HOLD. Reward is used to evaluate the results of the action taken by the agent. Here, image reconstruction loss L_R and time consumption T are both considered. If the agent chooses the action of ADAPT, T is set to -1, otherwise it is 1. By adjusting the weight κ between image reconstruction loss and time consumption, the percentage of adaption can be controlled. Here. The reward equation is as follows:

$$R = \frac{1}{e^{L_R}} + \kappa T. \tag{5}$$

Deep Q-Network. We use the DQN proposed in [34] to train the agent and improve the performance by referring to [36]. The DQN is a combination of deep learning and Q-learning, using DNN to predict the Q value $Q(s, a)$ of each action a for the input state s. There are two networks in DQN, one called target_net, to get the value of q_{target}, and the other, called eval_net, to get the value of q_{eval}. The target_net parameters θ^- are only updated with the eval_net parameters θ every few steps and are keep fixed between individual updates. This reduces the correlations between the q_{eval} and the q_{target} and significantly improved the stability of learning. The q_{target} is defined as:

$$q_{target} = r + \gamma Q(s', argmax_a(s', a; \theta); \theta^-), \tag{6}$$

where r is the reward, γ is the discount factor, s' represents the state of next step. The loss function is defined as the difference between q_{target} and q_{eval}:

$$Loss(\theta) = E[(r + \gamma Q(s', argmax_a(s', a; \theta); \theta^-) - Q(s, a; \theta))^2]. \tag{7}$$

The training data is randomly extracted from the memory buffer, where each record (s, a, r, s') includes the current state, action, corresponding reward, and next state. The size of memory buffer is limited, so the records will be overwritten as the network updates. By randomly extracting records from memory for learning, the correlation between experiences is disrupted, making the neural network updating more efficient.

4   Experiment

In this section, we first describe the implementation details and then conduct benchmark comparisons with our teacher algorithm ELAS, a supervised algorithm DispNet and a online self-adaptive algorithm MADNet. After that, we performed some ablation experiments to prove the effectiveness of KRD and AOH. For the KRD, we compare the performance of different loss functions. These experiments are made on two different kinds of datasets, one is KITTI 2012 and KITTI 2015 which provides discrete images, but the label has a higher density. The other is a continuous video of [9], which is more suitable for online learning. In the meantime, we make an experiment to analyze the sparsity and accuracy of the preserved predicted labels under different texture threshold. As for AOH, we designed a detailed comparison experiment, including not only fine-tuning in advance and adapting all the time, but also three other typical strategies are designed. The details will be shown below.

4.1   Implementation Details

We adopt MADNet [8] as the backbone of the proposed AoHNet. In order to achieve the real-time performance of the ELAS algorithm, we reduce the input image to a quarter, calculate the disparity map, and finally linear interpolation to the original resolution. In our experiments, the texture threshold β is set to 50, left-right consistency threshold δ is 2 and the hyper-parameter λ trading off two loss objectives is 0.1. Following [28], α in L_R is 0.85.

The micro DQN only contains two hidden layers with 20 and 10 units respectively, followed by ReLU activation. The output layer has 2 nodes with no activation. The action chosen is determined according to the Q-function, which has the maximum value. The DQN is trained on the KITTI raw [9] in advance. The weight coefficient κ between image reconstruction loss and time consumption is set to 0.02. As for training, We set 5,000 as memory buffer size and 32 as batch size. 1000 pre-training steps are preceded to gather experience replay buffer. ϵ-greedy and the discount factor γ are set to 0.9. ϵ-greedy means the action is selected according to the learned network by the probability of ϵ and is randomly selected by the probability of $1 - \epsilon$. The target_net updates every 1000 steps. An RMSProp optimizer was used with a learning rate of 0.001.

Unless otherwise specified, for all experiments involved in this paper, the weights pre-trained on synthetic data [1] are used as a common initialization and evaluate the proposed method on real datasets KITTI [9,39,40]. As there is the same number of labeled images and unlabeled images in the training set of KITTI 2012 and KITTI 2015. We use unlabeled images to train and labeled images to test. For all experiments, both average End Point Error (EPE) and the percentage of pixels with disparity error larger than 3 (D1-all) are analyzed. Since the image format of each sequence is different, a central crop with a size of 320 × 1216 is extracted from each frame as proposed in [8]. Finally, we use Adam as the optimizer with a constant learning rate equal to 0.0001.

4.2   Benchmark Comparison

In this section, we conduct benchmark comparisons to demonstrate the superiority of AoHNet. We compare AoHNet with the following competitors: (1) ELAS [10], our teacher, a fast and relatively accurate traditional method; (2) DispNet [1], a supervised algorithm that uses ground-truth labels for training directly; (3) MADNet [8], the first online stereo method. (4) Recent self-supervised stereo methods. The network parameters of DispNet is obtained from [8] which have been fine-tuned on KITTI. For both MADnet and AoHNet, the networks are pre-trained on the synthetic data [1] and then fine-tuned on the unlabeled data of KITTI in a self-supervised way. Finally, we evaluate the performance of all algorithms on the labeled data of KITTI 2012 and KITTI 2015.

Experimental results are provided in Table 1. It can be seen that: (1) Compared with deep stereo models, the traditional algorithm ELAS [10] produces a much larger error in both KITTI 2012 and KITTI 2015; (2) The proposed model, albeit trained online in a self-supervised way, outperforms DispNet trained with ground-truth information, which means that our self-supervised method can even be comparable to some supervised methods; (3) Compared with MADNet, our approach exhibits significantly superior performance in both precision and speed thanks to the KRD loss and the AoH mechanism. (4) The SOTA [43] achieves the smallest D1-all error. Despite the higher accuracy, it runs 20 times slower

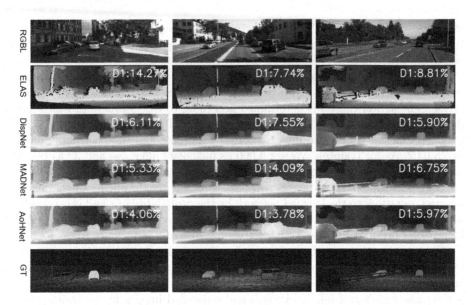

Fig. 4. Quantitative comparison of different methods on KITTI 2015.

Table 1. Comparison of different algorithms in KITTI 2012 and KITTI 2015.

KITTI	ELAS [10]	DispNet [1]	MADNet [8]	Zhou [41]	Li [42]	Aleotti [43]	AoHNet
2012 D1-all	17.12	9.53	9.25	9.91	8.60	–	8.64
2015 D1-all	14.78	7.87	8.53	–	8.98	4.06	7.76
FPS	3.34	16.67	14.26	2.56	1.37	2.44	28.95

than AoHNet. Besides, as it requires a monocular completion network to provide proxy labels in addition to the conventional algorithm, making it cumbersome to deploy in a real-time changing environment.

Figure 4 visualizes some examples produced by the above algorithms in three different scenarios on the KITTI 2015 dataset, from left to right are "City", "Resident" and "Road". The D1-all error is shown in the right corner of the disparity maps. As is shown in Fig. 4, the disparity maps generated by DispNet has a precise shape and smooth edges, but the overall error is somewhat significant. AoHNet yields lower total error and preserves better results in detail. For example, the isolation barrier in the middle of the road on the right image.

4.3 Ablation Study

In this section, we conduct ablation studies to validate the effectiveness of the KRD loss and AoH mechanism proposed in the paper.

Table 2. Comparison of different loss objectives on KITTI.

Model	Color	KITTI 2012			KITTI 2015		
		Frames	D1-all (%)	EPE	Frames	D1-all (%)	EPE
MADNet	Color	330	9.47	1.51	250	9.63	1.71
+KRD	Color	290	9.19	1.37	210	9.41	1.75
AoHNet⁻	Color	240	8.94	1.41	200	9.25	1.65
MADNet	Gray	150	7.49	1.31	190	7.98	1.39
+KRD	Gray	110	7.11	1.25	160	7.60	1.36
AoHNet⁻	Gray	**90**	**7.05**	**1.19**	**70**	**7.58**	**1.32**

With Versus Without KRD. In our method, we propose to adopt the KRD loss, together with the image reconstruction loss, to guide the learning of the deep stereo model. Table 2 reports the comparison of different loss objectives. MAD-Net [8] only uses image reconstruction loss as the self-supervised loss. "+KRD" means only using KRD loss and AoHNet⁻ means to adopt KRD loss together with image reconstruction loss, but AoH mechanism is removed. Here "Frames" means the number of frames required by the network to be adapted to KITTI from synthetic data [1] (If the accuracy is not improved after ten consecutive evaluations, the network is considered to have been adapted to the new scenario).

In [8], all experiments were performed on color images. However, we find that the network performs better on gray images than color images. Gray images means three channels are the same. We provide experimental results on both color images and gray images. On KITTI 2012, MADNet requires 330 frames to be fully adapted to the new scenario on the color images. However, less than half of the frames (150 frames) are needed on the gray images, and the D1-all error is lower.

To find out whether image reconstruction loss is still needed as supervision, we also do experiments that only used KRD loss. Table 2 shows that the performance of only using KRD loss is better than that of only using image reconstruction loss but slightly worse than that of the combination of the two losses. It may be because KRD loss only provides sparse supervision, and image reconstruction loss can help to learn the missing part of them.

Due to the use of a more powerful supervision KRD, no matter in color images or gray images, AoHNet⁻ is superior to MADNet in both the adaption speed and the accuracy. Finally, we only need less than 100 frames (90 frames in KITTI 2012 and 70 frames in KITTI 2015) to adjust the network from one domain to another. This implies that KRD loss not only improves the accuracy of the network but also makes the network adapting to new scenarios faster.

We also make experiments on a continuous video to analyze the effectiveness of KRD. Figure 5 plots the D1-all error across frame for MADNet and AoHNet⁻ on the 2011_09_30_drive_0028_sync sequence which is a 2500 frames residential video of KITTI [9]. The three color lines represent the three patterns. The red line presents the performance of MADNet fine-turned offline on KITTI, which is

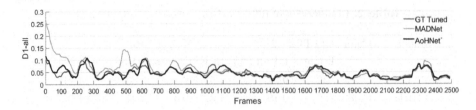

Fig. 5. D1-all error across frames on the 2011_09_30_drive_0028_sync sequence. (Color figure online)

Table 3. The performance of different texture thresholds on KITTI 2015.

Sparsity	NO	LR	S20	S50	S80	S100
Density (%)	77.56	71.71	61.33	43.64	32.54	27.20
D1-all (%)	4.43	4.79	4.23	**3.42**	3.43	3.48
Deep-D1-all (%)	7.72	7.72	8.28	**7.68**	7.80	8.05

used as a benchmark for comparison. The green and blue lines represent MADnet and AoHNet$^-$ respectively. The parameters of them are initialized on synthetic data [1]. Both lines improve their performances by back-propagation. After a period of adaption, they achieve comparable performance to the offline fine-tuned model (red). It shows that MADNet (green) needs about 900 frames to reach the similar performance to fine-tuning, while AoHNet$^-$ (blue) only needs less than 400 frames with the help of KRD loss.

Influence of Different Sparsity. We make use of left-right consistency detection and low-texture area removal to filter the noisy pixels. Different texture thresholds are set to analyze the sparsity and accuracy of the preserved labels on 200 images from KITTI 2015 [39].

As shown in the Table 3, "Density" represents the percentage of valid pixels in disparity maps. "No" represents the original outputs of ELAS, which the density of valid pixel is 77.56%. "LR" indicates that only left-right consistency detection is performed, and the D1-all error is largest. This means that only by left-right consistency detection, there are still many outliers that can't be detected. "S" plus number represents different texture threshold. For example, "S20" represents that the texture threshold is 20. As the texture threshold increases, from 20 to 100, the density of the valid pixels decreases. However, even when the texture threshold is set to 100, the density is still higher than 19.73% of the ground truth provided by KITTI 2015.

As the texture threshold increases, the D1-all error of the sparse disparity maps first decreases and then increases. When the texture threshold is 50, the D1-all error is minimized. This is because traditional methods tend to perform poorly in low-texture areas, so at low texture thresholds, more percentage of the low-confidence pixels are removed, causing D1-all error to decrease. As the

Table 4. Performance of AoH and other comparisons on the KITTI2015 sequence.

Model	MADNet			AoHNet					
	NO FT	GT	FULL	FULL	R-10	F250	E1-10	HAND	AoH
D1-all (%)	47.82	4.65	4.90	4.70	4.83	5.94	4.70	4.64	**4.51**
EPE	12.46	1.22	1.23	1.24	1.24	1.29	1.23	1.23	**1.19**
FPS	39.48	39.48	14.26	13.93	29.85	31.34	29.90	24.19	28.95

texture threshold increases, the percentage of high-confidence pixels is increasing, more pixels of high-confidence are removed, so the D1-all error increases.

We further experimented with the above data for network training. The networks are fine-tuned in the same way on the different sparsity disparity maps and then use the ground-truth labels of KITTI 2015 for evaluation. The results are shown in the "Deep-D1-all" row. Finally, the texture threshold is set to 50. Under this threshold, the valid pixel density of the disparity map is 43.64%, and the accuracy is 96.58%.

With Versus Without AoH. We have demonstrated the effectiveness of KRD, which adapts the network to a new scenario in less than 100 frames. However, fine-tuning the network all the time in the online environment comes with the side effect that back-propagation slows the network speed down to a third, which is unbearable for real application scenarios. What's more, it leads to another shortcoming that the model may become over-fitted if it continues training when it has already been adapted to the environment. To overcome the above problems, we propose an Adopt-or-Hold Mechanism that can automatically decide when the network needs adaption and when to stop adaption.

Table 4 shows performance of MADNet and AoHNet on a 2500 frames residential video of KITTI [9]. "NO FT" means that the network parameters are trained from synthetic data and have not been fine-tuned on KITTI. The error is large, which indicates that deep learning-based methods produce poor performance when the domain of data changes. "GT" means the results attained by the model that is fine-tuned offline on the target domain. "FULL" means that the network is fine-tuned all the time during the video. When AoHNet and MADNet work in the mode of "FULL", their speeds both drop to nearly one-third of the inference speeds. The error of AoHNet is smaller than MADNet due to the help of KRD loss. The AoH Mechanism performs excellent. Since the adaption is only made on 10% of the video frames in AoH Mechanism, the speed is one time faster compared to the "FULL" adaption. What's more, the D1-all error is even smaller than that of fine-tuning the network all the time.

According to the analysis, the AoH Mechanism updates about 250 frames across the entire video, so we designed three other methods for comparison. "R-10" means randomly choose 10% of frames for adaption. "F250" means only updating the network on the first 250 frames, and the rest frames only make an inference. "E1-10" means updating the network 1 frames every 10 frames,

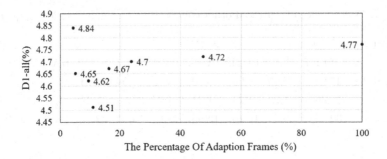

Fig. 6. The relationship between the percentage of adaption frames and the average D1-all error on the 2011_09_30_drive_0028_sync sequence.

a total of 250 frames are updated on the whole video. "HAND" is the method designed manually with image reconstruction loss. The error of "F250" is the largest, which is probably because of the environmental changes during the video. "HAND" is a little better than "R-10" and "E1-10". AoH produces superior results to all other methods, verifying the effectiveness of the AoH mechanism.

Furthermore, we did an experiment to analyze the relationship between the percentage of frames for adaption and the D1-all error on the whole video. The results are shown in the Fig. 6. As the percentage of the adaption frames increases, D1-all error decreases first and then increases. When the percentage of the adaption frames is about 11%, the error becomes the smallest. It implies that once the network has been adapted to the new environment, the adaption process should stop in time to avoid the model becoming over-fitted.

5   Conclusion and Future Work

In this paper, we proposed AoHNet, a real-time, self-supervised and self-adaptive online framework that can automatically adapt to new environments without the need for ground-truth labels. Two key components are introduced to improve the precision and the speed of deep stereo models: the Knowledge Reverse Distillation and the Adapt-or-Hold mechanism. Knowledge Reverse Distillation leverages the noisy predictions from lightweight traditional models (teachers) as supervision to guide the learning of the deep stereo model (student) and makes the student surpass the teacher. Adapt-or-Hold (AoH) mechanism based on Deep Q-Netwok can automatically determines when the deep stereo model adapts or holds in online environment. Experiments demonstrate that the proposed approach outperforms existing methods significantly in both speed and precision.

We believe that the direction of deep stereo matching in the future is that without the need for aligned labels, the network can adjust itself online according to the changing environment, rather than training a specific model for a particular scene. Besides, more attention will be paid on the embedded side, to bring the newest technology to the real practical applications.

References

1. Mayer, N., et al.: A large dataset to train convolutional networks for disparity, optical flow, and scene flow estimation. In: IEEE Conference on Computer Vision and Pattern Recognition (2016)
2. Pang, J., Sun, W., Ren, J.S., Yang, C., Yan, Q.: Cascade residual learning: a two-stage convolutional neural network for stereo matching. In: Proceedings of the IEEE International Conference on Computer Vision, pp. 887–895 (2017)
3. Chang, J.R., Chen, Y.S.: Pyramid stereo matching network. In: Proceedings of the IEEE Conference on Computer Vision and Pattern Recognition, pp. 5410–5418 (2018)
4. Guo, X., Yang, K., Yang, W., Wang, X., Li, H.: Group-wise correlation stereo network. In: Proceedings of the IEEE Conference on Computer Vision and Pattern Recognition, pp. 3273–3282 (2019)
5. Zhang, F., Prisacariu, V., Yang, R., Torr, P.H.: GA-net: guided aggregation net for end-to-end stereo matching. In: Proceedings of the IEEE Conference on Computer Vision and Pattern Recognition, pp. 185–194 (2019)
6. Tonioni, A., Poggi, M., Mattoccia, S., Di Stefano, L.: Unsupervised adaptation for deep stereo. In: IEEE International Conference on Computer Vision (2017)
7. Pang, J., et al.: Zoom and learn: generalizing deep stereo matching to novel domains. In: IEEE Conference on Computer Vision and Pattern Recognition (2018)
8. Tonioni, A., Tosi, F., Poggi, M., Mattoccia, S., Stefano, L.D.: Real-time self-adaptive deep stereo. In: Proceedings of the IEEE Conference on Computer Vision and Pattern Recognition, pp. 195–204 (2019)
9. Geiger, A., Lenz, P., Stiller, C., Urtasun, R.: Vision meets robotics: the KITTI dataset. Int. J. Robot. Res. **32**, 1231–1237 (2013)
10. Geiger, A., Roser, M., Urtasun, R.: Efficient large-scale stereo matching. In: Kimmel, R., Klette, R., Sugimoto, A. (eds.) ACCV 2010. LNCS, vol. 6492, pp. 25–38. Springer, Heidelberg (2011). https://doi.org/10.1007/978-3-642-19315-6_3
11. Wang, X., Li, Z., Tao, D.: Subspaces indexing model on grassmann manifold for image search. IEEE Trans. Image Process. **20**, 2627–2635 (2011)
12. Qiu, J., Wang, X., Maybank, S.J., Tao, D.: World from blur. In: IEEE Conference on Computer Vision and Pattern Recognition. In: CVPR, pp. 8493–8504 (2019)
13. Wang, X., Türetken, E., Fleuret, F., Fua, P.: Tracking interacting objects using intertwined flows. IEEE Trans. Pattern Anal. Mach. Intell. **38**, 2312–2326 (2016)
14. Lan, L., Wang, X., Hua, G., Huang, T.S., Tao, D.: Semi-online multi-people tracking by re-identification. Int. J. Comput. Vis. **128**, 1937–1955 (2020)
15. Scharstein, D., Szeliski, R.: A taxonomy and evaluation of dense two-frame stereo correspondence algorithms. Int. J. Comput. Vis. **47**, 7–42 (2002)
16. Klaus, A., Sormann, M., Karner, K.: Segment-based stereo matching using belief propagation and a self-adapting dissimilarity measure. In: 18th International Conference on Pattern Recognition (ICPR2006), vol. 3, pp. 15–18. IEEE (2006)
17. Kolmogorov, V., Zabih, R.: Computing visual correspondence with occlusions via graph cuts. Technical report, Cornell University (2001)
18. Yang, Y., Qiu, J., Song, M., Tao, D., Wang, X.: Distilling knowledge from graph convolutional networks. In: IEEE Conference on Computer Vision and Pattern Recognition (CVPR) (2020)
19. Zbontar, J., et al.: Stereo matching by training a convolutional neural network to compare image patches. J. Mach. Learn. Res. **17**, 2 (2016)

20. Kendall, A., et al.: End-to-end learning of geometry and context for deep stereo regression. In: IEEE International Conference on Computer Vision, pp. 66–75 (2017)

21. Wang, X., Türetken, E., Fleuret, F., Fua, P.: Tracking interacting objects optimally using integer programming. In: Fleet, D., Pajdla, T., Schiele, B., Tuytelaars, T. (eds.) ECCV 2014. LNCS, vol. 8689, pp. 17–32. Springer, Cham (2014). https://doi.org/10.1007/978-3-319-10590-1_2

22. Yu, X., Liu, T., Wang, X., Tao, D.: On compressing deep models by low rank and sparse decomposition. In: IEEE Conference on Computer Vision and Pattern Recognition (CVPR) (2017)

23. Yang, E., Deng, C., Li, C., Liu, W., Li, J., Tao, D.: Shared predictive cross-modal deep quantization. IEEE Trans. Neural Netw. Learn. Syst. **29**, 5292–5303 (2018)

24. Yin, X., Wang, X., Yu, J., Zhang, M., Fua, P., Tao, D.: FishEyeRecNet: a multi-context collaborative deep network for fisheye image rectification. In: Ferrari, V., Hebert, M., Sminchisescu, C., Weiss, Y. (eds.) ECCV 2018. LNCS, vol. 11214, pp. 475–490. Springer, Cham (2018). https://doi.org/10.1007/978-3-030-01249-6_29

25. Deng, C., Yang, E., Liu, T., Li, J., Liu, W., Tao, D.: Unsupervised semantic-preserving adversarial hashing for image search. IEEE Trans. Image Process. **28**, 4032–4044 (2019)

26. Wang, J., Huang, S., Wang, X., Tao, D.: Not all parts are created equal: 3D pose estimation by modeling bi-directional dependencies of body parts. In: IEEE International Conference on Computer Vision (ICCV) (2019)

27. Garg, R., B.G., V.K., Carneiro, G., Reid, I.: Unsupervised CNN for single view depth estimation: geometry to the rescue. In: Leibe, B., Matas, J., Sebe, N., Welling, M. (eds.) ECCV 2016. LNCS, vol. 9912, pp. 740–756. Springer, Cham (2016). https://doi.org/10.1007/978-3-319-46484-8_45

28. Godard, C., Mac Aodha, O., Brostow, G.J.: Unsupervised monocular depth estimation with left-right consistency. In: Proceedings of the IEEE Conference on Computer Vision and Pattern Recognition, pp. 270–279 (2017)

29. Ye, J., Ji, Y., Wang, X., Ou, K., Tao, D., Song, M.: Student becoming the master: knowledge amalgamation for joint scene parsing, depth estimation, and more. In: IEEE Conference on Computer Vision and Pattern Recognition (CVPR) (2019)

30. Poggi, M., Mattoccia, S.: Learning from scratch a confidence measure. In: BMVC (2016)

31. Zhong, Y., Li, H., Dai, Y.: Open-world stereo video matching with deep RNN. In: Ferrari, V., Hebert, M., Sminchisescu, C., Weiss, Y. (eds.) ECCV 2018. LNCS, vol. 11206, pp. 104–119. Springer, Cham (2018). https://doi.org/10.1007/978-3-030-01216-8_7

32. Zhao, H., Gallo, O., Frosio, I., Kautz, J.: Loss functions for image restoration with neural networks. IEEE Trans. Comput. Imaging **3**, 47–57 (2016)

33. Mnih, V., et al.: Playing atari with deep reinforcement learning. arXiv preprint arXiv:1312.5602 (2013)

34. Mnih, V., et al.: Human-level control through deep reinforcement learning. Nature **518**, 529 (2015)

35. Schaul, T., Quan, J., Antonoglou, I., Silver, D.: Prioritized experience replay. arXiv preprint arXiv:1511.05952 (2015)

36. Van Hasselt, H., Guez, A., Silver, D.: Deep reinforcement learning with double q-learning. In: Thirtieth AAAI Conference on Artificial Intelligence (2016)

37. Wang, Z., et al.: Dueling network architectures for deep reinforcement learning. arXiv preprint arXiv:1511.06581 (2015)

38. Wang, Z., Bovik, A.C., Sheikh, H.R., Simoncelli, E.P., et al.: Image quality assessment: from error visibility to structural similarity. IEEE Trans. Image Process. **13**, 600–612 (2004)
39. Menze, M., Geiger, A.: Object scene flow for autonomous vehicles. In: IEEE Conference on Computer Vision and Pattern Recognition, pp. 3061–3070 (2015)
40. Geiger, A., Lenz, P., Urtasun, R.: Are we ready for autonomous driving? the kitti vision benchmark suite. In: 2012 IEEE Conference on Computer Vision and Pattern Recognition, pp. 3354–3361. IEEE (2012)
41. Zhou, T., Brown, M., Snavely, N., Lowe, D.G.: Unsupervised learning of depth and ego-motion from video. In: Proceedings of the IEEE Conference on Computer Vision and Pattern Recognition, pp. 1851–1858 (2017)
42. Li, A., Yuan, Z.: Occlusion aware stereo matching via cooperative unsupervised learning. In: Jawahar, C.V., Li, H., Mori, G., Schindler, K. (eds.) ACCV 2018. LNCS, vol. 11366, pp. 197–213. Springer, Cham (2019). https://doi.org/10.1007/978-3-030-20876-9_13
43. Aleotti, F., Tosi, F., Zhang, L., Poggi, M., Mattoccia, S.: Reversing the cycle: self-supervised deep stereo through enhanced monocular distillation. arXiv preprint arXiv:2008.07130 (2020)

AFN: Attentional Feedback Network Based 3D Terrain Super-Resolution

Ashish Kubade[✉], Diptiben Patel, Avinash Sharma, and K. S. Rajan

International Institute of Information Technology, Hyderabad, India
{ashish.kubade,dipti.patel}@research.iiit.ac.in,
{asharma,rajan}@iiit.ac.in

Abstract. Terrain, representing features of an earth surface, plays a crucial role in many applications such as simulations, route planning, analysis of surface dynamics, computer graphics-based games, entertainment, films, to name a few. With recent advancements in digital technology, these applications demand the presence of high resolution details in the terrain. In this paper, we propose a novel fully convolutional neural network based super-resolution architecture to increase the resolution of low-resolution Digital Elevation Model (LRDEM) with the help of information extracted from the corresponding aerial image as a complementary modality. We perform the super-resolution of LRDEM using an attention based feedback mechanism named 'Attentional Feedback Network' (AFN), which selectively fuses the information from LRDEM and aerial image to enhance and infuse the high-frequency features and to produce the terrain realistically. We compare the proposed architecture with existing state-of-the-art DEM super-resolution methods and show that the proposed architecture outperforms enhancing the resolution of input LRDEM accurately and in a realistic manner.

1 Introduction

Real-world terrain is a complex structure consisting of bare land, high range mountains, river paths, arcs, canyons and many more. The terrains and their surface geology are digitally represented using Digital Elevation Models (DEM) or volumetric models. The terrain data coupled with Geographical Information Systems (GIS) extract topological information for various applications including modeling water flow or mass movements, analyse the dynamic behaviour of the earth surface, perform disaster mitigation planning such as flood modeling, landslides, etc. Real-time simulations of terrains are used for fast adaptation and route planning of aerial vehicles such as drones, aircrafts and helicopters, to name a few. Realistic terrain rendering also finds its application in ranging simulations, entertainment, gaming, and many more. As the visual detail and depth in many of these applications, mentioned above, demand terrain information of high resolution and fidelity, capturing or generating such information, as accurately as possible, is the need of the hour.

© Springer Nature Switzerland AG 2021
H. Ishikawa et al. (Eds.): ACCV 2020, LNCS 12622, pp. 192–208, 2021.
https://doi.org/10.1007/978-3-030-69525-5_12

Diversity and combinations of the complex topological structures make capture/synthesis and analysis of the terrain a challenging task while taking realism into consideration. For instance, computer games with high realistic graphic environments include terrain features for users to experience better realism and allow for detailed exploration. The synthetic or amplified terrain can be used as a background for science fantasy films as well, as the synthetic terrain does not exist and amplified terrain may be difficult for the filming process.

However, DEMs captured with recent remote sensing sensors are still of relatively low-resolution (>2 m per pixel) and very few geographical locations are captured in high-resolution using airborne LiDAR technology due to high processing requirements. An alternate solution to this problem is to transform the captured low-resolution DEMs (LRDEM) to super-resolved DEMs termed as terrain modeling in general. Existing terrain modeling process can be broadly classified as terrain amplification and terrain synthesis. Terrain amplification enhances the high frequency 3D texture details of the scanned low resolution terrain captured from the real world, thereby making it as close as possible to actual ground truth terrain. On the other hand, terrain synthesis deals with generation of terrain with specific user controls giving a near-realistic appearance.

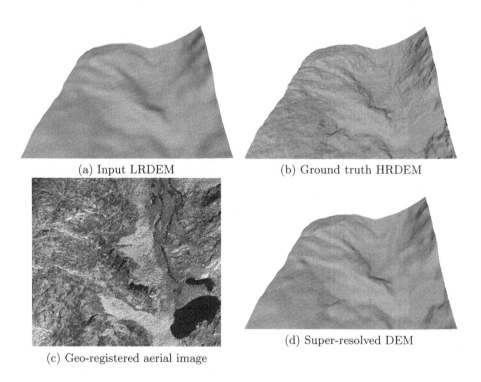

(a) Input LRDEM   (b) Ground truth HRDEM

(c) Geo-registered aerial image

(d) Super-resolved DEM

Fig. 1. Views of the terrain at different resolutions and corresponding aerial image.

Our primary focus in this work is on terrain amplification of LRDEM (Fig. 1(a)) with aim to obtain super-resolved DEM (Fig. 1(d)) terrain models with high fidelity to the ground-truth (Fig. 1(b)) terrain structures.

Some of the earliest methods for terrain amplification employed dictionary of exemplars to synthesis high resolution terrains [1,2], while some other efforts in the literature used erosion simulations to mimic the terrain degradation effects [3,4]. Owing to recent advancements in deep learning literature for super-resolution of real world RGB images [5–10], some recent efforts have adopted these ideas for DEM super-resolution. DEM Super Resolution with Feedback Block (DSRFB) [11] is one such method that attempts to incrementally add high frequency terrain details to the LRDEM in high dimensional feature space using deep learning framework. Another line of work attempted to exploit the terrain information from alternate modalities like aerial (RGB) images (Fig. 1(c)) that are geo-registered with low resolution DEMs by performing fusion in feature space, e.g., Fully Convolutional Networks (FCN) proposed in [12]. However, despite using RGB information in DEM super-resolution task, such methods perform poorly in cases of land regions covered with dense vegetation or heavy snowfall. On the other hand, by not availing such modalities (like in DSRFB), we may refrain from exploiting the complementary information captured by RGB images primarily for bare terrain.

In this paper, we aim to utilize these complementary modalities in a more efficient and effective manner using the concept of selective fusion in feature space. Attention networks, applied to applications like image captioning [13], allow such selective fusion in deep learning framework. Therefore, we aim to design an integrated attention module that enables learning of selective information fusion from multiple modalities. In our setup, where we have two modalities viz aerial image and DEM, we use attention mechanism to selectively pick high frequency details from one modality and discard from the other. Our joint attentional module generates attention mask, which serves as a weight factor deciding the contribution of each modality.

Thus, we propose a novel terrain amplification method for the DEM representation of real world terrains. We propose supervised learning based fully convolutional neural network (CNN) with LRDEM and corresponding high resolution aerial image as an input and Super-resolved DEM as an output. The architecture of the CNN constitutes a feedback neural network with attention mechanism where the attention mask itself is also allowed to refine its response over the iterations. The high frequency details are added to the DEM using the features extracted from the corresponding high resolution aerial image using the Feature Extraction module. In order to capture high frequency details, we minimize the L1 loss. The overall architecture of the proposed Attentional Feedback Network (AFN) is shown in Fig. 2.

We compare the performance of the proposed methods with other state-of-the-art super-resolution methods for DEM in a quantitative and qualitative manner and are able to achieve better performance in terms of reduced number of parameters as well as inference time. More precisely, proposed AFN solution shares the parameters across feedback loop for incremental fusion in feature space with just 7M parameters whereas other SOTA architectures like [12] use an order of 20M parameters. Being leaner model, it achieves better performance 50% faster than the average inference time required by [12] on similar hardware.

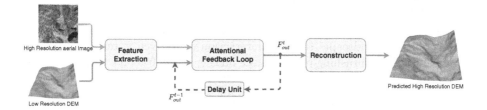

Fig. 2. Proposed attentional feedback network architecture

2   Related Work

Generating high-resolution of DEM from a low-resolution DEM can be thought of as enhancing or adding the high frequency details like texture patterns, sharp edges, and small curves which often are lost or absent in the low-resolution DEM. With recent success of deep learning, super-resolution of natural RGB images has achieved state-of-the-art performance. However, very few attempts have been made to apply super-resolution to enhance the resolution of DEMs. The possible reasons for fewer attempts could be difference of underlying features, size of features, different textures, and salient objects. Earlier attempts by [12] have explored the new paths to apply super-resolution to DEMs and successfully demonstrated that deep learning solutions can be adapted to DEMs as well. To understand the challenges in this cross domain task, we would like to highlight some of the major works in respective domains in detail. This section presents a focused overview of terrain modeling, super-resolution methods for images in general and deep learning based feedback network as individual components used in computer vision community.

2.1   Terrain Modeling

Based on the underlying process acquired for terrain modeling, it is classified into three categories: procedural generation methods, physically-based simulation methods, and example-based methods. Procedural generation methods consist of algorithms that use the intrinsic properties of a terrain from the observation of the real world. Physically-based simulation methods execute computer simulations of a geomorphological process that modifies physical properties and surface aspects of a terrain. Example-based methods extract the information from scanned heightfield real world terrains and combine these information for the generation or amplification purpose. The detailed review of existing terrain modeling processes can be referred from [14].

Procedural generation methods use self repeating fractal patterns to mimic the self repeating property of a real world terrain at different scales. Perlin et al. [15] proposed the use of generating such fractal patterns for terrain modeling. By using combinations of octaves of noises and thereby creating various scales of noise and smoothness, [3] offers variations in the fractal dimensions. Analogous to mountains, rivers can also be modeled with procedural modeling and incorporated into the landscape [16]. User interaction is involved in terrain modeling using painting and brushing on gray-scale images as the fractal's basis functions for editing in [17]. Primitive features in the form of silhouette and shadows, vector based features in the form of ridge lines, riverbeds, cliffs have been used to generate the terrain in [18] and [19], respectively. Hierarchical combination of the primitives such as riverbed, cliffs, hills is used as a tree objects in [20]. However, terrains generated using procedural methods lack the effect of natural phenomenon like erosion in their appearances. Hence, a terrain generated by procedural methods is often combined with simulation operations.

Simulation based methods use physical processes such as diffusion, erosion, temperature aided contraction, expansion, hydrological factors aided smoothening, and wind aided gradual abrasion to generate more realistic terrain. [3] presented hydraulic and thermal erosion and combined with ecosystems such as vegetation modeling. However, the heightfield is unable to represent the arches and caves present in the terrain as heightfield can represent only topmost surface in a terrain. [21] introduced layered representation for such structures with multiple layers. These structural representations have also enabled stacking multiple layers for effects of various physical and biological phenomenon. One such integration has been represented by [22], where they fused the interaction between the growing vegetation and terrain erosion by representing them into different layers.

Example-based methods are data-driven methods utilizing the information available in scanned data of real-world terrain. Sample terrain is transformed to desired terrain using user defined sketch in [4]. Patch based terrain synthesis by using a dictionary of exemplars is performed in [1,2]. With recently successful deep learning based Generative Adversarial Networks (GANs), [23] used Conditional GANs to translate a sample terrain using interactive user sketch.

2.2   Super-Resolution of Images

Different interpolations from neighbourhood information such as linear, bilinear or bicubic are trivial solutions for super-resolution of an image. However, interpolation without high frequency information leads to average out the sharp edges resulting in blur image. Sharp edges and high frequency textures are preserved using Edge Directed Interpolation suggested in [24]. Alternatively, patch based solutions [25–27] reconstruct high-resolution patches using a learned mapping between LR and HR patches. While learning the mapping between LR and HR patches, patch consistency is a major issue with patch based approaches.

In order to avoid patch inconsistency, mapping between LR and HR images is learned considering an image as a single patch and extracting hand-crafted features using convolutional operators [28], gradient profile prior [29,30], Kernel Ridge Regressions (KRR) [31].

Super-resolution task using deep learning is attempted in [5,32] to learn the mapping between LR and HR. With ResNet overcoming the vanishing gradient problem by using skips connections in deeper networks, super-resolution of images using residual blocks is achieved by DRCN [6], SRResNet [33], Residual of Residual (RoR) [34], Residual Dense Network (RDN) [7], to name a few. With an emerging interest in generative adversarial networks, super-resolution of an image is attempted by [8,34]. While the trend was to go deeper apathetic to the number of parameters, DRRN [35] formulated a recursive structure to fuse features across all depths.

2.3   DEM Super-Resolution with Neural Networks

Though RDN [7], DRRN [35] were able to effectively utilize the low level features, the flow of information was only in forward direction, i.e., from initial layers to deeper layers. The low level features are used repeatedly, limiting the reconstruction ability of lower features in the super-resolution task of the network.

SRFBN (Super-Resolution Feedback Network) [10] was proposed to tackle this problem. SRFBN used a feedback mechanism adapting from Feedback Networks [36] in their architecture. Using a feedback mechanism has another advantage with respect to size (number of parameters) of the model. Using a recurrent structure and thereby reusing the parameters has been one of the major techniques in deep learning. Recurrent structures also helps realizing a feedback mechanism easily as recurrent structure can save states of a layer which helps in implementing the feedback component. This approach of super-resolution has been effectively utilized in [11] for DEM super-resolution task. [11] have also suggested using overlapped prediction to remove artifacts observed at patch boundaries due to discontinued structures. Even though performing comparable with then state-of-the-art, [11] network can not avail any additionally available modalities, and hence performance of their method is limited to information cues available in low-resolution DEM only. A Method based on fully convolutional networks by [12] (referred as FCN, here onwards) extract complementary information from aerial images. However, in their feed-forward setup, there is no control over features learned by initial layers of network. Also, it has been shown that FCN could perform poorly in case of unexposed land regions covered with dense vegetation or areas with heavy snowfall. This motivates us to explore solutions that enable selective extraction of features from aerial images while focusing more on learning of initial layers of the network. We propose the use of attention mechanism for adaptive utilization of features selected respectively from aerial images and DEM. Integrating attention mechanism with feedback network enables the proposed network to learn more refined lower level features.

3 Method

Despite using RGB information in super-resolution task, FCN [12] performs poorly in cases of dense vegetation or heavy snowfall. However, by not availing such modalities, like in DSRFB [11], we may refrain ourselves from improvements in super-resolution systems. We utilize these additional modalities in complementary fashion. Inspired from attentional networks applied to applications like image captioning [13], we design a module that lets system learn to focus and extract selective information. In our setup, where we have two modalities viz aerial image and DEM, we use attention mechanism to selectively pick high frequency details from one modality and discard from the other. Our joint attentional module generates attention mask, which serves as a weight factor deciding the contribution of each modality.

Moreover, our interest is in recovering the lower level details (alternately 'high frequency' details) as edges, texture, sharp changes, etc. In a typical Convolutional Neural Network (CNN), these features are captured by the initial layers of the network. To refine the features captured by the shallow layers, we design our attention network in recursive fashion and introduce part of deep features as input back to the shallow layers. This also enables our attention mask to get updated with each time step. Thus, our network becomes a feedback network enabled with attention, we call it as 'Attentional Feedback Network' (AFN). The implementation of the feedback module is based on an RNN with T states. With each state, our model refines the lower level features learned by initial layers and enables the reconstruction of SR at each time step. The overall network architecture, once unrolled over time, has the structure as shown in Fig. 3. In next section, we explain the architectural details of each component.

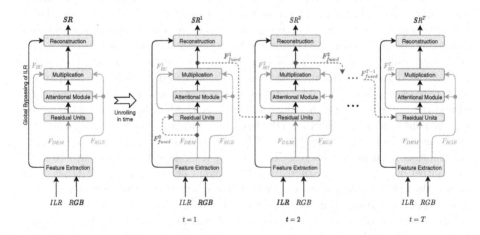

Fig. 3. Unrolled model structure

3.1 Proposed Attentional Feedback Network Architecture

As shown in Fig. 3, unfolded network across time comprises of three components: A Feature Extraction Module, Attentional Feedback Module (AFM) and Reconstruction Block. We also introduce following notations used throughout this paper.

- m denotes the base number of filters
- $Conv(m, k)$ denotes a convolutional layer with output number of channels m and kernel size k
- T denotes the number of steps in feedback loop

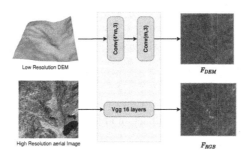

Fig. 4. Feature extraction module (Color figure online)

Input to the **Feature Extraction Module** (FE) is a pair of geo-registered LRDEM and aerial image. As shown in Fig. 4, the FE module consists of two branches of layers. Input to the first branch is LRDEM. It comprises of two convolutional layers as $Conv(4*m, 3)$ and $Conv(m, 3)$. The output of this branch is denoted by F_{DEM} (shown with blue outline). Second branch operates on aerial image. We use first two layers from pre-trained VGG-16 network [37] on Imagenet dataset to extract aerial image features. To reduce the domain shift from the aerial images to the images from Imagenet data, we fine-tune these VGG layers during training. The choice of layers has been done empirically by comparing the feature responses of the layers. First two layers are sufficient to extract most of the high frequency details. We denote the output of VGG layers as F_{RGB} (shown with green outline).

We feed the F_{DEM} and F_{RGB} to **Attentional Feedback Module** (AFM) which is the heart of our algorithm. As shown in Fig. 5, AFM consists of two sub-modules: A stack of residual units and an attention module.

Each residual unit consists of a $Conv(m, 1)$ followed by a $Conv(m, 3)$. The $Conv(m, 1)$ allows the residual unit to adaptively fuse the information from previous residual units and $Conv(m, 3)$ layer produces new m channel features to be passed towards following residual units. The residual units are denoted with B_i, where $i \in \{1, N\}$, N being an even number. As implemented by [11], we use

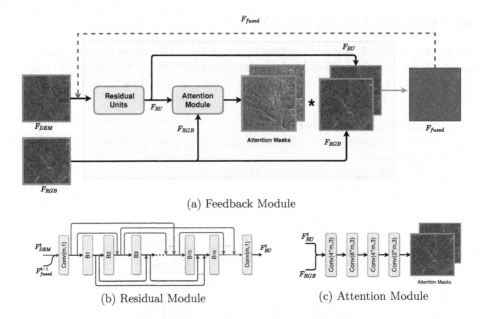

(a) Feedback Module

(b) Residual Module

(c) Attention Module

Fig. 5. Attentional feedback module (Color figure online)

two sets of skip connections to combine the features from residual blocks. The skip connections from $B1$ bypass the information to $\{B2, B4, B6, B8, \ldots, B_N\}$, from $B2$ to $\{B3, B5, B7, \ldots, B_{N-1}\}$, from $B3$ to $\{B4, B6, B8, \ldots, B_N\}$ and so on. Being inside the iterative feedback module, at each time step t, residual module receives a concatenated feature map of F_{DEM} and F_{fused}^{t-1}. This timely varying part F_{fused}^{t-1}, constitutes the feedback component of our network that we save at time step $t-1$ and is shown as red dashed line in Fig. 5(a). A $Conv(m, 1)$ layer has been used to compress F_{DEM} and F_{fused}^{t-1} before passing them to B1 at time step t. At current iteration, t, the outputs from units $\{B2, B4, \ldots, B_N\}$ are compressed by another $Conv(m, 1)$ layer to generate the output of residual module viz F_{RU}^t.

At each time step, t, the resultant output of residual module, denoted as F_{RU}^t, along with the features from the RGB branch i.e. F_{RGB}, are fed to the attention module.

Inspired from [38], attention masks generated from the attention module can be thought of as spatial probability maps. These spatial probability maps can be learnt using fully convolutional networks. Hence, attention module comprises of a small fully convolutional network of 4 layers.

As shown in Fig. 5(c), the attention module consists of $Conv(4 * m, 3)$, $Conv(4 * m, 3), Conv(8 * m, 3)$ and $Conv(2 * m, 3)$. The final output with $2 * m$ channels has been split into two units: $Attn_{DEM}^t$ and $Attn_{RGB}^t$ of m channels each which in turn act as an attention mask for the input features F_{RU}^t and F_{RGB}, respectively. Unlike [38], we use multi channel attention maps. We then use element wise channel multiplication to get a weighted set of features with attention channels. A channel-wise summation then fuses the two sets of features together into, F_{fused}^t, the final output of AFM as shown in Eq. (1).

$$F_{fused}^t = F_{RU}^t * Attn_{DEM}^t + \gamma * F_{RGB} * Attn_{RGB}^t \qquad (1)$$

where a learnable parameter γ is used for stable learning. γ has been initialized with 0 so as to focus on F_{RU} first and adaptively move the attention to F_{RGB}. To implement an iterative feedback, we store F_{fused}^t over current step and then concatenate it with F_{DEM} to be processed in next step as part of feedback. For the first step, i.e. at $t = 0$, as there will not be any F_{fused}, we use F_{DEM} itself as feedback information for step $t = 0$. We forward F_{fused}^t as input to the reconstruction block. Residing inside the feedback module, we let the attention maps to refine themselves as the iterations proceed. This timely varying attention units for same input also makes our attention module unique and different from [38].

We run the AFM module for T number of steps. For each step t, we get one set of features F_{fused}^t, which is improved version of itself as the iteration goes on.

We implement **Reconstruction Block** with two units of convolutional layers $Conv(m, 3)$ and $Conv(1, 3)$. For each step of the feedback unit, the reconstruction block takes in F_{fused}^t and produces a residual map denoted by I_{res}^t. The I_{res}^t are the higher frequency details we are interested in generating. We add this residual, I_{res}^t to DEM_{ILR} which we forward from input directly via a global skip connection shown in Fig. 3. The predicted super-resolved DEM at time step t is given by Eq. (2).

$$SR^t = I_{res}^t + DEM_{ILR} \quad \forall t \in \{1, T\} \qquad (2)$$

With a recursion of depth T, for each step of t for single data instance, we get one SR, forming an array of predicted SRDEMs with increasing amount of details.

We use $L1$ loss over HRDEM and SR^t for $t \in \{1, T\}$ as given by Eq. (3).

$$L = \sum_{t=1}^{T} |HRDEM - SR^t| \qquad (3)$$

The final loss L will be used for back-propagation and training the parameters.

4   Experimental Setup

4.1   Datasets

Our goal in this study is to selectively utilize the information from other modalities like aerial images. For fair comparison with existing methods such as [12] and [11], we train our model using dataset provided by Institut Cartogràfic i Geològic de Catalunya (ICC) [39] and Südtiroler Bürgernetz GeoKatalog

(SBG) [40]. The terrains provided by these institutes have been pre-processed by the authors of [12]. The dataset used for training comprises of geo-registered pairs of DEM and aerial images of several mountain regions named Pyrenees and Tyrol. DEM patches with a resolution of 2m/pixel have been used as ground truth (HRDEM) elevation maps. These HRDEMs have been downsampled to 15m/pixel to create a corresponding LRDEM. For convenient training, original DEM tiles have been split into patches of size 200×200 pixels, where each pixel intensity signifies terrain height. To effectively avail the aerial information, the resolution of aerial image has been set twice that of DEM, resulting in patches of size 400×400. From all the patches, 22000 patches have been chosen for training and 11000 patches for validation. Also, two regions from Pyrenees namely Bassiero and Forcanada, and two regions from Tyrol namely Durrenstein and Monte Magro have been set aside for testing the network performance. We suggest the reader to refer [12] for more details about the dataset.

4.2 Implementation Details

In this section, we explain the hyper-parameters and details about our experimental setup. We have used convolutional layers with kernel size of 3×3, unless explicitly stated. The parameters in these layers were initialized with *Kaiming* initialization protocol. All the convolutional layers are followed by PReLU activation. For the RGB branch in FE module, we have used first two convolution layers (pre-trained on ImageNet dataset) from VGG-16 network. Later, we allow to fine-tune their weights so as to adapt the weights according to DEM modality. We set m (the number of base channels) to 64 and T (number of steps in feedback loop) to 4. We have chosen T to be 4, as the gain performance in terms of PSNR and RMSE (Shown in Fig. 6) is getting stagnant around $T = 4$. We use N, i.e. the number of residual units, as 16. Since we have used LRDEM with resolution of 15 m (as stated in [11]), the effective super-resolution factor in our case is 7.5X. We have used a batch size of 4, the max supported with our 4 NVIDIA-1080Ti GPUs. We used learning rate of $\eta = 0.0001$ with multi-step degradation by parameter 0.5 with epoch intervals at [45, 60, 70]. Parameters were updated with *Adam* optimizer. We have implemented our network in PyTorch framework. After convergence of the network, the value learned by γ is 0.358.

During testing, similar to [11], we have adopted the technique of overlapped prediction with overlap of 25% on all sides of the patch.

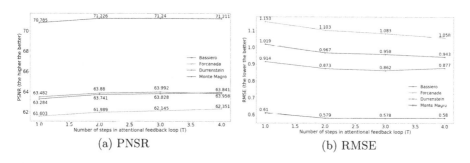

(a) PNSR   (b) RMSE

Fig. 6. Choice of parameter T (number of steps)

5   Results and Discussions

We use standard root mean squared error(RMSE) and peak signal-to-noise ratio (PSNR) metrics to compare the performance of our proposed method with existing SOTA methods, namely FCN [12] and DSRFB [11]. While RMSE helps understand the cumulative squared error between the prediction and ground truth, PSNR helps to gain the measure of peak error, PSNR and RMSE are complementary measures to compare the performance of SR methods. We also compare the performance with a variant of FCN, FCND which does not use aerial imagery as complementary source of information.

From Table 1, we can infer that our network AFN outperforms both FCN and DSRFB. Using the overlapped prediction, our variant, AFNO performs even better. Similar observation can be made from Table 2, where AFN has the best PSNR even without using overlapped prediction. Even though the quantitative performance in some areas seems marginal, the gains achieved by our method (over SOTA) in terms of absolute height values are around 0.5 to 1.0 m which is quite valuable.

Table 1. Comparison: RMSE values (in meters. The lower the better).

Input	Only LRDEM				LRDEM and RGB		
Region	Bicubic	DSRFB	DSRFO	FCND	FCN	AFN	AFNO
Bassiero	1.406	1.146	1.091	1.083	1.005	**0.943**	**0.926**
Forcanada	1.632	1.326	1.2702	1.259	1.097	**1.058**	**1.030**
Durrenstein	1.445	0.957	0.884	0.868	0.901	**0.877**	**0.854**
Monte Magro	0.917	0.632	0.589	0.581	0.587	**0.580**	**0.566**

Table 2. Comparison: PSNR values (The higher the better).

Input	Only LRDEM				LRDEM and RGB		
Region	Bicubic	DSRFB	DSRFO	FCND	FCN	AFN	AFNO
Bassiero	60.5	62.261	62.687	62.752	63.4	**63.958**	**64.113**
Forcanada	58.6	60.383	60.761	60.837	62.0	**62.351**	**62.574**
Durrenstein	59.5	63.076	63.766	63.924	63.6	**63.841**	**64.061**
Monte Magro	67.2	70.461	71.081	71.196	71.1	**71.211**	**71.417**

From our test regions, we pick one patch each based on certain geographical property, typically containing one major terrain feature. In Fig. 7, first row shows the aerial view of the selected terrain patches. From Bassiero, we select a highly varying terrain patch. From Forcanada, we choose a patch with bare surface. Patches from Durrenstein and Monte Magro respectively have terrains covered with dense vegetation and snow. From comparison results in Fig. 7, we can see that, for Bassiero, our method is able to recover most of the terrain variations in the terrain. In low resolution input of Forcanada, almost all terrain details have been lost, yet our method can recover most of the lost structure. In cases of covered terrains in Durrenstein and Monte Magro, where LRDEM is seen to have more variations, our method has introduced the least noise. Additional results are available in the supplementary video.

5.1   Ablation Studies

To justify the effectiveness of the Attention module, we thoroughly test our network by creating its variants around Attentional Feedback Module. We discuss four major studies in this section.

Without Attention Module: In this experiment, we remove the attention module from the network entirely. For fusing the features from two modalities, i.e. F_{DEM} and F_{RGB}, we use channel concatenation followed by $Conv(m, 1)$ layer. We keep the rest of the setup same as in AFN. The reduction in performance of the network can be seen in Table 3 which supports the role of attention module in selective feature extraction.

Static Attention Masks: In AFN, the attention masks for both F_{RU} and F_{RGB} get updated with iterations. In this study, we move the attention module outside the feedback network and use feedback module only for refining the F_{RU} features. So in this case, we denote the attention state as static and call this variant as AFN0. Comparison from Table 3 confirms that iterative attention can help the network learn more refined feature than fixed attention mask.

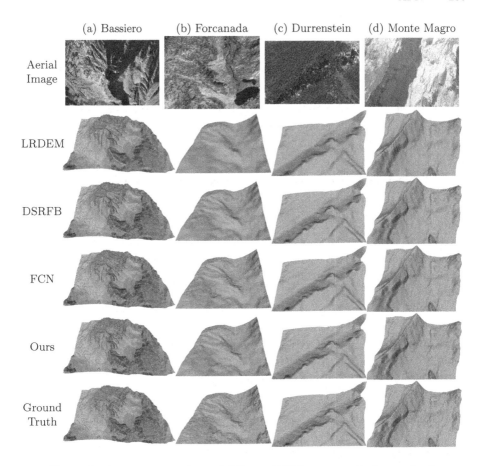

Fig. 7. Qualitative comparison of different DEM super-resolution methods

Number of Channels in Attention Module: To understand the contribution of AFM in performance gain, we changed hyper-parameters. We reduced the number of channels to 64 throughout the attention module. We denote AFN in this setup as AFN64. The proportional reduction in performance reflects the role of AFM in capturing the higher frequency details.

Performance Without Aerial Imagery: To test the flexibility and limitations of AFN, we study its performance in absence of aerial imagery. Getting aligned pair of aerial image and DEM could be challenging sometimes and hence we analyze the performance of AFN in absence of aerial image. In this exercise, we replace the input aerial image with an uniform prior image of same dimensions. We call this variant as AFND. Table 4 shows that despite trained with RGB images, while prediction, AFND selectively picks information from DEM modality and perform consistently better than FCND and almost comparable to DSRFB. Of course, DSRFB was designed to work without RGB. The marginal

Table 3. Ablation Studies.

Region	Without AFM		AFN0		AFN64		AFN	
	PSNR	RMSE	PSNR	RMSE	PSNR	RMSE	PSNR	RMSE
Bassiero	62.406	1.128	63.108	1.04	63.724	0.969	63.958	0.943
Forcanada	60.537	1.303	61.355	1.186	62.141	1.084	62.351	1.058
Durrenstein	62.994	0.967	63.769	0.884	64.116	0.85	63.841	0.877
Monte Magro	70.365	0.64	70.934	0.599	71.154	0.584	71.211	0.58

Table 4. Performance of AFND i.e. AFN without using aerial images.

Region	PSNR (in dB, the higher the better)				RMSE (in meters, the lower the better)			
	Bicubic	FCND	DSRFB	AFND	Bicubic	FCND	DSRFB	AFND
Bassiero	60.5	62.261	62.687	62.404	1.406	1.146	1.091	1.128
Forcanada	58.6	60.383	60.761	60.504	1.632	1.326	1.2702	1.308
Durrenstein	59.5	63.076	63.766	63.394	1.445	0.957	0.884	0.923
Monte Magro	67.2	70.461	71.081	70.768	0.917	0.632	0.589	0.611

decrease in performance of AFND compared with DSRFB can be attributed partially to the uniform prior acting as noise and causing the attention module to generate a biased attention response.

6   Conclusion

We have proposed a novel terrain amplification method called AFN for generating the DEM super-resolution. It uses low-resolution DEM and complementary information from corresponding aerial image by computing an attention mask from the attention module along with the feedback network to enhance the performance of the proposed architecture. While this architecture is able to learn well across different terrains, there is a need to further enhance some key features of terrains, especially in regions with high frequency. Hence, there might be a need to explore the use of multi-scale fusion as an extension to the proposed AFN. Also, similar to other computer vision applications, it might be interesting to generate high-resolution DEM using only aerial image as an input.

References

1. Guérin, E., Digne, J., Galin, E., Peytavie, A.: Sparse representation of terrains for procedural modeling. In: Computer Graphics Forum, vol. 35, pp. 177–187. Wiley Online Library (2016)
2. Kwatra, V., Schödl, A., Essa, I., Turk, G., Bobick, A.: Graphcut textures: image and video synthesis using graph cuts. ACM Trans. Graph. (ToG) **22**, 277–286 (2003)

3. Musgrave, F.K., Kolb, C.E., Mace, R.S.: The synthesis and rendering of eroded fractal terrains. ACM Siggraph Comput. Graph. **23**, 41–50 (1989)
4. Zhou, H., Sun, J., Turk, G., Rehg, J.M.: Terrain synthesis from digital elevation models. IEEE Trans. Vis. Comput. Graph. **13**, 834–848 (2007)
5. Dong, C., Loy, C.C., Tang, X.: Accelerating the super-resolution convolutional neural network. In: Leibe, B., Matas, J., Sebe, N., Welling, M. (eds.) ECCV 2016. LNCS, vol. 9906, pp. 391–407. Springer, Cham (2016). https://doi.org/10.1007/978-3-319-46475-6_25
6. Kim, J., Lee, J.K., Lee, K.M.: Deeply-recursive convolutional network for image super-resolution. In: Proceedings of the IEEE Conference on Computer Vision and Pattern Recognition, pp. 1637–1645 (2016)
7. Zhang, Y., Tian, Y., Kong, Y., Zhong, B., Fu, Y.: Residual dense network for image super-resolution. In: Proceedings of the IEEE Conference on Computer Vision and Pattern Recognition, pp. 2472–2481 (2018)
8. Johnson, J., Alahi, A., Fei-Fei, L.: Perceptual losses for real-time style transfer and super-resolution. In: Leibe, B., Matas, J., Sebe, N., Welling, M. (eds.) ECCV 2016. LNCS, vol. 9906, pp. 694–711. Springer, Cham (2016). https://doi.org/10.1007/978-3-319-46475-6_43
9. Wang, X., et al.: ESRGAN: enhanced super-resolution generative adversarial networks. In: Leal-Taixé, L., Roth, S. (eds.) ECCV 2018. LNCS, vol. 11133, pp. 63–79. Springer, Cham (2019). https://doi.org/10.1007/978-3-030-11021-5_5
10. Li, Z., Yang, J., Liu, Z., Yang, X., Jeon, G., Wu, W.: Feedback network for image super-resolution. In: Proceedings of the IEEE Conference on Computer Vision and Pattern Recognition, pp. 3867–3876 (2019)
11. Kubade, A., Sharma, A., Rajan, K.S.: Feedback neural network based super-resolution of DEM for generating high fidelity features (2020)
12. Argudo, O., Chica, A., Andujar, C.: Terrain super-resolution through aerial imagery and fully convolutional networks. In: Computer Graphics Forum, vol. 37, pp. 101–110. Wiley Online Library (2018)
13. Xu, K., et al.: Show, attend and tell: neural image caption generation with visual attention. In: International Conference on Machine Learning, pp. 2048–2057 (2015)
14. Galin, E., et al.: A review of digital terrain modeling. In: Computer Graphics Forum, vol. 38, pp. 553–577. Wiley Online Library (2019)
15. Perlin, K.: An image synthesizer. ACM Siggraph Comput. Graph. **19**, 287–296 (1985)
16. Génevaux, J.D., Galin, É., Guérin, E., Peytavie, A., Benes, B.: Terrain generation using procedural models based on hydrology. ACM Trans. Graph. (TOG) **32**, 1–13 (2013)
17. Schneider, J., Boldte, T., Westermann, R.: Real-time editing, synthesis, and rendering of infinite landscapes on GPUs. In: Vision, Modeling and Visualization 2006, pp. 145–152 (2006)
18. Gain, J., Marais, P., Straßer, W.: Terrain sketching. In: Proceedings of the 2009 Symposium on Interactive 3D Graphics and Games, pp. 31–38 (2009)
19. Hnaidi, H., Guérin, E., Akkouche, S., Peytavie, A., Galin, E.: Feature based terrain generation using diffusion equation. In: Computer Graphics Forum, vol. 29, pp. 2179–2186. Wiley Online Library (2010)
20. Génevaux, J.D., et al.: Terrain modelling from feature primitives. In: Computer Graphics Forum, vol. 34, pp. 198–210. Wiley Online Library (2015)
21. Benes, B., Forsbach, R.: Layered data representation for visual simulation of terrain erosion. In: Proceedings Spring Conference on Computer Graphics, pp. 80–86. IEEE (2001)

22. Cordonnier, G., et al.: Authoring landscapes by combining ecosystem and terrain erosion simulation. ACM Trans. Graph. (TOG) **36**, 1–12 (2017)
23. Guérin, É., et al.: Interactive example-based terrain authoring with conditional generative adversarial networks. ACM Trans. Graph. (TOG) **36**, 1–13 (2017)
24. Allebach, J., Wong, P.W.: Edge-directed interpolation. In: Proceedings of 3rd IEEE International Conference on Image Processing, vol. 3, pp. 707–710. IEEE (1996)
25. Freeman, W.T., Pasztor, E.C., Carmichael, O.T.: Learning low-level vision. Int. J. Comput. Vis. **40**, 25–47 (2000). https://doi.org/10.1023/A:1026501619075
26. Freeman, W.T., Jones, T.R., Pasztor, E.C.: Example-based super-resolution. IEEE Comput. Graph. Appl. **22**, 56–65 (2002)
27. Huang, J.B., Singh, A., Ahuja, N.: Single image super-resolution from transformed self-exemplars. In: Proceedings of the IEEE Conference on Computer Vision and Pattern Recognition, pp. 5197–5206 (2015)
28. Gu, S., Zuo, W., Xie, Q., Meng, D., Feng, X., Zhang, L.: Convolutional sparse coding for image super-resolution. In: Proceedings of the IEEE International Conference on Computer Vision, pp. 1823–1831 (2015)
29. Tai, Y.W., Liu, S., Brown, M.S., Lin, S.: Super resolution using edge prior and single image detail synthesis. In: 2010 IEEE Computer Society Conference on Computer Vision and Pattern Recognition, pp. 2400–2407. IEEE (2010)
30. Sun, J., Xu, Z., Shum, H.Y.: Image super-resolution using gradient profile prior. In: 2008 IEEE Conference on Computer Vision and Pattern Recognition, pp. 1–8. IEEE (2008)
31. Kim, K.I., Kwon, Y.: Single-image super-resolution using sparse regression and natural image prior. IEEE Trans. Pattern Anal. Mach. Intell. **32**, 1127–1133 (2010)
32. Wang, Z., Liu, D., Yang, J., Han, W., Huang, T.: Deep networks for image super-resolution with sparse prior. In: Proceedings of the IEEE International Conference on Computer Vision, pp. 370–378 (2015)
33. Ledig, C., et al.: Photo-realistic single image super-resolution using a generative adversarial network. In: Proceedings of the IEEE Conference on Computer Vision and Pattern Recognition, pp. 4681–4690 (2017)
34. Zhang, K., Sun, M., Han, T.X., Yuan, X., Guo, L., Liu, T.: Residual networks of residual networks: multilevel residual networks. IEEE Trans. Circ. Syst. Video Technol. **28**, 1303–1314 (2017)
35. Tai, Y., Yang, J., Liu, X.: Image super-resolution via deep recursive residual network. In: Proceedings of the IEEE Conference on Computer Vision and Pattern Recognition, pp. 3147–3155 (2017)
36. Zamir, A.R., et al.: Feedback networks. In: Proceedings of the IEEE Conference on Computer Vision and Pattern Recognition, pp. 1308–1317 (2017)
37. Simonyan, K., Zisserman, A.: Very deep convolutional networks for large-scale image recognition. arXiv preprint arXiv:1409.1556 (2014)
38. Li, G., Xie, Y., Lin, L., Yu, Y.: Instance-level salient object segmentation. In: Proceedings of the IEEE Conference on Computer Vision and Pattern Recognition, pp. 2386–2395 (2017)
39. ICC: Institut cartogràfic i geològic de catalunya (ICC) (2020). http://www.icc.cat/vissir3. Accessed 2 Feb 2020
40. SBG: Südtiroler bürgernetz geokatalog (SBG) (2020). http://geokatalog.buergernetz.bz.it/geokatalog. Accessed 2 Feb 2020

Bi-Directional Attention for Joint Instance and Semantic Segmentation in Point Clouds

Guangnan Wu(ID), Zhiyi Pan(ID), Peng Jiang$^{(\boxtimes)}$(ID), and Changhe Tu$^{(\boxtimes)}$(ID)

Shandong University, Jinan, China
wuguangnan1006@gmail.com, panzhiyi1996@gmail.com, sdujump@gmail.com,
changhe.tu@gmail.com

Abstract. Instance segmentation in point clouds is one of the most fine-grained ways to understand the 3D scene. Due to its close relationship to semantic segmentation, many works approach these two tasks simultaneously and leverage the benefits of multi-task learning. However, most of them only considered simple strategies such as element-wise feature fusion, which may not lead to mutual promotion. In this work, we build a Bi-Directional Attention module on backbone neural networks for 3D point cloud perception, which uses similarity matrix measured from features for one task to help aggregate non-local information for the other task, avoiding the potential feature exclusion and task conflict. From comprehensive experiments on the three prevalent datasets, as well as ablation and efficiency studies, the superiority of our method is verified. Moreover, the mechanism of how bi-directional attention module helps joint instance and semantic segmentation is also analyzed.

1 Introduction

Among the tasks of computer vision, instance segmentation is one of the most challenge ones which requires understanding and perceiving the scene in unit and instance level. Notably, the vast demands for machines to interact with real scenarios, such as robotics and autonomous driving [1,2], make the instance segmentation in the 3D scene to be the hot research topic.

Though much progress has been made, 3D instance segmentation still lags far behind its 2D counterpart [3–8]. Unlike the 2D image, the 3D scene can be represented by many forms, such as multi-view projection images [9–13], volumes [14–17], and point clouds.

Since point clouds could represent a 3D scene more compactly and intuitively, and thus became more popular and drew more attention recently. The proposed PointNet [18] and some following works [19–28] could process the raw

Electronic supplementary material The online version of this chapter (https://doi.org/10.1007/978-3-030-69525-5_13) contains supplementary material, which is available to authorized users.

H. Ishikawa et al. (Eds.): ACCV 2020, LNCS 12622, pp. 209–226, 2021.
https://doi.org/10.1007/978-3-030-69525-5_13

point clouds directly, achieving remarkable performance on 3D classification and part segmentation tasks. The success brings the prospect for more fine-grained perception tasks in 3D point clouds, such as instance segmentation.

Instance segmentation in point clouds requires distinguishing category and instance belonging to each point. The most direct way is to regress further each instance's bounding box based on the semantic segmentation results, such as [29–31].

Due to the close relationship between instance segmentation and semantic segmentation, most of the recent works approach these two tasks simultaneously and use deep neural networks with two sub-branches for the two tasks, respectively [32–34]. Among them, many take feature fusion strategy letting features for one task promote the other task. However, in fact, the features of the two tasks are not completely compatible with each other. While points belong to different semantics must belong to different instances, points in the different instances are not necessarily of the different semantics. Obviously, directly concatenating or adding these two kinds of features in the model may lead to task conflict.

Actually, with simple element-wise feature fusion way such as concatenating and adding, only semantic features could always help distinguish instances in all the cases.

This situation poses a question, do we still need instance features for semantic segmentation and how to make these two tasks mutually promoted? In this work, we invest another way to incorporate features for semantic and instance segmentation. Instead of explicitly fusing features, we use similarity information implied in features for one task to assist the other task. Specifically, we first measure pair-wise similarity on semantic features to form the semantic similarity matrix, with which we propagate instance features. The propagation operation computes the response at a point as a weighted sum of the features at all points with semantic similarity as weight. Finally, the responses are further concatenated to the original instance features for instance segmentation. The same steps are also conducted in another direction that computing instance similarity matrix to propagate semantic features for semantic segmentation. The propagation operation could aggregate non-local information and is also referred to as attention [35–38]. Therefore, we name this kind of module as Bi-Directional Attention and call our networks as BAN.

The help of Bi-Directional Attention module lies in the following aspects. First, for aggregation operation applied to instance features for instance segmentation, semantic similarity matrix would help push instance features belonging to the different semantic apart. Though it will also pull instance features belonging to the same semantic together, the concatenated original instance features could still guarantee the difference distinguishable. Second, for aggregation operation applied on semantic features for semantic segmentation, instance similarity matrix would let semantic within each instance more consistent, thus improve the detail delineation. In addition to the positive effects when using bi-directional attention in a forward manner, the operation will also be good

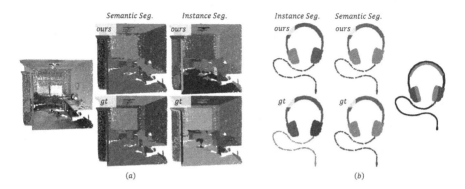

Semantic Seg.   Instance Seg.   Instance Seg.   Semantic Seg.
ours   ours   ours   ours
gt   gt   gt   gt

(a)   (b)

Fig. 1. Instance and semantic segmentation in point clouds using BAN. (a) Results on the S3DIS dataset, (b) Results on the PartNet dataset.

for back-propagating uniform gradients within the same semantic or instance. Consequently, our Bi-Directional Attention module could aggregate the features more properly and avoid potential task conflict.

We compare our BAN to state-of-the-art methods on prevalent 3D point cloud datasets, including S3DIS [39], PartNet [40] and ScanNetV2 [41]. Some instance and semantic segmentation results is shown in Fig. 1. In experiments, our method demonstrates consistent superiority according to most of the evaluation metrics. Moreover, we conduct detailed ablation, mechanism and efficiency studies, which suggest that the similarity matrices truly reflect the required pairwise semantic and instance similarities without too much computation complexity increase.

With attention operations from two directions together sequentially, BAN we can reach the best performance. Our code has been open sourced.

2   Related Works

Here, we mainly focus on methods that are most relevant to ours.

As well known, PointNet [18], for the first time, used neural networks to perceive point clouds and showed leading results on classification and semantic segmentation. However, it has difficulties in capturing local and fine-grained features. Correspondingly, many sequential works proposed to address this problem, such as [19–27].

Recently, instance segmentation in point clouds has drawn intense attention. Many works have been proposed and could be divided into two types in general, proposal-based and proposal-free. The former ones usually follow the scheme of Mask R-CNN [4] in 2D images, leading to a two-stage training, such as 3D-SIS [29] and GSPN [30]. Unlike them, BoNet [31] follows the one-stage scheme and regresses the bounding box directly. Nevertheless, the bounding box sometimes contains multiple objects or just a part of an object, making proposal-based methods hard to delineate the instance precisely. In contrast, the latter ones, *e.g.*, SGPN [42], 3D-BEVIS [43], JSIS3D [33], ASIS [32] and JSNet [34], directly produce representations to estimate the semantic categories and cluster the instance groups for each element, correspondingly, obtain more fine-grained perception.

It is worth to note that, whether for semantic segmentation or instance segmentation in 2D images, capturing long-range dependency and non-local information had been the consensus approach to improve accuracy. For this purpose, attention has been invented in [35], and become basic operation that applied prevalently [37,38]. However, this operation has not been well studied for 3D point cloud perception.

3   Motivation

In this work, we intend to propose a proposal-free type of joint instance and semantic segmentation method in point clouds. For this task, the key issue is how to incorporate the features of semantic and instance efficiently for mutual benefits. In view of the close relationship between instance and semantic segmentation, JSNet [34] fuses semantic and instance features to each other by simple aggregation strategies such as element-wise add and concatenate operations. In this way, the problem can be formalized as the following equations:

$$\mathcal{F}(\alpha(S_a, I_a)) \rightarrow C_a, \qquad \mathcal{F}(\alpha(S_b, I_b)) \rightarrow C_b,$$
$$\mathcal{H}(\alpha(S_a, I_a)) \rightarrow G_a, \qquad \mathcal{H}(\alpha(S_b, I_b)) \rightarrow G_b, \qquad (1)$$

where S_i and I_i represent semantic and instance features of point i respectively, and C_i and G_i are the semantic category and instance group of point i. α is some simple feature aggregating method. We use $\mathcal{F}$ and $\mathcal{H}$ to represent mapping functions for semantic and instance segmentation, respectively.

Ideally, there are three cases for two points a and b: (1) $C_a = C_b$ and $G_a \neq G_b$; (2) $C_a = C_b$ and $G_a = G_b$; (3) $C_a \neq C_b$ and $G_a \neq G_b$. In the first case, for semantic segmentation $\mathcal{F}$, aggregating S and I by α will make responses $\alpha(S_a, I_a)$ and $\alpha(S_b, I_b)$ far away. Thus C_a and C_b are hard to keep consistent, which is contrary to the case setting. In the second case, both $\mathcal{F}$ and $\mathcal{H}$ could get promoted by aggregating features of the same instance by α. The third case will not be considered when aggregating feature, because a and b are not relevant in either semantic or instance. So, with the simple aggregation strategy adopted by JSNet [34], there is a potential risk of task conflict in some specific cases.

Some works get rid of task conflict problem by introducing more complex feature aggregation strategies. JSIS3D [33] uses multi-value conditional random field to fuse semantic and instance, but it requires some approximation to optimize. ASIS [32] uses KNN to assemble more instance features from the neighborhood to each point and make the assembled feature more robust, but the KNN operation is non-differentiable and will break the back-propagation chain. The use of KNN in this work could be considered as proto non-local operation.

In summary, simple feature aggregation strategies such as element-wise add and concatenation will bring task conflict potential while other more complex feature aggregation strategies are far more satisfying.

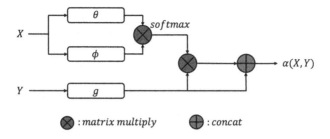

Fig. 2. Attention operation.

4 Methodology and Implementation

4.1 Methodology

As discussed in Sect. 3, for semantic segmentation, just adding or concatenating instance feature to semantic feature will be problematic. It poses a question, does instance feature has any help for semantic segmentation?

Here we suggest a way to use similarity information implied in the instance features to help semantic segmentation without any harm. To be specific, we propose to adjust the point's semantic feature as the weighted sum of semantic features of points belong to the same instance (with similar instance features). This way would make the semantic features robust and consistent within each instance, which will promote the details delineation.

To enable this function and take advantage of similar information in the instance features, we design the aggregation operation as:

$$\alpha(X, Y) = \{P \cdot g(Y), Y\},$$
$$P = softmax(\theta(X)\phi(X)^T),$$
(2)

where X and Y represent two kinds of features of size $N \times N_X$ and $N \times N_Y$ respectively (N is point number and N_i is number of channels for feature i). θ, ϕ and g are functions to re-weighted sum values in feature dimension with learned weights. Here, α is the concat operation. We measure similarities by inner-product of $\theta(X)$ and $\phi(X)$, which results into a matrix of size $N \times N$. We further apply $softmax$ on each row to get transition matrix which is our final similarity matrix P.

When X is instance features, and Y is semantic features, this operation propagates semantic features to other points by instance similarity matrix and the adjusted semantic features $P \cdot g(Y)$ will be more uniform in each instance than the original Y. Since there is no explicit element-wise adding or concatenating between semantic and instance features, using the final aggregation result $\alpha(X, Y)$ for semantic segmentation will not have the problems mentioned in the last section. Besides, this aggregation operation has the non-local characteristic naturally. For these reasons, we will also use it to fuse semantic features for instance segmentation. In other words, we will conduct another aggregation operation with X as semantic features and Y as instance features for instance segmentation. It is worth to note that though in this case, Eq. 2 will tend to pull instance features belonging to the same semantic together, the concatenated original instance features could still guarantee the difference distinguishable.

The above-defined operation has a similar form as attention in [35]. However, we have two of them with different architecture and goals. We have two different data flow directions, to aggregate semantic and instance features with the help of similarity inherent in features. Consequently, we name the proposed module as the Bi-Directional Attention module. The architecture of our module is illustrated in Fig. 2.

4.2   Implementation

Networks. By connecting the Bi-Directional Attention module to the end of the feature extracting backbone, we have the Bi-Directional Attention networks (BAN), which uses two attention operations to achieve information transmission and aggregation between instance branch and semantic branch. The full pipeline of our networks is illustrated in Fig. 3.

Our BAN is composed of a shared encoder, and two parallel decoders to produce representations for estimating the semantic categories and clustering the instance groups. Specifically, our backbone is PointNet++ [19]. Given input point clouds of size N, the backbone first extracts and encodes them into feature matrix which further decoded to semantic feature matrix S of size $N \times N_S$ and instance feature matrix I of $N \times N_I$.

The Bi-Directional Attention module takes these two feature matrices as input and will conduct two attention operations as defined by Eq. 2. We name the attention operation that computes semantic similarity matrix applied to instance features for instance segmentation as STOI, and attention operation that computes instance similarity matrix applied to semantic features for semantic segmentation as ITOS. The output of STOI is further passed to some simple fully connected layers (FC) to produces instance embedding space (of size $N \times N_E$), while the output of ITOS is further passed to some simple fully connected layers (FC) to give semantic prediction (of size $N \times N_C$). To get the instance groups, we cluster the produced instance embedding space by mean-shift method [44].

There are three kinds of sequences to conduct STOI and ITOS, and they are STOI first, ITOS first, and simultaneously. Here we use STOI first because we will use pixel-level regression loss for semantic segmentation and discriminative loss for instance segmentation, and we believe semantic features will converge faster than instance features. So, semantic features will give instance segmentation task more help at the beginning. This assumption will be verified in our ablation study in Sect. 5.

Loss Function. Our loss function $\mathcal{L}$ has two parts, semantic segmentation loss $\mathcal{L}_{sem}$ and instance segmentation loss $\mathcal{L}_{ins}$. These two parts are optimized at the same time:

$$\mathcal{L} = \mathcal{L}_{sem} + \mathcal{L}_{ins}. \tag{3}$$

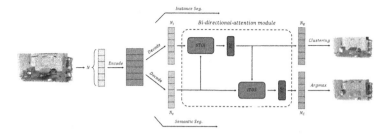

Fig. 3. The pipeline of proposed Bi-Directional Attention Networks (BAN).

We use cross-entropy loss for $\mathcal{L}_{sem}$, and choose discriminative loss for 2D images in [8] as $\mathcal{L}_{ins}$. The discriminative loss has been extended to 3D point clouds and used by many works [32–34]. $\mathcal{L}_{ins}$ will penalize the grouping of the points across different instances and bring the points belonging to the same instance closer in the embedding space. For the details, please check the supplementary.

Derivative Analysis. The above sections have explained how our module gives help in a forward manner. Here we further analyze the back-propagation of proposed Eq. 2. To simplify the problem, we first give a simple version of Eq. 2 without softmax, re-weight functions, and concatenation of original features:

$$Z = XX^TY. \tag{4}$$

where Z is the output of simplified attention operation.

In this case, the derivatives with respect to feature X and Y are:

$$
\begin{aligned}
vec(d\mathcal{L}) &= (\frac{\partial \mathcal{L}}{\partial Z})^T vec(dZ) \\
&= (\frac{\partial \mathcal{L}}{\partial Z})^T [vec(dXX^TY) + vec(XdX^TY)] \\
&= (\frac{\partial \mathcal{L}}{\partial Z})^T [(X^TY)^T \otimes E_N + (Y^T \otimes X)K_{NN_X}]vec(dX) \\
\frac{\partial \mathcal{L}}{\partial X} &= [(X^TY) \otimes E_N + K_{NN_X}(Y \otimes X^T)]\frac{\partial \mathcal{L}}{\partial Z}
\end{aligned}
\tag{5}
$$

$$
\begin{aligned}
vec(d\mathcal{L}) &= (\frac{\partial \mathcal{L}}{\partial Z})^T vec(dZ) \\
&= (\frac{\partial \mathcal{L}}{\partial Z})^T vec(XX^TdY) \\
&= (\frac{\partial \mathcal{L}}{\partial Z})^T (E_{N_Y} \otimes XX^T)vec(dY) \\
\frac{\partial \mathcal{L}}{\partial Y} &= (E_{N_Y} \otimes XX^T)\frac{\partial \mathcal{L}}{\partial Z}
\end{aligned}
\tag{6}
$$

where $vec()$ means matrix vectorization and $\otimes$ represents Kronecker Product, E is identity matrix and K is commutation matrix.

It can be seen, the similarity matrices also appear in $\frac{\partial \mathcal{L}}{\partial X}$ and $\frac{\partial \mathcal{L}}{\partial Y}$. As for XX^T in $\frac{\partial \mathcal{L}}{\partial Y}$, it will make the gradients uniform and robust within a similar region defined by X (semantic or instance), thus help optimization. As for $X^T Y$, it computes similarities between different features of X and Y other than points and provides another crucial information to extract robust and useful gradients.

In summary, the proposed Bi-Directional Attention module not only help joint instance and semantic segmentation by transmitting and aggregating information between instance features and semantic features, and also be good for back-propagating uniform and robust gradients.

5 Experiments

5.1 Experiments Setting

Datasets. We train and evaluate methods on three prevalent used datasets. *Stanford 3D Indoor Semantics (S3DIS)* [39] contains 3D scans in 6 areas including 271 rooms. Each scanned 3D point is associated with an instance label and a semantic label from 13 categories. *PartNet* [40] contains 573,585 fine-grained part instances with annotations and has 24 object categories. *ScanNetV2* [41] is an RGB-D video dataset containing 2.5 million views in more than 1500 scans.

Evaluation Metrics. For semantic segmentation, we compare our BAN with others by overall accuracy (oAcc), mean accuracy (mAcc), and mean IoU (mIoU).

As for instance segmentation, coverage (Cov) and weighted coverage (WCov) [45–47] are adopted.

Cov and Wcov are defined as:

$$Cov(\mathcal{G}, \mathcal{O}) = \sum_{i=1}^{|\mathcal{G}|} \frac{1}{|\mathcal{G}|} \max_j IoU(r_i^G, r_j^O) \tag{7}$$

$$WCov(\mathcal{G}, \mathcal{O}) = \sum_{i=1}^{|\mathcal{G}|} \frac{1}{|\mathcal{G}|} \omega_i \max_j IoU(r_i^G, r_j^O), \quad \omega_i = \frac{|r_i^G|}{\sum_k |r_k^G|} \tag{8}$$

where ground-truth is denoted as $\mathcal{G}$ and prediction is denoted as $\mathcal{O}$, $|r_i^G|$ is the number of points in ground-truth i. Besides, the classical metrics mean precision (mPrec), and mean recall (mRec) with IoU threshold 0.5 are also reported.

Hyper-parameters. To optimize the proposed BAN, we use Adam optimizer [48] with batch size 12 and set initial learning rate as 0.001 following the "divided by 2 every $300k$ iterations" learning rate policy. During training, we use the default parameter setting in [8] for $\mathcal{L}_{ins}$. At test time, bandwidth is set to 0.6 for mean-shift clustering. BlockMerging algorithm proposed by SGPN [42] is used to merge instances from different blocks. Please check supplementary for the training and testing details on the three datasets.

Table 1. Instance segmentation results on S3DIS dataset.

Method	Backbone	mCov	mWCov	mPrec	mRec
Test on 6-fold cross-validation					
PointNet	PointNet	43.0	46.3	50.6	39.2
PointNet++	PointNet++	49.6	53.4	62.7	45.8
SGPN	PointNet	37.9	40.8	38.2	31.2
ASIS	PointNet++	51.2	55.1	63.6	47.5
BoNet	PointNet++	46.0	50.2	**65.6**	47.6
JSNet	PointNet++	46.4	50.3	58.9	43.0
Ours	PointNet++	**52.1**	**56.2**	63.4	**51.0**

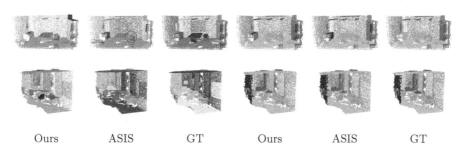

Ours   ASIS   GT   Ours   ASIS   GT

Fig. 4. Visual comparison of instance and semantic segmentation results on the S3DIS dataset. The first three columns are the instance segmentation results, while the last three columns show semantic segmentation results. (Color figure online)

5.2   S3DIS Results

In this section, we will compare our method (BAN) with other state-of-the-art methods, and the reported metric values are either from their papers or implemented and evaluated by ourselves when not available.

Instance Segmentation. In Table 1, six methods are compared, including PointNet [18], PointNet++ [19], SGPN [42], ASIS [32], BoNet [31] and our BAN. It's worth to note that, PointNet++ has the same architecture and settings as ours except the Bi-Directional Attention module, and thus can be treated as baseline. PointNet is similar to PointNet++ except the backbone. It can be seen, our BAN outperforms baseline (PointNet++) on all the metrics, and demonstrates significant superiority compared with others.

Semantic Segmentation. Since SGPN [42] and BoNet [31] do not provide semantic segmentation results. For semantic segmentation, we only compare PointNet [18], PointNet++ [19] and ASIS [32]. The evaluation results are shown in Table 2, from mAcc, mIoU, and oAcc, our method achieves the best performance consistently.

Table 2. Semantic segmentation results on S3DIS dataset.

Method	Backbone	mAcc	mIoU	oAcc
Test on 6-fold cross-validation				
PointNet	PointNet	60.7	49.5	80.4
PointNet++	PointNet++	69.0	58.2	85.9
ASIS	PointNet++	70.1	59.3	86.2
JSNet	PointNet++	65.5	56.3	85.5
Ours	PointNet++	**71.7**	**60.8**	**87.0**

Visual Comparison. We show some visual results of semantic and instance segmentation methods in Fig. 4. From results, we can see ours are more accurate and uniform compared with ASIS [32], especially for instance segmentation as marked by red circles. We believe it is because of the applying of attention operations and the introduction of non-local information. The more studies of attention mechanisms are in Sect. 6.

Table 3. Instance segmentation results on PartNet dataset.

Method	Backbone	mCov	mWCov	mPrec	mRec
PointNet++	PointNet++	42.0	43.1	51.2	44.7
ASIS	PointNet++	39.3	40.2	49.9	42.8
Ours	PointNet++	**42.7**	**44.2**	**52.8**	**45.3**

5.3 PartNet Results

In addition to object instance segmentation in indoor scenes, we further evaluate our method on part instance segmentation in objects using the PartNet dataset. This task is more fine-grained and thus requires more perception ability to understand the similarity between points.

The semantic and instance segmentation scores are listed in Tables 3, 4. We can see that the performance has a significant drop compared with the S3DIS. This is because the dataset contains many kinds of small semantic parts, which are difficult to perceive and predict, causing low semantic mIoU and instance mCov but relative high semantic oAcc.

For this kind of dataset with small semantic parts, ASIS [32] with KNN is difficult to adapt by a fixed range control parameter. However, with the Bi-Directional Attention module, our method could compute the similarities between any of two points and achieves better results.

The visual results on PartNet are shown in Fig. 5. Our method demonstrates obvious advantages compared with ASIS [32], and produces more accurate instance and semantic segmentation, especially for some small parts as marked by red circles. For other methods compared in S3DIS, their performance is not evaluated in this section, because we do not have their code or statistic report.

Table 4. Semantic segmentation results on PartNet dataset.

Method	Backbone	mAcc	mIoU	oAcc
PointNet++	PointNet++	53.4	43.4	78.4
ASIS	PointNet++	50.6	40.2	76.7
Ours	PointNet++	**56.1**	**44.9**	**80.3**

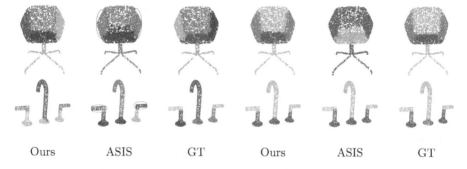

| Ours | ASIS | GT | Ours | ASIS | GT |

Fig. 5. Visual comparison of instance and semantic segmentation results on the Part-Net dataset. Columns are arranged as Fig. 4. (Color figure online)

5.4 ScanNetV2 Results

Finally, we evaluate the performance on the ScanNetV2 which is the biggest in-door 3D point cloud dataset by now. The quantitative results are listed in Table 5 and Table 6, while the qualitative results are shown in Fig. 6. We only evaluate the methods we have code or corresponding statistic report. All the results have verified the superiority of our method in the large scale dataset.

Table 5. Instance segmentation results on ScanNetV2 dataset.

Method	Backbone	mCov	mWCov	mPrec	mRec
PointNet++	PointNet++	39.0	40.1	46.0	40.1
ASIS	PointNet++	39.1	40.4	46.3	40.5
Ours	PointNet++	**40.4**	**41.7**	**48.2**	**42.2**

Table 6. Semantic segmentation results on ScanNetV2 dataset.

Method	Backbone	mAcc	mIoU	oAcc
PointNet++	PointNet++	58.3	47.1	82.3
ASIS	PointNet++	58.5	46.5	81.9
Ours	PointNet++	**60.8**	**48.8**	**82.7**

6   Discussion

In this section, we intend to show more evidence to justify the design and the mechanism of the proposed Bi-Directional Attention module.

6.1   Ablation Study

As mentioned in Sect. 4.2, there are three kinds of sequences to conduct STOI and ITOS in our Bi-Directional Attention module, and we gave an assumption to decide our design. Here, we will verify our choice and further prove the necessity to have both STOI and ITOS.

In Table 7, we give five rows of results for instance and semantic segmentation with different combinations and order of STOI and ITOS. The experiments are conducted on Area 5 of S3DIS [39]. We can see, by introducing STOI, the instance segmentation gets boosted. With ITOS, both instance and semantic segmentation demonstrate certain improvement, which suggests fusing instance

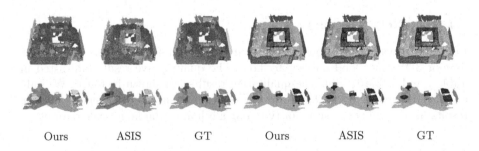

Ours   ASIS   GT   Ours   ASIS   GT

Fig. 6. Visual comparison of instance and semantic segmentation results on the Scan-NetV2 dataset. Columns are arranged as Fig. 4.

features for semantic segmentation in our way is very effective. Moreover, considering the potential task conflict when using simple element-wise feature aggregation strategies such as adding and concatenating, the improvement is more significant. Finally, with both STOI and ITOS, and STOI first, we achieve the best results. But, with an inverse order that ITOS first, the performance shows a large drop, even worse than results without STOI and ITOS. This phenomenon verified the importance of order to conduct STOI and ITOS and is worth to be studied further in the future.

Further, we test performance when $X = Y$ in Eq. 2 where our Bi-Directional Attention module is degraded to two independent self-attention operations [35]. The result is listed in the last row of Table 7. Obviously, without feature fusing, self-attention is not comparable to our method.

Table 7. Results of all ablation experiments on Area 5 of S3DIS.

Ablation		Instance segmentation				Semantic segmentation		
STOI	ITOS	mCov	mWCov	mPrec	mRec	mAcc	mIoU	oAcc
×	×	46.0	49.1	54.2	43.3	62.1	53.9	87.3
✓	×	47.1	50.1	55.3	43.6	61.2	53.4	87.0
×	✓	47.4	50.3	54.0	43.4	62.0	54.7	87.8
✓	✓	**49.0**	**52.1**	**56.7**	**45.9**	**62.5**	**55.2**	87.7
Inverse order		46.3	49.4	53.5	41.5	**62.5**	55.1	**87.9**
Self-attention		45.4	48.6	53.3	43.6	**62.5**	55.1	**87.9**

6.2 Mechanism Study

Here, we visualize the learned instance and semantic similarity matrices P defined in Eq. 2 to study and verify their mechanism. The similarity matrix is the key functional unit, which builds the pair-wise similarities and uses to weighted-sum non-local information. A good instance similarity matrix should accurately reflect the similarity relationship between all of the points, so P are of size $N \times N$. When the instance/semantic similarity matrix trained well, it will help generate uniform and robust semantic/instance features. Besides, good instance and semantic similarity matrices will also benefit the back-propagation process, as stated in Sect. 4.2.

In Fig. 7, for trained networks and each sample, we select the same row from instance similarity matrix and semantic similarity matrix, respectively, then reshape the row vector to the 3D point cloud. So, the value of each point here represents the similarity to the point corresponding to the selected row. For better visualization, we binarize the 3D point cloud to divide points into two groups, similar points (green) and dissimilar points (blue) and marked the point corresponding to the selected row by red circle. Each sample of Fig. 7 has

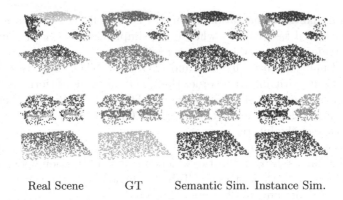

Real Scene   GT   Semantic Sim. Instance Sim.

Fig. 7. Visualization of instance and semantic similarity matrices. One row for each sample. From left to right, they are real scene blocks (each has two chairs), ground truth (instance), point cloud reflecting semantic similarity, point cloud reflecting instance similarity. (Color figure online)

two chairs in the scenes. We can see that the semantic similarity matrix could basically correctly reflect the semantic similarities, and the instance similarity matrix could highlight most of the points in the same instance.

Table 8. Speed and memory

Method	Backbone	Speed with/without clustering	GPU memory cost
Pointnet++	PointNet++	1859/**322** s	4500 MB
ASIS	PointNet++	2146/501 s	4500 MB+64 MB
Our model	PointNet++	**1649**/361 s	4500 MB+64 MB

6.3 Efficiency Study

In Table 8, we report the computation speed and memory cost of ours and some other methods. For memory cost, with size of 4096×4096 and single precision, our similarity matrix will cost $64M$ memory. Though we have two similarity matrices, they are constructed sequentially, so the maximum cost of GPU memory is $4500M+64M$. ASIS also has a matrix of size 4096 × 4096. The storage of the similarity matrix can be further reduced with one-way/three-way, criss-cross connection operations [49,50].

For computation speed, ASIS is the slowest one, because it needs another KNN step. Though our method will spend more time on network feed-forward (without cluster op) than the backbone, we are faster over the whole process (with cluster op) because we divide the features of different instances far apart and make mean-shift converge quickly. In summary, our similarity matrices do not cost too much computation and memory.

7   Conclusion

We present Bi-Directional Attention Networks (BAN) for joint instance and semantic segmentation. Instead of element-wised fusing features for two tasks, our Bi-Directional Attention module builds instance and semantic similarity matrices from the instance and semantic features, respectively, with which two attention operations are conducted to bi-directionally aggregate features implicitly, introduce non-local information and avoid potential task conflict. Experiments on the three prevalent datasets S3DIS, PartNet and ScanNetV2 and method analysis suggest that the Bi-Directional Attention module could help give uniform and robust results within the same semantic or instance regions, and would also help to back-propagate uniform and robust gradients for optimization. Our BAN demonstrates significant superiority compared with baseline and other state-of-the-art works on the instance and semantic segmentation tasks consistently. Moreover, the ablation, mechanism and efficiency study further verifies the design and effectiveness of the Bi-Directional Attention module.

Acknowledgment. This work was funded by National Key Research & Development Plan of China (No. 2017YFB1002603), National Natural Science Foundation of China (61702301, 61772318) and Fundamental Research Funds of Shandong University.

References

1. Nguyen, A., Le, B.: 3D point cloud segmentation: a survey. In: 2013 6th IEEE Conference on Robotics, Automation and Mechatronics (RAM), pp. 225–230. IEEE (2013)
2. Ioannidou, A., Chatzilari, E., Nikolopoulos, S., Kompatsiaris, I.: Deep learning advances in computer vision with 3D data: a survey. ACM Comput. Surv. (CSUR) **50**, 1–38 (2017)
3. Pinheiro, P.O., Collobert, R., Dollár, P.: Learning to segment object candidates. In: Advances in Neural Information Processing Systems, pp. 1990–1998 (2015)
4. He, K., Gkioxari, G., Dollár, P., Girshick, R.: Mask R-CNN. In: Proceedings of the IEEE International Conference on Computer Vision, pp. 2961–2969 (2017)
5. Li, Y., Qi, H., Dai, J., Ji, X., Wei, Y.: Fully convolutional instance-aware semantic segmentation. In: Proceedings of the IEEE Conference on Computer Vision and Pattern Recognition, pp. 2359–2367 (2017)
6. Dai, J., He, K., Sun, J.: Instance-aware semantic segmentation via multi-task network cascades. In: Proceedings of the IEEE Conference on Computer Vision and Pattern Recognition, pp. 3150–3158 (2016)
7. Dai, J., He, K., Li, Y., Ren, S., Sun, J.: Instance-sensitive fully convolutional networks. In: Leibe, B., Matas, J., Sebe, N., Welling, M. (eds.) ECCV 2016. LNCS, vol. 9910, pp. 534–549. Springer, Cham (2016). https://doi.org/10.1007/978-3-319-46466-4_32
8. De Brabandere, B., Neven, D., Van Gool, L.: Semantic instance segmentation with a discriminative loss function. arXiv preprint arXiv:1708.02551 (2017)
9. Su, H., Maji, S., Kalogerakis, E., Learned-Miller, E.: Multi-view convolutional neural networks for 3D shape recognition. In: Proceedings of the IEEE International Conference on Computer Vision, pp. 945–953 (2015)

10. Qi, C.R., Su, H., Nießner, M., Dai, A., Yan, M., Guibas, L.J.: Volumetric and multi-view CNNs for object classification on 3D data. In: Proceedings of the IEEE Conference on Computer Vision and Pattern Recognition, pp. 5648–5656 (2016)
11. Shi, B., Bai, S., Zhou, Z., Bai, X.: DeepPano: deep panoramic representation for 3-D shape recognition. IEEE Sig. Process. Lett. **22**, 2339–2343 (2015)
12. Guerry, J., Boulch, A., Le Saux, B., Moras, J., Plyer, A., Filliat, D.: SnapNet-R: consistent 3D multi-view semantic labeling for robotics. In: Proceedings of the IEEE International Conference on Computer Vision Workshops, pp. 669–678 (2017)
13. Nguyen, D.T., Hua, B.S., Tran, K., Pham, Q.H., Yeung, S.K.: A field model for repairing 3D shapes. In: Proceedings of the IEEE Conference on Computer Vision and Pattern Recognition, pp. 5676–5684 (2016)
14. Wu, Z., et al.: 3D ShapeNets: a deep representation for volumetric shapes. In: Proceedings of the IEEE Conference on Computer Vision and Pattern Recognition, pp. 1912–1920 (2015)
15. Maturana, D., Scherer, S.: VoxNet: a 3D convolutional neural network for real-time object recognition. In: 2015 IEEE/RSJ International Conference on Intelligent Robots and Systems (IROS), pp. 922–928. IEEE (2015)
16. Riegler, G., Osman Ulusoy, A., Geiger, A.: OctNet: learning deep 3D representations at high resolutions. In: Proceedings of the IEEE Conference on Computer Vision and Pattern Recognition, pp. 3577–3586 (2017)
17. Wang, P.S., Liu, Y., Guo, Y.X., Sun, C.Y., Tong, X.: O-CNN: octree-based convolutional neural networks for 3D shape analysis. ACM Trans. Graph. (TOG) **36**, 1–11 (2017)
18. Qi, C.R., Su, H., Mo, K., Guibas, L.J.: PointNet: deep learning on point sets for 3D classification and segmentation. In: Proceedings of the IEEE Conference on Computer Vision and Pattern Recognition, pp. 652–660 (2017)
19. Qi, C.R., Yi, L., Su, H., Guibas, L.J.: PointNet++: deep hierarchical feature learning on point sets in a metric space. In: Advances in Neural Information Processing Systems, pp. 5099–5108 (2017)
20. Huang, Q., Wang, W., Neumann, U.: Recurrent slice networks for 3D segmentation of point clouds. In: Proceedings of the IEEE Conference on Computer Vision and Pattern Recognition, pp. 2626–2635 (2018)
21. Wang, Y., Sun, Y., Liu, Z., Sarma, S.E., Bronstein, M.M., Solomon, J.M.: Dynamic graph CNN for learning on point clouds. ACM Trans. Graph. (TOG) **38**, 1–12 (2019)
22. Landrieu, L., Simonovsky, M.: Large-scale point cloud semantic segmentation with superpoint graphs. In: Proceedings of the IEEE Conference on Computer Vision and Pattern Recognition, pp. 4558–4567 (2018)
23. Hua, B.S., Tran, M.K., Yeung, S.K.: Pointwise convolutional neural networks. In: Proceedings of the IEEE Conference on Computer Vision and Pattern Recognition, pp. 984–993 (2018)
24. Li, Y., Bu, R., Sun, M., Wu, W., Di, X., Chen, B.: PointCNN: convolution on X-transformed points. In: Advances in Neural Information Processing Systems, pp. 820–830 (2018)
25. Ye, X., Li, J., Huang, H., Du, L., Zhang, X.: 3D recurrent neural networks with context fusion for point cloud semantic segmentation. In: Proceedings of the European Conference on Computer Vision (ECCV), pp. 403–417 (2018)
26. Rethage, D., Wald, J., Sturm, J., Navab, N., Tombari, F.: Fully-convolutional point networks for large-scale point clouds. In: Proceedings of the European Conference on Computer Vision (ECCV), pp. 596–611 (2018)

27. Wu, W., Qi, Z., Fuxin, L.: PointConv: deep convolutional networks on 3D point clouds. In: Proceedings of the IEEE Conference on Computer Vision and Pattern Recognition, pp. 9621–9630 (2019)
28. Yan, X., Zheng, C., Li, Z., Wang, S., Cui, S.: PointASNL: robust point clouds processing using nonlocal neural networks with adaptive sampling. In: Proceedings of the IEEE Conference on Computer Vision and Pattern Recognition, pp. 5588–5597 (2020)
29. Hou, J., Dai, A., Nießner, M.: 3D-SIS: 3D semantic instance segmentation of RGB-D scans. In: Proceedings of the IEEE Conference on Computer Vision and Pattern Recognition, pp. 4421–4430 (2019)
30. Yi, L., Zhao, W., Wang, H., Sung, M., Guibas, L.J.: GSPN: generative shape proposal network for 3D instance segmentation in point cloud. In: Proceedings of the IEEE Conference on Computer Vision and Pattern Recognition, pp. 3947–3956 (2019)
31. Yang, B., et al.: Learning object bounding boxes for 3D instance segmentation on point clouds. In: Advances in Neural Information Processing Systems, pp. 6737–6746 (2019)
32. Wang, X., Liu, S., Shen, X., Shen, C., Jia, J.: Associatively segmenting instances and semantics in point clouds. In: Proceedings of the IEEE Conference on Computer Vision and Pattern Recognition, pp. 4096–4105 (2019)
33. Pham, Q.H., Nguyen, T., Hua, B.S., Roig, G., Yeung, S.K.: JSIS3D: joint semantic-instance segmentation of 3D point clouds with multi-task pointwise networks and multi-value conditional random fields. In: Proceedings of the IEEE Conference on Computer Vision and Pattern Recognition, pp. 8827–8836 (2019)
34. Zhao, L., Tao, W.: JSNet: joint instance and semantic segmentation of 3D point clouds. In: Thirty-Fourth AAAI Conference on Artificial Intelligence, pp. 12951–12958 (2020)
35. Wang, X., Girshick, R., Gupta, A., He, K.: Non-local neural networks. In: Proceedings of the IEEE Conference on Computer Vision and Pattern Recognition, pp. 7794–7803 (2018)
36. Vaswani, A., et al.: Attention is all you need. In: Advances in Neural Information Processing Systems, pp. 5998–6008 (2017)
37. Zhao, H., et al.: PSANet: point-wise spatial attention network for scene parsing. In: Proceedings of the European Conference on Computer Vision (ECCV), pp. 267–283 (2018)
38. Fu, J., et al.: Dual attention network for scene segmentation. In: Proceedings of the IEEE Conference on Computer Vision and Pattern Recognition, pp. 3146–3154 (2019)
39. Armeni, I., et al.: 3D semantic parsing of large-scale indoor spaces. In: Proceedings of the IEEE Conference on Computer Vision and Pattern Recognition, pp. 1534–1543 (2016)
40. Mo, K., et al.: PartNet: a large-scale benchmark for fine-grained and hierarchical part-level 3D object understanding. In: Proceedings of the IEEE Conference on Computer Vision and Pattern Recognition, pp. 909–918 (2019)
41. Dai, A., Chang, A.X., Savva, M., Halber, M., Funkhouser, T., Nießner, M.: ScanNet: richly-annotated 3D reconstructions of indoor scenes. In: Proceedings of the IEEE Conference on Computer Vision and Pattern Recognition, pp. 5828–5839 (2017)
42. Wang, W., Yu, R., Huang, Q., Neumann, U.: SGPN: similarity group proposal network for 3D point cloud instance segmentation. In: Proceedings of the IEEE Conference on Computer Vision and Pattern Recognition, pp. 2569–2578 (2018)

43. Elich, C., Engelmann, F., Schult, J., Kontogianni, T., Leibe, B.: 3D-BEVIS: birds-eye-view instance segmentation. arXiv preprint arXiv:1904.02199 (2019)

44. Cheng, Y.: Mean shift, mode seeking, and clustering. IEEE Trans. Pattern Anal. Mach. Intell. **17**, 790–799 (1995)

45. Ren, M., Zemel, R.S.: End-to-end instance segmentation with recurrent attention. In: Proceedings of the IEEE Conference on Computer Vision and Pattern Recognition, pp. 6656–6664 (2017)

46. Liu, S., Jia, J., Fidler, S., Urtasun, R.: SGN: sequential grouping networks for instance segmentation. In: Proceedings of the IEEE International Conference on Computer Vision, pp. 3496–3504 (2017)

47. Zhuo, W., Salzmann, M., He, X., Liu, M.: Indoor scene parsing with instance segmentation, semantic labeling and support relationship inference. In: Proceedings of the IEEE Conference on Computer Vision and Pattern Recognition, pp. 5429–5437 (2017)

48. Kingma, D.P., Ba, J.: Adam: a method for stochastic optimization (2015)

49. Liu, S., De Mello, S., Gu, J., Zhong, G., Yang, M.H., Kautz, J.: Learning affinity via spatial propagation networks. In: Advances in Neural Information Processing Systems, pp. 1520–1530 (2017)

50. Huang, Z., Wang, X., Huang, L., Huang, C., Wei, Y., Liu, W.: CCNet: criss-cross attention for semantic segmentation. In: Proceedings of the IEEE International Conference on Computer Vision, pp. 603–612 (2019)

Anatomy and Geometry Constrained One-Stage Framework for 3D Human Pose Estimation

Xin Cao[1,2] and Xu Zhao[1,2(✉)]

[1] Department of Automation, Shanghai Jiao Tong University, Shanghai, China
[2] Institute of Medical Robotics, Shanghai Jiao Tong University, Shanghai, China
{xinc1024,zhaoxu}@sjtu.edu.cn

Abstract. Although significant progress has been achieved in monocular 3D human pose estimation, the correlation between body parts and cross-view geometry consistency have not been well studied. In this work, to fully explore the priors on body structure and view-relationship for 3D human pose estimation, we propose an anatomy and geometry constrained one-stage framework. First of all, we define a kinematic structure model in deep learning framework which represents the joint positions in a tree-structure model. Then we propose bone-length and bone-symmetry losses based on the anatomy prior, to encode the body structure information. To further explore the cross-view geometry information, we introduce a novel training mechanism for multi-view consistency constraints, which effectively reduces unnatural and implausible estimation results. The proposed approach achieves state-of-the-art results on both Human3.6M and MPI-INF-3DHP data sets.

1 Introduction

Human pose estimation is a fundamental task in computer vision and has been studied for decades. It refers to estimating human anatomical key points or parts and supports many applications, such as human-computer interaction, video surveillance, augmented reality, sports performance analysis and so forth [1].

In traditional way, some approaches try to learn a concise low-dimensional embedding [2] of high-dimensional 3D pose structure space to solve this problem. Pictorial structure model [3] is another representative way to model body structure, where the joints and their relations are represented as vertexes and edges respectively in a non-circular graph. Actually, tree-structured model is the

This work has been supported in part by the funding from NSFC (61673269, 61273285) and the project funding of the Institute of Medical Robotics at Shanghai Jiao Tong University.

Electronic supplementary material The online version of this chapter (https://doi.org/10.1007/978-3-030-69525-5_14) contains supplementary material, which is available to authorized users.

H. Ishikawa et al. (Eds.): ACCV 2020, LNCS 12622, pp. 227–243, 2021.
https://doi.org/10.1007/978-3-030-69525-5_14

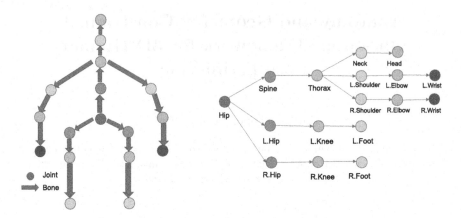

Fig. 1. Representation of human joints and bones in a body tree structure, different colors indicate different hierarchy levels. (Color figure online)

most popular pose representation and had been well studied in the traditional methods. For example, Yub et al. [4] proposed a kinematic tree pose estimation method along with the RTW expectation, where the joint positions are determined sequentially according to the typical skeletal topology.

Recently with the development of Deep Learning (DL) and the emergence of large scale 3D pose data sets [2,5], many state-of-the-art methods [6–10] have been proposed for 3D human pose estimation. These methods can be simply divided into two categories. In the first category, 3D pose positions are directly regressed from raw images. While in the second category, usually a well-trained 2D pose network is used to estimate 2D joint positions, and then a following 2D-3D lifting network is used to further acquire 3D poses.

Despite the remarkable progress that has been achieved, we argue that most of the existing 3D human pose estimation methods in DL framework treated the body joints independently and overlooked the structure information and the correlation between body parts. Seldom method utilizes kinematic structure information. Besides, current popular 3D human pose data sets like Human3.6M [2] and MPI-INF-3DHP [11] are captured in multi-view settings. However, the geometry information that can be extracted via multi-view consistency constrains have not been well studied yet.

To address the above mentioned issues, we propose an anatomy and geometry constrained one-stage framework which impose the anatomy prior and fully explore the geometry relationship for 3D human pose estimation.

In fact, the human body is like a tree structure. Suppose that the hip joint is a root node, according to the distance to the root joint, we can define six hierarchical levels of human body joints as illustrated in Fig. 1. Usually the motion range of the leaf node joint is larger than its parent node joint, so it is more difficult to estimate its 3D joint locations. Therefore it is intuitive to infer the location of the child node joint as a dependent valuable of its parent node joint's location and hence get more plausible results. To this end, we first define a **kinematic structure model** in a deep learning framework which represents human joint positions by the root joint position and each joints' transformation matrices relative to their parent joints. In this way, we can obtain the position of a joint by multiplying the transformation matrix to its parent joint along the way to the root joint following a kinematic tree. To simplify the learning process, we further decompose the transformation matrices into rotation angles and translation parameters.

To avoid the error accumulation with the expansion of the kinematic tree, following the idea of Newell et al. [12], we adopt **bone-length loss** [13], which usually is reliable information and acts as intermediate supervision during the training process. In addition, we bring up a novel **bone-symmetry loss** function based on the symmetry of human's left/right parts to penalize the inequality between the left/right limbs. These two loss functions are both based on body anatomy prior and with which some implausible results are effectively removed.

Besides, in order to fully explore the cross-view geometry relationship, we propose a **multi-view consistency constraints** algorithm to study the latent pose representation. Pose estimation results of the same person from different camera views are mapped to a latent space to encode the pose information and then the similarity between them is computed. In this way, the model is required to output the same pose representation for multi-view inputs, which implicitly explores the geometry information from different views and strengthen the generalization ability of the model.

Our contributions can be summarized as follows:

- We propose a one-stage deep learning framework with anatomy-aware kinematic structure model, by which human body structure information and anatomy prior can be captured effectively.
- We show that adding multi-view consistency constraints into the one-stage framework is able to explore the geometry relationship and reduce implausible results for 3D human pose estimation.
- Quantitative and qualitative experiments are conducted on public 3D human pose estimation data-sets, and the results demonstrate the effectiveness of our proposed method.

2   Related Work

Here we will briefly review the two main streams of 3D pose estimation solutions, the *one-stage* methods and the *two-stage* ones.

2.1   One Stage Methods

One-stage methods usually directly regresses 3D pose positions from raw images [6–9,13,14]. According to the final representation of human pose, this method can be further divided into regression-based and detection-based sub-categories.

Regression based methods directly map the input image space to the output joint positions. Li et al. [15] proposed a multi-task learning task which simultaneously conducted joint point regression and joint point detection tasks. Tekin et al. [16] introduced an auto-decoder model to learn a high-dimensional latent pose representation and account for joint dependencies. After that, the latent representation was mapped back to the original pose space using the decoder. The regression based method usually obtained unsatisfactory performance, because mapping raw image to the pose space is a highly non-linear process and ignores the spatial relationship between body parts. Besides, the detection based methods regard the human pose estimation problem as a detection problem and usually output a heatmap for each joint. Pavlakos et al. [17] proposed a fine discretization of the 3D space around the human body subject and trained a convNet to predict per voxel likelihoods for each joint. To improve the initial estimation positions, they used a coarse-to-fine scheme to further improve the results. In order to overcome the quantization error of the argmax operation, Sun et al. [7] proposed an integral regression method to take the expectation of the heatmap as the output 3D joint locations.

Due to the lack of large-scale in-the-wild 3D human pose datasets, there are also some researches for weakly-supervised and unsupervised 3D human pose estimation. Zhou et al. [6] used mixed 2D and 3D labels in a deep neural network which presented a two-stage cascaded structure. 2D datasets does not have 3D labels but with diverse in-the-wild images, and hence acted as weak labels for 3D pose estimation. Yang et al. [8] proposed a multi-source discriminator to distinguish the predicted 3D pose from the ground truth. Rhogin et al. [18] introduced multi-view constraints as weak supervision and trained the system to predict the same pose from all views.

As for the kinematic related works, Mount et al. [19] defined the kinematics or forward kinematic as the problem of determining where a point is transformed as a result of the rotations associated with individual joints. For the deep learning based method, Zhou et al. [20] developed a new layer to realize the non-linear forward kinematics in human hand pose estimation and obtained geometrically valid results. Zhou et al. [21] introduced the kinematic structure model for 3D human pose estimation and demonstrated its effectiveness. In fact, our method takes the inspiration from this work but have several improvements.

- In the work of [21], the root joint is simply fixed at the origin point and the bone length is set as the average of the training subject with a global scale. However, it will reduce the generality of the method and lead to intrinsic errors because scale is unknown for the test phase. Therefore, we add the root joint position and bone length as learnable parameters in the network and optimized with the training data.
- We introduce body bone length and symmetry loss which is able to express the anatomy prior and also act as intermediate supervision to avoid the accumulation of errors in the kinematic tree.

2.2   Two Stage Methods

While the two-stage methods usually first used a well-trained 2D pose network to estimate 2D pose positions, then trained a 2D-3D lifting network to further acquire 3D joint positions [10, 22–26]. Thanks to the available of large scale 2D human pose datasets, these methods were able to acquire accurate 2D pose results and focused on the 2D-to-3D mapping process.

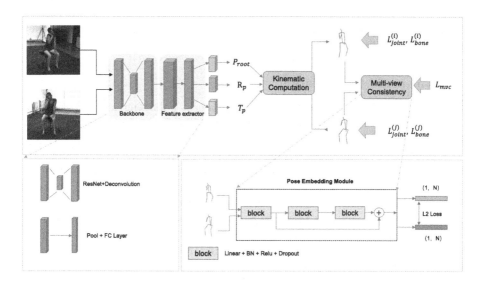

Fig. 2. Diagram of the proposed anatomy and geometry constrained framework. During training, a pair of images of different views (I_i, I_j) taken from the same person are sent to the network and acquire the corresponding root joint locations, rotation parameters and translation parameters. Then with the kinematic computation module we can compute the joint locations with the predefined process. The output of the network is optimized by the joint loss, body bone loss and multi-view consistency loss which is implemented by the pose embedding module. During inference, the network takes a single image as input and output its 3D joint locations.

Chen et al. [22] proposed to first generate a 2d pose result and then estimate its depth by matching to a library of 3d pose. Martinez et al. [23] used several residual blocks to learn the mapping from 2D joints to 3D joints, and found that a large portion of the error of modern deep 3d pose estimation systems stems from their visual analysis. Li et al. [10] proposed a multi-modal mixture density network to generate multiple hypothesis of the 3D pose for 2D joints. Drover et al. [24] utilized an adversarial framework to impose a prior on the 3D structure which is learned solely from their random 2D projections. Zhao et al. [27] proposed a semantic graph convolutional network to infer 3D joint locations from 2D joints.

3   Method

Given a cropped image $I \in \mathbb{R}^{W \times H \times 3}$, we aim to learn a mapping function θ, such that $\theta(I) = P_K$, where $P_K \in \mathbb{R}^{3 \times K}$ is the estimated position of K joints. We assume that x, y are in image pixel coordinates while z is the relative depth value to the root joint in camera coordinates.

The diagram of our proposed anatomy and geometry constrained framework is illustrated in Fig. 2. In this section, we will first introduce the kinematic computation process and the kinematic structure model. Then we will explain the bone-length and bone-symmetry loss as well as the multi-view consistency constraints. Finally we will demonstrate the total loss function for training.

3.1   Kinematic Computation

A human body is composed of joints and bones. Following a kinematic tree structure, we can reach any position of body joints from root joint with body structure information.

Suppose that the hip joint is a root node in a tree structure, we can categorize the body joints into different hierarchies according to the distance to the root joint. For example, the left hip, right hip and spine joint can be considered as the second hierarchy because they can reach the root joint without passing any other joints. Following this idea, we can define six hierarchy levels of human body joints as illustrated in Fig. 1, the circle dots indicate the 17 body joints while different colors demonstrate different hierarchy levels in a tree structure. Besides, we use arrows to define bone structures which start from parent joint and heads to its child joint.

Following the idea of [21], we can obtain the position of a child joint with its parent joint's position and the corresponding rotation and translation matrix in Eq. 1, where $\mathbf{R}_p \in \mathbb{R}^{3 \times 3}$ and $\mathbf{T}_p \in \mathbb{R}^{3 \times 3}$ indicate the rotation and translation matrices and $P_{parent} \in \mathbb{R}^{3 \times 1}$ is the coordinate of the parent joint. In a similar fashion, the position P_k of joint k can be represented following the path from the root joint to itself, where $\mathcal{P}_{(k)}$ indicates the set of parent joints along the way, and P_{root} is the position of the root joint.

For example, if we want to calculate the 3D positions of the left wrist (lw), we need to calculate the transformation matrix from the root joint to itself. With the predefined Eq. 2, we can set $\mathcal{P}_{(k)} = \{$left hip (lh), spine (sp), left shoulder (ls), left elbow (le), left wrist $(lw)\}$. Then the location of the left wrist joint can be calculated with Eq. 3.

$$P_{child} = (\mathbf{R}_p \cdot \mathbf{T}_p) \cdot P_{parent} \tag{1}$$

$$P_k = \left(\prod_{a \in \mathcal{P}_{(k)}} \mathbf{R}_a \cdot \mathbf{T}_a \right) \cdot P_{root} \tag{2}$$

$$P_{lw} = (\mathbf{R}_{lw} \cdot \mathbf{T}_{lw}) \cdot (\mathbf{R}_{le} \cdot \mathbf{T}_{le}) \cdot (\mathbf{R}_{ls} \cdot \mathbf{T}_{ls}) \cdot (\mathbf{R}_{sp} \cdot \mathbf{T}_{sp}) \cdot (\mathbf{R}_{lh} \cdot \mathbf{T}_{lh}) \cdot P_{root} \tag{3}$$

3.2   Kinematic Structure Model

According to the kinematic computation process, we first design a kinematic structure model in a deep learning framework which is illustrated in Fig. 2. Multi-view input images are first passed to a shared backbone network to extract representative contextual features. Then we use a feature extractor to output root joint positions $P_{root} \in \mathbb{R}^{3 \times 1}$, rotation parameters $R_p \in \mathbb{R}^{3 \times K}$, and translation parameters $T_p \in \mathbb{R}^K$. For the $i^{(th)}$ joint, suppose its translation parameter is l_i and the rotation parameter is α_i, β_i and γ_i, we can acquire the translation matrix and rotation matrix with the following equation. Finally together with the root joint position, Eq. 2 is applied to obtain the 3D joint positions. All the defined computing process are differentiable which allowed our model to be trained end-to-end.

$$\mathbf{T}_i = \begin{pmatrix} 1 & 0 & l_i \\ 0 & 1 & 0 \\ 0 & 0 & 1 \end{pmatrix}, \mathbf{R}_i = \begin{pmatrix} \cos \alpha_i & -\sin \alpha_i & 0 \\ \sin \alpha_i & \cos \alpha_i & 0 \\ 0 & 0 & 1 \end{pmatrix} \cdot \begin{pmatrix} \cos \beta_i & 0 & \sin \beta_i \\ 0 & 1 & 0 \\ -\sin \beta_i & 0 & \cos \beta_i \end{pmatrix} \cdot \begin{pmatrix} 1 & 0 & 0 \\ 0 & \cos \gamma_i & -\sin \gamma_i \\ 0 & \sin \gamma_i & \cos \gamma_i \end{pmatrix}$$

3.3   Bone-Length and Bone-Symmetry Loss

One drawback of the kinematic structure model is that joint errors may accumulate following the kinematic tree. Apart from joint position loss which is usually adopted in current 3D pose estimation methods, we also calculate the difference between the predicted bone length and the ground truth which can be considered as intermediate supervisions [12]. For the $k^{(th)}$ joint, we define its parent joint's index as $parent(k^{(th)})$, then the associated bone can be represented as Eq. 4. In general, bone representation is more stable and able to cover geometry constraints [13].

$$\mathcal{B}_k = P_{parent(k^{(th)})} - P_{(k^{(th)})} \qquad (4)$$

Besides, considering that human body is a symmetry structure. As illustrated in Fig. 3, we define four groups of symmetry bones and make a statistic for the symmetry bone length errors in Human3.6m dataset [2]. Then, we devise a loss function to penalize the inequality between the predefined symmetry left and right parts. These two loss functions are both based on body structure

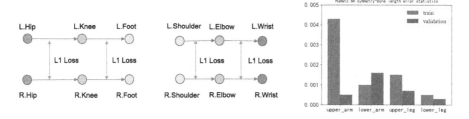

Fig. 3. Definition of the bone-symmetry loss and the statistic results in Human3.6m dataset

information and therefore able to implicitly impose the anatomy prior into the kinematic structure model.

The total bone loss is defined in Eq. 5, here $\mathcal{L}_p = \{$left lower/upper arm, left lower/upper leg$\}$, $\mathcal{R}_p = \{$right lower/upper arm, right lower/upper leg$\}$.

$$L_{bone} = \sum_{k=1}^{K-1}(\| \hat{\mathcal{B}}_k - \mathcal{B}_k{}^{gt} \|_2) + \sum_{i=1}^{4}(\| \mathcal{B}_{\hat{\mathcal{L}}_p(i)} - \mathcal{B}_{\hat{\mathcal{R}}_p(i)} \|_2) \tag{5}$$

3.4 Multi-view Consistency Constraints

To further explore the geometry relationship between multiple views, we propose a pose embedding module to represent the latent pose information. To this end, pose estimation results of the same person at the same time across multiple views are mapped to a latent space, then we computed the similarity between the cross-view encoding results. To be specific, suppose the 3D joint estimation of image i and image j are $P_K^i \in \mathbb{R}^{3 \times K}$ and $P_K^j \in \mathbb{R}^{3 \times K}$. Here we use a residual block to encode the joint locations into geometry latent vectors $g^{(i)} \in \mathbb{R}^{1 \times N}$ and $g^{(j)} \in \mathbb{R}^{1 \times N}$, where N is the length of the latent vector. Then we apply a L2 loss to compute the similarity between two geometry latent representations.

The general idea behind this computation is that P_K^i and P_K^j should be the same pose representation under global world coordinate, and then mapped to the corresponding camera coordinate. In this way, the consistency constraints will enforce the network to output the same pose embedding results across multiple views and effectively filter out implausible predictions. Moreover, our training mechanism doesn't need camera extrinsic parameters and can be implemented to any multi-view datasets. In a word, it is a multi-view and self-supervised method during training, and a single view method during inference.

The loss function is defined in Eq. 6, where $\mathcal{F}$ is the multi-view structure information encoding function, i and j indicate different camera views of the same person, and P^i and P^j represent joint positions from camera view i and j.

$$L_{mvc} = \| \mathcal{F}(P^i) - \mathcal{F}(P^j) \|_2 \tag{6}$$

3.5 Loss Function

Our total loss function includes the joint loss, body bone loss and multi-view consistency loss. Here joint loss L_{joint} is defined as the smooth L_1 loss between the predicted and ground truth joint positions.

$$L_{joint} = \sum_{i=1}^{K} \begin{cases} \frac{1}{2}(\hat{P}_{i(th)} - P_{i(th)}{}^{gt})^2 & if \mid \hat{P}_{i(th)} - P_{i(th)}{}^{gt} \mid < 1 \\ \mid \hat{P}_{i(th)} - P_{i(th)}{}^{gt} \mid -0.5 & otherwise \end{cases} \tag{7}$$

And the total loss function is in Eq. 8, where λ and β are loss weights for body bone loss and multi-view consistency loss, M is the total training samples and N is the total multi-view training sample pairs.

$$L = \sum_{i=1}^{M} \frac{1}{M} (L_{joint}(i) + \lambda L_{bone}(i)) + \sum_{j=1}^{N} \frac{1}{N} \beta L_{mvc}(j) \qquad (8)$$

4 Experiment

In this part, we first introduce the datasets and evaluation metrics, then we will provide the implementation details and augmentation operations during training. And next we will show the ablation studies as well as comparisons with the state-of-the-art results.

4.1 Datasets

We conduct quantitative experiments on two publicly available 3D human pose estimation datasets: Human3.6M dataset and MPI-INF-3DHP dataset. To demonstrate the generality of the proposed model, we also provide some qualitative results on the MPII dataset, which is a challenging public outdoor 2D human pose dataset.

Human3.6M. [2] is one of the most publicly used dataset in 3D human pose estimation. It captures 3.6 million images and there are 11 subjects performing daily activities from 4 camera views in a lab environment. The 3D ground truth is obtained by the motion capture system and the camera intrinsic and extrinsic parameters are also provided.

Following the standard, we use subject 1, 5, 6, 7, 8 for training and and evaluate on every 64th frame for subject 9 and 11. The evaluation metric is the mean per joint position error (MPJPE) between the estimated and the ground-truth joint positions after aligning the root position.

MPI-INF-3DHP. [5] is a recently released dataset which includes both indoor and outdoor scenes. Following the common practice, we use the 3D Percentage of Correct Keypoints (3DPCK@150 mm) and Area Under Curve (AUC) as the evaluation metrics.

MPII. [28] is a 2D dataset which provides 22k in-the-wild dataset, we demonstrate the qualitative results on this dataset to reveal the generality of our proposed method.

4.2 Implementation Details

We use ResNet-50 followed by three deconvolution layers as our backbone network to extract representative features. For the multi-view consistency module,

Table 1. Ablation study for MPJPE on Human3.6M dataset.

Model	Bone loss	Multi-view consistency loss	MPJPE (mm)
Kinematic Model	✗	✗	62.01
	✓	✗	58.69
	✗	✓	57.33
	✓	✓	**56.18**

*Here bone loss indicates bone-length and bone-symmetry loss

Table 2. Ablation study for joint location errors on Human3.6M dataset.

Method	LShoulder	LElbow	LWrist	RShoulder	RElbow	Rwrist
baseline	64.8	75.9	96.5	64.9	81.8	102.2
baseline+bone	62.2	75.2	94.4	**57.2**	**69.3**	93.8
baseline+bone+mvc	**61.3**	**67.7**	**85.7**	58.2	70.9	**89.5**

*Here bone and mvc indicate bone loss and multi-view consistency loss

we adopt a residual block [23] followed by a fully connected layer as the mapping function. As for the total loss function weights, we set $\lambda = 1e-3$ and $\beta = 1e-4$ after cross-validation experiments. For the Human3.6M dataset, we randomly select two views from the total four views and form six pairs of multi-view inputs. In the same way, there are four pairs of multi-view inputs for the MPI-INF-3DHP dataset.

Input images are cropped with the ground truth bbox to extract the human body region and then resized to 256×256. Augmentation of random rotate and flip are used for both datasets. Besides we utilize synthetic occlusions [29] to make the network robust to occluded joints. For the MPI-INF-3DHP dataset, we also apply clothing and background augmentation.

During training, we use batch size of 64. Each model was trained for 140 epochs with an initial learning rate of $1e-3$ which dropped at steps 90 and 120. The ADAM optimizer is used for all the training steps. Our code was implemented with PyTorch [30] and the proposed model was trained for 8 h with 2 Nvidia 1080Ti GPUS.

4.3 Experiment Results on Human3.6M Dataset

Ablation Study. We conduct an ablation study to explore the contribution of the proposed anatomy prior and the multi-view consistency constraints.

The experiment results are demonstrated on Table 1. We notice that multi-view consistency loss had a very noticeable impact on the precision, and improving the MPJPE by 4.7 mm. This finding implies that including multi-view constraints is able to learn the geometry information and produce more reliable results.

Table 3. Ablation study for bone length error in Human3.6m datasets. Here LU indicates left upper, LL indicates left lower, RU indicates right upper and RL indicates right lower.

Method	LU arm	LL arm	RU arm	RL arm	LU leg	LL leg	RU leg	RL leg
baseline	10.8	17.3	10.9	17.2	16.0	13.8	14.4	13.1
baseline+bone	**10.2**	**15.5**	10.2	20.1	**12.9**	11.3	**12.5**	10.9
baseline+bone+mvc	10.6	15.7	**9.2**	**14.0**	13.9	**9.6**	13.0	**8.9**

Table 4. Ablation study for bone symmetry error on Human3.6M dataset.

Method	Upper arm	Lower arm	Upper leg	Lower leg
baseline	11.1	21.9	14.8	11.8
baseline+bone-loss	11.0	22.9	11.0	11.4
baseline+bone-loss+mvc-loss	**8.6**	**14.4**	**9.7**	**10.7**

Also, bone loss was shown to be of considerable benefit to the result with a decrease of MPJPE by 3.3 mm, proving the effectiveness of the proposed anatomy prior constraints.

Discussion. To further analyse the effect of the proposed anatomy and geometry constraints, we also calculate the high-hierarchy joint errors together with the bone-length and bone-symmetry errors in Human3.6M dataset. The quantitative results are illustrated in Table 2, 3 and 4.

Here we choose six joints which are far from the root joint and analyse the effect of the proposed two loss functions. We notice that for the right elbow and right wrist joint, adding bone-length and bone-symmetry loss significantly reduced the joint location errors, which indicated that bone information was able to express the anatomy prior and reduce the location errors of the high-hierarchy joints.

As for the bone length and bone symmetry errors, the results are illustrated in Table 3. Similarly introducing bone loss and multi-view consistency loss will eventually lead to smaller errors especially for the legs.

Visualization Results. In Fig. 4, we present some hard examples on the Human3.6m datasets, and make a qualitative comparison of the visualization results. These pictures include some occluded and severely deformed actions like Sitting down and Lying. Our baseline kinematic structure model is already able to output plausible results. After adding bone loss and multi-view consistency loss, some details will be further refined. For example, in the fourth picture, introducing the anatomy prior and multi-view consistency supervision will revise the unreasonable leg positions of the baseline model. More details are outlined by the green circles.

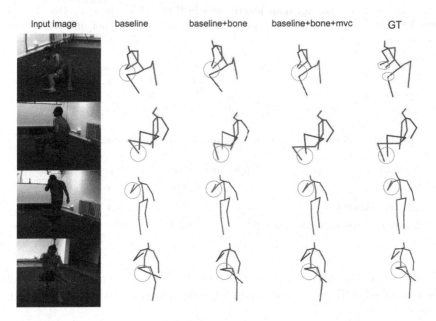

Fig. 4. Some visualization results on Human3.6m dataset. Here bone indicates bone-length and bone-symmetry loss and mvc indicates multi-view consistency loss. (Color figure online)

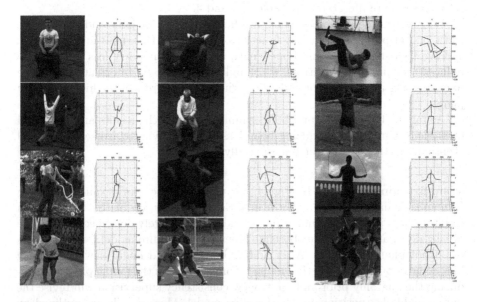

Fig. 5. Qualitative results. The first and second rows show results on MPI-INF-3DHP dataset, while the third and forth rows demonstrate results on MPII datasets.

Table 5. Comparison with the state-of-the-art on Human3.6M dataset.

Method	Dir	Disc	Eat	Greet	Phone	Photo	Pose	Purch
Chen et al. [22]	89.9	97.6	90.0	107.9	107.3	139.2	93.6	136.1
Zhou et al. [21]	91.8	102.4	96.9	98.7	113.3	125.2	90.0	93.8
Rogez et al. [31]	76.2	80.2	75.8	83.3	92.2	105.7	79.0	71.1
Pavlakos et al. [17]	67.4	71.9	66.7	69.1	72	77	65	68
Zhou et al. [6]‡	54.8	60.7	58.2	71.4	62	65.5	53.8	55.6
Martinez et al. [23]	51.8	56.2	58.1	59	69.5	78.4	55.2	58.1
Yang et al. [8]‡	51.5	58.9	<u>50.4</u>	<u>57.0</u>	62.1	65.4	49.8	<u>52.7</u>
Sun et al. [7]‡	<u>46.5</u>	<u>48.1</u>	**49.9**	**51.1**	**47.3**	**43.2**	**45.9**	57
PVH-TSP [32]§	92.7	85.9	72.3	93.2	86.2	101.2	75.1	78.0
Trumble et al. [33]§	**41.7**	**43.2**	52.9	70.0	64.9	83.0	57.3	63.5
Ours	51.4	53.0	52.4	66.6	<u>52.9</u>	<u>57.1</u>	<u>46.6</u>	**47.5**
Method	Sit	SitD	Smoke	Wait	WalkD	Walk	WalkT	Avg
Chen et al. [22]	133.1	240.1	106.7	106.2	114.1	87.0	90.6	114.2
Zhou et al. [21]	132.1	158.9	106.9	94.4	126.0	79.0	98.9	107.2
Rogez et al. [31]	105.9	127.1	88.0	83.7	86.6	64.9	84.0	87.7
Pavlakos et al. [17]	83	96.5	71.7	65.8	74.9	59.1	63.2	71.9
Zhou et al. [6]‡	75.2	111.6	64.1	66	51.4	63.2	55.3	64.9
Martinez et al. [23]	74	94.6	62.3	59.1	65.1	<u>49.5</u>	52.4	62.9
Yang et al. [8]‡	69.2	<u>85.2</u>	57.4	<u>58.4</u>	<u>43.6</u>	60.1	47.7	58.6
Sun et al. [7]‡	77.6	**47.9**	<u>54.9</u>	**46.9**	**37.1**	49.8	**41.2**	**49.8**
PVH-TSP [32]§	83.5	94.8	85.8	82.0	114.6	94.9	79.7	87.3
Trumble et al. [33]§	**61.0**	95.0	70.0	62.3	66.2	53.7	52.4	62.5
Ours	<u>62.9</u>	92.5	**53.0**	62.5	52.3	**41.6**	<u>45.2</u>	<u>56.1</u>

*Here § indicates multi-view methods, ‡ indicates methods training with extra 2D Pose Datasets. A lower value is better for MPJPE. The results are taken from corresponding papers. The best results are marked in bold while the second best approach is underlined.

Comparison with the State-of-the-Art. In Table 5 we compare the prediction results of our proposed 3D pose models with current state-of-the-art methods. Recall that our models are trained in a multi-view setting without any camera information and tested in single view, to make a fair comparison, we also consider results from multi-view input approaches.

Even though our model is trained with only 3D datasets, our method still outperform most of the benchmark results and is only inferior to the model by Sun et al. [7] which is a high-memory required heatmap-based model and trained with extra 2D dataset. Besides, we also make a comparison of the per-action joint errors and demonstrate the effectiveness of the proposed model.

Table 6. Comparison with the state-of-the-art results on MPI-INF-3DHP dataset.

Method	3DPCK	AUC
VNect [11]	**76.6**	**40.4**
Mehta et al. [34]	75.2	37.8
SPIN [35]	76.4	36.1
Ching-Hang Chen et al. [36]	71.1	36.3
LCR-Net [31]	59.6	27.6
Zhou et al. [6]	69.2	32.5
Ours	72.0	37.3

*A higher value is better for 3DPCK and AUC.
The results are taken from corresponding papers.

We notice that in some actions like purchasing, photoing and sitting where extensive movements may appear in body parts, our model got the lowest error. This finding provides compelling empirical evidence for the benefits of our proposed bone loss and multi-view consistency constraints which effectively encodes geometry structure information and thus reduces implausible results.

4.4 Experiment Results on MPI-INF-3DHP Dataset

MPI-INF-3DHP Dataset contains a mixture of indoor and outdoor scenes in test set, and we also evaluate our method on this challenging dataset. As can be seen from Table 6, we achieved a comparable result of 72.0 in 3DPCK and 37.3 in AUC, which indicated the strong robustness of our proposed model.

Besides, we provide some visualization results on the test set in Fig. 5. Even in some severely movable action and unseen outdoor scenes, our model still provides satisfactory results.

4.5 Qualitative Results on MPII Dataset

To demonstrate the cross-domain generalization ability of our proposed model, we also test our method on the MPII dataset. Note that our model is only trained on the Human3.6m dataset which contains constrained data in indoor environment. Since the ground truth 3D pose results are not available, we only give qualitative results on the third and forth rows of Fig. 5. We can see that our model can output plausible results and generalize well on unseen scenes.

5   Conclusion

In this paper, we propose an anatomy and geometry constrained one-stage framework which imposes the anatomy prior and fully explore the geometry relationship for 3D human pose estimation. We first define a kinematic structure model in a deep learning framework, then we introduce bone loss which utilizes bone-length and bone-symmetry property to capture the anatomy prior. In addition, we show that adding a multi-view consistency constraints during training can improve the performance and reduce implausible results. We conduct quantitative experiments on two 3D benchmark datasets and achieve state-of-the-art results.

References

1. Sarafianos, N., Boteanu, B., Ionescu, B., Kakadiaris, I.A.: 3D human pose estimation: a review of the literature and analysis of covariates. Comput. Vis. Image Underst. **152**, 1–20 (2016)
2. Ionescu, C., Papava, D., Olaru, V., Sminchisescu, C.: Human3.6m: large scale datasets and predictive methods for 3D human sensing in natural environments. IEEE Trans. Pattern Anal. Mach. Intell. **36**, 1325–1339 (2014)
3. Felzenszwalb, P.F., Huttenlocher, D.P.: Pictorial structures for object recognition. Int. J. Comput. Vis. **61**, 55–79 (2005)
4. Yub Jung, H., Lee, S., Seok Heo, Y., Dong Yun, I.: Random tree walk toward instantaneous 3D human pose estimation. In: Proceedings of the IEEE Conference on Computer Vision and Pattern Recognition, pp. 2467–2474 (2015)
5. Mehta, D., et al.: Monocular 3D human pose estimation in the wild using improved CNN supervision. In: 2017 Fifth International Conference on 3D Vision (3DV). IEEE (2017)
6. Zhou, X., Huang, Q., Sun, X., Xue, X., Wei, Y.: Towards 3D human pose estimation in the wild: a weakly-supervised approach. In: Proceedings of the IEEE International Conference on Computer Vision, pp. 398–407 (2017)
7. Sun, X., Xiao, B., Wei, F., Liang, S., Wei, Y.: Integral human pose regression. In: Ferrari, V., Hebert, M., Sminchisescu, C., Weiss, Y. (eds.) ECCV 2018. LNCS, vol. 11210, pp. 536–553. Springer, Cham (2018). https://doi.org/10.1007/978-3-030-01231-1_33
8. Yang, W., Ouyang, W., Wang, X., Ren, J., Li, H., Wang, X.: 3D human pose estimation in the wild by adversarial learning. In: Proceedings of the IEEE Conference on Computer Vision and Pattern Recognition, pp. 5255–5264 (2018)
9. Rhodin, H., Salzmann, M., Fua, P.: Unsupervised geometry-aware representation for 3D human pose estimation. In: Proceedings of the European Conference on Computer Vision (ECCV), pp. 750–767 (2018)
10. Li, C., Lee, G.H.: Generating multiple hypotheses for 3D human pose estimation with mixture density network. In: Proceedings of the IEEE Conference on Computer Vision and Pattern Recognition, pp. 9887–9895 (2019)
11. Mehta, D., et al.: VNect: real-time 3D human pose estimation with a single RGB camera. ACM Trans. Graph. **36**, 44 (2017)
12. Newell, A., Yang, K., Deng, J.: Stacked hourglass networks for human pose estimation. In: Leibe, B., Matas, J., Sebe, N., Welling, M. (eds.) ECCV 2016. LNCS, vol. 9912, pp. 483–499. Springer, Cham (2016). https://doi.org/10.1007/978-3-319-46484-8_29
13. Sun, X., Shang, J., Liang, S., Wei, Y.: Compositional human pose regression. In: Proceedings of the IEEE International Conference on Computer Vision, pp. 2602–2611 (2017)

14. Habibie, I., Xu, W., Mehta, D., Pons-Moll, G., Theobalt, C.: In the wild human pose estimation using explicit 2D features and intermediate 3D representations. In: Proceedings of the IEEE Conference on Computer Vision and Pattern Recognition, pp. 10905–10914 (2019)
15. Li, S., Chan, A.B.: 3D human pose estimation from monocular images with deep convolutional neural network. In: Cremers, D., Reid, I., Saito, H., Yang, M.-H. (eds.) ACCV 2014. LNCS, vol. 9004, pp. 332–347. Springer, Cham (2015). https://doi.org/10.1007/978-3-319-16808-1_23
16. Tekin, B., Katircioglu, I., Salzmann, M., Lepetit, V., Fua, P.: Structured prediction of 3D human pose with deep neural networks. arXiv preprint arXiv:1605.05180 (2016)
17. Pavlakos, G., Zhou, X., Derpanis, K.G., Daniilidis, K.: Coarse-to-fine volumetric prediction for single-image 3D human pose. In: Proceedings of the IEEE Conference on Computer Vision and Pattern Recognition, pp. 7025–7034 (2017)
18. Rhodin, H., et al.: Learning monocular 3D human pose estimation from multi-view images. In: Proceedings of the IEEE Conference on Computer Vision and Pattern Recognition, pp. 8437–8446 (2018)
19. Mount, D.M.: CMSC 425 game programming (2013)
20. Zhou, X., Wan, Q., Zhang, W., Xue, X., Wei, Y.: Model-based deep hand pose estimation. arXiv preprint arXiv:1606.06854 (2016)
21. Zhou, X., Sun, X., Zhang, W., Liang, S., Wei, Y.: Deep kinematic pose regression. In: Hua, G., Jégou, H. (eds.) ECCV 2016. LNCS, vol. 9915, pp. 186–201. Springer, Cham (2016). https://doi.org/10.1007/978-3-319-49409-8_17
22. Chen, C.H., Ramanan, D.: 3D human pose estimation = 2D pose estimation + matching. In: 2017 IEEE Conference on Computer Vision and Pattern Recognition (CVPR) (2017)
23. Martinez, J., Hossain, R., Romero, J., Little, J.J.: A simple yet effective baseline for 3D human pose estimation. In: Proceedings of the IEEE International Conference on Computer Vision, pp. 2640–2649 (2017)
24. Drover, D., Rohith, M.V., Chen, C.-H., Agrawal, A., Tyagi, A., Huynh, C.P.: Can 3D pose be learned from 2D projections alone? In: Leal-Taixé, L., Roth, S. (eds.) ECCV 2018. LNCS, vol. 11132, pp. 78–94. Springer, Cham (2019). https://doi.org/10.1007/978-3-030-11018-5_7
25. Wandt, B., Rosenhahn, B.: RepNet: weakly supervised training of an adversarial reprojection network for 3D human pose estimation. In: Proceedings of the IEEE Conference on Computer Vision and Pattern Recognition, pp. 7782–7791 (2019)
26. Akhter, I., Black, M.J.: Pose-conditioned joint angle limits for 3D human pose reconstruction. In: Proceedings of the IEEE Conference on Computer Vision and Pattern Recognition, pp. 1446–1455 (2015)
27. Zhao, L., Peng, X., Tian, Y., Kapadia, M., Metaxas, D.N.: Semantic graph convolutional networks for 3D human pose regression. In: Proceedings of the IEEE Conference on Computer Vision and Pattern Recognition, pp. 3425–3435 (2019)
28. Andriluka, M., Pishchulin, L., Gehler, P., Schiele, B.: 2D human pose estimation: new benchmark and state of the art analysis. In: Proceedings of the IEEE Conference on computer Vision and Pattern Recognition, pp. 3686–3693 (2014)
29. Sárándi, I., Linder, T., Arras, K.O., Leibe, B.: How robust is 3D human pose estimation to occlusion? arXiv preprint arXiv:1808.09316 (2018)
30. Paszke, A., et al.: Pytorch: an imperative style, high-performance deep learning library. In: Advances in Neural Information Processing Systems, pp. 8024–8035 (2019)

31. Rogez, G., Weinzaepfel, P., Schmid, C.: LCR- Net: localization-classification-regression for human pose. In: IEEE Computer Society Conference on Computer Vision and Pattern Recognition (CVPR) (2017)

32. Trumble, M., Gilbert, A., Malleson, C., Hilton, A., Collomosse, J.: Total capture: 3D human pose estimation fusing video and inertial sensors. In: British Machine Vision Conference 2017 (2017)

33. Trumble, M., Gilbert, A., Hilton, A., Collomosse, J.: Deep autoencoder for combined human pose estimation and body model upscaling. In: Ferrari, V., Hebert, M., Sminchisescu, C., Weiss, Y. (eds.) ECCV 2018. LNCS, vol. 11214, pp. 800–816. Springer, Cham (2018). https://doi.org/10.1007/978-3-030-01249-6_48

34. Mehta, D., Sotnychenko, O., Mueller, F., Xu, W., Theobalt, C.: Single-shot multi-person 3D pose estimation from monocular RGB. In: 2018 International Conference on 3D Vision (3DV) (2018)

35. Kolotouros, N., Pavlakos, G., Black, M.J., Daniilidis, K.: Learning to reconstruct 3D human pose and shape via model-fitting in the loop. In: Proceedings of the IEEE International Conference on Computer Vision, pp. 2252–2261 (2019)

36. Chen, C.H., Tyagi, A., Agrawal, A., Drover, D., Stojanov, S., Rehg, J.M.: Unsupervised 3D pose estimation with geometric self-supervision. In: Proceedings of the IEEE Conference on Computer Vision and Pattern Recognition, pp. 5714–5724 (2019)

DeepVoxels++: Enhancing the Fidelity of Novel View Synthesis from 3D Voxel Embeddings

Tong He[1(✉)], John Collomosse[2,3], Hailin Jin[2], and Stefano Soatto[1]

[1] University of California, Los Angeles, USA
{simpleig,soatto}@cs.ucla.edu
[2] Creative Intelligence Lab, Adobe Research, London, UK
{collomos,hljin}@adobe.com
[3] CVSSP, University of Surrey, Guildford, UK

Abstract. We present a novel view synthesis method based upon latent voxel embeddings of an object, which encode both shape and appearance information and are learned without explicit 3D occupancy supervision. Our method uses an encoder-decoder architecture to learn such deep volumetric representations from a set of images taken at multiple viewpoints. Compared with DeepVoxels, our DeepVoxels++ applies a series of enhancements: a) a patch-based image feature extraction and neural rendering scheme that learns local shape and texture patterns, and enables neural rendering at high resolution; b) learned view-dependent feature transformation kernels to explicitly model perspective transformations induced by viewpoint changes; c) a recurrent-concurrent aggregation technique to alleviate single-view update bias of the voxel embeddings recurrent learning process. Combined with d) a simple yet effective implementation trick of frustum representation sufficient sampling, we achieve improved visual quality over the prior deep voxel-based methods (33% SSIM error reduction and 22% PSNR improvement) on 360° novel-view synthesis benchmarks.

1 Introduction

A physical scene is far more complex than any number of images of it, so it is challenging to just "reconstruct *it*". The question of how to evaluate a *model* of a scene depends on whether one has access to additional sensors (*e.g.* tactile), or prior knowledge (*e.g.* scale of objects). In the absence of any side information, one often utilized measure of quality of a model built from data is its ability to predict data that the model can generate [1,2]. Hence, view synthesis is a critical step in building and evaluating models of physical scenes from images. There are also practical ramifications of novel-view synthesis to video compression, graphics

---

Electronic supplementary material The online version of this chapter (https://doi.org/10.1007/978-3-030-69525-5_15) contains supplementary material, which is available to authorized users.

© Springer Nature Switzerland AG 2021
H. Ishikawa et al. (Eds.): ACCV 2020, LNCS 12622, pp. 244–260, 2021.
https://doi.org/10.1007/978-3-030-69525-5_15

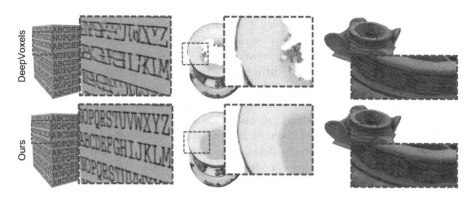

Fig. 1. Rendering results of our model have sharper details (*e.g.* text, fine-grained shapes) and fewer artifacts (*e.g.* aliasing, holes) than DeepVoxels [5].

rendering and reinforcement learning. Before deep learning, novel-view synthesis was either approached as a pipeline of motion estimation, sparse reconstruction, topology estimation, meshing, and texture mapping [3], or directly by resampling the plenoptic function [4]. More recently, Sitzmann *et al.* [5] proposed DeepVoxels – an approach employing a 3D grid of persistent features integrated over input images along with 2D lifting and projection networks.

We learn 3D voxel embeddings of object shape and appearance based on image patches, whose pose can be directly controlled to generate novel views at high resolution. Our method is based on DeepVoxels [5], but with improved rendering quality leveraging a series of enhancements and a simple yet effective implementation trick of 3D embeddings sampling. Specifically, DeepVoxels++ is different from DeepVoxels in four aspects:

1. **Low-complexity patch modelling.** We adopt a patch-based training and inference scheme that halves the 2D U-Net parameters used in image feature extraction and neural rendering. It reduces the complexity of large image context modeling (*e.g.* $512 \times 512 \times 3$ full image vs. $128 \times 128 \times 3$ small patch) by learning local patterns, and enables image modeling as well as rendering at high resolution in sliding window manner.
2. **View-dependent voxel feature transformations.** Viewpoint changes can cause perspective transformations in the images (see Fig. 3). We directly learn view-dependent feature transformation kernels in the lifting/projection steps to model such perspective effect. We transform the features from input patches to the 3D voxel embeddings and then from the voxels to output patches based on the relative voxel-camera poses. We demonstrate this idea on objects of diffuse reflection, delicate shapes and limited training views.
3. **Recurrent-concurrent voxel feature aggregation.** We aggregate 3D voxel embeddings utilizing both recurrent gated-fusion and concurrent max-pooling. It differs from existing works which treat multi-view images as a sequence and solely rely on recurrent networks [5–7]. Our method increases

surface coverage of an object during each iteration of voxel feature aggregation and improves data utilization rate. For example, our model can outperform DeepVoxels [5] under different training data size configurations.

4. **Frustum representation sufficient sampling.** Sampling the 3D voxel embeddings into a frustum of the target pose is a critical step in decoding the learned volumetric representation into a rendered image. We empirically found that sufficient frustum sampling is a simple yet effective implementation trick to alleviate the issue of limited voxel resolution, reduce blurring artifacts, and preserve sharp details. It enforces the voxel feature learning process which in turn helps encode fine-scale details in the learned 3D voxel embeddings.

Overall, our approach improves over DeepVoxels [5] upon the visual quality of novel-view rendering at various poses (by up to 33% SSIM error reduction and 22% PSNR performance boost). We use the same 360° novel-view synthesis benchmarks as [5], which contain 512×512 color images of delicate shapes and textures. In contrast, other object based novel-view synthesis methods [8–11] mainly use the 256×256 ShapeNet images that consist of mostly mono-color flat surfaces and do not evaluate rendering results at 360° densely sampled poses.

2 Related Work

Our work is related to multiple fields in 3D computer vision and graphics: image-based modeling, deep learning for view generation, 3D representation learning and neural-rendering, *and* deep learning with feature structure constraints.

Image-Based Modeling. Image-based modeling and rendering techniques [3] are the early approaches to the novel view synthesis problem. Modern approaches, such as [12,13, ?], are able to obtain high-quality results even for challenging scenarios with hand-held cameras. However these methods usually require multiple steps to (soft) reconstruct the object or learn image blending weights, and therefore they are prone to accumulative errors. They do not take full advantage of large scale multi-view datasets for 3D latent embedding learning and (adversarial) image generation training from the learned embeddings.

Deep Learning for View Generation. With the advent of deep convolutional neural networks (CNNs), data-driven methods are gaining popularity for novel view generation [5,8–10,14–23]. The early methods overlook inherent 3D object structures/constraints and rely heavily on optical flow estimation [8] and generative adversarial networks [17]. The former can maintain fine details in generated images while the latter are good at handling large pose changes for view synthesis. There are also hybrid approaches that combine the benefits of both sides [9,10]. However, these methods usually lack a learned latent representation of the object that is geometrically persistent, and thus tend to produce inconsistent images across output poses [5,24].

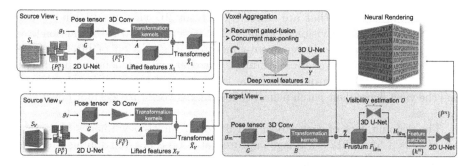

Fig. 2. DeepVoxels++ pipeline. Red: view-dependent patch feature extraction from V views. Blue: 3D voxel embeddings aggregation with recurrent gated-fusion and concurrent max-pooling. Green: view-dependent image patch rendering. Full network architectures are in the supplementary material. The networks are trained jointly with L^1 image reconstruction losses upon rendered views. (Color figure online)

3D Representation Learning and Rendering. 3D representation learning and neural-rendering with deep networks is a problem studied in 3D Deep Learning. Various approaches have been proposed using point clouds [25], implicit neural functions [20], voxel grids [26], multi-plane images [18,19,22,27,28], and *etc.* We follow the line of work using voxel grids [5,6,11,26] which offer a geometrically persistent structure to integrate visual information across multiple poses around the object. In particular Sitzmann *et al.* [5] demonstrate promising results for novel-view rendering utilizing a learned deep voxel representation. In this work, we achieve greatly improved visual quality for 360° novel-view synthesis than [5] via a series of enhancements on feature extraction, transformation and aggregation, *and* a simple yet effective implementation trick of voxel embeddings sufficient sampling when rendering images.

Learning with Feature Structure Constraints. Our work is also related to the emerging direction of introducing explicit structure constraints upon deep features to data-driven deep networks [29–32]. For example, Worrall *et al.* [30] impose a 3×3 rotation matrix constraint on high-dimensional features by length dividing and sub-vector multiplication to learn an interpretable representation for rotation/scaling factors. In this work, we propose to learn voxel feature transformation kernels conditioning on the relative voxel-camera poses. The learned kernels are used to model perspective transformations of the observed/rendered images induced by viewpoint changes under diffuse reflectance.

3 Method

Our model, DeepVoxels++, learns latent 3D voxel embeddings using color images of an object from multiple viewpoints. Our deep network architecture can be perceived as: an encoder-decoder with a geometrically consistent voxel feature space as the latent representation. As shown in Fig. 2, the architecture comprises three stages that are trained jointly by 2D view prediction without any 3D occupancy supervision: (*encoder*) view-dependent feature extraction from image patches, (*bottleneck*) recurrent-concurrent aggregation of lifted features to form the latent 3D voxel embeddings, (*decoder*) view-dependent patch rendering. At *test time* we only need the learned voxel embeddings (*bottleneck*) and the view-dependent patch neural-rendering network (*decoder*) for novel-view synthesis.

The training data of each object consists of M multi-view images $\{I_i, g_i\}_{i=1}^M$, where I_i is a $512 \times 512 \times 3$ image captured at a pose g_i. At training time, the multi-view images are sampled into tuples of $\left\{S_i, T_i^0, T_i^1\right\}_{i=1}^M$. During each training step, the networks are updated with L^1 reconstruction losses upon the predicted target views $\{(\hat{T}_j^0, \hat{T}_j^1)\}_{j=1}^V$, accepting multiple source images $\{S_j\}_{j=1}^V$ as input. We aggregate information from V (*e.g.* 1, 4, 8, and *etc.*) views concurrently during training, making use of 3D-GRU and max-pooling at the bottleneck stage. This training methodology is to ensure large coverage of the object surface within each recurrent-concurrent step of 3D voxel embeddings aggregation. A degenerate case is DeepVoxels, which only conducts recurrent aggregation (strictly $V = 1$); *i.e.* without concurrent consideration of views. The previous training strategy induces single-view observation caused latent voxel feature update bias, and thus has low data utilization efficiency.

3.1 View-Dependent Patch Feature Extraction

To learn deep 3D voxel embeddings from multi-view images, we first sample image patches from training images in sliding window manner. We then extract 2D feature maps from the set of image patches and accumulate these features in voxel space of pre-defined resolution, via view-dependent feature lifting.

Patch Feature Extraction. We subdivide each source image S_i into small-size patches $\{P_i^n\}_{n=1}^N$ via a sliding window with overlaps. Patches are encoded via a 2D U-Net with skip connections for feature extraction: $P_i^n \mapsto F_i^n$. For very large images, if GPU memory sizes prohibit training on all N patches at one pass, we can sample a subset $\{P_i^n\}_{n=1}^{N'}$. In our experiments, we randomly sample 80% patches, but note the possibility of sampling heuristically *e.g.* sampling patches containing high-frequency/fine-scale content more frequently [33]. Compared with the full-image based prior methods, the patch-based scheme enables our method to better learn (and render) local image patterns.

View-Dependent Feature Lifting. We first define a $s \times s \times s$ cubic voxel space for aggregating feature patch lifting obtained voxel-shape features $X_i \in \mathbb{R}^{c \times s \times s \times s}$. Next, we project each voxel onto the feature patches $\{F_i^n\}_{n=1}^{N'}$ and conduct differentiable bilinear feature sampling to get the lifted voxel features. The projection operation, approximated via a pin-hole camera model, is also differentiable. Note that the intrinsic matrix $K \in \mathbb{R}^{3 \times 3}$ *wrt. the image patches* P_i^n has to be rectified to get K_r in order to correctly map world-coordinate locations onto *the extracted feature patches* F_i^n. Because an image patch and its corresponding feature patch have different sizes.

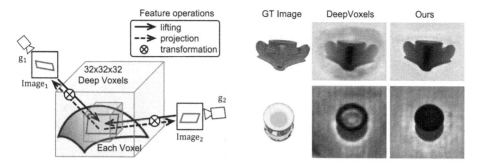

Fig. 3. A voxel that encodes a parallelogram pattern looks different at two poses due to perspective projection effects under diffuse reflectance.

Fig. 4. Pseudo-depth maps visualized using estimated frustum visibility values. Our results are sharper than DeepVoxels and have less artifacts.

$$K_r = \begin{bmatrix} \alpha f_x & & \alpha c_x \\ & \beta f_y & \beta c_y \\ & & 1 \end{bmatrix} \tag{1}$$

where (f_x, f_y, c_x, c_y) belong to K. K_r is the rectified intrinsic matrix used in voxel projection, and (α, β) are (width, height) ratios between F_i^n and P_i^n.

The voxel space used to accumulate the lifted features X_i is typically of low resolution (*e.g.* $32 \times 32 \times 32$). Therefore, each voxel can be thought of modeling a local surface region of the object, as illustrated in Fig. 3. It explains the motivation for perspective projection effect modeling by voxel feature transformations during the lifting (and projection) steps. We apply learned convolutional feature transformation kernels $A(\cdot) \in \mathbb{R}^{c \times c \times 1 \times 1 \times 1}$ on the lifted features X_i.

$$\bar{X}_i = A(G(g_i)) \circledast X_i \tag{2}$$

in which $\bar{X}_i \in \mathbb{R}^{c \times s \times s \times s}$ are the transformed features and $\circledast$ represents 3D convolution operation. As shown in Fig. 2, the kernel estimation network $A(\cdot)$ is implemented as several 3D convolution layers that take relative voxel-camera poses $G(g_i) \in \mathbb{R}^{6 \times s \times s \times s}$ as input and estimate convolutional feature transformation kernels. The reason why $G(g_i)$ is a 3D shape tensor is because each entry of it consists of the relative voxel-camera translation and the camera pose rotation vector. Note that voxels has different relative voxel-camera translations but share the same camera rotation vector. We adopt this encoding format of relative voxel-camera poses based on empirical studies.

3.2 Recurrent-Concurrent Voxel Feature Aggregation

The lifted and transformed features $\bar{X}_i$ from one source image S_i only provide a single-view observation of the object at pose g_i. To learn holistic 3D voxel embeddings $Z \in \mathbb{R}^{c \times s \times s \times s}$ we need to integrate features extracted from all the

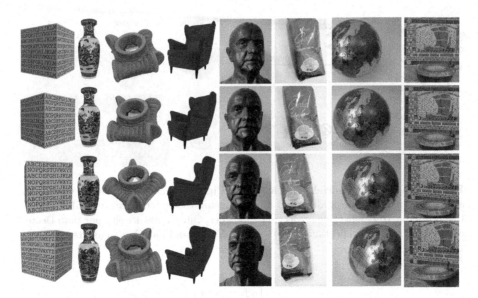

Fig. 5. Novel-view synthesis results of DeepVoxels++ on objects with large viewpoint changes and complex shape/texture patterns. Our model is proposed for diffuse objects but we also show a few preliminary results on objects with specularities and shadows.

training views, which have about 500 images and thus cannot be aggregated into the voxels at one time. We address this challenge by aggregating $\{\bar{X}_j^k\}_{j=1}^V$ from V different views within each iteration (indexed by k) of voxel representation updates, via both recurrent gated-fusion and concurrent max-pooling. Note that the prior methods only integrate features from a single-view into Z at each feature update iteration, and therefore suffer from single-view observation bias. Our aggregation approach provides a large surface coverage of the object during each voxel representation update and improves data utilization rate.

Recurrent Gated-Fusion. We first use 3D-GRU [7] to separately fuse each single-view obtained $\bar{X}_j^k$ into the holistic 3D voxel embeddings Z^{k-1} that are obtained from the previous training iteration: $Z_j^k = \mathrm{GRU}(\bar{X}_j^k, Z^{k-1})$. The 3D object representation Z is modeled as the hidden voxel embeddings of 3D-GRU and will be recurrently updated when more views come in. At the first round of voxel aggregation, we initialize Z^0 with zeros. However, within each step of voxel embedding update, recurrent gated-fusion only aggregates features from a single-view observation. To tackle the single-view update bias, we further utilize a multi-view based max-pooling operation upon the 3D voxel embeddings.

Concurrent Max-Pooling. Now we need to aggregate a set of deep voxel embeddings $\{Z_j^k\}_{j=1}^V$ obtained separately by recurrent gated-fusion from $V > 1$ views. Inspired by Multi-view CNN [34], we use the max-pooling operation: $Z^k = \mathrm{Max}(Z_1^k, Z_2^k, ..., Z_V^k)$. $\mathrm{Max}(\cdot)$ means applying max-pooling operations along the first dimension (*i.e.* the feature channel) of the 3D voxel embeddings

$Z_j^k \in \mathbb{R}^{c \times s \times s \times s}$. The obtained latent voxel representation Z^k (*i.e.* the 3D-GRU hidden embedding at the k-th iteration) will be passed into the next iteration of recurrent-concurrent voxel feature update until the end of training.

3.3   View-Dependent Patch Rendering

Rendering a target image $T_{|g_m}$ from the 3D voxel embeddings $Z_{(j)}^{(k)}$[1] at any given pose g_m around the object involves three steps: view-dependent frustum feature sampling, depth dimension reduction and patch-based neural rendering.

View-Dependent Frustum Sampling. For each target camera pose g_m, we define a $d \times h \times w$ frustum space to enclose the $s \times s \times s$ cubic voxels where the volumetric embeddings Z are saved. While voxels are usually of low spatial resolution (*e.g.* $32 \times 32 \times 32$) due to GPU size constraint, the rendering visual quality from these deep voxel embeddings can be substantially improved by sufficient frustum sampling. Namely, we utilize large 2D sampling sizes $h \times w$ (*e.g.* 128×128 vs. 32×32). The depth axis d is collapsed when rendering image patches. We found that this is a simple yet effective implementation trick for deep voxels-based high quality view synthesis. Ablation studies in the experiments section support this argument (see Fig. 7 and Table 3). Specifically, we can map the frustum into the voxel space by inverse-perspective projection and sample the transformed voxel features $\bar{Z} \in \mathbb{R}^{c \times s \times s \times s}$ by differentiable trilinear interpolation.

$$\bar{Z} = B(G(g_m)) \circledast Y(Z) \tag{3}$$

here $Y(\cdot)$ is a 3D U-Net that further refines the 3D voxel embeddings Z. As shown in Fig. 3, we need to conduct voxel feature transformations at both lifting and projection steps due to the corresponding perspective projection effect in the observed/rendered images. Thus, similar to Eq. 2, we use a kernel estimation network $B(\cdot)$ to directly take the relative voxel-camera poses $G(g_m) \in \mathbb{R}^{6 \times s \times s \times s}$ as input and estimate convolutional feature transformation kernels. $B(\cdot)$ is also implemented as several 3D convolution layers. The sufficiently sampled frustum features from $\bar{Z}$ are denoted as $F_{|g_m} \in \mathbb{R}^{c \times d \times h \times w}$. Note that, as per Eq. 1, we use a rectified camera intrinsic matrix when conducting inverse-perspective projection for frustum representation sufficient sampling. In this case, scaling factors (α, β) are (width, height) ratios between the frustum and the target image.

Depth Dimension Reduction. Rather than directly utilizing the frustum representation $F_{|g_m}$ for patch neural-rendering, we follow [5] and first collapse it into depth dimension reduced features $H_{|g_m} \in \mathbb{R}^{c \times h \times w}$ by weighted average feature pooling upon the depth dimension: $H_{|g_m} = \text{Avg}[F_{|g_m} \otimes O(F_{|g_m})]_{|dim=1}$. Here $\text{Avg}[\cdot]_{|dim=1}$ indicates weighted average feature pooling along the second dimension (*i.e.* depth) of the $c \times d \times h \times w$ input tensor. $\otimes$ means element-wise multiplication with broadcasting between $F_{|g_m} \in \mathbb{R}^{c \times d \times h \times w}$ and $O(\cdot) \in$

---

[1] During training gradients are back-propagated to Z_j^k. At test time we use the converged Z for rendering. We use Z for convenience from here.

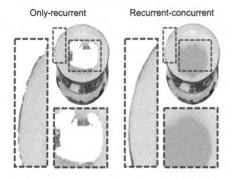

Fig. 6. 3D voxel embeddings aggregation: only-recurrent vs. recurrent-concurrent.

Fig. 7. Frustum representation sampling sizes: small (32×32) vs. large (128×128).

$\mathbb{R}^{1 \times d \times h \times w}$. $O(\cdot)$ is implemented as a 3D U-Net with skip connections, whose output can be treated as frustum visibility estimation *wrt.* a viewpoint g_m and adds interpretability to the rendering process. Because it enables the computation of pseudo-depth maps which explain several rendering artifacts of the prior methods (see Fig. 4). Specifically, inaccurate visibility estimation, induced by incorrectly up-weighting (in)visible surfaces and empty space within the frustum, can cause DeepVoxels' rendering artifacts like aliasing and holes.

Patch-Based Neural Rendering. The final step of the model is to render patches from $H_{|g_m}$. Recall that during the encoder stage, we explained the benefits of *patch-based feature extraction* (Subsect. 3.1). During the decoding step we conduct patch-based neural rendering, for the same purposes of utilizing fewer 2D U-Net parameters, reducing the complexity of large image context modeling and being able to model/render images at high resolution. Similar to patch-based feature extraction, we subdivide $H_{|g_m}$ into small-size feature patches $\{h^n\}_{n=1}^N$ by a sliding window with overlaps, and then conduct patch neural rendering using a 2D U-Net with skip connections: $h^n \mapsto P^n$. At training time, we apply random sampling to retain N' feature patches (*e.g.* 80% of N) to save GPU memory. We use L^1 reconstruction losses upon rendered image patches to enable joint training for the complete network architectures as shown in Fig. 2.

$$L(\hat{P}^n, P^n) = \frac{\sum_{n=1}^{N'} \sum_{a,b} \left\| \hat{P}_{a,b}^n - P_{a,b}^n \right\|_1}{N' * D} \tag{4}$$

where $\hat{P}^n$ is a rendered image patch and P^n is a ground-truth patch. (a, b) are pixel indices within an image patch and D is the pixel number of a patch. At test time, we composite all N rendered patches $\{\hat{P}^n\}_{n=1}^N$ into the target image raster, and crop overlapped regions. The stitched patches comprise the final 512×512 color rendered image $\hat{T}_{|g_m}$.

Table 1. 360° novel-view synthesis benchmark of objects with diffuse reflectance. Higher values of PSNR and SSIM indicate better rendering quality. Our method DeepVoxels++ surpasses DeepVoxels and other competing methods by large margins.

Method	Vase	Pedestal	Chair	Cube	Mean
	PSNR/SSIM	PSNR/SSIM	PSNR/SSIM	PSNR/SSIM	PSNR/SSIM
Nearest Neighbor	23.26/0.92	21.49/0.87	20.69/0.94	18.32/0.83	20.94/0.89
Tatarchenko *et al.* [37]	22.28/0.91	23.25/0.89	20.22/0.95	19.12/0.84	21.22/0.90
Worrall *et al.* [30]	23.41/0.92	22.70/0.89	19.52/0.94	19.23/0.85	21.22/0.90
Pix2Pix [38]	26.36/0.95	25.41/0.91	23.04/0.96	19.69/0.86	23.63/0.92
Neural Volumes [39]	20.39/0.84	36.47/**0.99**	35.15/**0.99**	26.48/0.96	29.62/0.95
DeepVoxels [5]	27.99/0.96	32.35/0.97	33.45/**0.99**	28.42/0.97	30.55/0.97
Ours	**32.91/0.98**	**38.93**/0.98	**40.87/0.99**	**36.51/0.99**	**37.31/0.99**

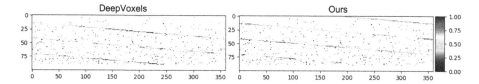

Fig. 8. Normalized azimuth-elevation PSNR maps on Cube. More objects are visualized in supplementary. Horizontal: [0°, 360°] azimuth. Vertical: [0°, 100°] elevation. Black dots are the training poses. Colored spiral lines are the test pose trajectories. Red color means large PSNR value and blue means small. These plots showcase smooth viewpoint interpolation paths between training views (*i.e.* black dots), showing consistent improvement over DeepVoxels across different novel views. (Color figure online)

3.4   Implementation Details

We implement our approach using PyTorch [35]. The networks are trained with the ADAM optimizer [36] using an initial learning rate of 0.0004. For different benchmark objects, we use the same set of hyper-parameters and stop the training at 400 epochs, which takes about 4 days. More details of our network architectures can be found in supplementary.

4   Experiments and Discussion

We evaluate DeepVoxels++ on 360° novel-view synthesis benchmarks against several competing methods: a Nearest Neighbor baseline, Tatarchenko et al. [37], Worrall et al. [30], Pix2Pix [38], Neural Volumes [39], SRN [20] and DeepVoxels [5]. To add interpretability of our model, we also conduct ablation studies to reveal the impact of our series of enhancements.

4.1   Dataset and Metrics

For fairness of comparison, we use the same dataset and evaluation metrics (*e.g.* the Structural Similarity Index (SSIM), the Peak Signal-to-noise Ratio (PSNR))

Table 2. Better rendering quality can be achieved when more multi-view images V are aggregated in each round of recurrent-concurrent latent 3D voxel embedding updates.

V	Vase	Pedestal	Chair	Cube	Mean PSNR	Mean SSIM
1	27.99	32.35	33.45	28.42	30.55	0.97
4	**30.30**	34.64	35.97	**31.97**	33.22	**0.98**
8	29.45	**35.54**	**37.79**	31.65	**33.61**	**0.98**

as DeepVoxels [5]. The dataset contains 512×512 color images of delicate shapes and appearance (*e.g.* pedestal, vase). For each object, the dataset has about 500 training images and 1000 test views as ground truth. The test views are densely sampled from a 360° spiral curve enclosing the object at different angles and distances, for evaluating smoothness and fidelity as the viewpoint changes. This contrasts with recent object based novel-view synthesis papers which mainly use the 256×256 ShapeNet image dataset. ShapeNet lacks the aforementioned appearance complexity, and does not evaluate novel-view rendering results at densely sampled test poses. Though not the purpose of our method, we also show a few results on objects with specular reflectance and shadows in order to shed light on future work.

4.2   Evaluating 360° Novel View Synthesis

Once trained on multi-view images of an object, we no longer requires those views at *test time* as reference-view input; a requirement of some recent methods [8–10]. Rather, we can directly use the learned 3D voxel embeddings Z to render high-resolution images at novel views. Table 1 shows our method Deep-Voxels++ to outperform DeepVoxels [5] by 22% PSNR improvement and 33% SSIM error reduction. Both DeepVoxels and Neural Volumes [39] are based on (deep) voxel representations. Our method also surpasses a recent implicit neural representation method SRN [20] but it only reported mean results: 33.03 PSNR, 0.97 SSIM. We further visualize normalized azimuth-elevation PSNR maps in Fig. 8 to prove that our improvement is due to consistently improved rendering quality across 1000 dense test views of the object, not caused by over-fitting at certain viewpoints that are close to the training data. This capability to smoothly interpolate between training views at high fidelity contrasts with DeepVoxels.

Figures 1 and 5 present rendering results on diverse objects. While the competing methods and our approach are proposed for and benchmarked on objects of diffuse reflectance, in the figures we also show some preliminary results on specularity and shadow modeling. Our rendered images contain sharper details and fewer rendering artifacts such as blur, aliasing and holes than DeepVoxels.

4.3   Ablation Studies

Voxel Feature Aggregation. Previous deep voxel methods [5,6] use 3D-GRU [40,41] for image-based modeling by adopting a structured voxel space

Table 3. Frustum representation sufficient sampling from the low spatial resolution deep voxels can substantially improve the $360°$ novel-view synthesis performance.

Sampling sizes $h \times w$	Vase	Pedestal	Chair	Cube	Mean PSNR	Mean SSIM
32×32	27.16	27.93	32.99	27.35	28.86	0.95
64×64	30.30	34.64	35.97	31.97	33.22	0.98
128×128	**32.62**	**38.75**	**38.73**	**35.35**	**36.36**	**0.99**

as the hidden embedding and treating hundreds of multi-view images of an object as a video sequence. However, this type of single-view based *sequential* update manner can cause inefficiency and bias of 3D voxel embeddings learning. Because it imposes an ordering on viewpoints and biases training when only a single-view observation is aggregated during each recurrent step. Inspired by Multi-view CNN [34], we address these challenges by conducting voxel feature aggregation at two different dimensions jointly: recurrent gated-fusion and concurrent max-pooling. This provides a large surface coverage of the object during each iteration of voxel feature updates and improves data utilization rate. Results in Table 2 verify our arguments. Figure 6 further demonstrates that our aggregation method helps to reduce DeepVoxels' rendering artifacts such as aliasing and holes. Better rendering quality and faster training can be achieved with more views aggregated by max-pooling in each round of voxel feature updates, which is most effective when view number increases from 1 to 4 and starts to become less effective when it reaches 8 views. Thus, in our benchmark results we use 4 views considering the trade-off between performance gains and GPU memory size constraints.

Frustum Sufficient Sampling. To decode the learned 3D voxel embeddings and render an image at a target pose g_m, we need to first project the deep voxel features into a frustum. As explained in Subsect. 3.3 the projection procedure essentially is feature sampling from the voxel space to the frustum space. Table 3 and Fig. 7 show that while voxels are usually of $32 \times 32 \times 32$ low spatial resolution due to GPU memory constraints, sufficient frustum sampling can substantially improve the visual quality of rendered images with sharper details than DeepVoxels. The frustum representation sampling sizes are determined by height/width of the depth dimension reduced frustum feature maps. We use 128×128 sampling sizes in our main results. Frustum representation sufficient sampling is *a simple yet effective implementation trick* that addresses the low voxel resolution problem. One explanation is that though voxels have low spatial resolution, they contain high dimensional latent 3D embeddings, encoding objects' appearance and shape information. Meanwhile, the differentiable trilinear interpolation-based frustum sufficient sampling enforces strong supervision on the deep voxel features (*i.e.* rich gradient signals), and eventually helps to encode more fine-scale details into the learned latent 3D embeddings.

Table 4. Our patch-based scheme reduces the complexity of large image context modeling and improves the rendering results by learning local shape patterns.

Method	Mean PSNR	2D U-Net parameters (M)	
		Feature extraction	Neural rendering
Full-image	36.36	92.2	108.9
Patch	**36.99**	**40.3**	**56.9**

Table 5. Comparisons between without/with voxel feature transformations. With the learned feature transformation kernels, we achieve better performance on objects of delicate shapes (*e.g.* pedestal, chair) and limited training views (*e.g.* 30 images).

Method	Vase	Pedestal	Chair	Cube	Mean PSNR	Mean SSIM
Without	**26.05**	29.84	28.89	25.19	27.49	0.93
With	25.76	**30.83**	**29.45**	**25.43**	**27.87**	**0.94**

Low-Complexity Patch Modeling. The patch-based training/inference scheme has multiple advantages over the previous full-image based one, which are also demonstrated in other problems like point-cloud upsampling [42], image restoration [43]. Besides reducing the complexity of modeling large image context and therefore improving fine-scale patch synthesis quality (see Table 4), our approach requires only half the 2D U-Net parameters used in image feature extraction and neural rendering of prior methods due to small-size input. Furthermore, the patch-based scheme enables us to model and render images of high resolution at low GPU memory cost, whereas full-image based methods are not easily trainable. Though small patch sizes enable the network to reduce its receptive field and capture local shape patterns, too small sizes can harm the learning and rendering results due to lacking sufficient image context. Therefore, there is a sweet spot of patch sizes. We tested 3 different patch sizes on Cube (512×512, 128×128, 64×64) and the PSNR/SSIM are: 35.35/0.992, 36.27/0.993, 32.08/0.980. We kept the 128×128 patch size as our default configuration.

View-Dependent Voxel Feature Transformation. Figure 3 illustrates how 3D voxel embeddings that encode shape and appearance of an object's local surface plane can be mapped to different patterns, due to the corresponding perspective projection effect induced by viewpoint changes. Such perspective transformation in the observed/rendered images is explicitly modeled via learned feature transformation kernels from relative voxel-camera poses. In contrast, previous methods rely on voxel volume changes caused by vantage point changes to infer view-dependency. But voxel volume differences are constrained by low voxel spatial resolutions and only implicitly reflect viewpoints. Table 5 shows that explicit voxel feature transformation modeling is critical for objects with delicate shapes (*e.g.* pedestal) and limited training views (*e.g.* 30 images), where

Table 6. Our model surpasses DeepVoxels under different data size configurations by large gaps in mean PSNR. The results indicate that DeepVoxels++ is data efficient.

Method	Training data sizes			
	Full	1/3	1/16	1/48
DeepVoxels	30.55	28.09	26.06	19.35
Ours	**37.31**	**33.34**	**27.87**	**20.71**

voxel volume changes are less continuous and less effective to model the corresponding perspective transformation caused by viewpoint changes under diffuse reflectance.

Number of Training Views. While DeepVoxels requires around 500 multi-view images to learn faithful 3D voxel embeddings of an object, DeepVoxels++ can learn to synthesize high fidelity novel views even with a limited number of training images. In Table 6, we experiment on full-size, 1/3, 1/16 and 1/48 training data. Our method outperforms DeepVoxels in all conditions, demonstrating promising results for real-world applications where only few images are available for 3D object representation learning and novel view synthesis. For example, camera rig-based image capture systems.

5 Conclusion and Limitations

We have proposed a novel view modeling and rendering technique that learns latent 3D voxel embeddings from multi-view images of an object without 3D occupancy supervision. Our approach outperforms previous deep voxel-based methods by large margins on 360° novel-view synthesis benchmarks. We show that our results contain more fine-scale details and less rendering artifacts than DeepVoxels [5]. We also conduct multiple ablation studies to show the impact of our series of improvements in achieving this enhanced rendering fidelity.

Although the benchmark mainly evaluates objects with diffuse reflectance, our proposed method of learning voxel feature transformation kernels potentially can also model other view-dependent effects (*e.g.* specularity) besides image-plane perspective transformations of diffuse surfaces. We demonstrate some preliminary visual results for specularity and shadow modeling in Fig. 5 and the supplementary material. But it is worth considering extending the current dataset with objects of non-Lambertian reflectance and conducting evaluations under various lighting situations. Novel-view rendering for non-rigid objects leveraging dynamic volumes is another challenging and important problem. In brief, future work could consider various scenarios that are not explicitly modeled or extensively evaluated by the current deep voxel-based methods, such as lighting and specular reflectance, multi-object scenes, dynamic objects and so on.

Acknowledgment. Research supported in part by ONR N00014-17-1-2072, N00014-13-1-034, ARO W911NF-17-1-0304, and Adobe.

References

1. Anderson, B.D., Moore, J.B., Hawkes, R.: Model approximations via prediction error identification. Automatica **14**, 615–622 (1978)
2. Astrom, K.: Maximum likelihood and prediction error methods. IFAC Proc. Vol. **12**, 551–574 (1979)
3. Kang, S.B., Li, Y., Tong, X., Shum, H.Y.: Image-based rendering. Found. Trends Comput. Graph. Vision (2006)
4. Gortler, S.J., Grzeszczuk, R., Szeliski, R., Cohen, M.F.: The Lumigraph. In: SIG-GRAPH vol. 96, pp. 43–54 (1996)
5. Sitzmann, V., Thies, J., Heide, F., Nießner, M., Wetzstein, G., Zollhofer, M.: Deep-Voxels: learning persistent 3D feature embeddings. In: Proceedings of the IEEE Conference on Computer Vision and Pattern Recognition, pp. 2437–2446 (2019)
6. Tung, H.Y.F., Cheng, R., Fragkiadaki, K.: Learning spatial common sense with geometry-aware recurrent networks. In: Proceedings of the IEEE Conference on Computer Vision and Pattern Recognition, pp. 2595–2603 (2019)
7. Cho, K., et al.: Learning phrase representations using RNN encoder-decoder for statistical machine translation. arXiv preprint arXiv:1406.1078 (2014)
8. Zhou, T., Tulsiani, S., Sun, W., Malik, J., Efros, A.A.: View synthesis by appearance flow. In: Leibe, B., Matas, J., Sebe, N., Welling, M. (eds.) ECCV 2016. LNCS, vol. 9908, pp. 286–301. Springer, Cham (2016). https://doi.org/10.1007/978-3-319-46493-0_18
9. Park, E., Yang, J., Yumer, E., Ceylan, D., Berg, A.C.: Transformation-grounded image generation network for novel 3D view synthesis. In: Proceedings of the IEEE Conference on Computer Vision and Pattern Recognition, pp. 3500–3509 (2017)
10. Sun, S.H., Huh, M., Liao, Y.H., Zhang, N., Lim, J.J.: Multi-view to novel view: synthesizing novel views with self-learned confidence. In: Proceedings of the European Conference on Computer Vision (ECCV), pp. 155–171 (2018)
11. Olszewski, K., Tulyakov, S., Woodford, O., Li, H., Luo, L.: Transformable bottleneck networks. arXiv preprint arXiv:1904.06458 (2019)
12. Hedman, P., Philip, J., Price, T., Frahm, J.M., Drettakis, G., Brostow, G.J.: Deep blending for free-viewpoint image-based rendering. ACM Trans. Graph. **37**, 1–15 (2018)
13. Penner, E., Zhang, L.: Soft 3D reconstruction for view synthesis. ACM Trans. Graph. **36**, 1–11 (2017)
14. Flynn, J., Neulander, I., Philbin, J., Snavely, N.: DeepStereo: learning to predict new views from the world's imagery. In: CVPR (2016)
15. Ji, D., Kwon, J., McFarland, M., Savarese, S.: Deep view morphing. In: CVPR (2017)
16. Meshry, M., et al.: Neural rerendering in the wild. In: Proceedings of the IEEE Conference on Computer Vision and Pattern Recognition, pp. 6878–6887 (2019)
17. Yin, X., Wei, H., Wang, X., Chen, Q., et al.: Novel view synthesis for large-scale scene using adversarial loss. arXiv preprint arXiv:1802.07064 (2018)
18. Zhou, T., Tucker, R., Flynn, J., Fyffe, G., Snavely, N.: Stereo magnification: learning view synthesis using multiplane images. ACM Trans. Graph. **37**, 65 (2018)
19. Flynn, J., et al.: DeepView: view synthesis with learned gradient descent. In: CVPR (2019)
20. Sitzmann, V., Zollhofer, M., Wetzstein, G.: Scene representation networks: continuous 3D-strcuture-aware neural scene representations. In: NeurIPS (2019)

21. Thies, J., Zollhöfer, M., Nießner, M.: Deferred neural rendering: image synthesis using neural textures. ACM Trans. Graph. **38**, 1–12 (2019)
22. Srinivasan, P.P., Tucker, R., Barron, J.T., Ramamoorthi, R., Ng, R., Snavely, N.: Pushing the boundaries of view extrapolation with multiplane images. In: CVPR (2019)
23. Thies, J., Zollhöfer, M., Theobalt, C., Stamminger, M., Nießner, M.: IGNOR: image-guided neural object rendering. arXiv (2018)
24. Sitzmann, V., Thies, J., Heide, F., Nießner, M., Wetzstein, G., Zollhofer, M.: Deep-Voxels: learning persistent 3D feature embeddings video demo (2019). https://youtu.be/-Vto65Yxt8s?t=228
25. Qi, C.R., Su, H., Mo, K., Guibas, L.J.: PointNet: deep learning on point sets for 3D classification and segmentation. In: CVPR (2017)
26. Kar, A., Hane, C., Malik, J.: Learning a multi-view stereo machine. In: NIPS (2017)
27. Mildenhall, B., et al.: Local light field fusion: practical view synthesis with prescriptive sampling guidelines. ACM Trans. Graph. (TOG) **38**, 1–14 (2019)
28. Kalantari, N.K., Wang, T.C., Ramamoorthi, R.: Learning-based view synthesis for light field cameras. ACM Trans. Graph. (TOG) **35**, 1–10 (2016)
29. Yang, J., Reed, S.E., Yang, M.H., Lee, H.: Weakly-supervised disentangling with recurrent transformations for 3D view synthesis. In: Advances in Neural Information Processing Systems, pp. 1099–1107 (2015)
30. Worrall, D.E., Garbin, S.J., Turmukhambetov, D., Brostow, G.J.: Interpretable transformations with encoder-decoder networks. In: Proceedings of the IEEE International Conference on Computer Vision, pp. 5726–5735 (2017)
31. Nguyen-Phuoc, T., Li, C., Theis, L., Richardt, C., Yang, Y.L.: HoloGAN: unsupervised learning of 3D representations from natural images. In: Proceedings of the IEEE International Conference on Computer Vision, pp. 7588–7597 (2019)
32. Xu, X., Chen, Y.C., Jia, J.: View independent generative adversarial network for novel view synthesis. In: Proceedings of the IEEE International Conference on Computer Vision, pp. 7791–7800 (2019)
33. Schaul, T., Quan, J., Antonoglou, I., Silver, D.: Prioritized experience replay. CoRR abs/1511.05952 (2015)
34. Su, H., Maji, S., Kalogerakis, E., Learned-Miller, E.: Multi-view convolutional neural networks for 3D shape recognition. In: Proceedings of the IEEE International Conference on Computer Vision, pp. 945–953 (2015)
35. Paszke, A., et al.: Automatic differentiation in PyTorch. In: NIPS Autodiff Workshop (2017)
36. Kingma, D.P., Ba, J.: Adam: a method for stochastic optimization. arXiv preprint arXiv:1412.6980 (2014)
37. Tatarchenko, M., Dosovitskiy, A., Brox, T.: Single-view to multi-view: reconstructing unseen views with a convolutional network. arXiv preprint arXiv:1511.06702 6 (2015)
38. Isola, P., Zhu, J.Y., Zhou, T., Efros, A.A.: Image-to-image translation with conditional adversarial networks. In: Proceedings of the IEEE Conference on Computer Vision and Pattern Recognition, pp. 1125–1134 (2017)
39. Lombardi, S., Simon, T., Saragih, J., Schwartz, G., Lehrmann, A., Sheikh, Y.: Neural volumes: learning dynamic renderable volumes from images. ACM Trans. Graph. (TOG) **38**, 65 (2019)
40. Chung, J., Gulcehre, C., Cho, K., Bengio, Y.: Gated feedback recurrent neural networks. In: International Conference on Machine Learning, pp. 2067–2075 (2015)
41. Hochreiter, S., Schmidhuber, J.: Long short-term memory. Neural Comput. **9**, 1735–1780 (1997)

42. Yu, L., Li, X., Fu, C.W., Cohen-Or, D., Heng, P.A.: PU-Net: point cloud upsampling network. In: Proceedings of the IEEE Conference on Computer Vision and Pattern Recognition, pp. 2790–2799 (2018)
43. Papyan, V., Elad, M.: Multi-scale patch-based image restoration. IEEE Trans. Image Process. **25**, 249–261 (2015)

Dehazing Cost Volume for Deep Multi-view Stereo in Scattering Media

Yuki Fujimura$^{(\boxtimes)}$, Motoharu Sonogashira , and Masaaki Iiyama

Kyoto University, Kyoto-shi 606-8501, Japan
{fujimura,sonogashira,iiyama}@mm.media.kyoto-u.ac.jp

Abstract. We propose a learning-based multi-view stereo (MVS) method in scattering media such as fog or smoke with a novel cost volume, called the dehazing cost volume. An image captured in scattering media degrades due to light scattering and attenuation caused by suspended particles. This degradation depends on scene depth; thus it is difficult for MVS to evaluate photometric consistency because the depth is unknown before three-dimensional reconstruction. Our dehazing cost volume can solve this chicken-and-egg problem of depth and scattering estimation by computing the scattering effect using swept planes in the cost volume. Experimental results on synthesized hazy images indicate the effectiveness of our dehazing cost volume against the ordinary cost volume regarding scattering media. We also demonstrated the applicability of our dehazing cost volume to real foggy scenes.

1 Introduction

Three-dimensional (3D) reconstruction from 2D images is important in computer vision. However, images captured in scattering media, such as fog or smoke, degrade due to light scattering and attenuation caused by suspended particles. For example, Fig. 1(a) shows a synthesized hazy image, the contrast of which is reduced due to light scattering. Traditional 3D reconstruction techniques that exploit observed pixel intensity cannot work in such environments.

We propose a learning-based multi-view stereo (MVS) method in scattering media. MVS [1] is a method for reconstructing the 3D geometry of a scene from multiple images. Recently, learning-based MVS methods have been proposed and provided highly accurate results [2–4]. The proposed method is based on MVDepthNet [5], which is one such MVS method.

MVDepthNet estimates scene depth by taking a cost volume as input for the network. The cost volume is based on a plane sweep volume [6], i.e., it is constructed by sweeping a fronto-parallel plane to a camera in the scene and evaluates the photometric consistency between multiple cameras under the assumptions that the scene lies on each plane. As described above, however, an image captured in scattering media degrades; thus, using the ordinary cost volume leads to undesirable results, as shown in Fig. 1(c).

To address this problem, we propose a novel cost volume for scattering media, called *the dehazing cost volume*. In scattering media, light bouncing off a scene is

© Springer Nature Switzerland AG 2021
H. Ishikawa et al. (Eds.): ACCV 2020, LNCS 12622, pp. 261–277, 2021.
https://doi.org/10.1007/978-3-030-69525-5_16

(a)   (b)   (c)   (d)

Fig. 1. (a) synthesized hazy image due to scattering medium. (b) ground truth depth. (c) output depth of fine-tuned MVDepthNet [5] with ordinary cost volume. (d) output depth of network with our dehazing cost volume.

attenuated exponentially relative to the depth. On the other hand, scattered light observed with a camera increases with depth. This means that the degradation due to a scattering medium depends on the scene depth. Our dehazing cost volume can restore images with such depth-dependent degradation and compute the effective cost of photometric consistency simultaneously. It enables robust 3D reconstruction in scattering media, as shown in Fig. 1(d).

In summary, the primary contribution of this paper is to design a novel cost volume for scattering media, which *avoids the chicken-and-egg problem of depth and scattering estimation by computing degradation with the depth of each swept plane in the cost volume.* Accordingly, our dehazing cost volume will accelerate the real-time applicability of 3D reconstruction in scattering media.

2 Related Work

2.1 Multi-view Stereo

As mentioned above, MVS [1] is a method of reconstructing 3D geometry using multiple cameras. In general, it exploits the dense pixel correspondence between multiple images for 3D reconstruction. The correspondence is referred to as photometric consistency and computed on the basis of the similarity measure of pixel intensity. One of the difficulties in the computation of photometric consistency is occlusion, i.e., the surface of a target object is occluded from certain cameras. This leads to incorrect correspondence and inaccurate 3D reconstruction. To address this problem, methods have been proposed for simultaneous view selection to compute effective photometric consistency and 3D reconstruction with MVS, achieving highly accurate 3D reconstruction [7,8].

Along with the above issue, there are many cases in which it is difficult to obtain accurate 3D geometry with traditional MVS methods. A textureless surface and an object with a view-dependent reflectance property, such as specular reflection, are typical cases. Learning-based MVS methods have recently been used to learn semantic information on large-scale training data and enable robust 3D reconstruction in such scenes.

Learning-based MVS methods often construct a cost volume to constrain 3D geometry between multiple cameras. For example, Wang and Shen [5] proposed

MVDepthNet, which constructs a cost volume from multi-view images setting one of the images as a reference image. It can take an arbitrary number of input images to construct the cost volume. The convolutional neural network takes the reference image and cost volume as input then estimates the depth map of the reference camera. DeepMVS proposed by Huang et al. [3] first constructs a plane sweep volume, then the patch matching network is applied to the reference image and each slice of the volume to extract features to measure the correspondence, which is followed by feature aggregation networks and depth refinement with a fully connected conditional random field. Yao et al. [2] and Im et al. [4] respectively proposed MVSNet and DPSNet, in which input images are first passed through the networks to extract features, then the features are warped instead of constructing the cost volume in the image space. Our proposed method is based on MVDepthNet [5], which is the simplest and light-weight method, and we extended the ordinary cost volume for scattering media.

2.2   Dehazing

In scattering media, a captured image degrades due to light scattering and attenuation. To enhance the quality of an image captured in scattering media, dehazing and defogging methods have been proposed [9–12]. These studies introduced the priors of latent clear images to solve the ill-posed nature of the problem. For example, He et al. [9] proposed a dark channel prior with which a clear image having a dark pixel in a local image patch is assumed. Berman et al. [12] proposed a haze-line prior with which the same intensity pixels of the latent clear image forms a line in RGB space. Many learning-based methods using neural networks have also been proposed recently [13–18]. Dehazing can improve computer vision tasks in scattering media such as object detection [19].

2.3   3D Reconstruction in Scattering Media

Our goal is to reconstruct 3D geometry directly from degraded images by scattering media instead of recovering the latent clear images. There has been research focusing on the same problem as in our study. For example, Narasimhan et al. [20] proposed a 3D reconstruction method using structured light in scattering media. Photometric stereo methods have also been proposed for scattering media [21–23]. However, these methods require active light sources, which limits real-world applicability. Instead of using an ordinary camera, Heide et al. [24] and Satat et al. [25] respectively used a time-of-flight camera and single photon avalanche diode for scattering media. Wang et al. [26] combined a line sensor and line laser to generate a programmable light curtain that can suppress the backscatter effect. However, the use of these methods is hindered due to the requirement of expensive sensors or special hardware settings.

The proposed method is based on stereo 3D reconstruction requiring neither active light sources nor special hardware settings. Caraffa et al. [27] proposed a binocular stereo method in scattering media. With this method, image enhancement and stereo reconstruction are simultaneously modeled on the basis of a Markov random field. Song et al. [28] proposed a learning-based binocular stereo method in scattering media, where dehazing and stereo reconstruction are trained as multi-task learning. The features from the networks of each task are simply concatenated at the intermediate layer. The most related method to ours is the MVS method proposed by Li et al. [29]. They modeled dehazing and MVS simultaneously, and the output depth was regularized using an ordering constraint, which was based on a transmission map that was the output of dehazing with Laplacian smoothing. With all these methods, homogeneous scattering media is assumed; thus, we followed the same assumption. It is left open to apply these methods to inhomogeneous media.

These previous studies [27,29] designed photometric consistency measures considering the scattering effect. However, this requires scene depth because degradation due to scattering media depends on this depth. Thus, they relied on iterative implementation of an MVS method and dehazing, which leads to large computation cost. In contrast, our dehazing cost volume can solve this chicken-and-egg problem by computing the scattering effect in the cost volume. The scene depth is then estimated effectively by taking the cost volume as input for a convolutional neural network, making fast inference possible.

3   Multi-view Stereo in Scattering Media

In this section, we describe MVS in scattering media with our dehazing cost volume. First, we introduce an image formation model in scattering media then give an overview of the proposed method, followed by a discussion on an ordinary cost volume and our dehazing cost volume.

3.1   Image Formation Model

We use an atmospheric scattering model [30] for image observation in scattering media. This model is used for many dehazing methods and describes the degradation of an observed image in scattering media in daylight. Let an RGB value at the pixel (u, v) of a degraded image captured in scattering media and its latent clear image be $I(u, v) \in \mathbb{R}^3$ and $J(u, v) \in \mathbb{R}^3$, respectively. We assume that the pixel value of each color channel is within 0 and 1. The observation process of this model is given as

$$I(u, v) = J(u, v)e^{-\beta z(u,v)} + A(1 - e^{-\beta z(u,v)}), \tag{1}$$

where $z(u, v) \in \mathbb{R}$ is the depth at pixel (u, v), $\beta \in \mathbb{R}$ is a scattering coefficient that represents the density of a medium, and $A \in \mathbb{R}$ is global airlight. The first term is a component that describes reflected light in a scene. This reflected component becomes attenuated exponentially with respect to the scene depth. The second term is a scattering component, which consists of scattered light that arrives at a camera without reflecting on objects. In contrast to the reflected component, this component increases with depth. Therefore, image degradation due to scattering media depends on the scene depth.

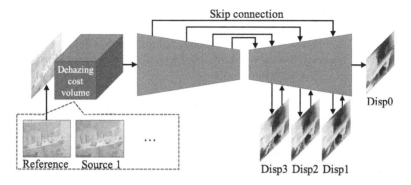

Fig. 2. Input of network is reference image captured in scattering medium and our dehazing cost volume. Our dehazing cost volume is constructed from reference image and source images. Network architecture of our method is same as that of MVDepthNet [5], which has encoder-decoder with skip connections. Output of network is disparity maps (inverse depth maps) at different resolutions.

In the context of image restoration, we aim to estimate unknown parameters J, z, scattering coefficient β, and airlight A from an observed image I, and the estimation of all these parameters at the same time is an ill-posed problem. Previous studies developed methods for estimating A from a single image [9,31]. In addition, Li et al. [29] estimated β under a multi-view setting at a structure-from-motion (SfM) step. This is the same problem setting as in our study. In the rest of this paper, therefore, we assume that A and β have already been estimated unless otherwise noted. At the end of Sect. 4, we discuss the effect of the estimation error of these parameters.

3.2 Overview

MVS methods are roughly categorized by output representation, e.g., point-cloud, volume, or mesh-based reconstruction. The proposed method is formulated as a depth map estimation, i.e., given multiple cameras, we estimate a depth map for one of the cameras. In this paper, a target camera to estimate a depth map is referred to as a reference camera r and the other cameras are referred to as source cameras $s \in \{1, \cdots, S\}$, and images captured with these cameras are denoted as a reference image I_r and source images I_s. We assume that the camera parameters are calibrated beforehand.

An overview of the proposed method is shown in Fig. 2. Our dehazing cost volume is constructed from a hazy reference image and source images captured in a scattering medium. The network takes the reference image and our dehazing cost volume as input then outputs a disparity map (inverse depth map) of the reference image. The network architecture is the same as that of MVDepthNet [5], while the ordinary cost volume used in MVDepthNet is replaced with our dehazing cost volume for scattering media.

3.3 Dehazing Cost Volume

In this section, we explain our dehazing cost volume, which is taken as input to the network. The dehazing cost volume enables effective computation of photometric consistency in scattering media.

Before explaining our dehazing cost volume, we show the computation of the ordinary cost volume in Fig. 3(a). We first sample the 3D space in the reference camera coordinate by sweeping a fronto-parallel plane. We then back-project source images onto each sampled plane. Finally, we take the residual between the reference image and each warped source image, which corresponds to the cost of photometric consistency on the hypothesis that the scene exists on the plane. Let the image size be $W \times H$ and number of sampled depths be N. We denote the cost volume by $\mathcal{V} : \{1, \cdots, W\} \times \{1, \cdots, H\} \times \{1, \cdots, N\} \to \mathbb{R}$, and each element of the cost volume is given as follows:

$$\mathcal{V}(u, v, i) = \frac{1}{S} \sum_{s} \|I_r(u, v) - I_s(\pi_{r \to s}(u, v; z_i))\|_1, \tag{2}$$

where z_i is the depth value of the i-th plane. The operator $\pi_{r \to s} : \mathbb{R}^2 \to \mathbb{R}^2$ projects the camera pixel (u, v) of the reference camera r onto the source image I_s with the given depth, which is defined as follows:

$$\begin{bmatrix} \pi_{r \to s}(u, v; z) \\ 1 \end{bmatrix} \sim z \mathbf{K}_s \mathbf{R}_{r \to s} \mathbf{K}_r^{-1} \begin{bmatrix} u \\ v \\ 1 \end{bmatrix} + \mathbf{K}_s \mathbf{t}_{r \to s}, \tag{3}$$

where $\mathbf{K}_r$ and $\mathbf{K}_s$ are the intrinsic parameters of r and the source camera s, and $\mathbf{R}_{r \to s}$ and $\mathbf{t}_{r \to s}$ are a rotation matrix and translation vector from r to s. The cost volume evaluates the photometric consistency of each pixel with respect to the sampled depth; thus, the element of the cost volume with correct depth ideally becomes zero.

An observed image captured in scattering media degrades in the manner described in Eq. (1), and the ordinary cost volume defined in Eq. (2) leads to undesirable results. In contrast, our dehazing cost volume dehazes the image and computes photometric consistency cost simultaneously. As described in Sect. 3.1, degradation due to scattering media depends on scene depth; thus, our dehazing cost volume restores degraded images using the depth of a swept plane.

Figure 3(b) shows the computation of our dehazing cost volume. A reference image is dehazed directly using the depth of a swept plane. A source image is dehazed using the swept plane from a source camera view, then the dehazed source image is warped to the reference camera coordinate. Similar to the ordinary cost volume, we define our dehazing cost volume as $\mathcal{D} : \{1, \cdots, W\} \times \{1, \cdots, H\} \times \{1, \cdots, N\} \to \mathbb{R}$, and each element of our dehazing cost volume is given as

$$\mathcal{D}(u, v, i) = \frac{1}{S} \sum_{s} \|J_r(u, v; z_i) - J_s(\pi_{r \to s}(u, v; z_i))\|_1, \tag{4}$$

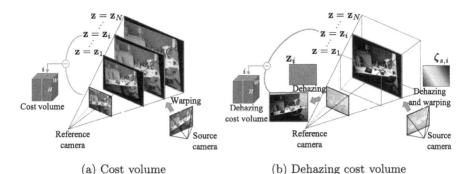

(a) Cost volume   (b) Dehazing cost volume

Fig. 3. (a) Ordinary cost volume is constructed by sweeping fronto-parallel plane in reference-camera coordinate. Cost of photometric consistency is simply computed as residual between reference image and warped source image on each swept plane $\mathbf{z} = \mathbf{z}_i$. (b) In our dehazing cost volume, reference image is dehazed using sampled depth, $\mathbf{z}_i$, which is constant over all pixels. Source image is dehazed using depth of swept plane from source-camera view, then dehazed source image is back-projected onto plane. Cost is computed by taking residual between both dehazed images.

where $J_r(u, v; z_i)$ and $J_s(\pi_{t \to s}(u, v; z_i))$ are dehazed reference and source images, and from Eq. (1), they are computed as follows:

$$J_r(u, v; z_i) = \frac{I_r(u, v) - A}{e^{-\beta z_i}} + A, \tag{5}$$

$$J_s(\pi_{r \to s}(u, v; z_i)) = \frac{I_s(\pi_{r \to s}(u, v; z_i)) - A}{e^{-\beta \zeta_{s,i}(\pi_{r \to s}(u, v; z_i))}} + A. \tag{6}$$

As shown in Fig. 3(b), the reference image is dehazed using the swept plane with depth z_i, whose depth map is denoted as $\mathbf{z}_i$. On the other hand, the source image is dehazed using $\zeta_{s,i}$, which is a depth map of the swept plane from the source camera view. The depth $\zeta_{s,i}(\pi_{r \to s}(u, v; z_i))$ is used for the cost computation of the pixel (u, v) of the reference camera because the pixel $\pi_{r \to s}(u, v; z_i)$ on the source camera corresponds to pixel (u, v) of the reference camera. Our dehazing cost volume exploits the dehazed images with much more contrast than the degraded ones; thus, the computed cost is robust even in scattering media. According to this definition of our dehazing cost volume, the photometric consistency between the latent clear images is preserved.

Our dehazing cost volume computes photometric consistency with dehazed images in the cost volume. This is similar to the previous methods [27,29] that compute photometric consistency considering scattering effect. However, this is a chicken-and-egg problem because the effect of scattering media depends on scene depth, and they rely on iterative implementation of MVS and dehazing to compute the scattering effect. Our method, on the other hand, can compute the scattering effect using a depth hypothesis of a swept plane without an explicit scene depth, which can eliminate the iterative optimization.

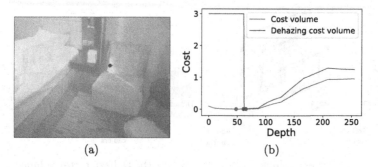

(a)   (b)

Fig. 4. Visualization of our dehazing cost volume. (b) shows values of ordinary cost volume and our dehazing cost volume at red point in (a), respectively.

Our dehazing cost volume restores an image using all depth hypotheses; thus, image dehazing with depth that greatly differs from the correct scene depth results in an unexpected image. The extreme case is when a dehazed image has negative values at certain pixels. This includes the possibility that a computed cost using Eq. (4) becomes very large. To avoid such cases, we revise the definition of our dehazing cost volume as follows:

$$\mathcal{D}(u,v,i) = \frac{1}{S}\sum_s \begin{cases} \|J_r(u,v;z_i) - J_s(\pi_{r\to s}(u,v;z_i))\|_1 \\ \quad if\ 0 \le J_r^c(u,v;z_i) \le 1\ and \\ \quad 0 \le J_s^c(\pi_{r\to s}(u,v;z_i)) \le 1\ c \in \{r,g,b\} \\ \gamma\ otherwise, \end{cases} \tag{7}$$

where $J_r^c(u,v;z_i)$ and $J_s^c(\pi_{r\to s}(u,v;z_i))$ are the pixel values of the channel $c \in \{r,g,b\}$ of the reconstructed clear images. A constant γ is a parameter that is set as a penalty cost when the dehazed result is not contained in the domain of definition. This makes the training of the network stable because our dehazing cost volume is upper bounded by γ. We can also reduce the search space of depth by explicitly giving the penalty cost. In this study, we set $\gamma = 3$, which is the maximum value of the ordinary cost volume defined in Eq. (2) when the pixel value of each color channel is within 0 and 1.

Figure 4 (b) visualizes the ordinary cost volume and our dehazing cost volume at the red point in (a). Each point in (b) indicates a minimum, and the red point in (b) indicates ground truth depth. The curve of the cost volume is smoother than our dehazing cost volume due to the degradation of the image contrast, which leads to a depth error. In addition, our dehazing cost volume can reduce the search space with the dehazing constraint γ on the left part in (b).

3.4   Network Architecture and Loss Function

As shown in Fig. 2, the network takes a reference image and our dehazing cost volume as input. To compute our dehazing cost volume, we should predetermine the target 3D space for scene reconstruction and number of depth hypotheses for plane sweep. We uniformly sample the depth on the disparity space between 0.02 and 2 and set the number of samples to $N = 256$. The network architecture is the same as that of MVDepthNet [5], which has an encoder-decoder architecture with skip connections. The network outputs disparity maps at different resolutions. The training loss is defined as the sum of L1 loss between these estimated disparity maps and the ground truth disparity map. For more details, please refer to [5].

4   Experiments

In this study, we used MVDepthNet [5] as a baseline method. As mentioned previously, the ordinary cost volume is replaced with our dehazing cost volume in the proposed method, so we can directly evaluate the effect of our dehazing cost volume by comparing our method with this baseline method. We also compared the proposed method to simple sequential methods of dehazing and 3D reconstruction using the baseline method. DPSNet [4], whose architecture is more complicated such as a multi-scale feature extractor, 3D convolutions, and a cost aggregation module, was also trained on hazy images for further comparison. In addition to the experiments with synthetic data, we give an example of applying the proposed method to actual foggy scenes. At the end of this section, we discuss the effect of the estimation errors of scattering parameters.

4.1   Dataset

We used the DeMoN dataset [32] for training. This dataset consists of the SUN3D [33], RGB-D SLAM [34], and MVS datasets [35], which have sequences of real images. The DeMoN dataset also has the Scenes11 dataset [32,36], which consists of synthetic images. Each image sequence in the DeMoN dataset includes RGB images, depth maps, and camera parameters. In the real-image datasets, most of the depth maps have missing regions due to sensor sensibility. As we discuss later, we synthesized hazy images from the DeMoN dataset for training the proposed method, which requires a dense depth map without missing regions. Therefore, we first trained the baseline method using clear images then compensated for the missing regions of each depth map with the output depth of the baseline method. To suppress boundary discontinuities and sensor noise around missing regions, we applied a median filter after inpainting each depth map. For the MVS dataset, which has larger noise than other datasets, we reduced the noise simply by thresholding before inpainting. Note that the training loss was computed using only pixels that originally had valid depth values. We generated 419,046 and 8,842 samples for training and test data, respectively. Each sample contained one reference image and one source image. All images were resized to 256×192.

We synthesized a hazy-image dataset for training the proposed method from clear images. The procedure of generating a hazy image is based on Eq. (1). For A, we randomly sampled $A \in [0.7, 1.0]$ for each data sample. For β, we randomly sampled $\beta \in [0.4, 0.8], [0.4, 0.8], [0.05, 0.15]$ for the SUN3D, RGB-D SLAM, and

Scenes11 datasets, respectively. We found that for the MVS dataset, it was difficult to determine the same sampling range of β for all images because it contains various scenes with different depth scales. Therefore, we determined the sampling range of β for each sample of the MVS dataset as follows: first, we set the range of a transmission map $e^{-\beta z}$ to $e^{-\beta z} \in [0.2, 0.4]$ for all samples then computed the median of a depth map z_{med} for each sample. Finally, we determined the β range for each sample as $\beta \in [-\log(0.4)/z_{med}, -\log(0.2)/z_{med}]$.

Similar to [5], we adopted data augmentation to enable the network to reconstruct a wide depth range. The depth of each sample was scaled by a factor between 0.5 and 1.5 together with the translation vector of the camera. Note that when training the proposed method, β should also be scaled by the inverse of the scale factor.

4.2 Training Details

All networks were implemented in PyTorch. The training was done on a NVIDIA V100 GPU with 32-GB memory. The size of a minibatch was 32 for all training.

We first trained the baseline method from scratch on the clear image dataset. We used Adam with a learning rate of 1.0×10^{-4}. After the initial 100K iterations, the learning rate was reduced by 20% after every 20K iterations. The method was trained for about 260K iterations in total.

We then fine-tuned the baseline method on hazy images and trained the proposed method with our dehazing cost volume. The parameters of both methods were initialized by that of the trained baseline method on clear images. The initial learning rate was set to 1.0×10^{-4} and reduced by 20% after every 20K iterations. The fine-tuned baseline and proposed methods were trained for about 196K and 144K iterations, respectively.

We also trained the dehazing methods, AOD-Net [19] and FFA-Net [18], and DPSNet [4] on our hazy image dataset for comparison. The dehazing networks were followed by the baseline method trained on clear images for depth estimation. DPSNet was trained with the same loss function and learning schedule as in the original paper [4].

4.3 Results

Table 1 shows the quantitative evaluation of each method. We used four evaluation metrics following [5]: L1-rel is the mean of the relative L1 error between the ground truth depth and estimated depth, L1-inv is the mean of the L1 error between ground truth inverse depth and estimated inverse depth, sc-inv is the scale-invariant error of depth proposed by Eigen et al. [37], and correctly estimated depth percentage (C.P.) [38] is the percentage of pixels whose relative L1 error is within 10%. The bold and italic values are the best and second-best, respectively. The proposed method was compared to the baseline method [5] fine-tuned on hazy images, the sequential method of dehazing [19] and baseline method [5], and DPSNet [4] trained on hazy images. In most evaluation metrics,

Table 1. Quantitative results. We compared proposed method to baseline method [5] fine-tuned on hazy images, simple sequential methods of dehazing [18,19] and depth estimation with baseline method, and DPSNet [4] trained on hazy images. Bold and italic values are best and second-best, respectively.

Dataset	Method	L1-rel	L1-inv	sc-inv	C.P. (%)
SUN3D	AOD-Net [19] + Baseline [5]	0.249	0.132	0.250	47.8
	FFA-Net [18] + Baseline [5]	0.180	0.111	0.211	55.5
	Fine-tuned [5]	0.155	0.093	0.184	60.3
	DPSNet [4]	*0.145*	*0.082*	*0.183*	*64.7*
	Proposed	**0.100**	**0.058**	**0.161**	**79.0**
RGB-D SLAM	AOD-Net [19] + Baseline [5]	0.205	0.127	0.315	58.9
	FFA-Net [18] + Baseline [5]	0.179	0.114	0.288	65.0
	Fine-tuned [5]	*0.157*	0.091	0.254	*70.7*
	DPSNet [4]	**0.152**	*0.090*	*0.234*	**71.6**
	Proposed	0.162	**0.089**	**0.231**	68.8
MVS	AOD-Net [19] + Baseline [5]	0.323	0.123	0.309	51.9
	FFA-Net [18] + Baseline [5]	0.215	0.112	0.288	55.6
	Fine-tuned [5]	*0.184*	0.100	0.241	57.1
	DPSNet [4]	0.191	**0.088**	*0.239*	**67.9**
	Proposed	**0.160**	*0.091*	**0.222**	*58.1*
Scenes11	AOD-Net [19] + Baseline [5]	0.330	0.036	0.539	52.3
	FFA-Net [18] + Baseline [5]	0.377	0.041	0.600	51.3
	Fine-tuned [5]	0.151	0.022	*0.279*	64.0
	DPSNet [4]	**0.105**	**0.018**	0.381	**81.8**
	Proposed	*0.134*	*0.019*	**0.216**	*72.3*

the proposed method outperformed the fine-tuned baseline method, demonstrating the effectiveness of our dehazing cost volume. For the RGB-D SLAM dataset, the fine-tuned baseline method was comparable to the proposed method. This is because many scenes in the RGB-D SLAM dataset are close to a camera. In this case, the degradation of an observed image is small and exists uniformly in the image, which has little effect on photometric consistency. The proposed method also performed better than the sequential methods of dehazing [18,19] and baseline method [5]. Therefore, we can see that the simultaneous modeling of dehazing and 3D reconstruction based on our dehazing cost volume is effective. DPSNet [4] first extracts feature maps from input images, and then constructs a cost volume in the feature space. Thus, the feature extractor might be able to deal with image degradation caused by light scattering. Nevertheless, our dehazing cost volume allows considering image degradation with a simple network architecture.

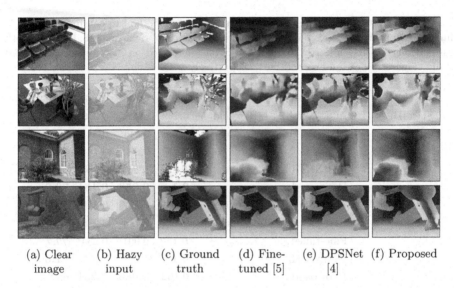

(a) Clear   (b) Hazy   (c) Ground   (d) Fine-   (e) DPSNet   (f) Proposed
   image   input   truth   tuned [5]   [4]

Fig. 5. Qualitative results. (a) clear image, (b) hazy input, (c) ground-truth depth, (d) output of fine-tuned baseline [5], (e) output of DPSNet [4], and (f) output of proposed method. From top to bottom, each row shows results of input images in SUN3D, RGB-D SLAM, MVS, and Scenes11 datasets, respectively. Values below each estimated depth represent error values (L1-rel/L1-inv/sc-inv/C.P.).

The output depth of each method is shown in Fig. 5. From top to bottom, each row shows the results of the input images in the SUN3D, RGB-D SLAM, MVS, and Scenes11 datasets, respectively. DPSNet failed to construct correspondence in some scenes, although it has the multi-scale feature extractor. Note that the results from the Scenes11 dataset indicate that the proposed method can reconstruct the 3D geometry of a distant scene where the image is heavily degraded due to scattering media.

4.4   Experiments with Actual Data

We applied the proposed method to actual scenes including scattering media. The captured images are shown in Figs. 6(a) and (b). We generated fog artificially with a fog generator. Differing from the synthetic data, A and β were unknown. We applied a previous method [31] to both the reference and source images to estimate A as pre-processing. We then applied COLMAP [8,39] to estimate extrinsic parameters and an initial depth map, which was very sparse due to image degradation, as shown in Fig. 6(c). This sparse depth was used for the estimating β in a similar manner to [29]. The results of depth estimation are shown in Figs. 6(d)–(f). The proposed method also estimated depth effectively in these actual hazy scenes. DPSNet estimated edge-preserved depth, which was achieved due to its cost aggregation module.

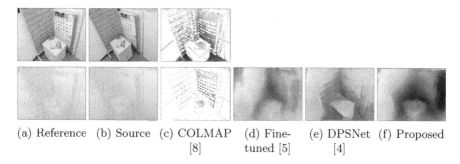

(a) Reference   (b) Source   (c) COLMAP   (d) Fine-   (e) DPSNet   (f) Proposed
                             [8]   tuned [5]   [4]

Fig. 6. Experimental results with actual foggy scenes. Top and bottom rows show clear and hazy scenes, respectively. (a) Reference image, (b) source image, (c) output of COLMAP [8], (d) output of fine-tuned baseline [5], (e) output of DPSNet [4], and (f) output of proposed method.

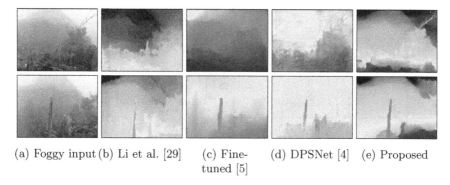

(a) Foggy input (b) Li et al. [29]   (c) Fine-   (d) DPSNet [4]   (e) Proposed
                                     tuned [5]

Fig. 7. Experimental results on actual outdoor foggy scenes. (a) foggy input, (b) estimated depth of [29], (c) output of fine-tuned baseline method [5], (d) output of DPSNet [4], and (e) output of proposed method.

We also applied the proposed method to actual outdoor scenes including scattering media. We used the image sequence *bali* [29] for the actual data. We rescaled the camera parameters so that the scene depth is contained within the target 3D space of our dehazing cost volume. In this experiment, the network took five images as input, one as a reference image and the others as source images. For A and β, we used the estimated values presented in a previous paper [29].

The results are shown in Fig. 7. These scenes are very difficult for learning-based methods due to a large domain gap. The fine-tuned baseline method and DPSNet did not perform well in these scenes. In contrast, the proposed method is more robust and the estimated depth is the closest to that of [29], though the details of the near objects were lost. However, the method proposed by Li et al. [29] requires iterative graph-cut optimization, so it takes a few minutes to estimate depth for one image. Our method, on the other hand, requires only a few seconds to estimate depth for one reference image.

4.5   Discusssion on Errors of Scattering Parameters

In this study, scattering parameters A and β are assumed to be estimated beforehand. However, this assumption is sometimes too strict especially for β because the estimation method [29] that uses sparse point clouds obtained at a SfM step and the corresponding pixel intensity is not necessarily numerically stable. However, our dehazing cost volume is parameterized by β, that is, the output depth can be regarded as a function of one variable β. Thus, β can be easily adjusted so that the output depth corresponds to the sparse SfM depth. Figure 8(b) is the SfM depth of (a). (c) shows the L1 error between the sparse depth and output depth with each β. The green dashed line, which represents the ground truth β, corresponds to the global minimum. The final output depth (d) is obtained with this value.

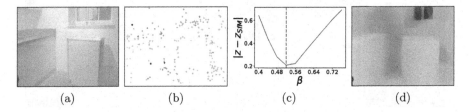

(a)   (b)   (c)   (d)

Fig. 8. Discusssion on errors of β. β can be adjusted so that output depth corresponds to sparse SfM depth.

5   Conclusion

We proposed a learning-based MVS method with a novel cost volume, called the dehazing cost volume, which enables MVS methods to be used in scattering media. Differing from the ordinary cost volume, our dehazing cost volume can compute the cost of photometric consistency by taking into account image degradation due to scattering media. This is the first paper to solve the chicken-and-egg problem of depth and scattering estimation by computing the scattering effect using each swept plane in the cost volume without explicit scene depth. The experimental results on synthesized hazy images indicate the effectiveness of our dehazing cost volume in scattering media. We also demonstrated its applicability using the images captured in actual foggy scenes. For future work, we will include the estimation of the scattering coefficient and airlight in our method. We will also extend the proposed method to depth-dependent degradation, other than light scattering, such as defocus blur [40, 41].

Acknowledgements. This work was supported by JSPS KAKENHI Grant Number 18H03263 and 19J10003.

References

1. Furukawa, Y., Hernández, C.: Multi-view stereo: a tutorial. Found. Trends® Comput. Graph. Vis. **9**, 1–148 (2015)
2. Yao, Y., Luo, Z., Li, S., Fang, T., Quan, L.: MVSNet: depth inference for unstructured multi-view stereo. In: The European Conference on Computer Vision (ECCV), pp. 767–783 (2018)
3. Huang, P., Matzen, K., Kopf, J., Ahuja, N., Huang, J.: DeepMVS: learning multi-view stereopsis. In: The IEEE Conference on Computer Vision and Pattern Recognition (CVPR), pp. 2821–2830 (2018)
4. Im, S., Jeon, H., Lin, S., Kweon, I.S.: DPSNet: end-to-end deep plane sweep stereo (2019)
5. Wang, K., Shen, S.: Mvdepthnet: real-time multiview depth estimation neural network. In: International Conference on 3D Vision (3DV), pp. 248–257 (2018)
6. Collins, R.T.: A space-sweep approach to true multi-image matching. In: The IEEE Conference on Computer Vision and Pattern Recognition (CVPR), pp. 358–363 (1996)
7. Zheng, E., Dunn, E., Jojic, V., Frahm, J.: PatchMatch based joint view selection and depthmap estimation. In: The IEEE Conference on Computer Vision and Pattern Recognition (CVPR), pp. 1510–1517 (2014)
8. Schönberger, J.L., Zheng, E., Pollefeys, M., Frahm, J.: Pixelwise view selection for unstructured multi-view stereo. In: The European Conference on Computer Vision (ECCV), pp. 501–518 (2016)
9. He, K., Sun, J., Tang, X.: Single image haze removal using dark channel prior. IEEE Trans. Pattern Anal. Mach. Intell. **33**, 2341–2353 (2011)
10. Nishino, K., Kratz, L., Lombardi, S.: Bayesian defogging. Int. J. Comput. Vision **98**, 263–278 (2012)
11. Fattal, R.: Dehazing using color-lines. ACM Trans. Graph. (TOG) **34**, 1–14 (2014)
12. Berman, D., Treibitz, T., Avidan, S.: Non-local image dehazing. In: The IEEE Conference on Computer Vision and Pattern Recognition (CVPR), pp. 1674–1682 (2016)
13. Cai, B., Xu, X., Jia, K., Qing, C., Tao, D.: DehazeNet: an end-to-end system for single image haze removal. IEEE Trans. Image Process. **25**, 5187–5198 (2016)
14. Ren, W., Liu, S., Zhang, H., Pan, J., Cao, X., Yang, M.-H.: Single image dehazing via multi-scale convolutional neural networks. In: Leibe, B., Matas, J., Sebe, N., Welling, M. (eds.) ECCV 2016. LNCS, vol. 9906, pp. 154–169. Springer, Cham (2016). https://doi.org/10.1007/978-3-319-46475-6_10
15. Zhang, H., Patel, V.M.: Densely connected pyramid dehazing network. In: The IEEE Conference on Computer Vision and Pattern Recognition (CVPR), pp. 3194–3203 (2018)
16. Yang, D., Sun, J.: Proximal Dehaze-Net: a prior learning-based deep network for single image dehazing. In: Ferrari, V., Hebert, M., Sminchisescu, C., Weiss, Y. (eds.) ECCV 2018. LNCS, vol. 11211, pp. 729–746. Springer, Cham (2018). https://doi.org/10.1007/978-3-030-01234-2_43
17. Liu, Y., Pan, J., Ren, J., Su, Z.: Learning deep priors for image dehazing. In: The IEEE International Conference on Computer Vision (ICCV), pp. 2492–2500 (2019)
18. Qin, X., Wang, Z., Bai, Y., Xie, X., Jia, H.: FFA-Net: feature fusion attention network for single image dehazing. In: The Thirty-Fourth AAAI Conference on Artificial Intelligence (AAAI 2020), pp. 11908–11915 (2020)

19. Li, B., Peng, X., Wang, Z., Xu, J., Feng, D.: AOD-Net: all-in-one dehazing network. In: The IEEE International Conference on Computer Vision (ICCV), pp. 4770–4778 (2017)
20. Narasimhan, S.G., Nayar, S.K., Sun, B., Koppal, S.J.: Structured light in scattering media. In: Proceedings of the Tenth IEEE International Conference on Computer Vision, vol. I, pp. 420–427 (2005)
21. Tsiotsios, C., Angelopoulou, M.E., Kim, T., Davison, A.J.: Backscatter compensated photometric stereo with 3 sources. In: The IEEE Conference on Computer Vision and Pattern Recognition (CVPR), pp. 2259–2266 (2014)
22. Murez, Z., Treibitz, T., Ramamoorthi, R., Kriegman, D.J.: Photometric stereo in a scattering medium. IEEE Trans. Pattern Anal. Mach. Intell. **39**, 1880–1891 (2017)
23. Fujimura, Y., Iiyama, M., Hashimoto, A., Minoh, M.: Photometric stereo in participating media considering shape-dependent forward scatter. In: The IEEE Conference on Computer Vision and Pattern Recognition (CVPR), pp. 7445–7453 (2018)
24. Heide, F., Xiao, L., Kolb, A., Hullin, M.B., Heidrich, W.: Imaging in scattering media using correlation image sensors and sparse convolutional coding. Opt. Express **22**, 26338–26350 (2014)
25. Satat, G., Tancik, M., Rasker, R.: Towards photography through realistic fog. In: The IEEE International Conference on Computational Photography (ICCP), pp. 1–10 (2018)
26. Wang, J., Bartels, J., Whittaker, W., Sankaranarayanan, A.C., Narasimhan, S.G.: Programmable triangulation light curtains. In: Ferrari, V., Hebert, M., Sminchisescu, C., Weiss, Y. (eds.) ECCV 2018. LNCS, vol. 11207, pp. 20–35. Springer, Cham (2018). https://doi.org/10.1007/978-3-030-01219-9_2
27. Caraffa, L., Tarel, J.: Stereo reconstruction and contrast restoration in daytime fog. In: Asian Conference on Computer Vision (ACCV), pp. 13–25 (2012)
28. Song, T., Kim, Y., Oh, C., Sohn, K.: Deep network for simultaneous stereo matching and dehazing. In: British Machine Vision Conference (BMVC) (2018)
29. Li, Z., Tan, P., Tang, R.T., Zou, D., Zhou, S.Z., Cheong, L.: Simultaneous video defogging and stereo reconstruction. In: The IEEE Conference on Computer Vision and Pattern Recognition (CVPR), pp. 4988–4997 (2015)
30. Tan, R.T.: Visibility in bad weather from a single image. In: The IEEE Conference on Computer Vision and Pattern Recognition (CVPR), pp. 1–8 (2008)
31. Berman, D., Treibitz, T., Avidan, S.: Air-light estimation using haze-lines. In: The IEEE International Conference on Computational Photography (ICCP) (2017)
32. Ummenhofer, B., et al.: DeMoN: depth and motion network for learning monocular stereo. In: The IEEE Conference on Computer Vision and Pattern Recognition (CVPR), pp. 5038–5047 (2017)
33. Xiao, J., Owens, A., Torralba, A.: SUN3D: a database of big spaces reconstructed using SFM and object labels. In: The IEEE International Conference on Computer Vision (ICCV), pp. 1625–1632 (2013)
34. Sturm, J., Engelhard, N., Endres, F., Burgard, W., Cremers, D.: A benchmark for the evaluation of RGB-D SLAM systems. In: The International Conference on Intelligent Robot Systems (IROS) (2012)
35. Fuhrmann, S., Langguth, F., Goesel, M.: MVE: a multi-view reconstruction environment. Eurographics Workshop on Graphics and Cultural Heritage, pp. 11–18 (2014)
36. Chang, A.X., et al.: ShapeNet: an information-rich 3D model repository. arXiv:1512.03012 (2015)

37. Eigen, D., Puhrsch, C., Fergus, R.: Depth map prediction from a single image using a multi-scale deep network. In: Twenty-eighth Conference on Neural Information Processing Systems (NeurIPS) (2014)
38. Tateno, K., Tombari, F., Laina, I., Navab, N.: CNN-SLAM: real-time dense monocular slam with learned depth prediction. In: The IEEE Conference on Computer Vision and Pattern Recognition (CVPR), pp. 6243–6252 (2017)
39. Schönberger, J.L., Frahm, J.M.: Structure-from-motion revisited. In: The IEEE Conference on Computer Vision and Pattern Recognition (CVPR), pp. 4104–4113 (2016)
40. Gur, S., Wolf, L.: Single image depth estimation trained via depth from defocus cues. In: The IEEE Conference on Computer Vision and Pattern Recognition (CVPR), pp. 7683–7692 (2019)
41. Maximov, M., Galim, K., Leal-Taixe, L.: Focus on defocus: bridging the synthetic to real domain gap for depth estimation. In: The IEEE/CVF Conference on Computer Vision and Pattern Recognition (CVPR), pp. 1071–1080 (2020)

Homography-Based Egomotion Estimation Using Gravity and SIFT Features

Yaqing Ding[1]([⊠]), Daniel Barath[2,3], and Zuzana Kukelova[3]

[1] Nanjing University of Science and Technology, Nanjing, China
dingyaqing@njust.edu.cn
[2] Machine Perception Research Laboratory, SZTAKI in Budapest,
Budapest, Hungary
barath.daniel@sztaki.mta.hu
[3] VRG, Faculty of Electrical Engineering, Czech Technical University in Prague,
Prague, Czechia
kukelova@cmp.felk.cvut.cz

Abstract. Camera systems used, e.g., in cars, UAVs, smartphones, and tablets, are typically equipped with IMUs (inertial measurement units) that can measure the gravity vector. Using the information from an IMU, the y-axes of cameras can be aligned with the gravity, reducing their relative orientation to a single DOF (degree of freedom). In this paper, we use the gravity information to derive extremely efficient minimal solvers for homography-based egomotion estimation from orientation- and scale-covariant features. We use the fact that orientation- and scale-covariant features, such as SIFT or ORB, provide additional constraints on the homography. Based on the prior knowledge about the target plane (horizontal/vertical/general plane, w.r.t. the gravity direction) and using the SIFT/ORB constraints, we derive new minimal solvers that require fewer correspondences than traditional approaches and, thus, speed up the robust estimation procedure significantly. The proposed solvers are compared with the state-of-the-art point-based solvers on both synthetic data and real images, showing comparable accuracy and significant improvement in terms of speed. The implementation of our solvers is available at https://github.com/yaqding/relativepose-sift-gravity.

1 Introduction

Estimating the relative camera motion from two views is a fundamental problem in computer vision [1], which usually is approached by applying a minimal solver combined with a robust estimator, e.g., RANSAC [2]. Using a minimal set of point correspondences is important since the processing time of robust

Electronic supplementary material The online version of this chapter (https://doi.org/10.1007/978-3-030-69525-5_17) contains supplementary material, which is available to authorized users.

estimation depends exponentially on the sample size. The well-known five-point solver [3], which uses only the point coordinate information, is a minimal solution to the relative pose estimation problem with calibrated cameras. In order to reduce the number of necessary points, we usually need to exploit additional prior knowledge about the underlying camera motion or scene geometry. Such a prior is, for example, the assumption that the camera moves on a plane – e.g., it is mounted to a vehicle – and, therefore, only a single rotation and two translation parameters have to be estimated [4,5]. Recently, largely motivated by the availability of camera-IMU systems, smart phones and tablets, which have accelerometers to measure the gravity direction, point-plus-direction solvers have shown a number of benefits [6–14]. Using this measurement, the y-axes of the cameras can be aligned with the gravity direction, reducing the relative orientation of two cameras from three to a single degree of freedom (DOF). This allows using only three point correspondences to obtain the relative camera motion (the DOF of the estimated essential matrix reduces from five to three) [7].

Scenes containing large planar surfaces, e.g., floor, walls, doors, street or other general structures, are very common in man-made environments. Thus, homography-based methods [1] also play an important role in relative pose estimation. For a known gravity direction, Saurer et al. [6] show that planes, in such environments, can be divided into three categories: horizontal, vertical and general planes. Using the orientation prior, the number of correspondences required for the estimation is reduced: to two point correspondences for the ground and a vertical plane with known normal, and 2.5 point correspondences for vertical planes with unknown normals. For a general plane, the homography-based relative pose estimation is equivalent to the epipolar geometry (the essential matrix estimation), and therefore, it requires three point correspondences (note that three points always lie on a general plane). In [15], the authors propose a homography-based relative pose estimation approach assuming a known vertical direction with points on the horizontal line.

Affine correspondences encode higher-order information about the underlying scene geometry. Thus, fewer features are needed for model estimation compared to point-based methods. Barath et al. [16,17] show that two affine correspondences are enough for relative pose estimation when the focal length is fixed and unknown. Recently, it has been shown that the relative pose can be estimated from one affine correspondence with known gravity direction or under the planar motion assumption [18,19]. However, a major drawback of using such features in practice is that obtaining them, e.g., via Affine-SIFT [20] or Harris-Affine [21], is time-consuming. This severely restricts the applicability of these techniques, especially for real-time applications. Nevertheless, parts of the affine features can be obtained from widely-used feature detectors. For example, SIFT [22] and SURF [23] provide orientation- and scale-covariant features, which allows homography estimation from two correspondences [24]. ORB [25] provides oriented features, and has been successfully used for fundamental matrix estimation [26].

In this paper, we investigate the case where the camera is equipped with an IMU to align the y-axes with the gravity direction. After aligning the camera coordinate system, we may have some information about the normal of the target plane, e.g., the ground plane usually becomes parallel to the XZ plane of the aligned system. Since the scale and rotation of the feature is known at no cost when using most of the widely-used feature detectors, e.g., SIFT or SURF, we propose minimal solvers for homography estimation in man-made environments based on orientation- and scale-covariant features. Our work builds on top of the work of Saurer et al. [6] and Barath et al. [24]. Our new solvers exploit the orientation and scale constraints on Euclidean homographies introduced in [24] and apply them for homography-based egomotion estimation with a known vertical direction. In contrast to the point correspondences used in the solvers of Saurer et al. [6], our solvers require fewer correspondences. Thus, the new solvers speed up the robust estimation procedure significantly. We support this claim by extensive experiments, where we show that the new solvers have comparable accuracy and notable improvement in speed over point-based solvers [3,6].

The main **contributions** of this paper are: (i) Since the affine transformations will change after the cameras are aligned with the gravity direction, the scale and orientation from features detected in the original image cannot be directly used for the aligned cameras. We thus investigate the relationship between the original and aligned views so that the scale and orientation from the original views can give constraints on the aligned views. (ii) When the points lie on the ground plane, we show that the relative pose problem can be solved from a single orientation- and scale-covariant feature. (iii) In addition, we prove that the rotation estimation is independent of the feature scale for this case. (iv) If the points are on a vertical plane, we show that a single orientation-covariant feature and one point correspondence are sufficient to estimate the camera motion. (v) In the case that the normal of the plane is completely unknown, we derive a minimal solution using only two orientation-covariant features for general homography estimation. For more details on this solver we refer the reader to the supplementary material.

2   Background

Suppose that we are given a point on a 3D plane and its two projections, $\mathbf{m}_1 = [u_1, v_1, 1]^\top$ and $\mathbf{m}_2 = [u_2, v_2, 1]^\top$, with respect to two camera frames. These two image points are related by a Euclidean homography matrix $\mathbf{H} \in \mathbb{R}^{3 \times 3}$ as

$$\gamma \mathbf{K}_2^{-1} \mathbf{m}_2 = \mathbf{H} \mathbf{K}_1^{-1} \mathbf{m}_1, \tag{1}$$

where $\gamma \in \mathbb{R}$ is a scaling factor, and $\mathbf{K}_1, \mathbf{K}_2 \in \mathbb{R}^{3 \times 3}$ are the camera intrinsic matrices. The homography matrix $\mathbf{H}$ relates the normalized image points $\mathbf{K}_1^{-1} \mathbf{m}_1$ and $\mathbf{K}_2^{-1} \mathbf{m}_2$. $\mathbf{H}$ is related to the rotation $\mathbf{R}$, translation $\mathbf{T}$, and distance d from the camera frame to the target plane, and the normal $\mathbf{N}$ of the plane via

$$\mathbf{H} = (\mathbf{R} + \mathbf{T} \mathbf{N}^\top), \tag{2}$$

where we can absorb the distance d into the translation $\mathbf{T}$. Here, we assume that the gravity direction is known. The gravity direction can be calculated, e.g., from the IMU data or vanishing points [1]. With this assumption, and without loss of generality, we can rotate the points so that the y-axes of the cameras are aligned with the gravity direction (Fig. 1(a)). Let R_1, R_2 be the rotation matrices that were used for the alignment of the first and the second camera. Applying the rotations to the normalized image points, Eq. (1) becomes

$$\gamma R_2 K_2^{-1} m_2 = H_y R_1 K_1^{-1} m_1, \tag{3}$$

with

$$H_y = (R_y + t n^\top). \tag{4}$$

Here, t is the translation (the distance is absorbed into t) after the alignment and R_y is an unknown rotation around the y-axis of the form

$$R_y = \begin{bmatrix} \cos\theta & 0 & \sin\theta \\ 0 & 1 & 0 \\ -\sin\theta & 0 & \cos\theta \end{bmatrix}, \tag{5}$$

where θ is the unknown yaw angle. The relationship between H and H_y is given by the following formula:

$$H = R_2^\top H_y R_1. \tag{6}$$

Hence, the full relative rotation and translation between the two views are

$$R = R_2^\top R_y R_1, \quad T = R_2^\top t. \tag{7}$$

In this case, H_y can be used to get the 5-DOF relative pose between the views.

2.1 DOF Analysis

It is well-known that the general Euclidean homography matrix has 8° of freedom originating from the three parameters of rotation R, two unknowns describing the orientation of the unit plane normal n, the distance d of the plane from the camera, and two DOF from the direction of t.

In our case, when the coordinate system is aligned, the DOF of R is reduced to one, i.e., the angle of rotation around the vertical axis. In general configurations, the relative translation t between the two cameras has only two degrees of freedom since it can only be recovered up to scale, due to the nature of perspective projection [1]. However, since the distance d of the observed plane is absorbed into t to achieve the special form of H_y, t cannot be arbitrarily scaled and, thus, it has three degrees of freedom. As a consequence, we will be estimating all three parameters of t and, also, the unknown rotation angle.

2.2 Orientation- and Scale-Covariant Feature Constraints

In this paper, we use orientation- and scale-covariant features to estimate the unknown homography. Most of the widely-used feature detectors, e.g., SIFT and SURF, not only provide point correspondences but also additional information about each feature's scale and rotation. This means that an orientation- and scale-covariant feature correspondence can be considered as a correspondence of triplets $(\mathbf{m}_1, \varphi_1, q_1) \leftrightarrow (\mathbf{m}_2, \varphi_2, q_2)$, where $\mathbf{m}_1 \leftrightarrow \mathbf{m}_2$ is a point correspondence, and φ_i and q_i, $i = 1, 2$ are, respectively, the orientation and the scale of the feature.

For the point correspondence part, Eq. (1) holds and can be rewritten as

$$\gamma \mathbf{m}_2 = \mathbf{G} \mathbf{m}_1, \tag{8}$$

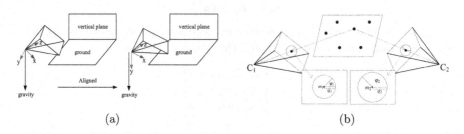

(a)   (b)

Fig. 1. (a) Illustration of the coordinate systems used in this paper. We can align the y-axis of the camera with the gravity based on the IMU readings. (b) Visualization of orientation- and scale-covariant features.

where $\mathbf{G}$ is a homography matrix which relates uncalibrated image points $\mathbf{m}_1$ and $\mathbf{m}_2$, i.e., $\mathbf{G} = \mathbf{K}_2 \mathbf{H} \mathbf{K}_1^{-1}$. This means that each point correspondence yields the following two linear constraints on $\mathbf{G}$:

$$\begin{bmatrix} 0 & 0 & 0 & -u_1 & -v_1 & -1 & v_2 u_1 & v_2 v_1 & v_2 \\ u_1 & v_1 & 1 & 0 & 0 & 0 & -u_2 u_1 & -u_2 v_1 & -u_2 \end{bmatrix} \mathbf{g} = 0, \tag{9}$$

$$\mathbf{g} = \begin{bmatrix} g_1 & g_2 & g_3 & g_4 & g_5 & g_6 & g_7 & g_8 & g_9 \end{bmatrix}^{\top}, \tag{10}$$

where $g_1, g_2, ..., g_9$ are the elements of the homography $\mathbf{G}$ in a row-major order.

In [24], two constraints that relate the homography matrix to the scales and rotations of the orientation- and scale-covariant features, e.g., SIFTs, in the first and second image are derived. These constraints have the form

$$g_8 u_2 s_1 s_2 + g_7 u_2 s_2 c_1 - g_8 v_2 s_1 c_2 - g_7 v_2 c_1 c_2 + \tag{11}$$
$$-g_2 s_1 s_2 - g_1 s_2 c_1 + g_5 s_1 c_2 + g_4 c_1 c_2 = 0,$$
$$g_7^2 u_1^2 q_2 + 2 g_7 g_8 u_1 v_1 q_2 + g_8^2 v_1^2 q_2 + g_5 g_7 u_2 q_1 + \tag{12}$$
$$-g_4 g_8 u_2 q_1 - g_2 g_7 v_2 q_1 + g_1 g_8 v_2 q_1 + 2 g_7 g_9 u_1 q_2 +$$
$$2 g_8 g_9 v_1 q_2 + g_2 g_4 q_1 - g_1 g_5 q_1 + g_9^2 q_2 = 0,$$

where $c_i = \cos(\varphi_i)$, $s_i = \sin(\varphi_i)$. Note that the first constraint (11) is not dependent on scales. It can thus also be used for features that are orientation- but not scale-covariant, e.g., ORB features [25].

This means that each SIFT correspondence gives four constraints on the homography matrix $\mathbf{G}$ (three linear ones from (9) and (11) and one quadratic one from (12)) and each ORB correspondence gives just three linear constraints ((9) and (11)). Our objective is to estimate the camera motion by estimating a homography from a combination of SIFT/ORB and point correspondences. Note, that constraints (11) and (12) were derived for a general homography. In our case, the y-axes of the cameras are aligned with the gravity direction. This changes not only the point coordinates, but also affects the orientation and scale of the features. Thus, the constraints (11) and (12) cannot be directly applied when estimating the Euclidean homography matrix H_y via Eq. (3). Next, we describe how to use the orientation and scale constraints to estimate the homography H_y under different assumptions about the camera motion and observed plane.

3   Pose Estimation

Based on (1), (6) and (8), the relationship between the Euclidean homography matrix H_y and the standard homography matrix G can be formulated as

$$H_y \sim \widehat{H}_y = R_2 K_2^{-1} G K_1 R_1^\top, \tag{13}$$

where $\sim$ indicates equality up to a scaling factor, i.e., $\widehat{H}_y = \lambda H_y$, for some scale $\lambda \neq 0$. In order to find the constraints on the Euclidean homography matrix H_y, we first consider the matrix B defined as

$$B = \widehat{H}_y - \lambda R_y = \lambda t n^\top. \tag{14}$$

B is the difference between the homography $\widehat{H}_y$ and the corresponding rotation R_y (we have to add a scalar λ because (13) holds up to scale). Matrix λR_y can be written as

$$\lambda R_y = \begin{bmatrix} \alpha & 0 & \beta \\ 0 & \lambda & 0 \\ -\beta & 0 & \alpha \end{bmatrix}, \tag{15}$$

where $\alpha = \lambda \cos\theta$, $\beta = \lambda \sin\theta$, and θ is the yaw angle associated with R_y. Matrix B in (14) can then be rewritten as

$$B = \begin{bmatrix} h_1 - \alpha & h_2 & h_3 - \beta \\ h_4 & h_5 - \lambda & h_6 \\ h_7 + \beta & h_8 & h_9 - \alpha \end{bmatrix}, \tag{16}$$

where h_i are the elements of the matrix $\widehat{H}_y$.

Next, we consider two different cases based on prior knowledge of the type of target plane, i.e., situations where our points lie on a horizontal or a vertical plane. The third case, i.e., a general plane, is discussed in the supplementary material. The prior knowledge of the type of target plane gives additional constraints on the form of the matrix B that simplify the computation of H_y.

3.1   Points on a Horizontal Plane

An important case arises when the points lie on a horizontal plane. This is practical and relevant when a camera is mounted on a vehicle/robot or a UAV mounted with a bird-view camera, since the ground plane is virtually always available. In this case, $n = [0\ 1\ 0]^\top$, and we have a 4-DOF problem with respect to $[\theta, t_x, t_y, t_z]$. Hence, this problem can be solved from a single SIFT correspondence which yields four independent constraints. From Eq. (14), it follows that the matrix B has the form

$$B = \lambda \begin{bmatrix} 0 & t_x & 0 \\ 0 & t_y & 0 \\ 0 & t_z & 0 \end{bmatrix}. \tag{17}$$

Using (16) and (17), we obtain six constraints on the elements of the homography matrix $\widehat{H}_y$, i.e.,

$$h_4 = 0,\ h_6 = 0,\ h_1 - \alpha = 0,\ h_3 - \beta = 0,\ h_9 - \alpha = 0,\ h_7 + \beta = 0. \tag{18}$$

After eliminating the parameters $\{\alpha, \beta\}$ based on the last four equations in (18), we obtain four constraints

$$h_4 = 0,\ \ h_6 = 0,\ \ h_1 - h_9 = 0,\ \ h_3 + h_7 = 0 \tag{19}$$

which generally hold for this type of homographies. Given a single SIFT correspondence, we have three linear constraints (from (9) and (11)) on the homography matrix G. These constraints can be written in a matrix form

$$Mg = 0, \tag{20}$$

where M is a 3×9 coefficient matrix and the vector g contains the elements of G (cf. (10)). Vector g can be written as a linear combination of the six basis vectors from the 6-dimensional null space of the matrix M as

$$g = x_1 g_a + x_2 g_b + x_3 g_c + x_4 g_d + x_5 g_e + x_6 g_f, \tag{21}$$

where $x_1, \ldots, x_6$ are new unknowns. Note that since G is given only up to scale, we can fix one of the unknowns, e.g., $x_6 = 1$. Substituting (21) into (13) yields $\widehat{H}_y = R_2 K_2^{-1} G K_1 R_1^\top$. The Euclidean homography matrix $\widehat{H}_y$, for calibrated cameras, can be parameterized using five unknowns $\{x_1, x_2, x_3, x_4, x_5\}$. Since there are four linear constraints (19) on the elements of $\widehat{H}_y$, we can use these ones to express four from the five unknowns, e.g., $x_1, \ldots, x_4$ as a linear functions of x_5. This leads to a parameterization of the homography matrix G (21), as well as $\widehat{H}_y$, using just one unknown, i.e., x_5. This parameterization is finally substituted into the SIFT constraint (12), leading to one quadratic equation in x_5. After solving this equation, $\widehat{H}_y$ and, subsequently, R_y and t can be recovered. Although we can directly decompose G into R and T using the SVD-based method, there will be two possible rotations for a standard homography matrix G. By contrast, each $\widehat{H}_y$ corresponds to a unique rotation, where the redundant solution is eliminated.

3.2   Points on a Vertical Plane

As a complement to the case where points are on a horizontal plane, we address the case where they lie on a vertical plane with unknown normal. This is also practical, since walls and building facades in man-made environments are usually parallel to the gravity direction. In this case, $\mathbf{n} = [n_x \ 0 \ n_z]^\top$ and we have a 5-DOF problem w.r.t. $\{\theta, t_x, t_y, t_z, n_x, n_z\}$ (the unit vector $\mathbf{n}$ has two parameters and one DOF). We need at least one SIFT or ORB and one point correspondences to solve this problem compared to the 2.5 point correspondences of the point-based solver [6]. Note that one SIFT and one point correspondence provide 6 independent constraints which result in an over-constrained system. We choose to only use the orientation constraint (11) from the feature (SIFT/ORB) correspondence since, in practice, the scale is usually more noise-sensitive. Moreover, the orientation constraint (11) is linear compared to the quadratic constraint (12). The new solver only requires oriented features and thus also works with ORB [25] features. Under the vertical plane constraint, matrix $\mathbf{B}$ in (14) becomes

$$\mathbf{B} = \lambda \begin{bmatrix} t_x n_x & 0 & t_x n_z \\ t_y n_x & 0 & t_y n_z \\ t_z n_x & 0 & t_z n_z \end{bmatrix}. \tag{22}$$

There are 6 constraints on the matrix $\mathbf{B}$ as follows:

$$\begin{aligned} & \mathbf{B}(1,2) = 0, \ \mathbf{B}(2,2) = 0, \ \mathbf{B}(3,2) = 0, \\ & \mathbf{B}(1,1)\mathbf{B}(2,3) = \mathbf{B}(1,3)\mathbf{B}(2,1), \\ & \mathbf{B}(1,1)\mathbf{B}(3,3) = \mathbf{B}(1,3)\mathbf{B}(3,1), \\ & \mathbf{B}(2,1)\mathbf{B}(3,3) = \mathbf{B}(2,3)\mathbf{B}(3,1). \end{aligned} \tag{23}$$

Substituting (16) into (23), we have the following 6 equations

$$\begin{aligned} & h_2 = 0, \ h_8 = 0, \ h_5 - \lambda = 0, \ h_4(h_9 - \alpha) - h_6(h_7 + \beta) = 0, \\ & h_6(h_1 - \alpha) - h_4(h_3 - \beta) = 0, \ (h_1 - \alpha)(h_9 - \alpha) - (h_3 - \beta)(h_7 + \beta) = 0. \end{aligned} \tag{24}$$

Similar to the case where points are on a horizontal plane, we find that two of the equations in (24) (forth and fifth) are linear in α and β. Thus, we can use them to express α and β using h_i. Substituting the formulation into the last equation of (24), we obtain the following constraint without parameters $\{\lambda, \alpha, \beta\}$:

$$(h_1 h_6 - h_3 h_4)^2 + (h_4 h_9 - h_6 h_7)^2 - h_5^2(h_4^2 + h_6^2) = 0. \tag{25}$$

Together with $h_2 = 0$, $h_8 = 0$, we obtain three constraints for the vertical plane-induced Euclidean homography matrix H_y. Given one SIFT/ORB and one point correspondences, we have $3 + 2$ linear constraints ((9) and (11)) on the homography matrix $\mathbf{G}$. These constraints can be written in a matrix form

$$\mathbf{Mg} = 0, \tag{26}$$

where M is a 5×9 coefficient matrix and the vector $\mathbf{g}$ contains the elements of G. The vector $\mathbf{g}$ can be written as a linear combination of the four basis vectors from the 4-dimensional null space of the matrix M as

$$\mathbf{g} = x_1 \mathbf{g}_a + x_2 \mathbf{g}_b + x_3 \mathbf{g}_c + x_4 \mathbf{g}_d, \tag{27}$$

where x_1, x_2, x_3, x_4 are new unknowns. Again, we fix one of the unknowns, e.g., $x_4 = 1$. Substituting (27) into (13) yields $\widehat{\mathbf{H}}_y = \mathbf{R}_2 \mathbf{K}_2^{-1} \mathbf{G} \mathbf{K}_1 \mathbf{R}_1^\top$. The Euclidean homography matrix $\widehat{\mathbf{H}}_y$, for calibrated cameras, can be parameterized using three unknowns $\{x_1, x_2, x_3\}$. We can use $h_2 = 0$, $h_8 = 0$ to express two from these three unknowns, e.g., x_1, x_2 as a linear functions of x_3. This leads to a parameterization of the homography matrix G, as well as $\widehat{\mathbf{H}}_y$, using just one unknown x_3. This parameterization is finally substituted into the Euclidean homography constraint (25), leading to one quartic equation in x_3. The remaining steps are the same as for the case where points lie on the horizontal plane.

Table 1. Theoretical computational complexity of solvers (gray – proposed).

Solver	SVD	QR	Eigen	Operations	Total operations with outliers			
					0.25	0.50	0.75	0.90
1SIFT Ground	3×9	4×4	–	145	482	964	2321	6338
2PC Ground [6]	4×5	–	–	80	446	1281	5709	$3.6 * 10^4$
1SIFT+1PC Vert.	5×9	2×2	4×4	297	1655	4755	$2.1 * 10^4$	$1.3 * 10^5$
3PC Vertical [6]	5×6	–	4×4	214	1799	7381	$6.2 * 10^4$	$9.8 * 10^5$
3PC Essential [7]	3×6	6×6	4×4	334	2807	$1.1 * 10^4$	$9.7 * 10^4$	$1.5 * 10^6$
5PC [3]		5×9 10×10	10×10	2225	$3.8 * 10^4$	$3.2 * 10^5$	$\sim 10^7$	$\sim 10^9$

4   Experiments

In this section, we study the performance of our solvers on both synthetic data and real images. We compare our solvers with the most closely related work by Saurer et al. [6] and the three-point essential matrix-based solver [7]. Since in [6], the authors have shown that the five-point essential matrix-based solver [3] outperforms the four-point homography algorithm [1], we only compare with the five-point algorithm. Note that there are several different solvers for the five-point relative pose problem [27–29] and three-point relative problem [7,9,11,12,14,30], respectively. However, solving the same problem from the same data using stable solvers, the results should be almost equal. We thus only compare against one solver per problem.

4.1   Computational Complexity

Table 1 shows the theoretical computational complexity of each solver. The number of operations for one RANSAC iteration for each solver is calculated based on the solvers' major computations, including SVD, QR and Eigenvalue decomposition. The total number of operations (last four columns) are given as the number of operations for one iteration multiplied by the number of RANSAC iterations for different percentage of outliers. We can see that our solvers need significant fewer operations than the other techniques.

4.2   Synthetic Evaluation

We chose the following setup that is similar to [6] to generate synthetic data. 100 spatial points were distributed uniformly on two planes, a horizontal plane and a vertical plane. The focal length f_g of the camera was set to 500 pixels and the resolution of the image to 1000×1000 pixels. We focused on two practical motions: forward motion (along the z-axis) and sideways motion (along the x-axis). The Euclidean distance between the two cameras was set to be 10 percent of the average scene distance. In addition, the two cameras were rotated around every axis. It was guaranteed that each 3D point was observed by two cameras – however, it is theoretically not required. This is similar to [6,7]. We generated 10,000 pairs of images with different transformations. To simulate the SIFT orientations and scales, the affine transformations were calculated from the homography using the 4-point algorithm. Then the affine transformations

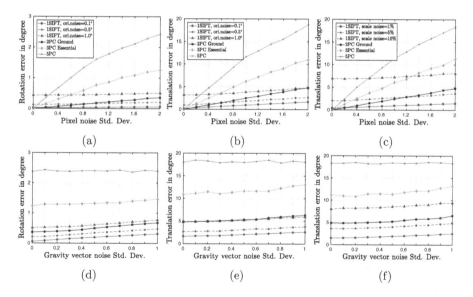

Fig. 2. Comparing the proposed 1SIFT solver with the 2PC Ground solver [6], 3PC Essential solver [7] and the 5PC solver [3]. **Top**: increasing image noise. (a, b) Rotation and translation errors with additional noise added to SIFT orientations. (c) Translation error with additional noise added to SIFT scales. **Bottom**: increasing gravity vector noise and fixed image noise (2 px std.). (d, e) Rotation and translation errors with noise added to SIFT orientations. (f) Translation error with noise added to SIFT scales.

were decomposed into SIFT orientations and scales based on [24]. The rotation error was defined as the angle difference between the estimated rotation and the true rotation: $\arccos\left(\left(\operatorname{tr}(R_g R_e^\top) - 1\right)/2\right)$, where R_g and R_e represent the true and estimated rotations, respectively. The translation error was measured as the angle between the estimated and true translation vectors, since the estimated translation is only defined up to scale. We only show the results for forward motion. Results for sideways motion are shown in the supplementary material.

Figure 2 reports the rotation and translation errors for points on the ground plane. The top row shows the performance under image noise with different standard deviations. We also add different levels of noise to the SIFT orientations and scales (see the legend). We ran 10,000 trials per data point in the plots and the first quartile of the rotation and translation errors are plotted. This measure is an appropriate performance criterion when the method is used for RANSAC or other robust statistics [6]. The bottom row shows the performance with increased gravity vector noise and constant image noise of 2 pixel standard deviation. As we can see, for different levels of noise, our 1SIFT solver performs well and obtains promising results. As shown in previous studies, e.g., [7], smartphones in 2009 such as Nokia N900 and iPhone 4 had a maximum gravity vector error of 1°, which is the maximum tested value in our synthetic experiments. For 1°, the new solvers provide stable results and thus, are useful even for low-cost

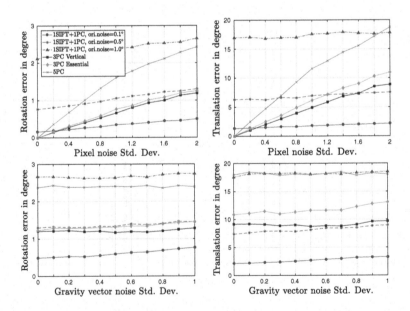

Fig. 3. Comparing the proposed 1SIFT+1PC solver with 3PC Vertical [6], 3PC Essential [7] and 5PC [3]. **Top:** rotation and translation errors under image noise. **Bottom:** rotation and translation errors under gravity vector noise and fixed image noise (2 px std.).

sensors. Nowadays, accelerometers used in cars and modern smartphones have noise levels around $0.06°$ (and expensive "good" accelerometers have $<0.02°$) [7].

Note that, we do not report the rotation error under SIFT scale noise, since there is a special property for our 1SIFT solver: the rotation estimation is independent of the scale. The proof is given in the supplementary material.

Figure 3 reports the rotation and translation errors for points on a vertical plane. The top row shows the performance under image noise with different standard deviations. Since this solver does not use the scale information from SIFT, we only need to add noise to the SIFT orientations. The bottom row shows the performance with increased gravity vector noise and constant image noise of 2 pixel standard deviation. In this case, our vertical plane-based solver is slightly sensitive to orientation noise. However, with the image noise increased, it is still comparable to other solvers.

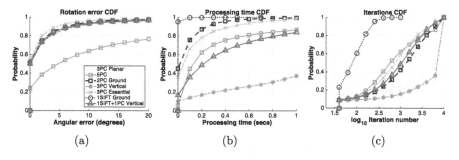

Fig. 4. The cumulative distribution function of the rotation errors; processing time; and $\log_{10}$ iteration number of GC-RANSAC. The values were calculated from a total of $9{,}064$ image pairs (15 scenes from the Malaga dataset). Being more accurate or faster is interpreted as a curve close to the top-left corner.

4.3   Camera Mounted to a Moving Vehicle

In order to test the proposed technique on real-world data, we chose the `Malaga`[1] dataset [31]. This dataset was gathered entirely in urban scenarios with car-mounted sensors, including one high-resolution stereo camera and five laser scanners. We used the sequences of one high-resolution camera and every 10th frame from each sequence. The proposed method was applied to every consecutive image pair. The ground truth paths were composed using the GPS coordinates provided in the dataset. Each consecutive frame-pair was processed independently and we did not run any optimization minimizing the error on the whole path or detecting loop-closures. The estimated relative poses of the consecutive frames were simply concatenated. In total, $9{,}064$ image pairs were used.

Considering that the orientation and scale of local features are often noisier than their point coordinates, we chose to use a locally optimized RANSAC,

---

[1]   https://www.mrpt.org/MalagaUrbanDataset.

i.e., Graph-Cut RANSAC[2] [32] (GC-RANSAC), as the robust estimator, where the local optimization is applied to only the point coordinates, similarly as in [24]. In GC-RANSAC (and other RANSAC-like methods), two different solvers are used: (a) one for fitting to a minimal sample and (b) one for fitting to a non-minimal sample when doing model polishing on all inliers or in the local optimization step. For (a), the main objective is to solve the problem using as few data points as possible since the processing time depends exponentially on the number of points required for the model estimation. The proposed and compared solvers were included in this part of the robust estimator. Also, we observed that the considered special planes usually have lower inlier ratio, being localized in the image, compared to general ones. Therefore, instead of verifying the homography in the RANSAC loop, we composed the essential matrix immediately from the recovered pose parameters and did not use the homography itself. For (b), we applied the planar 3PC essential matrix solver [7] to estimate the relative pose from all inlier correspondences. Note that, when testing a solver aiming to find a particular plane (e.g., ground), we let GC-RANSAC decide which sample is good by immediately decomposing H to the pose and validating the essential

Table 2. The avg. angular error (degrees) and processing time (seconds) of the pose estimation on 13 scenes (columns) of the Malaga dataset using different minimal solvers and GC-RANSAC as robust estimator [32]. The compared methods are the planar solver of [33] (3PC), essential matrix solver of [7] (3PC Ess.), solver of [3] (5PC), ground (2PC Ground) and vertical plane (3PC Vert.) solvers of [6], and the proposed two SIFT-based solvers assuming points on the ground (1SIFT) or vertical plane (1SIFT+1PC). The CDFs are in shown Fig. 4.

	1	2	3	4	5	6	7	8	9	10	11	12	13	Avg
	Angular error (°)													
3PC	2.6	3.4	2.9	4.6	3.8	**4.2**	3.9	1.8	4.4	6.3	2.8	2.8	6.2	3.6
3PC Ess.	**2.4**	**2.5**	**1.3**	**1.9**	3.2	**4.2**	3.5	1.6	**3.2**	5.8	1.4	**2.7**	**5.0**	**2.7**
5PC	5.5	14.8	18.6	18.1	10.7	9.3	13.2	18.0	22.0	13.1	18.2	13.2	24.9	16.5
2PC Ground	2.5	3.0	2.2	2.1	3.8	**4.2**	4.1	2.5	4.3	6.8	2.1	2.8	5.7	3.5
3PC Vert.	2.5	3.6	4.5	3.5	4.1	4.4	4.3	2.9	8.5	5.9	2.5	3.9	6.9	4.4
1SIFT+1PC	2.5	3.6	4.0	3.1	4.1	4.3	4.2	3.1	5.2	7.0	3.2	3.5	6.7	4.2
1SIFT	**2.4**	3.5	2.0	2.5	4.0	4.3	**3.5**	2.1	3.9	6.3	2.2	3.2	6.4	3.5
	Time (seconds)													
3PC	0.20	0.22	0.15	0.19	0.21	0.15	0.18	0.24	0.17	0.20	0.14	0.19	0.24	0.19
3PC Ess.	0.17	0.27	0.06	0.20	0.22	0.09	0.12	0.16	0.08	0.24	0.09	0.10	0.21	0.19
5PC	0.28	0.48	0.26	0.76	0.29	0.27	0.21	0.23	0.10	0.22	0.50	0.18	0.41	0.31
2PC Ground	0.06	0.14	0.03	0.11	0.17	0.03	0.09	0.07	0.08	0.21	0.05	0.09	0.13	0.09
3PC Vert.	1.28	1.68	0.68	1.31	1.89	0.60	1.34	1.55	1.47	2.05	0.95	1.40	1.73	1.35
1SIFT+1PC	0.32	0.68	0.15	0.61	0.79	0.11	0.44	0.37	0.37	1.12	0.23	0.44	0.62	0.47
1SIFT	**0.02**	**0.02**	**0.01**	**0.02**	**0.03**	**0.01**	**0.01**	**0.02**	**0.02**	**0.03**	**0.01**	**0.01**	**0.02**	**0.02**

---

[2] https://github.com/danini/graph-cut-ransac.

matrix. Thus, the proposed solvers can be applied without a-priori knowing what types of planes are present in the scene.

The cumulative distribution functions of the rotation errors (in degrees) of the compared methods are shown in the left plot of Fig. 4. A method being accurate is interpreted as the curve being close to the top-left corner. Both of the proposed solvers are among the best performing ones. The cumulative distribution functions of the processing times and iteration numbers of the whole robust estimation procedure are shown in the right two plots of Fig. 4. The proposed 1SIFT ground solver leads to significantly faster robust estimation than the other algorithms. The average errors and processing times, for each scene, are reported in Table 2. It can be seen that the proposed 1SIFT ground solver is the fastest one on all scenes while being the second most accurate one.

4.4 Smart Phone Images

We captured two videos, at a resolution of 1920×1080 30 Hz using an iPhone 6S, observing the ground or a vertical wall. The corresponding IMU data were captured 100 Hz. The frames and IMU data were synchronized based on their timestamps. The intrinsic camera parameters were obtained by using a Matlab toolbox. We applied the RealityCapture [34] software to acquire camera poses which we can use as ground truth when evaluating the solvers. For the sequence showing the ground, we used every consecutive images. For the video of the wall, we used every 5th image. In total, the methods were tested on $1,247$ image pairs from the videos.

The results are reported in Table 3. For the video observing the ground, the proposed 1SIFT solver is marginally – by $0.2°$ – less accurate than the 2PC solver of [6]. However, it leads to the most efficient robust estimation, being 0.3 seconds faster than the second fastest solver, i.e., 2PC Ground. For the video showing a wall, the proposed 1SIFT+1PC methods marginally leads to the most accurate solutions while being faster than the other algorithms. Furthermore, our solvers can be combined in a RANSAC loop to improve the performance.

Table 3. The average rotation error (in degrees), processing time (in seconds) and iteration numbers required for GC-RANSAC are reported.

Video 1 (ground)				Video 2 (wall)			
Solver	Error (°)	Time (s)	Iter. #	Solver	Error (°)	Time (s)	Iter. #
1SIFT	0.627	**0.571**	**286**	**1SIFT+1PC**	**5.364**	**0.219**	**233**
2PC Ground	**0.438**	0.842	973	3PC Vert.	5.391	0.420	853
5PC	1.875	2.966	5208	5PC	11.162	1.071	4104

5 Conclusions

We propose three new minimal solvers for estimating the egomotion of cameras with known vertical orientation and considering special target planes.

The methods use orientation- and scale-covariant features, thus reducing the sample size at no cost when the features are obtained by the most commonly used detectors, e.g., SIFT. The proposed solvers are compared with state-of-the-art point-based approaches on both synthetic data and real images, showing comparable accuracy and significant improvements in computation times. Based on our experiments, the most promising method is the one which estimates the homography from a single correspondence if it originates from the ground plane. We believe that the proposed solvers will be useful for the community.

Acknowledgement. The research reported in this paper was supported by the OP VVV project Research Center for Informatics No. CZ.02.1.01/0.0/0.0/16_019/0000765 and by the project: Exploring the Mathematical Foundations of Artificial Intelligence 2018-1.2.1-NKP-00008.

References

1. Hartley, R., Zisserman, A.: Multiple View Geometry in Computer Vision. Cambridge University Press, Cambridge (2003)
2. Fischler, M.A., Bolles, R.C.: Random sample consensus: a paradigm for model fitting with applications to image analysis and automated cartography. Commun. ACM **24**, 381–395 (1981)
3. Nistér, D.: An efficient solution to the five-point relative pose problem. IEEE Trans. Pattern Anal. Mach. Intell. **26**, 756–770 (2004)
4. Scaramuzza, D.: 1-point-RANSAC structure from motion for vehicle-mounted cameras by exploiting non-holonomic constraints. Int. J. Comput. Vision **95**, 74–85 (2011). https://doi.org/10.1007/s11263-011-0441-3
5. Choi, S., Kim, J.: Fast and reliable minimal relative pose estimation under planar motion. Image Vis. Comput. **69**, 103–112 (2018)
6. Saurer, O., Vasseur, P., Boutteau, R., Demonceaux, C., Pollefeys, M., Fraundorfer, F.: Homography based egomotion estimation with a common direction. IEEE Trans. Pattern Anal. Mach. Intell. **39**, 327–341 (2017)
7. Fraundorfer, F., Tanskanen, P., Pollefeys, M.: A minimal case solution to the calibrated relative pose problem for the case of two known orientation angles. In: Daniilidis, K., Maragos, P., Paragios, N. (eds.) ECCV 2010. LNCS, vol. 6314, pp. 269–282. Springer, Heidelberg (2010). https://doi.org/10.1007/978-3-642-15561-1_20
8. Saurer, O., Fraundorfer, F., Pollefeys, M.: Homography based visual odometry with known vertical direction and weak Manhattan world assumption. In: Vicomor Workshop at IROS, vol. 2012 (2012)
9. Naroditsky, O., Zhou, X.S., Gallier, J., Roumeliotis, S.I., Daniilidis, K.: Two efficient solutions for visual odometry using directional correspondence. IEEE Trans. Pattern Anal. Mach. Intell. **34**, 818–824 (2012)
10. Hee Lee, G., Pollefeys, M., Fraundorfer, F.: Relative pose estimation for a multi-camera system with known vertical direction. In: Proceedings of the IEEE Conference on Computer Vision and Pattern Recognition, pp. 540–547 (2014)
11. Ding, Y., Yang, J., Ponce, J., Kong, H.: An efficient solution to the homography-based relative pose problem with a common reference direction. In: The IEEE International Conference on Computer Vision (ICCV) (2019)

12. Ding, Y., Yang, J., Kong, H.: An efficient solution to the relative pose estimation with a common direction. In: 2020 IEEE International Conference on Robotics and Automation (ICRA), pp. 11053–11059. IEEE (2020)
13. Ding, Y., Yang, J., Ponce, J., Kong, H.: Minimal solutions to relative pose estimation from two views sharing a common direction with unknown focal length. In: IEEE/CVF Conference on Computer Vision and Pattern Recognition (CVPR) (2020)
14. Ding, Y., Yang, J., Ponce, J., Kong, H.: Homography-based minimal-case relative pose estimation with known gravity direction. IEEE Trans. Pattern Anal. Mach. Intell. (2020)
15. Guan, B., Vasseur, P., Demonceaux, C., Fraundorfer, F.: Visual odometry using a homography formulation with decoupled rotation and translation estimation using minimal solutions. In: 2018 IEEE International Conference on Robotics and Automation (ICRA), pp. 2320–2327. IEEE (2018)
16. Barath, D., Toth, T., Hajder, L.: A minimal solution for two-view focal-length estimation using two affine correspondences. In: Proceedings of the IEEE Conference on Computer Vision and Pattern Recognition, pp. 6003–6011 (2017)
17. Barath, D., Hajder, L.: Efficient recovery of essential matrix from two affine correspondences. IEEE Trans. Image Process. **27**, 5328–5337 (2018)
18. Guan, B., Zhao, J., Li, Z., Sun, F., Fraundorfer, F.: Minimal solutions for relative pose with a single affine correspondence. In: Proceedings of the IEEE/CVF Conference on Computer Vision and Pattern Recognition, pp. 1929–1938 (2020)
19. Hajder, L., Barath, D.: Relative planar motion for vehicle-mounted cameras from a single affine correspondence (2020)
20. Morel, J.M., Yu, G.: ASIFT: a new framework for fully affine invariant image comparison. SIAM J. Imaging Sci. **2**, 438–469 (2009)
21. Mikolajczyk, K., et al.: A comparison of affine region detectors. Int. J. Comput. Vision **65**, 43–72 (2005)
22. Lowe, D.G.: Distinctive image features from scale-invariant keypoints. Int. J. Comput. Vision **60**, 91–110 (2004)
23. Bay, H., Tuytelaars, T., Van Gool, L.: SURF: speeded up robust features. In: Leonardis, A., Bischof, H., Pinz, A. (eds.) ECCV 2006. LNCS, vol. 3951, pp. 404–417. Springer, Heidelberg (2006). https://doi.org/10.1007/11744023_32
24. Barath, D., Kukelova, Z.: Homography from two orientation- and scale-covariant features. In: The IEEE International Conference on Computer Vision (ICCV) (2019)
25. Rublee, E., Rabaud, V., Konolige, K., Bradski, G.: ORB: an efficient alternative to sift or surf. In: International Conference on Computer Vision, pp. 2564–2571. IEEE (2011)
26. Barath, D.: Five-point fundamental matrix estimation for uncalibrated cameras. In: Proceedings of the IEEE Conference on Computer Vision and Pattern Recognition, pp. 235–243 (2018)
27. Stewenius, H., Engels, C., Nistér, D.: Recent developments on direct relative orientation. ISPRS J. Photogramm. Remote Sens. **60**, 284–294 (2006)
28. Hartley, R., Li, H.: An efficient hidden variable approach to minimal-case camera motion estimation. IEEE Trans. Pattern Anal. Mach. Intell. **34**, 2303–2314 (2012)
29. Kukelova, Z., Bujnak, M., Pajdla, T.: Polynomial eigenvalue solutions to minimal problems in computer vision. IEEE Trans. Pattern Anal. Mach. Intell. **34**, 1381–1393 (2012)
30. Sweeney, C., Flynn, J., Turk, M.: Solving for relative pose with a partially known rotation is a quadratic eigenvalue problem. In: 3DV, vol. 2, p. 5 (2014)

31. Blanco-Claraco, J., Moreno-Dueñas, F., Jiménez, J.G.: The Málaga urban dataset: high-rate stereo and lidar in a realistic urban scenario. Int. J. Robot. Res. **33**, 207–214 (2014)
32. Barath, D., Matas, J.: Graph-cut RANSAC. In: The IEEE Conference on Computer Vision and Pattern Recognition (CVPR) (2018)
33. Ortin, D., Montiel, J.M.M.: Indoor robot motion based on monocular images. Robotica **19**, 331–342 (2001)
34. Capturing Reality: RealityCapture (2020). http://www.capturingreality.com

Mapping of Sparse 3D Data Using Alternating Projection

Siddhant Ranade[1]([⊠]), Xin Yu[1], Shantnu Kakkar[2], Pedro Miraldo[3], and Srikumar Ramalingam[1]

[1] University of Utah, Salt Lake City, UT 84112, USA
{sidra,xiny,srikumar}@cs.utah.edu
[2] Trimble, Sunnyvale, CA 94085, USA
shantnu_kakkar@trimble.com
[3] Instituto Superior Técnico, University of Lisboa, Lisbon, Portugal
pedro.miraldo@tecnico.ulisboa.pt

Abstract. We propose a novel technique to register sparse 3D scans in the absence of texture. While existing methods such as KinectFusion or Iterative Closest Points (ICP) heavily rely on dense point clouds, this task is particularly challenging under sparse conditions without RGB data. Sparse texture-less data does not come with high-quality boundary signal, and this prohibits the use of correspondences from corners, junctions, or boundary lines. Moreover, in the case of sparse data, it is incorrect to assume that the same point will be captured in two consecutive scans. We take a different approach and first re-parameterize the point-cloud using a large number of line segments. In this re-parameterized data, there exists a large number of line intersection (and not correspondence) constraints that allow us to solve the registration task. We propose the use of a two-step alternating projection algorithm by formulating the registration as the simultaneous satisfaction of intersection and rigidity constraints. The proposed approach outperforms other top-scoring algorithms on both Kinect and LiDAR datasets. In Kinect, we can use 100X downsampled sparse data and still outperform competing methods operating on full-resolution data.

Keywords: LiDAR · 3D registration · Line intersection · Generalized relative pose estimation

1 Introduction

The last few years have witnessed the rise of inexpensive 3D sensors for both indoor (e.g., Microsoft Kinect) and outdoor scenes (e.g., Velodyne's VLP-16

S. Ranade and X. Yu—Indicates equal contribution.

Electronic supplementary material The online version of this chapter (https://doi.org/10.1007/978-3-030-69525-5_18) contains supplementary material, which is available to authorized users.

© Springer Nature Switzerland AG 2021
H. Ishikawa et al. (Eds.): ACCV 2020, LNCS 12622, pp. 295–313, 2021.
https://doi.org/10.1007/978-3-030-69525-5_18

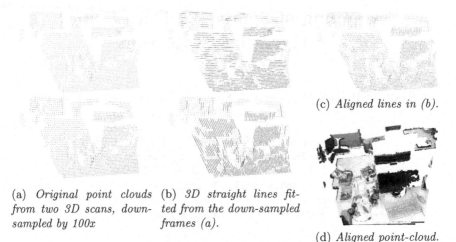

(c) *Aligned lines in (b).*

(a) *Original point clouds from two 3D scans, down-sampled by 100x* (b) *3D straight lines fitted from the down-sampled frames (a).*

(d) *Aligned point-cloud.*

Fig. 1. Illustration of the proposed method. (a) shows 100× down-sampled Kinect depth data (64 × 48). We fit 3D line segments to rows in the first and columns in the second frames as shown in (c). We identify line-to-line intersection correspondences and use alternating projection [1] to get the 3D scan alignment (c). (d) shows the registered point-cloud in original resolution with color. The average error is 0.53° for rotations, 7.58 mm for the translation, an improvement of 1.82× for the translation and 1.35× for the rotation, compared to FGR [2] which uses the full resolution Kinect data (640 × 480) for registration.

LITE LIDAR, ZED stereo camera). The algebraic centerpiece of all 3D problems is the 3D point cloud registration. This problem is well studied in the case of dense settings and scenarios with point correspondences extracted from RGB components. Solutions include recent deep learning machinery [3], the celebrated iterative closest point (ICP) [4], and half a century old orthogonal Procrustes method [5] that is universally used till date. In this work, we study the problem of aligning highly sparse 3D scans without RGB information. In this setting, we lack boundary information, and without RGB components, it is hard to obtain any form of correspondences based on corners or line segments for registration.

We show the basic idea of our technique in Fig. 1. We fit lines to the data and represent the point-cloud using a large number of line segments. The original data hardly contains any correspondence constraints. On the contrary, in the re-parameterized line-based representation, there exists a rich set of line intersection constraints. Our strategy is to exploit these constraints to solve the registration problem. We consider 100× down-sampled Kinect data without RGB components. We show that the proposed algorithm can outperform competing Kinect registration algorithms that use full resolution (see Table 1).

There is an interesting connection between our approach and the relative pose estimation for generalized cameras. The problem of relative pose estimation involves finding rotation and translation between two cameras such that the projection rays associated with corresponding 2D points intersect with each other. In the case of perspective cameras, we can find the motion up to a scale, and the associated projection rays are central [6]. In the case of generalized cameras [7], the projection rays are unconstrained, and we are looking at the alignment of two sets of line segments such that the corresponding line segments intersect with each other. In our problem, we compute line segments from the point cloud representing the 3D scene. In both settings, we try to satisfy line intersection constraints (which essentially amounts to placing four 3D points on a plane), where the four 3D points are the endpoints of the intersecting line segments. While minimal solvers typically produce robust solutions in general, the 6-point minimal solver for generalized relative pose [8] has degeneracy problems (i.e., the constraints are sometimes insufficient to produce a unique solution, and thereby lead to infinite number of poses). The algorithm is supposed to produce unique pose for truly unconstrained set of projection rays (two or more projection rays from the same camera can not be parallel or coplanar). It is hard to expect that the line segments re-parameterizing the point-cloud will satisfy them. Thereby, we solve the registration using an alternating projection [1] method (AP) with seven pairs of line intersection constraints (one additional constraint is used since six intersection constraints can have up to 64 different solutions [8]).

In addition to line intersection constraints, we also utilize constraints that corner points, occurring in the boundary regions, are incident with edge lines in the scene. The highlights of the paper are the following:

1. We propose an AP [1] algorithm for the problem of scan alignment by showing that it is equivalent to the generalized relative pose estimation, i.e., pose estimation by satisfying intersection constraints among six or more pairs of corresponding line segments.
2. We show a family of registration algorithms that, additionally, exploit corner points in sparse point clouds and utilize collinearity (corner points lying on corner lines) constraints.
3. We outperform other registration algorithms such as fast global registration (FGR) and Super4PCS, despite using 100X down-sampled point-cloud and not relying on the color information.
4. In 6 out of 11 KITTI LiDAR sequences, we outperform LOAM [9], a competing LiDAR registration algorithm that minimizes point-to-line and point-to-plane distances in a Levenberg Marquardt framework for registration.
5. On down-sampled KITTI data, we outperform LOAM in all 11 sequences.

2   Related Work

3D scan alignment is a classical problem in the computer vision and robotics communities, and there is a rich body of literature on this topic.

Iterative Techniques: Iterative Closest Point (ICP) and its variants [4,10–14] are the most applied scan alignment algorithm, and it works well for dense point-clouds with good initialization. ICP [4], the gold standard for dense point-to-point registration, is an alternating minimization algorithm, alternating between finding closest correspondences and computing the rigid transformation. Alternating minimization and projection algorithms [1] have been used for human pose and other geometrical problems [15–19].

Techniques for finding globally optimal solutions combine local or probabilistic methods with graph optimization [20] and branch-and-bound [21,22]. A closely related work is LOAM [9,23], which is a top-ranking LiDAR alignment algorithm. We differ with LOAM as follows: 1) LOAM uses a distortion correction step for addressing the motion of the sensor at low frame-rate. This effect is similar to the rolling shutter effect in cameras. 2) LOAM uses the Levenberg Marquardt method for non-minimal registration, while we develop AP algorithm for near-minimal configurations and utilize the RANSAC framework. 3) LOAM additionally utilize IMU, and we rely only on sparse 3D points.

Several global methods have been proposed in the literature, such as [24,25]. One of the problems with these methods is the high computation requirement for doing the branch and optimization. To overcome this, one line of research attempts to decompose the task of finding the relative transformation into first finding the rotation and then obtaining the translation given the optimal rotation [26,27]. Further, [28] proposes Rotation Invariant Features (RIF) to ease the task of decoupling rotation solution from the translation. However, none of the methods have been tested on LiDAR data.

Minimal Solvers: Other popular scan alignment methods in the absence of good initialization include minimal 3-point solvers in a RANSAC framework. The most common approaches to remove outliers from the data are based on the use of RANSAC [29] plus some 3D point correspondences solver, such as [5,30]. In addition to points, several registration algorithms have utilized other features on beam-based environment modeling [31], 3D planes [32–37], 3D line segments [33,38], implicit surface representation [39], and edges [40]. A detailed survey on 3D SLAM methods can be found in [41,42].

Our approach for the registration of 3D scans is tightly connected with minimal solvers for relative pose estimation. In particular, we have relative pose estimation algorithms for calibrated perspective cameras [6,43], with known relative rotation angle [44], with known directions [45,46], with unknown focal lengths [47,48], solutions invariant to translation [49], and generalized relative pose [8,50]. Recently, a minimal hybrid solver considers relative and absolute poses [51]. In the case of absolute poses, we have perspective [52–55], and multi-perspective systems [56,57]. For 3D scans, we have the Procrustes solver for a pairwise alignement [5], and solutions to the mini-loop alignments in [30]. It was recently shown that the generalized relative pose estimation [8,58–61] can be used in privacy-preserving pose estimation from 3D pointclouds [62].

Deep Scan Alignment: Deep neural networks (DNNs) for solving 3D registration problems have increased significantly in the last few years. Several methods have been developed to extract local 3D geometric structures, such as [63–68].

There have been a few recent algorithms for LiDAR registration [63,69] using deep neural networks, but they are mostly applicable to dense point clouds.

A technique for registering 3D point clouds given a set of point correspondences is proposed in [3]. Floor plan reconstruction using deep networks has been shown in [36]. The PointNet [70] is used in [71], together with Lukas-Kanade algorithm in a single network. The proposed method works in an iterative fashion, similar to ICP. In [68,72], a differential SVD layer is coupled with DNNs for generating matching. DNNs also prove to be helpful for solving other kind of problems such as multi-scan transformation averaging [73]. [74] utilizes deep neural networks to compute the weights for different pairwise relative pose estimates and [69] use two networks, for pose and scene estimation.

3   Problem Statement

Given two sparse 3D point sets $\{p_1^1, \ldots, p_{n_1}^1\}$ and $\{p_1^2, \ldots, p_{n_2}^2\}$, our goal is to compute $T = (R, \mathbf{t})$, such that $\{p_1^1, \ldots, p_{n_1}^1\}$ and the transformed point set $\{Rp_1^2 + \mathbf{t}, \ldots, Rp_{n_2}^2 + \mathbf{t}\}$ would model or represent the same 3D scene in the first coordinate frame.

We model the scene using a set of 3D line segments on planar surfaces and the detection of a few informative 3D corner points, and 3D edge lines. Concretely, the first point set $\{p_1^1, \ldots, p_{n_1}^1\}$ is re-parameterized as $\{l_1^1, \ldots, l_{m_l}^1, k_1^1, \ldots, k_{c_1}^1\}$, where l denotes *lines* and k are *corners* (obtained by line fitting and corner estimation respectively, see Sect. 5.1). The second point set $\{p_1^2, \ldots, p_{n_2}^2\}$ is re-parameterized as $\{g_1^2, \ldots, g_{m_2}^2, q_1^2, \ldots, q_{c_2}^2\}$, where g denotes *lines* and q are *edges* (obtained by line fitting and edge line estimation respectively, see Sect. 5.1). In the original point set representation, we can not identify any point correspondences due to sparsity. The re-parameterization allows us to obtain a rich set of line intersections (e.g., lines l_i^1 and g_i^2 intersect) and incidence relations (e.g., an edge q_j^2 passes through a corner point k_j^1).

Our implementation considers line intersections, and corner-edge, edge-corner incidences. For clarity of illustration, we will only look at lines and corners from the first frame, and lines and edges from the second.

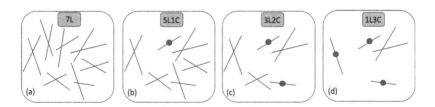

Fig. 2. The four sets of constraints addressed in this paper are denoted by 7L, 5L1C, 3L2C, and 1L3C. For example, 3L2C in (c) denotes a total of five constraints (three line-to-line intersections, and two corner-to-line incidences). For simplicity, we consider the corners only from the first frame. The primitives from the first and the second frame are shown in blue and red, respectively. (Color figure online)

In Fig. 2 we show the different sets of constraints used in the paper. The line-to-line intersection constraint enforces that the four end-points of two intersecting line segments are coplanar, i.e., lie on the same plane. The corner-to-line incidence constraint enforces that a corner point lies on a line. It is always a useful exercise to check the degrees of freedom (DOF) of the unknowns and the number of available constraints. Our goal is to compute 6 DOF pose $(R, \mathbf{t})$ using line-to-line intersections and point-to-line incidences. Each constraint of line-to-line intersection and point-to-line incidences takes away 1 DOF (See [8]) and 2 DOFs (See [6,43]), respectively. The algebraic methods that employ exact minimal solvers (where the DOFs from the constraints and the unknowns are equal) typically produce multiple solutions for poses corresponding to the multiple roots of the higher degree polynomial systems. Consequently, it needs a second step with additional correspondence constraints to pick the correct pose from the multiple solutions. In contrast to the algebraic solvers, we use the AP algorithm on near-minimal cases (i.e. each of the 4 sets of constraints shown in Fig. 2 has one DOF extra over the six unknowns), and the over-constrained setting leads to a single pose.

4   Alternating Projection (AP)

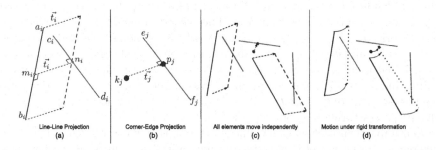

Fig. 3. One AP iteration on a set of line-line and corer-edge pairs has two steps: 1) To satisfy their **intersection** constraints, it translates elements (lines, corners) from the first frame towards their counterparts (lines, edges) in the second frame, independent of the other pairs, as illustrated in (a), (b), and (c). 2) To preserve the **rigidity** for the first frame elements as a whole, it computes a single rigid transformation that takes all elements in this frame as close as possible to their position after the independent translation, as shown in (d). (Color figure online)

We briefly explain the general approach used in AP [1]. We compute a point (a higher dimensional vector denoting the unknowns) in the intersection of sets (denote the various constraint sets) by a sequence of projections onto the sets. Let us denote our unknown parameter vector as $x \in \mathbb{R}^n$, and the two sets as C and D in $\mathbb{R}^n$, respectively. Let P_C and P_D be projection operators. Given a point $x \in \mathbb{R}^n$, the projection operator $P_C(x)$ produces a point $x' \in C$ such that

$|x - x'|$ is minimum. The key elements of the AP are the constraints and the projection operations.

In our registration setting, given a set of candidate line intersections and corner-edge incidences, the goal of AP is to estimate a rigid transformation which satisfies the given intersection/incidence constraints (henceforth referred to simply as intersection constraints). Thus the solver needs to compute the unknowns $(R, \mathbf{t})$ to satisfy two constraint sets: **intersection**, and **rigidity**. The projection operators for intersection and rigidity constraints are shown in Fig. 3.

Algorithm 1. Alternating Projection

Require: $S^1 = \{l_1^1, .., l_M^1, k_1^1, .., k_N^1\}$, $S^2 = \{g_1^2, .., g_M^2, q_1^2, .., q_N^2\}$
Ensure: T
1: **repeat**
2:　　$\overrightarrow{t_i} = \text{LineLineProjection}(l_i^1, g_i^2)$ for i $\in 1, ..., M$　　▷ as shown in Fig. 3(a)
3:　　$\overrightarrow{t_j} = \text{CornerEdgeProjection}(k_j^1, q_j^2)$ for j $\in 1, ..., N$　　▷ as shown in Fig. 3(b)
4:　　$l_i'^1 = l_i^1 + \overrightarrow{t_i}$ for i $\in 1, ..., M$　　▷ as shown in Fig. 3(c)
5:　　$k_j'^1 = k_j^1 + \overrightarrow{t_j}$ for j $\in 1, ..., N$
6:　　$S'^1 = \{l_1'^1, .., l_M'^1, k_1'^1, .., k_N'^1\}$
7:　　$T = \text{RigidAlign}(S^1, S'^1)$
8:　　Update $l_i^1 = T \cdot l_i^1$ for i $\in 1,...,M$　　▷ as shown in Fig. 3(d)
9:　　Update $k_j^1 = T \cdot k_j^1$ for j $\in 1,...,N$
10:　　$\delta = \max_{i,j}(dist(l_i^1, g_i^2), dist(k_j^1, q_j^2))$
11: **until** $\delta \leq \epsilon$ or max iterations reached　　▷ ϵ is a distance threshold
12: **return** T

Formally, let us denote the lines from the first frame with $l_i^1 = (a_i, b_i)$ (where a_i and b_i are the end-points), and those from the second frame by $g_i^2 = (c_i, d_i)$, for $i \in \{1, ..., M\}$, i.e. each (l_i^1, g_i^2) is a candidate pair of lines, where M is the number of line intersections used by that particular solver. For simplicity, let's consider only corners from the first frame k_j^1 and edges $q_j^2 = (e_j, f_j)$ from the second, for $j \in \{1, ... N\}$, such that each (k_j^1, q_i^2) is a candidate corner-edge pair, where N is the number of corner-edge incidence constraints used by the solver. In this paper, we solve the cases $(M, N) \in \{(7, 0), (5, 1), (3, 2), (1, 3)\}$, corresponding to our solvers 7L, 5L1C, 3L2C, and 1L3C respectively. Please note that edges are also line segments, but they are extracted in a different manner compared to regular line segments (see Sect. 5).

We illustrate our AP solver in Fig. 3 with a simple scenario that considers only two intersection constraints (one line-to-line and one corner-to-edge). In Fig. 3(a), the closest points on the line segments are denoted by m_i and n_i respectively. The line segment from the first frame (blue) is moved by the smallest distance so that the two line segments intersect. In Fig. 3(b), p_j denotes the point on the edge-line q_j closest to the corner point k_j, i.e. p_j is the projection of point k_j on the line q_j. After applying this projection operation to frame 1 (blue) in (c), we get their projected position. For the rigid alignment between frame 1 (lines, corners) and their projected positions, we estimate translation by aligning their centroids and then estimate rotation using Orthogonal Procrustes, as shown in Fig. 3(d). We repeat these two steps (intersections followed by rigid transform estimation) until the update is lower than a threshold. The complete algorithm is illustrated in Algorithm 1. In our implementation, we move both elements of each pair towards each other, rather than moving only elements from the first frame towards those from the second.

5 Implementation Details

5.1 Pre-processing

Organized Point Clouds: Our algorithms require line fitting outputs, which we find is easiest done on organized point clouds. In the case of Kinect data, the input is already organized in the form of a depth image, and no further action is necessary. In the case of the KITTI data, we use the sensor calibration parameters to organize the raw input points into a grid-like structure by azimuth and elevation. In the experiments involving down-sampling of this data, we select points at appropriate indices from these organized point clouds. For instance, Fig. 4 shows a point-cloud down-sampled by a factor of 6 along both horizontal and vertical directions, to retain roughly $1/36^{th}$ the points.

(a) original scan

(b) 1/36 downsampling

Fig. 4. Single frames from KITTI at (a) original resolution and (b) 1/36 down-sampled.

Line Fitting: Given a set of 3D points in a regular grid (with some points missing due to sensor noise), we consider horizontal and vertical scan-lines in this organized point cloud and use RANSAC to fit lines to every scan-line. We call lines that come from horizontal scan-lines "H-lines", and the ones coming from vertical scan lines are called "V-lines".

For instance, in Fig. 5, H-lines are represented by the color red, and V-lines by blue. H and V do not refer to the orientations of the lines in 3D, only the scan-line they come from; the blue lines on the ground plane in this figure are actually V-lines.

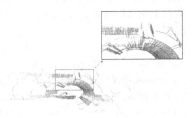

Fig. 5. Line fitting on one KITTI frame. Red lines come from horizontal scan-lines(H-lines) and blue from vertical(V-lines). (Color figure online)

Corner Points and Edge Lines: We use a similar formulation to [9] for esti-
mating corner points. Let $\{x_i | i \in W\}$ denote the coordinates of the (ordered)
points in a single scan-line in an organized point cloud in the local coordinate
frame, where W is the total number of points in the scan-line. We define a local
smoothness term for each point i based on K neighbors on either side of i as

$$c_i = \frac{1}{2K \|x_i\|} \| \sum_{j=-K, j\neq 0}^{K} (x_i - x_j) \|, \tag{1}$$

where a higher c value indicates lower smoothness. We divide each scan-line into
4 zones, and select two points with the highest c as corner points. We fit lines
to corner points from successive scanes in the same frame to get the edge lines.

5.2   Full Meta-algorithm with RANSAC

At each step, we estimate the frame-to-frame transformations between successive
frames. We designate the local frame of the first scan to be the world coordinate
frame, and compose (multiply) these transformations to obtain transformation
matrices for all frames with respect to the first frame.

The proposed solvers (7L, 5L1C, 3L2C, 1L3C) produce a transformation matrix given a small number of inputs. We apply these solvers in a
RANSAC framework to obtain the best possible transformation matrices. At
each RANSAC iteration, we pick a solver at random (all 4 solvers are selected
with the same probability, i.e., 0.25), and select candidates for that solver as
appropriate.

Candidates for RANSAC: We identify candidates for (a) line intersection
constraints based on the distance between line segments in the first and second
scans, and (b) corner point-edge line incidence constraints based on the distances
between corner points from one scan and edge lines from the other. We select
from among these candidates at random in every RANSAC iteration. This simple
approach assumes that the relative transformation is close to identity, but we
observe that this works well in practice.

Inlier Counting: From the set of candidates pairs of lines, we count the number
of pairs that have a distance less than another threshold (2 cm on KITTI dataset
5 mm on TUM here) after applying the computed transformation.

In addition, we find that we get better results by running the full algorithm
described above thrice, each time using the best transformation from the previous
step as the initial guess for candidate estimation. With improved initialization
we obtain better candidates for line intersection constraints. Both ICP and our
algorithm iteratively update the relative transformation between two frames, but
there are some important differences: (a) our algorithm needs only 3 iterations,
while ICP typically needs many more, (b) within each iteration, our algorithm
uses RANSAC, the AP solver works with near-minimal sets of constraints, while
ICP uses correspondence constraints involving all primitives.

6   Experiments

We evaluated the proposed algorithms on two datasets: TUM [42] and KITTI [75].

Relative Pose Error (RPE): As proposed in [42], we compute the error in the relative pose between successive frames, and report the translation error in meters and rotation error in degrees respectively.

Translation and Rotation Error Along the Trajectory: This metric is used in [75] and on their online leaderboard. For all sub-sequences of length 100 m, 200 m, ..., 800 m, we compute the translation and rotation errors per unit length of the trajectory. Translation error is reported as a percentage value, and rotation error in degrees per meter.

Kinect Data: TUM Dataset [42] consists of sequences of Kinect RGBD data captured in an indoor environment. The sensor resolution is 640×480, at 30 fps. The sequences come with a ground truth trajectory of the sensor, obtained from a high-accuracy motion-capture system. We test our algorithm on 7 sequences from the TUM dataset, down-sampled by a factor of 10 in both dimensions (i.e., $1/100^{th}$ the points). The error values for all three sequences are presented in Table 1 (on page 304). We use two baseline methods: Super4PCS [76] + ICP and fast global registration (FGR) [2] methods. Super4PCS works with point clouds without any point correspondences, and FGR uses point correspondences from the depth maps of the Kinect data. Both these methods are tested on full resolution Kinect data, whereas our approach only takes the sparsified input (down-sampled by a factor of 100). As shown in Table 1, we outperform the baselines in 6 out of the 7 sequences, despite using down-sampled data.

Table 1. Results on 7 sequences of the TUM RGBD dataset. Our method uses only the depth-maps, down-sampled by a factor of 100. Super4PCS + ICP and FGR use full resolution depth maps. Mean rotation and translation error between successive frames is reported.

Sequence	Proposed		Super4PCS+ICP		FGR	
	tra. [mm]	rot. [°]	tra. [mm]	rot. [°]	tra. [mm]	rot. [°]
fr1/xyz	**3.86**	**0.46**	12.99	0.49	9.51	0.70
fr1/360	17.67	0.82	22.89	0.79	**14.76**	**0.76**
fr3/sitting_xyz	**6.09**	0.41	9.47	**0.39**	9.09	0.46
fr1/room	**7.25**	**0.52**	15.29	0.73	11.82	0.70
fr1/plant	**6.47**	**0.61**	14.23	0.74	11.86	0.68
fr3/cabinet	**7.25**	**0.55**	16.56	0.64	16.63	0.84
fr3/structure_nn	**4.49**	**0.35**	8.28	0.53	9.77	0.67

LiDAR Data: KITTI dataset [75] consists of LiDAR point-clouds collected from the top of a moving vehicle. The LiDAR sensor captures roughly 10 fps (frames per second), with about 100k points per frame.

Table 2. Mean translation and rotation errors between successive frames, and translation, rotation errors over the trajectory for KITTI sequences. Proposed method has a lower error than LOAM in many sequences.

Seq.	Proposed				LOAM			
	Mean errors		KITTI metrics		Mean errors		KITTI metrics	
	tra. [m]	rot. [°]	tra. [%]	rot. [°/m]	tra. [m]	rot. [°]	tra. [%]	rot. [°/m]
00	**0.024**	**0.105**	**1.612**	**0.007**	0.061	0.457	2.865	0.015
01	2.125	2.432	91.139	0.327	**0.651**	**0.245**	**25.711**	**0.022**
02	0.198	**0.325**	17.361	0.057	**0.165**	0.396	**8.567**	**0.033**
03	**0.035**	**0.106**	**2.291**	0.023	0.103	0.361	9.861	**0.021**
04	0.698	0.247	57.950	0.091	**0.138**	**0.213**	**1.927**	**0.009**
05	**0.018**	**0.096**	**1.407**	**0.009**	0.048	0.312	1.721	0.011
06	**0.023**	**0.079**	**0.818**	**0.006**	0.063	0.211	1.884	0.010
07	**0.018**	**0.084**	**0.999**	**0.006**	0.042	0.321	2.080	0.014
08	**0.044**	**0.105**	3.064	**0.011**	0.064	0.348	**2.705**	0.013
09	0.249	0.366	18.654	0.054	**0.109**	**0.328**	**5.196**	**0.031**
10	**0.074**	**0.289**	10.558	0.047	0.093	0.432	**9.727**	**0.038**

Table 3. Under extreme sparsity: Mean translation and rotation errors between successive frames, and translation, rotation errors over the trajectory for KITTI sequences at low resolution ($1/36^{\text{th}}$ the points). Proposed method outperforms LOAM in all sequences.

Seq.	Proposed				LOAM			
	Mean errors		KITTI metrics		Mean errors		KITTI metrics	
	tra. [m]	rot. [°]	tra. [%]	rot. [°/m]	tra. [m]	rot. [°]	tra. [%]	rot. [°/m]
00	**0.202**	**0.191**	**14.937**	**0.033**	0.446	1.343	38.939	0.176
01	**2.196**	**0.936**	**94.428**	**0.134**	2.205	1.602	95.274	0.212
02	**0.544**	**0.396**	**36.003**	**0.065**	0.833	1.488	62.246	0.194
03	**0.277**	**0.300**	**33.545**	**0.064**	0.583	1.573	89.949	0.491
04	**1.329**	**0.400**	**92.768**	**0.074**	1.386	1.762	97.335	0.352
05	**0.172**	**0.180**	**14.139**	**0.038**	0.527	2.041	54.738	0.280
06	**0.615**	**0.466**	**37.981**	**0.094**	0.956	2.813	60.321	0.370
07	**0.123**	**0.123**	**14.522**	**0.038**	0.334	1.491	36.841	0.209
08	**0.290**	**0.346**	**26.796**	**0.101**	0.479	2.081	58.518	0.272
09	**0.551**	**0.541**	**44.765**	**0.134**	0.781	1.921	66.405	0.255
10	**0.188**	**0.311**	**19.770**	**0.071**	0.384	1.444	36.346	0.189

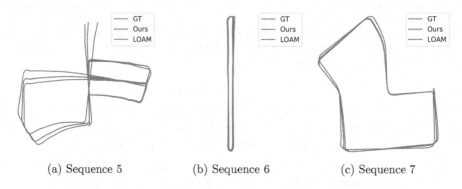

(a) Sequence 5   (b) Sequence 6   (c) Sequence 7

Fig. 6. Computed trajectories on KITTI Sequences at original resolution. The trajectory from the proposed method is closer to the ground truth than LOAM.

We compare our results against the LOAM Algorithm [9], which is currently highly ranked on the online leaderboard. The computed trajectories on these sequences are shown in Fig. 6, the relative pose error between consecutive frames, and the error along the trajectory is reported in Table 2 (on page 305). Selected full point-clouds after registration are presented in Fig. 7 (on page 307).

The results of LOAM here differ from those on the leaderboard because we run LOAM by ourselves, without using IMU data, for a fair comparison. As the official version is unavailable, we use the open-source version of LOAM[1].

Comparison of Our Algorithms: We test all our algorithms separately on sequence 03 of the KITTI dataset. The combined approach produces the best translation and 5L1C produces the best rotation (Table 4). All of these approaches have their own strengths and weaknesses. For example, line intersection constraints handle planar regions better, and the methods utilizing corner points are supposed to handle scenes containing vegetation and other non-planar regions.

Algorithm	tra. err. [%]	rot. err. [deg/m]
7L	2.628	0.021
5L1C	2.452	**0.017**
3L2C	2.589	0.025
1L3C	2.794	0.021
Combined	**2.291**	0.023

Table 4. Comparison of our algorithms

Under Extreme Sparsity: We test our approach on LiDAR data down-sampled by a factor of 6 in both dimensions, $1/36^{th}$ of all points (see Fig. 4, page 302) and compare our results with LOAM on the KITTI dataset. We show a trajectory in Fig. 8, and the errors are reported in Table 3 (on page 305). While both our algorithm and LOAM deteriorate as we increase the sparsity, our algorithm significantly outperforms LOAM.

Fig. 8. 1/36 down-sampled KITTI sequence 7

---

[1] https://github.com/laboshinl/loam_velodyne.

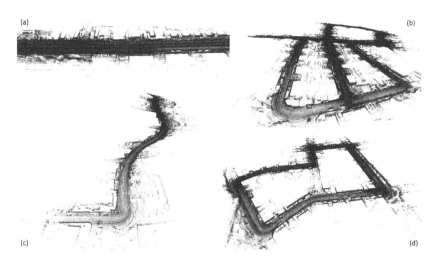

Fig. 7. Visualization of the fully registered point-clouds from KITTI sequences (a) 06, (b) 05, (c) 03, and (d) 07.

Performance and Speed: Our code is implemented in C++. The average computation time on KITTI dataset at full resolution for various operations (running on 1 core of Intel i7-8700K) is as follows: 22 ms for the AP solver; 2 ms for the inlier counting; and 3 s for the line fitting. The time taken by inlier counting varies with the number of detected lines; these are typically observed values. The total runtime of the entire algorithm depends on the number of RANSAC iterations and can be brought down to 30 s by paralleling on 10 threads.

We use a threshold (2 cm on KITTI, 5 mm on TUM) as well as max number of iterations (30K iterations) for terminating the AP. In the future, we will explore certain extrapolated projection techniques for further speedup [77].

6.1   Sensitivity Analysis

We conducted some experiments to study the robustness of our algorithm to large motion and sparse settings.

Convergence Under Large Motion: We generate a pair of frames by taking the first frame of KITTI's sequence 7 and apply large translation and rotation to it. Then we use the same fitting strategy to get pairs of lines and edge/corner candidates from the two frames. We repeat the process 100 times and applied the AP solver for registration. We count a success when

tra. [m]	succ. rate	rot. [deg]	succ. rate
0.5	94%	0.5	97%
2	86%	2	91%
8	79%	8	83%
32	65%	32	78%
128	60%	128	49%

Table 5. Robustness to large translations and rotation by augmenting them in noisy LiDAR data.

the registration has rotation error smaller than 0.5° and translation error within

0.1 m. The success rate is the number of success out of 100 trials. As shown in Table 5, the success rate is monotonic and RANSAC only needs some good hypotheses. For comparison, the maximum translation, rotation between two frames in KITTI is 1.5 m and 5° respectively.

Robustness of Intersection Constraints Under Sparsity: Under sparsity, line intersection constraints continue to exist while point correspondences diminish significantly. We take two consecutive frames of KITTI's sequence 7 and align them using the ground truth. For each line/point in the first frame, we find the closest line/point in the second frame. We fixed a threshold for the line/point distance for inlier counting and vary the down-sampling factor (sparsity). As observed in Fig. 9, the per-

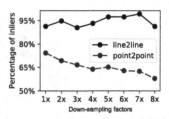

Fig. 9. Inlier ratio of point correspondence vs. intersected lines as sparsity increases.

centage of inliers using line intersections (line2line in Fig. 9) is not affected by sparsity. On the other hand, the percentage of inliers using point correspondences (point2point in Fig. 9) decreases considerably. This means that point-based methods like ICP are more sensitive to the inlier threshold.

7   Discussion

The proposed algorithm applies to sensors on a moving platform and we make smoothness assumption for obtaining line intersection constraints, although our algorithm is robust to outliers due to the use of near-minimal solvers in a RANSAC framework. While we outperform LOAM in 6 out of 11 sequences, our method can further be improved by following LOAM and correcting for distortions obtained from moving platforms [9]. We also show that we outperform LOAM in all the KITTI sequences under extreme sparsity. Note that the proposed method is not customized to a specific sensor. After handling the challenges in LiDAR, we ported to Kinect datasets with almost zero-development cost and outperformed all baselines in 6 out of 7 sequences using 1/100th of the data, without texture.

At the heart of our technique, we hinge on two elements to achieve the superior performance. First, we exploit interior regional information (by fitting line segments on the point-cloud and generating rich line intersection constraints) in addition to the boundary information (through the extraction of corners and edges) typically used by classical methods. Every line intersection adds a planarity constraint implicitly on the four end points. Compared to plane detection, intersected lines is easier to find in sparse point cloud. Plane detection in sparse settings with sensor motion distortion can be brittle, and finding enough planes in near-degenerate situations will be challenging (e.g., many road scenes with buildings on both sides or highways may not provide enough planes to lock the pose from sliding). Second, despite the simplicity, AP should not be treated as a trivial endeavour. In addition to several vision related problems [15–19], variants of AP have also been used to solve computationally hard problems such protein folding, sphere packing, and Sudoku [78, 79].

In our work, we observed that AP can solve near-minimal problems that are known to be hard for algebraic solvers. From the formulations used in this paper, it is not difficult to see that the proposed approach can be easily extended to other geometric vision problems as well. We show a video demonstration of our algorithm in the Supplementary Materials.

References

1. Bauschke, H.H., Borwein, J.M.: On projection algorithms for solving convex feasibility problems. SIAM Rev. **38**, 367–426 (1996)
2. Zhou, Q.-Y., Park, J., Koltun, V.: Fast global registration. In: Leibe, B., Matas, J., Sebe, N., Welling, M. (eds.) ECCV 2016. LNCS, vol. 9906, pp. 766–782. Springer, Cham (2016). https://doi.org/10.1007/978-3-319-46475-6_47
3. Pais, G.D., Miraldo, P., Ramalingam, S., Govindu, V.M., Nascimento, J.C., Chellappa, R.: 3DRegNet: a deep neural network for 3D point registration. In: IEEE Conference on Computer Vision and Pattern Recognition (CVPR) (2020)
4. Besl, P.J., McKay, N.: A method for registration of 3-D shapes. IEEE Trans. Pattern Anal. Mach. Intell. (T-PAMI) **14**, 239–256 (1992)
5. Schönemann, P.H.: A generalized solution of the orthogonal procrustes problem. Psychometrika **31**, 1–10 (1966). https://doi.org/10.1007/BF02289451
6. Nister, D.: An efficient solution to the five-point relative pose problem. In: IEEE Conference on Computer Vision and Pattern Recognition (CVPR) (2003)
7. Grossberg, M.D., Nayar, S.K.: A general imaging model and a method for finding its parameters. In: IEEE International Conference on Computer Vision (ICCV) (2001)
8. Stewenius, H., Oskarsson, M., Astrom, K., Nister, D.: Solutions to minimal generalized relative pose problems. In: Workshop on Omnidirectional Vision (OMNIVIS) (2005)
9. Zhang, J., Singh, S.: LOAM: lidar odometry and mapping in real-time. In: Robotics: Science and Systems (RSS) (2014)
10. Arun, K.S., Huang, T.S., Blostein, S.D.: Least-squares fitting of two 3-D point sets. IEEE Trans. Pattern Anal. Mach. Intell. (T-PAMI) **9**, 698–700 (1987)
11. Horn, B.K.P.: Closed-form solution of absolute orientation using unit quaternions. J. Opt. Soc. Am. A: **4**, 629–642 (1987)
12. Umeyama, S.: Least-squares estimation of transformation parameters between two point patterns. IEEE Trans. Pattern Anal. Mach. Intell. (T-PAMI) **13**, 376–380 (1991)
13. Penney, G.P., Edwards, P.J., King, A.P., Blackall, J.M., Batchelor, P.G., Hawkes, D.J.: A stochastic iterative closest point algorithm (stochastICP). In: Niessen, W.J., Viergever, M.A. (eds.) MICCAI 2001. LNCS, vol. 2208, pp. 762–769. Springer, Heidelberg (2001). https://doi.org/10.1007/3-540-45468-3_91
14. Colas, F., Pomerleau, F., Siegwart, R.: A review of point cloud registration algorithms for mobile robotics. Found. Trends® Robot. **4**, 1–104 (2015)
15. Zhou, X., Leonardos, S., Hu, X., Daniilidis, K.: 3D shape reconstruction from 2D landmarks: a convex formulation. In: IEEE Conference on Computer Vision and Pattern Recognition (CVPR) (2015)

16. Zhou, X., Zhu, M., Daniilidis, K.: Multi-image matching via fast alternating minimization. In: IEEE International Conference on Computer Vision (ICCV) (2015)
17. Yan, J., Wang, J., Zha, H., Yang, X., Chu, S.M.: Multi-view point registration via alternating optimization. In: AAAI Conference on Artificial Intelligence (2015)
18. Schops, T., Sattler, T., Pollefeys, M.: BAD SLAM: bundle adjusted direct RGB-D SLAM. In: IEEE Conference on Computer Vision and Pattern Recognition (CVPR) (2019)
19. Campos, J., Cardoso, J., Miraldo, P.: POSEAMM: a unified framework for solving pose problems using an alternating minimization method. In: IEEE International Conference on Robotics and Automation (ICRA) (2019)
20. Theiler, P.W., Wegner, J.D., Schindler, K.: Globally consistent registration of terrestrial laser scans via graph optimization. ISPRS J. Photogramm. Remote Sens. **109**, 126–138 (2015)
21. Campbell, D., Petersson, L.: GOGMA: globally-optimal gaussian mixture alignment. In: IEEE Conference on Computer Vision and Pattern Recognition (CVPR), pp. 5685–5694 (2016)
22. Li, H., Hartley, R.: The 3D–3D registration problem revisited. In: IEEE International Conference on Computer Vision (ICCV), pp. 1–8 (2017)
23. Zhang, J., Singh, S.: Low-drift and real-time lidar odometry and mapping. Auton. Robots **41**, 401–416 (2017). https://doi.org/10.1007/s10514-016-9548-2
24. Yang, J., Li, H., Jia, Y.: Go-ICP: solving 3D registration efficiently and globally optimally. In: IEEE International Conference on Computer Vision (ICCV), pp. 1457–1464 (2013)
25. Yang, J., Li, H., Campbell, D., Jia, Y.: Go-ICP: a globally optimal solution to 3D ICP point-set registration. IEEE Trans. Pattern Anal. Mach. Intell. (T-PAMI) **38**, 2241–2254 (2016)
26. Makadia, A., Patterson, A., Daniilidis, K.: Fully automatic registration of 3D point clouds. In: IEEE Conference on Computer Vision and Pattern Recognition (CVPR), vol. 1, pp. 1297–1304 (2006)
27. Straub, J., Campbell, T., How, J.P., Fisher III, J.W.: Efficient global point cloud alignment using Bayesian nonparametric mixtures. In: IEEE Conference on Computer Vision and Pattern Recognition (CVPR), pp. 2403–2412 (2017)
28. Liu, Y., Wang, C., Song, Z., Wang, M.: Efficient global point cloud registration by matching rotation invariant features through translation search. In: Ferrari, V., Hebert, M., Sminchisescu, C., Weiss, Y. (eds.) ECCV 2018. LNCS, vol. 11216, pp. 460–474. Springer, Cham (2018). https://doi.org/10.1007/978-3-030-01258-8_28
29. Fischler, M.A., Bolles, R.C.: Random sample consensus: a paradigm for model fitting with applications to image analysis and automated cartography. Commun. ACM **24**, 381–395 (1981)
30. Miraldo, P., Saha, S., Ramalingam, S.: Minimal solvers for mini-loop closures in 3D multi-scan alignment. In: IEEE Conference on Computer Vision and Pattern Recognition (CVPR) (2019)
31. Endres, F., Hess, J., Sturm, J., Cremers, D., Burgard, W.: 3-D mapping with an RGB-D camera. IEEE Trans. Robot. (T-RO) **30**, 177–187 (2014)
32. Raposo, C., Lourenço, M., Barreto, J.P., Antunes, M.: Plane-based odometry using an RGB-D camera. In: British Machine Vision Conference (BMVC) (2013)
33. Zhou, L., Li, Z., Kaess, M.: Automatic extrinsic calibration of a camera and a 3D lidar using line and plane correspondences. In: IEEE/RSJ International Conference on Intelligent Robots and Systems (IROS) (2018)

34. Ma, L., Kerl, C., Stuckler, J., Cremers, D.: CPA-SLAM: consistent plane-model alignment for direct RGB-D SLAM. In: IEEE International Conference on Robotics and Automation (ICRA), pp. 1285–1291 (2016)
35. Bhattacharya, U., Veerawal, S., Govindu, V.M.: Fast multiview 3D scan registration using planar structures. In: International Conference on 3D Vision (3DV), pp. 548–556 (2017)
36. Liu, C., Wu, J., Furukawa, Y.: FloorNet: a unified framework for floorplan reconstruction from 3D scans. In: Ferrari, V., Hebert, M., Sminchisescu, C., Weiss, Y. (eds.) ECCV 2018. LNCS, vol. 11210, pp. 203–219. Springer, Cham (2018). https://doi.org/10.1007/978-3-030-01231-1_13
37. Grant, W.S., Voorhies, R.C., Itti, L.: Efficient velodyne SLAM with point and plane features. Auton. Robots **43**(5), 1207–1224 (2018). https://doi.org/10.1007/s10514-018-9794-6
38. Lu, Y., Song, D.: Robust RGB-D odometry using point and line features. In: IEEE International Conference on Computer Vision (ICCV), pp. 3934–3942 (2015)
39. Deschaud, J.E.: IMLS-SLAM: scan-to-model matching based on 3D data. In: IEEE International Conference on Robotics and Automation (ICRA), pp. 2480–2485 (2018)
40. Choi, C., Trevor, A.J.B., Christensen, H.I.: RGB-D edge detection and edge-based registration. In: IEEE/RSJ International Conference on Intelligent Robots and Systems (IROS), pp. 1568–1575 (2013)
41. Endres, F., Hess, J., Engelhard, N., Sturm, J., Cremers, D., Burgard, W.: An evaluation of the RGB-D SLAM system. In: IEEE International Conference on Robotics and Automation (ICRA), pp. 1691–1696 (2012)
42. Sturm, J., Engelhard, N., Endres, F., Burgard, W., Cremers, D.: A benchmark for the evaluation of RGB-D SLAM systems. In: IEEE/RSJ International Conference on Intelligent Robots and Systems (IROS), pp. 573–580 (2012)
43. Li, H., Hartley, R.: Five-point motion estimation made easy. In: International Conference on Pattern Recognition (ICPR), vol. 1, pp. 630–633 (2006)
44. Li, B., Heng, L., Lee, G.H., Pollefeys, M.: A 4-point algorithm for relative pose estimation of a calibrated camera with a known relative rotation angle. In: IEEE/RSJ International Conference on Intelligent Robots and Systems (IROS), pp. 1595–1601 (2013)
45. Fraundorfer, F., Tanskanen, P., Pollefeys, M.: A minimal case solution to the calibrated relative pose problem for the case of two known orientation angles. In: Daniilidis, K., Maragos, P., Paragios, N. (eds.) ECCV 2010. LNCS, vol. 6314, pp. 269–282. Springer, Heidelberg (2010). https://doi.org/10.1007/978-3-642-15561-1_20
46. Saurer, O., Vasseur, P., Demonceaux, C., Fraundorfer, F.: A homography formulation to the 3pt plus a common direction relative pose problem. In: Cremers, D., Reid, I., Saito, H., Yang, M.-H. (eds.) ACCV 2014. LNCS, vol. 9004, pp. 288–301. Springer, Cham (2015). https://doi.org/10.1007/978-3-319-16808-1_20
47. Stewenius, H., Nister, D., Kahl, F., Schaffalitzky, F.: A minimal solution for relative pose with unknown focal length. In: IEEE Conference on Computer Vision and Pattern Recognition (CVPR), vol. 2, pp. 789–794 (2005)
48. Li, H.: A simple solution to the six-point two-view focal-length problem. In: Leonardis, A., Bischof, H., Pinz, A. (eds.) ECCV 2006. LNCS, vol. 3954, pp. 200–213. Springer, Heidelberg (2006). https://doi.org/10.1007/11744085_16

49. Kneip, L., Siegwart, R., Pollefeys, M.: Finding the exact rotation between two images independently of the translation. In: Fitzgibbon, A., Lazebnik, S., Perona, P., Sato, Y., Schmid, C. (eds.) ECCV 2012. LNCS, vol. 7577, pp. 696–709. Springer, Heidelberg (2012). https://doi.org/10.1007/978-3-642-33783-3_50

50. Ventura, J., Arth, C., Lepetit, V.: An efficient minimal solution for multi-camera motion. In: IEEE International Conference on Computer Vision (ICCV), pp. 747–755 (2015)

51. Camposeco, F., Cohen, A., Pollefeys, M., Sattler, T.: Hybrid camera pose estimation. In: IEEE Conference on Computer Vision and Pattern Recognition (CVPR), pp. 136–144 (2018)

52. Kneip, L., Scaramuzza, D., Siegwart, R.: A novel parametrization of the perspective-three-point problem for a direct computation of absolute camera position and orientation. In: IEEE Conference on Computer Vision and Pattern Recognition (CVPR), pp. 2969–2976 (2011)

53. Ke, T., Roumeliotis, S.I.: An efficient algebraic solution to the perspective-three-point problem. In: IEEE Conference on Computer Vision and Pattern Recognition (CVPR), pp. 4618–4626 (2017)

54. Wang, P., Xu, G., Wang, Z., Cheng, Y.: An efficient solution to the perspective-three-point pose problem. Comput. Vis. Image Underst. (CVIU) **166**, 81–87 (2018)

55. Persson, M., Nordberg, K.: Lambda twist: an accurate fast robust perspective three point (P3P) solver. In: Ferrari, V., Hebert, M., Sminchisescu, C., Weiss, Y. (eds.) ECCV 2018. LNCS, vol. 11208, pp. 334–349. Springer, Cham (2018). https://doi.org/10.1007/978-3-030-01225-0_20

56. Ventura, J., Arth, C., Reitmayr, G., Schmalstieg, D.: A minimal solution to the generalized pose-and-scale problem. In: IEEE Conference on Computer Vision and Pattern Recognition (CVPR), pp. 422–429 (2014)

57. Camposeco, F., Sattler, T., Pollefeys, M.: Minimal solvers for generalized pose and scale estimation from two rays and one point. In: Leibe, B., Matas, J., Sebe, N., Welling, M. (eds.) ECCV 2016. LNCS, vol. 9909, pp. 202–218. Springer, Cham (2016). https://doi.org/10.1007/978-3-319-46454-1_13

58. Pless, R.: Using many cameras as one. In: IEEE Conference on Computer Vision and Pattern Recognition (CVPR), vol. 2, p. 587 (2003)

59. Sturm, P.: Multi-view geometry for general camera models. In: IEEE Conference on Computer Vision and Pattern Recognition (CVPR) (2005)

60. Li, H., Hartley, R., Kim, J.: A linear approach to motion estimation using generalized camera models. In: IEEE Conference on Computer Vision and Pattern Recognition (CVPR) (2008)

61. Kneip, L., Li, H.: Efficient computation of relative pose for multi-camera systems. In: 2014 IEEE Conference on Computer Vision and Pattern Recognition (2014)

62. Pittaluga, F., Koppal, S.J., Kang, S.B., Sinha, S.N.: Revealing scenes by inverting structure from motion reconstructions. In: CVPR (2019)

63. Elbaz, G., Avraham, T., Fischer, A.: 3D point cloud registration for localization using a deep neural network auto-encoder. In: IEEE Conference on Computer Vision and Pattern Recognition (CVPR), pp. 2472–2481 (2017)

64. Khoury, M., Zhou, Q.Y., Koltun, V.: Learning compact geometric features. In: IEEE International Conference on Computer Vision (ICCV), pp. 153–161 (2017)

65. Zhou, L., et al.: Learning and matching multi-view descriptors for registration of point clouds. In: European Conference on Computer Vision (ECCV), pp. 505–522 (2018)

66. Deng, H., Birdal, T., Ilic, S.: PPF-FoldNet: unsupervised learning of rotation invariant 3D local descriptors. In: European Conference on Computer Vision (ECCV), pp. 602–618 (2018)
67. Deng, H., Birdal, T., Ilic, S.: 3D local features for direct pairwise registration. In: IEEE Conference on Computer Vision and Pattern Recognition (CVPR) (2019)
68. Lu, W., Wan, G., Zhou, Y., Fu, X., Yuan, P., Song, S.: DeepVCP: an end-to-end deep neural network for point cloud registration. In: IEEE International Conference on Computer Vision (ICCV) (2019)
69. Ding, L., Feng, C.: DeepMapping: unsupervised map estimation from multiple point clouds. In: IEEE Conference on Computer Vision and Pattern Recognition (CVPR) (2019)
70. Qi, C.R., Su, H., Mo, K., Guibas, L.J.: PointNet: deep learning on point sets for 3D classification and segmentation. In: IEEE Conference on Computer Vision and Pattern Recognition (CVPR), pp. 652–660 (2017)
71. Aoki, Y., Goforth, H., Srivatsan, R.A., Lucey, S.: PointNetLK: robust & efficient point cloud registration using PointNet. In: IEEE Conference on Computer Vision and Pattern Recognition (CVPR), pp. 7163–7172 (2019)
72. Wang, Y., Solomon, J.M.: Deep closest point: learning representations for point cloud registration. In: IEEE International Conference on Computer Vision (ICCV) (2019)
73. Chatterjee, A., Govindu, V.M.: Robust relative rotation averaging. IEEE Trans. Pattern Anal. Mach. Intell. (T-PAMI) **40**, 958–972 (2018)
74. Huang, X., Liang, Z., Zhou, X., Xie, Y., Guibas, L., Huang, Q.: Learning transformation synchronization. In: IEEE Conference on Computer Vision and Pattern Recognition (CVPR) (2019)
75. Geiger, A., Lenz, P., Urtasun, R.: Are we ready for autonomous driving? The KITTI vision benchmark suite. In: IEEE Conference on Computer Vision and Pattern Recognition (CVPR) (2012)
76. Mellado, N., Mitra, N., Aiger, D.: SUPER 4PCS: fast global pointcloud registration via smart indexing. In: Computer Graphics Forum (Proceedings of the EUROGRAPHICS), vol. 33, pp. 205–215 (2014)
77. Censor, Y., Chen, W., Combettes, P.L., Davidi, R., Herman, G.T.: On the effectiveness of projection methods for convex feasibility problems with linear inequality constraints. Comput. Optim. Appl. **51**, 1065–1088 (2012). https://doi.org/10.1007/s10589-011-9401-7
78. Gravel, S., Elser, V.: Divide and concur: a general approach to constraint satisfaction. Phys. Rev. E **78**, 036706 (2008)
79. Elser, V., Rankenburg, I., Thibault, P.: Searching with iterated maps. Proc. Natl. Acad. Sci. U.S.A. (PNAS) **104**, 418–423 (2007)

Best Buddies Registration for Point Clouds

Amnon Drory[✉], Tal Shomer, Shai Avidan, and Raja Giryes

Tel Aviv University, Tel Aviv-Yafo, Israel
`amnondrory@mail.tau.ac.il`

Abstract. We propose new, and robust, loss functions for the point cloud registration problem. Our loss functions are inspired by the Best Buddies Similarity (BBS) measure that counts the number of mutual nearest neighbors between two point sets. This measure has been shown to be robust to outliers and missing data in the case of template matching for images. We present several algorithms, collectively named *Best Buddy Registration (BBR)*, where each algorithm consists of optimizing one of these loss functions with Adam gradient descent. The loss functions differ in several ways, including the distance function used (point-to-point vs. point-to-plane), and how the BBS measure is combined with the actual distances between pairs of points. Experiments on various data sets, both synthetic and real, demonstrate the effectiveness of the BBR algorithms, showing that they are quite robust to noise, outliers, and distractors, and cope well with extremely sparse point clouds. One variant, BBR-F, achieves state-of-the-art accuracy in the registration of automotive lidar scans taken up to several seconds apart, from the KITTI and Apollo-Southbay datasets.

1 Introduction

Fig. 1. Best-Buddies Pairs: The BBR methods perform point cloud registration by iteratively optimizing (with gradient descent) a loss defined by a set of soft or hard *best buddy pairs*. Blue and Green points denote the original point clouds to register. Best buddy pairs are marked in purple. From left to right: iteration 1, 2, 4, 80 and the last iteration (120). (Color figure online)

Electronic supplementary material The online version of this chapter (https://doi.org/10.1007/978-3-030-69525-5_19) contains supplementary material, which is available to authorized users.

© Springer Nature Switzerland AG 2021
H. Ishikawa et al. (Eds.): ACCV 2020, LNCS 12622, pp. 314–329, 2021.
https://doi.org/10.1007/978-3-030-69525-5_19

Point clouds registration is an important task in 3D computer vision. The same object or scene is scanned from two view points, e.g. with a laser scanner, and the goal is to recover the rigid transformation (rotation and translation) that aligns the two scans to each other. Realistic scenarios add complications: measurement noise, occlusions due to the change in view point, and outliers due to independent motions of free moving objects in the scene (*distractors*). This makes robustness a central issue for point cloud registration algorithms.

Probably the most popular approach to solve the problem is using some variant of the Iterative Closest Point (ICP) algorithm [1]. This method works by iterating between two stages: first match pairs of points between the two clouds, and then apply the transformation that minimizes a loss defined by the distance between the two points in each pair. The simplest version of ICP uses the Euclidean distance between points, but later versions make use of more complex distance measures to achieve faster and more accurate convergence. Some of the most popular and successful variants use local normals to define point-to-plane distance measures. ICP-like methods are typically sensitive to noise, requiring the use of steps such as explicit outlier removal to improve their robustness.

Recently, Oron *et al.* introduced the Best-Buddies Similarity (BBS) measure [2]. BBS counts the number of mutual nearest-neighbors between two point sets. This simple measure was used for template matching between images and proved to be resilient to outliers and occluders. This success motivated us to study how the BBS measure could be adapted to the task of point cloud registration. We suggest several differentiable loss functions inspired by BBS. Our registration algorithms consist of optimizing over these losses with a variant of gradient descent (Adam [3]), to recover the parameters of the aligning transformation. We collectively name the resulting algorithms *Best Buddy Registration (BBR)*, and demonstrate their high level of robustness to noise, occlusions and distractors, as well as an ability to cope with extremely sparse point clouds. Some of the algorithms are able to achieve very high accuracy in noisy settings where robustness is essential.

Deep neural networks (DNN) have increasingly been used for the processing of point clouds lately. BBR can easily be integrated into such DNNs as a registration stage, and be optimized as part of the overall gradient descent optimization of the network.[1] To facilitate this, we implemented BBR in Pytorch[2], which also makes it possible to run the algorithms on widely available neural network infrastructure, such as GPUs. (See diagram in supplementary material).

The main contributions of this paper are:

1. A robust and accurate point cloud registration algorithm that is especially useful in realistic scenarios with a large time offset between the pair of point clouds, meaning large occlusions and outlier motions.

---

[1] For example, the DeepMapping network [4] includes a registration stage based on the non-robust Chamfer distance, which could be replaced by BBR.

[2] https://github.com/AmnonDrory/BestBuddiesRegistration.

2. The algorithm naturally fits into the deep learning settings as a component: it can be implemented using operations that already exist in deep learning frameworks, and optimized using Adam gradient descent, which is commonly used for neural network optimization.

2   Related Work

There are various approaches to the problem of point cloud registration. These algorithms can be divided into classic (i.e., non-deep) and deep methods.

Classic Methods. ICP was introduced by Besl and Mckay [1], and Chen and Medioni [5]. See the survey of Rusinkiewicz and Levoy [6] or the recent review of the topic by Pomerelo *et al.* [7]. The basic ICP algorithm deals with point-to-point registration, but already [5] considered point-to-plane registration to improve accuracy. This, however, requires the use of normals as an additional source of information.

Segal *et al.* [8] later extended ICP to a full plane-to-plane formulation and gave it a probabilistic interpretation. Jian and Vemuri [9] proposed a robust point set registration. Their approach reformulated ICP as the problem of aligning two Gaussian mixtures such that a statistical discrepancy measure between the two corresponding mixtures is minimized. It was recently accelerated by Eckart *et al.* [10] who introduced a Hierarchical multi-scale Gaussian Mixture Representation (HGMR) of the point clouds. Similarly, FilterReg [11] is a probabilistic point-set registration method that is considerably faster than alternative methods due to its computationally-efficient probabilistic model. Their key idea is to treat registration as a maximum likelihood estimation, which can be solved using the EM algorithm. With a simple augmentation, they formulate the E step as a filtering problem and solve it using advances in efficient Gaussian filters.

ICP is prone to errors due to outliers and missing data. Thus, a variety of heuristics, as well as more principled methods, were introduced to deal with it. Chetverikov *et al.* [12] proposed a robust version of ICP, termed Trimmed ICP, which is based on Least Trimmed Squares that is designed to robustify the minimization of the error function. Bouaziz *et al.* [13] used sparse inducing norms to cope with missing points and outliers.

Rusinkiewicz [14] recently introduced a symmetric objective function for ICP that approximated a locally-second-order surface centered around the corresponding points. The proposed objective function achieved a larger basin of convergence, compared to regular ICP, while providing state-of-the-art accuracy.

Fitzgibbon [15] replaces ICP with a general-purpose nonlinear optimization (the Levenberg-Marquardt algorithm) that minimizes the registration error directly. His surprising finding is that his technique is comparable in speed to the special-purpose ICP algorithm.

Another line of research gives the correspondence problem a probabilistic interpretation. Instead of assuming a one-to-one correspondence, assignments are assumed to be probabilistic. Similar to us, these methods, described next, use gradient descent to find the optimal registration between two point clouds.

The differentiable approximation we take resembles that taken in SoftAssign [16]. There, they solve the correspondence problem, as an intermediate step, using a permutation matrix. Because that matrix is non-differentiable it is replaced with a Doubly-Stochastic Matrix.

EM-ICP [17] treats point matches as hidden variables and suggests a method that corresponds to an ICP with multiple matches weighted by normalized Gaussian weights, giving birth to the EM-ICP acronym of the method.

In KCReg [18], the authors take an information theoretic approach to the problem. First, they define a kernel correlation that measures affinity between every pair of points. Then, they use that to measure the compactness of a point set and then show that registering two point sets minimizes the overall compactness. In addition, they show that this is equivalent to minimizing Renyi's Quadratic Entropy. In fact, the only difference between the gradients of KCReg [18] and EM-ICP [17] is the normalization term.

Deep Methods. The introduction of PointNet [19] for processing unordered point clouds led to the development of PointNet-based registration algorithms.

PointNetLK [20] maps the two point clouds to some latent space in which it applies the Lucas-Kanade registration [21]. To do that, they define a supervised learning problem that takes two rotated versions of the same point cloud and produces the rotation between the two. The method is implemented using a Recurrent Neural Network, and avoids the costly step of point correspondence. On the downside, it requires a training phase to learn the embedding space, unlike our work that requires no training at all.

Deep Closest Point [22] consists of three parts: a point cloud embedding network, an attention-based module combined with a pointer generation layer [23] to approximate combinatorial matching, and a differentiable singular value decomposition (SVD) layer to extract the final rigid transformation. PointGMM [24] represents the data via a hierarchical Gaussian mixture and learns to perform registration by transforming shapes to their canonical position. DeepVCP [25], for *Virtual Corresponding Points*, trains a network to detect keypoints, match them probabilistically, and recover the registration using them.

A major drawback of deep learning based registration methods is that they strongly depend on the data that they have been trained on. A registration network that is trained for a given dataset does not necessarily generalize well to other datasets [26]. As we do not have a training step, our approach does not suffer from this problem.

Our approach builds on the work of Oron *et al.* [2] and that of Plötz and Roth [27]. Oron *et al.* introduced the concept of the best-buddies similarity measure as a robust method for template matching in images. The idea was to map image patches to points in some high dimensional space and count the number of mutual nearest neighbor matches between the two point sets. This was shown to converge to the χ^2 error measure when the number of points tends to infinity.

Plötz and Roth [27] proposed an approximation scheme to the nearest neighbor problem. Instead of selecting a particular element to be the nearest neighbor to a query point, they use a soft approximation that is governed by a temperature parameter. When the temperature goes to zero, the approximation converges to the deterministic nearest neighbor. Similarly to ICP and its variants, the best-buddies similarity relies on nearest neighbor search, and we use this nearest neighbor approximation in our work.

3   Method

We consider two point clouds $P = \{p_i\}_{i=1}^n$, $Q = \{q_i\}_{i=1}^m$, where $p_i, q_j \in \mathbb{R}^3$. We wish to find the transformation that aligns them, and in this work we assume this is a rigid transformation with 6 degrees of freedom (6DOF). We define several differentiable loss functions inspired by the *Best Buddy Similarity measure (BBS)*. We collectively name our registration algorithms *Best Buddy Registration (BBR)*. For each loss function L, the algorithm *BBR-L* works by optimizing over this loss function to find the aligning transformation:

$$\arg\min_{R,t,\alpha} \mathcal{L}(P, RQ + t), \tag{1}$$

where R is a 3D rotation matrix, t a 3D translation vector, and α a temperature parameter (discussed ahead). We parameterize the rotation using Euler angles: $R = R(\theta, \phi, \psi)$. We next describe the four variants of our algorithm: *BBR-softBBS, BBR-softBD, BBR-N* and *BBR-F*.

We start by defining the BBS measure: Let $D \in \mathbb{R}^{n \times m}$ denote the distance matrix between points in P and points in Q. A best buddies matrix B determines if a pair of points p_i and q_j are mutual nearest neighbors:

$$B_{ij} = [\![i = \arg\min_{i'} D_{i'j}]\!] \cdot [\![j = \arg\min_{j'} D_{ij'}]\!], \tag{2}$$

where $[\![\cdot]\!]$ equals 1 if the term in the brackets is true and zero otherwise.

The Best-Buddies Similarity (BBS) loss $\mathcal{L}_{BBS}(P, Q)$ is negative the number of best buddies pairs[3]:

$$\mathcal{L}_{BBS}(P, Q) = -\sum_{i,j} B_{ij}. \tag{3}$$

The best-buddies similarity measure was shown to be very robust to outliers and missing data [2], in the context of template matching for images. We bring it to 3D point clouds. $\mathcal{L}_{BBS}$ is a robust measure for the quality of the matching between two point clouds P and Q. However, it cannot be used for gradient-descent optimization, because it uses the non-differentiable argmin operator. To overcome this, we use the soft argmin approximation introduced by [27] for Neural Nearest Neighbors Networks. Specifically, $\bar{B}$ approximates B as follows:

$$\bar{B}_{ij} = \frac{e^{-D_{ij}/\alpha}}{\epsilon + \sum_j e^{-D_{ij}/\alpha}} \cdot \frac{e^{-D_{ij}/\alpha}}{\epsilon + \sum_i e^{-D_{ij}/\alpha}}, \tag{4}$$

where α is a temperature parameter (see ahead), and ϵ is a small constant used for numerical stability. The matrix $\bar{B}$ is the element-wise multiplication of

---

[3] In the original definition [2], BBS is normalized by nm. We omit that here.

row-wise and column-wise soft argmin of the distance matrix D. Observe how it corresponds to the brackets in Eq. (2). The *softBBS* loss is now given by:

$$\mathcal{L}_{softBBS}(P,Q) = - \sum_i \sum_j \bar{B}_{i,j}. \tag{5}$$

$\mathcal{L}_{softBBS}$ is not only a differentiable approximation to $\mathcal{L}_{BBS}$, but also a generalization. While B_{ij} is only non-zero if p_i and q_j are mutual nearest neighbors, $\bar{B}_{ij}$ can also be non-zero when, for example, p_i is q_j's 3rd nearest neighbor, while q_j is p_i's 4th nearest neighbor. The value of the temperature parameter, α, controls this behaviour. The smaller it is, the more strict $\bar{B}_{ij}$ becomes, meaning more similar to B_{ij}. α is also learned during the optimization (together with the other optimized parameters, R and t). However, we find it important to initialize it with a reasonable value. A bad choice of α can result in a flat loss, unsuitable for gradient descent. In all our experiments we set $\alpha_{init} = 1e{-}2$ as it generally provides a smooth approximation to $\mathcal{L}_{BBS}$, but with a good slope near the minimum. For numerical stability, we allow it to decrease down to $\alpha_{final} = 1e{-}8$.

The next loss we suggest is the *soft buddy distance* loss, or $\mathcal{L}_{softBD}$, which makes use of the distance between the two points in each pair. This is in contrast to the BBS measure, which only counts the *number* of best-buddies, and softBBS loss, which is a soft approximation to that. We define *softBD* as follows:

$$\mathcal{L}_{softBD}(P,Q) = \frac{\sum_i \sum_j \bar{B}_{i,j} D_{ij}}{\sum_i \sum_j \bar{B}_{i,j}}. \tag{6}$$

The next loss is *softBD with normals* loss, or $\mathcal{L}_N$, which uses a point-to-plane distance measure calculated from local normals. Such a distance measure is used in some of the most popular and successful ICP variants, such as generalized ICP [8], and symmetric ICP [14]. In the previous methods we suggested, we used the Euclidean point-to-point distance to create the distance matrix D. In *BBR-N* we replace that with the following symmetric point-to-plane distance, based on Rusinkievicz [14]:

$$D_{i,j}^n = dist(Rq_i + t, p_j) = |\langle Rq_i + t - p_j, Rn_{q_i} + n_{p_j}\rangle|. \tag{7}$$

where n_{q_i} is the normal at point q_i, n_{p_j} is the normal at point p_j, and D^n denotes the version of the distance matrix calculated using this distance. The loss function is then calculated as in *softBD*, except using D^n instead D. This distance is symmetric in the sense that it uses the normals from both points, unlike algorithms such as point-to-plane ICP [5] that only use normals from one of the point clouds.[4]

The final loss we present is the *best-buddy filtering* loss, or $\mathcal{L}_F$. At the heart of the BBS measure lies the robustness achieved by using mutual nearest neighbors. *BBR-F* translates this idea into *best buddy filtering*: using only pairs that are

---

[4] This is not to be confused with the symmetric nature of the best-buddies similarity measure that we introduce here.

mutual nearest neighbors. In addition, it follows the trend in ICP-like algorithms, in that it uses both point-to-point and point-to-plane distance measures: the Euclidean point-to-point distance is used for the stage of matching pairs between the two point clouds. Then the symmetric point-to-plane distance between these pairs is used to define the following loss:

$$\mathcal{L}_F(P,Q) = -\sum_i \sum_j B_{i,j} \cdot D_{i,j}^n. \tag{8}$$

Notice that in this variant of BBR we have a hard selection of pairs, which isn't optimized during gradient descent. Instead, the *distances* between the points in each pair are minimized.

The central difference between *BBR-F* and symmetric ICP [14] is that best buddy filtering replaces explicit outlier rejection. This removes the necessity to calibrate outlier-rejection parameters, while resulting in better accuracy in settings where robustness is important, as Sect. 4 shows. Another difference is that *BBR-F* uses Adam gradient descent for optimization, while symmetric ICP uses a closed form solution to an approximate linearized version of the symmetric point-to-plane distance measure.

BBR-F is especially useful for very large point clouds, where memory and running time become a constraint, because it does not require the full distance matrix D or D^n. For the pair matching step, we use the KD-tree method [28], and then calculate the point-to-plane distances only for best-buddy pairs. See supplementary material for run time measurements.

4   Experiments

We present experiments that are designed to analyze the behaviour of the BBR methods, and evaluate them on several datasets including Stanford [29], TUM RGBD [30], KITTI Odometry [31], and Apollo-Southbay [32]. We compare our approach to several established alternatives, focusing on classic approaches (e.g., ICP) as opposed to learned methods, as the latter do not necessarily generalize well across datasets [26].

Figure 1 shows the best-buddies pairs during a typical run of *BBR-softBBS* on the Stanford Bunny model [29]. The algorithm converges after 120 iterations. At first, there are few best-buddies pairs, but as time progresses their number grows until convergence.

4.1   Performance Evaluation Setup

We conduct a set of experiments to evaluate accuracy and robustness. To do that, we apply different rotations, translations, sub-sampling, and noise, to each point cloud. We compare ourselves to the following popular point cloud registration algorithms: (i) HGMR [10], a GMM based method; (ii) Coherent Point Drift (CPD) [33], a probabilistic algorithm based on GMM; (iii) Generalized ICP (G-ICP) [8], a very popular and accurate ICP variant that uses local normals, and (iv) Symmetric ICP (Sym-ICP) [14], which provides state-of-the-art performance on several point cloud registration challenges. Additional experiments with different ranges of noise and motions appear in the supplementary material, as do the definitions we use for translational and angular error.

ICP algorithms are sensitive to noise, and therefore commonly employ a set of standard practices for outlier rejection. Our BBR methods require no such processes.

Setting. We test the 4 variants of our algorithm: *BBR-softBBS*, *BBR-softBD*, *BBR-N* and *BBR-F*. *BBR-softBBS* tends to be less accurate than the others, and therefore we omit it from most experiments.

The local normals that are used in *BBR-N* and *BBR-F* are estimated by calculating the principal axis of a neighborhood of $k = 13$ neighbors around each point in the full cloud (before subsampling). For consistency, Sym-ICP was given the same normals used for *BBR-N*. G-ICP calculates its own normals on-the-fly, from the subsampled point cloud that it takes as input. For all BBR methods, the optimization is performed by running Adam for a pre-defined number of iterations.

We use the Probreg[5] library's implementation of *HGMR* and *CPD*, and the original *SymICP* implementation, for all of which we use the default parameters. We use the Point Cloud Library's [34] implementation of *G-ICP*, setting the parameters as in [25].

4.2 Comparing Accuracy and Robustness Between BBR Variants

We start by comparing the different variants of BBR in a simple experiment, testing their accuracy and ability to converge with different initial rotations: 5, 10, 30, 60 and 90°. For each angle, we repeat 20 times: select two random subsets of 500 points from the Stanford Bunny point cloud, rotate the target point cloud around a random axis, perform registration and measure the angular error. We consider registration to have failed if the final error is over 5°. Results are shown in Fig. 2. *BBR-softBBS* is the clear leader in robustness to large initial error. Unlike the others, it is able to handle initial rotations of 90° with hardly any failures. Notice that BBR-N is especially sensitive to large initial rotations, due to its reliance on normals to recognize best-buddies. When the initial rotation is large, the same object will have very different normals in each of the two scans. For all algorithms, large initial rotations do not cause degradation in accuracy - for the attempts that did succeed. When looking at the accuracy of the successful attempts, it's clear that the methods that make use of local normals (*BBR-N* and *BBR-F*) are significantly more accurate.

4.3 Accuracy

The experiments shown in Fig. 3 demonstrate our ability to register point clouds with random rotation and translation, using the Bunny, Horse, and Dragon point

---

[5] https://github.com/neka-nat/probreg.

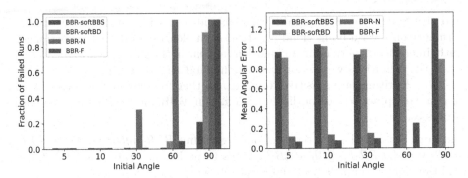

Fig. 2. Accuracy and Robustness to Initial Error Comparison among the BBR methods using the Stanford Bunny point cloud. Left - the fraction out of 20 registration attempts that failed, Right - accuracy as measured by the mean angular error of the successful attempts. *BBR-softBBS* is the best at converging from a large initial error. *BBR-N* and *BBR-F*, that make use of local normals, are the most accurate.

clouds from [29]. We randomly select a source and target subset from the original point cloud, each containing M points. The target point cloud is rotated around a randomly selected axis by an angle of θ_{rot}. It is then translated along a random axis to a distance of Δ_{trans}. We then run the registration algorithms on the point-cloud pair and record their translational and angular error. We repeat the experiment T times and report the median error for each algorithm and each cardinality M of the point clouds.

For all experiments in Fig. 3 we set $\Delta_{trans} = 0.005$ m and $T = 20$. The other parameters are: Bunny: $M \in \{200, 300, \ldots, 1000\}$, $\theta_{rot} = 8°$. Horse: $150 \leq M \leq 1000$, $\theta_{rot} = 10°$. Dragon: M up to 2000, $\theta_{rot} = 5°$. *BBR-F* achieves the lowest error rate, across almost all point cloud sizes. It is followed closely by *BBR-N*. Only when the point density is high, Sym-ICP performs on-par with *BBR-N*. This demonstrate BBR's ability to work well with very sparse point clouds. It should also be pointed out that *BBR-softBD* outperforms the comparable registration method that do not use normals (as well as G-ICP).

4.4   Robustness

The next experiments demonstrate the resistance of the algorithm to a variety of challenges, including occlusions, the presence of a distractor, measurement noise, and a large initial error.

Partial Overlap and Occlusion. The experiment shown in Fig. 4 evaluates the resistance to partial overlap and occlusion. We perform registration between two partial scans of the Stanford Bunny, *bun000* and *bun090*, each captured from a different view point. Following Rusinkiewicz's [14] experimental setup, we first align the scans according to the ground truth motion. Then we follow the same experimental method as in Sect. 4.3, with $M \in \{200, 300, \ldots, 1000\}$, $\theta_{rot} = 5°$ and $\Delta_{trans} = 0.005$ m. *BBR-F* achieves the most accurate results, followed by

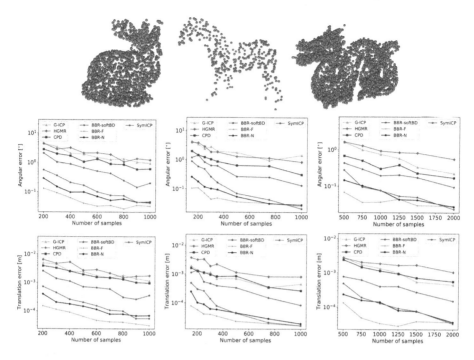

Fig. 3. Accuracy test: Top Row - Point clouds examples as used in the accuracy test. Middle and bottom rows - angular and translation error as a function of the number of points. *BBR-F* achieves the most accurate results in all scenarios, followed closely by *BBR-N*. *SymICP* becomes competitive only when the number of points increases.

BBR-N and *Sym-ICP*. However, *Sym-ICP* deteriorates considerably when given a very sparse point cloud, while both of our algorithms cope with it very well.

Resistance to Distractors. This experiment evaluates the effects of distractor noise. This is the case where in addition to the main object of interest, the scene also contains a second object with a different motion. In this synthetic experiment, the main object, a large horse, was randomly translated and rotated as in Sect. 4.3, with $T = 20$, $\theta_{rot} = 10°$ and $\Delta_{trans} = 0.005\,\mathrm{m}$. The distractor object, a small horse, underwent a different motion. Such a situation may occur when attempting to estimate the ego-motion of a vehicle, using scans that include other independently moving vehicles. The main object contains 1000 points, and we vary the number of points in the distractor object from 200 up to 900. In Fig. 5 we show the median error as a function of the number of points in the distractor. *BBR-F* shows a strong resistance to distractor noise in this experiment, while *Sym-ICP* is quite susceptible to it. Among methods that do not make use of normals, *BBR-softBD* is the most accurate.

Measurement Noise. The TUM RGB-D dataset [30] contains point clouds of indoor scenes captured with the Kinect sensor. It contains natural measurement noise, due to the warp and scanning noise from the Kinect sensor. It has

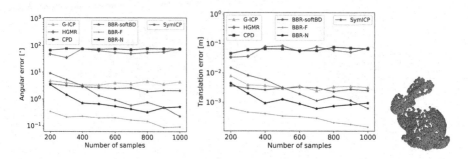

Fig. 4. Robustness to point of view changes: Right - aligned *bun000* and *bun090* with 1000 points, with overlap of less than 30%. Left - angular and translation error for varying number of points. *BBR-softBD*, *BBR-N* and *BBR-F* all outperform Sym-ICP [14] when the number of samples is low.

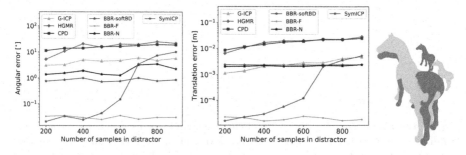

Fig. 5. Distractor noise: Right - an example of our experimental setting: The main object (large horse) has moved differently than the distractor (small horse). Left and center - the angular and translation errors for varying distractor strengths. The BBR algorithms are able to ignore the distractor and focus on the motion of the main object.

been noted by Rusinkiewicz [14] that this dataset poses a qualitatively different challenge than the bunny point cloud. He demonstrates his algorithm on a specific pair of partially-overlapping scans from this dataset. We use the same pair, 1305031104.030279 and 1305031108.503548 of the freiburg1_xyz sequence from the TUM RGB-D (See image in supplementary material), sample 1000 points from each, and experiment with adding a random rotation of up to 5° around a random axis. We repeat this 50 times and perform registration for each, showing the cumulative distribution of the final errors in Fig. 6. The BBR algorithms perform better than all competing methods.

Large Initial Error with Partial Overlap. In this experiment we evaluate the ability to converge when the source and target point clouds are only partially overlapping, and starting from a large initial error. We use two scans of the bunny point cloud, *bun180* and *bun270*, that were captured from significantly different view points. As before, we first align them, sample 1000 points from each, and

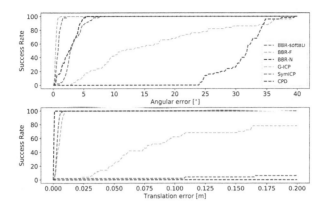

Fig. 6. Convergence Analysis (TUM): The cumulative distribution of errors over 50 repeats. x-axis: the error threshold; y axis: the fraction of results that achieved an error smaller than this threshold. For example, *G-ICP* has 20% of its registration results with an angular error lower than 5°, *SymICP* has 90% of its results under 5°, and the BBR algorithms have 100% of their errors under 5°.

then apply a random motion to one of them. In this experiment the motion is large: a random rotation in the range [30, 50] degrees, around a random axis, and a translation of half the extent of the point cloud (0.05 m) along a random direction. Figure 7 shows the cumulative distribution of errors over 50 repeats. *BBR-softBD* performs considerably better than all other algorithms.

4.5   Odometry

In this section we present experiments in the realistic setting of vehicle navigation, specifically focusing on a difficult setting where the separation between the two clouds is relatively large, leading to significant occlusions and outliers caused by independently moving objects in the scene. We use two datasets of high-resolution Lidar scans: KITTI Odometry [31], and Apollo-Southbay [32], both of which consist of large point clouds of over 100K points. We follow the experimental setup of [25], where the test set consists of pairs of clouds scanned by the same vehicle at two times, during which the vehicle has travelled up to 5 m, for up to 2 s (KITTI) or even 5 s (Apollo-Southbay). An initial estimate for the motion is assumed to be available, which is inaccurate by up to 1 m in each of x, y, z, and up to 1° in each of θ, ϕ, ψ. We report the mean translation and angular errors, as well as the maximum (worst case).

For this test, we use the *BBR-F* variant of our BBR algorithm. Normals are estimated from neighborhoods of $k = 94$ points in the full cloud. To achieve high accuracy, we only moderately subsample the point clouds to 30K points, uniformly at random.

Tables 1 and 2 compare our results to those reported in [25], and to those of Sym-ICP [14]. In both experiments, *BBR-F* achieves state of the art accuracy

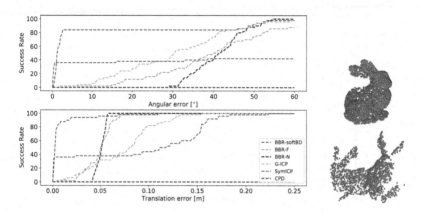

Fig. 7. Convergence Analysis (partially-overlapping Bunny): Right: *bun180* and *bun270*, aligned (top), and in their initial position: rotated in 50° and translated by a factor of 0.05 m (bottom). Left: the cumulative distribution of errors over 50 repeats. The x-axis is the error threshold and the y axis is fraction of registration results whose error is smaller than this threshold.

Table 1. The KITTI odometry dataset. Our algorithm achieves state of the art results for almost all accuracy measures.

Method	Angular error (°)		Translation error (m)	
	Mean	Max	Mean	Max
ICP-Po2Po [1]	0.139	1.176	0.089	2.017
ICP-Po2Pl [1]	0.084	1.693	0.065	2.050
G-ICP [8]	0.067	0.375	0.065	2.045
AA-ICP [35]	0.145	1.406	0.088	2.020
NDT-P2D [36]	0.101	4.369	0.071	2.000
CPD [33]	0.461	5.076	0.804	7.301
3DFeat-Net [37]	0.199	2.428	0.116	4.972
DeepVCP-Base [25]	0.195	1.700	0.073	**0.482**
DeepVCP-Duplication [25]	0.164	1.212	0.071	**0.482**
Sym-ICP [14]	0.066	0.422	**0.058**	0.863
BBR-F (ours)	**0.065**	**0.356**	**0.058**	0.730

by three of the four accuracy measures. This demonstrates BBR's capabilities of achieving high accuracy in realistic scenarios that include occlusions, outlier motions and measurement noise.

Table 2. The Apollo-SouthBay odometry dataset. Our algorithm achieves state of the art results for almost all accuracy measures.

Method	Angular error (°)		Translation error (m)	
	Mean	Max	Mean	Max
ICP-Po2Po [1]	0.051	0.678	0.089	3.298
ICP-Po2Pl [1]	0.026	0.543	0.024	4.448
G-ICP [8]	0.025	0.562	0.014	1.540
AA-ICP [35]	0.054	1.087	0.109	5.243
NDT-P2D [36]	0.045	1.762	0.045	1.778
CPD [33]	0.054	1.177	0.210	5.578
3DFeat-Net [37]	0.076	1.180	0.061	6.492
DeepVCP-Base [25]	0.135	1.882	0.024	**0.875**
DeepVCP-Duplication [25]	0.056	0.875	0.018	0.932
Sym-ICP [14]	0.018	2.589	0.010	6.625
BBR-F (ours)	**0.015**	**0.308**	**0.007**	2.517

5   Conclusions

We proposed *Best Buddy Registration (BBR)* algorithms for point cloud registration inspired by the Best Buddy Similarity (BBS) measure. First we show that registration can be performed by running gradient descent on a differential approximation to the negated BBS measure. This results in an algorithm that is quite robust to noise, occlusions and distractions, and able to cope with very sparse point clouds. We then present additional algorithms that achieve higher accuracy while maintaining robustness, by incorporating point-to-point and point-to-plane distances into the loss function. Finally, we present the *BBR-F* algorithm that uses *best buddy filtering* to achieves state of the art accuracy on challenges that include significant noise, occlusions and distractors, including registration of automotive lidar scans that are relatively widely separated in time. Our algorithms are implemented in Pytorch and optimized with Adam gradient descent, allowing them to be incorporated as a registration stage in Deep Neural Networks for processing point clouds.

Acknowledgements. This research was supported by ERC-StG grant no. 757497 (SPADE) and by ISF grant number 1549/19.

References

1. Besl, P.J., McKay, N.D.: A method for registration of 3-D shapes. IEEE Trans. Pattern Anal. Mach. Intell. **14**, 239–256 (1992)
2. Oron, S., Dekel, T., Xue, T., Freeman, W.T., Avidan, S.: Best-buddies similarity-robust template matching using mutual nearest neighbors. IEEE Trans. Pattern Anal. Mach. Intell. **40**, 1799–1813 (2018)

3. Kingma, D., Ba, J.: Adam: a method for stochastic optimization. In: International Conference on Learning Representations (2014)
4. Ding, L., Feng, C.: DeepMapping: unsupervised map estimation from multiple point clouds. In: The IEEE Conference on Computer Vision and Pattern Recognition (CVPR) (2019)
5. Chen, Y., Medioni, G.: Object modelling by registration of multiple range images. Image Vis. Comput. **10**, 145–155 (1992)
6. Rusinkiewicz, S., Levoy, M.: Efficient variants of the ICP algorithm. In: Proceedings Third International Conference on 3-D Digital Imaging and Modeling, pp. 145–152 (2001)
7. Pomerleau, F., Colas, F., Siegwart, R.: A review of point cloud registration algorithms for mobile robotics (2015)
8. Segal, A., Hähnel, D., Thrun, S.: Generalized-ICP. In: Trinkle, J., Matsuoka, Y., Castellanos, J.A. (eds.) Robotics: Science and Systems. The MIT Press (2009)
9. Jian, B., Vemuri, B.C.: Robust point set registration using Gaussian mixture models. IEEE Trans. Pattern Anal. Mach. Intell. **33**, 1633–1645 (2011)
10. Eckart, B., Kim, K., Kautz, J.: HGMR: hierarchical gaussian mixtures for adaptive 3D registration. In: Ferrari, V., Hebert, M., Sminchisescu, C., Weiss, Y. (eds.) ECCV 2018. LNCS, vol. 11219, pp. 730–746. Springer, Cham (2018). https://doi.org/10.1007/978-3-030-01267-0_43
11. Gao, W., Tedrake, R.: FilterReg: robust and efficient probabilistic point-set registration using Gaussian filter and twist parameterization. In: IEEE Conference on Computer Vision and Pattern Recognition, CVPR, Computer Vision Foundation/IEEE, pp. 11095–11104 (2019)
12. Chetverikov, D., Stepanov, D., Krsek, P.: Robust Euclidean alignment of 3D point sets: the trimmed iterative closest point algorithm. Image Vis. Comput. **23**, 299–309 (2005)
13. Bouaziz, S., Tagliasacchi, A., Pauly, M.: Sparse iterative closest point. In: Proceedings of the Eleventh Eurographics/ACMSIGGRAPH Symposium on Geometry Processing, SGP 2013, pp. 113–123 (2013)
14. Rusinkiewicz, S.: A symmetric objective function for ICP. ACM Trans. Graph. **38**, 1–7 (2019). (Proc. SIGGRAPH)
15. Fitzgibbon, A.W.: Robust registration of 2D and 3D point sets. In: British Machine Vision Conference, pp. 662–670 (2001)
16. Rangarajan, A., Chui, H., Bookstein, F.L.: The softassign procrustes matching algorithm. In: Duncan, J., Gindi, G. (eds.) IPMI 1997. LNCS, vol. 1230, pp. 29–42. Springer, Heidelberg (1997). https://doi.org/10.1007/3-540-63046-5_3
17. Granger, S., Pennec, X.: Multi-scale EM-ICP: a fast and robust approach for surface registration. In: Heyden, A., Sparr, G., Nielsen, M., Johansen, P. (eds.) ECCV 2002. LNCS, vol. 2353, pp. 418–432. Springer, Heidelberg (2002). https://doi.org/10.1007/3-540-47979-1_28
18. Tsin, Y., Kanade, T.: A correlation-based approach to robust point set registration. In: Pajdla, T., Matas, J. (eds.) ECCV 2004. LNCS, vol. 3023, pp. 558–569. Springer, Heidelberg (2004). https://doi.org/10.1007/978-3-540-24672-5_44
19. Qi, C.R., Su, H., Mo, K., Guibas, L.J.: PointNet: deep learning on point sets for 3D classification and segmentation. In: Proceedings of the IEEE Conference on Computer Vision and Pattern Recognition (CVPR), pp. 652–660 (2017)
20. Aoki, Y., Goforth, H., Srivatsan, R.A., Lucey, S.: PointNetLK: robust & efficient point cloud registration using PointNet. In: The IEEE Conference on Computer Vision and Pattern Recognition (CVPR) (2019)

21. Lucas, B.D., Kanade, T.: An iterative image registration technique with an application to stereo vision. In: Proceedings of the 7th International Joint Conference on Artificial Intelligence, IJCAI 1981, vol. 2, pp. 674–679 (1981)
22. Wang, Y., Solomon, J.M.: Deep closest point: learning representations for point cloud registration. In: The IEEE International Conference on Computer Vision (ICCV) (2019)
23. Vinyals, O., Fortunato, M., Jaitly, N.: Pointer networks. In: Cortcs, C., Lawrence, N.D., Lee, D.D., Sugiyama, M., Garnett, R. (eds.) Advances in Neural Information Processing Systems, vol. 28., pp. 2692–2700 (2015)
24. Hertz, A., Hanocka, R., Giryes, R., Cohen-Or, D.: PointGMM: a neural gmm network for point clouds. In: IEEE/CVF Conference on Computer Vision and Pattern Recognition (CVPR), pp. 12051–12060 (2020)
25. Lu, W., Wan, G., Zhou, Y., Fu, X., Yuan, P., Song, S.: DeepVCP: an end-to-end deep neural network for point cloud registration. In: The IEEE International Conference on Computer Vision (ICCV) (2019)
26. Sarode, V., et al.: PCRNet: point cloud registration network using PointNet encoding. ArXiv abs/1908.07906 (2019)
27. Plötz, T., Roth, S.: Neural Nearest Neighbors Networks. In: Proceedings of Advances in Neural Information Processing Systems (NeuralIPS) (2018)
28. Bentley, J.L.: Multidimensional binary search trees used for associative searching. Commun. ACM **18**, 509–517 (1975)
29. Turk, G., Levoy, M.: Zippered polygon meshes from range images. In: Proceedings of the 21st Annual Conference on Computer Graphics and Interactive Techniques, SIGGRAPH 1994, pp. 311–318. ACM (1994)
30. Sturm, J., Engelhard, N., Endres, F., Burgard, W., Cremers, D.: A benchmark for the evaluation of RGB-D SLAM systems. In: IEEE/RSJ International Conference on Intelligent Robots and Systems, IROS, Vilamoura, Algarve, Portugal, 7–12 October 2012, pp. 573–580 (2012)
31. Geiger, A., Lenz, P., Urtasun, R.: Are we ready for autonomous driving? The kitti vision benchmark suite. In: Conference on Computer Vision and Pattern Recognition (CVPR) (2012)
32. Lu, W., Zhou, Y., Wan, G., Hou, S., Song, S.: L3-Net: towards learning based LiDAR localization for autonomous driving. In: IEEE Conference on Computer Vision and Pattern Recognition (CVPR). IEEE (2019)
33. Myronenko, A., Song, X.: Point set registration: coherent point drift. IEEE Trans. Pattern Anal. Mach. Intell. **32**, 2262–2275 (2010)
34. Rusu, R.B., Cousins, S.: 3D is here: point cloud library (PCL). In: IEEE International Conference on Robotics and Automation (ICRA), Shanghai, China (2011)
35. Pavlov, A.L., Ovchinnikov, G.W., Derbyshev, D.Y., Tsetserukou, D., Oseledets, I.V.: AA-ICP: iterative closest point with anderson acceleration. In: 2018 IEEE International Conference on Robotics and Automation (ICRA), pp. 3407–3412 (2018)
36. Stoyanov, T., Magnusson, M., Andreasson, H., Lilienthal, A.J.: Fast and accurate scan registration through minimization of the distance between compact 3D NDT representations. Int. J. Robotics Res. **31**, 1377–1393 (2012)
37. Yew, Z.J., Lee, G.H.: 3DFeat-Net: weakly supervised local 3D features for point cloud registration. In: Ferrari, V., Hebert, M., Sminchisescu, C., Weiss, Y. (eds.) ECCV 2018. LNCS, vol. 11219, pp. 630–646. Springer, Cham (2018). https://doi.org/10.1007/978-3-030-01267-0_37

Project to Adapt: Domain Adaptation for Depth Completion from Noisy and Sparse Sensor Data

Adrian Lopez-Rodriguez[1](✉)(iD), Benjamin Busam[2,3](iD),
and Krystian Mikolajczyk[1](iD)

[1] Imperial College London, London, UK
{al4415,k.mikolajczyk}@imperial.ac.uk
[2] Huawei Noah's Ark Lab, London, UK
[3] Technical University of Munich, Munich, Germany
b.busam@tum.de

Abstract. Depth completion aims to predict a dense depth map from a sparse depth input. The acquisition of dense ground truth annotations for depth completion settings can be difficult and, at the same time, a significant domain gap between real LiDAR measurements and synthetic data has prevented from successful training of models in virtual settings. We propose a domain adaptation approach for sparse-to-dense depth completion that is trained from synthetic data, without annotations in the real domain or additional sensors. Our approach simulates the real sensor noise in an RGB + LiDAR set-up, and consists of three modules: simulating the real LiDAR input in the synthetic domain via projections, filtering the real noisy LiDAR for supervision and adapting the synthetic RGB image using a CycleGAN approach. We extensively evaluate these modules against the state-of-the-art in the KITTI depth completion benchmark, showing significant improvements.

1 Introduction

Motivation. Active sensors such as LiDAR determine the distance of objects within a specified range via a sparse sampling of the environment whose density decreases quadratically with the distance. RGB cameras densely capture their field of view, however, monocular depth estimation from RGB is an ill-posed problem that can be solved only up to a geometric scale. The combination of RGB and depth modalities form a rich source for mutual improvements where each sensor can benefit from the advantage of the other.

Many pipelines have been proposed for a fusion of these two inputs [1–6]. Ground truth annotations for this task, however, require elaborate techniques,

---

Electronic supplementary material The online version of this chapter (https://doi.org/10.1007/978-3-030-69525-5_20) contains supplementary material, which is available to authorized users.

H. Ishikawa et al. (Eds.): ACCV 2020, LNCS 12622, pp. 330–348, 2021.
https://doi.org/10.1007/978-3-030-69525-5_20

manual adjustments and are subject to hardware noise or costly and time-consuming labeling. The most prominent publicly available data for this task [7] creates a ground truth by aligning consecutive raw LiDAR scans that are cleaned from measurement errors, occlusions, and motion artifacts in a post-processing step involving classical stereo reconstruction. Even after the use of this additional data and tedious processing, the signal is not noise-free as discussed in [7]. To avoid such annotations, some methods perform self-supervision [4,5,8], where a photometric loss is employed with stereo or video data. The dependence on additional data such as stereo or temporal sequences brings other problems such as line-of-sight issues and motion artifacts from incoherently moving objects. Modern 3D engines can render highly realistic virtual environments [9–11] with perfect ground truth. However, a significant domain gap between real and virtual scenes prevents from successful training on synthetic data only.

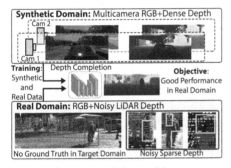
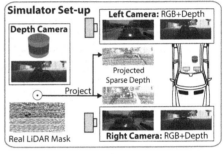

Overview of the problem   Multicamera set-up in CARLA

Fig. 1. We investigate the depth completion problem without ground truth in the real domain, which contains paired noisy and sparse depth measurements and RGB images. We highlight some noise present in the real data: see-through on the tree trunk and bicycle, self-occlusion on the bicycle and missing points on the van. We leverage synthetic data with multicamera dense depth and RGB images. An overview of the multicamera set-up in CARLA used to simulate the real projection LiDAR artifacts is included. The *Depth Camera* acts as a virtual LiDAR and collects a dense depth, which is sparsified using real LiDAR binary masks and projected to either the *Left Camera* or *Right Camera* reference frame. Both the *Left Camera* and the *Right Camera* collect RGB information, used as part of the input data, and a dense depth map, used for supervision.

Contributions and Outline. In contrast to the self-supervised methods [4,5,8], we propose to use a domain adaptation approach to address the depth completion problem without real data ground truth as shown in Fig. 1. We train our method from the synthetic data generated with the driving simulator CARLA [11] and evaluate it on the real KITTI depth completion benchmark [7]. The real LiDAR data is noisy with the main source of noise being the see-through artifacts that occur after projecting the LiDAR's point cloud to the RGB cameras. We aim to generate synthetic LiDAR data with a noise distribution similar to the real LiDAR data. Hence, we propose an approach to simulate the see-through artifacts by generating data in CARLA using a multicamera set-up, employing random masks from the real LiDAR to sparsify the virtual LiDAR sensor, and projecting from the virtual LiDAR camera to the RGB reference frame. We further improve the model by filtering the noisy input in the real domain, thus obtaining a set of reliable points that are used as supervision. Finally, to reduce the domain gap between the RGB images, we use a CycleGAN [12] to transfer the image style from the real domain to the synthetic one.

We compare our approach to other state-of-the-art depth completion methods and provide a detailed analysis of the proposed components. The proposed domain adaptation for RGB-guided sparse-to-dense depth completion is a novel approach for the task of depth completion, which leads to significant improvements as demonstrated by the results. To this end, our main contributions are:

1. A novel domain adaptation method for depth completion that includes geometric and data-driven sensor mimicking, noise filtering and image style adaptation. We demonstrate that adapting the synthetic sparse depth is crucial for improving the performance, whereas RGB adaptation is secondary.
2. An improvement of 6.4% RMSE, and 9.2% RMSE when combining our pipeline with video self-supervision, over the state-of-the-art in the KITTI depth completion benchmark amongst ground truth free methods.

2   Related Work

We first review related works on depth estimation using either RGB or LiDAR, and then discuss depth completion methods from both RGB and LiDAR.

2.1   Unimodal Approaches

RGB Images. RGB based depth estimation has a long history [13–15] reaching from temporal Structure from Motion (SfM) [16,17] and SLAM [18–20] to recent approaches that estimate depth from a static image [21–25]. Networks are either trained with full supervision [21,26] or use additional cameras to exploit photometric consistency during training [22,27]. Some monocular depth estimators leverage a pre-computation stage with an SfM pipeline to provide supervision for both camera pose and depth [28,29] or incorporate hints from stereo algorithms [30]. These approaches are in general tailored for a specific use case and suffer from domain shift errors, which has been addressed with stereo proxies [23] or various publicly available pre-training sources [24].

Sparse Depth. While recent advantages in depth super-resolution [31,32] show good performance, they are not directly applicable to LiDAR data which is sparsely and irregularly distributed within the image. Similar to super-resolution, a rectangular grid for the sampling was assumed in [33]. The sampling grid of the sparse depth signal is crucial for the depth completion task [7], which can be provided as a mask to the network, thus helping to densify the input. While classical image processing techniques are used in [34], an encoder-decoder architecture is applied for this task in [35]. Other approaches [36,37] design more efficient architectures to improve the runtime performance.

2.2 Depth Completion from RGB and LiDAR

Most recent solutions to depth completion leverage deep neural networks. These can be divided into supervised and self-supervised approaches.

Supervision and Ground Truth. Usually, an encoder-decoder network is used to encode the different input signals into a common latent space where feature fusion is possible and a decoder reconstructs an output depth map [1–3,6,38]. Different additional random sampling strategies can increase the density of the input signal [1] while fusing 2D and 3D representations [39] can improve depth boundaries. The noise problem has been targeted with local and global information in [2]. Other methods [3,6] leverage different input modalities such as surface normals to increase the amount of diversity in the input data. The publicly available dataset KITTI [7,40] includes real driving scenes where a stereo RGB camera system is fixed on the roof of a car along with a LiDAR scanner that acquires data while the car is driving. A post-processing stage fuses several LiDAR scans and filters outliers with the help of stereo vision to provide labeled ground truth. While this process is intricate and time-consuming, further error is accumulated from calibration and alignment [7].

Self-supervised Approaches. Another view either from a second camera or a video sequence can be used for self-supervision. Temporal information and mutually predicted poses between RGB frames were used in [4] for self-supervision with a photometric loss on the reprojected image. A probabilistic formulation was proposed in [5] with a conditional prior within a maximum a posteriori (MAP) estimation, which also leverages stereo information. A non-learning method was used in [8] to form a spatially dense but coarse depth approximation from the sparse points, where the coarse approximation was then refined using another network. A photometric loss was also used in [8], where a separate network predicted the poses between RGB frames obtained from a video sequence.

Synthetic Data. For monocular depth estimation, two domain adaptation approaches used style-transfer methods [41,42]. Sparse-to-dense methods, however, have used synthetic data without any adaptation [3,5,43] so far. Training on synthetic data requires a high rendering quality [44]. To this end, synthesizing driving scenarios has also been researched: SYNTHIA [9] provides synthetic urban images together with semantic annotations, while Virtual KITTI [10] gives synthetic renderings that closely match the videos of the KITTI dataset [40] including semantic and depth ground truth. A LiDAR simulator using ray-casting and a learning process to drop points was proposed in [45], which was tested in detection and segmentation tasks, but is not publicly available. The CARLA simulator [11] allows for photo-realistic simulations of driving scenarios, which we utilize to generate realistic RGB images. While LiDAR scans can be simulated with CARLA via ray-casting, the car shapes are approximated with cuboids, thus losing detail. We leverage the simulator z-buffer to obtain fine-granular depth and then sparsify the signal to simulate LiDAR scans.

3   Method

Our method, shown in Fig. 2, consists of two main components that include an adaptation of the synthetic data to make it similar to the real data, as well as a retrieval of reliable supervision from the real but noisy LiDAR signal.

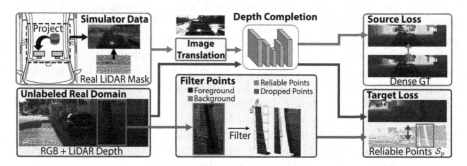

Fig. 2. Overview of our method. We use a simulator with a multicamera set-up and real LiDAR binary masks to transform the synthetic dense depth map into a noisy and sparse depth map. We train in two steps: green blocks are used in the 1st and 2nd step of training while blue blocks in the 2nd step only. In the filtering block, green points are the reliable points S_p and red points are dropped. The *Image Translation* network is pretrained using a CycleGAN approach [12].

3.1   Data Generation via Projections

Supervised depth completion methods strongly rely on the sparse depth input, achieving good performance without RGB information [2,4]. To train a completion model from synthetic data that works well in the real domain we need to generate a synthetic sparse input that reflects the real domain distribution. Instead of simulating a LiDAR via ray-casting, which is computationally expensive and hard to implement [46], we leverage the z-buffer of our synthetic rendering engine to provide a dense depth ground truth at first. Now, we aim to transform this synthetic dense data into a sparse depth resembling a real LiDAR sparse input.

Previous approaches used synthetic sparse data to evaluate a model in indoor scenes or synthetic outdoor scenes [5,35,47]. To sparsify the data a Bernoulli distribution per pixel is used in some works [1,35,47] which, given a probability p_B and a dense depth image x_D, samples each of the pixels $x_{D,k}$ by either keeping the value $x_{D,k}$ with probability p_B or setting its value to 0 with probability $(1 - p_B)$, thus generating the sparse depth $x_D^{s_B}$. We argue that a model trained with $x_D^{s_B}$ does not perform well in the real domain, and our results in Sect. 4 support this observation. There are two reasons for the drop of performance in the real LiDAR data. Firstly, the distribution of the points $x_D^{s_B}$ does not follow the LiDAR sparse distribution. Secondly, there is no noise in the sampled points, as we directly sample from the ground truth. We now address these two issues.

Mimicking LiDAR Sampling Distribution. To simulate a pattern similar to a real LiDAR, we propose to sample at random the real LiDAR inputs $x_{R,D}^s$ from the real domain similarly to [43]. We use $x_{R,D}^s$ to generate a binary mask M_L, which is 1 in $M_{L,k}$ if $x_{R,D,k}^s > 0$ and 0 if $x_{R,D,k}^s = 0$. We then apply the masks to the dense synthetic depth data by $x_D^{s_M} = M_L \odot x_D$. This approach adapts the synthetic data directly to the sparsity level in the real domain without the need to tune it depending on the LiDAR used.

Fig. 3. *Left:* example of the generated projection artifacts in the simulator. The zoomed-in areas marked with red rectangles correspond to $x_D^{s_M}$ and the zoomed-in areas marked with green rectangles to $x_D^{s_P}$, where we can see simulated projection artifacts, *e.g.*, see-through points on the left side of the motorcyclist. *Right:* we reduce the domain gap in the RGB modality using a CycleGAN approach. We show synthetic CARLA images and the resulting adapted images.

Generating Projection Artifacts. Previous works use noise-free sparse data to pre-train [3] or evaluate a model [35] with synthetic data. However, simulating the noise of real sparse data can reduce the domain gap and improve the adaptation result. Real LiDAR depth contains noise from several sources including the asynchronous acquisition due to the rotation of lasers, dropping of points due to low surface reflectance and projection errors. Simulating a LiDAR sampling process by modelling all of these noise sources can be costly and technically difficult as a physics-based rendering engine with additional material properties is necessary to simulate the photon reflections individually. We propose a more pragmatic solution and use the z-buffer of a simulator by assuming that the dominating noise is a consequence of the point cloud projection to the RGB camera reference frame. For such a simulation, the error becomes twofold. Firstly, the

3D points are not exactly projected on the pixel center which produces a minor quantization error. Secondly, as we are projecting a sparse point cloud arising from another viewpoint, we do not have a way to filter the overlapping points by depth. This creates the see-through patterns that do not respect occlusions as shown in Fig. 3 which is also observed in the real domain [48]. Therefore, a simple point drawing from a depth map at the RGB reference cannot recreate this effect and such method does not perform well in the real domain.

To recreate this pattern, we use the CARLA simulator [11], which allows us to capture multicamera synchronized synthetic data. Our CARLA set-up mimics the camera distances in KITTI [40], as our benchmark is the KITTI depth completion dataset [7]. Instead of a LiDAR, we use a virtual dense depth camera. The set-up is illustrated in Fig. 1. As the data is synthetic, the intrinsic and extrinsic parameters needed for the projections are known. After obtaining the depth from the virtual LiDAR camera, we sparsify it using the LiDAR masks resulting in $x_D^{s_M}$, which is then projected onto the RGB reference with

$$x_D^{s_P} = K_{RGB} P_{RGB}^L K_L^{-1} x_D^{s_M} \tag{1}$$

where K_L, K_{RGB} are the LiDAR and RGB camera intrinsics and P_{RGB}^L is the rigid transformation between the LiDAR and RGB reference frame. The resulting $x_D^{s_P}$ is the projected sparse input to either left or right camera.

3.2 RGB Adaptation

Similarly to domain adaptation for depth estimation methods [41,42,49], we address the domain gap in the RGB modality with style translation from synthetic to real images. Due to the complexity of adapting high-resolution images, we first train a model to translate from synthetic to real using a CycleGAN [12] approach. The generator is not further trained and is used to translate the synthetic images to the style of real images, thus reducing the domain gap as shown in Fig. 3.

3.3 Filtering Projection Artifacts for Supervision

In a depth completion setting, the given LiDAR depth can also be used as supervision data, as in [4]. The approach in [4] did not take into account the noise present in the data. The given real-domain LiDAR input is precise in most points with an error of only a few centimeters. However, due to the noise present, some points cannot be used for supervision, such as the see-through points, which have errors in the order of meters. Another method [48] also used the sparse input as guidance for LiDAR-stereo fusion while filtering the noisy points using stereo data. We propose to filter the real-domain noisy input without using additional data such as a stereo pair as this may not always be available.

Our goal is to find a set of reliable sparse points $\mathcal{S}_p$, likely to be correct, for supervision in the real-domain based on the assumption used in Sect. 3.1, i.e., the main source of error are the see-through points after projection. We assume that in any given local window there are two modes of depth distribution, approximated by a closer and a further plane. We show an overview of the idea in Fig. 2. The points from the closer plane are more likely to be correct as part of the occluding objects. To retrieve $\mathcal{S}_p$ we apply a minimum pooling with window size w_p yielding a minimum depth value d_m per window. Then, we include in $\mathcal{S}_p$ the points $s \in [d_m, d_m + \theta]$ where θ is a local thickness parameter of an object. The number of noisy points not filtered out depends on the window w_p and object thickness θ, e.g., larger windows remove more points but the remaining points are more reliable. We use the noise rate η, which is the fraction of noisy points as introduced in noisy labels literature [50–52], to select w_p and θ in the synthetic validation set, thus not requiring any ground truth in the real domain. Section 4 shows that using a large object thickness parameter θ or a small window size w_p leads to a higher noise rate due to an increased tolerance of the filter.

After the filtering step, a certain number of false positives remains. The noisy points in $\mathcal{S}_p$ are more likely to be further away from the dense depth prediction $\hat{y}$, hence the Reverse Huber (BerHu) loss [53] used in the synthetic domain will give more weight to those outliers. To provide extra robustness against these false positives, we use in the real domain a Mean Absolute Error (MAE) loss, as MAE weights all values equally, showing more robustness to the noise.

3.4 Summary of Losses

Our proposed loss is

$$\mathcal{L} = \lambda_S \mathcal{L}_S + \lambda_R \mathcal{L}_R \tag{2}$$

where $\mathcal{L}_S$ is the loss used for the synthetic data, $\mathcal{L}_R$ the loss used for the real data and λ_S and λ_R are hyperparameters.

We use a two-step training approach similar to past domain adaptation works using pseudo-labels [54,55], aiming first for good performance in the synthetic data before introducing noise in the labels. First, we set $\lambda_S = 1.0$ and $\lambda_R = 0.0$, to train only from the synthetic data. For $\mathcal{L}_S$ we use a Reverse Huber loss [53], which works well for depth estimation problems [21]. Hence, we define $\mathcal{L}_S$ as

$$\mathcal{L}_S = \frac{1}{b_S} \sum_i \frac{1}{n_i} \sum_k \mathcal{L}_{bh}(\hat{y}_k, y_k) \tag{3}$$

where b_S is the synthetic batch size, n_i the number of ground truth points in image i, $\hat{y}$ is the predicted dense depth, y is the ground truth depth and $\mathcal{L}_{bh}$ is the Reverse Huber loss.

In the second step we set $\lambda_S = 1.0$ and $\lambda_R = 1.0$ as we introduce real domain data into the training process using $\mathcal{S}_p$ for supervision. We define $\mathcal{L}_R$ as

$$\mathcal{L}_R = \frac{1}{b_R} \sum_i \frac{1}{\#(\mathcal{S}_{p,i})} \sum_k |\hat{y}_k - y_k| \tag{4}$$

where b_R is the real domain batch size and $\#(\mathcal{S}_{p,i})$ is the cardinality of the set of reliable points $\mathcal{S}_p$ for an image i.

Table 1. Ablation study on the selected validation set. *BerHu* refers to using BerHu for real data supervision. All of *2nd Step* results use *LiDAR Mask + Proj + CycleGAN RGB*. We use Bernoulli with $p_B = 0.062$ as the KITTI LiDAR density for the crop used is approximately 6.2%. RMSE and MAE are reported in mm, and iRMSE and iMAE in 1/km.

Model	RMSE	MAE	iRMSE	iMAE
1st Step: only synthetic supervision				
Syn. Baseline 1: Bernoulli ($p_B = 0.062$)	1735.59	392.81	7.68	1.73
+ Proj.	3617.98	1411.36	23.42	9.06
Syn. Baseline 2: LiDAR Mask	1608.32	386.49	7.13	1.76
+ Proj.	1335.00	342.16	5.41	1.55
+ Proj. + CycleGAN RGB	1247.53	308.08	4.54	1.34
2nd Step: adding real data				
No Filter	1315.74	315.40	4.70	1.40
$\mathcal{S}_p$+BerHu	1328.76	320.23	4.25	1.33
Full Pipeline: $\mathcal{S}_p$	**1150.27**	**281.94**	**3.84**	**1.20**
Real GT supervision	802.49	214.04	2.24	0.91

4   Experiments

We use PyTorch 1.3.1 [56] and an NVIDIA 1080 Ti GPU, as well as the official implementation of FusionNet [2] as our sparse-to-dense architecture. The batch size is set to 4 and we use Adam [57] with a learning rate of 0.001. For the synthetic data, we train by randomly projecting to the left or right camera with the same probability. In the first step of training, we use only synthetic data (*i.e.*, $\lambda_S = 1.0$, $\lambda_R = 0.0$, $b_S = 4$ and $b_R = 0$) until performance plateaus in the synthetic validation set. In the second step, we mix real and synthetic data setting $\lambda_S = 1.0$, $\lambda_R = 1.0$, $b_S = 2$, $b_R = 2$, the filter's window size to $w_p = 16$ pixels, the filter's object thickness to $\theta = 0.5$ m, and train for 40,000 iterations.

To test our approach, data from a real LiDAR+RGB set-up is needed as we address the artifacts arising from projecting the LiDAR to the RGB camera. There are no standard real LiDAR+RGB indoor depth completion datasets available. In NYUv2 [58] the dense ground-truth is synthetically sparsified using Bernoulli sampling, while VOID [8] provides sparse depth from visual inertial odometry that contains no projection artifacts. Thus, the KITTI depth completion benchmark [7] is our real domain dataset, as it provides paired real noisy LiDAR depth with RGB images, along with denser depth ground truth for testing. We evaluate our method in the selected validation set and test set, each containing 1,000 images. Following [2], we train using images of 1216 × 256 by cropping their top part. We evaluate on the full resolution images of 1216 × 356. The metrics used are Root Mean Squared Error (RMSE) and Mean Absolute

Error (MAE), reported in mm, and inverse RMSE (iRMSE) and inverse MAE (iMAE), in 1/km.

Synthetic Data. We employ CARLA 0.84 [11] to generate synthetic data using the camera set-up in Fig. 1. We collect images from 154 episodes resulting in 18,022 multicamera images for training and 3,800 for validation. An episode is defined as an expert agent placed at random in the map and driving around while collecting left and right depth+RGB images, as well as the virtual LiDAR depth. We use for the virtual LiDAR camera a regular dense depth camera instead of the provided LiDAR sensor in CARLA because the objects in the LiDAR view are simplified (*e.g.*, CARLA approximates the cars using cuboids). The resolution of the images is 1392×1392 with a Field Of View of $90°$. To match the view and image resolution in KITTI, we first crop the center 1216×356 of the image and then the upper part of 1216×256. To adapt the synthetic RGB images, we train the original implementation of CycleGAN [12] for 180,000 iterations.

Table 2. Results in the validation set depending on the input type for the whole pipeline. RMSE and MAE are reported in mm, and iRMSE and iMAE in 1/km.

Input data	RMSE	MAE	iRMSE	iMAE
Only sparse depth	1175.54	290.51	4.11	1.27
+ RGB	1167.83	289.86	3.87	1.28
+ Img. transfer from [42]	1184.39	306.66	3.99	1.36
+ CycleGAN RGB	**1150.27**	**281.94**	**3.84**	**1.20**

4.1 Ablation Study

We include an ablation study in Table 1 using the validation set. For the result of the whole pipeline, we average the results of three different runs to account for training variability. All of the proposed modules provide an increase in accuracy.

CARLA Adaptation. Table 1 shows that projecting the sparse depth is as important as matching the LiDAR sampling pattern, decreasing the RMSE by 23.1% when used jointly. Table 1 also shows that using Bernoulli sampling and then projecting the sparse depth results in worse performance compared to training only with Bernoulli sampling, showing that it is the combination of using a LiDAR distribution of points and projection to another camera which reduces the domain gap. Even though CycleGAN mostly adapts the brightness, contrast and colors of the images as shown in Fig. 3, using image translation further reduces the RMSE by 6.6% when used jointly with real LiDAR masks sampling and projections. Figure 4 includes some predictions for examples with projection artifacts, showing that simulating the see-through artifacts via projections in the synthetic images is crucial to deal with the noisy input in the real domain.

Introducing Real Domain Data. Using the reliable points S_p as supervision in the real domain alongside the MAE loss function increases the performance as Table 1 shows. If we use BerHu along with reliable points supervision, the method deteriorates as the noisy points are likely to dominate the loss. Using MAE without filtering also drops the performance due to the high noise rate η. These results show that using the noisy LiDAR points for supervision as in [4,8] is detrimental to the performance. If we define a point to be noisy if its difference with the ground-truth is more than 0.3 m, the noise rate η for the unfiltered depth is 5.8%, and with our filtering method is reduced to 1.7% while dropping 45.8% of input points. The results suggest that η in S_p is more important than the total amount of points used for supervision. Supervising with real filtered data (*Full Pipeline*) improves both synthetic baselines (*Syn. Baseline*) in Table 1.

Impact of RGB Modality. Contrary to self-supervised methods, which use RGB information to compute a photometric loss, we do not require the RGB image for good performance as shown in Table 2. Including RGB information reduces the error by 0.7% in RMSE, and by using the CycleGAN RGB images the RMSE is reduced by 2.1%. In a fully supervised manner the difference is 16.3% for FusionNet [2], showing that methods aiming to further reduce the RGB domain gap may increase the overall performance. Due to computational constraints, we train the CycleGAN model in a separate step. To test an end-to-end approach, we use the method in [42], which does not use cycle-consistency, but we obtained lower-quality translated images and larger error as Table 2 shows.

Table 3. Comparison of results in the KITTI selected validation set and the official online test set. *DA Base* is our Domain Adaptation baseline formed by CycleGAN [12] + LiDAR Masks. RMSE and MAE are reported in mm, and iRMSE and iMAE in 1/km.

Model	Param.	Validation set				Online test set			
		RMSE	MAE	iRMSE	iMAE	RMSE	MAE	iRMSE	iMAE
Unsuperv.									
DDP [5]	18.8M	1325.79	355.86	–	–	1285.14	353.16	3.69	1.37
Self-Sup.									
SS-S2D [4]	27.8M	1384.85	358.92	4.32	1.60	1299.85	350.32	4.07	1.57
DDP+St. [5]	18.8M	1310.03	347.17	–	–	1263.19	343.46	3.58	1.32
VOICED [8]	9.7M	1239.06	305.06	3.71	1.21	1169.97	299.41	3.56	1.20
Dom. Ada.									
DA Base	2.6M	1630.31	423.70	6.64	1.98	–	–	–	–
+ D. Out.	2.6M	1636.89	390.59	6.78	1.78	–	–	–	–
+ D. Feat.	2.6M	1617.41	389.88	7.01	1.79	–	–	–	–
Ours	2.6M	1150.27	281.94	3.84	1.20	1095.26	280.42	3.53	1.19
Ours-S2D	16.0M	1211.97	296.19	4.24	1.33	–	–	–	–
+ Self-Sup.									
Ours+SS [4]	2.6M	**1112.83**	**268.79**	**3.27**	**1.12**	1062.48	268.37	3.12	1.13
Supervised									
S-S2D [4]	27.8M	878.56	260.90	3.25	1.34	814.73	249.95	2.80	1.21
FusionNet [2]	2.6M	802.49	214.04	2.24	0.91	772.87	215.02	2.19	0.93
DDP [5]	18.8M	–	–	–	–	836.00	205.40	2.12	0.86

4.2   Method Evaluation

Comparison to State-of-the-Art. In Table 3 we compare our method, *Ours*, with the real domain GT-free state-of-the-art. In the test set our method decreases the RMSE by 6.4%, the MAE by 6.3% and obtains better results for iRMSE and iMAE compared to VOICED [8]. Note that these improvements upon previous methods are obtained by using an architecture with fewer parameters. Table 1 and Table 3 show that we achieve similar results to [8] by training only with synthetic data, *i.e.*, in the first training step, which validates the observation that the main source of error to simulate are the see-through points. DDP [29] uses synthetic ground truth from Virtual KITTI [10] for training, however no adaptation is performed on the synthetic data, resulting in worse results compared to our method even when using stereo pairs (*DDP+St.*). Both VOICED [8] and SS-S2D [4] use, besides video self-supervision, the noisy sparse input as supervision with no filtering, reducing the achievable performance as shown in Table 1 in *No Filter*.

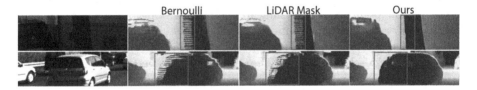

Fig. 4. Qualitative results with different training methodologies. *Bernoulli* refers to training using $x_D^{s_B}$, *LiDAR Mask* to training using $x_D^{s_M}$ and *Ours* to our full pipeline. Both rows show projection artifacts which we deal with correctly.

Domain Adaptation Baselines. Following synthetic-to-real depth estimation methods [41,42], we use as a domain adaptation baseline a CycleGAN [12] to adapt the images. To sparsify the synthetic depth, we use the real LiDAR masks [43], shown in Table 1 to perform better than Bernoulli sampling. The performance of this domain adaptation baseline is presented in Table 3 in *DA Base*. We explore the use of adversarial approaches to match synthetic and real distributions on top of the *DA Base*. *DA Base + D. Out.* in Table 3 uses an output discriminator using the architecture in [59], with an adversarial loss weight of 0.001 similarly to [60]. Following [42], we also tested a feature discriminator in the model bottleneck in *DA Base + D. Feat.* with weight 0.01. Table 3 shows that the use of discriminators has a small performance impact and that standard domain adaptation pipelines are not capable of bridging the domain gap.

Semi-supervised Learning. In some settings, a subset of the real data may be annotated. Our full pipeline mimics the noise in the real sparse depth and takes advantage of the unannotated data by using the filtered reliable points $\mathcal{S}_p$ for supervision. This provides a good initialization for further finetuning with any

Table 4. Semi-supervised results in the selected validation set for different pretraining strategies before finetuning on available annotations. S and I are the number of annotated sequences and images respectively. For *Only supervised*, the weights are randomly initialized. RMSE and MAE are reported in mm, and iRMSE and iMAE in 1/km.

Pretraining strategy	S:1/I:196		S:3/I:1508		S:5/I:2690	
	RMSE	MAE	RMSE	MAE	RMSE	MAE
Only supervised	2578.72	1175.78	1177.90	302.30	1042.75	295.73
DA baseline	1130.79	310.68	1042.70	255.56	986.09	244.94
Ours	**1106.30**	**262.29**	**996.28**	**247.00**	**949.63**	**242.61**

available annotations as Table 4 shows. Compared to pretraining using the *DA Baseline*, our method achieves in all cases a better performance after finetuning.

Hyper-parameter Selection. We do not tune the loss weights λ_S and λ_R. The projected points x_D^{sP} in the synthetic validation set are used to choose the filter window size w_p and the filter object thickness θ by employing the noise rate η in the reliable points S_p as the indicator for the filtering process performance. Figure 5 shows the noise percentage depending on w_p and θ, where we see that curves for the noise rate η follow a similar pattern in both the synthetic and real domain. We first select w_p and then θ as the gain in performance is lower for θ. The optimal values found are $w_p = 16$ pixels and $\theta = 0.5$ m. Figure 5 also shows the MAE depending on the number of iterations in the second step. After 40,000 training iterations, we did not see any improvement.

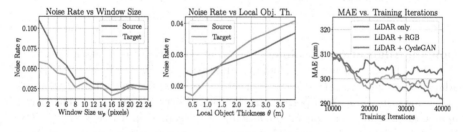

Fig. 5. Hyperparameter analysis. The two left images show the noise rate η vs. w_p ($\theta = 0.5$ m) and θ ($w_p = 16$ pixels). The right plot shows MAE vs. number of training iterations in the second step, where we evaluate every 400 iterations, use a moving average with window size 25 and average 3 runs to reduce the variance.

Adding Self-supervision. When real domain video data is available, our approach can be combined with self-supervised methods [4,8]. *Ours+SS* in Table 3 adds the photometric loss $\lambda_{ph}\mathcal{L}_{ph}$ from [4] to our pipeline during the second step of training for the real data, with $\lambda_{ph} = 10$ to have similar loss values as $\mathcal{L}_S + \mathcal{L}_R$. *Ours+SS* further reduces the error in the test set and achieves, compared to VOICED [8], a lower RMSE by 9.2% and a lower MAE by 10.4%.

Fig. 6. Qualitative results in PandaSet [61] for our *DA Baseline* and full method (*Ours*) trained in CARLA and KITTI. RGB images also show sparse depth input.

Model Agnosticism. We chose FusionNet [2] as our main architecture, but we test our approach with the 18-layers architecture from [4] to show our method is robust to changes of architecture. Due to memory constraints we use the 18-layers architecture instead of the 34-layers model from [4], which accounts for the different parameter count in Table 3 between *Ours-S2D* and *SS-S2D*. We set the batch size to 2, increase the number of iterations in the second step to 90,000 (the last 20,000 iterations use a lower learning rate of 10^{-4}), and freeze the batch normalization statistics in the second step. The result is given in Table 3 in *Ours w/S2D arch.*, which achieves state-of-the-art RMSE and MAE.

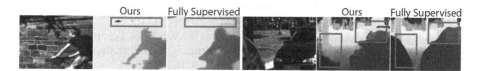

Fig. 7. Failure cases of our method in KITTI, which cannot correct all types of noise. The left side example shows a set of noisy inputs on the wall. The right side example shows dropping of points due to low-reflectance black surfaces.

Qualitative Results in PandaSet [61] are shown in Fig. 6 for our full method compared to the DA Baseline trained for CARLA and KITTI without further tuning. PandaSet contains a different camera set-up and physical distances compared to the one used in training, *e.g.*, top row in Fig. 6 corresponds to a back camera not present in KITTI. Our method is still capable of better correcting projection artifacts (top row and middle row) and completing the missing data (bottom row) compared to the DA Baseline. PandaSet does not provide depth completion ground-truth, thus no quantitative results can be computed.

Limitations. While we addressed see-through artifacts, other types of noise can be present in the real sparse depth as Fig. 7 shows. The left side example shows a set of noisy inputs on the wall that is not corrected. The right side example shows missing points in the prediction due to the lack of data in the black hood surface. The fully supervised model deals properly with these cases, suggesting that approaches focused on other types of noise could further decrease the error.

5   Conclusions

We proposed a domain adaptation method for sparse depth completion using data-driven masking and projections to imitate real noisy and sparse depth in synthetic data. The main source of noise in a joint RGB + LiDAR set-up was assumed to be the see-through artifacts due to projection from the LiDAR to the RGB reference frame. We also found a set of reliable points in the real data that are used for additional supervision, which helped to reduce the domain gap and to improve the performance of our model. A promising direction is to investigate the use of orthogonal domain adaptation techniques capable of leveraging the RGB inputs even more to correct also other types of error in the LiDAR co-modality.

Acknowledgements. This research was supported by UK EPSRC IPALM project EP/S032398/1.

References

1. Mal, F., Karaman, S.: Sparse-to-dense: depth prediction from sparse depth samples and a single image. In: 2018 IEEE International Conference on Robotics and Automation (ICRA), pp. 1–8. IEEE (2018)
2. Van Gansbeke, W., Neven, D., De Brabandere, B., Van Gool, L.: Sparse and noisy lidar completion with RGB guidance and uncertainty. In: International Conference on Machine Vision Applications (MVA), pp. 1–6. IEEE (2019)
3. Qiu, J., et al.: DeepLiDAR: deep surface normal guided depth prediction for outdoor scene from sparse lidar data and single color image. In: Proceedings of the IEEE/CVF Conference on Computer Vision and Pattern Recognition (CVPR), pp. 3313–3322 (2019)
4. Ma, F., Cavalheiro, G.V., Karaman, S.: Self-supervised sparse-to-dense: self-supervised depth completion from LiDAR and monocular camera. In: 2019 International Conference on Robotics and Automation (ICRA), pp. 3288–3295. IEEE (2019)
5. Yang, Y., Wong, A., Soatto, S.: Dense depth posterior (DDP) from single image and sparse range. In: Proceedings of the IEEE/CVF Conference on Computer Vision and Pattern Recognition (CVPR), pp. 3353–3362 (2019)
6. Xu, Y., Zhu, X., Shi, J., Zhang, G., Bao, H., Li, H.: Depth completion from sparse LiDAR data with depth-normal constraints. In: Proceedings of the IEEE/CVF International Conference on Computer Vision (ICCV), pp. 2811–2820 (2019)
7. Uhrig, J., Schneider, N., Schneider, L., Franke, U., Brox, T., Geiger, A.: Sparsity invariant CNNs. In: Proceedings of the International Conference on 3D Vision (3DV)), pp. 11–20. IEEE (2017)
8. Wong, A., Fei, X., Tsuei, S., Soatto, S.: Unsupervised depth completion from visual inertial odometry. IEEE Robot. Autom. Lett. **5**, 1899–1906 (2020)

9. Ros, G., Sellart, L., Materzynska, J., Vazquez, D., Lopez, A.M.: The SYNTHIA dataset: a large collection of synthetic images for semantic segmentation of urban scenes. In: Proceedings of the IEEE/CVF Conference on Computer Vision and Pattern Recognition (CVPR), pp. 3234–3243 (2016)

10. Gaidon, A., Wang, Q., Cabon, Y., Vig, E.: Virtual worlds as proxy for multi-objcct tracking analysis. In: Proceedings of the IEEE/CVF Conference on Computer Vision and Pattern Recognition (CVPR) (2016)

11. Dosovitskiy, A., Ros, G., Codevilla, F., Lopez, A., Koltun, V.: CARLA: an open urban driving simulator. In: Proceedings of the Conference on Robot Learning (CoRL), pp. 1–16 (2017)

12. Zhu, J.Y., Park, T., Isola, P., Efros, A.A.: Unpaired image-to-image translation using cycle-consistent adversarial networks. In: Proceedings of the IEEE/CVF International Conference on Computer Vision (ICCV), pp. 2223–2232 (2017)

13. Scharstein, D., Szeliski, R.: A taxonomy and evaluation of dense two-frame stereo correspondence algorithms. Int. J. Comput. Vision (IJCV) **47**, 7–42 (2002)

14. Lazaros, N., Sirakoulis, G.C., Gasteratos, A.: Review of stereo vision algorithms: from software to hardware. Int. J. Optomechatronics **2**, 435–462 (2008)

15. Tippetts, B., Lee, D.J., Lillywhite, K., Archibald, J.: Review of stereo vision algorithms and their suitability for resource-limited systems. J. Real-Time Image Proc. (JRTIP) **11**, 5–25 (2016)

16. Faugeras, O.D., Lustman, F.: Motion and structure from motion in a piecewise planar environment. Int. J. Pattern Recognit. Artif. Intell. (IJPRAI) **2**, 485–508 (1988)

17. Huang, T.S., Netravali, A.N.: Motion and structure from feature correspondences: a review. In: Advances In Image Processing And Understanding, pp. 331–347. World Scientific (2002)

18. Handa, A., Whelan, T., McDonald, J., Davison, A.J.: A benchmark for RGB-D visual odometry, 3D reconstruction and slam. In: Proceedings of the IEEE International Conference on Robotics and Automation (ICRA), pp. 1524–1531. IEEE (2014)

19. Mur-Artal, R., Tardós, J.D.: ORB-SLAM2: an open-source slam system for monocular, stereo, and RGB-D cameras. IEEE Trans. Rob. (T-RO) **33**, 1255–1262 (2017)

20. Engel, J., Koltun, V., Cremers, D.: Direct sparse odometry. IEEE Trans. Pattern Anal. Mach. Intell. (TPAMI) **40**, 611–625 (2018)

21. Laina, I., Rupprecht, C., Belagiannis, V., Tombari, F., Navab, N.: Deeper depth prediction with fully convolutional residual networks. In: Proceedings of the International Conference on 3D Vision (3DV), pp. 239–248. IEEE (2016)

22. Godard, C., Mac, O., Gabriel, A., Brostow, J.: UCL_unsupervised monocular depth estimation with left-right consistency. In: Proceedings of the IEEE/CVF Conference on Computer Vision and Pattern Recognition (CVPR), p. 7 (2017)

23. Guo, X., Li, H., Yi, S., Ren, J., Wang, X.: Learning monocular depth by distilling cross-domain stereo networks. In: Ferrari, V., Hebert, M., Sminchisescu, C., Weiss, Y. (eds.) ECCV 2018. LNCS, vol. 11215, pp. 506–523. Springer, Cham (2018). https://doi.org/10.1007/978-3-030-01252-6_30

24. Li, Z., Snavely, N.: MegaDepth: learning single-view depth prediction from internet photos. In: Proceedings of the IEEE/CVF Conference on Computer Vision and Pattern Recognition (CVPR), pp. 2041–2050 (2018)

25. Godard, C., Aodha, O.M., Firman, M., Brostow, G.J.: Digging into self-supervised monocular depth estimation. In: Proceedings of the IEEE/CVF International Conference on Computer Vision (ICCV), pp. 3828–3838 (2019)

26. Eigen, D., Puhrsch, C., Fergus, R.: Depth map prediction from a single image using a multi-scale deep network. In: Advances in Neural Information Processing Systems (NIPS), pp. 2366–2374 (2014)

27. Poggi, M., Tosi, F., Mattoccia, S.: Learning monocular depth estimation with unsupervised trinocular assumptions. In: Proceedings of the International Conference on 3D Vision (3DV) (2018)

28. Klodt, M., Vedaldi, A.: Supervising the new with the old: learning SFM from SFM. In: Ferrari, V., Hebert, M., Sminchisescu, C., Weiss, Y. (eds.) ECCV 2018. LNCS, vol. 11214, pp. 713–728. Springer, Cham (2018). https://doi.org/10.1007/978-3-030-01249-6_43

29. Yang, N., Wang, R., Stückler, J., Cremers, D.: Deep virtual stereo odometry: leveraging deep depth prediction for monocular direct sparse odometry. In: Ferrari, V., Hebert, M., Sminchisescu, C., Weiss, Y. (eds.) ECCV 2018. LNCS, vol. 11212, pp. 835–852. Springer, Cham (2018). https://doi.org/10.1007/978-3-030-01237-3_50

30. Watson, J., Firman, M., Brostow, G.J., Turmukhambetov, D.: Self-supervised monocular depth hints. In: Proceedings of the IEEE/CVF International Conference on Computer Vision (ICCV), pp. 2162–2171 (2019)

31. Voynov, O., et al.: Perceptual deep depth super-resolution. In: Proceedings of the IEEE/CVF International Conference on Computer Vision (ICCV), pp. 5653–5663 (2019)

32. Lutio, R.d., D'Aronco, S., Wegner, J.D., Schindler, K.: Guided super-resolution as pixel-to-pixel transformation. In: Proceedings of the IEEE/CVF International Conference on Computer Vision (ICCV), pp. 8829–8837 (2019)

33. Riegler, G., Rüther, M., Bischof, H.: ATGV-Net: accurate depth super-resolution. In: Leibe, B., Matas, J., Sebe, N., Welling, M. (eds.) ECCV 2016. LNCS, vol. 9907, pp. 268–284. Springer, Cham (2016). https://doi.org/10.1007/978-3-319-46487-9_17

34. Ku, J., Harakeh, A., Waslander, S.L.: In defense of classical image processing: fast depth completion on the CPU. In: Proceedings of the Conference on Computer and Robot Vision (CRV), pp. 16–22.. IEEE (2018)

35. Jaritz, M., De Charette, R., Wirbel, E., Perrotton, X., Nashashibi, F.: Sparse and dense data with CNNs: depth completion and semantic segmentation. In: Proceedings of the International Conference on 3D Vision (3DV), pp. 52–60. IEEE (2018)

36. Chodosh, N., Wang, C., Lucey, S.: Deep convolutional compressed sensing for LiDAR depth completion. In: Jawahar, C.V., Li, H., Mori, G., Schindler, K. (eds.) ACCV 2018. LNCS, vol. 11361, pp. 499–513. Springer, Cham (2019). https://doi.org/10.1007/978-3-030-20887-5_31

37. Eldesokey, A., Felsberg, M., Khan, F.S.: Confidence propagation through CNNs for guided sparse depth regression. IEEE Trans. Pattern Anal. Mach. Intell. (TPAMI) **42**, 2423–2436 (2019)

38. Lee, B.U., Jeon, H.G., Im, S., Kweon, I.S.: Depth completion with deep geometry and context guidance. In: Proceedings of the International Conference on Robotics and Automation (ICRA), pp. 3281–3287. IEEE (2019)

39. Chen, Y., Yang, B., Liang, M., Urtasun, R.: Learning joint 2D–3D representations for depth completion. In: Proceedings of the IEEE/CVF International Conference on Computer Vision (ICCV) (2019)

40. Geiger, A., Lenz, P., Urtasun, R.: Are we ready for autonomous driving? The KITTI vision benchmark suite. In: Proceedings of the IEEE/CVF Conference on Computer Vision and Pattern Recognition (CVPR), pp. 3354–3361. IEEE (2012)

41. Atapour-Abarghouei, A., Breckon, T.P.: Real-time monocular depth estimation using synthetic data with domain adaptation via image style transfer. In: Proceedings of the IEEE/CVF Conference on Computer Vision and Pattern Recognition (CVPR), pp. 2800–2810 (2018)

42. Zheng, C., Cham, T.-J., Cai, J.: T^2Net: synthetic-to-realistic translation for solving single-image depth estimation tasks. In: Ferrari, V., Hebert, M., Sminchisescu, C., Weiss, Y. (eds.) ECCV 2018. LNCS, vol. 11211, pp. 798–814. Springer, Cham (2018). https://doi.org/10.1007/978-3-030-01234-2_47

43. Atapour-Abarghouei, A., Breckon, T.P.: To complete or to estimate, that is the question: a multi-task approach to depth completion and monocular depth estimation. In: Proceedings of the International Conference on 3D Vision (3DV), pp. 183–193. IEEE (2019)

44. Mayer, N., et al.: What makes good synthetic training data for learning disparity and optical flow estimation? Int. J. Comput. Vision (IJCV) **126**, 942–960 (2018)

45. Manivasagam, S., et al.: LiDARsim: realistic lidar simulation by leveraging the real world. In: Proceedings of the IEEE/CVF Conference on Computer Vision and Pattern Recognition (CVPR), pp. 11167–11176 (2020)

46. Yue, X., Wu, B., Seshia, S.A., Keutzer, K., Sangiovanni-Vincentelli, A.L.: A LiDAR point cloud generator: from a virtual world to autonomous driving. In: Proceedings of the 2018 ACM on International Conference on Multimedia Retrieval (ICMR), pp. 458–464. ACM (2018)

47. Huang, Z., Fan, J., Yi, S., Wang, X., Li, H.: HMS-Net: hierarchical multi-scale sparsity-invariant network for sparse depth completion. arXiv preprint arXiv:1808.08685 (2018)

48. Cheng, X., Zhong, Y., Dai, Y., Ji, P., Li, H.: Noise-aware unsupervised deep Lidar-stereo fusion. In: Proceedings of the IEEE/CVF Conference on Computer Vision and Pattern Recognition (CVPR), pp. 6339–6348 (2019)

49. Zhao, S., Fu, H., Gong, M., Tao, D.: Geometry-aware symmetric domain adaptation for monocular depth estimation. In: Proceedings of the IEEE/CVF Conference on Computer Vision and Pattern Recognition (CVPR), pp. 9788–9798 (2019)

50. Li, J., Wong, Y., Zhao, Q., Kankanhalli, M.S.: Learning to learn from noisy labeled data. In: Proceedings of the IEEE/CVF Conference on Computer Vision and Pattern Recognition (CVPR), pp. 5051–5059 (2019)

51. Han, B., et al.: Co-teaching: robust training of deep neural networks with extremely noisy labels. In: Advances in Neural Information Processing Systems (NIPS), pp. 8527–8537 (2018)

52. Zhang, Z., Sabuncu, M.: Generalized cross entropy loss for training deep neural networks with noisy labels. In: Advances in Neural Information Processing Systems (NIPS), pp. 8778–8788 (2018)

53. Zwald, L., Lambert-Lacroix, S.: The BerHu penalty and the grouped effect. arXiv preprint arXiv:1207.6868 (2012)

54. Zou, Y., Yu, Z., Vijaya Kumar, B.V.K., Wang, J.: Unsupervised domain adaptation for semantic segmentation via class-balanced self-training. In: Ferrari, V., Hebert, M., Sminchisescu, C., Weiss, Y. (eds.) ECCV 2018. LNCS, vol. 11207, pp. 297–313. Springer, Cham (2018). https://doi.org/10.1007/978-3-030-01219-9_18

55. Tang, K., Ramanathan, V., Fei-Fei, L., Koller, D.: Shifting weights: adapting object detectors from image to video. In: Advances in Neural Information Processing Systems (NIPS), pp. 638–646 (2012)

56. Paszke, A., et al.: Automatic differentiation in PyTorch. In: Advances in Neural Information Processing Systems (NIPS), Autodiff Workshop (2017)

57. Kingma, D.P., Ba, J.: Adam: a method for stochastic optimization. In: Proceedings of the International Conference on Learning Representations (ICLR) (2015)
58. Silberman, N., Hoiem, D., Kohli, P., Fergus, R.: Indoor segmentation and support inference from RGBD images. In: Fitzgibbon, A., Lazebnik, S., Perona, P., Sato, Y., Schmid, C. (eds.) ECCV 2012. LNCS, vol. 7576, pp. 746–760. Springer, Heidelberg (2012). https://doi.org/10.1007/978-3-642-33715-4_54
59. Pilzer, A., Xu, D., Puscas, M., Ricci, E., Sebe, N.: Unsupervised adversarial depth estimation using cycled generative networks. In: Proceedings of the International Conference on 3D Vision (3DV), pp. 587–595. IEEE (2018)
60. Tsai, Y.H., Hung, W.C., Schulter, S., Sohn, K., Yang, M.H., Chandraker, M.: Learning to adapt structured output space for semantic segmentation. In: Proceedings of the IEEE/CVF Conference on Computer Vision and Pattern Recognition (CVPR), pp. 7472–7481 (2018)
61. Scale AI: Pandaset (2020). https://scale.com/open-datasets/pandaset

Dynamic Depth Fusion and Transformation for Monocular 3D Object Detection

Erli Ouyang[1], Li Zhang[1], Mohan Chen[1], Anurag Arnab[2], and Yanwei Fu[1(✉)]

[1] School of Data Science, and MOE Frontiers Center for Brain Science, Shanghai Key Lab of Intelligent Information Processing, Fudan University, Shanghai, China
{eouyang18,lizhangfd,mhchen19,yanweifu}@fudan.edu.cn
[2] University of Oxford, Oxford, UK

Abstract. Visual-based 3D detection is drawing a lot of attention recently. Despite the best efforts from the computer vision researchers visual-based 3D detection remains a largely unsolved problem. This is primarily due to the lack of accurate depth perception provided by LiDAR sensors. Previous works struggle to fuse 3D spatial information and the RGB image effectively. In this paper, we propose a novel monocular 3D detection framework to address this problem. Specifically, we propose to primary contributions: (i) We design an *Adaptive Depth-guided Instance Normalization* layer to leverage depth features to guide RGB features for high quality estimation of 3D properties. (ii) We introduce a *Dynamic Depth Transformation* module to better recover accurate depth according to semantic context learning and thus facilitate the removal of depth ambiguities that exist in the RGB image. Experiments show that our approach achieves state-of-the-art on KITTI 3D detection benchmark among current monocular 3D detection works.

Keywords: 3D object detection · Monocular

1 Introduction

3D object detection from images plays an essential role in self-driving cars and robotics. Powered by the effective deep point clouds processing techniques [1,2], recent LiDAR-based 3D detectors [3–8] have achieved superior performance through exploiting accurate depth information scanned by sensors. However, LiDAR is too expensive for some low cost scenarios and has a limited perception range, i.e., usually less than 100 m. On the other hand, 3D from 2D is a fundamentally ill-posed problem, and estimating 3D bounding boxes from images remains a challenging task, due to the difficulty in drawing missing spatial information in 2D images. In spite of this, recent image-based 3D detectors have

E. Ouyang, L. Zhang—Authors contributed equally to this paper.
This work was supported in part by NSFC Projects (U62076067), Science and Technology Commission of Shanghai Municipality Projects (19511120700, 19ZR1471800).

© Springer Nature Switzerland AG 2021
H. Ishikawa et al. (Eds.): ACCV 2020, LNCS 12622, pp. 349–364, 2021.
https://doi.org/10.1007/978-3-030-69525-5_21

Ours   Pseudo-LiDAR

Depth map from DORN   Ground truth

Fig. 1. We propose a novel monocular 3D detection approach. Pseudo-LidAR point cloud-based methods, i.e., Pseudo-LidAR [19], rely much on the quality of depth map (DORN [23]) and our methods fuse depth information and color context for more accurate object 3D properties. Our approach also handle occlusion issue well. (As shown in zoomed in region, where Pseudo-LidAR is affected by serious occlusion problem.) (Color figure online)

made some progress with the help of carefully designed network architectures. However, there still exists a huge performance gap between them and LiDAR-based approaches due to the ambiguities of 2D color images. Thus, predicted depth maps are introduced to help resolve context vagueness.

Some early monocular image 3D detection approaches [9–11] either utilize additional input features for more context information such as instance/semantic segmentation [12–18] or directly regress the 3D bounding boxes by 2D convolutional layers. However, it is still hard for them to recover 3D from 2D inputs, which leads to relatively poor results. Recent work [19,20] transfers the generated depth map into point clouds, and show that the depth data representation matters in the 3D detection task. However, they are sensitive to input depth quality and the procedure is complex as a result of point clouds processing, e.g., segmenting an object's point cloud from its surroundings.

The dense disparity (inverse of depth) map could be inferred by stereo matching equipped with convolutional neural networks, which motivates some stereo-based 3D detection works [21,22]. However, their accuracy still falls behind LiDAR-methods and camera calibration is also needed, i.e., stereo cameras must be maintained at the same horizontal level. Therefore, monocular methods [9–11,19,20] fit in more various scenarios where stereo is not available or practical.

In this paper, we propose a novel image-based 3D detection framework, aiming to address the following key issues in monocular 3D detection field: (1) Inefficient utilization for generated depth maps. For methods [19,20] using pseudo-LiDAR point clouds, they rely heavily on the accuracy of depth maps. Moreover, depth maps generated from state-of-the-art deep networks still tend to be blurry on the objects boundary and thus re-projected point clouds are noisy, which makes results sensitive. (2) Inaccurate spatial location estimation for occluded objects. Occlusion happens in typical autonomous driving scenes, and these cases affect detector performance greatly because it is difficult for traditional 2D convolution to capture correct depth information of occluded objects. To solve these aforementioned problems, we propose two effective modules respectively for each of the issues as shown in Fig. 1. Specifically, we first propose an Adaptive Depth-guided Instance Normalization (AdaDIN) layer to fuse depth features and color features in a more effective way, where the depth features are utilized as an adaptive guidance to normalize color features to recover hidden depth message from the 2D color map. Secondly, we design a novel Dynamic Depth Transformation (DDT) module to address the object occlusion problem, in which we sample and transfer depth values dynamically from tje depth map in the target objects' region by using deformable kernels generated over fused features.

To summarize, this works makes the following contributions:

- We propose an AdaDIN layer, where color features are adaptively normalized by depth feature to recover 3D spatial information.
- We design a novel Dynamic Depth transformation module to sample depth value from target region to determine object spatial location properly.
- Evaluation on KITTI datasets [24] shows that our proposed method achieves the state-of-the-art among all monocular approaches on 3D detection and Bird's eye view detection.

2   Related Work

For 3D objects detection task, the methods could be grouped into two classes: LiDAR-based and image-based. Here we briefly review relevant works.

Image-Based 3D Object Detection. For lack of accurate depth information, 3D object detectors using only monocular/stereo image data is generally worse than those using LiDAR data. For monocular input, early works [9,10] take a strategy of aligning 2D-3D bounding boxes, predicting 3D proposals based on the 2D detection results and additional features extracted from segmentation, shape, context and location. Since the image-based 3D detection is an ill-posed problem, more recent works [25–27] utilize objects prior like objects shape and geometry constraints to predict the results. GS3D [25] generates refined detection results by an estimated coarse basic cuboid from 2D results. M3D-RPN [26] is a one stage detector, where a depth-aware convolutional layer is designed to learn features related to depth. In contrast, our approach adopt a depth map estimated from monocular as well as color image to fully utilize depth information for better results.

As for stereo, there are a small number of arts compared with monocular so far. 3DOP [21] generates 3D box proposals by exploiting object size priors, ground plane and a variety of depth informed features (e.g., point cloud density).

Finally they combine a CNN to score the proposal boxes. Stereo R-CNN [22] first estimates 2D bounding box and key-point information and solves the 3D boxes by optimizing a group of geometry constraints equations.

Nevertheless, the traditional 2D convolution does not have enough capability to resolve the 3D spatial message from 2D features, and there is no effective signal transformation ways from depth to color image, which limits the 3D detection performance. Pseudo-LiDAR [19] brings another important option to imaged-based detectors, in which the generated depth map from monocular are re-projected into point clouds and then existing LiDAR-based approaches are applied to point clouds data for 3D results. AM3D [20] further aggregates RGB information into re-projected point clouds for a higher performance. However, point clouds-based methods are sensitive to the quality of input depth maps. In contrast, we normalize color features with depth features, which helps 3D spatial information transfer from depth to color.

LiDAR-Based 3D Object Detection. Most of state-of-the-art 3D object detection methods use LiDAR data. VoxelNet [3] learns a feature representation from point clouds and predict the results. The general point clouds processing architectures [1,2] provide the basic tools for LiDAR-based approaches [4,5] to generate accurate 3D proposals. However, the high price device and large space consumption limit LiDAR-based methods in many scenarios. In this paper, our proposed method takes easily available monocular image and depth map estimated from the same color image as input to produce superior 3D detection results.

3   Methodology

We describe our proposed one-stage monocular 3D detection method in this section. Compared with two-stage approach [20] that also takes the monocular input and depth map as input, our method facilitates a simplified detection procedure while also achieving a higher performance. We first introduce our overall framework, and then we give the details of each key module of our approach.

3.1   Approach Overview

The overall framework of our approach is shown in Fig. 2. The network mainly consists of these modules: image and depth feature extractors, Adaptive Depth-guide instance normalization, Dynamic Depth transformation and 3D detection heads. Our network takes monocular RGB image $\mathcal{I} \in \mathbb{R}^{H \times W \times 3}$ and the corresponding generated depth map $\mathcal{D} \in \mathbb{R}^{H \times W \times 1}$ as input, then extracts the features of both depth map and image, and the depth map feature is utilized to guide feature representation of RGB image by our Depth-guide instance normalization module, which could effectively transfer the depth message to the color feature for accurate 3D bounding box estimation. Afterwards, the depth map is further transformed by our Dynamic Depth transformation to solve occlusion issue which often occurs in autonomous scenes. Our network outputs are generated from 5

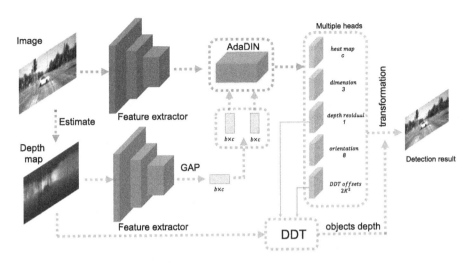

Fig. 2. Overall framework of proposed approach. The color image and the depth map are feed into two feature extractor, and then AdaDIN layer is applied to fuse depth information into color context feature. Multi-heads are attached for 3D bounding box estimation with the help of DDF which address occlusion issue effectively. Note that for simplicity, we omit the two offsets heads (2D center offset and 2D-3D offset) in above figure. The numbers below the multiple heads names are channels of each head.

main independent heads (shown in Fig. 2) and 2 center point offsets heads, and each main head stands for a property of 3D bounding box, e.g., dimension, location, rotation, object center position and its depth. During testing, we parse all the outputs of multiple heads to obtain the final 3D objects bounding boxes as described in Sect. 3.4.

3.2 Adaptive Depth-Guided Instance Normalization

In this section, we introduce our Adaptive Depth-guided Instance Normalization (AdaDIN).

AdaDIN layer is designed to normalize color features by exploiting depth map features. Due to the lack of depth information, it is hard for color feature to estimate 3D properties of objects (i.e., 3D dimension and depth), and how to fuse depth information from depth feature into color features effectively is a key issue for monocular 3D detection. In this work, inspired by [28,29], we normalize the color feature across the spatial dimensions independently for each channel and instance, then the normalized feature is modulated with learned scale γ and bias β generated from the depth feature. Specifically, assume that $\mathcal{F}_I^i \in \mathbb{R}^{C' \times H' \times W'}$ is the extracted feature for image i, where $H' = H/4, W' = W/4$ is feature size, C' is number of feature channel, and note that we omit the mini-batch size for simplicity. $\mathcal{F}_D^i$ is the corresponding depth map feature with the same shape of $\mathcal{F}_I^i$. Then we apply the following normalization ($j \in \{1, \ldots, H'\}, k \in \{1, \ldots, W'\}, c \in \{1, \ldots, C'\}, f_{c,j,k}^i \in \mathcal{F}_I^i,$):

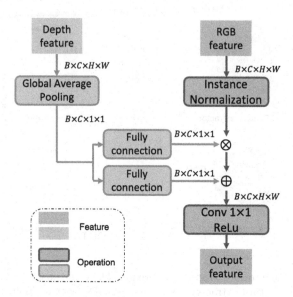

Fig. 3. Adaptive depth-guided instance normalization. The feature from depth map are applied to generate channel-wise affine parameters γ and β for color feature after instance normalization. We first apply a Global Average Pooling to the depth feature, then two independent fully connection layers are utilized to generate two affine parameters for every RGB channel.

$$\mu_c^i = \frac{1}{H' \times W'} \sum_{j,k} f_{c,j,k}^i \tag{1}$$

$$\sigma_c^i = \sqrt{\frac{1}{H' \times W'} \sum_{j,k} \left(f_{c,j,k}^i - \mu_c^i \right)^2 + \epsilon} \tag{2}$$

$$\text{AdaDIN}(f_{c,j,k}^i, \mathcal{F}_D^i) = \gamma_c(\mathcal{F}_D^i) \left(\frac{f_{c,j,k} - \mu_c^i}{\sigma_c^i} \right) + \beta_c(\mathcal{F}_D^i) \tag{3}$$

Where affine parameters γ, β are generated from depth map feature $\mathcal{F}_D^i$. As shown in Fig. 3, the depth map feature is fed into two fully connection layers after a Global Average Pooling (GAP), and the outputs of these two fully connections layers are applied to as affine parameters γ and β for color feature, respectively.

3.3 Dynamic Depth Transformation

Another crucial module of our proposed approach is Dynamic Depth Transformation (DDT). The depth value ($Z-$coordinate in camera coordinate system, in meters) estimation of 3D object is challenging for image-based 3D detectors. The difficulty lies in the domain gap between 2D RGB context and 3D spatial location. Our AdaDIN module effectively transforms the spatial message from depth map to RGB feature for learning more accurate 3D spatial properties, i.e., 3D object dimension and rotation. Furthermore, to determine the exact depth value of a 3D bounding box, we design a novel Dynamic Depth Transformation module.

 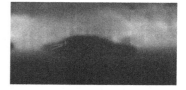

Fig. 4. The intuitive explanation for DDT. When the target object (the car behind) is occluded, we hope to perceive depth value of its center position (red cross) from unoccluded region. (Color figure online)

To fully utilize the depth map which is the most explicit representation of 3D data to estimate the depth value of a target object, we first learn to generate a depth residual map by a head branch attached to the image features, then we sum this estimated depth residual and the input depth map together. To obtain the depth of 3D bounding box center, we select the depth value in summed map indexed by the corresponding object location. The intuition behind this summation is that, when we have the relatively accurate dense depth map that stands for the depth values of object surface, we only need to an additional "depth residual" from the surface of objects to their 3D bounding box centers. However, in real world scenes, objects like cars are often occluded by another one, and this means that the depth value of the target center point is inaccurately represented by the one who occludes it, which makes it hard to learn an accurate depth residual and would harm the performance of center depth estimation, see Fig. 4.

To address this problem, we propose a Dynamic Depth Transformation module, which can dynamically sample and transfer the proper depth values for the target object from surrounding positions who are not occluded, see Fig. 5. Inspired by the [30], we learn a group dynamic offsets conditional on the local input to help a sampling kernel grasp proper depth values.

To start with simple case, for a non-dynamic uniform sampling, we apply a regular grid $\mathcal{R}$ over the dense depth map $D = \{d(p)\}$, where p is 2D index of depth map, for example,

$$\mathcal{R} = \{(-1, -1), (-1, 0), \ldots, (0, 1), (1, 1)\} \tag{4}$$

is a 3×3 sampling kernel with dilation 1. We can get the estimated depth value $\hat{d}(p_0)$ by this uniform kernel at the position p_0:

$$\hat{d}(p_0) = \sum_{p_n \in \mathcal{R}} w(p_n) \cdot d(p_0 + p_n) \tag{5}$$

where w are learnable weights shared by all position p_0.

We can further augment this regular grid $\mathcal{R}$ with offsets $\{\Delta p_n\}$:

$$\hat{d}(p_0) = \sum_{p_n \in \mathcal{R}} w(p_n) \cdot d(p_0 + p_n + \Delta p_n) \tag{6}$$

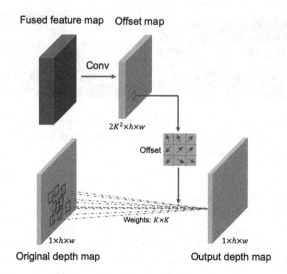

Fig. 5. Dynamic Depth Transformation (DDT). The fused color feature generates offsets for the kernel at every local position and input depth map sample.

Δp_n is dynamically generated conditional on specific sample and local context, which enable network to avoid incorrect depth value in occluded region. The final estimated depth value $d_{obj}(p_0)$ of object 3D bounding box center is:

$$d_{obj}(p_0) = \hat{d}(p_0) + d_{res}(p_0) \tag{7}$$

where d_{res} is estimated depth residual from a 1-channel head. Different from [30], in which the dynamic offsets are obtained by a convolutional layer over the same input feature map, instead, our offsets are estimated over the final RGB features by an attached head. After fusing with depth information by our AdaDIN layers, the final RGB features provide more sufficient local semantic content as well as spatial depth information than raw depth map for obtaining kernel offsets when encountering occlusion.

Note that the offsets of a single location need $K \times K \times 2$ scalars, where K is the size of sample kernel, hence our dynamic offsets head makes a $2K^2$-channel offsets prediction (18 for $K = 3$).

3.4   3D Bounding Box Estimation

To estimate 3D objects bounding boxes, we need the following properties: locations, dimensions and orientation. Locations is determined by the depth and projected 3D location in image plane; Dimensions is the size of bounding boxes (height, width and length); Orientation is the rotation angle of bounding box around $y-$axis (perpendicular to ground). Therefore, we attach multiple heads to the feature extractors to produce a group of 3D predictions, see Fig. 2. Specifically, in addition to the object distance $D \in \mathbb{R}^{H' \times W' \times 1}$ and depth transformation offset $O_{depth} \in \mathbb{R}^{H' \times W' \times 18}$, which have been discussed in Sect. 3.3, the complete model produce a objects 2D center heat-map $\mathcal{H} \in \mathbb{R}^{H' \times W' \times C}$, 2D center offset $O_{2D} \in \mathbb{R}^{H' \times W' \times 2}$, 2D-3D offsets $O_{2D-3D} \in \mathbb{R}^{H' \times W' \times 2}$, objects dimensions $S \in \mathbb{R}^{H' \times W' \times 3}$ and objects rotations $R \in \mathbb{R}^{H' \times W' \times 8}$, where $H' = H/4, W' = W/4$ are the size of output feature and C is the number of objects classes. Next we explain these predictions and corresponding loss objective one by one.

Firstly, to determine the position of object i that belongs to class c ($c = 1, \cdots, C$) in the image plane, we regard 2D centers (x_i^c, y_i^c) of objects as key-points and solve these key-points through estimating a C-channel heat-map $\mathcal{H}$, similar to human pose estimation [31–33]. The 2D center offset O_{2D} is predicted to recover the discretization error caused by the output stride of feature extractor networks. It's worth noting that the 2D center and the projected 3D center on the image plane is not necessarily the same point, i.e., there is an offset from object 2D center to its corresponding projected 3D center, therefore, another output head is desired to predict this offset O_{2D-3D}. In particular, the projected 3D center may not lie in the actual image (i.e., for objects which partially missed lying on the edge of image), and our offset O_{2D-3D} could lead to the correct out-of-image 3D center. All classes share the same offsets O_{2D} and O_{2D-3D}. For an object i, our final prediction of projected 3D center on the image plane is obtained by:

$$(\hat{x}_i^c, \hat{y}_i^c) = (_{int}\hat{x}_i^c + \hat{o}_i^x + \hat{o'}_i^x, {}_{int}\hat{y}_i^c + \hat{o}_i^y + \hat{o'}_i^y) \tag{8}$$

where $(_{int}\hat{x}_i^c, {}_{int}\hat{y}_i^c)$ is integer image coordinate generated from heat-map $\mathcal{H}$, $(\hat{o}_i^x, \hat{o}_i^y)$ is the estimated 2D offset obtained from O_{2D} and $(\hat{o'}_i^x, \hat{o'}_i^y)$ is 2D-3D offset obtained from O_{2D-3D}.

Note that the above object 3D center coordinate is represented on the 2D image plane, to lift it to the 3D space, we can simply re-project the center point to the 3D space by its depth Z_i (obtained from our dynamic depth transformation module) and camera intrinsics which is assumed known from the datasets:

$$Z_i \cdot [x_i, y_i, 1]^\top = K \cdot [X_i, Y_i, Z_i, 1]^\top \tag{9}$$

where $K \in \mathbb{R}^{3 \times 4}$ is camera intrinsics assumed to be known as in [20,33], $[x_i, y_i, 1]^\top$ and $[X_i, Y_i, Z_i, 1]^\top$ are homogeneous coordinates of 3D object center in 2D image plane and 3D space, respectively.

In addition to 3D coordinate of object center, we still need the orientation and object dimension to get the exact 3D bounding boxes. For orientation α, we actually estimate the viewpoint angle, which is more intuitive for humans. Since it is not easy to regress a single orientation value directly, we encode it into 8 scalars lying in 2 bins, with 4 scalars for each bin and then apply a in-bin regression, like [10]. Our orientation head thus outputs a 8-channel prediction R. For object dimension, we regress the height, width and length (h_i, w_i, l_i) for each object with a 3-channel head prediction S.

Loss Objective. Our overall loss is

$$\mathcal{L} = \mathcal{L}_\mathcal{H} + \mathcal{L}_{O,2D} + \mathcal{L}_{O,3D-2D} + \mathcal{L}_{depth} + \mathcal{L}_{dim} + \mathcal{L}_{rotation} \tag{10}$$

For simplicity, we omit the weighting factors for each loss term. Where heatmap loss $\mathcal{L}_{\mathcal{H}}$ is a penalty-reduced pixel-wise logistic regression with focal loss, following [33, 34] $\mathcal{L}_{rotation}$ is orientation regression loss. 2D offset loss $\mathcal{L}_{O,2D}$, 3D-2D offset loss $\mathcal{L}_{O,3D-2D}$, object depth loss $\mathcal{L}_{depth}$ and object dimension loss $\mathcal{L}_{dim}$ are defined as L1-loss ($\mathcal{L}_{dim}$ is in meters and $\mathcal{L}_{O,3D-2D}, \mathcal{L}_{O,2D}$ are in pixels):

$$
\begin{aligned}
\mathcal{L}_{O,2D} &= \tfrac{1}{N} \sum_{i=1}^{N} (o_i^x - \hat{o}_i^x) + (o_i^y - \hat{o}_i^y) \\
\mathcal{L}_{O,3D-2D} &= \tfrac{1}{N} \sum_{i=1}^{N} (o'^x_i - \hat{o}'^x_i) + (o'^y_i - \hat{o}'^y_i) \\
\mathcal{L}_{depth} &= \tfrac{1}{N} \sum_{i=1}^{N} (d_i - \hat{d}_i) \\
\mathcal{L}_{dim} &= \tfrac{1}{N} \sum_{i=1}^{N} (h_i - \hat{h}_i) + (w_i - \hat{w}_i) + (l_i - \hat{l}_i)
\end{aligned}
\tag{11}
$$

where $(o_i^x, o_i^y), (o'^x_i, o'^y_i)$ is ground truth 2D offset and 3D-2D offset of object i, $\hat{h}_i, \hat{w}_i, \hat{l}_i$ are estimated size of object i and N is the number of objects.

3.5 Feature Extraction

In principle, any deep network is suitable for our feature extractor. In our experiments, we adopt Deep Layer Aggregation [35] (DLA-34) architecture as our image and depth feature extractors because DLA balances speed and accuracy well. Original DLA network is designed for image classification task with hierarchical skip connections and we adapt it to our 3D detection framework. Inspired by [33], we adopt a fully convolutional upsampling version of DLA-34 with network stride of 4, and the 3×3 deformable convolution [30] is applied at upsampling layers to replace normal convolution. We have two similar feature extraction networks for RGB image and depth map respectively, and the image and depth map share the same input size $H \times W \times 3$. Note that we tile the original 1-channel depth map three times to form a 3-channel input. The size of output feature is $H/4 \times W/4 \times 64$.

After RGB image and depth map are fed into two DLA-34 feature extractors separately, the feature of depth map is utilized as a guidance for image feature through fusing 3D spatial message from depth map by our Adaptive Depth-guided instance normalization module, which is introduced in Sect. 3.2.

3.6 Implementation Details

Our proposed approach is implemented in PyTorch framework and takes about 12 h to train on 2 NIVIDIA TITAN X GPUs for KITTI. We train our networks for 70 epochs with batch size of 14. For input, we normalize each RGB channel of color image with means and standard deviations calculated over all training data. The input depth maps are inferenced by DORN [23], and are tiled into 3-channel images before fed into feature extractor. The input depth are also normalized with depth mean and standard deviation. When training, encoder of our feature extractor is initialized with ImageNet pretrained weights, and the

Fig. 6. Qualitative results of our 3D detection results on KITTI. Bounding boxes from different class are drawn in different color. (Color figure online)

Adam optimizer is applied with $\beta = [0.9, 0.999]$. Learning rate is initialized with 1.25e−4 and decays at epoch 45 and 60 with 0.1×. All loss weighting factors are set to 1. When testing, we apply non-maximal suppression (NMS) on center point heat-map with the threshold of 0.2.

Table 1. Bird's eye view and 3D detection results: Average Precision (in %) of bird's eye view boxes and 3D bounding boxes on KITTI *validation* set at IoU ≥ 0.5. In Data column, **M** means only taking monocular image as input; **M+D** means taking both monocular image and generated depth map as input.

Method	Data	AP_{BEV}			AP_{3D}		
		Easy	Moderate	Hard	Easy	Moderate	Hard
Mono3D [9]	M	30.50	22.39	19.16	25.19	18.20	15.52
Deep3DBox [10]	M	30.02	23.77	18.83	27.04	20.55	15.88
Monogrnet [36]	M	54.21	39.69	33.06	50.51	36.97	30.82
Multi-fusion [11]	M	55.02	36.73	31.27	47.88	29.48	26.44
M3D-RPN [26]	M	55.37	**42.49**	35.29	48.96	**39.57**	33.01
Ours	M	**56.8**	42.3	**35.9**	**51.60**	38.9	**33.7**
Pseudo-LiDAR [19]	M+D	70.8	49.4	42.7	66.30	42.30	38.50
AM3D [20]	M+D	**72.64**	51.82	44.21	68.86	49.19	42.24
Ours	M+D	71.35	**53.54**	**45.74**	**67.01**	**49.77**	**43.09**

4   Experiments

Datasets. We evaluate our approach on the widely used KITTI 3D detection benchmark [24]. The **KITTI** datasets contains 7,481 RGB images sampled from different scenes with corresponding 3D objects annotations and LiDAR data for training and 7,518 for testing. The calibration parameters are also provided for each frame and the objects are labeled into three classes for evaluation: Car, Pedestrian and Cyclist. To compare with previous works, we split out 3,769 images for validation and remaining 3,712 for training our networks, following [21]. Samples from the same sequence are avoided being included in both training and validation set.

Evaluation Metric. For KITTI, average precision (AP) calculated from precision-recall curves of two tasks are evaluated in our experiments: Bird's Eye View (BEV) and 3D Object Detection. According to the occlusion/truncation and the size of an object in the 2D image, the evaluation has three difficulty setting of easy, moderate and hard under IoU ≥ 0.5 or 0.7 per class. We show the major results on Car to compare with previous works.

4.1   Results on KITTI

We conduct our experiments on KITTI split [21]. The results on KITTI *validation* set are shown in Table 1 and Table 2 (IoU ≥ 0.5 and IoU ≥ 0.7, respectively). We only list the monocular image-based methods here for fair comparison. For our model without depth map input, we just remove our DDT (Dynamic Depth transformation) module and replace Adaptive Depth-guided Instance Normalization (AdaDIN) layer with normal Instance Normalization.

Then our results still outperforms all approaches who take only single image as input under easy and hard difficulty, and we also show a close accuracy with M3D-RPN [26] under moderate difficulty.

For our full model, we achieve state-of-the-art among all methods under moderate and hard difficulty at IoU $\geq$ 0.5, and also performs closely with AM3D [20]. For results at IoU $\geq$ 0.7, we can observe that comparing with previous works, our method improves the performance by a large margin from Table 2. Some qualitative examples are shown in Fig. 6. We also report our full model results on KITTI *test* set at IoU $\geq$ 0.7 in Fig. 3, showing superior performance to previous works.

Table 2. Bird's eye view and 3D detection results: Average Precision (in %) of bird's eye view boxes and 3D bounding boxes on KITTI *validation* set at IoU $\geq$ 0.7

Method	AP_{BEV}			AP_{3D}		
	Easy	Moderate	Hard	Easy	Moderate	Hard
MonoDIS [37]	18.45	12.58	10.66	11.06	7.60	6.37
M3D-RPN [26]	20.85	15.62	11.88	14.53	11.07	8.65
Ki3D [38]	27.83	19.72	15.10	19.76	14.10	10.47
Ours	**34.97**	**26.01**	**21.78**	**23.12**	**17.10**	**14.29**

Table 3. Evaluation results on KITTI *test* set at IoU $\geq$ 0.7.

Method	AP_{BEV}			AP_{3D}		
	Easy	Moderate	Hard	Easy	Moderate	Hard
FQNet [39]	5.40	3.23	2.46	2.77	1.51	1.01
ROI-10D [27]	9.78	4.91	3.74	4.32	2.02	1.46
GS3D [25]	8.41	6.08	4.94	4.47	2.90	2.47
MonoPSR [40]	18.33	12.58	9.91	10.76	7.25	5.85
Ours	**18.71**	**13.03**	**11.02**	**11.52**	**8.26**	**6.97**

4.2 Ablation Study

We conduct our ablation study and experiment analysis on KITTI split [21] on Car class. We adopt moderate setting on Bird's eye view detection and 3D detection task to show our analysis results.

Adaptive Depth-Guided Instance Normalization. AdaDIN is designed to adaptively transfer spatial depth information to the color context feature. We compare three versions of our methods to verify its effectiveness: (1). **Base** model. The baseline model of our approach, where the AdaDIN and DDT are removed. (2). **Base+AdaDIN**. Our baseline model with AdaDIN layer, and this model needs generated monocular depth map as input for AdaDIN layer. From Table 4, we can observe that our AdaDIN greatly increases the performance of 3D detection performance thanks to the information transferred from depth feature.

Table 4. Comparisons of models with each component. The validation results on KITTI 3D detection results are shown.

Method	Easy	Moderate	Hard
Base	51.6	38.9	33.7
Base+DDT	59.53	44.30	40.82
Base+AdaDIN	62.37	45.08	37.61
Full model	**67.01**	**49.77**	**43.09**

Table 5. Comparison of our dynamic offsets generation strategy and deformable convolution.

Method	Easy	Moderate	Hard
Deformable [30]	33.34	27.58	23.49
Ours	67.01	49.77	43.09

Dynamic Depth Transformation. Our Dynamic depth transformation (DDT) module is able to address occlusion issue in very common urban scenes. From Table 4, we can see that DDT also shows improvements for 3D detection.

Offsets in DDT Module. As elaborated in Sect. 3.3, to tackle occlusion problem, we apply a dynamic offset to a uniform sampling kernel for recovering correct object depth. Different to Deformable Convolution [30], our kernel offsets are generated from image feature and then apply to another source input – raw depth map. We compare these two strategies and show the result in Table 5.

We can observe from Table 5 that our offset generation strategy outperforms Deformable convolution with a large margin. The reason is that our RGB normalized feature affined with parameters generated from depth map feature contains not only high level color context but also 3D depth information. On the other hand, very limited information could be exacted by a few convolution layers from raw depth map. Therefore, more accurate local depth offset could be estimated by our approach.

5   Conclusion

In this paper, we proposed a novel monocular 3D detection approach. One of our key components is Adaptive Depth-guided Instance Normalization, which could effectively fuse 3D spatial information obtained from depth map features with the color context message from RGB features for accurate 3D detection. Another crucial module is Dynamic Depth transformation, which is helpful when the detector encounters occlusions. Extensive experiments show our method achieves state-of-the-art performance on the KITTI 3D detection benchmark among other monocular image-based methods.

References

1. Qi, C.R., Su, H., Mo, K., Guibas, L.J.: PointNet: deep learning on point sets for 3D classification and segmentation. In: CVPR (2017)
2. Qi, C.R., Yi, L., Su, H., Guibas, L.J.: PointNet++: deep hierarchical feature learning on point sets in a metric space. In: NeurIPS (2017)
3. Zhou, Y., Tuzel, O.: VoxelNet: end-to-end learning for point cloud based 3D object detection. In: CVPR (2018)
4. Qi, C.R., Liu, W., Wu, C., Su, H., Guibas, L.J.: Frustum PointNets for 3D object detection from RGB-D data. In: CVPR (2018)
5. Shi, S., Wang, X., Li, H.: PointRCNN: 3D object proposal generation and detection from point cloud. In: CVPR (2019)
6. Chen, X., Ma, H., Wan, J., Li, B., Xia, T.: Multi-view 3D object detection network for autonomous driving. In: CVPR (2017)
7. Liang, M., Yang, B., Wang, S., Urtasun, R.: Deep continuous fusion for multi-sensor 3D object detection. In: ECCV (2018)
8. Yang, B., Luo, W., Urtasun, R.: Pixor: real-time 3D object detection from point clouds. In: CVPR (2018)
9. Chen, X., Kundu, K., Zhang, Z., Ma, H., Fidler, S., Urtasun, R.: Monocular 3D object detection for autonomous driving. In: CVPR (2016)
10. Mousavian, A., Anguelov, D., Flynn, J., Kosecka, J.: 3D bounding box estimation using deep learning and geometry. In: CVPR (2017)
11. Xu, B., Chen, Z.: Multi-level fusion based 3D object detection from monocular images. In: CVPR (2018)
12. Zhang, L., Li, X., Arnab, A., Yang, K., Tong, Y., Torr, P.H.: Dual graph convolutional network for semantic segmentation. In: BMVC (2019)
13. Zhang, L., Xu, D., Arnab, A., Torr, P.H.: Dynamic graph message passing networks. In: CVPR (2020)
14. Hou, Q., Zhang, L., Cheng, M.M., Feng, J.: Strip pooling: rethinking spatial pooling for scene parsing. In: CVPR (2020)
15. Li, X., Zhang, L., You, A., Yang, M., Yang, K., Tong, Y.: Global aggregation then local distribution in fully convolutional networks. In: BMVC (2019)
16. Li, X., et al.: Improving semantic segmentation via decoupled body and edge supervision. In: ECCV (2020)
17. Wang, Q., Zhang, L., Bertinetto, L., Hu, W., Torr, P.H.: Fast online object tracking and segmentation: a unifying approach. In: CVPR (2019)
18. Zhu, F., Zhang, L., Fu, Y., Guo, G., Xie, W.: Self-supervised video object segmentation. arXiv preprint (2020)
19. Wang, Y., Chao, W.L., Garg, D., Hariharan, B., Campbell, M., Weinberger, K.: Pseudo-LiDAR from visual depth estimation: bridging the gap in 3D object detection for autonomous driving. In: CVPR (2019)

20. Ma, X., Wang, Z., Li, H., Zhang, P., Ouyang, W., Fan, X.: Accurate monocular 3D object detection via color-embedded 3D reconstruction for autonomous driving. In: ICCV (2019)
21. Chen, X., et al.: 3D object proposals for accurate object class detection. In: NeurIPS (2015)
22. Li, P., Chen, X., Shen, S.: Stereo R-CNN based 3D object detection for autonomous driving. In: CVPR (2019)
23. Fu, H., Gong, M., Wang, C., Batmanghelich, K., Tao, D.: Deep ordinal regression network for monocular depth estimation. In: CVPR (2018)
24. Geiger, A., Lenz, P., Urtasun, R.: Are we ready for autonomous driving? The kitti vision benchmark suite. In: CVPR (2012)
25. Li, B., Ouyang, W., Sheng, L., Zeng, X., Wang, X.: GS3D: an efficient 3D object detection framework for autonomous driving. In: CVPR (2019)
26. Brazil, G., Liu, X.: M3D-RPN: monocular 3D region proposal network for object detection. In: ICCV (2019)
27. Manhardt, F., Kehl, W., Gaidon, A.: ROI-10D: monocular lifting of 2D detection to 6D pose and metric shape. In: CVPR (2019)
28. Huang, X., Belongie, S.: Arbitrary style transfer in real-time with adaptive instance normalization. In: CVPR (2017)
29. Park, T., Liu, M.Y., Wang, T.C., Zhu, J.Y.: Semantic image synthesis with spatially-adaptive normalization. In: CVPR (2019)
30. Dai, J., et al.: Deformable convolutional networks. In: CVPR (2017)
31. Newell, A., Yang, K., Deng, J.: Stacked hourglass networks for human pose estimation. In: Leibe, B., Matas, J., Sebe, N., Welling, M. (eds.) ECCV 2016. LNCS, vol. 9912, pp. 483–499. Springer, Cham (2016). https://doi.org/10.1007/978-3-319-46484-8_29
32. Wei, S.E., Ramakrishna, V., Kanade, T., Sheikh, Y.: Convolutional pose machines. In: CVPR (2016)
33. Zhou, X., Wang, D., Krähenbühl, P.: Objects as points. In: arXiv preprint (2019)
34. Lin, T.Y., Goyal, P., Girshick, R., He, K., Dollár, P.: Focal loss for dense object detection. In: CVPR (2017)
35. Yu, F., Wang, D., Shelhamer, E., Darrell, T.: Deep layer aggregation. In: CVPR (2018)
36. Qin, Z., Wang, J., Lu, Y.: MonoGRNet: a geometric reasoning network for monocular 3D object localization. In: AAAI (2019)
37. Simonelli, A., Bulo, S.R., Porzi, L., López-Antequera, M., Kontschieder, P.: Disentangling monocular 3D object detection. In: CVPR (2019)
38. Brazil, G., Pons-Moll, G., Liu, X., Schiele, B.: Kinematic 3D object detection in monocular video. In: Vedaldi, A., Bischof, H., Brox, T., Frahm, J.-M. (eds.) ECCV 2020. LNCS, vol. 12368, pp. 135–152. Springer, Cham (2020). https://doi.org/10.1007/978-3-030-58592-1_9
39. Liu, L., Lu, J., Xu, C., Tian, Q., Zhou, J.: Deep fitting degree scoring network for monocular 3D object detection. In: CVPR (2019)
40. Ku, J., Pon, A.D., Waslander, S.L.: Monocular 3D object detection leveraging accurate proposals and shape reconstruction. In: CVPR (2019)

Attention-Aware Feature Aggregation for Real-Time Stereo Matching on Edge Devices

Jia-Ren Chang[1,2], Pei-Chun Chang[1], and Yong-Sheng Chen[1(✉)]

[1] Department of Computer Science, National Chiao Tung University,
Hsinchu, Taiwan
{followwar.cs00g,maplepig.cs05g,yschen}@nctu.edu.tw
[2] aetherAI, Taipei, Taiwan

Abstract. Recent works have demonstrated superior results for depth estimation from a stereo pair of images using convolutional neural networks. However, these methods require large amounts of computational resources and are not suited to real-time applications on edge devices. In this work, we propose a novel method for real-time stereo matching on edge devices, which consists of an efficient backbone for feature extraction, an attention-aware feature aggregation, and a cascaded 3D CNN architecture for multi-scale disparity estimation. The efficient backbone is designed to generate multi-scale feature maps with constrained computational power. The multi-scale feature maps are further adaptively aggregated via the proposed attention-aware feature aggregation module to improve representational capacity of features. Multi-scale cost volumes are constructed using aggregated feature maps and regularized using a cascaded 3D CNN architecture to estimate disparity maps in anytime settings. The network infers a disparity map at low resolution and then progressively refines the disparity maps at higher resolutions by calculating the disparity residuals. Because of the efficient extraction and aggregation of informative features, the proposed method can achieve accurate depth estimation in real-time inference. Experimental results demonstrated that the proposed method processed stereo image pairs with resolution 1242×375 at 12–33 fps on an NVIDIA Jetson TX2 module and achieved competitive accuracy in depth estimation. The code is available at https://github.com/JiaRenChang/RealtimeStereo.

1 Introduction

Depth estimation from stereo images is an essential task for computer vision applications, including autonomous driving for vehicles, 3D model reconstruction, and object detection and recognition [1,2]. Given a pair of rectified stereo images, the goal of depth estimation is to compute the disparity d for each pixel in the reference image. Disparity refers to the horizontal displacement between a pair of corresponding pixels in the left and right images. If the corresponding point for pixel (x, y) in the left image is found at $(x - d, y)$ in the right image,

© Springer Nature Switzerland AG 2021
H. Ishikawa et al. (Eds.): ACCV 2020, LNCS 12622, pp. 365–380, 2021.
https://doi.org/10.1007/978-3-030-69525-5_22

then the depth of this pixel is calculated by $\frac{fB}{d}$, where f is the focal length of the camera and B is the distance between two camera centers.

The typical pipeline for stereo matching involves finding the corresponding points based on matching cost and post-processing [3]. Recently, convolutional neural networks (CNNs) have been applied to learn to compute the matching cost between two image patches in MC-CNN [4]. Early approaches using CNNs treat the problem of correspondence estimation as similarity computation [4–6], where CNNs compute the similarity score for a pair of image patches to further determine whether they are matched. Further studies propose more complex network architectures for better matching cost computation. Some studies propose end-to-end networks for stereo depth estimation. Specifically, these studies first extract image features via a CNN, use features to form a cost volume, and further process the cost volume with a 3D CNN. GC-Net [7] develops an encoder-decoder architecture of 3D CNN for learning context of cost volume. PSMNet [8] exploits pyramid features via spatial pyramid pooling and a stacked hourglass 3D CNN for regularizing cost volume. GA-Net [9] integrates semi-global matching [10] into 3D CNN for cost filtering. Further studies, such as AANet [11] and DeepPruner [12], are attempts to reduce the latency during inference by removing 3D convolutions or reducing disparity searching space, respectively. These end-to-end approaches demonstrated the state-of-the-art performance on stereo matching. However, difficulties still remain in issues such as robustness, generalization ability, and computational cost.

One major problem with current CNN-based stereo matching methods is how to efficiently perform inference using low-budget devices which has limited computational resources. As an example, PSMNet [8], which is one of the current state-of-the-art methods for stereo depth estimation, runs at a frame rate below 0.16 fps on an NVIDIA Jetson TX2 module. This is far from real-time applications on drones or robots. AnyNet [13] is proposed as a trade-off between computation and accuracy at inference time. It can run 10–35 fps on an NVIDIA Jetson TX2, at the expense of marginal accuracy on stereo matching.

In this paper, we propose a novel method for real-time stereo matching on edge devices in anytime settings, as shown in Fig. 1. Inspired by designing efficient CNNs on edge devices [14–16], we first build an efficient backbone to extract multi-scale features. We further propose an attention-aware feature aggregation module to learn adaptive fusion of multi-scale features. The aggregated features are utilized to construct multi-scale cost volumes. These cost volumes are regularized via a cascaded 3D CNN architecture to perform depth estimation in anytime settings. Similar to other coarse-to-fine approaches [13,17], the proposed method begins by estimating disparity maps at a low resolution and further refines the upsampled disparity maps. A wide range of possible frame rates are attainable (12–33 fps on an NVIDIA Jetson TX2 module) while still preserving accurate disparity estimation in a high-latency setting.

We evaluate the proposed method on several datasets and the major contributions of this work are:

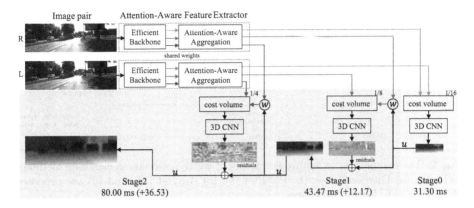

Fig. 1. Architecture overview of the proposed method. Left and right input stereo images are fed to two weight-sharing attention-aware feature extractor, consisting of an efficient backbone and an attention-aware feature aggregation. The left and right feature maps are then used to form a cost volume, which is fed into a cascaded 3D CNN architecture for cost volume regularization. The operator u indicates bilinear upsampling and the operator $+$ indicates element-wise summation. The warping function w uses the upsampled disparity map from previous stage to pixel-wise align the image pairs. The network can be queried to output its current best estimate in anytime settings. For example, a coarse disparity map can be obtained at 31.3 ms while a fine disparity map can be obtained at 80 ms on an NVIDIA Jetson TX2 for 1242×375 input image pairs.

- We propose a novel architecture to efficiently extract informative features by adaptively incorporating multi-resolutional information into the encoded features via cross-scale connections.
- We demonstrate that the proposed method considers both computational cost and accuracy at inference time and runs at real-time on low-budget devices.
- We show that the proposed method achieves competitive results compared to state-of-the-art methods.

2   Methods

The proposed network consists of an efficient backbone for feature extraction, an attention-aware aggregation module for feature fusion, and a cascaded 3D CNN architecture for estimating disparity maps and residuals, as illustrated in Fig. 1.

2.1   Attention-Aware Feature Extraction

We propose an attention-aware feature extractor to obtain multi-scale feature maps from stereo image pairs. As shown in Fig. 2, we compare the proposed feature extractor with those of other widely-used stereo matching architectures. The DispNetC [18] directly adopted different scales of feature maps. The PSMNet [8]

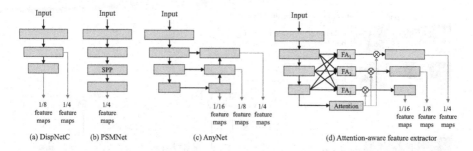

Fig. 2. The comparison of feature extractors of widely-used stereo matching methods, including (a) DispNetC [18], (b) PSMNet [8], (c) AnyNet [13], and (d) the proposed attention-aware feature extractor.

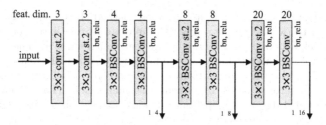

Fig. 3. The architecture of the proposed efficient backbone for feature extraction. The feat. dim. indicates the number of output feature maps. Each convolution follows batch normalization [19] and ReLU except the first one.

introduced spatial pyramid pooling (SPP) to incorporate pyramid representations. The AnyNet [13] adopted the U-Net architecture [20] to learn top-down features. By contrast, the proposed attention-aware feature extractor can adaptively aggregate information from different scales into the encoded features with attention mechanism. As shown in Fig. 2(d), the attention-aware feature extractor consists of an efficient backbone, three feature aggregation modules, and an attention module. We describe these components of the proposed method in the following.

Efficient Backbone. Previous studies [14–16] have developed efficient network architecture on limited resource devices. Remarkably, the depthwise separable convolution (DSConv) [14, 16] can balance the tradeoff between computation and accuracy, which factorizes a standard convolution into a depthwise convolution and a 1 × 1 convolution. The blueprint separable convolutions (BSConv) [15] further provides a justification for DSConv by analysing intra-kernel correlations of vanilla CNNs. As shown in Fig. 3, two strided 3 × 3 convolutions are used to extract coarse features of input image, and several stacked BSConvs are applied to distill information from these features with less computational cost. In order to obtain multi-scale representation, the strided BSConv are utilized to reduce the size of feature maps and to obtain multi-scale feature maps sequentially. Note

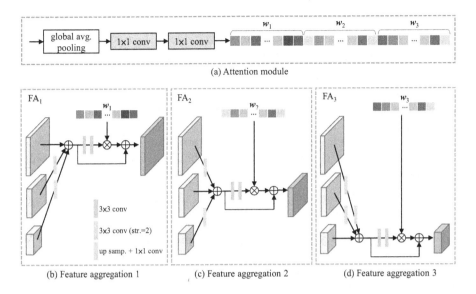

(a) Attention module

(b) Feature aggregation 1   (c) Feature aggregation 2   (d) Feature aggregation 3

Fig. 4. The architecture of the proposed attention-aware feature aggregation module. The feature aggregation modules FA_1, FA_2 and FA_3 are correspond to modules illustrated in Fig. 2(d). Each convolution follows batch normalization [19] and ReLU except in the attention module.

that these multi-scale feature maps are parallelly aggregated using the attention-aware feature aggregation module described in the next section, and only the 1/16 feature map is used to learn all channel-wised weights across multi-scale information.

Attention-Aware Feature Aggregation. As shown in Fig. 2, feature information at different scales is propagated sequentially in state-of-the-art stereo matching architectures. In stead of sequential propagation from coarse to fine levels such as U-Net [20], the proposed method parallelly aggregate information from all levels. There are three levels $(1/4, 1/8, 1/16$ size) of output feature maps from the efficient backbone. As shown in Fig. 4(b), (c) and (d), we proposed three parallel aggregation modules for these three level of features. We formulate the aggregation module in the following:

$$\hat{F}^s = \sum_{k=1}^{S} f_k(F^k), \qquad s = 1, 2, ..., S ,$$

(1)

where S is the level number of feature maps ($S = 3$ in this work) and F^k is the output feature map of the efficient backbone at level k. Similar to HRNet [21], we adopt the definition of f_k to calculate feature maps depending on their resolutions:

$$f_k = \begin{cases} I, & k = s, \\ (s-k) \; 3 \times 3 \text{ conv with stride 2}, & k < s, \\ \text{bilinear upsampling and } 1 \times 1 \text{ conv}, & k > s, \end{cases} \quad (2)$$

where I denotes the identity function, $s-k$ convolutions with stride 2 are used for downsampling the feature maps to achieve consistent size. Bilinear upsampling is applied to achieve consistent size followed by a 1×1 convolution to align the number of channels.

Inspired by SENet [22], we propose an attention module, as shown in Fig. 4(a), to recalibrate channel importance for boosting feature discriminability. The recalibrated feature maps $\tilde{F}^s$ can be formulated as:

$$\tilde{F}^s = \phi_s(\hat{F}^s) \cdot w_s + \hat{F}^s, \qquad s = 1, 2, ..., S , \quad (3)$$

where ϕ_s consists of two 3×3 convolutions with batch normalization and ReLU, and w_s is the attention weights learnt from the proposed attention module. We apply global average pooling on the final output feature maps of the efficient backbone, followed by two 1×1 convolutions to compute channel-wise attention weights w_s for multi-scale feature maps. The final recalibrated feature maps at each level are utilized to form cost volumes for disparity estimation.

2.2   Cost Volume

The GC-Net [7] and PSMNet [8] approaches concatenate left and right features to learn matching cost estimation using 3D CNNs. For real-time constraints, we adopt a distance metric to form a cost volume by computing the L_1 distance of left feature maps with their corresponding right feature maps across each disparity level, resulting in a 4D volume (height × width × disparity × 1).

A crucial aspect of the proposed architecture is that we compute the full disparity map only at a very low resolution in Stage 0 and compute disparity residuals in Stages 1 and 2. By focusing on residuals, that is, correction of existing disparities, we can greatly reduce the range of searching correspondences to $D = 5$ (that is, offsets $-2, -1, 0, 1, 2$) and obtain significant speedups. As shown in Fig. 1, in order to compute the residuals in Stages 1 and 2, we first upscale the coarse disparity map and use it to warp the input features at the higher scale by applying the disparity estimation in pixel-wise manner. If the current disparity estimate is correct, the updated right feature maps should match the left feature maps. Because of the coarseness of the low resolution inputs, mismatch may occur but may be corrected by computing residual disparity maps. Estimation of the residual disparity is accomplished similarly to the full disparity map computation. The only difference is that the residual disparity map is limited to -2 to 2, and the resulting residual disparity map is added to the upscaled disparity map from the previous stage.

2.3   Cascaded 3D CNN Architecture

The attention-aware feature extractor facilitates stereo matching by taking into account multi-resolution information and channel-wise recalibration. To aggregate the feature information along the disparity dimension as well as spatial dimensions, we follow the design in [13] to construct a cascaded 3D CNN architecture for cost volume regularization. The cascaded 3D CNN architecture contains three subnetworks depending on spatial resolutions, and each subnetwork has five 3 × 3 × 3 convolutions followed by batch normalization and ReLU except the final one. The subnetworks are further used for regularizing cost volume at each level. We then apply regression to calculate the disparity map, which is introduced in Sect. 2.4. Finally, we upsample the disparity map to the original image size.

2.4   Disparity Regression

We use disparity regression as proposed in [7] to estimate the continuous disparity map. The probability of each disparity d is calculated from the calculated cost c_d via the softmax operation $\sigma(\cdot)$. The disparity $\hat{d}$ is calculated as the sum of each disparity d weighted by its probability, as

$$\hat{d} = \sum_{d=0}^{D_{max}} d \times \sigma(-c_d) \,. \tag{4}$$

As reported in [7], the above disparity regression is more robust than classification-based stereo matching methods.

3   Experiments

We evaluated our method on three stereo datasets: Scene Flow [18], KITTI 2012, and KITTI 2015 [23].

3.1   Datasets

1. Scene Flow: a large-scale synthetic dataset containing 35,454 training and 4,370 testing images with $H = 540$ and $W = 960$. This dataset provides dense and elaborate disparity maps as ground truth. Some pixels have large disparities and are excluded in the loss computation if the disparity is larger than the limits set in our experiment.
2. KITTI 2012/2015: a real-world dataset with street views from a driving car. KITTI2012 contains 194 training stereo image pairs with sparse ground-truth disparities obtained using LiDAR and 195 testing image pairs without ground-truth disparities. KITTI2015 contains 200 training stereo image pairs with sparse ground-truth disparities obtained using LiDAR and another 200 testing image pairs without ground-truth disparities. Image size is $H = 376$ and $W = 1240$. We further divided the whole training data into a training set (80%) and a validation set (20%).

3.2 Implementation Details

The proposed method was implemented using PyTorch. All models were end-to-end trained with Adam ($\beta_1 = 0.9, \beta_2 = 0.999$). We performed color normalization as in [8] on the entire dataset for data preprocessing. During training, images were randomly cropped to size $H = 288$ and $W = 576$. The maximum disparity (D) was set to 192. We trained our models from scratch using the Scene Flow dataset with a learning rate of 0.0005 for 10 epochs. For Scene Flow, the trained model was directly used for testing. For KITTI validation, we used the model trained with Scene Flow after fine-tuning on the KITTI training set for 300 epochs. The learning rate of this fine-tuning began at 0.0005 for the first 200 epochs and 0.00005 for the remaining 100 epochs. For KITTI submission, we fine-tuned the pre-trained model on the combination of KITTI 2012/2015 for 500 epochs. The learning rate of this fine-tuning began at 0.0005 for the first 300 epochs and 0.0001 for the remaining 200 epochs. Then another 500 epochs were trained on the separate KITTI 2012/2015 training set, and the learning rate schedule remained the same. The batch size was set to 6 for Scene Flow and 4 for KITTI for the training on an NVIDIA Titan-Xp GPU. We adopted smooth L_1 loss as in [8]. The loss weights of three output stages were set to 0.25, 0.5, and 1.0. We calculated end-point-error (EPE) for Scene Flow dataset and three pixel error (3-px err.) for KITTI dataset.

3.3 Ablation Studies

To validate the effectiveness of each component proposed in this paper, we conducted controlled experiments on Scene Flow test set and KITTI 2015 validation set.

Components: As shown in Table 1, removing the feature aggregation and attention module leads to significant performance drop. The best performance is obtained by integrating these two modules.

Usage of Convolution: As described in Sect. 2.1, we adopt BSConv [15] to design the efficient backbone for feature extraction. As shown in Table 2, we compare the performance of vanilla convolution, DSConv [14], and BSConv [15] in our backbone. We used full architecture of the proposed method, and only replaced the convolutions in backbone. The results demonstrate that the BSConv can achieve the best performance with moderate FLOPs and number of parameters.

Cost Metric: We form cost volumes by computing the L_1 distance of left feature maps with their corresponding right feature maps, as described in Sect. 2.2. As shown in Table 3, we evaluated the performance with other metrics, such as L_2 distance and correlation. The results demonstrate that the usages of L_1 and L_2 distance have similar performance, but the correlation has the worst performance.

Table 1. Ablation study of feature aggregation (Feat. Agg.) and attention (Att.) modules. The best performance is obtained by integrating these two modules. S0, S1, and S2 indicate Stage 0, Stage 1, and Stage 2, respectively.

	Feat. Agg.	Att.	Scene flow (EPE)			KITTI 2015 (3-px err.)		
			S0	S1	S2	S0	S1	S2
Baseline			4.49	4.26	4.07	10.95	9.27	7.28
+Agg.	√		4.44	4.26	4.03	10.78	9.07	7.07
Ours	√	√	**4.34**	**4.14**	**3.90**	**11.03**	**9.15**	**6.76**

Table 2. Ablation study of convolution usage in efficient backbone. The best performance is obtained by using BSConv [15].

	Scene flow (EPE)			FLOPs (B)	Params
Conv type	S0	S1	S2		
Vanilla Conv	4.40	4.17	3.98	0.578	28,054
DSConv	4.62	4.40	4.18	0.543	23,005
BSConv	**4.34**	**4.14**	**3.90**	0.548	23,158

3.4 Evaluation Results

We evaluated the proposed method on KITTI 2012/2015 validation set for anytime estimation and test set for benchmarking.

Anytime Setting Estimation. The proposed method performs anytime depth estimation that balance the tradeoff between accuracy and speed. It can output three stages of disparity maps with progressive precision and runtime. As shown in Table 4, we clocked the running time of each stage on a low-budget NVIDIA Jetson TX2 with 1242×375 image pairs.

We further compare our results to other state-of-the-art approaches, such as AnyNet [13], PSMNet [8] and StereoNet [24], as shown in Table 4. For a fair comparison, we adopted their public codes and trained on the same train/validation split. Note that in the results of PSMNet [8], the evaluation of intermediate output in stacked hourglass 3D CNN are also reported. As shown in Fig. 5, the

Table 3. Ablation study of cost metric. The best performance for forming cost volume is achieved by computing the L_1 distance.

	Scene flow (EPE)		
Cost metric	S0	S1	S2
Correlation	4.7	4.44	4.20
L_2 distance	4.37	4.19	3.92
L_1 distance	**4.34**	**4.14**	**3.90**

Table 4. The evaluation results (3-px error) of the proposed method on KITTI 2012/2015 validation set. The runtime is clocked on an NVIDIA Jetson TX2 with 1242 × 375 image pairs. It clearly demonstrates that the proposed method can produce accurate disparity maps in real-time on edge device.

	KITTI 2012			KITTI 2015			FLOPs	Params	Runtime (ms)		
	S0	S1	S2	S0	S1	S2	(B)	(M)	S0	S1	S2
StereoNet-16× [24]	–	–	–	–	–	6.32	59.82	0.425	–	–	727.3
PSMNet [8]	1.72	1.45	1.39	2.24	1.86	1.77	937.9	5.224	3995	5072	6131
AnyNet [13]	14.61	11.92	8.26	14.24	12.11	8.51	1.339	0.043	29.00	48.80	87.90
Ours	9.75	8.09	6.01	11.03	9.15	6.76	0.548	0.023	31.30	43.47	80.00

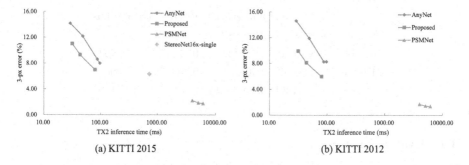

(a) KITTI 2015   (b) KITTI 2012

Fig. 5. The proposed method runs significantly faster than other approaches, such as AnyNet [13] and PSMNet [8], on a low-budget device (TX2) with competitive performance.

proposed method balanced best tradeoff between accuracy and runtime. It can achieve similar performance but runs 9× faster compared with StereoNet [24]. The proposed method can outperform AnyNet [13] by a notable margin with only half of FLOPs and parameters compared to AnyNet. PSMNet [8] can produce very accurate results; however, it needs high computational costs and cannot run in real-time for applications. We also compared qualitative results in Fig. 6. The yellow squares show that the proposed method can produce more sharp results than AnyNet [13]. The results demonstrate that the progressive refinement of the proposed method efficiently improves the quality of disparity maps at a low computational cost.

Benchmark Results. We further evaluated the proposed method on KITTI 2012/2015 test set for benchmarking. According to the online leaderboard, as shown in Table 5, the overall three-pixel-error for the proposed method was 6.94 on KITTI 2012 and 7.54% on KITII 2015, which is comparable to state-of-the-art methods with very low computational costs. We also clocked the runtime for each method on a Jetson TX2 according to their public codes. We found that GC-Net [7] and GA-Net-15 [9] cannot run on TX2 due to the problem of

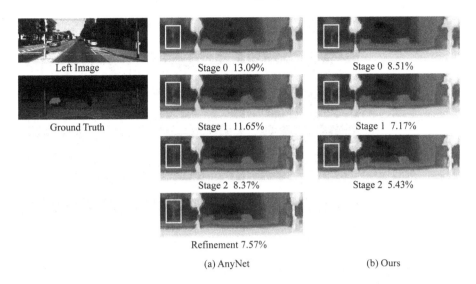

Left Image

Ground Truth

Stage 0 13.09%

Stage 1 11.65%

Stage 2 8.37%

Refinement 7.57%

Stage 0 8.51%

Stage 1 7.17%

Stage 2 5.43%

(a) AnyNet

(b) Ours

Fig. 6. The comparison of stage outputs between AnyNet [13] and the proposed method. The 3-px error is shown below each disparity map. The yellow squares depict that the proposed method can produce sharper results than those of AnyNet. Moreover, the accuracy in terms of 3-px error is progressively improved from Stage 0 to Stage 2. (Color figure online)

out of memory (OOM). Other state-of-the-art approaches, such as PSMNet [8], DeepPruner-Best [12], HD^3 [25] and GwcNet [26], can produce accurate results; however, they have very high latency (>2000 ms) and cannot be applied for real-time applications.

There are some approaches designed for real-time applications, such as MAD-Net [27], DispNetC [18] and DeepPruner-Fast [12]. They can run in real-time in a high-budget device (NVIDIA 1080ti or higher), but still have noticeable latency on edge devices (>100 ms in an NVIDIA Jetson TX2). In contrast, the proposed method can achieve competitive performance of anytime depth estimation at 12–33 fps on an NVIDIA Jetson TX2. As shown in Fig. 7, we compare the qualitative results adopted from KITTI 2015 leaderboard with MADNet [27] and DispNetC [18]. It suggests that the proposed method can produce accurate disparity maps for real-world applications with very low amount of model parameters and computational costs.

3.5 Generalization

We further test the generalization ability of the proposed method on ETH3D dataset [28]. Specifically, we directly use our KITTI fine-tuned model to estimate the disparity map on ETH3D without further training. As shown in Fig. 8, the proposed method can generalize to other domains and can produce accurate disparity maps.

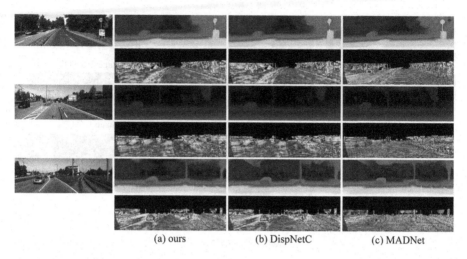

(a) ours   (b) DispNetC   (c) MADNet

Fig. 7. The qualitative comparisons between (a) the proposed method, (b) Disp-NetC [18], and MADNet [27]. The first row of each left image is the predicted disparity map and the second row is the 3-px error map. The proposed method can produce accurate disparity of objects and background, and gives the possibility of real-time dense depth estimation on the low-budget devices.

Left image   Right image   Stage 2 Output

Fig. 8. Generalization on ETH3D dataset. The proposed method can produce accurate disparity maps, indicating its potential for practical applications, such as obstacle avoidance.

3.6   Role of Attention

To have a profound understanding of the proposed attention-aware feature aggregation, we illustrate the weighting modulation of attention module in this section. From the Scene Flow test dataset, we chose three pairs of images exhibiting diverse disparity distribution and their attention activation profiles are illustrated in Fig. 9.

Table 5. We evaluate the proposed method on KITTI 2012/2015 test set. These results are adopted from KITTI leaderboard except the runtime. We clocked the runtime for each method on an Jetson TX2 according to their public codes with 1242×375 image pairs. The runtime ratios of the proposed method to other methods are also provided in the last column. Notably, our approach takes 61.5% time of DisPNetC [18]. The OOM indicates that the method cannot run on TX2 caused by out of memory.

Method	KITTI 2012		KITTI 2015		Params (M)	Time (ms)	Ratio (%)
	Noc	All	Noc	All			
GC-Net [7]	1.77	2.30	2.61	2.87	2.84	OOM	–
PSMNet [8]	1.49	1.89	2.14	2.32	5.22	6131	1.3
DeepPruner-Best [12]	–	–	1.95	2.15	7.39	3239	2.4
HD^3 [25]	1.40	1.80	1.87	2.02	39.50	2396	3.3
GwcNet [26]	1.32	1.70	1.92	2.11	6.52	3366	2.4
GA-Net-15 [9]	1.36	1.80	1.73	1.93	2.30	OOM	–
MADNet [27]	–	–	4.27	4.66	3.82	328	24.4
DispNetC [18]	4.11	4.65	4.05	4.34	38.14	130	61.5
DeepPruner-Fast [12]	–	–	2.35	2.59	7.47	1208	6.6
AANet [11]	1.91	2.42	2.32	2.55	4.00	1575	5.1
Ours	6.10	6.94	7.12	7.54	0.023	80	

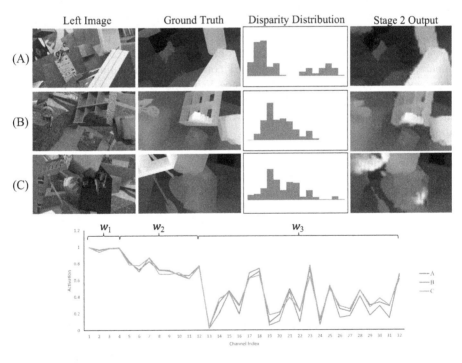

Fig. 9. Activation induced by the proposed attention module on Scene Flow test dataset. Note that the proposed module is a top-down attention which splits activation weights to w_1, w_2, and w_3 for modulating all three levels of feature maps.

The role of attention module can be observed from two aspects. First, the activation across different disparity distributions is nearly identical in lower feature level, that is, w_1. This suggests that the importance of feature channels in the early stage of the network is prone to be fixed in estimating disparity maps. Second, the channel weights of high level feature maps, w_2 and w_3, tend to be disparity-specific because different disparity distribution exhibit different preferences to the weighting values of feature maps. These observations are consistent with findings in previous work [22]. That is, lower layer features are typically more general whereas higher layer features have greater specificity, suggesting the importance of recalibration during feature extraction in stereo matching.

4 Conclusion

Recent studies using CNNs for stereo matching have achieved prominent performance. Nevertheless, it remains intractable to estimate disparity in real-time on low-budget devices for practical applications. In this work, we proposed a novel network architecture that can perform anytime depth estimation of 12–33 fps with competitive accuracy on an edge device (NVIDIA Jetson TX2). Specifically, we designed an efficient backbone for balancing the trade-off between speed and accuracy. Furthermore, an attention-aware feature aggregation is proposed to improve the representational capacity of features. A cascaded 3D CNN architecture is further used to estimate disparity maps in multiple spatial resolutions according to the constraints of computational costs. In our experiments, the proposed method achieved competitive performance in terms of accuracy and stat-of-the-art performance in terms of speed which was evaluated on an low-budget device. The estimated disparity maps clearly demonstrate that the proposed method can produce accurate depth estimation for practical applications.

Acknowledgments. This work was supported in part by the Taiwan Ministry of Science and Technology (Grants MOST-109-2218-E-002-038 and MOST-109-2634-F-009-015), Pervasive Artificial Intelligence Research (PAIR) Labs, Qualcomm Technologies Inc., and the Center for Emergent Functional Matter Science of National Chiao Tung University from the Featured Areas Research Center Program within the framework of the Higher Education Sprout Project by the Ministry of Education in Taiwan.

References

1. Chen, X., et al.: 3D object proposals for accurate object class detection. In: Advances in Neural Information Processing Systems, pp. 424–432 (2015)
2. Zhang, C., Li, Z., Cheng, Y., Cai, R., Chao, H., Rui, Y.: MeshStereo: a global stereo model with mesh alignment regularization for view interpolation. In: Proceedings of the IEEE International Conference on Computer Vision, pp. 2057–2065 (2015)
3. Scharstein, D., Szeliski, R.: A taxonomy and evaluation of dense two-frame stereo correspondence algorithms. Int. J. Comput. Vision **47**, 7–42 (2002)

4. Zbontar, J., LeCun, Y.: Stereo matching by training a convolutional neural network to compare image patches. J. Mach. Learn. Res. **17**, 2 (2016)
5. Shaked, A., Wolf, L.: Improved stereo matching with constant highway networks and reflective confidence learning. In: The IEEE Conference on Computer Vision and Pattern Recognition (CVPR) (2017)
6. Seki, A., Pollefeys, M.: SGM-Nets: semi-global matching with neural networks. In: The IEEE Conference on Computer Vision and Pattern Recognition (CVPR) (2017)
7. Kendall, A., et al.: End-to-end learning of geometry and context for deep stereo regression. In: The IEEE International Conference on Computer Vision (ICCV) (2017)
8. Chang, J.R., Chen, Y.S.: Pyramid stereo matching network. In: Proceedings of the IEEE Conference on Computer Vision and Pattern Recognition (CVPR), pp. 5410–5418 (2018)
9. Zhang, F., Prisacariu, V., Yang, R., Torr, P.H.: GA-Net: guided aggregation net for end-to-end stereo matching. In: Proceedings of the IEEE Conference on Computer Vision and Pattern Recognition, pp. 185–194 (2019)
10. Hirschmuller, H.: Accurate and efficient stereo processing by semi-global matching and mutual information. In: IEEE Computer Society Conference on Computer Vision and Pattern Recognition, 2005. CVPR 2005, vol. 2, pp. 807–814. IEEE (2005)
11. Xu, H., Zhang, J.: AANet: adaptive aggregation network for efficient stereo matching. In: Proceedings of the IEEE/CVF Conference on Computer Vision and Pattern Recognition, pp. 1959–1968 (2020)
12. Duggal, S., Wang, S., Ma, W.C., Hu, R., Urtasun, R.: DeepPruner: learning efficient stereo matching via differentiable PatchMatch. In: Proceedings of the IEEE International Conference on Computer Vision, pp. 4384–4393 (2019)
13. Wang, Y., et al.: Anytime stereo image depth estimation on mobile devices. In: International Conference on Robotics and Automation (ICRA) (2019)
14. Sandler, M., Howard, A., Zhu, M., Zhmoginov, A., Chen, L.C.: MobileNetV2: inverted residuals and linear bottlenecks. In: Proceedings of the IEEE Conference on Computer Vision and Pattern Recognition, pp. 4510–4520 (2018)
15. Haase, D., Amthor, M.: Rethinking depthwise separable convolutions: how intra-kernel correlations lead to improved MobileNets. In: Proceedings of the IEEE/CVF Conference on Computer Vision and Pattern Recognition, pp. 14600–14609 (2020)
16. Ma, N., Zhang, X., Zheng, H.T., Sun, J.: ShuffleNet V2: practical guidelines for efficient CNN architecture design. In: Proceedings of the European Conference on Computer Vision (ECCV), pp. 116–131 (2018)
17. Sun, D., Yang, X., Liu, M.Y., Kautz, J.: PWC-Net: CNNs for optical flow using pyramid, warping, and cost volume. In: Proceedings of the IEEE Conference on Computer Vision and Pattern Recognition (CVPR), pp. 8934–8943 (2018)
18. Mayer, N., et al.: A large dataset to train convolutional networks for disparity, optical flow, and scene flow estimation. In: The IEEE Conference on Computer Vision and Pattern Recognition (CVPR) (2016)
19. Ioffe, S., Szegedy, C.: Batch normalization: accelerating deep network training by reducing internal covariate shift. arXiv preprint arXiv:1502.03167 (2015)
20. Ronneberger, O., Fischer, P., Brox, T.: U-Net: convolutional networks for biomedical image segmentation. In: Navab, N., Hornegger, J., Wells, W.M., Frangi, A.F. (eds.) MICCAI 2015. LNCS, vol. 9351, pp. 234–241. Springer, Cham (2015). https://doi.org/10.1007/978-3-319-24574-4_28

21. Sun, K., Xiao, B., Liu, D., Wang, J.: Deep high-resolution representation learning for human pose estimation. In: Proceedings of the IEEE Conference on Computer Vision and Pattern Recognition, pp. 5693–5703 (2019)
22. Hu, J., Shen, L., Sun, G.: Squeeze-and-excitation networks. In: Proceedings of the IEEE Conference on Computer Vision and Pattern Recognition, pp. 7132–7141 (2018)
23. Menze, M., Geiger, A.: Object scene flow for autonomous vehicles. In: Proceedings of the IEEE Conference on Computer Vision and Pattern Recognition, pp. 3061–3070 (2015)
24. Khamis, S., Fanello, S., Rhemann, C., Kowdle, A., Valentin, J., Izadi, S.: StereoNet: guided hierarchical refinement for real-time edge-aware depth prediction. In: Proceedings of the European Conference on Computer Vision (ECCV), pp. 573–590 (2018)
25. Yin, Z., Darrell, T., Yu, F.: Hierarchical discrete distribution decomposition for match density estimation. In: Proceedings of the IEEE Conference on Computer Vision and Pattern Recognition, pp. 6044–6053 (2019)
26. Guo, X., Yang, K., Yang, W., Wang, X., Li, H.: Group-wise correlation stereo network. In: Proceedings of the IEEE Conference on Computer Vision and Pattern Recognition, pp. 3273–3282 (2019)
27. Tonioni, A., Tosi, F., Poggi, M., Mattoccia, S., Stefano, L.D.: Real-time self-adaptive deep stereo. In: Proceedings of the IEEE Conference on Computer Vision and Pattern Recognition, pp. 195–204 (2019)
28. Schops, T., et al.: A multi-view stereo benchmark with high-resolution images and multi-camera videos. In: Proceedings of the IEEE Conference on Computer Vision and Pattern Recognition, pp. 3260–3269 (2017)

FKAConv: Feature-Kernel Alignment for Point Cloud Convolution

Alexandre Boulch[1(✉)], Gilles Puy[1], and Renaud Marlet[1,2]

[1] valeo.ai, Paris, France
{alexandre.boulch,gilles.puy,renaud.marlet}@valeo.com
[2] LIGM, Ecole des Ponts, Univ Gustave Eiffel, CNRS, Marne-la-Vallée, France

Abstract. Recent state-of-the-art methods for point cloud processing are based on the notion of point convolution, for which several approaches have been proposed. In this paper, inspired by discrete convolution in image processing, we provide a formulation to relate and analyze a number of point convolution methods. We also propose our own convolution variant, that separates the estimation of geometry-less kernel weights and their alignment to the spatial support of features. Additionally, we define a point sampling strategy for convolution that is both effective and fast. Finally, using our convolution and sampling strategy, we show competitive results on classification and semantic segmentation benchmarks while being time and memory efficient.

1 Introduction

Convolutional Neural Networks (CNNs) have been a breakthrough in machine learning for image processing [7,19]. The discrete formulation of convolution allows a very efficient processing of grid-structured data such as images in 2D or videos in 3D. Yet a number of tasks require processing unstructured data such as point clouds, meshes or graphs, with application domains such as autonomous driving, robotics or urban modeling. However discrete convolution does not directly apply to point clouds as 3D points are not usually sampled on a grid.

The most straightforward workaround is to voxelize the 3D space to use discrete CNNs [31]. However, as 3D points are usually sampled on a surface, most of the voxels are empty. For efficient large-scale processing, a sparse formulation is thus required [37,60]. Other deep learning approaches generalize convolution to less structured data, such as graphs or meshes [5,41], but applying them to point clouds requires addressing the issue of sensible graph construction first.

Deep-learning techniques that directly process raw data have been developed to overcome the problem of point cloud pre-processing [33,50]. Just as for structured data, such networks are usually designed as a stack of layers and are optimized using stochastic gradient descent and back-propagation. Key issues when designing these networks include speed and memory efficiency.

Electronic supplementary material The online version of this chapter (https://doi.org/10.1007/978-3-030-69525-5_23) contains supplementary material, which is available to authorized users.

© Springer Nature Switzerland AG 2021
H. Ishikawa et al. (Eds.): ACCV 2020, LNCS 12622, pp. 381–399, 2021.
https://doi.org/10.1007/978-3-030-69525-5_23

In this context, we propose a new convolution method for point cloud processing. It is a mixed discrete-continuous formulation that disentangles the geometry of the convolution kernel and the spatial support of the features: using a geometry-less kernel domain, we stick to a discrete convolution scheme, which is efficient and has been successful on grid data; the spatial domain however keeps its continuous flavor, as point clouds are generally sampled on manifolds.

Our contributions are the following: (1) we provide a formulation to relate and analyze existing point convolution methods; (2) we propose a new convolution method (FKAConv) that explicitly separates the estimation of geometry-less kernel weights and their alignment to the spatial support of features; (3) we define a point sampling strategy for convolution that is both efficient and fast; (4) experiments on large-scale datasets for classification and semantic segmentation show we reach the state of the art, while being memory and time efficient.

2   Related Work

Projection in 2D. Some methods project the point cloud in a space suitable for using standard discrete CNNs. 2D CNNs have been use for 3D data converted as range images [13,29] or viewed from virtual viewpoints [4,21,44]. As neighboring points in the resulting image can be far away in 3D space, 2D CNNs often fail to capture well 3D relations. 2D CNNs can also be applied locally to point-specific neighborhoods by projecting data on the tangent plane [45]; the result is then highly dependant on the tangent plane estimation. Other approaches use a volumetric data representation, such as voxels [31,34,39,54]. These approaches however suffer from encoding mostly empty volumes, calling for sparsity handling, e.g., with octree-based 3D-CNNs [37] or sparse convolution [11,12].

Graph Convolution, Geometric Deep Learning. Graph Neural Networks (GNNs) [5,41] extend neural networks to irregular structures (not on a grid), using edges between nodes for message passing [10,24] or defining convolution in the spectral domain [6,9,18]. Point convolution using GNNs requires first explicitly building a graph from the point cloud [36]. To scale to large point clouds, SPG [20] defines a graph over nodes corresponding to point segments. In contrast, our approach directly applies to the raw point cloud, with no predefined relation between points, somehow making point association as part of the method.

MLP Processing. PointNet [33] directly processes point coordinates with a multi-layer perceptron (MLP), gathering context information with a permutation-invariant max-pooling. PointNet++ [35] and So-Net [22] reduce the loss of local information due to subsampling with a cascade of MLPs at different scales.

Point Convolution. A first line of work considers an explicit spatial location for the kernel, in the same space as the point cloud. Kernel elements can be located on a regular grid (voxels) [16], at the vertices of a polyhedron [47] or randomly sampled and optimized at training [3]. In KPConv [47], an adjustment of the kernel locations may also be predicted at test time to better fit the data.

Another type of approaches models kernel locations implicitly. The kernel can be a family of polynomials like in SpiderCNN [55], or it can be estimated with an MLP, like in PCCN [50], RSConv [27] or PointConv [53]. The weights of the input features are then directly estimated based on the local geometry of points. In contrast, we learn the weights of a discrete kernel and, at inference time, we only estimate the spatial relation between the kernel and input points. PointConv [53] reweights the input features based on local point densities. Our method reaches state-of-the-art performances without the need of such a mechanism.

Finally, PointCNN [23] shares apparent similarities with our work as one of its main components is the estimation of a matrix, that actually differs from ours. Besides, geometric information in [23] is lifted to the feature space and used as additional features. Our work shows it is sufficient to use the geometry only for features-kernel alignment, mimicking the discrete convolution on a regular grid.

Our approach lies in between these lines of work. On the one hand, our kernel weights are explicitly modeled as in [3,16,47], which gives a discrete flavor to our method; on the other hand, we estimate a transformation of input points to apply the convolution as in [27,50,53], which operates in the continuous domain, avoiding kernel spatialization. The key is that, contrary to fully-continuous approaches that re-estimate at inference time how to weigh given sets of points to operate the convolution, we estimate separately a kernel while learning, and we predict the relation between the kernel and input points while testing. Besides, we perform the convolution with a direct matrix multiplication rather than getting indirectly results from a network output. This separation and the explicit matrix multiplication (outside the network) allows a better learning of kernel weights and spatial relations, without the burden and inaccuracy of estimating their composition, resulting in a time and memory efficient method.

Point Sampling. Like PointNet [33], several methods maintain point clouds at full resolution during the whole processing [26,28,56]. These methods suffer from a high memory cost, which requires to either limit the input size [33,56], split the input into parts [26], or use a coarse voxel grid [28]. Other approaches [3,23,35], as ours, use an internal sub-sampling of the point cloud. The choice of sampled points forming a good support is a key step for this reduction. *Furthest point sampling* (FPS) [35], where points are chosen iteratively by selecting the furthest point from all the previously picked points at each iteration, yields very good performance but is slow and its performance depends on the initialization. In [56], point sampling is based on a learned attention, which induces a high memory cost. Our sampling strategy, based on the quantization of the 3D space, ensures a good sampling of the space, like FPS, and is fast and memory efficient.

3   A General Formulation of Point Cloud Convolution

We base our convolution formulation on the discrete convolution used in image or voxel grid processing. The formulation is general enough to cover a wide range of state-of-the-art convolution methods for point clouds, and to relate them.

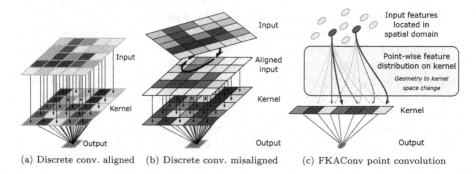

(a) Discrete conv. aligned (b) Discrete conv. misaligned   (c) FKAConv point convolution

Fig. 1. Kernel-input alignment for grid inputs (a, b) and point clouds (c).

Discrete Convolution. Let F be the dimension of the input feature space, d the spatial dimension (e.g., 2 for images, 3 for voxel grids), $\mathbf{K}$ the convolution kernel, and $\mathbf{f}$ the input features. The classical discrete convolution, noted $\mathbf{h}$, is:

$$\mathbf{h}[n] = \sum_{f\in\{1,\dots,F\}} \sum_{m\in\{-M/2,\dots,M/2\}^d} \mathbf{K}_f[m]\,\mathbf{f}_f[n+m], \tag{1}$$

where M^d is the grid kernel size, f indexes the feature space, n is the spatial index, and $\mathbf{K}_f[m]$ and $\mathbf{f}_f[n+m]$ are scalars. Defining vectors $\mathbf{K}_f = (K_f[m],\ m \in \{-M/2,\dots,M/2\}^d\})$ and $\mathbf{f}_f(n) = (\mathbf{f}_f[n+m],\ m \in \{-M/2,\dots,M/2\}^d)$, we can highlight the separation between the kernel space ($\mathbf{K}$) and the feature space ($\mathbf{f}$):

$$\mathbf{h}[n] = \sum_{f\in\{1,\dots,F\}} \underbrace{\mathbf{K}_f^\top}_{\text{Kernel space}} \underbrace{\mathbf{f}_f(n)}_{\text{Feature space}} . \tag{2}$$

The kernel $\mathbf{K}_f$ and the features $\mathbf{f}_f(n)$ are perfectly aligned: the grid index m associates a kernel element $\mathbf{K}_f[m]$ with a single input element $\mathbf{f}_f[n+m]$ (Fig. 1(a)).

Point Convolution. To generalize this discrete convolution to point clouds, we first consider a hypothetical misalignment between the feature and kernel spaces, assuming the feature grid is rotated with respect to the kernel grid (Fig. 1(b)), thus obfuscating the correspondence between kernel elements and feature elements. Yet, provided that the rotation matrix $\mathbf{A} \in \mathbb{R}^{M^d} \times \mathbb{R}^{M^d}$ is known, the correspondences can be recovered by rotating the support points of features:

$$\mathbf{h}[n] = \sum_{f\in\{1,\dots,F\}} \mathbf{K}_f^\top \mathbf{A}\, \mathbf{f}_f(n). \tag{3}$$

This equation actually holds in a more general setting, with an arbitrary linear transformation between the feature space and the kernel space; $\mathbf{A}$ is then the *alignment matrix* that associates the feature values to the kernel elements.

The discrete convolution on a regular grid becomes a particular case of Eq. (3), with $\mathbf{A} = \mathbf{I}_{M^d}$, the identity matrix. In the case of a point cloud, $\mathbf{f}_f(n)$ is the feature associated to the point at spatial location n, typically computed on a neighborhood $\mathbf{N}[n]$. These features are generally not grid-aligned. But Eq. (3) can still apply, provided we can estimate an alignment matrix $\mathbf{A}$ that distributes each input point onto the kernel elements (Fig. 1(c)).

In this context, a fixed matrix $\mathbf{A}$ is suboptimal as it cannot cope well with both a regular grid ($\mathbf{A} = \mathbf{I}_{M^d}$) and arbitrary point configurations in a point cloud. $\mathbf{A}$ thus has to be a function of the input points, which in practice have to be limited to neighbors $\mathbf{N}[n]$ at location n. The convolution becomes:

$$\mathbf{h}[n] = \sum_{f \in \{1,\dots,F\}} \mathbf{K}_f^\top \mathbf{A}(\mathbf{N}[n]) \, \mathbf{f}_f(n). \tag{4}$$

It is a mixed discrete-continuous formulation: $\mathbf{K}_f$ and $\mathbf{f}_f(n)$ have a discrete support and continuous values, while $\mathbf{A}(\mathbf{N}[n])$ provides a continuous mapping.

Analysis of Exiting Methods. This formulation happens to be generic enough to describe a range of existing methods for point convolution [3,23,43, 47,50].

Using Spatial Kernel Points. The most common approach to discrete convolution on a point cloud assigns a spatial point to each kernel element. The distribution of features on kernel elements is then based on the distance between kernel points and points in $\mathbf{N}[n]$, corresponding to an association matrix $\mathbf{A}$ invariant by rotation. A simple method would be to assign the features to the nearest kernel point, but it is unstable as a small perturbation in the point position may result in a different kernel point attribution. A workaround is to distribute the input points to several close kernel points. In SplatNet [43], an interpolation distribute points onto the kernel space. However, this handcrafted assignment is arbitrary and heavily relies on the geometry of kernel points. KPConv [47] chooses to distribute the input points over all the neighboring kernel points, with a weight inversely proportional to their distance to kernel points. Moreover, KPConv allows deformable kernels, for which local shifts of kernel points are estimated, offering more adaptation to input points. Yet, this handcrafted distribution is still arbitrary and still relies on the geometry of kernel points. ConvPoint [3] randomly samples the kernel points, and their position is learned along with an assignment function $\mathbf{A}$, with an MLP is applied to the kernel points represented in the coordinate system centered on the input points. All these methods [3,43, 47] raise the issue of defining and optimizing the position of kernel points.

Feature Combination and Geometry Lifting. In PointCNN [23], geometric information is extracted with an MLP_δ, parameterized by δ, and concatenated with the input features to create mixed spectral-geometric features. The summands in Eq. (4) become $\mathbf{K}^\top \mathbf{A}(\mathbf{N}[n])[\mathbf{f}_f(n), \mathrm{MLP}_\delta(\mathbf{N}[n])]$.

Joint Estimation of $\mathbf{K}^\top \mathbf{A}(\mathbf{N}[n])$. In fully implicit approaches [3,47,50], MLPs are used to directly estimate the weights $\mathbf{W}(n)$ to apply to input features $\mathbf{f}_f(n)$, i.e., not separating $\mathbf{W}(n)$ into a product $\mathbf{K}^\top \times \mathbf{A}(\mathbf{N}[n])$, and thus mixing estimations in the spatial and feature domains.

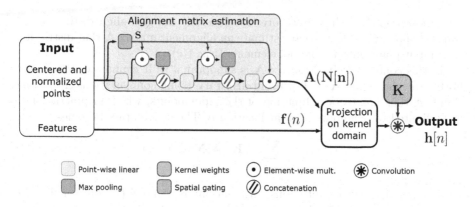

Fig. 2. FKAConv convolutional layer.

Kernel Separation. As acknowledged by the authors of PCCN themselves [50], a direct estimation of $\mathbf{W}(n) = \mathbf{K}^\top \mathbf{A}(\mathbf{N}[n])$ is too computationally expensive to be used in practice. Instead, they resort to an implementation which falls into our formulation: for N_{out} output channels, they consider N_{out} parallel convolution layers with a size-1 kernel, corresponding to using a different $\mathbf{A}$ for each filter. In PointCNN [23], the extra features generated by the geometry lifting induce a larger kernel (1/4 more weights with default parameters [23]), thus an increased memory footprint. To overcome this issue, [23] also chooses to factorize the kernel as the product of two smaller matrices. Notice that this kernel separation trick can be implemented in any method that uses explicit kernel weights. Although we could as well, we do not need to resort to that trick in our method.

4   Our Method: Estimating a Feature-Kernel Alignment

Our own convolution method is also based on Eq. (4). However, contrary to preceding approaches, we do not use kernel points. Instead, we estimate a soft alignment matrix $\mathbf{A}$ based on the coordinates of neighboring points in $\mathbf{N}[n]$. Our convolutional layer is illustrated on Fig. 2.

Neighborhood Normalization. To be globally invariant to translation, all coordinates of the points of $\mathbf{N}[n]$ are expressed in the local coordinates system of n. This is particularly important for scene segmentation: the network should behave the same way for similar objects at different spatial locations. Please notice that it is not the case in RSConv [27] where absolute coordinates are used, making it appropriate for shape analysis, not for scene processing.

$\mathbf{N}[n]$ is typically defined as the k-nearest neighbors (k-NNs) of n, or as all points in a ball around n. Both definitions have pros and cons. Using k-NNs is relatively fast, but the radius of the encompassing ball is (potentially highly) variable. As observed in [47], it may degrade spatial consistency compared to using a ball with a fixed radius. But searching within a radius is slower and yields (potentially widely) different numbers of neighbors, requiring strategies to deal with variable sizes, e.g., large tensor sizes and size tracking as in [47].

We propose an intermediate approach based on the k nearest neighbors, with a form a rescaling. As opposed to [3,23,35], we do not normalize the neighborhood to a unit sphere regardless of its actual size in the original space. We estimate a normalization radius r_t of the neighborhood at the layer level using the exponential moving average of Eq. (5) computed at training time, where t is the update step, m is a momentum parameter and $\hat{r}_t$ is the average neighborhood radius of the current batch. Let $\mathbf{q}$ be the support point associated to n, and $\mathbf{p}_i$ the i-th point of $\mathbf{N}[n]$. The points $(\hat{\mathbf{p}}_i)_i$ actually used for the estimating $\mathbf{A}$ are the points $(\mathbf{p}_i)_i$ centered and normalized using $\mathbf{q}$ and r_t as follows:

$$r_t = \hat{r}_t * m + r_{t-1} * (1 - m), \tag{5}$$

$$\hat{\mathbf{p}}_i = (\mathbf{p}_i - \mathbf{q})/r_t. \tag{6}$$

At inference time, this normalization ensures that all neighborhood are processed at the same scale while on average, neighborhoods are mapped to the unit ball.

Gating Mechanism on Distance to Support Point. While solving the problem of the neighborhood scale, this normalization strategy does not prevent points far away from the support point (the neighborhood center) to influence negatively the result. One could use hard-thresholding on the distance based on the estimated normalization radius r to filter these points, but this approach may cut too much information from the neighborhood, particularly in the case of high variance in neighborhood radii. Instead, we propose a gating mechanism to reduce, if needed, the effect of such faraway points. Given $(\hat{\mathbf{p}}_i)_i$ as defined in Eq. (6), the spatial gate weight $\mathbf{s} = (s_i)_i$ satisfies

$$s_i = \sigma(\beta - \alpha||\hat{\mathbf{p}}_i||_2), \tag{7}$$

where $\sigma(\cdot)$ is the sigmoid function, β is the cutoff distance (50% of the maximal value) and α parametrize the slope of the transition between 0 (points filtered out) and 1 (points kept). Both α and β are learned layer-wise.

Estimation of $\mathbf{A}$. As underlined in [33], a point cloud is invariant by point permutation: changing the order of points should not change the point cloud properties. Hence, the product $\mathbf{A}\mathbf{f}_f(n)$ must be invariant by permutation of the inputs. This can be achieved by estimating independently each line $\mathbf{A}_j$ of the matrix $\mathbf{A}$ using only the corresponding point $\mathbf{p}_j \in \mathbf{N}[n]$, with an MLP shared across all points. But it does not take the neighborhood into account, and thus may ignore useful information such as the local normal or curvature. To address point permutation invariance, PointNet [33] uses a max-pooling operation. Likewise, we use a three-layer point-wise MLP with max-pooling after the first two layers. To reduce the influence of outliers, max-pooling inputs are weighted with $\mathbf{s}$. The output is then concatenated to the point-wise features and given as input to the next fully-connected layer. This series of computations is illustrated in Fig. 2 in the block called "alignment matrix estimation."

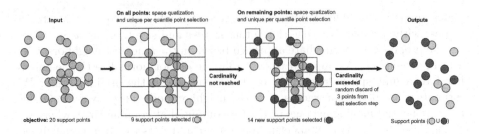

Fig. 3. Point sampling with space quantization.

5   Efficient Point Sampling with Space Quantization

Networks architectures for point cloud processing operates at full resolution through the entire network [50], or have an encoder/decoder structure [3,23] similar to networks used in image processing, e.g., U-Net [38]. While the former maintain a maximum of information through the network, the later are usually faster as convolutions are applied to smaller point sets. However, decreasing the size of the point cloud requires to select *the support points*, i.e., the points at the center of the neighborhoods used in the convolution.

PointNet++ [35] introduces farthest point sampling, an iterative sampling procedure where the next sampled point is the farthest from the already picked points. The main advantage of this sampling is to ensure a somewhat spatially uniform distribution which favors extreme points (e.g., at wing extremities for planes) as they are usually important for shape recognition. However, it requires to keep track of distances between all pairs of points, which is costly and increases the computation time, in particular when dealing with large point clouds.

In ConvPoint [3], the point-picking strategy only takes into account seen and unseen points, without distance consideration. Points are randomly picked among points that were not previously seen (picked points and points in the neighborhood of these points). While being much faster than farthest point sampling, it appears to be less efficient (see experiments in Sect. 6). In particular, the sampling is dependent of the neighborhood size: the sampling is done outside the neighborhoods of the previously picked support points. A very small neighborhood size reduces the method to a pure random sampling.

Space Quantization. We propose an alternative approach that ensures a better sampling than [3] while being much faster than [35]. The procedure is illustrated on Fig. 3. We discretize the space using a regular voxel grid. Each point is associated to the grid cube it falls in. In each non-empty grid cube, one point is selected. We continue with the non-selected points and a voxel size divided by two, and repeat the process until the desired number of sampled points is reached or exceeded. In the later case, some points selected at the last iteration are discarded at random to reduce the cardinality of Q, the set selected points.

Quantization Step Estimation. Our approach is voxel-size dependent. On the one hand, a coarse grid leads to many iterations in the selection procedure, at the expense of computation time. On the other hand, a fine grid reduces to random sampling. Finding the optimal voxel size could be achieved using a exhaustive search (for $|Q|$ filled voxels at a single quantization step), but it is very slow. Instead, we propose to estimate the voxel size via a rule of thumb derived by considering a simple configuration where a plane is intersecting a cube of unit length divided by a voxel grid of size $a \times a \times a$. If the plane is axis aligned, it intersects a^2 voxels. A sensible sampling would pick a support point in each intersected voxel, $i.e.$, $|Q| = a^2$. This indicates that letting the length $v = 1/a$ of a voxel be proportional to $1/\sqrt{|Q|}$ is a reasonable choice for the voxel size. We found experimentally that choosing the diagonal length of the bounding box of the point cloud, denoted hereafter by diag, as factor of proportionality is usually a good choice (see Sect. 6.2). The voxel size is thus set to

$$v = \text{diag}/\sqrt{|Q|}. \tag{8}$$

6   Experiments

In this section, we evaluate our convolutional layer on shape classification, part segmentation and semantic segmentation, reaching the state of the art regarding task metrics while being efficient regarding computation time and memory usage.

Network Architectures. In our experiments, we use a simple yet effective residual network for classification and semantic segmentation. We mimic the architecture of [47], except that ours is designed for k-NN convolution, i.e., we do not need to add phantom points and features to equalize the size of data tensor due to a variable number of points in radius search. The network has an encoder-decoder structure. The encoder is composed of an alternation of residual blocks maintaining the resolution and residual blocks with down-sampling. The decoder is a stack of fully-connected and nearest-neighbor upsampling layers. The classification network is the encoder of the previously described network followed by a global average pooling. For large scale semantic segmentation, we use either input modality dropout [47] or dual network fusion [3], as indicated in tables.

Experimental Setup. Our formulation (and code) allows a variable input size, but in order to use optimization with mini-batches, with train the networks with fixed input sizes. As every operations of FKAConv are differentiable, all parameters are optimized via gradient descent (including the spatial gating parameters α's and β's). Finally, we use a standard cross-entropy loss.

6.1   Benchmark Results

Shape Classification. The classification task is evaluated on ModelNet40 [54]. As the spatial pooling process is stochastic, multiple predictions with the same point cloud might lead to different outcomes. We aggregate 16 predictions for each point cloud and select the most predicted shape (we use a similar approach for part segmentation). On the classification task (Table 1(a)), we present average

Table 1. Classification and part segmentation benchmarks.

(a) ModelNet40

Methods	Num. points	OA	AA
Mesh or voxels			
Subvolume [34]	-	89.2	-
MVCNN [44]	-	90.1	-
Points			
DGCNN [52]	1024	92.2	**90.2**
PointNet [33]	1024	89.2	86.2
PointNet++ [35]	1024	90.7	-
PointCNN [23]	1024	92.2	88.1
ConvPoint [3]	2048	92.5	89.6
KPConv [47]	2048	**92.9**	-
Ours		Average±std. (best run)	
FKAConv	1024	92.3±0.2 (92.5) 89.6±0.3 (89.9)	
	2048	92.5±0.1 (92.5) 89.5±0.1 (89.7)	

(b) ShapeNet

Method	mcIoU	mIoU
PointNet++ [35]	81.9	85.1
SubSparseCN [12]	83.3	86.0
SPLATNet [43]	83.7	85.4
SpiderCNN [55]	81.7	85.3
SO-Net [22]	81.0	84.9
PCNN [2]	81.8	85.1
KCNet [42]	82.2	83.7
SpecGCN [49]	-	85.4
RSNet [17]	81.4	84.9
DGCNN [52]	82.3	85.1
SGPN [51]	82.8	85.8
PointCNN [23]	84.6	86.1
ConvPoint [3]	83.4	85.8
KPConv [47]	**85.1**	**86.4**
FKAConv (Ours)	84.8	85.7

(and best) results over five runs. For fair comparison, we train with 1024 (resp. 2048) points. We rank first (resp. second) among the method trained with 1024 (resp. 2048) points. We mainly observe that increasing the number points of reduces the standard deviation of the performances.

Part Segmentation. On ShapeNet [57], the network is trained with 2048 input points and 50 outputs (one for each part). The loss and scores are computed per object category (16 object categories with 2- to 6-part labels). The results are presented in Table 1(b). We rank among the best methods: top-2 or top-5 depending on the metric used, i.e., mean class intersection over union (mcIoU) or instance average intersection over union (mIoU); we are only 0.3 point mcIoU and 0.7 point mIoU behind the best method. It is interesting to notice that we are as good as or better than several methods for which the convolution falls into our formalism, such as ConvPoint [3] or SPLATNet [43].

Semantic Segmentation. Three datasets are used for semantic segmentation corresponding to three different use cases. S3DIS [1] is an indoor dataset acquired with an RGBD camera. The evaluation is done using a 6-fold cross validation. NPM3D [40] is an outdoor dataset acquired in four sites using a lidar-equipped car. Finally, Semantic8 [14] contains 30 lidar scenes acquired statically. NPM3D and Semantic8 are datasets with hidden test labels. Scores in the tables are reported from the official evaluation servers.

We use 8192 input points but, as subsampling the whole scene produces a significant loss of information, we select instead points in vertical pillars with a square footprint of 2 m for S3DIS, and 8 m for NPM3D and Semantic8. The center point of the pillar is selected randomly at training time and using a sliding

Table 2. Semantic segmentation benchmarks.

(a) S3DIS

Method	Search	IoU	ceil.	floor	wall	beam	col.	wind.	door	chair	table	book.	sofa	board	clut.
Pointnet [33]	Knn	47.6	88.0	88.7	69.3	42.4	23.1	47.5	51.6	42.0	54.1	38.2	9.6	29.4	35.2
RSNet [17]	-	56.5	92.5	92.8	78.6	32.8	34.4	51.6	68.1	60.1	59.7	50.2	16.4	44.9	52.0
PCCN [50]	-	58.3	92.3	96.2	75.9	0.27	6.0	69.5	63.5	65.6	66.9	68.9	47.3	59.1	46.2
SPGraph [20]	Super pt.	62.1	89.9	95.1	76.4	62 8	47.1	55.3	68.4	73.5	69.2	63.2	45.9	8.7	52.9
PointCNN [23]	Knn	65.4	94.8	97.3	75.8	63.3	51.7	58.4	57.2	71.6	69.1	39.1	61.2	52.2	58.6
PointWeb [59]	Knn	66.7	93.5	94.2	80.8	52.4	41.3	64.9	68.1	71.4	67.1	50.3	62.7	**62.2**	58.5
ShellNet [58]	Knn	66.8	90.2	93.6	79.9	60.4	44.1	64.9	52.9	71.6	84.7	53.8	64.6	48.6	59.4
ConvPoint [3]	Knn	68.2	**95.0**	97.3	81.7	47.1	34.6	63.2	73.2	75.3	**71.8**	64.9	59.2	57.6	65.0
KPConv [47]	Radius	**70.6**	93.6	92.4	**83.1**	**63.9**	**54.3**	66.1	**76.6**	57.8	64.0	**69.3**	**74.9**	61.3	60.3
FKAConv (Ours *RGB only*)	Knn	64.9	94.0	97.8	80.5	38.5	48.5	49.8	68.0	79.4	70.7	48.4	43.7	62.9	61.4
FKAConv (Ours *RGB drop.*)	Knn	66.6	94.4	97.8	81.5	38.7	43.3	56.4	71.6	80.2	71.8	63.5	54.1	50.6	62.5
FKAConv (Ours *fusion*)	Knn	68.4	94.5	**98.0**	82.9	41.0	46.0	57.8	74.1	**77.7**	71.7	65.0	60.3	55.0	**65.5**
Rank		2	3	1	2	7	4	6	2	1	2	3	4	5	1

(b) NPM3D

Method	Av.IoU	Ground	Building	Pole	Bollard	Trash can	Barrier	Pedestrian	Car	Natural
RF MSSF [46]	56.3	99.3	88.6	47.8	67.3	2.3	27.1	20.6	74.8	78.8
MS3 DVS [39]	66.9	99.0	94.8	52.4	38.1	36.0	49.3	52.6	91.3	88.6
HDGCN [25]	68.3	99.4	93.0	67.7	75.7	25.7	44.7	37.1	81.9	89.6
ConvPoint [3]	75.9	99.5	95.1	71.6	88.7	46.7	52.9	53.5	89.4	85.4
KPConv [47]	82.0	99.5	94.0	71.3	83.1	**78.7**	47.7	**78.2**	94.4	91.4
FKAConv (ours *fusion*)	**82.7**	**99.6**	**98.1**	**77.2**	**91.1**	64.7	**66.5**	58.1	**95.6**	**93.9**
Rank	1	1	1	1	1	2	1	2	1	1

Note: We report here only the published methods at the time of writing.

(c) Semantic3D

Method	Av. IoU	OA	Man made	Nat. veg.	High veg.	Low veg.	Build.	Hard scape	Art.	Cars
TML-PC [32]	39.1	74.5	80.4	66.1	42.3	41.2	64.7	12.4	0.	5.8
TMLC-MS [15]	49.4	85.0	91.1	69.5	32.8	21.6	87.6	25.9	11.3	55.3
PointNet++ [35]	63.1	85.7	81.9	78.1	64.3	51.7	75.9	36.4	43.7	72.6
EdgeConv [8]	64.4	89.6	91.1	69.5	65.0	56.0	89.7	30.0	43..8	69.7
SnapNet [4]	67.4	91.0	89.6	79.5	74.8	56.1	90.9	36.5	34.3	77.2
PointGCR [30]	69.5	92.1	93.8	80.0	64.4	66.4	93.2	34.3	34.3	85.3
FPCR [48]	72.0	90.6	86.4	70.3	69.5	68.0	96.9	43.4	52.3	89.5
SPGraph [20]	76.2	92.9	91.5	75.6	**78.3**	71.7	94.4	**56.8**	52.9	88.4
ConvPoint [3]	**76.5**	93.4	92.1	80.6	76.0	**71.9**	**95.6**	47.3	**61.1**	87.7
FKAConv* (ours *fusion*)	74.6	**94.1**	**94.7**	**85.2**	77.4	70.4	94.0	52.9	29.4	**92.6**
Rank	3	1	1	1	2	3	5	2	9	1

Note: We report here only the published methods at the time of writing.

*In the official benchmark, the entry corresponding to our method is called LightConvPoint,
which refers to the framework used for our implementation.

window at test time. If a point is seen several times, the prediction scores are summed and the most probable class is selected afterward.

The results are presented in Fig. 4 and Table 2. We use S3DIS (Table 2(a)) to study the impact of the training strategy. As underlined in [3,47], direct learning with colored points yields a model relying too much on color information, at the expense of geometric information. We train three models. The first is the baseline model trained with color information, the second uses color dropout as in [47], and the third is a dual model with a fusion module [3]. We observe that fusion gives the best results. In practice, the model trained with modality dropout tends to select one of the two modalities, either color or geometry, depending on what

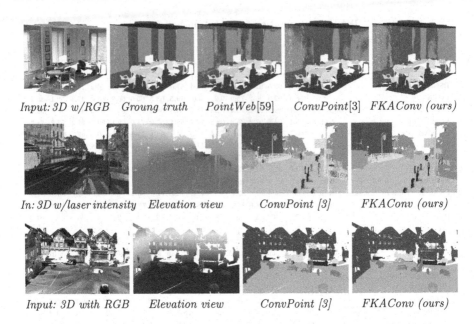

Input: 3D w/RGB   Groung truth   PointWeb[59]   ConvPoint[3]   FKAConv (ours)

In: 3D w/laser intensity   Elevation view   ConvPoint [3]   FKAConv (ours)

Input: 3D with RGB   Elevation view   ConvPoint [3]   FKAConv (ours)

Fig. 4. Visual results of semantic segmentation: S3DIS (1st row), NPM3D (2nd row) and Semantic3D (3rd row). Ground truth of test data publicly unavailable for last two.

modality gives the best results. On the contrary, the fusion technique uses two networks each trained with a different modality, resulting in a lot larger network, but ensuring that the information of both modalities is taken into account.

Our network is second on S3DIS, first on NPM3D and third on Semantic8. On S3DIS, it is the best approach for 3 out of 13 categories and it performs well on the remaining ones. We are only outperformed by KPConv, which is based on radius search. On NPM3D, we reach an average intersection over union (av. IoU) of 82.7, which is 0.7 point above the second best method. On Semantic8, we place third according to average IoU, and first on overall accuracy among the published and arXiv methods. We obtain the best scores in 3 out 8 categories (the top-3 for 6 categories out of 8). More interestingly, we exceed the scores of ConvPoint [3] on 5 categories. The only downside is the very low score on the category of artefacts. One possible explanation could be that the architecture used in this paper (the residual network) is not suitable to learn a reject class (the artefact class is mainly all the points that do not belong to the 7 other classes, i.e., pedestrians but also scanning outliers). It is future work to train the ConvPoint network with our convolution layer to support this hypothesis.

6.2 Support Point Sampling: Discretization Parameter

The rule of thumb in Eq. (8) was derived in a simplistic case: a point cloud sampled from an axis aligned plane crossing a regular voxel grid. In practice, planar

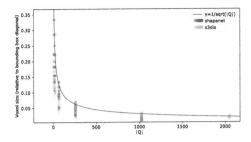

Fig. 5. Empirical validation of voxel size estimation: ShapeNet (blue), S3DIS (orange). Each dot is the empirical optimal voxel size obtained by dichotomic search. The red line is the voxel size defined as the inverse square root of the number of support points. (Color figure online)

Table 3. Computation time and memory consumption.

(a) Computation times for different sampling strategies.

Method	Sampling time (ms)			ShapeNet
	1k pts	5k pts	10k pts	(mIoU)
Random	1.66	8.6	18.6	84.4
(baseline)	(-60%)	(-89%)	(-94%)	
ConvPoint [3]	2.60	25.4	88.2	84.6
	(-37%)	(-68%)	(-71%)	
Farthest [35]	4.12	79.8	310.2	84.7
	(-)	(-)	(-)	
FKAConv sampling	1.93	10.3	20.4	84.6
	(-53%)	(-87%)	(-93%)	

(time for n inputs points, $n/2$ support points, 16 neighbors, averaged over 5000 iterations).

(b) Time and memory consumption for a segmentation network, with 8192 points.

Convolution	Training		Test	
Layer	Time	Memory	Time	Memory
	(ms)	(GB)	(ms)	(GB)
ConvPoint [3]	85.7	10.1	65	2.9
ConvPoint*	**12.2**	**4.3**	4.29	1.6
PointCNN* [23]	33.6	3.5	6.23	1.7
PCCN* [50]	31.1	4.9	10.2	2.3
PCCN** (bs4)	64.2	6.4	19.7	2.6
FKAConv (Ours)	19.1	5.6	**4.9**	**1.4**

*: reimplemented in our framework.

**: original formulation without separation trick, differs from code used for experiments in [50].

surfaces are very common, particularly in semantic segmentation (walls, floors, etc.), but are not a good model for most of the object of the scenes (chairs, cars, vegetation, *etc.*). To validate Eq. (8), we compute the optimal quantization parameter (i.e., the parameter with the largest value leading to the desired number of support points in a single quantization) computed using a dichotomic search on the parameter space and compare it to the derived expression. Figure 5 presents the results of the experiment. For each point cloud, the optimal voxel size is represented by a semi-transparent disk (blue for ShapeNet, orange for S3DIS) and can be compared to the derived expression (red curve). In our setting, a curve under the colored disks is not desired; it is an over-quantization. We prefer a curve above these disks, possibly leading to extra iterations, but not affecting performance. We observe that Eq. (8) provides a good estimate of the voxel size, especially for S3DIS which is a dataset containing a lot of planes. For ShapeNet, we observe a higher variance, due to the great variability of shapes. Because of numerous objects that cannot be modeled well by planes in ShapeNet, we slightly overestimate the voxel size, leading only to one spurious iteration, which only slightly slows down the operation.

Low-level features　　　　　　　　High-level features

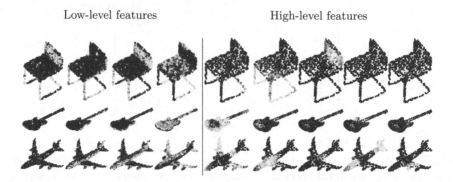

Fig. 6. FKAConv filter response for different input shapes on ModelNet40. Low-level features are extracted from the first layer (4 filters), and high-level features from the fourth layer (5 filters). The colormap represents the filter response for the shape, from blue (low response) to red (high response). (Color figure online)

6.3 Support Point Sampling: Computation Times

To assess our sampling approach, we run two experiments. First, in Table 3(a), we compare the sampling time as a function of the size of the input point cloud. The number of support points is half the input point cloud size, and the number of neighbors is 16. The scores are averaged over 5000 random points clouds sampled in a cube. We also report the ShapeNet scores to relate the performance and the computation times. We compare our sampling strategy with farthest point sampling [35], with iterative neighborhood rejection [3] and with a random baseline. As farthest point sampling [35] is the reference of several state-of-the-art methods, we give the gain relatively to this method in percentage. Our quantized sampling is almost as fast as random sampling and much more efficient than farthest point sampling. In fact, our sampling has almost a linear complexity, compared to farthest point sampling, that has a quadratic complexity.

6.4 Inference Time and Memory Consumption

We present in Table 3(b) the performance of our convolution layer and compare it to other convolutional layers. All computation times and memory usage are given for the segmentation network architecture and for one point cloud. The measures were done with 8192 points in each point cloud and a batch size of 16 (except for PCCN** for which the batch size is reduce to 4 to fit in the 11 GB GPU memory). Computational times are given per point cloud in milliseconds, and memory usage is reported in gigabytes.

We observe that our computation times at inference are very similar to those of ConvPoint [3], which is expected as it falls into our same general formulation. The same would probably be observed for a k-NN version of the KPConv [47]. Then, we remark that PointCNN [23] and PCCN [50] are up to twice slower for inference. PCCN uses the separable kernel trick to improve memory performance (cf. Sect. 3). In this form, it is similar to N_{out} (N_{out} being the number of filters of the layer) parallel instances of our layer with one kernel element, i.e., it is equivalent to estimating a different $\mathbf{A}$ for each $f \in \{1, \ldots, F\}$. We also report in Table 3(b) the performance for PCCN**, which is the purely continuous convolution described in PCCN [50], but without the separable kernel trick.

6.5 Filter Visualization

Our method FKAConv was derived from the discrete convolution on regular grids. The behavior of our 3D filters should thus be comparable to their 2D counterparts. In Fig. 6, we present the outputs of early and deep filters for the classification network on ModelNet40. For easier visualization, the features at coarse scales (high level/deep features) have been upsampled at the full point-cloud resolution. We notice that early layers produce features based on surface orientation. This is consistent with the small receptive field of early layers, that yields fine-scale features. On the contrary, deep layers produces shape-related features detecting objects parts, such as people heads or airplane bodies.

7   Conclusion

We presented a formulation for convolution on point clouds that unifies a range of existing convolutional layers and suggests a new point convolution approach. The core of the method is the estimation of an alignment matrix between the input points and the kernel. We also introduced an alternative point sampling strategy to farthest point sampling by using a progressive voxelization of the input space. While being almost as efficient as farthest point sampling, it is nearly as fast as random sampling. With these conceptually simple and easy to implement ideas, we obtained state-of-the-art results on several classification and semantic segmentation benchmarks among methods based on k-NN search, while being among the fastest and most memory-efficient approaches.

References

1. Armeni, I., et al.: 3D semantic parsing of large-scale indoor spaces. In: IEEE Conference on Computer Vision and Pattern Recognition (CVPR), pp. 1534–1543 (2016)
2. Atzmon, M., Maron, H., Lipman, Y.: Point convolutional neural networks by extension operators. ACM Trans. Graph. (TOG) **37**(4) (2018). SIGRAPH
3. Boulch, A.: ConvPoint: continuous convolutions for point cloud processing. Comput. Graph. **88**, 24–34 (2020)
4. Boulch, A., Guerry, J., Le Saux, B., Audebert, N.: SnapNet: 3D point cloud semantic labeling with 2D deep segmentation networks. Comput. Graph. **71**, 189–198 (2018)
5. Bronstein, M.M., Bruna, J., LeCun, Y., Szlam, A., Vandergheynst, P.: Geometric deep learning: going beyond Euclidean data. IEEE Signal Process. Mag. **34**(4), 18–42 (2017)

6. Bruna, J., Zaremba, W., Szlam, A., LeCun, Y.: Spectral networks and locally connected networks on graphs. In: International Conference on Learning Representation (ICLR) (2014)
7. Cireşan, D.C., Meier, U., Masci, J., Gambardella, L.M., Schmidhuber, J.: Flexible, high performance convolutional neural networks for image classification. In: 22nd International Joint Conference on Artificial Intelligence (IJCAI), pp. 1237–1242 (2011)
8. Contreras, J., Denzler, J.: Edge-convolution point net for semantic segmentation of large-scale point clouds. In: IEEE International Geoscience and Remote Sensing Symposium (IGARSS), pp. 5236–5239 (2019)
9. Defferrard, M., Bresson, X., Vandergheynst, P.: Convolutional neural networks on graphs with fast localized spectral filtering. In: Advances in Neural Information Processing Systems (NeurIPS), pp. 3844–3852 (2016)
10. Gilmer, J., Schoenholz, S.S., Riley, P.F., Vinyals, O., Dahl, G.E.: Neural message passing for quantum chemistry. In: International Conference on Machine Learning (ICML) (2017)
11. Graham, B.: Spatially-sparse convolutional neural networks. arXiv preprint arXiv:1409.6070 (2014)
12. Graham, B., Engelcke, M., van der Maaten, L.: 3D semantic segmentation with submanifold sparse convolutional networks. In: IEEE Conference on Computer Vision and Pattern Recognition (CVPR), pp. 9224–9232 (2018)
13. Gupta, S., Girshick, R., Arbeláez, P., Malik, J.: Learning rich features from RGB-D images for object detection and segmentation. In: Fleet, D., Pajdla, T., Schiele, B., Tuytelaars, T. (eds.) ECCV 2014. LNCS, vol. 8695, pp. 345–360. Springer, Cham (2014). https://doi.org/10.1007/978-3-319-10584-0_23
14. Hackel, T., Savinov, N., Ladicky, L., Wegner, J.D., Schindler, K., Pollefeys, M.: Semantic3D.net: a new large-scale point cloud classification benchmark. In: ISPRS Annals of the Photogrammetry, Remote Sensing and Spatial Information Sciences (ISPRS Annals), vol. IV-1-W1, pp. 91–98 (2017)
15. Hackel, T., Wegner, J.D., Schindler, K.: Fast semantic segmentation of 3D point clouds with strongly varying density. ISPRS Ann. Photogram. Remote Sens. Spat. Inf. Sci. (ISPRS Annals) 3(3) (2016)
16. Hua, B.S., Tran, M.K., Yeung, S.K.: Pointwise convolutional neural networks. In: IEEE Conference on Computer Vision and Pattern Recognition (CVPR), pp. 984–993 (2018)
17. Huang, Q., Wang, W., Neumann, U.: Recurrent slice networks for 3D segmentation of point clouds. In: IEEE Conference on Computer Vision and Pattern Recognition (CVPR), pp. 2626–2635 (2018)
18. Kipf, T.N., Welling, M.: Semi-supervised classification with graph convolutional networks. In: International Conference on Machine Learning (ICML) (2017)
19. Krizhevsky, A., Sutskever, I., Hinton, G.E.: ImageNet classification with deep convolutional neural networks. In: Advances in Neural Information Processing Systems (NeurIPS), pp. 1097–1105 (2012)
20. Landrieu, L., Simonovsky, M.: Large-scale point cloud semantic segmentation with superpoint graphs. In: IEEE Conference on Computer Vision and Pattern Recognition (CVPR), pp. 4558–4567 (2018)
21. Lawin, F.J., Danelljan, M., Tosteberg, P., Bhat, G., Khan, F.S., Felsberg, M.: Deep projective 3D semantic segmentation. In: Felsberg, M., Heyden, A., Krüger, N. (eds.) CAIP 2017. LNCS, vol. 10424, pp. 95–107. Springer, Cham (2017). https://doi.org/10.1007/978-3-319-64689-3_8

22. Li, J., Chen, B.M., Hee Lee, G.: SO-Net: self-organizing network for point cloud analysis. In: IEEE Conference on Computer Vision and Pattern Recognition (CVPR), pp. 9397–9406 (2018)
23. Li, Y., Bu, R., Sun, M., Wu, W., Di, X., Chen, B.: PointCNN: convolution on X-transformed points. In: Advances in Neural Information Processing Systems (NeurIPS), pp. 820–830 (2018)
24. Li, Y., Tarlow, D., Brockschmidt, M., Zemel, R.: Gated graph sequence neural networks. In: International Conference on Learning Representations (ICLR) (2016)
25. Liang, Z., Yang, M., Deng, L., Wang, C., Wang, B.: Hierarchical depthwise graph convolutional neural network for 3D semantic segmentation of point clouds. In: IEEE International Conference on Robotics and Automation (ICRA), pp. 8152–8158 (2019)
26. Liu, J., Ni, B., Li, C., Yang, J., Tian, Q.: Dynamic points agglomeration for hierarchical point sets learning. In: IEEE International Conference on Computer Vision (ICCV), pp. 7546–7555 (2019)
27. Liu, Y., Fan, B., Xiang, S., Pan, C.: Relation-shape convolutional neural network for point cloud analysis. In: IEEE Conference on Computer Vision and Pattern Recognition (CVPR), pp. 8895–8904 (2019)
28. Liu, Z., Tang, H., Lin, Y., Han, S.: Point-voxel CNN for efficient 3D deep learning. In: Advances in Neural Information Processing Systems (NeurIPS), pp. 965–975 (2019)
29. Long, J., Shelhamer, E., Darrell, T.: Fully convolutional networks for semantic segmentation. In: IEEE Conference on Computer Vision and Pattern Recognition (CVPR), pp. 3431–3440 (2015)
30. Ma, Y., Guo, Y., Liu, H., Lei, Y., Wen, G.: Global context reasoning for semantic segmentation of 3D point clouds. In: IEEE Winter Conference on Applications of Computer Vision (WACV), pp. 2931–2940 (2020)
31. Maturana, D., Scherer, S.: VoxNet: a 3D convolutional neural network for real-time object recognition. In: IEEE/RSJ International Conference on Intelligent Robots and Systems (IROS), pp. 922–928 (2015)
32. Montoya-Zegarra, J.A., Wegner, J.D., Ladický, Ľ., Schindler, K.: Mind the gap: modeling local and global context in (road) networks. In: Jiang, X., Hornegger, J., Koch, R. (eds.) GCPR 2014. LNCS, vol. 8753, pp. 212–223. Springer, Cham (2014). https://doi.org/10.1007/978-3-319-11752-2_17
33. Qi, C.R., Su, H., Mo, K., Guibas, L.J.: PointNet: deep learning on point sets for 3D classification and segmentation. In: IEEE Conference on Computer Vision and Pattern Recognition (CVPR) (2017)
34. Qi, C.R., Su, H., Nießner, M., Dai, A., Yan, M., Guibas, L.J.: Volumetric and multi-view CNNs for object classification on 3D data. In: IEEE Conference on Computer Vision and Pattern Recognition (CVPR), pp. 5648–5656 (2016)
35. Qi, C.R., Yi, L., Su, H., Guibas, L.J.: PointNet++: deep hierarchical feature learning on point sets in a metric space. In: Advances in Neural Information Processing Systems (NeurIPS), pp. 5105–5114 (2017)
36. Qi, X., Liao, R., Jia, J., Fidler, S., Urtasun, R.: 3D graph neural networks for RGDB semantic segmentation. In: IEEE International Conference on Computer Vision (ICCV), pp. 5199–5208 (2017)
37. Riegler, G., Osman Ulusoy, A., Geiger, A.: OctNet: learning deep 3D representations at high resolutions. In: IEEE Conference on Computer Vision and Pattern Recognition (CVPR), pp. 3577–3586 (2017)

38. Ronneberger, O., Fischer, P., Brox, T.: U-Net: convolutional networks for biomedical image segmentation. In: Navab, N., Hornegger, J., Wells, W.M., Frangi, A.F. (eds.) MICCAI 2015. LNCS, vol. 9351, pp. 234–241. Springer, Cham (2015). https://doi.org/10.1007/978-3-319-24574-4_28
39. Roynard, X., Deschaud, J.E., Goulette, F.: Classification of point cloud scenes with multiscale voxel deep network. arXiv preprint arXiv:1804.03583 (2018)
40. Roynard, X., Deschaud, J.E., Goulette, F.: Paris-Lille-3D: a large and high-quality ground-truth urban point cloud dataset for automatic segmentation and classification. Int. J. Robot. Res. (IJRR) **37**(6), 545–557 (2018)
41. Scarselli, F., Gori, M., Tsoi, A.C., Hagenbuchner, M., Monfardini, G.: The graph neural network model. IEEE Trans. Neural Netw. **20**(1), 61–80 (2008)
42. Shen, Y., Feng, C., Yang, Y., Tian, D.: Mining point cloud local structures by kernel correlation and graph pooling. In: IEEE Conference on Computer Vision and Pattern Recognition (CVPR), vol. 4 (2018)
43. Su, H., et al.: SPLATNet: sparse lattice networks for point cloud processing. In: IEEE Conference on Computer Vision and Pattern Recognition (CVPR), pp. 2530–2539 (2018)
44. Su, H., Maji, S., Kalogerakis, E., Learned-Miller, E.: Multi-view convolutional neural networks for 3D shape recognition. In: IEEE International Conference on Computer Vision (ICCV), pp. 945–953 (2015)
45. Tatarchenko, M., Park, J., Koltun, V., Zhou, Q.Y.: Tangent convolutions for dense prediction in 3D. In: IEEE Conference on Computer Vision and Pattern Recognition (CVPR), pp. 3887–3896 (2018)
46. Thomas, H., Goulette, F., Deschaud, J.E., Marcotegui, B.: Semantic classification of 3D point clouds with multiscale spherical neighborhoods. In: IEEE International Conference on 3D Vision (3DV), pp. 390–398 (2018)
47. Thomas, H., Qi, C.R., Deschaud, J.E., Marcotegui, B., Goulette, F., Guibas, L.J.: KPConv: flexible and deformable convolution for point clouds. In: IEEE International Conference on Computer Vision (ICCV) (2019)
48. Truong, G., Gilani, S.Z., Islam, S.M.S., Suter, D.: Fast point cloud registration using semantic segmentation. In: IEEE Digital Image Computing: Techniques and Applications (DICTA) (2019)
49. Wang, C., Samari, B., Siddiqi, K.: Local spectral graph convolution for point set feature learning. In: European Conference on Computer Vision (ECCV), pp. 52–66 (2018)
50. Wang, S., Suo, S., Ma, W.C., Pokrovsky, A., Urtasun, R.: Deep parametric continuous convolutional neural networks. In: IEEE Conference on Computer Vision and Pattern Recognition (CVPR), pp. 2589–2597 (2018)
51. Wang, W., Yu, R., Huang, Q., Neumann, U.: SGPN: similarity group proposal network for 3D point cloud instance segmentation. In: IEEE Conference on Computer Vision and Pattern Recognition (CVPR), pp. 2569–2578 (2018)
52. Wang, Y., Sun, Y., Liu, Z., Sarma, S.E., Bronstein, M.M., Solomon, J.M.: Dynamic graph CNN for learning on point clouds. ACM Trans. Graph. (TOG) **38**(5), 1–12 (2019)
53. Wu, W., Qi, Z., Fuxin, L.: PointConv: deep convolutional networks on 3D point clouds. In: IEEE Conference on Computer Vision and Pattern Recognition (CVPR), pp. 9621–9630 (2019)
54. Wu, Z., et al.: 3D ShapeNets: a deep representation for volumetric shapes. In: IEEE Conference on Computer Vision and Pattern Recognition (CVPR), pp. 1912–1920 (2015)

55. Xu, Y., Fan, T., Xu, M., Zeng, L., Qiao, Y.: SpiderCNN: deep learning on point sets with parameterized convolutional filters. In: European Conference on Computer Vision (ECCV), pp. 87–102 (2018)

56. Yang, J., et al.: Modeling point clouds with self-attention and Gumbel subset sampling. In: IEEE Conference on Computer Vision and Pattern Recognition (CVPR), pp. 3323–3332 (2019)

57. Yi, L., et al.: A scalable active framework for region annotation in 3D shape collections. ACM Trans. Graph. (TOG) **35**(6), 210 (2016)

58. Zhang, Z., Hua, B.S., Yeung, S.K.: ShellNet: efficient point cloud convolutional neural networks using concentric shells statistics. In: IEEE International Conference on Computer Vision (ICCV), pp. 1607–1616 (2019)

59. Zhao, H., Jiang, L., Fu, C.W., Jia, J.: PointWeb: enhancing local neighborhood features for point cloud processing. In: IEEE Conference on Computer Vision and Pattern Recognition (CVPR), pp. 5565–5573 (2019)

60. Zhou, Y., Tuzel, O.: VoxelNet: end-to-end learning for point cloud based 3D object detection. In: IEEE Conference on Computer Vision and Pattern Recognition (CVPR), pp. 4490–4499 (2018)

Sparse Convolutions on Continuous Domains for Point Cloud and Event Stream Networks

Dominic Jack[1]([✉]) [iD], Frederic Maire[1] [iD], Simon Denman[1] [iD],
and Anders Eriksson[2] [iD]

[1] Queensland University of Technology, Brisbane, QLD, Australia
thedomjack@gmail.com, {f.maire,s.denman}@qut.edu.au
[2] University of Queensland, Brisbane, QLD, Australia
a.eriksson@uq.edu.au

Abstract. Image convolutions have been a cornerstone of a great number of deep learning advances in computer vision. The research community is yet to settle on an equivalent operator for sparse, unstructured continuous data like point clouds and event streams however. We present an elegant sparse matrix-based interpretation of the convolution operator for these cases, which is consistent with the mathematical definition of convolution and efficient during training. On benchmark point cloud classification problems we demonstrate networks built with these operations can train an order of magnitude or more faster than top existing methods, whilst maintaining comparable accuracy and requiring a tiny fraction of the memory. We also apply our operator to event stream processing, achieving state-of-the-art results on multiple tasks with streams of hundreds of thousands of events.

Keywords: Convolution · Point clouds · Event cameras · Deep learning

1 Introduction

Deep learning has exploded in popularity since AlexNet [1] achieved groundbreaking results in image classification [2]. The field now boasts state-of-the-art performance in fields as diverse as medical imaging [3], natural language processing [4], and molecular design [5].

Robotics [6] applications are of particular interest due to their capacity to revolutionize society in the near future. Driverless cars [7] specifically have

This research was supported by the Australian Research Council through the grant ARC FT170100072.

Electronic supplementary material The online version of this chapter (https://doi.org/10.1007/978-3-030-69525-5_24) contains supplementary material, which is available to authorized users.

H. Ishikawa et al. (Eds.): ACCV 2020, LNCS 12622, pp. 400–416, 2021.
https://doi.org/10.1007/978-3-030-69525-5_24

attracted enormous amounts of research funding, with advanced systems being built with multi-camera setups [8], active LiDAR sensors [9], and sensor fusion approaches [10].

At the other end of the spectrum, small mobile robotics applications and mobile devices benefit from an accurate 3D understanding of the world. These platforms generally don't have access to large battery stores or computationally hefty hardware, so efficient computation is essential. Even where compute is available, the cost of energy alone can be prohibitive, and the research community is beginning to appreciate the environmental cost of training massive power-hungry algorithms in data centres [11].

The convolution operator has been a critical component of almost all recent advances in deep learning for computer vision. However, implementations designed for use with images cannot be used for data types that are not defined on a regular grid. Consider for example event cameras, a new type of sensor which shows great promise, particularly in the area of mobile robotics. Rather than reporting average intensities of every pixel at a uniform frame rate, pixels in an event camera fire individual events when they observe an intensity change. The result is a sparse signal with very fast response time, high dynamic range and low power usage. Despite the potential, this vastly different data encoding means that a traditional 2D convolution operation is no longer appropriate.

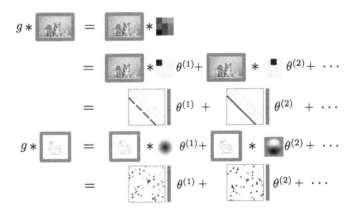

Fig. 1. Learned image convolutions can be thought of as linear combinations of static basis convolutions, where the linear combination is learned. Each basis convolution can be expressed as a sparse-dense matrix product. We take the same approach with point clouds and event streams.

In this work, we investigate how the convolution operator can be applied to two non-image input sources: point clouds and event streams. In particular, our contributions are as follows.

1. We implement a convolution operator for sparse inputs on continuous domains using only matrix products and addition during training. While others have

proposed such an operator, we believe we are the first to *implement* one without compromising the mathematical definition of convolution.

2. We discuss implementation details essential to the feasible training and deployment of networks using our operator on modest hardware. We demonstrate speed-ups of an order of magnitude or more compared to similar methods with a memory foot-print that allows for batch sizes in the thousands.

3. For point clouds, we discuss modifications that lead to desirable properties like robustness to varying density and continuity, and demonstrate that relatively small convolutional networks can perform competitively with much larger, more expensive networks.

4. For event streams, we demonstrate that convolutions can be used to learn features from spiking network spike trains. By principled design of our kernels, we propose two implementations of the same networks: one for learning that takes advantage of modern accelerator hardware, and another for asynchronous deployment which can provide features or inferences associated with events as they arrive. We demonstrate the effectiveness of our learned implementation by achieving state-of-the-art results on multiple classification benchmarks, including a 44% reduction in error rate on sign language classification [12].

2   Prior Work

Point Clouds. Early works in point cloud processing – Pointnet [13] and Deep Sets [14] – use point-wise shared subnetworks and order invariant pooling operations. The successor to Pointnet, Pointnet++ [15] was (to the best of our knowledge) the first to take a hierarchical approach, applying Pointnet submodels to local neighborhoods.

SO-Net [16] takes a similar hierarchical approach to Pointnet++, though uses a different method for sampling and grouping based on self-organizing maps. DGCNN [17] applies graph convolutions to point clouds with edges based on spatial proximity. KCNet [18] uses dynamic kernel points in correlation layers that aim to learn features that encapsulate the relationships between those kernel points and the input cloud. While most approaches treat point clouds as unordered sets by using order-invariant operations, PointCNN [19] takes the approach of learning a canonical ordering over which an order-dependent operation is applied. SpiderCNN [20] and FlexConv [21] each bring their own unique interpretation to generalizing image convolutions to irregular grids. While SpiderCNN focuses on large networks for relatively small classification and segmentation problems, FlexConv utilizes a specialized GPU kernel to apply their method to point clouds with millions of points.

Event Stream Networks. Compared to standard images, relatively little research has been done with event networks. Interest has started to grow recently with the availability of a number of event-based cameras [22,23] and publicly available datasets [12,23–26].

A number of approaches utilize the extensive research in standard image processing by converting event streams to images [25,27]. While these can leverage existing libraries and cheap hardware optimized for image processing, the necessity to accumulate synchronous frames prevents them from taking advantage of many potential benefits of the data format. Other approaches look to biologically-inspired spiking neural networks (SNNs) [28–30]. While promising, these networks are difficult to train due to the discrete nature of the spikes.

Other notable approaches include the work of Lagorce *et al.* [31], who introduce hierarchical time-surfaces to describe spatio-temporal patterns; Sironi *et al.* [26], who show histograms of these time surfaces can be used for object classification; and Bi *et al.* [12], who use graph convolution techniques operating over graphs formed by connecting close events in space-time.

Sparse Convolutions. Sparse convolutions have been used in a variety of ways in deep learning before. Liu *et al.* [32] and Park *et al.* [33] demonstrate improved speed from using implementations optimized for sparse kernel on discrete domains, while there are various voxel-based approaches [34–36] that look at convolutions on discrete sparse inputs and dense kernels. Other approaches involve performing dense discrete convolutions on interpolated projections [37,38].

3   Method Overview

For simplicity, we formulate continuous domain convolutions in the context of physical point clouds in Sect. 3.1, before modifying the approach for event streams in Sect. 3.2. A summary of notation used in this section is provided in the supplementary material.

3.1   Point Cloud Convolutions

We begin by considering the mathematical definition of a convolution of a function h with a kernel g,

$$(h * g)(t) = \int_{\mathcal{D}} h(\tau)g(t - \tau) \, d\tau. \tag{1}$$

We wish to evaluate the convolution of a function with values defined at fixed points x_j in an input cloud $\mathcal{X}$ of size S, at a finite set of points x_i' in an output cloud $\mathcal{X}'$ of size S'. We denote a single feature for each point in these clouds $f \in \mathbb{R}^S$ and $f' \in \mathbb{R}^{S'}$ respectively. For the moment we assume coordinates for both input and output clouds are given. In practice it is often the case that only the input coordinates are given. We discuss choices of output clouds in subsequent sections.

By considering our convolved function h to be the sum of scaled Dirac delta functions δ centred at the point coordinates,

$$h(x) = \sum_j f_j \delta(x - x_j), \tag{2}$$

Equation 1 reduces to

$$f'_i = \sum_{x_j \in \mathcal{N}_i} f_j g(x'_i - x_j), \tag{3}$$

where $\mathcal{N}_i$ is the set of points in the input cloud within some neighborhood of the output point x'_i. We refer to pairs of points $\{x_j, x'_i\}$ where $x_j \in \mathcal{N}_i$ as an *edge*, and the difference in coordinates $\Delta x_{ij} = x'_i - x_j$ as the *edge vector*.

Like Groh *et al.* [21], we use a kernel made up of a linear combination of M unlearned basis functions p_m,

$$g(\Delta x; \theta) = \sum_m p_m(\Delta x)\theta_m, \tag{4}$$

where θ_m are learnable parameters. As with Groh *et al.*, we use geometric monomials for our basis function. Substituting this into Eq. 3 and reordering summations yields

$$f'_i = \sum_m \sum_{x_j \in \mathcal{N}_i} p_m(\Delta x_{ij})f_j\theta_m. \tag{5}$$

We note the inner summation can be expressed as a sparse-dense matrix product,

$$f' = \sum_m N^{(m)} f\theta_m, \tag{6}$$

This is visualized in Fig. 1. Neighborhood matrices $N^{(m)}$ have the same sparsity structure for all m. Values $n_{ij}^{(m)}$ are given by the corresponding basis functions evaluated at edge vectors,

$$n_{ij}^{(m)} = \begin{cases} p_m(\Delta x_{ij}) & x_j \in \mathcal{N}_i, \\ 0 & \text{otherwise.} \end{cases} \tag{7}$$

Generalizing to multi-channel input and output features $F \in \mathbb{R}^{S \times Q}$ and $F' \in \mathbb{R}^{S' \times P}$ respectively, this can be expressed as a sum of matrix products,

$$F' = \sum_m N^{(m)} F\Theta^{(m)}, \tag{8}$$

where $\Theta^{(m)} \in \mathbb{R}^{Q \times P}$ is a matrix of learned parameters.

The elegance of this representation should not be understated. $N^{(m)}$ is a sparse matrix defined purely by relative point coordinates and choice of basis functions. $\Theta^{(m)}$ is a dense matrix of parameter weights much like traditional convolutional layers, and F' and F are feature matrices with the same structure, allowing networks to be constructed in much the same way as image CNNs.

We now identify three implementations with analogues to common image convolutions. A summary is provided in Table 1.

Down-Sampling Convolutions. Convolutions in which there are fewer output points than input points and more output channels than input channels are more efficiently computed left-to-right, *i.e.* as $(N^{(m)}F)\Theta^{(s)}$. These are analogous to conventional strided image convolutions.

Up-Sampling Convolutions. Convolutions in which there are more output points than input points and fewer output channels than input channels are more efficiently computed right-to-left, i.e. $N^{(m)}\left(F\Theta^{(m)}\right)$. These are analogous to conventional fractionally strided or transposed image convolutions.

Featureless Convolutions. The initial convolutions in image CNNs typically have large receptive fields and a large increase in the number of filters. For point clouds, there are often no input features at all – just coordinates. In this instance the convolution reduces to a sum of kernel values over the neighborhood. In the multi-input/output channel context this is given by

$$Z = \tilde{G}\Phi_0, \tag{9}$$

where $\Phi_0 \in \mathbb{R}^{S \times Q}$ is the learned matrix and $\tilde{G} \in \mathbb{R}^{N' \times S}$ is a dense matrix of summed monomial values

$$\tilde{g}_{is} = \sum_j \hat{n}_{ij}^{(m)}. \tag{10}$$

Table 1. Time complexity of different point cloud convolution operations and theoretical space complexity of intermediate terms (Mem). The matrix product for in place convolutions can be evaluated in either order.

	Opt. cond.	Form	Mult. adds	Mem.
In place	$Q = P$ $S' = S$	$\sum_m N^{(m)}F\Theta^{(m)}$	$MP(E + SP)$	SP
Down-sample	$Q < P$ $S' < S$	$\sum_m \left(N^{(m)}F\right)\Theta^{(m)}$	$MQ(E + S'P)$	$S'Q$
Up-sample	$Q > P$ $S' > S$	$\sum_m N^{(m)}\left(F\Theta^{(m)}\right)$	$MP(E + SQ)$	SP
Featureless	$F = 1$	$\tilde{G}\Phi_0$	MSP	–

Neighborhoods. To be consistent with the mathematical definition of convolution, the neighborhood of each point should be fixed, which precludes the use of k-nearest neighbors (kNN), despite its prevalence in the literature [15,20,21,39]. The obvious choice of a neighborhood is a ball. Equation 8 can be implemented trivially using either kNN or ball neighborhoods, though from a deep learning perspective each neighborhood has its own advantages and disadvantages.

Predictable Computation Time: The sparse-dense matrix products have computation proportional to the number of edges. For kNN this is proportional to the output cloud size, but is less predictable when using ball-searches.

Robustness to Point Density: Implementations based on each neighborhood react differently to variations in point density. As the density increases, kNN implementations shrink their receptive field. On the other hand, ball-search implementations suffer from increased computation time and output values proportional to the density.

Discontinuity in Point Coordinates: Both neighborhood types result in operations that are discontinuous in point coordinates. kNN convolutions are discontinuous as the kth and $(k+1)^{\text{th}}$ neighbors of each point pass each other. Ball-search convolutions have a discontinuity at the ball-search radius.

Symmetry: Connectedness in ball-neighborhoods is symmetric – i.e. if $x_i' \in \mathcal{N}_j$ then $x_j \in \mathcal{N}_i$ for neighborhood functions with the same radius. This means the neighborhood matrix N_{IJ} between sets $\mathcal{X}_I$ and $\mathcal{X}_J$ is related to the reversed neighborhood by $N_{IJ} = N_{JI}^T$ (up to a possible difference in sign due to the monomial value). This allows for shared computation between different layers.

Transposed Neighborhood Occupancy: For kNN, all neighborhood matrices are guaranteed to have k entries in each row. This guarantees there will be no empty rows, and hence no empty neighborhoods. Ball search neighborhoods do not share this property, and there is no guarantee points will have any neighbors. This is important for transposed convolutions, where points may rely on neighbors from a lower resolution cloud to seed their features.

Subsampling. Thus far we have remained silent as to how the S' output points making up $\mathcal{X}'$ are chosen. In-place convolutions can be performed with the same input and output clouds, but to construct networks we would like to reduce the number of points as we increase the number of channels in a similar way to image CNNs. We adopt a similar approach to Pointnet++ [15] in that we sample a set of points from the input cloud. Pointnet++ [15] selects points based on the first S' points in iterative farthest point (IFP) ordering, whereby a fixed number of points are iteratively selected based on being farthest from the currently selected points. For each point selected, the distance to all other points has to be computed, resulting in an $\mathcal{O}(S'S)$ implementation.

To improve upon this, we begin by updating distances only to points within a ball neighborhood – a neighborhood that may have already been computed for the previous convolution. By storing the minimum distances in a priority queue, this sampling process still gives relatively uniform coverage like the original IFP, but can be computed in $\mathcal{O}(S'\bar{k})$, where $\bar{k}$ is the average number of neighbors of each point.

We also propose to terminate searching once this set of neighborless candidates has been exhausted, rather than iterating for a fixed number of steps. We refer to this as *rejection sampling*. This results in point clouds of different sizes, but leads to a more consistent number of edges in subsequent neighborhood matrices. It also guarantees all points in the input cloud will have a neighbor in the output cloud. We provide pseudo-code for these algorithms and illustrations in the supplementary material.

Weighted Convolutions. To address both the discontinuity at the ball radius and the neighbor count variation inherent to using balls, we propose using a weighted average convolution by weighting neighboring values by some continuous function w which decreases to zero at the ball radius,

$$\hat{n}_{ij}^{(m)} = \frac{1}{W_i} w_{ij} n_{ij}^{(m)} \tag{11}$$

where $w_{ij} = w(|\Delta x_{ij}|)$ and $W_i = \sum_j w_{ij}$. We use $w(x) = 1 - x/r$ for our experiments, where r is the search radius.

Comparison to Existing Methods. We are not the first to propose hierarchical convolution-like operators for learning on point clouds. In this section we look at a number of other implementations and identify key differences.

Pointnet++ [15] and SpiderCNN [20] each use feature kernels which are nonlinear with respect to the learned parameters. This means these methods have a large memory usage which increases as they create edge features from point features, before reducing those edge features back to point features.

Pointnet++ claims to use a ball neighborhood – and show results are improved using this over kNN. However, their implementation is based on a truncated kNNsearch with fixed k, meaning padding edges are created in sparse regions and meaningful edges are cropped out in dense regions. The cropping is partially offset by the use of max pooling over the neighborhood and IFP ordering, since the first k neighbors found are relatively spread out over the neighborhood. As discussed however, IFP is $\mathcal{O}(SS')$ in time, but removing this means results in the truncated ball search will no longer necessarily be evenly distributed. Also, the padding of sparse neighborhoods leads to an inefficient implementation, as edge features are computed despite never being used.

FlexConv [21] present a very similar derivation to our own. However, they implement Eq. 5 with a custom GPU kernel that only supports kNN.

On the whole, we are unable to find any existing learned approaches that perform true ball searches, nor make any attempt to deal with the discontinuity inherent to kNN. We accept models are capable of learning robustness to such discontinuities, but feel enforcing it at the design stage warrants consideration.

Data Pipeline. There are two aspects of the data processing that are critical to the efficient implementation of our point cloud convolution networks.

Neighborhood Preprocessing. The neighborhood matrices $N^{(m)}$ are functions of relative point coordinates and the choice of unlearned basis functions – they do not depend on any learned parameters. This means they can be pre-computed, either online on CPUs as the previous batch utilizes available accelerators, or offline prior to training. In practice we only pre-compute the neighborhood indices and calculate the relative coordinates and basis functions on the accelerator. This additional computation on the accelerator(s) takes negligible time and reduces the amount of memory that needs to be stored, loaded and shipped.

Ragged Batching. During the batching process, the uneven number of points in each cloud for each example can be concatenated, rather than padded to a uniform size, and sparse matrices block diagonalized. For environments where fixed-sized inputs are required, additional padding can occur at the *batch* level, rather than the individual example level, where variance in the average size will be smaller.

Unlike standard dataset preprocessing, our networks require network-specific preprocessing – preprocessing dependent on *e.g.* the size of the ball searches at each layer, the number of layers *etc.*. To facilitate testing and rapid prototyping, we developed a meta-network module for creating separate pre- and post-batch preprocessing, while simultaneously building learned network stages based on a single conceptual network architecture. This is illustrated in Fig. 2.

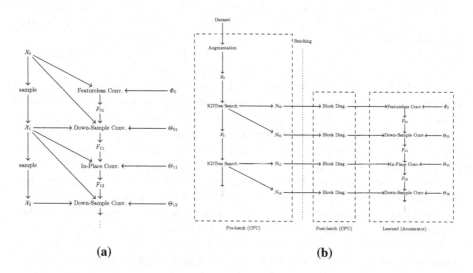

Fig. 2. (a) Conceptual network vs (b) separate computation graphs.

3.2   Event Stream Convolutions

Event streams from cameras can be thought of as 3D point clouds in (x, y, t) space. However, only the most fundamental of physicists would consider space and time equivalent dimensions, and in practice their use cases are significantly different. For event cameras in particular,

- spatial coordinates of events are discrete and occur on a fixed size grid corresponding to the pixels of the camera;
  the time coordinate is effectively continuous and unbounded; and
- events come in time-sorted order.

We aim to formulate a model with the following requirements:

- *Intermediate results*: we would like our model to provide a stream of predictions, updated as more information comes in, rather than having to wait for the end of a sequence before making an inference.
- *Run indefinitely*: we would like to deploy these models in systems which can run for long periods of time. As such, our memory and computational requirements must be $\mathcal{O}(1)$ and $\mathcal{O}(E)$ respectively, with respect to the number of events.

Unfortunately, these requirements are difficult to enforce while making good use of modern deep learning frameworks and hardware accelerators. That said, just because we desire these properties in our end system does not mean we need them during training. By using convolutions with a domain of integration extending *backwards in time only* and using an exponentially decaying kernel, we can train using accelerators on sparse matrices and have an alternative deployment implementation which respects the above requirements.

Formally, we propose neighborhoods defined over small spatial neighborhood of size M_u – similar to image convolutions – extending backwards in time – with a kernel given by

$$g(u, \Delta t) = \sum_v \exp(-\lambda_{uv} \Delta t)\theta_{uv}, \tag{12}$$

where u corresponds to the pixel offset between events and v sums over some fixed temporal kernel size M_v, λ_{uv} is a learned temporal decay term enforced to be positive, θ_{uv} is a learned parameter and u extends over the spatial neighborhood. A temporal domain of integration extending backwards in time only ensures $\Delta t \geq 0$, hence we ensure the effects of events on features decay over time.

Dual Implementations For training, the kernel function of Eq. 12 can be used in Eq. 5 and reduced to a form similar to Eq. 8, where $M = M_u M_v$. This can be implemented in the same way as our point cloud convolutions. Unfortunately, this requires us to construct the entire sparse matrix, removing any chance of getting intermediate results when they are relevant, and also breaks our $\mathcal{O}(1)$ memory constraint with respect to the number of events.

As such, we additionally propose a deployment implementation that updates features at pixels using exponential moving averages in response to events. As an input events come in, we decay the current values of the corresponding pixel by the time since it was last updated and add the new input features. When the features for an output event are required, the features of the pixels in the receptive field can be decayed and then transformed by $\Theta^{(uv)}$, and reduced like a standard image convolution. Formally, we initialize $\mathbf{z}_x^{(uv)} = \mathbf{0} \in \mathbb{R}^Q$ and $\tau_x = 0$ for all pixels x. For each input event (x, t) with features $\mathbf{f}$, we perform the following updates:

$$\mathbf{z}_x^{(uv)} \leftarrow \mathbf{f} + \exp(-\lambda_{uv}(t - \tau_x))\mathbf{z}_x^{(uv)} \tag{13}$$

$$\tau_x \leftarrow t. \tag{14}$$

Features $\mathbf{f}'$ for output event at (x', t') can thus be computed by

$$\mathbf{f}' = \sum_{u,v} \exp(-\lambda_{uv}(t' - \tau_{x'-u}))\mathbf{z}_{x'-u}^{(uv)}{}^T \Theta^{(uv)}. \tag{15}$$

This requires $\mathcal{O}(M_u M_v Q)$ operations per input event, $\mathcal{O}(M_u M_v P Q)$ operations per output event and $\mathcal{O}(M_u M_v Q)$ space per pixel. Alternatively, the linear transform can be applied to $\mathbf{f}$ during the $\mathbf{z}_x^{(uv)}$ update (equivalent to up-sampling convolutions) for subtly different space and computational requirements. Either way, our requirements are satisfied.

Subsampling. As with our point cloud formulation, we would like a hierarchical model with convolutions joining multiple streams with successively lower resolution and higher dimensional features. We propose using an unlearned leaky-integrate-and-fire (LIF) model due to the simplicity of the implementation and its prevalence in SNN literature [40].

LIF models transform input spike trains by tracking a theoretical voltage at each location or "neuron". These voltages exponentially decay over time, but are increased discontinuously by input events in some receptive field. If the voltage at a location exceeds a certain threshold, the voltage at that neuron is reset, and an output event is fired. SNNs generally learn the sensitivity of each output neuron to input spikes. We take a simpler approach, using a fixed voltage increase of $1/n$ as a result of an input spike, where n is the number of output neurons affected by the input event. Note we do not suggest this is optimal for our use case – particularly the unlearned nature of it – though we leave additional investigation of this idea to future work.

4   Experiments

We perform experiments on various classification tasks across point clouds and event streams. We provide a brief overview of network structures here. Model diagrams and technical details about the training procedure are provided in the supplementary material.

We investigate our point cloud operator in the context of ModelNet40 [41], a 40-class classification problem with 9840 training examples and 2468 testing examples. We use the first 1024 points provided by Pointnet++ [15] and use the same point dropout, random jittering and off-axis rotation, uniform scaling and shuffling data augmentation policies.

We construct two networks based loosely on Resnet [42]. Our larger model consists of an in-place convolution with 32 output channels, followed by 3 alternating down-sampling and in-place residual blocks, with the number of filters increasing by a factor of 2 in each down-sampling block. Our in-place ball radii start at 0.1125 and increase by a factor of 2 each level. Our down-sample radii are $\sqrt{2}$ larger than the previous in-place convolution. This results in sampled point clouds with roughly 25% of the original points on average, roughly 10 neighbors per in-place output point and 20 neighbors per down-sample output point. After our final in-place convolution block we use a single point-wise convolution to increase the number of filters by a factor of 4 before max pooling across the point dimension. We feed this into a single hidden layer classifier with 256 hidden units. All convolutions use monomial basis functions up to 2nd order. We use dropout, batch normalization and L2 regularization throughout. Our smaller model is similar, but skips the initial in-place convolution and has half the number of filters at each level. Both are trained using a batch size of 128 using Adam optimizer [43] and with the learning rate reduced by a factor of 5 after 20 epochs without an improvement to training accuracy.

For event streams, we consider 5 classification tasks – N-MNIST and N-Caltech101 from Orchard et al. [24], MNIST-DVS and CIFAR10-DVS from Serrano et al. [23]) and ASL-DVS from Bi et al. [12].

All our event models share the same general structure, with an initial 3 × 3 convolution with stride 2 followed by alternating in-place resnet/inception-inspired convolution blocks and down-sample convolutions (also 3 × 3 with stride 2), finishing with a final in-place block. We doubled the number of filters and the LIF decay time at each down sampling.

The result is multiple streams, with each event in each stream having its own features. The features of any event in any stream could be used as inputs to a classifier, but in order to compare to other work we choose to pool our streams by averaging over (x, y, t) voxels at our three lowest resolutions. For example, our CIFAR-10 model had streams with learned features at 64 × 64 down to 4 × 4. We voxelized the 16 × 16 stream to 16 × 16 × 4, the 8 × 8 stream into an 8 × 8 × 2 grid and the final stream into a 4 × 4 × 1. Each voxel grid beyond the first receives inputs from the lower resolution voxel grid (via a strided 2 × 2 × 2 voxel convolution), and from the average of the event stream. In this way, examples with relatively few events that result in zero events at the final stream still resulted in predictions (empty voxels are assigned the value $\mathbf{0}$). Hyperparameters associated with stream propagation (decay rate, spike threshold and reset potential) were hand-selected via an extremely crude search that aimed to achieve a modest number of events in the final stream for most examples. These hyperparameters, along with further details on training and data augmentation are provided in the supplementary material.

5 Results

5.1 Point Clouds

We begin by benchmarking our implementations of Eq. 8. We implement the outer summation in two ways: a parallel implementation which unstacks the relevant tensors and computes matrix-vector products in parallel, and a map-reduce variant which accumulates intermediate values. Both are written entirely in the high-level python interface to Tensorflow 2.0.

We compare with the work of Groh *et al.* [21] who provide benchmarks for their own tensorflow implementation, as well as a custom CUDA implementation that only supports kNN. Our implementations are written entirely in the high-level Tensorflow 2 python interface and can handle arbitrary neighborhoods. Computation time and memory requirements are shown in Table 2. Values do not include neighborhood calculations. Despite our implementation being more flexible, our forward pass is almost an order of magnitude faster, and our full training pass is sped up more than 60-fold. Our implementation does require more memory. We also see significant improvements by using Tensorflow's accelerated linear algebra just-in-time (JIT) compilation module, particularly in terms of memory usage.

Table 2. Equation 8 implementations vs. FlexConv benchmarks on an Nvidia GTX-1080Ti. $M = 4$, $P = Q = 64$, $S = S' = 4096$, 9 neighbors and batch size of 8. Backward passes compute gradients w.r.t. learned parameters and input features (F and Θ). JIT rows correspond to just-in-time compiled implementations excluding compile time.

	Time (ms)		GPU Mem (Mb)	
	Forward	Backward	Forward	Backward
TF [21]	1829	2738	34G	63G
Custom [21]	24.0	265.0	**8.4**	**8.7**
$(NF)\Theta$	2.9	5.1	57.3	105.0
$(NF)\Theta$-JIT	**2.7**	5.0	41.0	41.0
$N(F\Theta)$	2.9	4.3	56.0	56.2
$N(F\Theta)$-JIT	**2.7**	**4.1**	40.0	49.0

Next we look at training times and capacity of our model on the ModelNet40 classification task using 1024 input points. Table 3 shows performance at various possible batch sizes and training times for our standard model compared to various other methods. For fair comparison, we do not use XLA compilation.

Clearly our model runs significantly faster than those we compare to. Just as clear is the fact that our models which compute neighborhood information online are CPU-constrained. This preprocessing is not particularly slow – a modest 8-core desktop is capable of completing the 7 neighborhood searches and 3 rejection samplings associated with each example on our large model at 800 Hz, which

Table 3. Time to train 1 epoch of ModelNet40 classification on an Nvidia GTX-1080Ti. Online/offline refers to preprocessing.

Model	Batch size	Epoch time (s)	
		Online	Offline
SpiderCNN [20]	24	196	–
Pointnet++ [15]	32	56	–
	64	56	–
PointCNN [19]	32	35	–
	64	33	–
	128	33	–
Ours (large)	32	12.9	6.80
	64	11.8	5.10
	128	11.2	4.13
	1024	12.4	3.60
	4096	11.5	**3.35**
Ours (small)	32	12.0	4.35
	64	11.4	2.83
	128	11.2	2.06
	1024	11.4	**1.38**
	4096	11.5	1.41
	9840	13.0	1.39

Table 4. Top-1 instance accuracy on ModelNet40, sorted by mean of 10 runs according to Koguciuk *et al.* [44], for our large model with batch size 128. Reported/Best are those values reported by other papers, and the best of 10 runs for our models.

Model	Reported/Best	Mean
Ours (small)	88.77	87.94
Pointnet [13]	89.20	88.65
KCNet [18]	91.00	89.62
DeepSets [14]	90.30	89.71
Pointnet++ [15]	90.70	90.14
Ours (large)	91.08	90.34
DGCNN [17]	92.20	91.55
PointCNN [19]	92.20	91.82
SO-Net [16]	**93.40**	**92.65**

results in training that is still an order of magnitude faster than the closest competitor – but in the context of an accelerator-based training loop that runs at up 3000 Hz this is a major bottleneck.

One might expect such a speed-up to come at the cost of inference accuracy. Top-1 accuracy is given in Table 4. We observe a slight drop in performance compared to recent state-of-the-art methods, though our large model is still competitive with well established methods like Pointnet++. Our small model performs distinctly worse, though still respectably.

5.2 Event Camera Streams

Table 5 shows results for our method on the selected classification tasks. We see minor improvements over current state-of-the art methods on the straightforward MNIST variants, though acknowledge the questionable value of such minor improvements on datasets like these. We see a modest improvement on CIFAR-10, though perform relatively poorly on N-Caltech101. Our ASL-DVS model significantly out-performs the current state-of-the-art, with a 44% reduction in error rate. We attribute the greater success on this last dataset compared to others to the significantly larger number of examples available during training (~80,000 vs ~10,000).

Table 5. Top-1 classification accuracy (%) for event stream classification tasks.

Model	N-MNIST	MNIST-DVS	CIFAR-DVS	NCaltech101	ASL-DVS
HATS [26]	99.1	98.4	52.4	64.2	–
RG-CNN [12]	99.0	98.6	54.0	**65.7**	90.1
Ours	**99.2**	**99.1**	**56.6**	63.0	**94.6**

References

1. Krizhevsky, A., Sutskever, I., Hinton, G.E.: ImageNet classification with deep convolutional neural networks. In: Pereira, F., Burges, C.J.C., Bottou, L., Weinberger, K.Q. (eds.) Advances in Neural Information Processing Systems, vol. 25, pp. 1097–1105. Curran Associates, Inc. (2012)
2. Deng, J., Dong, W., Socher, R., Li, L.J., Li, K., Fei-Fei, L.: ImageNet: a large-scale hierarchical image database. In: IEEE Conference on Computer Vision and Pattern Recognition, pp. 248–255. IEEE (2009)
3. Erickson, B.J., Korfiatis, P., Akkus, Z., Kline, T.L.: Machine learning for medical imaging. Radiographics **37**, 505–515 (2017)
4. Devlin, J., Chang, M.W., Lee, K., Toutanova, K.: BERT: pre-training of deep bidirectional transformers for language understanding. arXiv preprint arXiv:1810.04805 (2018)
5. Elton, D.C., Boukouvalas, Z., Fuge, M.D., Chung, P.W.: Deep learning for molecular design-a review of the state of the art. Mol. Syst. Design Engi. **4**, 828–849 (2019)
6. Pierson, H.A., Gashler, M.S.: Deep learning in robotics: a review of recent research. Adv. Robot. **31**, 821–835 (2017)
7. Grigorescu, S., Trasnea, B., Cocias, T., Macesanu, G.: A survey of deep learning techniques for autonomous driving. arXiv preprint arXiv:1910.07738 (2019)
8. Heng, L., et al.: Project AutoVision: localization and 3D scene perception for an autonomous vehicle with a multi-camera system. In: 2019 International Conference on Robotics and Automation (ICRA), pp. 4695–4702. IEEE (2019)
9. Li, B., Zhang, T., Xia, T.: Vehicle detection from 3D lidar using fully convolutional network. arXiv preprint arXiv:1608.07916 (2016)
10. Gao, H., Cheng, B., Wang, J., Li, K., Zhao, J., Li, D.: Object classification using CNN-based fusion of vision and lidar in autonomous vehicle environment. IEEE Trans. Industr. Inf. **14**, 4224–4231 (2018)
11. García-Martín, E., Rodrigues, C.F., Riley, G., Grahn, H.: Estimation of energy consumption in machine learning. J. Parallel Distrib. Comput. **134**, 75–88 (2019)
12. Bi, Y., Chadha, A., Abbas, A., Bourtsoulatze, E., Andreopoulos, Y.: Graph-based spatial-temporal feature learning for neuromorphic vision sensing. arXiv preprint arXiv:1910.03579 (2019)
13. Qi, C.R., Su, H., Mo, K., Guibas, L.J.: PointNet: deep learning on point sets for 3D classification and segmentation. In: Proceedings of the IEEE Conference on Computer Vision and Pattern Recognition, pp. 652–660 (2017)
14. Zaheer, M., Kottur, S., Ravanbakhsh, S., Poczos, B., Salakhutdinov, R.R., Smola, A.J.: Deep sets. In: Advances in Neural Information Processing Systems, pp. 3391–3401 (2017)

15. Qi, C.R., Yi, L., Su, H., Guibas, L.J.: PointNet++: deep hierarchical feature learning on point sets in a metric space. In: Advances in Neural Information Processing Systems, pp. 5099–5108 (2017)
16. Li, J., Chen, B.M., Hee Lee, G.: SO-Net: self-organizing network for point cloud analysis. In: Proceedings of the IEEE Conference on Computer Vision and Pattern Recognition, pp. 9397–9406 (2018)
17. Wang, Y., Sun, Y., Liu, Z., Sarma, S.E., Bronstein, M.M., Solomon, J.M.: Dynamic graph CNN for learning on point clouds. ACM Trans. Graph. (TOG) **38**, 146 (2019)
18. Shen, Y., Feng, C., Yang, Y., Tian, D.: Mining point cloud local structures by kernel correlation and graph pooling. In: Proceedings of the IEEE Conference on Computer Vision and Pattern Recognition, pp. 4548–4557 (2018)
19. Li, Y., Bu, R., Sun, M., Wu, W., Di, X., Chen, B.: PointCNN: convolution on X-transformed points. In: Advances in Neural Information Processing Systems, pp. 820–830 (2018)
20. Xu, Y., Fan, T., Xu, M., Zeng, L., Qiao, Y.: SpiderCNN: deep learning on point sets with parameterized convolutional filters. CoRR abs/1803.11527 (2018)
21. Groh, F., Wieschollek, P., Lensch, H.P.A.: Flex-convolution (deep learning beyond grid-worlds). CoRR abs/1803.07289 (2018)
22. Posch, C., Matolin, D., Wohlgenannt, R.: A QVGA 143 dB dynamic range frame-free PWM image sensor with lossless pixel-level video compression and time-domain CDS. IEEE J. Solid-State Circ. **46**, 259–275 (2010)
23. Serrano-Gotarredona, T., Linares-Barranco, B.: A 128 *times* 128 1.5% contrast sensitivity 0.9% FPN 3 μs latency 4 mW asynchronous frame-free dynamic vision sensor using transimpedance preamplifiers. IEEE J. Solid-State Circ. **48**, 827–838 (2013)
24. Orchard, G., Jayawant, A., Cohen, G.K., Thakor, N.: Converting static image datasets to spiking neuromorphic datasets using saccades. Front. Neurosci. **9**, 437 (2015)
25. Maqueda, A.I., Loquercio, A., Gallego, G., García, N., Scaramuzza, D.: Event-based vision meets deep learning on steering prediction for self-driving cars. In: Proceedings of the IEEE Conference on Computer Vision and Pattern Recognition, pp. 5419–5427 (2018)
26. Sironi, A., Brambilla, M., Bourdis, N., Lagorce, X., Benosman, R.: HATS: histograms of averaged time surfaces for robust event-based object classification. In: Proceedings of the IEEE Conference on Computer Vision and Pattern Recognition, pp. 1731–1740 (2018)
27. Nguyen, A., Do, T.T., Caldwell, D.G., Tsagarakis, N.G.: Real-time 6dof pose relocalization for event cameras with stacked spatial LSTM networks. In: Proceedings of the IEEE Conference on Computer Vision and Pattern Recognition Workshops (2019)
28. Bohte, S.M., Kok, J.N., La Poutre, H.: Error-backpropagation in temporally encoded networks of spiking neurons. Neurocomputing **48**, 17–37 (2002)
29. Russell, A., et al.: Optimization methods for spiking neurons and networks. IEEE Trans. Neural Networks **21**, 1950–1962 (2010)
30. Cao, Y., Chen, Y., Khosla, D.: Spiking deep convolutional neural networks for energy-efficient object recognition. Int. J. Comput. Vision **113**, 54–66 (2015)
31. Lagorce, X., Orchard, G., Galluppi, F., Shi, B.E., Benosman, R.B.: HOTS: a hierarchy of event-based time-surfaces for pattern recognition. IEEE Trans. Pattern Anal. Mach. Intell. **39**, 1346–1359 (2016)

32. Liu, B., Wang, M., Foroosh, H., Tappen, M., Pensky, M.: Sparse convolutional neural networks. In: Proceedings of the IEEE Conference on Computer Vision and Pattern Recognition, pp. 806–814 (2015)
33. Park, J., et al.: Faster CNNs with direct sparse convolutions and guided pruning. arXiv preprint arXiv:1608.01409 (2016)
34. Graham, B., van der Maaten, L.: Submanifold sparse convolutional networks. arXiv preprint arXiv:1706.01307 (2017)
35. Graham, B., Engelcke, M., Van Der Maaten, L.: 3D semantic segmentation with submanifold sparse convolutional networks. In: Proceedings of the IEEE Conference on Computer Vision and Pattern Recognition, pp. 9224–9232 (2018)
36. Choy, C., Gwak, J., Savarese, S.: 4D spatio-temporal convnets: Minkowski convolutional neural networks. In: Proceedings of the IEEE Conference on Computer Vision and Pattern Recognition, pp. 3075–3084 (2019)
37. Jampani, V., Kiefel, M., Gehler, P.V.: Learning sparse high dimensional filters: image filtering, dense CRFs and bilateral neural networks. In: Proceedings of the IEEE Conference on Computer Vision and Pattern Recognition, pp. 4452–4461 (2016)
38. Su, H., et al.: SPLATNet: sparse lattice networks for point cloud processing. In: Proceedings of the IEEE Conference on Computer Vision and Pattern Recognition, pp. 2530–2539 (2018)
39. Boulch, A.: ConvPoint: continuous convolutions for point cloud processing. Comput. Graph. **88**, 24–34 (2020)
40. Koch, C., Segev, I., et al.: Methods in Neuronal Modeling: From Ions to Networks. MIT Press, Cambridge (1998)
41. Wu, Z., et al.: 3d ShapeNets: a deep representation for volumetric shapes. In: Proceedings of the IEEE Conference on Computer Vision and Pattern Recognition, pp. 1912–1920 (2015)
42. He, K., Zhang, X., Ren, S., Sun, J.: Deep residual learning for image recognition. In: 2016 IEEE Conference on Computer Vision and Pattern Recognition (CVPR), pp. 770–778 (2016)
43. Kingma, D.P., Ba, J.: Adam: a method for stochastic optimization. arXiv preprint arXiv:1412.6980 (2014)
44. Koguciuk, D., Chechliński, Ł., El-Gaaly, T.: 3D object recognition with ensemble learning—a study of point cloud-based deep learning models. In: Bebis, G., et al. (eds.) ISVC 2019. LNCS, vol. 11845, pp. 100–114. Springer, Cham (2019). https://doi.org/10.1007/978-3-030-33723-0_9

IAFA: Instance-Aware Feature Aggregation for 3D Object Detection from a Single Image

Dingfu Zhou[1,2($\boxtimes$)], Xibin Song[1,2], Yuchao Dai[3], Junbo Yin[1,4], Feixiang Lu[1,2], Miao Liao[1], Jin Fang[1,2], and Liangjun Zhang[1]

[1] Baidu Research, Beijing, China
zhoudingfu@baidu.com
[2] National Engineering Laboratory of Deep Learning Technology and Application, Beijing, China
[3] Northwestern Polytechnical University, Xi'an, China
[4] Beijing Institute of Technology, Beijing, China

Abstract. 3D object detection from a single image is an important task in Autonomous Driving (AD), where various approaches have been proposed. However, the task is intrinsically ambiguous and challenging as single image depth estimation is already an ill-posed problem. In this paper, we propose an instance-aware approach to aggregate useful information for improving the accuracy of 3D object detection with the following contributions. First, an instance-aware feature aggregation (IAFA) module is proposed to collect local and global features for 3D bounding boxes regression. Second, we empirically find that the spatial attention module can be well learned by taking coarse-level instance annotations as a supervision signal. The proposed module has significantly boosted the performance of the baseline method on both 3D detection and 2D bird-eye's view of vehicle detection among all three categories. Third, our proposed method outperforms all single image-based approaches (even these methods trained with depth as auxiliary inputs) and achieves state-of-the-art 3D detection performance on the KITTI benchmark.

1 Introduction

Accurate perception of surrounding environment is particularly important for Autonomous Driving [1,2], and robot systems. In AD pipeline, the perception 3D positions and orientation of surrounding obstacles (e.g., vehicle, pedestrian, and cyclist) are essential for the downstream navigation and control modules. 3D object detection with depth sensors (e.g., RGBD camera, LiDAR) is relatively easy and has been well studied recently. Especially, with the development of deep learning techniques in 3D point cloud, a wide variety of 3D object detectors have

Electronic supplementary material The online version of this chapter (https://doi.org/10.1007/978-3-030-69525-5_25) contains supplementary material, which is available to authorized users.

H. Ishikawa et al. (Eds.): ACCV 2020, LNCS 12622, pp. 417–435, 2021.
https://doi.org/10.1007/978-3-030-69525-5_25

Fig. 1. An example of center-point-based object representation. The red points in the left sub-image are the projected 3D center of the objects on the 2D image. The numbers in the blue text box represent the "ID" of vehicles. The red points are the projected 3D vehicle centers onto the 2D image plane. The number in the red text boxes represents which vehicle that the center point belongs to. (Color figure online)

sprung up including point-based methods [3,4], voxel-based methods [5–7] and hybrid-point-voxel-based methods [8,9].

Although depth sensors have been widely used in different scenarios, their drawbacks are also obvious: expensive prices, high-energy consumption, and less structure information. Recently, 3D object detection from passive sensors such as monocular or stereo cameras has attracted many researchers' attention and some of them achieved impressive detection performance. Compared with the active sensors, the most significant bottleneck of 2D image-based approaches [10] is how to recover the depth of these obstacles. For stereo rig, the depth (or disparity) map can be recovered by traditional geometric matching [11] or learned by deep neural networks [12]. By using traditional geometric techniques, it's really difficult to estimate the depth map from a single image without any prior information while this problem has been partly solved with deep learning based methods, [13]. With the estimated depth map, the 3D point cloud (pseudo LiDAR point cloud) can be easily reconstructed via pre-calibrated intrinsic (or extrinsic) camera parameters. Any 3D detectors designed for LiDAR point cloud can be use directly on pseudo LiDAR point cloud [14–16] and [17]. Furthermore, in [14], the depth estimation and 3D object detection network has been integrated together in an end-to-end manner.

Recently, center-based (anchor-free) frameworks become popular for 2D object detection. Two representative frameworks are "CenterNet" [18] and "FCOS" [19]. Inspired by these 2D detectors, some advanced anchor-free 3D object detectors have been proposed such as "SMOKE" [20] and "RTM3D" [21]. In the center-based frameworks, an object is represented as a center point and object detection has been transferred as a problem of point classification and its corresponding attributes (e.g., size, offsets, depth, etc.) regression.

Although the center-based representation is very compact and effective, it also has some drawbacks. In the left sub-figure of Fig. 1, the vehicles are represented with center points, where the red points are the projected 3D object centers on the 2D image plane. The white numbers in the blue text boxes represent the "ID" of the vehicles and the white numbers in the red text boxes are the vehicle "ID"s that these points belong to. From this image, we can easily find that the projected 3D centers of vehicle "2" is on the surface of vehicle "1". Similarly, the projected 3D centers of vehicle "3" is on the surface of vehicle "2". Particularly, this kind of misalignment commonly happens in the AD scenario in the case of occlusion. Taking vehicle "2" as an example, its projected 3D center is on the surface of vehicle "1" and most of its surrounding pixels are from vehicle "1". During the training, the network may be confused about which pixels (or features) should be used for this center classification and its attributes regression. This problem becomes much more serious for the depth regression because the real depth of the 2D center point (on the surface of vehicle "1") is totally different from its ground truth value-the depth of its 3D Bounding Box's (BBox's) center.

In order to well handle this kind of misalignment or to alleviate this kind of confusion during the network learning process, we propose to learn an additional attention map for each center point during training and explicitly tell the network that which pixels belong to this object and they should contribute more for the center classification and attributes regression. Intuitively, the learning of the attention map can be guided by the instance mask of the object. By adding this kind of attention map estimation, we can achieve the following advantages: first of all, the occluded objects, attention map can guide the network to use the features on the corresponding objects and suppress these features that belong to the other object; second, for these visible objects, the proposed module is also able to aggregate the features from different locations to help the object detection task. The contributions of our work can be summarized as follows:

1. First, we propose a novel deep learning branch termed as Instance-Aware Features Aggregation (IAFA) to collect all the pixels belong to the same object for contributing to the object detection task. Specifically, the proposed branch explicitly learns an attention map to automatically aggregate useful information for each object.
2. Second, we empirically find that the coarse instance annotations from other instance segmentation networks can provide good supervision to generate the features aggregation attention maps.
3. The experimental results on the public benchmark show that the performance of the baseline can be significantly improved by adding the proposed branch. In addition, the boosted framework outperforms all other monocular-based 3D object detectors among all the three categories ("Easy", "Moderate" and "Hard").

2   Related Work

LiDAR-Based 3D Detection: 3D object detection in traffic scenario becomes popular with the development of range sensor and the AD techniques. Inspired by 2D detection, earlier 3D object detectors project point cloud into 2D (e.g., bird-eye-view [22] or front-view [23]) to obtain the 2D object bounding boxes first and then re-project them into 3D. With the development of 3D convolution techniques, the recently proposed approaches can be generally divided into two categories: volumetric convolution-based methods and points-based methods. Voxel-net [5] and PointNet [24] are two pioneers for these methods, respectively. How to balance the GPU memory consumption and the voxel's resolution is one bottleneck of voxel-based approach. At the beginning, the voxel resolution is relative large as $0.4\,m \times 0.2\,m \times 0.2\,m$ due the limitation of GPU memory. Now this issue has been almost solved due to the development of GPU hardware and some sparse convolution techniques, e.g., SECOND [25] and PointPillars [6]. At the same time, points-based methods [26] also have been well explored and achieved good performance on the public benchmarks.

Camera-Based 3D Object Detection: Due to the cheaper price and less power consumption, many different approaches have been proposed recently for 3D object detection from camera sensor. A simple but effective idea is to reconstruct the 3D information of the environment first and then any point cloud-based detectors can be employed to detect objects from the reconstructed point clouds (which is also called "Pseudo-LiDAR") directly. For depth estimation (or 3D reconstruction), either classical geometric-based approaches or deep-learning based approaches can be used. Based on this idea, many approaches have been proposed for either monocular [16] or stereo cameras [14,15,17,27]. Rather than transforming the depth map into point clouds, many approaches propose using the depth estimation map directly in the framework to enhance the 3D object detection. In M3D-RPN [28] and [29], the pre-estimated depth map has been used to guide the 2D convolution, which is called as "Depth-Aware Convolution". In addition, in order to well benefit the prior knowledge, some approaches are also proposed to integrate the shape information into the object detection task via sparse key-points [30] or dense 2D and 3D mapping.

Direct Regression-Based Methods: Although these methods mentioned above achieved impressive results, they all need auxiliary information to aid the object detection, such as "Depth Map" or "Pseudo Point Cloud". Other approaches are direct regression-based methods. Similar to the 2D detectors, the direct regression based methods can be roughly divided into anchor-based or anchor-free methods. Anchor-based methods such as [31–34] need to detect 2D object bounding boxes first and then ROI align technique is used to crop the related information in both original image domain or extracted feature domain for corresponded 3D attributes regression. Inspired by the development of center-point-based (anchor free) methods in 2D object detection [18,19] and instance segmentation [35,36], some researchers have proposed center-point-based methods for 3D object detection task [20,21] and [34]. In [18], the object has been represented as a center point with associated attributes (e.g., object's size, category class, etc.). In addition, they extend this representation into 3D and achieve reasonable performance. Based on this framework, Liu et al. [20] modify the baseline 3D detector by adding the group-normalization in backbone network and propose a multi-step disentangling approach for constructing the 3D bounding box. With these modifications, the training speed and detection performances have been significantly improved. Instead of representing the object as a single point, Li et al. [21] propose to use nine points which are center point plus eight vertexes of the 3D bounding box. First, the network is designed to detect all the key-points and a post-processing step is required for solving the object pose as an optimization problem.

Attention-Based Feature Aggregation: Recently, attention-based feature aggregation strategies have proven their effectiveness in many areas, such as image super-resolution [37], image translation [38,39], GAN based methods [40], semantic segmentation [41]. According to previous work, the attention strategies can efficiently enhance extracted features in several manners, including: channel attention aggregation [42] and spatial attention based aggregation [37,41]. The channel attention based aggregation strategy aims to learn the weight of each channel of feature maps to aggregate the features in channel-level, while spatial attention based aggregation aims to learn the weight of each pixel in feature maps to aggregate the features in pixel-level.

3   Definition and Baseline Method

Before the introduction of the proposed approach, the 3D object detection problem and the baseline center-based framework will be discussed first.

3.1   Problem Definition

For easy understanding, the camera coordinate is set as the reference coordinate and all the objects are defined based on it. In deep-learning-based approaches, an object is generally represented as a rotated 3D BBox as

$$\mathbf{c}, \mathbf{d}, \mathbf{r} = (c_x, c_y, c_z), (l, w, h), (r_x, r_y, r_z), \tag{1}$$

in which $\mathbf{c}$, $\mathbf{d}$, $\mathbf{r}$ represent the centroid, dimension and orientation of the BBox respectively. In AD scenario, the road surface that the objects lie on is almost flat locally, therefore the orientation parameters are reduced from three to one by keeping only the yaw angle r_y around the Y-axis. In this case, the BBox is simply represented as $(c_x, c_y, c_z, l, w, h, r_y)$.

3.2   Center-Based 3D Object Detector

Center-based (anchor-free) approaches have been widely employed for 2D object detection and instance segmentation recently. In these methods, an object is represented as a center with associated attributes (e.g., dimensions and center offsets) which are obtained with a classification and regression branches simultaneously. Based on the 2D centernet, Liu et al. [20] modified and improved it for 3D object detection, where the object center is the projection of 3D BBox's

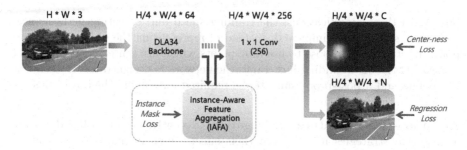

Fig. 2. A sketch description of the proposed Instance-Aware Feature Aggregation (IAFA) module integrated with the baseline 3D object detector. In which, the structure inside the dotted bordered rectangle is the proposed IAFA and "C" and "N" at the end of the frameworks are the number of "categories" and regression parameters respectively.

centroid and the associated attributes are 3d dimensions, depth and object's orientation etc.

A sketch of baseline 3D object detector is illustrated in Fig. 2. By passing the backbone network (e.g., DLA34 [43]), a feature map $\mathbf{F}_{\text{backbone}}$ with the size of $\frac{W}{4} \times \frac{H}{4} \times 64$ is generated from the input image $\mathbf{I}$ ($W \times H \times 3$). After a specific $1 \times 1 \times 256$ convolution layer, two separate branches are designed for center classification and corresponding attributes regression. Due to anchor-free, the classification and regressions are generated densely for all points of the feature map. In center classification branch, a point is classified as positive if its response is higher than a certain threshold. At the same time, its associated attributes can be obtained correspondingly according to its location index.

3D BBox Recovery: Assuming that a point (x_i, y_i) is classified as an object's center and its associated attributes usually includes $(x_{\text{offset}}, y_{\text{offset}})$, *depth*, (l, w, h) and $(\sin\theta, \cos\theta)$, where d is the depth of object, (l, w, h) is 3D BBox's dimension. Similar to [44], θ is an alternative representation of r_y for easy regression and $(x_{\text{offset}}, y_{\text{offset}})$ is estimated discretization residuals due to feature map downsampling operation. Based on the 2D center and its attributes, the 3D centroid (c_x, c_y, c_z) of the object can be recovered via

$$[c_x, c_y, c_z]^{\text{T}} = \mathbf{K}^{-1} * [x_i + x_{\text{offset}}, y_i + y_{\text{offset}}, 1]^{\text{T}} * \text{depth}, \tag{2}$$

where $\mathbf{K}$ is the camera intrinsic parameter.

Loss Function: During training, for each ground truth center p_k of class j, its corresponding low-resolution point $\hat{p}_j$ in the down-sampled feature map is computed first. To increase the positive sample ratio, all the ground truth centers are splat onto a heatmap $\mathbf{h} \in [0, 1]$ with the size of $\frac{W}{4} \times \frac{H}{4} \times C$ using a Gaussian kernel $h_{xyj} = \exp(-\frac{(x-\hat{p}_x)^2 + (y-\hat{p}_y)^2}{2\sigma_p^2})$, where σ_p is an object size-adaptive standard deviation. If two Gaussians of the same class overlap, the element-wise maximum is employed here. The training loss for center point classification branch is defined as

$$L_{\text{center-ness}} = \frac{1}{M} \sum_{xyj} \begin{cases} (1 - \hat{h}_{xyj})^\alpha \log(\hat{h}_{xyj}) & if\ h_{xyj} = 1, \\ (1 - h_{xyj})^\beta (\hat{h}_{xyj})^\alpha \log(1 - \hat{h}_{xyj}) & \text{otherwise.} \end{cases} \quad (3)$$

where α and β are hyper-parameters of the focal loss [45] and M is the number of all positive center points.

Although the attributes regression is computed densely for each location in the feature map, the loss function is only defined sparsely on the ground truth centers. Usually, a general expression of regression loss is defined as

$$L_{reg} = \frac{1}{N} \sum_{i=1}^{N} (\mathbb{1}_{p_i} l_{reg}), \quad \mathbb{1}_{p_i} = \begin{cases} 1\ if\ p_i\ \text{is an object center,} \\ 0\ \text{otherwise.} \end{cases} \quad (4)$$

where l_{reg} is a general definition of regression loss which can be defined as L_1 or $smooth - L_1$ loss defined on the prediction directly, $corners$ loss [20] on the vertex of the recovered 3D BBox, IoU loss [46] on 3D BBoxes or disentangling detection loss [47] etc.

4   Proposed Approach

We propose the IAFA network to gather all the useful information related to a certain object for 3D pose regression. It generates a pixel-wise spatial attention map to aggregate all the features belongs to the objects together for contributing the center classification and its attribution regression. The proposed branch is a light-weight and plug-and-play module, which can be integrated into any one-stage based 3D object detection framework.

4.1   IAFA Module

The proposed IAFA branch is highlighted with dotted box in Fig. 2, which aims at collecting all the useful information (e.g., related to a certain object) together to help 3D object detection task. Specifically, for a feature map $\mathbf{F}^s$ in a certain level, with the size of $W^s \times H^s \times C^s$, the IAFA module will generate a high-dimension matrix $\mathbf{G}$ with the size of $W^s \times H^s \times D$, where $D = W^s \times H^s$. For a certain location (i, j) of $\mathbf{G}$, the vector $\mathbf{G}_{ij} \in \mathbb{R}^{1 \times D}$ encodes a dense relationship map of the target point $p(i, j)$ with all the other locations (including itself). Intuitively, these pixels belonging to the same object should have closer relationship than those pixels that don't belong to the object and therefore they should give more contribution for the 3D object detection task.

To achieve this purpose, we propose to use the corresponding object instance mask as a supervised signal for learning this attention map $\mathbf{G}$. For efficient computation, this supervision signal is only sparsely added to object's centers. Some learned attention vectors $\mathbf{G}(i, j)$ (reshaped as images with the size of $W^s \times H^s$ for easy understanding) are displayed in Fig. 4, in which three maps correspond to three objects' centers.

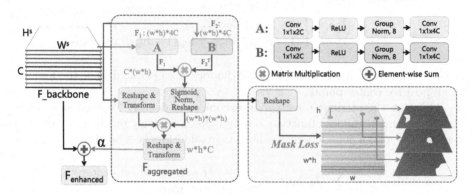

Fig. 3. The proposed IAFA module. The input $\mathbf{F}_{\text{backbone}}$ will be enhanced by collecting the features from the corresponding instance to generate the output $\mathbf{F}_{\text{enhanced}}$.

4.2   Detailed IAFA Structure

The detailed structure of the proposed IAFA branch is illustrated in Fig. 3. The input of IAFA is the feature map $\mathbf{F}_{\text{backbone}} \in \mathbb{R}^{W^s \times H^s \times C}$ from the backbone network and the output of the module is the enhanced feature $\mathbf{F}_{\text{enhanced}} \in \mathbb{R}^{W^s \times H^s \times C}$ which has the same dimension with the input feature map. The enhanced feature $\mathbf{F}_{\text{enhanced}}$ can be obtained as

$$\mathbf{F}_{\text{enhanced}} = \mathbf{F}_{\text{backbone}} + \alpha * \mathbf{F}_{\text{aggregated}}, \tag{5}$$

where $\mathbf{F}_{\text{aggregated}}$ is the aggregated features from other locations and α is a learnable parameter initialized with zero to balance the importance of $\mathbf{F}_{\text{aggregated}}$ and $\mathbf{F}_{\text{backbone}}$. The building of the $\mathbf{F}_{\text{aggregated}}$ has been highlighted with red dotted rectangle in Fig. 3. If needed, the input $\mathbf{F}_{\text{backbone}}$ can be downsampled to an appropriate size for saving the GPU memory and upsampled to the same size of $\mathbf{F}_{\text{backbone}}$ after aggregation. For general representation, we assume the input features size is $w \times h \times C$. First of all, two new feature maps $\{\mathbf{F}_1, \mathbf{F}_2\} \in \mathbb{R}^{w \times h \times 4C}$ are generated with a series of convolutions operations which are represented with "Operation" $\mathbf{A}$ and $\mathbf{B}$ in short. Here $\mathbf{A}$ and $\mathbf{B}$ share the same structure with different parameters. Specifically, both of them contain two 1×1 convolution layers, one non-linear activation layer (e.g., ReLU) and one group normalization layer. Detailed convolution kernel information and group size information are given in right top of Fig. 3. Then both of them are reshaped to $\mathbb{R}^{d \times 4C}$, where $d = w \times h$ is the number of the pixels in $\mathbf{F}_1$ or $\mathbf{F}_2$. Assuming the two reshaped tensors are $\mathbf{F}_1'$ and $\mathbf{F}_2'$, then the high-dimension relation map $\mathbf{G}$ can be obtained as

$$\mathbf{G} = Norm\{Sigmoid(\mathbf{F}_1 \otimes (\mathbf{F}_2')^{\mathrm{T}})\}, \tag{6}$$

where $\otimes$ represent the matrix multiplication, "Sigmoid" represent the *Sigmoid* function to re-scale the element's value from $(-\infty, +\infty)$ to $(0, +1)$ and Norm represent the normalization operation along the row dimension. Then we reshape this relationship map $\mathbf{G}$ from $\mathbb{R}^{d \times d}$ to $\mathbb{R}^{W^s \times H^s \times d}$ and each vector of $\mathbf{G}(i, j)$ gives the relationship of current pixel (i, j) with all other pixels. With the estimated $\mathbf{G}$, $\mathbf{F}_{\text{aggregated}}$ can be computed as

$$\mathbf{F}_{\text{aggregated}} = \mathbf{G} \otimes \mathcal{F}\{\mathbf{F}'_{\text{backbone}}\}, \tag{7}$$

here $\mathcal{F}\{.\}$ operation is used for transforming the downsampled $\mathbf{F}'_{\text{backbone}}$ from the shape of $w \times h \times C$ to the shape of $d \times C$. Finally, the $\mathbf{F}_{\text{aggregated}}$ can be upsampled to $W^s \times H^s$, the same size as $\mathbf{F}_{\text{backbone}}$.

4.3 Loss Function for Instance Mask

Three loss functions are used for training the framework which are $L_{\text{center-ness}}$, L_{reg} and L_{mask}. Here, we choose the smooth-L1 loss on the 3D BBox's 8 corners for regression loss L_{reg}. Consequently, the whole loss function is formulated as

$$L = \gamma_0 L_{\text{center-ness}} + \gamma_1 L_{\text{reg}} + \gamma_2 L_{\text{mask}}, \tag{8}$$

where γ_0, γ_1 and γ_3 are hype-parameters for balancing the contributions of different parts. As shown in the green dotted box in Fig. 3, the loss for mask is only activated sparsely on the center points. Due to the unbalance between the foreground and background pixels, focal loss is also applied here. Similar to (3), the L_{mask} is defined with focal loss as

$$L_{\text{mask}} = -\frac{1}{N} \sum_{j=0}^{N} \frac{1}{M_j} \sum_{i=0}^{M_j} (1 - \hat{y}_i)^\alpha \log(\hat{y}_i) \tag{9}$$

where $\hat{y}_i$ is the predicted probability that a pixel i belongs to a certain instance j, N is the number of instance per batch and M_j is the number of pixels for instance j.

4.4 Coarse Instance Annotation Generation

For training the mask attention module, dense pixel-wise instance segmentation annotation is needed. However, for most of the 3D object detection dataset (e.g., KITTI [1]), only the 2D/3D bounding boxes are provided and the instance-level segmentation annotation is not provided. In our experiment, we just used the output of the commonly used instance segmentation framework "Mask R-CNN [48]" as the coarse label. Surprisingly, we find that the performance can also be boosted evenly with this kind of noise label.

5 Experimental Results

We implement our approach and evaluate it on the public KITTI [1] 3D object detection benchmark.

5.1   Dataset and Implementation Details

Dataset: The KIITI data is collected from the real traffic environment in Europe streets. The whole dataset has been divided into training and testing two subsets, which consist of $7,481$ and $7,518$ frames, respectively. Since the ground truth for the testing set is not available, we divide the training data into a training and validation set as in [5,25], and obtain $3,712$ data samples for training and $3,769$ data samples for validation to refine our model. On the KITTI benchmark, the objects have been categorized into "Easy", "Moderate" and "Hard" based on their height in the image and occlusion ratio, etc. For each frame, both the camera image and the LiDAR point cloud have been provided, while only RGB image has been used for object detection and the point cloud is only used for visualization purposes.

Evaluation Metric: We focus on the evaluation on "Car" category because it has been considered most in the previous approaches. In addition, the number of the training data for "Pedestrain" and "Cyclist" is too small for training a stable model. For evaluation, the average precision (AP) with Intersection over Union (IoU) is used as the metric for evaluation. Specifically, before October 8, 2019, the KITTI test sever used the 11 recall positions for comparison. After that the test sever change the evaluation criterion from 11-points to 40-points because the latter one is proved to be more stable than the former [47]. Therefore, we use the 40-points criterion on the test sever, while we keep the 11-points criterion on validation dataset because most of previous methods only report their performance using 11-points criterion.

Implementation Details: For each original image, we pad it symmetrically to 1280×384 for both training and inference. Before training, these ground truth BBoxes whose depth larger than 50m or whose 2D projected center is out of the image range are eliminated and all the rest are used for training our model. Similar to [20], three types of data-augmentation strategies have been applied here: random horizontal flip, random scale and shift. The scale ratio is set to 9 steps from 0.6 to 1.4, and the shift ratio is set to 5 steps from -0.2 to 0.2. To be clear, the scale and shift augmentation haven't been used for the regression branch because the 3D information is inconsistent after these transformations.

Parameters Setting: For each object, the "depth" prediction is defined as $depth = a_0 + b_0 x$, where a_0, b_0 are two predefined constants and x is the output of the network. Here, we set $a_0 = b_0 = 12.5$ experimentally and re-scale the output $x \in [-1.0, 1.0]$. For the focal loss in (3) and (9), we set $\alpha = 2.0$ and $\beta = 4.0$ for all the experiments. The group number for normalization in IAFA module is set to 8. For decreasing the GPU consumption, we set $\text{w} = \frac{1}{2}\text{W}^s$ and $\text{h} = \frac{1}{2}\text{H}^s$ in the IAFA module.

Training: Adam [49] together with L1 weights regularization is used for optimizing our model. The network is trained with a batch size of 42 on 7 T V100 for

160 epochs. The learning rate is set at 2.5×10^{-4} and drops at 80 and 120 epochs by a factor of 10. The total training process requires about 12 h. During testing, top 100 center points with response above 0.25 are chosen as valid detection. No data augmentation is applied during inference process.

5.2 Evaluation on the "Test" Split

First of all, we evaluate our methods with other monocular based 3D object detectors on the KITTI testing benchmark. Due the limited space, we only list the results with public publications. For fair comparison, all the numbers are collected directly from the official benchmark website[1]. Here, we show the Bird-Eye-View (BEV) and 3D results with threshold of 0.7.

Table 1. Comparison with other public methods on the KITTI testing sever for 3D "Car" detection. For the "direct" methods, we represent the "Modality" with "Mono" only. For the other methods, we use *, † to indicate that the "depth" or "3D model" have been used by these methods during training or inference procedure. For each column, we have highlighted the top numbers in bold and the second best is shown in blue. The numbers in red represent the absolute improvements compared with the baseline.

Methods	Modality	$AP_{3D}70$ (%)			$AP_{BEV}70$ (%)			Time (s)
		Moderate	Easy	Hard	Moderate	Easy	Hard	
FQNet [32]	Mono	1.51	2.77	1.01	3.23	5.40	2.46	0.50
GS3D [31]	Mono	2.90	4.47	2.47	6.08	8.41	4.94	2.0
MVRA [50]	Mono	3.27	5.19	2.49	5.84	9.05	4.50	0.18
Shift R-CNN [51]	Mono	3.87	6.88	2.83	6.82	11.84	5.27	0.25
MonoGRNet [52]	Mono	5.74	9.61	4.25	11.17	18.19	8.73	0.04
SMOKE [20]	Mono	9.76	14.03	7.84	14.49	20.83	12.75	0.03
MonoPair [34]	Mono	9.99	13.04	8.65	14.83	19.28	12.89	0.06
RTM3D [21]	Mono	10.34	14.41	8.77	14.20	19.17	11.99	0.05
ROI-10D [53]	Mono*†	2.02	4.32	1.46	4.91	9.78	3.74	0.20
MonoFENet [54]	Mono*	5.14	8.35	4.10	11.03	17.03	9.05	0.15
Decoupled-3D [55]	Mono*	7.02	11.08	5.63	14.82	23.16	11.25	0.08
MonoPSR [56]	Mono*	7.25	10.76	5.85	12.58	18.33	9.91	0.20
AM3D [27]	Mono*	10.74	16.50	9.52	17.32	25.03	14.91	0.40
RefinedMPL [17]	Mono*	11.14	**18.09**	8.94	17.60	**28.08**	13.95	0.15
D4LCN [29]	Mono*	11.72	16.65	9.51	16.02	22.51	12.55	0.20
Baseline [20]	Mono	9.76	14.03	7.84	14.49	20.83	12.75	
Proposed Method	Mono	**12.01**	17.81	**10.61**	**17.88**	25.88	**15.35**	0.034
Improvement	–	+2.25	+3.78	+2.77	+3.39	+5.05	+2.6	

Comparison with SOTA Methods: We make our results public on the KITTI benchmark sever and the comparison with other methods are listed in Table 1.

---

[1] http://www.cvlibs.net/datasets/kitti/eval_object.php?obj_benchmark=3d.

For fair comparison, the monocular-based methods can also be divided into two groups, which are illustrated in the top and middle rows of Table 1, respectively. The former is called the "direct"-based method, which only uses a single image during the training and inference. In the latter type, other information such as depth or 3D model is used as an auxiliary during the training or inference. Our proposed method belongs to the former.

Similar to the official benchmark website, all the results are displayed in ascending order based on the values of "Moderate" $AP_{3D}70$. From the table, we can find that the proposed method outperforms all the "direct"-based method with a big margin among all the three categories. For example, for "Easy" $AP_{BEV}70$, our method achieved 5.05 points improvements than the best method of SMOKE [20]. The minimum improvement happens on "Moderate" $AP_{3D}70$, even so, we also obtained 1.67 points of improvements than RTM3D [21].

Based on the evaluation criterion defined by KITTI (ranking based on values of "Moderate" $AP_{3D}70$), our method achieved the first place among all the monocular-based 3D object detectors[2] up to the submission of this manuscript (Jul. 8, 2020), including these models trained with depth or 3D models. Specifically, the proposed method achieved four first places, two second places among all the six sub-items. The run time of different methods is also provided in the last column of Table 1. Compared with other methods, we also show superiority on efficiency. By using the DAL34 as the backbone network, our methods can achieve 29 fps on Tesla V-100 with a resolution of 384×1280.

Comparison with Baseline: From the table, we also can find that the proposed method significantly boosts the baseline method on both the BEV and 3D evaluation among all the six sub-items. Especially, for "Easy" category, we have achieved 3.78 and 5.05 points improvements for AP_{3D} and AP_{BEV} respectively. For the other four sub-items, the proposed method achieves more 2.0 points improvement. The minimal improvement we have achieved is for "Moderate" $AP_{3D}70$, while it also provides 2.25 points of improvement.

5.3 Evaluation on "Validation" Split

We also evaluate our proposed method on the validation split. The detailed comparison is given in Table 2. As mentioned in [15], the 200 training images of KITTI stereo 2015 overlap with the validation images of KITTI object detection. That is to say, some LiDAR point cloud in the object detection validation split has been used for training the depth estimation networks. That is the reason why some 3D object detectors (with depth for training) achieved very good performances while obtained unsatisfactory results on the test dataset. Therefore, we only list the "direct"-based methods for comparison here. Compared with the baseline method, the proposed method achieves significant improvements among all the six sub-items. Especially, we achieve more than 3.0 points improvement

---

[2] Only these methods with publications have been listed for comparison here.

Table 2. Comparison with other public methods on the KITTI "val" split for 3D "Car" detection, where "–" represent the values are not provided in their papers. For easy understanding, we have highlighted the top number in bold for each column and the second best is shown in blue. The numbers in red represent the absolute improvements compared with the baseline.

Methods	Modality	$AP_{3D}70$ (%)			$AP_{BEV}70$ (%)		
		Mod	Easy	Hard	Mod	Easy	Hard
CenterNet [18]	Mono	1.06	0.86	0.66	3.23	4.46	3.53
Mono3D [22]	Mono	2.31	2.53	2.31	5.19	5.22	4.13
OFTNet [57]	Mono	3.27	4.07	3.29	8.79	11.06	8.91
GS3D [31]	Mono	10.51	11.63	10.51	–	–	–
MonoGRNet [52]	Mono	10.19	13.88	7.62	–	–	–
ROI-10D [53]	Mono	6.63	9.61	6.29	9.91	14.50	8.73
MonoDIS [47]	Mono	14.98	18.05	13.42	18.43	24.26	16.95
M3D-RPN [28]	Mono	**16.48**	**20.40**	13.34	21.15	**26.86**	17.14
Baseline [20]	Mono	12.85	14.76	11.50	15.61	19.99	15.28
Proposed	Mono	14.96	18.95	**14.84**	19.60	22.75	**19.21**
Improvements		+2.11	+4.19	+3.34	+3.998	+2.76	+3.94

in four items and the improvements for all the items are above 2.0 points. Comparison with other methods, we achieve 2 first places, 2 second places and 2 third places among all the 6 sub-items.

5.4 Ablation Studies

In addition, we also have designed a set of ablation experiments to verify the effectiveness of each module of our proposed method (Table 3).

Table 3. Comparison with other public methods on the KITTI testing sever for 3D "Car" detection. For easy understanding, we have highlighted the top two numbers in bold and italic for each column and the second best is shown in blue. All the numbers are the higher the better.

Methods	$AP_{3D}70$ (%)			$AP_{BEV}70$ (%)		
	Mod	Easy	Hard	Mod	Easy	Hard
Baseline	12.85	14.76	11.50	15.61	19.99	15.28
w/o supervision	12.98	14.59	11.76	15.79	20.12	14.98
w supervision	14.96	18.95	14.84	19.60	22.75	19.21

Supervision of the Instance Mask: Self-attention strategy is commonly used for in semantic segmentation [32,41] and object detection [58] etc. To highlight the influence of the supervision of the instance mask, we compare the performance of the proposed module with and without the supervision signal. From the table, we can easily found that the supervision signal is particularly useful for training IAFA module. Without the supervision, the detection performance nearly unchanged. The positive effect of the instance supervision signal is obvious. Furthermore, we also illustrated some examples of the learned attention maps in Fig. 4, where the bottom sub-figures are the corresponding attention maps for the three instances respectively. From the figure, we can see that the maximum value is at the center of object and it decreases gradually with the increasing of its distance to the object center.

Fig. 4. An example of feature map for IAFA module. Different brightness reveals different importance related to the target point (red dot). (Color figure online)

5.5   Qualitative Results

Some qualitative detection results on the test split are displayed in Fig. 5. For better visualization and comparison, we also draw the 3D BBoxes in point cloud and BEV-view images. The results clearly demonstrate that the proposed framework can recover objects' 3D information accurately.

Fig. 5. Three examples of 3D detection results. The "top", "Middle" and "Bottom" are results are drawn in RGB image, 3D Point cloud and BEV-view respectively. The point cloud is only used for visualization purposes here.

6   Conclusions and Future Works

In this paper, we have proposed a simple but effective instance-aware feature aggregation (IAFA) module to collect all the related information for the task of single image-based 3D object detection. The proposed module is an easily implemented plug-and-play module that can be incorporated into any one-stage object detection framework. In addition, we find out that the IAFA module can achieve satisfactory performance even though the coarsely annotated instance masks are used as supervision signals.

In the future, we plan to implement the proposed framework for real-world AD applications. Our proposed framework can also be extended to a multi-camera configuration to handle the detection from 360°- viewpoints. In addition, extending the detector to multi-frame is also an interesting direction, which can boost the detection performances of distant instances.

References

1. Geiger, A., Lenz, P., Urtasun, R.: Are we ready for autonomous driving? The KITTI vision benchmark suite. In: 2012 IEEE Conference on Computer Vision and Pattern Recognition, pp. 3354–3361. IEEE (2012)
2. Wang, P., Huang, X., Cheng, X., Zhou, D., Geng, Q., Yang, R.: The ApolloScape open dataset for autonomous driving and its application. IEEE Trans. Pattern Anal. Mach. Intell. **42**, 2702–2719 (2019)
3. Qi, C.R., Liu, W., Wu, C., Su, H., Guibas, L.J.: Frustum PointNets for 3D object detection from RGB-D data. In: Proceedings of the IEEE Conference on Computer Vision and Pattern Recognition, pp. 918–927 (2018)
4. Shi, S., Wang, X., Li, H.: PointRCNN: 3D object proposal generation and detection from point cloud. In: Proceedings of the IEEE Conference on Computer Vision and Pattern Recognition, pp. 770–779 (2019)

5. Zhou, Y., Tuzel, O.: VoxelNet: end-to-end learning for point cloud based 3D object detection. In: Proceedings of the IEEE Conference on Computer Vision and Pattern Recognition, pp. 4490–4499 (2018)
6. Lang, A.H., Vora, S., Caesar, H., Zhou, L., Yang, J., Beijbom, O.: PointPillars: fast encoders for object detection from point clouds. arXiv preprint arXiv:1812.05784 (2018)
7. Yin, J., Shen, J., Guan, C., Zhou, D., Yang, R.: LiDAR-based online 3D video object detection with graph-based message passing and spatiotemporal transformer attention. In: Proceedings of the IEEE/CVF Conference on Computer Vision and Pattern Recognition, pp. 11495–11504 (2020)
8. Yang, Z., Sun, Y., Liu, S., Shen, X., Jia, J.: STD: sparse-to-dense 3D object detector for point cloud. In: Proceedings of the IEEE International Conference on Computer Vision, pp. 1951–1960 (2019)
9. Shi, S., Guo, C., Jiang, L., Wang, Z., Shi, J., Wang, X., Li, H.: PV-RCNN: point-voxel feature set abstraction for 3D object detection. In: Proceedings of the IEEE/CVF Conference on Computer Vision and Pattern Recognition, pp. 10529–10538 (2020)
10. Zhou, D., Frémont, V., Quost, B., Dai, Y., Li, H.: Moving object detection and segmentation in urban environments from a moving platform. Image Vis. Comput. **68**, 76–87 (2017)
11. Hernandez, C., Vogiatzis, G., Cipolla, R.: Multiview photometric stereo. IEEE Trans. Pattern Anal. Mach. Intell. **30**, 548–554 (2008)
12. Luo, W., Schwing, A.G., Urtasun, R.: Efficient deep learning for stereo matching. In: Proceedings of the IEEE Conference on Computer Vision and Pattern Recognition, pp. 5695–5703 (2016)
13. Godard, C., Mac Aodha, O., Firman, M., Brostow, G.J.: Digging into self-supervised monocular depth estimation. In: Proceedings of the IEEE International Conference on Computer Vision, pp. 3828–3838 (2019)
14. Qian, R., et al.: End-to-end pseudo-lidar for image-based 3D object detection. arXiv preprint arXiv:2004.03080 (2020)
15. Wang, Y., Chao, W.L., Garg, D., Hariharan, B., Campbell, M., Weinberger, K.Q.: Pseudo-LiDAR from visual depth estimation: bridging the gap in 3D object detection for autonomous driving. In: Proceedings of the IEEE Conference on Computer Vision and Pattern Recognition, pp. 8445–8453 (2019)
16. Weng, X., Kitani, K.: Monocular 3D object detection with pseudo-LiDAR point cloud. In: Proceedings of the IEEE International Conference on Computer Vision Workshops (2019)
17. Vianney, J.M.U., Aich, S., Liu, B.: RefinedMPL: refined monocular PseudoLiDAR for 3D object detection in autonomous driving. arXiv preprint arXiv:1911.09712 (2019)
18. Zhou, X., Wang, D., Krähenbühl, P.: Objects as points. arXiv preprint arXiv:1904.07850 (2019)
19. Tian, Z., Shen, C., Chen, H., He, T.: FCOS: fully convolutional one-stage object detection. In: Proceedings of the IEEE International Conference on Computer Vision, pp. 9627–9636 (2019)
20. Liu, Z., Wu, Z., Tóth, R.: SMOKE: single-stage monocular 3D object detection via keypoint estimation. arXiv preprint arXiv:2002.10111 (2020)
21. Li, P., Zhao, H., Liu, P., Cao, F.: RTM3D: real-time monocular 3D detection from object keypoints for autonomous driving. arXiv preprint arXiv:2001.03343 (2020)

22. Chen, X., Kundu, K., Zhang, Z., Ma, H., Fidler, S., Urtasun, R.: Monocular 3D object detection for autonomous driving. In: Proceedings of the IEEE Conference on Computer Vision and Pattern Recognition, pp. 2147–2156 (2016)

23. Wu, B., Wan, A., Yue, X., Keutzer, K.: SqueezeSeg: convolutional neural nets with recurrent CRF for real-time road-object segmentation from 3D LiDAR point cloud. In: 2018 IEEE International Conference on Robotics and Automation (ICRA), pp. 1887–1893. IEEE (2018)

24. Qi, C.R., Su, H., Mo, K., Guibas, L.J.: PointNet: deep learning on point sets for 3D classification and segmentation. Proc. Computer Vision and Pattern Recognition (CVPR), vol. 4, p. 4. IEEE (2017)

25. Yan, Y., Mao, Y., Li, B.: SECOND: sparsely embedded convolutional detection. Sensors **18**, 3337 (2018)

26. Zhou, D., et al.: Joint 3D instance segmentation and object detection for autonomous driving. In: Proceedings of the IEEE/CVF Conference on Computer Vision and Pattern Recognition, pp. 1839–1849 (2020)

27. Ma, X., Wang, Z., Li, H., Zhang, P., Ouyang, W., Fan, X.: Accurate monocular 3D object detection via color-embedded 3D reconstruction for autonomous driving. In: Proceedings of the IEEE International Conference on Computer Vision, pp. 6851–6860 (2019)

28. Brazil, G., Liu, X.: M3D-RPN: monocular 3D region proposal network for object detection. In: Proceedings of the IEEE International Conference on Computer Vision, pp. 9287–9296 (2019)

29. Ding, M., et al.: Learning depth-guided convolutions for monocular 3D object detection. In: Proceedings of the IEEE/CVF Conference on Computer Vision and Pattern Recognition Workshops, pp. 1000–1001 (2020)

30. Song, X., et al.: ApolloCar3D: a large 3D car instance understanding benchmark for autonomous driving. In: Proceedings of the IEEE Conference on Computer Vision and Pattern Recognition, pp. 5452–5462 (2019)

31. Li, B., Ouyang, W., Sheng, L., Zeng, X., Wang, X.: GS3D: an efficient 3D object detection framework for autonomous driving. In: Proceedings of the IEEE Conference on Computer Vision and Pattern Recognition, pp. 1019–1028 (2019)

32. Liu, L., Lu, J., Xu, C., Tian, Q., Zhou, J.: Deep fitting degree scoring network for monocular 3D object detection. In: Proceedings of the IEEE Conference on Computer Vision and Pattern Recognition, pp. 1057–1066 (2019)

33. Jörgensen, E., Zach, C., Kahl, F.: Monocular 3D object detection and box fitting trained end-to-end using intersection-over-union loss. arXiv preprint arXiv:1906.08070 (2019)

34. Chen, Y., Tai, L., Sun, K., Li, M.: MonoPair: monocular 3D object detection using pairwise spatial relationships. arXiv preprint arXiv:2003.00504 (2020)

35. Lee, Y., Park, J.: CenterMask: real-time anchor-free instance segmentation. In: Proceedings of the IEEE/CVF Conference on Computer Vision and Pattern Recognition, pp. 13906–13915 (2020)

36. Wang, Y., Xu, Z., Shen, H., Cheng, B., Yang, L.: CenterMask: single shot instance segmentation with point representation. In: Proceedings of the IEEE/CVF Conference on Computer Vision and Pattern Recognition, pp. 9313–9321 (2020)

37. Liu, Z.S., Wang, L.W., Li, C.T., Siu, W.C., Chan, Y.L.: Image super-resolution via attention based back projection networks. In: 2019 IEEE/CVF International Conference on Computer Vision Workshop (ICCVW), pp. 3517–3525. IEEE (2019)

38. Tang, H., Xu, D., Sebe, N., Wang, Y., Corso, J.J., Yan, Y.: Multi-channel attention selection GAN with cascaded semantic guidance for cross-view image translation. In: The IEEE Conference on Computer Vision and Pattern Recognition (CVPR) (2019)
39. Sun, S., Zhao, B., Chen, X., Mateen, M., Wen, J.: Channel attention networks for image translation. IEEE Access **7**, 95751–95761 (2019)
40. Zhang, H., Goodfellow, I., Metaxas, D., Odena, A.: Self-attention generative adversarial networks. In: International Conference on Machine Learning, pp. 7354–7363 (2019)
41. Fu, J., et al.: Dual attention network for scene segmentation. In: Proceedings of the IEEE Conference on Computer Vision and Pattern Recognition, pp. 3146–3154 (2019)
42. Song, X., et al.: Channel attention based iterative residual learning for depth map super-resolution. In: Proceedings of the IEEE/CVF Conference on Computer Vision and Pattern Recognition, pp. 5631–5640 (2020)
43. Yu, F., Wang, D., Shelhamer, E., Darrell, T.: Deep layer aggregation. In: Proceedings of the IEEE Conference on Computer Vision and Pattern Recognition, pp. 2403–2412 (2018)
44. Mousavian, A., Anguelov, D., Flynn, J., Kosecka, J.: 3D bounding box estimation using deep learning and geometry. In: Proceedings of the IEEE Conference on Computer Vision and Pattern Recognition, pp. 7074–7082 (2017)
45. Lin, T.Y., Goyal, P., Girshick, R., He, K., Dollár, P.: Focal loss for dense object detection. In: Proceedings of the IEEE International Conference on Computer Vision, pp. 2980–2988 (2017)
46. Zhou, D., et al.: IoU loss for 2D/3D object detection. In: 2019 International Conference on 3D Vision (3DV), pp. 85–94. IEEE (2019)
47. Simonelli, A., Bulo, S.R., Porzi, L., López-Antequera, M., Kontschieder, P.: Disentangling monocular 3D object detection. In: Proceedings of the IEEE International Conference on Computer Vision, pp. 1991–1999 (2019)
48. He, K., Gkioxari, G., Dollár, P., Girshick, R.: Mask R-CNN. In: Proceedings of the IEEE International Conference on Computer Vision, pp. 2961–2969 (2017)
49. Kingma, D.P., Ba, J.: Adam: a method for stochastic optimization. arXiv preprint arXiv:1412.6980 (2014)
50. Choi, H.M., Kang, H., Hyun, Y.: Multi-view reprojection architecture for orientation estimation. In: 2019 IEEE/CVF International Conference on Computer Vision Workshop (ICCVW), pp. 2357–2366. IEEE (2019)
51. Naiden, A., Paunescu, V., Kim, G., Jeon, B., Leordeanu, M.: Shift R-CNN: deep monocular 3D object detection with closed-form geometric constraints. In: 2019 IEEE International Conference on Image Processing (ICIP), pp. 61–65. IEEE (2019)
52. Qin, Z., Wang, J., Lu, Y.: MonoGRNet: a geometric reasoning network for monocular 3D object localization. In: Proceedings of the AAAI Conference on Artificial Intelligence, vol. 33, pp. 8851–8858 (2019)
53. Manhardt, F., Kehl, W., Gaidon, A.: ROI-10D: monocular lifting of 2D detection to 6D pose and metric shape. In: Proceedings of the IEEE Conference on Computer Vision and Pattern Recognition, pp. 2069–2078 (2019)
54. Bao, W., Xu, B., Chen, Z.: MonoFENet: monocular 3D object detection with feature enhancement networks. IEEE Trans. Image Process. **29**, 2753–2765 (2019)
55. Cai, Y., Li, B., Jiao, Z., Li, H., Zeng, X., Wang, X.: Monocular 3D object detection with decoupled structured polygon estimation and height-guided depth estimation. In: AAAI, pp. 10478–10485 (2020)

56. Ku, J., Pon, A.D., Waslander, S.L.: Monocular 3D object detection leveraging accurate proposals and shape reconstruction. In: Proccedings of the IEEE Conference on Computer Vision and Pattern Recognition, pp. 11867–11876 (2019)
57. Roddick, T., Kendall, A., Cipolla, R.: Orthographic feature transform for monocular 3D object detection. arXiv preprint arXiv:1811.08188 (2018)
58. Gu, J., Hu, H., Wang, L., Wei, Y., Dai, J.: Learning region features for object detection. In: Proceedings of the European Conference on Computer Vision (ECCV), pp. 381–395 (2018)

Attended-Auxiliary Supervision Representation for Face Anti-spoofing

Son Minh Nguyen[✉], Linh Duy Tran, and Masayuki Arai

Graduate School of Science and Engineering Teikyo University,
Utsunomiya, Tochigi 320-8551, Japan
nguyenminhson1110@gmail.com, duylinh161287@gmail.com,
arai@ics.teikyo-u.ac.jp

Abstract. Recent face anti-spoofing methods have achieved impressive performance in recognizing the subtle discrepancies between live and spoof faces. However, due to directly holistic extraction and the resulting ineffective clues used for the models' perception, the previous methods are still subject to setbacks of not being generalizable to the diversity of presentation attacks. In this paper, we present an attended-auxiliary supervision approach for radical exploitation, which automatically concentrates on the most important regions of the input, that is, those that make significant contributions towards distinguishing the spoof cases from live faces. Through a multi-task learning approach, the proposed network is able to locate the most relevant/attended/highly selective regions more accurately than previous methods, leading to notable improvements in performance. We also suggest that introducing spatial attention mechanisms can greatly enhance our model's perception of the important information, partly intensifying the resilience of our model against diverse types of face anti-spoofing attacks. We carried out extensive experiments on publicly available face anti-spoofing datasets, showing that our approach and hypothesis converge to some extent and demonstrating state-of-the-art performance.

Keywords: Face anti-spoofing · Multi-task learning · Feature extraction · Self-attention

1 Introduction

Face recognition expertise is currently one of the most prominent subjects attracting a lot of research attention and large collaborations due to its potential for convenient effectiveness in biometric-based security applications. Due to organizations' endeavors, current state-of-the-art modalities have been achieving tremendous accuracy beyond that of human ability. However, the related applications have been generally turned into objects appealing to illegal access of the so-called facial spoofing attacks, due to their incompetence in identifying imposters. As a result, these systems are really vulnerable to such impersonating attacks, *e.g.*, replayed videos or photographs, which are perfectly recorded

© Springer Nature Switzerland AG 2021
H. Ishikawa et al. (Eds.): ACCV 2020, LNCS 12622, pp. 436–452, 2021.
https://doi.org/10.1007/978-3-030-69525-5_26

by sophisticated devices. Face anti-spoofing (FAS) techniques are thus being urgently developed for assurances of face recognition system operation.

There have been many attempts at enhancing effective solutions for preventing facial impostures in recent years. At first, the previous methods [1] used image distortion analysis to capture optical textural differences between presentation attacks (PAs) and live faces. Other methods [2,3] focused on local binary patterns to identify distinguishable features for further improvements, while some techniques [4,5] attained some success. However, the nature of the handcrafted features that these methods exploited are not generalized traits, the resulting models hence showed limitations on practical environments, and are prone to dramatically degraded performance in peculiar media.

Most recent studies have obtained significant achievements based on convolutional neural networks (CNNs) along with supplemental dependencies. Luo *et al.* [6] adopted a CNN long short-term memory (LSTM) architecture to learn spatiotemporal patterns in sequential frames for distinguishing genuine cases from spoof activities, whereas LSTM was previously used almost for sequence-related tasks. Atoum *et al.* [7] used an auxiliary supervision associated with a patch-scored modality, and then fed the result into a support vector machine-based classifier for PA detection. Compared with previous work, an algorithm [8] that relied on the extra remote photoplethysmography (rPPG) pattern in addition to the auxiliary supervision [7] made an advance to some extent. Recently, Yang *et al.* attempted to provide enhanced spatiotemporal patterns with the help of a pretrained CNN-LSTM model augmented by an attention mechanism and their own synthetic data [9].

However, it seems that these techniques might not radically capture essential characteristics for genuine and counterfeit case analysis. For instance, the models in [8,10] put a lot of effort into the full scope of auxiliary supervision, namely facial depth maps and rPPG signals, without any highly selective approaches. In other words, such learning holistic representations of input images might lead to the excessive exploitation and thus guide the models' focus onto redundant/irrelevant information, interfering with the models' perception. Similarly to auxiliary cases, the binary supervision-based networks [2,9] did not enable the networks to capture sufficient distinct features needed to discern spoof faces. On the contrary, that induces the networks to have a great tendency towards inconsistent features, raising the high possibility of being overfitted and poor performance in most test cases.

To tackle these problems, we developed the idea of radically capturing the most relevant locations, but still making the best use of auxiliary supervision because of its undeniable contribution in prior methods. Hence, we propose an attended-auxiliary supervision (AAS) architecture in which the attended-auxiliary information is comprehensively used in both the highly selective region proposal and inference stages. We represent this AAS/patch-driven facial depth map supervision for live and spoof images. To invigorate the adoption of the AAS, the patches used to estimate these partial depth maps are intended to be sampled from highly selective regions of input images based on their contribution to model's decision. In order to make these regions identifiable, we built a two-module model. The first module uses a pretrained network integrated with squeeze-and-excitation network (SENet) blocks [11], which are useful for describing the nature of channels in feature blocks, to extract the more distinguishable spatial properties. Then, the employed LSTM network converts the resulting embeddings into temporal information for sequential frame-driven classification. The second module is processed within reciprocal stages. The *Region Proposal Stage* (RPS) is in charge of best aligning initial advice given by the first module with the model's situation, and then proposing the ensuing highly selective regions to the *Attended-Auxiliary Execution Stage* (AAES). In the AAES, the highly selective regions are fully exploited through the corresponding patch-driven depth map regression, which stimulates the network to explore sufficient generalizable representations of both spoof and live images.

Our main contributions are summarized as follows:

- We present a practical solution to radically exploit the most relevant regions of input images based on the patch-driven depth map supervision in both channel and region attention scenarios for 2D PAs. Such AAS adoption has the purpose of partially influencing the network to learn adequate salient information of input images, thereby alleviating the performance degradation caused by irrelevant information.
- To this end, we designed the AAS framework towards a multi-task learning fashion to further advance the model's perception of highly selective regions.
- We demonstrate the reliability of our model and arguments by evaluating our framework on publicly available FAS datasets. Our experimental results show the FAS community another potential concept to resolve ongoing issues in FAS.

2   Prior Work

Traditional Approaches. Distinguishable features are the most fundamental keys to recognize spoof cases. Many prior patterns have been, to a degree, flourishingly built upon such ideas since several years ago. However, these patterns are still essentially handcrafted feature representations, such as local binary patterns [12–14], HOG [15,16], and SIFT [17], which produce modest outcomes via conventional classifiers, namely support vector machines and linear discriminant analysis. The handcrafted-feature-based methods thus showed limitations regarding generalizable representation in PA detection. To cope with these difficulties, researchers have approached these problems in another way that maps input images onto other domains, namely HSV, YCbCr [18,19], temporal domains [20,21], and Fourier spectra [22].

In lieu of using a mere single frame, researchers have attempted to exploit the traits of facial motions in several consecutive frames, such as determining "facial liveness" with eye-blinking detection[5,23] and mouth and lip motions [4].

Deep Learning-Based Approaches. During the deep learning era, the FAS modalities have thrived dramatically on prior difficulties. Some of the modern

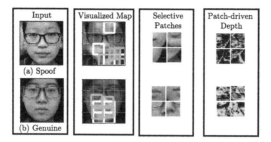

Fig. 1. Translation offsets of the orange regions, given the white initial locations of the AM, are thoroughly regularized based not only on binary supervision, but also on the attended auxiliary supervision in a multi-task learning manner. (Color figure online)

CNNs[24,25] have been used as feature extractors to discriminate live and spoof images. In [26], Jourabloo *et al.* tackled anti-spoofing in a particular way that treats PAs as decomposition issues, inversely decomposes a spoof face into spoof noise and a live face, and then uses the spoof noise for classification. At that point, Liu *et al.* [8] attempted to holistically estimate depth maps and rPPG signals from live and spoof faces through a recurrent neural network-CNN model based on ground truths predefined with dense face alignment [27]. Inspired by auxiliary supervision [8], Kim *et al.* [10] introduced an additional auxiliary supervision by extending the reflection map into PAs, which intensified the resilience of their model on PA types. Additionally, some works have proposed spatiotemporal features. In particular, Yang *et al.* [9] adopted spatiotemporal features extracted from discriminative regions for PA detection using a CNN-LSTM structure, which was already pretrained on their own synthetic data.

Motivated by [9,28], we partly used a CNN-LSTM model, but with advanced subnets in order to precisely interpret temporal features, as an *Advisor Module* (AM), supporting the rest of network in determining where to look first. Furthermore, we imposed extra essential constraints towards a multitask-learning scheme on the proposed model, so that the representation regularization of refined subtle offsets, mentioned in Subsect.3.2, should be more vigorous than its predecessor [9]. As shown in Fig. 1, the AM and the rest of the model share similar considerations in genuine cases, but spoof activities cause a large displacement.

3 Proposed Method

The main objective of our approach is to direct the network to autonomously centralize regions of input images possessing the model's decision, rather than digesting completely unprocessed full scope of inputs, which avoids redundant information causing noise and detrimental effects on performance. In contrast with previous auxiliary supervision-based methods, the most striking feature of our approach, as aforementioned, is that we meticulously exploit the patch-driven facial depth map supervision for both live and spoof faces on the basis

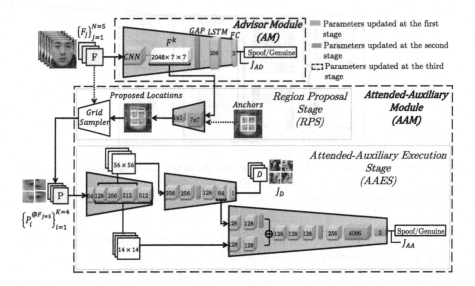

Fig. 2. Proposed framework constituted by interdependent attending modules. The AM plays a main role in providing the AAM with its experience in discerning spoof from genuine images. The AAM, in turn, draws attention to the received advice and sequentially processes images with reciprocal stages. For the architecture interpretation, the white, yellow, and green blocks represent feature blocks, sequential filters followed by a BatchNorm, and a rectified linear unit (RELU) activation function, respectively, each with a given size of 3×3 and pooling layers. Apart from that, the gray blocks are depth-wise convolutions with size 7×7 and point-wise convolutions with size 1×1. At the AAES, the patches proposed by the RPS are used to extract and to synthesize coarse to fine features with the help of the patch-driven depth map supervision D for PA detection. The figured is best viewed online in color. (Color figure online)

of the patches. As shown in Fig. 2, the proposed architecture comprises two main interdependent attending modules. The AM bases the fabric of a CNN-LSTM incorporated with SENets on performing the classification task itself and conveying its initial advice to the *Attended-Auxiliary Module* (AAM) for spotting which part of the input is plausible to look into (hereafter referred to as initial regions). The AAM with reciprocal stages thereafter build its attention to the most relevant regions upon the initial regions.

3.1 Auxiliary Supervision

Depth Map. The fundamental disparity between basic PAs, such as print and replay attacks, and live faces is basically manifested in the depth, the distance from points of an object to a capturing device. In practice, such spoof cases, which were previously recorded for several times by diverse devices, are often presented in even and flat facial surfaces, e.g. electronic displays and print materials. However, live faces, which are captured directly in front of the camera, are not completely analogous to PA properties, with differences in the color distribution and illumination reconstructions, but more importantly, the depth due to the irregular geometry of live faces. According to this point, we consider the basic PAs and genuine faces as flat images and depth maps, respectively. However, due to a shortage of related ground truth labels for the depth maps in spoof datasets, PRNET [29] was used to produce the corresponding ground truth labels by estimating the depth maps for genuine images. Specifically, the ground truth depth maps D estimated at facial regions are defined as follows:

$$D(I|y) = \begin{cases} 0, & \text{if y is spoof,} \\ \frac{1}{|D|}d(I), & \text{if y is genuine,} \end{cases} \tag{1}$$

where I is a given input image with label y of either 0 or 1. The depth map distance $d(I)$ is normalized from 0 to 1 by the intensity maximum $|D|$, where values of 0 and 1 represent the farthest and closest points to the camera, respectively. Based on the Eq. 1, the spoof cases' supervision is also regarded as depth maps, but with all distance values of zero.

3.2   Network Architecture

The previous model [9] used a simple CNN-LSTM architecture for initial advice providing, and weight-shared CNNs worked under the binary classification for attended region mining, resulting in the exploitation of weak features and the inefficient utilization. To resolve this weakness, our architecture is further advanced by an effective combination of two interdependent attending modules with the use of the patch-driven depth map supervision, which enables the whole network to exploit enough generalized clues that are supposed to strongly boost the model perception. Apart from that, we are still able to achieve robust performance without the use of bipartite auxiliary supervision, as in [10], which requires very time-consuming preparation. Typically, we process the input as video classification by feeding N sequential frames directly into the AM to teach it spatiotemporal information, largely helping the module to accurately converge on key regions.

Advisor Module (AM). Let $\{V_i, y_i\}_{i=1}^{k}$ describe the set of training data, where V_i is the i-th training video among k training videos and y_i is the corresponding label where 0 or 1 represents the attribute of V_i, namely genuine or spoof, respectively. As aforementioned, the CNN presented in Fig. 2 takes as input N sequential frames from $\{V_i\} = \{F_i\}_{j=1}^{m}$, where F_j^i denotes the j-th frame among m frames extracted from the i-th video. We are aware of the main role of the AM, which must be powerful to correctly provide the AAM with the initial regions. Accordingly, we use a pretrained model, a 101-layer residual network (Resnet) pretrained on the ImageNet dataset for the CNN, into which minor SENet subnets were integrated for the channel attention.

SENets. With the SENet functionality, the informative channels of each feature map are remarkably intensified, whereas the less useful ones are greatly

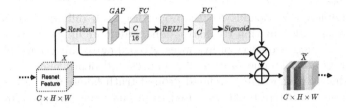

Fig. 3. Fundamental structure of a squeeze-and-excitation block, attached to each of the 101 residual blocks as a channel-wise enhancement submodule.

suppressed, as opposed to being equally treated by conventional models. Each feature map from each residual block particularly undergoes the squeeze-and-excitation process for channel analysis and enhancement. As illustrated in Fig. 3, a feature map X is firstly shrunk to a C-sized vector by the global average pooling (GAP) layer at the squeeze stage for the purpose of channel analysis. The shrunk feature is then transferred to the excitation stage, where the channel enhancement is represented by two fully connected (FC) layers, before sending it back to X, with channel-wise weighting thereafter to obtain the augmented feature map $\tilde{X}$. Taking advantage of the subnets increases the confidence in avoiding overfitting caused by unnecessary channels. In addition, the aforesaid LSTM introduced behind the GAP is accountable for interpreting spatial information in the CNN as temporal patterns, which aims to make discrete spatial information more mutually dependent and have a closer relationship between sequential frames.

Attended-Auxiliary Module (AAM). The workings of this module consist in the region attention mechanism with reciprocal functions, both of which are observed in the RPS and AAES.

Region Proposal Stage (RPS). Motivated by [28], which used a spatial transformer network to be sensitive to spatial changes of input, the AAM is thus offered the differentiable attention to any spatial transformation, and it learns to align the initial regions with locations of the most relevant regions via learnable parameters. Because of the difficulties in directly determining these locations, we thus let the model be automated to adjust the learnable parameters as translation offsets, which are subsequently associated with the anchors in order to locate the most relevant regions. To enable the model to optimize the offset parameters during the training period, these were set up as the affine transformation M, whose resulting patches are then manipulated and collected by a grid sampler in the RPS as follows:

$$M = \begin{bmatrix} s_x & 0 & t_x \\ 0 & s_y & t_y \end{bmatrix}, \tag{2}$$

where s_x, s_y must be constant scaling ratios of an image in the x and y-axes, respectively, in order to achieve K constant-sized patches. In contrast, t_x and t_y along the corresponding axes are adaptive translation offsets for every epoch.

As indicated in Fig. 2, these offsets are achieved by attaching two extra filters, namely a 7×7 depth-wise layer followed by a 1×1 point-wise layer, to the $2,048 \times 7 \times 7$ feature map F_k behind the GAP layer. Deriving the $K \times 2$ output of $[t_x, t_y]$ from these filters is, however, far more efficient in reducing the complexity of the number of parameters and operations than that from FC layers [28], thereby casing degradation in performance more greatly.

The anchors, which are locations of the initial regions given by the AM, are recommended to the RPS for subsequent proposed patches through the effect of Gradcam [30]. In effect, we used Gradcam to enhance the analytical capability of the AM to interpret its concentration on specific regions of the input image, with regard to the considered label, for the provision of the anchors. According to Gradcam, F^k with the predicted label-related score y_c is extracted for the gradient α_k^c in terms of F^k.

$$\alpha_k^c = \frac{1}{z} \sum_i \sum_j \frac{\delta y_c}{\delta F_{ij}^k}, \tag{3}$$

where z is a normalizing constant. After that, a 7×7 Gradcam map S_k is obtained by applying a RELU layer to the weighted feature map,

$$S_k = RELU(\sum_k \alpha_c^k F^k). \tag{4}$$

The 7×7 Gradcam map shows the important regions, with respect to y_c, which are of interest to the AM's performance. To enhance visualization, we turn the Gradcam map into a score map whose size is upsampled to be similar to that of the input, mentioned in Subsect. 4.2, using bilinear interpolation. An averaged pooling layer overlaid on the score map results in a 4×4 grid, which is used to identify the K highest scored regions in the grid cells. Finally, the anchors extracted from the K regions are transferred to the RPS for the above-mentioned alignment.

In fact, although the RPS is implemented with all the above initial inspirations [9,28,30], the offset-regularizing effects of the surroundings, namely the AM and the AAES, on the RPS are far more intensive and extensive than that of the prior approaches in channel interaction and supervision, respectively.

Attended-Auxiliary Execution Stage (AAES). The proposed patches from the RPS are fetched by the AAES coupled with bypass connections, which aim to conflate both low-level and high-level features collectively. Given the obvious benefits of the RPS for the AAES, the partial depth map regression with the corresponding attended patches of a face is much less demanding than the straightforward generation of a full depth map from the face. In addition, based on closely related constraints of regression and classification in a multi-task learning manner, the AAES is fully able to extract enough related features and to ignore the less useful context, helping the RPS quickly converge on optimal offsets. To be more effective, the 14×14 low-level features at the first layers are channel-wise associated with the high-level features to preserve the depth

Table 1. Ablation study using Protocol 1 of the OULU-NPU dataset.

Model	Channel Attention	Region Attention	AAS	APCER (%)	BPCER (%)	ACER (%)
Model A		✓	✓	2.0	0.7	1.4
Model B	✓			1.6	0.2	0.9
Model C	✓	✓		1.6	**0.0**	0.8
Model D	✓	✓	✓	**1.1**	0.1	**0.6**

of information because some distinct information existing at the low-level stage might be significantly attenuated or virtually vanish after further processing. The inferred scores behind the softmax layer of the AM that need to receive a greater emphasis by an exponential transformation are eventually fused with probabilistic results of the AAM for the final decision.

Objective Functions. To enable the AAS, we employed a depth loss to supervise regression of the partial depth maps from the corresponding patches.

$$J_D = \frac{1}{M} \sum_{i=1}^{M} \sum_{j=1}^{K} \| CNN_{AAM}(P_i^j, \Theta_D) - D_i^j \|_1^2, \tag{5}$$

where J_D depicts the regression loss between the partial depth maps estimated from the corresponding patches P and the ground truth label D, while Θ_D, K, and M are CNN_{AAM} parameters at the AAES, the number of patches, and batch size of training images, respectively. In addition, the losses of both the AM and the AAM trained in a multi-task learning manner need to be attached to different levels of importance.

$$J_{overall} = \lambda_1 J_D + \lambda_2 J_{AD} + \lambda_3 J_{AA}, \tag{6}$$

where $J_{overall}$, J_{AA}, and J_{AD} refer to the overall loss, the softmax cross-entropy losses designed for the AAM, and the AM. During each training stage, we accommodate the magnitudes of weights λ to the stage so as to balance the involved losses.

4   Experiments

4.1   Datasets and Metrics

Datasets. We evaluated the performance of our model by using two publicly available datasets. Specifically, the assessments were conducted on only the SiW [8] and OULU [31] datasets, which are new datasets with very high resolution and a wide variety of practical protocols covering subject, pose, illumination, medium, and attack variations. These protocols can rigorously verify quality

Table 2. Intra-testing results on three SiW protocols.

Protocol	Method	APCER (%)	BPCER (%)	ACER (%)
1	Auxiliary [8]	3.58	3.58	3.51
	STASN [9]	–	–	1.00
	DepthFreq [33]	0.80	0.50	0.67
	BASN [10]	–	–	0.37
	Ours	**0.21**	**0.03**	**0.12**
2	Auxiliary [8]	0.57 ± 0.69	0.57 ± 0.69	0.57 ± 0.69
	DepthFreq [33]	$\mathbf{0.00 \pm 0.00}$	0.75 ± 0.96	0.38 ± 0.48
	STASN [9]	–	–	0.28 ± 0.05
	BASN [10]	–	–	0.12 ± 0.03
	Ours	0.03 ± 0.02	$\mathbf{0.10 \pm 0.10}$	$\mathbf{0.07 \pm 0.06}$
3	STASN [9]	–	–	12.10 ± 1.50
	Auxiliary [8]	8.31 ± 3.81	8.31 ± 3.80	8.31 ± 3.81
	DepthFreq [33]	9.50 ± 1.20	5.30 ± 2.10	7.40 ± 2.90
	BASN [10]	–	–	6.45 ± 1.80
	Ours	$\mathbf{3.35 \pm 2.62}$	$\mathbf{4.15 \pm 1.50}$	$\mathbf{3.75 \pm 2.05}$

and efficiency of a model through cross-testing in media, pose, and unknown attacks.

Evaluation Metrics. To make comparisons with prior works, we report our results with the following metrics: attack presentation classification error rate (APCER) [32]; bona fide presentation classification error rate (BPCER) [32]; and average classification error rate (ACER), which equals (APCER+BPCER)/2 [32].

4.2   Implementation Details

The input fed to the network was sequential frames ($N = 5$) of 224×224 pixels. Four patches K with size of 56×56 pixels and s_x, s_y of 0.25 were selected in our experiments. Our architecture was trained on a single GeForce GTX 1080 GPU and implemented in the PyTorch framework with a learning rate of $5e - 5$ for the first two training stages, and $5e - 6$ for the last. In addition, λ_1, λ_2, and λ_3 were set as 0.5, 10, and 10 in turn.

Multi-step Approach for Training. In this case, we used a training procedure similar to that used in [9] to divide the progression of training into three main stages. During the first stage, the AM was trained with a learning rate of $5e - 5$ over 10 epochs. Likewise, the AAM was trained with the same learning rate for another 10 epochs while the AM's parameters were not updated. Both of them were then trained together over 6 epochs with the learning rate reduced by 10 times to ensure that they fit with each other.

4.3 Ablation Study

We used OULU's Protocol 1 to conduct an ablation study to verify the effectiveness of separate modules from the proposed network in four configurations, as shown in Table 1:

(i) Model A: The proposed model, but with SENet integration excluded. This model was designed to explicitly recognize the power of the channel-attention.

(ii) Model B: The independent AM was trained with a softmax loss. Accordingly, the feature maps that Model B extracted were merely able to accommodate to channel interaction, but they did not respond with region attention.

(ii) Model C: The AM was connected with the AAM, but the advantages of the AAS were removed. *(iv) Model D*: This is the complete proposed model in which the attention is comprehensively and remarkably boosted in both channel and region spaces by means of SENets and the attended regions provided by the AAM through the adaptive translation offsets. Therefore, the performance has far more potential than that of the other three models.

Advantage of SENets. Similarly to Model A with the mere region attention, Model D, however offered with the extra understanding of channel interactions, achieves the superiority (ACER of 0.6% to 1.4%) over its rival, Model A. This dominance demonstrates the impact of SENets on the model's perception in which the subnets greatly strengthen the power of the AM.

Advantage of the AAS. It can be seen clearly that Model D far outweighs Model C by an overwhelming margin of 0.2 percentage points due to the main effectiveness of the AAS.

Advantage of the AAM. In our approach, we used the AAS supervised by the regression loss J_D to alleviate difficulties in accommodating offsets to the optimal locations. Therefore, Model D with the channel and region attention, obtained 0.3% ACER lower than Model B with the deficiency of the region attention, indicating the impact of the AAM on the exploitation of the most relevant regions.

4.4 Intra-testing

Intra-testing was performed on the OULU-NPU and SiW datasets, which have a variety of practical protocols that we rigorously followed. The resulting comparison is shown in Tables 2 and 3.

SiW. In Table 2, the results show that our method outperforms all of the state-of-the-art methods with a remarkable advantage, demonstrating considerable ameliorations in tackling or at least mitigating variations in media. To be more specific, the proposed model brings out a promising improvement at Protocol 3, which is the most demanding protocol for generalizability verification, with a reduction of nearly 42% compared with the next best method.

OULU-NPU. The numerical results in Table 3 demonstrate that our approach significantly surpasses all of the existing methods with the 1st position. Notably,

Table 3. Intra-testing results on four protocols of OULU-NPU.

Protocol	Method	APCER (%)	BPCER (%)	ACER (%)
1	GRADIENT [34]	1.3	12.5	6.9
	BASN [10]	1.5	5.8	3.6
	STASN [9]	1.2	2.5	1.9
	Auxiliaɪy [8]	1.6	1.6	1.6
	FaceDe-S [26]	1.2	1.7	1.5
	Ours	**1.1**	**0.1**	**0.6**
2	MixedFASNet [34]	9.7	2.5	6.1
	Auxiliary [8]	2.7	2.7	2.7
	BASN [10]	**2.4**	3.1	2.7
	GRADIANT	3.1	1.9	2.5
	STASN [9]	4.2	**0.3**	2.2
	Ours	2.7	1.0	**1.9**
3	GRADIENT	2.6 ± 3.9	5.0 ± 5.3	3.8 ± 2.4
	FaceDe-S [26]	4.0 ± 1.8	3.8 ± 1.2	3.6 ± 1.6
	Auxiliary [8]	2.7 ± 1.3	3.1 ± 1.7	2.9 ± 1.5
	STASN [9]	4.7 ± 3.9	**0.9 ± 1.2**	2.8 ± 1.6
	BASN [10]	**1.8 ± 1.1**	3.6 ± 3.5	2.7 ± 1.6
	Ours	1.9 ± 1.4	2.5 ± 2.1	**2.2 ± 1.7**
4	GRADIENT	5.0 ± 4.5	15.0 ± 7.1	10.0 ± 5.0
	Auxiliary [8]	9.3 ± 5.6	10.4 ± 6.0	9.5 ± 6.0
	STASN [9]	6.7 ± 10.6	8.3 ± 8.4	7.5 ± 4.7
	FaceDe-S [26]	**1.2 ± 6.3**	6.1 ± 5.1	5.6 ± 5.7
	BASN [10]	6.4 ± 8.6	**3.2 ± 5.3**	4.8 ± 6.4
	Ours	1.3 ± 1.1	5.1 ± 2.0	**3.2 ± 0.9**

Table 4. Cross-testing results on SiW and OULU-NPU.

Training	Test	Method	ACER (%)
SiW	OULU 1	Auxiliary [8]	10.0
		DepthFreq [33]	9.3
		Ours	**3.8**
	OULU 2	Auxiliary [8]	14.0
		DepthFreq [33]	**7.8**
		Ours	11.0
	OULU 3	Auxiliary [8]	13.8 ± 5.7
		DepthFreq [33]	16.2 ± 5.0
		Ours	**9.7 ± 1.6**
	OULU 4	Auxiliary [8]	10.0 ± 8.8
		DepthFreq [33]	14.1 ± 8.3
		Ours	**1.9 ± 0.6**
OULU	SiW 1	DepthFreq	**7.28**
		Ours	8.90
	SiW 2	DepthFreq [33]	6.9 ± 1.1
		Ours	**6.7 ± 0.9**
	SiW 3	DepthFreq [33]	11.6 ± 4.7
		Ours	**6.1 ± 0.02**

we achieved state-of-the-art success over the former best methods at Protocols 1 and 4 by large margins, of around 60% and 33%, respectively. In spite of a high BPCER of 5.1% at Protocol 4, which is the most challenging protocol verifying the generalizability under variations of unknown sessions and capturing devices, the proposed model still dominate the others with the lowest ACER. The results partly suggest the robustness of our approach under PA variations in terms of pose, illumination, and capture device.

4.5   Cross-testing

We evaluated the effectiveness of our model on cross-datasets, in which the network alternately is trained on OULU-NPU and assessed on SiW and vice-versa, via the ACER metric. Our improvements of deeply mining AAS representations are more confident and transparent as some of the best results are shown. As shown in Table 4, our model achieved slightly worse results compared with the best model by approximately 41% and 22% at SiW with OULU's Protocol 2 and OULU with SiW's Protocol 1, respectively. We hypothesize that the reason is that the features extracted in the frequency domain by the above competitor have more correlations between both datasets. However, the rest still outweighs state-of-the-art results to a great extent, and especially the ACER of 1.9% for SiW with OULU's Protocol 4 declines by five times compared with the best result. This verifies that our network is indeed competent at radically exploiting necessary information for PA detection based on both the AM and RPS with the multi-level fused features.

5   Discussion

Our approach provided notable improvement through outperforming the previous model by far [9], which determines the attended regions based only on binary supervision. Due to the simple constraints on supervision and the heavy reliance on the weak CNN-LSTM, the previous model has a great tendency to investigate inferior outer regions for the spoof cases, namely facial borders and backgrounds that may have no related clues for differentiation between genuine and spoof cases. As a result, we are aware of the issue that the effectiveness of the lower module, namely the AAM, relies heavily on the accuracy of the AM. Accordingly, we boosted the AM's performance to a great extent by adopting SENets that increase the interaction in channel. The offsets are also more likely to coincide with optimal locations due to the introduction of the AAS in a multi-task learning manner.

To better understand the effect of the AAS, the distribution of our multi-level fused feature at the channel-wise addition stage and that of a conventional CNN-LSTM on OULU-NPU's Protocol 1 is illustrated in Fig. 4 through t-SNE [35]. It can be clearly observed that our model represents multi-level fused features with far better well-clustered properties than those of the conventional model. From the revealed information in the ablation study and the 3D visual distribution, our approach with the main purpose of fully resolving the issues of the excessive and inadequate exploitations in FAS partly yields effectiveness

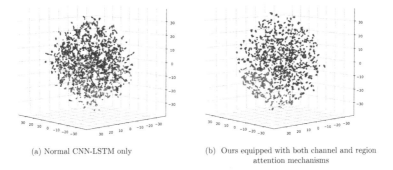

(a) Normal CNN-LSTM only

(b) Ours equipped with both channel and region attention mechanisms

Fig. 4. 3D visualization of feature distribution extracted from the last layer next to the classification block of (a) a vanilla CNN-LSTM and (b) our model comprising the AM, intensified with SENets for channel interaction, and the AAM, enhanced with region attention. Red points represent genuine cases and blue points are spoof cases. The figure is best viewed online in color. (Color figure online)

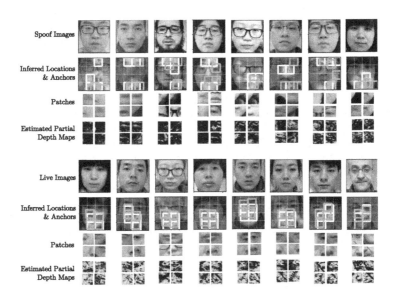

Fig. 5. Illustration of the model's perception of live and spoof cases in OULU-NPU Protocol 1. The first four columns in the first row are print attack cases, followed by four replay attack cases. (Color figure online)

and obvious advancements in assuaging PA variations. Additional insight is presented in Fig. 5, where the attention to live images located by the AAM (orange boxes) has close ties to that of the AM (white boxes). However, the locations to discern spoof images in both modules are inconsistent with each other, proving that the initial advice of the AM is not always appropriate for the AAM to follow up.

Despite the benefits of our approach, it has some drawbacks. The model complexity means that training time is slightly longer than conventional ones as a result of the multi-step approach to guarantee the unified modules efficiently work together. Additionally, more memory must be allocated as well because of the module-driven scheme, but it is a worthwhile trade-off to improve classification performance.

6   Conclusions

In this paper, we have described a novel initiative to overcome or at least mitigate the dilemma of PA variations in FAS expertise by leaving anxiety of the excessive and inadequate exploitations of the input behind. Specifically, introducing the extra channel interaction to the AM and the region attention to the AAM with the use of the AAS bears witness its feasibility in guiding the model to mine adequate distinct properties that it needs for PA detection. Our experimental outcomes also reflect a practical perspective that raising the model's consciousness to PA variations using attention mechanisms much more forceful than broadening the model's horizons in PA variations with some synthetic data.

References

1. Wen, D., Han, H., Jain, A.K.: Face spoof detection with image distortion analysis. IEEE Trans. Inf. Forensics Secur. **10**, 746–761 (2015)
2. Chingovska, I., Anjos, A., Marcel, S.: On the effectiveness of local binary patterns in face anti-spoofing. In, : BIOSIG-Proceedings of the International Conference of Biometrics Special Interest Group (BIOSIG), vol. 2012, pp. 1–7. IEEE (2012)
3. Kim, W., Suh, S., Han, J.J.: Face liveness detection from a single image via diffusion speed model. IEEE Trans. Image Process. **24**, 2456–2465 (2015)
4. Kollreider, K., Fronthaler, H., Faraj, M.I., Bigun, J.: Real-time face detection and motion analysis with application in "liveness" assessment. IEEE Trans. Inf. Forensics Secur. **2**, 548–558 (2007)
5. Pan, G., Sun, L., Wu, Z., Lao, S.: Eyeblink-based anti-spoofing in face recognition from a generic web camera. In: 2007 IEEE 11th International Conference on Computer Vision, pp. 1–8. IEEE (2007)
6. Luo, S., Kan, M., Wu, S., Chen, X., Shan, S.: Face anti-spoofing with multiscale information. In: 2018 24th International Conference on Pattern Recognition (ICPR), pp. 3402–3407. IEEE (2018)
7. Atoum, Y., Liu, Y., Jourabloo, A., Liu, X.: Face anti-spoofing using patch and depth-based CNNs. In: 2017 IEEE International Joint Conference on Biometrics (IJCB), pp. 319–328. IEEE (2017)
8. Liu, Y., Jourabloo, A., Liu, X.: Learning deep models for face anti-spoofing: binary or auxiliary supervision. In: Proceedings of the IEEE Conference on Computer Vision and Pattern Recognition, pp. 389–398 (2018)
9. Yang, X., et al.: Face anti-spoofing: model matters, so does data. In: Proceedings of the IEEE Conference on Computer Vision and Pattern Recognition, pp. 3507–3516 (2019)

10. Kim, T., Kim, Y., Kim, I., Kim, D.: Basn: enriching feature representation using bipartite auxiliary supervisions for face anti-spoofing. In: Proceedings of the IEEE International Conference on Computer Vision Workshops (2019)
11. Hu, J., Shen, L., Sun, G.: Squeeze-and-excitation networks. In: The IEEE Conference on Computer Vision and Pattern Recognition (CVPR) (2018)
12. Määttä, J., Hadid, A., Pietikäinen, M.: Face spoofing detection from single images using micro-texture analysis. In: International Joint Conference on Biometrics (IJCB), vol. 2011, pp. 1–7. IEEE (2011)
13. de Freitas Pereira, T., Anjos, A., De Martino, J.M., Marcel, S.: *LBP - TOP* based countermeasure against face spoofing attacks. In: Park, J.-I., Kim, J. (eds.) ACCV 2012. LNCS, vol. 7728, pp. 121–132. Springer, Heidelberg (2013). https://doi.org/10.1007/978-3-642-37410-4_11
14. de Freitas Pereira, T., Anjos, A., De Martino, J.M., Marcel, S.: Can face anti-spoofing countermeasures work in a real world scenario? In: International Conference on Biometrics (ICB), vol. 2013, pp. 1–8. IEEE (2013)
15. Yang, J., Lei, Z., Liao, S., Li, S.Z.: Face liveness detection with component dependent descriptor. In: 2013 International Conference on Biometrics (ICB), pp. 1–6. IEEE (2013)
16. Komulainen, J., Hadid, A., Pietikäinen, M.: Context based face anti-spoofing. In: 2013 IEEE Sixth International Conference on Biometrics: Theory, Applications and Systems (BTAS), pp. 1–8. IEEE (2013)
17. Patel, K., Han, H., Jain, A.K.: Secure face unlock: spoof detection on smartphones. IEEE Trans. Inf. Forensics Secur. **11**, 2268–2283 (2016)
18. Boulkenafet, Z., Komulainen, J., Hadid, A.: Face anti-spoofing based on color texture analysis. In: IEEE International Conference on Image Processing (ICIP), vol. 2015, pp. 2636–2640. IEEE (2015)
19. Boulkenafet, Z., Komulainen, J., Hadid, A.: Face spoofing detection using color texture analysis. IEEE Trans. Inf. Forensics Secur. **11**, 1818–1830 (2016)
20. Bao, W., Li, H., Li, N., Jiang, W.: A liveness detection method for face recognition based on optical flow field. In: 2009 International Conference on Image Analysis and Signal Processing, pp. 233–236. IEEE (2009)
21. Siddiqui, T.A., et al.: Face anti-spoofing with multi feature videolet aggregation. In: 2016 23rd International Conference on Pattern Recognition (ICPR), pp. 1035–1040. IEEE (2016)
22. Li, J., Wang, Y., Tan, T., Jain, A.K.: Live face detection based on the analysis of fourier spectra. In: Biometric Technology for Human Identification, vol. 5404, pp. 296–303, International Society for Optics and Photonics (2004)
23. Sun, L., Pan, G., Wu, Z., Lao, S.: Blinking-based live face detection using conditional random fields. In: Lee, S.-W., Li, S.Z. (eds.) ICB 2007. LNCS, vol. 4642, pp. 252–260. Springer, Heidelberg (2007). https://doi.org/10.1007/978-3-540-74549-5_27
24. Li, L., Feng, X., Boulkenafet, Z., Xia, Z., Li, M., Hadid, A.: An original face anti-spoofing approach using partial convolutional neural network. In: 2016 Sixth International Conference on Image Processing Theory, Tools and Applications (IPTA), pp. 1–6. IEEE (2016)
25. Patel, K., Han, H., Jain, A.K.: Cross-database face antispoofing with robust feature representation. In: You, Z., et al. (eds.) CCBR 2016. LNCS, vol. 9967, pp. 611–619. Springer, Cham (2016). https://doi.org/10.1007/978-3-319-46654-5_67
26. Jourabloo, A., Liu, Y., Liu, X.: Face de-spoofing: anti-spoofing via noise modeling. In: Proceedings of the European Conference on Computer Vision (ECCV), pp. 290–306 (2018)

27. Liu, Y., Jourabloo, A., Ren, W., Liu, X.: Dense face alignment. In: Proceedings of the IEEE International Conference on Computer Vision Workshops, pp. 1619–1628 (2017)
28. Jaderberg, M., Simonyan, K., Zisserman, A., et al.: Spatial transformer networks. In: Advances in Neural Information Processing Systems, pp. 2017–2025 (2015)
29. Feng, Y., Wu, F., Shao, X., Wang, Y., Zhou, X.: Joint 3D face reconstruction and dense alignment with position map regression network. In: ECCV (2018)
30. Selvaraju, R.R., Cogswell, M., Das, A., Vedantam, R., Parikh, D., Batra, D.: Grad-cam: visual explanations from deep networks via gradient-based localization. In: Proceedings of the IEEE International Conference on Computer Vision, pp. 618–626 (2017)
31. Boulkenafet, Z., Komulainen, J., Li, L., Feng, X., Hadid, A.: Oulu-npu: a mobile face presentation attack database with real-world variations. In: 2017 12th IEEE International Conference on Automatic Face and Gesture Recognition (FG 2017), pp. 612–618. IEEE (2017)
32. ISO/IEC JTC 1/SC 37 Biometrics.: information technology biometric presentation attack detection part 1: Framework (2006). https://www.iso.org/obp/ui/iso
33. Huang, Y., Zhang, W., Wang, J.: Deep frequent spatial temporal learning for face anti-spoofing. arXiv preprint arXiv:2002.03723 (2020)
34. Boulkenafet, Z., et al.: A competition on generalized software-based face presentation attack detection in mobile scenarios. In: 2017 IEEE International Joint Conference on Biometrics (IJCB), pp. 688–696. IEEE (2017)
35. Maaten, L.v., Hinton, G.: Visualizing data using t-sne. J. Mach. Learn. Res. **9**, 2579–2605 (2008)

3D Object Detection from Consecutive Monocular Images

Chia-Chun Cheng[1]([✉])[ID] and Shang-Hong Lai[1,2][ID]

[1] National Tsing Hua University, Hsinchu, Taiwan
ms0365647@gmail.com, lai@cs.nthu.edu.tw
[2] Microsoft AI R&D Center, Taipei, Taiwan
shlai@microsoft.com

Abstract. Detecting objects in 3D space plays an important role in scene understanding for real applications, such as autonomous driving and mobile robot navigation. Many image-based methods have been proposed due to the high cost of LiDAR. However, monocular images are lack of depth information and difficult to detect objects with occlusion. In this paper, we propose to integrate 2D/3D object detection and 3D motion estimation for consecutive monocular images to overcome these problems. Additionally, we estimate the relative motion of the object between frames to reconstruct the scene in the previous timestamp. To learn motion estimation from unlabeled data, we propose an unsupervised motion loss which learns 3D motion estimation from consecutive images. Our experiments on KITTI dataset show that the proposed method outperforms the state-of-the-art methods for 3D Pedestrian and Cyclist detection and achieves competitive results for 3D Car detection.

1 Introduction

Detecting objects and their motions in 3D space plays an important role in scene understanding for applications such as autonomous driving [1] and mobile robot navigation [2]. Previous methods [3] on 3D object detection rely heavily on LiDAR device which provides precise depth information. However, due to the high cost of LiDAR, many monocular image-based approaches were proposed. Specifically, image-based approaches can be categorized into image-only [4] and pseudo-LiDAR methods [5]. The image-only methods typically leverage geometric constraints such as object shape and key points. Pseudo-LiDAR approaches relied on external sub-networks such as state-of-the-art depth prediction network to obtain depth cues. The drawback of these approaches is the upper-bound for the framework limited by the additional network due to the persistent output noise. On the other hand, unsupervised depth prediction methods [6] using sequential monocular frames have achieved state-of-the-art performance compared to the supervised approaches, which makes it possible to solve the core problem in 3D object detection for the lack of depth information. Furthermore, due to the single view observation, monocular image-based approaches typically fail to detect objects with occlusion and truncation, which may occur in real-world driving scenarios. Therefore, the lack of depth information and occlusion

© Springer Nature Switzerland AG 2021
H. Ishikawa et al. (Eds.): ACCV 2020, LNCS 12622, pp. 453–468, 2021.
https://doi.org/10.1007/978-3-030-69525-5_27

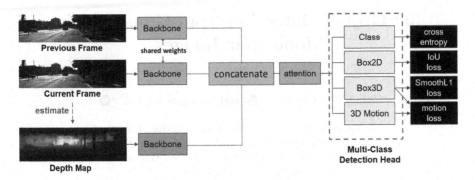

Fig. 1. The overall architecture of the proposed network that integrates 2D/3D object detection and 3D object motion estimation for multi-frame monocular images. The outputs are for current frame.

cause large performance gap between LiDAR-based methods and monocular approaches, thus making 3D object detection from monocular images still a challenging problem.

The 3D object detection aims to classify the object category and estimate 3D bounding boxes of physical objects. Specifically, for each detected 3D bounding box, 3D centroid coordinates (x, y, z), orientation (rotation y) and sizes (l, h, w) are given according to the camera coordinate system. Particularly, monocular image-based approaches only take monocular frames as input instead of 3D point cloud data, and the calibration parameters for each image are usually provided.

In this work, we focus on addressing two key challenges in monocular 3D object detection. First, depth prediction is considerably the most challenging problem in monocular image-only 3D object detection. Previous approaches typically use projection geometric constraint [7], prior knowledge [4,8] or external pre-trained depth estimation network [9] to solve this problem. In addition, occlusion or truncation often occurs in driving scenes, especially in the scenarios with lots of cars on the road. Thus, an accurate 3D object detector is highly demanded for real-world autonomous driving applications.

Motivating by [6], which learns depth prediction from unlabeled monocular videos, we propose another way to address the above problems by using sequential frames from a single monocular camera. Specifically, we use consecutive frames to detect objects in 3D space. To utilize consecutive frames, we not only predict 3D bounding boxes, but also their 3D relative motions to reconstruct their 3D positions in the previous timestamp. Thus, we can recover depth cues from multi-view geometric constraints. Overall, we propose a novel three-streamed convolutional neural network based on [4], which takes consecutive frames and an estimated depth map as inputs and additionally estimates 3D relative motion for each object. The overall architecture of the proposed integrated network is depicted in Fig. 1.

To better capture object motion between consecutive frames, we adopt channel attention mechanism [10] in our proposed network. Due to the lack of labels in previous frames, unsupervised training is adopted to learn 3D object motion. Notably, we propose a motion loss which projects the 3D object onto the current frame and the previous frame according to the estimated depth and motion, and then calculate the absolute error and structural similarity error [11] between two projected patches.

The main contributions of this work include: (1) We propose a three-streamed network which combines the local features and motion features to address the depth estimation problem in 3D object detection. (2) Channel attention is applied to capture motion features between consecutive frames. (3) Moreover, we additionally estimate the relative 3D motions for objects in 3D space to help us better understand the surroundings in real-world driving scenes. (4) To estimate 3D motions, we propose a unsupervised motion loss which projects the 3D object onto both current and previous frames, and then computes the structure similarity error. In the experimental evaluation, we show that our method outperforms the state-of-the-art methods in both 3D Pedestrian and Cyclist detection and achieves competitive results for 3D Car detection on the KITTI [12] dataset.

2   Related Work

2.1   LiDAR-Based 3D Object Detection

Typically, LiDAR-based 3D object detection can be categorized into point-based and voxel-based according to the feature representations. Zhou *et al.* [13] divided point clouds into equally spaced 3D voxels and transform a group of points within each voxel into a unified feature representation. In [14], Wang *et al.* implemented FPN technique on voxel-based networks. On the other hand, PointNets [15] can directly extract features from raw point clouds, which leads to many point-based approaches being proposed. Qi *et al.* [16] leveraged mature 2D object detectors and extracted point clouds from 2D detection frustum. In [3], Shi *et al.* proposed to segment point clouds into foreground and background and generate high-quality 3D proposals. The drawbacks of LiDAR are its high cost and sensitivity to adverse weather conditions, which limit its application to real-world scenarios.

2.2   Pseudo LiDAR-Based 3D Object Detection

Ma *et al.* [17] first transformed the input data from 2D image plane to 3D point clouds space for a better input representation and embedded the complementary RGB cue into the generated point clouds representation. In [18], Wang *et al.* converted image-based depth maps to pseudo-LiDAR, which can apply different existing LiDAR-based detection algorithms. Following the pipeline of two-stage 3D detection algorithms, Weng *et al.* [19] detected 2D object proposals in the input image and extracted a point cloud frustum from the pseudo-LiDAR for each proposal. However, pseudo-LiDAR relies heavily on the additional predicted depth map, which limits the upper bound of the performance.

2.3   Image-Based Monocular 3D Object Detection

Liu *et al.* [20] predicted a 3D bounding box for each detected object by combining a single keypoint estimate with regressed 3D variables and proposed a multi-step disentangling approach for constructing the 3D bounding box, which significantly improves both training convergence and detection accuracy. Qin *et al.* [21] proposed a unified network composed of four task-specific subnetworks, responsible for 2D object detection, instance depth estimation (IDE), 3D localization and local corner regression. In [4], Brazil *et al.* proposed 2D-3D anchor architecture for region proposal network, which initializes all anchors with prior statistics for each of its 3D parameters. Additionally, depth-aware convolutional layers are proposed to better capture depth information. To increase 2D-3D consistency and achieve better orientation prediction, a post-optimization algorithm is applied after region proposal network. Ding *et al.* [9] indicated that conventional 2D convolutions are unsuitable for 3D object detection due to the failed capture of local object and its scale information. Therefore, a new local convolutional network (LCN), termed Depth-guided Dynamic-Depthwise-Dilated LCN, was proposed, where the filters and their receptive fields can be automatically learned from image-based depth maps, making different pixels of different images have different filters. However, single 2D image can not fully represent the 3D structure of each object and fail to restore the accurate 3D information.

In this paper, we use consecutive monocular images to recover depth information through multi-view geometric constraints. To reconstruct the previous scene, we not only predict 3D bounding box for each object but also predict its 3D relative motion. In addition, we use channel attention mechanism to capture motion information between consecutive frames. Notably, we do not need extra labels to train the estimation of relative object motions. The motion is trained through unsupervised learning.

3   Proposed Method

As a multi-class 3D object detector, the proposed network is comprised of three key components: a backbone, an attention module and a multi-class detection head. Following [9], we apply DORN [22] to generate our depth maps. Figure 1 illustrates the overall architecture of the proposed network. First, our network takes two consecutive RGB frames and an estimated depth map of the current frame as inputs. Then, the features are concatenated along the channel dimension after the backbone feature extraction. The channel attention mechanism is applied after the feature concatenation. Last, the attention module is followed by a multi-class detection head. Details of the three components are described below.

3.1   Backbone

To better utilize previous frames and depth maps, we design the backbone with a three-branch network. The first two branches are the RGB images feature extraction networks with shared weights for the previous frame and current frame. The

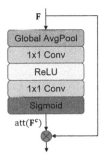

Fig. 2. Illustration of channel attention block

third branch is the depth feature extraction network which takes the estimated depth map of the current image as input. After the feature extraction, these three feature maps are merged via concatenating along the channel dimension. Inspired by [9], the backbone of the feature extraction network is ResNet-50 [23] without the FC and average pooling layers. The all subsequent convolutional layers in block4 are replaced by dilated convolutional layers (the dilation rate is 2) to obtain a larger receptive field.

3.2   Attention Module

Attention mechanism helps the neural network to highlight distinctive features. Consecutive frames contain redundant information such as background in both spatial and temporal dimensions, which should not be treated as equally important in our detection network. In addition, attention mechanism allows our network to focus on object motions and bring out better depth reconstruction effects. Thus, we adopt the channel attention [10] mechanism to predict relative object motion and aggregate more robust features in consecutive frames. The output of the attention module can be considered as the weighted sum of the feature maps along the channel dimension.

The backbone features are followed by three residual groups [10], each of which consists of 12 residual attention blocks, having totally 36 channel attention blocks. Figure 2 illustrates the architecture of the channel attention block. First, global average pooling is applied on the input feature map to aggregate the statistics of each channel. Then, we used two 1×1 convolutional layers to capture the inter-channel relationship. To make sure the weights are in the range between 0 and 1, sigmoid is applied. The output of channel attention block is calculated as an element-wise product of the input feature $\mathbf{F}$ and att($\mathbf{F}^c$) along the channel dimension.

3.3   Multi-class Detection Head

Inspired by [4,9], the proposed framework is based on the region proposal network (RPN) with shared 2D-3D anchor boxes. The region proposal network locates the predefined anchors at every spatial location of an image and generates proposals where the object matches the templates of the predefined anchors. Then, the parameters of the estimated objects are regressed from the generated proposals.

Formulation: The input feature maps of our detection head has a network stride factor of 16 to the input image. Following the practice, the 3D-to-2D projection matrix for each image is given both at training and test time. The projection matrix $\mathbf{P} \in \mathbb{R}^{3 \times 4}$ can be written as:

$$\begin{bmatrix} x \\ y \\ 1 \end{bmatrix}_P \cdot z_{3D} = \mathbf{P} \cdot \begin{bmatrix} x \\ y \\ z \\ 1 \end{bmatrix}_{3D} , \tag{1}$$

where $[x, y, z]_{3D}$ denotes the 3D point in camera coordinates, and $[x, y]_P$ denotes the projected 2D point of the 3D point in image coordinates.

Let us denote n_a to be the number of anchors, n_c the number of classes, h and w the height and width of the input feature maps, respectively. The output represents the anchor-based transformation. Our detection head predicts $n_c + 14$ parameters per anchor for each position (i, j) in the input feature maps as: $\mathbf{c}, [t_x, t_y, t_w, t_h]_{2D}, [t_x, t_y]_P, [t_w, t_h, t_l, t_z, t_\alpha]_{3D}, [t_x, t_y, t_z]_{motion}$, where $\mathbf{c}$ denotes the confidence score of each class, and $[t_x, t_y, t_w, t_h]_{2D}$ is the estimated 2D box, $[t_x, t_y]_P$ denotes the projected 2D point of the 3D object center, $[t_w, t_h, t_l, t_z, t_\alpha]_{3D}$ denotes the estimated 3D shape, depth and rotation, $[t_x, t_y, t_z]_{motion}$ denotes the 3D relative motion of the object between two frames in camera coordinates. The total size of the output is $w \times h \times n_a \times (14 + n_c)$.

2D-3D Anchor: We utilize our 2D anchors with 3D parameters. Specifically, the 2D-3D anchors are defined on the 2D space. For each anchor, the default values of the 3D parameters are the mean statistics calculated from the training dataset as the corresponding priors. A template anchor is defined using parameters of both 2D and 3D spaces: $[x, y, w, h]_{2D}, [x, y]_P, [w, h, l, z, \alpha]_{3D}$, where $[x, y, w, h]_{2D}$ denotes the 2D box, $[x, y]_P$ denotes the projected 3D center in image coordinates, $[w, h, l]_{3D}$ denotes the shape of the 3D box, z_{3D} denotes the depth, and α_{3D} denotes the observation viewing angle.

For 2D anchors, we use 12 anchor scales ranging from 30 to 400 pixels and 3 ratios (0.5, 1.0, 1.5) to define our total 36 anchors for each cell in the output feature maps. Note that $[x, y]_{2D}$ and $[x, y]_P$ share the same anchor parameters. To calculate the default priors for the 3D parameters, we project all 3D ground truth boxes to the 2D space. Then, for each projected box, we assign it to the 2D anchors whose intersection over union (IoU) with it are greater than 0.5. Afterwards, the 3D parameters $[w, h, l, z, \alpha]_{3D}$ are the statistics across all matching 3D ground truth boxes.

Motion Scale Parameter: For the relative object motion, since the 2D convolution is a spatially-invariant operation and does not consider the depth dimension, it is difficult for convolutional kernels to predict 3D object motions between frames. On the other hand, due to the perspective projection, the moving distance for an object in the monocular view would be different.

To address these problems, we predefine our motion scale parameter s_{motion} for each anchor based on its depth prior. Specifically, the motion scale parameter is applied to the estimated relative object motion to obtain the final object motion in the 3D space. The transformation is further detailed in Data Transformation. Generally, the anchor with the larger depth prior has larger motion scale parameter. To calculate the motion scale parameter, we first define two fixed points in image coordinates and back-project these two points from image coordinates to camera coordinates based on the depth prior of each anchor. Then, we calculate the distance between the two points in the 3D space. We thus define a motion scale parameter for each anchor based on the ratio of its distance difference in the 3D space to the smallest one among all anchors.

Data Transformation: The output of our network represents the anchor-based transformation. Following [4], the data transformation is applied to obtain the final results:

$$
\begin{aligned}
[x', y']_{2D} &= [x, y]_{2D} + [t_x, t_y]_{2D} \cdot [w, h]_{2D} \\
[w', h']_{2D} &= [w, h]_{2D} \cdot exp([t_w, t_h]_{2D}) \\
[x', y']_P &= [x, y]_P + [t_x, t_y]_P \cdot [w, h]_{2D} \\
[w', h', l']_{3D} &= [w, h, l]_{3D} \cdot exp([t_w, t_h, t_l]_{3D}) \\
[z', \alpha']_{3D} &= [z, \alpha]_{3D} + [t_z, t_\alpha]_{3D} \\
[x', y', z']_{motion} &= [s_{motion}, 1, s_{motion}] \cdot [t_x, t_y, t_z]_{motion},
\end{aligned}
\tag{2}
$$

where $[*']$ denotes the transformed parameter, $[*]$ denotes the parameter of the predefined anchor, s_{motion} denotes the motion scale parameter, $[t_*]$ is the output of our network. Notably, since the difference in vertical motion of an object is usually small, the motion scale parameter is applied to the horizontal and depth axes in camera coordinates.

3.4 Loss Function

The loss of our network is formed as a multi-task learning task, which contains a classification loss L_{class}, a 2D box regression loss L_{2D}, a 3D box regression loss L_{3D} and a relative object motion regression loss L_{motion}. Let b'_{2D} denote $[x', y', w', h']_{2D}$, b'_{3D} denote $[x', y']_P$ and $[w', h', l', z', \alpha']_{3D}$. Following [24], to generate the ground truth target $\hat{b}_{2D}, \hat{b}_{3D}$ for each anchor, we check if any ground truth 2D box matches the predefined 2D anchors with at least 0.5 IoU. We thus define the target of the anchor with the best matching ground truth.

For the classification loss, we employ the cross-entropy loss:

$$
L_{class} = -log(softmax(\mathbf{c})). \tag{3}
$$

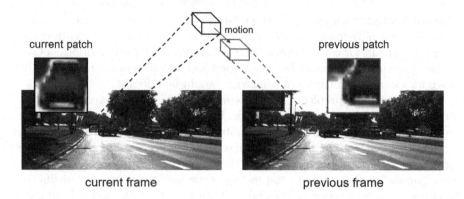

current frame   previous frame

Fig. 3. Illustration of motion loss

For 2D box, we use the negative logistic IoU loss for transformed b'_{2D}:

$$L_{2D} = -log(IoU(b'_{2D}, \hat{b}_{2D})).\tag{4}$$

We use Smooth L1 loss for each transformed parameter in b'_{3D}:

$$L_{3D} = SmoothL1(b'_{3D}, \hat{b}_{3D}).\tag{5}$$

For the target of relative 3D object motion, due to the lack of labels, we adopt an unsupervised learning mechanism to learn 3D object relative motion in camera coordinates. As shown in Fig. 3, for each foreground anchor, we project the target 3D bounding box onto the image in the current timestamp to obtain a 2D image patch $\hat{patch}_{curr}$. Then, we shift the estimated 3D box with estimated 3D relative motion to reconstruct the object location in the previous timestamp, and obtain another 2D patch $patch'_{prev}$ through 3D-to-2D projection. We finally calculate the SSIM loss and the L1 loss between the two patches to supervise the motion learning.

The motion loss L_{motion} is denoted as:

$$L_{motion} = SSIM(\hat{patch}_{curr}, patch'_{prev}) + L1(\hat{patch}_{curr}, patch'_{prev}).\tag{6}$$

Overall, the weighted loss of our multi-task network is defined as:

$$L = \lambda_1 L_{class} + \lambda_2 L_{2D} + L_{3D} + \lambda_3 L_{motion}.\tag{7}$$

4 Experimental Results

4.1 Dataset

KITTI: The KITTI [12] dataset is a widely used autonomous driving dataset, which provides the 3D object detection and the bird's eye view (BEV) benchmarks for 3D localization evaluation. In BEV task evaluation, all 3D boxes are projected to the ground plane, and 2D object detection is applied to compute the evaluation results. The official dataset consists of 7,481 training samples and 7,518 test samples, including images, corresponding point clouds, 3 temporally preceding frames, camera calibration matrices, and 2D-3D annotations for three object classes: Car, Pedestrian, and Cyclist. For each object in annotations, one of the three difficulty levels (easy, moderate, hard) is given based on the occlusion and truncation levels of the object.

Since the annotations of the official test dataset are not available, we split the training dataset into a *training* set and a *validation* set described in [25] for comprehensive evaluation. The split renders 3,712 *training* and 3,769 *validation* samples, and avoids overlapping sequences in both sets.

4.2 Evaluation Metrics

Following [12], for each difficulty level and class, we compute the precision-recall curve and average precision (AP) for evaluation with IoU threshold 0.7 (Car) and 0.5 (Pedestrian, Cyclist). Notably, all methods on the official KITTI leaderboard are ranked based on the moderately difficult results. Before Aug. 2019, 11 recall points are applied to compute interpolated average precision, denotes as $\text{AP}|_{R_{11}}$. After [26] released, the official evaluation uses 40 recall points instead of 11 recall points in the benchmark, denoted as $\text{AP}|_{R_{40}}$. Particularly, since the early methods only report the results under old metric, we compare our results on *validation* set using $\text{AP}|_{R_{11}}$ for fair comparison.

4.3 Implementation Details

In our motion loss, we generate two projection patches in the previous frame to supervise both motion and depth. Particularly, to better supervise motion, we use the ground truth 3D box $\hat{b}_{3D}$ and the estimated motion $[x', y', z']_{motion}$ to obtain the patch in the previous frame. On the other hand, to supervise both depth and motion, we replace the depth parameter in $\hat{b}_{3D}$ with estimated depth z'_{3D} and obtain another previous patch with the estimated motion $[x', y', z']_{motion}$. Both patches are used to compute SSIM and L1 loss with the current patch. All patches are scaled to 32×32. We set $\lambda_1 = \lambda_2 = 1$, $\lambda_3 = 0.05$.

A dropout layer with a dropout rate of 0.2 is applied after the channel attention module. We adopt non-maximum suppression with an IoU threshold of 0.4 on our output in 2D space. Horizontal flipping is used for data augmentation. The input images are scaled to 512×1760. Following [4], a hill climbing post-processing is applied for optimizing the estimated rotation α'_{3D}.

The model is trained with SGD optimizer with a learning rate 0.01, a momentum 0.9, a weight decay 0.0005, and mini-batches of size 8. We adopt the 'one-cycle' learning policy [27] with a maximum learning rate 0.01 and a minimum learning rate 0.000001. The model has 263,283,080 trainable parameters and the inference time is 0.4 s. We train our network on 4 NVIDIA Tesla V100 GPUs for 50,000 iterations.

Fig. 4. Qualitative examples

Fig. 5. Visualization results of reconstructed object positions in previous frames.

4.4   Experimental Results

In this section, we present evaluation results on the KITTI *validation* set [25]. We compare our results with existing monocular methods in 3D object detection and bird's eye view (BEV) benchmarks. For fair comparison, all results are reported in $AP|_{R_{11}}$. We visualize our qualitative examples in Fig. 4. In Fig. 5, the second row shows the scene in the previous timestamp corresponding to the first row. Since we only predict the results in the current timestamp, the reconstructed results from the estimated object motions in the previous timestamp show that our model can estimate the object motion.

Car: Table 1 and Table 2 show the comparative results in Car at IoU threshold 0.7 and 0.5, respectively. Our methods achieve competitive results both in AP_{3D} and AP_{BEV}. As mentioned in [9], pseudo-LiDAR based methods [17,19] fail to detect other classes in their single model, while our model is a multi-class detector. In addition, [17,19] used the additional 2D detector to obtain the better 2D results in their model and resort to multi-stage training. However, our multi-task model is trained end-to-end. The 2D detection results are shown in Table 3.

Pedestrian & Cyclist: For Pedestrian and Cyclist, our method achieves the state-of-the-art results in both 3D object detection and bird's eye view benchmarks (Table 4 and Table 5). Notably, due to the non-rigid body and small size, pedestrians and cyclists are particularly hard to detect in 3D space. Most methods fail to detect these two classes in their models. However, our proposed

Table 1. Comparative results on *validation* set at 0.7 IoU threshold for Car.

Method	AP_{3D}			AP_{BEV}		
	Easy	Moderate	Hard	Easy	Moderate	Hard
Shift R-CNN [28]	13.84	11.29	11.08	18.61	14.71	13.57
MonoGRNet [21]	13.88	10.19	7.62	24.97	19.44	16.30
MonoPSR [29]	12.75	11.48	8.59	20.63	18.67	14.45
Multi-Fusion [30]	10.53	5.69	5.39	22.03	13.63	11.60
Mono3D-PLiDAR [19]	31.50	21.00	17.50	41.90	28.30	**24.50**
AM3D [17]	**32.23**	21.09	17.26	**43.75**	**28.39**	23.87
MonoDIS [26]	18.05	14.98	13.42	24.26	18.43	16.95
M3D-RPN [4]	20.27	17.06	15.21	25.94	21.18	17.90
SMOKE [20]	14.76	12.85	11.50	19.99	15.61	15.28
D4LCN [9]	26.97	**21.71**	**18.22**	34.82	25.83	23.53
Ours	25.49	18.86	17.15	33.69	25.02	20.38

Table 2. Comparative results on *validation* set at 0.5 IoU threshold for Car.

Method	AP_{3D}			AP_{BEV}		
	Easy	Moderate	Hard	Easy	Moderate	Hard
MonoGRNet [21]	50.51	36.97	30.82	54.21	39.69	33.06
MonoPSR [29]	49.65	41.71	29.95	56.97	43.39	36.00
Multi-Fusion [30]	47.88	29.48	26.44	55.02	36.73	31.27
Mono3D-PLiDAR [19]	68.40	48.30	**43.00**	72.10	**53.10**	**44.60**
AM3D [17]	**68.86**	**49.19**	42.24	**72.64**	51.82	44.21
M3D-RPN [4]	48.96	39.57	33.01	55.37	42.49	35.29
Ours	59.00	44.29	36.72	66.38	46.32	38.48

Table 3. Comparative 2D detection results on *validation* set at 0.7 IoU threshold for Car.

Method	AP_{2D}		
	Easy	Moderate	Hard
AM3D [17]	90.50	**89.90**	80.70
Mono3D-PLiDAR [19]	**96.50**	**90.30**	**87.60**
Ours	87.32	82.42	66.51

multi-class 3D detection model outperforms all previous methods with a large margin. Particularly, we achieve 10.46% relative improvement (12.46 vs. 11.23) in Pedestrian AP_{3D} under the moderate setting.

Table 4. Comparative results on *validation* set at 0.5 IoU threshold for Pedestrian.

Method	AP_{3D}			AP_{BEV}		
	Easy	Moderate	Hard	Easy	Moderate	Hard
Shift R-CNN [28]	7.55	6.80	6.12	8.24	7.50	6.73
MonoPSR [29]	10.64	8.18	7.18	11.68	10.05	8.14
Mono3D-PLiDAR [19]	11.60	11.20	10.90	14.40	**13.80**	12.00
AM3D [17]	11.29	9.01	7.04	14.30	11.26	9.23
MonoDIS [26]	10.79	10.39	9.22	11.04	10.94	10.59
M3D-RPN [4]	-	11.28	-	-	11.44	-
D4LCN [9]	12.95	11.23	11.05	-	-	-
Ours	**14.19**	**12.46**	**11.82**	**14.98**	12.73	**12.40**

Table 5. Comparative results on *validation* set at 0.5 IoU threshold for Cyclist.

Method	AP_{3D}			AP_{BEV}		
	Easy	Moderate	Hard	Easy	Moderate	Hard
Shift R-CNN [28]	1.85	1.08	1.10	2.30	2.00	2.11
MonoPSR [29]	10.88	9.93	9.93	11.18	10.18	10.03
Mono3D-PLiDAR [19]	8.50	6.50	6.50	11.00	7.70	6.80
AM3D [17]	8.90	4.81	4.52	10.12	6.39	5.63
MonoDIS [26]	5.27	4.55	4.55	5.52	4.66	4.55
M3D-RPN [4]	-	10.01	-	-	10.13	-
D4LCN [9]	5.85	4.41	4.14	-	-	-
Ours	**10.94**	**10.39**	**10.43**	**12.31**	**10.76**	**10.76**

4.5 Ablations

To verify the effect of each component in our model, we conduct ablation study on *validation* set. We only modify the target components and keep other settings in our study. We evaluate the performance in both AP_{3D} and AP_{BEV} using $AP|_{R_{11}}$.

Effect of Multi-frame Input: In Table 6, we compare models trained with the different numbers of input frames. The model trained with 2 frames and 3 frames which additionally use one and two preceding frames as inputs, respectively. The model with 2-frame input outperforms others in Car and Pedestrian. In Cyclist, 3-frame input achieves the best. We present the contribution of consecutive frames in monocular 3D object detection task. Particularly, for hard difficulty, we observe that the performance increases when using more frames as input, which shows the effect of preceding frames on highly occluded objects as well.

Table 6. Comparisons of different number of frames as input on *validation* set

Class	Input	AP$_{3D}$			AP$_{BEV}$		
		Easy	Moderate	Hard	Easy	Moderate	Hard
Car	1-frame	24.09	18.05	15.08	31.23	23.36	18.95
	2-frame	**25.49**	**18.86**	**17.15**	**33.69**	**25.02**	**20.38**
	3-frame	23.88	18.05	16.46	30.82	23.73	19.30
Pedestrian	1-frame	7.15	5.84	5.28	8.01	6.29	6.22
	2-frame	**14.19**	**12.46**	**11.82**	**14.98**	**12.72**	**12.40**
	3-frame	13.14	11.51	11.12	13.46	11.73	11.48
Cyclist	1-frame	4.06	3.52	3.60	5.71	3.96	3.86
	2-frame	10.84	10.39	10.43	12.31	10.76	**10.76**
	3-frame	**12.50**	**10.44**	**10.46**	**12.87**	**10.83**	10.74

Table 7. Comparisons of the effect of motion loss L_{motion} on *validation* set

Class	L_{motion}	AP$_{3D}$			AP$_{BEV}$		
		Easy	Moderate	Hard	Easy	Moderate	Hard
Car	✗	23.93	18.13	15.87	32.10	23.92	19.58
	✓	**25.49**	**18.86**	**17.15**	**33.69**	**25.02**	**20.38**
Pedestrian	✗	6.86	6.06	5.51	7.61	5.97	6.02
	✓	**14.19**	**12.46**	**11.82**	**14.98**	**12.72**	**12.40**
Cyclist	✗	6.83	5.97	6.02	9.25	6.68	6.39
	✓	**10.84**	**10.39**	**10.43**	**12.31**	**10.76**	**10.76**

Table 8. Comparisons of the number of attention groups in the moderate difficulty on *validation* set

Num of attention groups	AP$_{3D}$			AP$_{BEV}$		
	Car	Pedestrian	Cyclist	Car	Pedestrian	Cyclist
0	17.66	10.99	10.15	23.31	11.36	10.23
1	18.11	5.81	5.49	23.75	11.96	5.65
2	18.54	11.33	3.75	24.21	12.09	4.09
3	**18.86**	**12.46**	**10.39**	**25.02**	**12.72**	**10.76**

Effect of Motion Loss: To better utilize two consecutive frames, we add motion loss L_{motion} to train our model. Therefore, we ablate L_{motion} in Table 7 to observe the contribution in our model. We show that L_{motion} improves the performance with large margin especially for Pedestrian and Cyclist. Since the movement of pedestrians and cyclists is much smaller than cars, it is easier to predict their motions and achieve large improvement.

Table 9. Comparisons of patch sizes in the moderate difficulty on *validation* set

Patch size	AP_{3D}			AP_{BEV}		
	Car	Pedestrian	Cyclist	Car	Pedestrian	Cyclist
8 × 8	18.80	5.16	3.82	24.81	6.27	4.64
16 × 16	18.61	5.43	4.71	24.80	7.47	5.11
32 × 32	**18.86**	**12.46**	**10.39**	**25.02**	**12.72**	**10.76**

Effect of Attention Module: In this part, we compare the model trained with the different numbers of attention groups in Table 8. We report the results at moderate difficulty level for better viewing. We observe that the performance of Car detection in both AP_{3D} and AP_{BEV} becomes larger as the number of attention groups increases. Notably, due to the small shapes of pedestrians and cyclists, it is hard to detect them in 3D space and is more sensitive to the hyperparameters. Overall, all categories achieve the best performances under 3 attention groups.

Effect of Patch Size: Table 9 shows the effect of different patch sizes used in motion loss. We observe that the performance of Pedestrian detection and Cyclist detection becomes better as the patch size increases. All categories achieve the best performance when patch size is 32 × 32.

5   Conclusions

In this paper, we proposed a three-streamed network which additionally estimates relative object motions to recover depth cues for 3D object detection from monocular images. We observe that depth prediction and occlusion are the most important issues in monocular-based methods. Thus, we take consecutive monocular images as inputs to overcome the above problems. To better utilize consecutive frames, we proposed an unsupervised motion loss and applied the attention mechanism. Our model is a multi-class detector which is more robust in real-world scenes than existing pseudo LiDAR-based methods. Additionally, our model also estimates the relative 3D motions for the detected objects, which provides more information for the surrounding environment in driving scenarios. Our experiments show that the proposed model outperforms existing methods with a large margin for Pedestrian and Cyclist detection and achieves competitive results for Car detection on the KITTI dataset.

References

1. Behl, A., Hosseini Jafari, O., Karthik Mustikovela, S., Abu Alhaija, H., Rother, C., Geiger, A.: Bounding boxes, segmentations and object coordinates: how important is recognition for 3D scene flow estimation in autonomous driving scenarios? In: Proceedings of the IEEE International Conference on Computer Vision, pp. 2574–2583 (2017)

2. Guerry, J., Boulch, A., Le Saux, B., Moras, J., Plyer, A., Filliat, D.: Snapnet-r: Consistent 3D multi-view semantic labeling for robotics. In: Proceedings of the IEEE International Conference on Computer Vision Workshops, pp. 669–678 (2017)

3. Shi, S., Wang, X., Li, H.: PointRCNN: 3D object proposal generation and detection from point cloud. In: Proceedings of the IEEE Conference on Computer Vision and Pattern Recognition, pp. 770–779 (2019)

4. Brazil, G., Liu, X.: M3D-RPN: monocular 3D region proposal network for object detection. In: Proceedings of the IEEE International Conference on Computer Vision, pp. 9287–9296 (2019)

5. You, Y., et al.: Pseudo-lidar++: accurate depth for 3D object detection in autonomous driving. arXiv preprint arXiv:1906.06310 (2019)

6. Casser, V., Pirk, S., Mahjourian, R., Angelova, A.: Depth prediction without the sensors: Leveraging structure for unsupervised learning from monocular videos. In: Proceedings of the AAAI Conference on Artificial Intelligence, vol. 33, pp. 8001–8008 (2019)

7. Mousavian, A., Anguelov, D., Flynn, J., Kosecka, J.: 3D bounding box estimation using deep learning and geometry. In: Proceedings of the IEEE Conference on Computer Vision and Pattern Recognition, pp. 7074–7082 (2017)

8. Chen, X., Kundu, K., Zhang, Z., Ma, H., Fidler, S., Urtasun, R.: Monocular 3D object detection for autonomous driving. In: Proceedings of the IEEE Conference on Computer Vision and Pattern Recognition, pp. 2147–2156 (2016)

9. Ding, M., et al.: Learning depth-guided convolutions for monocular 3D object detection. arXiv preprint arXiv:1912.04799 (2019)

10. Choi, M., Kim, H., Han, B., Xu, N., Lee, K.M.: Channel attention is all you need for video frame interpolation, AAAI (2020)

11. Wang, Z., Bovik, A.C., Sheikh, H.R., Simoncelli, E.P.: Image quality assessment: from error visibility to structural similarity. IEEE Trans. Image Process. **13**, 600–612 (2004)

12. Geiger, A., Lenz, P., Urtasun, R.: Are we ready for autonomous driving? the kitti vision benchmark suite. In: 2012 IEEE Conference on Computer Vision and Pattern Recognition, pp. 3354–3361. IEEE (2012)

13. Zhou, Y., Tuzel, O.: Voxelnet: End-to-end learning for point cloud based 3D object detection. In: Proceedings of the IEEE Conference on Computer Vision and Pattern Recognition, pp. 4490–4499 (2018)

14. Wang, B., An, J., Cao, J.: Voxel-FPN: multi-scale voxel feature aggregation in 3D object detection from point clouds. arXiv preprint arXiv:1907.05286 (2019)

15. Qi, C.R., Su, H., Mo, K., Guibas, L.J.: Pointnet: deep learning on point sets for 3D classification and segmentation. In: Proceedings of the IEEE Conference on Computer Vision and Pattern Recognition, pp. 652–660 (2017)

16. Qi, C.R., Liu, W., Wu, C., Su, H., Guibas, L.J.: Frustum pointnets for 3D object detection from RGB-d data. In: Proceedings of the IEEE Conference on Computer Vision and Pattern Recognition, pp. 918–927 (2018)

17. Ma, X., Wang, Z., Li, H., Zhang, P., Ouyang, W., Fan, X.: Accurate monocular 3D object detection via color-embedded 3D reconstruction for autonomous driving. In: Proceedings of the IEEE International Conference on Computer Vision, pp. 6851–6860 (2019)
18. Wang, Y., Chao, W.L., Garg, D., Hariharan, B., Campbell, M., Weinberger, K.Q.: Pseudo-lidar from visual depth estimation: bridging the gap in 3D object detection for autonomous driving. In: Proceedings of the IEEE Conference on Computer Vision and Pattern Recognition, pp. 8445–8453 (2019)
19. Weng, X., Kitani, K.: Monocular 3D object detection with pseudo-lidar point cloud. In: Proceedings of the IEEE International Conference on Computer Vision Workshops (2019)
20. Liu, Z., Wu, Z., Tóth, R.: Smoke: single-stage monocular 3D object detection via keypoint estimation. arXiv preprint arXiv:2002.10111 (2020)
21. Qin, Z., Wang, J., Lu, Y.: Monogrnet: a geometric reasoning network for monocular 3D object localization. In: Proceedings of the AAAI Conference on Artificial Intelligence, vol. 33, pp. 8851–8858 (2019)
22. Fu, H., Gong, M., Wang, C., Batmanghelich, K., Tao, D.: Deep ordinal regression network for monocular depth estimation. In: Proceedings of the IEEE Conference on Computer Vision and Pattern Recognition, pp. 2002–2011 (2018)
23. He, K., Zhang, X., Ren, S., Sun, J.: Deep residual learning for image recognition. In: Proceedings of the IEEE Conference on Computer Vision and Pattern Recognition, pp. 770–778 (2016)
24. Ren, S., He, K., Girshick, R., Sun, J.: Faster R-CNN: towards real-time object detection with region proposal networks. In: Advances in Neural Information Processing Systems, pp. 91–99 (2015)
25. Chen, X., et al.: 3D object proposals for accurate object class detection. In: Advances in Neural Information Processing Systems, pp. 424–432 (2015)
26. Simonelli, A., Bulo, S.R., Porzi, L., López-Antequera, M., Kontschieder, P.: Disentangling monocular 3D object detection. In: Proceedings of the IEEE International Conference on Computer Vision, pp. 1991–1999 (2019)
27. Smith, L.N., Topin, N.: Super-convergence: very fast training of neural networks using large learning rates. In: Artificial Intelligence and Machine Learning for Multi-Domain Operations Applications, vol. 11006, p. 1100612, International Society for Optics and Photonics (2019)
28. Naiden, A., Paunescu, V., Kim, G., Jeon, B., Leordeanu, M.: Shift R-CNN: deep monocular 3D object detection with closed-form geometric constraints. In: 2019 IEEE International Conference on Image Processing (ICIP), pp. 61–65. IEEE (2019)
29. Ku, J., Pon, A.D., Waslander, S.L.: Monocular 3D object detection leveraging accurate proposals and shape reconstruction. In: Proceedings of the IEEE Conference on Computer Vision and Pattern Recognition, pp. 11867–11876 (2019)
30. Xu, B., Chen, Z.: Multi-level fusion based 3D object detection from monocular images. In: Proceedings of the IEEE conference on computer vision and pattern recognition, pp. 2345–2353 (2018)

Data-Efficient Ranking Distillation
for Image Retrieval

Zakaria Laskar[✉] and Juho Kannala

Aalto University, Espoo, Finland
{zakaria.laskar,juho.kannala}@aalto.fi

Abstract. Recent advances in deep learning has lead to rapid developments in the field of image retrieval. However, the best performing architectures incur significant computational cost. The paper addresses this issue using knowledge distillation for metric learning problems. Unlike previous approaches, our proposed method jointly addresses the following constraints: i) limited queries to teacher model, ii) black box teacher model with access to the final output representation, and iii) small fraction of original training data without any ground-truth labels. In addition, the distillation method does not require the student and teacher to have same dimensionality. The key idea is to augment the original training set with additional samples by performing linear interpolation in the final output representation space. In low training sample settings, our approach outperforms the fully supervised baseline approach on ROxford5k and RParis6k with the least possible teacher supervision.

1 Introduction

Instance level image retrieval have dramatically improved with the advent of Convolutional Neural Networks (CNN) [1–3]. The improvement in performance is particularly driven by deeper networks such as VGG [4], ResNet [5] family of networks. However, with the increased accuracy also comes higher inference time and computational burden at test time. There are two main ideas that have been proposed to address this challenge. One is to quantize (and/or prune) the trained bigger network to a lighter version with reduced precision and weights but with the same depth [6]. The other direction is to transfer knowledge from the bigger network (teacher model) to a different but much smaller and lighter network (student model). In this paper, we focus on the second direction, popularly known as Knowledge Distillation (KD) [7,8], although it can be applied to the former case as well.

The idea of using information from a teacher model(s) to train a student model was first proposed by Caruana [7], and, was later improved upon by Hinton [8]. Instead of providing a one hot vector as target or ground-truth class label, KD aims to distill additional information from the teacher to the student model. Such additional knowledge is usually constituted by the output at various layers of the teacher model, e.g. logits from the layer before the softmax

© Springer Nature Switzerland AG 2021
H. Ishikawa et al. (Eds.): ACCV 2020, LNCS 12622, pp. 469–484, 2021.
https://doi.org/10.1007/978-3-030-69525-5_28

in the teacher constitute softer targets for the student. Traditionally proposed for classification problem, KD was later extended to the metric learning scenario [9,10]. However, the knowledge being distilled was addressed differently as traditional KD methods did not perform well in this setting [9,10]. While [9] proposed to distill the teacher ranking, [10] proposed to distill the teacher distance for a given query-database sample(s). In both cases, the student model tries to learn the relation (rank/distance) between query-database samples instead of learning the exact input-output mapping. This allows the student network to maintain its own output dimensionality. We refer to these methods as Metric Knowledge Distillation (MKD) methods.

In this paper we address MKD from the perspective of data-efficiency. While existing distillation approaches [9,10] have addressed test time efficiency by compressing the knowledge from cumbersome models onto compact ones, they have failed to address training time efficiency. We address this issue by defining the training time efficiency as i) the number of queries to the teacher model to obtain teacher knowledge (pseudo ground-truth) in the form of final output representation or logits, and ii) the number of training samples required to distill the teacher knowledge onto the student model. In this paper we propose an MKD method under the above mentioned budget constraints while operating under the setting of black-box teacher models, preserving student-teacher dimensionality and achieving comparable performance to the no-budget scenario. Large scale datasets are costly in terms of memory (storage), computation (training) and economic (data accumulation/labelling). In addition private data such as trained teacher models or full training dataset can have limited or partial access due to privacy concerns. Our proposed method reduces the dependency on large scale datasets for learning new models while being efficient also during training.

The key ingredient in our proposed method is the idea of mixup [11,12]. Using mixup, one can augment a small original training set with large number of additional samples by convex combination of the training samples. Such idea has been recently used in [13] to address data-efficient knowledge distillation using mixup based data augmentations. While the existing mixup based methods have addressed classification problems, we extend the idea to the problem of metric learning. In contrast to [11–13], we perform mixup at the global image representation level. That is, each image is represented by a global representation vector obtained by spatial encoding of 2D representation maps from a CNN. Thereafter, augmented representations are obtained by linearly interpolating between representations from original samples. We then perform distillation between teacher and student models in the joint space of original and augmented global representations. In particular we train the student model to mimic the teacher ranking for each sample in the joint representation space of respective models using the recently proposed ranking loss [14]. Representation level mixup requires orders of magnitude less queries to the teacher model compared to mixup at the input image level [13]. In the process our proposed method still achieves comparable performance to fully supervised models trained on the full training dataset.

2   Related Work

We describe the image retrieval and knowledge distillation based related work in this section

Image Retrieval. Before the advent of CNNs, earlier works addressed the image retrieval problem using SIFT [15] based local descriptors [16], and additionally encoded into global representations [17,18] followed by geometric verification [19]. Since then CNN based methods [1–3,20–22] have improved the performance on challenging benchmarks such as Oxford5k and Paris6k [23]. The success can be attributed to large datasets [24], improved global encoding methods [22,25–27], and robust ranking loss functions [2,14,28,29]. In particular, the Average Precision (AP) loss [14] has the least training compute overhead by avoiding hard negative mining with joint ranking supervision over large batches of images.

Knowledge Distillation. Knowledge distillation can be traced back to the work of Breiman *et al.* [30] where the knowledge of multiple tree models were distilled onto a single model. The term knowledge distillation (KD) was itself coined by Hinton *et al.* in his work [8]. In addition to the standard supervisory signals, the student model was additionally trained to match the softmax distribution of a heavier teacher model. Since then, several works have been proposed that provide additional information apart from the softmax logits. [31] and [32] propose to transfer attention maps. Self-distillation where the student and the teacher share the same network architecture have also been proposed [33,34].

For image retrieval and metric learning in general, Chen *et al.* [9] propose to transfer rank information. Similarly, Park *et al.* [10] proposed to distill distance information between teacher and student models. Both these methods show improvements over standard KD approaches.

Mixup. Mixup based regularizers were first proposed by [11,35]. Later, mixup based interpolation was extended to hidden representations of a CNN by several works [12,36]. Recently, [13] proposed mixup based augmentation for data-efficient knowledge distillation. For each mixed sample, the above approaches require a new feed-forward pass through the CNN. Instead our approach performs mixing of the global vector representations requiring just a single feed-forward pass. Mixed samples can be obtained by simply interpolating between original global representations.

3   Proposed Method

In this section we propose an algorithm to train a compact student model, S by distilling the knowledge from a cumbersome teacher model, T. The key idea of knowledge distillation in classification problem is to use soft labels from T as targets in addition to ground-truth hard labels. Soft labels encode semantic similarity by providing inter class similarity information. However, we consider a general scenario where ground-truth labels are not known apriori. In addition metric learning involves optimizing the representation space directly without explicit label prediction as in classification problems. Thus it is not clear how to generate and incorporate teacher soft labels for unsupervised knowledge distillation in the domain of metric learning problems.

First we present preliminaries followed by the data augmentation algorithm to address low training sample complexity. This is followed by teacher label generation and computing the ranking loss to train the student model. Finally, we present the algorithm combining the above steps in a single framework.

3.1   Preliminaries

Given a batch of images, $B = \{I_1, ..I_j..I_B\}$, we obtain teacher and student $l2$ normalized output representations, $f_B^T = \{f_b^T\}_{b=1}^{|B|} \in \mathbb{R}^{N_T \times |B|}$ and $f_B^S = \{f_b^S\}_{b=1}^{|B|} \in \mathbb{R}^{N_S \times |B|}$, where $f_b^T = e^T(T(I_b)) \in \mathbb{R}^{N_T}$, $f_b^S = e^S(S(I_b)) \in \mathbb{R}^{N_S}$. $T(.)$ and $S(.)$ are teacher and student convolutional neural networks respectively, with N_T, N_S being their respective final output dimensionality. As database size in image retrieval problems tends towards millions, it is common practise to store global representations per image by encoding the 3D representation map from the CNNs into 1D vectors. Popular encoding methods from literature include GeM [37], MAC [1], RMAC [26]. As we consider the teacher model as black-box with access to the final vector encoded global representation, we represent the student and teacher encoding functions separately with e^T and e^S respectively. These encoding functions can represent any of the above mentioned encoding methods. As the global representations are $l2$ normalized, a simple dot product is used to compute similarity values.

3.2   Database Augmentation

Acquiring large training datasets and labelling the ground-truth incurs large computational resources, huge memory footprint and high economic costs. We address this using knowledge distillation by replacing large datasets with models trained on them and a small amount of the original training samples. This also addresses practical scenarios where teacher models have limited access rights, or the whole training set is not made public. Furthermore, extracting representations for the whole dataset using both the teacher and student model is inefficient as it leads to increased training costs.

Given a small amount of training samples, D, we extract both teacher and student global representations, f^T and f^S for a given batch, B. We augment the representations from each batch using mixup [11,12]. These works perform mixup at the local level, while we perform mixup at the global representation level. In particular, given representations for images, $I_i, I_j \in B$, we perform representation mixup as follows:

$$f_{ij} = \lambda f_i + (1 - \lambda)f_j, \tag{1}$$

where $\lambda \sim beta(\alpha, \alpha)$ is the mixing coefficient. Instead of sampling λ per training sample, we only sample a single value of λ per batch. The mixed representations are further $l2$ normalized.

There are several benefits to performing mixup at the global representation level. It is to be noted that since we consider black-box teacher models, we can only consider *InputMixup* [11] and not *ManifoldMixup* [12] as the later requires access to intermediate representation maps. However, *InputMixup* which performs mixup at the input image level, requires a new feed-forward pass of the mixed input image through the network to obtain representations. This increases the number of queries to the teacher model to be much more than $|D|$. The same applies for the student network, which in total significantly increase the training cost. The same costs applies for *ManifoldMixup* considering white-box teacher models. In contrast, global representation mixup only requires at most $|D|$ queries to the teacher model, and large amount additional representations can be obtained at a marginal overhead cost. To give the reader an estimate, given a batch of $B = 1000$ images, mixing each image with $R = 10$ other images from the batch will result in 10000 samples. For *InputMixup* this will require $10000 \times ep$ queries to the teacher model where ep is the number of training epochs. Our approach will only require 1000 queries.

3.3   Label Generation

Previously, mixup has been addressed in classification domains [11,12,38]. In such settings, the label of the mixed sample is obtained by linear interpolation of respective labels of the original samples by λ. In this section, we show how to generate labels for student model using global teacher representations.

Let the joint set of representations be $F^T = f_B^T \bigcup f_{B'}^T$, $F^S = f_B^S \bigcup f_{B'}^S$, where $f_{B'}^T, f_{B'}^S$ are the augmented teacher and student representations. Let $Z = \{1, 2, ..., (|B| + |B'|)\}$ be the joint sample index set. We are interested in computing a binary label matrix $Y \in \mathbb{R}^{|Z| \times |Z|}$, where each row $Y_q \in \mathbb{R}^{1 \times |Z|}$ represents the label vector corresponding to the qth representation. Before we explain how the binary values are computed for Y_q, we first formally define a positive index set $P_q \subseteq Z$ such that $\forall z \in Z$

$$Y_q(z) = \begin{cases} 1, & \text{if } z \in P_q \\ 0, & \text{otherwise} \end{cases} \tag{2}$$

The matrix Y is symmetric $(Y = Y^\intercal)$ i.e. $Y_q(z) = Y_z(q)$. The binary label 1 signifies the corresponding representations, f_q^T, f_z^T are similar. Consequently, the corresponding student representations, f_q^S, f_z^S are trained to be similar. The measure of similarity is defined next where we present methods to compute the elements of P_q.

Similarity Labelling (SL). The first measure of similarity is based on cosine similarity in the representation space. We first compute the teacher and student similarity matrices, $S^T = (F^T)^\intercal(F^T)$, $S^S = (F^S)^\intercal(F^S) \in \mathbb{R}^{|Z| \times |Z|}$. The positive set P_q constitutes the Euclidean Nearest Neighbors (ENN) and is computed as $P_q = \{z \mid S_q^T(z) > \tau\} \forall z \in Z$, where $\tau \in [0,1]$ is a similarity threshold. We call this similarity based labelling Similarity Labelling (SL). If τ is too high, P_q will only contain near duplicate representations, while keeping it too low will include too many false positives. We experiment with different values of τ and found that optimal performance is achieved with moderate values of τ (c.f. Sect. 6).

Mixup Labelling. As observed the positive set, P_q under similarity labelling is constituted by the ENN. Thus for representations falling in low density regions, the positive sets will be empty or have low cardinality. Empty positive sets means zero loss and thus no gradient to train the model. This becomes an issue if most of the samples fall in such low density regions (c.f. Sect. 7). To address this issue we introduce mixup labelling (ML) based on the following assumption: the global representations contain semantic concepts, so mixed representation will be closer to the positive sets of representations being mixed, than the other representations. Formally, if representations, f_k^T, f_r^T are mixed resulting in the corresponding mixed representation, f_{kr}^T indexed at $kr \in Z$, and the corresponding positive sets obtained from similarity labelling be P_k, P_r and P_{kr} respectively. Then $P_{kr} = P_{kr} \cup P_k \cup P_r$. Thereafter, using Eq. 2 the label matrix, Y is computed while maintaining matrix symmetry.

3.4 Loss Function

In this section we show how to compute the loss given the student similarity matrix, S^S and teacher label matrix, Y. To realize this, we use the listwise loss, known as Average Precision Loss (AP) [14]. The loss maximizes the distance between histogram of positive and negative similarity scores. For brevity we elaborate the loss function below:

The similarity interval $S_q^S = [0,1]^{1 \times |Z|}$ is divided into $C - 1$ bins of width $\Delta c = \frac{2}{C-1}$. Let $c_b = 1 - (b-1)\Delta c$, $b = 1...C$ represent the center of the bth bin. Average Precision is generally computed at each rank, $r = 1...|Z|$. However, as rank assignment is non-differentiable, the images are instead assigned to bins using the soft bin assignment as follows:

$$p(S_q^S(i), b) = \max\left(1 - \frac{|S_q^S(i) - c_b|}{\Delta}, 0\right). \tag{3}$$

Here, p represents the probability that the ith image occupies the bth bin conditioned on its similarity to the query, q based on S_q^S. The AP is then computed in each bin as follows:

$$Pr(S_q^S, Y_q, b) = \frac{\sum_{b'=1}^{b} p(S_q^S, b')^\top Y_q}{\sum_{b'=1}^{b} p(S_q^S, b')^\top \mathbf{1}}, \tag{4}$$

$$\Delta Rc(S_q^S, Y_q, b) = \frac{p(S_q^S, b)^\top Y_q}{N_q}, \tag{5}$$

Algorithm 1. Rank Distillation

REQUIRE: Teacher & Student representation $f_B^T = \{f_i^T\}_{i=1}^B, f_B^S = \{f_i^S\}_{i=1}^B$
REQUIRE: Labelling functions: $SL(.), ML(.)$
REQUIRE: Loss function: $AP(.)$
REQUIRE: τ, R, λ
OUTPUT: Loss value

1: Initialize $L = \{\}$ ▷ store loss values.
2: $S_o^T \leftarrow (f_B^T)^\intercal (f_B^T)$
3: $P_o \leftarrow SL(S_o^T, \tau)$. ▷ Initial positive set.
4: **for** $r = 1, 2..., R$ **do**
5:      Initialize $F^T = \{\}, F^S = \{\}$ ▷ store original & augmented samples.
6:      Initialize $MIX = \{\}$ ▷ store indices of mixing & mixed samples.
7:      $\{F_i^T\}_{i=1}^{|B|} \leftarrow \{f_i^T\}_{i=1}^{|B|}, \{F_i^S\}_{i=1}^{|B|} \leftarrow \{f_i^S\}_{i=1}^{|B|}$
8:      **for** $k = 1, 2..., |B|$ **do**
9:          Sample index r_k from range $(1, |B|)$
10:         $F_{|B|+K}^T \leftarrow \lambda f_k^T + (1 - \lambda) f_{r_k}^T$
11:         $F_{|B|+K}^S \leftarrow \lambda f_k^S + (1 - \lambda) f_{r_k}^S$
12:         $F_{|B|+K}^S$.requires_grad = False ▷ Restrict back-propagation.
13:         MIX.store$(k, r_k, |B| + k)$ ▷ Store mixing information.
14:      **end for**
15:      $S^T \leftarrow (F^T)^\intercal (F^T), S^S \leftarrow (F^S)^\intercal (F^S)$ ▷ Compute teacher & student similarity matrix.
16:      $P_s \leftarrow SL(S^T, \tau)$. ▷ Positive set based on SL.
17:      $P_m \leftarrow ML(P_o, MIX)$ ▷ Positive set based on ML.
18:      $P \leftarrow P_s \cup P_m$. ▷ Final positive set based.
19:      Compute Y using P ▷ Eq. 2
20:      $L_r \leftarrow AP(Y, S^S)$ ▷ Compute Average Precision Loss
21: **end for**
22: $L \leftarrow 1/R \sum_{r=1}^R L_r$ ▷ Total loss
23: **return** L

The AP loss for each q is computed as:

$$AP(q) = 1 - \sum_{b=1}^{C} Pr(S_q^S, Y_q, b) \; \Delta Rc(S_q^S, Y_q, b). \tag{6}$$

The final loss function to be optimized is defined as:

$$L = \frac{1}{|Z|} \sum_{q=1}^{|Z|} AP(q) \tag{7}$$

3.5 Algorithm

Given the training set, D we first extract all the teacher representations, $f_D^T = \{f_i^T\}_{i=1}^{|D|}$. Thereafter for each epoch, ep, we sample a batch of B images from D.

We then extract the student representations, $f_B^S = \{f_b^S\}_{b=1}^{|B|}$ and from f_D^T obtain the teacher representations $f_B^T = \{f_b^T\}_{b=1}^{|B|}$. We now proceed to compute the loss as described in Algorithm 1.

First, we compute the initial positive set, P_o based on similarity labelling (SL) and teacher representations, f_B^T. Next, we introduce the mixing iterator, R. In each iteration, $r = 1, 2, ...R$ we iterate over the following steps: 1) Mix each student and teacher representation, $f_k^T, f_k^S, k = 1, 2..|B|$ with the representation, $f_r^T \in f_B^T, f_{r_k}^S \in f_B^S$ of a random sample r_k. The mixed representations are concatenated with the original representations resulting in the joint representation set, $F^T \in \mathbb{R}^{N_T \times 2|B|}$, $F^S \in \mathbb{R}^{N_S \times 2|B|}$, where the first $N \times |B|$ are the original representations while the bottom $N \times |B|$ are mixed representations respectively. 2) Simultaneously with the previous step we store the index information of mixing samples (k, r_k) and the mixed sample $(|B| + k), \forall k = 1...|B|$ in the variable, MIX. 3) Given F^T, F^S we compute the teacher and student similarity matrices, S^T, S^S. 4) Next we proceed to label generation. Using the similarity threshold, τ and S^T we first compute the positive set, $P_s = \{P_k\}_{k=1}^{2|B|}$ based on similarity labelling (SL). Thereafter, using the mixing information in MIX and P_o we perform mixup labelling (ML) to compute the mixup positive set, $P_m = \{P_k\}_{k=|B|}^{2|B|}$. The final positive set, P is obtained by combining similarity and mixup positive sets. The label matrix, $Y \in \mathbb{R}^{2|B| \times 2|B|}$ is formed using P. 5) Finally, we compute the Average Precision (AP) loss, L_r using teacher label matrix, Y and student similarity matrix, S^S. After r iterations we have R loss values, $\{L_r\}_{r=1}^R$ which are then averaged followed by back-propagation. It is to be noted that the mixed representations are not used to back-propagate gradients (line 12 in Algorithm 1).

We now explain the rationale behind introducing R. Under the current setting, the number of mixed representations used to compute the final loss is $|B|R$. If these mixed representations were jointly used in computing the final loss the size of the similarity and label matrices will be $((|B| + |B|R)^2)$. For values of $|B| = 1000, R = 10$ used in this work, the size will be $\sim 10000^2$. Loss and gradient computation becomes considerably slow under this setting. Instead, by dividing the loss computation into R steps, we are still able to leverage $|B|R$ mixed representations, while the final similarity matrices are of size $(2|B|)^2 \sim 2000^2$. This leads to comparable performance while increasing training efficiency.

4   Implementation Details

Training Dataset. We use the training dataset used in [1]. The dataset was initially introduced in [24] and consists of 7.4 million internet photo collections of popular landmarks around the world. The images are passed through an SfM pipeline [1] to create clusters of images (class labels). This process results in 163k images clustered into about 700 classes. Training dataset consists of randomly selected 550 classes containing 133k images. We refer to this dataset as *SfMFr*.

Network Training. We used the publicly available trained Resnet101 models by Radenovic *et al.* [37] trained on *SfMFr* as teacher models, T. MobileNetV2

Table 1. Different networks with the number of respective parameters and time taken to process 1 image in multi-scale mode.

Method	Param	Time/Image
ResNet101	42M	60 ms
ResNet34	21M	20 ms
MVNetV2	1.8M	10 ms

(MVNetV2) and Resnet34 pre-trained on ImageNet [39] are used as the student models S1 and S2 respectively. We randomly sample $D = 4000$ images from *SfMFr*. The network is trained with a batch size, $B = 1000$ which are randomly sampled from the training set, D. We used Adam [40] optimizer with an initial learning rate of $l_0 = 1 \times 10^{-4}$, exponential decay $l_0 \exp(-0.01 \times ep)$ every epoch, ep. Weight decay was set to 1×10^{-6}. Images were rescaled to 362 pixels on the longest side while maintaining the aspect ratio. Training is done for 30 epochs on GeForce RTX GPU with 11 GB memory. We use generalized mean pooling (GeM) [37] to obtain global representations for each image. The global descriptors are subsequently $l2$ normalized.

We list the hyper-parameters associated with our algorithm are $\tau = 0.75$, $R = 10$. We use the same hyper-parameter settings for both the student networks, S1 and S2.

Baselines. We train MVNetV2, Resnet34 using contrastive loss (CL) and Average Precision (AP) loss on *SfMFr* dataset. For CL, we mine hard negatives every epoch from a random pool of 22K images, and keep top 5 negatives. Margin is set to 0.65. Batch size are 5 and 4000 for CL and AP respectively. The learning rate was set to 5×10^{-7} for CL and 1×10^{-4} for AP.

Test Dataset. We evaluate our approaches on standard image retrieval benchmark datasets, Oxford5k (Oxf) [41], Paris6k (Par) [42], ROxford5k (ROxf) [23], and RParis (RPar) [23] datasets. The evaluation metric is mean Average Precision (mAP). The test sets consists of 55 queries and several thousand database images (Oxf: 5k, Par: 6k), while their revisited counterparts have 70 queries each with 4k and 6k database images respectively. The revisited datasets also have 3 splits: Easy (E), Medium (M), and Hard (H) defining the difficulty level of retrieving the corresponding database images in the set. The queries are annotated with a bounding box specifying the landmark of interest. Similar to prior works, we crop the query images with bounding box.

During evaluation, we extract multi-scale global representations with the scales: 1, $1/\sqrt{2}$, and $1/2$. The resulting descriptors are combined using GeM pooling. The resulting vector is $l2$ normalized. Furthermore, due to low sample complexity we do not use any validation data during training. Instead, we perform weight averaging [43] to combine model performances from different epochs. In particular, the final student network used for evaluation is obtained by averaging the weights of the trained student models from the 20th and 30th epoch.

The number of parameters and average multi-scale inference time during evaluation are presented in Table 1 for teacher and student models.

Table 2. Performance comparison of compact student networks MobileNetV2 (S1, MVnetV2) and Resnet34 (S2, ResNet34) trained using our method, and baseline methods : without augmentation (no -aug), Average Precision (AP), contrastive loss (CL). Evaluation is done on image retrieval datasets : Oxford (Oxf), Paris (Par), ROxford (ROxf), RParis (RPar). The revisited datasets, ROxf, RPar are evaluated using Easy (E), Medium (M) and Hard (H) splits. Evaluation metric is mAP. T/S denotes the teacher/student role of the model. Our method does not require training labels.

Method	$|D|$	Oxf	ROxf			Par	RPar		
			E	M	H		E	M	H
Resnet101 (T, CL)	120k	81.2	73.8	55.8	27.4	87.8	86.5	70.0	44.8
Compact student networks									
MVnetV2 (CL)	120k	74.5	66.5	48.9	20.8	85.7	**84.6**	**66.2**	39.0
MVnetV2 (AP)	120k	74.2	67.2	51.0	24.3	85.0	83.7	65.6	39.5
MVNetV2 (S1, no-aug)	4k	76.1	67.0	51.0	25.8	**84.6**	84.0	66.1	**40.4**
MVnetV2 (S1)	4k	**78.7**	**70.8**	**53.8**	**26.9**	84.0	82.1	65.0	39.4
ResNet34 (CL)	120k	77.9	70.7	51.9	23.1	**86.5**	**85.9**	**69.5**	**44.0**
ResNet34 (AP)	120k	79.6	70.5	53.3	24.9	86.3	**86.4**	69.2	43.1
ResNet34 (S2, no-aug)	4k	77.3	70.7	50.8	22.5	84.9	83.8	68.0	42.8
ResNet34 (S2)	4k	**78.1**	**74.1**	**55.1**	**25.9**	85.4	84.2	68.6	43.8

5   Results

In this section we compare our proposed algorithms on the standard retrieval datasets. In addition we also compare with baseline methods and perform detailed ablation study.

Baseline Comparison. We compare the performance of the student models, S1: MVNetV2, S2: ResNet34 trained using our proposed method with the teacher model, T: ResNet101 and the same student models trained without the proposed augmentation. In addition we also consider student models trained with ground-truth labels on the full dataset with loss functions: contrastive loss (CL) and average precision (AP). Results are presented in Table 2. Results show that student models using our proposed method are able to match the performance of the supervised counterparts. It is to be noted that our method was only trained on 4k images. Compared to it, the supervised models based on CL and AP losses were trained using the full dataset of 120k images. Among the student models, ResNet34 outperforms MVNetV2 by 2–3% on ROxford and RParis datasets. This can be attributed to the higher capacity of ResNet34 model (c.f. Table 1).

Table 3. Comparison of different mixup methods in terms of performance and computational costs. Mixed indicates the number of mixed samples generated. Cost represents the number of feed-forward pass required through the teacher model. Similar costs also extend to student model. The number of original training samples is 4k.

Method	Mixed	Cost	ROxf			RPar		
			E	M	H	E	M	H
Ours, no-aug	0k	4k	70.7	50.8	22.5	83.8	68.0	42.8
Inp Mix	1k	5k	71.9	52.3	24.4	83.1	67.1	40.5
Inp Mix	8k	12k	72.6	52.7	24.9	82.2	64.7	37.1
Inp Mix	32k	36k	73.4	53.1	24.5	81.7	65.0	38.2
Ours, with-aug	600k	4k	**74.1**	**55.1**	**25.9**	**84.2**	**68.6**	**43.8**

Furthermore, student models trained without the proposed global representation augmentation performs poorly compared to our proposed method with augmentation. Baseline student models trained only on $D = 4k$ dataset with AP loss and full ground-truth label supervision has similar performance to the no-augmentations setting. The decrease in performance in low sample setting can be attributed to the fact that in a randomly selected training set D, large number of samples, $q \in D$ have empty or very small sized positive set P_q. Thus, without any positives there is no error signal that can lead to learning representations from these images. Augmentation addresses this issue by generating positives from the mixed samples.

The computational gains of the proposed global mixup over the baseline input mixup approach is shown in Table 3. Generating more samples using input mixup leads to improvement in ROxford dataset while it decreases on RParis dataset. We hypothesize this is due to limited number of mixed samples.

Table 4. mAP performance on ROxford (ROxf) and RParis (RPar) datasets. We present alongside each method, the model architecture (R: ResNet101, V: VGG16, A: AlexNet, R34: ResNet34 and M: MobileNetV2). In addition we also show the dimension of the final global representation from each model. It is to be noted that our proposed method only requires a fraction of the full supervised dataset and a trained teacher.

Method	Nw	Dim	ROxf				RPar			
			M		H		M		H	
			mAP	mP@10	mAP	mP@10	mAP	mP@10	mAP	mP@10
GeM [37]	R101	2048	64.7	84.7	38.5	53.0	76.9	98.1	55.4	89.1
AP [14]	R101	2048	**67.5**	-	**42.8**	-	**80.1**	-	**60.5**	-
GeM [37]	V	512	60.9	82.7	32.9	51.0	69.3	97.9	44.2	83.7
NetVLAD [22]	V	512	37.1	56.5	13.8	23.3	59.8	94.0	35.0	73.7
Ours	R34	512	55.4	79.9	29.1	46.3	68.7	96.6	43.7	83.4
Ours	M	320	51.1	74.0	24.9	38.6	67.3	96.1	41.1	80.0

However, increasing the number of input mixup augmentations incurs significant computational costs.

State-of-the-Art. State-of-the-art methods are compared in Table 4. Whitening is a standard post-processing step in all standard image retrieval methods as it reduces the impact of correlated features. While some [14] use unsupervised whitening based on PCA, others [37] use supervised whitening. We use PCA based whitening. In particular we use the square rooted PCA [44]. Similar to traditional practices, we learn PCA on Paris6k for evaluating the network on Oxford5k and vice-versa. In addition to mAP, we also report mean precision @10 (mP@10). In RPar PCA does not bring any improvement. However, in ROxf, PCA brings significant improvement both in terms of mAP : ResNet34 (ROxf, M: 55.1 → 55.4, ROxf, H: 25.9 → 29.1), and mP@10: ResNet34 (ROxf, M: 76.6 → 79.9, ROxf, H: 39.8 → 46.3). However, there is an increase in the performance gap with the teacher model (GeM [37]). The performance difference can be attributed to the supervision in the whitening process. Compared to supervised models with similar dimensionality such as (GeM [37], V) that uses a VGG16 architecture, the performance gap is much smaller. Overall, the difference in student performance is well compensated by the reduced number of parameters and computation time for processing a single image in current multi-scale mode as shown in Table 1.

6 Hyper-parameter Ablation

In this section, we analyze and present detailed analysis on the impact of different hyper-parameters in retrieval performance. This is done by varying the concerned hyper-parameter while keeping the rest same as detailed in Sect. 4.

First we analyze the image retrieval performance by varying the size of the training set, D. In Fig. 1 we observe that our method consistently outperforms the baseline method trained without the representation augmentations. As the sample size increases, both the methods converge in performance.

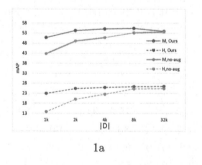
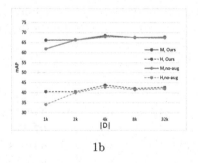

1a   1b

Fig. 1. Figure shows the impact of sample size, $|D|$ on (a) Roxford and (b) RParis datasets for methods with and without the proposed augmentation based global mixup method.

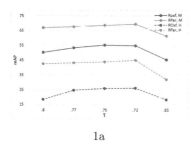
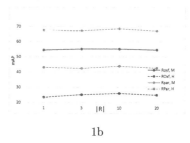

1a   1b

Fig. 2. Figure shows the impact of different hyper-parameters τ (a) and R (b) in retrieval performance.

In Fig. 2a we study the impact of size of similarity threshold τ on the retrieval performance. As mentioned earlier, τ controls the amount of semantic information that is distilled from teacher onto student model. From Fig. 2a we observe that retrieval performance increases as τ is decreased. As explained earlier, high values of τ selects easy positives in the positive set, P. As we decrease this threshold, the hardness of positives increases. However, decreasing τ too much will allow false positives to get included in P which will be detrimental to the learning process. This is evident by the sharp decrease in retrieval performance for $\tau = 0.65$.

Finally in Fig. 2b we study the impact of R. We notice a marginal but consistent improvement in retrieval performance across both datasets as R is increased. In particular for the Hard (H) setting, the performance improves by 2–3 % as R increases from 1 to 10. Beyond $R = 10$ there is a marginal drop in performance.

The above experiments are in line with our motivation to apply the given hyper-parameters and also shows that beyond certain values, our proposed methods are not sensitive to the choice of hyper-parameter values.

7   Training Ablation

In this section we study some of the key components in the training algorithm. In our experiments, the teacher model uses GeM encoding method. Both encoding methods GeM/MAC produce comparable performance on ROxf, M: 55.1/55.0, ROxf, H: 25.9/25.4, RPar, M: 68.6/67.1, and RPar, H: 43.8/42.2. This demonstrates that our algorithm is robust to the selected global encoding method.

Next, we analyze the retrieval performance of models trained on a dataset of size, $|D| = 2000$ with/without back-propagating gradients beyond the level of mixed global representations: ROxf, M: 54.3/49.7, ROxf, H: 25.2/21.8, RPar, M: 66.4/65.5, and RPar, H: 40.5/37.6. Back-propagating beyond mixed representations results in over-fitting and decrease in retrieval performance.

Thirdly, we analyze the scenario where the original teacher representations are sparesely connected. As such the mixed samples are located in low density regions resulting in most samples having empty positive sets from similarity

Table 5. mAP performance with and without mixup labelling (ML). Note that for this experiment, D was set to 2000.

Method	ROxf			RPar		
	E	M	H	E	M	H
ResNet34 ($\tau = 0.75$)	**71.5**	**50.9**	**21.9**	**83.6**	**64.6**	37.6
ResNet34 (no-ML, $\tau = 0.75$)	66.7	47.2	18.5	82.8	63.9	**37.8**
ResNet34 (no-ML, $\tau = 0.65$)	64.2	46.3	17.7	78.0	59.5	30.4
ResNet34 (no-ML, $\tau = 0.5$)	57.1	39.5	13.9	73.0	56.0	26.5
ResNet34 (no-aug, $\tau = 0.65$)	64.4	46.8	20.9	79.6	62.4	36.1

labels (SL) alone. In such settings we expect the mixup labeling (ML) to provide training signals that can drive the learning process. Results are shown in Table 5. For this setting, we sample 2000 images from the full dataset such that each sample has atmost 3 Euclidean Nearest Neighbors. Results demonstrate that the mixup labelling significantly improves the retrieval performance across all settings in ROxford5k dataset. On RParis6k, both methods have comparable performance. No ML setting is compared under different teacher similarity thresholds to demonstrate that simply decreasing τ to increase occupancy of positive set, P does not lead to improvement in performance. In addition, our method also outperforms the baseline setting without the proposed augmentations across both datasets.

8   Conclusion

We have presented a knowledge distillation approach based on ranking distillation. The proposed approach transfers the ranking knowledge of a list of images from a cumbersome teacher onto a compact student model. The proposed method introduces key algorithmic design choices that make the approach data-efficient under budget constraints w.r.t access to black-box teacher model and the number of training samples.

Our results are comparable or better than the standard supervised methods with the same network architecture that are trained using full dataset. Under the training budget constraints, the proposed method clearly outperforms the baseline methods on challenging image retrieval datasets. Our approach finds use case in settings where teacher models are hosted as public APIs with limited access.

References

1. Radenović, F., Tolias, G., Chum, O.: CNN image retrieval learns from BoW: unsupervised fine-tuning with hard examples. In: Leibe, B., Matas, J., Sebe, N., Welling, M. (eds.) ECCV 2016. LNCS, vol. 9905, pp. 3–20. Springer, Cham (2016). https://doi.org/10.1007/978-3-319-46448-0_1

2. Gordo, A., Almazán, J., Revaud, J., Larlus, D.: Deep image retrieval: learning global representations for image search. In: Leibe, B., Matas, J., Sebe, N., Welling, M. (eds.) ECCV 2016. LNCS, vol. 9910, pp. 241–257. Springer, Cham (2016). https://doi.org/10.1007/978-3-319-46466-4_15

3. Teichmann, M., Araujo, A., Zhu, M., Sim, J.: Detect-to-retrieve: efficient regional aggregation for image search. In: Proceedings CVPR (2019)

4. Simonyan, K., Zisserman, A.: Very deep convolutional networks for large-scale image recognition. arXiv preprint arXiv:1409.1556 (2014)

5. He, K., Zhang, X., Ren, S., Sun, J.: Deep residual learning for image recognition. In: Proceedings CVPR (2016)

6. Yang, J., et al.: Quantization networks. In: Proceedings CVPR (2019)

7. Buciluǎ, C., Caruana, R., Niculescu-Mizil, A.: Model compression. In: Proceedings SIGKDD (2006)

8. Hinton, G., Vinyals, O., Dean, J.: Distilling the knowledge in a neural network. In: Proceedings NIPSW (2015)

9. Chen, Y., Wang, N., Zhang, Z.: Darkrank: accelerating deep metric learning via cross sample similarities transfer. In: Proceedings AAAI (2018)

10. Park, W., Kim, D., Lu, Y., Cho, M.: Relational knowledge distillation. In: Proceedings CVPR (2019)

11. Zhang, H., Cisse, M., Dauphin, Y.N., Lopez-Paz, D.: mixup: beyond empirical risk minimization. In: Proceedings ICLR (2018)

12. Verma, V., et al.: Manifold mixup: better representations by interpolating hidden states. In: Proceedings ICML (2019)

13. Wang, D., Li, Y., Wang, L., Gong, B.: Neural networks are more productive teachers than human raters: active mixup for data-efficient knowledge distillation from a blackbox model. In: Proceedings CVPR (2020)

14. Revaud, J., Almazán, J., Rezende, R.S., de Souza, C.R.: Learning with average precision: training image retrieval with a listwise loss. In: Proceedings ICCV (2019)

15. Lowe, D.G.: Distinctive image features from scale-invariant keypoints. Int. J. Comput. Vis. (2004)

16. Sivic, J., Zisserman, A.: Video google: a text retrieval approach to object matching in videos. In: Proceedings ICCV (2003)

17. Sánchez, J., Perronnin, F., Mensink, T., Verbeek, J.: Image classification with the fisher vector: theory and practice. Int. J. Comput. Vis. 222–245 (2013)

18. Arandjelovic, R., Zisserman, A.: All about vlad. In: Proceedings CVPR (2013)

19. Perd'och, M., Chum, O., Matas, J.: Efficient representation of local geometry for large scale object retrieval. In: Proceedings CVPR (2009)

20. Sharif Razavian, A., Azizpour, H., Sullivan, J., Carlsson, S.: CNN features off-the-shelf: an astounding baseline for recognition. In: Proceedings CVPRW (2014)

21. Babenko, A., Slesarev, A., Chigorin, A., Lempitsky, V.: Neural codes for image retrieval. In: Fleet, D., Pajdla, T., Schiele, B., Tuytelaars, T. (eds.) ECCV 2014. LNCS, vol. 8689, pp. 584–599. Springer, Cham (2014). https://doi.org/10.1007/978-3-319-10590-1_38

22. Arandjelovic, R., Gronat, P., Torii, A., Pajdla, T., Sivic, J.: Netvlad: CNN architecture for weakly supervised place recognition. In: Proceedings CVPR (2016)

23. Radenović, F., Iscen, A., Tolias, G., Avrithis, Y., Chum, O.: Revisiting oxford and Paris: large-scale image retrieval benchmarking. In: Proceedings CVPR (2018)

24. Schonberger, J.L., Radenovic, F., Chum, O., Frahm, J.M.: From single image query to detailed 3D reconstruction. In: Proceedings CVPR (2015)

25. Perronnin, F., Larlus, D.: Fisher vectors meet neural networks: a hybrid classification architecture. In: Proceedings CVPR (2015)

26. Tolias, G., Sicre, R., Jegou, H.: Particular object retrieval with integral max-pooling of CNN activations. arXiv preprint arXiv:1511.05879 (2015)
27. Gong, Y., Wang, L., Guo, R., Lazebnik, S.: Multi-scale orderless pooling of deep convolutional activation features. In: Fleet, D., Pajdla, T., Schiele, B., Tuytelaars, T. (eds.) ECCV 2014. LNCS, vol. 8695, pp. 392–407. Springer, Cham (2014). https://doi.org/10.1007/978-3-319-10584-0_26
28. Oh Song, H., Xiang, Y., Jegelka, S., Savarese, S.: Deep metric learning via lifted structured feature embedding. In: Proceedings CVPR (2016)
29. Chen, W., Chen, X., Zhang, J., Huang, K.: Beyond triplet loss: a deep quadruplet network for person re-identification. In: Proceedings CVPR (2017)
30. Breiman, L., Shang, N.: Born again trees. In: Citeseer (1996)
31. Zagoruyko, S., Komodakis, N.: Paying more attention to attention: improving the performance of convolutional neural networks via attention transfer. arXiv preprint arXiv:1612.03928 (2016)
32. Huang, Z., Wang, N.: Like what you like: knowledge distill via neuron selectivity transfer. arXiv preprint arXiv:1707.01219 (2017)
33. Bagherinezhad, H., Horton, M., Rastegari, M., Farhadi, A.: Label refinery: improving imagenet classification through label progression. arXiv preprint arXiv:1805.02641 (2018)
34. Furlanello, T., Lipton, Z.C., Tschannen, M., Itti, L., Anandkumar, A.: Born again neural networks. arXiv preprint arXiv:1805.04770 (2018)
35. Tokozume, Y., Ushiku, Y., Harada, T.: Between-class learning for image classification. In: Proceedings CVPR (2018)
36. Cho, K., et al.: Retrieval-augmented convolutional neural networks against adversarial examples. In: Proceedings CVPR (2019)
37. Radenović, F., Tolias, G., Chum, O.: Fine-tuning CNN image retrieval with no human annotation. IEEE TPAMI (2018)
38. Verma, V., Lamb, A., Kannala, J., Bengio, Y., Lopez-Paz, D.: Interpolation consistency training for semi-supervised learning. In: Proceedings IJCAI (2019)
39. Krizhevsky, A., Sutskever, I., Hinton, G.E.: Imagenet classification with deep convolutional neural networks. In: Proceedings NIPS (2012)
40. Kingma, D.P., Ba, J.: Adam: a method for stochastic optimization. arXiv preprint arXiv:1412.6980 (2014)
41. Philbin, J., Chum, O., Isard, M., Sivic, J., Zisserman, A.: Lost in quantization: improving particular object retrieval in large scale image databases. In: IEEE Conference on Computer Vision and Pattern Recognition, vol. 2008, pp. 1–8. IEEE (2008)
42. Radenovic, F., Schonberger, J.L., Ji, D., Frahm, J.M., Chum, O., Matas, J.: From dusk till dawn: modeling in the dark. In: Proceedings CVPR (2016)
43. Izmailov, P., Podoprikhin, D., Garipov, T., Vetrov, D., Wilson, A.G.: Averaging weights leads to wider optima and better generalization. In: Proceedings UAI (2018)
44. Jégou, H., Chum, O.: Negative evidences and co-occurences in image retrieval: the benefit of PCA and whitening. In: Fitzgibbon, A., Lazebnik, S., Perona, P., Sato, Y., Schmid, C. (eds.) ECCV 2012. LNCS, vol. 7573, pp. 774–787. Springer, Heidelberg (2012). https://doi.org/10.1007/978-3-642-33709-3_55

Quantum Robust Fitting

Tat-Jun Chin[1]([✉])(iD), David Suter[2](iD), Shin-Fang Ch'ng[1](iD), and James Quach[3](iD)

[1] School of Computer Science, The University of Adelaide, Adelaide, Australia
{tat-jun.chin,shinfang.chng}@adelaide.edu.au
[2] School of Computing and Security, Edith Cowan University, Perth, Australia
d.suter@ecu.edu.au
[3] School of Physical Sciences, The University of Adelaide, Adelaide, Australia
quach.james@gmail.com

Abstract. Many computer vision applications need to recover structure from imperfect measurements of the real world. The task is often solved by robustly fitting a geometric model onto noisy and outlier-contaminated data. However, recent theoretical analyses indicate that many commonly used formulations of robust fitting in computer vision are not amenable to tractable solution and approximation. In this paper, we explore the usage of quantum computers for robust fitting. To do so, we examine and establish the practical usefulness of a robust fitting formulation inspired by the analysis of monotone Boolean functions. We then investigate a quantum algorithm to solve the formulation and analyse the computational speed-up possible over the classical algorithm. Our work thus proposes one of the first quantum treatments of robust fitting for computer vision.

1 Introduction

Curve fitting is vital to many computer vision capabilities [1]. We focus on the special case of "geometric" curve fitting [2], where the curves of interest derive from the fundamental constraints that govern image formation and the physical motions of objects in the scene. Geometric curve fitting is conducted on visual data that is usually contaminated by outliers, thus necessitating robust fitting.

To begin, let $\mathcal{M}$ be a geometric model parametrised by a vector $\mathbf{x} \in \mathbb{R}^d$. For now, we will keep $\mathcal{M}$ generic; specific examples will be given later. Our aim is to fit $\mathcal{M}$ onto N data points $\mathcal{D} = \{\mathbf{p}_i\}_{i=1}^{N}$, i.e., estimate $\mathbf{x}$ such that $\mathcal{M}$ describes $\mathcal{D}$ well. To this end, we employ a residual function

$$r_i(\mathbf{x}) \tag{1}$$

which gives the nonnegative error incurred on the i-th datum $\mathbf{p}_i$ by the instance of $\mathcal{M}$ that is defined by $\mathbf{x}$. Ideally we would like to find an $\mathbf{x}$ such that $r_i(\mathbf{x})$ is small for *all* i.

However, if $\mathcal{D}$ contains outliers, there are no $\mathbf{x}$ where all $r_i(\mathbf{x})$ can be simultaneously small. To deal with outliers, computer vision practitioners often maximise the consensus

© Springer Nature Switzerland AG 2021
H. Ishikawa et al. (Eds.): ACCV 2020, LNCS 12622, pp. 485–499, 2021.
https://doi.org/10.1007/978-3-030-69525-5_29

$$\Psi(\mathbf{x}) = \sum_{i=1}^{N} \mathbb{I}(r_i(\mathbf{x}) \le \epsilon) \tag{2}$$

of $\mathbf{x}$, where ϵ is a given inlier threshold, and $\mathbb{I}$ is the indicator function that returns 1 if the input predicate is true and 0 otherwise. Intuitively, $\Psi(\mathbf{x})$ counts the number of points that agree with $\mathbf{x}$ up to threshold ϵ, which is a robust criterion since points that disagree with $\mathbf{x}$ (the outliers) are ignored [3]. The maximiser $\mathbf{x}^*$, called the maximum consensus estimate, agrees with the most number of points.

To maximise consensus, computer vision practitioners often rely on randomised sampling techniques, i.e., RANSAC [4] and its variants [5]. However, random sampling cannot guarantee finding $\mathbf{x}^*$ or even a satisfactory alternative. In fact, recent analysis [6] indicates that there are no efficient algorithms that can find $\mathbf{x}^*$ or bounded-error approximations thereof. In the absence of algorithms with strong guarantees, practitioners can only rely on random sampling methods [4,5] with supporting heuristics to increase the chances of finding good solutions.

Robust fitting is in fact intractable in general. Beyond maximum consensus, the fundamental hardness of robust criteria which originated in the statistics community (e.g., least median squares, least trimmed squares) have also been established [7]. Analysis on robust objectives (e.g., minimally trimmed squares) used in robotics [8] also point to the intractability and inapproximability of robust fitting.

In this paper, we explore a robust fitting approach based on "influence" as a measure of outlyingness recently introduced by Suter et al. [9]. Specifically, we will establish

- The practical usefulness of the technique;
- A probabilistically convergent classical algorithm; and
- A quantum algorithm to speed up the classical method, thus realising quantum robust fitting.

1.1 Are All Quantum Computers the "Same"?

Before delving into the details, it would be useful to paint a broad picture of quantum computing due to the unfamiliarity of the general computer vision audience to the topic.

At the moment, there are no practical quantum computers, although there are several competing technologies under intensive research to realise quantum computers. The approaches can be broadly classified into "analog" and "digital" quantum computers. In the former type, adiabatic quantum computers (AQC) is a notable example. In the latter type, (universal) gate quantum computers (GQC) is the main subject of research, in part due to its theoretically proven capability to factorise integers in polynomial time (i.e., Shor's algorithm). Our work here is developed under the GQC framework.

There has been recent work to solve computer vision problems using quantum computers, in particular [10–12]. However, these have been developed under the AQC framework, hence, the algorithms are unlikely to be transferrable easily to our setting. Moreover, they were not aimed at robust fitting, which is our problem of interest.

2 Preliminaries

Henceforth, we will refer to a data point $\mathbf{p}_i$ via its index i. Thus, the overall set of data $\mathcal{D}$ is equivalent to $\{1, \ldots, N\}$ and subsets thereof are $\mathcal{C} \subseteq \mathcal{D} = \{1, \ldots, N\}$.

We restrict ourselves to residuals $r_i(\mathbf{x})$ that are quasiconvex [13] (note that this does not reduce the hardness of maximum consensus [6]). Formally, if the set

$$\{\mathbf{x} \in \mathbb{R}^d \mid r_i(\mathbf{x}) \leq \alpha\} \tag{3}$$

is convex for all $\alpha \geq 0$, then $r_i(\mathbf{x})$ is quasiconvex. It will be useful to consider the minimax problem

$$g(\mathcal{C}) = \min_{\mathbf{x} \in \mathbb{R}^d} \ \max_{i \in \mathcal{C}} \ r_i(\mathbf{x}), \tag{4}$$

where $g(\mathcal{C})$ is the minimised maximum residual for the points in the subset $\mathcal{C}$. If $r_i(\mathbf{x})$ is quasiconvex then (4) is tractable in general [14], and $g(\mathcal{C})$ is monotonic, viz.,

$$\mathcal{B} \subseteq \mathcal{C} \subseteq \mathcal{D} \implies g(\mathcal{B}) \leq g(\mathcal{C}) \leq g(\mathcal{D}). \tag{5}$$

Chin et al. [6,15] exploited the above properties to develop a fixed parameter tractable algorithm for maximum consensus, which scales exponentially with the outlier count.

A subset $\mathcal{I} \subseteq \mathcal{D}$ is a consensus set if there exists $\mathbf{x} \in \mathbb{R}^d$ such that $r_i(\mathbf{x}) \leq \epsilon$ for all $i \in \mathcal{I}$. Intuitively, $\mathcal{I}$ contains points that can be fitted within error ϵ. In other words

$$g(\mathcal{I}) \leq \epsilon \tag{6}$$

if $\mathcal{I}$ is a consensus set. The set of all consensus sets is thus

$$\mathbb{F} = \{\mathcal{I} \subseteq \mathcal{D} \mid g(\mathcal{I}) \leq \epsilon\}. \tag{7}$$

The consensus maximisation problem can be restated as

$$\mathcal{I}^* = \underset{\mathcal{I} \in \mathbb{F}}{\operatorname{argmax}} \ |\mathcal{I}|, \tag{8}$$

where $\mathcal{I}^*$ is the maximum consensus set. The maximum consensus estimate $\mathbf{x}^*$ is a "witness" of $\mathcal{I}^*$, i.e., $r_i(\mathbf{x}^*) \leq \epsilon$ for all $i \in \mathcal{I}^*$, and $|\mathcal{I}^*| = \Psi(\mathbf{x}^*)$.

3   Influence as an Outlying Measure

Define the binary vector

$$\mathbf{z} = [z_1, \ldots, z_N] \in \{0, 1\}^N \tag{9}$$

whose role is to select subsets of $\mathcal{D}$, where $z_i = 1$ implies that $\mathbf{p}_i$ is selected and $z_i = 0$ means otherwise. Define $\mathbf{z}_C$ as the binary vector which is all zero except at the positions where $i \in C$. A special case is

$$\mathbf{e}_i = \mathbf{z}_{\{i\}}, \tag{10}$$

i.e., the binary vector with all elements zero except the i-th one. Next, define

$$C_{\mathbf{z}} = \{i \in \mathcal{D} \mid z_i = 1\}, \tag{11}$$

i.e., the set of indices where the binary variables are 1 in $\mathbf{z}$.

Define *feasibility test* $f : \{0, 1\}^N \mapsto \{0, 1\}$ where

$$f(\mathbf{z}) = \begin{cases} 0 & \text{if } g(C_{\mathbf{z}}) \leq \epsilon; \\ 1 & \text{otherwise.} \end{cases} \tag{12}$$

Intuitively, $\mathbf{z}$ is feasible ($f(\mathbf{z})$ evaluates to 0) if $\mathbf{z}$ selects a consensus set of $\mathcal{D}$. The *influence* of a point $\mathbf{p}_i$ is

$$\begin{aligned} \alpha_i &= Pr\left[f(\mathbf{z} \oplus \mathbf{e}_i) \neq f(\mathbf{z})\right] \\ &= \frac{1}{2^N} \left|\{\mathbf{z} \in \{0, 1\}^N \mid f(\mathbf{z} \oplus \mathbf{e}_i) \neq f(\mathbf{z})\}\right|. \end{aligned} \tag{13}$$

In words, α_i is the probability of changing the feasibility of a subset $\mathbf{z}$ by inserting/removing $\mathbf{p}_i$ into/from $\mathbf{z}$. Note that (13) considers all 2^N instantiations of $\mathbf{z}$.

The utility of α_i as a measure of outlyingness was proposed in [9], as we further illustrate with examples below. Computing α_i will be discussed from Sect. 4 onwards.

Note that a basic requirement for α_i to be useful is that an appropriate ϵ can be input by the user. The prevalent usage of the consensus formulation (2) in computer vision [3] indicates that this is usually not a practical obstacle.

3.1   Examples

Line Fitting. The model $\mathcal{M}$ is a line parametrised by $\mathbf{x} \in \mathbb{R}^2$, and each $\mathbf{p}_i$ has the form

$$\mathbf{p}_i = (a_i, b_i). \tag{14}$$

The residual function evaluates the "vertical" distance

$$r_i(\mathbf{x}) = |[a_i, 1]\mathbf{x} - b_i| \tag{15}$$

from the line to $\mathbf{p}_i$. The associated minimax problem (4) is a linear program [16], hence $g(\mathcal{C})$ can be evaluated efficiently.

Figure 1(a) plots a data instance $\mathcal{D}$ with $N = 100$ points, while Fig. 1(b) plots the sorted normalised influences of the points. A clear dichotomy between inliers and outliers can be observed in the influence.

Multiple View Triangulation. Given observations $\mathcal{D}$ of a 3D scene point $\mathcal{M}$ in N calibrated cameras, we wish to estimate the coordinates $\mathbf{x} \in \mathbb{R}^3$ of $\mathcal{M}$. The i-th camera matrix is $\mathbf{P}_i \in \mathbb{R}^{3 \times 4}$, and each data point $\mathbf{p}_i$ has the form

$$\mathbf{p}_i = [u_i, v_i]^T. \tag{16}$$

The residual function is the reprojection error

$$r_i(\mathbf{x}) = \left\| \mathbf{p}_i - \frac{\mathbf{P}_i^{1:2}\tilde{\mathbf{x}}}{\mathbf{P}_i^3\tilde{\mathbf{x}}} \right\|_2, \tag{17}$$

where $\tilde{\mathbf{x}} = [\mathbf{x}^T, 1]^T$, and $\mathbf{P}_i^{1:2}$ and $\mathbf{P}_i^3$ are respectively the first-two rows and third row of $\mathbf{P}_i$. The reprojection error is quasiconvex in the region $\mathbf{P}_i^3\tilde{\mathbf{x}} > 0$ [13], and the associated minimax problem (4) can be solved using generalised linear programming [14] or specialised routines such as bisection with SOCP feasibility tests; see [13] for details.

Figure 1(c) shows a triangulation instance $\mathcal{D}$ with $N = 34$ image observations of the same scene point, while Fig. 1(d) plots the sorted normalised influences of the data. Again, a clear dichotomy between inliers and outliers can be seen.

Homography Estimation. Given a set of feature matches $\mathcal{D}$ across two images, we wish to estimate the homography $\mathcal{M}$ that aligns the feature matches. The homography is parametrised by a homogeneous 3×3 matrix $\mathbf{H}$ which is "dehomogenised" by fixing one element (specifically, the bottom right element) to a constant of 1, following [13]. The remaining elements thus form the parameter vector $\mathbf{x} \in \mathbb{R}^8$. Each data point $\mathbf{p}_i$ contains matching image coordinates

$$\mathbf{p}_i = (\mathbf{u}_i, \mathbf{v}_i). \tag{18}$$

The residual function is the transfer error

$$r_i(\mathbf{x}) = \frac{\|(\mathbf{H}^{1:2} - \mathbf{v}_i\mathbf{H}_3)\tilde{\mathbf{u}}_i\|_2}{\mathbf{H}^3\tilde{\mathbf{u}}_i}, \tag{19}$$

where $\tilde{\mathbf{u}}_i = [\mathbf{u}_i^T, 1]^T$, and $\mathbf{H}_i^{1:2}$ and $\mathbf{H}_i^3$ are respectively the first-two rows and third row of $\mathbf{H}_i$. The transfer error is quasiconvex in the region $\mathbf{H}^3\tilde{\mathbf{u}}_i > 0$ [13], which usually fits the case in real data; see [13] for more details. As in the case of triangulation, the associated minimax problem (4) for the transfer error can be solved efficiently.

Figure 1(e) shows a homography estimation instance $\mathcal{D}$ with $N = 20$ feature correspondences, while Fig. 1(f) plots the sorted normalised influences of the data. Again, a clear dichotomy between inliers and outliers can be observed.

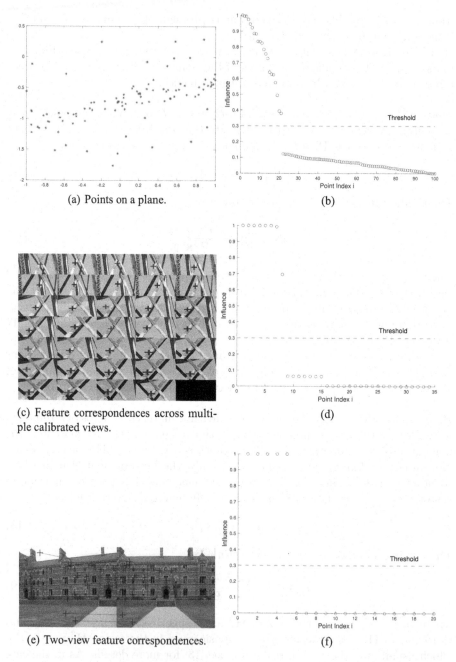

(a) Points on a plane.

(b)

(c) Feature correspondences across multiple calibrated views.

(d)

(e) Two-view feature correspondences.

(f)

Fig. 1. Data instances $\mathcal{D}$ with outliers (left column) and their normalised influences (right column). Row 1 shows a line fitting instance with $d = 2$ and $N = 100$; Row 2 shows a triangulation instance with $d = 3$ and $N = 34$; Row 3 shows a homography estimation instance with $d = 8$ and $N = 20$. In each result, the normalised influences were thresholded at 0.3 to separate the inliers (blue) and outliers (red). (Color figure online)

3.2   Robust Fitting Based on Influence

As noted in [9] and depicted above, the influence has a "natural ability" to separate inliers and outliers; specifically, outliers tend to have higher influences than inliers. A basic robust fitting algorithm can be designed as follows:

1. Compute influence $\{\alpha_i\}_{i=1}^N$ for $\mathcal{D}$ with a given ϵ.
2. Fit $\mathcal{M}$ (e.g., using least squares) onto the subset of $\mathcal{D}$ whose $\alpha_i \leq \gamma$, where γ is a predetermined threshold.

See Fig. 1 and Fig. 3 for results of this simple algorithm. A more sophisticated usage of the influences could be to devise inlier probabilities based on influences and supply them to algorithms such as PROSAC [17] or USAC [5].

In the rest of this paper (Sect. 4 onwards), we will mainly be concerned with computing the influences $\{\alpha_i\}_{i=1}^N$ as this is a major bottleneck in the robust fitting algorithm above. Note also that the algorithm assumes only a single structure in the data—for details on the behaviour of the influences under multiple structure data, see [9].

4   Classical Algorithm

The naive method to compute influence α_i by enumerating $\mathbf{z}$ is infeasible (although the enumeration technique was done in Fig. 1, the instances there are low-dimensional d or small in size N). A more practical solution is to sample a subset $\mathsf{Z} \subset \{0,1\}^N$ and approximate the influence as

$$\hat{\alpha}_i = \frac{1}{|\mathsf{Z}|} \left| \{\mathbf{z} \in \mathsf{Z} \mid f(\mathbf{z} \oplus \mathbf{e}_i) \neq f(\mathbf{z})\} \right|. \tag{20}$$

Further simplification can be obtained by appealing to the existence of bases in the minimax problem (4) with quasiconvex residuals [14]. Specifically, $\mathcal{B} \subseteq \mathcal{D}$ is a basis if

$$g(\mathcal{A}) < g(\mathcal{B}) \quad \forall \mathcal{A} \subset \mathcal{B}. \tag{21}$$

Also, each $\mathcal{C} \subseteq \mathcal{D}$ contains a basis $\mathcal{B} \subseteq \mathcal{C}$ such that

$$g(\mathcal{C}) = g(\mathcal{B}), \tag{22}$$

and, more importantly,

$$g(\mathcal{C} \cup \{i\}) = g(\mathcal{B} \cup \{i\}). \tag{23}$$

Amenta et al. [18] proved that the size of a basis (called the combinatorial dimension k) is at most $2d + 1$. For the examples in Sect. 3.1 with residuals that are continuously shrinking, $k = d + 1$. Small bases (usually $k \ll N$) enable quasiconvex problems to be solved efficiently [14,18,19]. In fact, some of the algorithms compute $g(\mathcal{C})$ by finding its basis $\mathcal{B}$.

It is thus sufficient to sample Z from the set of all k-subsets of $\mathcal{D}$. Algorithm 1 summarises the influence computation method for the quasiconvex case.

4.1   Analysis

For N data points and a total of M samples, the algorithm requires $\mathcal{O}(NM)$ calls of f, i.e., $\mathcal{O}(NM)$ instances of minimax (4) of size proportional to only k and d each.

How does the estimate $\hat{\alpha}_i$ deviate from the true influence α_i? To answer this question, note that since $\mathbf{Z}$ are random samples of $\{0,1\}^N$, the $X_i^{[1]}, \ldots, X_i^{[M]}$ calculated in Algorithm 1 (Steps 5 and 7) are effectively i.i.d. samples of

$$X_i \sim \text{Bernoulli}(\alpha_i); \tag{24}$$

cf. (13) and (20). Further, the estimate $\hat{\alpha}_i$ is the empirical mean of the M samples

$$\hat{\alpha}_i = \frac{1}{M} \sum_{m=1}^{M} X_i^{[m]}. \tag{25}$$

By Hoeffding's inequality [20], we have

$$Pr(|\hat{\alpha}_i - \alpha_i| < \delta) > 1 - 2e^{-2M\delta^2}, \tag{26}$$

where δ is a desired maximum deviation. In words, (26) states that as the number of samples M increases, $\hat{\alpha}_i$ converges probabilistically to the true influence α_i.

Algorithm 1. Classical algorithm to compute influence.

Require: N input data points $\mathcal{D}$, combinatorial dimension k, inlier threshold ϵ, number of iterations M.

1: **for** $m = 1, \ldots, M$ **do**
2:     $\mathbf{z}^{[m]} \leftarrow$ Randomly choose k-tuple from $\mathcal{D}$.
3:     **for** $i = 1, \ldots, N$ **do**
4:         **if** $f(\mathbf{z}^{[m]} \oplus \mathbf{e}_i) \neq f(\mathbf{z}^{[m]})$ **then**
5:             $X_i^{[m]} \leftarrow 1$.
6:         **else**
7:             $X_i^{[m]} \leftarrow 0$.
8:         **end if**
9:     **end for**
10: **end for**
11: **for** $i = 1, \ldots, N$ **do**
12:     $\hat{\alpha}_i \leftarrow \frac{1}{M} \sum_{m=1}^{M} X_i^{[m]}$.
13: **end for**
14: **return** $\{\hat{\alpha}_i\}_{i=1}^{N}$.

4.2 Results

Figure 2 illustrates the results of Algorithm 1 on the data in Fig. 1. Specifically, for each input instance, we plot in Fig. 2 the proportion of $\{\hat{\alpha}_i\}_{i=1}^{N}$ that are within distance $\delta = 0.05$ to the true $\{\alpha_i\}_{i=1}^{N}$, i.e.,

$$\frac{1}{N} \sum_{i=1}^{N} \mathbb{I}(|\hat{\alpha}_i - \alpha_i| < 0.05), \tag{27}$$

as a function of number of iterations M in Algorithm 1. The probabilistic lower bound $1 - 2e^{-2M\delta^2}$ is also plotted as a function of M. The convergence of the approximate influences is clearly as predicted by (26).

Figure 3 shows the approximate influences computed using Algorithm 1 on 3 larger input instances for homography estimation. Despite using a small number of iterations ($M \approx 800$), the inliers and outliers can be dichotomised well using the influences.

The runtimes of Algorithm 1 for the input data above are as follows:

Input data (figure)	1(a)	1(c)	1(e)	3(a)	3(c)	3(e)
Iterations (M)	5,000	5,000	5,000	800	800	800
Runtime (s)	609	4,921	8,085	2,199	5,518	14,080

The experiments were conducted in MATLAB on a standard desktop using unoptimised code, e.g., using `fmincon` to evaluate f instead of more specialised routines.

5 Quantum Algorithm

We describe a quantum version of Algorithm 1 for influence computation and investigate the speed-up provided.

5.1 Quantum Circuit

We use the Bernstein-Vazirani (BV) circuit [21] originally designed to solve linear Boolean functions; see Fig. 4.

For our application, our circuit builds an $(N + 1)$-qubit system, where N is the number of points $\mathcal{D}$. At the input stage, the system contains quantum registers

$$|\mathbf{z}\rangle \otimes |y\rangle = |\mathbf{z}\rangle |y\rangle, \tag{28}$$

where, as before, $\mathbf{z}$ is a binary vector indicating selection of points in $\mathcal{D}$, and y is a dummy input.

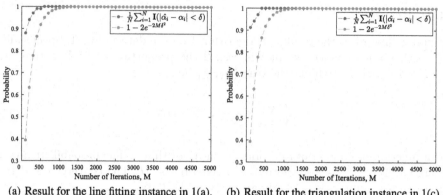

(a) Result for the line fitting instance in 1(a).   (b) Result for the triangulation instance in 1(c).

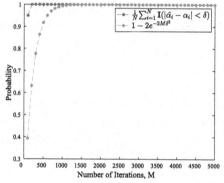

(c) Result for the homography estimation instance in 1(e).

Fig. 2. Comparing approximate influences from Algorithm 1 with the true influences (13), for the problem instances in Fig. 1. The error of the approximation (magenta) is within the probabilistic bound (green). See Sect. 4.2 on the error metric used. (Color figure online)

The Boolean function f (12) and the underlying data $\mathcal{D}$ are implemented in the quantum oracle U_f, where

$$U_f \, |\mathbf{z}\rangle \, |y\rangle = |\mathbf{z}\rangle \, |y \otimes f(\mathbf{z})\rangle \tag{29}$$

and $\oplus$ is bit-wise XOR. Recall that by considering only quasiconvex residual functions (Sect. 2), f is classically solvable in polynomial time, thus its quantum equivalent U_f will also have an efficient implementation (requiring polynomial number of quantum gates) [22, Sect. 3.25]. Following the analysis of the well-known quantum algorithms (e.g., Grover's search, Shor's factorisation algorithm), we will mainly be interested in the number of times we need to invoke U_f (i.e., the query complexity of the algorithm [23]) and not the implementation details of U_f (Sect. 5.4).

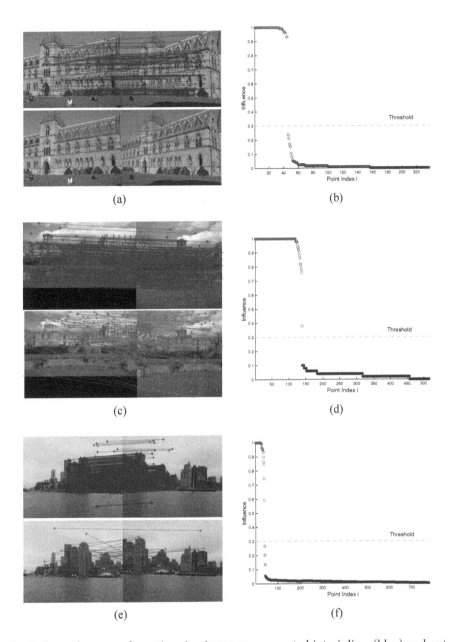

Fig. 3. Large homography estimation instances, separated into inliers (blue) and outliers (red) according to their normalised approximate influences (right column), which were computed using Algorithm 1. Note that only about $M = 800$ iterations were used in Algorithm 1 to achieve these results. Row 1 shows an instance with $N = 237$ correspondences; Row 2 shows an instance with $N = 516$ correspondences; Row 3 shows an instance with $N = 995$ correspondences. (Color figure online)

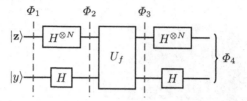

Fig. 4. Quantum circuit for influence computation.

5.2 Quantum Operations

Our usage of BV follows that of [24,25] (for basics of quantum operations, see [26, Chapter 5]). We initialise with $|\mathbf{z}\rangle = |\mathbf{0}\rangle$ and $|y\rangle = |1\rangle$ thus

$$\Phi_1 = |\mathbf{0}\rangle \, |1\rangle \,. \tag{30}$$

The next operation consists of $N+1$ Hadamard gates $H^{\otimes(N+1)}$; the behaviour of n Hadamard gates is as follows

$$H^{\otimes n} |\mathbf{q}\rangle = \frac{1}{\sqrt{2^n}} \sum_{\mathbf{t} \in \{0,1\}^n} (-1)^{\mathbf{q} \cdot \mathbf{t}} |\mathbf{t}\rangle \,, \tag{31}$$

hence

$$\Phi_2 = H^{\otimes(N+1)} \Phi_1 \tag{32}$$

$$= \frac{1}{\sqrt{2^N}} \sum_{\mathbf{t} \in \{0,1\}^N} |\mathbf{t}\rangle \, \frac{|0\rangle - |1\rangle}{\sqrt{2}}. \tag{33}$$

Applying U_f, we have

$$\Phi_3 = U_f \Phi_2 \tag{34}$$

$$= \frac{1}{\sqrt{2^N}} \sum_{\mathbf{t} \in \{0,1\}^N} (-1)^{f(\mathbf{t})} |\mathbf{t}\rangle \, \frac{|0\rangle - |1\rangle}{\sqrt{2}}. \tag{35}$$

Applying the Hadamard gates $H^{\otimes(N+1)}$ again,

$$\Phi_4 = H^{\otimes(N+1)} \Phi_3 \tag{36}$$

$$= \frac{1}{2^N} \sum_{\mathbf{s} \in \{0,1\}^N} \sum_{\mathbf{t} \in \{0,1\}^N} (-1)^{f(\mathbf{t}) + \mathbf{s} \cdot \mathbf{t}} |\mathbf{s}\rangle \, |1\rangle \,. \tag{37}$$

Focussing on the top-N qubits in Φ_4, we have

$$\sum_{\mathbf{s}\in\{0,1\}^N} I(\mathbf{s})\,|\mathbf{s}\rangle\,, \tag{38}$$

where

$$I(\mathbf{s}) := \sum_{\mathbf{t}\in\{0,1\}^N} (-1)^{f(\mathbf{t})+\mathbf{s}\cdot\mathbf{t}}. \tag{39}$$

The significance of this result is as follows.

Theorem 1. *Let* $\mathbf{s} = [s_1,\ldots,s_N] \in \{0,1\}^N$. *Then*

$$\alpha_i = \sum_{s_i=1} I(\mathbf{s})^2. \tag{40}$$

Proof. See [25, Sect. 3].

The theorem shows that the influences $\{\alpha_i\}_{i=1}^N$ are "direct outputs" of the quantum algorithm. However, physical laws permit us to access the information indirectly via quantum measurements only [26, Sect. 4]. Namely, if we measure in the standard basis, we get a realisation $\mathbf{s}$ with probability $I(\mathbf{s})^2$. The probability of getting $s_i = 1$ is

$$Pr(s_i = 1) = \sum_{s_i=1} I(\mathbf{s})^2 = \alpha_i. \tag{41}$$

Note that the above steps involve only one "call" to U_f. However, as soon as Φ_4 is measured, the quantum state collapses and the encoded probabilities vanish.

5.3 The Algorithm

Based on the setup above, running the BV algorithm *once* provides a *single* observation of *all* $\{\alpha_i\}_{i=1}^N$. This provides a basis for a quantum version of the classical Algorithm 1; see Algorithm 2. The algorithm runs the BV algorithm M times, each time terminating with a measurement of $\mathbf{s}$, to produce M realisations $\mathbf{s}^{[1]},\ldots,\mathbf{s}^{[M]}$. Approximate estimates $\{\hat\alpha_i\}_{i=1}^N$ of the influences are then obtained by collating the results of the quantum measurements.

5.4 Analysis

A clear difference between Algorithms 1 and 2 is the lack of an "inner loop" in the latter. Moreover, in each (main) iteration of the quantum algorithm, the BV algorithm is executed only once; hence, the Boolean function f is also called just once in each iteration. The overall query complexity of Algorithm 2 is thus $\mathcal{O}(M)$, which is a speed-up over Algorithm 1 by a factor of N. For example,

---

Algorithm 2. Quantum algorithm to compute influence [24,25].

Require: N input data points $\mathcal{D}$, inlier threshold ϵ, number of iterations M.
1: **for** $m = 1, \ldots, M$ **do**
2:    $\mathbf{s}^{[m]} \leftarrow$ Run BV algorithm with $\mathcal{D}$ and ϵ and measure top-N qubits in standard basis.
3: **end for**
4: **for** $i = 1, \ldots, N$ **do**
5:    $\hat{\alpha}_i \leftarrow \frac{1}{M} \sum_{m=1}^{M} s_i^{[m]}$.
6: **end for**
7: **return** $\{\hat{\alpha}_i\}_{i=1}^{N}$.

---

in the case of the homography estimation instance in Fig. 3, this represents a sizeable speed-up factor of 516.

In some sense, the BV algorithm computes the influences exactly in one invocation of f; however, limitations placed by nature allows us to "access" the results using probabilistic measurements only, thus delivering only approximate solutions. Thankfully, the same arguments in Sect. 4.1 can be made for Algorithm 2 to yield the probabilistic error bound (26) for the results of the quantum version.

As alluded to in Sect. 5, the computational gain is based on analysing the query complexity of the algorithm [23], i.e., the number of times U_f needs to be invoked, which in turn rests on the knowledge that any polynomial-time classical algorithm can be implemented as a quantum function f efficiently, i.e., with a polynomial number of gates (see [22, Chap. 3.25] and [26, Chap. 6]). In short, the computational analysis presented is consistent with the literature on the analysis of quantum algorithms.

6   Conclusions and Future Work

We proposed one of the first quantum robust fitting algorithms and established its practical usefulness in the computer vision setting. Future work includes devising quantum robust fitting algorithms that have better speed-up factors and tighter approximation bounds. Implementing the algorithm on a quantum computer will also be pursued.

References

1. Hartnett, K.: Q&A with Judea Pearl: to build truly intelligent machines, teach them cause and effect. (https://www.quantamagazine.org/to-build-truly-intelligent-machines-teach-them-cause-and-effect-20180515/. Accessed 30 May 2020
2. Kanatani, K., Sugaya, Y., Kanazawa, Y.: Ellipse fitting for computer vision: implementation and applications. Synth. Lect. Comput. Vis. **6**(1), 1–141 (2016)
3. Chin, T.J., Suter, D.: The maximum consensus problem: recent algorithmic advances. Synth. Lect. Comput. Vis. **7**(2), 1–194 (2017)

4. Fischler, M.A., Bolles, R.C.: Random sample consensus: a paradigm for model fitting with applications to image analysis and automated cartography. Commun. ACM **24**, 381–395 (1981)

5. Raguram, R., Chum, O., Pollefeys, M., Matas, J., Frahm, J.M.: USAC: a universal framework for random sample consensus. IEEE Trans. Pattern Anal. Mach. Intell. **35**, 2022–2038 (2013)

6. Chin, T.J., Cai, Z., Neumann, F.: Robust fitting in computer vision: easy or hard? In: European Conference on Computer Vision (ECCV) (2018)

7. Bernholt, T.: Robust estimators are hard to compute. Technical Report 52, Technische Universität Dortmund (2005)

8. Touzmas, V., Antonante, P., Carlone, L.: Outlier-robust spatial perception: hardness, general-purpose algorithms, and guarantees. In: IEEE/RSJ International Conference on Intelligent Robots and Systems (IROS) (2019)

9. Suter, D., Tennakoon, R., Zhang, E., Chin, T.J., Bab-Hadiashar, A.: Monotone boolean functions, feasibility/infeasibility, LP-type problems and MaxCon (2020)

10. Neven, H., Rose, G., Macready, W.G.: Image recognition with an adiabatic quantum computer I. Mapping to quadratic unconstrained binary optimization. arXiv:0804.4457 (2008)

11. Nguyen, N.T.T., Kenyon, G.T.: Image classification using quantum inference on the D-Wave 2X. arXiv:1905.13215 (2019)

12. Golyanik, V., Theobalt, C.: A quantum computational approach to correspondence problems on point sets. In: IEEE Computer Society Conference on Computer Vision and Pattern Recognition (CVPR) (2020)

13. Kahl, F., Hartley, R.: Multiple-view geometry under the l_∞-norm. IEEE Trans. Pattern Anal. Mach. Intell. **30**, 1603–1617 (2008)

14. Eppstein, D.: Quasiconvex programming. Comb. Comput. Geom. **25** (2005)

15. Chin, T.J., Purkait, P., Eriksson, A., Suter, D.: Efficient globally optimal consensus maximisation with tree search. In: IEEE Computer Society Conference on Computer Vision and Pattern Recognition (CVPR) (2015)

16. Cheney, E.W.: Introduction to Approximation Theory. McGraw-Hill, United States (1966)

17. Chum, O., Matas, J.: Matching with PROSAC - progressive sample consensus. In: IEEE Computer Society Conference on Computer Vision and Pattern Recognition (CVPR) (2005)

18. Amenta, N., Bern, M., Eppstein, D.: Optimal point placement for mesh smoothing. J. Algorithms **30**, 302–322 (1999)

19. Matoušek, J., Sharir, M., Welzl, E.: A subexponential bound for linear programming. Algorithmica **16**, 498–516 (1996)

20. (https://en.wikipedia.org/wiki/Hoeffding%27s_inequality)

21. Bernstein, E., Vazirani, U.: Quantum complexity theory. SIAM J. Comput. **26**, 1411–1473 (1997)

22. Nielsen, M.A., Chuang, I.L.: Quantum Computation and Quantum Information. Cambridge University Press, Cambridge (2010)

23. Ambainis, A.: Understanding quantum algorithms via query complexity. Int. Congr. Math. **4**, 3283–3304 (2018)

24. Floess, D.F., Andersson, E., Hillery, M.: Quantum algorithms for testing Boolean functions. Math. Struc. Comput. Sci. **23**, 386–398 (2013)

25. Li, H., Yang, L.: A quantum algorithm for approximating the influences of boolean functions and its applications. Quantum Inf. Process. **14**, 1787–1797 (2015)

26. Rieffel, E., Polak, W.: Quantum Computing: A Gentle Introduction. The MIT Press, United States (2014)

HDD-Net: Hybrid Detector Descriptor with Mutual Interactive Learning

Axel Barroso-Laguna[1(✉)], Yannick Verdie[2], Benjamin Busam[2,3],
and Krystian Mikolajczyk[1]

[1] Imperial College London, London, UK
{axel.barroso17,k.mikolajczyk}@imperial.ac.uk
[2] Huawei Noah's Ark Lab, London, UK
{yannick.verdie,benjamin.busam}@huawei.com
[3] Technical University of Munich, Munich, Germany

Abstract. Local feature extraction remains an active research area due to the advances in fields such as SLAM, 3D reconstructions, or AR applications. The success in these applications relies on the performance of the feature detector, descriptor, and its matching process. While the trend of detector-descriptor interaction of most methods is based on unifying the two into a single network, we propose an alternative approach that treats both components independently and focuses on their interaction during the learning process. We formulate the classical hard-mining triplet loss as a new detector optimisation term to improve keypoint positions based on the descriptor map. Moreover, we introduce a dense descriptor that uses a multi-scale approach within the architecture and a hybrid combination of hand-crafted and learnt features to obtain rotation and scale robustness by design. We evaluate our method extensively on several benchmarks and show improvements over the state of the art in terms of image matching and 3D reconstruction quality while keeping on par in camera localisation tasks.

1 Introduction

At its core, a feature extraction method identifies locations within a scene that are repeatable and distinctive, so that they can be detected with high localisation accuracy under different camera conditions and be matched between different views. The results in vision applications such as image retrieval [1], 3D reconstruction [2], camera pose regression [3], or medical applications [4], among others, have shown the advantage of using sparse features over direct methods.

Classical methods [5–7] independently compute keypoints and descriptors. For instance, SIFT [5] focused on finding blobs on images and extracting gradient histograms as descriptors. Recently proposed descriptors, especially the patch-based [8–11], are often trained for DoG keypoints [5], and although they may perform well with other detectors [12], their performance can be further improved if the models are trained with patches extracted by the same detector.

© Springer Nature Switzerland AG 2021
H. Ishikawa et al. (Eds.): ACCV 2020, LNCS 12622, pp. 500–516, 2021.
https://doi.org/10.1007/978-3-030-69525-5_30

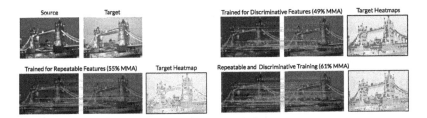

Fig. 1. Effect of different training strategies on the result. Correct matches and target detection response maps on *London Bridge* sequence (HPatches) when optimising the detector's features to be repetitive, discriminative, or both.

Similarly, detectors can benefit by training jointly with their associated descriptor [13]. Therefore, following the trend of using the descriptor information to infer the detections [13–16], we reformulate the descriptor hard-mining triplet cost function [9] as a new detector loss. The new detector term can be combined with any repeatability loss, and consequently, keypoint locations can be optimised based on the descriptor performance jointly with the detector repeatability. This approach leads to finding in a single score map both, repeatable and discriminative features, as shown in Fig. 1. We extend the network trainings to a multi-scale framework, such that the detector/descriptor learns to use different levels of detail when making predictions.

Our two-networks approach is motivated by the observations that jointly learnt detector-descriptor models [14,17] lack keypoint localisation accuracy, which is critical for SLAM, SfM, or pose estimations [12], and the fact that keypoints are typically well localised on simple structures such as edges or corners, while descriptors require more context to be discriminative. We argue that despite the recent tendency for end-to-end and joint detector-descriptor methods, separate extractors allow for shallow models that can perform well in terms of accuracy and efficiency, which has recently been observed in [12]. Besides that, in contrast to patch-based descriptors, dense image descriptors make it more difficult to locally rectify the image regions for invariance. To address this issue, we introduce an approach based on a block of hand-crafted features and a multi-scale representation within the descriptor architecture, making our network robust to small rotations and scale changes. We term our approach as HDD-Net: Hybrid Detector and Descriptor Network.

In summary, our contributions are:

- A new detector loss based on the hard-mining triplet cost function. Although the hard-mining triplet is widely used for descriptors, it has not been adapted to improve the keypoint detectors.
- A novel multi-scale sampling scheme to jointly train both architectures at multiple scales by combining local and global detections and descriptors.

- We improve the robustness to rotation and scale changes with a new dense descriptor architecture that leverages hand-crafted features together with multi-scale representations.

2   Related Work

We focus the review of related work on learnt methods, and refer to [12,18–22] for further details.

Detectors. Machine learning detectors were introduced with FAST [23], a learnt algorithm to speed up the detection of corners in images. Later, TILDE [24] proposed to train multiple piecewise regressors that were robust under photometric changes in images. DNET [25] and TCDET [26] based its learning on a formulation of the covariant constraint, enforcing the architecture to propose the same feature location in corresponding patches. Key.Net [27] expanded the covariant constraint to a multi-scale formulation, and used a hybrid architecture composed of hand-crafted and learnt feature blocks. More details about the latest keypoint detectors can be found in [21], which provides an extensive detector evaluation.

Descriptors. Descriptors have attracted more attention than detectors, particularly patch-based methods [8,9,28] due to the simplicity of the task and available benchmarks. TFeat [28] moved from loss functions built upon pairs of examples to a triplet based loss to learn more robust representations. In [8], L2-Net architecture was introduced. L2-Net has been adopted in the following works due to its good optimisation and performance. HardNet [9] introduced the hard-mining strategy, selecting only the hardest examples as negatives in the triplet loss function. SOSNet [10] added a regularisation term to the triplet loss to include second-order similarity relationships among descriptors. DOAP [29] reformulated the training of descriptors as a ranking problem, by optimising the mean average precision instead of the distance between patches. GeoDesc [11] integrated geometry constraints to obtain better training data.

Joint Detectors and Descriptors. LIFT [15] was the first CNN based method to integrate detection, orientation estimation, and description. LIFT was trained on quadruplet patches which were previously extracted with SIFT detector. SuperPoint [17] used a single encoder and two decoders to perform dense feature detection and description. It was first pretrained to detect corners on a synthetic dataset and then improved by applying random homographies to the training images. This improves the stability of the ground truth positions under different viewpoints. Similar to LIFT, LF-Net [30] and RF-Net [31] computed position, scale, orientation, and description. LF-Net trained its detector score and scale estimator in full images without external keypoint supervision, and RF-Net extended LF-Net by exploiting the information provided by its receptive fields. D2-Net [14] proposed to perform feature detection in the descriptor space, showing that an already pre-trained network could be used for feature extraction even though it was optimized for a different task. R2D2 [13] introduced a dense version of the L2-Net [8] architecture to predict descriptors and two keypoint score maps, which were each based on their repeatability and reliability. ASLFeat [16] proposed an accurate detector and invariant descriptor with multi-level connections and deformable convolutional networks [32, 33].

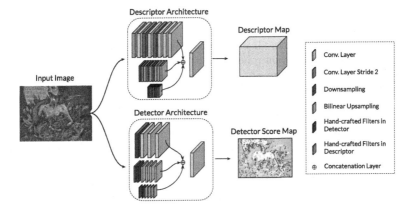

Fig. 2. HDD-Net architecture. HDD-Net is composed by two independent architectures. Instead of sharing a common feature extractor as in [13, 14, 16, 17], HDD-Net focuses its detector-descriptor interaction at the learning level.

3   Method

3.1   HDD-Net Architecture

HDD-Net consists of two independent architectures for inferring the keypoint and descriptor maps, allowing to use different hand-crafted blocks that are designed specifically for each of these two tasks. Figure 2 shows the two independent blocks within the HDD-Net's feature extraction pipeline.

Descriptor. As our method estimates dense descriptors in the entire image, an affine rectification of independent patches or rotation invariance by construction [34] is not possible. To circumvent this, we design a hand-crafted block that explicitly addresses the robustness to rotation. We incorporate this block before the architecture based on L2-Net [8]. As in the original L2-Net, we use stride convolutions to increase the size of its receptive field, however, we replace the last convolutional layer by a bilinear upsampling operator to upscale the map to its original image resolution. Moreover, we use a multi-scale image representation to extract features from resized images, which provides the network with details from different resolutions. After feature upsampling, multi-scale L2-Net features are concatenated and fused into a final descriptor map by a final convolutional layer. The top part of Fig. 2 shows the proposed descriptor architecture.

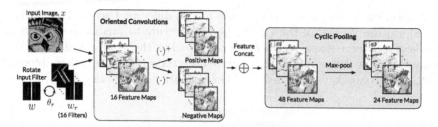

Fig. 3. Hand-crafted block. Given an input image, x, a designed filter, w, and a set of orientations, θ_r, the rotation robustness is given by extracting and features from x with each of the oriented filters, w_r. Additionally, $(\cdot)^+$ and $(\cdot)^-$ operators split positive and negative maps before the cyclic max-pooling block.

Rotation Robustness. Transformation equivariance in CNNs has been extensively discussed in [35–39]. The two main approaches differ whether the transformations are applied to the input image [40] or the filters [39,41], we follow the latest methods and decide to rotate the filters. Rotating filters is more efficient since they are smaller than the input images, and therefore, have fewer memory requirements. Unlike [41], our rotational filter is not learnt. We show in Sect. 4.1 that the pre-designed filters offer a strong feature set that benefits the learning of consecutive CNN blocks. Moreover, in contrast to [41], which applies the rotation to all the layers in their convolutional model, we only focus on the input filter, which further reduces the computational complexity. However, we apply more rotations than [41] to the input filter to provide sufficient robustness. In [39], authors proposed a method that applied multiple rotations to each convolutional filter. Different than estimating a pixel-wise vector field to describe angle and orientation [39], our rotation block returns multiple maxima through a cyclic pooling. The cyclic pooling operator returns local maxima every three neighbouring angles. We experimentally found that returning their local maxima provides better results than only using the global one. Thence, our hand-crafted block applies our input filter, w, at $R = 16$ orientations, each corresponding to the following angles:

$$\theta_r = \frac{360}{R}r \quad \text{and} \quad r \in [1, 2, ..., R]. \tag{1}$$

A rotated filter is generated by rotating θ_r degrees around the input filter's center. Since our rotated filter is obtained by bilinear interpolation, we apply a circular mask to avoid possible artifacts on the filter's corners:

$$w_r = m \cdot f(w, \theta_r), \tag{2}$$

with m as a circular mask around filter's center and f denoting the bilinear interpolation when rotating the filter, w, by θ_r degrees. Given an input image I, and our designed filter, w, we obtain a set of features $h(I)$ such as:

$$h_r(I) = (I * w_r) \quad \text{and} \quad r \in [1, 2, ..., R], \tag{3}$$

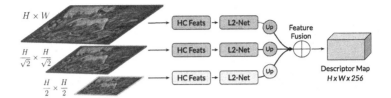

Fig. 4. Multi-scale hybrid descriptor. Gaussian pyramid is fed into our multi-scale descriptor. Each of the re-scaled input images go into one stream, which is composed by the hand-crafted block detailed in Sect. 3.1 and a L2-Net architecture. At the end, multi-scale L2-Net features are upsampled and combined through a final convolution.

where $*$ denotes the convolution operator. Before the cyclic max-pooling block, and because max-pool is driven to positive values, we additionally split and concatenate the feature maps in a similar fashion to Descriptor Fields [42]:

$$\mathcal{H}_r(I) = [h_r(I),\ (h_r(I))^+, \text{-}1 \cdot (h_r(I))^-], \tag{4}$$

with $(\cdot)^+$ and $(\cdot)^-$ operators respectively keeping the positive and negative parts of the feature map $h_r(I)$. Descriptor Fields proved to be effective under varying illumination conditions [42]. Our new set of features, $\mathcal{H}_r(I)$, are concatenated into a single feature map, $\mathcal{H}(I)$. Finally, we apply a cyclic max-pooling block on $\mathcal{H}(I)$. Instead of defining a spatial max-pooling, our cyclic pooling is applied in the channel depth, where each channel dimension represents one orientation, θ_r, of the input filter. Cyclic max-pooling is applied every three neighbouring feature maps with a channel-wise stride of two, meaning that each feature map after max-pooling represents the local maxima among three neighbouring orientations. The full hand-crafted feature block is illustrated in Fig. 3.

Scale Robustness. Gaussian scale-space has been extensively exploited for local feature extraction [6,15,43]. In [27,30,31], the scale-space representation was used not only to extract multi-scale features but also to learn to combine their information. However, the fusion of multi-scale features is only used during the detection, while, in deep descriptors, it is either implemented via consecutive convolutional layers [17] or by applying the networks on multiple resized images and combining the detections at the end [13,14,16]. In contrast to [14,16], we extend the Gaussian pyramid to the descriptor part by designing a network that takes a Gaussian pyramid as input and fuses the multi-scale features before inferring the final descriptor. To fuse the extracted features, the network upsamples them into the original image resolution in each of the streams. Afterward, features are concatenated and fed into the last convolution, which maps the multi-scale features towards the desired descriptor size dimension as shown in Fig. 4. The descriptor encoder shares the weights on each multi-scale branch, hence, boosting its ability to extract features robust to scale changes.

Detector. We adopt the architecture of Key.Net [27] as shown in Fig. 2. Key.Net combines specific hand-crafted filters for feature detection and a multi-scale shal-

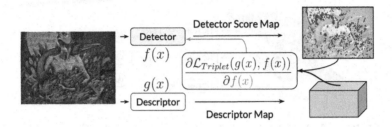

Fig. 5. Detector-descriptor interaction. The proposed triplet loss detector term optimises keypoint locations based on the descriptor map, refining the feature candidates towards more discriminative positions.

low network. It has recently shown to achieve the state of the art results in repeatability [12,27]. Key.Net extended the covariant loss function proposed in [25] to a multi-scale level, which was termed M-SIP. M-SIP splits the input images into smaller windows of size $s_1 \times s_1$ and formulates the loss as the difference between soft-argmaximum positions in corresponding regions. M-SIP repeats the process multiple times but splitting the images each time with different window sizes, $s_n \times s_n$. The final loss function proposed by M-SIP between two images, A and B, with their matrix transformation, $H_{b,a}$, is computed as the loss of all windows from all defined scale levels:

$$\mathcal{L}_{M-SIP}(A, B) = \sum_i \| [u_i, v_i]_a^T - H_{b,a}[u_i, v_i]_b^T \|^2. \tag{5}$$

We refer to [27] for further details.

3.2 Descriptor-Detector Training

The detector learning has focused on localising features that are repeatable in a sequence of images [17,21,24,27,30,31], with a few works that determine whether these features are adequate for the matching stage [13–15,44]. Since a good feature should be repeatable as well as discriminative [18], we formulate the descriptor triplet loss function as a new detector learning term to refine the feature candidates towards more discriminative positions. Unlike AffNet [44], which estimates the affine shape of the features, we refine only their locations, as these are the main parameters that are often used for end tasks such as SfM, SLAM, or AR. R2D2 [13] inferred two independent response maps, seeking for discriminativeness of the features and their repeatability. Our approach combines both objectives into a single detection map. LIFT [15] training was based on finding the locations with closest descriptors, in contrast, we propose a function based on a triplet loss with a hard-negative mining strategy. D2-Net [14] directly extracts detections from its dense descriptor map, meanwhile, we use Key.Net [27] architecture to compute a score map that represents repeatable as well as discriminative features.

Detector Learning with Triplet Loss. Hard-negative triplet learning maximises the Euclidean distance between a positive pair and their closest negative sample. In the original work [9], the optimisation happens in the descriptor part, however, we propose to freeze the descriptor such that the sampling locations proposed by the detector are updated to minimise the loss term as shown in Fig. 5. Then, given a pair of corresponding images, we create a grid on each image with a fixed window size of $s_1 \times s_1$. From each window, we extract a soft-descriptor and its positive and negative samples as illustrated in Fig. 6. To compute the soft-descriptor, we aggregate all the descriptors within the window based on the detection score map, so that the final soft-descriptor and the scores within a window are entangled. Note that if Non-Maximum Suppression (NMS) was used to select the maximum coordinates and its descriptor, we would only be able to back-propagate through the selected pixels and not the entire map. Consider a window w of size $s_1 \times s_1$ with the score value r_i at each coordinate $[u, v]$ within the window. A softmax provides:

$$p(u, v) = \frac{e^{r(u,v)}}{\sum_{j,k}^{s_1} e^{r(j,k)}}. \tag{6}$$

The window w has the associated descriptor vector d_i at each coordinate $[u, v]$ within the window. We compute the soft-score, $\bar{r}$, and soft-descriptor, $\bar{d}$, as:

$$\bar{r} = \sum_{u,v}^{s_1} r(u, v) \odot p(u, v) \quad \text{and} \quad \bar{d} = \sum_{u,v}^{s_1} d(u, v) \odot p(u, v). \tag{7}$$

We use L2 normalisation after computing the soft-descriptor. Similar to previous works [31,45], we sample the hardest negative candidate from a non-neighbouring region. This geometric constraint is illustrated in Fig. 6. We can define our detector triplet loss with soft-descriptors in window w as:

$$\mathcal{L}(w) = \mathcal{L}(\delta^+, \delta^-, \bar{r}, \mu) = \bar{r} \ max(0, \mu + \delta^+ - \delta^-), \tag{8}$$

where μ is a margin parameter, and δ^+ and δ^- are the Euclidean distances between positive and negative soft-descriptors pairs. Moreover, we weight the contribution of each window by its soft-score to control the participation of meaningless windows $e.g.$, flat areas. The final loss is defined as the aggregation of losses on all N_1 windows of size $s_1 \times s_1$:

$$\mathcal{L}_{Trip}(s_1) = \sum_{n}^{N_1} \mathcal{L}(w_n) = \sum_{n}^{N_1} \mathcal{L}(\delta_n^+, \delta_n^-, \bar{r}_n, \mu). \tag{9}$$

Multi-Scale Context Aggregation. We extend Eq. 9 to a multi-scale approach to learn features that are discriminative across a range of scales. Multi-scale learning was used in keypoint detection [27,30,31], however, we extend these works by using the multi-scale sampling strategy not only on the detector but also on the descriptor training. Thus, we sample local soft-descriptors with

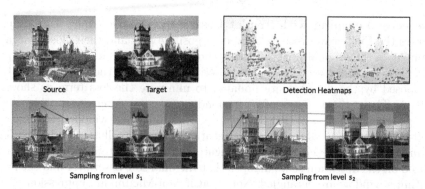

Fig. 6. Triplet formation pipeline. Soft-descriptors are extracted from each window together with their respective positives and the hardest negatives. The negatives are extracted only from non-neighbouring areas (non-red areas). (Color figure online)

varying window sizes, s_j with $j \in [1, 2, ..., S]$, as shown in Fig. 6, and combine their losses with control parameters λ_j in a final term:

$$\mathcal{L}_{MS-Trip} = \sum_j \lambda_j \mathcal{L}_{Trip}(s_j), \tag{10}$$

Repeatable and Discriminative. The detector triplet loss optimises the model to find locations that can potentially be matched. As stated in [18], discriminativeness is not sufficient to train a suitable detector. Therefore, we combine our discriminative loss and the repeatability term M-SIP proposed in [27] with control parameter β to balance their contributions:

$$\mathcal{L}_{R\,\&D} = \mathcal{L}_{M-SIP} + \beta \mathcal{L}_{MS-Trip}, \tag{11}$$

Entangled Detector-Descriptor Learning. We frame our joint optimisation strategy as follows. The detector is optimised by Eq. 11, meanwhile, the descriptor learning is based on the hard-mining triplet loss [9]. For the descriptor learning, we use the same sampling approach as in Fig. 6, however, instead of sampling soft-descriptors, we sample a point-wise descriptor per window. The location to sample the descriptor is provided by an NMS on the detector score map. Hence, the descriptor learning is conditioned by the detector score map sampling, meanwhile, our triplet detector loss term refines its candidate positions using the descriptor space. The interaction between parts tightly couples the two tasks and allows for mutual refinement. We alternate the detector and descriptor optimisation steps during training until a mutual convergence is reached.

3.3 Implementation Details

Training Dataset. We synthetically create pairs of images by cropping and applying random homography transformations to ImageNet images [46]. The

Table 1. Ablation study. Mean matching accuracy (MMA) on Heinly dataset [48] for different descriptor designs. Best results are obtained with Gabor filters in the hand-crafted block, $(\cdot)^+$ and $(\cdot)^-$ operators, and multi-scale feature fusion.

Dense-L2Net	1st order	2nd order	Gabor filter	Fully learnt	$(\cdot)^+$ & $(\cdot)^-$	Multi-scale	MMA (%)
✓	–	–	–	✓	–	–	41.8
✓	–	–	–	–	–	–	42.0
✓	✓	–	–	–	–	–	42.5
✓	–	✓	–	–	–	–	43.1
✓	–	–	✓	–	–	–	43.3
✓	–	–	–	–	–	✓	43.4
✓	–	–	✓	–	✓	–	43.6
✓	–	–	✓	–	–	✓	44.1
✓	–	–	✓	–	✓	✓	**44.5**

image's dimensions after cropping are 192×192, and the random homography parameters are: rotation $[-30°, 30°]$, scale $[0.5, 2.0]$, and skew $[-0.6, 0.6]$. However, illumination changes are harder to perform synthetically, and therefore, for tackling the illumination variations, we use the AMOS dataset [47], which contains outdoor webcam sequences of images taken from the same position at different times of the year. We experimentally observed that removing long-term or extreme variations *i.e.*, winter-summer, helps the training of HDD-Net. Thus, we filter AMOS dataset such that we keep only images that are taken during summertime between sunrise and midnight. We generate a total of 12,000 and 4,000 images for training and validation, respectively.

HDD-Net Training and Testing. Although the detector triplet loss function is applied to the full image, we only use the top K detections for training the descriptor. We select $K = 20$ with a batch size of 8. Thus, in every training batch, there is a total of 160 triplets for training the descriptor. On the detector site, we use $j = [8, 16, 24, 32]$, $\lambda_j = [64, 16, 4, 1]$, and set $\beta = 0.4$. The hyper-parameter search was done on the validation set. We fix HDD-Net descriptor size to a 256 dimension since it is a good compromise between performance and computational time. Note that the latest joint detector-descriptor methods do not have a standard descriptor size, while [13] is derived from 128-d L2-Net [8], the works in [17,30] use 256-d and [14] is 512-d. During test time, we apply a 15×15 NMS to select candidate locations on the detector score map. HDD-Net is implemented in TensorFlow 1.15 and is available on GitHub[1].

4   Experimental Evaluation

This section presents the evaluation results of our method in several application scenarios. Due to the numerous possible combinations of independent detectors and patch-based descriptors, the comparison focuses against end-to-end and joint detector-descriptor state of the art approaches.

---

[1]   https://github.com/axelBarroso/HDD-Net.

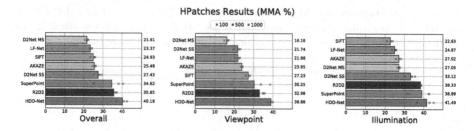

Fig. 7. Mean Matching Accuracy (MMA) on HPatches dataset for top 100, 500 and 1,000 points. HDD-Net gets the best results on both, viewpoint and illumination sequences.

4.1 Architecture Design

Dataset. We use the Heinly dataset [48] to validate our architecture design choices. We focus on its homography set and use only the sequences that are not part of HPatches [20]. We compute the Mean Matching Accuracy (MMA) [49] as the ratio of correctly matched features within a threshold of 5 pixels and the total number of detected features.

Ablation Study. We evaluate a set of hand-crafted filters for extracting features that are robust to rotation. Specifically, 1st and 2nd order derivatives as well as a Gabor filter. Besides, we further test a fully learnt approach without the hand-crafted filters. We also report results showing the impact of splitting the hand-crafted positive and negative features. Finally, our multi-scale approach is tested against a single-pass architecture without multi-scale feature fusion.

Results in Table 1 show that the Gabor filter obtains better results than 1st or 2nd order derivatives. Gabor filters are especially effective for rotation since they are designed to detect patterns under specific orientations. Besides, results without constraining the rotational block to any specific filter are slightly lower than the baseline. The fully learnt model could be improved by adding more filters, but if we restrict the design to a single filter, hand-crafted filter with $(\cdot)^{+}$ and $(\cdot)^{-}$ operators give the best performance. Lastly, a notable boost over the baseline comes from our proposed multi-scale pyramid and feature fusion within the descriptor architecture.

4.2 Image Matching

Dataset. We use the HPatches [20] dataset with 116 sequences, including viewpoint and illumination changes. We compute results for sequences with image resolution smaller than 1200 × 1600 following the approach in [14]. To demonstrate the impact of the detector and to make a fair comparison between different methods, we extend the detector evaluation protocol proposed in [21] to the matching metrics by computing the MMA score for the top 100, 500, and 1,000

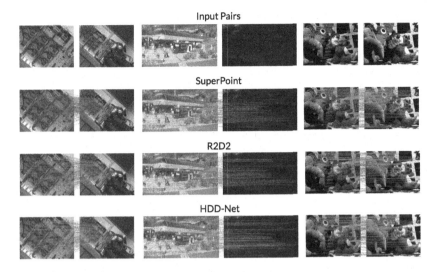

Fig. 8. Qualitative examples on *v_bip*, *i_bridger*, and *i_smurf* from the HPatches dataset. Illustrated sequences display extreme scale and rotation changes, as well as outdoor and indoor illumination variations.

keypoints. As in Sect. 4.1, MMA is computed as the ratio of correctly matched features within a threshold of 5 pixels and the total number of detected features.

Effect of Triplet Learning on Detector. Table 2 shows HDD-Net results when training its detections to be repeatable ($\mathcal{L}_{M-SIP}$) or/and discriminative ($\mathcal{L}_{MS-Trip}$). The performance of $\mathcal{L}_{MS-Trip}$ only is lower than $\mathcal{L}_{M-SIP}$, which is in line with [13]. Being able to detect repeatable features is crucial for matching images, however, best results are obtained with $\mathcal{L}_{R\,\&D}$, which combines $\mathcal{L}_{M-SIP}$ and $\mathcal{L}_{MS-Trip}$ with $\beta = 0.4$, and shows the benefits of merging both principles into a single detection map.

Table 2. MMA (%) results for different detector optimisations.

	HPatches (MMA)	
	View	Illum
$\mathcal{L}_{MS-Trip}$	26.4	34.9
$\mathcal{L}_{M-SIP}$	38.3	35.5
$\mathcal{L}_{R\,\&D}$ (Eq. 11)	**38.9**	**41.5**

Comparison to SOTA. Figure 7 compares our HDD-Net to different algorithms. HDD-Net outperforms all the other methods for viewpoint and illumination sequences on every threshold, excelling especially in the viewpoint change, that includes the scale and rotation transformations for which HDD-Net was designed. SuperPoint [17] performance is lower when using only the top 100 keypoints, and even though no method was trained with such constraint, the other models keep their performance very close to their 500 or 1,000 results. When constraining the number of keypoints, D2Net-SS [14] results are higher than for its multi-scale version D2Net-MS. D2Net-MS was reported in [14] to achieve higher performance when using an unlimited number of features. In Fig. 8, we

Table 3. 3D Reconstruction results on the ETH 3D benchmark. Dash symbol (–) means that COLMAP could not reconstruct any model.

	Madrid Metropolis (448 Images)				Gendarmenmarkt (488 Images)				Tower of London (526 Images)			
	Reg. Ims	Sp. Pts	Track Len	Rep. Err.	Reg. Ims	Sp. Pts	Track Len	Rep. Err.	Reg. Ims	Sp. Pts	Track Len	Rep. Err.
SIFT	27	1140	4.34	0.69	132	5332	3.68	**0.86**	75	4621	3.21	0.71
LF-Net	19	467	4.22	**0.62**	99	3460	4.65	0.90	76	3847	4.63	**0.56**
SuperPoint	39	1258	5.08	0.96	**156**	**6470**	5.93	1.21	111	5760	5.41	0.75
D2Net-SS	–	–	–	–	17	610	3.31	1.04	10	360	2.93	0.94
D2Net-MS	–	–	–	–	14	460	3.02	0.99	10	64	5.95	0.93
R2D2	22	984	4.85	0.88	115	3834	**7.12**	1.05	81	3756	**6.02**	1.03
HDD-Net	**43**	**1374**	**5.25**	0.80	154	6174	6.30	0.98	**116**	**6039**	5.45	0.80

show matching results for the three best-performing methods on hard examples from HPatches. Even though those examples present extreme viewpoint or illumination changes, HDD-Net can match correctly most of its features.

4.3   3D Reconstruction

Dataset. We use the ETH SfM benchmark [50] for the 3D reconstruction task. We select three sequences; *Madrid Metropolis, Gendarmenmarkt,* and *Tower of London.* We report results in terms of registered images (Re.g. Ims), sparse points (Sp. Pts), track length (Track Len), and reprojection error (Rep. Err.). Top 2,048 points are used as in [12], which still provides a fair comparison between methods at a much lower cost. The reconstruction is performed using COLMAP [2] software where we used one-third of the images to reduce the computational time.

Results. Table 3 presents the results for the 3D reconstruction experiments. HDD-Net and SuperPoint obtain the best results overall. While HDD-Net recovers more sparse points and registers more images in *Madrid* and *London,* SuperPoint does it for *Geendarmenmarkt.* D2-Net features did not allow to reconstruct any model on *Madrid* within the evaluation protocol *i.e.,* small regime on the number of extracted keypoints. Due to challenging examples with moving objects and in distant views, recovering a 3D model from a subset of keypoints makes the reconstruction task even harder. In terms of a track length, that is the number of images in which at least one feature was successfully tracked, R2D2 and HDD-Net outperform all the other methods. LF-Net reports a smaller reprojection error followed by SIFT and HDD-Net. Although the reprojection error is small in LF-Net, their number of sparse points and registered images are below other competitors.

4.4   Camera Localisation

Dataset. The Aachen Day-Night [51] contains more than 5,000 images, with separate queries for day and night[2]. Due to the challenging data, and to avoid convergence issues, we increase the number of keypoints to 8,000. Despite that, LF-Net features did not converge and are not included in Table 4.

Results. The best results for the most permissive error threshold are reported by D2-Net networks and R2D2. Note that D2-Net and R2D2 are trained on MegaDepth [52], and Aachen datasets, respectively, which contains real 3D scenes under similar geometric conditions. In contrast, SuperPoint and HDD-Net use synthetic training data, and while they perform better on image matching or 3D reconstruction, their performance is lower on localisation.

Table 4. Aachen Day-Night results on localisation. The higher the better.

	Aachen Day-Night		
	Correct Localised Queries (%)		
Threshold	0.5 m, 2°	1 m, 5°	5 m, 10°
SIFT [5]	33.7	52.0	65.3
SuperPoint [17]	42.9	61.2	85.7
D2-Net SS [14]	44.9	65.3	**88.8**
D2-Net MS [14]	41.8	**68.4**	**88.8**
R2D2 [13]	**45.9**	66.3	**88.8**
HDD-Net	43.9	62.2	82.7

As a remark, results are much closer in the most restrictive error, showing that HDD-Net and SuperPoint are on par with their competitors for more accurate camera localisation.

5   Conclusion

In this paper, we have introduced a new detector-descriptor method based on a hand-crafted block and multi-scale image representation within the descriptor. Moreover, we have formulated the triplet loss function to not only learn the descriptor part but also to improve the accuracy of the keypoint locations proposed by the detector. We validate our contributions in the image matching task, where HDD-Net outperforms the baseline with a wide margin. Furthermore, we show through extensive experiments across different tasks that our approach outperforms or performs as well as the top joint detector-descriptor algorithms in terms of matching accuracy and 3D reconstruction, despite using only synthetic viewpoint changes and much fewer data samples for training.

Acknowledgements. This research was supported by UK EPSRC IPALM project EP/S032398/1.

References

1. Teichmann, M., Araujo, A., Zhu, M., Sim, J.: Detect-to-retrieve: efficient regional aggregation for image search. In: Proceedings of the IEEE Conference on Computer Vision and Pattern Recognition, pp. 5109–5118 (2019)

---

[2] We use the benchmark from the CVPR 2019 workshop on Long-term Visual Localization.

2. Schonberger, J.L., Frahm, J.M.: Structure-from-motion revisited. In: Proceedings of the IEEE Conference on Computer Vision and Pattern Recognition, pp. 4104–4113 (2016)
3. Sattler, T., Zhou, Q., Pollefeys, M., Leal-Taixe, L.: Understanding the limitations of CNN-based absolute camera pose regression. In: Proceedings of the IEEE Conference on Computer Vision and Pattern Recognition, pp. 3302–3312 (2019)
4. Busam, B., et al.: Markerless inside-out tracking for 3D ultrasound compounding. In: Stoyanov, D., et al. (eds.) POCUS/BIVPCS/CuRIOUS/CPM -2018. LNCS, vol. 11042, pp. 56–64. Springer, Cham (2018). https://doi.org/10.1007/978-3-030-01045-4_7
5. Lowe, D.G.: Distinctive image features from scale-invariant keypoints. Int. J. Comput. Vis. **60**, 91–110 (2004)
6. Alcantarilla, P.F., Nuevo, J., Bartoli, A.: Fast explicit diffusion for accelerated features in nonlinear scale spaces. In: BMVC (2013)
7. Leutenegger, S., Chli, M., Siegwart, R.: Brisk: binary robust invariant scalable keypoints. In: IEEE International Conference on Computer Vision (ICCV), vol. 2011, pp. 2548–2555. IEEE (2011)
8. Tian, Y., Fan, B., Wu, F.: L2-net: deep learning of discriminative patch descriptor in euclidean space. In: Proceedings of the IEEE Conference on Computer Vision and Pattern Recognition, pp. 661–669 (2017)
9. Mishchuk, A., Mishkin, D., Radenovic, F., Matas, J.: Working hard to know your neighbor's margins: local descriptor learning loss. In: Advances in Neural Information Processing Systems, pp. 4826–4837 (2017)
10. Tian, Y., Yu, X., Fan, B., Wu, F., Heijnen, H., Balntas, V.: SOSNet: second order similarity regularization for local descriptor learning. In: Proceedings of the IEEE Conference on Computer Vision and Pattern Recognition, pp. 11016–11025 (2019)
11. Luo, Z., et al.: Geodesc: learning local descriptors by integrating geometry constraints. In: Proceedings of the European Conference on Computer Vision (ECCV), pp. 168–183 (2018)
12. Yuhe, J., et al.: Image matching across wide baselines: from paper to practice. arXiv preprint arXiv:2003.01587 (2020)
13. Revaud, J., et al.: R2d2: repeatable and reliable detector and descriptor. In: Advances in Neural Information Processing Systems (2019)
14. Dusmanu, M., et al.: D2-net: a trainable CNN for joint detection and description of local features. In: Proceedings of the IEEE Conference on Computer Vision and Pattern Recognition (2019)
15. Yi, K.M., Trulls, E., Lepetit, V., Fua, P.: LIFT: learned invariant feature transform. In: Leibe, B., Matas, J., Sebe, N., Welling, M. (eds.) ECCV 2016. LNCS, vol. 9910, pp. 467–483. Springer, Cham (2016). https://doi.org/10.1007/978-3-319-46466-4_28
16. Luo, Z., et al.: Aslfeat: learning local features of accurate shape and localization. In: Proceedings of the IEEE Conference on Computer Vision and Pattern Recognition (2020)
17. DeTone, D., Malisiewicz, T., Rabinovich, A.: Superpoint: self-supervised interest point detection and description. In: Proceedings of the IEEE Conference on Computer Vision and Pattern Recognition Workshops, pp. 224–236 (2018)
18. Tuytelaars, T., Mikolajczyk, K.: Local invariant feature detectors: a survey. Foundations and Trends in Computer Graphics and Vision (2008)
19. Csurka, G., Dance, C.R., Humenberger, M.: From handcrafted to deep local features. arXiv preprint arXiv:1807.10254 (2018)

20. Balntas, V., Lenc, K., Vedaldi, A., Mikolajczyk, K.: Hpatches: a benchmark and evaluation of handcrafted and learned local descriptors. In: Proceedings of the IEEE Conference on Computer Vision and Pattern Recognition, pp. 5173–5182 (2017)

21. Lenc, K., Vedaldi, A.: Large scale evaluation of local image feature detectors on homography datasets. In: BMVC (2018)

22. Bojanić, D., Bartol, K., Pribanić, T., Petković, T., Donoso, Y.D., Mas, J.S.: On the comparison of classic and deep keypoint detector and descriptor methods. In: 11th International Symposium on Image and Signal Processing and Analysis (ISPA), vol. 2019, pp. 64–69. IEEE (2019)

23. Rosten, E., Drummond, T.: Machine learning for high-speed corner detection. In: Leonardis, A., Bischof, H., Pinz, A. (eds.) ECCV 2006. LNCS, vol. 3951, pp. 430–443. Springer, Heidelberg (2006). https://doi.org/10.1007/11744023_34

24. Verdie, Y., Yi, K., Fua, P., Lepetit, V.: Tilde: a temporally invariant learned detector. In: Proceedings of the IEEE Conference on Computer Vision and Pattern Recognition, pp. 5279–5288 (2015)

25. Lenc, K., Vedaldi, A.: Learning covariant feature detectors. In: Hua, G., Jégou, H. (eds.) ECCV 2016. LNCS, vol. 9915, pp. 100–117. Springer, Cham (2016). https://doi.org/10.1007/978-3-319-49409-8_11

26. Zhang, X., Yu, F.X., Karaman, S., Chang, S.F.: Learning discriminative and transformation covariant local feature detectors. In: Proceedings of the IEEE Conference on Computer Vision and Pattern Recognition, pp. 6818–6826 (2017)

27. Barroso-Laguna, A., Riba, E., Ponsa, D., Mikolajczyk, K.: Key.net: keypoint detection by handcrafted and learned CNN filters, pp. 5836–5844 (2019)

28. Balntas, V., Riba, E., Ponsa, D., Mikolajczyk, K.: Learning local feature descriptors with triplets and shallow convolutional neural networks. In: BMVC, vol. 1, p. 3 (2016)

29. He, K., Lu, Y., Sclaroff, S.: Local descriptors optimized for average precision. In: Proceedings of the IEEE Conference on Computer Vision and Pattern Recognition, pp. 596–605 (2018)

30. Ono, Y., Trulls, E., Fua, P., Yi, K.M.: LF-net: learning local features from images. In: Advances in Neural Information Processing Systems, pp. 6234–6244 (2018)

31. Shen, X., et al.: RF-net: an end-to-end image matching network based on receptive field. In: Proceedings of the IEEE Conference on Computer Vision and Pattern Recognition, pp. 8132–8140 (2019)

32. Dai, J., et al.: Deformable convolutional networks. In: Proceedings of the IEEE International Conference on Computer Vision, pp. 764–773 (2017)

33. Zhu, X., Hu, H., Lin, S., Dai, J.: Deformable convnets v2: more deformable, better results. In: Proceedings of the IEEE Conference on Computer Vision and Pattern Recognition, pp. 9308–9316 (2019)

34. Ebel, P., Mishchuk, A., Yi, K.M., Fua, P., Trulls, E.: Beyond cartesian representations for local descriptors. In: Proceedings of the IEEE International Conference on Computer Vision, pp. 253–262 (2019)

35. Cohen, T., Welling, M.: Group equivariant convolutional networks. In: International Conference on Machine Learning, pp. 2990–2999 (2016)

36. Follmann, P., Bottger, T.: A rotationally-invariant convolution module by feature map back-rotation. In: 2018 IEEE Winter Conference on Applications of Computer Vision (WACV), pp. 784–792. IEEE (2018)

37. Worrall, D.E., Welling, M.: Deep scale-spaces: equivariance over scale. In: Advances in Neural Information Processing Systems (2019)

38. Dieleman, S., Willett, K.W., Dambre, J.: Rotation-invariant convolutional neural networks for galaxy morphology prediction. Mon. Not. R. Astron. Soc. Lett. **450**, 1441–1459 (2015)
39. Marcos, D., Volpi, M., Komodakis, N., Tuia, D.: Rotation equivariant vector field networks. In: Proceedings of the IEEE International Conference on Computer Vision, pp. 5048–5057 (2017)
40. Jaderberg, M., Simonyan, K., Zisserman, A., et al.: Spatial transformer networks. In: Advances in Neural Information Processing Systems, pp. 2017–2025 (2015)
41. Dieleman, S., De Fauw, J., Kavukcuoglu, K.: Exploiting cyclic symmetry in convolutional neural networks. In: ICML (2016)
42. Crivellaro, A., Lepetit, V.: Robust 3D tracking with descriptor fields. In: Proceedings of the IEEE Conference on Computer Vision and Pattern Recognition, pp. 3414–3421 (2014)
43. Mikolajczyk, K., Schmid, C.: Indexing based on scale invariant interest points. In: ICCV (2001)
44. Mishkin, D., Radenovic, F., Matas, J.: Repeatability is not enough: learning affine regions via discriminability. In: Proceedings of the European Conference on Computer Vision (ECCV), pp. 284–300 (2018)
45. Mishkin, D., Matas, J., Perdoch, M.: MODS: fast and robust method for two-view matching. Comput. Vis. Image Underst. **141**, 81–93 (2015)
46. Krizhevsky, A., Sutskever, I., Hinton, G.E.: Imagenet classification with deep convolutional neural networks. In: Advances in Neural Information Processing Systems, pp. 1097–1105 (2012)
47. Pultar, M., Mishkin, D., Matas, J.: Leveraging outdoor webcams for local descriptor learning. Proc. CVWW 2019 (2019)
48. Heinly, J., Dunn, E., Frahm, J.-M.: Comparative evaluation of binary features. In: Fitzgibbon, A., Lazebnik, S., Perona, P., Sato, Y., Schmid, C. (eds.) ECCV 2012. LNCS, vol. 7573, pp. 759–773. Springer, Heidelberg (2012). https://doi.org/10.1007/978-3-642-33709-3_54
49. Mikolajczyk, K., Schmid, C.: A performance evaluation of local descriptors. IEEE Trans. Pattern Anal. Mach. Intell. **27**, 1615–1630 (2005)
50. Schonberger, J.L., Hardmeier, H., Sattler, T., Pollefeys, M.: Comparative evaluation of hand-crafted and learned local features. In: Proceedings of the IEEE Conference on Computer Vision and Pattern Recognition, pp. 1482–1491 (2017)
51. Sattler, T., et al.: Benchmarking 6DoF outdoor visual localization in changing conditions. In: Proceedings of the IEEE Conference on Computer Vision and Pattern Recognition, pp. 8601–8610 (2018)
52. Li, Z., Snavely, N., Megadepth: learning single-view depth prediction from internet photos. In: Proceedings of the IEEE Conference on Computer Vision and Pattern Recognition, pp. 2041–2050 (2018)

Segmentation and Grouping

RGB-D Co-attention Network
for Semantic Segmentation

Hao Zhou[1,3], Lu Qi[2], Zhaoliang Wan[1,3], Hai Huang[1(✉)], and Xu Yang[3(✉)]

[1] National Key Laboratory of Science and Technology of Underwater Vehicle,
Harbin Engineering University, Harbin, China
zhouhao94@yahoo.com, wan.zhaoliang@icloud.com, haihus@163.com
[2] The Chinese University of Hong Kong, Hong Kong, China
luqi@cse.cuhk.edu.hk
[3] State Key Laboratory of Management and Control for Complex System,
Institute of Automation, Chinese Academy of Sciences, Beijing, China
xu.yang@ia.ac.cn

Abstract. Incorporating the depth (D) information for RGB images has
proven the effectiveness and robustness in semantic segmentation. However, the fusion between them is still a challenge due to their meaning
discrepancy, in which RGB represents the color but D depth information.
In this paper, we propose a co-attention Network (CANet) to capture
the fine-grained interplay between RGB' and D' features. The key part
in our CANet is co-attention fusion part. It includes three modules. At
first, the position and channel co-attention fusion modules adaptively
fuse color and depth features in spatial and channel dimension. Finally,
a final fusion module integrates the outputs of the two co-attention fusion
modules for forming a more representative feature. Our extensive experiments validate the effectiveness of CANet in fusing RGB and D features,
achieving the state-of-the-art performance on two challenging RGB-D
semantic segmentation datasets, i.e., NYUDv2, SUN-RGBD.

1 Introduction

Semantic segmentation aims to assign each pixel into different categories (e.g.
desk, sofa, wall, floor). It is fundamental in computer vision and benefits a large
number of applications, such as automatic driving, robotic sensing, visual SLAM
and so on. Despite the community's great achievement in semantic segmentation
[1–8], most of the researches only used the RGB images. The RGB information
provides models with robust color and texture but not geometric information. It
makes hard to discriminate instances and context which shares the similar color
and texture. As shown in Fig. 1, pillows on a bed with similar color of the bed,
cushion on a sofa with similar color of the sofa.

To solve the problems described above, some researches begin to leverage
depth information in assisting semantic segmentation [9–14]. The combination

---

H. Zhou and L. Qi—Contributed equally to this work.

© Springer Nature Switzerland AG 2021
H. Ishikawa et al. (Eds.): ACCV 2020, LNCS 12622, pp. 519–536, 2021.
https://doi.org/10.1007/978-3-030-69525-5_31

Fig. 1. Some hard samples of semantic segmentation only by RGB image. Left: pillows on a bed with similar color of the bed. Right: cushion on a sofa with similar color of the sofa. (Color figure online)

of RGB and depth images is vital significance in many aspects. On one hand, depth images provide necessary geometric information and can enrich the representation of RGB images. On the other hand, depth images are robust to environment disturbances, such as illumination, fog, etc. However, it is not trivial to fuse the color and depth images well duo to the data discrepancy between color and depth information, where depth image embedding geometric information and color image embedding texture information.

Remarkable efforts have been invested on this task RGB-D semantic segmentation. For example, [9–12] use depth image as an extra channel for the input. [13,14] respectively extract features from RGB and depth images and then fuse them. [15–20] jointly learn the correlation between depth features and color features. Albeit efficient for these approaches, that mainly focus on the local feature fusing and do not take the long-range dependencies into consideration.

Instead of designing heuristic fusion module of local features, we prefer to design self-supervised fusion module for global information. Based on this idea, There are two requirements need to consider: the fused features should have strong representation ability and the fusion method can automatically learn the long-range dependencies between different modalities. According to the analysis, we propose a CANet that contains three parts, encoder, co-attention fusion part and decoder. The encoder has three parallel branches to extract depth, color and mixture features respectively. This parallel design avoids the influence between the extracted depth and color feature while brings a CNN learned mixture feature. The co-attention fusion part, inspired by self-attention [21], is proposed to sovle the data discrepancy problem and effectively fuse RGB and depth features. The decoder is an up-sampled ResNet that decodes the fused feature for the final segmentation

The co-attention fusion part consists of three modules, position co-attention fusion module (PCFM), channel co-attention fusion module (CCFM) and final fusion module (FFM). PCFM and CCFM are proposed to fuse color and depth features in spatial and channel dimension. The FFM, is designed to effectively integrate the PCFM and CCFM and produces the final fused feature. For PCFM and CCFM, co-attention is first used to model long-range dependendencies between RGB and depth. Then, the learned long-range dependencies are used to tranform the depth information into color feature space. Finally, the transformed depth feature is added with the orginal color feature. The key idea of co-attention fusion method can described as using a color feature query and a set of depth feature key-value pairs to transform the depth feature into color feature space and then fuse with corresponding local color feature.

The main contributions of our CANet can be summarized as below:

- We propose a novel Co-attention Network (CANet) for RGB-D semantic segmentation.
- The key part, co-attention fusion part, consisting of PCFM, CCFM and FFM. PCFM and CCFM are propposed to solve the data discrepany problem and effectively fusion color and depth features at position and channel dimensions respectively. FFM is used to integrate PCFM and CCFM.
- We perform extensive experiments on the NYUDv2 [22] and the SUN-RGBD [23] datasets. CANet significantly improves RGB-D semantic segmentation results, achieving state-of-the-art on the two popular RGB-D benchmarks.

2   Related Works

2.1   Attention Modules

The attention mechanism [24–28] is widely used to model the global dependencies of features. There are many representations for attention mechanism. Among them, self-attention [29,30] could capture the long-range dependencies in a sequence. The work [21] is the first one that proves simply using self-attention in machine translation models could achieve state-of-the-art results. Owing to the modeling capability of long-range dependencies, self-attention module benefits in many tasks [31–38].

Inspired by the great success in NLP, self-attention module also gets focuses in computer vision field [39–45]. SENet [40] proposes channel attention modules that adaptively recalibrate channel-wise feature responses. NLNet [39] proposes non-local operations for capturing long-range dependencies. GCNet [41] creates a simplified network of NLNet based on a query-independent formulation. SAGAN [42] uses position attention modules that models the long-range dependency in generative adversarial networks for image generation tasks. SCA-CNN [43], DANet [44] and ABD-Net [45] incorporate spatial and channel-wise attention on image captioning, sementic segmentation and person re-identification tasks respoecitvely. Different from previous works, we extend the attention mechanism to color-depth features fusion. We design two attention based fusion modules for long-range dependencies between features from different modalities.

We name our attention mechanism as co-attention. The concept of co-attention is widely used in Visual Question Answer (VQA) task. The work [46] presents a novel co-attention mechanism to inference for the question and the image consequently. The work [47] develops a co-attention mechanism to jointly learn both the image and question attentions. The work [48] proves that co-attention mechanism enables dense, bi-directional interactions between image and text modalities. DANs [49] jointly leverages visual and textual attention mechanisms to create a fine-grained interplay between vision and language.

The above-mentioned works learn the visual and textual attentions separately. Different from that, we use co-attention to acquire the global dependencies between color and depth modalities.

2.2 RGB-D Semantic Segmentation

Different from color image semantic segmentation, RGB-D semantic segmentation is provided with a piece of additional depth information by depth Image. In the early stage, works [22,50,51] design handcrafted features tailored for RGB with depth information. Recently, with the benefit of CNN in color image semantic segmentation, deep-learning-based RGB-D semantic segmentation methods [9–20] have been proposed. Some works [9–12] use depth information as an additional channel of RGB channels. However, simply using depth image as an extra channel of RGB image cannot take full advantage of the depth information.

To better exploit the depth context, multimodal feature fusion-based methods [13–19] are proposed for RGB-D semantic segmentation. FuseNet [13] introduces a fuse layer to fuse depth features into color features maps. RDFNet [15] uses multi-modal feature fusion blocks and multi-level feature refinement blocks to capture RGB-D features. LSD-GF [16] introduces a gated fusion layer to adjust the contributions of RGB and depth over each pixel. Depth-aware CNN [17] presents depth-aware convolution and depth-aware pooling to incorporate geometry information into color features. CFN [18] and SCN [19] use the available depth to split the image into layers with the common visual characteristics.

Nevertheless, the aforementioned existing works mainly focus on local feature fusion and do not take the long-range dependencies into consideratin. We propose a new idea, to use an attention mechanism to model the long-range dependencies between color and depth features. Then, the learned long-range dependencies are used to transform the depth feature into color feature space. Finally, the transformed depth feature is added with the original color feature.

3   Co-attention Network

In this section, we first present the overall architecture of CANet (Sect. 3.1), including a standard encoder-decoder structure and our proposed co-attention fusion part. Then we introduce the modules of co-attention fusion part in Sect. 3.2, 3.3 and 3.4 respectively. At last, we describe our multi-scale loss function in Sect. 3.5.

3.1   Network Architecture Overview

Inspired by Unet [53], our CANet adopts an encoder-decoder structure for RGB-D semantic segmentation. The encoder is used to extract latent features, and then the decoder decodes them for final segmentation. For this structure, the robustness and effectiveness of latent features should directly influence the segmentation quality. As such, we proposed a co-attention fusion method to enhance

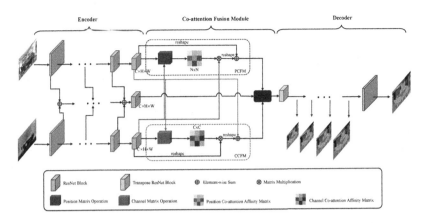

Fig. 2. Architecture of CANet. CANet mainly consists of three parts: 1) encoder (color encoder, depth encoder, mixture encoder). This paper adopts ResNet [52] as the backbone. 2) decoder, a upsample ResNet with standard residual building block. 3) co-attention fusion part, consists of PCFM, CCFM and FFM, are used to effectively fuse color features, depth features and mixture features.

our latent feature by fusing color and depth features. At first, we elaborately design the encoder to extract robust features from both color and depth information, which serves as the input for our co-attention method. Then, these features are adaptively fused by co-attention in different feature dimension.

As shown in Fig. 2, the encoder has three CNN branches. The first two, namely the RGB and D branch, are used to extract features of the color and depth image. Another CNN branch combines intermediate features from both RGB and D branches. For the decoder, it is an up-sampled ResNet with a series of the standard residual blocks. For fair comparison for other methods [14,15], we extract the multiple up-sampled features to generate semantic maps for multi-scale supervision.

Apart from our multi-branch structure in encoder-decoder, we also propose a co-attention fusion method to fuse these encoded features. It has three modules, including position co-attention fusion module (PCFM), channel co-attention fusion module (CCFM) and final fusion module (FFM). The first two use co-attention to fuse color and depth features in spatial and channel dimension. And the last one wraps the features with high consistency.

The PCFM captures the spatial dependencies between any two positions from color and depth feature maps respectively. For the color feature at a certain position, it is aggregated by depth features at all spatial locations with a learnable weighted summation. It is similar to CCFM except for fusing features among channels. Finally, FFM is designed to effectively integrate the outputs of these two co-attention modules.

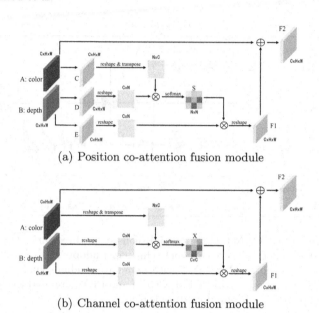

(a) Position co-attention fusion module

(b) Channel co-attention fusion module

Fig. 3. The detailed structure of position co-attention fusion module and channel co-attention fusion module

3.2 Position Co-attention Fusion Module

Enriching the local features with context by attention has been widely used in RGB semantic segmentation. However, RGB and Depth features have different semantic information, meaning, making it hard to adopt a similar strategy for RGB-D images. Inspired by the independent embed features adopted in NLP [21], we introduce color, depth and mixture features by three branches. Each branch represents a unique embed feature. We fuse them step by step for better feature consistency.

We firstly introduce a position co-attention fusion module to adaptively fuse depth and color features. By this way, PCFM uses a spatial query of color feature and a set of spatial key-value pairs of depth feature to transform the global depth feature into color feature space and then fuse with corresponding local color feature.

The detail of PCFM is illustrated in Fig. 3(a). The input color feature maps $\mathbf{A} \in \mathbb{R}^{C \times H \times W}$ are fed into one convolution layer with batch normalization and ReLU activation to a feature map $\mathbf{C} \in \mathbb{R}^{C \times H \times W}$. C, H, W are channel, height and width of features respectively. A similar process is conducted in the input depth feature map $\mathbf{B} \in \mathbb{R}^{C \times H \times W}$ by two times, producing the two new feature maps $\mathbf{D}, \mathbf{E} \in \mathbb{R}^{C \times H \times W}$. Then we flatten the $\mathbf{C}, \mathbf{D}, \mathbf{E}$ feature maps in $C \times N$ format, where $N = H \times W$. All of $\mathbf{C}, \mathbf{D}, \mathbf{E}$ share the same feature embedding with the original feature but with different characteristics. As such, we could use them for forming our position co-attention affinity matrix.

For detail, the position co-attention affinity matrix $\mathbf{S} \in \mathbb{R}^{N \times N}$ between $\mathbf{C}$ and $\mathbf{D}$ is calculated by the matrix multiplication and softmax layer:

$$s_{ji} = \frac{\exp\left(C_i^T \times D_j\right)}{\sum_{j=1}^{N} \exp\left(C_i^T \cdot D_j\right)}, i, j \in \{1, \cdots, N\} \tag{1}$$

Where s_{ji} represents the impact of ith position of color feature maps on j^{th} position of depth feature maps. In other words, s_{ji} is the correlation for pixel-level features at i^{th} and j^{th} positions from different feature maps. Secondly, we obtain the co-attention feature maps $\mathbf{F}1$ by matrix production between $\mathbf{E}$ and $\mathbf{S}$. The $\mathbf{F}1$ adaptively aggregated depth feature of each position. At last, we perform the element-wise sum operation between the co-attention feature maps $\mathbf{F}1$ and original color feature maps $\mathbf{A}$:

$$F2_j = \alpha \sum_{i=1}^{N} (E_i s_{ji}) + A_j, j \in \{1, \cdots, N\} \tag{2}$$

We are noting that a learnable scale parameter α in this sum operation, dynamically balancing the contribution of these two features.

Equation (2) shows that each position of the fused feature maps $\mathbf{F}2$ is obtained by adding the local color feature with weighted sum of global depth features in spatial dimension. Hence, the fused feature maps have a global view of depth feature maps, and it selectively fuses spatial depth contexts according to the position co-attention affinity matrix.

3.3   Channel Co-attention Fusion Module

Each channel plays different role in RGB recognition tasks, which has been comprehensively explored in SENet [40]. Inspired by this, we propose a channel co-attention fusion module to fuse the channel features step by step. In this module, we adopt a similar method with our PCFM, except we operate and fuse features in channel dimension.

As illustrated in Fig. 3(b), our channel co-attention fusion module is similar to our position fusion module in Sect. 3.2. We flatten the input color and depth feature maps $\mathbf{A}, \mathbf{B}$ into the new feature maps with $C \times N$, where $N = H \times W$. They could be calculated to get the co-attention affinity matrix.

At first, the channel co-attention affinity matrix $\mathbf{X} \in \mathbb{R}^{C \times C}$ between $\mathbf{A}$ and $\mathbf{B}$ is calculated by matrix multiplication and softmax layer:

$$x_{ji} = \frac{\exp\left(B_i \times A_j^T\right)}{\sum_{j=1}^{N} \exp\left(B_i \cdot A_j^T\right)}, i, j \in \{1, \cdots, C\} \tag{3}$$

Where, x_{ji} represents the impact of the jth channel of color feature maps on the ith channel of depth feature maps. In other words, x_{ji} is the correlation for the channel-level features at i^{th} and j^{th} channels from different feature maps.

Secondly, we obtain the co-attention feature maps **F**1 by matrix production between **X** and **B**. The **F**1 brings adaptively aggregated depth feature of each channel. Finally, we perform an element-wise sum operation between the co-attention feature maps **F**1 and original color feature maps **A**:

$$F2_j = \beta \sum_{i=1}^{N} (x_{ji}B_i) + A_j, j \in \{1, \cdots, C\} \tag{4}$$

Noting that a learnable scale parameter β is added in this sum operation to modify the contribution of these two features.

Equation (4) indicates that each channel of the fusion feature maps **F**2 is obtained by adding the local color feature with weighted sum of global depth features in channel dimension. Hence, the fused feature maps have a global view of all the channel feature maps of depth, and it selectively aggregates channel feature map according to the channel co-attention affinity matrix.

3.4 Final Fusion Module

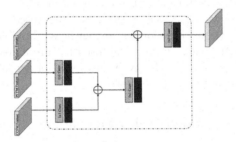

Fig. 4. Final Fusion Module (FFM)

FFM is used to integrate the output of PCFM, CCFM, and the mixture branch. The proposed FFM is implemented by four convolution layers followed by batch normalization and element-wise sum operation. The detailed structure of the FFM is shown in Fig. 4. The features of PCFM and CCFM are first convolved followed by batch normalization (a conv unit). The output channel of these convolutions is 2048, expanding the channel dimension of original features. Then we fuse the expanded attentions features with element-wise addition. After that, we smooth the added features by an extra conv unit. By addition again between smoothed and mixture features and then convolution, we obtain the final features.

3.5 Loss Function

The Fig. 2 illustrates our multi-scale loss function. At the training period, pyramid supervision introduces four intermediate side outputs from the features of the four unsampled residual unit except of the final output. The side outputs have 1/2, 1/4, 1/8, and 1/16 the height and width of the final outputs, respectively. A cross-entropy loss function is used on the four side and final outputs as follows:

$$J(F_1, \ldots F_5) = \sum_{k=1}^{K} J_k(F_k) \tag{5}$$

where

$$J_k(F_k) = \sum_{(h,w) \in \Omega_k} L(y_k^*(h, w), y_k(h, w)) \tag{6}$$

J_k is the objective function for the side output or final output. The Ω_k denotes the set of pixels of side output or final output. The function L is cross entropy loss function. The whole network is trained by optimizing Eq. (5) with back propagation.

4   Experiments

4.1   Comparison with the State-of-the-Art

4.2   Datasets and Metrics

In this section, we evaluate our network through comprehensive experiments. We use two public datasets:

- NYUDv2 [22]: The NYUDv2 dataset contains 1449 RGB-D images. We follow the 40-class settings [51] and the standard split [22] by involves 795 images for training and 654 images for testing.
- SUN RGB-D [23]: The SUN RGB-D dataset consists of 10335 RGB-D image pairs with 37 categories. We use the standard training/testing split [23] with 5285 as training and 5050 as testing.

Three common metrics [1] are used for evaluation, including pixel accuracy (PixAcc.), mean accuracy (mAcc.) and mean intersection over union (mIoU).

4.3   Implementation Details

We implement our network using the PyTorch deep learning framework [54]. All the models are trained with Nvidia Tesla V100 GPU. We use the pre-trained ResNet-50/ResNet-101 [52] as our three backbone branches in the encoder. Except for the backbones, the weights of other layers in our network are initialized by a normal distribution with zero mean and 0.01 variance, while the biases are padded with zero. The SGD is used as our optimizer, with momentum 0.9 and weight decay 0.0005. The learning rate is 0.001 (NYUDv2) or 0.0005 (SUN RGB-D) for the backbone and 0.01 for the other parts at the early stage, and it decays by a factor of 0.8 in every 100 (NYUDv2) or 20 (SUN RGB-D) epochs.

Table 1. Comparison with state-of-the-arts on the NYUDv2 dataset. Results are reported in terms of percentage (%) of pixel accuracy, mean accuracy, and mean IoU.

Method	Backbone	PixAcc.	mAcc.	mIoU
Gupta et al. [51]	–	60.3	35.1	28.6
Deng et al. [55]	–	63.8	–	31.5
FCN [1]	VGG-16	65.4	46.1	34.0
Eigen [56]	–	65.6	45.1	34.1
STD2P [57]	–	70.1	53.8	40.1
3DGNN [58]	ResNet-101	–	55.7	43.1
LSD-GF [16]	VGG-16	71.9	60.7	45.9
CFN [18]	ResNet-152	–	–	47.7
D-CNN [17]	ResNet-152	–	61.1	48.4
SCN [19]	ResNet-152	–	–	49.6
RDFNet [15]	ResNet-152	76.0	62.8	50.1
CANet	ResNet-50	75.7	62.6	49.6
CANet	ResNet-101	76.6	63.8	51.2

In the training period, we resize the inputs including RGB images, depth images and ground truth labels to size 480×640. We are noting that, the ground truth labels are further resized into four down-sampled maps from 240×320 to 30×40 for pyramid supervision of the side output. For fair comparison with other methods, we adopt the multi-scale and crop as our data augmentation strategy. Each image is also processed with random hue, brightness, and satura-

Table 2. Comparison with state-of-the-arts on the NYUDv2 dataset. Results are reported in terms of percentage (%) IoU. The best performance for per class is marked in bold.

Method	wall	floor	cabinet	bed	chair	sofa	table	door	window	bookshelf	picture	counter	blinds	desk	shelves	curtain	dresser	pillow	mirror	floormat
FCN [1]	69.9	79.4	50.3	66.0	47.5	53.2	32.8	22.1	39.0	36.1	50.5	54.2	45.8	11.9	8.6	32.5	31.0	37.5	22.4	13.6
Gupta et al. [51]	68.0	81.3	44.9	65.0	47.9	29.9	20.3	32.6	39.0	18.1	40.3	51.3	42.0	11.3	3.5	29.1	34.8	34.4	16.4	28.0
Deng et al. [55]	65.6	79.2	51.9	66.7	41.0	55.7	36.5	20.3	33.2	32.6	44.6	53.6	49.1	10.8	9.1	47.6	27.6	42.5	30.2	32.7
STD2P [57]	72.7	85.7	55.4	**73.6**	58.5	60.1	42.7	30.2	42.1	41.9	52.9	59.7	46.7	13.5	9.4	40.7	44.1	42.0	34.5	35.6
LSD-GF [16]	78.5	87.1	56.6	70.1	**65.2**	63.9	46.9	35.9	47.1	**48.9**	54.3	66.3	51.7	20.6	13.7	49.8	43.2	50.4	48.5	32.2
RDFNet [15]	79.7	87.0	60.9	73.4	64.6	**65.4**	**50.7**	39.9	**49.6**	44.9	61.2	67.1	**63.9**	**28.6**	14.2	**59.7**	49.0	49.9	**54.3**	**39.4**
CANet (ResNet-50)	79.6	87.5	61.1	70.7	63.7	64.7	46.8	44.6	46.5	45.1	61.2	68.9	58.0	22.4	14.1	56.1	47.0	48.6	49.1	32.0
CANet (ResNet-101)	**80.1**	**88.3**	**61.7**	72.8	63.9	**65.4**	48.0	**46.5**	48.3	44.4	**61.4**	**69.9**	59.5	27.2	**16.8**	57.3	**50.6**	**50.9**	51.3	38.6

Method	clothes	ceiling	books	fridge	tv	paper	towel	shower	box	board	person	nightstand	toilet	sink	lamp	bathtub	bag	ot. stuct.	ot. furn.	ot. props
FCN [1]	18.3	59.1	27.3	27.0	41.9	15.9	26.1	14.1	6.5	12.9	57.6	30.1	61.3	44.8	32.1	39.2	4.8	15.2	7.7	30.0
Gupta et al. [51]	4.7	60.5	6.4	14.5	31.0	14.3	16.3	4.2	2.1	14.2	0.2	27.2	55.1	37.5	34.8	38.2	0.2	7.1	6.1	23.1
Deng et al. [55]	12.6	56.7	8.9	21.6	19.2	28.0	28.6	22.9	1.6	1.0	9.6	30.6	48.4	41.8	28.1	27.6	0	9.8	7.6	24.5
STD2P [57]	22.2	55.9	29.8	41.7	52.5	21.1	34.4	15.5	7.8	29.2	60.7	42.2	62.7	47.4	38.6	28.5	7.3	18.8	15.1	31.4
LSD-GF [16]	24.7	62.0	34.2	45.3	53.4	27.7	42.6	23.9	11.2	58.8	53.2	**54.1**	80.4	59.2	45.5	52.6	15.9	12.7	16.4	29.3
RDFNet [15]	**26.9**	69.1	**35.0**	**58.5**	**63.8**	34.1	41.6	38.5	11.6	54.0	80.0	45.3	65.7	62.1	47.1	57.3	**19.1**	**30.7**	20.6	39.0
CANet (ResNet-50)	22.9	79.0	32.7	51.8	60.4	32.7	38.4	**41.3**	14.7	81.9	**81.0**	39.0	78.0	61.9	**49.5**	53.5	9.3	28.1	20.1	**39.3**
CANet (ResNet-101)	25.1	**79.5**	33.5	56.0	60.8	31.7	**47.7**	25.3	14.8	**83.7**	77.6	40.2	**83.8**	**67.3**	48.2	**66.2**	11.0	30.6	**21.2**	39.2

tion adjustment. The mean and standard deviation of RGB and Depth images are calculated to normalize our input data.

As shown in Tables 1, 2 and 3, we compare CANet with other state-of-the-art methods on the two RGB-D datasets. The performance is reported with different backbones ResNet-50 and ResNet-101.

NYUDv2 Dataset. We evaluate the three aforementioned metrics on our network for 40 classes on the NYUDv2 dataset. As illustrated in Table 1, we achieve the new state-of-the-art results on all three metrics. We owe the better performance to the RGB-D co-attention fusion module. The two fusion modules could effectively fuse the two modality features by capturing the long-range dependencies between RGB and D information. On the most important metric mean IoU, we achieve 51.2% with a slightly 2.2% improvement over the recent state-of-the-art method RDFNet [15].

On the NYUDv2 dataset, the distribution of semantic labels is long tail, with the number of some labels are very few. To evaluate the performance of our model on the imbalanced distributed dataset, we also show the category-wise results on each category, as in Table 2. Our method performs better than other methods over 18 classes (40 classes in total), especially in some 'hard' categories (e.g., shelves, box, ot. furn.), which demonstrate the robustness of our method among different categories with imbalanced training data.

Table 3. Comparison with state-of-the-arts on the SUN RGB-D dataset. Results are reported in terms of percentage (%) of pixel accuracy, mean accuracy, and mean IoU

Method	Backbone	PixAcc.	mAcc.	mIoU
FCN [1]	VGG-16	–	–	35.1
FuseNet [13]	VGG-16	76.3	48.3	37.3
Jiang et al. [59]	–	76.6	50.6	39.3
D-CNN [17]	ResNet-152	–	53.5	42.0
3DGNN [58]	ResNet-101	–	57.0	45.9
LSD-GF [16]	VGG-16	–	58.0	–
RDFNet [15]	ResNet-152	81.5	60.1	47.7
CFN [18]	ResNet-152	–	–	48.1
CANet	ResNet-50	81.6	59.0	48.1
CANet	ResNet-101	82.5	60.5	49.3

SUN RGB-D Dataset. Following the same test pattern on the NYUDv2 dataset. We also compare our method with state-of-the-art methods on the large-scale SUN RGB-D dataset. The test results are shown in Table 3. Our methods outperform existing RGB-D semantic segmentation methods and is the state-of-the-art with all three evaluation metrics. The comparison on this large-scale dataset again validates the effectiveness of our proposed method.

Table 4. Ablation study of CANet on the NYUDv2 dataset. Results are reported in terms of percentage (%) of pixel accuracy, mean accuracy, and mean IoU.

Method	Backbone	PixAcc.	mAcc.	mIoU
Basel.	ResNet-50	74.1	60.1	46.6
Basel. + PCFM	ResNet-50	75.4	61.6	48.9
Basel. + CCFM	ResNet-50	74.9	62.0	48.4
CANet	ResNet-50	75.7	62.6	49.6
Basel.	ResNet-101	75.2	62.2	48.5
Basel. + PCFM	ResNet-101	76.0	62.9	49.6
Basel. + CCFM	ResNet-101	75.5	63.0	50.2
CANet	ResNet-101	76.6	63.8	51.2

4.4 Ablation Study

To verify the performances of co-attention fusion modules, we conduct an ablation study on the NYUDv2 dataset. Each experiment is ablated with the same hypermeter setting at both training and testing period. For fair comparison, we regard the simple element-wise sum fusion as our baseline. The performance of each component is shown in Table 4. When using ResNet-50 as the backbone, the PCFM achieves 48.9 in mIoU with 5.0% improvement over the baseline method, and the CCFM improves 3.9% over the baseline method. When integrating the two modules, we gain further improvements 6.4% over the baseline, which demonstrating their complementary power over utilizing either alone. Furthermore, the usage of a deeper backbone network (ResNet-101) can still bring large improvements, which demonstrates our proposed modules are not limited to stronger backbones.

4.5 Visualizations

Semantic Segmentation Qualitative Visual Results: Figure 5 is the visualization for our sampled examples in RGB-D indoor semantic segmentation with Baseline, Baseline + PCFM, Baseline + CCFM, and Baseline + PCFM + CCFM (CANet) on the NYUDv2 dataset, which involves cluttered objects from various indoor scenes. Compared to Baseline we can see that both the PCFM and CCFM promotes the semantic segmentation results on details and misclassification problems. Moreover, the integration of PCFM and CCFM gets better segmentation results than the use of PCFM or CCFM individually.

Co-attention Affinity Matrix Visualization: The position co-attention affinity matrix has the shape of $HW \times HW$. For each point in the color features, a sub-co-attention affinity matrix ($1 \times HW$) is used to multiply with depth features maps. The aggregated depth feature then is added to the color feature of that point. In Fig. 6, we choose two points (p1, p2) and visualize their sub-co-attention matrices. We could clearly see that sub-co-attention affinity

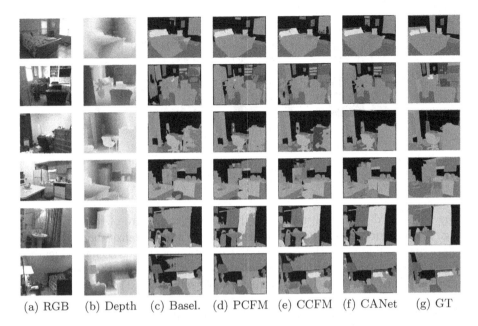

(a) RGB   (b) Depth   (c) Basel.   (d) PCFM   (e) CCFM   (f) CANet   (g) GT

Fig. 5. Semantic Segmentation Qualitative Visual Results on the NYUDv2 dataset. (a), (b) and (g) are the input color images, depth images and ground truth labels, respectively. (c) are the results of Baseline. (d) are the result of Baseline + PCFM. (e) are the results of Baseline + CCFM. (f) are the results of proposed CANet.

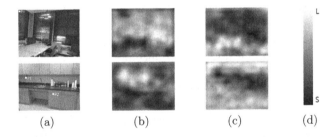

(a)   (b)   (c)   (d)

Fig. 6. Visualization of position co-attention affinity matrix. (a) Original image; (b) Sub affinity matrix of p1; (c) Sub affinity matrix of p2; (d) Color bar.

matrix puts more attention on the areas with the same labels even when some of them are far away from that point. For example, in the first row, the co-attention affinity matrix of p1 focuses on most regions which is labeled as 'window', and p2 focuses the attention on the regions labeled as 'table'. The visualization results show the co-attention affinity matrix could capture long-range depth features with the same semantic label.

The channel co-attention affinity matrix is with the shape of $C \times C$. For the feature map of each channel, a sub-co-attention affinity matrix $(1 \times C)$ is a weight matrix of depth feature maps and is used to aggregate the depth features.

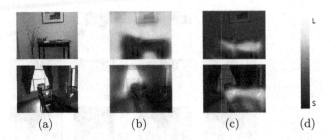

(a)   (b)   (c)   (d)

Fig. 7. Visualization of channel co-attention affinity matrix. (a) Original images; (b) Fused feature map of c1; (c) Fused feature map of c2; (d) Color bar.

The aggregated depth feature is added to the color feature of that channel. In Fig. 7, we randomly select two channels (c1, c2) and visualize their aggregated depth feature maps. As Fig. 7 shown, the attention of the fused channel features focuses more on areas with the same label. For example, in the first row, the attention of c1 are focused on the regions of 'wall', and c2 focus attentions on 'bed' areas. The visualization results demonstrate that the channel co-attention affinity matrix could capture the class-aware long-range cross channel depth features.

5   Conclusion

In this paper, we propose a novel CANet method that learns more representative, robust and discriminative feature embeddings for RGB-D semantic segmentation. In CANet, co-attention is used to adaptively aggregate depth features with color features. Specifically, we introduce position co-attention fusion module (PCFM) and channel co-attention fusion module (CCFM) to capture intermodality long-range dependencies in spatial and channel dimensions respectively. Meantime, we design a final fusion module (FFM) to effectively integrate of position co-attention fusion module and channel co-attention fusion module. The ablation study and visualization results illustrate the importance of each component. The experiments on the NYUDv2 and the SUN RGB-D datasets demonstrate that the proposed CANet outperforms existing RGB-D semantic segmentation methods. The interdependency between different modality feature will be further explored in the future.

Acknowledgement. This work is supported partly by the National Natural Science Foundation (NSFC) of China (grants 61973301, 61972020, 61633009, 51579053 and U1613213), partly by the National Key R&D Program of China (grants 2016YFC0300801 and 2017YFB1300202), partly by the Field Fund of the 13th Five-Year Plan for Equipment Pre-research Fund (No. 61403120301), partly by Beijing Science and Technology Plan Project, partly by the Key Basic Research Project of Shanghai Science and Technology Innovation Plan (No. 15JC1403300), and partly by Meituan Open R&D Fund.

References

1. Long, J., Shelhamer, E., Darrell, T.: Fully convolutional networks for semantic segmentation. In: Proceedings of the IEEE Conference on Computer Vision and Pattern Recognition, pp. 3431–3440 (2015)
2. Badrinarayanan, V., Kendall, A., Cipolla, R.: SegNet: a deep convolutional encoder-decoder architecture for image segmentation. IEEE Trans. Pattern Anal. Mach. Intell. **39**, 2481–2495 (2017)
3. Qi, L., Jiang, L., Liu, S., Shen, X., Jia, J.: Amodal instance segmentation with kins dataset. In: Proceedings of the IEEE Conference on Computer Vision and Pattern Recognition, pp. 3014–3023 (2019)
4. Yu, F., Koltun, V.: Multi-scale context aggregation by dilated convolutions. arXiv preprint arXiv:1511.07122 (2015)
5. Chen, L.C., Papandreou, G., Kokkinos, I., Murphy, K., Yuille, A.L.: DeepLab: semantic image segmentation with deep convolutional nets, atrous convolution, and fully connected CRFs. IEEE Trans. Pattern Anal. Mach. Intell. **40**, 834–848 (2017)
6. Lin, G., Milan, A., Shen, C., Reid, I.: RefineNet: multi-path refinement networks for high-resolution semantic segmentation. In: Proceedings of the IEEE Conference on Computer Vision and Pattern Recognition, pp. 1925–1934 (2017)
7. Peng, C., Zhang, X., Yu, G., Luo, G., Sun, J.: Large kernel matters-improve semantic segmentation by global convolutional network. In: Proceedings of the IEEE Conference on Computer Vision and Pattern Recognition, pp. 4353–4361 (2017)
8. Chen, L.C., Papandreou, G., Schroff, F., Adam, H.: Rethinking atrous convolution for semantic image segmentation. arXiv preprint arXiv:1706.05587 (2017)
9. Gupta, S., Girshick, R., Arbeláez, P., Malik, J.: Learning rich features from RGB-D images for object detection and segmentation. In: Fleet, D., Pajdla, T., Schiele, B., Tuytelaars, T. (eds.) ECCV 2014. LNCS, vol. 8695, pp. 345–360. Springer, Cham (2014). https://doi.org/10.1007/978-3-319-10584-0_23
10. He, Y., Chiu, W.C., Keuper, M., Fritz, M.: RGBD semantic segmentation using spatio-temporal data-driven pooling. arXiv preprint arXiv:1604.02388 (2016)
11. Wang, J., Wang, Z., Tao, D., See, S., Wang, G.: Learning common and specific features for RGB-D semantic segmentation with deconvolutional networks. In: Leibe, B., Matas, J., Sebe, N., Welling, M. (eds.) ECCV 2016. LNCS, vol. 9909, pp. 664–679. Springer, Cham (2016). https://doi.org/10.1007/978-3-319-46454-1_40
12. Husain, F., Schulz, H., Dellen, B., Torras, C., Behnke, S.: Combining semantic and geometric features for object class segmentation of indoor scenes. IEEE Robot. Autom. Lett. **2**, 49–55 (2016)
13. Hazirbas, C., Ma, L., Domokos, C., Cremers, D.: FuseNet: incorporating depth into semantic segmentation via fusion-based CNN architecture. In: Lai, S.-H., Lepetit, V., Nishino, K., Sato, Y. (eds.) ACCV 2016. LNCS, vol. 10111, pp. 213–228. Springer, Cham (2017). https://doi.org/10.1007/978-3-319-54181-5_14
14. Jiang, J., Zheng, L., Luo, F., Zhang, Z.: RedNet: residual encoder-decoder network for indoor RGB-D semantic segmentation. arXiv preprint arXiv:1806.01054 (2018)
15. Park, S.J., Hong, K.S., Lee, S.: RdfNet: RGB-D multi-level residual feature fusion for indoor semantic segmentation. In: Proceedings of the IEEE International Conference on Computer Vision, pp. 4980–4989 (2017)
16. Cheng, Y., Cai, R., Li, Z., Zhao, X., Huang, K.: Locality-sensitive deconvolution networks with gated fusion for RGB-D indoor semantic segmentation. In: Proceedings of the IEEE Conference on Computer Vision and Pattern Recognition, pp. 3029–3037 (2017)

17. Wang, W., Neumann, U.: Depth-aware CNN for RGB-D segmentation. In: Ferrari, V., Hebert, M., Sminchisescu, C., Weiss, Y. (eds.) ECCV 2018. LNCS, vol. 11215, pp. 144–161. Springer, Cham (2018). https://doi.org/10.1007/978-3-030-01252-6_9
18. Lin, D., Chen, G., Cohen-Or, D., Heng, P.A., Huang, H.: Cascaded feature network for semantic segmentation of RGB-D images. In: Proceedings of the IEEE International Conference on Computer Vision, pp. 1311–1319 (2017)
19. Lin, D., Zhang, R., Ji, Y., Li, P., Huang, H.: SCN: switchable context network for semantic segmentation of RGB-D images. IEEE Trans. Cybern. **50**(3), 1120–1131 (2018)
20. Hu, X., Yang, K., Fei, L., Wang, K.: ACNET: attention based network to exploit complementary features for RGBD semantic segmentation. In: 2019 IEEE International Conference on Image Processing (ICIP), pp. 1440–1444. IEEE (2019)
21. Vaswani, A., et al.: Attention is all you need. In: Advances in Neural Information Processing Systems, pp. 5998–6008 (2017)
22. Silberman, N., Hoiem, D., Kohli, P., Fergus, R.: Indoor segmentation and support inference from RGBD images. In: Fitzgibbon, A., Lazebnik, S., Perona, P., Sato, Y., Schmid, C. (eds.) ECCV 2012. LNCS, vol. 7576, pp. 746–760. Springer, Heidelberg (2012). https://doi.org/10.1007/978-3-642-33715-4_54
23. Song, S., Lichtenberg, S.P., Xiao, J.: Sun RGB-D: a RGB-D scene understanding benchmark suite. In: Proceedings of the IEEE Conference on Computer Vision and Pattern Recognition, pp. 567–576 (2015)
24. Bahdanau, D., Cho, K., Bengio, Y.: Neural machine translation by jointly learning to align and translate. arXiv preprint arXiv:1409.0473 (2014)
25. Xu, K., et al.: Show, attend and tell: neural image caption generation with visual attention. In: International Conference on Machine Learning, pp. 2048–2057 (2015)
26. Yang, Z., He, X., Gao, J., Deng, L., Smola, A.: Stacked attention networks for image question answering. In: Proceedings of the IEEE Conference on Computer Vision and Pattern Recognition, pp. 21–29 (2016)
27. Gregor, K., Danihelka, I., Graves, A., Rezende, D.J., Wierstra, D.: Draw: a recurrent neural network for image generation. arXiv preprint arXiv:1502.04623 (2015)
28. Chen, X., Mishra, N., Rohaninejad, M., Abbeel, P.: Pixelsnail: an improved autoregressive generative model. arXiv preprint arXiv:1712.09763 (2017)
29. Cheng, J., Dong, L., Lapata, M.: Long short-term memory-networks for machine reading. arXiv preprint arXiv:1601.06733 (2016)
30. Parikh, A.P., Täckström, O., Das, D., Uszkoreit, J.: A decomposable attention model for natural language inference. arXiv preprint arXiv:1606.01933 (2016)
31. Tang, J., Jin, L., Li, Z., Gao, S.: RGB-D object recognition via incorporating latent data structure and prior knowledge. IEEE Trans. Multimedia **17**, 1899–1908 (2015)
32. Lin, G., Shen, C., Van Den Hengel, A., Reid, I.: Efficient piecewise training of deep structured models for semantic segmentation. In: Proceedings of the IEEE Conference on Computer Vision and Pattern Recognition, pp. 3194–3203 (2016)
33. Lin, Z., et al.: A structured self-attentive sentence embedding. arXiv preprint arXiv:1703.03130 (2017)
34. Shen, T., Zhou, T., Long, G., Jiang, J., Pan, S., Zhang, C.: DISAN: directional self-attention network for RNN/CNN-free language understanding. In: Thirty-Second AAAI Conference on Artificial Intelligence (2018)
35. Qi, L., Liu, S., Shi, J., Jia, J.: Sequential context encoding for duplicate removal. In: Advances in Neural Information Processing Systems, pp. 2049–2058 (2018)
36. Zhu, Y., Wang, J., Xie, L., Zheng, L.: Attention-based pyramid aggregation network for visual place recognition. In: Proceedings of the 26th ACM International Conference on Multimedia, pp. 99–107 (2018)

37. Song, X., Zhang, S., Hua, Y., Jiang, S.: Aberrance-aware gradient-sensitive attentions for scene recognition with RGB-D videos. In: Proceedings of the 27th ACM International Conference on Multimedia, pp. 1286–1294 (2019)
38. Li, W., Tao, X., Guo, T., Qi, L., Lu, J., Jia, J.: MUCAN: multi-correspondence aggregation network for video super-resolution. arXiv preprint arXiv:2007.11803 (2020)
39. Wang, X., Girshick, R., Gupta, A., He, K.: Non-local neural networks. In: Proceedings of the IEEE Conference on Computer Vision and Pattern Recognition, pp. 7794–7803 (2018)
40. Hu, J., Shen, L., Sun, G.: Squeeze-and-excitation networks. In: Proceedings of the IEEE Conference on Computer Vision and Pattern Recognition, pp. 7132–7141 (2018)
41. Cao, Y., Xu, J., Lin, S., Wei, F., Hu, H.: GCNET: non-local networks meet squeeze-excitation networks and beyond. In: Proceedings of the IEEE International Conference on Computer Vision Workshops (2019)
42. Zhang, H., Goodfellow, I., Metaxas, D., Odena, A.: Self-attention generative adversarial networks. arXiv preprint arXiv:1805.08318 (2018)
43. Chen, L., et al.: SCA-CNN: spatial and channel-wise attention in convolutional networks for image captioning. In: Proceedings of the IEEE Conference on Computer Vision and Pattern Recognition, pp. 5659–5667 (2017)
44. Fu, J., et al.: Dual attention network for scene segmentation. In: Proceedings of the IEEE Conference on Computer Vision and Pattern Recognition, pp. 3146–3154 (2019)
45. Chen, T., et al.: ABD-NET: attentive but diverse person re-identification. In: Proceedings of the IEEE International Conference on Computer Vision, pp. 8351–8361 (2019)
46. Lu, J., Yang, J., Batra, D., Parikh, D.: Hierarchical question-image co-attention for visual question answering. In: Advances in Neural Information Processing Systems, pp. 289–297 (2016)
47. Yu, Z., Yu, J., Fan, J., Tao, D.: Multi-modal factorized bilinear pooling with co-attention learning for visual question answering. In: Proceedings of the IEEE International Conference on Computer Vision, pp. 1821–1830 (2017)
48. Nguyen, D.K., Okatani, T.: Improved fusion of visual and language representations by dense symmetric co-attention for visual question answering. In: Proceedings of the IEEE Conference on Computer Vision and Pattern Recognition, pp. 6087–6096 (2018)
49. Nam, H., Ha, J.W., Kim, J.: Dual attention networks for multimodal reasoning and matching. In: Proceedings of the IEEE Conference on Computer Vision and Pattern Recognition, pp. 299–307 (2017)
50. Ren, X., Bo, L., Fox, D.: RGB-(D) scene labeling: features and algorithms. In: 2012 IEEE Conference on Computer Vision and Pattern Recognition, pp. 2759–2766. IEEE (2012)
51. Gupta, S., Arbelaez, P., Malik, J.: Perceptual organization and recognition of indoor scenes from RGB-D images. In: Proceedings of the IEEE Conference on Computer Vision and Pattern Recognition, pp. 564–571 (2013)
52. He, K., Zhang, X., Ren, S., Sun, J.: Deep residual learning for image recognition. In: Proceedings of the IEEE Conference on Computer Vision and Pattern Recognition, pp. 770–778 (2016)

53. Ronneberger, O., Fischer, P., Brox, T.: U-Net: convolutional networks for biomedical image segmentation. In: Navab, N., Hornegger, J., Wells, W.M., Frangi, A.F. (eds.) MICCAI 2015. LNCS, vol. 9351, pp. 234–241. Springer, Cham (2015). https://doi.org/10.1007/978-3-319-24574-4_28

54. Paszke, A., et al.: Pytorch: an imperative style, high-performance deep learning library. In: Advances in Neural Information Processing Systems, pp. 8024–8035 (2019)

55. Deng, Z., Todorovic, S., Jan Latecki, L.: Semantic segmentation of RGBD images with mutex constraints. In: Proceedings of the IEEE International Conference on Computer Vision, pp. 1733–1741 (2015)

56. Eigen, D., Fergus, R.: Predicting depth, surface normals and semantic labels with a common multi-scale convolutional architecture. In: Proceedings of the IEEE International Conference on Computer Vision, pp. 2650–2658 (2015)

57. He, Y., Chiu, W.C., Keuper, M., Fritz, M.: STD2P: RGBD semantic segmentation using spatio-temporal data-driven pooling. In: Proceedings of the IEEE Conference on Computer Vision and Pattern Recognition, pp. 4837–4846 (2017)

58. Qi, X., Liao, R., Jia, J., Fidler, S., Urtasun, R.: 3D graph neural networks for RGBD semantic segmentation. In: Proceedings of the IEEE International Conference on Computer Vision, pp. 5199–5208 (2017)

59. Jiang, J., Zhang, Z., Huang, Y., Zheng, L.: Incorporating depth into both CNN and CRF for indoor semantic segmentation. In: 2017 8th IEEE International Conference on Software Engineering and Service Science (ICSESS), pp. 525–530. IEEE (2017)

Semantics Through Time: Semi-supervised Segmentation of Aerial Videos with Iterative Label Propagation

Alina Marcu[1,2(✉)], Vlad Licaret[1], Dragos Costea[1,2], and Marius Leordeanu[1,2]

[1] University Politehnica of Bucharest, 313 Splaiul Independentei,
Bucharest, Romania
[2] Institute of Mathematics of the Romanian Academy, 21 Calea Grivitei,
Bucharest, Romania
{alina.marcu,vlad.licaret,dragos.costea,marius.leordeanu}@upb.ro

Abstract. Semantic segmentation is a crucial task for robot navigation and safety. However, current supervised methods require a large amount of pixelwise annotations to yield accurate results. Labeling is a tedious and time consuming process that has hampered progress in low altitude UAV applications. This paper makes an important step towards automatic annotation by introducing *SegProp*, a novel iterative flow-based method, with a direct connection to spectral clustering in space and time, to propagate the semantic labels to frames that lack human annotations. The labels are further used in semi-supervised learning scenarios. Motivated by the lack of a large video aerial dataset, we also introduce *Ruralscapes*, a new dataset with high resolution (4K) images and manually-annotated dense labels every 50 frames - the largest of its kind, to the best of our knowledge. Our novel SegProp automatically annotates the remaining unlabeled 98% of frames with an accuracy exceeding 90% (F-measure), significantly outperforming other state-of-the-art label propagation methods. Moreover, when integrating other methods as modules inside SegProp's iterative label propagation loop, we achieve a significant boost over the baseline labels. Finally, we test SegProp in a full semi-supervised setting: we train several state-of-the-art deep neural networks on the SegProp-automatically-labeled training frames and test them on completely novel videos. We convincingly demonstrate, every time, a significant improvement over the supervised scenario.

1 Introduction

While ground vehicles are restricted to movements in 2D, aerial robots are free to navigate in three dimensions. This allows them to capture images of objects from a wide range of scales and angles, with richer views than the ones available

Electronic supplementary material The online version of this chapter (https://doi.org/10.1007/978-3-030-69525-5_32) contains supplementary material, which is available to authorized users.

© Springer Nature Switzerland AG 2021
H. Ishikawa et al. (Eds.): ACCV 2020, LNCS 12622, pp. 537–552, 2021.
https://doi.org/10.1007/978-3-030-69525-5_32

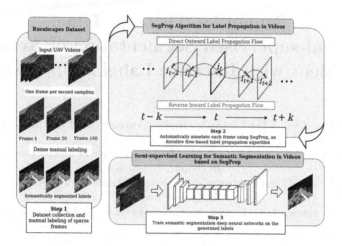

Fig. 1. SegProp: our method for automatic propagation of semantic labels in the context of semi-supervised segmentation in aerial videos. **Step 1.** First, we sample the UAV videos, at regular intervals (e.g. one or two frames per second). The resulting frames are then manually labeled. **Step 2.** We automatically propagate labels to the remaining unlabeled frames using our SegProp algorithm - based on class voting, at the pixel level, according to inward and outward label propagation flows between the current frame and an annotated frame. The propagation flows could be based on optical flow, homography transformation or other propagation method, as shown in experiments. SegProp propagates iteratively the segmentation class voting until convergence, improving performance over iterations. **Step 3.** We then mix all the generated annotations with the ground truth manual labels to train powerful deep networks for semantic segmentation and significantly improve performance in unseen videos.

in datasets collected on the ground. Unfortunately, this unconstrained movement imposes significant challenges for accurate semantic segmentation, mostly due to the aforementioned variation in object scale and viewpoint. Classic semantic segmentation approaches are focused on ground scenes. More recent work tackled imagery from the limited viewpoints of specialized scenes, such as ground-views of urban environments (from vehicles) and direct overhead views (from orbital satellites). Nevertheless, recent advances in aerial robotics allows us to capture previously unexplored viewpoints and diverse environments more easily. Given the current state of technology, in order to evaluate the performance of autonomous systems, the human component is considered a reference. However, the manual segmentation annotations in supervised learning is a laborious and time consuming process. In the context of video segmentation, it is impractical to manually label each frame independently, especially considering there is relatively little change from one to the next. In this context, the ability to perform automatic annotation would be extremely valuable.

SegProp - Automated Semantic Propagation in Videos. In this paper we present SegProp (Sect. 2), an iterative flow-based method to propagate, through space and time, the semantic segmentation labels to video frames that lack human annotations. SegProp propagates labels in an iterative fashion, forward and backward in time from annotated frames, by looping several times through the video and accumulating class votes at each iteration. At convergence the majority class wins. From a theoretical point of view, SegProp relates to spectral MAP labeling in graphical models and has convergence and improvement guarantees (Sect. 2.1). In practice, we demonstrate the effectiveness of SegProp in several ways (Sect. 4). First, we show that SegProp is able to propagate labels to unlabeled frames with an accuracy that outperforms competition by a significant margin (Sect. 4.1). Second, we show that other methods for label propagation could be immediately integrated as modules inside the SegProp propagation loop, with a significant boost in performance (Sect. 4.3). And third, we demonstrate SegProp's effectiveness in a semi-supervised learning scenario (Sect. 4.2), in which several state-of-the-art deep networks for semantic segmentation are trained on the automatically annotated frames and tested on novel videos, with an important improvement over the supervised case.

Label Propagation Methods. Our method is not limited to single-object maks propagation [1]. Methods that are most related to ours perform total scene, multi-class label propagation [2]. One such method, also propagates labels between two frames, in the context of ground navigation and low resolution images (320 × 240) [3]. They employ an occlusion-aware algorithm coupled with an uncertainty estimation method. Their approach is less useful in our case, where we have very high resolution images (4k) at a high frame rate (50fps) and dense optical flow can be accurately computed. Earlier works, exploring the idea of propagating ground truth labels using an optical flow based method [4], have shown that it could be useful to treat pseudo-labels differently than the ground truth ones, during training. That idea builds upon other work that addresses occlusion errors [5]. More recent methods for automatic label propagation use a single human annotated frame and extend the label to nearby frames, such as it is the work of Zhu et al. [6], with sate-of-the-art results on Cityscapes and KITTI [7]. The main limitation of [6] is that the performance drops drastically when increasing the number of propagated frames, as we confirm in our tests (Fig. 5). Budvytis et al. [8] use semi-supervised learning to improve the intermediate labels and Reza et al. [9] integrate depth and camera pose and formulate the problem as energy minimization in Conditional Random Fields.

Ruralscapes Dataset for Semantic Segmentation in UAV Videos. In this paper we also introduce *Ruralscapes*, the largest high resolution video dataset (20 high quality 4K videos) for aerial semantic segmentation, taken in flight over rural areas in Europe (Sect. 3). We manually annotate a relatively small subset (2%) of frames in a video and use SegProp, our novel iterative label propagation algorithm, to automatically annotate the whole sequence. Given a start and an end frame of a video sequence, SegProp finds pixelwise correspondences between labeled and unlabeled frames, to assign a class for each pixel in the video based on an iterative class voting procedure. In this way we generate large amounts of labeled data (over 50k densely segmented frames) to use in semi-supervised training deep neural networks and show that training on the automatically generated labels, boosts the performance at test time significantly. Our pipeline can be divided into three steps (see Fig. 1). The first and most important is the data labeling step. We leverage the advantages of high quality 4K aerial videos, such as small frame-to-frame changes (50 frames per second) and manually annotate a relatively small fraction of frames, sampled at 1 frame per second. We then automatically generate labels for each intermediate frame, between two labeled ones using SegProp, our proposed algorithm (Sect. 2), such that the whole video is labeled. In our last step, we use the manually and automatically annotated frames together for semi-supervised training.

Datasets for Semantic Segmentation in Video. Since most work is focused on ground navigation, the largest datasets with real-world scenarios are ground-based. Earlier image-based segmentation datasets, such as Microsoft's COCO [10], contained rough labels, but the large number of images (123k) and classes (80), made it a very popular choice. Cityscapes [11] was among the first large-scale dataset for ground-level semantic and instance segmentation. Year after year, the datasets increased in volume and task complexity, culminating with Apolloscape [12], which is, to the best of our knowledge, the largest real ground-level dataset. Compared to its predecessors, it also includes longer video shots, not just snippets. It comprises of 74,555 annotated video frames. To help reduce the labeling effort, a depth and flow-based annotation tool is used. Aeroscapes [13] is a UAV dataset that contains real-world videos and semantic annotations for each frame and it is closer to what we aim to achieve. Unfortunately, the size of the dataset is rather small, with video snippets ranging from 2 to 125 frames. The most similar dataset to ours is UAVid [14]. The dataset contains set of 4K UAV videos, that captures urban street scenes, with 300 images manually-labeled with 8 classes, compared to our dataset that has 60% more frames, manually-labeled with 12 classes. Since labeling real-world data (especially video) is difficult, a common practice is to use synthetic videos from a simulated environment. Such examples are Playing for Benchmarks [15], for ground-level navigation and the recently released Mid-air [16], for low-altitude navigation. Mid-air has more than 420k training video frames. The diversity of the flight scenarios and classes is reduced - mostly mountain areas with roads - but the availability of multiple seasons and weather conditions is a plus.

Main contributions: 1) We present SegProp, an iterative semantic label propagation method in video, which outperforms the current state-of-the-art (Sect. 2). **2)** We introduce Ruralscapes, the largest high-res (4K) video dataset for aerial semantic segmentation with 50,835 fully annotated frames and 12 semantic classes (Sect. 3). **3)** SegProp can be easily integrated with other label propagation methods and further improve their initial segmentation results (Sect. 4.3). **4)** We test SegProp in semi-supervised learning scenarios and compare with state-of-the-art deep neural nets for semantic segmentation (Sect. 4.2).

2   SegProp: Semantic Propagation Through Time

We now present SegProp, our iterative, voting-based label propagation method (Algorithm 2), which takes advantage of the temporal coherence and symmetry present in videos. Before presenting the full method, we first show how labels are propagated between two labeled frames to the intermediate initially unlabeled ones (in one iteration). Let P_k be an intermediate (initially unlabeled) video frame between two (manually) labeled key frames P_i and P_j. We first extract optical flow both forward $F_{i \to j}$ and backward $F_{j \to i}$ through time, between subsequent frames. Then, we use the dense pixel motion trajectories formed by the optical flow and map pixels from the annotated frames towards the unlabeled P_k. Since the optical flow mapping is not bijective (mapping from P_k to P_j could differ from mapping from P_j to P_k), we take both forward and backward mappings into account. Thus, for each pixel in P_k we have 4 correspondence maps that will vote for a certain class: two votes are collected based on the direct outward maps from P_k to its nearby key labeled frames $(P_{k \to i}, P_{k \to j})$ and two are based on the reversed inward maps $(P_{i \to k}, P_{j \to k})$. Since motion errors are expected to increase with the length of the temporal distance between frames, we weigh these votes with exponential decay, decreasing with the distance (Algorithm 1).

Notation. P_k is a 3-dimensional segmentation map, of the same two dimensions as the frame, but with a third dimension corresponding to the class label. Thus, votes for a given class are accumulated on the channel corresponding to that specific class. With a slight notation abuse, by $P_{k \to i}$ we denote either the flow propagation directed from frame k to frame i as well as the class vote cast by the labeled frame (in this case, i) onto the unlabeled frame k at the corresponding locations in k, according to the flow propagation map $P_{k \to i}$.

Algorithm 1. Label propagation between labeled frames in one iteration

---

Input: Two labeled frames P_i and P_j, optical flow maps $F_{i \to j}$ and $F_{j \to i}$.
Output: P_k, an intermediate, automatically labeled frame ($i < k < j$).
1) Compute 4 segmentations P_{kn} ($n = \overline{1,4}$) by casting class votes $(P_{k \to i}, P_{k \to j})$ and $(P_{i \to k}, P_{j \to k})$ according to direct outward flow and reverse inward flow, respectively.
2) Gather weighted votes from all four P_{kn} for each pixel (x, y):
   $p_k(x, y, :) = \sum_{n=1}^{4} w_n p_{kn}(x, y, :)$,
   where $w_n \propto e^{-\lambda * dist_n(k, q_n)}$ and $dist_n(k, q_n)$ is the distance between frame k and corresponding labeled frame $q_n \in i, j$. Weights w_n are normalized to sum to 1.
3) Compute final P_k by class majority voting for each pixel.

Iterative SegProp Algorithm. A similar label propagation procedure (as in Algorithm 1) could be repeated for several iterations (as in Algorithm 2) by considering all frames labelled from previous iterations and cast votes between nearby ones. The intuition is that after the initial voting, we can establish better temporal coherence among neighbouring frames and improve consistency by

---

Algorithm 2. Iterative SegProp Algorithm for Label Propagation

---

1) For a given frame k, perform **Step 1** from **Algorithm 1** considering of $2f$ neighbouring frames, symmetrically spaced around k. *Optional: replace or augment the optical flow votes by another propagation procedure.*

2) Gather all available votes for each class, including the ones from frame k's previous iteration:

$$p_k(x, y, :) = \sum_{n=1}^{4f+1} w_n p_{kn}(x, y, :)$$

3) Return to Step 1 and repeat several iterations, for all frames, until convergence.

4) Return final segmentation by class majority voting: $class_k(x, y) = max(p_k(x, y, :))$

---

iteratively propagating class votes between each other. The iterative SegProp (Algorithm 2) results in better local consensus, with smoother and more accurate labels. In Sect. 2.1 we also show that SegProp has interesting theoretical properties such as convergence to an improved segmentation objective score.

Integrating Other Propagation Methods into SegProp. We can use SegProp as a meta-procedure on top of other label propagation solutions (such as [6] or homography-based propagation), resulting in further improvement of the initial results, as shown in our experiments (Sect. 4). Segprop could in principle start from any initial solution (soft or hard) and then, at each iteration, replace or augment the class voting with votes from any other label propagation module.

Final Segmentation Space-Time 3D Filtering. As final post-processing step we smooth out the segmentation noise as follows: we propagate P_k along optical flow vectors for a number of steps, forward and backward through time, and concatenate the results into a local 3D spatiotemporal voting volume, one per class. We then apply a 3D (2D + time) Gaussian filter kernel to the 3D volume and obtain an average of the votes, one per each class, independently. Then we finally set hard per-pixel classes by class majority voting.

2.1 Mathematical Interpretation and Properties of SegProp

From a more theoretical point of view, SegProp can be seen as a Maximum A Posteriori (MAP) label inference method for graphical models [17], strongly related to other, more classical iterative optimization techniques for labeling problems with pairwise terms, such as relaxation labeling [18], deterministic and self annealing [19], spectral MAP inference [20] and iterative conditional modes [21]. Conceptually, we could think of the video as a graph of pixels in space and time, with a node for each pixel. Then, each node in the graph can get one class label out of several. A multi-class segmentation solution at the entire video level, could be represented with a single vector $\mathbf{p}$, with N × C elements (N - total number of nodes, C - number of possible classes per node). Thus, for a unique pixel i in the video and potential label a, we get a unique index ia. A final hard segmentation could then be expressed as an indicator vector $\mathbf{p}$, such that $p_{ia} = 1$ if pixel i has class a and $p_{ia} = 0$, otherwise.

We consider the space-time graph edge structure as given by the flow based links between neighbouring pixels as presented in Algorithms 1 and 2. Thus, any two pixels (i, j) connected through an optical flow link that vote for the same class (where pixel i is from one frame and pixel j from another) establish an undirected edge between them. These edges define the structure of the graph, with adjacency matrix $\mathbf{M}$.

Then, the weighted class voting can be expressed by correctly defining $\mathbf{M}$, such that $\mathbf{M}_{ia,jb} = w_{ij} = e^{-\lambda * dist(i,j)}$ if and only if (i, j) are connected and class a is the same as class b (class a from frame of pixel i can only vote for the same class in frame of pixel j). One can then show that the iterative voting procedure (Algorithm 2) can be written in simplified matrix form as:

$$\mathbf{p}_{ia}^{(t+1)} \leftarrow \sum_{j \in N_i} \mathbf{M}_{ia,ja} \mathbf{p}_{ja}^{(t)} \tag{1}$$

Note that the sum above is exactly the accumulation of votes coming from the neighbouring frames (labeled at the previous iteration). Also note that as the number of votes per node over all classes is constant (equal to the total number of votes), the vector $\mathbf{p}$ remains $L1$-normalized from one iteration to the next, both at the local level of nodes ($\sum_a \mathbf{p}_{ia} = N_{votes}$) and overall $\sum_{ia} \mathbf{p}_{ia} = N_{pixels} * N_{votes}$. One could immediately observe that Eq. 1 above is the power iteration method for computing the principal eigenvector of matrix $\mathbf{M}$, which must have positive elements since matrix M has positive elements, according to Perron-Frobenius theorem. It also means that the final solution of SegProp should, in principle, always converge to the same solution regardless of initialization as it depends only on $\mathbf{M}$, which is defined by the propagation flow of labels (e.g.. optical flow) and the initial manually labeled frames. Note that those frames should never change their solution and never accumulate votes, a condition that can be easily enforced through the way we set up $\mathbf{M}$.

It is also well known that the principal eigenvector of $\mathbf{M}$ maximizes a segmentation score $S_L(\mathbf{p}) = \mathbf{p}^T \mathbf{M} \mathbf{p}$, under L2-norm constraints on $\mathbf{p}$. In other words, SegProp should converge to $\mathbf{p}^* = \text{argmax}_p S(\mathbf{p}) = \sum_{ia} \sum_{jb} \mathbf{M}_{ia,jb} \mathbf{p}_{ia} \mathbf{p}_{jb}$. Now, if we use the definition of our pairwise terms in $\mathbf{M}$ we can also show that: $S_L(\mathbf{p}) = \sum_{j \in N_i} \mathbf{M}_{ia(i),ja(i)} \mathbf{p}_{ia(i)} \mathbf{p}_{ja(i)} = \sum_i N_i(a(i))$, where $N_i(a(i))$ are the number of neighbours of node i, which have the same label $a(i)$ as i. Thus, maximizing the segmentation score has a natural and intuitive meaning: we will find the segmentation $\mathbf{p}$ that encourages connected nodes to have the same label.

SegProp Theoretical Properties. In summary, we expect SegProp to converge and maximize the quadratic soft-segmentation score with pairwise links $S_L(\mathbf{p}) = \mathbf{p}^T \mathbf{M} \mathbf{p}$, under L2-norm constraints on $\mathbf{p}$. It should do so regardless of the initialization as it only depends on $\mathbf{M}$, defined by the propagation flow and the initial manually labeled frames. Initialization should, however, affect the speed of convergence, as also observed in experiments (Sect. 4.1). Since the segmentation $\mathbf{p}$ has constant L1 norm, we also expect it to converge to the stationary distribution of the random walk, as defined by the transition adjacency matrix $\mathbf{M}$. Thus, the solution, which is the principal eigenvector of $\mathbf{M}$, strongly relates SegProp to spectral clustering [22] and spectral MAP inference [20], a fact that could help us better understand its behaviour in practice.

3   The Ruralscapes Dataset

Manual Annotation Tool. In order to manually annotate the sampled frames, we designed a user-friendly tool that facilitates drawing the contour of objects (in the form of polygons). For each selected polygon we can assign one of the 12 available classes, which include background regions: forest, land, hill, sky, residential, road or water, and also foreground, countable objects: person, church, haystack, fence and car. In the context of total scene segmentation, we assume that the image needs to be fully segmented (e.g., no 'other' class). While there are other annotation tools available [23,24], ours has several novel convenient features for rapid annotation that go beyond simple polygonal annotation.

Our software is suited for high resolution images. Furthermore, it offers support for hybrid contour and point segmentation - the user can alternate between point-based and contour-based segmentation during a single polygon. The most time-saving feature is a 'send to back' functionality to copy the border from the already segmented class to the new one being drawn. This tool is mostly useful in cases when smaller objects are on top of bigger ones (such as cars on the road). Instead of delineating the area surrounding the car twice, one can firstly contour the road and on top that polygon, segment the car.

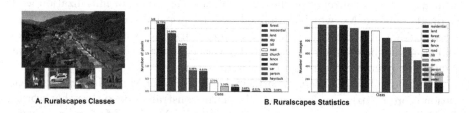

A. Ruralscapes Classes   **B. Ruralscapes Statistics**

Fig. 2. A. Ruralscapes classes. Labels overlaid over RGB image with detail magnification, offering a good level of detail. Ruralscapes also offers large variation in object scale. **B. Ruralscapes statistics.** (Left) Class pixels' distribution. Being a rural landscape, the dominant classes are buildings, land and forest. Due to high altitude, smaller classes such as haystack, car and person hold a very small percentage. (Right) Number of labeled images in which each class is present.

Dataset Details and Statistics. We have collected 20 high quality 4 K videos portraying rural areas. Ruralscapes comprises of various landscapes, different flying scenarios at multiple altitudes and objects across a wide span of scales. The video sequence length varies from 11 s up to 2 min and 45 s. The dataset consists of 17 min of drone flight, resulting in a total of 50,835 fully annotated frames with 12 classes. Of those, 1,047 were manually annotated, once every second. To the best of our knowledge, it is the largest dataset for semantic segmentation from real UAV videos. The distribution of classes in terms of occupied area is shown in Fig. 2(B). Background classes such as forest, land and residential are dominant, while smaller ones such as person and haystack are at the opposite spectrum.

Details Regarding the Annotation Process. Labels offer a good level of detail, but, due to the reduced spatial resolution of the small objects, accurate segmentation is difficult, as seen in the sample label from Fig. 2(A). Some classes, such as haystack, are very small by the nature of the dataset, others such as person, also feature close-ups. Manual labeling is a time consuming process. Based on the feedback received from the 21 volunteers that segmented the dataset, it took them on average 45 min to label an entire frame. This translates into 846 human hours needed to segment the manually labeled 1,047 frames.

4   Experimental Analysis

We evaluate the performance of our proposed method and compare the results to the current state-of-the-art for label propagation [6]. We also train three widely adopted segmentation networks on the automatically generated segmentation labels and report the results compared to the baseline supervised training.

Dataset Split. The whole 20 densely labeled video sequences are divided into 13 training and 7 testing video subsets. We divided the dataset in such a way to be representative enough for the variability of different flying scenarios. We selected the videos in such a manner that the scenes were equally distributed between the training and testing sets. We never have the same exact scene in both train and test. When two videos have similar scenes (w.r.t classes, viewpoint and altitude), we select the longer video for train and the other for test (happened only once). The 7 test videos ($\approx$29.61% of the total frames from the dataset) have 311 manually-labeled frames (used for evaluation metrics) out of a total of 15,051 frames. The 13 training videos have 736 manually-labeled frames out of a total of 35,784 frames that we automatically annotate, starting from the initial manually labeled ones, using SegProp for the semi-supervised learning tests.

For experimental purposes, we sample manually labeled frames every 2 s (every 100th frame, starting with the first) from the training set, and term this set *TrainEven*. The remaining manually-labeled frames, the ones at odd seconds marks, form the *TrainOdd* set, which are used, as explained later, to test the performance of label propagation on the training set itself, before semi-supervised deep learning and evaluation on the unseen test videos. We conducted a more detailed analysis of the influence of having larger temporal gaps between labeled frames over the segmentation performance, shown in Fig. 5(B).

4.1   Comparisons to Other Label Propagation Methods

We use every pair of consecutive ground truth labels, from *TrainEven*, to populate with segmentation labels the remaining 99 frames in between and evaluate

Fig. 3. Qualitative results of our label propagation method. Our iterative SegProp method provides labels that are less noisy and more consistent for larger propagation distances. Also, by looking both forward and backward in time we can better handle occlusion: this is easily visible on the second row in the bottom of the image where forward camera movement obscures a bridge.

on the center frame (from *TrainOdd*), the one that is maximally distant from both manual labels and for which we have ground truth.

We compare our label propagation results with a state-of-the-art method recently proposed by Zhu et al. [6]. We use their method to similarly propagate ground truth labels. Since Zhu et al.'s method works with only one temporal direction at test time, we extract label estimations first forward and then backwards in time, up to a maximum of 50 frames, thus populating all 99 frames in between while keeping the propagation distance minimal. For a fair comparison, we used the same optical flow as [6], namely FlowNet2 [25]. We test our SegProp (Sect. 2) method against [6] and provide results in Table 1. In Fig. 3 we also present some visual comparative results. We also show the effect of initialization on SegProp, when we start it with the solution from [6] vs. initializing with Algorithm 1. SegProp improves in both cases and converges towards the same solution, but at different speeds. Finally, we apply our 3D filtering as a final step to further remove noisy labels and observe another final jump in F-measure.

We have tested different connectivity between frames for the iterative Seg-Prop (Algorithm 2) and settled on the structure which connects the center frame k to frames $[k-10, k-5, k, k+5, k+10]$. As computational costs increase both with the number of frames included in the set and with the distance between them, we find this to be a good compromise between width (inter-frame distance) and depth (number of iterations we can run). Note that P_{k-10} at iteration 3 will have included propagated votes from P_{k-20} on iteration 2, so width indirectly increases with iteration depth.

4.2   Semi-supervised Learning with Automatically Generated Labels

In order to assess the gain brought by the generated labels with SegProp, we train 3 different deep convolutional networks, two of which are widely adopted semantic segmentation models, namely Unet [26] and DeepLabV3+ [27], and

Table 1. Automatic label propagation comparisons. We measure mean F1-score and mean IOU over all classes. We present Zhu et al. [6] (which has only 1 iteration) vs. SegProp starting either from [6] or from Algorithm 1 (our full SegProp Version). An interesting result, which confirms our theoretical expectation is that SegProp (Algorithm 2) seems to converge to the same global relaxed solution, regardless of initialization ([6] to Algorithm 1), albeit with different convergence rates. The final output depends only on the structure of the graph (defined by the flow links) and the manually labeled frames, as expected.

Methods	Iterations								
		1	2	3	4	5	6	7	+ Filt
Zhu et al. [6]	mF1	.846	–	–	–	–	–	–	–
	mIOU	.747	–	–	–	–	–	–	–
SegProp from [6]	mF1	.846	.874	.877	.885	.888	.891	.893	.896
	mIOU	.747	.785	.790	.801	.805	.810	.813	.818
SegProp from Algorithm 1	mF1	.884	.894	.896	**.897**	**.897**	**.897**	**.897**	**.903**
	mIOU	.801	.817	.819	**.821**	**.821**	**.821**	**.821**	**.829**

a model that has previously shown to yield good segmentation results on similar problems, in UAV flying scenarios [28]. Our approach, however, is agnostic of the chosen architecture and could work with any semantic segmentation method. We chose to train Unet since is the de facto standard for semantic segmentation networks and has been widely applied in many scenarios. Ultimately, our goal is to be able to deploy the model and use it on the UAV. Therefore, we trained two embeddable-hardware compatible deep convolutional networks, namely DeepLabv3+ with a MobileNetv2 [29] backbone and SafeUAV-Net Large.

Supervised Baselines. We also trained the same models only on the manually-labeled frames from *TrainEven*. To compensate for the differences in terms of training volume, only for baselines, we apply data augmentation in the form of random rotations, color jittering and random flips, online, during training.

Training Details. Models were trained using the same learning setup. Our deep learning framework of choice is Keras with a backend of Tensorflow. We use RMSprop optimizer with a learning rate starting from $1e-4$ and decreasing it, no more than five times when optimization reaches a plateau. Training is done using the early stopping paradigm. We monitor the error on the validation set and suspend the training when the loss has not decayed for 10 epochs. The models were trained with RGB frames at a spatial resolution of 2048×1080px, rescaled from the original 4K resolution (4096×2160px).

Quantitative results on the testing set are reported in Table 2. We compare our results with reference to the ground truth (manually given labels) from the testing set. The overall score was computed as mean F-measure over the whole classes. Some of the classes were not predicted at all in the supervised baseline case and were marked with .000. It is clear that all methods trained

Table 2. Quantitative results after training the neural networks on the generated labels. We report mean F-measure over all videos from the testing set, for each individual class: (1) - land, (2) - forest, (3) - residential, (4) - haystack, (5) - road, (6) - church, (7) - car, (8) - water, (9) - sky, (10) - hill, (11) - person, (12) - fence and the average over the all classes. The best results for each class and each trained model, are bolded. Results clearly show a significant performance boost over the baseline, when training with SegProp. (*) Due to space limitations we abbreviate SegProp with SP in the table.

Methods	SP*	(1)	(2)	(3)	(4)	(5)	(6)	(7)	(8)	(9)	(10)	(11)	(12)	All
Unet	✗	.681	.497	.834	.000	.000	.000	.000	.000	**.967**	.000	.000	.000	.248
[26]	✓	**.757**	**.544**	**.838**	.000	**.556**	**.672**	.000	.000	.900	**.454**	.000	.000	**.393**
DeepLab	✗	.500	.416	.745	.000	.220	.073	.000	.000	.909	.242	.000	.000	.259
v3+ [27]	✓	**.570**	**.452**	**.776**	**.022**	**.369**	**.122**	**.007**	.000	**.926**	**.272**	**.004**	**.043**	**.297**
SafeUAV	✗	.713	.475	.757	.000	.371	.640	.000	.000	.953	**.260**	.000	.003	.348
Net [28]	✓	**.783**	**.488**	**.836**	**.364**	**.552**	**.748**	**.031**	**.428**	**.973**	.176	**.481**	**.610**	**.515**

in a semi-supervised fashion on the SegProp generated labels (marked with SP) strongly benefit from the label propagation procedure. The relative performance boost, compared to the supervised case, varies from 3.8% for DeepLabv3+ with MobileNetv2 backbone, 14.5% for Unet, and up to 16.7% for SafeUAV-Net. The results also show that small classes experience a significant boost. The "secret" behind recovering classes that are completely lost lies in the label propagation algorithm that is able to add significantly more evidence for classes that are initially not well represented in the ground truth frames: appearing rarely, being very small or often occluded. The ambiguity for the land, forest and hill classes is reflected in our results. Well represented classes in the dataset such as residential areas and land, yield the best results.

Qualitative results on our testing set are shown in Fig. 4. They exhibit good spatial coherency, even though the neural networks process each frame individually. The quality of segmentation is affected by sudden scene geometry changes, cases not well represented in the training videos and motion blur.

4.3   Ablation Studies: The Effect of the Propagation Module

Homography Propagation Module. Even state-of-the-art optical flow is prone to noise. In order to obtain more robust results, we test with the idea of incorporating geometric constraints to improve the class propagation. Thus, we compute two additional class voting maps coming from connected class regions in the labeled frames that are transformed with a homography and placed on the current frame of interest. The homography is estimated in a robust way, with RANSAC, using as correspondences the already computed flow maps between the labeled frames and the current one. Adding the homography based votes to the optical flow votes improves the results (Table 3) even from the first propagation iteration. Then, by applying our 3D filtering step on top, we further

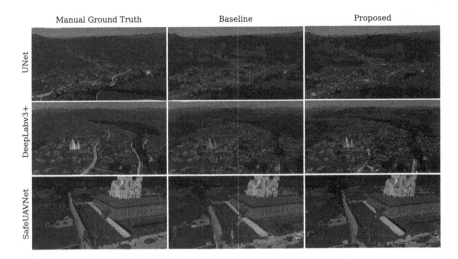

Fig. 4. Qualitative results on the testing set. The results show that our proposed method leads to significantly more accurate segmentation in the semi-supervised scenario rather than the supervised case. SegProp clearly benefits the smaller, not well represented, classes such as person (third row).

improve performance. While the homography based voting is clearly superior it is also much more computationally intensive, reason for which we did not include it in the other experiments presented in the paper. Note that voting propagation based on homography is particularly useful for edge preservation, where the CNN-based optical flow generally lacks precision (see Fig. 5(A)).

Other Vote Propagation Modules. As mentioned in Sect. 2 we could in principle use any label propagation method to bring in more votes. Thus, in the same way we added homography voting to the initial optical flow ones, we also added two more class votes by using the method of Zhu et al. [6] to propagate class labels from the manually labeled frames to each unlabeled one. We weighted the votes with a validated parameter ($w = 0.25$) and observed another additional performance gain (see Table 3), even from the first iteration. Since it would have

Table 3. Ablation studies comparison. We run SegProp including other votes next to our optical flow based mappings, measuring mean F-measure over all classes. For the version with homography voting we also run the final filtering step. The bolded values are the best results.

Method	Iteration	Overall
Zhu et al. [6]	1	.846
SegProp	1	.884
SegProp + Zhu et al. [6]	1	.892
SegProp + Homography	1	.894
SegProp + Homography + Filtering	1	**.904**

been computationally expensive to re-apply the method in [6] for voting, we have only tested with one iteration. Optical flow voting, while not the most accurate, remains very fast (computed only once at the start) and enables SegProp to achieve a significant boost over iterations.

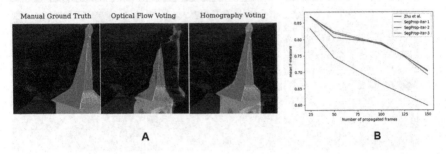

Fig. 5. A. Label propagation example showing typical optical flow voting difficulties. From left to right: RGB frame with manual white label overlaid, flow-based voting, homography-based voting. **B.** The influence of increasingly larger temporal gaps between labeled frames over the segmentation performance (mean F-measure over all classes on a subset of videos labeled with a frequency of 25 frames).

Influence of Temporal Propagation Length. We measured the degradation in performance as the propagation temporal length increases, from 25 frames to 150 frames and also compared with Zhu et al. [6] (Fig. 5(B)). We performed the study on a subset of clips that are annotated every 25 frames (1/3 of the dataset), such that the evaluation can be done at every 25 frames as the propagation period increases. We measure mean F-measure over all classes from the selected videos. Note that our performance degrades slower than that of [6].

5   Conclusions

We introduced SegProp, an efficient iterative label propagation algorithm for semi-supervised semantic segmentation in aerial videos. We also introduced Ruralscapes, the largest high resolution (4 K) dataset for dense semantic segmentation in aerial videos from real UAV flights - which we make publicly available alongside a fast segmentation tool and our label propagation code[1], in a bid to help aerial segmentation algorithms. We have demonstrated in extensive experiments that SegProp outperforms other published labeled propagation algorithms, while also being able to work in conjunction with similar methods. Moreover, we have showed in semi-supervised learning experiments that deep neural networks for semantic image segmentation could extensively benefit

---

[1] We make our code, dataset and annotation tool publicly available at: https:// sites.google.com/site/aerialimageunderstanding/semantics-through-time-semi-supervised-segmentation-of-aerial-videos.

(by up to 16% increase in F-measure) from the added training labels using the proposed label propagation algorithm. SegProp is fast (it only needs to compute the optical flow once) and flexible, being able to integrate other label propagation methods. Furthermore, it has provable convergence and optimality properties. We believe that our work, introducing a well-needed dataset and algorithm, with strong experimental results, could bring a solid contribution to semantic segmentation in video and UAV research.

Acknowledgements. This work was funded by UEFISCDI, under Projects EEA-RO-2018-0496 and PN-III-P1-1.2-PCCDI-2017-0734. We express our sincere thanks to Aurelian Marcu and The Center for Advanced Laser Technologies (CETAL) for providing access to their GPU computational resources.

References

1. Le, H., Nguyen, V., Yu, C.-P., Samaras, D.: Geodesic distance histogram feature for video segmentation. In: Lai, S.-H., Lepetit, V., Nishino, K., Sato, Y. (eds.) ACCV 2016. LNCS, vol. 10111, pp. 275–290. Springer, Cham (2017). https://doi.org/10.1007/978-3-319-54181-5_18
2. Galasso, F., Cipolla, R., Schiele, B.: Video segmentation with superpixels. In: Lee, K.M., Matsushita, Y., Rehg, J.M., Hu, Z. (eds.) ACCV 2012. LNCS, vol. 7724, pp. 760–774. Springer, Heidelberg (2013). https://doi.org/10.1007/978-3-642-37331-2_57
3. Budvytis, I., Sauer, P., Roddick, T., Breen, K., Cipolla, R.: Large scale labelled video data augmentation for semantic segmentation in driving scenarios. In: Proceedings of the IEEE International Conference on Computer Vision, pp. 230–237 (2017)
4. Mustikovela, S.K., Yang, M.Y., Rother, C.: Can ground truth label propagation from video help semantic segmentation? In: European Conference on Computer Vision, Springer, pp. 804–820 (2016)
5. Chen, A.Y., Corso, J.J.: Propagating multi-class pixel labels throughout video frames. In: 2010 Western New York Image Processing Workshop, pp. 14–17. IEEE (2010)
6. Zhu, Y., et al.: Improving semantic segmentation via video propagation and label relaxation. In: Proceedings of the IEEE Conference on Computer Vision and Pattern Recognition, pp. 8856–8865 (2019)
7. Geiger, A., Lenz, P., Stiller, C., Urtasun, R.: Vision meets robotics: the KITTI dataset. Int. J. Robot. Res. **32**, 1231–1237 (2013)
8. Budvytis, I., Badrinarayanan, V., Cipolla, R.: Label propagation in complex video sequences using semi-supervised learning. BMVC **2257**, 2258–2259 (2010)
9. Reza, M.A., Zheng, H., Georgakis, G., Košecká, J.: Label propagation in RGB-D video. In: 2017 IEEE/RSJ International Conference on Intelligent Robots and Systems (IROS), pp. 4917–4922. IEEE (2017)
10. Lin, T.Y., et al.: Microsoft COCO: common objects in context. In: Fleet, D., Pajdla, T., Schiele, B., Tuytelaars, T. (eds.) ECCV 2014. LNCS, vol. 8693, pp. 740–755. Springer, Cham (2014). https://doi.org/10.1007/978-3-319-10602-1_48
11. Cordts, M., et al.: The cityscapes dataset for semantic urban scene understanding. In: Proceeding of the IEEE Conference on Computer Vision and Pattern Recognition (CVPR) (2016)

12. Huang, X., et al.: The apolloscape dataset for autonomous driving. In: Proceedings of the IEEE Conference on Computer Vision and Pattern Recognition Workshops, pp. 954–960 (2018)
13. Nigam, I., Huang, C., Ramanan, D.: Ensemble knowledge transfer for semantic segmentation. In: 2018 IEEE Winter Conference on Applications of Computer Vision (WACV), pp. 1499–1508. IEEE (2018)
14. Lyu, Y., Vosselman, G., Xia, G., Yilmaz, A., Yang, M.Y.: The uavid dataset for video semantic segmentation. arXiv preprint arXiv:1810.10438 (2018)
15. Richter, S.R., Hayder, Z., Koltun, V.: Playing for benchmarks. In: Proceedings of the IEEE International Conference on Computer Vision, pp. 2213–2222 (2017)
16. Fonder, M., Droogenbroeck, M.V.: Mid-air: a multi-modal dataset for extremely low altitude drone flights. In: Conference on Computer Vision and Pattern Recognition Workshop (CVPRW) (2019)
17. Li, S.Z.: Markov random field models in computer vision. In: Eklundh, J.-O. (ed.) ECCV 1994. LNCS, vol. 801, pp. 361–370. Springer, Heidelberg (1994). https://doi.org/10.1007/BFb0028368
18. Hummel, R.A., Zucker, S.W.: On the foundations of relaxation labeling processes. IEEE Trans. Pattern Anal. Mach. Intell. **3**, 267–287 (1983)
19. Rangarajan, A.: Self-annealing and self-annihilation: unifying deterministic annealing and relaxation labeling. Pattern Recogn. **33**, 635–649 (2000)
20. Leordeanu, M., Hebert, M.: Efficient map approximation for dense energy functions. In: Proceedings of the 23rd International Conference on Machine Learning, pp. 545–552 (2006)
21. Besag, J.: On the statistical analysis of dirty pictures. J. Royal Stat. Soc. Ser. B (Methodol.) **48**, 259–279 (1986)
22. Meila, M., Shi, J.: A random walks view of spectral segmentation. In: AISTATS (2001)
23. Brooks, J.: COCO Annotator (2019). https://github.com/jsbroks/coco-annotator/
24. Russell, B.C., Torralba, A., Murphy, K.P., Freeman, W.T.: LabelMe: a database and web-based tool for image annotation. Int. J. Comput. Vis. **77**, 157–173 (2008)
25. Ilg, E., Mayer, N., Saikia, T., Keuper, M., Dosovitskiy, A., Brox, T.: FlowNet 2.0: evolution of optical flow estimation with deep networks. In: Proceedings of the IEEE Conference on Computer Vision and Pattern Recognition, pp. 2462–2470 (2017)
26. Ronneberger, O., Fischer, P., Brox, T.: U-Net: convolutional networks for biomedical image segmentation. In: Navab, N., Hornegger, J., Wells, W.M., Frangi, A.F. (eds.) MICCAI 2015. LNCS, vol. 9351, pp. 234–241. Springer, Cham (2015). https://doi.org/10.1007/978-3-319-24574-4_28
27. Chen, L.-C., Zhu, Y., Papandreou, G., Schroff, F., Adam, H.: Encoder-decoder with atrous separable convolution for semantic image segmentation. In: Ferrari, V., Hebert, M., Sminchisescu, C., Weiss, Y. (eds.) ECCV 2018. LNCS, vol. 11211, pp. 833–851. Springer, Cham (2018). https://doi.org/10.1007/978-3-030-01234-2_49
28. Marcu, A., Costea, D., Licaret, V., Pîrvu, M., Slusanschi, E., Leordeanu, M.: SafeUAV: learning to estimate depth and safe landing areas for UAVs from synthetic data. In: Proceedings of the European Conference on Computer Vision (ECCV) (2018)
29. Sandler, M., Howard, A., Zhu, M., Zhmoginov, A., Chen, L.C.: MobileNetV2: inverted residuals and linear bottlenecks. In: Proceedings of the IEEE Conference on Computer Vision and Pattern Recognition, pp. 4510–4520 (2018)

Dense Dual-Path Network for Real-Time Semantic Segmentation

Xinneng Yang[1], Yan Wu[1(✉)], Junqiao Zhao[1,2], and Feilin Liu[1]

[1] College of Electronics and Information Engineering, Tongji University,
Shanghai, China
yanwu@tongji.edu.cn
[2] Institute of Intelligent Vehicle, Tongji University, Shanghai, China

Abstract. Semantic segmentation has achieved remarkable results with high computational cost and a large number of parameters. However, real-world applications require efficient inference speed on embedded devices. Most previous works address the challenge by reducing depth, width and layer capacity of network, which leads to poor performance. In this paper, we introduce a novel Dense Dual-Path Network (DDP-Net) for real-time semantic segmentation under resource constraints. We design a light-weight and powerful backbone with dense connectivity to facilitate feature reuse throughout the whole network and the proposed Dual-Path module (DPM) to sufficiently aggregate multi-scale contexts. Meanwhile, a simple and effective framework is built with a skip architecture utilizing the high-resolution feature maps to refine the segmentation output and an upsampling module leveraging context information from the feature maps to refine the heatmaps. The proposed DDPNet shows an obvious advantage in balancing accuracy and speed. Specifically, on Cityscapes test dataset, DDPNet achieves 75.3% mIoU with 52.6 FPS for an input of 1024×2048 resolution on a single GTX 1080Ti card. Compared with other state-of-the-art methods, DDPNet achieves a significant better accuracy with a comparable speed and fewer parameters.

1 Introduction

Semantic segmentation is a fundamental task in computer vision, the purpose of which is to assign semantic labels to each image pixel. It has many potential applications in the fields of autonomous driving, video surveillance, robot sensing and so on. Existing methods mainly focus on improving accuracy. However, these real-world applications require efficient inference speed on high-resolution images.

Previous works [1–6] have already obtained outstanding performances on various benchmarks [7–11]. By analyzing existing state-of-the-art semantic segmentation methods, we find the keys to achieving high accuracy. 1) The backbone

Electronic supplementary material The online version of this chapter (https://doi.org/10.1007/978-3-030-69525-5_33) contains supplementary material, which is available to authorized users.

of these methods has a powerful feature extraction capability, such as ResNet [12], ResNeXt [13], DenseNet [14], which is usually pre-trained on ImageNet [15]. These backbones have a strong generalization capability and thus are adapted to many computer vision tasks. 2) These methods aggregate multi-scale context information sufficiently. There are many objects in semantic segmentation that are difficult to be distinguished only by their appearance, such as 'field' and 'grass', 'building' and 'wall'. Due to multiple scales, occlusion and illumination, some objects like 'car' and 'person' require multi-scale context information to be correctly identified. To address above issues, dilated convolution and pooling operation are often used to enlarge the receptive field. Even though the theoretical receptive field is large enough, it still can't fully exploit the capability of global context information. Therefore, some approaches [1,4,6,16,17] aggregate multi-scale contexts via fusing feature maps generated by parallel dilated convolutions and pooling operations to robustly segment objects at multiple scales. 3) These methods recover spatial information effectively. Downsampling enlarges the receptive field and decreases the size of feature maps. It enriches high-level features, but loses spatial details. However, detailed spatial information is essential for semantic segmentation. In order to preserve spatial information, most works [1,3,4,6] remove the last two pooling operations and replace the subsequent convolutions with dilated convolutions to keep the receptive field unchanged at the expense of computational efficiency. Unlike them, [2,5,18–22] utilize upsampling methods and self-designed skip connection to refine the boundaries of objects and small objects.

Based on the above analysis, we summarize the keys to achieving high accuracy in semantic segmentation as follows:

- Backbone with a powerful feature extraction capability.
- Sufficient aggregation of context information.
- Effective recovery of spatial information.

Recently, real-time semantic segmentation methods [23–28] have shown prom-ising results. [29,30] reduce the input size to accelerate the model, while easily losing the spatial details around boundaries and small objects. [31,32] remove some of downsampling operations to create an extremely small model. Nevertheless, the receptive field of these models is not sufficient to cover large objects, resulting in a poor performance. To achieve real-time speed, some works [23,25,31–33] design a specialized network for semantic segmentation as backbone. Differently, some works [24,26–28,34] adopt a light-weight classification network as backbone, such as MobileNets [35–37], ShuffleNets [38,39], ResNet-18 [12]. Convolution factorization refers to the decomposition of a large convolution operation into several smaller operations, such as factorized convolution and depth-wise separable convolution, which is widely adopted in these backbones to reduce the computational cost and the number of parameters. However, convolution factorization is not conducive to GPU parallel processing, which results in a much slower inference speed under the same computational budget. On the other hand, these backbones have a limited capability due to fewer convolution operations and feature maps. Recent works [27,30,40] propose a two-column network which consists of a deep network for encoding context information and a shallow network for capturing spatial information. However, the extra network on high-resolution images limits the inference speed, and the independence between networks limits the performance of the model.

To strike a better balance between accuracy and efficiency, we follow the principle of simplicity in designing the model. A complicated and sophisticated work may improve accuracy, but in most cases it hurts efficiency significantly. A simple and clean framework can make it easier to re-implement and improve. Therefore, we propose a light-weight yet powerful backbone and a simple yet effective framework for fast and accurate semantic segmentation. The proposed Dense Dual-Path Network (DDPNet) achieves 75.3% mIoU with merely 2.53M parameters on Cityscapes test dataset. It can run on high-resolution images (1024×2048) at 52.6 FPS on a single GTX 1080Ti card. DDPNet is superior to most of the state-of-the-art real-time semantic segmentation methods in accuracy and speed, and requires fewer parameters.

Our main contributions are summarized as follows:

- We design a light-weight and powerful backbone with dense connectivity to facilitate feature reuse throughout the whole network and the proposed Dual-Path module (DPM) to sufficiently aggregate multi-scale contexts.
- We propose a simple and effective framework with a skip architecture utilizing the high-resolution feature maps to refine the segmentation output and an upsampling module leveraging context information from the feature maps to refine the heatmaps.
- We conduct a series of experiments on two standard benchmarks, Cityscapes and CamVid, to investigate the effectiveness of each component of our proposed DDPNet and compare accuracy and efficiency with other state-of-the-art methods.

2   Related Work

Recently, FCN [20] based methods have greatly improved the performance of semantic segmentation. Most of them focus on encoding content information and recovering spatial information.

Real-Time Segmentation: The goal of real-time semantic segmentation is to achieve the best trade off between accuracy and efficiency. In order to reach a real-time speed, SegNet [41] and U-Net [42] perform multiple downsampling operations to significantly reduce the feature map size. SegNet designs a symmetric encoder-decoder architecture to carefully recover feature maps. U-Net proposes a symmetric architecture with skip connection to enable precise localization. Differently, E-Net [32] constructs an extremely light-weight network with fewer downsampling operations to boost the inference speed. ERFNet [33] focuses on a better accuracy with a deeper network that uses residual connection and factorized convolution. ESPNet [31] proposes a light-weight network with efficient spatial pyramid module. ICNet [30] uses an image cascade network to capture objects of different sizes from multi-scale images. BiSeNet [27] designs a spatial path to preserve spatial information and a context path to obtain sufficient receptive field. Based on multi-scale feature propagation, DFANet [24] reduces the number of parameters and maintains high accuracy.

Context Information: Semantic segmentation needs to sufficiently obtain context information to correctly identify objects that are similar in appearance but belong to different categories and objects that are different in appearance but belong to the same category. Most works capture diverse context information by using different dilation convolutions to enlarge the receptive field. DeepLab [16] proposes an atrous spatial pyramid pooling module to aggregate multi-scale contexts. In the follow-up work, [17] further improves performance by extending the previously proposed atrous spatial pyramid pooling module with a global average pool, which is able to capture the global context of images. Similarly, PSPNet [6] proposes a pyramid pooling module which consists of different sizes of average pooling operations to aggregate multi-scale contexts. [43] designs a scale-adaptive convolution to acquire flexible-size receptive fields. PAN [44] combines attention mechanism and spatial pyramid to learn a better feature representation. DMNet [4] adaptively captures multi-scale contents with multiple dynamic convolutional modules arranged in parallel.

Spatial Information: Semantic segmentation requires spatial details to restore the boundaries of objects and small objects. The reason for the loss of spatial details is downsampling operations in the convolutional network. Downsampling is essential for convolutional networks because it can reduce the size of feature maps and enlarge the receptive field. Most works reduce the number of downsampling operations to preserve spatial details, which leads to slow inference speed. Differently, [21,32,33,41] construct an encoder-decoder structure with unpooling and deconvolution to recover spatial details. However, this structure still can not effectively recover the loss of spatial details and have high computational complexity. Skip connection is first introduced in FCN [20], which combines semantic information from a deep layer with appearance information from a shallow layer to produce accurate and detailed segmentation result. Based on FCNs, RefineNet [19] presents a multi-path refinement network that refines high-level semantic features using long-range residual connection. BiseNet [27] and Fast-SCNN [40] explicitly acquire spatial information at a fast inference speed using a light-weight spatial path.

3 Dense Dual-Path Network

In this section, we introduce the backbone of DDPNet and the proposed framework for real-time semantic segmentation. Furthermore, we elaborate the design choices and motivations in detail.

3.1 Dense Connectivity

The backbone of DDPNet is a variant of densely connected convolutional network, which adopts dense connectivity to stack convolution operations.

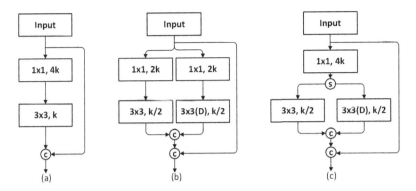

Fig. 1. Depiction of the dense layer originally proposed in DenseNet [14], and our proposed Dual-Path module (DPM). "k": the growth rate. "D": dilated convolution. "c": channel concatenate operation. "s": channel split operation. In the convolutional blocks, "$s1 \times s2, n_o$" indicates their kernel sizes (s_1, s_2) and the number of output feature maps (n_o). (a) Original dense layer. (b, c) Dual-Path Module. For brevity, we omit normalization and activation function.

Dense connectivity is originally proposed by DenseNet [14], in which each layer has direct connections to all subsequent layers. Formally, the mth layer takes feature maps from all preceding layers as input:

$$x_m = H_m([x_0, x_1, ..., x_{m-1}]) \tag{1}$$

where x_n, $n \in [1, 2, ..., m]$ refers to the output of nth layer. x_0 refers to the input of dense block, bracket indicates concatenation operation, and H is a composite function of three consecutive operations: batch normalization [45], followed by a rectified linear unit [46] and a convolution operation.

Some works [47,48] utilize dense connectivity in the network to boost the performance of semantic segmentation. However, they focus on accuracy rather than speed. Dense connectivity allows for the reuse of features throughout the network and significantly reduces the number of parameters, which contributes to the implementation of light-weight models. Therefore, we use dense connectivity to build a light-weight and powerful backbone for real-time semantic segmentation. Following PeleeNet [49], we use post-activation as composite function, which conducts convolution operation before batch normalization, for improving inference speed.

3.2 Dual-Path Module

Dual-Path module (DPM) is the basic unit of dense block. Motivated by the diversity of object scales in semantic segmentation, we propose a specific Dual-Path module composed of two bottleneck layers in parallel. One of the bottleneck layers uses a point-wise convolution to reduce the number of input feature maps, followed by a 3×3 convolution to produce $\frac{k}{2}$ new feature maps. k refers to the growth rate. The other bottleneck layer replaces the 3 × 3 convolution with dilation convolutions to learn visual patterns for large objects. The structural details are shown in Fig. 1(b). We refer this structure as DPM-b. Notice that the point-wise convolutions in both branches have the same input. Therefore, we combine the two point-wise convolutions into one, and split the output of the convolution into two independent inputs for the two branches, as depicted in Fig. 1(c). We refer this structure as DPM-c. The two implementations are functionally identical but differ in efficiency. DPM-c is more efficient than DPM-b in GPU parallel processing. For this reason, we adopt the structure of DPM-c as our final implementation of DPM. Finally, the output of two branches is concatenated, followed by a dropout layer [50].

As can be seen from Fig. 1, Dual-Path module has a larger effective receptive field than the original dense layer. With an extra dilated branch in dense layer, Dual-Path module can extract features from different scales. Intuitively, more branches can aggregate multi-scale contexts more effectively, such as ASPP in [16]. However, the decomposition of a single convolution into multiple parallel convolutions is not conducive to the acceleration of the model. Due to the ability to effectively aggregate feature maps at different scales, Dual-Path module significantly improves the capacity of backbone.

3.3   Backbone Design

In this subsection, we discuss the main components and algorithms used to build the backbone of Dense Dual-Path Network. In this work, we aim to design an architecture that gets the best possible trade-off between accuracy and efficiency. Many approaches that focus on designing a light-weight architecture largely adopt depth-wise separable convolution and factorized convolution which lack efficient implementation. Instead of using depth-wise separable convolution or factorized convolution, Dense Dual-Path Network is build with traditional convolution.

Transition Layer. Transition layer is used to reduce the size of feature maps and compress the model. It is composed of a point-wise convolution followed by a 2 × 2 average pooling layer. In order to fully exploit dense connectivity, DDPNet keeps the number of input channels and output channels the same in all transition layers. This design facilitates feature reuse throughout the whole network.

Initial Block. Initial block is used to reduce the input size, which typically involves several downsampling operations. Due to direct operation on the original image, initial block is often computationally expensive. However, a well-designed initial block can effectively improve feature expression and preserve rich spatial information. The initial block of DPPNet is motivated by ENet [32] and PeleeNet [49], which preserves rich spatial information and takes full advantage of feature reuse. In our initial block, a 3 × 3 convolution with stride 2 is performed on the original image, followed by two branches. One of the branches is a 3 × 3 convolution with stride 2. The other branch is a 2×2 max pooling layer with stride 2. Finally, the output of two branches is concatenated.

Table 1. The backbone of our proposed DDPNet. "$DenseLayer\,(or\,DPM) \times n_d, k$" indicates the operation in dense block is the original dense layer ($DenseLayer$) or the proposed Dual-Path module (DPM), the number of layers (n_d) and the growth rate (k). Input size is ($1024 \times 2048 \times 3$).

Type	Operator	Output shape
Initial block		$256 \times 512 \times 64$
Dense block	Dense Layer $\times$ 2, k = 32	$256 \times 512 \times 128$
Transition layer	1×1 conv, stride 1	$128 \times 256 \times 128$
	2×2 average pool, stride 2	
Dense block	Dense layer $\times$ 4, k = 32	$128 \times 256 \times 256$
Transition layer	1×1 conv, stride 1	$64 \times 128 \times 256$
	2×2 average pool, stride 2	
Dense block	DPM $\times$ 8, k = 32	$64 \times 128 \times 512$
Transition layer	1×1 conv, stride 1	$32 \times 64 \times 512$
	2×2 average pool, stride 2	
Dense block	DPM $\times$ 8, k = 32	$32 \times 64 \times 768$
Transition layer	1×1 conv, stride 1	$32 \times 64 \times 768$

Architecture Detail. The backbone of our proposed DDPNet is shown in Table 1. The entire architecture consists of an initial block and four dense blocks followed by a transition layer. To maintain a better balance between accuracy and computational cost, DDPNet first reduces spatial resolution twice in the initial block and performs downsampling operation in each transition layer (except for the last one). Except for the last block, DDPNet doubles the number of feature maps in each dense block.

In DenseNet [14], each layer produces k new feature maps, where k refers to as the growth rate. The growth rate is usually a small constant due to feature reuse. With a fixed number of output channels and a fixed growth rate, we can get the number of layers in a certain block. For example, the nth block has $\frac{(n_{out}-n_{in})}{k}$ layers, where n_{out} is the number of channels at the end of the block, and n_{in} is the number of channels in the input layer. As mentioned in [14,51], convolution layers in a deeper block tend to rely more on high-level features than on low-level features. Based on this observation, DDPNet produces more new feature maps in deeper blocks, which means that more layers are needed in deeper blocks.

Since the feature maps from a higher layer contain more semantic information and less spatial information, we adopt the original dense layer in the first two blocks and replace the original dense layer with Dual-Path module in the last two blocks. We explore further in the experiment section. A larger growth rate requires fewer layers to generate new feature maps, which can boost the inference speed. However, a smaller growth rate forms a denser connections, which improves the quality of feature maps. To strike a better balance between accuracy and efficiency, we set the growth rate to 32 in DDPNet.

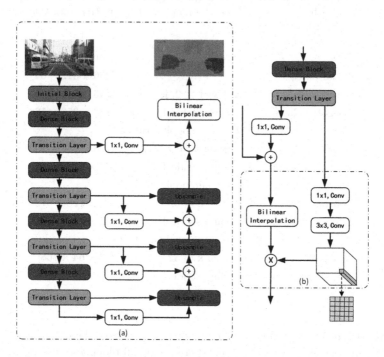

Fig. 2. (a) Framework of the proposed DDPNet. (b) Architecture details of the usampling module. Note that the feature maps used to generate heatmaps are the output of the point-wise convolution in transition layer before downsampling. For brevity, we refer to these feature maps as the output of transition layer in this diagram. "+": element-wise addition. "×": weighted sum operation.

3.4   Framework for Real-Time Semantic Segmentation

In this subsection, we propose a simple and effective framework for real-time semantic segmentation. Figure 2(a) shows the overall framework. The proposed backbone and the framework are adopted to construct the DDPNet. The backbone can be other classification networks, such as ResNet [13]. Most of the frameworks used for real-time semantic segmentation adopt an encoder-decoder architecture. The encoder is used to provide information for the final classification and reduce the computational cost by downsampling. The main purpose of the decoder is to recover the spatial details lost during the downsampling process.

Skip Architecture. DDPNet employs an asymmetric sequential architecture, where an extreme light-weight decoder is adopted to upsample the feature maps to match the input resolution. The decoder of DDPNet is a skip architecture, which utilizes the high-resolution feature maps to refine the segmentation output. In U-Net [42], skip connection is performed on the feature space, which is very computational expensive because it is directly affected by the number of channels. To accelerate the inference speed, DDPNet adopts skip connection on heatmaps in the label space, similar to FCN [20]. The output of each transition layer is followed by a point-wise convolution to map from feature space to label space, resulting in a heatmap corresponding to each class. Note that the feature maps used to generate heatmaps are the output of the point-wise convolution in transition layer before downsampling. For convenience, we refer to these feature maps as the output of transition layer in the following paper. A low-resolution heatmap is upsampled by an upsampling module, and then element-wise addition is performed between this heatmap and a high-resolution heatmap. After three skip connections, a bilinear interpolation with stride 4 is adopted to produce the final output. Figure 2(a) shows the overall framework of DDPNet.

Upsampling Module. The commonly used upsampling methods in semantic segmentation are bilinear interpolation and deconvolution. Bilinear interpolation is computationally cheap, but only leverages the distance information between pixels. Deconvolution uses fixed kernels to perform upsampling, which has been proved to be limited and inefficient. The upsampling module of DDPNet is modified from [22] to save a lot of computation by performing upsampling on label space instead of upsampling on feature space. More specifically, DDPNet uses a bilinear interpolation to upsample the heatmap and refine the upsampled heatmap with a dynamic filtering layer. Dynamic filtering layer is originally proposed in dynamic filter networks [52]. In dynamic filter networks, a dynamic filter module consists of a filter generating path that produces filters based on one input, and a dynamic filtering layer that applies the generated filters to another input. In the upsampling module of DDPNet, the filter generating path takes the output of transition layer as input, then compresses the input feature channel with a point-wise convolution. Finally, a 3×3 convolution followed by a pixel shuffle operation and a softmax is used to generate the filters. In dynamic filtering layer, the generated filters are applied to refine the upsampled heatmap, which is a weighted sum operation. Formally, the upsampling module can be written as

$$\mathbf{Y} = U(\mathbf{X_1}) \otimes \delta(S(N(F^1(w_{3 \times 3}, \sigma(N(F^2(w_{1 \times 1}, \mathbf{X_2}))))))) \tag{2}$$

where Y and X are the output and input of the upsampling module respectively. X_1 and X_2 refer to the input of dynamic filtering layer and filter generating path. U denotes bilinear interpolation, $\otimes$ indicates weighted sum operation, F and N represent convolution operation and batch normalization, S refers to pixel shuffle operation, σ and δ indicate ReLU and softmax activation. $w_{n \times n}$ is convolutional parameter and n represents kernel size. Figure 2(b) shows the detailed architecture of the upsampling module.

4   Experiment

In this section, we evaluate the proposed DDPNet on Cityscapes [8] and CamVid [7] benchmarks. We first introduce the datasets and the implementation proto-col. Then, we conduct a series of experiments on Cityscapes validation set to investigate the effectiveness of each component of our proposed method. Finally, we report the accuracy and efficiency results compared with other state-of-the-art methods. All accuracy results are reported using the commonly used mean Intersection-over-Union (IoU) metric. Runtime evaluations are performed on a single 1080Ti card. To eliminate the error fluctuation, we report an average of 5000 frames for the frames per second (FPS) measurement.

Cityscapes. The Cityscapes dataset is a large urban street scene dataset which is collected from 50 different cities. It contains 5000 fine annotated images, which are split into three sets: 2975 images for training, 500 images for validation, and 1525 images for testing. For fair a comparison, the 1525 test images is offered without ground-truth. There is another set of 19,998 images with coarse annotation, but we only use the fine annotated images for all experiments. All images have a resolution of 1024×2048, in which each pixel is annotated to pre-defined 19 classes.

CamVid. The CamVid dataset is another street scene dataset which is extracted from video sequences. It contains 701 images, which are split into three sets: 367 images for training, 101 images for validation, and 233 images for testing. All images have a resolution of 720×960 and 11 semantic categories. Following the general settings, we reduce the image resolution to 360×480 and use the training set and the validation set to train our model, then test it on the test set.

4.1   Implementation Protocol

We conduct all experiments using PyTorch with CUDA 10.0 and cuDNN back-ends on a single 1080Ti card. We use Adam optimizer [53] with batch size 8 and weight decay $2e^{-4}$ in training. For learning rate schedule, we use the learning rate warmup strategy suggested by [54] and the cosine learning rate decay policy. The learning rate l_i is computed as:

$$l_i = \frac{1}{2} \times \left(1 + \cos \frac{i \times \pi}{T} \right) \times l_{base} \tag{3}$$

where i refers to current epoch, the maximum number of epochs T is set to 350 for training on Cityscapes and 700 for training on CamVid, the initial learning rate l_{base} is $5e^{-4}$. As for data augmentation, we employ mean subtraction, random horizontal flip and random scale on the input images during training. A random parameter between $[0.75, 2]$ is used to transform the images to different scales. Finally, we randomly crop the images into fixed size for training.

4.2   Ablation Study

In this subsection, we perform a series of experiments to evaluate the effectiveness of each component in our proposed DDPNet. All ablation studies are trained on Cityscapes training set and evaluated on Cityscapes validation set. We reduce the image size to 768×1536 to accelerate the training process and evaluate the accuracy and efficiency of our models. For a fair comparison, we use the same training settings for all models.

Table 2. Ablation studies for dense connectivity and DPM. All models are trained from scratch on Cityscapes training set and evaluated on Cityscapes validation set. The numbers in brackets denote the performance improvement over the baseline. The bold entries are the final settings for DDPNet.

Model	mIoU (%)	Time (ms)	FPS	Para	FLOPs	Memory
Baseline	72.8	9.5	105.7	2.7M	13.7G	333 MB
ResNet [12]	70.9	9.8	101.6	11.2M	41.7G	287 MB
PeleeNet [49]	72.5	11.7	85.3	2.1M	12.3G	406 MB
+ $DPM \times 1$	74.6 (+1.8)	10.3	97.4	2.6M	13.5G	333 MB
+ DPM $\times$ 2	75.5 (+2.7)	11.2	89.4	2.4M	12.8G	333 MB
+ $DPM \times 4$	74.7 (+1.9)	11.7	85.5	2.4M	11.5G	333 MB

Ablation Study for Dense Connectivity and DPM. We first explore the effects of dense connectivity and Dual-Path module specifically. A densely connected convolutional network without compression in transition layer is built as our backbone. The growth rate is set to 32. The proposed initial block and a skip architecture are adopted to construct a baseline for semantic segmentation. We replace the backbone with the frequently used ResNet-18 [12] to make a comparison between two different connection mechanisms. As suggested by [54], we adopt a modified ResNet, which replace the 1×1 convolution with stride 2 in downsampling block with a 2×2 average pooling layer with stride 2 followed by a 1×1 convolution with stride 1. As can be seen from Table 2, our baseline is far more accurate (72.8% VS 70.9%) and efficient than ResNet. Due to feature reuse, our baseline has 4× fewer parameters and 3× fewer FLOPs than ResNet, which results in a much lower power consumption. To better understand the DPM, we replace the original dense layer with the proposed DPM stage by stage. Equipping the DPM in the last stage alone can boost the baseline by 1.8% (72.8% → 74.6%) in accuracy with a slight drop in inference speed. We continue to adopt the DPM in the third stage, which brings in 2.7% (72.8% → 75.5%) improvement to the baseline. However, adopting more DPMs at early stages does not yield further benefits. It verifies that feature maps from an early stage contain more spatial details, which is essential for further feature representation. Therefore, we adopt the original dense layer in the first two blocks and replace the original dense layer with the proposed DPM in the last two blocks as the backbone of DDPNet. Here, we adopt an increasing dilation rate in dense blocks to fully explore the ability to aggregate feature maps at different scales. For example, the dilation rate sequence of the third dense block is set to {2, 4, 8, 16, 2, 4, 8, 16}. We also try to set all dilation rates to a fixed number, or increase them gradually in different ways, which all lead to a slight decrease in accuracy. We compare DDPNet with PeleeNet [49], which utilizes a different way to aggregate multi-scale representations. Table 2 shows that DDPNet is superior to PeleeNet (75.5% VS 72.5%).

Table 3. Ablation studies for skip architecture and upsampling module. All models are trained from scratch on Cityscapes training set and evaluated on Cityscapes validation set. The numbers in brackets denote the performance improvement or degradation over the baseline. The bold entries are the final settings for DDPNet.

Model	mIoU (%)	Time (ms)	FPS	Para	FLOPs	Memory
Baseline	69.7	10.7	93.4	2.4M	12.5G	326 MB
+ Skip architecture	75.5 (+5.8)	11.2 (+0.5)	89.4	2.4M	12.8G	333 MB
+ Upsampling module	76.2 (+6.5)	11.7 (+1.0)	85.4	2.5M	13.2G	412 MB
+ U-Net architecture	75.2 (+5.5)	11.7 (+1.0)	85.6	2.5M	13.7G	356 MB
+ CARAFE [22]	76.2 (+6.5)	14.8 (+4.1)	67.4	2.5M	14.0G	601 MB

Ablation Study for Skip Architecture and Upsampling Module. Here, we demonstrate the effectiveness of our proposed framework for real-time semantic segmentation. The proposed backbone is adopted as the encoder of baseline and the output heatmap is directly upsampled to the original image size, which leads to poor segmentation of boundaries and small objects. We compare two different decoder structures, skip architecture and U-Net architecture, which perform skip connection on label space and feature space respectively. As can be seen from Table 3, skip architecture is more efficient than U-Net architecture and has a comparable accuracy (75.5% VS 75.2%). By gradually restoring spatial information, skip architecture significantly improves the baseline by 5.8% (69.7% → 75.5%) in accuracy. Furthermore, we adopt the proposed upsampling module that leverages context information from feature maps to refine the heatmaps. DDPNet with the proposed framework boosts the baseline by 6.5% (69.7% → 76.2%) in accuracy with a negligible drop in inference speed (1.0 ms). We compare another upsampling method CARAFE [22], which performs upsampling on feature space. We directly adopt CARAFE in U-Net architecture and compare it with DDPNet. Table 3 shows that the proposed framework has a comparable accuracy, but 4 times faster (1.0 ms VS 4.1 ms). Some visual results and analyses are provided in the supplementary file.

4.3 Accuracy and Efficiency Analysis

In this subsection, we compare the proposed DDPNet with other existing state-of-the-art real-time segmentation models on Cityscapes dataset. For a fair comparison, we measure the mIoU without any evaluation tricks like multi-crop, multi-scale, etc.

Table 4. Accuracy and efficiency results on Cityscapes test dataset. "-" indicates that the corresponding result is not provided by the method. "†" indicates that the model is evaluated on Cityscapes validation set.

Method	Pretrain	Input size	#Params	FLOPs	GPU	FPS	mIoU(%)
SegNet [41]	ImageNet	640 × 360	29.5M	286G	TitanX M	14.6	56.1
ENet [32]	No	512 × 1024	0.4M	4.4G	TitanX M	76.9	58.3
ESPNet [31]	No	512 × 1024	0.4M	4.7G	TitanX	112	60.3
ERFNet [33]	No	512 × 1024	2.1M	–	TitanX M	41.7	68.0
ICNet [30]	ImageNet	1024 × 2048	26.5M	29.8G	TitanX M	30.3	69.5
BiSeNet1 [27]	ImageNet	768 × 1536	5.8M	14.8G	TitanX	72.3	68.4
BiSeNet2 [27]	ImageNet	768 × 1536	49.0M	55.3G	TitanX	45.7	74.7
DABNet [23]	No	1024 × 2048	0.8M	–	1080Ti	27.7	70.1
DFANet [24]	ImageNet	1024 × 1024	7.8M	3.4G	TitanX	100	71.3
SwiftNet† [26]	No	1024 × 2048	11.8M	104G	1080Ti	39.9	70.4
SwiftNet [26]	ImageNet	1024 × 2048	11.8M	104G	1080Ti	39.9	75.5
ShelfNet [28]	ImageNet	1024 × 2048	–	–	1080Ti	36.9	74.8
DDPNet†	No	768 × 1536	2.52M	13.2G	1080Ti	85.4	76.2
DDPNet†	No	1024 × 2048	2.52M	23.5G	1080Ti	52.6	77.2
DDPNet	No	768 × 1536	2.52M	13.2G	1080Ti	85.4	74.0
DDPNet	No	1024 × 2048	2.52M	23.5G	1080Ti	52.6	75.3

The comparison of the accuracy (class mIoU) and efficiency (FLOPs, FPS) is shown in Table 4. Our DDPNet outperforms most existing real-time semantic segmentation methods in accuracy, and maintains a superior inference speed. Specifically, DDPNet achieves 75.3% mIoU with 52.6 FPS for an input of 1024 × 2048 resolution and 74.0% mIoU with 85.4 FPS for an input of 768 × 1536 resolution on Cityscapes test set. ShelfNet [28] and SwiftNet [26] are recent published state-of-the-art models. Compared to ShelfNet, DDPNet is faster (52.6 FPS VS 36.9 FPS) and more accurate (75.3% VS 74.8%). SwiftNet has a slightly better accuracy than DDPNet (75.5% VS 75.3%). However, DDPNet is trained with only Cityscapes fine-annotated images, without using any extra data. For a fair comparison, we compare the results of SwiftNet and DDPNet trained from scratch and evaluated on Cityscapes validation set. As can be seen from Table 4, DDPNet achieves significant better results in accuracy (77.2% VS 70.4%) and inference speed (52.6 FPS VS 39.9 FPS). Note that DDPNet has fewer parameters and smaller FLOPs than most methods. The reason is that most real-time semantic segmentation methods adopt ResNet-18 as their backbone, while DDP-Net designs a light-weight and powerful backbone with fewer parameters.

Table 5. Accuracy results on CamVid test dataset.

Method	Pretrain	#Params	mIoU (%)
SegNet [41]	ImageNet	29.5M	55.6
ENet [32]	No	0.4M	51.3
ICNet [30]	ImageNet	26.5M	67.1
BiSeNet1 [27]	ImageNet	5.8M	65.6
BiSeNet2 [27]	ImageNet	49.0M	68.7
DABNet [23]	No	0.8M	66.4
FPENet [25]	No	0.4M	65.4
DFANet [24]	ImageNet	7.8M	64.7
SwiftNet [26]	No	11.8M	63.3
SwiftNet [26]	ImageNet	11.8M	72.6
FC-HarDNet [55]	No	1.4M	62.9
DDPNet	No	1.1M	67.3
DDPNet	Cityscapes	1.1M	73.8

4.4 Result on Other Dataset

To verify the generality of our proposed DDPNet, we conduct experiments on CamVid dataset. We modify the DDPNet to better fit the image resolution by replacing the initial block with a 3×3 convolution and removing the last dense block. As can be seen from Table 5, DDPNet achieves impressive results with only 1.1 M parameters. Besides, we investigate the effect of the pre-training datasets on CamVid. The last two rows of Table 5 show that pre-training on Cityscapes can significantly improve the accuracy over 6.5% (67.3% → 73.8%).

5   Conclusion

In this paper, we propose a novel Dense Dual-Path Network (DDPNet) for real-time semantic segmentation on high-resolution images. The proposed DDPNet achieves a significant better accuracy with a comparable speed and fewer parameters than most real-time semantic segmentation methods.

Acknowledgement. This work is supported by the National Key This work is supported by the National Key Research and Development Program of China (No. 2018YFB0105103, No. 2017YFA0603104, No. 2018YFB0505400), the National Natural Science Foundation of China (No. U19A2069, No. U1764261, No. 41801335, No. 41871370), the Shanghai Science and Technology Development Foundation (No. 17DZ1100202, No. 16DZ1100701) and the Fundamental Research Funds for the Central Universities (No. 22120180095).

References

1. Chen, L.C., Zhu, Y., Papandreou, G., Schroff, F., Adam, H.: Encoder-decoder with Atrous separable convolution for semantic image segmentation. In: Proceedings of the European Conference on Computer Vision (ECCV), pp. 801–818 (2018)
2. Cheng, B., et al.: SPGNet: semantic prediction guidance for scene parsing. In: Proceedings of the IEEE International Conference on Computer Vision, pp. 5218–5228 (2019)
3. Fu, J., et al.: Dual attention network for scene segmentation. In: Proceedings of the IEEE Conference on Computer Vision and Pattern Recognition, pp. 3146–3154 (2019)
4. He, J., Deng, Z., Qiao, Y.: Dynamic multi-scale filters for semantic segmentation. In: Proceedings of the IEEE International Conference on Computer Vision, pp. 3562–3572 (2019)
5. Tian, Z., He, T., Shen, C., Yan, Y.: Decoders matter for semantic segmentation: data-dependent decoding enables flexible feature aggregation. In: Proceedings of the IEEE Conference on Computer Vision and Pattern Recognition, pp. 3126–3135 (2019)
6. Zhao, H., Shi, J., Qi, X., Wang, X., Jia, J.: Pyramid scene parsing network. In: Proceedings of the IEEE Conference on Computer Vision and Pattern Recognition, pp. 2881–2890 (2017)
7. Brostow, G.J., Fauqueur, J., Cipolla, R.: Semantic object classes in video: a high-definition ground truth database. Pattern Recogn. Lett. **30**, 88–97 (2009)
8. Cordts, M., et al.: The cityscapes dataset for semantic urban scene understanding. In: Proceedings of the IEEE Conference on Computer Vision and Pattern Recognition, pp. 3213–3223 (2016)
9. Everingham, M., Van Gool, L., Williams, C.K., Winn, J., Zisserman, A.: The pascal visual object classes (VOC) challenge. Int. J. Comput. Vis. **88**, 303–338 (2010)
10. Lin, T.-Y., et al.: Microsoft COCO: common objects in context. In: Fleet, D., Pajdla, T., Schiele, B., Tuytelaars, T. (eds.) ECCV 2014. LNCS, vol. 8693, pp. 740–755. Springer, Cham (2014). https://doi.org/10.1007/978-3-319-10602-1_48
11. Zhou, B., Zhao, H., Puig, X., Fidler, S., Barriuso, A., Torralba, A.: Scene parsing through ADE20K dataset. In: Proceedings of the IEEE Conference on Computer Vision and Pattern Recognition, pp. 633–641 (2017)
12. He, K., Zhang, X., Ren, S., Sun, J.: Deep residual learning for image recognition. In: Proceedings of the IEEE Conference on Computer Vision and Pattern Recognition, pp. 770–778 (2016)
13. Xie, S., Girshick, R., Dollár, P., Tu, Z., He, K.: Aggregated residual transformations for deep neural networks. In: Proceedings of the IEEE Conference on Computer Vision and Pattern Recognition, pp. 1492–1500 (2017)
14. Huang, G., Liu, Z., Van Der Maaten, L., Weinberger, K.Q.: Densely connected convolutional networks. In: Proceedings of the IEEE Conference on Computer Vision and Pattern Recognition, pp. 4700–4708 (2017)
15. Deng, J., Dong, W., Socher, R., Li, L.J., Li, K., Fei-Fei, L.: ImageNet: a large-scale hierarchical image database. In: IEEE Conference on Computer Vision and Pattern Recognition, pp. 248–255. IEEE (2009)
16. Chen, L.C., Papandreou, G., Kokkinos, I., Murphy, K., Yuille, A.L.: DeepLab: semantic image segmentation with deep convolutional nets, Atrous convolution, and fully connected CRFs. IEEE Trans. Pattern Anal. Mach. Intell. **40**, 834–848 (2017)

17. Chen, L.C., Papandreou, G., Schroff, F., Adam, H.: Rethinking atrous convolution for semantic image segmentation. arXiv preprint arXiv:1706.05587 (2017)

18. Fu, J., et al.: Adaptive context network for scene parsing. In: Proceedings of the IEEE International Conference on Computer Vision, pp. 6748–6757 (2019)

19. Lin, G., Milan, A., Shen, C., Reid, I.: RefineNet: multi-path refinement networks for high-resolution semantic segmentation. In: Proceedings of the IEEE Conference on Computer Vision and Pattern Recognition, pp. 1925–1934 (2017)

20. Long, J., Shelhamer, E., Darrell, T.: Fully convolutional networks for semantic segmentation. In: Proceedings of the IEEE Conference on Computer Vision and Pattern Recognition, pp. 3431–3440 (2015)

21. Noh, H., Hong, S., Han, B.: Learning deconvolution network for semantic segmentation. In: Proceedings of the IEEE International Conference on Computer Vision, pp. 1520–1528 (2015)

22. Wang, J., Chen, K., Xu, R., Liu, Z., Loy, C.C., Lin, D.: CARAFE: content-aware reassembly of features. arXiv preprint arXiv:1905.02188 (2019)

23. Li, G., Yun, I., Kim, J., Kim, J.: DABNet: depth-wise asymmetric bottleneck for real-time semantic segmentation. arXiv preprint arXiv:1907.11357 (2019)

24. Li, H., Xiong, P., Fan, H., Sun, J.: DFANet: deep feature aggregation for real-time semantic segmentation. In: Proceedings of the IEEE Conference on Computer Vision and Pattern Recognition, pp. 9522–9531 (2019)

25. Liu, M., Yin, H.: Feature pyramid encoding network for real-time semantic segmentation. arXiv preprint arXiv:1909.08599 (2019)

26. Orsic, M., Kreso, I., Bevandic, P., Segvic, S.: In defense of pre-trained ImageNet architectures for real-time semantic segmentation of road-driving images. In: Proceedings of the IEEE Conference on Computer Vision and Pattern Recognition, pp. 12607–12616 (2019)

27. Yu, C., Wang, J., Peng, C., Gao, C., Yu, G., Sang, N.: BiSeNet: bilateral segmentation network for real-time semantic segmentation. In: Ferrari, V., Hebert, M., Sminchisescu, C., Weiss, Y. (eds.) ECCV 2018. LNCS, vol. 11217, pp. 334–349. Springer, Cham (2018). https://doi.org/10.1007/978-3-030-01261-8_20

28. Zhuang, J., Yang, J., Gu, L., Dvornek, N.: ShelfNet for fast semantic segmentation. In: Proceedings of the IEEE International Conference on Computer Vision Workshops (2019)

29. Wu, Z., Shen, C., Hengel, A.V.D.: Real-time semantic image segmentation via spatial sparsity. arXiv preprint arXiv:1712.00213 (2017)

30. Zhao, H., Qi, X., Shen, X., Shi, J., Jia, J.: ICNet for real-time semantic segmentation on high-resolution images. In: Ferrari, V., Hebert, M., Sminchisescu, C., Weiss, Y. (eds.) ECCV 2018. LNCS, vol. 11207, pp. 418–434. Springer, Cham (2018). https://doi.org/10.1007/978-3-030-01219-9_25

31. Mehta, S., Rastegari, M., Caspi, A., Shapiro, L., Hajishirzi, H.: ESPNet: efficient spatial pyramid of dilated convolutions for semantic segmentation. In: Proceedings of the European Conference on Computer Vision (ECCV), pp. 552–568 (2018)

32. Paszke, A., Chaurasia, A., Kim, S., Culurciello, E.: ENet: a deep neural network architecture for real-time semantic segmentation. arXiv preprint arXiv:1606.02147 (2016)

33. Romera, E., Alvarez, J.M., Bergasa, L.M., Arroyo, R.: ERFNet: efficient residual factorized convnet for real-time semantic segmentation. IEEE Trans. Intell. Transp. Syst. 19, 263–272 (2017)

34. Siam, M., Gamal, M., Abdel-Razek, M., Yogamani, S., Jagersand, M., Zhang, H.: A comparative study of real-time semantic segmentation for autonomous driving. In: Proceedings of the IEEE Conference on Computer Vision and Pattern Recognition Workshops, pp. 587–597 (2018)

35. Howard, A., et al.: Searching for MobileNetV3. arXiv preprint arXiv:1905.02244 (2019)

36. Howard, A.G., et al.: MobileNets: efficient convolutional neural networks for mobile vision applications. arXiv preprint arXiv:1704.04861 (2017)

37. Sandler, M., Howard, A., Zhu, M., Zhmoginov, A., Chen, L.C.: MobileNetV2: inverted residuals and linear bottlenecks. In: Proceedings of the IEEE Conference on Computer Vision and Pattern Recognition, pp. 4510–4520 (2018)

38. Ma, N., Zhang, X., Zheng, H.T., Sun, J.: ShuffleNet V2: practical guidelines for efficient CNN architecture design. In: Proceedings of the European Conference on Computer Vision (ECCV), pp. 116–131 (2018)

39. Zhang, X., Zhou, X., Lin, M., Sun, J.: ShuffleNet: an extremely efficient convolutional neural network for mobile devices. In: Proceedings of the IEEE Conference on Computer Vision and Pattern Recognition, pp. 6848–6856 (2018)

40. Poudel, R.P., Liwicki, S., Cipolla, R.: Fast-SCNN: fast semantic segmentation network. arXiv preprint arXiv:1902.04502 (2019)

41. Badrinarayanan, V., Kendall, A., Cipolla, R.: SegNet: a deep convolutional encoder-decoder architecture for image segmentation. IEEE Trans. Pattern Anal. Mach. Intell. **39**, 2481–2495 (2017)

42. Ronneberger, O., Fischer, P., Brox, T.: U-Net: convolutional networks for biomedical image segmentation. In: Navab, N., Hornegger, J., Wells, W.M., Frangi, A.F. (eds.) MICCAI 2015. LNCS, vol. 9351, pp. 234–241. Springer, Cham (2015). https://doi.org/10.1007/978-3-319-24574-4_28

43. Zhang, R., Tang, S., Zhang, Y., Li, J., Yan, S.: Scale-adaptive convolutions for scene parsing. In: Proceedings of the IEEE International Conference on Computer Vision, pp. 2031–2039 (2017)

44. Li, H., Xiong, P., An, J., Wang, L.: Pyramid attention network for semantic segmentation. arXiv preprint arXiv:1805.10180 (2018)

45. Ioffe, S., Szegedy, C.: Batch normalization: accelerating deep network training by reducing internal covariate shift. arXiv preprint arXiv:1502.03167 (2015)

46. Glorot, X., Bordes, A., Bengio, Y.: Deep sparse rectifier neural networks. In: Proceedings of the Fourteenth International Conference on Artificial Intelligence and Statistics, pp. 315–323 (2011)

47. Jégou, S., Drozdzal, M., Vazquez, D., Romero, A., Bengio, Y.: The one hundred layers Tiramisu: fully convolutional DenseNets for semantic segmentation. In: Proceedings of the IEEE Conference on Computer Vision and Pattern Recognition Workshops, pp. 11–19 (2017)

48. Yang, M., Yu, K., Zhang, C., Li, Z., Yang, K.: DenseASPP for semantic segmentation in street scenes. In: Proceedings of the IEEE Conference on Computer Vision and Pattern Recognition, pp. 3684–3692 (2018)

49. Wang, R.J., Li, X., Ling, C.X.: Pelee: a real-time object detection system on mobile devices. In: Advances in Neural Information Processing Systems, pp. 1963–1972 (2018)

50. Srivastava, N., Hinton, G., Krizhevsky, A., Sutskever, I., Salakhutdinov, R.: Dropout: a simple way to prevent neural networks from overfitting. J. Mach. Learn. Res. **15**, 1929–1958 (2014)

51. Huang, G., Liu, S., Van der Maaten, L., Weinberger, K.Q.: CondenseNet: an efficient DenseNet using learned group convolutions. In: Proceedings of the IEEE Conference on Computer Vision and Pattern Recognition, pp. 2752–2761 (2018)
52. Jia, X., De Brabandere, B., Tuytelaars, T., Gool, L.V.: Dynamic filter networks. In: Advances in Neural Information Processing Systems, pp. 667–675 (2016)
53. Kingma, D.P., Ba, J.: Adam: a method for stochastic optimization. arXiv preprint arXiv:1412.6980 (2014)
54. He, T., Zhang, Z., Zhang, H., Zhang, Z., Xie, J., Li, M.: Bag of tricks for image classification with convolutional neural networks. In: Proceedings of the IEEE Conference on Computer Vision and Pattern Recognition, pp. 558–567 (2019)
55. Chao, P., Kao, C.Y., Ruan, Y.S., Huang, C.H., Lin, Y.L.: HarDNet: a low memory traffic network. In: Proceedings of the IEEE International Conference on Computer Vision, pp. 3552–3561(2019)

Learning More Accurate Features for Semantic Segmentation in CycleNet

Linzi Qu, Lihuo He[✉], Junji Ke, Xinbo Gao, and Wen Lu

School of Electronic Engineering, Xidian University, Xi'an, China
lhhe@mail.xidian.edu.cn

Abstract. Contextual information is essential for computer vision tasks, especially semantic segmentation. Previous works generally focus on how to collect contextual information by enlarging the size of receptive field, such as PSPNet, DenseASPP. In contrast to previous works, this paper proposes a new network – CycleNet, which considers assigning a more accurate representative for every pixel. It consists of two modules, Cycle Atrous Spatial Pyramid Pooling (CycleASPP) and Alignment with Deformable Convolution (ADC). The former realizes dense connections between a series of atrous convolution layers with different dilation rates. Not only the forward connections can aggregate more contextual information, but also the backward connections can pay more attention to important information by transferring high-level features to low-level layers. Besides, ADC generates accurate information during the decoding process. It draws support from deformable convolution to select and recombine features from different blocks, thus improving the misalignment issues caused by simple interpolation. A set of experiments have been conducted on Cityscapes and ADE20K to demonstrate the effectiveness of CycleNet. In particular, our model achieved 46.14% mIoU on ADE20K validation set.

1 Introduction

Semantic segmentation is a great challenge in dense image classification where the resolution of output labels is the same as that of the input images. Each pixel in the image needs a semantic label. This task has been widely used in video surveillance, automotive driving, medical image processing and other fields. Traditional segmentation methods aim to extract handicraft features of image regions which is not only complicated, but also lead to inaccurate results.

With the development of deep learning, especially Convolution Neural Networks (CNN), a landmark framework – Fully Convolutional Networks (FCN) has emerged in the field of semantic segmentation. Based on it, most of the subsequent works train model end to end to obtain representative image features automatically. FCNs use pooling layers to expand receptive fields and further achieve high-level information. However, these methods ignore the negative impact of down-sampling on the resolution, which is crucial for semantic segmentation.

© Springer Nature Switzerland AG 2021
H. Ishikawa et al. (Eds.): ACCV 2020, LNCS 12622, pp. 571–584, 2021.
https://doi.org/10.1007/978-3-030-69525-5_34

In order to obtain larger receptive fields and richer contextual information, recent works mainly rely on atrous convolution [1] or attention mechanism. Deeplab [2] and DenseASPP [3] concatenated features from a cascade of atrous convolution layers with different dilation rates. PSPNet [4] proposed pyramid pooling module to aggregate information from multi-scale features after pooling layers. However, a neglected issue in these works is whether a large receptive field is equally important for every pixel in the image. For example, a pixel in a semantic object requires a larger receptive field to see the entire object, but when a pixel approaches the boundary, a larger receptive field may bring more information about other categories, leading to incorrect segmentation. At the same time, the attention-based methods are designed to capture long-range context without being limited by the fixed size of convolution kernel. But it's time-consuming because more useful information mainly locates around the pixels, meaning that numbers of computation is unnecessary. In addition, in the process of obtaining high-level information, the size of models' output like [3,5] is 1/8 of the input size, and then interpolated to the same size of input. Simple methods of restoring resolution can lead to misalignment issue.

In this paper, an elaborate CycleNet is proposed to provide precise features for each pixel, on the premise of adequate receptive fields. CycleNet is mainly composed of two sub-modules CycleASPP and ADC. CycleNet is a DenseASPP-like method. They all consist of a backbone to encode features followed by a series of atrous convolution layers. The difference is that there are both forward and backward connections between any atrous convolution layers in CycleASPP, but DenseASPP only has forward connections. To be specific, the first time of an atrous convolution begins with the concatenation of all the previous layers' output, just like DenseASPP, to successively produce multi-scale features. Inspired by CliqueNet [6], the feedback mechanism is able to enhance the representation of models. Thus, CycleASPP applies backward connections to refine features. After the first time, outputs of update layers then are concatenated to be inputs of the previous layers, as illustrated in Fig. 1. By backward connections, the high-level information is fed back to previous layers. Benefits from this, CycleASPP not only refines the filters, but also produces more accurate features. Moreover, an ADC module is proposed to prevent the loss of accurate information caused by down-sampling. Deformable convolution layers are used to learn the positional correspondence between different resolution features.

Our main contributions are summarized as follows:

1. We introduce CycleASPP, which continuously refines the representativeness of asrous convolution layers through feedback mechanism.
2. ADC module is proposed to compensate for the misalignment issue caused by down-sampling.
3. The visualization between different parts of CycleASPP shows the backward connections can refine filters.
4. We verify CycleNet on two semantic segmentation benchmark datasets, Cityscapes [7] and ADE20K [8]. The experiments show that our model

achieves the state-of-the-art results including 82.0% mIoU on Cityscapes test set and 46.14% mIoU on ADE20K validation set.

2   Related Work

2.1   Context Model in Semantic Segmentation

Recent studies have shown that semantic segmentation benefits from rich contextual information. Although the emergence of FCN has made some progress in semantic segmentation, it can not produce enough contextual information by a single receptive field. PSPNet [4] designed a spatial pyramid pooling model to collect contextual information from different pooling layers. ASPP [2] utilized atrous convolutions to enlarge receptive fields thus further fusing different contextual information. Inspired by DenseNet [9], DenseASPP [3] added dense connections between a cascade of atrous convolution layers to capture multiscale context. Some other works focused on attention-based methods. Contextual information in DANet [10] is collected by calculating the similarity between each pixel in image. To improve efficiency, CCNet [5] adopted criss-cross attention module which only computing pixels on the criss-cross path.

2.2   Recurrent Neural Network

Recurrent neural networks, such as LSTM [11] and GRU [12], which benefited from feature-usage and iterative learning, are mainly used for sequential tasks, especially natural language processing (NLP). In image classification tasks, to simulate feedback loops in human brain, I. Caswell [13] proposed loopy neural networks that allow the information flow from deeper layers to lower layers, CliqueNet [6] incorporated forwards and backwards connections between every layers in a block to maximize the information flow and realize spatial attention. RNN-like model also improved the ability of long-dependencies between pixels in semantic segmentation. Like, ReSeg [14] proposed a recurrent layer containing four RNN, which first horizontally computed the image patches, and then vertically computed the output of the hidden states, so as to efficiently collect contextual information.

2.3   Multi-level Features Fusion

Encoder-decoder structures are presented to balance the high-level semantic features with high resolution. Common methods are to add or concatenate low-level features with high-level features after interpolated. GFF [15] is inspired by the gate mechanism of LSTM to assign different weights to different features according to their validity, because multi-level features are not equally important to the results. Considering the misalignment of different layers, enlightened by the optical flow, Alignseg [16] proposed a learnable interpolation method to precisely align high and low level features. Different from other works, [17] firstly down-sampling the low-level features to the same size as the high-level features, and then aggregated all the features at the low resolution. Finally, a data-based DUpsampling method is designed to reproduce the original size.

3   Method

3.1   Cycle Atrous Spatial Pyramid Pooling (CycleASPP)

DenseASPP. The purpose of atrous convolution layers is to balance the problem of large receptive fields and high resolution in semantic segmentation. It can be represented as follows:

$$Y[k] = \sum_{i=1}^{I} X[k + r \cdot i] \cdot w[i] \tag{1}$$

where $Y[k]$ is the output features, $X[k]$ is the input features, $w[i]$ is a parameter of convolution filter, and r is the dilation rate, and I denotes the filter size. We adopt $f_r(X)$ to represent atrous convolution to simplify symbolization.

Since the features generated by the simple atrous convolutional layer are difficult to cover a scale range, DenseASPP adopted atrous convolution layers with different rates, which not only realizes lager receptive fields, but also produces dense scale-range features. However, a lager receptive field is unable to benefit all the pixels in image, especially those near the boundaries. A larger receptive field means more information from adjacent objects, which sometimes confuse the model. Inspired by CliqueNet [6], we added the backward connections between every atrous convolution layer to ensure that each pixel is able to focus on its own accurate features, on the premise that it receives a sufficient receptive field.

CycleASPP. CycleASPP is a DenseASPP-like module that contains a series of sequential atrous convolution layers with increasing atrous rates. In particular, there are bidirectional connections in CycleASPP, whereas DenseASPP only has forward connections.

As depicted in Fig. 1, CycleASPP consists of two parts. In the Part I, input features are concatenated with output of previous layers, and then all the features are utilized to update the next layer. In part I, each atrous layer can be defined as:

$$Y_j^0 = f_{r_j}(concate[Y_{j-1}^0, Y_{j-2}^0, \cdots, Y_0^0]) \tag{2}$$

where Y^0 is the output of atrous convolution in part I, r_j represents the $j-th$ atrous convolution layers in CycleASPP, and $concate[\cdots]$ is concatenation operation.

After that, feedback features from Part I is used to refine the atrous convolution layers. In the part II, all the features from the Part I are concatenated as input except for the output of current layer. What is more noteworthy is that the atrous convolution layers are updated sequentially, so some of aggregate features are from Part I and others are from Part II, which can be formulated as:

$$Y_{j,j\neq 1}^{k} = f_{r_j}(concate[Y_J^{k-1}, Y_{J-1}^{k-1}, \cdots, Y_{j+1}^{k-1}, Y_{j-1}^{k}, \cdots, Y_1^k]) \qquad (3)$$

where k denotes feedback times in Part II. $k = 0$ represents only forward connections.

In CycleASPP, the latest outputs from each atrous convolution layer are used together to generate the final feature maps. This recurrent structure has two main benefits: the first is to refine the convolution filters to attain more accurate representative features, and the second is to maximize information flow.

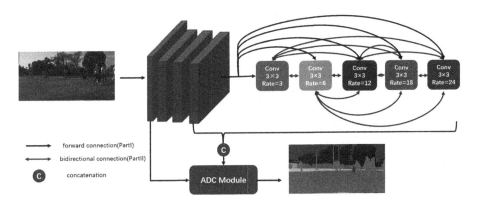

Fig. 1. Overview of CycleNet. Given an input image, we use a CNN model to generate high-level features. Then, CycleASPP including a series of atrous convolution layers with different rates is used to learn rich and accurate contextual features. The outputs of CycleASPP are concatenated with low-level features. To align multi-scale features, we proposed Alignment with Deformable Convolution (ADC) module.

3.2   Alignment with Deformable Convolution (ADC)

Restoration of image resolution caused by pooling layers is an inevitable procedure of semantic segmentation. At the decoding stage, the low-resolution feature maps firstly are interpolated to the same size of high-resolution ones, and then a simple concatenating way results in spatial misalignment. Considering that the deformable convolution layers are able to automatically learn the position offset which enhance the different features fusion. We exploit modulated deformable module [18] and it is obtained by:

$$Y[l_0] = \sum_{n=1}^{N} w_n \cdot X[l_0 + l_n + \triangle l_n] \cdot \triangle m_n \qquad (4)$$

N is sampling positions, w_n and l_n respectively denote the weight and the predefined offsets for l_0. Supposing a 3×3 deformable convolution, N is 9 and

$l_n \in [(-1,-1),(-1,0),\cdots,(1,1)]$. Besides, the offset $\triangle l_n$ and the modulation scalar $\triangle m_n$ are based on data.

In this module, we firstly perform bilinear interpolation on the features X_{high} generated by CycleASPP to the same size with low-level features X_{low}. Then, these features are combined, followed by several convolutions to generate the learnable offset $\triangle l_n$ and modulation scalar $\triangle m_n$ which are required by the modulated deformable module. Finally, our aligned context features $Y_{context}$ could be defined as follow:

$$Y_{context} = f(concate[X_{low}, \widetilde{X}_{high}]) \tag{5}$$

where $\widetilde{X}_{high}$ denotes the aligned features by deformable convolution, and f is conventional convolution layers (Fig. 2).

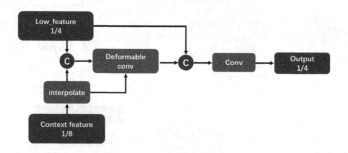

Fig. 2. An elaborate show of Alignment with Deformable Convolution (ADC) module. It takes two parts features respectively from Backbone and CycleASPP, and then exploit deformable convolution to align these features.

4   Experimental Evaluation

A large number of experiments are conducted to evaluate the effectiveness of CycleNet on two benchmark datasets Cityscapes [7] and ADE20K [8]. Results are evaluated with mean of class-wise Intersection over Union (mIoU) and pixel accuracy.

4.1   Implementation Details and Datasets

Network Structure. Our method adopts ResNet101 [19] pre-trained on ImageNet [20]. The last two pooling layers and the fully-connected layers of model are removed. At the same time, the convolution layers in the last two blocks are replaced by atrous convolution layers with atrous rates of 2 and 4, respectively.

Training Settings. We train our model with stochastic gradient descent training method. The initial learning rate is initialized as 1e−2 for Cityscapes and 2e−2 for ADE20K. The momentum and weight decay are set as 0.9 and 1e−4, respectively. According to the prior work [5,10], we utilize a poly learning rate policy where the initial learning rate is multiplied by 0.9. Synchronized Batch Normalization [21] is employed to synchronize the mean and standard variation. For Cityscapes (only use 2975 finely annotated images), we train the model with 8 mini-batch size and 180 epochs. The input is randomly cropped to 796796 from the original image. For ADE20K, we train the model with 16 mini-batch size, 120 epochs and the input is cropped to 512512. During training, data augmentation including random horizontal flipping, random cropping, and random scaling in the range of [0.75, 2] are used to avoid overfitting. As for loss, we adopt the auxiliary supervision, as [22,23].

Cityscapes. The Cityscapes dataset is designed for understanding of urban street scenes. It contains 5000 images with finely annotations and 20000 images with coarse annotations. The annotations include 30 categories such as road, tree and person. Only 19 categories are commonly used for training and evaluation. The 5000 finely annotated images are split into 2975 images for training, 500 images for validation and 1525 images for testing.

ADE20K. ADE20K is a complex scene parsing dataset including 150 categories involved objects and stuff. It contains 25000 images which consist of 20000 training images, 2000 validation images and 3000 testing images.

4.2 Experiments on Cityscapes

Ablation Study. To evaluate the effectiveness of proposed model, we implement ablation experiments on Cityscapes validation set. We choose atrous ResNet101 mentioned above as the baseline network which down-samples the input size to 1/8 of its original size. The baseline model reaches 76.25% mIoU. All components are based on baseline model and continuously improve the performance.

Effectiveness of CycleASPP. All evaluation of CycleASPP are equal without ADC module. There are two important components in CycleASPP, one is atrous convolution layers and the other is recurrent connections. First, we compare several methods of atrous convolution layers with different numbers at different dilation rates, as shown in Table 1. It is obvious that adding more atrous convolution layers and increasing dilation rates can both improve the performance, because the model achieves larger receptive fields and gains more contextual information. As DenseASPP [3] demonstrates when the receptive field goes larger than the feature map, the results begin to decrease. Thus, there is no need to add more convolutions. For subsequent evaluation of the recurrent connections, which is proposed to refine filters. In order to be fair, we compare

Table 1. The contrast experiments between ASPP, DenseASPP and CycleASPP with various atrous dilation rates.

Method	Backbone	mIoU(%)	GFLOPs
ASPP (6, 12, 18)	ResNet101	78.18	–
DensASPP (3, 6, 12, 18, 24)	ResNet101	78.45	539.1
DenseASPP (3, 6, 12, 18, 24, 30)	ResNet101	78.57	555.5
CycleASPP (6, 12, 18, 24)	ResNet101	78.54	530.8
CycleASPP (3, 6, 12, 18, 24)	ResNet101	78.93	551.5
CycleASPP (3, 6, 12, 18, 24, 30)	ResNet101	78.95	574.0

the results from DenseASPP and CycleASPP with same dilation rates. The performance in Table 1 shows that segmentation results with same receptive fields from CycleASPP outperform these from DenseASPP. CycleASPP (6, 12, 18, 24) achieves the almost same result as DenseASPP (3, 6, 12, 18, 24, 30) while at low GFLOPs. In other words, CycleASPP improves the accuracy of our method without much loss of speed. To ensure the follow-up experiments' performance, we utilize atrous convolution layers with dilation rates (3, 6, 12, 18, 24, 30) and only once feedback connection for the further experiments. As is illustrated in Table 2, the CycleASPP module brings 2.70% mIoU improvements compared with baseline, proving the effectiveness of the introduced module.

Effectiveness of ADC. The use of ADC module to retrieve location information from high-level features missing from the pooling layers has been detailed in Sect. 3.2. We select the low-level features from block1 of atrous ResNet101, which are 1/4 the size of the input image. Compared to the previous models in Table 2, the performance gains 1.60% mIoU improvement when adding this part.

Effectiveness of extra trick. In order to boost the results, we also incorporate a trick used in many works, like [22,23]. Multi-scale inference (MS): this trick is only used in inference. The final segmentation results are obtained by averaging the output probability maps at different scales which vary between [0.75, 1, 1.25, 1.5, 1.75]. From Table 2, we can see that MS brings 0.69% mIoU improvements.

Table 2. Ablation experiments on Cityscapes validation dataset. We evaluated the improvements of each proposed model.

ResNet101	CycleASPP	ADC	MS	mIoU(%)
✓	–	–	–	76.25
✓	✓	–	–	78.95
✓	✓	✓	–	80.55
✓	✓	✓	✓	81.26

Compare with State of the Arts. We compare our CycleNet with previous state-of-arts works such as DenseASPP [3], CCNet [5], DANet [10] and so on Cityscapes test set in Table 3. For fair comparison, we only train the model with fine annotated dataset and evaluate the results by the evaluation server. The CycleNet consists of CycleASPP which set the dilation rates as (3, 6, 12, 18, 24, 30), only once feedback connection and ADC module. Then, we boost the performance by MS. Finally, our approach achieves 82.0% mIoU which outperforms DANet 0.5% mIoU.

Table 3. Results on Cityscapes test dataset.

Method	Backbone	mIoU(%)
RefineNet [24]	ResNet101	73.6
PSPNet [4]	ResNet101	78.4
BiSeNet [25]	ResNet101	78.9
DSSPN [26]	ResNet101	77.8
PSANet [22]	ResNet101	80.1
DenseASPP [3]	DenseNet161	80.6
CCNet [5]	ResNet101	81.4
DANet [10]	ResNet101	81.5
CycleNet (ours)	ResNet101	82.0

4.3   Experiments on ADE20K

Compare with State of the Arts. Here, we further experiment with our method on ADE20K. As shown in Table 4, we compare our work with PSPNet [4], EncNet [21], DSSPN [26], PSANet [22], CCNet [5] and SPNet [23] on the ADE20K validation set. We also adopt atrous ResNet101 as our backbone, and the dilation rates of CycleASPP are set as (3, 6, 12, 18, 24) because of the small input size. Both 46.14% mIoU and 82.20% pixel accuracy are achieves state-of-art results.

5   Visualization

The CycleNet mainly benefits from two modules mentioned above, CycleASPP and ADC. To further analyze the reason, we visualize features'similarity maps and class activation maps to realize a clear understanding.

Table 4. Results on ADE20K validation dataset.

Method	Backbone	mIoU(%)	Pixel Acc.(%)
PSPNet [4]	ResNet101	43.29	81.39
EncNet [21]	ResNet101	44.65	81.69
DSSPN [26]	ResNet101	43.68	81.13
PSANet [22]	ResNet101	43.77	81.51
CCNet [5]	ResNet101	45.22	–
SPNet [23]	ResNet101	45.60	82.09
DenseASPP [3]	ResNet101	43.03	80.73
CycleNet (ours)	ResNet101	46.14	82.20

5.1 Results of Two Datasets

We visualize some results under different settings of the proposed approach in Fig. 3. The red square show the more difficult to distinguish regions. Obviously to find, CycleASPP can correct the misclassified pixels in DensASPP. Such as 'truck' or 'car' in the second example and 'building' or 'wall' in third example. Then, as in first example, CycleASPP can make sure that the pixels on the

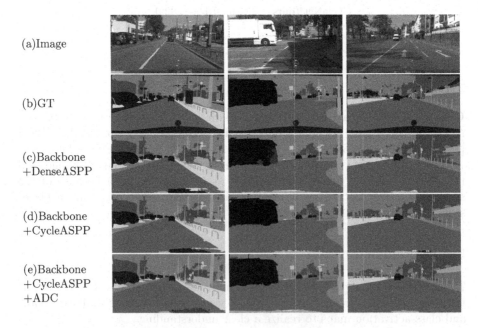

Fig. 3. Visualization of segmentation results among different approaches on Cityscapes validation sets. The first to the fifth rows respectively are original image, ground truth results, results from Backbone+DenseASPP, results from Backbone+CycleASPP, results from Backbone+CycleASPP+ADC.

edge are not disturbed by the rich information from the large receptive fields. From the third example, compared the segmentation results of 'pole' from different methods, obviously, Backbone+CycleASPP equipped with ADC is able to exactly segment tiny objects.

5.2 Features in Different Parts

In CycleASPP, each layer benefits from backwards high-level information. In order to show the refinement more clearly, we calculated the similarity maps, as shown in Fig. 4(b) and (c). With the help of backward connections, features of the same objects are more similar and features of different objects are more discriminative. Grad-CAM [27] are used to visualize the activation maps of two

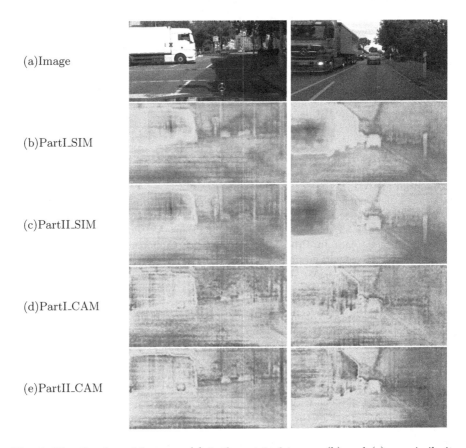

Fig. 4. Visualization of features. (a) is the original image. (b) and (c) are similarity maps with red pixel in original images. Hotter color denotes more similar in feature level. (d) and (e) are class activation maps. Hotter color means larger in the degree of activation.

parts. As shown in Fig. 4(d) and (e), we only use one pixel exactly as red symbol in Fig. 4(a) to produce a class activation map. It is obvious that our module can see targets.

6   Conclusion

In this work, we present CycleNet to deal with the semantic segmentation task in complex scene. CycleNet contains two significant parts, CycleASPP and ADC. CycleASPP adds recurrent connections to dense forward connections like DenseASPP that help model gain more accurate information. Since deformable convolution can collect the information from unfixed positions, ADC develops the decoding procedure that is different from the simple interpolation. As a result, the possibility maps can better aligned with input image. Experiments on Cityscapes and ADE20K demonstrate the effectiveness of the proposed approach.

Acknowledgements. This research was supported in part by the National Key Research and Development Program of China (Grant No. 2018AAA0102702), the National Natural Science Foundation of China (Grant Nos. 61876146, 62036007, 61871311).

References

1. Yu, F., Koltun, V.: Multi-scale context aggregation by dilated convolutions. arXiv preprint arXiv:1511.07122 (2015)
2. Chen, L.C., Papandreou, G., Schroff, F., Adam, H.: Rethinking atrous convolution for semantic image segmentation. arXiv preprint arXiv:1706.05587 (2017)
3. Yang, M., Yu, K., Zhang, C., Li, Z., Yang, K.: DenseASPP for semantic segmentation in street scenes. In: Proceedings of the IEEE Conference on Computer Vision and Pattern Recognition, pp. 3684–3692 (2018)
4. Zhao, H., Shi, J., Qi, X., Wang, X., Jia, J.: Pyramid scene parsing network. In: Proceedings of the IEEE Conference on Computer Vision and Pattern Recognition, pp. 2881–2890 (2017)
5. Huang, Z., Wang, X., Huang, L., Huang, C., Wei, Y., Liu, W.: CCNet: criss-cross attention for semantic segmentation. In: Proceedings of the IEEE International Conference on Computer Vision, pp. 603–612 (2019)
6. Yang, Y., Zhong, Z., Shen, T., Lin, Z.: Convolutional neural networks with alternately updated clique. In: Proceedings of the IEEE Conference on Computer Vision and Pattern Recognition, pp. 2413–2422 (2018)
7. Cordts, M., et al.: The Cityscapes dataset for semantic urban scene understanding. In: Proceedings of the IEEE Conference on Computer Vision and Pattern Recognition, pp. 3213–3223 (2016)
8. Zhou, B., Zhao, H., Puig, X., Fidler, S., Barriuso, A., Torralba, A.: Scene parsing through ADE20K dataset. In: Proceedings of the IEEE Conference on Computer Vision and Pattern Recognition, pp. 633–641 (2017)
9. Huang, G., Liu, Z., Van Der Maaten, L., Weinberger, K.Q.: Densely connected convolutional networks. In: Proceedings of the IEEE Conference on Computer Vision and Pattern Recognition, pp. 4700–4708 (2017)

10. Fu, J., et al.: Dual attention network for scene segmentation. In: Proceedings of the IEEE Conference on Computer Vision and Pattern Recognition, pp. 3146–3154 (2019)

11. Zaremba, W., Sutskever, I., Vinyals, O.: Recurrent neural network regularization. arXiv preprint arXiv:1409.2329 (2014)

12. Chung, J., Gulcehre, C., Cho, K., Bengio, Y.: Empirical evaluation of gated recurrent neural networks on sequence modeling. arXiv preprint arXiv:1412.3555 (2014)

13. Caswell, I., Shen, C., Wang, L.: Loopy neural nets: imitating feedback loops in the human brain. Technical report (2016)

14. Visin, F., et al.: ReSeg: a recurrent neural network-based model for semantic segmentation. In: Proceedings of the IEEE Conference on Computer Vision and Pattern Recognition Workshops, pp. 41–48 (2016)

15. Li, X., Zhao, H., Han, L., Tong, Y., Yang, K.: GFF: gated fully fusion for semantic segmentation. arXiv preprint arXiv:1904.01803 (2019)

16. Huang, Z., Wei, Y., Wang, X., Shi, H., Liu, W., Huang, T.S.: AlignSeg: feature-aligned segmentation networks. arXiv preprint arXiv:2003.00872 (2020)

17. Tian, Z., He, T., Shen, C., Yan, Y.: Decoders matter for semantic segmentation: data-dependent decoding enables flexible feature aggregation. In: Proceedings of the IEEE Conference on Computer Vision and Pattern Recognition, pp. 3126–3135 (2019)

18. Zhu, X., Hu, H., Lin, S., Dai, J.: Deformable ConvNets V2: more deformable, better results. In: Proceedings of the IEEE Conference on Computer Vision and Pattern Recognition, pp. 9308–9316 (2019)

19. He, K., Zhang, X., Ren, S., Sun, J.: Deep residual learning for image recognition. In: Proceedings of the IEEE Conference on Computer Vision and Pattern Recognition, pp. 770–778 (2016)

20. Deng, J., Dong, W., Socher, R., Li, L.J., Li, K., Fei-Fei, L.: ImageNet: a large-scale hierarchical image database. In: 2009 IEEE Conference on Computer Vision and Pattern Recognition, pp. 248–255. IEEE (2009)

21. Zhang, H., et al.: Context encoding for semantic segmentation. In: Proceedings of the IEEE Conference on Computer Vision and Pattern Recognition, pp. 7151–7160 (2018)

22. Zhao, H., et al.: PSANet: point-wise spatial attention network for scene parsing. In: Ferrari, V., Hebert, M., Sminchisescu, C., Weiss, Y. (eds.) ECCV 2018. LNCS, vol. 11213, pp. 270–286. Springer, Cham (2018). https://doi.org/10.1007/978-3-030-01240-3_17

23. Hou, Q., Zhang, L., Cheng, M.M., Feng, J.: Strip pooling: rethinking spatial pooling for scene parsing. In: Proceedings of the IEEE/CVF Conference on Computer Vision and Pattern Recognition, pp. 4003–4012 (2020)

24. Lin, G., Milan, A., Shen, C., Reid, I.: RefineNet: multi-path refinement networks for high-resolution semantic segmentation. In: Proceedings of the IEEE Conference on Computer Vision and Pattern Recognition, pp. 1925–1934 (2017)

25. Yu, C., Wang, J., Peng, C., Gao, C., Yu, G., Sang, N.: BiSeNet: bilateral segmentation network for real-time semantic segmentation. In: Ferrari, V., Hebert, M., Sminchisescu, C., Weiss, Y. (eds.) ECCV 2018. LNCS, vol. 11217, pp. 334–349. Springer, Cham (2018). https://doi.org/10.1007/978-3-030-01261-8_20

26. Liang, X., Zhou, H., Xing, E.: Dynamic-structured semantic propagation network. In: Proceedings of the IEEE Conference on Computer Vision and Pattern Recognition, pp. 752–761 (2018)
27. Selvaraju, R.R., Cogswell, M., Das, A., Vedantam, R., Parikh, D., Batra, D.: Grad-CAM: visual explanations from deep networks via gradient-based localization. In: Proceedings of the IEEE International Conference on Computer Vision, pp. 618–626 (2017)

3D Guided Weakly Supervised Semantic Segmentation

Weixuan Sun[1,2](✉), Jing Zhang[1,2], and Nick Barnes[1]

[1] Australian National University, Canberra, Australia
weixuansun7@outlook.com
[2] CSIRO, Data61, Canberra, Australia

Abstract. Pixel-wise clean annotation is necessary for fully-supervised semantic segmentation, which is laborious and expensive to obtain. In this paper, we propose a weakly supervised 2D semantic segmentation model by incorporating sparse bounding box labels with available 3D information, which is much easier to obtain with advanced sensors. We introduce a 2D-3D inference module to generate accurate pixel-wise segment proposal masks. Guided by 3D information, we first generate a point cloud of objects and calculate a per class objectness probability score for each point using projected bounding-boxes. Then we project the point cloud with objectness probabilities back to the 2D images followed by a refinement step to obtain segment proposals, which are treated as pseudo labels to train a semantic segmentation network. Our method works in a recursive manner to gradually refine the above-mentioned segment proposals. We conducted extensive experimental results on the 2D-3D-S dataset where we manually labeled a subset of images with bounding boxes. We show that the proposed method can generate accurate segment proposals when bounding box labels are available on only a small subset of training images. Performance comparison with recent state-of-the-art methods further illustrates the effectiveness of our method.

Keywords: Semantic segmentation · Weak supervision · 3D guidance

1 Introduction

Recent work on 2D image semantic segmentation has achieved great progress via adopting deep fully convolutional neural networks (FCN) [1]. The success of these models [2–6] arises from large training datasets with pixel-wise labels, which are laborious and expensive to obtain. For example, the cost of pixel-wise segmentation labeling is 15 times larger than bounding box labeling and 60 times larger than image-level labeling [7].

Electronic supplementary material The online version of this chapter (https://doi.org/10.1007/978-3-030-69525-5_35) contains supplementary material, which is available to authorized users.

ⓒ Springer Nature Switzerland AG 2021
H. Ishikawa et al. (Eds.): ACCV 2020, LNCS 12622, pp. 585–602, 2021.
https://doi.org/10.1007/978-3-030-69525-5_35

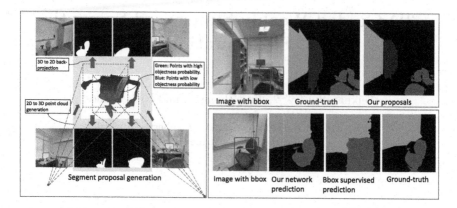

Fig. 1. Left: Our segment proposal generation pipeline. Top right: Example images of our segment proposals compared with ground-truth. Bottom right: Network prediction example supervised with our segment proposals compared with prediction supervised with bounding box masks and ground-truth segmentation map. The sample images are from the 2D-3D-S dataset [8]. (Color figure online)

Unlabeled or weakly-labeled data can be collected in a much faster and cheaper manner, which makes weakly supervised semantic segmentation a promising direction to develop. Multiple types of weak labels have been studied, including image-level labels [9–12], points [13], scribbles [14–16], and bounding boxes [17–21]. Bounding box annotation offers a simple yet intuitive direction, that is relatively inexpensive, while still offering rich semantic regional information. Current bounding box based methods [17–21] usually adopt non-learning methods like Conditional Random Fields (CRF) [22], GrabCut [23] or Multiscale Combinatorial Grouping (MCG) [24] to obtain segment proposals, which are then treated as pseudo labels to train semantic segmentation models.

It has been argued that 3D information plays an important role in scene understanding, but most previous semantic segmentation approaches operate only on individual 2D images. With more recent data collection technology and sensors, collection of large scale 3D datasets is no longer a cumbersome process. Not only 2D RGB information but also accurate corresponding 3D information like depth maps, camera trajectories, and point clouds are collected. Especially for indoor scene understanding, datasets like 2D-3D-S [8], SUN3D [25], ScanNet [26] are available. For outdoor autonomous driving there are datasets like Kitti [27], ApolloScape [28] and the Waymo open dataset [29]. With the above-mentioned widely available data, it's natural to raise a question: *"Can we retain comparably good performance while only labeling a few images by using box-level weak supervision together with 3D information?"*

In this paper, we investigate the task of combining bounding box labels with 3D information for weakly supervised semantic segmentation, aiming at reducing annotation cost by leveraging available 3D information. We investigate this by using the Stanford 2D-3D-Semantics dataset (2D-3D-S) [8]. We propose a novel 3D guided weakly supervised semantic segmentation approach, where a small number

of images are labeled with bounding boxes and these images have their corresponding 3D data. Our approach can extract segment proposals from bounding boxes on
labeled images and creates new segment proposals on unlabeled images of the same
object instance. These proposals are then used to train a semantic segmentation
network. Further, our approach works in a recursive manner to gradually refine the
above-mentioned segment proposals, leading to improved segmentation results.

The proposed pipeline (2D-3D inference module) is shown in the left of Fig. 1,
where we use a chair as an example. First, we label the chair from two camera
viewpoints and extrude bounding boxes from 2D to 3D space to generate a point
cloud of the chair. Then we perform 3D inference to compute an objectness probability for each 3D point, representing the possibility of each point belonging to
an object. The objectness probability is computed based on detection frequency
across bounding boxes to enhance correct points and suppress noise. As displayed in the left image of Fig. 1, green and blue points have high and low
objectness probability respectively. We then project from the point cloud with
objectness probabilities back to the 2D images to obtain objectness probability
masks. Besides the labeled images, we can also back-project the point cloud to
new images without labels. During projection, we propose a novel strategy by
using depth maps to deal with occlusion. Finally, we refine the objectness probability masks to obtain our final segment proposals. We evaluate our method on
the 2D-3D-S dataset [8], and experimental results show that our method considerably outperforms the competing methods using bounding box labels. We
summarize our contributions as follows:

- We propose a 3D-guided, 2D weakly supervised semantic segmentation
  method. Our method leverages information that is widely available from 3D
  sensors without hand annotation to yield improved semantic segmentation
  with lower annotation cost.
- We present a novel 2D-3D probabilistic inference algorithm, which combines
  bounding-box labels and 3D information to simultaneously infer pixel-wise
  segment proposals for the labeled bounding boxes and unlabeled images.
- Our 3D weakly supervised semantic segmentation model learns an initial classifier from segment proposals, then uses the 2D-3D inference to transductively
  generate new segment proposals, resulting in further improvements to network
  performance in an iterative learning manner.
- To the best of our knowledge, it is the first work that uses 3D information to
  assist weakly supervised semantic segmentation. To evaluate our method we
  augment the 2D-3D-S dataset [8] with bounding box labels. We demonstrate
  that our method outperforms competing methods with fewer labeled images.

2   Related Work

We briefly introduce existing fully and weakly supervised semantic segmentation
models, and 3D information guided models.

Fully Supervised Semantic Segmentation. A series of work has been done
based on FCN [1] for fully supervised semantic segmentation. [1,30,31] use skip

architectures to connect earlier convolutional layers with deconvolutional layers, to reconstruct fine-grained segmentation shapes. The DeepLab series [3,4,6] use dilated (atrous) convolution in the encoder, which increases the receptive field to consider more spatial information. In addition, many methods [2,3,5,32–37] improve semantic segmentation performance by adopting context information. [2] proposes pyramid pooling to obtain both global and local context information. An adaptive pyramid context network is proposed in [36] to estimate adaptive context vectors for each local position.

Weakly Supervised Semantic Segmentation. A large number of weakly supervised semantic segmentation methods have been proposed to achieve a trade-off between labeling efficiency and network accuracy. They usually take low-cost annotation as a supervision signal, including image-level labels [9–12,18], scribbles [14–16], points [13], and bounding boxes [17–21]. Current bounding-box based methods extract object segment proposals from bounding boxes, which are then used as a network supervision signal. WSSL [18] proposes an expectation-maximization algorithm with a bias to enable refined estimated segmentation maps throughout training. BoxSup [17] proposes a recursive training procedure, which uses generated proposals as supervision in every iteration. [19] generates segment proposals by incorporating GrabCut [23] and MCG [24]. Most recently, [21] generate segment proposals with dense CRF [22], and proposes box-driven class-wise masking with a filling rate guided adaptive loss in the training procedure. However, none of the above methods adopt 3D information.

3D Information Guided Semantic Segmentation. Different from classic 2D RGB semantic segmentation, some work adopts 3D information such as depth maps and point clouds. [38–40] design handcrafted features tailored for RGB with depth information, extracted features are fed into further models. [1,41] take the depth map as an extra input channel with the RGB images. More recently, [42–45] encode depth maps into three-dimensional HHA (horizontal disparity, height above ground, and angle with gravity). [46] employs 3D convolutions to extract 3D geometry and 3D colour features from point clouds and project them back to 2D images for segmentation. Meanwhile, 3D data is becoming increasingly available from advanced 3D sensors, *e.g.*, [8,25–29,47–49] without requiring human intervention. Which offers opportunity to reduce labeling cost by exploiting automatically obtained 3D information. We propose to bring in 3D information to assist proposal generation from bounding boxes and propose a 3D guided weakly supervised semantic segmentation network. As far as we know, this is the first work that combines box-level labels and 3D information for weakly supervised semantic segmentation.

3   Proposed Approach

We propose a 3D information guided bounding-box based weakly supervised semantic segmentation network. Specifically, our method consists of two modules: 1) a segment proposal generation module that adopts the 3D information

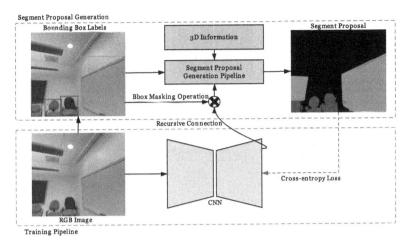

Fig. 2. Pipeline of the proposed method. We first hand-label a subset of all RGB images with bounding box, which is then fed into a 3D semantic projection module to generate segment proposals assisted by 3D information. The generated segment proposals are used as supervision signal for our semantic segmentation network. Meanwhile, the network predictions can also be fed back into the 3D semantic projection module after the bounding box masking operation in a recursive manner. The details of segment proposal generation pipeline are shown in Fig. 3.

and bounding box labels, and 2) a semantic segmentation network, which takes 2D images as training data. First, we feed images with box-level labels and their corresponding 3D information into our segment proposal generation framework, which extracts pixel-wise segment proposals from labeled bounding boxes and generates proposals on new images without labels. Then, the segment proposals are fed into the training pipeline as a supervision signal to train a semantic segmentation network. The network predictions are then fed back into the segment proposal generation module, which generates new segment proposals in a recursive manner. The entire procedure is shown in Fig. 2.

Considering a collection of images $X = \{X_1, ..., X_i, ..., X_N\}$, each image has corresponding 3D information, *i.e.*, camera parameters $M_i = (R_i, \tilde{C}_i, f_i)$ and a depth map X_{depth}, where R_i is camera rotation matrix, $\tilde{C}_i$ is camera position and f_i is focal length. In our method, we assume that only a subset of all images are labelled with bounding boxes, where $X_b \subset X$. During labeling, we label images from different camera viewpoints. Then we feed the labels into our segment proposal generation framework with their corresponding camera parameters and depth maps. We present our segment proposal generation module as a function $S = F(X, X_b, M_i, X_{depth})$, where S is the collection of all segment proposals $S = \{S_1, ..., S_i, ..., S_N\}$. Then the segment proposals S are used supervise the semantic segmentation network: $L = L_s(X_p, S)$, where L_s denotes segmentation loss and Y_p denotes network prediction. In addition, in the recursive process, images labeled with bounding boxes X_b can be replaced

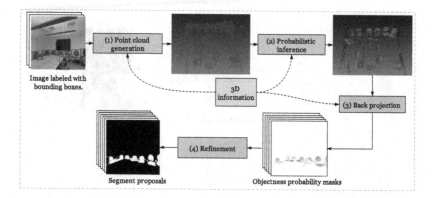

Fig. 3. Our segment proposal generation pipeline. Taking the class of chair as an example, we first project the point cloud for chairs in this room from bounding box labels. Then, we calculate each point's objectness score. Finally, we back-project the point cloud with probabilities to 2D images followed by refinement to get final segment proposals. Note that we can obtain segment proposals on extra images, which means we only need to label a small portion of images. (Color figure online)

with the network predictions X_p from the previous iteration, which is displayed as a recursive connection in Fig. 2. The recursive process is introduced in detail in Sect. 3.2.

3.1   Segment Proposal Generation:

Given a set of images X with corresponding 3D information, and annotated bounding boxes for a subset X_b of the images, our framework can learn semantic masks S (segment proposals) for all images of a room. As shown in Fig. 3, our approach uses a sequence consisting of four components: (1) bounding boxes to 3D projection to generate point clouds; (2) 3D probabilistic inference to accentuate correct points and diminish noise; (3) point-wise 3D to 2D projection to generate scattered objectness probability masks; and (4) mask refinement to get final segment proposals. We introduce each component in the following.

Point Cloud Generation from Bounding Boxes. This process aggregates label information from different camera viewpoints into a globally consistent 3D space[1]. Concretely, given an image X_i, pixels inside bounding boxes are represented as x^i. For one single pixel at position j inside the bounding boxes $x^i_j \in x^i$, we project it into 3D by:

---

[1] 3D information provided by the 2D-3D-S dataset [8] is determinate, and SLAM reconstruction is mature, so high quality 3D information is assumed. Our method is not based on SLAM and every point is projected independently so we don't need to handle accumulated errors.

$$P_j^i = [R_i \mid -R_i\tilde{C}_i]^{-1}K_i^{-1} * x_j^i * d_j^i, \quad \text{where} \quad K_i^{-1} = \begin{bmatrix} \frac{1}{f^i} & & -\frac{p_x^i}{f^i} \\ & \frac{1}{f^i} & -\frac{p_y^i}{f^i} \\ & & 1 \end{bmatrix}. \quad (1)$$

We follow the finite camera projection model [50] to project the pixel x_j^i into 3D space, K_i^{-1} denotes inverse camera matrix which projects pixels from the 2D image to camera coordinate, f^i is focal length and $[p_x^i, p_y^i]$ is principal point. $[R_i \mid -R_i\tilde{C}_i]^{-1}$ transforms points from camera coordinates to world coordinates, where R_i is a 3×3 rotation matrix representing the orientation of the camera coordinates, and $\tilde{C}_i$ denotes the position of the camera in world coordinates. d_j^i denotes depth information at position j of image i. Then we combine the projected 3D point clouds P^i from different camera views together in world coordinate to obtain a class-specific point cloud. We perform projection for each labeled bounding box, label information from different directions and classes is fused into a single 3D point cloud. By adopting depth maps, only points nearest to the camera are projected, which ensure accurate object shapes and occluded points are ignored. The class of every point is decided by the class of the projecting bounding box, so the point clouds are semantically classified. As shown in Fig. 3, the red point cloud displays all chairs in the environment.

Point Cloud Probabilistic Inference. Bounding boxes consist of object and background regions. When we project pixels in the bounding boxes into 3D space, the background regions are also projected as background noise. As shown by the red point clouds of Fig. 3, wall and table are also projected and wrongly categorized as chair. In order to distinguish points that belong to objects or background, we take advantage of our multiple views and 3D information.

We propose a novel method to sum objectness confidence across multiple views, which emphasizes the correct points and weakens the irrelevant points (background noise). We quantitatively present every point's correctness with a score called the objectness score. Inspired by [51], given that the projection matrix and depth map are known, we can get a 3D bounding frustum from a 2D bounding box, which is the "visible space" of that bounding box. All points inside this 3D bounding frustum can be projected back into the bounding box on 2D image. Thus, we make an assumption that, for some camera viewpoints, if a point projected from one camera viewpoint can also be "seen" by other camera viewpoints, i.e., the point can be projected back into the bounding boxes of other images, the objectness score of the point is higher. In this case, with multiple bounding boxes on a single object, the 3D points with a higher objectness score are more likely to belong to this object than to the background. Specifically, for a 3D point P_j of class c, its objectness score O_j is defined as:

$$O_j(P_j \mid B_c) = \sum_{k=1}^{K} F_o(P_j, b_k), \quad (2)$$

where B_c denotes bounding boxes of class c in this room and $F_o(P_j, b_k)$ is:

$$F_o(P_j, b_k) = \begin{cases} 1 & \text{if back-projected } P_j \text{ is inside } b_k \\ 0 & \text{otherwise} \end{cases}. \tag{3}$$

O_j in Eq. 2 indicates the frequency that the point P_j is projected back to bounding boxes across all the images from different viewpoints. We implement the above method for each class independently, then normalize objectness scores for each class to obtain an objectness probability $p(O_j)$: $p(O_j) = \frac{O_j}{max(O^c)}$, where O^c denotes the collection of objectness scores of all points that belong to class c. Points with higher objectness scores have more confidence to belong to objects. By doing so, label information from different camera viewpoints are aggregated on points to compose their objectness probability, and reveal objects' shapes. As shown in the top right figure of Fig. 3, after probabilistic inference, the chairs stand out from background noise, while wall and tables are suppressed.

Segment Proposal Generation by Point Cloud Back-Projection. In this stage, we apply 3D to 2D back-projection to generate prototype objectness score masks. Specifically, given a single point P_j in the point cloud, we project it to a image at camera viewpoint i [50]:

$$x_j^i = K_i[R_i \mid -R_i \tilde{C}_i]P_j, \quad \text{where} \quad K_i = \begin{bmatrix} f_i & p_x^i \\ & f_i & p_y^i \\ & & 1 \end{bmatrix}. \tag{4}$$

We project all points with their objectness probabilities and semantic labels onto 2D images. All 3D points are in the same world coordinate system and can be back-projected to 2D images at any camera viewpoints, no matter whether the images are labeled or not. Therefore, we only need to label a small portion of the images, which can significantly alleviate annotation cost. In addition, since the point cloud is sparse in 3D space, we get 2D masks with scattered points and every point represents normalized objectness probability, which are named objectness probability masks, as shown in the third column of Fig. 5.

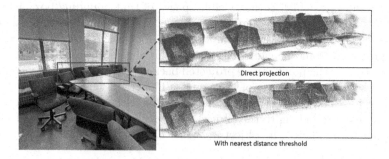

Fig. 4. Illustration of the proposed nearest distance threshold. As shown in the left RGB image, some parts of the chairs are occluded under the table. With direct projection, the occluded parts of the chairs are still wrongly projected. After applying our nearest distance threshold, occluded areas are properly ignored.

Nearest Distance Threshold. Occlusion may occur during the back projection, *i.e.*, when objects are overlapped facing a camera, points belong to both visible objects and occluded objects are projected to the same region. To address this issue, we propose a nearest distance threshold. by using the depth map. Depth represents the nearest surface to the camera, all 3D points behind the surface are occluded which should not be projected to 2D. Concretely, for a 3D point P_j, we calculate its distance to the camera as z_j. Then we project the 3D point back to 2D at camera viewpoint i at position x_j^i and obtain the depth threshold d_j^i at that position. Only points with $z_j <= d_j^i$ can be projected to generate objectness score masks. Sample results are shown in Fig. 4.

Segment Proposals Refinement. In this section, we propose a method to refine scattered objectness probability masks into segment proposals. We take the chair class as an example and display results in Fig. 5. As shown in the third column of Fig. 5, the objectness probability mask displays accurate object localization and objectness probability. However, the projected masks are sparse and cannot directly be used as a supervision. To address this issue, we adopt a morphological operation followed by a fully-connected CRF [22] to recover dense segment proposals from the scattered masks.

First, we follow [52] to binarize the projected objectness probability mask, then apply an image close operation. Then, we follow [4] to adopt a fully connected CRF [22] to refine local boundary areas of our segment proposals. Referring to the fourth column of Fig. 5, it shows the recovery of image object boundaries based on 2D features, resulting in accurate segment proposals.

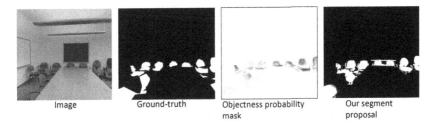

| Image | Ground-truth | Objectness probability mask | Our segment proposal |

Fig. 5. Examples of the segment proposals for the class of chair, where we reverse the grayscale of objectness probability masks for better visualization.

3.2 Recursive Procedure

We observe that the generated segment proposals capture the object shape significantly better than bounding boxes, which inspires us to adopt a recursive training procedure of transductive segmentation.

First, we generate segment proposals with bounding box labels. Then, after fully training the segmentation network with the segment proposals, the segment

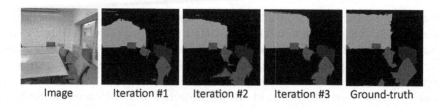

| Image | Iteration #1 | Iteration #2 | Iteration #3 | Ground-truth |

Fig. 6. Recursive updating of the segment proposals, which are progressively refined in each iteration, and then treated as supervision for the next iteration.

predictions are fed back into our pipeline to generate new segment proposals, where the input is segmentation masks instead of bounding boxes. New segment proposals are then used as supervision for the next iteration of training. By cycles of segment proposal generation, learning a semantic segmentation network, and using the learned network to find improved masks on previously seen images, we iteratively improve segment proposals and segmentation network.

Moreover, we use the bounding box labels to constrain our network predictions, $i.e.$, bounding box labels ensure that regions outside do not contain any object. So we employ bounding box masks to apply binary masking on our network predictions, which effectively removes false positive areas: $\Phi_p = X_b \otimes X_p$, where $\otimes$ means spatial-wise masking, X_b denotes masks generated by bounding boxes, X_p denotes original network predictions. We feed the masked network predictions Φ_p into our segment proposal generation module as shown in the recursive connection in Fig. 2.

3.3   Data Annotation

Currently, there exists no dataset available with multi-view camera parameters, depth data, and bounding box labels. Hence, we augment a subset of dataset 2D-3D-S [8] with hand labeled bounding boxes. 2D-3D-S [8] is an indoor dataset with multiple modalities from 2D, 2.5D and 3D domains, with instance-level semantic and geometric annotations. The dataset is collected in 6 large-scale indoor areas that originate from 3 buildings. The dataset provides a corresponding depth map, camera parameters for each 2D image, we adopt them as 3D information. They also provide 2D segmentation ground-truth projected from semantically labeled 3D mesh model. We pick four common indoor object classes (with clutter as the fifth class) to validate our method, including chair, bookcase, sofa and board as they are well defined and suitable for bounding box labels.

In this paper, we use data from area 1 to validate our method. Since there is no dataset contains both multi-view information and bounding box labels. We manually label bounding boxes on a subset of 1822 images and obtain segment proposals on all training images by adopting our proposed algorithm. Here we introduce the process that how we select a subset of images. First, since 2D images are separated by rooms, in order to obtain more object instances, we choose rooms where our objects are present and correctly labeled in the dataset.

Second, in each room, there are several camera locations, we ensure that the labeled images include images with views of the objects from different camera viewpoints to support our assumption of images over a wide baseline. Then, the generated segment proposals are used as a supervision signal during training. It is worth noting that the annotation signal is entirely derived from the box-level labels. Moreover, our bounding box labels can be used to train a prior 2D detector, *i.e.*, we can automate bounding boxes generation on more data, which further extends our method to a larger scale of data.

4 Experiments

4.1 Setup

We evaluate the proposed method on the 2D-3D-S [8] dataset. The dataset and annotation details are introduced in Sect. 3.3. We adopt the publicly available DeepLabV3+ [53] model as our backbone network. DeepLabv3+ is a recent state-of-the-art segmentation pipeline that uses a ResNet head [54], pre-trained on ImageNet [55]. We keep network structure unchanged, and train models under different supervision conditions to validate the effectiveness of our method. During training, the initial learning rate is 0.01 and is decreased by a factor of 10 after every 10 epochs. SGD is used as our optimizer with momentum of 0.9 and weight decay of 0.0001. All the training data are augmented by random cropping and horizontal flipping. We do not adopt a fully-connected CRF for post-processing of our network predictions. Results reported in Table 1, Table 2 and Fig. 8 are all from the first iteration without our recursive method. The evaluation performance is measured in terms of pixel intersection-over-union (mIoU). All experiments were conducted using PyTorch.

4.2 Comparison with Other Methods

In Table 1, comparisons are made to evaluate the impact of different levels of supervision. In our own method, we label bounding boxes on 1822 images and use our approach to obtain segment proposals on 4028 images as our training set, the performances are evaluated on a randomly selected validation set without overlapping without the training set. As a naive baseline, *Bounding boxes 1822*, we fill the bounding boxes of the labeled images as masks and use the filled masks as supervision. We form a second baseline, *CRF refined boxes 1822*, by directly applying a CRF on the bounding boxes to generate segment proposals. Moreover, we adopt GrabCut [23] to directly extract segment proposals from bounding boxes as *GrabCut 1822*. Then we evaluate performance in fully-supervised mode where the ground-truth is provided by the 2D-3D-S [8]. We report performances of the models supervised with both 1822 pixel-wise ground-truth, *pixel-wise 1882* and full 4028 pixel-wise ground-truth, *pixel-wise 4028*. We also report the performance in semi-supervised mode. We randomly select 400 images from the 4028 training set images, replace supervision with the ground-truth provided by [8]. which is called *semi 1822+400* in Table 1.

In addition, we compare with two state-of-the-art methods, *i.e.*, SDI [19], WSSL [18]. For bounding box based weakly supervised semantic segmentation, the state-of-the-art methods are: [21], BoxSup [17], SDI [19] and WSSL [18]. However, [17,19,21] did not release the official implementation code. Further, the released code for [18] was based on another deep framework. We re-implement SDI [19] and WSSL [18] with Pytorch as their performance is still competitive with SOTA and have clear and explicit implementation details. Our implementations will be made publicly available.

Table 1. Comparison of performances under different supervision conditions. The number after the method name means the number of images with human annotations that were used in this setting. $M \cap G+$: using the masks where both MCG and GrabCut agree. In bold is the best performing of the bounding box supervised methods. Our method outperforms competing box supervised methods and is midway to the fully supervised methods.

Modes	Method	Sofa	Board	Chair	Bookcase	Clutter	mIoU
Full	Pixel-wise 4028	62.77	89.57	70.58	77.77	96.23	79.38
	Pixel-wise 1822	54.44	85.29	66.78	74.64	95.37	75.30
Box	Bounding boxes 1822	34.23	71.23	45.30	67.65	90.46	61.78
	CRF refined boxes 1822	31.47	73.13	49.09	68.26	91.48	62.69
	GrabCut 1822	41.38	79.79	56.91	70.76	93.89	68.55
	WSSL [18] 1822	55.52	75.58	53.43	67.14	93.95	69.06
	SDI [19] $M \cap G+$ 1822	47.28	81.10	56.47	66.94	93.74	69.11
	Ours 1822	63.24	81.23	60.31	62.10	94.45	**72.27**
Semi	Semi 1822+400	61.98	80.33	62.77	67.09	94.64	73.36

Table 1 shows the results of our segment proposals compared with other methods. The bounding-box based baseline achieves 61.78 of mIoU while CRF refined bounding boxes improve the performance to 62.69. To explore the upper-bound on weakly supervised performance, we include results with a fully supervised model, trained using 1822 and 4028 pixel-wise ground-truth images respectively, the scores are 75.30 and 79.38. Our method achieves 72.27, which outperforms all the compared bounding-box based methods with a clear margin and is approaching the 1822 pixel-wise supervised baseline. This validates that our proposed method is effective. By labeling a subset of the dataset, we can extract accurate segment proposals on labeled and unlabeled images. Finally, in semi-supervised mode, we achieve 73.36 mIoU through replacing segment proposals of 400 images (10% of the training set) with pixel-level ground truth, where the performance is comparable with fully supervised models. The performance of our semi-supervised model indicates that we can achieve even better performance if additional supervision information is provided.

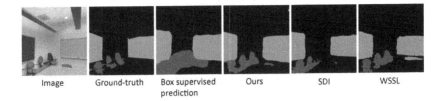

Image   Ground-truth   Box supervised   Ours   SDI   WSSL
                               prediction

Fig. 7. Examples of semantic segmentation prediction results.

Table 2. Comparison of performances on the test set.

Modes	Supervision	mIoU
Full	Pixel-wise 1822	63.62
Box	Bounding boxes 1822	53.57
	CRF refined boxes 1822	54.82
	Ours 1822	**57.61**
Semi	Semi 1822+1000	59.24

Table 3. Evaluate effectiveness of the recursive training method.

Supervision	Iteration 1	Iteration 2	Iteration 3
Ours	57.61	59.12	59.83

4.3   Experiments on Data from Unseen Areas

In our procedure, we label a subset of all images and get segment proposals for all those images by adopting 3D information. However, images from the same room may view the same object instances across the training and validation sets. To validate the effectiveness of our proposed method, we randomly select 2000 images from new areas to assemble a test set. These new areas are "unseen", which means none of the images in these areas are labeled nor seen in the training or validation. We test our trained model on this test set without fine-tuning. As shown in Table 2, our method outperforms the model trained with only bounding box masks, and achieves comparable performance to the fully supervised model. Thus, it validates that our method captures precise object information, and provides similar general class-wise features as the pixel-wise ground-truth.

4.4   Recursive Training Performance

As introduced in Sect. 3.2, we may apply our proposed method in a recursive manner. In the recursive procedure, the network predictions are fed into our segment proposal generation pipeline to generate new segment proposals. Although we achieve good results in the first iteration, the recursive training

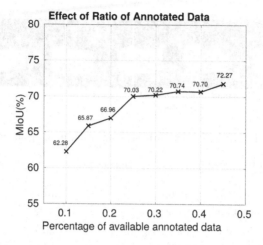

Fig. 8. Performance of our method when we randomly select different percentages of available annotated data. Reasonable segmentation is possible when just 10% of the training set is annotated. We can observe clear improvement when more annotation is provided, trailing off above 25%.

process transductively refines the new segment proposals and improves our network progressively. As shown in Table 3, we evaluate performance on the test set, the performance in every iteration is gradually improved.

4.5   Ablation: Effect of Ratio of Annotated Data

Our proposed method labels only a small portion of the dataset and obtains segment proposals on all images, which drastically decreases the cost of annotation. In this section, we investigate how the percentage of available annotated data affects performance, and attempt to achieve a balance between annotation cost and network performance. 1822 labeled images make up 45% of 4028 training images. We randomly select images from these to get different ratios of available labeled images. Selected labels are then fed into the same pipeline to generate segment proposals on the training set and report results in Fig. 8. As shown, more annotation data leads to manifest performance improvements which indicates the effectiveness of our method. When trained using only 25% of training images, we achieve 70.03 mIoU which already outperforms all competing methods (trained on 45%). Moreover, our method still gets a reasonably good results when only 10% of the training data is labeled with bounding boxes.

5   Conclusion

In this paper, we propose a novel 3D weakly supervised semantic segmentation approach, which incorporates box-level labels with corresponding 3D information. By only labeling a small number of images with bounding boxes, our approach extracts segment proposals on labeled and unlabeled images. Then we use the obtained segment proposals to train a semantic segmentation model. Moreover, our method can work in a recursive manner, which further refines our segment proposals. Our proposed method achieves competitive semantic segmentation results with less annotation effort. We evaluate the proposed method on the 2D-3D-S [8] dataset, extensive experimental results show that our proposed method is effective. Our annotations and source code will be made publicly available for future research endeavors in this field.

References

1. Long, J., Shelhamer, E., Darrell, T.: Fully convolutional networks for semantic segmentation. In: Proceeding IEEE Conference Computer Vision Pattern Recognition, pp. 3431–3440 (2015)
2. Zhao, H., Shi, J., Qi, X., Wang, X., Jia, J.: Pyramid scene parsing network. In: Proceeding IEEE Conference Computer Vision Pattern Recognition, pp. 2881–2890 (2017)
3. Chen, L.C., Papandreou, G., Kokkinos, I., Murphy, K., Yuille, A.L.: DeepLab: semantic image segmentation with deep convolutional nets, atrous convolution, and fully connected CRFs. IEEE Trans. Pattern Anal. Mach. Intell. **40**, 834–848 (2017)
4. Chen, L.C., Papandreou, G., Kokkinos, I., Murphy, K., Yuille, A.L.: Semantic image segmentation with deep convolutional nets and fully connected CRFs. ArXiv e-prints (2014)
5. Zhao, H., et al.: PSANet: point-wise spatial attention network for scene parsing. In: Ferrari, V., Hebert, M., Sminchisescu, C., Weiss, Y. (eds.) ECCV 2018. LNCS, vol. 11213, pp. 270–286. Springer, Cham (2018). https://doi.org/10.1007/978-3-030-01240-3_17
6. Chen, L.C., Papandreou, G., Schroff, F., Adam, H.: Rethinking atrous convolution for semantic image segmentation. ArXiv e-prints (2017)
7. Lin, T.-Y., et al.: Microsoft COCO: common objects in context. In: Fleet, D., Pajdla, T., Schiele, B., Tuytelaars, T. (eds.) ECCV 2014. LNCS, vol. 8693, pp. 740–755. Springer, Cham (2014). https://doi.org/10.1007/978-3-319-10602-1_48
8. Armeni, I., Sax, A., Zamir, A.R., Savarese, S.: Joint 2D–3D-semantic data for indoor scene understanding. ArXiv e-prints (2017)
9. Huang, Z., Wang, X., Wang, J., Liu, W., Wang, J.: Weakly-supervised semantic segmentation network with deep seeded region growing. In: Proceedings of the IEEE Conference on Computer Vision and Pattern Recognition, pp. 7014–7023 (2018)
10. Wei, Y., Xiao, H., Shi, H., Jie, Z., Feng, J., Huang, T.S.: Revisiting dilated convolution: a simple approach for weakly-and semi-supervised semantic segmentation. In: Proceedings of the IEEE Conference on Computer Vision and Pattern Recognition, pp. 7268–7277 (2018)
11. Ahn, J., Kwak, S.: Learning pixel-level semantic affinity with image-level supervision for weakly supervised semantic segmentation. In: Proceedings of the IEEE Conference on Computer Vision and Pattern Recognition, pp. 4981–4990 (2018)
12. Fan, J., Zhang, Z., Tan, T.: Cian: cross-image affinity net for weakly supervised semantic segmentation. ArXiv e-prints (2018)

13. Bearman, A., Russakovsky, O., Ferrari, V., Fei-Fei, L.: What's the point: semantic segmentation with point supervision. In: Leibe, B., Matas, J., Sebe, N., Welling, M. (eds.) ECCV 2016. LNCS, vol. 9911, pp. 549–565. Springer, Cham (2016). https://doi.org/10.1007/978-3-319-46478-7_34

14. Vernaza, P., Chandraker, M.: Learning random-walk label propagation for weakly-supervised semantic segmentation. In: Proceedings of the IEEE Conference on Computer Vision and Pattern Recognition, pp. 7158–7166 (2017)

15. Lin, D., Dai, J., Jia, J., He, K., Sun, J.: ScribbleSup: scribble-supervised convolutional networks for semantic segmentation. In: Proceedings of the IEEE Conference on Computer Vision and Pattern Recognition, pp. 3159–3167 (2016)

16. Tang, M., Perazzi, F., Djelouah, A., Ayed, I.B., Schroers, C., Boykov, Y.: On regularized losses for weakly-supervised CNN segmentation. In: Ferrari, V., Hebert, M., Sminchisescu, C., Weiss, Y. (eds.) ECCV 2018. LNCS, vol. 11220, pp. 524–540. Springer, Cham (2018). https://doi.org/10.1007/978-3-030-01270-0_31

17. Dai, J., He, K., Sun, J.: BoxSup: exploiting bounding boxes to supervise convolutional networks for semantic segmentation. In: Proceedings of the IEEE Conference on Computer Vision, pp. 1635–1643 (2015)

18. Papandreou, G., Chen, L.C., Murphy, K.P., Yuille, A.L.: Weakly-and semi-supervised learning of a deep convolutional network for semantic image segmentation. In: Proceedings of the IEEE Conference on Computer Vision, pp. 1742–1750 (2015)

19. Khoreva, A., Benenson, R., Hosang, J., Hein, M., Schiele, B.: Simple does it: weakly supervised instance and semantic segmentation. In: Proceedings of the IEEE Conference on Computer Vision and Pattern Recognition, pp. 876–885 (2017)

20. Li, Q., Arnab, A., Torr, P.H.: Weakly-and semi-supervised panoptic segmentation. In: Proceedings of the IEEE Conference on Computer Vision, pp. 102–118 (2018)

21. Song, C., Huang, Y., Ouyang, W., Wang, L.: Box-driven class-wise region masking and filling rate guided loss for weakly supervised semantic segmentation. In: Proceedings of the IEEE Conference on Computer Vision and Pattern Recognition, pp. 3136–3145 (2019)

22. Krähenbühl, P., Koltun, V.: Efficient inference in fully connected CRFs with gaussian edge potentials. In: Proceeding of Advance Neural Information Processing System, pp. 109–117 (2011)

23. Rother, C., Kolmogorov, V., Blake, A.: GrabCut: interactive foreground extraction using iterated graph cuts. ACM Trans. Graph. (TOG) **23**, 309–314 (2004)

24. Pont-Tuset, J., Arbelaez, P., Barron, J.T., Marques, F., Malik, J.: Multiscale combinatorial grouping for image segmentation and object proposal generation. IEEE Trans. Pattern Anal. Mach. Intell. **39**, 128–140 (2016)

25. Xiao, J., Owens, A., Torralba, A.: Sun3D: a database of big spaces reconstructed using SFM and object labels. In: Proceedings of the IEEE Conference on Computer Vision, pp. 1625–1632 (2013)

26. Dai, A., Chang, A.X., Savva, M., Halber, M., Funkhouser, T., Nießner, M.: Scan-Net: richly-annotated 3D reconstructions of indoor scenes. In: Proceedings of the IEEE Conference on Computer Vision and Pattern Recognition, pp. 5828–5839 (2017)

27. Geiger, A., Lenz, P., Stiller, C., Urtasun, R.: Vision meets robotics: the KITTI dataset. Int. J. Robot. Res. (IJRR) (2013)

28. Huang, X., et al.: The apolloscape dataset for autonomous driving. In: Proceedings of the IEEE Conference on Computer Vision and Pattern Recognition. Workshops, pp. 954–960 (2018)

29. Sun, P., et al.: Scalability in perception for autonomous driving: waymo open dataset. In: Proceedings of the IEEE/CVF Conference on Computer Vision and Pattern Recognition, pp. 2446–2454 (2020)
30. Ronneberger, O., Fischer, P., Brox, T.: U-Net: convolutional networks for biomedical image segmentation. In: Navab, N., Hornegger, J., Wells, W.M., Frangi, A.F. (eds.) MICCAI 2015. LNCS, vol. 9351, pp. 234–241. Springer, Cham (2015). https://doi.org/10.1007/978-3-319-24574-4_28
31. Badrinarayanan, V., Kendall, A., Cipolla, R.: SegNet: a deep convolutional encoder-decoder architecture for image segmentation. IEEE Trans. Pattern Anal. Mach. Intell. **39**, 2481–2495 (2017)
32. Liu, W., Rabinovich, A., Berg, A.C.: ParseNet: looking wider to see better. ArXiv e-prints (2015)
33. Yuan, Y., Wang, J.: OCNET: object context network for scene parsing. ArXiv e-prints (2018)
34. Zhang, H., Zhang, H., Wang, C., Xie, J.: Co-occurrent features in semantic segmentation. In: Proceedings of the IEEE Conference on Computer Vision and Pattern Recognition, pp. 548–557 (2019)
35. Zhou, Y., Sun, X., Zha, Z.J., Zeng, W.: Context-reinforced semantic segmentation. In: Proceedings of the IEEE Conference on Computer Vision and Pattern Recognition, pp. 4046–4055 (2019)
36. He, J., Deng, Z., Zhou, L., Wang, Y., Qiao, Y.: Adaptive pyramid context network for semantic segmentation. In: Proceedings of the IEEE Conference on Computer Vision and Pattern Recognition, pp. 7519–7528 (2019)
37. Fu, J., et al.: Dual attention network for scene segmentation. In: Proceedings of the IEEE Conference on Computer Vision and Pattern Recognition, pp. 3146–3154 (2019)
38. Ren, X., Bo, L., Fox, D.: RGB-(D) scene labeling: features and algorithms. In: Proceedings of the IEEE Conference on Computer Vision and Pattern Recognition, pp. 2759–2766 (2012)
39. Gupta, S., Arbelaez, P., Malik, J.: Perceptual organization and recognition of indoor scenes from RGB-D images. In: Proceedings of the IEEE Conference on Computer Vision and Pattern Recognition, pp. 564–571 (2013)
40. Silberman, N., Hoiem, D., Kohli, P., Fergus, R.: Indoor segmentation and support inference from RGBD images. In: Fitzgibbon, A., Lazebnik, S., Perona, P., Sato, Y., Schmid, C. (eds.) ECCV 2012. LNCS, vol. 7576, pp. 746–760. Springer, Heidelberg (2012). https://doi.org/10.1007/978-3-642-33715-4_54
41. Eigen, D., Fergus, R.: Predicting depth, surface normals and semantic labels with a common multi-scale convolutional architecture. In: Proceedings of the IEEE Conference on Computer , pp. 2650–2658 (2015)
42. Gupta, S., Girshick, R., Arbeláez, P., Malik, J.: Learning rich features from RGB-D images for object detection and segmentation. In: Fleet, D., Pajdla, T., Schiele, B., Tuytelaars, T. (eds.) ECCV 2014. LNCS, vol. 8695, pp. 345–360. Springer, Cham (2014). https://doi.org/10.1007/978-3-319-10584-0_23
43. Qi, X., Liao, R., Jia, J., Fidler, S., Urtasun, R.: 3D graph neural networks for RGBD semantic segmentation. In: Proceedings of the IEEE Conference on Computer Vision, pp. 5199–5208 (2017)
44. Park, S.J., Hong, K.S., Lee, S.: RDfNet: RGB-D multi-level residual feature fusion for indoor semantic segmentation. In: Proceedings of the IEEE Conference on Computer Vision, pp. 4980–4989 (2017)

45. Wang, W., Neumann, U.: Depth-aware CNN for RGB-D segmentation. In: Ferrari, V., Hebert, M., Sminchisescu, C., Weiss, Y. (eds.) ECCV 2018. LNCS, vol. 11215, pp. 144–161. Springer, Cham (2018). https://doi.org/10.1007/978-3-030-01252-6_9

46. Hou, J., Dai, A., Nießner, M.: 3D-SIS: 3D semantic instance segmentation of RGB-D scans. In: Proceedings of the IEEE Conference on Computer Vision and Pattern Recognition, pp. 4421–4430 (2019)

47. Vechersky, P., Cox, M., Borges, P., Lowe, T.: Colourising point clouds using independent cameras. IEEE Robot. Autom. Lett. **3**, 3575–3582 (2018)

48. Chen, D.Z., Chang, A.X., Nießner, M.: ScanRefer: 3D object localization in RGB-D Scans using natural language. arXiv preprint arXiv:1912.08830 (2019)

49. Chang, A., et al.: Matterport3D: learning from RGB-D data in indoor environments. In: International Conference on 3D Vision (3DV) (2017)

50. Hartley, R., Zisserman, A.: Multiple View Geometry in Computer Vision. Cambridge University Press, Cambridge (2003)

51. Qi, C.R., Liu, W., Wu, C., Su, H., Guibas, L.J.: Frustum pointnets for 3D object detection from RGB-D data. In: Proceeding of IEEE Conference Computer Vision Pattern Recognition, pp. 918–927 (2018)

52. Otsu, N.: A threshold selection method from gray-level histograms. IEEE Trans. Syst. Man, Cybern. **9**, 62–66 (1979)

53. Chen, L.-C., Zhu, Y., Papandreou, G., Schroff, F., Adam, H.: Encoder-decoder with atrous separable convolution for semantic image segmentation. In: Ferrari, V., Hebert, M., Sminchisescu, C., Weiss, Y. (eds.) ECCV 2018. LNCS, vol. 11211, pp. 833–851. Springer, Cham (2018). https://doi.org/10.1007/978-3-030-01234-2_49

54. He, K., Zhang, X., Ren, S., Sun, J.: Deep residual learning for image recognition. In: Proceeding of IEEE Conference Computer Vision and Pattern Recognition (2016)

55. Deng, J., Dong, W., Socher, R., Li, L.J., Li, K., Fei-Fei, L.: ImageNet: a large-scale hierarchical image database. In: Proceeding of IEEE Conference Computer Vision and Pattern Recognition, pp. 248–255 (2009)

Real-Time Segmentation Networks
Should be Latency Aware

Evann Courdier[1,2]([✉]) [ID] and François Fleuret[2,3] [ID]

[1] Idiap Research Institute, Martigny, Switzerland
evann.courdier@idiap.ch
[2] EPFL, Lausanne, Switzerland
[3] University of Geneva, Geneva, Switzerland
francois.fleuret@unige.ch

Abstract. As scene segmentation systems reach visually accurate results, many recent papers focus on making these network architectures faster, smaller and more efficient. In particular, studies often aim at designing 'real-time' systems. Achieving this goal is particularly relevant in the context of real-time video understanding for autonomous vehicles, and robots.

In this paper, we argue that the commonly used performance metric of mean Intersection over Union (mIoU) does not fully capture the information required to estimate the true performance of these networks when they operate in 'real-time'. We propose a change of objective in the segmentation task, and its associated metric that encapsulates this missing information in the following way: We propose to predict the future output segmentation map that will match the *future* input frame at the time when the network finishes the processing. We introduce the associated latency-aware metric, from which we can determine a ranking.

We perform latency timing experiments of some recent networks on different hardware and assess the performances of these networks on our proposed task. We propose improvements to scene segmentation networks to better perform on our task by using multi-frames input and increasing capacity in the initial convolutional layers.

1 Introduction

Recent image segmentation networks achieve near-human level performance due to their expressive power, and more focus is on designing architectures that are faster, and can run on smaller hardware with less memory and computing power. In particular, enabling real-time segmentation is critical for applications in robotics, autonomous driving or medical imaging during surgery.

The primary way currently used to assess performance is a task whose objective is the prediction of the input frame's segmentation, which is compared to the input frame's ground-truth segmentation using a given metric (*e.g.* mIoU).

Work done when F. Fleuret was at Idiap Research Institute.

© Springer Nature Switzerland AG 2021
H. Ishikawa et al. (Eds.): ACCV 2020, LNCS 12622, pp. 603–619, 2021.
https://doi.org/10.1007/978-3-030-69525-5_36

In what follows, we will use 'accuracy' to refer to such a metric. For networks aiming at low-latency, researchers also estimate efficiency with the *Frames Per Second* (FPS) metric, or its inverse the Seconds Per Frame metric, also called *latency*.

On real-time segmentation benchmarks, networks are ranked according either to some accuracy metric or latency. Often, accuracy-latency charts also allows to quickly estimate a new network overall performances. However, we claim there still is critical information missing to the practitioner: What is the actual accuracy of the system when deployed and used in practice? In other terms, we want to help answer the question of how the system's latency will affect the relevance of its predictions.

We propose an intuitive extension to the usual video segmentation task by introducing a change in the objective. We change the goal from predicting input frame segmentation to predicting future frame segmentation. Going beyond introducing a useful metric, our 'latency-aware' task aims at encouraging researchers to focus on a more relevant goal for real-time contexts, i.e. designing *anticipatory* networks.

The change we propose in the objective definition is straightforwardly applicable to a wide range of problem domains (*e.g.* object tracking, object detection, object segmentation, pose estimation). In the remainder of this paper, we will focus on the scene semantic segmentation task and perform our experiments on it.

Our contributions are as follows:

- We propose a simple, and relevant task that aims to assess actual performance of real-time networks,
- we highlight the associated metric and discuss its benefits,
- we analyse the relevance of the metric through multiple experiments on different scene segmentation networks,
- we propose improvements to a fast image-segmentation network for better performance on our task by taking multiple frames as input and increasing the number of channels of early convolutional layers.

We will make our code publicly available at the time of the conference.

2   Related Work

2.1   Image Semantic Segmentation

Most popular approaches for tackling Semantic Segmentation use a variant of powerful deep classification networks that are made fully convolutional, with all final fully connected layers replaced by convolutions. That seminal idea is at the core of the FCN paper [1].

The main issue coming with this technique is that it significantly reduces the image resolution in order to retrieve semantic information. Subsequent models for semantic segmentation are built as a "fully convolutional network" and attempt to cope with the dimension reductions, while increasing the Receptive Field.

One commonly used techniques is to use a *decoder network* plugged after the FCN to upsample the segmentation map using transposed convolution, as first did [2] and [3] with SegNet and U-Net. This setup allows to merge spatially rich shallow layers into semantically rich deeper layers.

DeepLab v2 [4] later proposed to use *dilated convolutions* [5] to avoid down-sampling. This allows to process images with a large field of view without having to reduce them, but it comes with a larger computational complexity.

Finally, [6] proposed to use a *"Spatial Pyramidal Pooling"* (SPP) module [7] for segmentation. SPP pools the image simultaneously at different resolutions over a grid, therefore enlarging the Receptive Field. This allows to incorporate a larger context, and take into account higher-level semantic.

Many works followed with techniques to produce high-quality segmentation [8–11], including better ways to extract features [12–15] and to take into account context [16,17]. Some recent works also proposed attention-based methods [18–23] and neural architecture search for image segmentation [24–26].

On a different application domain, similarly to the change we propose, back-bones with enlarged front-end have been used with success for object detection [27] were the authors are training their network without ImageNet pretraining.

2.2 Real-Time Semantic Segmentation

Reducing the computational cost and the memory cost of deep segmentation systems is critical for many applications that need to run real-time on slow hardware. A precursor in fast segmentation is ICNet [28], which is a fast network that uses multi-scale processing with a special fuse block to merge multi-scale information.

One way of optimising neural network architecture for speed is by using factorised convolutional blocks, *e.g.*. factorizing kernels $k \times k$ into $1 \times k$ and $k \times 1$ kernels as does ERFNet [29]. It can also be achieved using group convolutions, and methods such as ShuffleNet [30] propose different ways to create connections between groups.

One can also use depthwise separable convolution (DSC), which are the combination of depthwise and pointwise convolutions. These DSC are used to lower the number of parameters and makes the inference faster, at the cost of accuracy. They are used broadly in MobileNets [31,32].

Another important idea of these networks is to quickly downsample images in order to perform most of the processing at a smaller resolution and avoid full resolution processing. This idea is key to the design of ENet [33].

BiSeNet and BisenetV2 [34,35] proposed a way to separate the localization problem from the semantic extraction problem, and then to merge the two information appropriately.

Recent work such as FasterSeg network [36] also use Neural Architecture Search to successfully discover fast neural architectures for semantic segmentation.

Among fast segmentation networks, Swiftnet [37] is another recent work that proposes an architecture with a light-weight ImageNet-pretrained Resnet followed by a simple decoder using lateral connections similarly to U-Net. For our work, we choose SwiftNet as one of our base networks for its simplicity and its speed.

2.3 Video Scene Segmentation Networks

Another part of the literature focuses on designing *video* segmentation systems. More specifically, these works try to leverage the temporal correlation of consecutive frames in a video to improve the next-frame prediction and reduce computation and latency. However, most works in this domain are more focused on improving segmentation accuracy than reducing the latency.

The Clockwork net in [38] is a model that leverages temporal correlation by running different parts of the network at each time-step conditionally to how much the video has changed from the previous frame. This technique has the disadvantage of not providing a fixed frame-rate.

Another direction to address the problem is to try propagating previous features to consecutive frames to avoid recomputing very similar features for following frames, as is done in [39], even though their design is not meant for real-time.

The work [40] built on these two previous ideas. Their network decides at each frame whether to propagate previous features or to recompute the entire segmentation map. They improved the clockwork design to reduce the maximum latency but did not reach real-time.

Other works use predictive learning, that is predicting future frames or flow motion using past frames and segmentations to help current segmentation [41–43].

Video temporal coherence is also used along with representation warping to produce better future segmentation maps. Warping is either applied at the feature level [44,45] or directly at the segmentation map level [46], and possibly combined with existing features to produce the output. However, these works are not focused on time efficiency.

A Bayesian approach for multi-modal future prediction of scene segmentation was also proposed in [47] that allows to take into account model and observation uncertainty.

Recently, Temporally Distributed Network [48] was introduced for fast video segmentation. It uses a teacher-student design where fast student networks have to predict - in turns - part of the feature map of the teacher network.

3 A New Task for Real-Time Networks

3.1 Motivation for Latency Awareness

Real-time network performance is usually assessed through accuracy-latency charts that help in understanding a network's trade-offs. These charts provide *instant accuracy* of networks, *i.e.* the accuracy between the network's prediction and the input's ground truth. In practice however, networks may need a few seconds before they make a prediction. During that time, the scene has changed and the network prediction does not match that change. It is then particularly useful to compare the network prediction with this new scene's segmentation. This important comparison is missing from latency-accuracy charts as they do not provide the actual accuracy (compensated for time-delay) that one will get in practice. More, it does not provide neither a total order relation nor a ranking to compare various real-time networks, as can be seen on benchmark websites such as *paperswithcode.com*[1], We believe that it is therefore relevant to introduce a new objective for the segmentation task that takes into account network latency. This allows to get a meaningful accuracy information and practical benchmarking of networks.

3.2 Defining a New Objective for Real-Time Networks

We propose to change the objective of the segmentation task: currently, the objective of the task is to predict the input frame segmentation. Instead, we propose as objective to predict the segmentation of the "future" frame *at the time the network finishes its computation.*

Formally, let us consider a video sequence and let I_t and S_t denote respectively the frame at time t and its ground truth segmentation. Let F denote the operation of a network (say semantic segmentation) that takes l_F milliseconds to process the current input I_t. The common objective is to improve the metric:

$$\text{acc}\,(F(I_t), S_t) \tag{1}$$

while our task proposes to optimise for:

$$\text{acc}\,(F(I_t), S_{t+l_F}) \tag{2}$$

Instead of predicting the segmentation of the input frame, our task expects systems to predict the segmentation of a future frame, thus acknowledging the network latency.

This objective is particularly relevant for real-time applications in which we are usually more interested in what is currently happening than in what was a few seconds before: it is useful compare the information we get at a given time t using a network $(F(I_{t-l_F}))$ with the information we ideally would like to get at that time (S_t).

As said earlier, this change of objective is applicable to a whole range of different tasks such as object segmentation, object detection, object tracking, pose detection, etc. We focus on the scene segmentation task for this work.

3.3 Corresponding Latency-Aware Metric

For scene semantic segmentation, the metric commonly used is the mean Intersection over Union (mIoU). Our new task naturally defines a metric that depends

---

[1] https://paperswithcode.com/task/video-object-segmentation.

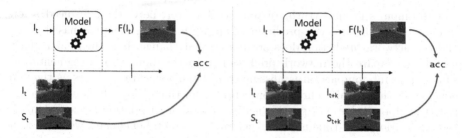

Fig. 1. Left: How mIoU is computed now; the output of the network is compared to the ground truth segmentation of the *image in input of the network*. Right: Our proposed way to measure mIoU; the output of the network is compared to the ground truth segmentation of the *future image* when network finishes processing.

on the latency of the network. We term it "Latency-Aware mIoU" (LAmIoU), which is defined as per Eq. (2).

Considering this metric is interesting as it carries an additional practical meaning compared to the classical instant mIoU: the accuracy (LAmIoU) that this metric outputs is the accuracy that one will see in practice when running this network in a real-time setting on the given hardware device.

3.4   Use with Video Datasets

In practice, a video sequence is collected with a specific sampling frequency (there is some time delay d between two sampled frames), and thus the dataset does not have a frame for every time t. For our task we therefore use the frame sampled just *after* the model has output a prediction as shown in Fig. 2.

More precisely, let's assume that $t = 0$ when frame of index 0 enters the network and consider a video sequence with a delay d between two frames (fps $= 1/d$). Then, the index of the segmentation map that the metric would use as ground truth is:

$$k_F = \lceil l_F/d \rceil \tag{3}$$

In what follows, when we refer to $t + k_F \times d$, we will simplify notation and write $t + k_F$.

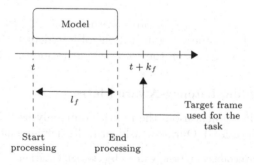

Fig. 2. Target frame used for our proposed objective

Note that the performance on this task is hardware-dependent. Indeed, as network latency depends on the device, the frame used for metric computation depends on it as well. Knowing the value of this metric for a network on multiple hardware allows one to pick the right network and hardware depending on precision needs.

4 Dataset, Models and Experimental Setup

4.1 Dataset

Dense pixel-level manual annotation of videos for scene segmentation is not feasible due to the time and economic costs involved. Cityscapes dataset [49] was estimated to take about 90 min per-frame for annotation and verification, and thus only provides sparse annotations of one frame per video sequence. We choose this dataset to conduct our experiments as it contains video sequences and its use is widespread as a segmentation benchmark.

This dataset contains 2,975 training, 500 validation and 1,525 testing video sequences. Each sequence contains 30 frames, and the 20th frame is annotated with fine pixel-level class labels for 19 object categories. A sequence is 1.8 s long, therefore the frame rate is approximately 16.6 fps and there is about 60 ms between each frame. As Cityscapes contains only the ground truth segmentation for one image per sequence, we process as follows:

1. We time the latency l_F of the network
2. We determine how many frames of offset k_F this time corresponds to: $k_F = \lceil l_F/0.06 \rceil$ (0.06 = 60 ms)
3. We use as input of the network the frame of index $20 - k_F$, as we only have the 20th frame's ground truth segmentation

Note that the Cityscapes framerate is about half of the one usually encountered in videos. This may be slightly detrimental as the higher the framerate is, the more precise the latency-aware metric will be.

4.2 Networks

For our experiments, we choose two image segmentation networks: SwiftNet [37] and DeepLab-V3+ [50] with 2 different encoders : ResNet-101 and MobileNet v2 [32].

SwiftNet. SwiftNet is a state-of-the-art network in real-time segmentation. For our experiments, we build this network as detailed in the original paper and describe it below. It is a network with an encoder-decoder structure:

– The encoder backbone is a classical ResNet-18 whose fully connected layers have been removed to make it fully convolutional.

- A Spatial Pyramidal Pooling Module with 4 different pooling layers of grid size (1, 2, 4, 8) is plugged in output of the encoder to increase its receptive field.
- Finally, a decoder with 3 upsampling modules recovers original image resolution. An upsampling module upsamples the previous layer's output and then merges it with a skip connection coming from the encoder.

We will refer to it as **SwiftNet-R18**. It has approximately 12M parameters. On Cityscapes validation set, it reaches 75% mIoU and runs at about 40 fps on a GTX 1080 Ti. On this hardware, SwiftNet has a latency of 26 ms. This means we have to use $k_F = \lceil 26/60 \rceil = 1$ frame offset to compute the latency-aware mIoU.

DeepLab v3+. DeepLab v3+ is a state of the art network for image segmentation. It has an encoder-decoder architecture very similar to that of SwiftNet:

- We use two different encoder backbones :

- A dilated ResNet-101 network stripped of its fully connected layers. We use an output stride of 16, so the last two residual blocks make use of dilated convolutions to enlarge the receptive field.
- A MobileNet-V2 network as described in [32]. It uses depthwise separable convolutions within "inverted" residuals blocks separated by linear bottlenecks.

- An Atrous Spatial Pyramidal Pooling module is plugged after this encoder. It convolves the encoder output with 4 atrous convolutions using different dilation rates: (1, 6, 12, 18).
- Finally, a small decoder upsamples the ASPP output and concatenates it with low-level features from the encoder. The decoder blends them with a convolution and upsamples the output to the original input image size.

When using a ResNet-101 as backbone, the whole network has approximately 60M parameters and reaches 77% mIoU on Cityscapes validation set and runs at 5 fps. We will refer to it as **DeepLab-R101**. On our hardware, it has a latency of 195 ms, which means we have to use $k_F = \lceil 195/60 \rceil = 4$ frame offsets to compute the latency-aware mIoU.

When using a MobileNet backbone, the model has about 5.5M parameters. It reaches 72% mIoU on Cityscapes and runs at 13 fps. We will refer to it as **DeepLab-MN.** It has a latency of 76 ms, so we have to use $k_F = \lceil 76/60 \rceil = 2$ frame offsets.

4.3   Adapting SwiftNet for Our Task

As we will discuss further, it is useful to input previous frames along with the current frame when training to predict a future segmentation map (that corresponds to the latency-aware objective). When we added more input channels to the first layer of the network, we noticed it is beneficial to increase the initial layers capacity by enlarging the number of channels. We construct a variant of SwiftNet that takes multiple frames in input, and where we expand the number of kernels in the initial convolution layers to deal with the increased input size. Specifically, in the case of two input frames, we replace the first layer:

$$\text{conv}(3, 64, 7 \times 7, s = 2)$$

with the following block of four layers:

$$\text{conv}(6, 130, 7 \times 7, s = 2)$$
$$\text{BN}(130)$$
$$\text{ReLU}$$
$$\text{conv}(130, 64, 3 \times 3, s = 1)$$

Note that we cannot introduce changes affecting multiple encoder layers as this would prevent us from reusing pretrained weights for the ResNet encoder, which represents SwiftNet's main strength. We have experimented with non-pretrained ResNet and observed a 6% mIoU drop on average.

The newly created convolutions were initialized using He's initialization [51] rule. We will refer to our extended SwiftNet version as **SwiftNet-R18-X**.

4.4   Training

All experiments are performed with the PyTorch framework. We use ImageNet-1k pretrained weights for all encoders in our networks.

Data Augmentation. We use image crops of 768×768. We do standard image augmentation with random horizontal flip, random scaling from 0.75 to 1.5 and random Gaussian blur.

SwiftNet. For SwiftNet, we use a batch size of 12 and train using the Adam optimiser with default parameters. We use a learning rate of $5e{-}4$ and a weight decay of $1e{-}4$. We also set a smaller learning rate of $1e{-}4$ for the part that is ImageNet-pretrained. We train the network for 200 epochs and use a cosine annealing schedule with $\eta_{min} = 1e{-}6$.

DeepLab v3+. For DeepLab, we use a batch size of 10 and train using the SGD optimiser with momentum of 0.9. We use a learning rate of $5e{-}2$ and a weight decay of $5e{-}4$. We similarly set a smaller learning rate of $5e{-}3$ for the part that is ImageNet-pretrained. We train the network for 200 epochs and use a poly schedule with a power of 3.

5   Experiments and Results

We perform experiments to evaluate the effect of network latency on the LAmIoU and to understand the changes in the training to suit the proposed objective.

5.1   Effect of Latency on the LAmIoU

The experiments described in this subsection are performed with *DeepLab-R101* and *SwiftNet-R18*. These two networks are modified to accept in input 2 frames X_{t-1}, X_t, as will be detailed later.

Decay of the LAmIoU with the Frame Offset. In Fig. 3, we plot the LAmIoU vs frame offsets. The two networks considered here are both trained and evaluated on the future segmentation map (with offset).

We notice that the LAmIoU drops quickly and the decrease is consistent between networks: an offset of 2 frames is enough to lose 10% mIoU for both networks on Cityscapes. In practice, we can expect this order of magnitude of mIoU drop, depending on the hardware.

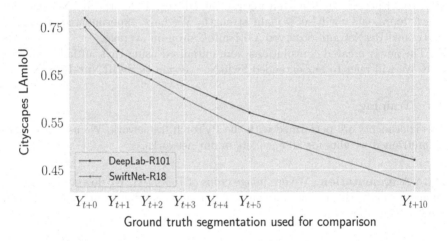

Fig. 3. LAmIoU decay with different offsets in the objective on Cityscapes validation set

Decay of the LAmIoU with the Hardware. Each network has a different latency per hardware. Therefore, the frame offset used for training and computing the metric is also different per hardware.

We perform timing experiments on *Tesla V100*, *GTX 1080 Ti* and *Tesla K80* GPUs for our two networks. We estimate latencies on these hardware and then train the networks with the corresponding frame offsets. In Fig. 4, we report the LAmIoU with respect to the inverse hardware speed (inverse of flops).

This plot exhibits an interesting and foreseeable fact: the slower deeplab network, whose "instant" mIoU is higher, performs worse than the faster SwiftNet network on slow hardware when measuring the LAmIoU. This graph illustrates the need for a latency aware metric in real-time contexts, which allows for a simple and fairer comparison of networks.

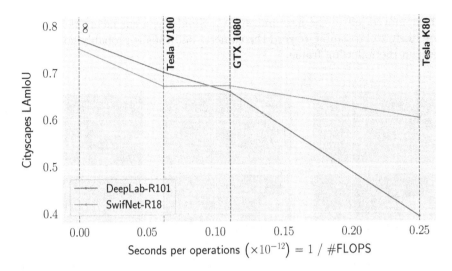

Fig. 4. LAmIoU decay with hardware speed on Cityscapes validation set

5.2 Optimising Network Training for Our Latency-Aware Objective

In this subsection, we investigate how changing the inputs and training target affects the LAmIoU. Precisely, we train using three different configurations and comment on the differences in the networks output. These experiments are performed on a *GTX 1080 Ti* GPU for each of the four networks described in Sect. 4.2.

First Configuration. First, we evaluate the four networks when trained with the usual objective (input I_t and target S_t) but evaluated with LAmIoU. The results are reported in second line of Table 1. Compared to their instant mIoU, we notice a significant drop between 10% and 30%.

Second Configuration. We train the networks for the proposed objective of predicting the future segmentation ground-truth used by the LAmIoU (input I_t and target S_{t+k}). The value of k is different for each network since each has a different latency. Therefore, they are trained and evaluated with a differently offset ground-truth.

The results are reported in third line of Table 1. We can see a slight but consistent increase of the LAmIoU metric for all networks. In Fig. 5, we show some qualitative results of SwiftNet-R18 overlaying images I_t and I_{t+1}. We notice that the segmentation mask is slightly blurry, as one would expect. However, we note that the blur is often surprisingly anisotropic, *i.e.* the segmentation blur is not surrounding the object, but favours a specific direction.

We conjecture that the network is able to predict some objects' movement based on their orientation. For instance, a person facing left in image I_t is likely to have moved left in the next image I_{t+1}. Similarly, a car facing the camera is more likely to be coming toward the camera, and thus is probably going to look bigger in the following frame.

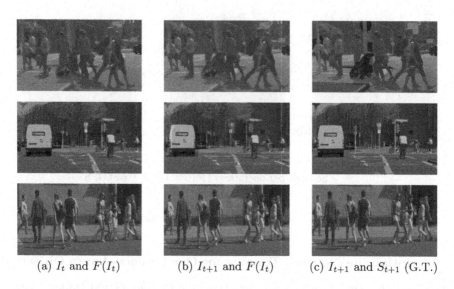

(a) I_t and $F(I_t)$ (b) I_{t+1} and $F(I_t)$ (c) I_{t+1} and S_{t+1} (G.T.)

Fig. 5. Output segmentation of SwiftNet-R18 trained to predict S_{t+1} from I_t. We observe anisotropic blur as the network is able to infer some objects movement directions from their orientation.

Third Configuration Finally, in order to allow the networks to infer speeds and directions, we train them using both I_{t-1} and I_t as inputs. The training objective remains to predict the future segmentation ground-truth S_{t+k}. Results reported in fourth line of Table 1 show a consistent improvement of the LAmIoU metric. These numbers confirms the relevance of using previous frames for our latency-aware objective. We reported in Fig. 6 examples of the output segmentation of SwiftNet-R18 overlaid on image I_t and I_{t+1} where it is clear that using an additional input is useful to produce sharper and more accurate segmentation maps.

For practical applications, we have seen that it is relevant to consider a future ground-truth as objective. When doing so, we need to change our training objective, and the result of this last configuration shows that it becomes necessary to use previous frames to get better predictions. While this result may not be surprising, the great majority of real-time scene segmentation works only use the current input when designing and training their networks. This last result emphasises the fact that networks constructed for real-time contexts should use previous frames to better predict a future target.

(a) I_t and $F(I_t)$ (b) I_{t+1} and $F(I_t)$ (c) I_{t+1} and S_{t+1} (G.T.)

Fig. 6. Output segmentation of SwiftNet-R18 trained to predict S_{t+1} from (I_{t-1}, I_t). We observe a more precise segmentation as the network has a way to infer relative speeds and directions.

5.3 Input Translations Experiment for Increased Receptive Field

When processing simultaneously images from different time-steps I_{t-1} and I_t, it is important for the network to have a large receptive field (to be able to map objects from one frame to the other). To do so without the need of big kernels, we try to offset this load on the input. The idea is to trade part of the computational cost usually associated with the use of big convolutional kernels for the memory cost of having more inputs.

Practically, we concatenate to the current input of the network various translations of the previous image I_{t-1}. When introducing translations, we want to compensate for the use of big kernels by allowing the model to simultaneously attend different parts of the image that a normal convolution kernel would not process simultaneously. Particularly, we change the inputs $\{I_{t-1}, I_t\}$ of the previous experiment to $\{T_1(I_{t-1}), \cdots, T_N(I_{t-1}), I_{t-1}, I_t\}$. corresponding to N different fixed translations T_i. The translations offsets were chosen to span a regular grid around the origin.

While initial experiments seemed promising, we further discovered that the only reason for improved LAmIoU was the additional convolutional layer with higher number of kernels that we added at the head of the model to handle the translations where we had replaced the first convolution layer $\text{conv}(3, 64, 7 \times 7, s = 2)$ with the following block:

$$\text{conv}(6 + 3 \times N, 8 \times N, 7 \times 7, s = 2)$$
$$\text{BN}(8 \times N)$$
$$\text{ReLU}$$
$$\text{conv}(8 \times N, 64, 3 \times 3, s = 1).$$

Table 1. Results for the 3 training configurations for the 4 networks. The first line gives the instant mIoU, the next three lines reports value of the LAmIoU metric for different training configurations. The last three lines give information about latency, frame offset used for the network as explained in Sect. 4.1, and fps of these networks when using a GTX 1080 Ti. Note that the k temporal offset depends on the network, hardware and on the dataset framerate: this offset is greater and leads to poorer performance for slow processing.

	Input	Target (train)	Target (test)	DeepLab-R101	DeepLab-MN	SwiftNet-R18	SwiftNet-R18-X
LAmIoU	I_t	S_t	S_t	**0.77**	0.72	0.75	0.74
	I_t	S_t	S_{t+k}	0.50	0.56	**0.64**	0.63
	I_t	S_{t+k}	S_{t+k}	0.53	0.57	**0.65**	0.64
	I_{t-1}, I_t	S_{t+k}	S_{t+k}	0.60	0.58	0.67	**0.69**
		Frame offset (k)		4	2	1	1
		Latency (ms)		195	76	26	38
		FPS		5	13	38	26

with N the number of translations. Noticing that using additional inputs requires increasing capacity in the early convolutional layers eventually lead to the design of SwiftNet-R18-X presented in Sect. 4.3 in which we increased the number of kernels in the first two layers.

6   Conclusion

We proposed a change in the usual objective of the segmentation task that makes real-time networks account for their latency when making their predictions. In addition to providing a new latency-aware ranking, the associated LAmIoU metric is of particular practical relevance as it represents the actual mIoU value one may obtain on a given hardware when taking into account network latency.

We argued the reasons why real-time networks should be latency-aware and we believe introducing a new latency-aware segmentation objective encourages research in anticipatory networks. With this objective in mind, we also proposed addition to networks and training in order to perform better under this new metric. While the focus of this paper is specifically toward video scene segmentation, the same change of objective is relevant and applicable to a wide range of other "real-time tasks" not limited to computer vision.

Acknowledgements. We thank Prabhu Teja for his help and relevant remarks on this manuscript. Evann Courdier was supported by the "Swiss Center for Drones and Robotics - SCDR" of the Swiss Department of Defence, Civil Protection and Sport via armasuisse S+T under project No 050-38.

References

1. Long, J., Shelhamer, E., Darrell, T.: Fully convolutional networks for semantic segmentation. In: Proceedings of the IEEE Conference on Computer Vision and Pattern Recognition, pp. 3431–3440 (2015)
2. Ronneberger, O., Fischer, P., Brox, T.: U-Net: convolutional networks for biomedical image segmentation. In: Navab, N., Hornegger, J., Wells, W.M., Frangi, A.F. (eds.) MICCAI 2015. LNCS, vol. 9351, pp. 234–241. Springer, Cham (2015). https://doi.org/10.1007/978-3-319-24574-4_28
3. Badrinarayanan, V., Kendall, A., Cipolla, R.: Segnet: a deep convolutional encoder-decoder architecture for image segmentation. IEEE Trans. Pattern Anal. Mach. Intell. **39**, 2481–2495 (2017)
4. Chen, L.C., Papandreou, G., Kokkinos, I., Murphy, K., Yuille, A.L.: Deeplab: Semantic image segmentation with deep convolutional nets, atrous convolution, and fully connected crfs. IEEE Trans. Pattern Anal. Mach. Intell. **40**, 834–848 (2017)
5. Yu, F., Koltun, V., Funkhouser, T.: Dilated residual networks. In: Proceedings of the IEEE Conference on Computer Vision and Pattern Recognition, pp. 472–480 (2017)
6. Zhao, H., Shi, J., Qi, X., Wang, X., Jia, J.: Pyramid Scene Parsing Network (PSP-Net). arXiv:1612.01105 (2016)
7. He, K., Zhang, X., Ren, S., Sun, J.: Spatial pyramid pooling in deep convolutional networks for visual recognition. IEEE Trans. Pattern Anal. Mach. Intell. **37**, 1904–1916 (2015)
8. Tang, M., Perazzi, F., Djelouah, A., Ben Ayed, I., Schroers, C., Boykov, Y.: On regularized losses for weakly-supervised CNN segmentation. In: Proceedings of the European Conference on Computer Vision (ECCV), pp. 507–522 (2018)
9. Takikawa, T., Acuna, D., Jampani, V., Fidler, S.: Gated-scnn: Gated shape CNNs for semantic segmentation. In: Proceedings of the IEEE International Conference on Computer Vision, pp. 5229–5238 (2019)
10. Zhu, Y., et al.: Improving semantic segmentation via video propagation and label relaxation. In: Proceedings of the IEEE Conference on Computer Vision and Pattern Recognition, pp. 856–8865 (2019)
11. Valada, A., Mohan, R., Burgard, W.: Self-supervised model adaptation for multi-modal semantic segmentation. Int. J. Comput. Vis. 1–47 (2019)
12. Peng, C., Zhang, X., Yu, G., Luo, G., Sun, J.: Large kernel matters-improve semantic segmentation by global convolutional network. In: Proceedings of the IEEE Conference on Computer Vision and Pattern Recognition, pp. 4353–4361 (2017)
13. Zhang, Z., Zhang, X., Peng, C., Xue, X., Sun, J.: Exfuse: enhancing feature fusion for semantic segmentation. In: Proceedings of the European Conference on Computer Vision (ECCV), pp. 269–284 (2018)
14. He, J., Deng, Z., Qiao, Y.: Dynamic multi-scale filters for semantic segmentation. In: Proceedings of the IEEE International Conference on Computer Vision, pp. 3562–3572 (2019)
15. Wu, H., Zhang, J., Huang, K., Liang, K., Yu, Y.: Fastfcn: rethinking dilated convolution in the backbone for semantic segmentation. arXiv preprint arXiv:1903.11816 (2019)
16. Ding, H., Jiang, X., Shuai, B., Qun Liu, A., Wang, G.: Context contrasted feature and gated multi-scale aggregation for scene segmentation. In: Proceedings of the IEEE Conference on Computer Vision and Pattern Recognition, pp. 2393–2402 (2018)

17. Yuan, Y., Chen, X., Wang, J.: Object-contextual representations for semantic segmentation. arXiv preprint arXiv:1909.11065 (2019)
18. Li, Y., Chen, X., Zhu, Z., Xie, L., Huang, G., Du, D., Wang, X.: Attention-guided unified network for panoptic segmentation. In: Proceedings of the IEEE Conference on Computer Vision and Pattern Recognition, pp. 7026–7035 (2019)
19. Fu, J., Liu, J., Tian, H., Li, Y., Bao, Y., Fang, Z., Lu, H.: Dual attention network for scene segmentation. In: Proceedings of the IEEE Conference on Computer Vision and Pattern Recognition, pp. 3146–3154(2019)
20. Huang, Z., Wang, X., Huang, L., Huang, C., Wei, Y., Liu, W.: Ccnet: criss-cross attention for semantic segmentation. In: Proceedings of the IEEE International Conference on Computer Vision, pp. 603–612 (2019)
21. Tao, A., Sapra, K., Catanzaro, B.: Hierarchical multi-scale attention for semantic segmentation. arXiv preprint arXiv:2005.10821 (2020)
22. Zhang, H., et al.: Resnest: split-attention networks. arXiv preprint arXiv:2004.08955 (2020)
23. Choi, S., Kim, J.T., Choo, J.: Cars can't fly up in the sky: improving urban-scene segmentation via height-driven attention networks. In: Proceedings of the IEEE/CVF Conference on Computer Vision and Pattern Recognition, pp. 9373–9383 (2020)
24. Liu, C., et al.: Auto-deeplab: hierarchical neural architecture search for semantic image segmentation. In: Proceedings of the IEEE Conference on Computer Vision and Pattern Recognition, pp. 82–92 (2019)
25. Zhang, X., Xu, H., Mo, H., Tan, J., Yang, C., Ren, W.: Dcnas: densely connected neural architecture search for semantic image segmentation. arXiv preprint arXiv:2003.11883 (2020)
26. Nekrasov, V., Chen, H., Shen, C., Reid, I.: Architecture search of dynamic cells for semantic video segmentation. In: The IEEE Winter Conference on Applications of Computer Vision, pp. 1970–1979 (2020)
27. Zhu, R., et al.: Scratchdet: training single-shot object detectors from scratch. In: Proceedings of the IEEE Conference on Computer Vision and Pattern Recognition, pp. 2268–2277 (2019)
28. Zhao, H., Qi, X., Shen, X., Shi, J., Jia, J.: ICNet for Real-Time Semantic Segmentation on High-Resolution Images. arXiv:1704.08545 (2017)
29. Romera, E., Alvarez, J.M., Bergasa, L.M., Arroyo, R.: Erfnet: efficient residual factorized convnet for real-time semantic segmentation. IEEE Trans. Intell. Transp. Syst. **19**, 263–272 (2017)
30. Zhang, X., Zhou, X., Lin, M., Sun, J.: Shufflenet: an extremely efficient convolutional neural network for mobile devices. In: Proceedings of the IEEE Conference on Computer Vision and Pattern Recognition, pp. 6848–6856 (2018)
31. Howard, A.G., et al.: MobileNets: Efficient Convolutional Neural Networks for Mobile Vision Applications. arXiv:1704.04861 (2017)
32. Sandler, M., Howard, A., Zhu, M., Zhmoginov, A., Chen, L.C.: Mobilenetv 2: inverted residuals and linear bottlenecks. In: Proceedings of the IEEE Conference on Computer Vision and Pattern Recognition, pp. 4510–4520 (2018)
33. Paszke, A., Chaurasia, A., Kim, S., Culurciello, E.: Enet: a deep neural network architecture for real-time semantic segmentation. arXiv preprint arXiv:1606.02147 (2016)
34. Yu, C., Wang, J., Peng, C., Gao, C., Yu, G., Sang, N.: BiSeNet: Bilateral Segmentation Network for Real-time Semantic Segmentation. arXiv:1808.00897 (2018)

35. Yu, C., Gao, C., Wang, J., Yu, G., Shen, C., Sang, N.: Bisenet v2: Bilateral network with guided aggregation for real-time semantic segmentation. arXiv preprint arXiv:2004.02147 (2020)
36. Chen, W., Gong, X., Liu, X., Zhang, Q., Li, Y., Wang, Z.: Fasterseg: searching for faster real-time semantic segmentation. arXiv preprint arXiv:1912.10917 (2019)
37. Orsic, M., Kreso, I., Bevandic, P., Segvic, S.: In defense of pre-trained imagenet architectures for real-time semantic segmentation of road-driving images. In: Proceedings of the IEEE Conference on Computer Vision and Pattern Recognition, pp. 12607–12616 (2019)
38. Shelhamer, E., Rakelly, K., Hoffman, J., Darrell, T.: Clockwork Convnets for Video Semantic Segmentation. arXiv:1608.03609 (2016)
39. Zhu, X., Xiong, Y., Dai, J., Yuan, L., Wei, Y.: Deep Feature Flow for Video Recognition. arXiv:1611.07715 (2016)
40. Li, Y., Shi, J., Lin, D.: Low-latency video semantic segmentation. In: Proceedings of the IEEE Conference on Computer Vision and Pattern Recognition, pp. 5997–6005 (2018)
41. Luc, P., Neverova, N., Couprie, C., Verbeek, J., LeCun, Y.: Predicting deeper into the future of semantic segmentation. In: Proceedings of the IEEE International Conference on Computer Vision, pp. 648–657 (2017)
42. Jin, X., et al.: Video scene parsing with predictive feature learning. In: Proceedings of the IEEE International Conference on Computer Vision, pp. 5580–5588 (2017)
43. Jin, X., et al.: Predicting scene parsing and motion dynamics in the future. In: Advances in Neural Information Processing Systems, pp. 6915–6924 (2017)
44. Saric, J., Orsic, M., Antunovic, T., Vrazic, S., Segvic, S.: Warp to the future: joint forecasting of features and feature motion. In: Proceedings of the IEEE/CVF Conference on Computer Vision and Pattern Recognition, pp. 10648–10657 (2020)
45. Gadde, R., Jampani, V., Gehler, P.V.: Semantic Video CNNs through Representation Warping. arXiv:1708.03088 (2017)
46. Terwilliger, A., Brazil, G., Liu, X.: Recurrent flow-guided semantic forecasting. In: 2019 IEEE Winter Conference on Applications of Computer Vision (WACV), pp. 1703–1712. IEEE (2019)
47. Bhattacharyya, A., Fritz, M., Schiele, B.: Bayesian prediction of future street scenes using synthetic likelihoods. arXiv preprint arXiv:1810.00746 (2018)
48. Hu, P., Caba, F., Wang, O., Lin, Z., Sclaroff, S., Perazzi, F.: Temporally distributed networks for fast video semantic segmentation. In: Proceedings of the IEEE/CVF Conference on Computer Vision and Pattern Recognition, pp. 8818–8827 (2020)
49. Cordts, M., et al.: The cityscapes dataset for semantic urban scene understanding. In: Proceedings of the IEEE Conference on Computer Vision and Pattern Recognition, pp. 3213–3223 (2016)
50. Chen, L.C., Zhu, Y., Papandreou, G., Schroff, F., Adam, H.: Encoder-Decoder with Atrous Separable Convolution for Semantic Image Segmentation (DeepLabv3+). arXiv:1802.02611 (2018)
51. He, K., Zhang, X., Ren, S., Sun, J.: Delving deep into rectifiers: Surpassing human-level performance on imagenet classification. In: Proceedings of the IEEE International Conference on Computer Vision, pp. 1026–1034 (2015)

Mask-Ranking Network for Semi-supervised Video Object Segmentation

Wenjing Li, Xiang Zhang$^{(\boxtimes)}$, Yujie Hu, and Yingqi Tang

University of Electronic Science and Technology of China, Chengdu, China
{liwenjing,huyujie,tangyingqi}@std.uestc.edu.cn, uestchero@uestc.edu.cn

Abstract. Video object segmentation is the fundamental problem of video analysis and many methods based on mask propagation and matching have been proposed in recent years. However, the two strategies are highly dependent on the last mask or the fixed mask given in the first frame and hence cannot adapt well to high deformation and rapid motion of objects. In this paper, we proposed a novel architecture named Mask-Ranking Network (MRNet), which takes advantage of both the propagation-based method and the matching-based method, to address the above problem. Specifically, in order to make better use of the long-term previous masks, we propose a novel propagation mechanism to make the network comprehensively consider the previous information. Under a unified encoder-decoder framework, we track the pixel-wise similarity of the object activation area in a long-term manner and explore the correlation between frames. In contrast to propagation-based only or matching-based only techniques, our method reduces the accumulation of errors in the propagation process and effectively uses the long-term previous frame information. In the video object segmentation task, MRNet can better handle the deformation of the objects, and make the segmentation result more accurate. We validate the effectiveness of the proposed method on the DAVIS 2016 and DAVIS 2017 dataset. Experiment results show that our method achieve state-of-the-art performance without using online fine-tuning and is robust to long-term propagation.

1 Introduction

Video Object Segmentation (VOS) aims to separate the object(s) of interest from the background pixels throughout a given video. With the rapid development of deep learning in recent years, as the basis of video analysis and subsequent video processing, this fundamental task has been applied to various fields, such as scene analysis, autonomous driving, action recognition and so on. In the aspect of setup, two main types of this problem are unsupervised and semi-supervised which differ from each other in whether the object annotation(s) in the first frame of the video is provided. In this paper, we consider the semi-supervised setting, in which the groundtruth segmentation of one or multiple objects are given

© Springer Nature Switzerland AG 2021
H. Ishikawa et al. (Eds.): ACCV 2020, LNCS 12622, pp. 620–636, 2021.
https://doi.org/10.1007/978-3-030-69525-5_37

in the first frame of the video, and then the methods automatically estimate the segmentation results in the rest of video. However, even with some prior knowledge in the process of inference, this is still a challenging task because the appearance of the object can drastically change throughout the video due to the deformation, occlusion and illumination change, greatly deteriorated the segmentation results.

To tackle the aforementioned challenges, many algorithms based on deep learning have been proposed in recent years. Some algorithms regard the VOS as a mask-refinement process, which belongs to the mask-propagation based method. This type of algorithm uses a neural network to learn the deformation from the previous output to the query frame, starting from the first frame. These networks learn the features of the previous mask prediction and adjust it to fit the current frame, usually are simple in structure and performing well on the smooth deformation. However, they are susceptible to rapid motion and suffer from error accumulation during propagation. Another type of method focuses on finding the connection between the query frame and the first frame, which belongs to the matching-based method. The standard strategy is to extract the features of the current frame and the reference through neural network and do high-dimensional pixel-wise metric matching. These methods avoid the loss of information in the mask propagation process, but directly using the k-nearest neighbour results as the final classification makes the segmentation rougher.

In this paper, we proposed a novel neural network Mask-Ranking Network (MRNet) for semi-supervised VOS task that integrate the advantages of both propagation-based and matching-based methods. We conduct a Mask-Ranking Module (MRM), to dynamically and rapidly select the most conductive mask to guiding the segmentation in the intermediate process of mask-propagation. Through MRM, the network can not only avoid the absoluteness of the hard classification based on the matching method, but also continuously modify the propagation results during the inference process. With our framework, the network is no longer limited to relying only on the first frame annotation and the previous output, as the conductive information can be easily added. The proposed network is also highly efficient as there is no need of fine-tuning in the test time, which is a truly end-to-end training network.

The major contributions of this paper are: (i) We proposed a novel network Mask-Ranking Network (MRNet) for semi-supervised video object segmentation, which can easily and continuously add conductive information to refine the segmentation result. (ii) We conduct a Mask-Ranking Module to dynamically and rapidly guiding the segmentation in the intermediate process of inference. (iii) Experiments on DAVIS 2016 and DAVIS 2017 show that the proposed method exceed the state-of-the-art performance.

2   Related Work

2.1   Unsupervised and Semi-supervised Video Object Segmentation

Video object segmentation can be divided into two types: unsupervised and semi-supervised, which differ from each other in whether the first frame groundtruth is provided. Methods based on unsupervised setting [1–4] mainly explore the dense optical flow and object appearance features to do pixel-wise prediction. However, the object of interest is not specified in the video, making the segmentation result is ambiguous. In this paper, we focus on the semi-supervised algorithms. Many semi-supervised approach rely on fine-tuning on the first frame during testing in order to obtain better performance [5–13]. It has shown that fine-tuning on the first frame significantly improves the accuracy. OSVOS [6] fine-tunes the pre-trained convolutional network on the annotated first-frame at test time. OnAVOS [12] and OSVOS-S [11] are build on the OSVOS. OnAVOS employs an online adaption mechanism by treat the segmentation results as new training examples to update the network online during the test time. OSVOS-S transfer the generic semantic information learned on ImageNet to the segmentation task based on a fully convolutional neural network. However, the expensive computation and time-delay extremely limit the real-time processing applications. Therefore, there are several recent works aim to achieve a better run time and usability by avoiding online learning [14–18]. FRTM [17] is composed of appearance model and segmentation model. The target adaption process of FRTM is fully simulated during the offline training stage. SAT [18] treats each target object as a tracklet, avoiding the effect of online fine-tuning to achieve real-time segmentation. In this paper, we explore an end-to-end network structure, which dynamically selects necessary information during the intermediate process of forward propagation to improve the segmentation effect, completely avoiding online training.

2.2   Matching-Based Methods

Matching-based method is to exploit the appearance similarity between the current frame and reference frame. They directly segment each pixel based on the result of pixel-level matching [19–29]. PML [25] treats the video object segmentation as pixel-wise retrieval problem. They first trained an embedding layer with triplet loss and then predict each pixel by nearest-neighbour matching result to the first frame. However, this type of hard classification often results in noisy segmentation. VideoMatch [26] adopts a soft matching mechanism which is similar to PML. It uses a soft matching layer to produce the foreground and background similarity maps and consider the k nearest neighbours of each pixel for segmentation. However, the result is still derived from the matching score, making the segmentation unsatisfactory. FEELVOS [28] uses an embedding layer to calculate global and local pixel-wise matching in the internal of network, but suffering the lose of the information from similarity maps due to the propagation. RANet [27] learns pixel-wise similarity maps to explore the similarity between the first frame and the current frame by a ranking attention module. Recently, Zhang et al. [29] proposed a transductive method TVOS, that takes a label propagation methods where the labels are propagate based on feature similarity in an embedding space. Different from the previous works, we tried to make use of the information of more previous frames, instead of just selecting

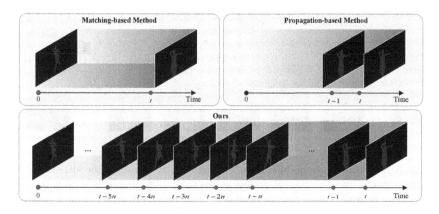

Fig. 1. A simple comparison of propagation-based methods, matching-based methods and our framework. The time marked with red dots represents the information at that moment is used to guide the segmentation of current frame. (Color figure online)

the first frame as guidance or directly taking the nearest neighbour matching as the final segmentation decision.

2.3   Propagation-Based Methods

The propagation-based methods [3,8,29–38] mainly rely on the segmentation of the previous frame to improve the performance of the current frame. VPN [39] propagates structure information through the entire video by a unified framework of temporal bilateral network and spatial refinement network. OSMN [40] combines a segmentation network with two modulators, which manipulate the intermediate layers of the segmentation network and learning the annotated first frame and spatial location of the previous frame, respectively. RGMP [34] constructs the network as a Siamese encoder-decoder structure, in which the weights of the encoder part are shared between two streams. One of the encoder stream takes the current frame with previous mask estimation as input. The other stream takes the first frame and its annotation as input. The architecture of RGMP is similar with ours, as we also utilize the Siamese network in the encoder part. However, instead of simply stacking the feature maps, we dynamically select the most conductive mask by proposed Mask-Ranking Module in the intermediate process and feed it into the decoder. Recently, TVOS [29] uses the previous segmentation as training data for discriminative model. The mask of the previous frame is feed into the target module to generate the low-resolution score map during the inference process. RANet [27] uses a ranking attention module to filter the similarity maps and then feed them together with the previous mask estimation into the decoder, which makes it easier for the network to capture useful information. However, directly feeding the previous segmentation into the decoder can easily lead to the error accumulation.

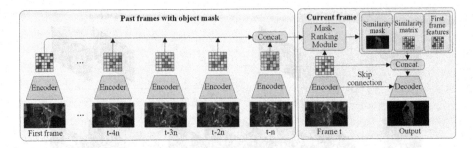

Fig. 2. An overview of our architecture. The network contains two encoders that encode the past frames and the current frame, respectively. The features of past frames (in orange) are concatenated, and then passed into the matching layer to calculate the correlation with the feature of the current frame (in green). Finally, the similarity mask, similarity matrix (in grey) and the first frame features (in blue) is concatenated and passed into decoder together with current frame features that skip connection. (Color figure online)

3   Method

Given the annotation of the first frame, many previous semi-supervised video object segmentation methods mainly explore the relationship between the current frame and the previous or first frame. In this paper, we proposed a novel architecture named Mask-Ranking Network(MRNet) for semi-supervised video object segmentation task. The motivation of our method is illustrated in Fig. 1. The key idea of our method is to explore more information from all of the previous frames while without any online learning. Our method can constantly update the content of reference to make it more consistent with the current frame. It combines the advantages of the propagation-based method and the matching-based method, so that the network can constantly correct errors during the inference process and be robust to long-term videos.

In this section, we first provide an overview of the proposed MRNet in Sect. 3.1. In Sect. 3.2, we describe the proposed Mask-Ranking Module in details. In Sect. 3.3, we discuss the details during the inference. Finally, the extension for multi-object is presented in Sect. 3.4.

3.1   Overview of the Architecture

Our MRNet can be divided into two parts: the part processing the past frames and the part processing the current frame. An illustration of our MRNet is shown in Fig. 2.

Processing the Past Frames. In the left part of Fig. 2, we exhibit the processing of a series of past frames. Each encoder takes a RGB image and mask as input and the weights of the encoders are shared. Among them, the first frame and its annotation are the reference frame and reference mask of this video,

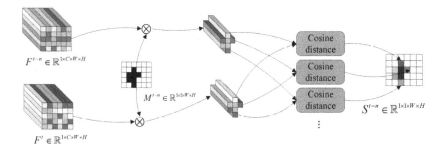

Fig. 3. An illustration of the process of mask similarity matching. $F^t \in \mathbb{R}^{1 \times C \times W \times H}$ represents the features of the current frame at time t. $F^{t-n} \in \mathbb{R}^{1 \times C \times W \times H}$ represents the features of the past frame at time $t - n$. $M^{t-n} \in \mathbb{R}^{1 \times 1 \times W \times H}$ represents the mask of the frame at time $t-n$. $S^{t-n} \in \mathbb{R}^{1 \times 1 \times W \times H}$ represents the similarity matrix between the current frame and the past frame at time $t - n$.

respectively. For other past frames, they are combined with the mask of their previous frame as the input of the encoder. In order to reduce the computation cost, the past frames are selected at an interval n. After getting the features of all the past frames, we concatenate all of the features and passed them to the matching layer for subsequent matching and selection. Specifically, we choose ResNet50 [41] as the shared feature extractor. The number of input channels has been adjusted to 4 to receive the input we set, containing 3 channel RGB image and 1 channel mask. The weights of the network are initialized from the ImageNet pretrained model.

Processing the Current Frame. The current video frame is processed by an encoder-decoder structure on the whole. The inputs of encoder are an RGB image and the mask from the previous frame. Features extracted by the backbone are stored and fed into the Mask-Ranking Module to learn the similarity with the past frame features. The output of Mask-Ranking Module contains three parts, the similarity mask, similarity matrix and the stored first frame features, which we will discuss in details in the Sect. 3.2. Then, the three outputs are concatenated with the current frame high-dimensional features and passed through our pipeline. The decoder consists of three refinement modules [42], which take the concatenated features and the skip connections features as input. What is different from the original architecture is that the convolution layers have been changed into residual blocks [43]. We first up-sample the deep layer features of by bilinear interpolation, and then concatenate them with shallow features of current frame from the encoder. In this way, the features of different depths in the encoder are fed into the decoder to obtain a more comprehensive segmentation result.

3.2   Mask-Ranking Module

The propagation-based method uses the previous frame to guide the segmentation of the current frame, and the matching-based method explores the

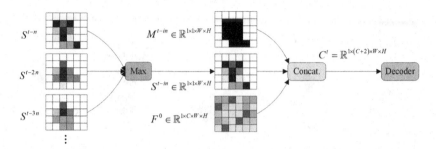

Fig. 4. An illustration of the process of mask ranking. After computing the similarity matrix, we choose the mask with the highest similarity matrix value. We choose the mask with the largest similarity matrix value, and feed it to the decoder with the similarity matrix and the mask of the first frame. S, M and the F^0 denote the similarity map, mask and the first frame feature, respectively. C^t represent s the concatenate features, with a dimension of $1 \times (C + 2) \times W \times H$.

relationship between the current frame and the first frame. However, just propagating the mask throughout the video without any refinement will lead to a poor performance in the long-term video. And the deformation of the object makes it difficult for the network to perform an accurate pixel-wise binary classification just through the similarity with the first frame. In order to use the features from the semantically related region in the past frames to help refine the current frame segmentation, we propose a Mask-Ranking Module, which synthesizes the advantages of the propagation-based and matching-based video segmentation methods. There are mainly two operations in our Mask-Ranking Module, one is the process of mask similarity matching based on the object activate region, and the other is the mask ranking operation to rank and select the previous masks and similarity matrices.

Mask Similarity Matching. A schematic illustrating details of the process of mask similarity matching is given in Fig. 3. Different from other matching-based methods that based on Euclidean distance to obtain pixel-wise similarity, we choose cosine similarity for our mask similarity matching. For a given object, we match the semantic activate region features between the current frame and the past frames to obtain the similarity matrices. Denote the current frame is at time t, the past frame features is defined as:

$$F = \{F^0, F^1, \cdots, F^{t-1}\} \tag{1}$$

Due to the similarity between adjacent frames, we balance the amount of calculation and the amount of information in past frames, and choose to perform mask similarity matching every n frames. In order to ensure a fixed number of channels, k feature maps are selected for calculation each time. Then, the features to be matched are $\{F^{t-kn}, \cdots, F^{t-2n}, F^{t-n}\}$. The masks of the selected features are $\{M^{t-kn}, \cdots, M^{t-2n}, M^{t-n}\}$. We denote the foreground feature vector at location (i, j) of the F^{t-kn} as m_{t-kn}^{ij}. The feature vector at the corresponding position (i, j) of the current frame feature map F^t is x_t^{ij}. The similarity matrix between the current frame and the past frame at time $t - kn$ is denoted as $S^{t-kn} \subset \mathbb{R}^{1 \times 1 \times W \times H}$. We denote the foreground similarity value at location (i, j) as s_{t-kn}^{ij}. The background pixels similarity value is set to 0. The cosine similarity between the two feature vectors m_{t-kn}^{ij} and x_t^{ij} is formulated as:

$$s_{t-kn}^{ij} = \frac{m_{t-kn}^{ij} x_t^{ij}}{\left\| m_{t-kn}^{ij} \right\| \left\| x_t^{ij} \right\|} \tag{2}$$

Mask Ranking. The process of mask ranking is shown in Fig. 4. After the calculating of the similarity matrix between the past frame features $\{F^{t-kn}, \cdots, F^{t-2n}, F^{t-n}\}$ and the current frame feature F^t, we rank the similarity matrix according to the value sum of them. The similarity matrix is obtained by cosine similarity between two vectors m_{t-kn}^{ij} and x_t^{ij}, where a larger value represents the higher the similarity of the feature vectors at the pixel. The similarity matrices are denoted as $\{S^{t-kn}, \cdots, S^{t-2n}, S^{t-n}\}$, and the dimension is $1 \times 1 \times W \times H$. The value sum of S^{t-kn} is calculated as:

$$V_{t-kn} = \sum_{i=1}^{H} \sum_{j=1}^{W} s_{t-kn}^{ij} \tag{3}$$

However, if we just make decision by the value V_{t-kn}, a similarity matrix with a large number of foreground pixels is easier to be selected because its similarity matrix value may be relatively larger. So, we use the average of V_{t-kn} to rank:

$$averageV_{t-kn} = \frac{1}{\sum_{i=1}^{H} \sum_{j=1}^{W} m_{t-kn}^{ij}} V_{t-kn} \tag{4}$$

We denoted the time with the largest $averageV_{t-kn}$ as $t - in$. The similarity matrix S^{t-in}, similarity mask M^{t-in} and the first frame feature map F^0 are concatenated to the feature $C^t \in \mathbb{R}^{1 \times (C+2) \times W \times H}$ and fed into the decoder.

3.3   Inference

The inference of the proposed MRNet is straight forward in an end-to-end manner. Given the first frame annotation, the network can automatically propagate the mask throughout the video with the dynamic mask ranking internal operation. When we segment the frame at time t, k feature maps are selected from the past frames according to the time interval n to learn the similarity with the current frame. Then the similarity matrix and mask with the largest similarity matrix $averageV_{t-kn}$ value are selected to refine the segmentation result of the current frame. Every feature map is calculate only once in the pipeline, making the technique efficient enough. In particular, two frames with long time intervals have low similarity, and two frames with short time intervals are usually similar.

Table 1. Past frames selection criteria

Current frame time	Selected past frames time
$t \leq 5$	0
$5 < t \leq 10$	$0, t - 5$
$10 < t \leq 15$	$0, t - 5, t - 10$
$15 < t \leq 20$	$0, t - 5, t - 10, t - 15$
$t > 20$	$0, t - 5, t - 10, t - 15, t - 20$

In order to avoid redundancy of information and waste of calculation, the k is set to 4 and the n is set to 5 in our implementation. In this way, if the time t of the current frame is greater than 20, the interval reference time for past frames is 20 frames. When t is less than 20, we increase the available past frames as the video passed through the network frame-by-frame. Specifically, if $t \leq 5$, we only consider the first frame; if $5 < t \leq 10$, we consider the first frame and the frame $t - 5$; if $10 < t \leq 15$, we consider the frame $t - 5$, $t - 10$ and the first frame; if $15 < t \leq 20$, we consider the frame $t - 5$, $t - 10$, $t - 15$ and the first frame. The past frames selection criteria is shown in Table 1.

3.4 Extension for Multi-object VOS

The extension from single-object video object segmentation to multi-object video object segmentation is to run each object independently. In the proposed MRNet, we individually match the feature vector of each object between the past frames and current frame. As for N objects in a frame, in order to keep the number of output channels of the Mask-Ranking Module unchanged, we unify the N similarity matrix of each object into one. Specifically, taking two objects as an example, the final similarity matrix $A \in {}^{1 \times 1 \times W \times H}$ is the average of the two similarity matrices $S_{t-kn,1}^{ij}$ and $S_{t-kn,2}^{ij}$. Each pixel value is calculated as:

$$A^{ij} = \frac{1}{2} \left(S_{t-kn,1}^{ij} + S_{t-kn,2}^{ij} \right) \tag{5}$$

The subscript $t - kn$ of $S_{t-kn,N}^{ij}$ represents the frame index, and the subscript N represents the object index in the frame.

4 Experiments

4.1 Implementation Details

Training Datasets. The DAVIS 2016 [44] dataset is for single-object segmentation which contains a total of 50 sequences, 3455 frames with densely pixel-wise annotations. The 50 sequences are divided into a training set with 30 sequences, and a validation set with 20 sequences. The DAVIS 2017 [45] dataset is the

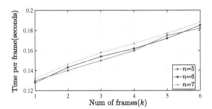

	$\mathcal{J}\&\mathcal{F}$
Baseline	81.1
+MRM(without Sim-map)	82.6
+MRM(with Sim-map)	85.0

Fig. 5. Visualization of Similarity matrix on DAVIS 2016 dataset.

Fig. 6. Ablation study of the proposed network on DAVIS 2016 dataset.

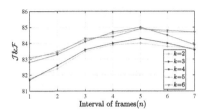

Fig. 7. The impact of k.

Fig. 8. The impact of n.

extension of multi-object segmentation, which contains a training set with 60 sequences and a validation set of 30 videos. Each sequence from DAVIS 2016 and DAVIS 2017 has a temporal extent about 2–4 s, that all major challenges in longer video sequences are included.

Network Settings and Training Details. We use the ResNet50 [41] as the encoder feature extractor, and the parameters of it is initialized by a pre-trained model on ImageNet. The weights of the entire network are shared between process of the past frames and the current frames. The channels of the encoder output are 2048, and the input channels of the decoder are $(2048 \times 2 + 2)$, which contain the channels of the current frame features, the first frame reference features, selected similarity matrix and mask. During the training process, we adopt the thought of BPTT [46], the length of it is taken as 12. The entire network runs on a single NVIDIA GeForce GTX 1080Ti GPU and is trained end-to-end using the Adam optimizer [47]. The weight decay factor is 0.0005 and the initial learning rate is set to 10^{-5} and gradually decreases overtime.

Evaluation Metrics. Following the suggestion of DAVIS [44], we use three standard metrics: the region similarity $\mathcal{J}$ Mean, the contour accuracy $\mathcal{F}$ Mean and $\mathcal{J}\&\mathcal{F}$, which is the average of $\mathcal{J}$ Mean and the $\mathcal{F}$ Mean. The Jaccard index $\mathcal{J}$ mean is calculated as the mean of the intersection over union $(mIoU)$ between the network output M and the groundtruth G, thus the metric represents the region similarity. As for the metric $\mathcal{F}$ mean, we consider it as a good trade-off between the *Precision* and the TP_{rate}. The definitions are as follows:

$$Precision = \frac{TP}{TP + FP} \tag{6}$$

$$TP_{rate} = \frac{TP}{TP + FN} \tag{7}$$

$$\mathcal{F} = \frac{2 \times Precision \times TP_{rate}}{Precision + TP_{rate}} \tag{8}$$

$$\mathcal{J} = \frac{M \cap G}{M \cup G} \tag{9}$$

where TP, FP and FN are the numbers of true positives, false positives and false negatives, respectively.

4.2 Ablation Study

We perform an extensive ablations on DAVIS 2016 validation set to confirm the effectiveness of our proposed method. In our ablative experiments, we first analyze the impact of proposed Mask Ranking Module (MRM) by totally removing it from our network. Then we verify the effectiveness of Similarity Matrix by leave its calculation out of decoder. Finally, we conduct a experiments on the impact of k and n. Ablation study results are shown in Fig. 6.

The Effectiveness of the Mask Ranking Module. Firstly, we remove the proposed Mask Ranking Module to analyze its impact, which leads to a dramatic reduction that the $\mathcal{J}\&\mathcal{F}$ reduce from the 85% to 81.1%, which is shown in the first row and the bottom row in Fig. 6. This results clearly demonstrate that the Mask Ranking Module we proposed plays an important role in our framework.

The Effectiveness of the Similarity Map. As for the effectiveness of the similarity matrix, we leave its calculation from the decoder, that the inputs of decoder only include the current frame feature, the first frame feature, the similarity mask and the skip-connection features from the encoder. As shown in the second row in Fig. 6, the $\mathcal{J}\&\mathcal{F}$ reduce from the 85% to 82.6%, and only 1.5% higher than baseline. This results demonstrate that the similarity matrix made a major contribution to the total accuracy. The visualization of the Similarity Matrix is shown in Fig. 5, we can find that the Similarity Matrix can provide conductive information for segmentation.

The Impact of the k and n. The larger the n, the longer the time we consider, but the object may have a larger deformation during this time, which is of little guiding significance for current frame. The larger the k, the larger number of similar frame to be calculated, and the greater the amount of calculation. Therefore, we conducted experiments for choosing k and n. Figure 7 shows the impact of k. We can see that the time process one frame go longer as the k increases. Figure 8 shows the impact of n, and we can see that when n increase, the $\mathcal{J}\&\mathcal{F}$ first increases and then decrease. That is because the similarity become smaller when two frames are too far apart.

4.3 Comparison to the State-of-the-Art

Comparison Methods. We compare our MRNet with a total of 20 methods that contains 9 online based methods (OSVOS [6], MaskRCNN [33],

Table 2. The quantitative comparison on the DAVIS 2016 and DAVIS 2017 validation sets. The results are sorted for online (OL) and non-online methods respectively. The highest scores in each category are highlighted in bold.

Method	OL	DAVIS 2016				DAVIS 2017		
		$\mathcal{J}$&$\mathcal{F}$	$\mathcal{J}$ mean	$\mathcal{F}$ mean	Time	$\mathcal{J}$&$\mathcal{F}$	$\mathcal{J}$ mean	$\mathcal{F}$ mean
OSVOS [6]	✓	80.2	79.8	80.6	9 s	60.3	56.6	63.9
MaskRCNN [33]	✓	80.8	80.7	80.9	-	-	60.5	-
Lucid [5]	✓	83	83.9	82.0	>100 s	66.6	63.4	69.9
OSVOS-S [11]	✓	86.6	85.6	87.5	**4.5 s**	68.0	64.7	71.3
CINM [32]	✓	84.2	83.4	85.0	>30 s	70.7	67.2	74.2
SegFlow [7]	✓	75.4	74.8	76.0	7.9 s	-	-	-
MSK [10]	✓	77.6	79.7	75.4	12 s	-	-	-
OnAVOS [12]	✓	85.5	86.1	84.9	13 s	67.9	64.5	71.2
PReMVOS [35]	✓	**86.8**	**84.9**	**88.6**	32.8 s	**77.8**	**73.9**	**81.7**
Videomatch [26]	✗	80.9	81.0	80.8	0.32 s	62.4	56.5	68.2
PML [25]	✗	77.4	75.5	79.3	0.28 s	-	-	-
VPN [39]	✗	67.9	70.2	65.5	0.63 s	-	-	-
OSMN [40]	✗	73.5	74.0	72.9	0.13 s	54.8	52.5	57.1
FEELVOS [28]	✗	81.7	80.3	83.1	0.5 s	69.1	65.9	72.3
RGMP[34]	✗	81.8	81.5	82.0	0.13 s	66.7	64.8	68.6
A-GAME [30]	✗	82.1	82.0	82.2	0.07 s	70.0	67.2	72.7
FAVOS [15]	✗	81.0	82.4	79.5	1.8 s	58.2	54.6	61.8
TVOS [29]	✗	-	-	-	-	72.3	69.9	74.7
SAT [18]	✗	83.1	82.6	83.6	**0.03 s**	72.3	68.6	76.0
FRTM [17]	✗	81.6	-	-	0.07 s	69.2	-	-
MRNet (ours)	✗	**85.0**	**85.1**	**84.9**	0.16 s	**73.4**	**70.4**	**76.3**

Lucid [5], OSVOS-S [11], CINM [32], SegFlow [7], MSK [10], OnAVOS [12], PReMVOS [35]) and 11 offline methods (Videomatch [26], PML [25], VPN [39], OSMN [40], FEELVOS [28], RGMP [34], A-GAME [30], FAVOS [15], TVOS [29], SAT [18], FRTM [17]).

Results on DAVIS 2016. Table 2 compares our methods on the DAVIS 2016 validation set to other state-of-the-art methods. Our MRNet achieves a $\mathcal{J}$&$\mathcal{F}$ Mean of 85%. Among all the methods without OL techniques, the performance of the proposed MRNet is the best. Considering all the methods listed in Table 2, the online learning based method PReMVOS [35] has a $\mathcal{J}$&$\mathcal{F}$ Mean of 86.8%, which is 1.8% higher than our MRNet. However, the time processing one frame of 32.8s is much longer than MRNet of 0.16s. Using additional training data and employing online learning lead to a low processing speed of PReMVOS. While our MRNet avoid the online learning operation and post-processing, obtaining a efficient performance on the DAVIS 2016 validation set.

Results on DAVIS 2017. For the task of multi-object segmentation, we evaluate our method on DAVIS 2017 validation set. Table 2 shows a comparison to

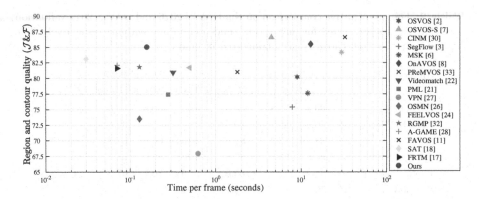

Fig. 9. A comparison of performance and speed for semi-supervised video object segmentation on the DAVIS 2016 validation set. The better methods are located at the upper-left corner. The proposed MRNet shows a good speed/accuracy trade-off.

other state-of-the-art methods. Experiments shows that our MRNet achieves a $\mathcal{J}\&\mathcal{F}$ Mean of 73.4%, which is the best among all of the methods without OL technique, demonstrating the superiority of the proposed MRNet on the multi-object segmentation.

Speed. A comparison of performance and speed for semi-supervised video object segmentation on the DAVIS 2016 validation set is shown in Fig. 9. The horizontal axis represents the time it takes the network to process a frame, and the vertical axis represents the metric $\mathcal{J}\&\mathcal{F}$ Mean. The method with less processing time and higher accuracy is superior. Therefore, the better methods are located at the uppper-left corner. The proposed MRNet shows a good speed/accuracy trade-off.

4.4   Qualitative Result

Figure 10 shows qualitative results of our MRNet on DAVIS 2016 and DAVIS 2017 validation set. It can be seen in many cases such as appearance changes, object fast motion, occlusion and so on, MRNet is able to produce accurate and robust segmentation results. While in some cases, the segmentation result of MRNet is not complete, this may be because the similar masks found by cosine similarity are not the most similar to the current frame in the global.

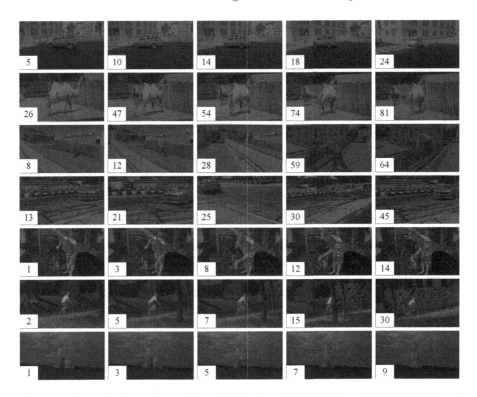

Fig. 10. The qualitative results of our MRNet on DAVIS 2016 and DAVIS 2017 validation set.

5   Conclusion

In this paper, we present a novel end-to-end architecture Mask-Ranking Network(MRNet) for semi-supervised video object segmentation, which take both the advantage of propagation-based methods and matching-based methods and avoiding online fine-tuning. A Mask-Ranking Module is proposed to make a internal guidance for the current frame processing. During the inference, the most conductive information will be selected from the past frames to refine the current segmentation. Experiments on DAVIS 2016 and DAVIS 2017 dataset demonstrate that our MRNet achieves state-of-the-art performance. Overall, MRNet is a practical useful method for video object segmentation.

The future research direction of this problem can be explored from multiple aspects. First, in our MRNet, we calculate the pixel-wise similarity using cosine similarity. There may be other effective similarity measurement methods between frames. Moreover, we measure the similarity for specific candidate frames(every 5 frames). The selection of candidate frames is also a problem worthy of further study. Finally, the mechanism of dynamically exploring long-term similarities between frames can be applied to other video processing tasks. We hope our method can serve as a solid baseline for future research.

Acknowledgements. This work was supported by the National Key Research and Development Program of China (2018YFE0203900), National Science Foundation of China (U1733111, U19A2052), and Sichuan Science and Technology Achievement Transformation project (2020ZHCG0015).

References

1. Brox, T., Malik, J.: Object segmentation by long term analysis of point trajectories. In: Daniilidis, K., Maragos, P., Paragios, N. (eds.) ECCV 2010. LNCS, vol. 6315, pp. 282–295. Springer, Heidelberg (2010). https://doi.org/10.1007/978-3-642-15555-0_21
2. Grundmann, M., Kwatra, V., Mei, H., Essa, I.: Efficient hierarchical graph-based video segmentation. In: 2010 IEEE Conference on Computer Vision and Pattern Recognition (CVPR) (2010)
3. Tokmakov, P., Alahari, K., Schmid, C.: Learning motion patterns in videos. In: 2017 IEEE Conference on Computer Vision and Pattern Recognition (CVPR), pp. 531–539 (2017)
4. Wang, W., Shen, J., Porikli, F.: Saliency-aware geodesic video object segmentation. In: 2015 IEEE Conference on Computer Vision and Pattern Recognition (CVPR) (2015)
5. Khoreva, A., Benenson, R., Ilg, E., Brox, T., Schiele, B.: Lucid data dreaming for video object segmentation. Int. J. Comput. Vis. **127**(9), 1175–1197 (2019). https://doi.org/10.1007/s11263-019-01164-6
6. Caelles, S., Maninis, K.K., Pont-Tuset, J., Leal-Taixe, L., Cremers, D., Van Gool, L.: One-shot video object segmentation. In: The IEEE Conference on Computer Vision and Pattern Recognition (CVPR) (2017)
7. Cheng, J., Tsai, Y.H., Wang, S., Yang, M.H.: SegFlow: joint learning for video object segmentation and optical flow. In: The IEEE International Conference on Computer Vision (ICCV) (2017)
8. Ci, H., Wang, C., Wang, Y.: Video object segmentation by learning location-sensitive embeddings. In: Ferrari, V., Hebert, M., Sminchisescu, C., Weiss, Y. (eds.) ECCV 2018. LNCS, vol. 11215, pp. 524–539. Springer, Cham (2018). https://doi.org/10.1007/978-3-030-01252-6_31
9. Hu, P., Wang, G., Kong, X., Kuen, J., Tan, Y.: Motion-guided cascaded refinement network for video object segmentation. IEEE Trans. Pattern Anal. Mach. Intell. **42**(8), 1957–1967 (2020)
10. Khoreva, A., Perazzi, F., Benenson, R., Schiele, B., Sorkine-Hornung, A.: Learning video object segmentation from static images. In: 2017 IEEE Conference on Computer Vision and Pattern Recognition (CVPR) (2017)
11. Maninis, K.K., et al.: Video object segmentation without temporal information. IEEE Trans. Pattern Anal. Mach. Intell. **41**(6), 1515–1530 (2018)
12. Voigtlaender, P., Leibe, B.: Online adaptation of convolutional neural networks for video object segmentation. arXiv preprint arXiv:1706.09364 (2017)
13. Jang, W.D., Kim, C.S.: Online video object segmentation via convolutional trident network. In: 2017 IEEE Conference on Computer Vision and Pattern Recognition (CVPR) (2017)
14. Johnander, J., Danelljan, M., Brissman, E., Khan, F.S., Felsberg, M.: A generative appearance model for end-to-end video object segmentation. In: 2019 IEEE/CVF Conference on Computer Vision and Pattern Recognition (CVPR) (2019)

15. Cheng, J., Tsai, Y.H., Hung, W.C., Wang, S., Yang, M.H.: Fast and accurate online video object segmentation via tracking parts (2018)
16. Ventura, C., Bellver, M., Girbau, A., Salvador, A., Marques, F., Giro-i Nicto, X.: RVOS: end-to-end recurrent network for video object segmentation (2019)
17. Robinson, A., Lawin, F.J., Danelljan, M., Khan, F.S., Felsberg, M.: Learning fast and robust target models for video object segmentation. In: Proceedings of the IEEE/CVF Conference on Computer Vision and Pattern Recognition, pp. 9384–9393 (2020)
18. Chen, X., Li, Z., Yuan, Y., Yu, G., Shen, J., Qi, D.: State-aware tracker for real-time video object segmentation. In: Proceedings of the IEEE/CVF Conference on Computer Vision and Pattern Recognition, pp. 9384–9393 (2020)
19. Sun, Y., Wang, X., Tang, X.: Deep learning face representation by joint identification-verification. In: Advances in Neural Information Processing Systems (2014)
20. Liu, Y., et al.: DEL: deep embedding learning for efficient image segmentation. In: Proceedings of the Twenty-Seventh International Joint Conference on Artificial Intelligence, IJCAI-2018, pp. 864–870. International Joint Conferences on Artificial Intelligence Organization (2018)
21. Liu, W., Wen, Y., Yu, Z., Li, M., Raj, B., Song, L.: SphereFace: deep hypersphere embedding for face recognition (2017)
22. Chen, B., Deng, W.: Deep embedding learning with adaptive large margin N-pair loss for image retrieval and clustering. Pattern Recogn. **93**, 353–364 (2019)
23. Guo, H., Wang, J., Gao, Y., Li, J., Lu, H.: Multi-view 3D object retrieval with deep embedding network. IEEE Trans. Image Process. **25**, 5526–5537 (2016)
24. Li, Z., Tang, J., Mei, T.: Deep collaborative embedding for social image understanding. IEEE Trans. Pattern Anal. Mach. Intell. **41**, 2070–2083 (2019)
25. Chen, Y., Pont-Tuset, J., Montes, A., Van Gool, L.: Blazingly fast video object segmentation with pixel-wise metric learning. In: Proceedings of the IEEE Conference on Computer Vision and Pattern Recognition, pp. 1189–1198 (2018)
26. Hu, Y.-T., Huang, J.-B., Schwing, A.G.: VideoMatch: matching based video object segmentation. In: Ferrari, V., Hebert, M., Sminchisescu, C., Weiss, Y. (eds.) ECCV 2018. LNCS, vol. 11212, pp. 56–73. Springer, Cham (2018). https://doi.org/10.1007/978-3-030-01237-3_4
27. Wang, Z., Xu, J., Liu, L., Zhu, F., Shao, L.: RANet: ranking attention network for fast video object segmentation. In: Proceedings of the IEEE International Conference on Computer Vision, pp. 3978–3987 (2019)
28. Voigtlaender, P., Chai, Y., Schroff, F., Adam, H., Leibe, B., Chen, L.C.: FEELVOS: fast end-to-end embedding learning for video object segmentation. In: Proceedings of the IEEE Conference on Computer Vision and Pattern Recognition, pp. 9481–9490 (2019)
29. Zhang, Y., Wu, Z., Peng, H., Lin, S.: A transductive approach for video object segmentation. In: Proceedings of the IEEE/CVF Conference on Computer Vision and Pattern Recognition, pp. 6949–6958 (2020)
30. Johnander, J., Danelljan, M., Brissman, E., Khan, F.S., Felsberg, M.: A generative appearance model for end-to-end video object segmentation. In: 2019 IEEE/CVF Conference on Computer Vision and Pattern Recognition (CVPR), pp. 8945–8954 (2019)
31. Wang, W., et al.: Learning unsupervised video object segmentation through visual attention (2019)

32. Bao, L., Wu, B., Liu, W.: CNN in MRF: video object segmentation via inference in a CNN-based higher-order spatio-temporal MRF. In: The IEEE Conference on Computer Vision and Pattern Recognition (CVPR) (2018)

33. Hu, Y., Huang, J., Schwing, A.G.: MaskRNN: instance level video object segmentation, pp. 325–334 (2017)

34. Oh, S.W., Lee, J.Y., Sunkavalli, K., Kim, S.J.: Fast video object segmentation by reference-guided mask propagation. In: Proceedings of the IEEE Conference on Computer Vision and Pattern Recognition, pp. 7376–7385 (2018)

35. Luiten, J., Voigtlaender, P., Leibe, B.: PReMVOS: proposal-generation, refinement and merging for video object segmentation. In: Jawahar, C.V., Li, H., Mori, G., Schindler, K. (eds.) ACCV 2018. LNCS, vol. 11364, pp. 565–580. Springer, Cham (2019). https://doi.org/10.1007/978-3-030-20870-7_35

36. Li, X., Loy, C.C.: Video object segmentation with joint re-identification and attention-aware mask propagation. In: Ferrari, V., Hebert, M., Sminchisescu, C., Weiss, Y. (eds.) ECCV 2018. LNCS, vol. 11207, pp. 93–110. Springer, Cham (2018). https://doi.org/10.1007/978-3-030-01219-9_6

37. Oh, S.W., Lee, J., Xu, N., Kim, S.J.: Video object segmentation using space-time memory networks. In: 2019 IEEE/CVF International Conference on Computer Vision (ICCV), pp. 9225–9234 (2019)

38. Xu, S., Liu, D., Bao, L., Liu, W., Zhou, P.: MHP-VOS: multiple hypotheses propagation for video object segmentation. In: 2019 IEEE/CVF Conference on Computer Vision and Pattern Recognition (CVPR), pp. 314–323 (2019)

39. Jampani, V., Gadde, R., Gehler, P.V.: Video propagation networks. In: The IEEE Conference on Computer Vision and Pattern Recognition (CVPR) (2017)

40. Yang, L., Wang, Y., Xiong, X., Yang, J., Katsaggelos, A.K.: Efficient video object segmentation via network modulation. In: Proceedings of the IEEE Conference on Computer Vision and Pattern Recognition, pp. 6499–6507 (2018)

41. He, K., Zhang, X., Ren, S., Sun, J.: Deep residual learning for image recognition. In: 2016 IEEE Conference on Computer Vision and Pattern Recognition (CVPR), pp. 770–778 (2016)

42. Pinheiro, P.O., Lin, T.-Y., Collobert, R., Dollár, P.: Learning to refine object segments. In: Leibe, B., Matas, J., Sebe, N., Welling, M. (eds.) ECCV 2016. LNCS, vol. 9905, pp. 75–91. Springer, Cham (2016). https://doi.org/10.1007/978-3-319-46448-0_5

43. He, K., Zhang, X., Ren, S., Sun, J.: Identity mappings in deep residual networks. In: Leibe, B., Matas, J., Sebe, N., Welling, M. (eds.) ECCV 2016. LNCS, vol. 9908, pp. 630–645. Springer, Cham (2016). https://doi.org/10.1007/978-3-319-46493-0_38

44. Perazzi, F., Pont-Tuset, J., Mcwilliams, B., Gool, L.V., Sorkine-Hornung, A.: A benchmark dataset and evaluation methodology for video object segmentation. In: 2016 IEEE Conference on Computer Vision and Pattern Recognition (CVPR) (2016)

45. Pont-Tuset, J., Perazzi, F., Caelles, S., Arbeláez, P., Sorkine-Hornung, A., Van Gool, L.: The 2017 DAVIS challenge on video object segmentation. arXiv preprint arXiv:1704.00675 (2017)

46. Werbos, P.J.: Backpropagation through time: what it does and how to do it. Proc. IEEE **78**, 1550–1560 (1990)

47. Kingma, D., Ba, J.: Adam: a method for stochastic optimization. Computer Science (2014)

SDCNet: Size Divide and Conquer Network for Salient Object Detection

Senbo Yan[1], Xiaowen Song[1($\boxtimes$)], and Chuer Yu[2]

[1] State Key Laboratory of Fluid Power and Mechatronic Systems,
Zhejiang University, Hangzhou 310027, China
{3140100833,songxw}@zju.edu.cn
[2] College of Computer Science and Technology,
Zhejiang University, Hangzhou 310027, China
11721080@zju.edu.cn

Abstract. The fully convolutional neural network (FCN) based methods achieve great performances in salient object detection (SOD). However, most existing methods have difficulty in detecting small or large objects. To solve this problem, we propose Size Divide and Conquer Network (SDCNet) which learning the features of salient objects of different sizes separately for better detection. Specifically, SDCNet contains two main aspects: (1) We calculate the proportion of objects in the image (with the ground truth of pixel-level) and train a size inference module to predict the size of salient objects. (2) We propose a novel Multi-channel Size Divide Module (MSDM) to learning the features of salient objects with different sizes, respectively. In detail, we employ MSDM following each block of the backbone network and use different channels to extract features of salient objects within different size range at various resolutions. Unlike coupling additional features, we encode the network based on the idea of divide and conquer for different data distributions, and learn the features of salient objects of different sizes specifically. The experimental results show that SDCNet outperforms 14 state-of-the-art methods on five benchmark datasets without using other auxiliary techniques.

1 Introduction

Salient object detection (SOD), which aims to find the distinctive objects in the image, plays an important role in many computer vision tasks, such as weakly supervised semantic segmentation [1], object recognition [2], image parsing [3] and image retrieval [4]. Besides, there is a lot of work focused on RGB-D salient object detection [5–8] and video salient object detection [9,10]. One main problem of SOD is that the salient objects in different images have extremely different sizes. As shown in Fig. 1, the size of salient objects under the same dataset varies greatly. We define the pixel-wise ratio between the salient objects and the entire image as salient object proportion (SOP). We show the SOP distribution of 10 benchmark datasets in Table 1 and Fig. 2. It is observed that 25% of images have

© Springer Nature Switzerland AG 2021
H. Ishikawa et al. (Eds.): ACCV 2020, LNCS 12622, pp. 637–653, 2021.
https://doi.org/10.1007/978-3-030-69525-5_38

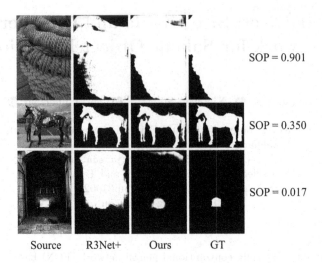

SOP = 0.901

SOP = 0.350

SOP = 0.017

Source   R3Net+   Ours   GT

Fig. 1. Saliency detection results for salient objects with different size by different methods. We use salient object proportion (SOP) to indicates the proportion of objects in the whole image.

the SOP less than 0.1, while 10% of images have the SOP larger than 0.4. The size difference of salient objects is ubiquitous in SOD datasets.

Some FPN-based complex multi-level feature fusion methods [11–13] try to alleviate the perplex caused by huge size deviation. However, multiscale feature fusion methods generally ignore the difference in data distribution determined by the huge size deviation, which leads to differences in the features that need to be learned. These methods have been proved cannot completely solve the problem of the size difference. [14] proved that performances of SOD methods generally decreased in small objects (SOP between 0 to 0.1) or large objects (SOP above 0.5). Our method is based on a basic fact: for a network with the same structure, if only small-size (or large-size) objects are used for training, the model performance in small-size (or large-size) objects detection will be better than using the entire dataset for training. Moreover, the size difference of the salient objects has an intuitive impact. For example, the detection of small objects depends more on local information, while large objects contain more global semantic information. Existing SOD methods ignore the size difference of salient objects. We argue that divide and conquer objects of different sizes can lead to a more robust model and better performances.

In this paper, we regard the size information as a beneficial supplement to the salient object information and propose a novel method to divide and conquer salient objects of different sizes. Firstly, we establish an FPN-based side output architecture to realize the fusion of features at high and low levels. The only reason we employ multi-resolution fusion is to make a fair comparison with SOTA methods that generally uses feature fusion to improve performance. Secondly, we obtain the size inference of salient objects through a Size Inference Module (SIM) which shares the same backbone with SDCNet. SIM generates a

Table 1. Distribution of salient object proportion (SOP) in 10 benchmark datasets without non-saliency images. The size range is divided into five categories according to SOP. "–10%" means SOP between 0 to 0.1.

Dataset	–10%	10%–20%	20%–30%	30%–40%	40%–	Total
MSRA10K	1020	3646	3060	1756	518	10000
ECSSD	154	326	244	130	136	1000
DUT-O	2307	1387	818	418	238	5168
DUTS-TR	1239	2656	2553	1994	2111	10553
DUTS-TE	2299	1506	626	234	354	5019
HKU-IS	983	1580	1179	510	195	4447
PASCAL-S	204	187	168	139	146	844
SED2	34	27	18	5	16	100
SOD	54	70	68	37	69	298
THUR-15K	2616	2083	779	429	326	6233
Total	11681	14036	9920	5948	4477	48462

binarized rough saliency inference and the predicted size range of salient objects is obtained by calculating SOP. As shown in Table 1, we classify the size range into five categories according to the SOP (0–10%, 10%–20%, 20%–30, 30%–40% and above 40%). In the side output structure, we add MSDM in the process of feature fusion up-to-down. MSDM divides feature maps of each side layer into size-independent stream and size-dependent stream. As shown in Fig. 4, we put the size-independent stream into a common convolutional layer and put size-dependent stream into multi-channel convolutional layers. Each channel of multi-channel convolutional layers corresponds to a specific size range. We integrate size-independent features with complementary size-dependent features.

Finally, we refer to [15] and add a one-to-one guidance module based on low-level feature maps to enhance the network sensitivity to small-size objects. In summary, the main contributions of this paper include three folds:

1. We propose a novel network design method that divides and conquers different data distributions. MSDM can learn the features of salient objects in different size ranges separately. This network design based on data characteristics is meaningful.
2. We provide an effective idea of solving the huge size deviation between salient objects, which significantly improves the accuracy of saliency maps.
3. We compare the proposed method with 14 state-of-the-art methods on five benchmark datasets. Our method achieves better performances over three evaluation metrics without pre-processing and post-processing.

2   Related Work

In the last few years, lots of methods have been proposed to detect salient objects in images. The early methods mainly used hand-craft low-level features, such

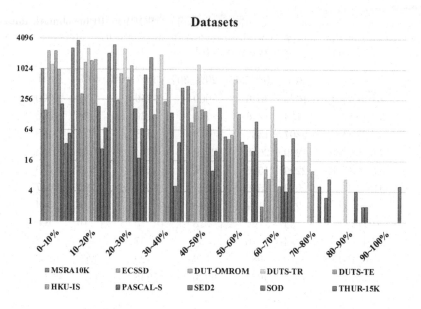

Fig. 2. Size distribution in 10 benchmark datasets

as color contrast [16], local contrast [17], and global contrast [18]. In recent years, FCN-based methods [19] have completely surpassed traditional methods. Most of FCN-based methods are devoted to better integrate multi-level features or enhance the utilization of important features so as to improve the performance [11,15,20–23]. [13] improves the traditional progressive structure of FPN. It aggregates multi-scale features from different layers and distributes the aggregated features to all the involved layers to gain access to richer context. For fair comparison, we employ the original FPN architecture in our network.

[11] designed a HED-based side output structure which using the short connection to integrate the low-level features in the shallow side layer and high-level features in the deep side layer to improve the effect of saliency prediction. Instead of using layer skipped dense short connections, we retain multi-channel concatenation layer by layer as our basic architecture.

Recently, methods based on edge feature enhancement have been widely studied. [24] proposed to learn the local context information of each spatial location to refine the boundaries. [15] proposed to use the complementarity of edge information and saliency information to enhance the accuracy of boundary and help to locate salient objects. [20] fused the boundary and internal features of salient objects through selectivity or invariance mechanism. Because edge information has a significant effect in improving the pixel-wise edge accuracy of salient objects, a lot of edge information enhancement methods have been proposed [15,20,25,26]. [21] have also used edge information as an important way to enhance the performance of network. These methods utilize additional edge information to solve the issue of rough edge prediction of salient objects

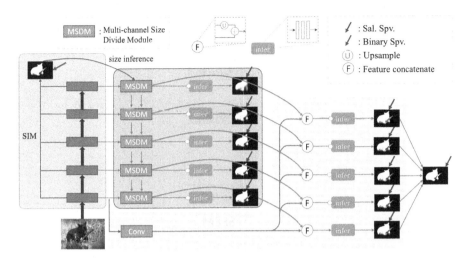

Fig. 3. Main pipeline of the proposed method. We integrate MSDM into improved FPN structure. Two parallel arrows between MSDM indicate the flow of size-independent and size-dependent features respectively. The green block on the left represents the size inference module (SIM) and yellow block represents the size guide module (SGM). (Color figure online)

in previous methods. These researches inspire us to explore the usage of size information of salient objects, which is equally important and facing difficulties currently. However, these two problems are opposite. Edge information is the common feature of salient objects, while size information emphasizes the feature difference between salient objects. Moreover, edge detection can be easily integrated into saliency detection tasks by multi-learning. Correlation of size categories and saliency detection by multi-learning directly does not make sense. Therefore, we combined the divide-and-conquer algorithm and designed MSDM to extract the corresponding features of salient objects of different sizes. It uses the size categories as high-dimensional information, activates different convolution channels to extract the features of salient objects of different sizes, and effectively solves the problem of the confusion of salient object sizes.

3   Methodology

The performance decline of SOD methods at small objects and large objects indicates that we need different features in detecting salient objects with huge size difference. Ignoring the size difference of saliency objects will suppress learning of features that are related to specific size. Accordingly, we design a MSDM for our improved FPN structure. The overall structure of SDCNet is shown in Fig. 3.

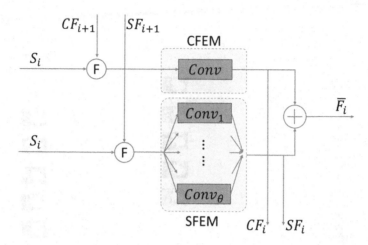

Fig. 4. Structure of MSDM. We use Common Feature Extract Module (CFEM) to get size-independent features and Size Feature Extract Module (SFEM) to get size-dependent features. We activate different convolutional channel in SFEM according to the size inference θ. The details are introduced in the Sect. 3.2.

3.1   Overall Pipeline

Our proposed network is independent of the specific backbone network. In practice, we use ResNet [27] as backbone for feature extraction. We remove the last pooling layer and fully connection layer and get 5 side features F_1, F_2, F_3, F_4, F_5 which including 64, 256, 512, 1024 and 2048 channels respectively as our side output path S_1, S_2, S_3, S_4, S_5. The side outputs of these different layers contain low-level details and high-level semantic information respectively. We employ Atrous Spatial Pyramid Pooling (ASPP) in processing two high-level feature maps F_4, F_5 to expand receptive field of convolutional layer. We use SIM to provide size inference. MSDM is added to each layer of the up-to-down structure to replace the simple feature fusion module. The main function of MSDM is to activate different convolution channels through the high-dimensional size information provided by SIM to learn the feature of salient objects of different sizes. It integrates basic function of upsample and concatenate as well. Finally, we add an one-to-one guidance module with low-level features to retain more information of small size salient objects. Our network is end-to-end, training and inference are both one-stage. The details of the convolutional layers could be found in Table 2.

3.2   Multi-channel Size Divide Module

The MSDM is mainly composed of the common saliency feature extraction module (CFEM) and size-dependent feature extraction module (SFEM). The structure of MSDM can be found in Fig. 4. CEFM is a single set of convolutional layers, while SEFM is a combination of multiple sets of parallel convolutional

Table 2. Details of kernels in SDCNet. We use ResNet50 for example. "3×3, 256" means the keneral size is 3×3 and channel number is 256. Each Conv layer follow with BN and PRelu and each side-layer share the same setting.

SIM	Backbone	CFEM	SFEM	SGM
$3 \times 3, 256$	Conv1_1	$3 \times 3, 256$	$(3 \times 3, 256)$	$3 \times 3, 256$
$3 \times 3, 256$		$3 \times 3, 256$	$(3 \times 3, 256)$	$3 \times 3, 256$
$1 \times 1, 128$		$1 \times 1, 128$	$(1 \times 1, 128) \times 5$	$1 \times 1, 128$
	Conv2_3			
	Conv3_4			
	Conv4_6			
	Conv5_3			

layers. In CFEM, we extract size-independent features through a common convolutional layer. CFEM remains active for salient objects of all sizes, that is, it learns common features that are not related to size differences. In SFEM, we activate different convolutional set to independently extract size-dependent features according to the specific size categories. We integrate these two complementary features to generate saliency maps in each side path S_1, S_2, S_3, S_4, S_5 up-to-down. The size-independent and size-dependent features of each layer are denoted as follows:

$$CF_i = f_{conv}^{(i)}(Cat(F_i, Up(CF_{(i+1)}; F_i))), \tag{1}$$

$$SF_i = f_{(conv,\theta)}^{(i)}(Cat(F_i, Up(SF_{(i+1)}; F_i)), \theta), \tag{2}$$

where CF_i represents size-independent feature maps, SF_i represents size-dependent feature maps. $Up(*; F_i)$ means up-sampling $*$ to the same size of F_i through bilinear interpolation. $Cat(A, B)$ means concatenation of feature maps A and B. $f_{conv}^{(i)}$ represents CFEM which is composed by three convolutional layers and nonlinear activation function. The structure of $f_{(conv,\theta)}^{(i)}$ is composed by several parallel $f_{conv}^{(i)}$, and we activate one of them for each image according to size inference θ. $f_{(conv,\theta)}^{(i)}$ is applied to extract size-dependent features. θ represents size inference, which provided by SIM. Specific characteristics of θ are as follows:

$$\theta = \frac{1}{W \times H} \sum_{x=1}^{W} \sum_{y=1}^{H} |S(x, y)|, \tag{3}$$

where W and H represent the width and height of the image respectively, and $S(x, y)$ represents the binarized pixel-wise value of saliency maps. In practice, size inference θ is divided into five categories according to the value. More details are shown in Table 1.

Deep supervision is applied on each side path S_i. We integrate CF_i and SF_i to make saliency inference P_i and impose the supervision signal each layer. The specific expression is as follows:

$$\begin{cases} \bar{F}_i = Cat(CF_i, SF_i, P_{(i+1)}), & 1 \le i \le 4, \\ \bar{F}_i = Cat(CF_i, SF_i), & i = 5, \end{cases} \tag{4}$$

$$P_i = Sig(Up(Pred^{(i)}_{conv}(F_i); S_{img})), \tag{5}$$

where P_i denotes the salieny prediction of i-th side layer. $\bar{F}_i$ represents feature maps aggregated by size-independent features and size-dependent features. Similar to $f^{(i)}_{conv}$, $Pred^{(i)}_{conv}$ is a series of convolutional layers for salient object prediction. S_{img} denotes the size of source image. $Up(*; S_{img})$ means up-sampling the saliency prediction * to the same size as source image. $Sig(*)$ means sigmoid function.

To realize the supervision in various resolutions, we design loss function for each side output based on the cross-entropy loss function. The formula is as follows:

$$\mathbb{L}_i(G, P_i) = -\frac{w_i}{W \times H} \sum_{x=1}^{W} \sum_{y=1}^{H} [g^{xy} \log p_i^{xy}$$
$$+ (1 - g^{xy}) \log(1 - p_i^{xy})], \qquad i \in [1, 5], \tag{6}$$

where G denotes the input image GT. g^{xy} and p_i^{xy} represent the pixel-wise value of GT and the normalized saliency prediction. w_i is used to represent the weight of loss function of each layer and the value is 1. For the MSDM, our total loss function can be expressed as:

$$\Theta = \sum_{i=1}^{5} \mathbb{L}_i(G, P_i). \tag{7}$$

3.3 Size Inference Module

As shown in Fig. 3, We generate binary predictions of salient objects through multi-level feature fusion. SIM share the same backbone with the main network and the loss function of SIM is similar to the loss function in Sect. 3.2. Unlike the usual non-binary saliency inference, we get a tensor of size (2, H, W). Channel 1 represents the salient objects and Channel 2 represents the background. We directly generate a binarized inference to conveniently calculate the SOP of the images pixel by pixel. For example, for an input data with a batchsize of 8, we separately infer the salient object area of each image, and calculate the SOP. According to the SOP, we generates a vector of length 8, which represents the predicted size category of each image. This size category is determined by the five size ranges shown in Table 1. This is a rough size estimate, but they all belong to the same category within a certain range, so the size category is usually accurate. The accuracy rate of the inference of the salient object size categories on different data sets is shown in Table 6. Finally, we employ this size category inference as high-dimensional information to guide the activation of different channels in MSDM.

3.4   Size Guidance Module

Since small objects suffer more information loss during the down-sampling, we use side path $\bar{F}_0$ of the shallow layer as the guidance layer to provide more low-level features. The guidance layer $\bar{F}_0$ and the sub-side layer $\bar{F}_i^*$ can be expressed as follows respectively:

$$\bar{F}_0 = f_{conv}^{(1)}(F_1), \tag{8}$$

$$\bar{F}_i^* = f_{conv}^{*(i)}(Up(\bar{F}_i; \bar{F}_1) + \bar{F}_0). \tag{9}$$

similar to MSDM, we use a series of convolutional layers $f_{conv}^{*(i)}$ to generate aggregated feature maps. We employ an inference module to generate the second round of saliency predictions. The setting of inference module and the loss function are the same as those described in Sect. 3.2.

4   Experiments

4.1   Experiment Setup

Implementation Details. We implement the model with PyTorch 0.4.0 on Titan Xp. We use ResNet [27] and ResNeXt [28] as the backbone of our network, respectively. We use the SGD algorithm to optimize our model, where the batch size is 8, momentum is 0.9, weight decays is 5e–4. We set the initial learning rate to 1e–4 and adopt polynomial attenuation with the power of 0.9. We iterate our model for 30,000 times and do not set the validation set during training. We use the fused prediction maps of side output as the final saliency map.

Datasets. We have evaluated the proposed method on five benchmark datasets: DUTS-TE [29], ECSSD [30], PASCAL-S [31], HKU-IS [32], DUT-OMRON [33]. DUTS [29] is a large SOD dataset containing 10553 images for training (DUT-TR) and 5019 images for testing (DUT-TE). Most images are challenging with various locations and scales as well as complex backgrounds. ECSSD [30] contains 1000 images with complex structures and obvious semantically meaningful objects. PASCAL-S [31] is derived from PASCAL VOC 2010 segmentation dataset and contains 850 natural images. HKU-IS [32] contains 4447 images and many of which have multiple disconnected salient objects or salient objects that touch image boundaries. DUT-OMRON [33] contains 5168 high-quality but challenging images. These images are chosen from more than 140,000 natural images, each of which contains one or more salient objects and relatively complex backgrounds.

4.2   Evaluation Metrics

We adopt mean absolute error (MAE), Max F-measure (F_β^{Max}) [34], and a structure-based metric, S-measure [35], as our evaluation metrics. MAE reflects the average pixel-wise absolute difference between the normalized saliency maps and GT. MAE can be calculated by:

$$MAE = \frac{1}{W \times H} \sum_{x=1}^{W} \sum_{y=1}^{H} |P(x,y) - G(x,y)| \tag{10}$$

where W and H represent the width and height of images. $P(x,y)$ and $G(x,y)$ denote the saliency map and GT, respectively.

F-measure is a harmonic mean of average precision and average recall. We compute the F-measure by:

$$F_\beta = \frac{(1 + \beta^2) Precision \times Recall}{\beta^2 Precision + Recall} \tag{11}$$

we set $\beta^2 = 0.3$ to weigh more on precision than recall as suggested in [16]. Precision denotes the ratio of detected salient pixels in the predicted saliency map. Recall denotes the ratio of detected salient pixels in the GT. We normalize the predicted saliency maps into the range of [0, 255] and binarize the saliency maps with a threshold from 0 to 255. By comparing the binary maps with GT, we can get precision-recall pairs at each threshold and then evaluate the maximum F-measure from all precision-recall pairs as F_β^{Max}.

S-measure is proposed by [14], and it can be used to evaluate the structural information of non-binary foreground maps. This measurement is calculated by evaluating the region-aware and object-aware structural similarity between the saliency maps and GT.

4.3   Comparisons with State-of-the-Arts

In this section, we compare the proposed method with 14 state-of-the-art methods, including EGNet [15], BANet [20], RAS [37], RADF [38], R3Net [12], PiAC-Net [39], PAGRN [22], DGRL [24], BDMPM [40], SRM [41], NLDF [42], DSS [11], Amulet [43] and UCF [44]. All of these methods are proposed in the last three years. Saliency maps of the above methods are produced by running source codes with original implementation details or directly provided by the authors. We evaluating the saliency maps both in the code provide by [11] and by ourselves to guarantee the reliability of the results.

F-Measure, MAE, and S-Measure. We compared with 14 state-of-the-art saliency detection methods on five datasets. The comparison results are shown in Table 3. We can see that our method significantly outperforms other methods across all of the six benchmark datasets in MAE. Specifically, our method reduce MAE by 17.9%, 10.8%, 25.6%, 6.5% and 15.1% on DUTS-TE [29], ECSSD [30], PASCAL-S [31], HKU-IS [32] and DUT-OMRON [33] datasets, respectively. For the metrics where we get top two or three, we are only slightly behind the best edge-guide method. In fact, without using edge information, we achieved state-of-the-art performance comparable to the best model combining edge information.

Table 3. Comparison of 14 state-of-the-arts and the proposed method on Max F, MAE, and S-measure over five benchmark datasets. ↑ & ↓ denote higher better and lower better respectively. * means the results are post-processed by dense conditional random field (CRF) [36]. The best three results are marked in red, and green, blue. Our method achieves the state-of-the-art on these five benchmark datasets under three evaluation metrics.

Method	DUTS-TE			ECSSD			PASCAL-S			HKU-IS			DUT-O		
	Fm↑	MAE↓	S↑	Fm↑	MAE↓	S↑	Fm↑	MAE↓	S↑	Fm↑	MAE↓	S↑	Fm↑	MAE↓	S↑
VGG-based															
UCF	0.772	0.111	0.782	0.903	0.069	0.884	0.816	0.116	0.806	0.888	0.062	0.875	0.730	0.120	0.760
Amulet	0.778	0.084	0.804	0.915	0.059	0.894	0.830	0.100	0.818	0.897	0.051	0.886	0.743	0.098	0.781
NLDF	0.816	0.065	0.805	0.905	0.063	0.875	0.824	0.098	0.805	0.902	0.048	0.879	0.753	0.080	0.770
RAS	0.831	0.059	0.839	0.921	0.056	0.893	0.831	0.101	0.799	0.913	0.045	0.887	0.786	0.062	0.814
DSS*	0.825	0.061	0.812	0.921	0.052	0.882	0.833	0.093	0.799	0.916	0.040	0.878	0.781	0.063	0.790
RADF	–	–	–	0.923	0.049	0.894	0.832	0.097	0.802	0.914	0.039	0.889	0.791	0.062	0.815
PAGRN	0.854	0.055	0.839	0.927	0.061	0.889	0.849	0.089	0.822	0.918	0.048	0.887	0.771	0.071	0.775
BDMPM	0.854	0.048	0.862	0.930	0.045	0.911	0.858	0.074	0.844	0.922	0.039	0.907	0.793	0.064	0.809
ResNet-based															
SRM	0.826	0.058	0.836	0.917	0.054	0.895	0.840	0.084	0.834	0.906	0.046	0.887	0.769	0.069	0.798
DGRL	0.828	0.050	0.842	0.922	0.041	0.903	0.849	0.072	0.836	0.910	0.036	0.895	0.774	0.062	0.806
PiCA*	0.871	0.040	0.863	0.940	0.035	0.916	0.870	0.064	0.846	0.929	0.031	0.905	0.828	0.054	0.826
BANet	0.872	0.039	0.879	0.943	0.035	0.924	0.866	0.070	0.852	0.931	0.032	0.913	0.803	0.059	0.832
EGNet	0.889	0.039	0.887	0.943	0.037	0.925	0.869	0.074	0.852	0.937	0.031	0.918	0.843	0.053	0.841
Ours	0.888	0.052	0.884	0.943	0.033	0.922	0.871	0.055	0.863	0.933	0.029	0.914	0.835	0.045	0.839
ResNeXt-based															
R3Net*	0.879	0.037	0.873	0.938	0.036	0.913	0.867	0.063	0.851	0.930	0.032	0.910	0.818	0.057	0.819
Ours	0.896	0.030	0.890	0.948	0.029	0.926	0.880	0.048	0.872	0.937	0.026	0.918	0.845	0.041	0.844

Visual Comparison. We show some visualization results in Fig. 5. Those pictures have different SOP: 0.866, 0.570, 0.281, 0.167, 0.134, 0.0864, 0.042, 0.034, from up-to-down. It is obvious that our method has consistent performance for salient objects of different sizes. A significant advantage of our method is that we can locate the main area of salient objects more accurately. As shown in row 6 and row 8, when the salient objects share the same attributes with background or the background is relatively complex, our method can accurately segment the main objects and dropout the extra parts. Another advantage of our approach is that we retain more detail. In row 4, we preserve more details compare with other methods. It proves that the shallow feature guidance layer is effective for retaining detail information. In addition to achieving marvelous performance on small objects, we achieve impressive results on large objects as well (row 1–3). These observations indicate the size information of salient objects is crucial for identifying the salient objects and improving the robustness of the SOD methods at multiple scales.

4.4   Ablation Analysis

To explore the effectiveness of different components of the proposed method, we conduct experiments on five benchmark datasets to compare the performance

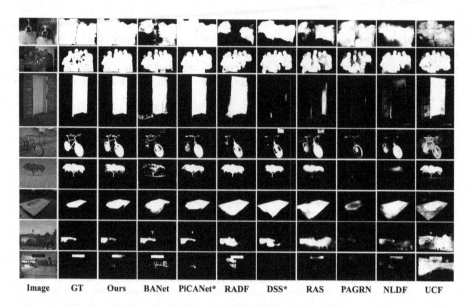

| Image | GT | Ours | BANet | PiCANet* | RADF | DSS* | RAS | PAGRN | NLDF | UCF |

Fig. 5. Qualitative comparisons with 8 state-of-the-art methods. We arrange those images from high to low SOP up-to-down. * means the results are post-processed by dense conditional random field (CRF).

variations of our methods with different experimental settings over the DUTS-TE [29], ECSSD [30], PASCAL-S [31] and DUT-OMRON [33]. Test results of different settings are shown in Table 4.

Effectiveness of MSDM. We explore the effectiveness of MSDM in this subsection. As shown in Table 4, CFEM denotes only remain CFEM in MSDM. SFEM denotes remain SFEM in MSDM. For better comparison, we kept other settings the same. The comparison between the first and third columns of Table 4 proves the effectiveness of SFEM and MSDM. It means that the divide-and-conquer module is effective in separately learning the features of salient objects of different sizes. By comparing the second and third columns we can find that retaining a common convolutional layer can better learning size-independent features and improve the network in a complementary way. MSDM+edge verifies the effectiveness of edge information. SDCNet achieved higher performance by combining edge information. Running time in CFEM, SFEM and CFEM+SFEM is 6.71, 6.58 and 6.06 FPS in Titan Xp with input size 300×300. In addition, MSAM can easily integrate into other lightweight networks.

Improvement on Small and Big Object Detection. To demonstrate the superiority of SDCNet in the detection of small and big salient objects, we compared the performance difference between the baseline network (the same as CFEM in Table 4) and SDCNet in the detection of small objects and large

Table 4. Ablation analyses on four datasets. CFEM, SFEM, MSDM are introduced in Sect. 3.2. MSAM+edge means add edge supervision to $\bar{F}_0$.

Model		CFEM	SFEM	MSDM (CFEM+SFEM)	MSDM+edge
DUTS-TE	MaxF↑	0.875	0.890	0.896	0.898
	MAE↓	0.042	0.033	0.030	0.028
ECSSD	MaxF↑	0.937	0.944	0.948	0.951
	MAE↓	0.035	0.031	0.029	0.027
PASCAL-S	MaxF↑	0.868	0.878	0.880	0.879
	MAE↓	0.067	0.058	0.058	0.058
DUT-O	MaxF↑	0.818	0.837	0.845	0.847
	MAE↓	0.063	0.045	0.041	0.040

Table 5. Performance improvement of SDCNet in small and big object detection. Small objects means SOP is less than 10%. Large objects refers to SOP more than 40%. We use the complete dataset to train the baseline and SDCNet, and test on large and small objects separately. Specific dataset means training with a dataset of the same size category as the test set.

Model			Baseline	SDCNet	Specific dataset
Small objects	DUTS-TE	MaxF↑	0.823	0.850	0.872
		MAE↓	0.038	0.027	0.015
	PASCAL-S	MaxF↑	0.766	0.794	0.820
		MAE↓	0.062	0.045	0.021
Big objects	DUTS-TE	MaxF↑	0.957	0.960	0.962
		MAE↓	0.056	0.052	0.048
	PASCAL-S	MaxF↑	0.923	0.933	0.932
		MAE↓	0.088	0.086	0.080

objects. The specific performance is shown in Table 5. SDCNet outperforms baseline in both small objects detection and large objects detection, while they sharing the same structure except SFEM. It demonstrates the superiority of the divide and conquer network in fitting actual data distribution. However, it still has performance differences compared to networks trained with specific data. The third column of Table 5 shows the best performance that can be achieved on small (or large) salient objects by dividing and conquering without changing other network structures.

Effectiveness of SIM. The performance of SIM determines whether we can accurately divide the image into the corresponding channel. We explore the effectiveness of SIM in this subsection. As shown in Tabel 6, Classification Network denotes train an individual ResNeXt101 to infer the size category of salient

Table 6. Accuracy of the size inference on benchmark datasets. The details are introduced in Sect. 4.4.

Dataset		ECSSD	DUT-TE	HKU-IS	DUT-O
Classification network (ResNeXt101)	acc (%)	74.8	71.7	72	69.6
SIM	acc (%)	85.4	83.6	84.7	80.2

objects. The results of the comparison show that the SIM module has a better accuracy of size inference than the independent size classification network. It indicates that it is more effective to calculate the size range of salient objects pixel by pixel than direct classification the size categories. The inference accuracy of SIM is about 80% to 85%. This does not seem completely satisfactory. But in fact, for those significant objects whose size range is wrongly estimated, the deviation is usually not large. The difference in features of salient objects in the size range of 30–40% and 40–50% is obviously smaller than that of the salient objects in the size range of 0–10%, so misclassification usually does not lead to worse performance. For those salient objects with large size inference deviation, the accuracy of labeling may be a more important reason. Moreover, the improvement space of SIM shows that SDCNet still has rich potential.

5 Conclusion

In this paper, we view size information as an important supplement of current SOD methods. We explored the application of divide-and-conquer networks in solving salient object detection with significant size differences. First, we counted the size distribution of salient objects in the benchmark datasets and trained a SIM to perform size inference using a pixel-by-pixel calculation. Second, we use an up-to-down multi-scale feature fusion network as the basic structure. We designed an MSDM, which activates different channels according to the size inference obtained by SIM, and learned the features of salient objects of different sizes. Finally, we utilize the low-level feature maps as one-to-one guidance to retain more information about small salient objects. Experimental results show that our method has a significant improvement in the detection performance of small-sized objects. Our method obtains state-of-the-art performance in five benchmark datasets under three evaluation metrics. Without using edge features, SDCNet can get results comparable to models that combine edge information. This impressive performance denotes the great effectiveness of our method. Furthermore, our method provides an original idea on how to overcome the inherent feature differences between task data and better solve the problems.

References

1. Hou, Q., Jiang, P., Wei, Y., Cheng, M.M.: Self-erasing network for integral object attention. In: Advances in Neural Information Processing Systems, pp. 549–559 (2018)

2. Ren, Z., Gao, S., Chia, L.T., Tsang, I.W.H.: Region-based saliency detection and its application in object recognition. IEEE Trans. Circ. Syst. Video Technol. **24**, 769–779 (2013)
3. Lai, B., Gong, X.: Saliency guided dictionary learning for weakly-supervised image parsing. In: Proceedings of the IEEE Conference on Computer Vision and Pattern Recognition, pp. 3630–3639 (2016)
4. He, J., et al.: Mobile product search with bag of hash bits and boundary reranking. In: 2012 IEEE Conference on Computer Vision and Pattern Recognition, pp. 3005–3012. IEEE (2012)
5. Piao, Y., Ji, W., Li, J., Zhang, M., Lu, H.: Depth-induced multi-scale recurrent attention network for saliency detection. In: Proceedings of the IEEE International Conference on Computer Vision, pp. 7254–7263 (2019)
6. Zhao, J.X., Cao, Y., Fan, D.P., Cheng, M.M., Li, X.Y., Zhang, L.: Contrast prior and fluid pyramid integration for RGBD salient object detection. In: Proceedings of the IEEE Conference on Computer Vision and Pattern Recognition, pp. 3927–3936 (2019)
7. Chen, H., Li, Y.: Three-stream attention-aware network for RGB-D salient object detection. IEEE Trans. Image Process. **28**, 2825–2835 (2019)
8. Chen, H., Li, Y., Su, D.: Multi-modal fusion network with multi-scale multi-path and cross-modal interactions for RGB-D salient object detection. Pattern Recogn. **86**, 376–385 (2019)
9. Fan, D.P., Wang, W., Cheng, M.M., Shen, J.: Shifting more attention to video salient object detection. In: Proceedings of the IEEE Conference on Computer Vision and Pattern Recognition, pp. 8554–8564 (2019)
10. Wang, Z., Xu, J., Liu, L., Zhu, F., Shao, L.: RANet: ranking attention network for fast video object segmentation. In: Proceedings of the IEEE International Conference on Computer Vision, pp. 3978–3987 (2019)
11. Hou, Q., Cheng, M.M., Hu, X., Borji, A., Tu, Z., Torr, P.H.: Deeply supervised salient object detection with short connections. In: Proceedings of the IEEE Conference on Computer Vision and Pattern Recognition, pp. 3203–3212 (2017)
12. Deng, Z., et al.: R^3Net: recurrent residual refinement network for saliency detection. In: Proceedings of the 27th International Joint Conference on Artificial Intelligence, pp. 684–690. AAAI Press (2018)
13. Li, Z., Lang, C., Liew, J., Hou, Q., Li, Y., Feng, J.: Cross-layer feature pyramid network for salient object detection. arXiv e-prints (2020). arXiv:2002.10864
14. Fan, D.-P., Cheng, M.-M., Liu, J.-J., Gao, S.-H., Hou, Q., Borji, A.: Salient objects in clutter: bringing salient object detection to the foreground. In: Ferrari, V., Hebert, M., Sminchisescu, C., Weiss, Y. (eds.) ECCV 2018. LNCS, vol. 11219, pp. 196–212. Springer, Cham (2018). https://doi.org/10.1007/978-3-030-01267-0_12
15. Zhao, J.X., Liu, J.J., Fan, D.P., Cao, Y., Yang, J., Cheng, M.M.: EGNet: edge guidance network for salient object detection. In: Proceedings of the IEEE International Conference on Computer Vision, pp. 8779–8788 (2019)
16. Achanta, R., Hemami, S., Estrada, F., Susstrunk, S.: Frequency-tuned salient region detection. In: 2009 IEEE Conference on Computer Vision and Pattern Recognition, pp. 1597–1604. IEEE (2009)
17. Klein, D.A., Frintrop, S.: Center-surround divergence of feature statistics for salient object detection. In: 2011 International Conference on Computer Vision, pp. 2214–2219. IEEE (2011)
18. Cheng, M.M., Mitra, N.J., Huang, X., Torr, P.H., Hu, S.M.: Global contrast based salient region detection. IEEE Trans. Pattern Anal. Mach. Intell. **37**, 569–582 (2014)

19. Long, J., Shelhamer, E., Darrell, T.: Fully convolutional networks for semantic segmentation. In: Proceedings of the IEEE Conference on Computer Vision and Pattern Recognition, pp. 3431–3440 (2015)

20. Su, J., Li, J., Zhang, Y., Xia, C., Tian, Y.: Selectivity or invariance: boundary-aware salient object detection. In: Proceedings of the IEEE International Conference on Computer Vision pp. 3799–3808 (2019)

21. Liu, J.J., Hou, Q., Cheng, M.M., Feng, J., Jiang, J.: A simple pooling-based design for real-time salient object detection. In: Proceedings of the IEEE Conference on Computer Vision and Pattern Recognition, pp. 3917–3926 (2019)

22. Zhang, X., Wang, T., Qi, J., Lu, H., Wang, G.: Progressive attention guided recurrent network for salient object detection. In: Proceedings of the IEEE Conference on Computer Vision and Pattern Recognition, pp. 714–722 (2018)

23. Wang, W., Shen, J., Cheng, M.M., Shao, L.: An iterative and cooperative top-down and bottom-up inference network for salient object detection. In: Proceedings of the IEEE Conference on Computer Vision and Pattern Recognition, pp. 5968–5977 (2019)

24. Wang, T., et al.: Detect globally, refine locally: a novel approach to saliency detection. In: Proceedings of the IEEE Conference on Computer Vision and Pattern Recognition, pp. 3127–3135 (2018)

25. Feng, M., Lu, H., Ding, E.: Attentive feedback network for boundary-aware salient object detection. In: Proceedings of the IEEE Conference on Computer Vision and Pattern Recognition, pp. 1623–1632 (2019)

26. Qin, X., Zhang, Z., Huang, C., Gao, C., Dehghan, M., Jagersand, M.: BASnet: boundary-aware salient object detection. In: Proceedings of the IEEE Conference on Computer Vision and Pattern Recognition, pp. 7479–7489 (2019)

27. He, K., Zhang, X., Ren, S., Sun, J.: Deep residual learning for image recognition. In: Proceedings of the IEEE Conference on Computer Vision and Pattern Recognition, pp. 770–778 (2016)

28. Xie, S., Girshick, R., Dollár, P., Tu, Z., He, K.: Aggregated residual transformations for deep neural networks. In: Proceedings of the IEEE Conference on Computer Vision and Pattern Recognition, pp. 1492–1500 (2017)

29. Wang, L., et al.: Learning to detect salient objects with image-level supervision. In: Proceedings of the IEEE Conference on Computer Vision and Pattern Recognition, pp. 136–145 (2017)

30. Yan, Q., Xu, L., Shi, J., Jia, J.: Hierarchical saliency detection. In: Proceedings of the IEEE Conference on Computer Vision and Pattern Recognition, pp. 1155–1162 (2013)

31. Li, Y., Hou, X., Koch, C., Rehg, J.M., Yuille, A.L.: The secrets of salient object segmentation. In: Proceedings of the IEEE Conference on Computer Vision and Pattern Recognition, pp. 280–287 (2014)

32. Li, G., Yu, Y.: Visual saliency based on multiscale deep features. In: Proceedings of the IEEE Conference on Computer Vision and Pattern Recognition, pp. 5455–5463 (2015)

33. Yang, C., Zhang, L., Lu, H., Ruan, X., Yang, M.H.: Saliency detection via graph-based manifold ranking. In: Proceedings of the IEEE Conference on Computer Vision and Pattern Recognition, pp. 3166–3173 (2013)

34. Margolin, R., Zelnik-Manor, L., Tal, A.: How to evaluate foreground maps? In: Proceedings of the IEEE Conference on Computer Vision and Pattern Recognition, pp. 248–255 (2014)

35. Fan, D.P., Cheng, M.M., Liu, Y., Li, T., Borji, A.: Structure-measure: a new way to evaluate foreground maps. In: Proceedings of the IEEE International Conference on Computer Vision, pp. 4548–4557 (2017)

36. Krähenbühl, P., Koltun, V.: Efficient inference in fully connected CRFs with Gaussian edge potentials. In: Advances in Neural Information Processing Systems, pp. 109–117 (2011)

37. Chen, S., Tan, X., Wang, B., Hu, X.: Reverse attention for salient object detection. In: Ferrari, V., Hebert, M., Sminchisescu, C., Weiss, Y. (eds.) ECCV 2018. LNCS, vol. 11213, pp. 236–252. Springer, Cham (2018). https://doi.org/10.1007/978-3-030-01240-3_15

38. Hu, X., Zhu, L., Qin, J., Fu, C.W., Heng, P.A.: Recurrently aggregating deep features for salient object detection. In: Thirty-Second AAAI Conference on Artificial Intelligence (2018)

39. Liu, N., Han, J., Yang, M.H.: PiCANet: learning pixel-wise contextual attention for saliency detection. In: Proceedings of the IEEE Conference on Computer Vision and Pattern Recognition, pp. 3089–3098 (2018)

40. Zhang, L., Dai, J., Lu, H., He, Y., Wang, G.: A bi-directional message passing model for salient object detection. In: Proceedings of the IEEE Conference on Computer Vision and Pattern Recognition, pp. 1741–1750 (2018)

41. Wang, T., Borji, A., Zhang, L., Zhang, P., Lu, H.: A stagewise refinement model for detecting salient objects in images. In: Proceedings of the IEEE International Conference on Computer Vision, pp. 4019–4028 (2017)

42. Luo, Z., Mishra, A., Achkar, A., Eichel, J., Li, S., Jodoin, P.M.: Non-local deep features for salient object detection. In: Proceedings of the IEEE Conference on Computer Vision and Pattern Recognition, pp. 6609–6617 (2017)

43. Zhang, P., Wang, D., Lu, H., Wang, H., Ruan, X.: Amulet: aggregating multi-level convolutional features for salient object detection. In: Proceedings of the IEEE International Conference on Computer Vision, pp. 202–211 (2017)

44. Zhang, P., Wang, D., Lu, H., Wang, H., Yin, B.: Learning uncertain convolutional features for accurate saliency detection. In: Proceedings of the IEEE International Conference on computer vision, pp. 212–221 (2017)

Bidirectional Pyramid Networks
for Semantic Segmentation

Dong Nie[1][(✉)], Jia Xue[2], and Xiaofeng Ren[1]

[1] Amap, Alibaba Group, Beijing, China
{dong.nie,x.ren}@alibaba-inc.com
[2] Rutgers University, New Brunswick, USA
jia.xue@rutgers.edu

Abstract. Semantic segmentation is a fundamental problem in computer vision that has attracted a lot of attention. Recent efforts have been devoted to network architecture innovations for efficient semantic segmentation that can run in real-time for autonomous driving and other applications. Information flow between scales is crucial because accurate segmentation needs both large context and fine detail. However, most existing approaches still rely on pretrained backbone models (e.g. ResNet on ImageNet). In this work, we propose to open up the backbone and design a simple yet effective multiscale network architecture, *Bidirectional Pyramid Network* (BPNet). BPNet takes the shape of a *pyramid*: information flows from bottom (high-resolution, small receptive field) to top (low-resolution, large receptive field), and from top to bottom, in a systematic manner, at every step of the processing. More importantly, fusion needs to be efficient; this is done through an add-and-multiply module with learned weights. We also apply a unary-pairwise attention mechanism to balance position sensitivity and context aggregation. Auxiliary loss is applied at multiple steps of the pyramid bottom. The resulting network achieves high accuracy with efficiency, without the need of pretraining. On the standard Cityscapes dataset, we achieve test mIoU 76.3 with 5.1M parameters and 36 fps (on Nvidia 2080 Ti), competitive with the state of the time real-time models. Meanwhile, our design is general and can be used to build heavier networks: a ResNet-101 equivalent version of BPNet achieves mIoU 81.9 on Cityscapes, competitive with the best published results. We further demonstrate the flexibility of BPNet on a prostate MRI segmentation task, achieving the state of the art with a 45× speed-up.

J. Xue—Work done during internship at Amap.
Code is available at https://github.com/ginobilinie/BPNet.

Electronic supplementary material The online version of this chapter (https://doi.org/10.1007/978-3-030-69525-5_39) contains supplementary material, which is available to authorized users.

© Springer Nature Switzerland AG 2021
H. Ishikawa et al. (Eds.): ACCV 2020, LNCS 12622, pp. 654–671, 2021.
https://doi.org/10.1007/978-3-030-69525-5_39

1   Introduction

Semantic segmentation, detailed semantic understanding of a scene, is a fundamental problem in computer vision. Great progress has been made in recent years
for semantic segmentation with convolutional neural networks (CNN), especially
with the encoder-decoder architecture [1,2]. In FCNs [1], convolution layers are
stacked with subsampling to form the encoder, and deconvolution layers are
stacked with upsampling to build the decoder. In such network architectures,
higher layers are usually thought to capture entire objects, and contexts beyond
objects, because they have larger receptive fields and go through more convolution steps; lower layers are more likely to capture local patterns, including part of
objects and fine details. However, accurate semantic segmentation requires both
large-scale contexts and small-scale details, and the integration of information
across scales has been a central topic of investigation. This is particularly important for efficient (real-time) segmentation because we cannot use heavyweight
backbones to preserve sufficient information in higher layers.

UNet [2], a successful architecture design that is still popular today, introduces skip connections between corresponding encoder and decoder layers to
better model small-scale details in the decoder. This general line of approach
has achieved good results with many improvements. VNet [3] proposes to use
a convolutional layer to enhance the raw skip connection. AttentionUNet [4]
utilizes an attention block to filter unrelated noise to improve the quality of
feature fusion. UNet++ [5] redesigns skip pathways to reduce the semantic gap
between the feature maps of the encoder and decoder. RefineNet [6] extracts
high-resolution semantic information which is both accurate in location and rich
in contextual information.

However, such skip connections cannot capture all useful interactions between
large-scale information and small-scale information as they flow through the
network. One major constraint is that most existing approaches use pre-trained
backbone networks in the encoder. Typically, a ResNet (or VGG) backbone
network is pre-trained on ImageNet on classification tasks, and then is fine-
tuned as part of the semantic segmentation network. Relying on pre-training
limits the possibility of adding interactions inside the backbone. Pre-training
can also be an issue when we look at different domains such as medical imaging.

In this work we aim to remove the need for pre-training, and open up the
backbone model to allow better flow of information across scales and processing
steps. We propose a simple yet effective architecture design called *Bidirectional
Pyramid Network* (**BPNet**), which symmetrically applies feature fusion between
successive layers (as we move up the resolution pyramid toward larger receptive
fields) and successive stages (as we apply more convolutions to extract segmentation cues on the same layer). With a very loose analogy, our BPNet design
looks similar to the *Pascal's Triangle*, where adjacent numbers are combined
to compute the next number. These cross-scale fusion "flows" are bidirectional:
not only can they go from higher layers (larger scale, lower resolution) to lower
layers (higher resolution); they can also go from lower layers to higher layers,
hence facilitating further integration of useful information. In addition to this

pyramid architecture, we also find it useful to employ a *parallel unary-pairwise attention* mechanism in order to help capture long-range dependencies and thin structures. An illustration of the BPNet design can be seen in Fig. 1.

Our BPNet design can be instantiated in different forms w.r.t. computational requirement, by changing the number of resolution layers (partly corresponding to input image resolution), and the number of channels at each convolution step. We find that systematic information fusion in BPNet is most effective for efficient semantic segmentation, when the network is light- to medium-weight. One lightweight version, BPNet-S3-W32, achieves mIoU 76.3 on Cityscapes running 36 fps on Nvidia 2080 Ti, outperforming BiSeNet and other state-of-the-art real-time networks. One heavyweight version, BPNet-S4, achieves mIoU 81.9 on Cityscapes, competitive with the best published results. We also achieve state-of-the-art results on other benchmarks such as Camvid [7] and PASCAL Context [8]. It is worth noting that we do not use pre-training or external datasets; all our models are trained from scratch on the individual datasets themselves. This is in contrast to related works including HRNet [9], which did not use standard backbones but still pre-trained their networks on ImageNet. Without needing pre-training, our networks can be more versatile; we demonstrate the flexibility of BPNet on a popular medical imaging task on prostate MRI segmentation [10], achieving the state of the art with a 45× speed-up (using 2D convolutions only instead of 3D).

2   Related Work

2.1   Balancing Resolution and Semantics

A widely used semantic segmentation framework is the encoder-decoder [1,2]. An encoder usually reduces the spatial resolution of feature maps to learn more abstract features. Correspondingly, the decoder recovers the spatial resolution of the input image from encoder so as to generate dense prediction maps. Fully convolutional network [1] is a typical encoder-decoder architecture which utilizes convolutions for encoding and deconvolutions for decoding to perform pixel-wise segmentation. UNet [2] combines shallow and deep features with skip connections to retain more details in the dense predictions. SharpMask [11] proposed a convolution in the skip connection between encoder and decoder layers to reduce the gap between semantics and localization. PANet [12] built a bottom-up connection between lower layers and the topmost layer to enhance the encoder-decoder's feature hierarchy with better localization and small-scale detail in the lower layers. HRNet [9] introduced multi-resolution convolution to fully fuse multi scale information, and the high-resolution pathway can well retain the localization information. In a related work on object detection, EfficientDet [13] proposed a weighted bi-directional feature pyramid network (BiFPN), showing that information flow in both directions (coarse-to-fine, and fine-to-coarse) are useful for feature fusion.

2.2   Context Aggregation

Context aggregation can be used to model long-range information dependency. Zhao et al. [14] proposed a pyramid pooling module to capture global contextual information. Chen et al. [15] used convolutions with different dilated ratios to harvest pixel-wise contextual information in different ranges. Wang et al. [16] developed a non-local module, which generates a pixel-wise attention mask by calculating pairwise similarity, so as to guide context aggregation. Yuan et al. [17] introduced an object context pooling (OCP) module to explore the relationship between a pixel and the object neighborhood. DANet [18] designed spatial-wise and channel-wise self-attention mechanism to harvest the contextual information. To reduce the computational complexity of non-local module, Huang [19] proposed criss-cross attention module which only computes correlation matrix between each pixel and the corresponding row and column of this pixel. Zhu et al. [20] proposed to sample typical pixels of a feature map as the basis to compute the correlation matrix, reducing computational cost for the non-local module. Li et al. [21] introduced EM algorithms to build a low-rank weight matrix to improve the efficiency of the context aggregation. Although pairwise attention is useful, Li et al. [22,23] found that long-range information in pairwise attention is usually dominated by features of large-scale patterns and inclined to oversmooth small-scale regions (e.g., boundaries and small objects). They proposed local distribution block to distribute global information adaptively over the feature map.

2.3   Efficient Segmentation

Many algorithms have been designed for efficient segmentation with reasonable accuracy, targeting real-time applications [24–29]. Some works dramatically reduced the resolution of the feature maps to achieve faster inference. For example, in ICNet [24], a cascade network was proposed with multi-scale inputs. Li et al. [25] used cross-level feature aggregation to boost accuracy on a lightweight backbone. Though effective, these methods had difficulty handling some small objects and boundaries of objects. Others tried to design light-weight networks to achieve efficiency. For example, BiSeNet [29] separated semantics and high-resolution details by introducing a spatial path and a semantic path. Different from these methods, we retain a high-resolution representation and encourage interactions between different levels of detail and abstraction.

3   Bidirectional Pyramid Networks

The architecture design of our BPNet is illustrated in Fig. 1, including a preliminary convolution step, a bidirectional pyramid network for cross-scale information fusion, then followed by a parallel unary-pairwise attention module for capturing long-range dependency and thin structures.

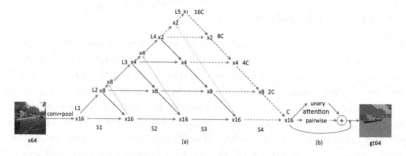

Fig. 1. Illustration of the architecture of the proposed BPNet. This framework consists of a pyramid network and a context aggregation module. (a) The pyramid network contains four stages, i.e., S1, S2, S3 and S4. Each stage is with a bidirectional information flow to boost communication between semantics and resolution, in which, top-down flow (red lines) propagate semantics to high-resolution features and bottom-up flow (yellow lines) passes high-resolution information to rich-semantic features. (b) Context aggregation module learns a pixel-wise unary attention for an emphasis on small patterns and a pairwise attention for long-range information dependency modeling. (Color figure online)

3.1 Pyramid Architecture

As shown in Fig. 1, our pyramid scheme of processing goes in two basic directions (blue arrows): one moves "up" in layers, from higher spatial resolution to lower resolution; the other moves "forward" in stages, maintaining spatial resolution while applying more convolution to extract information.

A typical instantiation of the BPNet model consists of 4 or 5 layers (3 or 4 steps of subsampling), and 3 or 4 stages of convolution at the bottom layer (highest resolution). If the input resolution is x64 (with x an arbitrary integer), the feature resolution of the lowest layer is x16. At the second lowest layer, the feature resolution is x8, and it goes through 3 stages of convolution at the x8 resolution. As we move up the "pyramid", following common practice, we reduce the feature resolution by half at each step, and increase the number of channels by two (as illustrated by the channel numbers C, $2C$, $4C$, etc. with C an integer). A "bird-eye" view of our network resembles a pyramid, or triangle. In the figure, we show a pyramid of 4 layers (with solid arrows), and a pyramid of 5 layers (with the added stage L5, and the dotted arrows on the right side of the triangle).

Note that this basic architecture (without the cross-scale flows, in red and yellow) is already different from a typical UNet structure (or, for that matter, that of a typical feature pyramid in object detection). There is no clearly defined encoder and decoder. We not only pass information, laterally, from various steps of the subsampling (L1, L2, to L5, left side of the triangle, reducing resolution) to the corresponding steps of upsampling (right side of the triangle, increasing resolution); for each lateral link, we add a varying number of stages, or convolution stages. As we move up the layers, fewer processing steps are needed laterally, as the information has already been through a number of convolutions in the subsampling process.

Top-Down Information Flow. With aforementioned basic architecture, we describe how we design information cross-scale flow in a systematic way. One key component is *top-down* information flow. As shown in Fig. 1 (in red arrows), information flows "down" the pyramid at each processing step. For example, the features at L2 (at resolution x8 and after one step of convolution with subsampling) are fed down the hierarchy to be integrated with S1, which is one step of convolution at the lowest layer (maintaining feature resolution x16). Similarly, the features at L3 (at resolution x4 and after two steps of convolution with subsampling) are fed down the hierarchy to the layer below, to be integrated with the output of one lateral step from L2. Other top-down flows are designed similarly across the pyramid.

Empirically, the number of layers (in the resolution hierarchy) and the number of stages (processing steps at the lowest layer) tend to be the same, which results in a "perfect" triangle pattern. In all the models we use in this work, the triangles are "perfect", as they produce good results across board. It is worth noting that the number of layers and the number of stages do not have to be exactly the same. We have experimented with "skewed" triangles and they can be effective under certain circumstances (such as when the input resolution is high but we want a lighter weight model).

Bottom-Up Information Flow. The top-down flows in our pyramid network enhances processing at the high resolutions (low layers) with more semantic and abstract information. However, the information flow does not have to be in only one direction. We can also add bottom-up information flows, as illustrated by yellow arrows in Fig. 1. For bottom-up flows, higher-resolution features (after top-down fusion) are fed upward to be integrated with lower-resolution features at the higher layers. This design completes our bidirectional pyramid network: information is free to flow laterally, upward, or downward, and they are fused at every step of the processing. In the ablation studies, we will show that both top-down flows and bottom-up flows are useful and improve accuracy without a heavy computational cost.

Feature Fusion Strategy. The bidirectional information flow in the pyramid network brings features with different characteristics together, where feature fusion plays a central role.

Typically, one of three feature fusion strategies is used in semantic segmentation: element-wise *addition*, element-wise *multiplication*, and *concatenation*. *Concatenation* is more flexible as it allows learned combination of the features at a later step, with a computational cost. On the other hand, element-wise *addition* and *multiplication* are more elementary operations: simple to compute, and do not increase the feature dimension.

We focus on how to effectively use the two elementary operations: *addition* and *multiplication*. Intuitively, *addition* can be viewed as an OR operation, combining individual signals from any of the two inputs; and *multiplication* can be viewed as an AND operation, selecting shared signals from both inputs. Using either of these two operations alone may not be sufficient for feature fusion. Therefore, we propose to use a combined fusion block *add-multiply-add* (**AMA**), a weighted combination of these operations, as described below and illustrated in Fig. 2.

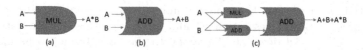

Fig. 2. Illustration of our feature fusion block *add-multiply-add* (**AMA**), which is more expressive than either **add** or **mul**, but does not increase feature dimension like **concat**.

Let A and B represent two input feature vectors at any fusion step of our pyramid network, A from the lower level (high-res, representing detail), and B from the higher level (low-res, representing context). Let A_i, B_i represent channel i of features A and B. Let $F(B)$ denote a transformation of B, including convolution, nonlinear activation, and also upsampling if there is a resolution mismatch between A and B. For element-wise addition **add**, our fusion function is $Y_i = A_i + F(B)_i$. Detail information is "summed" with context information directly. Intuitively, because context information in B has a low resolution, a direct sum tend to produce blurred boundaries. For element-wise multiplication **mul**, our fusion function is $Y_i = A_i \cdot F(B)_i$. Intuitively, this allows information both in A and B to reinforce each other, but unique signals in either A or B could be suppressed.

We find that either **add** or **mul** is not sufficient for feature fusion. Inspired by polynomial feature expansion, and related works such as Factorization Machine [30], we propose a simple yet effective feature fusion block called *add-multiply-add* (**AMA**):

$$Y_i = \alpha_i A_i + \beta_i F^a(B)_i + F^{ma}\left(A_i \cdot F^m(B)_i\right) \tag{1}$$

where F^a, F^m and F^{ma} are three transformations (convolutions) that bring the signals together, and α_i and β_i are learned weights.

In our ablation studies, we validate that the **AMA** fusion block is indeed more powerful and useful than either **add** or **mul**. As a comparison, we also explore a *concatenation* block **concat**, where the fusion function is $Y_i = conct(A_i, F(B)_i)$. Although *concatenation* is more expressive and incorporates *addition*, it cannot directly represent **multiplication**, and we find that it performs less well than the proposed **AMA** fusion, even with a higher computational cost.

3.2   Parallel Unary-Pairwise Attention

While our pyramid architecture is effective in modeling the fusion of small-scale and large-scale semantic cues, it operates locally and does not directly capture long-range dependency. Therefore, we feed the output of the pyramid model through a *Parallel Unary-Pairwise Attention* (**PUP**) module to further improve the effectiveness of the model.

We first use Asymmetric Pyramid Non-local Block (APNB) [20] to model long-range dependency through **pairwise attention**. APNB utilizes a pyramid sampling module into the nonlocal block to reduce computation and memory consumption. However, we find that pairwise attention context aggregation tends to be biased toward large-scale patterns and may harm small-scale patterns (also observed in [23]).

To mitigate the scale dilemma in APNB, we use a **unary attention** block parallel to the pairwise attention block, as shown in Fig. 3. Specifically, The input feature map first passes through a depth-wise 3×3 convolution, followed by a sigmoid function to transform them to "importance weights". Then we apply a learned importance matrix on the input feature map to generate a position-sensitive attention map. We conduct a simple element-wise addition to combine the position-sensitive attention map (from unary attention) and the long-range context-sensitive attention map (from pairwise attention), achieving effective context aggregation without losing signals for local regions. In our studies, we find that our PUP model, modeling unary and pairwise attention in parallel, performs better than pairwise attention alone.

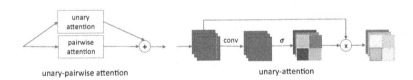

Fig. 3. Schematic illustration of unary-pairwise attention. This block receives a feature map from the pyramid network and outputs a feature map with global information aggregated and local signals retained.

3.3   Model Instantiations and Implementation Details

The model instance with 4 layers (L1 to L4) and 3 stages (i.e., S1 to S3), is called BPNet-S3. The model instance with 5 layers (L1 to L5) and 4 stages (i.e., S1 to S4), is called BPNet-S4.

We employ Kaiming initialization to initialize our proposed network. We use mini-batch stochastic gradient descent (SGD) with batch size 12, momentum 0.9 and weight decay $1e^{-4}$ during training. We apply the "poly" learning rate strategy in which the initial rate is multiplied by $(1 - \frac{iter}{maxiter})^{power}$ each iteration with power 0.9. The initial learning rate is set to $1e^{-2}$. We employ the mean subtraction, random horizontal flip and random scale on the input images to augment the dataset in training process. The scales contains {0.75, 1.0, 1.5, 1.75, 2.0}. Finally, we randomly crop the image into fix size for training. Implementation is done using TorchSeg [31].

4   Experiments

To evaluate the proposed BPNet models, we carry out experiments on Cityscapes dataset, CamVid, Pascal Context, and a medical image dataset (prostate MRI), with Cityscapes being our primary benchmark. Experimental results demonstrate that our BPNet achieves state-of-the-art performance on Cityscapes, particularly for real-time settings. Meanwhile, BPNet can compete with or outperform the state of the art on a number of other benchmarks, includign CamVid, Pascal context and prostate MRI. In this section, we first introduce the datasets, and then proceed to show our main results on Cityscapes, for both real-time and non-real-time settings. We then perform a series of ablation studies, also using the Cityscapes dataset, to valid various design choices in the BPNet. Finally, we report our results on Pascal Context, and a prostate MRI dataset.

4.1   Datasets and Evaluation Metrics

We use the standard *Mean IoU* (mean of class-wise intersection over union) for Cityscapes, Camvid, and Pascal Context. We use the Dice similarity score (DSC) for the prostate MRI dataset, as standard for that benchmark.

- Cityscapes [32] is tasked for urban segmentation, which contains 5,000 pixel-level finely annotated images captured from 50 different cities. Each image is with 1024×2048 resolution. The 5,000 finely annotated images are divided into 2,975/500/1,525 images for training, validation, and testing.
- CamVid [7] contains 701 road scenes with image resolution 720×960 extracted from driving videos, in which, 701 images are divided into training, validation and testing subsets with 367, 101 and 233 images, respectively. All images are pixel-wise annotated with 11 semantic classes.
- The PASCAL context dataset [8] includes 4, 998 scene images for training and 5, 105 images for testing with 59 semantic labels and 1 background label.
- PROMISE12-challenge dataset [10] is for MRI prostate segmentation, a widely used medical image segmentation benchmark. This dataset contains 50 labeled subjects where only prostate was annotated, and 30 extra subjects hose ground-truth label-maps are hidden from us.

4.2   Experiments on Cityscapes

We primarily carry out our experimental studies on the Cityscapes dataset. We first validate and compare the proposed models (our mediumweight network

BPNet-S3) with state-of-the-art real-time semantic segmentation methods that focus on efficiency. We then compare our heavyweight network (BPNet-S4) with state-of-the-art models that focus on accuracy. Furthermore, we conduct ablation studies to explore the impact of the various key components in the BPNet.

Comparison with State-of-the-Arts Real-Time Segmentation Methods. We first consider a lightweight model, i.e., BPNet-S3-W32, the S3 model with the base number of channels C equal to 32. (If not specified, the mediumweight BPNet-S3 has the base number of channels equal to 48). Results of other state-of-the-art real-time semantic segmentation solutions on cityscapes validation and test set (with single-scale inference strategy) are summarized in Table 1. The lightweight model, BPNet-S3-W32, presents the highest mIoU with a fast inference speed. This shows that BPNet-S3-W32 is a good choice for efficiency-demanding segmentation tasks.

Table 1. Semantic segmentation results on Cityscapes. The GFLOPs is calculated on the input size 1024×2048. * means FPS tested by ourselves on RTX 2080 TI.

Method	# params.	GFLOPs	FPS	mIoU	
				val	test
ICNet [24]	7.7	–	37.5*	70.6	69.5
BiSeNet (Res18) [29]	13.4	104.3	41.7*	74.8	74.7
DFANet [25]	7.8	–	58.8*	–	71.3
BPNet-S3-W32	5.1	74.2	36.5	77.2	76.3

Comparison with State-of-the-Art Segmentation Methods. We now show accuracy with our mediumweight and heavyweight models, i.e., BPNet-S3 and BPNet-S4. Results of other state-of-the-art semantic segmentation solutions on cityscapes validation set (with single-scale inference strategy) are summarized in Table 2. Among the approaches, DFN uses ResNet-101 [33] as backbone, Deeplabv3 [15] and PSPNet [14] both use Dilated-ResNet-101 as backbone and Deeplabv3+ [34] use stronger backbone. HRNet [9] utilizes imagenet to train a powerful pretrained model as the backbone for the segmentation tasks. The results show that the proposed BPNet-S3 can achieve similar performance with the DFN and DeepLabv3, but our model complexity is much lower (the number of parameters is about 5 times fewer). More importantly, the computational cost is about 10 times lower. In the meantime, our BPNet-S4 outperforms the DeepLabv3+, PSPNet and HRNetv2-W40. Again, BPNet-S4 has less parameters and needs much less computational resource. BPNet-S4 is also competitive to HRNetV2-W48, without using external data (e.g., Imagenet) for pretraining.

Table 2. Semantic segmentation results on Cityscapes validation with single-scale inference. The GFLOPs is calculated on the input size 1024 × 2048.

Method	Backbone	# params.	GFLOPs	mIoU
DFN [33]	ResNet-101	90.2M	2221.0	78.5
PSPNet [14]	Dilated-ResNet-101	65.9M	2017.6	79.7
DeepLabv3 [15]	Dilated-ResNet-101	58.0M	1778.7	78.5
DeepLabv3+ [34]	Dilated-Xception-71	43.5M	1444.6	79.6
HRNetV2-W40 [9]	–	45.2M	493.2	80.2
HRNetV2-W48 [33]	–	65.9M	747.3	81.1
BPNet-S3	–	11.8M	227.1	78.3
BPNet-S4	–	40.5M	307.5	80.3

Table 3. Semantic segmentation results on Cityscapes test (train and train+val as training set, respectively) with multi-scale inference.

Method	Backbone	Use pretraining	mIoU
With train set			
PSPNet [14]	Dilated-ResNet-101	Yes	78.4
PSANet [35]	Dilated-ResNet-101	Yes	78.6
HRNetV2-W48 [9]	–	Yes	80.4
BPNet-S4	–	**No**	80.5
With train+val set			
BiSeNet [29]	ResNet-101	Yes	78.9
DFN [33]	ResNet-101	Yes	79.3
PSANet [35]	Dilated-ResNet-101	Yes	80.1
PADNet [36]	Dilated-ResNet-101	Yes	80.3
DenseASPP [37]	WDenseNet-161	Yes	80.6
ANN [20]	ResNet-101	Yes	81.3
OCNet [17]	ResNet-101	Yes	81.7
OCR [38]	ResNet-101	Yes	81.8
HRNetv2-W48 [9]	–	Yes	81.6
BPNet-S4	–	**No**	81.9

In addition, we also evaluate our models on the test set (with multi-scale inference strategy) by submitting inference results to the official evaluation server. We use train+val as training set to train our model and report the mIoU on the test set. From Table 3, We see that BPNet-S4 achieve better mIoU than most of the methods, and achieve competitive performance compared to HRNetv2-W48, again without pre-training, and lower computational complexity.

Table 4. Investigation of bidirectional information flow.

Method	Fusion strategy	mIoU	ΔmIoU
BaseNet	–	73.7	–
+Top-Down	AMA	75.0	+1.3
+Bottom-Up	AMA	74.6	+0.9
+Bidirectional	AMA	76.1	+2.4
+Bidirectional	add	75.4	−0.7
+Bidirectional	mul	75.2	−0.9
+Bidirectional	concat	75.5	−0.6

Training Details. BPNet-S3-W32 and BPNet-S4 are trained with 240 epochs from scratch on Cityscapes, taking about 40 and 48 h with 4 RTX 2080 TI. The training time is not excessive, comparable to that of SOTA methods with pretrained models (e.g., PSPNet, DeepLab V3+, HRNet and so on).

Comparing to Other Methods. Scale and fusion are central topics in computer vision. Our work draws inspiration from many state-of-the-art algorithms, such as HRNet [9] and GridNet [39]. We take HRNet as an example to explain the difference. (1) Feature fusion design is quite different. (2) BPNet is much more efficient than HRNet. (3) Pretraining is not necessary for BPNet to achieve good performance. More details about the difference are introduced in the supplementary material (Sect. 5.3).

Ablation Studies. To validate design choices in the BPNet, we conduct ablation experiments on the validation set of Cityscapes with different settings. All ablation studies are conducted on BPNet-S3.

Impact of Bidirectional Information Flow. To investigate the effect of bidirectional information flow, we compare the following networks: (a) remove all top-down and bottom-up flows in the pyramid (denoted as 'BaseNet'); (b) add only top-down flow in the pyramid network (denoted as '+Top-Down'); (c) add only bottom-up flow (denoted as '+Bottom-Up') and (d) with both top-down and bottom-up flows (denoted as '+bidirectional').

In Table 4, both "+Top-Down" and "+Bottom-Up" can boost the base network to achieve better performance. Compared to bottom-up information flow, top-down information flow is more beneficial which means providing context to high-resolution processing is more important. With both the top-down and bottom-up links, the network can enjoy even more performance gain, demonstrating the merit of having information flow at every step of the processing, in both upward and downward directions.

Feature Fusion Strategy. As mentioned in Sect. 3, three popular feature fusion strategies are **add**, **mul** and **contact**. Our ablation studies focus on comparing these fusion approaches with our proposed **AMA** feature fusion in the bidirectional setting. Table 4 indicates that the proposed **AMA** works best for feature fusion, which outperforms the widely used **concat** as well as **add**.

Impact of Parallel Unary-Pairwise Attention. To validate the impact of our parallel unary-pairwise attention (PUP) mechanism for capturing both long-range dependency and thin structure, we conduct experiments with four different designs of attention mechanisms applied on the output of the pyramid network, respectively: (a) pairwise attention only (using APNB [20]) for context aggregation; (b) sequential integration of unary and pairwise attention, unary first, pairwise second; (c) sequential integration of unary and pairwise attention, pairwise first, unary second; (d) the proposed parallel unary-pairwise attention mechanism (PUP). We find that all four attention mechanisms are useful in improving accuracy, with parallel unary-pairwise attention mechanism (PUP) performs the best, significantly better than the two sequential mechanism (Fig. 4 and Table 5).

Table 5. Investigation of pairwise attention, unary attention, and their combinations.

Method	mIoU	Δ mIoU
pyramid (baseline)	76.1	–
+pairwise	77.5	+1.4
+unary+pairwise (sequential)	77.8	+1.7
+pairwise+unary (sequential)	78.1	+2.0
+PUP (parallel unary-pairwise)	78.3	+2.2

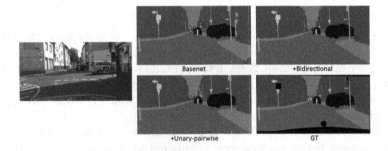

Fig. 4. An visual example of using the proposed modules in the BPNet. The bidirectional model significantly improves over the basenet, by removing wrong predictions on the building (right side), and improving upon one of the three lamps (upper middle). Adding attention, we see improvements over all three lamps with thin structures.

4.3 CamVid

In this subsection, we further validate our lightweight models on the CamVid dataset. The results on test set are listed in Table 6. BPNet-S3 can achieve a mIoU as high as 73.8. With a much smaller number of parameters (5.1M), BPNet-S3-W32 can achieve higher inference speed with competitive accuracy.

Table 6. Semantic segmentation results on CamVid test. Flops computed on 720×960.

Dataset	mIoU	# params	FLOPs	FPS
SegNet [40]	55.6	29.5	–	6.6*
ICNet [24]	67.1	7.7	–	41.9*
BiSeNet (Res18) [29]	68.7	13.4	34.5	–
BPNet-S3	73.8	11.8	56.9	34
BPNet-S3-W32	69.4	5.1	24.5	52

4.4 PASCAL Context

We keep the same data augmentation and learning rate policy in training are as Cityscapes. We set the initial learning rate to $4e^{-3}$ and weight decay to $1e^{-4}$ [41,42]. During inference, we follow the standard procedure as suggested in [41,42]. The comparison of our method with state-of-the-art methods is presented in Table 7. Our network performs competitively to previous state-of-the-arts without tuning of the hyper-parameters (same to those used for Cityscapes).

Table 7. Semantic segmentation results on PASCAL-context, evaluated on 59 classes.

Dataset	backbone	use pretraining	mIoU (59 classes)
PSPNet [14]	Dilated-ResNet-101	Yes	47.8
UNet++ [5]	ResNet-101	Yes	47.7
EncNet [42]	ResNet-152	Yes	52.6
HRNetv2-W48 [33]	–	Yes	54.0
BPNet-S4	–	**No**	52.7

4.5 Medical Image Data: Prostate Segmentation

Without the need for pre-training, BPNet has the potential to be useful for domains other than natural images. To show the versatility of BPNet, we conduct additional experiments on the PROMISE12-challenge dataset [10], a popular

MRI segmentation benchmark. The detailed comparison is provided in supplementary material due to page limit. Without specific adaptation, we can achieve a high DSC (91.1) in average based on five-fold cross validation, surpassing many existing 3D medical image segmentation algorithms with much less training and inference time. BPNet is competitive with nnUNet, a state-of-the-art 3D convolution model with the highest reported accuracy, but is 45× more efficient. These experimental results indicate that our models may find applications in many domains that need semantic segmentation.

5   Conclusions

We have presented our bidirectional pyramid network for semantic segmentation. Starting from scratch without standard backbones or pre-training, we designed a family of semantic segmentation models with several simple and yet effective components, i.e., pyramid network with top-down and bottom-up information flow, to enhance information interaction between large-scale contexts and small-scale details. We also propose a parallel unary-pairwise attention for context aggregation to help with long-range dependency and thin structure. Competitive results are produced on standard benchmarks and the proposed components are validated to be effective. With efficiency, and without pre-training, we believe our models have the potential to be used for many applications and have room for further improvements.

References

1. Long, J., Shelhamer, E., Darrell, T.: Fully convolutional networks for semantic segmentation. In: Proceedings of the IEEE Conference on Computer Vision and Pattern Recognition, pp. 3431–3440 (2015)
2. Ronneberger, O., Fischer, P., Brox, T.: U-Net: convolutional networks for biomedical image segmentation. In: Navab, N., Hornegger, J., Wells, W.M., Frangi, A.F. (eds.) MICCAI 2015. LNCS, vol. 9351, pp. 234–241. Springer, Cham (2015). https://doi.org/10.1007/978-3-319-24574-4_28
3. Milletari, F., Navab, N., Ahmadi, S.A.: V-Net: fully convolutional neural networks for volumetric medical image segmentation. In: 2016 Fourth International Conference on 3D Vision (3DV), pp. 565–571. IEEE (2016)
4. Oktay, O., et al.: Attention U-Net: learning where to look for the pancreas. arXiv preprint arXiv:1804.03999 (2018)
5. Zhou, Z., Rahman Siddiquee, M.M., Tajbakhsh, N., Liang, J.: UNet++: a nested U-Net architecture for medical image segmentation. In: Stoyanov, D., et al. (eds.) DLMIA/ML-CDS -2018. LNCS, vol. 11045, pp. 3–11. Springer, Cham (2018). https://doi.org/10.1007/978-3-030-00889-5_1
6. Lin, G., Milan, A., Shen, C., Reid, I.: RefineNet: multi-path refinement networks for high-resolution semantic segmentation. In: Proceedings of the IEEE Conference on Computer Vision and Pattern Recognition, pp. 1925–1934 (2017)
7. Brostow, G.J., Shotton, J., Fauqueur, J., Cipolla, R.: Segmentation and recognition using structure from motion point clouds. In: Forsyth, D., Torr, P., Zisserman, A. (eds.) ECCV 2008. LNCS, vol. 5302, pp. 44–57. Springer, Heidelberg (2008). https://doi.org/10.1007/978-3-540-88682-2_5

8. Mottaghi, R., et al.: The role of context for object detection and semantic segmentation in the wild. In: Proceedings of the IEEE Conference on Computer Vision and Pattern Recognition, pp. 891–898 (2014)

9. Sun, K., et al.: High-resolution representations for labeling pixels and regions. arXiv preprint arXiv:1904.04514 (2019)

10. Litjens, G., et al.: Evaluation of prostate segmentation algorithms for MRI: the PROMISE12 challenge. MedIA **18**, 359–373 (2014)

11. Pinheiro, P.O., Lin, T.-Y., Collobert, R., Dollár, P.: Learning to refine object segments. In: Leibe, B., Matas, J., Sebe, N., Welling, M. (eds.) ECCV 2016. LNCS, vol. 9905, pp. 75–91. Springer, Cham (2016). https://doi.org/10.1007/978-3-319-46448-0_5

12. Liu, S., Qi, L., Qin, H., Shi, J., Jia, J.: Path aggregation network for instance segmentation. In: Proceedings of the IEEE Conference on Computer Vision and Pattern Recognition, pp. 8759–8768 (2018)

13. Tan, M., Pang, R., Le, Q.V.: EfficientDet: scalable and efficient object detection. arXiv preprint arXiv:1911.09070 (2019)

14. Zhao, H., Shi, J., Qi, X., Wang, X., Jia, J.: Pyramid scene parsing network. In: Proceedings of the IEEE Conference on Computer Vision and Pattern Recognition, pp. 2881–2890 (2017)

15. Chen, L.C., Papandreou, G., Kokkinos, I., Murphy, K., Yuille, A.L.: DeepLab: semantic image segmentation with deep convolutional nets, atrous convolution, and fully connected CRFs. IEEE Trans. Pattern Anal. Mach. Intell. **40**, 834–848 (2017)

16. Wang, X., Girshick, R., Gupta, A., He, K.: Non-local neural networks. In: Proceedings of the IEEE Conference on Computer Vision and Pattern Recognition, pp. 7794–7803 (2018)

17. Yuan, Y., Wang, J.: OCNet: object context network for scene parsing. arXiv preprint arXiv:1809.00916 (2018)

18. Fu, J., et al.: Dual attention network for scene segmentation. In: Proceedings of the IEEE Conference on Computer Vision and Pattern Recognition, pp. 3146–3154 (2019)

19. Huang, Z., Wang, X., Huang, L., Huang, C., Wei, Y., Liu, W.: CCNet: criss-cross attention for semantic segmentation. In: Proceedings of the IEEE International Conference on Computer Vision, pp. 603–612 (2019)

20. Zhu, Z., Xu, M., Bai, S., Huang, T., Bai, X.: Asymmetric non-local neural networks for semantic segmentation. In: Proceedings of the IEEE International Conference on Computer Vision, pp. 593–602 (2019)

21. Li, X., Zhong, Z., Wu, J., Yang, Y., Lin, Z., Liu, H.: Expectation-maximization attention networks for semantic segmentation. In: Proceedings of the IEEE International Conference on Computer Vision, pp. 9167–9176 (2019)

22. Li, X., Zhao, H., Han, L., Tong, Y., Yang, K.: GFF: gated fully fusion for semantic segmentation. arXiv preprint arXiv:1904.01803 (2019)

23. Li, X., Zhang, L., You, A., Yang, M., Yang, K., Tong, Y.: Global aggregation then local distribution in fully convolutional networks. arXiv preprint arXiv:1909.07229 (2019)

24. Zhao, H., Qi, X., Shen, X., Shi, J., Jia, J.: ICNet for real-time semantic segmentation on high-resolution images. In: Ferrari, V., Hebert, M., Sminchisescu, C., Weiss, Y. (eds.) ECCV 2018. LNCS, vol. 11207, pp. 418–434. Springer, Cham (2018). https://doi.org/10.1007/978-3-030-01219-9_25

25. Li, H., Xiong, P., Fan, H., Sun, J.: DFANet: deep feature aggregation for real-time semantic segmentation. In: Proceedings of the IEEE Conference on Computer Vision and Pattern Recognition, pp. 9522–9531 (2019)

26. Li, X., Zhou, Y., Pan, Z., Feng, J.: Partial order pruning: for best speed/accuracy trade-off in neural architecture search. In: Proceedings of the IEEE Conference on Computer Vision and Pattern Recognition, pp. 9145–9153 (2019)

27. Orsic, M., Kreso, I., Bevandic, P., Segvic, S.: In defense of pre-trained imagenet architectures for real-time semantic segmentation of road-driving images. In: Proceedings of the IEEE Conference on Computer Vision and Pattern Recognition, pp. 12607–12616 (2019)

28. Howard, A., et al.: Searching for MobileNetV3. In: Proceedings of the IEEE International Conference on Computer Vision, pp. 1314–1324 (2019)

29. Yu, C., Wang, J., Peng, C., Gao, C., Yu, G., Sang, N.: BiSeNet: bilateral segmentation network for real-time semantic segmentation. In: Ferrari, V., Hebert, M., Sminchisescu, C., Weiss, Y. (eds.) ECCV 2018. LNCS, vol. 11217, pp. 334–349. Springer, Cham (2018). https://doi.org/10.1007/978-3-030-01261-8_20

30. Rendle, S.: Factorization machines. In: 2010 IEEE International Conference on Data Mining, pp. 995–1000. IEEE (2010)

31. Yu, C.: Torchseg (2019). https://github.com/ycszen/TorchSeg

32. Cordts, M., et al.: The cityscapes dataset for semantic urban scene understanding. In: Proceedings of the IEEE Conference on Computer Vision and Pattern Recognition, pp. 3213–3223 (2016)

33. Yu, C., Wang, J., Peng, C., Gao, C., Yu, G., Sang, N.: Learning a discriminative feature network for semantic segmentation. In: Proceedings of the IEEE Conference on Computer Vision and Pattern Recognition, pp. 1857–1866 (2018)

34. Chen, L.-C., Zhu, Y., Papandreou, G., Schroff, F., Adam, H.: Encoder-decoder with atrous separable convolution for semantic image segmentation. In: Ferrari, V., Hebert, M., Sminchisescu, C., Weiss, Y. (eds.) ECCV 2018. LNCS, vol. 11211, pp. 833–851. Springer, Cham (2018). https://doi.org/10.1007/978-3-030-01234-2_49

35. Zhao, H., et al.: PSANet: point-wise spatial attention network for scene parsing. In: Ferrari, V., Hebert, M., Sminchisescu, C., Weiss, Y. (eds.) ECCV 2018. LNCS, vol. 11213, pp. 270–286. Springer, Cham (2018). https://doi.org/10.1007/978-3-030-01240-3_17

36. Xu, D., Ouyang, W., Wang, X., Sebe, N.: PAD-Net: multi-tasks guided prediction-and-distillation network for simultaneous depth estimation and scene parsing. In: Proceedings of the IEEE Conference on Computer Vision and Pattern Recognition, pp. 675–684 (2018)

37. Yang, M., Yu, K., Zhang, C., Li, Z., Yang, K.: DenseASPP for semantic segmentation in street scenes. In: Proceedings of the IEEE Conference on Computer Vision and Pattern Recognition, pp. 3684–3692 (2018)

38. Yuan, Y., Chen, X., Wang, J.: Object-contextual representations for semantic segmentation. arXiv preprint arXiv:1909.11065 (2019)

39. Fourure, D., Emonet, R., Fromont, E., Muselet, D., Tremeau, A., Wolf, C.: Residual conv-deconv grid network for semantic segmentation. arXiv preprint arXiv:1707.07958 (2017)

40. Badrinarayanan, V., Kendall, A., Cipolla, R.: SegNet: a deep convolutional encoder-decoder architecture for image segmentation. IEEE Trans. Pattern Anal. Mach. Intell. **39**, 2481–2495 (2017)

41. Ding, H., Jiang, X., Shuai, B., Liu, A.Q., Wang, G.: Context contrasted feature and gated multi-scale aggregation for scene segmentation. In: Proceedings of the IEEE Conference on Computer Vision and Pattern Recognition, pp. 2393–2402 (2018)
42. Zhang, H., et al.: Context encoding for semantic segmentation. In: Proceedings of the IEEE Conference on Computer Vision and Pattern Recognition, pp. 7151–7160 (2018)

DEAL: Difficulty-Aware Active Learning for Semantic Segmentation

Shuai Xie, Zunlei Feng, Ying Chen, Songtao Sun, Chao Ma,
and Mingli Song$^{(\boxtimes)}$

Zhejiang University, Hangzhou, China
{shuaixie,zunleifeng,lynesychen,songtaosun,chaoma,brooksong}@zju.edu.cn

Abstract. Active learning aims to address the paucity of labeled data by finding the most informative samples. However, when applying to semantic segmentation, existing methods ignore the segmentation difficulty of different semantic areas, which leads to poor performance on those hard semantic areas such as tiny or slender objects. To deal with this problem, we propose a semantic Difficulty-awarE Active Learning (DEAL) network composed of two branches: the common segmentation branch and the semantic difficulty branch. For the latter branch, with the supervision of segmentation error between the segmentation result and GT, a pixel-wise probability attention module is introduced to learn the semantic difficulty scores for different semantic areas. Finally, two acquisition functions are devised to select the most valuable samples with semantic difficulty. Competitive results on semantic segmentation benchmarks demonstrate that DEAL achieves state-of-the-art active learning performance and improves the performance of the hard semantic areas in particular.

Keywords: Active learning · Semantic segmentation · Difficulty-aware

1 Introduction

Semantic segmentation is a fundamental task for various applications such as autonomous driving [1,2], biomedical image analysis [3–5], remote sensing [6] and robot manipulation [7]. Recently, data-driven methods have achieved great success with large-scale datasets [8,9]. However, tremendous annotation cost has become an obstacle for these methods to be widely applied in practical scenarios. Active Learning (AL) can be the right solution by finding the most informative samples. Annotating those selected samples can support sufficient supervision information and reduce the requirement of labeled samples dramatically.

Electronic supplementary material The online version of this chapter (https://doi.org/10.1007/978-3-030-69525-5_40) contains supplementary material, which is available to authorized users.

© Springer Nature Switzerland AG 2021
H. Ishikawa et al. (Eds.): ACCV 2020, LNCS 12622, pp. 672–688, 2021.
https://doi.org/10.1007/978-3-030-69525-5_40

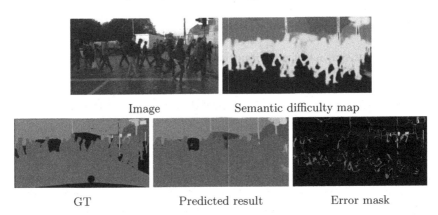

Image Semantic difficulty map

GT Predicted result Error mask

Fig. 1. (a) Image from Cityscapes [8]. (b) Semantic difficulty map. The colder color represents the easier semantic areas such as road, sky, and buildings. The warmer color represents the harder semantic areas such as poles and traffic signs. (c) GT. (d) Predicted result. (e) Error mask generated with (c) and (d) according to Eq. (1). It's a binary image, coloring for better visualization.

Previous methods can be mainly categorized into two families: uncertainty-based [10–13] and representation-based [14–16]. However, many works [10,12, 14,16] are only evaluated on image classification benchmarks. There has been considerably less work specially designed for semantic segmentation. Traditional uncertainty-based methods like Entropy [17] and Query-By-Committee (QBC) [18] have demonstrated their effectiveness in semantic segmentation [19,20]. However, all of them are solely based on the uncertainty reflected on each pixel, without considering the semantic difficulty and the actual labeling scenarios.

In this paper, we propose a semantic Difficulty-awarE Active Learning (DEAL) method taking the semantic difficulty into consideration. Due to the class imbalance and shape disparity, a noticeable semantic difficulty difference exists among the different semantic areas in an image. To capture this difference, we adopt a two-branch network composed of a semantic segmentation branch and a semantic difficulty branch. For the former branch, we adopt the common segmentation network. For the latter branch, we leverage the wrong predicted result as the supervision, which is termed as the *error mask*. It's a binary image where the right and wrong positions have a value 0 and 1, respectively. As illustrated in Fig. 1(e), we color these wrong positions for better visualization. Then, a pixel-wise probability attention module is introduced to aggregate similar pixels into areas and learn the proportion of misclassified pixels as the difficulty score for each area. Finally, we can obtain the semantic difficulty map in Fig. 1(b).

Then two acquisition functions are devised based on the map. One is Difficulty-aware uncertainty Score (DS) combining the uncertainty and difficulty. The other is Difficulty-aware semantic Entropy (DE) solely based on the difficulty. Experiments show that the learned difficulty scores have a strong connection with the standard evaluation metric IoU. And DEAL can effectively improve the overall AL performance and the IoU of the hard semantic classes in particular.

In summary, our major contributions are as follows: 1) Proposing a new AL framework incorporating the semantic difficulty to select the most informative samples for semantic segmentation. 2) Utilizing *error mask* to learn the semantic difficulty. 3) Competitive results on CamVid [21] and Cityscapes [8].

2   Related Work

AL for Semantic Segmentation. The core of AL is measuring the informativeness of the unlabelled samples. Modern AL methods can be mainly divided into two groups: uncertainty-based [10–13] and representation-based [14–16]. The latter views the AL process as an approximation of the entire data distribution and query samples to increase the data diversity, such as Core-set [14] and VAAL [15], which can be directly used in semantic segmentation. There are also some methods specially designed for semantic segmentation, which can also be divided into two groups: image-level [4, 11, 19, 22] and region-level [20, 23, 24].

Image-level methods use the complete image as the sampling unit. [4] propose suggestive annotation (SA) and train a group of models on various labeled sets obtained with bootstrap sampling and select samples with the highest variance. [11] employ MC dropout to measure uncertainty for melanoma segmentation. [19] adopt QBC strategy and propose a cost-sensitive active learning method for intracranial hemorrhage detection. [22] build a batch mode multi-clue method, incorporating edge information with QBC strategy and graph-based representativeness. All of them are based on a group of models and time-consuming when querying a large unlabeled data pool.

Region-level methods only sample the informative regions from images. [23] combines the MC dropout uncertainty with an effort estimation regressed from the annotation click patterns, which is hard to access for many datasets. [24] propose ViewAL and use the inconsistencies in model predictions across viewpoints to measure the uncertainty of super-pixels, which is specially designed for RGB-D data. [20] model a deep Q-network-based query network as a reinforcement learning agent, trying to learn sampling strategies based on prior AL experience. In this work, we incorporate the semantic difficulty to measure the informativeness and select samples at the image level. Region-level method will be studied in the future.

Self-attention Mechanism for Semantic Segmentation. The self-attention mechanism is first proposed by [25] in the machine translation task. Now, it has been widely used in many tasks [25–28] owing to its intuition, versatility and interpretability [29]. The ability to capture the long-range dependencies inspires many semantic segmentation works designing their attention modules. [30] use a point-wise spatial attention module to aggregate context information in a self-adaptive manner. [31] introduce an object context pooling scheme to better aggregate similar pixels belonging to the same object category. [32] replace the non-local operation [33] into two consecutive criss-cross operations and gather long-range contextual information in the horizontal and vertical directions. [34] design two types of attention modules to exploit the dependencies between pixels and channel maps. Our method also uses the pixel-wise positional attention mechanism in [34] to aggregate similar pixels.

3   Method

Before introducing our method, we first give the definition of the AL problem. Let (x^a, y^a) be an annotated sample from the initial annotated dataset $\mathcal{D}^a$ and x^u be an unlabeled sample from a much larger unlabeled data pool $\mathcal{D}^u$. AL aims to iteratively query a subset $\mathcal{D}^s$ containing the most informative m samples $\{x_1^u, x_2^u, ..., x_m^u\}$ from $\mathcal{D}^u$, where m is a fixed budget.

In what follows, we first give an overview of our difficulty-aware active learning framework, then detail the probability attention module and loss functions, finally define two acquisition functions.

3.1   Difficulty-Aware Active Learning

To learn the semantic difficulty, we exploit the *error mask* generated from the segmentation result. Our intuition is that these wrong predictions are what our model "feels" difficult to segment, which may have a relation with the semantic difficulty. Thus, we build a two-branch network generating semantic segmentation result and semantic difficulty map in a multi-task manner, best viewed in Fig. 2. The first branch is a common segmentation network, which can be used to generate the *error mask*. The second branch is devised to learn the semantic difficulty map with the guidance of *error mask*. This two-branch architecture is inspired by [13]. In their work, a loss prediction module is attached to the task model to predict a reliable loss for x^u and samples with the highest losses are selected. While in our task, we dig deeper into the scene and analyze the semantic difficulty of each area.

As illustrated in Fig. 2, the first branch can be any semantic segmentation network. Assume S^* is the output of softmax layer and S^p is the prediction result after the argmax operation. With the segmentation result S^p and GT S^g, the *error mask* M^e can be computed by:

$$M_k^e = \begin{cases} 1 & \text{if } S_k^p \neq S_k^g, \\ 0 & \text{otherwise,} \end{cases} \tag{1}$$

where S_k^p and S_k^g denote the kth pixel value of the segmentation result and GT, M_k^e is the kth pixel value of the *error mask*.

The second branch is composed of two parts: a probability attention module and a simple 1×1 convolution layer used for binary classification. The softmax output of the first branch S^* is directly used as the input of the second branch, which are C-channel probability maps and C is the number of classes. We denote it as $P \in \mathcal{R}^{C \times H \times W}$ and P_k is the probability vector for the kth pixel. Using probability maps is naive but accompanied with two advantages. First, pixels with similar difficulty tend to have similar P_k. Second, pixels of the same semantic tend to have similar P_k. Combined with a pixel-wise attention module, we can easily aggregate these similar pixels and learn similar difficulty scores for them. In our learning schema, the performance of the second branch depends much on the output of the first branch. However, there is no much difference if we branch these two tasks earlier and learn the independent features. We validate this opinion in Sect. 5.2.

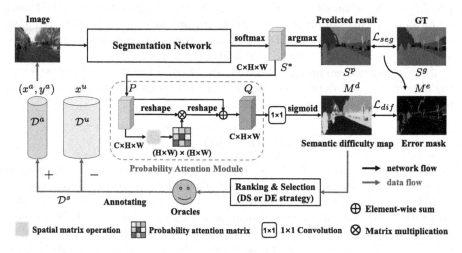

Fig. 2. Overview of our difficulty-aware active learning framework for semantic segmentation. The first branch is a common semantic segmentation network. The second branch is composed of a probability attention module and a 1×1 convolution. $\mathcal{D}^a$ and $\mathcal{D}^u$ are the annotated and unlabeled data, $\mathcal{D}^s$ is a subset selected from $\mathcal{D}^u$. P and Q are the probability maps before and after attention. $\mathcal{L}_{seg}$ and $\mathcal{L}_{dif}$ are the loss functions described in Eq. 3 and Eq. 4. DS and DE strategies are detailed in Sect. 3.4.

The semantic difficulty learning process can be imagined into two steps. Firstly, we learn a binary segmentation network with the supervision of *error mask* M^e. Each pixel will learn a semantic difficulty score. Secondly, similar pixels are aggregated into an area so that this score can be spread among them. Finally, we can obtain the semantic difficulty map M^d.

3.2   Probability Attention Module

In this section, we detail the probability attention module (PAM) in our task. Inspired by [34], we use this module to aggregate pixels with similar softmax probability. Given the probability maps $P \in \mathcal{R}^{C \times H \times W}$, we first reshape it to $P \in \mathcal{R}^{C \times K}$, where $K = H \times W$. Then the probability attention matrix $A \in \mathcal{R}^{K \times K}$ can be computed with $P^T P$ and a softmax operation as below:

Error inside the object   Error on the object boundary

Fig. 3. Two typical errors in semantic segmentation. The right and wrong areas are in blue and red, best viewed in color. (Color figure online)

$$A_{ji} = \frac{exp(P_i^T \cdot P_j)}{\sum_{i=1}^{K} exp(P_i^T \cdot P_j)},$$
$$Q_j = \gamma \sum_{i=1}^{K}(A_{ji}P_i) + P_j, \tag{2}$$

where A_{ji} is the ith pixel's impact on j^{th} pixel, P_j is the original probability vector of the jth pixel and Q_j is the one after attention, γ is a learnable weight factor. Finally, we can get the probability maps $Q \in \mathcal{R}^{C \times H \times W}$ after attention.

Let's take the segmentation result of the two bicyclists in Fig. 2 to explain the role of PAM as it reflects two typical errors in semantic segmentation: (1) error inside the object (the smaller one b_1); (2) error on the object boundary (the larger one b_2), as shown in Fig. 3. Assume our attention module can aggregate pixels from the same object together, the right part of the object learns 0 while the wrong part learns 1. Since b_1 has a larger part of wrong areas, it tends to learn larger difficulty scores than b_2. Similar to objects, pixels from the same semantic, such as road, sky and buildings can also learn similar difficulty scores. Ablation study in Sect. 5.1 also demonstrates that PAM can learn more smooth difficulty scores for various semantic areas.

Some traditional methods also employ the softmax probabilities to measure the uncertainty, such as least confidence (LC) [35], margin sampling (MS) [36] and Entropy [17]. The most significant difference between our method and these

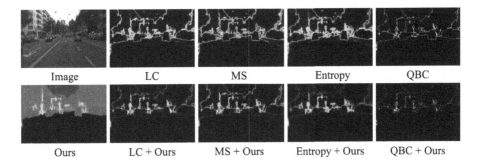

Fig. 4. First row: Image from Cityscapes [8] and traditional uncertainty maps. Second row: Our semantic difficulty map and difficulty-aware uncertainty maps. The warmer color means the higher uncertainty. (Color figure online)

methods is that we consider difficulty at the semantic level with an attention module, rather than measuring the uncertainty of each pixel alone. QBC [18] can use a group of models, but it still stays at the pixel level. To clearly see the difference, we compare our semantic difficulty map with the uncertainty maps of these methods in Fig. 4. The first row are uncertainty maps generated with these methods, which are loyal to the uncertainty of each pixel. For example, some pixels belonging to *sky* can have the same uncertainty with *traffic light* and *traffic sign*. Supposing an image has many pixels with high uncertainty belonging to the easier classes, it will be selected by these methods. While our semantic difficulty map (first in the second row) can serve as the difficulty attention and distinguish more valuable pixels. As illustrated in the second row, combined with our difficulty map, the uncertainty of the easier semantic areas like *sky* is suppressed while the harder semantic areas like *traffic sign* is reserved.

3.3   Loss Functions

Loss of Semantic Segmentation. To make an equitable comparison with other methods, we use the standard cross-entropy loss for the semantic segmentation branch, which is defined as:

$$\mathcal{L}_{seg}(S^*, S^g) = \frac{1}{K} \sum_{k=1}^{K} \ell(S_k^*, S_k^g) + R(\theta), \tag{3}$$

where S_k^* and S_k^g are the segmentation output and ground truth for pixel k, $\ell(\cdot)$ is the cross-entropy loss, K is the total pixel number, and R is the L2-norm regularization term.

Loss of Semantic Difficulty. For the semantic difficulty branch, we use an inverted weighted binary cross-entropy loss defined below, as there is a considerable imbalance between the right and wrong areas of *error mask*.

$$\mathcal{L}_{dif}(M^d, M^e) = -\frac{1}{K} \sum_{k=1}^{K} \lambda_1 M_k^e log(M_k^d) + \lambda_2 (1 - M_k^e) log(1 - M_k^d), \tag{4}$$

$$\lambda_1 = \frac{\sum_k^K \mathbf{1}(M_k^e = 0)}{K}, \lambda_2 = 1 - \lambda_1,$$

where M_k^d and M_k^e are the difficulty prediction and *error mask* ground truth for pixel k, $\mathbf{1}(\cdot)$ is the indicator function, and λ_1 and λ_2 are dynamic weight factors.

Final Loss. Our final training objective is a combination of Eq. 3 and Eq. 4, which is computed as:

$$\mathcal{L} = \mathcal{L}_{seg} + \alpha \mathcal{L}_{dif}, \tag{5}$$

where α is a weight factor and set to 1 in the experiments.

3.4   Acquisition Functions

Samples from $\mathcal{D}^u$ are usually ranked with a scalar score in AL. However, semantic segmentation is a dense-classification task, many methods output a score for each pixel on the image, including our semantic difficulty map. Thus, it's quite significant to design a proper acquisition function. Below are two functions we have designed.

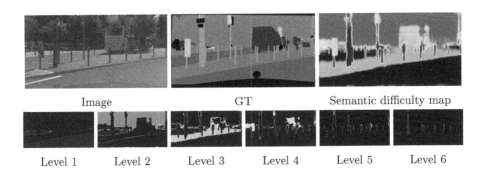

Fig. 5. Quantified difficulty levels. Semantics in (a) are quantified into 6 difficulty levels based on (c). (d) Level 1: road. (e) Level 2: vegetation. (f) Level 3: sidewalk and a part of bus. (g) Level 4: traffic light and the rear window of bus. (h) Level 5: boundaries of poles. (i) Level 6: poles. The background of images in (d–i) is in dark blue, representing pixels not falling in the corresponding level. (Color figure online)

Difficulty-Aware Uncertainty Score (DS). Assume M^c is the uncertainty map generated with traditional methods like Entropy, we can define the equation below to make each pixel aware of its semantic difficulty.

$$\mathcal{S}_{DS} = \frac{1}{K} \sum_{k=1}^{K} M_k^c \cdot M_k^d, \tag{6}$$

where M_k^c and M_k^d are the uncertainty score and difficulty score of the kth pixel, K is the total pixel number, $\mathcal{S}_{DS}$ is the average difficulty-aware uncertainty score for selecting samples with the highest uncertainty.

Difficulty-Aware Semantic Entropy (DE). This acquisition function is inspired by the laddered semantic difficulty reflected on M^d. Usually, pixels from the same semantic area have almost the same semantic difficulty scores, best viewed in Fig. 5(c). In this example, we quantify the difficulty of pixels in Fig. 5(a) into 6 levels in Fig. 5(d–i), with difficulty scores gradually increasing from level 1 to level 6. Generally, if we quantify the difficulty in an image into L levels, the difficulty entropy acquisition function can be defined below to query samples with more balanced semantic difficulty, which can be viewed as a representation-based method at the image scale.

$$\mathcal{S}_{DE} = -\sum_{l=1}^{l=L} \frac{K_l}{K} log(\frac{K_l}{K}), \qquad (7)$$

where K_l is the number of pixels falling in the lth difficulty level, K is the total pixel number, L is the quantified difficulty levels, $\mathcal{S}_{DE}$ is the difficulty-aware semantic entropy for selecting samples with more balanced semantic difficulty. Our full algorithm of DEAL is shown in Algorithm 1.

Algorithm 1: Difficulty-aware Active Learning Algorithm

Input: $\mathcal{D}^a$, $\mathcal{D}^u$, budget m, AL query times N, initialized network parameter Θ
Input: iterations T, weight factor α, quantified difficulty levels L (optional)
Output: $\mathcal{D}^a$, $\mathcal{D}^u$, Optimized Θ
for $n = 1, 2, ..., N$ **do**
    Train the two-branch difficulty learning network on $\mathcal{D}^a$;
    for $t = 1, 2, ..., T$ **do**
        Sample (x^a, y^a) from $\mathcal{D}^a$;
        Compute the segmentation output S^* and result S^p;
        Obtain M^e according to Eq. 1;
        Compute the difficulty prediction M^d;
        Compute $\mathcal{L}_{seg}$, $\mathcal{L}_{dif}$, $\mathcal{L}$ according to Eq. 3, Eq. 4, Eq. 5;
        Update Θ using gradient descent;
    end
    Rank x^u based on Eq. 6 or Eq. 7;
    Select $\mathcal{D}^s$ with top m samples;
    Annotate $\mathcal{D}^s$ by oralces;
    $\mathcal{D}^a \leftarrow \mathcal{D}^a + \mathcal{D}^s$;
    $\mathcal{D}^u \leftarrow \mathcal{D}^u - \mathcal{D}^s$;
end

---

4   Experiments and Results

In this section, we first describe the datasets we use to evaluate our method and the implementation details, then the baseline methods, finally compare our results with these baselines.

4.1   Experimental Setup

Datasets. We evaluate DEAL on two street scene semantic segmentation datasets: CamVid [21] and Cityscapes [8]. For Cityscapes, we randomly select 300 samples from the training set as the validation set, and the original validation set serves as the test set, same to [15]. The detailed configurations are list in Table 1. For each dataset, we first randomly sample 10% data from the training set as the initial annotated dataset $\mathcal{D}^a$, then iteratively query 5% new data $\mathcal{D}^s$ from the remaining training set, which serves as the unlabeled data pool $\mathcal{D}^u$. Considering samples in the street scenes have high similarities, we first randomly choose a subset from $\mathcal{D}^u$, then query m samples from the subset, same to [37].

Table 1. Evaluation datasets.

Dataset	Classes	Train	Valid	Test	Initial labeled	Budget	Image size
CamVid [21]	11	370	104	234	40	20	360×480
Cityscapes [8]	19	2675	300	500	300	150	688×688

Implementation Details. We adopt the Deeplabv3+ [38] architecture with a Mobilenetv2 [39] backbone. For each dataset, we use mini-batch SGD [40] with momentum 0.9 and weight decay $5e^{-4}$ in training. The batch size is 4 and 8 for CamVid and Cityscapes, respectively. For all methods and the upper bound method with the full training data, we train 100 epochs with an unweighted cross-entropy loss function. Similar to [38], we apply the "poly" learning rate strategy and the initial learning rate is 0.01 and multiplied by $(1 - \frac{iter}{max\_iter})^{0.9}$. To accelerate the calculation of the probability attention module, the input of the difficulty branch is resized to 80×60 and 86×86 for CamVid and Cityscapes.

4.2 Evaluated Methods

We compare DEAL with the following methods. *Random* is a simple baseline method. *Entropy* and *QBC* are two uncertainty-based methods. *Core-set* and *VAAL* are two representation-based methods. *DEAL (DS)* and *DEAL (DE)* are our methods with different acquisition functions.

- **Random**: each sample in $\mathcal{D}^u$ is queried with uniform probability.
- **Entropy** (Uncertainty): we query samples with max mean entropy of all pixels. [13] and [20] have verified this method is quite competitive in image classification and segmentation tasks.
- **QBC** (Uncertainty): previous methods designed for semantic segmentation, like [4,11,22,23], all use a group of models to measure uncertainty. We use the efficient MC dropout to represent these methods and report the best performance out of both the max-entropy and variation-ratio acquisition functions.
- **Core-set** (Representation): we query samples that can best cover the entire data distribution. We use the global average pooling operation on the encoder output features of Deeplabv3+ and get a feature vector for each sample. Then *k-Center-Greedy* strategy is used to query the most informative samples, and the distance metric is l_2 distance according to [14].
- **VAAL** (Representation): as a new state-of-the-art task-agnostic method, the sample query process of VAAL is totally separated from the task learner. We use this method to query samples that are most likely from $\mathcal{D}^u$ and then report the performance with our task model.
- **DEAL (DS)**: out method with DS acquisition function. We employ *Entropy* uncertainty maps in our experiments.
- **DEAL (DE)**: out method with DE acquisition function. The quantified difficulty levels L are set 8 and 10 for CamVid and Cityscapes, respectively.

4.3   Experimental Results

The mean Intersection over Union (mIoU) at each AL stage: 10%, 15%, 20%, 25%, 30%, 35%, 40% of the full training set, are adopted as the evaluation metric. Every method is run 5 times and the average mIoUs are reported.

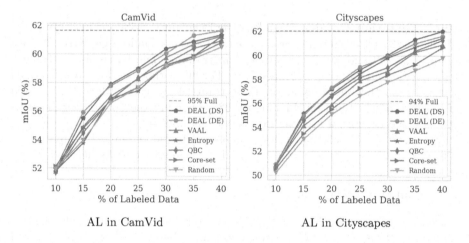

Fig. 6. DEAL performance on CamVid [21] and Cityscapes [8]. Every method is evaluated by the average mIoU of 5 runs. The dashed line represents the upper performance we can reach compared with the full training data.

Results on CamVid. Figure 6(a) shows results on a small dataset CamVid. Both *DEAL (DS)* and *DEAL (DE)* outperform baseline methods at each AL stage. We can obtain a performance of 61.64% mIoU with 40% training data, about 95% of the upper performance with full training data. *Entropy* can achieve good results at the last stage. However, it's quite unstable and depends much on the performance of current model, making it behave poorly and exceeded by *Random* at some stages. On the contrary, *DEAL (DS)* behaves better with the difficulty attention. *QBC* has a more stable growth curve as it depends less on the single model. Representation-based methods like *VAAL* and *Core-set* behave much better at earlier stages like 15% and 20%. However, *Core-set* lags behind later while *VAAL* still works well. Also, the experiment results suggest that the data diversity is more important when the entire dataset is small.

Results on Cityscapes. Figure 6(b) shows results on a larger dataset Cityscapes. The budget is 150 and all methods have more stable growth curves. When the budget is enough, *Entropy* can achieve better performance than other baseline methods. Consistently, with semantic difficulty, both *DEAL (DS)* and *DEAL (DE)* outperform other methods. Table 2 shows the per-class IoU for each method at the last AL stage (40% training data). Compared with *Entropy*, our method are more competitive on the difficult classes, such as *pole, traffic sign, rider* and *motorcycle*. For representation-based methods, the gap between *Core-set* and *VAAL* is more obvious, suggesting that *Core-set* is less effective when the input has a higher dimension. And *VAAL* is easily affected by the performance of the learned variational autoencoder, which introduces more uncertainty to the active learning system. If continue querying new data, our method will reach the upper performance of full training data with about 60% data.

Table 2. Per-class IoU of and mIoU [%] on Cityscapes original validation set with 40% training data. For clarity, only the average of 5 runs are reported, and the best and the second best results are highlighted in **bold** and **underline bold**.

Method	Road	Side-walk	Build-ing	Wall	Fence	Pole	Traffic Light	Traffic Sign	Vegetation	Terrain
Random	96.03	72.36	86.79	43.56	44.22	36.99	35.28	53.87	86.91	54.58
Core-set	96.12	72.76	87.03	44.86	**45.86**	35.84	34.81	53.07	87.18	53.49
VAAL	**96.22**	**73.27**	86.95	**47.27**	43.92	37.40	36.88	54.90	87.10	54.48
QBC	96.07	72.27	87.05	**46.89**	44.89	37.21	37.57	54.53	87.51	55.13
Entropy	**96.28**	**73.31**	**87.13**	43.82	43.87	38.10	**37.74**	55.39	**87.52**	53.68
DEAL (DS)	96.21	72.72	86.94	46.11	44.22	**38.18**	**37.62**	55.66	87.34	**55.62**
DEAL (DE)	95.89	71.69	**87.09**	45.61	**44.94**	38.29	36.51	**55.47**	87.53	56.90

	Sky	Pedestrian	Rider	Car	Truck	Bus	Train	Motor-cycle	Bicycle	mIoU
Random	91.47	62.74	37.51	88.05	54.64	61.00	43.69	30.58	55.67	59.79
Core-set	91.89	62.48	36.28	87.63	57.63	**67.02**	**56.59**	29.34	53.56	60.69
VAAL	91.63	63.44	38.92	87.92	50.15	63.70	52.36	35.99	54.97	60.92
QBC	91.87	63.79	38.76	88.04	53.88	65.92	**54.32**	32.68	56.15	61.29
Entropy	**92.05**	**63.96**	38.44	**88.38**	**59.38**	64.64	50.80	36.13	**57.10**	61.46
DEAL (DS)	92.10	63.92	40.39	87.87	59.85	67.32	52.30	**38.88**	55.44	62.04
DEAL (DE)	91.78	**64.25**	**39.77**	**88.11**	56.87	64.46	50.39	38.92	**56.69**	**61.64**

5 Ablation Study

5.1 Effect of PAM

To further understand the effect of PAM, we first visualize the attention heatmaps of the wrong predictions in Fig. 7. For each row, three points are selected from *error mask* and marked as $\{1, 2, 3\}$ in Fig. 7(a, b, c). In the first row, point 1 is from *road* and misclassified as *bicyclist*, we can observe that its related classes are *bicyclist, road* and *sidewalk* in Fig. 7(d). Point 2 is from *buildings* and misclassified as *bicyclist*, too. Point 3 is from *sign symbol* and misclassified as *tree*, we can also observe its related semantic areas in Fig. 7(f).

Then we conduct an ablation study by removing PAM and directly learning the semantic difficulty map without the attention among pixels. The qualitative results are shown in Fig. 8(a). Basically, without the long-range dependencies, pixels of the same semantic can learn quite different scores because the learned score of each pixel is more sensitive to its original uncertainty. Combined with PAM, we can learn more smooth difficulty map, which is more friendly to the annotators since the aggregated semantic areas are close to the labeling units in the real scenario. Also, we compare this ablation model with our original model on Cityscapes in Fig. 8(b). DEAL with PAM can achieve a better performance at each AL stage. DEAL without PAM fails to find samples with more balanced semantic difficulty, which makes it get a lower entropy of class distributions.

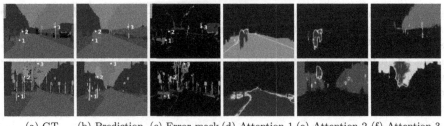

(a) GT   (b) Prediction   (c) Error mask (d) Attention 1 (e) Attention 2 (f) Attention 3

Fig. 7. Attention heatmaps of three selected wrong predicted pixels on CamVid [21]. (a) GT. (b) Prediction. (c) Error mask. (d, e, f) Attention heatmaps of the three selected points, which are marked as {1,2,3} in (a, b, c). The warmer color means the more dependency. (Color figure online)

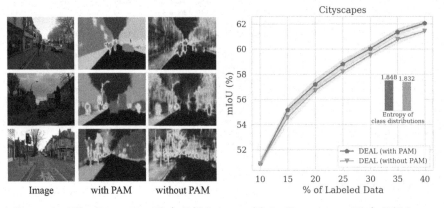

Semantic difficulty maps with/o PAM   AL in Cityscapes with/o PAM

Fig. 8. Ablation study on PAM. (a) The first column are images from CamVid [21], the second and third columns are semantic difficulty maps learned with and without PAM. (b) DEAL performance on Cityscapes [8] with and without PAM. We report the mean and standard deviation of 5 runs and the average entropy of class distributions of all AL stages.

5.2   Branch Position

In this section, we discuss the branch position of our framework. In our method above, the semantic difficulty branch is simply added after the segmentation branch. It may occur to us that if the segmentation branch performs poorly, the difficulty branch will perform poorly, too. These two tasks should be separated earlier and learn independent features. Thus, we modify our model architecture and branch out two tasks earlier at the boarder of encoder and decoder based on the Deeplabv3+ [38] architecture, as shown in Fig. 9(a). Also, we compare the AL performance on Cityscapes with both architectures in Fig. 9(b). The performance of the modified version is slightly poor than the original version

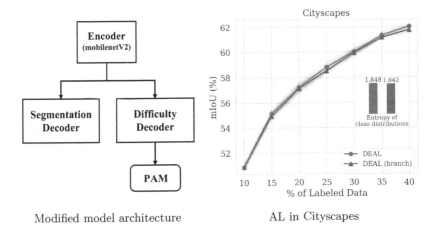

Modified model architecture   AL in Cityscapes

Fig. 9. Ablation study on branch position. (a) Modified model architecture. (b) DEAL performance on Cityscapes with different model architectures. *DEAL (branch)* is the modified version. We also report the mean and standard deviation of 5 runs and the average entropy of class distributions of all AL stages.

but still competitive with other methods. However, this modified version requires more computations, while our original version is simple yet effective and can be easily plugged into any segmentation networks.

6 Conclusion and Future Work

In this work, we have introduced a novel Difficulty-awarE Active Learning (DEAL) method for semantic segmentation, which incorporates the semantic difficulty to select the most informative samples. For any segmentation network, the *error mask* is firstly generated with the predicted segmentation result and GT. Then, with the guidance of *error mask*, the probability attention module is introduced to aggregate similar pixels and predict the semantic difficulty maps. Finally, two acquisition functions are devised. One is combining the uncertainty of segmentation result and the semantic difficulty. The other is solely based on the difficulty. Experiments on CamVid and Cityscapes demonstrate that the proposed DEAL achieves SOTA performance and can effectively improve the performance of hard semantic areas. In the future work, we will explore more possibilities with the semantic difficulty map and apply it to region-level active learning method for semantic segmentation.

Acknowledgments. This work is funded by National Key Research and Development Project (Grant No: 2018AAA0101503) and State Grid Corporation of China Scientific and Technology Project: Fundamental Theory of Human-in-the-loop Hybrid-Augmented Intelligence for Power Grid Dispatch and Control.

References

1. Teichmann, M., Weber, M., Zoellner, M., Cipolla, R., Urtasun, R.: MultiNet: real-time joint semantic reasoning for autonomous driving. In: IEEE Intelligent Vehicles Symposium (IV), pp. 1013–1020 (2018)
2. Feng, D., et al.: Deep multi-modal object detection and semantic segmentation for autonomous driving: datasets, methods, and challenges. IEEE Trans. Intell. Transp. Syst. (ITS) (2020)
3. Ronneberger, O., Fischer, P., Brox, T.: U-Net: convolutional networks for biomedical image segmentation. In: Navab, N., Hornegger, J., Wells, W.M., Frangi, A.F. (eds.) MICCAI 2015. LNCS, vol. 9351, pp. 234–241. Springer, Cham (2015). https://doi.org/10.1007/978-3-319-24574-4_28
4. Yang, L., Zhang, Y., Chen, J., Zhang, S., Chen, D.Z.: Suggestive annotation: a deep active learning framework for biomedical image segmentation. In: Descoteaux, M., Maier-Hein, L., Franz, A., Jannin, P., Collins, D.L., Duchesne, S. (eds.) MICCAI 2017. LNCS, vol. 10435, pp. 399–407. Springer, Cham (2017). https://doi.org/10.1007/978-3-319-66179-7_46
5. Zheng, Het al.: A new ensemble learning framework for 3D biomedical image segmentation. In: Proceedings of the AAAI Conference on Artificial Intelligence (AAAI), vol. 33, pp. 5909–5916 (2019)
6. Azimi, S.M., Henry, C., Sommer, L., Schumann, A., Vig, E.: Skyscapes fine-grained semantic understanding of aerial scenes. In: Proceedings of the IEEE International Conference on Computer Vision (ICCV), pp. 7393–7403 (2019)
7. Puang, E.Y., Lehner, P., Marton, Z.C., Durner, M., Triebel, R., Albu-Schäffer, A.: Visual repetition sampling for robot manipulation planning. In: International Conference on Robotics and Automation (ICRA), pp. 9236–9242 (2019)
8. Cordts, M., et al.: The cityscapes dataset for semantic urban scene understanding. In: Proceedings of the IEEE Conference on Computer Vision and Pattern Recognition (CVPR), pp. 3213–3223 (2016)
9. Zhou, B., Zhao, H., Puig, X., Fidler, S., Barriuso, A., Torralba, A.: Scene parsing through ade20k dataset. In: Proceedings of the IEEE Conference on Computer Vision and Pattern Recognition (CVPR), pp. 633–641 (2017)
10. Wang, K., Zhang, D., Li, Y., Zhang, R., Lin, L.: Cost-effective active learning for deep image classification. IEEE Trans. Circuits Syst. Video Technol. (CSVT) **27**, 2591–2600 (2016)
11. Gorriz, M., Carlier, A., Faure, E., Giro-i Nieto, X.: Cost-effective active learning for melanoma segmentation. In: Workshop of Advances in Neural Information Processing Systems (2017)
12. Gal, Y., Islam, R., Ghahramani, Z.: Deep Bayesian active learning with image data. In: Proceedings of the International Conference on Machine Learning (ICML), pp. 1183–1192 (2017)
13. Yoo, D., Kweon, I.S.: Learning loss for active learning. In: Proceedings of the IEEE Conference on Computer Vision and Pattern Recognition (CVPR), pp. 93–102 (2019)
14. Sener, O., Savarese, S.: Active learning for convolutional neural networks: a coreset approach. In: International Conference on Learning Representations (ICLR) (2017)
15. Sinha, S., Ebrahimi, S., Darrell, T.: Variational adversarial active learning. In: Proceedings of the IEEE International Conference on Computer Vision (ICCV), pp. 5972–5981 (2019)

16. Gissin, D., Shalev-Shwartz, S.: Discriminative active learning. arXiv preprint arXiv:1907.06347 (2019)
17. Shannon, C.E.: A mathematical theory of communication. Bell Syst. Tech. J. **27**, 379–423 (1948)
18. Seung, H.S., Opper, M., Sompolinsky, H.: Query by committee. In: Workshop on Computational Learning Theory, pp. 287–294 (1992)
19. Kuo, W., Häne, C., Yuh, E., Mukherjee, P., Malik, J.: Cost-sensitive active learning for intracranial hemorrhage detection. In: Frangi, A.F., Schnabel, J.A., Davatzikos, C., Alberola-López, C., Fichtinger, G. (eds.) MICCAI 2018. LNCS, vol. 11072, pp. 715–723. Springer, Cham (2018). https://doi.org/10.1007/978-3-030-00931-1_82
20. Casanova, A., Pinheiro, P.O., Rostamzadeh, N., Pal, C.J.: Reinforced active learning for image segmentation. In: International Conference on Learning Representations (ICLR) (2020)
21. Brostow, G.J., Fauqueur, J., Cipolla, R.: Semantic object classes in video: a high-definition ground truth database. Pattern Recogn. Lett. **30**, 88–97 (2009)
22. Tan, Y., Yang, L., Hu, Q., Du, Z.: Batch mode active learning for semantic segmentation based on multi-clue sample selection. In: Proceedings of the ACM International Conference on Information and Knowledge Management (CIKM), pp. 831–840 (2019)
23. Mackowiak, R., Lenz, P., Ghori, O., Diego, F., Lange, O., Rother, C.: CEREALS: cost-effective region-based active learning for semantic segmentation. In: British Machine Vision Conference (BMVC) (2018)
24. Siddiqui, Y., Valentin, J., Nießner, M.: ViewAL: active learning with viewpoint entropy for semantic segmentation. In: Proceedings of the IEEE Conference on Computer Vision and Pattern Recognition (CVPR), pp. 9433–9443 (2020)
25. Vaswani, A., et al.: Attention is all you need. In: Advances in neural information processing systems (NeurIPS), pp. 5998–6008 (2017)
26. Lin, Z., et al.: A structured self-attentive sentence embedding. In: International Conference on Learning Representations (ICLR) (2017)
27. Wang, Y., Huang, M., Zhu, X., Zhao, L.: Attention-based LSTM for aspect-level sentiment classification. In: Proceedings of Conference on Empirical Methods in Natural Language Processing (EMNLP), pp. 606–615 (2016)
28. Zhou, C., et al.: ATRank: an attention-based user behavior modeling framework for recommendation. In: Proceedings of the AAAI Conference on Artificial Intelligence (AAAI) (2018)
29. Chaudhari, S., Polatkan, G., Ramanath, R., Mithal, V.: An attentive survey of attention models. ArXiv abs/1904.02874 (2019)
30. Zhao, H., et al.: PSANet: point-wise spatial attention network for scene parsing. In: European Conference on Computer Vision (ECCV), pp. 267–283 (2018)
31. Yuan, Y., Wang, J.: OCNet: object context network for scene parsing. arXiv preprint arXiv:1809.00916 (2018)
32. Huang, Z., Wang, X., Huang, L., Huang, C., Wei, Y., Liu, W.: CCNet: criss-cross attention for semantic segmentation. In: Proceedings of the IEEE International Conference on Computer Vision, pp. 603–612 (ICCV) (2019)
33. Wang, X., Girshick, R.B., Gupta, A., He, K.: Non-local neural networks. IEEE Conference on Computer Vision and Pattern Recognition (CVPR), pp. 7794–7803 (2018)
34. Fu, J., et al.: Dual attention network for scene segmentation. In: Proceedings of the IEEE Conference on Computer Vision and Pattern Recognition (CVPR), pp. 3146–3154 (2019)

35. Settles, B.: Active learning literature survey. Technical report, University of Wisconsin-Madison Department of Computer Sciences (2009)
36. Scheffer, T., Decomain, C., Wrobel, S.: Active hidden Markov models for information extraction. In: Hoffmann, F., Hand, D.J., Adams, N., Fisher, D., Guimaraes, G. (eds.) IDA 2001. LNCS, vol. 2189, pp. 309–318. Springer, Heidelberg (2001). https://doi.org/10.1007/3-540-44816-0_31
37. Beluch, W.H., Genewein, T., Nürnberger, A., Köhler, J.M.: The power of ensembles for active learning in image classification. In: Proceedings of the IEEE Conference on Computer Vision and Pattern Recognition (CVPR), pp. 9368–9377 (2018)
38. Chen, L.C., Zhu, Y., Papandreou, G., Schroff, F., Adam, H.: Encoder-decoder with Atrous separable convolution for semantic image segmentation. In: European conference on computer vision (ECCV), pp. 801–818 (2018)
39. Sandler, M., Howard, A., Zhu, M., Zhmoginov, A., Chen, L.C.: MobileNetV2: inverted residuals and linear bottlenecks. In: Proceedings of the IEEE Conference on Computer Vision and Pattern Recognition (CVPR), pp. 4510–4520 (2018)
40. Krizhevsky, A., Sutskever, I., Hinton, G.E.: ImageNet classification with deep convolutional neural networks. In: Advances in Neural Information Processing Systems (NeurIPS), pp. 1097–1105 (2012)

EPSNet: Efficient Panoptic Segmentation Network with Cross-layer Attention Fusion

Chia-Yuan Chang[1], Shuo-En Chang[1], Pei-Yung Hsiao[2],
and Li-Chen Fu[1]([⊠])

[1] National Taiwan University, Taipei, Taiwan
{r07922102,r08922a02,lichen}@ntu.edu.tw
[2] National University of Kaohsiung, Kaohsiung, Taiwan
pyhsiao@nuk.edu.tw

Abstract. Panoptic segmentation is a scene parsing task which unifies semantic segmentation and instance segmentation into one single task. However, the current state-of-the-art studies did not take too much concern on inference time. In this work, we propose an Efficient Panoptic Segmentation Network (EPSNet) to tackle the panoptic segmentation tasks with fast inference speed. Basically, EPSNet generates masks based on simple linear combination of prototype masks and mask coefficients. The light-weight network branches for instance segmentation and semantic segmentation only need to predict mask coefficients and produce masks with the shared prototypes predicted by prototype network branch. Furthermore, to enhance the quality of shared prototypes, we adopt a module called "cross-layer attention fusion module", which aggregates the multi-scale features with attention mechanism helping them capture the long-range dependencies between each other. To validate the proposed work, we have conducted various experiments on the challenging COCO panoptic dataset, which achieve highly promising performance with significantly faster inference speed (51 ms on GPU).

1 Introduction

Due to Convolutional Neural Networks (CNNs) and other advances in deep learning, computer vision systems have achieved considerable success especially on computer vision tasks such as image recognition [1], semantic segmentation [2,3], object detection [4,5] and instance segmentation [6,7]. In particular, semantic segmentation aims to assign specific class label for each image pixel, whereas instance segmentation predicts foreground object masks. However, the former is not capable of separating objects of the same class, and the latter only focuses on segmenting of *things* (i.e countable objects such as people, animals, and tools) rather than *stuff* (i.e amorphous regions such as grass, sky, and road). To overcome the respective shortcomings, combination of semantic segmentation and instance segmentation leads to the so-called panoptic segmentation [8].

© Springer Nature Switzerland AG 2021
H. Ishikawa et al. (Eds.): ACCV 2020, LNCS 12622, pp. 689–705, 2021.
https://doi.org/10.1007/978-3-030-69525-5_41

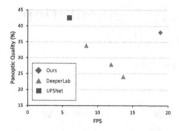

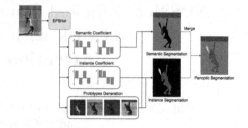

Fig. 1. Speed-performance trade-off of panoptic segmentation methods on COCO. The inference time is measured end-to-end from input image to panoptic segmentation output. Our approach achieves 19 fps and 38.6% PQ on COCO *val* set.

Fig. 2. Overview of Efficient Panoptic Network. EPSNet predicts prototypes and mask coefficients for semantic and instance segmentation. Both segmentation, obtained by linear combination of prototypes and mask coefficients, are fused using heuristic merging.

More specifically, the goal of panoptic segmentation is to assign a semantic label and an instance ID to every pixel in an image.

Several methods [9–14] have been proposed for panoptic segmentation in the literature. Detection-based approaches [9,12–14] usually exploit an instance segmentation network like Mask R-CNN [6] as the main stream and attach lightweight semantic segmentation branch after the shared backbone. Then, they combine those outputs by heuristic fusion [8] to generate the final panoptic prediction. Despite such detection-based fashions achieving the state-of-the-art results, they solely aim to improve the performance but may sacrifice the computation load and speed. In fact, detection-based methods suffer from several limitations. First, due to the two-stage detector, instance segmentation branch costs the major computation time and drags down the inference speed. Second, most detection-based approaches commonly employ the outputs of backbone, like feature pyramid network [15], as shared features without further enhancement, causing sub-optimality of features used by the following branches. Lastly, the independent branches unfortunately lead to inconsistency when generating final prediction.

To address the above problems, we propose a novel one-stage framework called Efficient Panoptic Segmentation Network (EPSNet), as shown in Fig. 2. It adopts parallel networks to generate prototype masks for the entire image and predicts a set of coefficients for instance and semantic segmentation. Instance and semantic segments can be easily generated by linearly combining the prototypes with predicted coefficients from the branches. The proposed semantic branch only needs to produce coefficients for each class instead of pixel-wise predictions. Moreover, the prototypes are shared by both branches, which save time for producing large-size masks and help them solve their tasks simultaneously. Further, we introduce an innovative fusion module called cross-layer attention fusion module, which enhances the quality of shared features with attention mechanism. Instead of directly using suboptimal features in FPN, we choose certain layer as the target feature and other layers as source features and then apply an attention module on them to capture spatial dependencies for any two positions of the feature maps. For each position in target feature, it is updated via aggregating source features at all positions with weighted summation. To verify the efficiency of EPSNet, we conduct experiments on COCO [16] dataset. The experimental results manifest that our method achieves competitive performances with much faster inference compared to current approaches, as shown in Fig. 1.

2   Related Work

2.1   Panoptic Segmentation

Panoptic segmentation is originally proposed by [8]. In panoptic segmentation tasks, each pixel in the image needs to be assigned a semantic label and an instance ID. In [8], separate networks are used for semantic segmentation and instance segmentation, respectively, and then the results are combined with heuristic rules. The recent approaches of panoptic segmentation train semantic and instance segmentation network in end-to-end fashion with shared backbone. These methods can be categorized into two groups, namely, detection-based methods and bottom-up methods.

Detection-Based. Most detection-based methods exploit Mask R-CNN [6] as their instance segmentation network and attach semantic segmentation branch with FCN [17] after shared backbone. These approaches are also considered as two-stage methods because of the additional stage to generate proposals. For instances, JSIS [18] firstly trains instance and semantic segmentation network jointly. TASCNet [19] ensures the consistency of stuff and thing prediction through binary mask. OANet [12] uses spatial ranking module to deal with the occlusion problem between the predicted instances. Panoptic FPN [14] endows Mask R-CNN [6] with a semantic segmentation branch. AUNet [13] adds RPN and thing segmentation mask attentions to stuff branch to provide object-level and pixel- level attentions. UPSNet [9] introduces a parameter-free panoptic head which solves the panoptic segmentation via pixel-wise classification. AdaptIS [10] adapts to the input point with a help of AdaIN layers [20] and produce masks for different objects on the same image. Although detection-based methods achieve better performance, they are usually slow in inference because of two-stage Mask R-CNN [6] in instance head. In addition, the inconsistency of semantic and instance segmentation needs to be solved when the two are merged into panoptic segmentation.

Bottom-Up. Unlike the above approaches, some methods tackle panoptic segmentation tasks by associating pixel-level predictions to each object instance [21–24]. In these approaches, they first predict the foreground mask with semantic segmentation, and then use several types of heatmaps to group foreground pixels into objects. DeeperLab [25] predicts instance keypoint as well as multi-range offset heatmap and then groups them into class-agnostic instance segmentation. In semantic segmentation head, they follow the design of DeepLab [3]. At the end, panoptic segmentation is generated by merging class-agnostic instance masks and semantic output. SSAP [26] groups pixels based on a pixel-pair affinity pyramid with an efficient graph partition method. Despite the single-shot architecture of bottom-up approaches, their post-processing step still needs major computational time. Also, the performance of the bottom-up methods usually is inferior to that of the detection-based methods.

Recently, the proposed methods obtain shared feature for semantic and instance head. The quality of shared feature is highly essential for the following network head to produce better results. Still, the proposed approaches do not take this into consideration, and they usually make use of the output of shared backbone as shared feature directly.

In this work, we aim to propose a panoptic segmentation network based on one-stage detector to attain fast inference speed and competitive performance. To increase the quality of shared feature, our proposed cross-layer attention fusion, which is a lightweight network, provides the target feature map with richer information in different feature pyramid layers using attention mechanism.

3   Efficient Panoptic Segmentation Network

3.1   Efficient Panoptic Segmentation Network

Our method consists of five major components including (1) shared backbone, (2) protohead for generating prototypes, (3) instance segmentation head, (4) semantic segmentation head, and (5) cross-layer attention fusion module.

Backbone. Our backbone exploits a deep residual network (ResNet) [1] with a feature pyramid network (FPN) [15], which takes a standard network with features at multiple spatial resolutions and adds a light top-down pathway with lateral connections. It generates a pyramid feature with scales from $1/8$ to $1/128$ resolution (F_3 to F_7) as in Fig. 3. For these features, F_7 is fed to the semantic head, and F_3 to F_5 are sent to instance head and protohead as inputs.

Protohead. Rather than producing masks with FCN [17], inspired by Yolact [27], we choose to combine prototypes and mask coefficients with linear combination to generate masks. Our network heads only need to deal with mask coefficients and construct masks with shared prototypes. The goal of protohead is to provide high-quality prototypes which contain semantic information and details of high-resolution feature.

To generate higher resolution prototypes with more semantic values, we perform cross-layer attention fusion module to aggregate multi-scale features in backbone into information-richer feature maps for protohead as inputs. Then, we apply three convolutional blocks, $2\times$ bilinear upsampling and 1×1 convolution to produce output prototypes which are at $1/4$ scale with k channels.

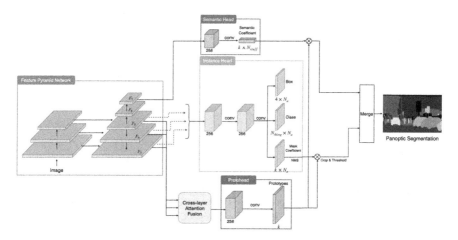

Fig. 3. Architecture of EPSNet. We adopt ResNet-101 [1] with FPN [15] as our backbone and only exploit F_3, F_4, F_5 for cross-layer attention fusion module. The prototypes are shared by semantic and instance head. k denotes the number of prototypes. N_a denotes the number of anchors. N_{thing} and N_{stuff} stands for the number of thing and stuff classes, respectively. $\otimes$ means matrix multiplication.

Instance Segmentation Head. In most panoptic segmentation networks, they adopt Mask R-CNN [6] as their instance segmentation branch. Yet, Mask R-CNN [6] needs to generate proposals first and then classify and segment those proposals in the second stage. Inspired by one-stage detector, Yolact [27], our instance head directly predicts object detection results and mask coefficients to make up the segmentation with prototypes without feature localization (e.g.. ROI Align [6]) and refinement.

The instance head aims to predict box regression, classification confidences and mask coefficients. There are three branches in instance head. Regression branch predicts 4 box regression values, classification branch predicts N_{thing} class confidences, and mask branch predicts k mask coefficients. Thus, there are totally $4 + N_{thing} + k$ values for each anchor. We perform a convolutional block on input features (F_3 to F_5) first and send them to each branch to predict respective results. In mask branch, we choose tanh as the activation function, which allows subtraction when linearly combining the coefficients.

In inference, we choose the mask coefficients whose corresponding bounding boxes survive after NMS procedure. Then, we combine mask coefficients and prototypes generated from protohead with linear combination followed by *sigmoid* to produce instance masks and crop final mask with predicted bounding box. During training, we crop mask with ground truth bounding box and divide mask segmentation loss by the area of ground truth bounding box.

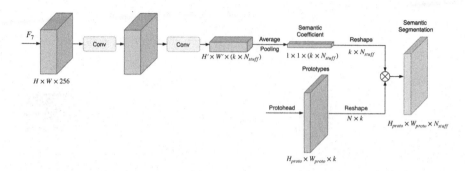

Fig. 4. Design of proposed semantic head. We adopt F_7 as input and apply two convolutional layers. The semantic coefficients are produced after average pooling, which predicts k mask coefficients for each stuff classes. $\otimes$ denotes matrix multiplication.

Semantic Segmentation Head. Usually, semantic segmentation masks are generated by decoder network [2,17,28,29], which applies FCN [17] networks and up-sampling layer on the features from backbone to make sure that the size of semantic segmentation outputs is similar to the original input size. However, due to the large feature maps, the computation speed is limited by image size.

To reduce the computation of large feature maps, we propose a novel semantic segmentation head which only produces mask coefficients for each class, see Fig. 4. The semantic masks can be easily generated by combining the coefficients and prototypes, and each semantic class only demands k mask coefficients. Therefore, with smaller feature maps, the proposed light-weight semantic head can achieve faster inference speed.

We adopt last layer F_7 from backbone as the input of semantic head. Two convolution blocks are performed. In the second convolution block, the output channel is set to $k \times N_{\text{stuff}}$ and tanh is used as activation function. Because of the channel size $k \times N_{\text{stuff}}$, every position in the feature map can predict k coefficients for each class to construct semantic segmentation. Accordingly, we perform average pooling to aggregate the mask coefficients from all positions to generate final semantic coefficients. Further, prototypes from protohead and semantic coefficients are reshaped to 2D matrix and applied with linear combination followed by *softmax* to produce semantic segmentation result. The operation is able to be implemented by matrix multiplication which is defined as

$$S = softmax(P \cdot Y), \tag{1}$$

where $P \in \mathbb{R}^{N \times k}$ denotes prototypes, $Y \in \mathbb{R}^{k \times N_{\text{stuff}}}$ stands for the reshaped semantic coefficients, and $S \in \mathbb{R}^{N \times N_{\text{stuff}}}$ is semantic segmentation result. N_{stuff} represents the number of stuff classes including 'other' class and N denotes the number of locations in prototypes.

The feature maps in semantic head are much smaller than the large feature maps in other approaches. Our semantic head provides faster semantic segmentation generation and less computation cost.

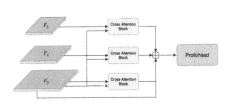

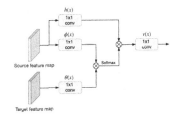

Fig. 5. The architecture of cross-layer attention module. The layers F_3, F_4 and F_5 in FPN are used. F_3 is considered as target feature, and all of them are set as source features. $\oplus$ denotes element-wise addition.

Fig. 6. The architecture of cross attention block. $\otimes$ denotes matrix multiplication.

Cross-layer Attention Fusion. Since all of the semantic or instance masks are derived from linear combination of mask coefficients and prototypes, the quality of prototypes significantly influences the generated masks. Hence, we decide to enrich the input features of protohead to help it produce preferable prototypes.

To enhance inputs of protohead, we propose a module called Cross-layer Attention (CLA) Fusion Module. This fusion module aims to efficiently aggregate the multi-scale feature maps in FPN layers. Certain layer within the module is chosen to be the target feature map and extract values from source feature maps with attention mechanism, as shown in Fig. 5. To provide high resolution details, the layer F_3, which is the highest resolution feature map in FPN, is selected as target feature map, and we choose other layers (e.g. F_3 to F_5) as source features to provide more semantic values for target.

Instead of directly merging multi-scale features with element-wise addition or concatenation [2,9,30,31], we combine them with a block called Cross Attention Block. Inspired by non-local [32] and self-attention [33–35], which are able to capture long-range dependencies efficiently in feature map, the proposed cross attention block follows their concepts and further finds the long-range relationships from two different feature maps, as shown in Fig. 6. Each position in target feature map is updated with the weighted sum of all positions in source feature, where attention weight is calculated by similarities between the corresponding positions.

For the target feature map $T \in \mathbb{R}^{C \times N}$ and source feature map $O \in \mathbb{R}^{C \times N'}$, we first transform these feature maps into two feature spaces $\theta(x) = W_\theta x$ and $\phi(x) = W_\phi x$ and calculate the attention score s with dot product as shown below

$$s_{i,j} = \theta(T_i)^T \phi(O_j), \tag{2}$$

where $s_{i,j}$ measures the attention score of position j in O and position i in T. Here, C denotes the number of channels, and N denotes the number of locations from feature maps. After that, we obtain the attention weight α by normalizing attention score for each position j with $softmax$

$$\alpha_{i,j} = \frac{\exp(s_{i,j})}{\sum_{j=1}^{N} \exp(s_{i,j})}, \tag{3}$$

where $\alpha_{i,j}$ stands for the normalized impact of position j in source feature map to position i in target feature map. Then, each position in output feature map $A \in \mathbb{R}^{C \times N}$ is produced by calculating weighted sum of source features across all positions. The operation is shown as follows

$$A_i = v(\sum_{j=1}^{N} \alpha_{i,j} h(O_j)). \tag{4}$$

Here, A_i denotes output feature on position i, and both $v(x) = W_v x$ and $h(x) = W_h x$ stand for embedding functions. The embedding functions θ, ϕ, h and v are implemented by 1×1 convolution, and their output channels are set to 128, which is $1/2$ of input channel to reduce computation cost. Finally, we apply cross attention block on each layer including F_5, F_4 and F_3 and consider F_3 as target feature map. The overall operation is defined as

$$Z = A^{F_3,F_5} + A^{F_3,F_4} + A^{F_3,F_3} + F_3, \tag{5}$$

where Z denotes the aggregated result from source and target features. Also, we adopt residual connection that makes a new cross attention block easier to insert without interfering the initial behaviors.

With the cross attention block, each position in the target feature is able to obtain spatial dependencies over all positions in feature maps from other layers. Moreover, we also select F_3 as source feature map even F_3 is target feature. In this case, it is same as self-attention, which helps target feature capture long-dependencies on its own feature map.

3.2   Training and Inference

During training, our EPSNet contains 4 loss functions in total, namely, classification loss $\mathcal{L}_c$, box regression loss $\mathcal{L}_b$, instance mask segmentation loss $\mathcal{L}_m$ and semantic segmentation loss $\mathcal{L}_s$. Because each loss function is in different scales and normalized policies, different weights on different loss functions actually affect the final performance on instance and semantic branch. Thus, we set several hyper-parameters on those loss functions, which is defined as $\mathcal{L} = \lambda_c \mathcal{L}_c + \lambda_b \mathcal{L}_b + \lambda_m \mathcal{L}_m + \lambda_s \mathcal{L}_s$.

In inference, since we won't allow overlaps on each pixel in panoptic segmentation, we resolve overlaps in instance segmentation with post-processing proposed in [8]. After getting non-overlapping instance segmentation results, we resolve possible overlaps between instance and semantic segmentation in favor of instance. Further, the stuff regions which are predicted as 'other' or under a predefined threshold are removed.

4 Experiments

In this section, we conduct experiments on COCO [16] panoptic dataset. Experimental results demonstrate that EPSNet achieves fast and competitive performance on COCO dataset.

4.1 Experimental Setup

Datasets. COCO [16] panoptic segmentation task consists of 80 thing classes and 53 stuff classes. There are approximately 118K images on training set and 5K on validation set.

Metrics. We adopt the evaluation metric called panoptic quality (PQ), which is introduced by [8]. Panoptic quality is defined as:

$$PQ = \underbrace{\frac{\sum_{(p,g)\in \text{TP}} \text{IoU}(p,g)}{|\text{TP}|}}_{\text{SQ}} \underbrace{\frac{|\text{TP}|}{|\text{TP}| + \frac{1}{2}|\text{FP}| + \frac{1}{2}|\text{FN}|}}_{\text{RQ}}, \tag{6}$$

which can be considered as the multiplication of semantic quality (SQ) and recognition quality (RQ). Here, p and g are predicted and ground truth segments. TP, FP and FN represent the set of true positives, false positives and false negatives, respectively.

Implementation Details. We implement our method based on Pytorch [36] with single GPU RTX 2080Ti. The models are trained with batch size 2. Owing to the small batch size, we freeze the batch normalization layers within backbone and add group normalization [37] layers in each head. The initial learning rate and weight decay are set to 10^{-3} and 5×10^{-4}. We train with SGD for 3200K iterations and decay the learning rate by a factor of 10 at 1120k, 2400K, 2800k and 3000k iterations and a momentum of 0.9. The loss weights λ_c, λ_b, λ_m and λ_s are 1, 1.5, 6.125 and 2, respectively.

Our models are trained with ResNet-101 [1] backbone using FPN with ImageNet [38] pre-trained weights. We adopt similar training strategies in backbone and instance segmentation head as Yolact [27]. The number of prototypes k is set to 32. Our instance head only predicts thing classes, and semantic head predicts stuff classes viewing thing class as other. The cross attention blocks are shared in cross-layer attention fusion module. The base image size is 550×550. We do not preserve aspect ratio in order to get consistent evaluation times per image. We perform random flipping, random cropping and random scaling on images for data augmentation. The image size is randomly scaled in range $[550, 825]$ and then randomly cropped into 550×550.

Table 1. Ablation study on COCO panoptic *val* set with panoptic quality (PQ), semantic quality (SQ) and recognition quality (RQ). PQ^{Th} and PQ^{St} indicate PQ on thing and stuff classes. *Data Aug* denotes data augmentation. *CLA Fusion* stands for cross-layer attention fusion.

Data Aug	CLA Fusion	Loss Balance	PQ	PQ^{Th}	PQ^{St}	SQ	RQ
			35.4	40.5	27.7	77.2	43.5
√			37.4	43.2	28.6	77.6	45.7
√	√		38.4	43.0	**31.4**	77.7	**47.6**
√	√	√	**38.6**	**43.5**	31.3	**77.9**	47.3

Table 2. Ablation study on number of prototypes.

Prototypes	PQ	PQ^{Th}	PQ^{St}	Inf time (ms)
16	38.4	43.4	30.8	**50.7**
32	**38.6**	**43.5**	**31.3**	51.1
64	38.4	43.2	31.2	52.4

4.2   Ablation Study

To verify the performance of training decisions and our cross-layer fusion attention module, we conduct the experiments with different settings in Table 1 on COCO panoptic *val* set. The empty cells in the table indicate that the corresponding component is not used.

Data Augmentation. We compare the model without using data augmentation during training. The first and second rows in Table 1 show that the model trained with data augmentation improves by 2% in PQ. It proves that data augmentation plays important role during training.

Cross-layer Attention Fusion. For the model without using cross-layer fusion module, it is replaced by another fusion module similar to Panoptic-FPN [14]. We adopt convolution blocks for different layers in backbone and combine them together. The layers F_5, F_4 and F_3 are attached with 3, 2 and 1 convolution blocks respectively and 2× bilinear upsampling layers between each block. Output features are obtained by combining them with element-wise addition. As shown in second and third rows in Table 1, the model employing the cross-layer attention fusion module yields 38.4% in PQ and 2.8% improvement in PQ^{St}.

Loss Balance. In order to balance the loss values in similar order of magnitude, we assign different weights for each loss during training. With loss balance, the weights are same as experimental setting. Without loss balance, all weights are set to 1. As shown in the third and fourth rows in Table 1, the model with loss balance performs better especially on PQ^{Th}.

Prototypes. We further conduct experiments on the number of prototypes. As shown in Table 2, the number of prototypes barely influence the overall performance. However, it will affect the inference and post-processing time. We choose 32 prototypes for the setting of EPSNet.

The ablation results show that our cross-layer attention fusion and training strategies bring significant improvement on panoptic segmentation.

Table 3. Performance comparison on different design of semantic head. *standard* denotes EPSNet with other design choice on semantic head, which directly generates semantic segmentation with convolutional layers. Note that, the EPSNet here does not use CLA fusion. M-adds denotes multiply-adds.

Method	PQ	PQ^{Th}	PQ^{St}	M-Adds (M)
Standard	37.2	42.9	28.5	33.8
Coefficients	**37.4**	**43.2**	**28.6**	**9.4**

Table 4. Performance comparison of using different options on semantic coefficients.

Method	PQ	PQ^{St}
Top-left	33.2	17.7
Top-right	33.4	18.1
Bottom-left	33.5	18.3
Bottom-right	33.6	18.5
Center	37.5	28.5
Max pooling	37.6	28.8
Average pooling	**38.6**	**31.3**

4.3 Analysis of Semantic Head

We further compare our semantic segmentation head to other design choice. In most proposed panoptic segmentation networks, they adopt feature maps in backbone and perform FCN [17] to obtain pixel-wise predictions. The semantic head of compared model is constructed by apply 1×1 convolutional layer on the the fused feature maps with the Panoptic-FPN fusion, whose size is same as F_3. Note that we only replace the semantic head in EPSNet without CLA fusion. We count the multiply-adds to evaluate the computation cost of different structures for semantic heads.

The experimental results in Table 3 show that the computation cost of the proposed semantic head is about 0.3 times less than the standard semantic head, although our semantic head is deeper. Unlike the standard semantic segmentation, because of the small input feature maps for computation, the proposed semantic head using mask coefficients does not slow down inference speed and outperforms the standard semantic head.

In semantic head, the coefficients $k \times N_{stuff}$ in each position is able to be used to generate semantic segmentation before average pooling. To verify the impact of coefficients from different position, we use the coefficients before average pooling from corner positions and center position to perform the semantic segmentations. In Table 4, the comparison shows that the result using coefficients from center position is superior than other positions. Moreover, we compare the different options on pooling operation. The coefficients produced by average pooling yield better performance than using max pooling, as shown in Table 4.

| Input Image | Ground Truth | Normal Fusion | CLA Fusion |

Fig. 7. Visualization results of cross-layer attention fusion on COCO panoptic *val* set. Normal fusion stands for the Panoptic-FPN [14] fusion with F_3, F_4 and F_5.

Table 5. Performance comparison on different strategies for fusion module. The inference time is measured without considering post-processing.

Method	PQ	PQTh	PQSt	Inf time
Panoptic-FPN fusion [14] (F_3, F_4, F_5)	37.4	43.2	28.6	23 ms
CLA fusion (F_3)	38.3	43.5	30.5	27 ms
CLA fusion (F_3, F_4, F_5)	**38.6**	**43.5**	**31.3**	29 ms

To sum up, the proposed semantic head predicts mask coefficients of each class with faster inference speed and efficiently exploits shared prototypes without dragging down panoptic segmentation performance.

4.4   Analysis of Cross-layer Attention Fusion Module

In this subsection, we investigate different strategies of using cross-layer attention (CLA) fusion. We compare our EPSNet to the model using other fusion method like Panoptic-FPN [14] with F_3, F_4 and F_5 and another model only employing F_3 as source feature map with CLA fusion module. As shown in Table 5, the model with CLA fusion outperforms the Panoptic-FPN fusion especsially on PQSt. Also, more layers are adopted in CLA fusion can yield slight improvement and inference time. The comparison of using cross-layer attention fusion can be visualized as Fig. 7. The details of background are much better and clearer. CLA fusion helps model generate higher quality segmentation especially for the stuff classes. For instance, the segments of the table in the first row and the ground in the second rows are much more complete.

To further understand what has been learned in CLA fusion module, we select two query points in input image in the first and fourth columns and visualize their corresponding sub-attention maps on other source features (F_3 and F_4) in remaining columns. In Fig. 8, we observe that CLA fusion module can capture long-range dependencies according to the similarity. For example, in first row, the red point #1 on bus pays more attention on positions labeled as bus (second

Image   Sub-attention Sub-attention   Image   Sub-attention Sub-attention
(point #1)   map (F_3)   map (F_4)   (point #2)   map (F_3)   map (F_4)

Fig. 8. Visualization results of cross attention block on COCO panoptic *val* set. In each row, we show the input images with different marked points in 1st and 4th columns and two sub-attention maps on source features (F_3 and F_4) corresponding to the marked point in 2nd, 3th, 5th and 6th columns.

and third columns). For the point # 2 on ground, it highlights most areas labeled as ground (fifth and sixth columns).

4.5   Comparison with Other Methods on COCO

We compare our method on COCO *val* set with panoptic quality and inference speed measured from input image to panoptic segmentation output including post-processing time. Specifically, our model is only trained on COCO training dataset with ResNet-101-FPN and tested using single-scale 550×550 image. As shown in Table 6, EPSNet outperforms every one-stage method and improves the performance over Real-time Panoptic Segmentation [39] with ResNet-50-FPN backbone and large input size by 1.5% PQ. Also, our inference speed is much faster than all existing panoptic segmentation methods. EPSNet only takes 51 ms for inference, which is 1.4× faster than DeeperLab with Light Wider MobileNet-V2 [40] backbone and 3.1× faster than UPSNet [9]. Compared to the two-stage methods, we bring better performance especially on PQ^{St}, which outperforms Panoptic-FPN [14] by 1.8%, indicating that our approach provides better results on semantic segmentation. Despite the one-stage detector of EPSNet, with the fusion module and efficient architecture, we not only achieve competitive result for panoptic segmentation but also boost the inference speed.

In COCO *test* set, the inference setting is the same as COCO *val* set experiment. As shown in Table 7, we outperform SSAP [26], which adopts horizontal flipping and multi-scale input images for testing, by 2% PQ. Without any additional tricks, we still achieve competitive result compared to other methods.

Table 6. Panoptic segmentation results on COCO *val* set. *LW-MNV2* denotes Light Wider MobileNet-V2.

Method	Backbone	Input size	PQ	PQ^{Th}	PQ^{St}	Inf time (ms)
Two stage						
JSIS [18]	ResNet-50	400×400	26.9	29.3	23.3	–
AUNet [13]	ResNet-50-FPN	–		39.6	49.1	25.2	–
Panoptic-FPN [14]	ResNet-101-FPN	–		40.3	47.5	29.5	–
AdaptIS [10]	ResNeXt-101	–		42.3	49.2	31.8	–
UPSNet [9]	ResNet-50-FPN	800×1333	42.5	48.6	33.4	167
Single stage						
DeeperLab [25]	LW-MNV2	641×641	24.1	–	–	73
DeeperLab [25]	Xception-71	641×641	33.8	–	–	119
SSAP [26]	ResNet-101	512×512	36.5	–	–	–
Real-time PS [39]	ResNet-50-FPN	800×1333	37.1	41.0	31.3	63
Ours	ResNet-101-FPN	550×550	**38.6**	**43.5**	31.3	**51**

Table 7. Panoptic segmentation results on COCO *test-dev* set. *Flip* and *MS* stands for horizontal flipping and multi-scale inputs during testing.

Method	Backbone	Flip	MS	PQ	PQ^{Th}	PQ^{St}
Two stage						
JSIS [18]	ResNet-50			27.2	29.6	23.4
Panoptic-FPN [14]	ResNet-101-FPN			40.9	48.3	29.7
AdaptIS [10]	ResNeXt-101	✓		42.8	50.1	31.8
AUNet [13]	ResNeXt-101-FPN		✓	46.5	55.8	32.5
UPSNet [9]	ResNet-101-FPN	✓	✓	46.6	53.2	36.7
Single stage						
DeeperLab [25]	Xception-71			34.3	37.5	29.6
SSAP [26]	ResNet-101	✓	✓	36.9	40.1	**32.0**
Ours	ResNet-101-FPN			**38.9**	**44.1**	31.0

5   Conclusions

In this paper, we present a one-stage Efficient Panoptic Segmentation Network. The masks are efficiently constructed by linear combination of prototypes generated by protohead and mask coefficients produced by instance and semantic branches. The proposed cross-layer attention fusion module aggregates multi-scale features in different layers with attention mechanism to enhance the quality of shared prototypes. The experiments show that our method achieves competitive performance on COCO panoptic dataset and outperforms other one-stage approaches. Also, EPSNet is significantly faster than the existing panoptic segmentation networks. In the future, We would like to explore a more effective way to replace the heuristic merging algorithm.

Acknowledgement. This work was partially sponsored by the Ministry of Science and Technology (MOST), Taiwan ROC, under Project 109–2634-F-002–027, 109–2634-F-002–040, and 109–2634-F-002–041. This research was also supported in part by the Center for AI & Advanced Robotics, National Taiwan University and the Joint Research Center for AI Technology and All Vista Healthcare under MOST.

References

1. He, K., Zhang, X., Ren, S., Sun, J.: Deep residual learning for image recognition. In: The IEEE Conference on Computer Vision and Pattern Recognition (CVPR), pp. 770–778 (2015)
2. Zhao, H., Shi, J., Qi, X., Wang, X., Jia, J.: Pyramid scene parsing network. In: The IEEE Conference on Computer Vision and Pattern Recognition (CVPR) (2017)
3. Chen, L.-C., Zhu, Y., Papandreou, G., Schroff, F., Adam, H.: Encoder-decoder with atrous separable convolution for semantic image segmentation. In: Ferrari, V., Hebert, M., Sminchisescu, C., Weiss, Y. (eds.) ECCV 2018. LNCS, vol. 11211, pp. 833–851. Springer, Cham (2018). https://doi.org/10.1007/978-3-030-01234-2_49
4. Ren, S., He, K., Girshick, R.B., Sun, J.: Faster R-CNN: towards real-time object detection with region proposal networks. IEEE Trans. Pattern Anal. Mach. Intell. **39**, 1137–1149 (2015)
5. Redmon, J., Farhadi, A.: Yolo9000: better, faster, stronger. In: The IEEE Conference on Computer Vision and Pattern Recognition (CVPR), pp. 6517–6525 (2016)
6. He, K., Gkioxari, G., Dollár, P., Girshick, R.B.: Mask R-CNN. In: The IEEE International Conference on Computer Vision (ICCV), pp. 2980–2988 (2017)
7. Liu, S., Qi, L., Qin, H., Shi, J., Jia, J.: Path aggregation network for instance segmentation. In: The IEEE Conference on Computer Vision and Pattern Recognition (CVPR), pp. 8759–8768 (2018)
8. Kirillov, A., He, K., Girshick, R.B., Rother, C., Dollár, P.: Panoptic segmentation. In: The IEEE Conference on Computer Vision and Pattern Recognition (CVPR), pp. 9396–9405 (2019)
9. Xiong, Y., et al.: UpsNet: a unified panoptic segmentation network. In: The IEEE Conference on Computer Vision and Pattern Recognition (CVPR) (2019)
10. Sofiiuk, K., Barinova, O., Konushin, A.: Adaptis: adaptive instance selection network. In: The IEEE International Conference on Computer Vision (ICCV) (2019)
11. Yang, Y., Li, H., Li, X., Zhao, Q., Wu, J., Lin, Z.: SOGNet: scene overlap graph network for panoptic segmentation. arXiv preprint arXiv:1911.07527 (2019)
12. Liu, H., et al.: An end-to-end network for panoptic segmentation. In: The IEEE Conference on Computer Vision and Pattern Recognition (CVPR), pp. 6165–6174 (2019)
13. Li, Y., et al.: Attention-guided unified network for panoptic segmentation. In: The IEEE Conference on Computer Vision and Pattern Recognition (CVPR), pp. 7019–7028 (2018)
14. Kirillov, A., Girshick, R., He, K., Dollar, P.: Panoptic feature pyramid networks. In: The IEEE Conference on Computer Vision and Pattern Recognition (CVPR) (2019)

15. Lin, T.Y., Dollár, P., Girshick, R.B., He, K., Hariharan, B., Belongie, S.J.: Feature pyramid networks for object detection. In: The IEEE Conference on Computer Vision and Pattern Recognition (CVPR), pp. 936–944 (2016)
16. Caesar, H., Uijlings, J., Ferrari, V.: Coco-stuff: thing and stuff classes in context. In: The IEEE Conference on Computer Vision and Pattern Recognition (CVPR) (2018)
17. Long, J., Shelhamer, E., Darrell, T.: Fully convolutional networks for semantic segmentation. In: The IEEE Conference on Computer Vision and Pattern Recognition (CVPR), pp. 3431–3440 (2015)
18. de Geus, D., Meletis, P., Dubbelman, G.: Panoptic Segmentation with a Joint Semantic and Instance Segmentation Network. arXiv preprint arXiv:1809.02110 (2018)
19. Li, J., Raventos, A., Bhargava, A., Tagawa, T., Gaidon, A.: Learning to fuse things and stuff. arXiv preprint arXiv:1812.01192 (2018)
20. Karras, T., Laine, S., Aila, T.: A style-based generator architecture for generative adversarial networks. In: The IEEE Conference on Computer Vision and Pattern Recognition (CVPR), pp. 4396–4405 (2018)
21. Zhang, Z., Fidler, S., Urtasun, R.: Instance-level segmentation for autonomous driving with deep densely connected MRFs. In: The IEEE Conference on Computer Vision and Pattern Recognition (CVPR), pp. 669–677 (2015)
22. Zhang, Z., Schwing, A.G., Fidler, S., Urtasun, R.: Monocular object instance segmentation and depth ordering with CNNs. In: The IEEE International Conference on Computer Vision (ICCV), pp. 2614–2622 (2015)
23. Uhrig, J., Cordts, M., Franke, U., Brox, T.: Pixel-level encoding and depth layering for instance-level semantic labeling. In: GCPR (2016)
24. Liang, X., Lin, L., Wei, Y., Shen, X., Yang, J., Yan, S.: Proposal-free network for instance-level object segmentation. IEEE Trans. Pattern Anal. Mach. Intell. **40**, 2978–2991 (2015)
25. Yang, T.J., et al.: DeeperLab: single-shot image parser. arXiv preprint arXiv:1902.05093 (2019)
26. Gao, N., et al.: Ssap: single-shot instance segmentation with affinity pyramid. In: The IEEE International Conference on Computer Vision (ICCV) (2019)
27. Bolya, D., Zhou, C., Xiao, F., Lee, Y.J.: Yolact: real-time instance segmentation. In: The IEEE International Conference on Computer Vision (ICCV) (2019)
28. Lin, G., Milan, A., Shen, C., Reid, I.D.: RefineNet: multi-path refinement networks for high-resolution semantic segmentation. In: The IEEE Conference on Computer Vision and Pattern Recognition (CVPR), pp. 5168–5177 (2016)
29. Zhang, Z., Zhang, X., Peng, C., Cheng, D., Sun, J.: Exfuse: enhancing feature fusion for semantic segmentation. In: The European Conference on Computer Vision (ECCV) (2018)
30. Pang, J., Chen, K., Shi, J., Feng, H., Ouyang, W., Lin, D.: Libra R-CNN: towards balanced learning for object detection. In: The IEEE Conference on Computer Vision and Pattern Recognition (CVPR) (2019)
31. Porzi, L., Bulo, S.R., Colovic, A., Kontschieder, P.: Seamless scene segmentation. In: The IEEE Conference on Computer Vision and Pattern Recognition (CVPR) (2019)
32. Wang, X., Girshick, R., Gupta, A., He, K.: Non-local neural networks. In: The IEEE Conference on Computer Vision and Pattern Recognition (CVPR) (2018)
33. Zhang, H., Goodfellow, I., Metaxas, D., Odena, A.: Self-attention generative adversarial networks. arXiv preprint arXiv:1805.08318 (2018)

34. Fu, J., et al.: Dual attention network for scene segmentation. In: The IEEE Conference on Computer Vision and Pattern Recognition (CVPR) (2019)
35. Vaswani, A., et al.: Attention is all you need. In: NIPS (2017)
36. Paszke, A., et al.: Pytorch: an imperative style, high-performance deep learning library. In: NeurIPS (2019)
37. Wu, Y., He, K.: Group normalization. In: The European Conference on Computer Vision (ECCV) (2018)
38. Russakovsky, O., et al.: ImageNet large scale visual recognition challenge. Int. J. Comput. Vis. **115**, 211–252 (2014)
39. Hou, R., et al.: Real-time panoptic segmentation from dense detections. In: 2020 IEEE/CVF Conference on Computer Vision and Pattern Recognition (CVPR), pp. 8520–8529 (2020)
40. Sandler, M., Howard, A.G., Zhu, M., Zhmoginov, A., Chen, L.C.: MobileNetV2: inverted residuals and linear bottlenecks. In: The IEEE Conference on Computer Vision and Pattern Recognition (CVPR), pp. 4510–4520 (2018)

Local Context Attention for Salient Object Segmentation

Jing Tan[(✉)], Pengfei Xiong, Zhengyi Lv, Kuntao Xiao, and Yuwen He

Megvii Technology Limited, Beijing, China
{tanjing,xiongpengfei,lvzhengyi,xiaokuntao,heyuwen}@megvii.com

Abstract. Salient object segmentation aims at distinguishing various salient objects from backgrounds. Despite the lack of semantic consistency, salient objects often have obvious texture and location characteristics in local area. Based on this priori, we propose a novel Local Context Attention Network (LCANet) to generate locally reinforcement feature maps in a uniform representational architecture. The proposed network introduces an Attentional Correlation Filter (ACF) module to generate explicit local attention by calculating the correlation feature map between coarse prediction and global context. Then it is expanded to a Local Context Block (LCB). Furthermore, a one-stage coarse-to-fine structure is implemented based on LCB to adaptively enhance the local context description ability. Comprehensive experiments are conducted on several salient object segmentation datasets, demonstrating the superior performance of the proposed LCANet against the state-of-the-art methods, especially with **0.883 max F-score** and **0.034 MAE** on DUTS-TE dataset.

1 Introduction

Salient object segmentation aims at locating the most obvious and salient objects from a given image. It has been widely used in various challenging fields like automatic focus, autonomous driving, scene understanding, image editing, etc. In the past decades, salient object segmentation approaches [1–12] have already obtained promising performances on various benchmarks [13–17]. Nevertheless, most of the previous salient object segmentation methods treat it as a general semantic segmentation problem, which improves the performance by increasing the semantic receptive field, optimizing the edge accuracy or other methods.

As a pixel-level classification problem, the intrinsic properties of salient object segmentation determine that it is different from traditional semantic segmentation. Salient objects usually do not belong to the same category, and their textures and shapes are various, which makes it hard to distinguish the salient objects and the background by simply increasing the receptive field.

In contrast, salient objects often have obvious local context characteristic of the image. Despite their various sizes and locations, their vivid texture are always quite different from the surrounding backgrounds. Based on this prior, we believe

© Springer Nature Switzerland AG 2021
H. Ishikawa et al. (Eds.): ACCV 2020, LNCS 12622, pp. 706–722, 2021.
https://doi.org/10.1007/978-3-030-69525-5_42

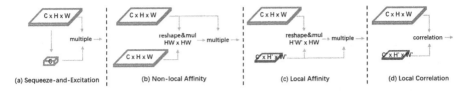

Fig. 1. Comparison of different attention approaches. From left to right: (a) Squeeze-and-Excitation [18]. (b) Non-local Affinity [19]. (c) Local Affinity and (d) Local Correlation Attention. It can be noticed that, Local Correlation is operated on the local context of global feature, instead of the entire feature map.

that the calculation of each pixel attention on an equal basis is computationally inefficient and out of focus in the previous approaches. Therefore, we rethink salient object segmentation task from a more macroscopic point of view, which separates the salient object from the distant irrelevant background, and then extracts local context features related to the object as supervision to enhance the distinguish ability of foreground object.

An intuitive way to extract local context features is to construct a coarse-to-fine architecture with multi-scale inputs [16, 20]. It generates an approximate prediction in the first stage, then crops the image as the input of a second refine network. Nevertheless, this method relies heavily on the accuracy of coarse predictions and does not make good use of the relationship between global and local contexts due to the cropping operation in the coarse stage. In addition, the increase of inference time makes the coarse-to-fine methods less favorable for practical applications. A global scene of the image can provide global semantic information, while local context around the target object produces the relationship between foreground and background. Both of them provides useful hints for inferring the content of the target. Therefore, how to strengthen local context features and retain global context features becomes the key to improve salient object segmentation accuracy. To this end, we propose a novel Local Context Attention Network (LCANet) to adapt the global and the local features with a uniform representational power.

Specifically, the proposed LCANet is mainly built upon a one-stage coarse-to-fine architecture. A coarse segmentation network is built from a standard classification model to extract the discriminant feature, which is up-scaled to generate the coarse feature map. Then an Attentional Correlation Filter (ACF) module is designed to generate local context attention. The local feature map is cropped based on the coarse location after image processing, and is regarded as the correlation filter to make a convolution with the whole feature map. With the help of convolution, the correlation feature map is taken as an attention map to concatenate with the original feature to explicitly enhance local context description ability. In contrast to other attention modules [18,19,21] exploring the channel or spatial weight, the proposed ACF module retains the global receptive field with local context enhanced in the surrounding areas, as shown in Fig. 2(d). Furthermore, ACF module is enhanced to Local Context Block (LCB) by

Multi-scale ACF operator and a Local Coordinate Convolution (LCC) layer. The LCC layer adopts the relative coordinates of the coarse prediction as another additional feature map to adaptively incorporate the local region context into the global scene context in the spatial dimension. Based on the enhanced LCB, a one-stage coarse-to-fine network is constructed in a type of encoder-decoder architecture as shown in Fig. 2. A multi-stage decoder is designed to aggregate the high-level information extracted by coarse network to gradually refine the segmentation results. The LCB is also implemented in the stages of decoder to handle with various sizes of salient objects.

In summary, there are three contributions in our paper:

– We rethink the salient object segmentation task from the intrinsic properties of salient object, and create a newly model structure, Local Context Attention Network (LCANet), to strengthen local context features by adaptively integrating local region context and global scene context in a one-stage coarse-to-fine architecture.
– We design a novel Local Context Block (LCB), on the basis of Attentional Correlation Filter (ACF). As a basic module, it can be used in many situations, instead of the traditional global and non-local attention map.
– Detailed experiments on five widely-used benchmarks indicate the effectiveness of our proposed modules and architecture in improving the accuracy. We achieve the state-of-the-art performance on all of these datasets with thorough ablation studies, especially a new record of **0.883 max F-score** and **0.034 MAE** without any other refinement steps on DUTS-TE dataset.

2   Related Work

Salient Object Segmentation: In the past decades, a number of approaches for saliency detection are developed. Most of them regard salient object segmentation as a special case of semantic segmentation, try to increase receptive field through multi-level features [4,6,22–25]. They think high-level features in deep layers encode the semantic information of an abstract description of objects, while low-level features keep spatial details for reconstructing the object boundaries. Some researchers think edge information is the key to improve segmentation accuracy. [5,22] adopt post-processing heuristics to obtain the refine predictions. DEA [26] simply uses an extra loss to emphasize the detection error for the pixels within the salient object boundaries, while others [27,28] consider semantic contour information from a pretrained contour detector. Although these methods are proved to be effective, no one analyzes the problem from the perspective of salient objects. Local context is easily overlooked in salient object segmentation.

Attention Module: Attention module is one of the most popular operations in recent neural networks to mimic the visual attention mechanism in the human visual system. SE-Net [18] explores a channel-wise attention map and has achieved state-of-the-art performance in image classification. In the field

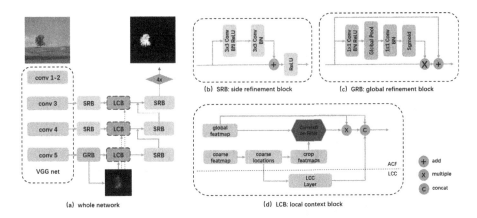

Fig. 2. Overview of our Local Context Attention Network (LCANet). A coarse network is built on a VGG network followed by GRB to generate coarse prediction of the input image. Then the feature map is entered into LCB to produce local context attention maps of the input global features. LCB consists of ACF and LCC modules. It can be implemented on multi-stage of decoder network, cooperating with SRB to gradually refine the final segmentation results.

of semantic segmentation, several methods [29–31] adopt multi-scale attention map to increase the receptive field of the high-level features. EncNet [32,33] introduces context encoding to enhance the prediction that is conditional on the encoded semantics. Non-Local [19,21] is further proposed self-attention with non-local affinity matrix for vision tasks. By contract, we apply the local context attention map on the output of encoder network to integrate the local region and global scene description.

Correlation Filter: Correlation filter [34–36] has proved to be effective in most of single object tracking methods. It takes advantage of the fact that they can specify the desired output of a linear classifier for several translations and image shifts based on the dot-product at different relative translations of two patches using only a fraction of the computational power. It is relevant to local similarity between the object and its local neighborhood and suitable for convolution operator. Naturally, encoding the local correlation feature as an attention map is an immediate thought.

Coarse-to-Fine: These also exist researchers finding the optimal coarse-to-fine solutions to deal with the scale-variation problem. However, most of them focus on the feature expression. DSS [6] proposes a saliency method by introducing short connections to the skip-layer structures within a multi-layer HED architecture. NLDF [37] combines the local and global information through a multi-resolution grid structure. Amulet [4] directly aggregates multi-level features by concatenating feature maps from different layers. Although the features from deeper layers help to locate the target, objects with different sizes cannot be represented in the same feature structure. A more proper way is to employ the multi-scale features in a coarse-to-fine fashion and gradually predict the final saliency map. However, the increase of inference time makes the coarse-to-fine methods less favorable for practical.

3   Methodology

In this section, we first detailedly introduce the idea of the Attentional Correlation Filter (ACF) module, and elaborate how this module specifically handles the local context issue. After that, we describe the complete Local Context Attention Network (LCANet) based on the Local Context Block (LCB), which builds a coarse-to-fine structure in a one-stage encoder-decoder architecture.

3.1   Attentional Correlation Filter

Let's revisit the main prior of salient object segmentation. Salient object usually has unique feature representations that are different from the surrounding background, such as vivid colors or clear boundaries. Pixels of salient object have strong correlation with its local context in physical space. Based on this observation and analysis, we propose an Attentional Correlation Filter (ACF) module to strengthen the salient features, which apply the attention mechanism to enhance feature expression ability of local context in global feature.

Correlation Filter. Given a target object $T \in \mathbb{R}^{H' \times W'}$ and an reference image $I \in \mathbb{R}^{H \times W}$. For each pixel $(x, y) \in I$, we have the correlation map $Corr$ between I and T is calculated as

$$Corr(I, T)_{x,y} = \sum_{v=-\frac{W'}{2}}^{\frac{W'}{2}} \sum_{u=-\frac{H'}{2}}^{\frac{H'}{2}} T[u, v] \odot I[x + u, y + v] \tag{1}$$

The correlation map can be generated according to the sliding window on the reference image. In the field of single object tracking [34–36], it is used widely to obtain the similarity degree between the tracking object and its neighborhood scene to search for the update object position in the next frame. The higher the correlation value, the higher the probability that two patches belong to the same object. The operation of the sliding window is similar to convolution. We regard the feature of the target object as convolution weight, then the correlation feature map can be generated by convolution on the original global feature.

Attentional Correlation Filter. We use the generated correlation feature map as an attention layer for subsequent processing. Given a local feature map $T \in \mathbb{R}^{C' \times H'W'}$ and a global feature map $I \in \mathbb{R}^{C \times HW}$, ACF can be generated as,

$$ACF = I \odot Sigmoid(Corr(I, T)) \tag{2}$$

There are many ways to implement attention map, as compared in Fig. 1. In the global attention [18] or the non-local affinity attention [19,21], features

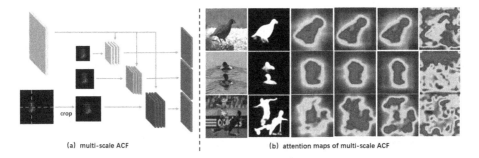

Fig. 3. Multi-scale ACF. In (a), multi-scale local feature maps are cropped based on coarse prediction and convoluted with the original feature to generate attention maps. In (b), attention maps of ACF with various scales (line 3,4,5) from coarse results (line 2) are compared with the attention map of non-local module (line 6).

are used to calculate the pixel similarity in channel or spatial dimensions. When it acts on the local area, the similar local affinity map can be generated by multiplying the local and global features. However, it is unreasonable that the correlation in channel dimensions loses the spatial relationship between pixels. The direct feature fusion will lead to the migration between features. In ACF, we crop the high-level features from encoder into local feature maps based on the coarse prediction. The coarse object location is calculated from the maximum and the minimum positions of the binarized course predictions. Then the coarse feature map is warped into a given size based on the affine transformation. The generated local context feature map is normalized to keep the same channel of global feature map and odd kernel size, and convoluted with the original feature to generate attention feature map. As shown in Fig. 3, the non-local attention map puts more emphasis on bright areas than significant areas, while the ACF significantly enhances the feature discrimination ability in the region of interest.

3.2 Local Context Block

We further extend the proposed ACF module to a more robust local context descriptor. Firstly, we introduce a Local Coordinate Convolution (LCC) layer to increase the local context information in the spatial perspective. Secondly, the ACF is extended to multi-scale ACF to better cope with the significant changes of different sizes of objects, and the inaccurate results of the coarse network.

Local Coordinate Convolution. The calculation of Local Coordinate Convolution Layer lcc_x, lcc_y of target pixel $p_t = I(x_t, y_t) \in I$ can be formulated as following:

$$lcc_x(x,y) = [1 - \frac{|x - x_t|}{H}], \ (x,y) \in H \times W \tag{3}$$

$$lcc_y(x,y) = [1 - \frac{|y - y_t|}{W}], \ (x,y) \in H \times W \tag{4}$$

we concatenate the LCC and I in channel dimension, and then send them into the convolution layer. The standard coordinate convolution is developed to provide an explicit relative position relationship on the spatial feature map. Based on the coarse location of the salient object, we modify it to further enhance local features in the perspective of physical space. lcc_x and lcc_y are respectively calculated through the distance of pixel relative to the center point of coarse prediction. The nearer the distance, the greater the value. LCC module, combined with ACF module, extracts the local context information of coarse results in the dimensions of feature and space dimensions, in order to complement each other in local area enhancement.

Multi-Scale ACF. Furthermore, in order to compensate the error of the coarse prediction, we apply the multi-scale attention maps. Based on the rough segmentation result, the original coarse feature map is warped into different scales. We extract local characteristics with scale changes by adjusting the expansion of the external rectangle of coarse predictions. All these multi-scale attention maps are respectively multipled and concatenated with the global features and to generate the local enhanced feature maps. As shown in Fig. 3, with the implementation of Multi-scale ACF, the significance of objects with different sizes is highlighted on different attention maps. On the contrary, the non-local attention more strengthens the distribution of global features, while ignores the salient objects.

3.3   Network Architecture

In the task of semantic segmentation, it has been proved that high-level features and multi-scale decoder are the main factors to improve the segmentation results. While the performance of LCB depends on the result of coarse network, the first stage of LCANet needs to obtain acceptable coarse prediction results under controllable computational complexity. Then a multi-stage decoder is needed to further refine the coarse results. Based on the above knowledge, we propose two complementary modules that are capable of capturing the positions of salient objects and refining their details from coarse level to fine level.

Coarse Network. The most direct way to integrate coarse and refined results is to share the encoder layers. High-level features generated from the encoder network already have preliminary classification ability in terms of distinguishing salient objects and backgrounds. We applied a standard VGG [38] network as the backbone network to extract multi-layer discriminating feature maps. Following the high-level semantic features from VGG, a Global Refinement Block (GRB) is applied to improve receptive field and change the weights of the features to enhance the semantic consistency. As illustrated in Fig. 2, two 1×1 convolutions and a global pooling operations are applied to reallocate the feature map and generate a spatial attention map onto the high-level features. This global attention map explicitly makes feature maps be aware of the locations of the salient objects. Then coarse prediction is generated by up-sampling this global strengthened features.

Coarse-to-Fine Network. Based on the coarse network and LCB, we construct a one-stage coarse-to-fine network. We build our network based on a type of classic U-shape architecture as shown in Fig. 2. Although GRB improves the receptive filed to capture the global information of the input images, the classification abilities in different stages of backbone network are ignored, which results in diverse consistency manifestation. So we design a residual structure named Side Refinement Block (SRB) to iteratively fuse discriminant features of different scales, which consists of two 3 × 3 convolution operations. Different from previous symmetrical encoder-decoder architectures, we only take the result of stage3 quadrupled as the final output. The last two abandoned up-sampling convolution blocks save a lot of computation, but improve the accuracy in our experiments. As mentioned above, the LCB is implemented cooperating with SRB to strengthen local context features of each stage before up-sampling. Similar to multi scale operations in feature level, multi-stage of LCB is also essential to adapt to the wrong predictions and scale variations as much as possible.

Loss Function. The LCANet is trained in an end-to-end manner with losses of coarse and refine outputs. we use the cross-entropy loss between the final saliency map and the ground truth. Besides that, we apply a boundary preservation loss to enhance the edge accuracy. Sobel operator is adopted to generate the edge of ground truth and the predication saliency map of network. Then the same cross-entropy loss is used to supervise the salient object boundaries. The similar boundary supervision is used and proved in several previous works [1,23,39]. Different from them, Sobel operator makes the model pay more attention to the junction of salient objects and background. The total loss function of the LCANet is the weighted sum of the above losses.

$$L = \lambda_0 L_{cs} + \lambda_1 L_{rf} + \lambda_2 L_{cs_{bd}} + \lambda_3 L_{rf_{bd}} \tag{5}$$

Where L_{cs} and L_{rf} denote the cross entropy loss function of the coarse and the coarse-to-fine predictions respectively, and $L_{cs_{bd}}$ and $L_{rf_{bd}}$ are their boundary preservation loss. An experimental weight are applied to combined them all. Also, online hard example mining [40] strategy is adopted with L_{cs} and L_{rf} respectively during training.

In contrast to other two-stage coarse-to-fine networks, LCANet is more like inserting a layer of local context attention into a standard encoder-decoder network. It doesn't separate the coarse and the fine networks with multi times inference. What's more, it adaptively combines the local surrounding context and the global scene information in a uniform feature description.

4 Experiments

In this section, we mainly investigate the effectiveness of the proposed LCB module. While the performance of the LCB depends on the result of coarse network, we first compare the effect of each module in the complete network structure. Then we conduct more experiments on the configurations of the LCB to analyze the influence of the LCB on local context in detail. Finally, we compare the proposed LCANet with other state-of-the-art approaches quantitatively and qualitatively.

4.1 Experimental Setup

Datasets. To evaluate the performance of the proposed approach, we conduct experiments on five popular benchmark datasets [13–17]. These datasets all contain a large number of images as well as well-segmented annotations and have been widely used in the filed of salient object segmentation. DUTS [14] is the largest dataset containing 10,553 images for training and 5,019 images for testing. Both training and test sets in DUTS contain very complex scenarios with high content variety. ECSSD [13] contains 1,000 natural images manually selected from the Internet. HKU-IS [16] includes 4447 images with multiple disconnected salient objects overlapping the image boundary. DUT-OMRON [15] has 5,168 images with many semantically meaningful and challenging structures. Images of this dataset have one or more salient objects and relatively complex background. PASCAL-S [17] contains 850 natural images that are free-viewed by 8 subjects in eye-tracking tests for salient object annotation.

Evaluation Metrics. In order to obtain a fair comparison with other state-of-the-art salient object segmentation approaches, we train the proposed networks on DUTS training set (DUTS-TR), and evaluate them on DUTS test set (DUTS-TE) and the other four datasets. For quantitative evaluation, two universally-agreed, standard metrics, mean absolute error (MAE) and maximum F-measure ($maxF$) are adopted respectively [6]. F-measure reflects the overall performance of pixel classification. It is computed by weighted harmonic mean of the precision and recall. MAE indicates the average pixel-wise absolute difference between the estimated salient map and ground-truth.

Implementation Details. All the networks mentioned below follow the same training strategy. A VGG-16 pre-trained on Imagenet [41] is used to initialize the convolution layers in the backbone network. The parameters in other convolution layers are randomly initialized. All training and test images are resized to 256×256 before being fed into the network. They are trained using mini-batch stochastic gradient descent (SGD) with batch size 48, momentum 0.9, weight decay 1e−5 and 300 epochs. As the common configuration, the "poly" learning rate policy is adopted where the initial rate is multiplied by $(1 - \frac{iter}{max\_iter})^{power}$ with power 0.9 and the base learning rate is set as 1e−4. Data augmentation contains mean subtraction, random horizontal flip, random resizing with scale ranges in [0.8, 1.2], and random cropping to keep most of the salient object intact for training.

4.2 Ablation Studies of Main Architecture

The main architecture is an encoder-decoder structure consisting of GRB, SRB and LCB. Besides that, boundary loss (BL) is verified here as part of main

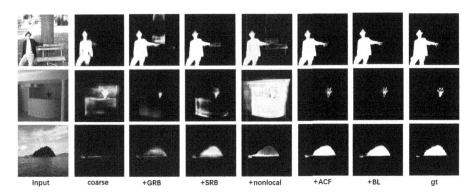

Fig. 4. Result comparisons of different modules in our proposed method. From left to right, each line depicts results of coarse backbone model, and the successive additions of GRB, SRB decoder, non-local attention map, ACF, boundary preservation loss (BL) and the ground truth.

network. We conduct ablation experiments on two challenging datasets DUTS-TE and ECSSD to demonstrate the effectiveness of each module separately.

GRB. Firstly, we verify the accuracy of coarse output. According to Table 1, the addition of GRB gives performance gains in term of both $maxF$ and MAE on the two datasets over the coarse network. While implemented on the coarse network, the $maxF$ of DUTS-TE is improved from 0.775 to 0.818. Also the performance is improved further to 0.843 while applied onto the coarse-to-fine network. The corresponding visual comparisons can be found in Fig. 4. The global pooling operator helps to increase the receptive field of the network and highlight the areas of interest.

SRB. Here SRB refers to the decoder network containing the SRB module. As can be observed as in Table 1, simply embedding of SRB decoder helps improve the performance on both $maxF$ and MAE. When GRB and SRB are superposed concurrently, the performance of the model is further enhanced, which indicates the effectiveness of multi-stage refinement for solving the aliasing effect of up-sampling.

ACF. Furthermore, we implement ACF onto the above encoder-decoder network. As the core of LCB module, ACF can well verify the effectiveness of local context attention. Here we only apply the simplest single-scale ACF onto the high-level features generated from coarse network. When it directly acts on the coarse prediction, the accuracy is only slightly improved. This proves from the side that a more reasonable local context is the key to improve the accuracy. When the coarse result is poor, ACF is similar to the attention map on the global context. When it is added to GRB and SRB in turn, the role of ACF is highlighted, and both $maxF$ and MAE on the two datasets are further improved. As shown in Fig. 4, the local guidance information generated by ACF allows our

Table 1. Ablation analysis for the main architecture on two popular datasets. All experiments are trained on the union set of DUTS-TR. No.1 depicts the encoder network, and the other modules are successively embedded. As can be observed, each proposed module plays an important role and contributes to the performance.

No.	GRB	SRB	ACF	BL	DUTS-TE		ECSSD	
					$maxF\uparrow$	$MAE\downarrow$	$maxF\uparrow$	$MAE\downarrow$
1					0.775	0.081	0.863	0.080
2	✓				0.818	0.051	0.883	0.066
3		✓			0.830	0.047	0.891	0.058
4	✓	✓			**0.843**	**0.046**	**0.915**	**0.054**
5			✓		0.781	0.077	0.871	0.078
6	✓		✓		0.847	0.044	0.904	0.051
7	✓	✓	✓		0.873	0.039	0.928	0.034
8	✓	✓	✓	✓	**0.875**	**0.038**	**0.931**	**0.033**

network to focus more on the salient objects, and greatly improve the quality of resulting salient maps.

BL. Finally, the boundary preservation loss (BL) is adopted to further improve the quality of boundary in the produced saliency map. Although the performance is only slightly improved, the upper edge of the visual results was optimized to be closer to the ground truth in Fig. 4.

4.3   Ablation Studies of LCB

To demonstrate the effectiveness of our proposed LCB, we adopt two basic networks. *coarse* depicts the GRB enhanced coarse network, and *baseline* is the combined model of GRB, SRB and BL, which has been verified in the previous section. We study the different variants of ACF and LCC modules in LCB, and compare them with other attention methods.

Coarse-to-Fine Structures. By introducing local context into the baseline network, the most direct way is to execute the model twice by cropping the predictions of the first network as the input of the second one. In Table 2, we conducted the experiments of executing the *coarse* and *baseline* twice respectively. The performance of $baseline \times 2$ is significantly improved both in terms of $maxF$ and MAE, while the accuracy of $coarse \times 2$ is slightly decreased. This is mainly because the refine network is heavily dependent on the results of coarse network. However, when $baseline + ACF$ integrates the local context attention and the global feature map in a joint training manner, the performance is greatly improved as shown in Table 2.

Other Attention Modules. Also we compare the proposed ACF module with other attention-based modules. Att_{se}, Att_{nl} and Att_{lf} are effective modules of

Table 2. Ablation analysis for the proposed main architecture on DUTS-TE. Different types of ACF and LCC modules are verified and compared with other attention modules. As can be noticed, ACF is superior to others, and LCC also contributes to the performance.

Model	$maxF\uparrow$	$MAE\downarrow$	Model	$maxF\uparrow$	$MAE\downarrow$
coarse × 2	0.813	0.050	baseline + $ACF_{0.1}$	0.874	0.038
baseline × 2	0.861	0.042	baseline + $ACF_{0.3}$	0.871	0.041
baseline + Att_{se}	0.845	0.047	baseline + $ACF_{0.5}$	0.875	0.038
baseline + Att_{lf}	0.847	0.046	baseline + ACF_{msz}	0.879	0.037
baseline + Att_{nl}	0.861	0.041	baseline + ACF_{msz} + LCC	0.882	0.041
baseline + ACF	**0.875**	**0.038**	baseline + $ACF_{msz+msa}$ + LCC	**0.883**	**0.034**

squeeze-and-excitiation [18], non-local affinity [19], and a modified local affinity depicted in Fig. 1. As can be observed from Table 2, although the accuracy can be improved by increasing the receptive field, these modules are still worse than the proposed ACF module. Att_{lf} is similar to ACF by generating the affinity matrix bewteen local context and global feature map. Nevertheless, the performance is even worse than results of *baseline* × 2, we think that the multiplication of affinity matrix in different feature space destroys the ability of feature description of both global and local feature map.

Multi-scale ACF. Furthermore, we investigates the effectiveness of Multi-scale ACF. Figure 3 depicts the visualization results of attention maps produces by the cropped feature maps with different sizes. Also the performance of Multi-scale ACF are showed in Table 2. It can be observed both in qualitative or quantitative analysis that different attention map corresponds to different size of salient object. And Also the unknown segmentation errors of coarse network also affect the performance of ACF. Although the accuracy of ACF with different scales fluctuates, Multi-scale ACF can cope with these accidental changes, and further improve the performance of both $maxF$ and MAE.

LCC. LCC is another complementary module in LCB. As present in Table 2, LCC further improves the result of Multi-scale ACF from 0.879 to 0.882. This proves the complementary relationship between ACF and LCC. Under the guidance of an explicit location provided by LCC, it realizes a more accurate and robust segmentation on the final result. The final LCB consists of Multi-scale ACF and LCC. It can be implemented onto the different stages of decoder to further enhance the final performance as $ACF_{msz+msa}$ depicted in Table 2.

4.4 Comparisons with the State-of-the-Arts

We compare the proposed LCANet with sixteen recent state-of-the-art methods including PoolNet [1], PFA [39], AFNet [2], MLMSNet [3], CPD [42], BDMPM [23], GRL [43], PAGRN [44], Amulet [4], SRM [45], UCF [46], DCL [5], DHS [47], DSS [6], ELD [24] and NLDF [37] on five datasets. We obtain the saliency maps

Table 3. Quantitative comparisons of the proposed approach and sixteen state-of-the-art CNN based salient object detection approaches on five datasets. The best two scores are shown in red and blue.

	DUTS-TE		ECSSD		HKU-IS		PASCAL-S		DUT-OM	
	$maxF$	MAE	$maxF$	MAE	$maxF$	MAE	$maxF$	MAE	$maxF$	MAE
ELD [24]	0.737	0.092	0.867	0.081	0.840	0.073	0.788	0.122	0.719	0.090
DHS [47]	0.811	0.065	0.904	0.062	0.890	0.053	0.845	0.096	–	–
DCL [5]	0.785	0.081	0.895	0.079	0.889	0.063	0.845	0.111	0.756	0.086
UCF [46]	0.772	0.111	0.901	0.070	0.887	0.062	0.849	0.109	0.729	0.120
SRM [45]	0.826	0.058	0.915	0.056	0.905	0.046	0.867	0.085	0.769	0.069
Amulet [4]	0.777	0.084	0.913	0.060	0.896	0.051	0.861	0.098	0.742	0.097
NLDF [37]	0.812	0.064	0.903	0.065	0.901	0.048	0.851	0.100	0.753	0.079
DSS [6]	0.813	0.064	0.895	0.064	0.901	0.047	0.850	0.099	0.760	0.075
PAGRN [44]	0.854	0.054	0.923	0.064	0.917	0.047	0.869	0.094	0.770	0.070
GRL [43]	0.834	0.050	0.923	0.044	0.913	0.037	0.881	0.079	0.778	0.063
BDMPM [23]	0.851	0.048	0.925	0.048	0.920	0.039	0.880	0.078	0.774	0.064
CPD [42]	0.864	0.043	0.936	0.040	0.924	0.033	0.866	0.074	0.794	0.057
MLMSNet [3]	0.851	0.049	0.928	0.045	0.921	0.039	0.862	0.074	0.774	0.064
AFNet [2]	0.862	0.046	0.935	0.042	0.923	0.036	0.868	0.071	0.797	0.057
PFA [39]	0.870	**0.040**	0.931	**0.032**	0.926	**0.032**	0.892	**0.067**	0.855	**0.041**
PoolNet [1]	**0.880**	0.041	**0.937**	0.044	**0.931**	0.033	0.865	0.072	0.821	0.056
LCANet	0.883	0.034	0.939	0.029	0.931	0.030	**0.889**	0.064	**0.843**	0.037

of these methods from authors or the deployment codes provided by authors for fair comparison.

Quantitative Evaluation. Table 3 shows the quantitative evaluation results of the proposed method and other state-of-the-art salient segmentation approaches in terms of $maxF$ and MAE. As present, our method outperforms other approaches across all these datasets. To be specific, LCANet achieves large improvement compared with the best existing approach on DUT-TE dataset. Both of $maxF$ and MAE are definitely increased from the ever best PoolNet [1] based on the VGG backbone. On PASCAL-S and DUT-OMRON, although the performance of $maxF$ is slightly lower than PFA [39], the MAE exceeds it. We find that objects in them are large or multi-subjects. When the object size is large, local context is almost the same as global context the, the role of LCANet will be correspondingly weakened. While the proposed approach is a simple one-stage structure, it can be further improved with multi-branch learning algorithms.

Qualitative Evaluation. To further explain the advantages of our approach, Fig. 5 provides a visual comparison of our method and other state-of-the-arts. From the former 5 rows of Fig. 5, it is clear that our method is obviously superior to others coping with small objects. While other methods are difficult to distinguish salient objects and background, LCANet obtains accurate segmentation results based on the coarse-to-fine guidance. This further verifies the effectiveness of local context in salient object location. More than this, we notice that

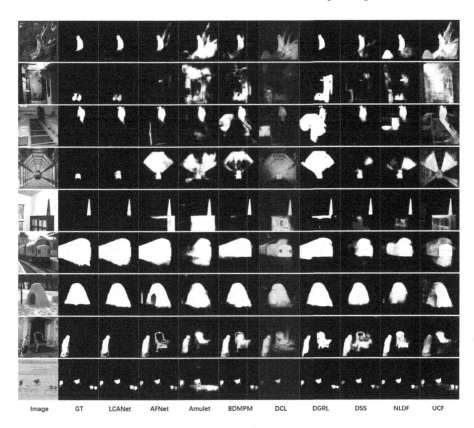

Fig. 5. Qualitative comparisons of the state-of-the-art algorithms and our proposed **LCANet**. GT means ground-truth masks of salient objects.

the consistency of larger objects is also preserved as shown in row 6,7 of Fig. 5. Even when salient objects are scattered in different places of the image, there is still a certain probability not be affected. Also it still obtains a good segmentation prediction when the salient object located in the side of the image. These observations indicate the intergration of local and global context information is important to deal with salient object segmentation, regardless of the position and size of the object.

5   Conclusion

In this paper, we propose a local context attention network to cope with salient object segmentation. Based on the prior that saliency object usually has unique feature representations that are different from the surrounding background, we proposed a Local Context Block consisting of an Attentional Correlation Filter and a Local Coordinate Convolution layer, in order to intergrate the local context information into the global scene features in a one-stage coarse-to-fine architecture. Detailed experiments verify the feasibility of the proposed LCANet. It achieves comparable performance with other state-of-the-art methods based on a simple baseline. We believe that this model will be useful for other scenarios.

References

1. Liu, J., Hou, Q., Cheng, M.M., Feng, J., Jiang, J.: A simple pooling-based design for real-time salient object detection. In: CVPR, pp. 3917–3926 (2019)
2. Feng, M., Lu, H., Ding, E.: Attentive feedback network for boundary-aware salient object detection. In: CVPR, pp. 1623–1632 (2019)
3. Wu, R., Feng, M., Guan, W., Wang, D., Lu, H., Ding, E.: A mutual learning method for salient object detection with intertwined multi-supervision. In: CVPR, pp. 8150–8159 (2019)
4. Zhang, P., Wang, D., Lu, H., Wang, H., Ruan, X.: Amulet: aggregating multi-level convolutional features for salient object detection. In: ICCV, pp. 202–211 (2017)
5. Li, G., Yu, Y.: Deep contrast learning for salient object detection. In: CVPR, pp. 478–487 (2016)
6. Hou, Q., Cheng, M.M., Hu, X., Borji, A., Tu, Z., Torr, P.H.S.: Deeply supervised salient object detection with short connections. In: CVPR, pp. 5300–5309 (2017)
7. Liu, Y., Zhang, Q., Zhang, D., Han, J.: Employing deep part-object relationships for salient object detection. In: ICCV, pp. 1232–1241 (2019)
8. Wang, W., Zhao, S., Shen, J., Hoi, S.C.H., Borji, A.: Salient object detection with pyramid attention and salient edges. In: CVPR, pp. 1448–1457 (2019)
9. Zeng, Y., Zhang, P., Zhang, J., Lin, Z.L., Lu, H.: Towards high-resolution salient object detection. In: ICCV (2019)
10. Zeng, Y., Zhuge, Y.Z., Lu, H., Zhang, L., Qian, M., Yu, Y.: Multi-source weak supervision for saliency detection. In: CVPR, pp. 6074–6083 (2019)
11. Zhang, L., Zhang, J., Lin, Z., Lu, H., He, Y.: CapSal: leveraging captioning to boost semantics for salient object detection. In: CVPR, pp. 6024–6033 (2019)
12. Zhao, J., Liu, J., Fan, D.P., Cao, Y., Yang, J., Cheng, M.M.: EGNet: edge guidance network for salient object detection. In: ICCV (2019)
13. Yan, Q., Xu, L., Shi, J., Jia, J.: Hierarchical saliency detection. In: CVPR, pp. 1155–1162 (2013)
14. Wang, L., et al.: Learning to detect salient objects with image-level supervision. In: CVPR, pp. 3796–3805 (2017)
15. Yang, C., Zhang, L., Lu, H., Ruan, X., Yang, M.H.: Saliency detection via graph-based manifold ranking. In: CVPR, pp. 3166–3173 (2013)
16. Li, G., Yu, Y.: Visual saliency based on multiscale deep features. In: CVPR, pp. 5455–5463 (2015)
17. Li, Y., Hou, X., Koch, C., Rehg, J.M., Yuille, A.L.: The secrets of salient object segmentation. In: CVPR, pp. 280–287 (2014)
18. Hu, J., Shen, L., Sun, G.: Squeeze-and-excitation networks. In: CVPR, pp. 7132–7141 (2018)
19. Wang, X., Girshick, R.B., Gupta, A., He, K.: Non-local neural networks. In: CVPR, pp. 7794–7803 (2018)
20. Piao, Y., Ji, W., Li, J., Zhang, M., Lu, H.: Depth-induced multi-scale recurrent attention network for saliency detection. In: ICCV (2019)
21. Yuan, Y., Wang, J.: OCNet: object context network for scene parsing (2019)

22. Wang, L., Wang, L., Lu, H., Zhang, P., Ruan, X.: Saliency detection with recurrent fully convolutional networks. In: ECCV, pp. 825–841 (2016)
23. Zhang, L., Dai, J., Lu, H., He, Y., Wang, G.: A bi-directional message passing model for salient object detection. In: CVPR (2018)
24. Lee, G., Tai, Y.W., Kim, J.: Deep saliency with encoded low level distance map and high level features. In: CVPR, pp. 660–668 (2016)
25. Tang, Y., Wu, X., Bu, W.: Deeply-supervised recurrent convolutional neural network for saliency detection. In: ACM Multimedia, pp. 397–401 (2016)
26. Zhang, J., Dai, Y., Porikli, F., He, M.: Deep edge-aware saliency detection (2017)
27. Li, X., Yang, F., Cheng, H., Liu, W., Shen, D.: Contour knowledge transfer for salient object detection. In: ECCV, pp. 370–385 (2018)
28. Yang, J., Price, B.L., Cohen, S., Lee, H., Yang, M.H.: Object contour detection with a fully convolutional encoder-decoder network. In: CVPR, pp. 193–202 (2016)
29. Zhao, H., Shi, J., Qi, X., Wang, X., Jia, J.: Pyramid scene parsing network. In: CVPR, pp. 6230–6239 (2017)
30. Chen, L.C., Zhu, Y., Papandreou, G., Schroff, F., Adam, H.: Encoder-decoder with atrous separable convolution for semantic image segmentation. In: ECCV, pp. 833–851 (2018)
31. Li, H., Xiong, P., An, J., Wang, L.: Pyramid attention network for semantic segmentation. In: BMVC (2018)
32. Zhang, H., et al.: Context encoding for semantic segmentation. In: CVPR, pp. 7151–7160 (2018)
33. Chen, L.C., Yang, Y., Wang, J., Xu, W., Yuille, A.L.: Attention to scale: scale-aware semantic image segmentation. In: CVPR, pp. 3640–3649 (2016)
34. Henriques, J.F., Caseiro, R., Martins, P., Batista, J.: High-speed tracking with kernelized correlation filters. IEEE Trans. Pattern Anal. Mach. Intell. **37**(3), 583–596 (2015)
35. Henriques, J.F., Caseiro, R., Martins, P., Batista, J.: Exploiting the circulant structure of tracking-by-detection with kernels. In: Fitzgibbon, A., Lazebnik, S., Perona, P., Sato, Y., Schmid, C. (eds.) ECCV 2012. LNCS, vol. 7575, pp. 702–715. Springer, Heidelberg (2012). https://doi.org/10.1007/978-3-642-33765-9_50
36. Bolme, D.S., Beveridge, J.R., Draper, B.A., Lui, Y.M.: Visual object tracking using adaptive correlation filters. In: CVPR, pp. 2544–2550 (2010)
37. Luo, Z., Mishra, A.K., Achkar, A., Eichel, J.A., Li, S., Jodoin, P.M.: Non-local deep features for salient object detection. In: CVPR, pp. 6593–6601 (2017)
38. Simonyan, K., Zisserman, A.: Very deep convolutional networks for large-scale image recognition. In: ICLR (2015)
39. Zhao, T., Wu, X.: Pyramid feature attention network for saliency detection. In: CVPR, pp. 3085–3094 (2019)
40. Shrivastava, A., Gupta, A., Girshick, R.B.: Training region-based object detectors with online hard example mining. In: CVPR, pp. 761–769 (2016)
41. Krizhevsky, A., Sutskever, I., Hinton, G.E.: ImageNet classification with deep convolutional neural networks. In: NIPS (2012)
42. Wu, Z., Su, L., Huang, Q.: Cascaded partial decoder for fast and accurate salient object detection. In: CVPR, pp. 3907–3916 (2019)
43. Wang, T., et al.: Detect globally, refine locally: a novel approach to saliency detection. In: CVPR (2018)
44. Zhang, X., Wang, T., Qi, J., Lu, H., Wang, G.: Progressive attention guided recurrent network for salient object detection. In: CVPR, pp. 714–722 (2018)
45. Wang, T., Borji, A., Zhang, L., Zhang, P., Lu, H.: A stagewise refinement model for detecting salient objects in images. In: ICCV (2017)

46. Zhang, P., Wang, D., Lu, H., Wang, H., Yin, B.: Learning uncertain convolutional features for accurate saliency detection. In: ICCV, pp. 212–221 (2017)
47. Liu, N., Han, J.: Deep hierarchical saliency network for salient object detection. In: CVPR, pp. 678–686 (2016)

Generic Image Segmentation in Fully Convolutional Networks by Superpixel Merging Map

Jin-Yu Huang$^{(\boxtimes)}$ and Jian-Jiun Ding

National Taiwan University, Taipei, Taiwan
{r07942085,jjding}@ntu.edu.tw

Abstract. Recently, the Fully Convolutional Network (FCN) has been adopted in image segmentation. However, existing FCN-based segmentation algorithms were designed for semantic segmentation. Before learning-based algorithms were developed, many advanced generic segmentation algorithms are superpixel-based. However, due to the irregular shape and size of superpixels, it is hard to apply deep learning to superpixel-based image segmentation directly. In this paper, we combined the merits of the FCN and superpixels and proposed a highly accurate and extremely fast generic image segmentation algorithm. We treated image segmentation as multiple superpixel merging decision problems and determined whether the boundary between two adjacent superpixels should be kept. In other words, if the boundary of two adjacent superpixels should be deleted, then the two superpixels will be merged. The network applies the colors, the edge map, and the superpixel information to make decision about merging suprepixels. By solving all the superpixel-merging subproblems with just one forward pass, the FCN facilitates the speed of the whole segmentation process by a wide margin meanwhile gaining higher accuracy. Simulations show that the proposed algorithm has favorable runtime, meanwhile achieving highly accurate segmentation results. It outperforms state-of-the-art image segmentation methods, including feature-based and learning-based methods, in all metrics.

1 Introduction

Image segmentation is fundamental and important in many image processing applications. There are many existing image segmentation algorithms, including the region growing method [1], the mean shift method [2], the watershed [3,4], the normalized cut [5,6], the graph-based method [7], and the superpixel-based method [8–10].

Electronic supplementary material The online version of this chapter (https:// doi.org/10.1007/978-3-030-69525-5_43) contains supplementary material, which is available to authorized users.

© Springer Nature Switzerland AG 2021
H. Ishikawa et al. (Eds.): ACCV 2020, LNCS 12622, pp. 723–737, 2021.
https://doi.org/10.1007/978-3-030-69525-5_43

In recent years, deep learning techniques have also been adopted in image segmentation [11–14]. With supplicated deep learning architectures, one can achieve good segmentation results with enough training time. However, these learning-based algorithms are used to produce semantic segmentation but not generic segmentation results.

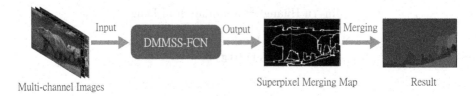

Fig. 1. Overview of the proposed DMMSS-FCN algorithm. Multiple feature maps including an original RGB image are stacked together to form the input data. Then, they are fed into the fully convolutional network. The output is the superpixel merging map that determines which boundaries should be kept. With such information, we perform superpixel merging based on the output of the model to produce the final segmentation result.

Before learning-based segmentation algorithms were developed, many advanced image segmentation algorithms are based on superpixels. However, due to the irregularity of sizes and shapes of superpixels, it is hard to apply superpixels in a learning-based generic segmentation architecture.

Therefore, in this study, we broke down the whole image segmentation problem into several superpixel merging decision problems. Furthermore, each superpixel merging process can be converted into a boundary keeping problem. That is, whether the boundaries between two adjacent superpixels should be deleted or not. We proposed a novel algorithm that leverages the Fully Convolutional Network (FCN) for learning generic image segmentation. We call it Deep Merging Models for Superpixel-Segmentation by Fully Convolutional Networks (DMMSS-FCN). With the use of FCN, all of those superpixel merging problems can be solved in just one forward pass. That is, it is extremely efficient. First, the proposed DMMSS-FCN model will predict whether the pixels along the boundary of two adjacent superpixels should be keep. Following, a majority voting technique will be applied to decide the existence of all superpixel boundaries. Therefore, the final image segmentation result will be produced with minimum effort.

We use 5-channel stacked images as the input, including an RGB image, a superpixel boundary map, an edge detection map. Since different superpixel algorithms will produce different superpixel boundary maps, by vary the parameters of different superpixel algorithms, numerous training data can be easily obtained. That is, our method does not require many human-annotated ground truth. Furthermore, our method is fully automatic, that is, user does not need to assign number of regions in prior.

We show the overview of the proposed DMMSS-FCN algorithm in Fig. 1. We will discuss the detail of DMMSS-FCN in Sect. 3.

2   Related Work

2.1   Superpixels

Superpixels are a group of pixels with similar colors and locations. There are many types of superpixels, including the entropy rate superpixel (ERS) [15] and the simple linear iterative clustering (SLIC) [16] superpixel. In [2], the superpixel generated by mean shift was proposed. It has good edge-preserving property and the number of superpixels have not to be specified in advance. Moreover, its boundaries highly match the borders of objects. Recently, deep learning-based superpixels like superpixel sampling network (SSN) [17], and segmentation-aware loss (SEAL) superpixels [18] were proposed. They both outperform non deep learning-based superpixels by a wide margin.

2.2   Classical Segmentation

Most classical segmentation methods utilize hand-crafted features such as color, histogram, gradient, or texture to perform segmentation. Many of them are still widely used today, such as the graph-based method [7] and the normalized cut [6]. Arbelaz et al. [3,4] proposed a method based on the global information to perform the oriented watershed transform and generated an ultra-metric contour map for hierarchical segmentation.

Moreover, superpixel-based segmentation algorithms like the method of segmentation by aggregating superpixels (SAS) [8] perform segmentation based on merging superpixels using some local grouping cues. Kim et al. [9] used a full range affinity model and Yang et al. [10] proposed a spectral clustering method based on Gaussian Kernel similarity measure for image segmentation. These superpixel-based segmentation algorithms have good performance. However, due to the irregular shapes and sizes of superpixels, it is hard to embed deep learning techniques in superpixels-based algorithms.

2.3   Deep Learning in Image Segmentation

Recently, many semantic segmentation algorithms applied the deep neural network were developed. In [12,13], the fully convolutional network (FCN) were proposed to improve the performance of image segmentation and object detection. In [14], the conditional random field (CRF) was applied in the pixel-wise segmentation method of DeepLab. In [11], Xia and Kulis proposed the W-Net based on the FCN to perform segmentation. In [19], Haeh et al. introduced a method based on the CNN to detect split error in segmented biomedical images. In [20], Chen et al. extracted deep features and used them for superpixel merging. In [21], Liu et al. applied the FCN for superpixel merging.

In this study, we integrate the merits of superpixel-based methods and state-of-the-art learning-based methods and propose a high accuracy image segmentation algorithm.

3   Proposed Algorithms: DMMSS-FCN

In this work, we proposed an effective way of integrating FCN with generic image segmentation. That is, with the use of superpixel, we can encode the superpixel merging problems with keeping of superpixel boundaries into generic image segmentation. In Fig. 2(a), the existence of boundary between two super-pixels implies that they are separated from each other, in other words, they are not merged. On the contrary, the disappearance of boundary means they are merged. Therefore, with the use of the FCN, we perform dense prediction on every adjacent boundaries. After one forward pass in the FCN, all the pixels along the boundaries are classified into two classes, *keeping or removing*. Then we measure the tendency of keeping a boundary by majority voting technique defined in (1) for quantization. Hence, we can easily recover the segmentation result.

$$BoundaryRate(i,j) = \frac{\# \text{ of pixels of } (keep \text{ label} \cap Bnd(i,j))}{\# \text{ of pixels of } Bnd(i,j)} \qquad (1)$$

where the *keeping* label indicates that the pixel is predicted to be on the boundary of some object and should be kept. For example in Fig. 2(b), there are 15 pixels along the boundary $Bnd(i,j)$, 10 of them are predicted as the *keeping* label (orange circles) while 5 of them (black circles) are of the *removing* label, resulting in a *BoundaryRate* of 2/3. Therefore, we can thresholding on the *BoundaryRate* to get the segmentation result from the FCN output.

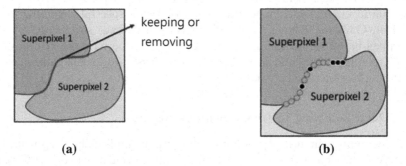

Fig. 2. (a) Converting superpixel merging problem into superpixel boundary keeping problem. (b) BoundaryRate example.

3.1   Five-Channel Input Data

We defined our input data by concatenating a RGB (3 channels) image with a superpixel boundary map (1 channel) and a edge-detection map (1 channel). The RGB image indicates the original image while the superpixel boundary map is a binary image with only the boundary between two adjacent superpixels are marked as positive (the *keeping* label). The superpixel boundary map generation is shown in Fig. 3. There are many advanced learning-based contour generation algorithms [22–24]. In this work, the RefineContourNet (RCN) [22] is adopted for edge detection. An example of the output of the RCN is shown in the right subfigure of Fig. 3.

Fig. 3. Component of input data. **Left**: superpixel result from SEAL-ERS [18]. **Middle**: binary image with superpixel boundaries marked as 1s, others are 0s. **Right**: Edges extracted by the RCN.

We have also tried different combination of concatenating input images. Ablation studies have been carried out to analyze the impact of different input channel in Sect. 4.2.

Since we want our model to be adaptive to any input superpixel type, the superpixel boundary map plays an important role in the whole process. That is, with any superpixel result as prior input, our model can determine which boundary should be keep, with the superpixel boundary map as attention mechanism.

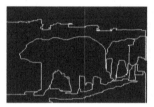

Fig. 4. Groundtruth generation. **Left**: SEAL-ERS superpixel result. **Middle**: perfect segmentation by oracle. **Right**: groundtruth superpixel boundary map by converting the resulting groundtruth into binary image.

3.2 GroundTruth Generation and Output

In [3], the Segmentation Covering (SC), the Probabilistic Rand Index (PRI), and the Variation of Information (VI) are proposed to be the standard evaluation metrics for generic image segmentation. Among all, the PRI as follows is often treated as the most important metric, where c_{ij} indicates the case where pixels i and j belong to the same region, p_{ij} is the probability, S is the resulting segmentation, and G_k is a set of groundtruth.

$$PRI\{S, G_k\} = \frac{1}{T} \sum_{i<j} [c_{ij}p_{ij} + (1 - c_{ij}) + (1 - p_{ij})] \tag{2}$$

That is, we use an oracleguided process to produce the highest achievable PRI score for a given oversegmentation (superpixel) result. From that, we can acquire the groundtruh by transforming the results into a binary boundary map called the superpixel merging map which is the ideal output of our model. The groundtruth generation result is shown in Fig. 4. Sufficient training data can be obtained by varying the parameters of superpixel generation algorithms. Therefore, the model is designed to be adaptive for different superpixel type. We use BoundaryRate to recover segmentation result. In Fig. 5, we show that for different superpixel type as prior input, our models will generate corresponding superpixel merging maps.

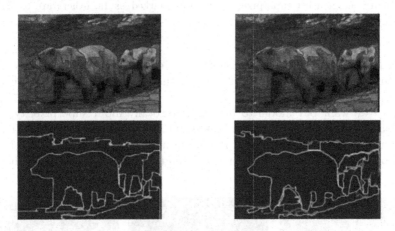

Fig. 5. Different superpixel boundary map input. **First Row**: superpixel boundaries overlapped with the original images. **Second Row**: superpixel merging maps overlapped with corresponding groundtruth merging maps.

3.3 Training Architecture

Since our goal is to perform pixel-wise prediction on the image, and examine the *BoundaryRate* along the boundary of two adjacent superpixels, the localization of predicted labels is crucial. Therefore, we adopted the DeepLab V3+ [25] FCN architecture proposed by Chen et al. The DeepLab V3+ utilized the atrous convolution in the encoder side for the better field of view and a simple but effective decoder with short cut skipped through the encoder part is added to this architecture, making it a highly accurate fully convolutional network structure while preserving good spacial information.

In this paper, we adopted the InceptionResNetV2 [26] as the hidden encoder architecture, and the output stride of encoder is set to 16. And the batch size is set to 13 with the size of input data is $321 \times 481 \times 5$.

Since this is a binary classification problem of two labels, *keeping or removing* labels, with the *keeping* class is far less than the other one, we applied the weighted binary cross entropy loss in the following equation to calculate the loss. Furthermore, Adam optimizer is adopted to update the parameters of the networks with initial learning rate of 0.0001 and divided by 0.5 for every 10 epochs, and stopped training after 100 epochs.

$$weighted\,BCE\,(T,S) = -\sum_i \left[\omega_0\,(T_i log S_i) + \omega_1 log\,(1 - S_i)\right] \qquad (3)$$

where S is the output superpixel merging map, and $S_i \in (0,1)$ denotes the predicted probability value at i^{th} pixel in S. T is the groundtruth merging map, and $T_i \in 0, 1$ denotes the groundtruth label in T. The weighting factors $\omega_0 = 1$ and $\omega_1 = 38$ is the ratio of two classes.

We applied the Berkeley Segmentation DataSet 500, with 200 test images, 200 training images, and 100 validation images. As we mentioned in Sect. 3.2, different superpixel algorithm can produce different superpixel and groundtruth pairs. Therefore, we adopted the SEAL-ERS [18] and the SSN [17] both with the number of superpixels set to 100, and 200 to generate the training data, resulting in 800 training images, and 400 validation images in total.

3.4 Inference and Superpixel Merging

As we shown in Fig. 6, we first concatenate RGB image with superpixel boundary map and RCN edge map to form the 5-channel input data. Then we perform

Fig. 6. Overview of DMMSS-FCN. We first form the 5-channel input data by concatenating a RGB (3 channels) image with a superpixel boundary map (1 channel) and an edge-detection map (1 channel). Then, the input is fed to perform pixel-wise prediction and output the superpixel merging map. Then, the BoundaryRate in (1) is used to threshold each superpixel boundary to perform superpixel merging and obtain the segmentation result.

one forward pass through the networks to obtain superpixel merging map. Afterwards, we use the *BoundaryRate* in (1) to measure how many predicted *keeping* label are on each boundary of adjacent superpixels. Then, we perform thresholding merging procedure as we by using the formula in (1). Here we adopted an adaptive thresholding technique which first start merging by thresholding with the lowest threshold values and increase the threshold values bit-by-bit until there are no candidates for merging. After the thresholding value (0.5 in this paper) is reached, the whole merging process stops and the final segmentation result is obtained.

4   Experiments

In this section, we carried out tons of experiments and ablation studies to justify that our proposed *DMMSS-FCN* can outperform many state-of-the-art algorithms, even compared to our own *DMMSS*, the proposed *DMMSS-FCN* can still surpass it in all evaluation metrics while boosting the speed, making *DMMSS-FCN* a highly accurate and efficient generic image segmentation algorithm.

Table 1. Results on the BSDS500 dataset.

Method	VI	PRI	SC
Ncuts	2.23	0.78	0.45
Canny-owt-ucm	2.19	0.79	0.49
Felz-Hutt	2.21	0.80	0.52
Mean Shift	1.85	0.79	0.54
Taylor	1.78	0.81	0.56
W-Net	1.76	0.81	0.57
fPb-owt-ucm	1.70	0.82	0.58
DC-Seg-full	1.68	0.82	0.59
W-Net+ucm	1.67	0.82	0.59
gPb-owt-ucm	1.69	0.83	0.59
cPb-owt-ucm	1.65	0.83	0.59
DMMSS (SSN)	**1.46**	**0.86**	**0.63**
DMMSS-FCN (SSN)	*1.38*	*0.87*	*0.66*
Human drawing	1.17	0.88	0.72

4.1   Segmentation Evaluation

To compare the proposed DMMSS-FCN algorithm to the existing methods, we evaluate the performance on the standard metrics of segmentation covering (SC), the probabilistic rand index (PRI), and the variation of information (VI) [3]. A higher SC and PRI and a lower VI mean better performance.

We compare the proposed DMMSS-FCN algorithm to the state-of-the-art methods, including the W-Net [11], gPb-owt-ucm [4], DC-Seg-full [27], Taylor [28], Felzenszwalb and Huttenlocher (Felz-Hutt) [7], Mean Shift [2], Canny-owtucm [4], Multiscale Normalized Cuts (NCuts) [5], fPb-owt-ucm [9], cPb-owtucm [9], and our own DMMSS. As the proposed algorithm, all the algorithms compared in Table 1 have not to assign the number of regions in prior.

4.2   Run Time Analysis

We then analyze the run time of the proposed *DMMSS-FCN* and compare it to the state-of-the-art segmentation algorithms of DC-Seg-full [27] and gPb-OWT-UCM [4]. The runtime includes the inference time of generating the superpixel boundary map and the edge map. We evaluate our algorithms on SEAL-ERS superpixels, and perform inference on the BSDS500 test set. In Table 2, the average run time of processing single image is presented. One can find out that the proposed *DMMSS-FCN* has drastically reduce the run time compare to gPb-OWT-UCM, decreasing the runtime up to 384x times less than the gPb-OWT-UCM and 227x times less than DC-Seg-full and meanwhile achieving higher accuracy. More on that, even we switch our *DMMSS-FCN* to CPU mode, our proposed *DMMSSFCN* still 12x faster than the gPb-OWT-UCM and 12x faster than the DC-Segfull.

Table 2. Run time on the BSDS500 test set.

Method	Mode	Time (s)
DMMSS-FCN (SEAL-ERS)	CPU+GPU	*0.26*
DMMSS-FCN (SEAL-ERS)	CPU	**8.2**
DC-Seg-full	CPU	59
gPb-OWT-UCM	CPU	100

4.3   Ablation Study

We then discuss the functionality of some key component in our proposed algorithm, and how they affect the overall performance. Including the different combination of input data, different superpixel generation algorithm, and different DeepLabV3 Plus implementation detail, furthermore, different inference techniques.

Combination of Input Data Following: We show that different combination of input data could have a great impact on the performance of the model. In this section, we mainly use the SEAL-ERS 100 as the underlying superpixel representation. In Table 3, we show the difference of concatenating different feature map as input data.

Table 3. Performance of different input data combination.

Input data	VI	PRI	SC
4-channel: RGB(3)+spixel bdry(1)	1.569	0.846	0.547
5-channel: RGB(3)+spixel bdry(1)+RCN edge(1)	**1.446**	**0.863**	**0.634**
5-channel: LAB(3)+spixel bdry(1)+RCN edge(1)	1.458	0.860	0.632
7-channel: RGB(3)+spixel bdry(1)+RCN edge(1)+AffinityXY(2)	1.472	0.861	0.629
7-channel: LAB(3)+spixel bdry(1)+RCN edge(1)+AffinityXY(2)	1.534	0.859	0.606

It is reasonable to think that concatenating another feature map as prior information might improve the performance. As we added the RCN edge-detection map, we got a huge gain in performance. Hence, we tried to concatenated more feature map or change RGB to CIE LAB color space to further improve the performance. For example, we use the Affinity map that generated from the SEAL-ERS as candidates for feature map concatenation. Nevertheless, from the experimental results in Table 3, more channels of feature maps do not imply better performance. In the end, we adopted the 5-channel with RGB image as the input of the model.

Superpixels: We measure the performance over different number of initial superpixels. In Fig. 7, the proposed *DMMSS-FCN*. Since our main superpixel boundary maps are collected from the initial number of superpixels set to 100, and 200, the peak performance is around 200. However, our proposed *DMMSS-FCN* still maintains great performance over different numbers of initial superpixels even if some of them are not included during training.

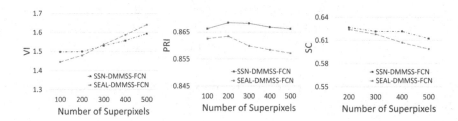

Fig. 7. Performance of different numbers of superpixels between SSN and SEALERS over *DMMSS-FCN*.

In Fig. 5, we show the performance of the proposed model on different types of superpixels, where yellow lines index that the prediction overlapped with the corresponding groundtruth superpixel boundary map, the light blue parts indicate that the model predicts the *keeping* label, and the dark blue parts represent the model predicts the *removing* label. Therefore, as we observe, different input superpixel type will lead the model to predict corresponding superpixel merging map.

DeepLabV3 Plus Variation: Chen et al. [25] proposed a powerful encoder-decoder-based fully convolutional networks. They suggested different variations of implementation details, including changing the output stride of the model or replacing hidden encoder architecture with any existing CNN architecture such as the ResNet [29] or Xception [30]. More on that, inference techniques like forwarding not one image but four up-down and right-left flipped images at once is also reported as legit method to gain performance. Therefore, we discuss the difference of the performance among the variation of DeepLabV3 Plus applied in our work. We choose SEAL-ERS 100 as the underlying superpixel representation to carry out the following experiments.

In Table 4, we reported the difference among two recent CNN architecture, the Xception [30] and the InceptionResNetV2 [26] with two different output stride setting. In [14], they indicated that smaller output stride could greatly increase the training time and memory usage with a negligible improvement which corresponds to our case here. As for different encoder architecture, InceptionResNetV2 has better performance over the Xception.

Furthermore, we also adopted the inference technique in [25] to improve the performance, that is, we generate extra images by flipped the original image, then feed them into the networks, then average the scores of the outputs to obtain the final superpixel merging map. In Table 5, we show that a simple but effective flipping technique could boost the performance.

Table 4. Performance of different encoder architecture and output stride.

Encoder architecture	Output stride	VI	PRI	SC
Xception	8	1.569	0.860	0.600
Xception	16	1.532	0.857	0.606
InceptionResNetV2	8	1.635	0.854	0.583
InceptionResNetV2	16	1.446	0.863	0.634

Table 5. Result of adopting flipping technique.

Encoder architecture	Flip	VI	PRI	SC
InceptionResNetV2	No	1.446	0.863	0.634
InceptionResNetV2	Yes	1.411	0.864	0.647

4.4   Visual Comparison

In this section, visual comparisons with other segmentation algorithms are presented. In addition to show the simulation results on the BSDS500, we also perform simulations on some real-world images to justify that under any circumstance, our proposed algorithm can be highly accurate and efficient to produce good generic image segmentation results.

BSDS500 Test Images Fig. 8 shows the comparison between the proposed methods and other methods like a deep-learning-based method, the DC-Seg-full method [27], and classical segmentation algorithm gPb-OWT-UCM [4]. As we can see, both the results of the proposed algorithms are much better than that of state-of-the-art algorithms, since ours can produce more general and compact segmentation results compared to the others.

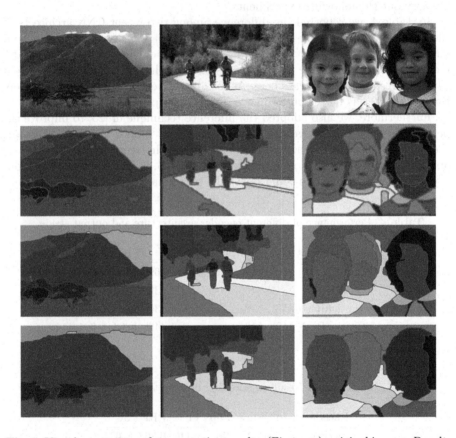

Fig. 8. Visual comparison of segmentation results. (First row): original images. Results produced by (Second row): DC-Seg-full [27]; (Third row): gPb-OWT-UCM [4]; (Fourth row): *DMMSS-FCN* (proposed).

Real-World Images: To further justify the robustness of our model, we pick some modern images that have never been in our training set. In this section, we show some segmentation results on the images taken in the night to test the capability of our proposed methods of handling dark view scenario. In Fig. 9(a) and Fig. 9(b) , one can see that, the proposed model well merges the superpixels

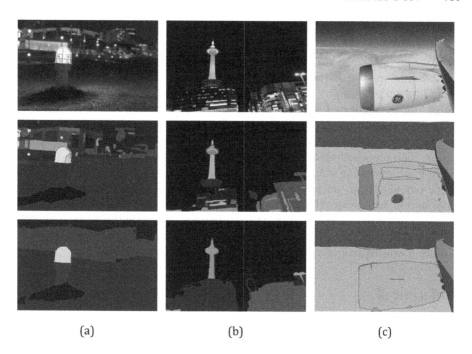

(a)   (b)   (c)

Fig. 9. Real-world image segmentation results. (First row): original images. Results produced by (Second row): gPb-OWT-UCM [4]; (Third row): *DMMSS-FCN* (proposed).

belonging to the same object into a region but the other method fails to do this and has severe segmentation leakage. Therefore, such examples prove that our models are robust not only in images taken under great exposures, but in those low-light and blurry scenarios. Additionally, we present simulations of an aircraft engine in Fig. 9(c), which is difficult for another algorithm to perform accurate segmentation on the boundary of engine itself since the background information is similar to the engine. Nevertheless, our proposed method can generate compact segmentation without losing edge information.

5   Conclusion

In this work, a novel image segmentation algorithm that integrates the merit of the Fully Convolutional Network and superpixel-based segmentation is proposed. We call it the *DMMSS-FCN*.

With the use of superpixel, which allows us to be able to solve the generic image segmentation by highly efficient networks. That is, we covert the merging decision into a boundary keeping problem across all superpixel pairs. Hence, with the use of Fully Convolutional Networks, we can solve all those boundary keeping problems with just one forward pass. As a result, the proposed *DMMSS-FCN* algorithm is not only vastly faster than the other state-of-the-art algorithms, but also has high score in accuracy close to human performance.

Additionally, one can obtain large quantity of training data by varying the parameters of existing superpixel algorithms to produce various superpixel boundary maps as input training data. That is, our method does not require a lot of human-annotated ground truth to be fully trained.

We proposed a simple but effective deep-learning-based generic image segmentation algorithm that leverages the FCN for learning generic image segmentation. The proposed algorithm is very effective and simulations show that it is capable of producing reliable segmentation results under many circumstances. Since our algorithm do not require any post-processing technique and further information from user, the simplicity makes it extremely efficient and reliable for any generic image segmentation task. Therefore, we hope this work could offer a great idea to be implemented in the downstream tasks, since segmentation is a quite useful technique in many computer vision applications.

References

1. Shih, F.Y., Cheng, S.: Automatic seeded region growing for color image segmentation. Image Vis. Comput. **23**(10), 877–886 (2005)
2. Comaniciu, D., Meer, P.: Mean shift: a robust approach toward feature space analysis. IEEE Trans. Pattern Anal. Mach. Intell. **24**(5), 603–619 (2002)
3. Arbelaez, P., Maire, M., Fowlkes, C., Malik, J.: From contours to regions: an empirical evaluation, pp. 2294–2301 (2009)
4. Arbelaez, P., Maire, M., Fowlkes, C., Malik, J.: Contour detection and hierarchical image segmentation. IEEE Trans. Pattern Anal. Mach. Intell. **33**, 898–916 (2010)
5. Cour, T., Benezit, F., Shi, J.: Spectral segmentation with multiscale graph decomposition. In: 2005 IEEE Computer Society Conference on Computer Vision and Pattern Recognition (CVPR'2005), vol. 2, pp. 1124–1131 (2005)
6. Shi, J., Malik, J.: Normalized cuts and image segmentation. IEEE Trans. Pattern Anal. Mach. Intell. **22**, 888–905 (2000)
7. Felzenszwalb, P.F., Huttenlocher, D.P.: Efficient graph-based image segmentation. Int. J. Comput. Vis. **59**, 167–181 (2004)
8. Li, Z., Wu, X.M., Chang, S.F.: Segmentation using superpixels: a bipartite graph partitioning approach. In: 2012 IEEE Conference on Computer Vision and Pattern Recognition, pp. 789–796 (2012)
9. Kim, T.H., Lee, K.M., Lee, S.U.: Learning full pairwise affinities for spectral segmentation. IEEE Trans. Pattern Anal. Mach. Intell. **35**, 1690–1703 (2012)
10. Yang, Y., Wang, Y., Xue, X.: A novel spectral clustering method with superpixels for image segmentation. Optik **127**, 161–167 (2016)
11. Xia, X., Kulis, B.: W-Net: a deep model for fully unsupervised image segmentation. arXiv preprint arXiv:1711.08506 (2017)
12. Noh, H., Hong, S., Han, B.: Learning deconvolution network for semantic segmentation, pp. 1520–1528 (2015)
13. Long, J., Shelhamer, E., Darrell, T.: Fully convolutional networks for semantic segmentation, pp. 3431–3440 (2015)

14. Chen, L.C., Papandreou, G., Kokkinos, I., Murphy, K., Yuille, A.L.: DeepLab: semantic image segmentation with deep convolutional nets, atrous convolution, and fully connected CRFs. IEEE Trans. Pattern Anal. Mach. Intell. **40**, 834–848 (2017)

15. Liu, M.Y., Tuzel, O., Ramalingam, S., Chellappa, R.: Entropy rate superpixel segmentation, pp. 2097–2104 (2011)

16. Achanta, R., Shaji, A., Smith, K., Lucchi, A., Fua, P., Süsstrunk, S.: Slic superpixels compared to state-of-the-art superpixel methods. IEEE Trans. Pattern Anal. Mach. Intell. **34**, 2274–2282 (2012)

17. Jampani, V., Sun, D., Liu, M.Y., Yang, M.H., Kautz, J.: Superpixel sampling networks. In: Proceedings of the European Conference on Computer Vision (ECCV), pp. 352–368 (2018)

18. Tu, W.C., et al.: Learning superpixels with segmentation-aware affinity loss. In: Proceedings of the IEEE Conference on Computer Vision and Pattern Recognition, pp. 568–576 (2018)

19. Haehn, D., Kaynig, V., Tompkin, J., Lichtman, J.W., Pfister, H.: Guided proofreading of automatic segmentations for connectomics. In: Proceedings of the IEEE Conference on Computer Vision and Pattern Recognition, pp. 9319–9328 (2018)

20. Cheng, M.M., et al.: HFS: hierarchical feature selection for efficient image segmentation. In: Leibe, B., Matas, J., Sebe, N., Welling, M. (eds.) ECCV 2016. LNCS, vol. 9907, pp. 867–882. Springer, Cham (2016). https://doi.org/10.1007/978-3-319-46487-9_53

21. Liu, Y., et al.: DEL: deep embedding learning for efficient image segmentation, vol. 864, p. 870 (2018)

22. Kelm, A.P., Rao, V.S., Zölzer, U.: Object contour and edge detection with RefineContourNet. In: Vento, M., Percannella, G. (eds.) CAIP 2019. LNCS, vol. 11678, pp. 246–258. Springer, Cham (2019). https://doi.org/10.1007/978-3-030-29888-3_20

23. Maninis, K.K., Pont-Tuset, J., Arbeláez, P., Van Gool, L.: Convolutional oriented boundaries: from image segmentation to high-level tasks. IEEE Trans. Pattern Anal. Mach. Intell. **40**, 819–833 (2017)

24. Liu, Y., Cheng, M.M., Hu, X., Wang, K., Bai, X.: Richer convolutional features for edge detection. In: Proceedings of the IEEE Conference on Computer Vision and Pattern Recognition, pp. 3000–3009 (2017)

25. Chen, L.C., Papandreou, G., Schroff, F., Adam, H.: Rethinking atrous convolution for semantic image segmentation. arXiv preprint arXiv:1706.05587 (2017)

26. Szegedy, C., Ioffe, S., Vanhoucke, V., Alemi, A.: Inception-v4, inception-ResNet and the impact of residual connections on learning. arXiv preprint arXiv:1602.07261 (2016)

27. Donoser, M., Schmalstieg, D.: Discrete-continuous gradient orientation estimation for faster image segmentation. In: Proceedings of the IEEE Conference on Computer Vision and Pattern Recognition, pp. 3158–3165 (2014)

28. Taylor, C.J.: Towards fast and accurate segmentation. In: Proceedings of the IEEE Conference on Computer Vision and Pattern Recognition, pp. 1916–1922 (2013)

29. He, K., Zhang, X., Ren, S., Sun, J.: Deep residual learning for image recognition. In: Proceedings of the IEEE Conference on Computer Vision and Pattern Recognition, pp. 770–778 (2016)

30. Chollet, F.: Xception: deep learning with depthwise separable convolutions. In: Proceedings of the IEEE Conference on Computer Vision and Pattern Recognition, pp. 1251–1258 (2017)

Author Index